Psychology

PSY 110 at University of Tennessee

James W. Kalat | Robert J. Sternberg | James S. Nairne, et al
Edited by Richard A. Saudargas

CENGAGE Learning™

Australia • Brazil • Japan • Korea • Mexico • Singapore • Spain • United Kingdom • United States

Psychology
PSY 110 at University of Tennessee

James W. Kalat | Robert J. Sternberg
James S. Nairne, et al
Edited by Richard A. Saudargas

Executive Editors:
Maureen Staudt
Michael Stranz

Senior Project Development Manager:
Linda DeStefano

Marketing Specialist:
Sara Mercurio
Lindsay Shapiro

Senior Production / Manufacturing Manager:
Donna M. Brown

PreMedia Supervisor:
Joel Brennecke

Rights & Permissions Specialist:
Kalina Hintz
Todd Osborne

Cover Image:
Getty Images*

ISBN-13: 978-1-4240-8176-9

ISBN-10: 1-4240-8176-9

Cengage Learning
5191 Natorp Boulevard
Mason, Ohio 45040
USA

Cengage Learning is a leading provider of customized learning solutions with office locations around the globe, including Singapore, the United Kingdom, Australia, Mexico, Brazil, and Japan. Locate your local office at: **international.cengage.com/region**

Cengage Learning products are represented in Canada by Nelson Education, Ltd.

For your lifelong learning solutions, visit **www.cengage.com/custom**

Visit our corporate website at **www.cengage.com**

Printed in the United States of America

Brief Contents

Contents

6 INTERPRETATION OF SENSORY INFORMATION 176

7 MOTIVATION AND EMOTION 208

8 CONSCIOUSNESS 256

Introduction

THIS CUSTOM edited introductory psychology textbook contains chapters from various introductory texts. Psychology is such a broad field of study that every area cannot be included in a one semester introductory course so chapters were selected that represent core areas of psychology. The order of the chapters is different from most introductory texts that typically begin with a chapter on psychology's history and major theoretical viewpoints. I believe students should immediately learn about psychology's main subject so the first chapter is human life span development. Learning about life span development sets the stage for learning about core topics that are researched by psychologists such as learning, intelligence, perception, memory, personality, and psychological disorders and therapies.

Study Questions and Vocabulary

Before each chapter are a series of study questions and vocabulary terms. Your instructor will let you know which of those study questions and vocabulary terms you should know and may provide additional questions or objectives from the text, readings, and lectures.

Practice Examinations

At the end of each chapter is a practice multiple choice test. You should do the practice tests ***after*** you have studied the chapter and answered the chapter questions, chapter vocabulary, and research article questions. Check your answers and review the material you missed.

Studying

One chapter in the book discusses talented people. Researchers discovered that the common factor among all the talented people was that they spent a lot of time to become an expert in their field. The more time you spend studying a subject the more you will learn and remember. It's really that simple. Every semester we ask students who fail the first exam how they studied and how long they studied. The answers reflect the fact that the students did not spend enough time studying—typical answers are: "I go to all the classes and I read my notes and the chapters over last night before I went to bed". "I spent about three hours studying the chapters". "I didn't have to study very much in high school and got good grades, I figured I could do the same here". The Memory chapter gives some helpful hints on studying for exams and the Motivation and Emotion chapter offers suggestions on coping with test anxiety.

Most of the material in this book will be new to you. There is a lot of information and a lot of new terms to learn. There are no shortcuts to learning—it takes time. Do not compare your study habits or how much time you spend studying with anyone else. Students learn different material at different rates and find different things interesting. Some of you will find psychology interesting but chemistry very difficult and boring. Others will find chemistry fun and exciting but psychology a drudge and difficult.

How You Should Study

1. Come to class having read the material in the chapter. The class lecture should review, clarify, amplify, and demonstrate material that is somewhat familiar to you. The best thing that can happen during a lecture is that you find yourself saying "I knew that."
2. Skim through the chapter to get an idea of what the chapter covers.
3. Read the chapter with the intent of getting involved in the material, not with trying to memorize information.
4. Take out the chapter study questions and vocabulary and begin to find the answers to the study questions and vocabulary in the chapter.
5. Students have different strategies for learning the answers to the study questions and vocabulary and you should use the strategy that works best for you.
   a. Underlining the appropriate text in the book.
   b. Highlighting the text
   c. Writing out the answers on note cards or a separate piece of paper.
   d. Outlining the chapter
6. Review some of the study questions and vocabulary every day or two.
7. When you sit down to study, set a specific learning goal, such as you will learn answers to 10 study questions and 5 vocabulary terms. Do not set a time limit.

ACKNOWLEDGEMENTS

I would like to thank the following people for their support and encouragement: my wife Barbara Skinner, Lori Gud, Linda Harper, and my children Katrice Morris and Alexis Saudargas whose art has graced the covers of these books.

CHAPTER 1: HUMAN DEVELOPMENT

QUESTIONS

1. What does extending the process of development over time help humans do?
2. What do developmental psychologists mean when they discuss development as a process of interaction?
3. What are the three stages of prenatal development?
4. What are the major hallmarks of each prenatal stage?
5. When is an embryo or fetus most susceptible to teratogens?
6. What might morning sickness be?
7. What happens to neurons during the first two years of life?
8. What does the plasticity principle mean for neuronal development?
9. What may account for individual differences in motor development?
10. What are the two physical changes that occur from toddlerhood to adolescence?
11. How does the onset of puberty represent the interactions of genes and the environment? What is an example of this interaction?
12. When do people begin to physically decline?
13. What occurs during menopause?
14. What were the results of the Buell and Coleman (1979) study?
15. What are three strategies researchers use to uncover the perceptual capabilities of infants?
16. What are advantages and disadvantages of longitudinal and cross-sectional research designs?
17. What kind of shapes do infants prefer?
18. How did researchers determine that babies track a face stimulus more than a blank or scrambled stimulus?
19. Why is the ability to have some preferences for shapes, sounds, and tastes important?
20. What happens to our sensory systems during childhood and adolescence?
21. What kinds of memory decline and do not decline with age?
22. What were the results of the memory and aging study?
23. What are two hypotheses as to why age related memory deficits are observed?
24. How did Piaget suggest people organize the world?
25. How do the two adaptive processes guide the process of cognitive development?
26. What are the Piaget's stages of cognitive development and the major characteristics and accomplishments and limitations of each stage?
27. What did Bower's (1982) study suggest about the timing of object permanence?
28. What is the major problem with a stage view of development?
29. What are examples of culture impacting on cognitive development?

30. What is the major criticism of Kohlberg's theory of moral development?
31. How does morality develop across the world?
32. What are three examples of culture differences with respect to morality?
33. What evidence suggests infants desire and need contact comfort?
34. How do psychologists explain infant temperament?
35. How do securely and insecurely attached infants react in the strange situation test?
36. What is one criticism of the strange situation test?
37. What is one methodological problem with showing that securely attached infants are securely attached at age 10 or 11?
38. What are 4 things one should do when selecting a day care center?
39. What did Erikson believe shaped a person's sense of self?
40. What are two of Erikson's contributions to development?
41. Why does Erikson's theory lack scientific rigor?
42. How does social learning explain gender role development?
43. How are gender schemas adaptive?
44. What are some common myths about the elderly?
45. Why was Kubler-Ross' work on death and dying important?
46. Why are trajectories preferred to stages when thinking about death and dying?
47. Why might it be difficult for a society to reach a policy concerning a person's end of life decision?
48. What do the theories of Piaget, Kohlberg, Erikson, and Kubler-Ross have in common? What is the main criticism of these kinds of theories?

VOCABULARY

1. accommodation
2. androgens
3. assimilation
4. attachments
5. cross-sectional design
6. dementia
7. development
8. gender roles
9. longitudinal design
10. menarche
11. menopause
12. morality
13. object permanence
14. personal identity
15. principle of conservation
16. schemata
17. teratogens
18. zygote

1 Human Development

Developing Physically

Developing Intellectually

Developing Socially and Personally

© Ariel Skelley/CORBIS

DO YOU EVER WISH you could hop into a time machine and start over? Maybe you could return to that point in the third grade where you tripped in front of the whole school, or to middle school where the answer you blurted out became the focus of jokes for months. In fact, while you're at it, why not return to early childhood? Maybe if your parents had been more sympathetic when you just couldn't get the hang of toilet training, things would be different now . . . right?

Psychologists believe that you are, in many ways, a product of your environment. Debate continues about the true origins of knowledge and behavior. If you could rerun your life, controlling your environment, would you really end up as a different person? Maybe, but remember that your personality—your likes and dislikes—also comes from the genetic recipe you inherited from your parents. The origins of thought and action don't lie exclusively in either the environment or in nature (genes), but always in both. So rerun your life a hundred times, and you might well end up with the same likes, dislikes, anxieties, and fears. Food for thought.

The topic of this chapter is human **development**, the age-related physical, intellectual, and social changes that occur throughout life. Why do humans develop? There's one very straightforward reason: There's no room for a full-sized adult in the mother's womb—nature is forced to start small. At the same time, however, extending the process of development over time enables us to fine-tune our physical, intellectual, and social capabilities to better meet the needs of varied environments.

development
the age-related physical, intellectual, social, and personal changes that occur throughout an individual's lifetime.

PREVIEW

Developmental Solutions

Nature has built a considerable amount of flexibility, or *plasticity,* into the developmental process. This flexibility has given us an exceptional degree of adaptability to environmental influences—in fact, as you'll soon see, the environment can change the course of development in profound ways (Greenough et al., 1987; Kolb et al., 2003). Keep the adaptive significance of development in mind as you consider the three main developmental problems that are the focus of this chapter.

© Eddie Soloway/Photographer's Choice/Getty Images

Developing physically

Developing Physically The environment helps shape the physical process of growth and can determine its ultimate outcome, but most physical changes are surprisingly consistent and predictable. We lift our heads before we crawl; we crawl before we can walk. In general, the timing of development is a product of evolutionary history and partly reflects the survival problems that our species has been required to solve.

© Layne Kennedy/CORBIS

Developing intellectually

Developing Intellectually The developmental changes that occur in how people think—what is called cognitive development—are of major importance to psychologists. Intellectually, the newborn is hardly an 'adultlet' (or miniature adult). You'll discover there are good reasons to believe that infants see and think about the world somewhat differently from adults. Infants are faced with infant problems, and these problems don't always overlap with those faced by adults.

© CORBIS

Developing socially and personally

Developing Socially and Personally Humans are social animals. We're continually interacting with each other, and these relationships help us adapt successfully to our environment. In this section we'll consider the milestones of social development, beginning with the formation of attachments to parents and caregivers and ending with a discussion of how relationships change in middle and late adulthood.

DEVELOPING PHYSICALLY

To a child, it seems to take forever to grow up. In fact, we do take a relatively long time to reach full physical maturity compared to other species. At birth a human newborn's brain has about 25% of its ultimate weight; the chimpanzee newborn's brain has about 60% (Corballis, 1991; Lenneberg, 1967). We do a lot of developing outside of the womb. Still, the main components of the body—the nervous system, the networks of glands, and so on—develop at an astonishingly rapid rate from the point of conception.

Guided by the genetic code and influenced by hormones released by the endocrine system, in the early years we change physically at rates that will never again be matched in our lifetimes. To place the growth rate in some perspective, if we continued to develop at the rate we show in the first 2 years of life, we'd end up over 12 feet tall and weighing several tons! Fortunately, things slow down considerably after the first few years of life; but they never completely stop—we continue to change physically until the very moment of death.

The Stages of Prenatal Development

Let's start at the beginning. The human developmental process begins with the union of egg and sperm at conception. Within the fertilized egg, or **zygote**, the 23 chromosomes from the father and the 23 chromosomes from the mother pair up to form the genetic recipe. Over the next 266 days or so (approximately 9 months), the newly formed organism undergoes a steady and quite remarkable transformation. It begins as a single cell and ends as an approximately 7-pound newborn composed of literally billions of cells. The period of development that occurs before birth is called *prenatal development,* and it's divided into three main stages: *germinal, embryonic,* and *fetal.*

zygote
the fertilized human egg, containing 23 chromosomes from the father and 23 chromosomes from the mother.

It takes about 2 weeks after conception for the zygote to migrate down from the mother's fallopian tubes (where the sperm and egg meet) and implant itself in the wall of the uterus (often called the womb). The period from conception to implantation is called the **germinal period**, and it's a make or break time for the fertilized egg. In fact, most fertilized eggs do not complete the process; well over half fail to achieve successful implantation, either because of abnormalities or because the implantation site is nutritionally inadequate for proper growth (Roberts & Lowe, 1975; Sigelman & Rider, 2004).

germinal period
the period in prenatal development from conception to implantation of the fertilized egg in the wall of the uterus.

If successful implantation occurs, the **embryonic period** begins. During the next 6 weeks, the human develops from an unrecognizable mass of cells to a somewhat familiar creature with arms, legs, fingers, toes, and a distinctly beating heart. Near the end of the embryonic period—in the 7th and 8th weeks after fertilization—sexual differentiation begins. Depending on whether the father has contributed an X or a Y chromosome (the mother always contributes an X), the embryo starts to develop either male or female sexual characteristics (see Figure 1.1). If the developing embryo has inherited a Y chromosome, it begins to secrete the sex hormone *testosterone,* which leads to the establishment of a male sexual reproductive system. In the absence of testosterone, the natural course of development in humans is to become female.

embryonic period
the period of prenatal development lasting from implantation to the end of the 8th week.

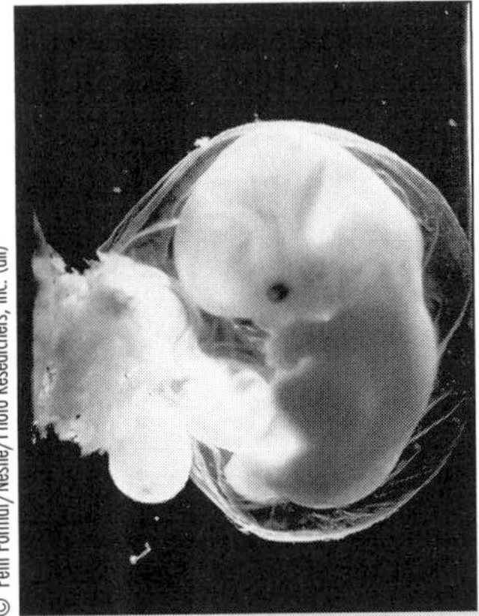

5–6 weeks postconception

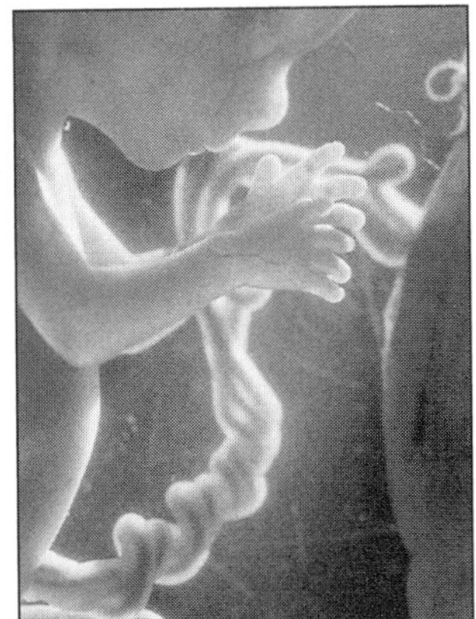

4 months

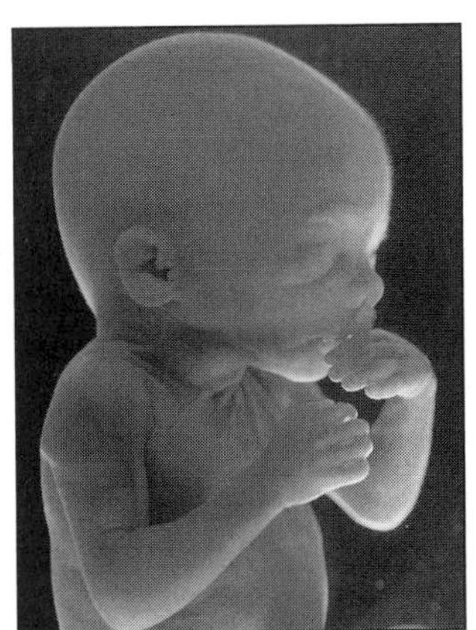

6 months

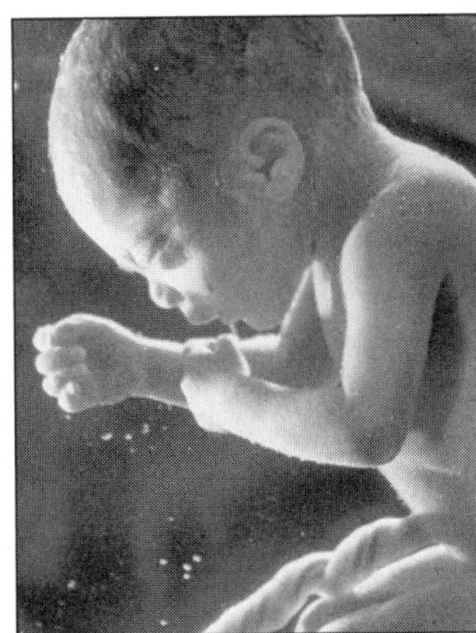

8 months

Prenatal human development

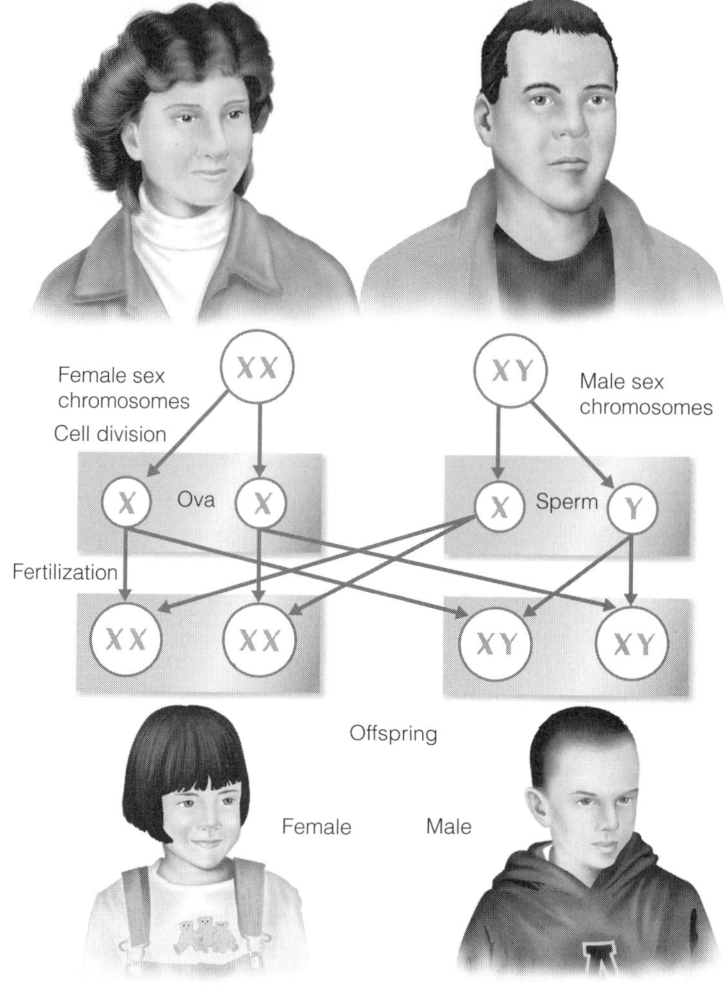

FIGURE 1.1

Genetic Determinants of Gender. If the father contributes an X chromosome, the child will be a girl; a Y chromosome from the father leads to the development of a boy.

fetal period
the period of prenatal development lasting from the 9th week until birth.

At the 9th week of prenatal development, the **fetal period** begins and continues until birth. Early in the period the bones and muscles of what is now called the *fetus* start to develop. By the end of the 3rd month, the skeletal and muscular systems allow for extensive movement—even somersaults—although the fetus at this point is still only about 3 inches long (Apgar & Beck, 1974). By the end of the 6th month, the fetus has grown to over a foot long, weighs in at about 2 pounds, and may be capable of survival if delivered prematurely. The last 3 months of prenatal development are marked by extremely rapid growth, both in body size and in the size and complexity of brain tissue. The fetus also develops a layer of fat under the skin during this period, which acts as protective insulation, and the lungs mature in preparation for the baby's first gasping breath of air.

Environmental Hazards Although the developing child is snugly tucked away within the confines of its mother's womb, it is by no means completely isolated from the effects of the environment. The mother's physical health and diet, as well as exposure to poisons in the environment, can seriously affect the developing child. Mother and child are linked physically, so if the mother gets sick, smokes, drinks, or uses drugs, the effects can transfer to the fetus or embryo. Some psychologists even believe that the mother's psychological state, such as her level of anxiety or stress during pregnancy, can exert an effect and may actually influence the personality of the child (Dawson et al., 2000; but see DiPietro, 2004).

Environmental agents that potentially damage the developing child are called **teratogens**. As a rule, the structures and systems of the fetus or embryo are most susceptible to teratogens during formation. For example, if the mother contracts German measles (rubella) during the first 6 weeks of pregnancy, the child is at risk for heart defects because it's during this period that the structures of the heart are formed. In general the embryonic period is the point of greatest susceptibility, although the critical structures of the central nervous system can be affected throughout prenatal development.

teratogens
environmental agents—such as disease organisms or drugs—that can potentially damage the developing embryo or fetus.

Interestingly, some researchers have suggested that morning sickness, which usually affects the mother during the first 3 months of pregnancy, may be a natural defense against the influence of teratogens (Profet, 1992). Pregnant women sometimes show increased sensitivity to foods and odors, and even develop aversions to certain tastes, which could help prevent potentially dangerous foods from being ingested. Remember, a food that's perfectly harmless to the adult mother might be damaging to the developing child. Morning sickness occurs across the world, in every culture, which suggests that it may be an evolutionary adaptation. Women who experience morning sickness are somewhat less likely to suffer miscarriages than women who do not (Flaxman & Sherman, 2000).

It's very important to recognize the powerful influence the environment can have on the developing child. If you're pregnant and drink heavily—five or more drinks a day—you're at least 30% more likely to give birth to a child suffering from *fetal alcohol syndrome,* a condition marked by physical deformities, a reduction in the size of certain brain structures, and an increased risk of mental retardation (Kaufman, 1997). Negative long-term effects can also result from drug consumption—including over-the-counter and prescription drugs—as well as from improper nutrition, smoking, and possibly excessive caffeine (Day & Richardson, 1994; Sussman & Levitt, 1989).

We can't predict with any certainty how an environmental agent will affect development because susceptibility is largely a matter of timing and genetics. Some mothers can abuse themselves terribly and still give birth to normal children; others who drink only moderately, perhaps as few as seven drinks a week, may produce a child with significant disabilities (Abel, 1981; Jacobson & Jacobson, 1994). Because the effects of maternal activities are impossible to predict in any particular case, most doctors recommend against playing Russian roulette with the developing fetus or embryo; it's best to stay sober, well fed, and under a doctor's care throughout pregnancy.

Growth During Infancy

Don't let all this bad news about the environment get you down too much—in the vast majority of cases the environment has a nurturing effect on the developing child. The internal conditions of the mother's uterus are perfectly "tuned" for physical development. The temperature is right, the fetus floats cushioned in a protective fluid, and regular nourishment is provided through the umbilical cord and placenta. More often than not, the result is a healthy baby who is ready to take on the world.

The average newborn weighs about 7 pounds and is roughly 20 inches in length. Over the next 2 years, as the child grows from baby to toddler, this weight will quadruple and the child will reach about half of his or her adult height. Along with the rest of the body, the brain continues its dramatic growth spurt during this period. As mentioned earlier, a newborn enters the world with a brain that is only 25% of its final weight; but by the second birthday, the percentage has increased to 75%. Remarkably, this increase in brain size is not due primarily to the formation of new neurons, as most of the cells that make up the cerebral cortex are in place well before birth (Nowakowski, 1987; Rakic, 1991). Instead, the cells grow in size and complexity, and a number of supporting glial cells are added. There is some

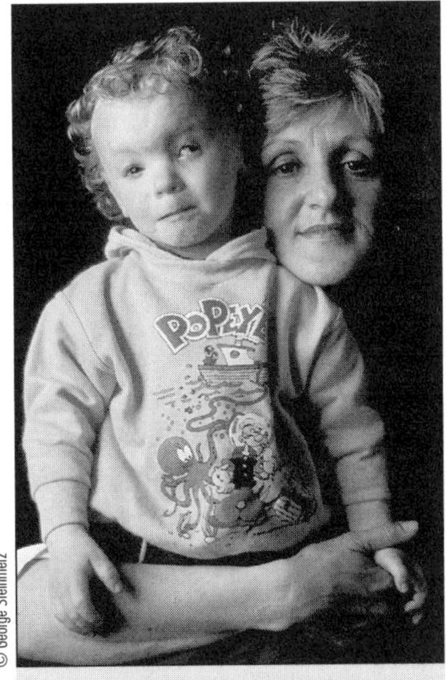

This child is one of thousands born each year with fetal alcohol syndrome.

evidence that new neurons may be added in the developing human brain through a process called *neurogenesis,* but this evidence remains controversial (see Gould et al., 1999; Nowakowski & Hayes, 2000).

Experience Matters The fact that substantial numbers of neurons are intact at birth does not mean that the brain of the newborn infant is mature—far from it. The brain still needs to build its vast internal communication network, and it requires experience to accomplish this task. During the final stages of prenatal development, and especially during the first year or two after birth, lots of changes occur in the neural circuitry. More branches (dendrites) sprout off from the existing cells, and the number of connections, or synapses, greatly increases. There is even a kind of neural pruning process in which neurons that are not used simply die (Dawson & Fischer, 1994).

Again, the key principle at work is plasticity. The genetic code does not rigidly fix the internal circuitry of the brain; instead, a kind of rough wiring pattern is established during prenatal development, which is filled in during the important first few years of life (Kolb et al., 2003). Studies with animals have shown that the quality of early experience may be extremely important during this period. For example, rats raised in enriched environments (with lots of social contact and external stimulation) show significantly more complex and better functioning brain tissue than rats raised in sterile, barren environments (Greenough et al., 1987; Rosenzweig, 1984). Rats also show better recovery of function after brain injury if their recovery time is spent in an enriched environment (van Rijzingen et al., 1997).

From Crawling to Walking

Of course, parents don't see their baby's burgeoning neural circuitry—what they notice are the observable things, such as when the baby begins to sit up, crawl, stand alone, and walk. Before a baby can do these things, however, both the brain and the neuron-to-muscle links that radiate throughout the body need to develop adequately.

For example, the insulated coating of the axons (myelin sheath), which helps speed up neural transmission, must develop properly. Generally, the nervous system matures in a "down and out" fashion—that is, from the head down and from the center out (Shirley, 1933). Infants can lift their heads before they can roll over because the neuron-to-muscle connections in the upper part of the body mature before those in the lower part of the body. Babies crawl before they walk because they're able to control their arms efficiently before they're able to control their legs.

Psychologists don't like to tie developmental milestones directly to age—because not all children develop at the same rate—but most children learn to crawl, then stand alone, and walk at about the same time. Figure 1.2 shows the major stages of infant motor development. The sequence of development is generally stable, orderly, and predictable. Also, notice that each stage is associated with a range of ages, although the range is not large. Roughly 90% of all babies can roll over at 5 months of age, sit without support at 8 months, and then walk alone by 15 months. One baby might stand alone consistently at 9 months, whereas another might not accomplish the same feat until nearly 14 months of age; both fall within the normal range of development.

Think About It

Given that the environment plays such an important role in shaping brain development, what advice would you give new parents to maximize enriched development of their baby's intellectual capabilities?

Why Is My Baby Different? What accounts for the individual differences? It's hard to tell for any particular case, but both nature and nurture contribute. Each person has a genetic recipe that determines when he or she will develop physically, although environmental experiences can speed up or slow down the process (Schmuckler, 1996). Some cultures place great value on early motor development and nurture

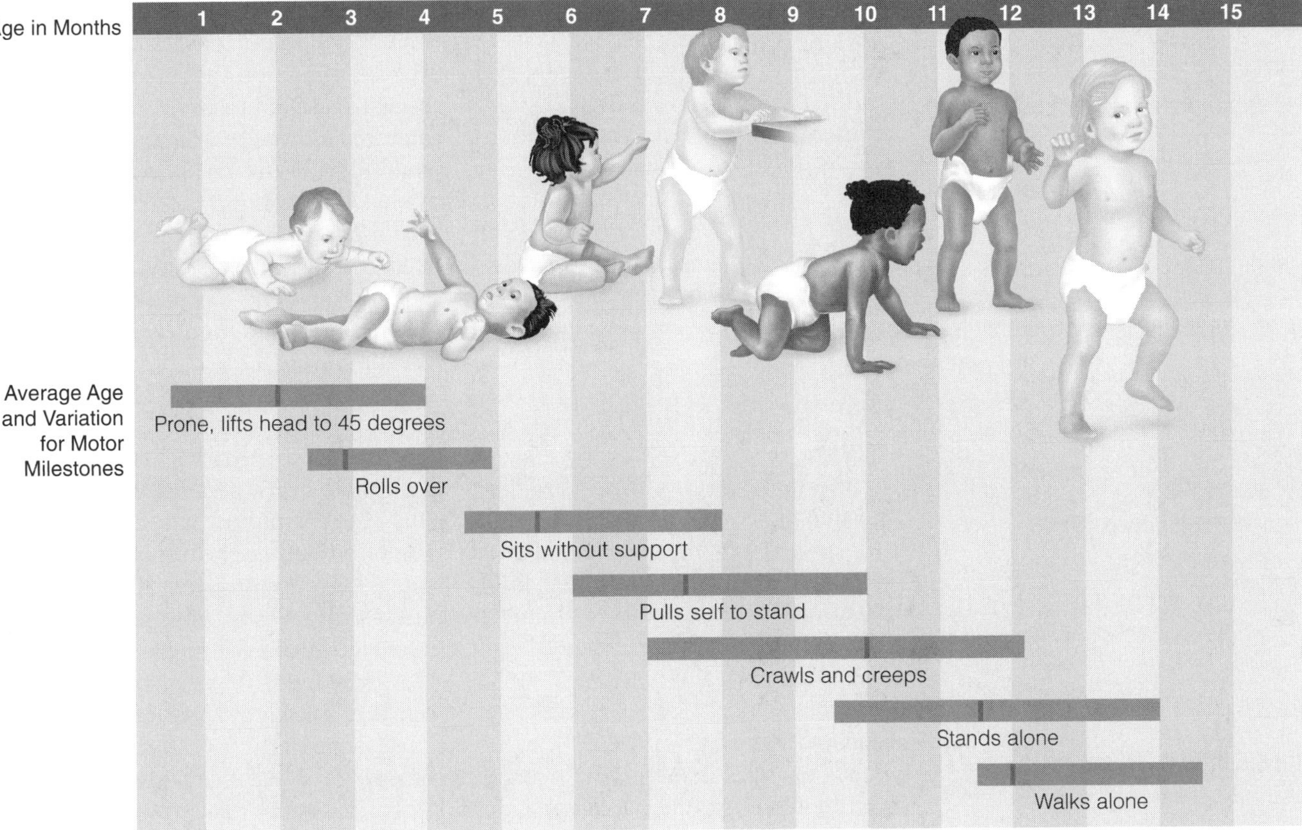

FIGURE 1.2

Major States of Motor Development. Although psychologists are reluctant to tie developmental milestones closely to age, most children learn to crawl, stand alone, and walk at about the same age.

such skills in children. If a baby is routinely exercised and handled during the early months of life, there is some evidence that he or she will progress through the landmark stages of motor development more quickly (Hopkins, 1991; Zelazo et al., 1972).

But these differences are usually small, and they play little, if any, role in determining final motor development. Hopi babies are traditionally swaddled and bound to cradleboards for much of the first year of life, yet these babies begin walking at roughly the same time as unbound babies (Dennis & Dennis, 1940). To learn to walk at a reasonable age, the baby simply needs to be given the opportunity to move around at some point—to "test the waters" and explore things on his or her own (Bertenthal et al., 1994). Hopi babies are bound to cradleboards for only their first 9 or 10 months; then they're given several months to explore their motor capabilities before they begin to walk (Shaffer, 2002).

Child-rearing practices reflect cultural differences. Hopi babies are traditionally swaddled and bound to cradleboards for much of the first year of life but show no developmental delays in walking.

From Toddlerhood to Adolescence

From the onset of toddlerhood through puberty, the growth rate continues, but at a less rapid pace. The average child grows several inches and puts on roughly 6 to 7 pounds annually. These are significant changes, but they're often hard for parents to detect because they represent only a small fraction of the child's current size (2 inches added to a 20-inch baby are far easier to spot than 2 inches added to someone who is 40 inches tall). More noticeable are the changes that occur in

© Bob Daemmrich/Stock Boston

Children reach the adolescent growth spurt at varying ages. Boys typically lag behind girls by as much as 2 years.

hand-to-eye coordination as the child matures. Three-year-olds lack the grace and coordination that are so obvious in 6-year-olds. The brain continues to mature, although again at a pace far slower than during prenatal development or during the first 2 years of life. General processing speed—how quickly we think and react to sudden changes in our environment—increases consistently throughout childhood (Kail, 1991; Kail & Salthouse, 1994).

Between the end of childhood and the beginning of young adulthood lies an important physical and psychological transition period called *adolescence*. Physically, the two most dramatic changes that occur during this time are the adolescent growth spurt and the onset of **puberty**, or sexual maturity (the word *puberty* is from the Latin for "to grow hairy"). Just like with crawling and walking, it's not possible to pinpoint the timing of these changes exactly, particularly for a specific individual, but changes usually start occurring for girls at around age 11 and for boys at about 13. Hormones released by the endocrine system rock us out of childhood by triggering a rapid increase in height and weight accompanied by the enlargement and maturation of internal and external sexual organs.

puberty
the period during which a person reaches sexual maturity and is potentially capable of producing offspring.

Maturing Sexually Puberty is the developmental period when we mature sexually and acquire the ability to reproduce. For the adolescent girl, high levels of *estrogen* in the body lead to external changes, such as breast development and broadening hips, and eventually to the beginning of *menarche* (the first menstrual flow) at around age 12 or 13. For boys, hormones called *androgens* lead to the appearance of facial hair, a lower voice, and the ability to ejaculate (release semen) at around age 13 or 14. Neither menarche nor the first ejaculation necessarily means that the adolescent is ready to reproduce—ovulation and sperm production may not occur until months later—but psychologically these "firsts" tend to be highly memorable and emotional events (Golub, 1992).

PhotoDisc

A strenuous daily exercise program may delay the onset of puberty.

The onset of puberty shows, yet again, the importance of both nature and nurture in development. Did you know that the average onset age for menarche has dropped from about 16 in the 1880s to the current 12 to 13? Physically, we're maturing earlier than in past generations, and it's not due to systematic changes in the genetic recipe. Instead, better nutrition, better living conditions, and improved medical care are responsible for the trend (Tanner, 1990). Even today, in parts of the world where living conditions are difficult, the average age of menarche is later than in industrialized countries such as the United States (Chumlea, 1982). Other factors, such as ethnicity and even family conflict, seem to matter as well (Romans et al., 2003). The environment does not cause sexual maturation—that's controlled by the genetic code—but the environment is clearly capable of accelerating or delaying the point when changes start to occur (Susman et al., 2003).

Becoming an Adult

The adolescent years are marked by dramatic changes in appearance and strength. Motor skills, including hand-to-eye coordination, improve to adult levels during the teenage years. As you know, there are world-class swimmers and tennis players who are barely into their teens. The brain reaches adult weight by about age 16, although the myelination of the neurons—so critical in early motor development—continues throughout the adolescent years (Benes, 1989; Benes et al., 1994). The continued development of the brain can also be seen in the gradual quickening of reaction times that occurs throughout adolescence (Kail, 1991).

When do we actually cross the threshold to adulthood? That's a tough question to answer because becoming an adult is, in some sense, a state of mind. There are differences in how the transition from adolescent to adult is defined across the world. Some cultures have specific rites of passage and others do not. Moreover, as you know, some adolescents are willing to accept the responsibilities of adulthood quite early and others are not (Eccles et al., 2003). Regardless, by the time we reach our 20s we're physically mature and at the height of our physical prowess.

The Aging Body Now for the downside. It's barely noticeable at first, but most of us begin slowly and steadily to decline physically, at least with respect to our peak levels of strength and agility, at some point during our 20s. The loss tends to be across the board, which means it applies to virtually all physical functions, from strength, to respiration rate, to the heart's pumping capacity (Whitbourne, 1985). Individual differences occur in the rate of decline, of course, depending on such factors as exercise, illness, and heredity. (I'm sure you can think of a 40-year-old who is in better physical shape than a 25-year-old.) But wrinkles, age spots, sagging flesh, and loss of muscle tone are all reliable and expected parts of the aging process.

By about age 50, the average woman begins **menopause**, the period when the menstrual cycle slows down and finally stops. Ovulation also stops, so women lose the ability to conceive children. These events are caused by hormonal changes, in particular by a decline in the level of female hormones in the body. Despite what you might have heard, menopause is not disruptive for all women, either physically or psychologically (McKinlay et al., 1992). The main physical symptoms, such as hot flashes, are not experienced by everyone, and the idea that women typically undergo a sustained period of depression or crankiness is simply a myth (Matthews, 1992). In fact, some women view menopause as a liberating experience, accompanied by an increased sense of sexual freedom (Lachman, 2004).

menopause
the period during which a woman's menstrual cycle slows down and finally stops.

The Aging Brain As we age, significant physical changes begin to occur in the brain as well. Some people suffer serious brain degeneration—the loss of brain cells—which leads to senility and, in some cases, to a disabling condition called Alzheimer's disease. The good news is that the majority of older people never experience these problems; fewer than 1% of people at age 65 are afflicted with **dementia**, the technical name for physically based loss in mental functioning. Although that percentage may rise to as much as 20% for individuals over age 80

dementia
physically based losses in mental functioning.

Think About It

How might you test the idea that mental activity or exercise helps to counteract the decline in mental skills that occurs with age? Can you make predictions based on choice of profession? Should people who choose intellectually challenging professions show less mental decline with age?

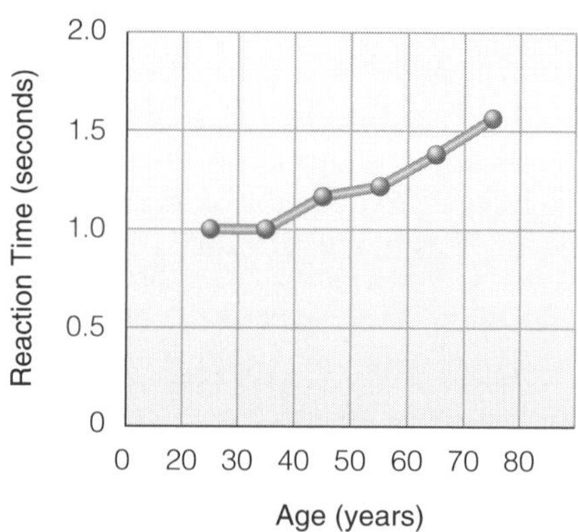

FIGURE 1.3

Age and Reaction Time. Average reaction time changes between ages 20 and 80, as demonstrated in a cognitive task requiring subjects to match numbers with symbols on a computer screen. Although reaction time gradually quickens from childhood through adolescence, it gradually slows after age 20. (Based on Salthouse, 1994)

(Cavanaugh & Blanchard-Fields, 2002), significant losses in mental functioning are still the exception rather than the rule. Everyone loses brain cells with age, and as you'll see later, declines also occur in certain kinds of memory, sensory ability, and reaction time (see Figure 1.3; Salthouse, 1994).

But the physical changes that occur in the aging brain are not all bad. Neurons are lost, and the loss may be permanent, but the remaining neurons sometimes increase in complexity. In a famous autopsy study by Buell and Coleman (1979), dendrites were significantly longer and more complex in samples of normal brain tissue taken from elderly adults when compared to those of middle-aged adults (see Figure 1.4). It appears that the brain may compensate for the losses it experiences by making better use of the structures that remain intact. Some researchers believe that sustained mental activity in later years helps promote neural growth, thereby counteracting some of the normal decline in mental skills and even reducing the risk of Alzheimer's disease (Wilson et al., 2002).

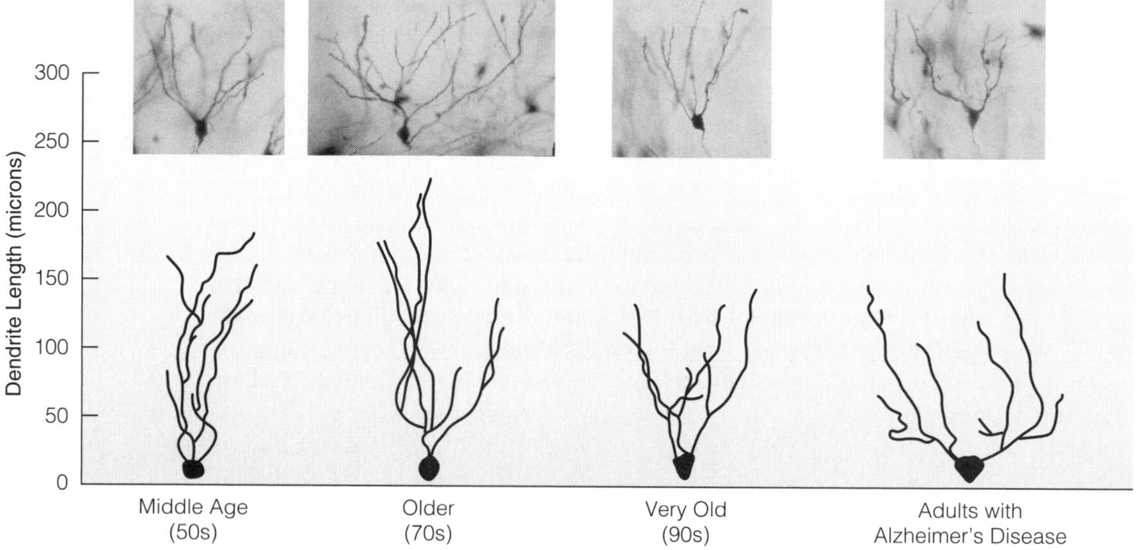

FIGURE 1.4

Aging Neurons. Notice that the dendrites of adult hippocampal neurons actually increase in length and complexity between 50 and 70, declining only in late old age or with Alzheimer's disease. (Photos courtesy Dr. Dorothy G. Flood/University of Rochester Medical Center)

DEVELOPING INTELLECTUALLY

As the brain changes physically in response to the environment, so too does mental functioning. Babies are not born seeing and thinking about the world as adults do (Flavell, 1999). Cognitive processes—how we think and perceive—develop over time. Like learning to walk, intellectual development depends on adequate physical development within the brain as well as on exposure to the right kinds of experiences. In this section, we'll consider three aspects of intellectual development: How do we learn to perceive and remember the world? How do thought processes change with age? How do we develop a sense of right and wrong?

The Tools of Investigation

What does the world look like to a newborn child? Is it a complex three-dimensional world, full of depth, color, and texture? Or is it a "blooming, buzzing confusion," as claimed by the early psychologist William James? Let's stop for a moment and think about how a psychologist might answer these questions. Detecting the perceptual capabilities of an infant is not a simple matter. Babies can't tell us what they see or hear.

Researchers who study development typically use two kinds of research design: *longitudinal* or *cross-sectional.* In a **longitudinal design**, you test the same person (or group of people) repeatedly over time, at various points in childhood or even through adulthood. If you wanted to study perceptual development, for instance, you would track the perceptual capabilities of baby Howard at various points in Howard's life. In a **cross-sectional design**, which is conducted over a more limited span of time, you assess the abilities of *different* people of different ages at the same time. So, rather than just testing Howard when he turns 2, 5, or 10, you would test groups of 2, 5, or 10-year-old children simultaneously. There are advantages and disadvantages associated with each research strategy.

longitudinal design
a research design in which the same people are studied or tested repeatedly over time.

cross-sectional design
a research design in which people of different ages are compared at the same time.

If you're interested in studying infants or small children, though, you face additional problems. Because infants don't communicate as adults do, the analysis of perceptual development (or any other intellectual capacity) requires some creative research methods. It's necessary to devise a way to infer perceptual capabilities from what are essentially immobile, largely uncommunicative infants. Fortunately, babies possess several characteristics that make the job a little easier: (1) they show *preferences,* which means they prefer some stimuli over others; (2) they notice *novelty,* which means they notice new or different things in their environment; and (3) they can *learn* to repeat activities that produce some kind of reward. As you'll see shortly, researchers have developed techniques that capitalize on each of these tendencies.

The Preference Technique In the "preference technique" developed by Robert Fantz (1961), an infant is presented with two visual displays simultaneously, and the investigator simply records how long the infant looks at each (see Figure 1.5).

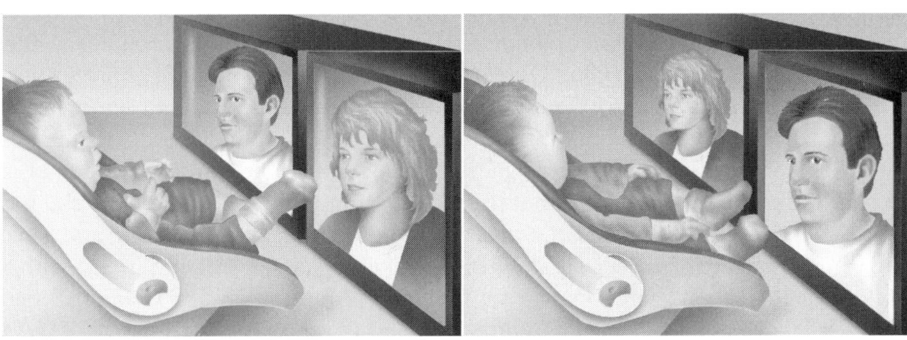

FIGURE 1.5
The Preference Technique. Babies prefer some visual stimuli over others. In this case, the infant demonstrates a preference for a female face by tracking its location across trials. (The preference can be determined by simply recording how long the baby looks at each face.)

Suppose one of the displays shows a male face and the other a female face, and the baby looks at the female face for a significantly longer period of time. By "choosing" to look longer at the female face, the infant has shown a preference. By itself, this preference indicates very little. To infer things about what the baby can really see, it's necessary to present the same two displays a number of times, switching their relative positions from trial to trial. If the baby continues to look longer at the female face even though it appears on the left on some trials and on the right on others, we can infer that the baby has the visual capability to differentiate between the two displays. The infant "tells" us that he or she can detect differences by exclusively tracking the female face. Notice that we didn't need to ask the baby anything—we simply inferred things about his or her visual system by measuring overt behavior.

Habituation Techniques One of the preferences babies consistently show is for novelty—they like to look at new things. But they tend to ignore events that occur repeatedly without consequence. For instance, if you show newborns a blue-colored card and track how their eyes move (or how their heart rate changes), you'll find that they spend a lot of time looking at the card when it first appears—it's something new. But if you present the same card over and over again, their interest wanes, and they'll begin to look at something else. This decline in responsiveness to repeated stimulation, called **habituation**, provides an effective tool for mapping out the infant's perceptual world (Bornstein, 1992; Colombo et al., 1997; Flavell et al., 1993). By acting bored, which is defined operationally by how long they look at the card, babies reveal that they remember the stimulus from its previous presentation and recognize that it hasn't changed. It's as if the baby is saying, "Oh, it's that blue card again."

habituation
the decline in responsiveness to a stimulus that is repeatedly presented.

Habituation can be used to discover specific information about how babies perceive and remember their world (DeSaint et al., 1997; Granrud, 1993). For example, suppose we wanted to discover whether newborns have the capacity to see color. We could show the blue card for a while, then suddenly switch to a green card that matches on all other visual dimensions (such as size and brightness). If the infant shows renewed interest in the card—treating the stimulus as if it was novel—we can infer that the baby can discriminate, or tell the difference, between blue and green. If, on the other hand, the baby continues to ignore the new green card, it suggests that perhaps the baby lacks color vision at this stage in development (although there may be other interpretations). We can also study memory by varying the time that elapses between presentations of the card. If the baby continues to act bored by the blue card even though we insert long pauses between successive presentations, we know that he or she is remembering the card over those particular time intervals.

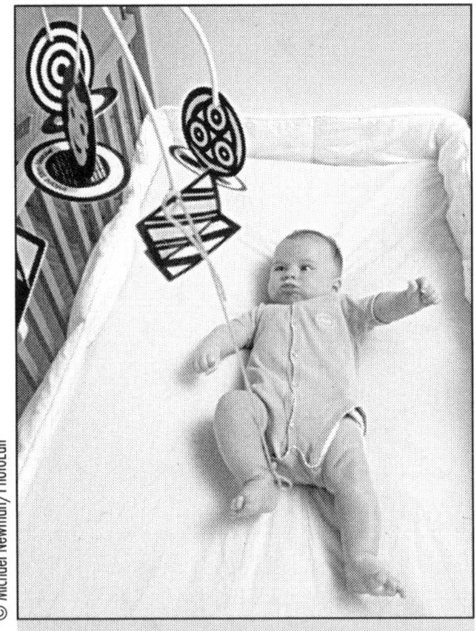

Researcher Carolyn Rovee-Collier showed that infants can learn to kick their legs to get an overhead mobile moving.

Using Rewards It's also possible to gain insight into what a baby sees, knows, and remembers by *rewarding* a simple motor movement, such as kicking a leg or sucking on an artificial nipple, in the presence of particular kinds of events (Siqueland & DeLucia, 1969). For example, in research by Carolyn Rovee-Collier (1993), 2- and 3-month-old infants were taught that kicking their legs could produce movement of a mobile hanging overhead. A moving mobile is quite rewarding to babies at this age, and they'll double or triple their rate of leg kicking in a matter of minutes if it leads to movement. We can then study cognitive abilities—such as memory—by taking the mobile away, waiting for some period of time, and then replacing the mobile. If the baby begins leg kicking again at rates comparable to those produced at the end of training, we can infer that the baby has remembered what he or she has learned. We can also change the characteristics of the mobile after training and learn things about a baby's perceptual abilities. For example, if we train an infant with a blue mobile and then switch to a green one, any differences in leg kicking should help to tell us whether the baby can discriminate between green and blue.

CONCEPT SUMMARY

Research Designs for Studying Development

TYPE OF DESIGN	OVERVIEW	ADVANTAGES AND DISADVANTAGES
Cross-sectional	Researchers compare performance of *different* people of different ages	**A:** Faster, more practical than longitudinal. **D:** Other variables may be *confounded* with age.
Longitudinal	Researchers test the *same* individuals repeatedly over time.	**A:** Can examine changes in *individuals*. **D:** Cost-intensive; subject loss over time.

The Growing Perceptual World

Using such techniques, researchers have discovered that babies greet the world with reasonably well-functioning sensory systems. Although none is operating at peak efficiency, because the biological equipment is still maturing, babies still see a world of color and shape (Banks & Shannon, 1993). They even arrive with built-in preferences. One-day-old babies, for example, respond more to patterned stimuli than to unpatterned ones. As shown in Figure 1.6 on the next page, they also prefer to look at correctly drawn faces rather than scrambled facial features (Johnson et al., 1991; see also Walton & Bower, 1993). It's likely that learning plays a role in some of these preferences (Turati, 2004), but reasonably sophisticated perceptual processing occurs soon after birth.

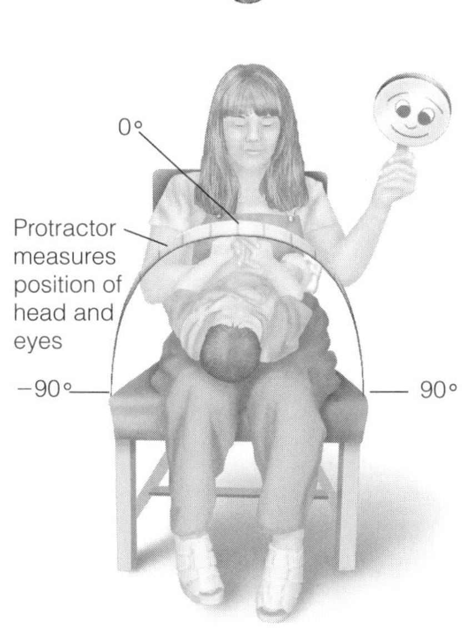

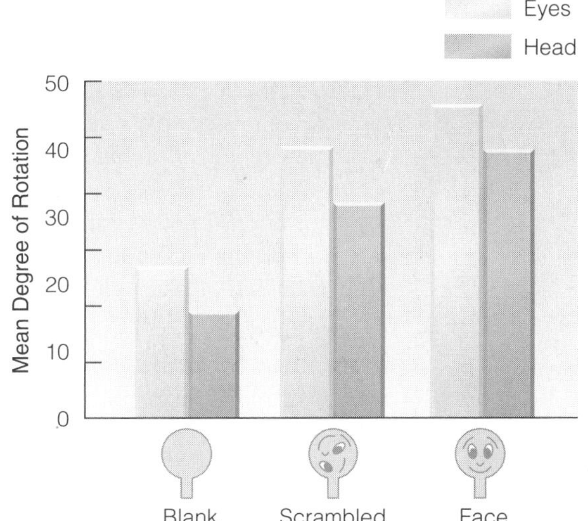

FIGURE 1.6

Infant Preferences. In this experiment, babies were shown either a blank stimulus, a stimulus with scrambled facial features, or a face. Each stimulus was first positioned over the baby's head and then moved from side to side. The dependent variable measured the extent to which the baby tracked each stimulus by head turning. As the results show, the babies tracked the face stimulus more than the others. (Graph adapted from Johnson et al., 1991)

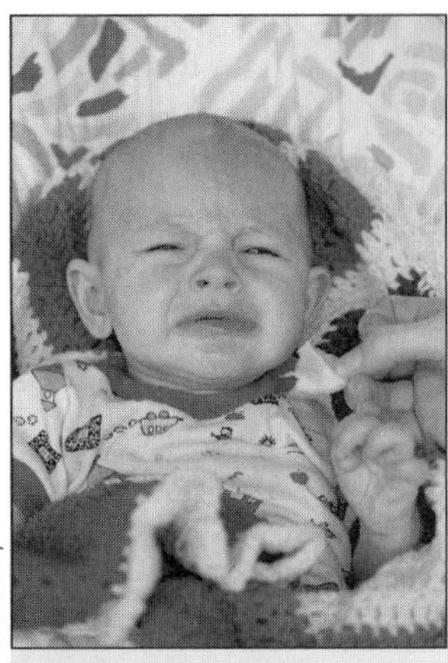

© John Livzey

This baby is a few months old, but even newborn infants show distinctive reactions to a variety of tastes (lemon, sugar, and salt are shown here).

Newborns also hear reasonably well, and they seem to recognize their mothers' voice within a day or two (DeCasper & Fifer, 1980). Remarkably, there is even evidence to suggest that newborns can hear and remember things that happen *prior* to birth. By the 28th week, fetuses will close their eyes in response to loud noises presented near the mother's abdomen (Parmelee & Sigman, 1983). Infants will also choose to suck on an artificial nipple that produces a recording of a story that was read aloud to them repeatedly before birth. It's unlikely that the baby is actually remembering the story—but it does indicate that babies are sensitive to particular experiences that happen in the womb (DeCasper & Spence, 1986). If you think about it, you'll realize this is an adaptive quality for the newborn. Remember, babies need nourishment and are dependent on others for survival. Consequently, those born into the world with a visual system that can detect shapes and forms and an auditory system tuned to the human voice have a better chance of survival.

In addition to sights and sounds, babies are quite sensitive to touch, smell, pain, and taste. Place a drop of lemon juice in the mouth of a newborn, and you'll see a distinctive grimace. Place a small amount of sugar in the baby's mouth, and the baby will smack his or her lips. These distinctive reactions are present at birth and are found even before the infant has had a single taste of food (Steiner, 1977). A baby's sense of smell is developed well enough that the newborn quickly learns to recognize the odor of its mother's breast (Porter et al., 1992). As for pain and touch, babies will reject a milk bottle that is too hot, and, as every parent knows, the right kind of pat on the baby's back is pleasurable enough to soothe the newborn into sleep.

© Enrico Ferorelli

In the visual cliff apparatus, a plate of glass covers an abrupt drop-off. From the age of approximately 6 months, babies are reluctant to cross the cliff to reach a beckoning parent.

Babies even seem to perceive a three-dimensional world. When placed on a visual cliff, such as the one shown in the photo, 6-month-old babies are reluctant to cross over the apparent drop-off, or cliff, to reach a parent (Gibson & Walk, 1960). Babies as young as 2 months show heart rate changes when they're placed on the glass portion covering the deep side of the visual cliff (Campos et al., 1970).

Still, these are infant perceptions, and the infant's world is not the same as that of an adult. Newborn babies cannot see as well as adults. They're not very good at discriminating fine detail in visual patterns: Compared with the ideal acuity level of 20/20, babies see a blurry world that is more on the order of 20/400, meaning that what newborns see at 20 feet is what adults with ideal vision see at 400 feet. In addition, newborns probably can't perceive shapes and forms in the same way adults do (Bornstein, 1992; Johnson, 1997), nor can they hear as well as adults. For example, infants seem to have some trouble listening selectively for certain kinds of sounds, and they require sounds to be louder than adults do before those sounds can be detected (Bargones & Werner, 1994).

Infants' perceptual systems improve markedly during the first few months, partly because of continued physical development but also because experience fine-tunes their sensory abilities. Research with nonhuman subjects, such as cats or chimpanzees, has shown that if animals are deprived of visual stimulation during the early weeks or months of life, permanent visual impairments can result (Gandelman, 1992). Thus perceptual development relies on experience as well as on physically mature sensory equipment.

By the time we leave infancy, our perceptual systems are reasonably intact. Most of the changes that occur during childhood and adolescence affect our ability to *use* the equipment we have. For example, as children grow older, their attention span improves, and they're better able to attend selectively to pertinent information. Memory improves throughout childhood, partly because kids learn strategies for organizing and maintaining information in memory (Courage & Howe, 2004). We use our general knowledge about people and events to help us interpret ambiguous stimuli and to remember things that happen in our lives. Perception and memory are influenced by the knowledge gained from experience, which is one of the reasons perceptual development is really a lifelong process.

Do We Lose Memory With Age?

By the time people hit their 40s or 50s, the odds are pretty good they'll start complaining about memory problems—maybe they'll have trouble coming up with the right word, or the name of someone they've recently met. These are normal trends, nothing to worry about, but overall, there isn't any simple or straightforward relationship between aging and memory. Some kinds of memory falter badly with age, but others do not.

For example, psychologists are now reasonably convinced that the ability to *recall* recent events, such as items from a grocery list, declines regularly with age. However, in other tests, such as *recognition,* where information is re-presented and the task is to tell whether it's been seen or heard before, little or no age differences might be found. So your 50-year-old Dad might fail to recall your best friend's name (it's on the tip of his tongue), but he'll easily recognize the name when he hears it. Age-related deficits are also restricted primarily to tasks that require conscious memory. If memory is tested in ways that don't require conscious awareness (such as testing whether your ability to solve a puzzle increases if you've seen it before), age-related differences largely disappear (see Balota et al., 2000).

Let's consider a specific example to illustrate how research in this area is typically done. Craik and McDowd (1987) used a cross-sectional design to compare recall and recognition performance for two age groups: a "young" group of college students, with an average age of 20.7 years; and an "old" group, volunteers from a senior citizen center, with an average age of 72.8 years. All of the participants were asked to learn memory lists that consisted of short phrases ("a body of water") presented together with associated target words ("pond"). The lists were followed by either (1) an immediate recall test in which the short phrase was given and the subject was to recall the target word or (2) a delayed recognition test that required the subjects to decide whether a word had or had not been presented in one of the earlier lists.

In such experiments, attempts are made to match the participants on as many variables as possible—such as educational level and verbal ability—so that the only difference between the groups is age. Any performance differences can then be attributed uniquely to the independent variable (age) and not to some other confounding factor. The results of the Craik and McDowd (1987) study are shown in Figure 1.7. As you can see, the younger group outperformed the older group on the test of recall, but the advantage vanished on the recognition test. So memory losses in the elderly depend importantly on how memory is actually tested.

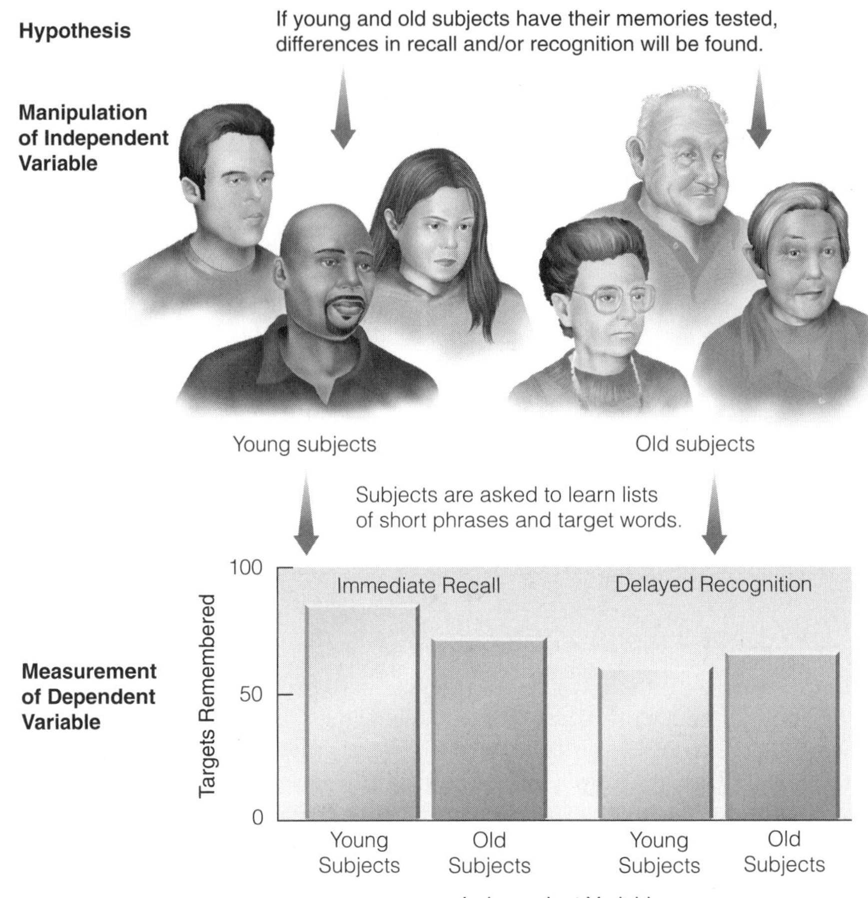

FIGURE 1.7

Memory and Aging. A group with an average age of 20.7 years and a group with an average age of 72.8 years were asked to learn and then recall or recognize target words. Although the younger subjects recalled more targets than the older subjects, the advantage disappeared for recognition. (Craik & McDowd, 1987)

Jean Piaget

Other studies have shown that performance also depends on the types of materials tested. When older individuals are asked to remember materials that fit naturally into their personal areas of expertise, they often perform better than their younger counterparts (Zacks & Hasher, 1994). Age-related memory problems can also be reduced, to a certain extent, if the elderly are given more time to study material and supportive cues are given at the time memory is required.

Researchers are actively trying to determine why age-related memory deficits occur (see Anderson & Craik, 2000). One possibility is that older adults lose the ability to suppress irrelevant thoughts or ignore irrelevant stimuli (Hasher et al., 1991). Because they're unable to focus selectively on the task at hand, they fail to process the to-be-remembered information in ways that help later recall (Craik, 1994). Memory depends greatly on the kinds of mental processing that occur during study. There's also some evidence that prior beliefs, or stereotypes, such as the belief that memory should decline with age, may influence memory performance in the aged. For example, there are generally fewer negative stereotypes about aging in mainland China, and Chinese residents tend to show smaller age-related memory differences than do residents of the United States (see Levy & Langer, 1994).

Piaget and the Development of Thought

Much of what we know about how thought develops during childhood comes from the collective works of a Swiss scholar named Jean Piaget (1896–1980). It was Piaget who first convinced psychologists that children think quite differently from adults. Children are not little adults, he argued, who simply lack knowledge and experience; instead, they view the world in a very unique way. Piaget believed that everyone is born with a natural tendency to organize the world meaningfully. People construct mental models of the world—called **schemata**—and use these schemata to guide and interpret their experiences. But these schemata are not very adult-like early in development—in fact, they tend not to reflect the world accurately—so much of early intellectual development is spent changing and fine-tuning our world-views. One of Piaget's primary contributions was to demonstrate that children's reasoning errors can provide a window into how the schema construction process is proceeding.

schemata
mental models of the world that we use to guide and interpret our experiences.

For example, consider the two tilted cups shown in the margin. If young children are asked to draw a line indicating how the water level in a tilted cup might look, they tend to draw a line that's parallel to the top and bottom of the cup, as shown in the cup on the left, rather than parallel to the ground, as shown in the cup on the right. This kind of error is important, Piaget argued, because children can't have learned such a thing directly from experience (water never tilts that way in real life). Instead, the error reflects a fundamental misconception of how the world is structured. Young children have an inaccurate internal view, or model, of the world.

Assimilation and Accommodation As their brains and bodies mature, children are able to use experience to build more sophisticated and correct mental models of the world. Piaget suggested that cognitive development is guided by two adaptive psychological processes: *assimilation* and *accommodation*. **Assimilation** is the process through which we fit—or assimilate—new experiences into our existing schemata. For example, suppose a small child who has been raised in a household full of cats mistakenly concludes that the neighbor's new rabbit is simply a kind of kitty. The new experience—the rabbit—has been assimilated into the child's existing view of the world: Small furry things are cats. The second function, **accommodation**, is the process through which we change or modify existing schemata to accommodate new experiences. When the child learns that the new "kitty" hops rather than walks and seems reluctant to purr, he or she will need to modify and revise the existing concept of small furry things; the child is forced to change the existing schemata to accommodate the new information. Notice that the child plays an active role in constructing schemata by interacting directly with the world (Piaget, 1929).

assimilation
the process through which we fit—or assimilate—new experiences into existing schemata.

accommodation
the process through which we change or modify existing schemata to accommodate new experiences.

Piaget believed that children develop an adult world-view by moving systematically through a series of four stages or developmental periods: *sensorimotor, preoperational, concrete operational,* and *formal operational.* Each of these periods is tied roughly to a particular age range—for example, the preoperational period usually lasts from age 2 to about age 7—but individual differences can occur in how quickly the child moves from one stage to the next. Although the timing may vary from child to child, Piaget believed that the *order* in which individuals progress through the stages is invariant—it remains the same for everyone. Let's consider these cognitive developmental periods in more detail.

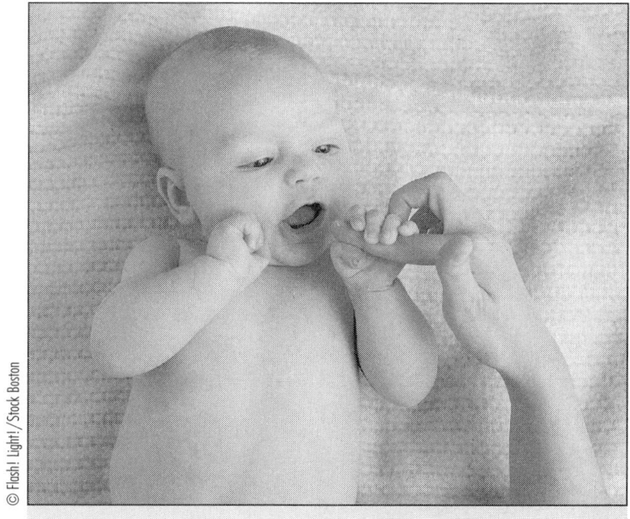

The rooting reflex is adaptive because it helps the newborn receive needed sustenance.

The Sensorimotor Period: Birth to Two Years

sensorimotor period
Piaget's first stage of cognitive development, lasting from birth to about 2 years of age; schemata revolve around sensory and motor abilities.

From birth to about age 2, schemata about the world revolve primarily around the infant's sensory and motor abilities (hence the name **sensorimotor period**). Babies initially interact with the world through a collection of survival reflexes. For example, they'll start sucking when an object is placed in their mouth (called the *sucking reflex*), and they'll automatically turn their head in the direction of a touch or brush on the cheek (called the *rooting reflex*). This behavior is different from an adult's, but it's adaptive for a newborn. These reflexes increase the likelihood that adequate nourishment will follow, and attaining adequate nourishment is a significant problem the newborn needs to solve.

object permanence
the ability to recognize that objects still exist when they're no longer in sight.

Object Permanence As infants develop intellectually over the first year, they use their maturing motor skills to understand how they can interact with the world voluntarily. Babies start to vocalize to gain attention; they learn they can kick their legs to make sounds; they acquire the ability to reach with their arms to touch or grasp objects. The initial stirrings of symbolic thought also begin during the sensorimotor period. The infant gradually develops the ability to construct internal mental images or symbols. Early in the first year, for example, babies lack **object permanence**, which means they fail to recognize that objects exist when they're no longer in sight. The photos below illustrate how psychologists have measured object permanence. Notice that the baby loses interest when the toy is covered, suggesting that the baby is only capable of thinking about objects that are directly in view. Babies at this point are unable to represent objects symbolically—out of sight equals out of mind. But by the end of the first year, Piaget argued, the child has a different reaction to the disappearance of a favored toy; as object permanence develops, the child will begin to search actively for the lost toy.

The Preoperational Period: Two to Seven Years

preoperational period
Piaget's second stage of cognitive development, lasting from ages 2 to about 7; children begin to think symbolically but often lack the ability to perform mental operations such as conservation.

From about ages 2 through 7, the child's schemata continue to grow in sophistication. Children in the **preoperational period** no longer have difficulty thinking about absent objects, and they can use one object to stand for another. A 4-year-old, for example, can effortlessly use a stick to represent a soaring airplane or a cardboard box for a stove. The child realizes these are not the real objects, but he or she can imagine them to be real for the purposes of play. At the same time, as Piaget demonstrated in a number of clever ways, the child still thinks about the

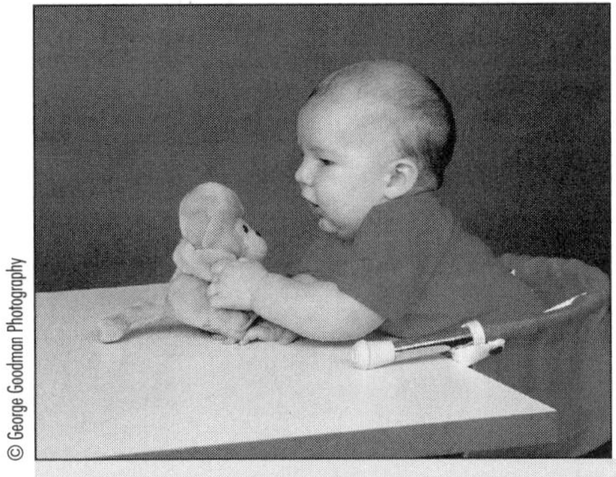

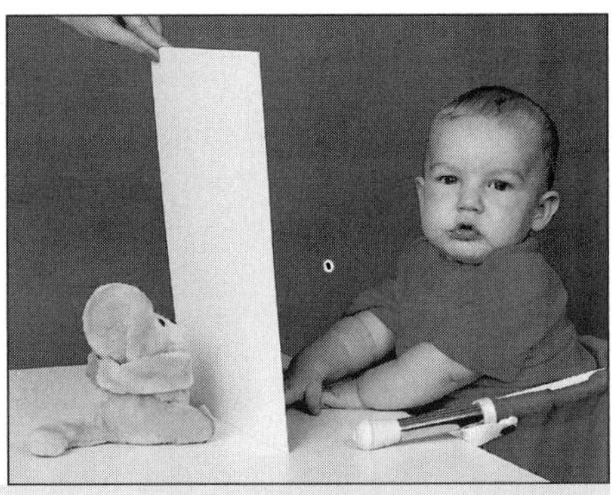

According to Piaget, babies who haven't yet mastered the concept of object permanence don't understand that objects still exist when they're no longer in view. Notice how this boy loses interest when he can no longer see his favorite toy.

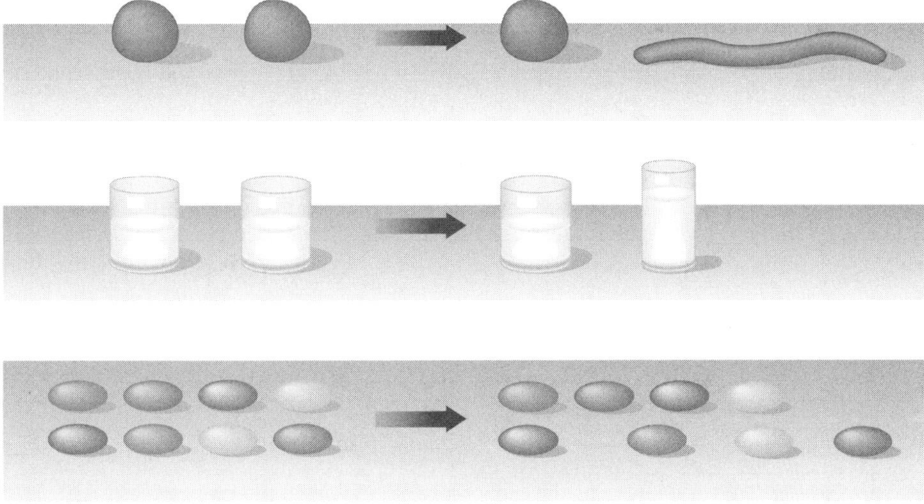

FIGURE 1.8

Examples of Conservation Problems. Understanding conservation means recognizing that the physical properties of objects remain the same even though the objects may superficially change in appearance. Preoperational children often fail conservation problems—they fail to detect, for example, that the objects to the right of the arrows still retain the same volume or number.

world quite differently from an adult. As you'll see momentarily, the child lacks the ability to perform certain basic mental operations—hence Piaget's use of the term *preoperational* to describe a child's mental abilities during this period.

Conservation Something that children at the preoperational stage often fail to understand is the **principle of conservation**. To understand conservation, one needs to be able to recognize that certain physical properties of an object remain the same despite superficial changes in its appearance (see Figure 1.8). If 4- or 5-year-old children are shown two playdough balls of exactly the same size and are asked which object contains more playdough, most of the children will say that the two balls contain the same amount. But if one of the balls is then rolled into a long sausage-like shape, the children are likely to think that the two quantities of playdough are no longer the same, saying that either the sausage or the ball has more playdough.

principle of conservation
the ability to recognize that the physical properties of an object remain the same despite superficial changes in the object's appearance.

Children at this age are unable to understand that a basic property of an object, in this case its mass, doesn't change as the object changes shape. Typically, preoperational children will fail to conserve a basic quantity even if they directly observe the change in appearance taking place. Suppose we ask 5-year-old Sam to pour a cup of water into each of two identical glasses. Sam performs the task and accepts that the two glasses now contain the same amount. We then instruct him to pour the water from one of the glasses into another glass that is tall and thin. Do the glasses now contain the same amount of water? "No," Sam explains, "now the tall one has more water." Sam is not showing any evidence of conservation; he does not yet recognize that how the water looks in the glass has no effect on its volume.

The reason children in the preoperational period make these kinds of errors, Piaget argued, is that they lack the capacity to think in truly adult-like ways. For example, preoperational children suffer from *centration*—they tend to focus their attention on one particular aspect of a situation and to ignore others. Sam is convinced that the tall glass has more water because he cannot simultaneously consider both the height and width of the glass; he focuses only on the height and therefore is convinced that the taller glass must contain more water. In addition, children at this age have difficulty understanding the concept of *reversibility*—that one kind of operation can produce change and that another kind of operation can undo that change. For example, Sam is unlikely to consider what will happen if the water from the tall glass is poured back into the original glass. The capacity to understand that operations are reversible doesn't develop until the next stage.

Piaget also discovered that children in the preoperational period tend to see the world, and the objects in it, from primarily one perspective: their own. Children at this stage have a tough time imagining themselves in another person's position. If you ask a child in the preoperational period to describe what another person will see or think, you're likely to find the child simply describing what he or she personally sees or thinks. Piaget called this characteristic **egocentrism**—the tendency to view the world from your own unique perspective only.

egocentrism
the tendency to see the world from one's own unique perspective only; a characteristic of thinking in the preoperational period of development.

The Concrete Operational Period: Seven to Eleven Years

concrete operational period
Piaget's third stage of cognitive development, lasting from ages 7 to 11. Children acquire the capacity to perform a number of mental operations but still lack the ability for abstract reasoning.

Between the ages of 7 and about 11, children enter the **concrete operational period** and acquire true mental *operations.* By mental operations, Piaget meant the ability to perform mental actions on objects—to verbalize, visualize, and mentally manipulate objects. A child of 8 can consider the consequences of rolling a long strip of playdough into a ball before the action is actually performed. Children in the concrete operational period have fewer difficulties with conservation problems because they are capable of reversing operations on objects—they can mentally consider the effects of both doing and undoing an action.

Children at the concrete operational stage also show the initial stirrings of logical thought, which means they can now mentally order and compare objects and perform more sophisticated classifications. These children can do simple math and solve problems that require elementary reasoning. Consider the following

CONCEPT SUMMARY

Piaget's Stages of Cognitive Development

STAGE	BASIC CHARACTERISTICS	ACCOMPLISHMENTS	LIMITATIONS
Sensorimotor period (birth–2 years)	Schemata about the world revolve primarily around sensory and motor abilities.	Child develops **object permanence;** learns how to control body; learns how to vocalize, and learns first words.	Schemata are limited primarily to simple sensory and motor function; problems in thinking about absent objects (early).
Preoperational period (2–7 years)	Schemata grow in sophistication. Children can think about absent objects, and can use one object to stand for another.	Children readily symbolize objects, and imaginary play is common; great strides in language development.	Children are pre-logical; they fail to understand **conservation,** due to **centration** and a failure to understand **reversibility;** children show **egocentricity** in thinking.
Concrete operational period (7–11 years)	Children gain the capacity for *true* mental operations, i.e., verbalizing, visualizing, mental manipulation.	Understand reversibility and other simple logical operations like categorizing and ordering.	Mental operations remain *concrete,* tied to actual objects in the real world. Difficulty with problems that do not flow from everyday experience.
Formal operational period (11 years–adulthood)	Mastery is gained over *abstract* thinking.	Adolescents can think and answer questions in general and abstract ways.	No limitations; development of reasoning is complete. However, not all reach this stage.

example: Martin is faster than Jose; Jose is faster than Conrad. Is Martin faster or slower than Conrad? Children of 9 or 10 have little trouble with this problem because they can keep track of ordered relations in their heads. Younger preoperational children will probably insist on actually seeing Martin and Conrad race—they can't easily solve the problem in their heads.

Although concrete operational children possess a growing array of mental operations, Piaget believed they are still limited intellectually in an important way. The mental operations they can perform remain *concrete,* or tied directly to actual objects in the real world. Children at this age have great difficulty with problems that do not flow directly from everyday experience. Ask an 8-year-old to solve a problem involving four-armed people and barking cats and you're likely to see a blank look on his or her face. Basically, if something can't be seen, heard, touched, tasted, or smelled, it's going to be tough for these children to think about (although they can imagine non-real-world objects they have encountered, for example, in cartoons or fairy tales). The ability to think truly abstractly doesn't develop until the final stage of cognitive development.

© David Young-Wolff/PhotoEdit

Most children reach the formal operational period by their teenage years, when they master abstract thinking.

The Formal Operational Period: Eleven to Adulthood

By the time children reach their teenage years, most will be in the formal operational period, during which thought processes become increasingly more like those of an adult. Neither teenagers nor adults have problems thinking about imaginary or artificial concepts; they can consider hypothetical outcomes, or make logical deductions about places they've never visited or that might not even exist. Teenagers can develop systematic strategies for solving problems—such as using trial and error—that are beyond the capability of most preteens.

The **formal operational period** is the stage at which we start to gain mastery over *abstract* thinking. Ask a concrete operational child about the meaning of education, and you'll be likely to hear about teachers and grades. The formal operational adolescent is able to answer the question in a general and abstract way, perhaps describing education as a system organized by parents and the government to foster the acquisition of useful knowledge. Piaget believed that the transition from concrete operational thinking to formal operational thinking probably occurs gradually, over several years, and may not be achieved by everyone (Piaget, 1970). Once reached, the adolescent is no longer tied to concrete, real-world constructs and can invent and experiment with the possible rather than just with the here and now.

formal operational period
Piaget's last stage of cognitive development; thought processes become adult-like, and people gain mastery over abstract thinking.

Challenges to Piaget's Theory

Piaget's contributions to our understanding of cognitive development were substantial. He successfully convinced the psychological community that children have unique internal schemata, and he provided convincing demonstrations that those schemata, once formed, tend to change systematically over time. However, not all of Piaget's ideas have withstood the rigors of experimental scrutiny. Researchers now commonly challenge the specifics of his theory, primarily his assumptions about what children really know and when they know it (Feldman, 2003).

It turns out that children and young infants are considerably more sophisticated in their models of the world than Piaget believed. For example, Piaget was convinced that object permanence doesn't develop until late in the child's first

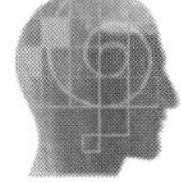

Think About It

Do you think Piaget's insights about cognitive development have any implications for education? For example, should teachers be giving first- and second-grade children abstract math problems to solve?

year. Although it's true that children will not search for a hidden toy in the first few months of life, more sensitive tests have revealed that even 1- to 4-month-old infants are capable of recognizing that vanished objects still exist (Baillargeon, 2004).

In research by child psychologist T. G. R. Bower (1982), very young infants watched as a screen was moved in front of a toy, blocking it from view (see Figure 1.9). Moments later, when the screen was removed, the infants acted surprised if the toy was absent (it could be secretly removed by the experimenter). If objects no longer exist when removed from view, then infants shouldn't be surprised by a sudden absence (see also Baillargeon, 1994; Hofstadter & Reznick, 1996). Other researchers have demonstrated that small infants can show symbolic thought—they understand, for instance, that objects move along continuous paths and do not jump around—and they gain this understanding at points in development far earlier than Piaget imagined (see Mandler, 1992; Spelke et al., 1992).

Piaget has also been criticized for sticking to the notion of distinct stages, or periods of development (Flavell et al., 1993). Piaget recognized that not all children develop at the same rate, but he remained convinced that a child's thought processes undergo sharp transitions from one stage to the next. Most developmental psychologists now believe that cognitive development is better viewed as a process of continual change and adaptation (Siegler, 1996). According to the stage view, once a child undergoes a stage transition—say, from the preoperational to the concrete operational—he or she should be able to perform a variety of new tasks relatively quickly. But this is not usually the case.

Children's thought processes do not seem to undergo rapid transitions; in fact, they often change slowly over long periods of time (Flavell, 1971). For example, it's not uncommon to find a 5-year-old who understands conservation of number but has no idea about conservation of mass or volume. A given child might show

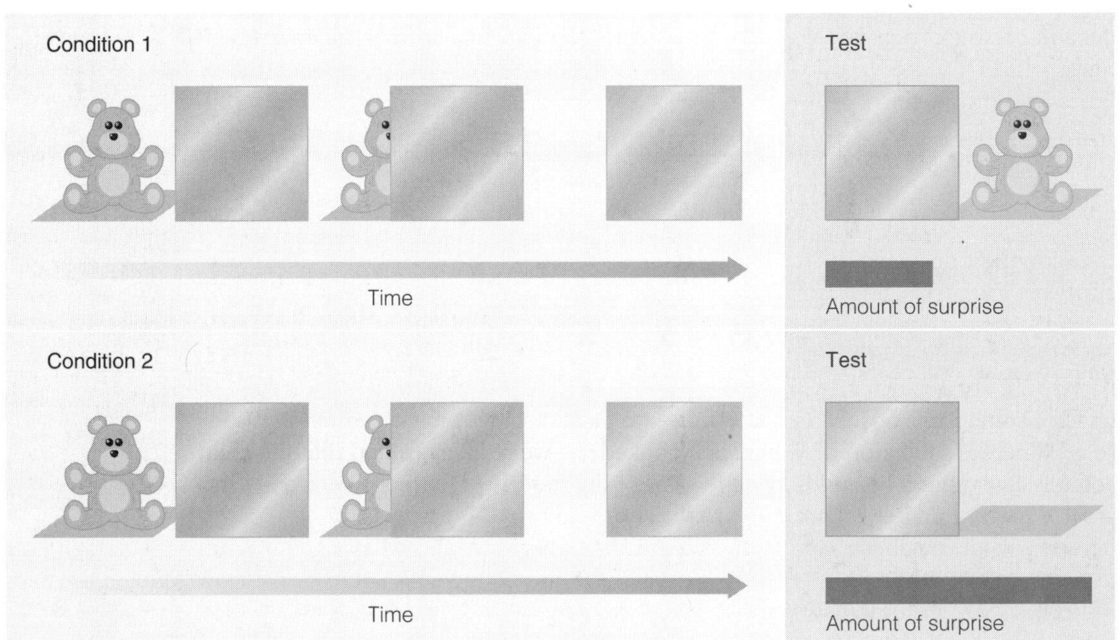

FIGURE 1.9

Reevaluating Object Permanence. In this experiment a screen was moved in front of a toy, blocking it from the infant's view. Moments later, when the screen was removed, the baby's level of surprise (defined as a change in heart rate) was measured. In one condition the toy appeared behind the screen; in a second condition it had vanished. Babies showed more surprise when the toy was absent, suggesting that object permanence may develop earlier than Piaget suspected. (Bower, 1982) mental schemata that are characteristic of more than one stage. Children are learning to adapt to their world, to tasks and problems that might occur only in particular situations, so it's not surprising that they don't always fit into a specific cognitive stage, or that the transitions from one developmental point to the next are not rapid and well-defined (Munakata et al., 1997).

The Role of Culture Piaget was rather fuzzy about the mechanisms that produce cognitive change. He recognized that infants, toddlers, and school-age children think in fundamentally different ways, but he never clearly accounted for the psychological processes that produce those changes (Siegler, 1994, 1996). He also largely ignored the importance of social context in explaining individual differences in cognitive ability. Cross-cultural research has shown that children across the world develop cognitively in similar ways, but significant cultural differences occur in the rate of development (Matsumoto, 1994). For example, children raised in nomadic societies, which move frequently from place to place, seem to acquire spatial skills (the ability to orient themselves in their environment) earlier than children raised in single, fixed locales. Schooling may also be a factor: Ample cross-cultural evidence indicates that people who never attend school may have a difficult time reaching the formal operational stage of thinking, at least as measured through traditional Piagetian tasks (Cole, 1992; Segall et al., 1990).

© Brian A. Vikander/CORBIS

Children in nomadic societies, who move from one place to another often, may be able to orient themselves in an environment faster and more efficiently than children raised in fixed locales.

The importance of social and cultural influences was promoted by a Russian psychologist, Lev Vygotsky, around the same time that Piaget was developing his theoretical ideas. Vygotsky died in 1934, after only a decade of work in psychology, but his ideas remain very influential (Mistry & Saraswathi, 2003). Vygotsky argued that cognitive abilities emerge directly out of our social interactions with others. He proposed, for example, that inner speech, which we use to think and plan activities, is a natural extension of the outer speech that we use to communicate. He was convinced that intellectual development is tied to social interaction—it grows out of each person's attempts to master social situations. Development can't be understood by considering the individual alone—you must always consider the individual in his or her social context (Vygotsky, 1978).

For example, imagine asking a 3-year-old child to describe how meals are prepared in the household. It's unlikely that you'll get much of a response—beyond, perhaps, a shrugging of the shoulders or shake of the head. Yet, if we engage the child in some form of social interaction—we provide clues or ask leading questions (e.g., Where is food stored? Where is it cooked?)—we're likely to find that the child actually has quite a bit of knowledge about how food is prepared. Every child has what Vygotsky called a "zone of proximal development," which is the difference between what the child can accomplish on his or her own and what he or she can do in the context of a social interaction (such as interacting with Mom or Dad). It is our social interactions, Vygotsky argued, that energize development and help to shape how we think.

© Bill Bachmann/PhotoEdit

According to Vygotsky, cognitive abilities arise directly out of children's social and verbal interactions with other people.

Moral Development: Learning Right From Wrong

Developing intellectually means more than learning to think logically and form correct internal models of the world. As children mature intellectually, they also need to develop *character*. They need to acquire a sense of **morality**, which provides them with a way to distinguish between appropriate and inappropriate actions. Piaget had

morality
the ability to distinguish between appropriate and inappropriate actions.

strong opinions on this topic, arguing that the sense of morality is closely tied to one's stage of cognitive development and to one's social experiences with peers. For example, from Piaget's perspective children in the concrete operational stage shouldn't show sophisticated moral reasoning skills because morality is basically an abstract concept—something that cannot be handled until the formal operational stage of development. Partly for this reason, most of the work on moral development has been conducted with adolescents and adults.

Kohlberg's Stage Theory The most influential theory of moral development is the stage theory proposed by Lawrence Kohlberg. Kohlberg was strongly influenced by Piaget, and like Piaget, he believed that people move through stages of moral development (Kohlberg, 1963, 1986). He would give people a moral dilemma, ask them to solve it, and use their reasoning to help identify their state of moral development. Let's consider an example, based on Kohlberg (1969):

> A woman is stricken with a rare and deadly form of cancer. There is a drug that can save her, a form of radium recently discovered by a druggist in town. But the druggist is charging $2,000 for the medicine, 10 times what the drug cost him to make. The sick woman's husband, Heinz, tries desperately to raise the money but can raise only half of the needed amount. He pleads with the druggist to sell him the drug at a reduced cost, or at least to allow him to pay for the drug over time, but the druggist refuses. "No," the druggist says, "I discovered the drug, and I'm going to make money from it." Frantic to save his wife, Heinz considers breaking into the druggist's office to steal the drug.

What do you think? Should the husband steal the drug? Why or why not? It is the *reasoning* behind your answer, the kind of intellectual justification you give, that was important to Kohlberg. He believed that people can be classified into stages of moral development based on how they answer such moral problems. Although Kohlberg's theory actually proposes as many as six stages of moral development, I'll focus on his three main levels only: *preconventional, conventional,* and *postconventional.*

preconventional level
in Kohlberg's theory, the lowest level of moral development, in which decisions about right and wrong are made primarily in terms of external consequences.

At the lowest level of moral development—the **preconventional level**—decisions about right and wrong are based primarily on external consequences. Young children will typically interpret the morality of a behavior in terms of its immediate individual consequences—that is, whether the act will lead directly to a reward or to a punishment: "Heinz shouldn't steal the drug because he might get caught and punished" or "Heinz should steal the drug because people will get mad at him if his wife dies." Notice the rationale is based on the immediate external consequences of the action rather than on some abstract moral principle.

conventional level
in Kohlberg's theory of moral development, the stage in which actions are judged to be right or wrong based on whether they maintain or disrupt the social order.

At the **conventional level** of moral reasoning, people justify their actions based on internalized rules. Now an action is right or wrong because it maintains or disrupts the *social order.* Someone at this level might argue that "Heinz shouldn't steal the drug because stealing is against the law" or that "Heinz should steal the drug because husbands have an obligation to protect their wives." Notice here that the moral reasoning has moved away from immediate individual consequences to societal consequences. Moral behavior is that which conforms to the rules and conventions of society. In general, people at the conventional level of moral reasoning tend to consider the appropriateness of their actions from the perspective of the resident authority figures in the culture.

postconventional level
Kohlberg's highest level of moral development, in which moral actions are judged on the basis of a personal code of ethics that is general and abstract and that may not agree with societal norms.

At the final level of moral development, the **postconventional level,** morality is based on abstract principles that may even conflict with accepted standards. The person adopts a moral standard not to seek approval from others or an authority figure but to follow some universal ethical principle. "An individual human life is more important than society's dictum against stealing," someone at this level might argue. In this case, moral actions are driven by general and abstract personal codes of ethics that may not agree with societal norms.

Evaluating Kohlberg's Theory Developmental psychologists continue to believe that we progress through periods of moral development, from an early focus on immediate individual consequences toward a final principled code of ethics. A number of observational studies have confirmed aspects of Kohlberg's views. For example, people do seem to move through the various types of moral reasoning in the sequence suggested by Kohlberg (Walker, 1989). Furthermore, the link that both Piaget and Kohlberg made between moral reasoning and level of cognitive development has clear merit. But Kolhberg's critics argue that he ties the concept of morality too closely to an abstract code of justice—that is, to the idea that moral acts are those that ensure fairness to the individual (Damon & Hart, 1992).

For example, suppose your sense of morality is not based on fairness but rather on concern for the welfare of others. You might believe that the appropriate action is always one that doesn't hurt anyone and takes into account the happiness of the affected individual. Under these conditions, as analyzed by Kohlberg, your behavior will appear to be driven more by an individual situation than by a consistent code of justice. Psychologist Carol Gilligan (1982) has argued that women in our culture often adopt such a view (a moral code based on caring), whereas men tend to make moral decisions on the basis of an abstract sense of justice. According to Kohlberg's theory, however, this means that women will tend to be classified at a lower level of moral development than men. Gilligan sees this as an unfair and unjustified gender bias.

Based on what you've learned about moral development, what advice would you give parents who are trying to teach their children about right and wrong?

The Role of Culture Gilligan may have overstated the case for sex differences in moral reasoning. Men and women often think in much the same way about the moral dilemmas studied by Kohlberg (Walker, 1989). At the same time, cross-cultural differences do occur in moral thinking that are not captured well by Kohlberg's classification system. For example, studies of moral decision making in India reveal striking differences from those typically found in Western cultures. Richard Shweder and his colleagues (1990) found that both Hindu children and adults are likely to find it morally acceptable for a husband to beat a disobedient wife—in fact, keeping disobedient family members in line is considered to be the moral obligation of the head of the family. In the United States, such actions would be widely condemned.

Western cultures also tend to place more value on individualism and stress individual goals more than other cultures, where the emphasis may be on collective goals. These kinds of cultural values must be factored into any complete theory of moral development (Miller, 1994). Moreover, the importance a culture places on teaching moral values can affect the speed with which moral development proceeds (Snarey, 1995). The bottom line: Morality seems to develop in a consistent manner across the world—that is, people tend to interpret morality first in terms of external consequences and only later in terms of abstract principles—but, not surprisingly, culture exerts its influence in powerful ways (Saltzstein, 1997).

Developmental psychologists also question whether the concept of morality can be easily captured by a simple analysis of reasoning. For example, Hart and Fegley (1995) interviewed inner-city adolescents who had been singled out by community leaders for exceptional volunteer work and commitment to social services. These kids expressed high degrees of moral commitment and often described themselves in terms of moral values, yet they didn't show a higher than average level of moral development when tested using Kohlberg's theory. Many developmental psychologists believe that we need to broaden our conception of morality to make it more representative of the diversity of social experiences (Arnold, 2000).

CONCEPT SUMMARY

Kohlberg's Stage Theory of Moral Development

STAGE	BASIS FOR MORAL JUDGMENT	POSSIBLE RESPONSE TO "WAS HEINZ RIGHT?"
Preconventional	External consequences	Yes: "He can't be happy without his wife." No: "If he gets caught, he'll be put in jail."
Conventional	Social order	Yes: "Spouses are responsible for protecting one another." No: "Stealing is against the law."
Postconventional	Abstract ethical principles	Yes: "Individual lives are more important than society's law against stealing." No: "Laws are necessary in a civilized society; they need to be followed by all to prevent chaos."

DEVELOPING SOCIALLY AND PERSONALLY

People do not develop in isolation. We're social animals, and the relationships we form with others affect how we act and view ourselves. For infants, relationships with caregivers—usually their parents—guarantee them adequate nourishment and a safe and secure environment. Children work hard to become part of a social group, learning how to get along with peers and to follow the rules and norms of society. For adults, whose social bonds become increasingly intimate, the task is to learn to accept responsibility for the care and support of others. As with most aspects of development, social and personal growth is shaped partly by biology and partly by what we learn from experience.

Forming Bonds With Others

attachments
strong emotional ties formed to one or more intimate companions.

Think again about the problems faced by the newborn infant: limited motor skills, somewhat fuzzy vision, yet a powerful sustained need for food, water, and warmth. To gain the nourishment needed to live, as well as protection from danger, the newborn relies on interactions with others—usually the mother. The newborn forms **attachments**, strong emotional ties to one or more intimate companions. The need for early attachments is so critical that researchers commonly argue that bonding behavior is built directly into our nature (Bowlby, 1969; Sable, 2004).

According to child psychiatrist John Bowlby, both caregiver and infant are preprogrammed from birth to respond to certain signals with attachment behavior. The newborn typically cries, coos, and smiles, and these behaviors lead naturally to attention and support from the caregiver. It's no accident that adults like to hear babies coo or watch them smile—these preferences may be built directly into the genetic code (Bowlby, 1969). At the same time, the baby arrives into the world with a bias to respond to care and particularly to comfort from the caregiver. Newborns imitate the facial expressions of their parents (Maratos, 1998), for example, which presumably enhances their social interactions with Mom and Dad (Bjorklund, 1997; Heimann, 1989).

Notice that both the infant and the caregiver are active participants—the attachment is formed because both parties are prepared to respond with bonding to the right kind of events. The bond usually is formed initially between baby and mother because it is the mother who provides most of the early care.

The Origins of Attachment

The idea that humans are built to form strong emotional attachments makes sense from an adaptive standpoint—it helps to guarantee survival. But what determines the strength or quality of the attachment? The quality of the bond that forms between infant and caregiver can vary enormously—some infants are securely attached to their caregivers, others are not. Research with animal subjects suggests that one very important factor is the amount of actual *contact comfort*—the degree of warm physical contact—provided by the caregiver.

© 2001 Laura Dwight

When a mother nurses her newborn child, she provides more than sustenance for survival. The "contact comfort" helps secure the bond of mutual attachment.

Contact Comfort In classic research on early attachment, psychologist Harry Harlow noticed that newborn rhesus monkeys, when separated from their mothers at birth, tended to become attached to soft cuddly objects left in their cages, such as baby blankets. If one of these blankets was removed for cleaning, the monkeys became extremely upset and would cling to it frantically when the blanket was returned. Intrigued, Harlow began a series of experiments in which he isolated newborn monkeys and raised them in cages with a variety of surrogate, or artificial, "mothers" (Harlow & Zimmerman, 1959). In one condition, baby monkeys were raised with a mother made simply of wire mesh and fitted with an artificial nipple that delivered food; in another condition, the babies were exposed to a nippleless cloth mother made of wire mesh that had been padded with foam rubber and wrapped in soft terrycloth.

Which of the two surrogate mothers did the monkeys prefer? If early attachments are formed primarily to caregivers who provide nourishment—that is, infants love the one who feeds them—we would expect the monkeys to prefer and cling to the wire mother because it provides the food. But in the vast majority of cases the monkeys preferred the cloth mother. If startled in some way, perhaps by the introduction of a foreign object into the cage, the monkeys ran immediately to the cloth mother, hung on tight, and showed no interest in the wire mother that provided the food. Harlow and his colleagues concluded that *contact comfort*—the warmth and softness provided by the terrycloth—was the primary motivator of attachment (Harlow et al., 1971).

© Martin Rogers/Stock Boston

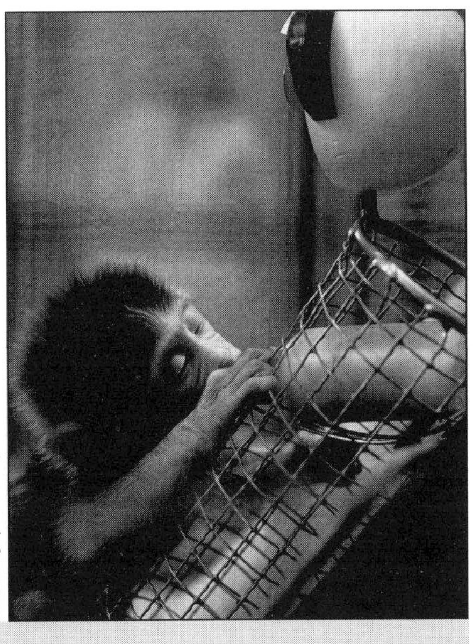

© Martin Rogers/Woodfin Camp & Associates

When forced to choose between surrogate mothers, baby monkeys prefer the soft and cuddly one, even when the wire "mother" provides the food.

Children orphaned by the 1989 war in Romania were sometimes housed in hospitals with very poor infant-to-caretaker ratios; not surprisingly, these children subsequently showed significant social and intellectual deficits compared to children reared at home.

For obvious reasons, similar experiments have never been conducted with human babies. However, we have every reason to believe that human infants are like rhesus infants in their desire and need for contact comfort. Many studies have looked at how children progress in institutional settings that provide relatively low levels of contact comfort (Hodges & Tizard, 1989; Provence & Lipton, 1962; Spitz, 1945). Children reared in orphanages with poor infant-to-caregiver ratios (e.g., one caregiver for every 10 to 20 infants) often show more developmental problems than children reared in less deprived environments (Shaffer, 2002).

Temperament Given that physical contact is such a necessary part of a secure attachment, what determines whether infants will receive the contact they need? One contributing factor may be a baby's **temperament**, the general level of his or her emotional reactivity. Difficult or fussy babies tend to get fewer comforting and responsive reactions, and the quality of the attachment between parent and child suffers as a result (Thomas & Chess, 1977). Links also exist between early temperament and various cognitive abilities, particularly language development (e.g., Dixon & Smith, 2000).

temperament
a child's general level of emotional reactivity.

Psychologists who study temperament find that infants can be categorized into types. As you might guess, some babies are *easy;* they're basically happy, readily establish daily routines, and tend not to get upset very easily. Other babies are *difficult;* they have trouble accepting new experiences, establishing routines, and maintaining a pleasant mood. Fortunately, only about 10% of babies fall into this difficult group, and about 40% of sampled babies are readily classified as easy (Thomas & Chess, 1977). The remaining 50% are more difficult to categorize. Some babies are "slow-to-warm-up," which means they roughly fall between easy and difficult and show a mixture of different temperaments.

Psychologists are convinced that these differences in moodiness, or temperament, can't be explained completely by the environment. Babies are probably born easy or difficult, although experience certainly plays some kind of role (Cummings et al., 2003). It's possible that biological factors, tied to specific structures in the brain, control a baby's degree of emotional reactivity. Jerome Kagan discovered that infants tend to be either *inhibited*—they're generally shy and fearful of unfamiliar people or new events—or *uninhibited,* which means they show little negative reaction to the unfamiliar or novel. Kagan has argued that natural differences in the activity levels of certain brain structures contribute to these inhibited and uninhibited temperaments (Kagan, 1997).

If temperament is based in biology, then you might expect it to remain stable across the life span. In other words, if you're a moody baby, then you should be a moody adolescent and a moody adult. In general, research has supported this conclusion (Caspi & Silva, 1995; Cummings et al., 2003). Infants who seem very shy or inhibited tend to remain so as they age. Identical twins, who share the same genes, also show more similarities in temperament than do fraternal twins or siblings raised in the same home (Braungart et al., 1992). As you'll see genetic factors probably influence many aspects of personality, not just temperament.

strange situation test
gradually subjecting a child to a stressful situation and observing his or her behavior toward the parent or caregiver. This test is used to classify children according to type of attachment—secure, resistant, avoidant, or disorganized/disoriented.

Types of Attachment

Not all attachments are created equal: There are systematic differences in the bonds that children form with their caregivers. To investigate these differences, psychologists often use a technique called the **strange situation test**. This test classifies 10- to 24-month-old children into four different attachment groups based on the children's reactions to stressful situations (Ainsworth & Wittig, 1969; Ainsworth et al., 1978). After arrival in the lab, the parent and child are ushered into a waiting room filled with toys; the child is encouraged to play with the toys. Various levels of infant stress are then introduced. A stranger might enter the room, or the parent might be asked to step out for a few moments leaving the child alone. Of main interest to the psychologist are the child's reactions: Initially, how willing is the child to move away from the parent and play with the toys? How much crying or distress does the child show when the parent leaves the room? How does the child react when the parent comes back into the room—does the child greet and cling to the parent, or does he or she move away?

Most infants—approximately 60 to 70%—react to the strange situation test with what psychologist Mary Ainsworth calls *secure attachment.* With the parent present, even if the situation is new and strange, these children play happily and are likely to explore the room looking for interesting toys or magazines to shred. But as the level of stress increases, they become increasingly uneasy and clingy. If the mother leaves the room, the child will probably start to cry but will calm down rapidly if the mother returns.

About 10% of children show a pattern called *resistant attachment;* these children react to stress in an ambiguous way, which may indicate a lack of trust for the parent. Resistant children will act wary in a strange situation, refusing to leave their mother's side and explore the room, and they do not deal well with the sudden appearance of strangers. They cry if the mother leaves the room, yet they're unlikely to greet her with affection on her return. Instead, these children act ambivalent, scorning their mother by temporarily resisting her affection.

A third group of children—about 20 to 25%—show a pattern of *avoidant attachment.* These children show no strong attachment to the mother in any aspect of the strange situation test. They're not particularly bothered by the appearance of strangers in the room, nor do they show much concern when the mother leaves the room or much interest when she returns. Ainsworth discovered that the parents of these children tend to be unresponsive and impatient when it comes to the child's needs and may even actively reject the child on a regular basis (Ainsworth, 1979).

The final attachment group—about 5 to 8%—is made up of children who show a pattern of *disorganized/disoriented attachment.* This fourth group was not part of Ainsworth's original classification scheme but was added to capture children with a history of possible abuse (Main & Soloman, 1990). These children react to the strange situation test with inconsistent responses. Sometimes they mimic securely attached children; sometimes they react with fear or anxiety to the returning mother. These children appear to have no consistent strategy for interacting with their caregivers.

What determines the kind of attachment a child will form? Unfortunately, there's no easy way to tell. The parent-child relationship depends on several factors: the particular personality characteristics of the parent, the temperament of the child, and the child-rearing practices of the culture. Although it might be tempting to conclude that the child's temperament matters most (e.g., "easy babies have secure attachments"), attachment and temperament are not the same thing (Vaughn & Bost, 1999). Like most complex psychological states, attachment is determined and controlled by multiple factors.

As a final note to parents, the strange situation test is a laboratory procedure and observations are made under carefully controlled conditions. You need to take care when drawing conclusions based on your own personal experiences. You shouldn't conclude that your child has an avoidant attachment, for example, just because he or she might not cry when left at day care. The strange situation test is not based on haphazard observations but on a careful examination of specific behaviors in a controlled setting.

Do you think the findings of the strange situation test would change if the test was conducted in the child's home? Why or why not?

Do Early Attachments Matter Later in Life?

Given that infants can be easily divided into these attachment groups by around age 1, it's reasonable to wonder about the long-term consequences. For instance, are the avoidant children doomed to a life of insecurity and failed relationships? There's some evidence to suggest that children with an early *secure* attachment do indeed have some social and intellectual advantages, at least throughout middle and later childhood. For example, teachers rate these children as more curious and self-directed in school (Waters et al., 1979). By age 10 or 11, securely attached children also tend to have more close and mature relationships with their peers than children who were classified as insecurely attached (Elicker et al., 1992).

However, early patterns of attachment are not perfect predictors of later behavior. One problem is stability: Sometimes a child who appears to be insecurely attached at 12 months can act quite differently in the strange situation test a few months later (Lamb et al., 1992). In addition, a child who has a particular kind of attachment to one parent may show quite a different pattern to the other. It's also important to remember that when psychologists talk about predicting later behavior based on early attachment patterns, they are referring mainly to correlational studies. It's not possible to draw firm conclusions about causality from simple correlational analyses. The fact that later behavior can be predicted from early attachment patterns does not mean that early bonding necessarily causes the later behavior patterns—other factors might be responsible. For instance, children who form secure attachments in infancy typically have caregivers who remain warm and responsive throughout childhood, adolescence, and adulthood. So it could be that securely attached infants tend to have successful relationships later in life because they live most of their lives in supportive environments.

Friendships Early attachments are important. But the relationships formed after infancy, especially during later childhood and adolescence, matter as well. Under the right circumstances, people can counteract negative experiences of infancy or childhood (Lamb et al., 1992). The significance of friendship is a case in point. Psychologists now recognize that a child's social network—the number and quality of his or her friends—has a tremendous impact on social development and well-being (Berndt, 2004; Hartup & Stevens, 1997).

Children with friends interact more confidently in social situations, they are more cooperative, and they report higher levels of self-esteem (Newcomb & Bagwell, 1995). Children with friends are also less likely to seek help for psychological problems, and they're more likely to be seen as well adjusted by teachers and adult caretakers. These trends are true for young children and adolescents, and they continue on into adulthood (Berndt & Keefe, 1995). You'll find that social support—particularly our network of friends—predicts how well we're able to cope and deal with stressful situations and how well we're able to recover from injury or disease. This is just as true for children as it is for adults (Hartup & Stevens, 1997).

Obviously, general conclusions like these need to be qualified a bit. For example, the quality (or closeness) of the friendship matters, but so does the identity of the friends. If you have very close friends who recommend drug use or a life of crime, the developmental consequences obviously will be less than ideal. We also don't know what aspects of friendship matter most. For instance, people often share similarities with their friends (such as common attitudes and values). Does this mean that friends merely play the role of reinforcing our values and making us more secure in our attitudes? In-depth research on friendships is ongoing, in part because psychologists recognize the value of friendship across the life span. When asked to rank what is most important in their lives, children, adolescents, and adults often pick "friends" as the answer (Klinger, 1977).

Child Care: A Cause for Concern?

What about child care and its long-term impact on development? Most parents of preschool children face a dilemma: Do I stay at home and provide full-time care for my child, or do I work outside the home and place my child in child care? In contemporary American society, *day care* often turns out to be the answer, although it's not always a choice made voluntarily. For many parents, day care has simply become an economic necessity. Over the last several decades there has been a steady rise in the number of mothers employed outside the home. In 1960, for example, 16.5% of mothers with children under 3 years of age worked outside the home; by the middle 1980s the figure had risen to more than 50%; by 1995 it was more than 60% (Hofferth, 1996; Lamb & Sternberg, 1990).

What are the long-term consequences of day care? Does leaving children in the hands of nonparental caretakers, often for many hours a day, have dire consequences on their social and mental development? Fortunately, the answer turns out to be "No" for most children, and day care may even have positive effects on social and cognitive development. Preschoolers who spend time in quality day-care centers adjust better in school—they are more sociable and popular among their classmates—than children who have received full-time care at home (Andersson, 1992). The day-care experience can also help speed up intellectual development, at least for some children. For example, Caughy and colleagues (1994) found that day-care participation during the first 3 years of life was positively associated with improved reading and math skills, although the results applied only to children who lived in home environments classified as low in emotional support and intellectual stimulation.

In the mid-1980s it was widely reported that children in day care are more likely to form insecure attachments (avoidant or resistant) than children who receive full-time home care (e.g., Belsky, 1988). More recent studies have failed to confirm these findings or have found the differences to be quite small (see Fitzgerald et al., 2003). At the same time, psychologists recognize that day care can have harmful effects under some circumstances. "Day care" is a multifaceted concept—the term can mean anything from occasional babysitting by a neighbor

Placing a child in day care is an economic necessity for many parents.

PRACTICAL SOLUTIONS

Choosing a Day-Care Center

If you decide to place your child in day care, it's important to choose a high-quality center. As noted in our discussion, you'll find considerable variation in the quality of existing day-care facilities. And, importantly, quality does matter: Factors such as the child-to-staff ratio, the size of the child's care group, and the education of the staff have been shown to correlate with measures of cognitive development (NICHD, 1999). Several professional organizations provide recommendations for assessing the quality of child care (e.g., Child Care Action Campaign, 1996). I've summarized some of the main recommendations here:

1. Check the physical environment. It's a must to visit the center and make sure the physical structure and play environments are safe. For example, are there fences around the grounds? Is the facility clean? Do you see the staff washing their hands regularly? Hands should be washed before and after diapering, after washing surfaces, and before any kind of food preparation. Is the play equipment well-constructed? Look to see if the electrical outlets are covered, and make certain there are no dangerous or toxic substances within reach of the children. Note: If you're restricted in any way from fully examining the environment, go someplace else for care.

2. Listen and watch. Spend some time watching the children who are currently enrolled. Do they look happy? Do they interact easily with each other and with the staff? Do the staff speak to the children in a positive and cheerful tone? Is the setting noisy? High noise levels can signal a lack of control on the part of the staff. If possible, also check with other parents and get their perspectives on the quality of the care.

3. Count group and staff sizes. As a general rule, the younger the child, the smaller should be the size of his or her care group. For infants or toddlers, no more than three to four children should be cared for by a single adult. For 2-year-olds, the size can increase to four to six; for 3-year-olds seven to eight; for 4-year-olds eight to nine; for 5-year-olds eight to ten children. If the child-to-staff ratios exceed these guidelines, the quality of your child's care may suffer.

4. Ask about staff training. Although legal requirements vary from state to state, it's a good idea to ask whether the center has been accredited by a professional organization. You should also inquire about the staff turnover rate. Qualified staff should have some specific training in early childhood education or child development. A number of studies have shown that caregiver background—specifically college training—influences the quality of the care provided (Howes, 1997). The better educated the staff, the more likely your child will be given activities that are appropriate for his or her developmental stage.

In a perfect world, all parents would be able to pick and choose the best from a wide array of child-care facilities. Unfortunately, high-quality centers are not always available or are too costly for the average parent or guardian. You can, however, be an active participant in choosing the best possible option. Take your time, use the guidelines listed here, and do your best to maximize a quality environment for your child.

for a few hours a week, to care by nonparental relatives, to extended care by licensed professionals in for-profit day-care centers. Consequently, it's difficult to draw general conclusions.

There are also wide variations in the quality of the service provided during day-care hours and in the quality of care that the child receives at home (see Melhuish, 2001). Factors such as how early in life the child enters a program and whether the child attends regularly or intermittently may be important (Lamb & Sternberg, 1990). As with most environmental effects, the role that day care plays in the life of a child will depend on many factors interacting together, including the individual characteristics of the child, the parents, the home environment, and the quality and quantity of the service provided. But the consensus among researchers is fairly positive at this point: For the vast majority of children, regular day care will have no negative long-term consequences on development, and it may even have substantial benefits (Scarr, 1998).

Forming a Personal Identity: Erikson's Crises of Development

© Bettmann/CORBIS

Erik Erikson

Another important aspect of social development is the formation of **personal identity**—a sense of self, of who you are as an individual and how well you measure up against peers. We recognize that we're unique people, different from others, quite early in our development. Children as young as 6 months will reach out and touch an image of themselves in a mirror; by a year and a half, if they look into a mirror and notice a smudge mark on their nose, they'll reach up and touch their own face (Butterworth, 1992; Lewis & Brooks-Gunn, 1979).

As noted earlier in the chapter, most psychologists are convinced that we use social interactions—primarily those with parents during childhood and with peers later in life—to help us come to grips with who we are as individuals. One of the most influential theories of how this process of identity formation proceeds is the stage theory of Erik Erikson. Erikson (1963, 1968, 1982) believed that our sense of self is shaped by a series of psychosocial *crises* that we confront at characteristic stages in development.

personal identity
a sense of who one is as an individual and how well one measures up against peers.

Infancy and Childhood As you know, for the first few years of life babies are largely at the mercy of others for their survival. According to Erikson, this overwhelming dependency leads infants to their first true psychosocial crisis, usually in the first year of life: *trust versus mistrust.* Psychologically and practically, babies face an important problem: Are there people out there in the world who will meet my survival needs? Resolution of this crisis leads to the formation of an initial sense of either trust or mistrust, and the infant begins to understand that people differ. Some people can be trusted and some can't. It's through social interactions, learning who to trust and who not to trust, that the newborn ultimately resolves the crisis and learns how to deal more effectively with the environment.

© Dan McCoy/Rainbow

Developing a personal identity is part of the process of maturing socially and individually. Ellen demonstrates self-awareness as she discovers her nose in the mirror.

As the child progresses through toddlerhood and on into childhood, other fundamental conflicts appear. During the "terrible twos," the child struggles with breaking his or her dependence on parents. The crisis at this point, according to Erikson, is *autonomy versus shame or doubt:* Am I capable of independent self-control of my actions, or am I generally inadequate? Between the ages of 3 and 6, the crisis becomes one of *initiative versus guilt:* Can I plan things on my own, with my own initiative, or should I feel guilty for trying to carry out my own bold plans for action? In late childhood, beginning around age 6 and ending at around age 12, the struggle is for a basic sense of *industry versus inferiority:* Can I learn and master new skills, can I be industrious and complete required tasks, or do I lack fundamental competence?

Again, what's important in determining how these crises are resolved is the quality of the child's interactions with parents, peers, and other significant role models. If 5-year-old Roberta's parents repeatedly scold her for taking the initiative to get her own drink of milk, she may develop strong feelings of guilt for trying to become independent. According to Erikson, children with highly critical parents or teachers can acquire a self-defeating attitude that carries over later in life. Children who resolve these crises positively learn to trust themselves and their abilities and acquire a strong positive sense of personal identity.

Adolescence and Young Adulthood By the time adolescence rolls around, our intellectual development has proceeded to the point where we begin to consider personal qualities that are pretty general and abstract. For example, Erikson argued, adolescents have to deal with the crisis of *identity versus role confusion.* They become concerned with testing roles and with finding their true identity: Who am I? What kind of person do I really represent? In a very real sense, the teenager acts as a kind of personality theorist, attempting to integrate various self-perceptions about abilities and limitations into a single unified concept of self. Erikson (1968) coined the term *identity crisis* to describe this transition period, which he believed can be filled with turmoil.

Observational studies of how adolescents come to grips with the identity crisis reveal many individual differences (Offer & Schonert-Reichl, 1992; Peterson, 1988). Not all teenagers become paralyzed with identity "angst" and anxiety—most, in fact, show no more anxiety during this transition period than at other points in their lives. Young people also vary widely in how they commit to a particular view of themselves (Marcia, 1966). Some adolescents choose an identity by modeling others: "I'm honest, open, and cooperative because that's the way I was brought up by my parents." Others develop a personal identity through a soul-searching evaluation of their feelings and abilities. Some adolescents even reject the crisis altogether, choosing instead not to commit to any particular view of themselves. The specific path an individual takes depends on many things, including his or her level of cognitive development, the quality of the parent-child relationship, and outside experiences (Compas et al., 1995).

Entrance into young adulthood is marked by the crisis of *intimacy versus isolation.* Resolution of the identity crisis causes us to question the meaning of our relationships with others: Am I willing or able to form an intimate, committed relationship with another person? Or will my insecurities and fears about losing independence lead to a lifetime of isolation and loneliness? People who lack an integrated conception of themselves, Erikson argued, cannot commit themselves to a shared identity with someone else. Some have argued that this particular conclusion may be more applicable to men than women (Gilligan, 1982). Historically, women have been forced to deal with intimate commitments—raising a family and running a home—either at the same time as, or before, the process of searching for a stable personal identity. Things are a bit different now, of course, because many women are establishing professional careers prior to marriage.

Adulthood, Middle Age, and Beyond With the establishment of career and family arrives the crisis of *generativity versus stagnation.* The focus at this point shifts from resolving intimacy to concern about children and future generations: Am I contributing successfully to the community at large? Am I doing enough to assure the survival and productivity of future generations? Failure to resolve this crisis can induce a sense of meaninglessness in middle life and beyond—a condition Erikson calls *stagnation.*

For some people, especially men in their 40s, this point in psychosocial development is marked by soul-searching questions about personal identity reminiscent of those faced in adolescence (Gould, 1978; Levinson et al., 1978). A "midlife crisis" arises as people begin to confront their own mortality—the inevitability of death—and as they come to grips with the fact that they may never achieve their lifelong dreams and goals. Although this can be an emotionally turbulent period for some, most of the evidence suggests that the midlife crisis is a relatively rare phenomenon. It gets a lot of attention in the media, and it's certainly consuming for those affected, but probably fewer than 5% of people in middle age undergo anything resembling a turbulent midlife crisis (McCrae & Costa, 2003).

The final stage in the process of psychosocial development, which occurs from late adulthood to the point of death, is the crisis of *integrity versus despair.* It's at this point in people's lives, Erikson believed, that they strive to accept themselves and their pasts—both failures and successes. Older people undergo a kind of life review in an effort to resolve conflicts in the past and to find ultimate meaning in their accomplishments. If successful in this objective search for meaning, they acquire wisdom; if unsuccessful, they wallow in despair and bitterness. An important part of the process is the preparation for death and dying, which I'll discuss in more detail near the end of the chapter.

Evaluating Erikson's Theory Erikson's stage theory of psychosocial crises has been quite influential in shaping how psychologists view personal identity development (see Steinberg & Morris, 2001). Among its most important contributions is the recognition that personal development is a lifelong process. Individuals don't simply establish a rigid identity around the time they reach Piaget's formal operational stage; the way people view themselves and their relationships changes regularly throughout their lives. Erikson's theory is also noteworthy for its emphasis on the role of social and cultural interactions in shaping human psychology. Human beings don't grow up in a psychological vacuum; the way we think and act is critically influenced by our interactions with others, as Erikson's theory fully acknowledges (Douvan, 1997; Eagle, 1997).

Nevertheless, Erikson's theory suffers from the same kinds of problems as any stage theory. Although there may be an orderly sequence of psychosocial crises, overlap occurs across the stages (Whitbourne et al., 1992). As noted earlier, the search for identity is not confined to one turbulent period in adolescence—it is likely to continue throughout a lifetime. Furthermore, like Piaget, Erikson never clearly articulated *how* a person actually moves from one crisis stage to the next: What are the psychological mechanisms that allow for conflict resolution, and what determines when and how they will operate (Achenbach, 1992)? Finally, Erikson's theory of identity development, although useful as a general organizing framework, lacks sufficient scientific rigor. His concepts are vague enough to make scientific testing difficult.

Think About It

How well do Erikson's ideas describe your own personal identity development? Are you going through any fundamental crisis at the moment, or are you aware of having solved one in the past?

Gender-Role Development

In our discussion of Erikson's theory, I touched briefly on the role of gender in establishing personal identity. Women are sometimes forced to struggle with questions about intimacy and relationships before addressing the identity crisis, as the task of establishing a home and rearing children typically falls on their shoulders. But gender is itself a kind of identity; children gain a sense of themselves as male or female quite early in life, and this *gender identity* has a long-lasting effect on how people behave and on how others behave toward them.

The rudimentary foundations of gender identity are already in place by the age of 2 or 3. Children at this age recognize that they're either a boy or a girl (Thompson, 1975), and they sometimes even give stereotypical responses about gender when asked. For example, when shown a picture of an infant labeled as either a boy or a girl, 3-year-olds are more likely to identify the infant "boy" as the one who is strong, big, or hard and the infant "girl" as the one who is weak, small, and soft (Cowan & Hoffman, 1986). Even so, children at this age have not developed sufficiently to recognize gender as a general and abstract characteristic of individuals. They might believe, for instance, that a boy can become a girl by changing hairstyle or clothing (Marcus & Overton, 1978). To understand that gender is a stable and unchanging condition requires some ability to conserve—to recognize that the qualities of objects remain the same despite superficial changes in appearance.

By the time children are firmly entrenched in elementary school, gender is seen as a permanent condition—"I'm a boy (or a girl) and I always will be." At this point, children tend to follow reasonably well-established **gender roles**—specific patterns of behavior consistent with society's dictums. As Martin and Ruble (2004) recently noted, children at this age become "gender detectives who search for cues about gender—who should and should not engage in a particular activity, who can play with whom, and why girls and boys are different" (p. 67). Can you

gender roles
specific patterns of behavior that are consistent with how society dictates makes and females should act.

CONCEPT SUMMARY

Erikson's Stages of Personal Identity Development

LIFE PERIOD	STAGE	CONFLICTS REVOLVE AROUND . . .
Infancy and childhood	Trust vs. mistrust (first year of life)	Developing a sense of trust in others: Will the people around me fulfill my needs?
	Autonomy vs. shame or doubt ("terrible twos")	Developing a sense of self-control: Am I in charge of my own actions?
	Initiative vs. guilt (ages 3–6)	Developing a sense of one's own drive and initiative: Can I carry out plans? Should I feel guilty for trying to carry out my own plans?
	Industry vs. inferiority (ages 6–12)	Developing a sense of personal ability and competence: Can I learn and develop new skills?
Adolescence and young adulthood	Identity vs. role confusion (adolescence)	Developing a single, unified concept of self, a sense of personal identity: Who am I?
	Intimacy vs. isolation (young adulthood)	Questioning the meaning of our relationships with others: Can I form a committed relationship with another person, or will my personal insecurities lead to isolation?
Adulthood and older adulthood	Generativity vs. stagnation	Concern over whether one has contributed to the success of children and future generations: Have I contributed to the community at large?
	Integrity vs. despair	Acceptance of one's life—successes and failures: Am I content, looking back on my life?

imagine the reaction a 7-year-old boy might receive if he walked into his second-grade class wearing a dress, or with his fingernails polished a bright shade of pink?

Children are often rewarded for behaving in ways that are gender-role appropriate.

Nature or Nurture? How do these firm ideas about gender roles develop? Are they due to biological differences between male and female brains, or do they grow out of experience? Although hormones released by the endocrine system early in development may account for some gender differences in behavior and thought (Kimura, 1999), psychologists are just as likely to appeal to the environment to explain gender-role development.

According to *social learning* accounts of gender-role development, children learn to act in a masculine or feminine manner because they grow up in environments that reward them for doing so. Parents across the world look for and reward specific kinds of behavior from their male and female children. The socialization process begins the moment the new parents learn the answer to their question, "Is it a boy or a girl?" Parents become preoccupied with dressing Adorable Ginnie in pink bows and Active Glenn in blue. Television and movies continue the process: Children are exposed to hour after hour of stereotypical children acting in gender-appropriate ways (Hansen, 1989; Lovdal, 1989). Studies have indicated, for example, that children who watch a lot of television are more likely to prefer toys that are "gender appropriate" than children who watch little television (McGhee & Frueh, 1980).

Growing up in societies with well-defined gender roles helps establish *gender schemas* (Bem, 1981). A gender schema is an organized set of beliefs and perceptions held about men and women. Gender schemas guide and direct how we view others, as well as our own behavior. For example, as a male, my gender schema leads me to interpret my own behavior, as well as the behavior of other males, in terms of concepts such as "strength," "aggression," and "masculinity." We encountered the concept of schemas (or schemata) earlier in the chapter when we talked about Piaget, and I'll have more to say in later chapters about schemas and the role they play in guiding behavior. For the moment, you can think of schemas as little knowledge packages that people carry around inside their heads. Gender schemas are acquired through learning. They set guidelines for behavior, and they help us decide whether actions are appropriate. As you can probably guess, gender schemas are generally adaptive—they help us interpret the behavior of others—but they can lead to inaccurate perceptions of specific individuals and even to discrimination.

Think About It

Do you think that we as a society should work hard to eliminate specific gender roles? Do you believe that men and women can ever be taught to think and act similarly?

Growing Old in Society

As Bette Davis once famously said, "Growing old ain't for sissies." True enough—the physical declines that accompany the aging process are certain to present new challenges for the developing individual. Yet not all of the changes that greet us in our older years are negative—far from it. In fact, some kinds of intelligence seem to increase with age. Marital satisfaction often grows (Carstensen, 1995), and many elderly people remain actively involved in the community and report high levels of contentment (Lawton et al., 1992). One survey found that people in their 70s report more confidence in their ability to perform tasks than do people in their 50s (Wallhagen et al., 1997)!

At the same time, there are definite hurdles in the pathways of the elderly, many related to health care. The elderly need more physical care, require more doctor visits, and can be at an economic disadvantage due to retirement. Although most elderly adults do not live in nursing homes, many are in need of continuing care. Whatever form it takes, it's likely to be expensive; the costs of nursing homes continue to rise (Belsky, 1999). To make matters worse, the bulk of the costs often must be borne by family members because Medicare (health care for the elderly funded by the federal government) doesn't cover custodial, or chronic, care. The scope of the problem is troubling, especially as the "graying of America" continues. Over the next 50 years, there's expected to be a huge increase (perhaps as much as sixfold) in the number of people over age 85.

Ageism The elderly face another problem as well: the potential for **ageism**, or prejudice against someone based on his or her age. For the moment, it is sufficient for you to understand that we all have beliefs about the traits and behaviors of individuals belonging to groups. The elderly comprise such a group, and our attitudes and beliefs toward the elderly can affect their ability to cope with the problems of everyday life.

ageism
discrimination or prejudice against an individual based on physical age.

Stereotypes about the elderly are complex and depend on cultural factors and the age of the individual holding the stereotype, but surveys often reveal beliefs that are inaccurate. Palmore (1990) has listed some of the more common myths, including the belief that most elderly people are sick, in mental decline, disabled and therefore unable to work, isolated and lonely, and depressed. In each of these cases, the negative stereotype is misleading or simply not true. Most elderly people are not sick or disabled and, as mentioned earlier, the elderly may often be more contented and less prone to depression than younger people (Lawton et al., 1992; Palmore, 1990). Not surprisingly, negative stereotypes can lead to negative consequences, including the fact that older people are generally evaluated less positively (Kite & Johnson, 1988) and may be subject to job discrimination (Kite, 1996).

As you'll learn, stereotypes can be quite adaptive. Like schemas, stereotypes help us organize and make predictions about the world, and some of the beliefs that accompany stereotypes are positive. For example, people tend to believe that the elderly are kinder, wiser, more dependable, and have more personal freedom than younger people (Palmore, 1990). Stereotypic beliefs such as these, although

© Jeff Greenberg/Index Stock Imagery

© Mark Gamba/CORBIS

Negative stereotypes about the elderly are very often false. Most elderly people are not sick or disabled but live active and productive lives.

not necessarily accurate, can lead to a kind of favorable discrimination that helps to counteract the negative stereotypes mentioned previously. One of the lessons of social psychology is that how we view others is often tied to our expectations; age can be a powerful determinant of what those expectations will be.

Death and Dying

As we close our discussion of the developmental process, it's fitting that we turn our attention to the final stage of life: death and dying. People commonly say that death is a part of living, but it's a part of living that most of us would choose to avoid. It's the process of death that troubles people most—the unpredictability, the uncertainty, the inability to understand what the end will be like. There are many psychological aspects to death and the dying process, including how people come to grips with their own mortality and how they grieve and accept the loss of others. One of the most influential approaches to the dying process is the stage theory of Elisabeth Kübler-Ross (1969, 1974).

Kübler-Ross proposed that people progress through five distinct psychological stages as they face death. Based on extensive interviews with hundreds of terminally ill patients, she found that people react to their own impending death via a characteristic sequence: (1) *denial*—"There must be some terrible mistake"; (2) *anger*—"Why is this happening to me?"; (3) *bargaining*—"What can I do to stop this terrible thing?"; (4) *depression*—"Blot out the sun because all is lost"; and (5) *acceptance*—"I am ready to die." As a stage theorist, Kübler-Ross believed that people move through each of these five stages, from denial to acceptance, as a normal part of their emotional acceptance of death.

Kübler-Ross' views on the dying process have been highly influential, in both psychological and medical circles, and rightly so. She was one of the first people to treat the topic of dying thoroughly and systematically. She sensitized legions of physicians to the idea that denial, anger, and depression are normal reactions to dying which should be treated with respect rather than dismissed out of hand.

However, many psychologists question whether people progress through a fixed set of orderly stages in exactly the way Kübler-Ross described. There are simply too many individual differences to support the theory. Not all dying people move through distinct emotional stages, and, even if they do, the stages don't seem to follow any particular set order. Stages might be skipped, might be experienced out of order, or might alternate, with the person being angry one day and accepting the next. In sum, there is no firm evidence to support a stage approach to the psychological aspects of dying.

Many psychologists find it more appropriate to talk about *dying trajectories.* A dying trajectory is the psychological path people travel as they face their impending death. Different people show different trajectories, and the shape and form of the path depends on the particular illness as well as on the personality of the patient (Bortz, 1990; Glaser & Strauss, 1968). Trajectories are preferred to stages because stages imply that all people react to impending death in fixed and characteristic ways. But there is no right or wrong way to deal with dying—some people may react with anger and denial, others with calm acceptance. Witnesses to the dying process can best serve the dying by offering support and allowing the individual to follow his or her own unique path.

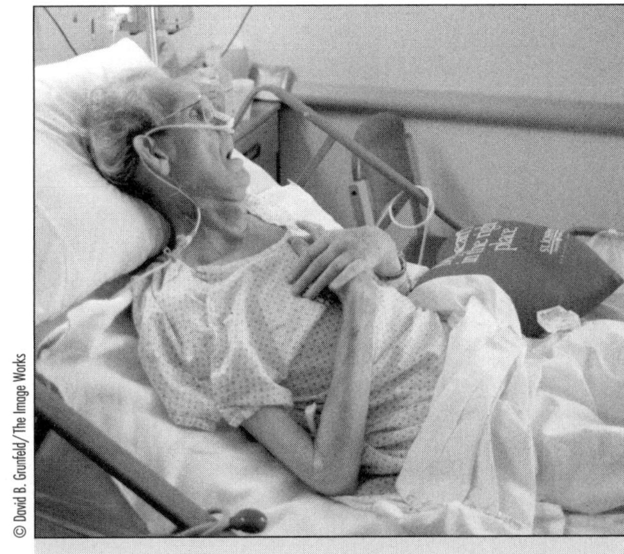

The dying trajectory depends on individual personality, the effects of age or illness, and what sort of care is received.

End-of-Life Decisions We end the chapter with a little controversy: the decision-making processes that surround the end of life. Should people have the right to control how and when they die, especially if they're faced with a poor quality of life (e.g., constant pain, immobility, or dependency)? Is suicide, assisted suicide, or "pulling the plug" justified under any circumstance? In some sense, these are legal and ethical questions rather than psychological ones, but questions about controlling the end of life occupy the attention of many people, especially the elderly.

Very little research has been conducted on the psychological factors that influence end-of-life decisions. It seems likely that religious convictions, value systems, life satisfaction, and even fear of death play a role in how people feel about end-of-life options. A study by Cicirelli (1997) confirms these expectations. Older adults, ranging in age from 60 to 100, were asked their views of various end-of-life options. Each person was given sample decision situations such as the following:

> Mrs. Lee is an elderly widow who has terminal bone cancer. She has had chemotherapy to try to cure the cancer, but it has not helped her, and the side effects from the chemotherapy itself have been difficult to deal with. She is slowly getting worse, and the pain is unbearable. Drugs for pain help some, but leave her in a stupor.

The participants were then asked to make judgments about various end-of-life options, such as strive to maintain life, refuse medical treatment or request that it be removed, commit suicide, or allow someone else to the make the decision about terminating life. Cicirelli (1997) found that people were often willing to endorse more than one option, but the majority opinion was to strive to continue life (51% of the participants endorsed this view). Psychosocial factors, such as religious convictions and fear of death, played a significant role in the decision-making process.

Death can mean many different things to the elderly (Cicirelli, 2002). For some older adults, death is associated with the beginning of the afterlife; for others

REVIEW

Psychology for a Reason

As we grow from infancy through childhood to adulthood, fundamental changes occur in physical, intellectual, and social functioning. Most of these changes serve adaptive functions. We're not biological machines, predestined to develop in fixed and inflexible ways from birth. Instead, we're born with a genetic recipe that mixes innate potential with the rigors and demands of the environment. It's nature via nurture and the final product is a better functioning person, someone who is fine-tuned to his or her environment.

In many ways this chapter acts as a concise summary of the topics you'll encounter throughout the book. Understanding human development requires that we take into account all aspects of the psychology of the individual: how people change physically, learn to perceive, think, and remember, and develop socially.

Developing Physically We begin life as a fertilized egg, or zygote, which contains genetic material packed into chromosomes received from the mother and father. During the prenatal period, we develop rapidly and are especially susceptible to environmental influences. Infancy and childhood are marked by rapid growth in height and weight and by a further maturing of the nervous system. One of the by-products of nerve cell maturation is motor development, the major milestones of which—crawling, standing alone, walking—tend to occur at similar times for most people, in part because the nervous system develops systematically.

As we move through adolescence and into early adulthood, our physical systems continue to change. During puberty people mature sexually and experience hormone-driven changes in physical appearance. Once people reach their 20s, their bodies become mature, and most begin a gradual decline in physical ability. Some declines occur in mental ability over time, especially in old age, although significant losses in mental functioning are the exception, not the rule.

Developing Intellectually Psychologists use the term *cognitive development* to refer to changes in intellectual functioning that accompany physical aging. Newborns have remarkably well-developed tools for investigating the world around them: they can see, hear, smell, feel, and taste, although not at the same level as they will in later childhood. We leave infancy with well-developed perceptual systems and use the experiences of childhood to help fine-tune our sensory equipment.

Much of what we know about thought processes during infancy and childhood comes from the work of Jean Piaget. Piaget's theory of cognitive development proposes that children use mental models of the world—called *schemata*—to guide and interpret ongoing experience. Central to the theory is the idea that as children grow and acquire new experiences their mental models of the world change. Piaget believed that children pass through a series of cognitive stages (sensorimotor, preoperational, concrete operational, and formal operational), each characterized by unique ways of thinking. Lawrence Kohlberg also proposed a stage theory, suggesting that individuals pass through levels of moral development that differ in the extent to which moral actions are seen as being driven by immediate external consequences or by general abstract principles. Not all psychologists agree that cognitive development progresses through fixed stages, but it's clear that qualitative differences in cognitive ability do occur over the course of development.

Developing Socially and Personally Our relationships with others help us solve problems that arise throughout development. Infants form attachments to gain the nourishment they need for survival. Both infant and caregiver are active participants in the attachment process and are prepared to respond, given the right kinds of environmental events, with mutual bonding. Ainsworth identified several categories of attachment based on the strange situation test. In general, the responsiveness of the parent early in life influences, but does not absolutely determine, the relationships formed by the child later in life.

Another aspect of social development is the formation of personal identity. Erik Erikson argued that personal identity is shaped by a series of psychosocial crises over the life span. During infancy and childhood, we address questions about our basic abilities and independence and learn to trust or mistrust others. During adolescence and adulthood, we deal with the identity crisis and come to grips with our roles as participants in intimate relationships. In later years we struggle with questions of accomplishment, concern for future generations, and meaning. Other important components of social development include learning gender roles, growing old in society, and confronting the important stages and decisions of dying.

it means complete extinction or annihilation. Not surprisingly, how one interprets death influences everyday living, reactions to death, and preparations for death. For those who believe that death provides the opportunity to be reunited with deceased friends and family in an afterlife, stressful end-of-life decisions are often easier to make. The fact that the elderly hold so many different personal meanings of death suggests that it will be difficult for society to reach consensus about the difficulties that surround end-of-life decisions.

CHAPTER 1 PRACTICE EXAM

____ 1. The second through the eighth weeks of a pregnancy is the :
a. fatal period
b. fetal period
c. critical period
d. embryonic period

____ 2. The embryonic period in a pregnancy is:
a. the second through the eighth weeks
b. the first two weeks
c. from the eighth week through to birth
d. From the thirtieth to the thirty-sixth week

____ 3. If a fetus with XX chromosomes who receives high levels of testosterone during the seventh and/or eighth weeks of pregnancy will likely develop:
a. a female reproductive system
b. Androgenous reproductive system
c. Superficial reproductive system
d. a male reproductive system

____ 4. A teratogen is:
a. a genetic defect
b. an environmental agent that can harm a fetus
c. a fertilized egg
d. a physical defect

____ 5. The typical temporal sequency of motor skills is:
a. rolling over, crawling, standing
b. sitting, rolling over, crawling
c. rolling over, sitting, crawling
d. sitting, crawling, rolling over

____ 6. What is one hypothesis why the age of puberty has decreased in the last 100 years?
a. Better medical care and living conditions
b. Alternative gene pools
c. Strict diets that are low in fatty acids
d. Increase emphasis on jogging

____ 7. Young infants consistently prefer to:
a. Familiar objects to look at to novelty
b. Novel objects to look at
c. Look at objects with their right eye closed
d. Look at objects with their left eye closed

____ 8. Bret who is four thinks the next door hamster is a puppy. Bret is using the process of _________
a. accommodation
b. assimilation
c. reversibility
d. centration

____ 9. Bret who is four now realizes that the hamster is not a puppy because the hamster doesn't bark. What process would Piaget suggest Bret showed?
a. assimilation
b. reductionism
c. centration
d. accommodation

____ 10. During the sensorimotor period:
a. children have a difficultly turing off their motors
b. schemata revolve around sensory and motor activities of the child
c. Concrete operations weight down the child's mind
d. Children discuss outcomes based on multi-modal senses

____ 11. Hospitals could encourage parent child attachment by having the parents:
a. Immediately give the newborn a bottle
b. Frequently cuddle the newborn
c. Wait until the baby cries before giving it any attention
d. Wait until the baby is hundgry before feeding it

____ 12. Gender identity appears to have it roots in place:
a. When the child is two to three years old
b. When the baby is six or seventh months old
c. At the end of the preoperational period
d. At the beginning of formal operations

____ 13. Around seventy percent of children typically show what kind of attachment?
a. resistant attachment
b. avoidant attachment
c. Insecure attachment
d. secure attachment

____ 14. Preschoolers enrolled in quality day care programs:
a. are not very sociable
b. adjust well to grade school
c. Have poor reading skills
d. Are very insecurely attached to their teachers

____ 15. In Kübler-Ross stage theory of dying a person who sees the illness as a mistake is in the _____ stage:
a. Pretrial stage
b. languid stage
c. denial stage
d. acceptance stage

Answers

1. D	5. C	9. D	13. D
2. A	6. A	10. B	14. B
3. D	7. B	11. B	15. C
4. B	8. B	12. B	

CHAPTER 2: PSYCHOLOGICAL RESEARCH

QUESTIONS

1. What are the four goals of psychology?
2. What are the five steps and examples of the scientific method?
3. What is an example of a predictive hypothesis?
4. What is an example of a causal hypothesis?
5. What is an example of naturalistic observation?
6. How would you conduct a study using naturalistic observation?
7. What is one problem with naturalistic observation?
8. What are case studies used for?
9. What is an example of a case study?
10. What are case studies valuable for?
11. What is the main disadvantage of a case study?
12. Why are correlational studies conducted?
13. What is the strength of a correlation?
14. What are some examples of positive and negative correlations?
15. What do correlational studies not allow researchers to do?
16. What is the third variable problem with correlational studies?
17. What are the two main features of an experiment?
18. What are examples of independent, dependent, and confounding variables?
19. What is the difference between a population of interest and a sample?
20. What is the difference between a random sample and a sample of convenience?
21. How does random assignment to experimental conditions work?
22. What are examples of quasi-experiments?
23. What are the advantages of using experiments?
24. What are three reasons experiments are not used in all research?
25. What are six parts of informed consent?
26. When is using deception research all right?
27. What are ethical guidelines for using animals in research?
28. What are five fallacies that prevent critical thinking and an example of each?

VOCABULARY

1. case study
2. causal hypothesis
3. confederates
4. confidentiality
5. confounding variable
6. correlation
7. correlation coefficient
8. debriefing
9. dependent variable
10. experiment
11. generalizability
12. independent variable
13. informed consent
14. institutional review board
15. naturalistic observations
16. negative correlation
17. population of interest
18 positive correlation
19. predictive hypothesis
20. quasi-experiment
21. random assignment
22. random sample
23. randomization
24. reactivity
25. representative sample
26. sample
27. sample of convenience

2 Psychological Research

The Scientific Method

Hypotheses

Research Methods

The Nature of Critical Thinking

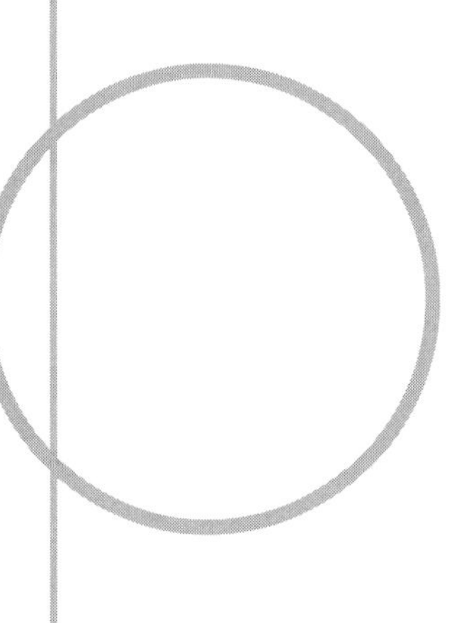

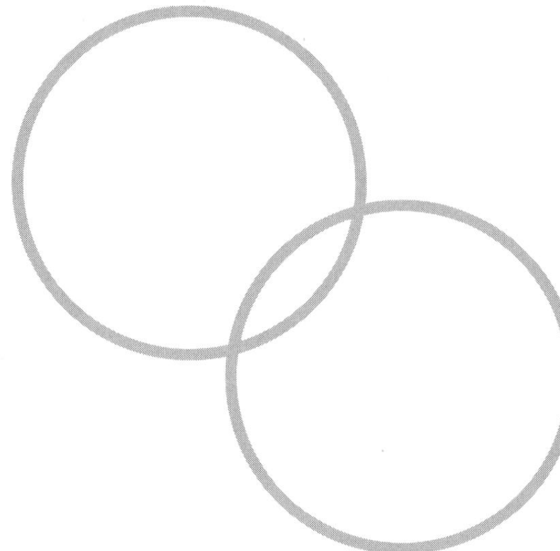

Courtesy of Andrew Whiten, Professor of Evolutionary and Developmental Psychology, University of St Andrews, Scotland

THOUGH PSYCHOLOGISTS in various subfields study and emphasize different aspects of behavior, they all share similar goals. The main goals of psychology and psychological research are:

- To describe behavior
- To predict behavior
- To explain behavior
- To control or change behavior

Description involves observing events and describing them. Typically, description is used to understand how events are related to one another. For example, you may notice that your health club tends to get more crowded in the months of January, February, and March. It seems you have to wait longer to use the weight machines or that there are more people in the kick boxing aerobic classes. This observation describes an event.

If you observe that two events occur together rather reliably or with a general frequency or regularity, you can make *predictions* about or anticipate what events may occur. From your observations, you may predict that the health club will be more crowded in January. You may arrive earlier for a parking spot or to get a place in the aerobics class. Another example is the relationship between standardized tests and college success. Many colleges use ACT or SAT achievement test scores as a criterion for admission. Why do they use these tests? Research shows that the scores on these tests and success in college are related (Hearn, 1984, 1990, 1991; U.S. Department of Education, 1995), therefore the tests reliably predict who will

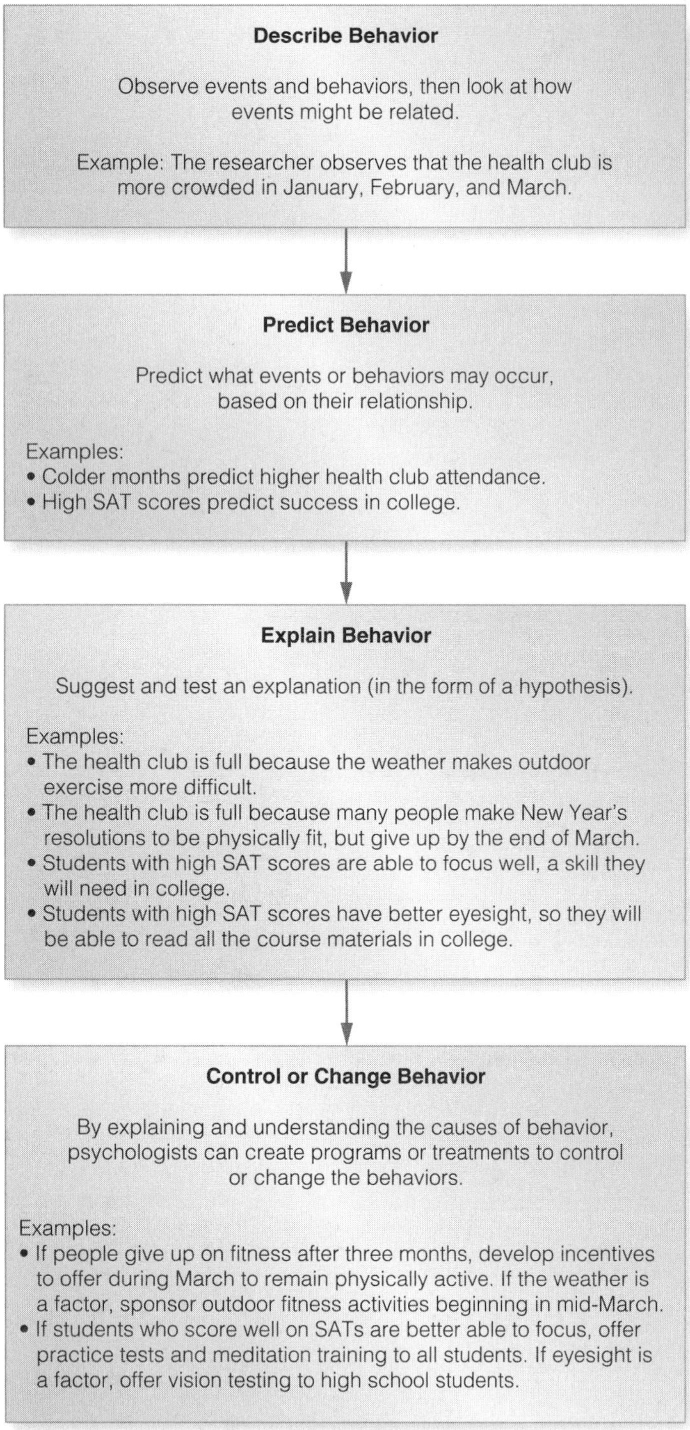

FIGURE 2.1

Goals of Psychology. Psychologists attempt to describe, predict, explain and, ultimately, control or change behavior.

do well in college. Consequently, a student's scores on these tests often influence college admission personnel in deciding who will be accepted and who will not (Davies & Guppy, 1997). The more academically rigorous colleges tend to admit students who score very high on these tests because it is predicted that they will do better than those with lower scores.

Although it may be known that two events regularly occur together, that doesn't tell us what caused a particular behavior to occur. Winter months do not cause health clubs to become crowded. Performing well on an SAT test on an early Saturday morning does not cause an individual to perform well in college. These two events are related, but one event does not cause the other. Therefore, an additional goal of psychology is to *explain* or understand the causes of behavior. As stated previously, psychologists usually put forth explanations of behavior in the form of theories. A theory is an explanation of why and how a particular behavior occurs. We introduced seven explanations, or perspectives of behavior, earlier in the chapter. For example, how do we explain higher health club attendance in the winter months? Is it a behavior that is influenced by the environment? Perhaps health clubs are more crowded because the weather makes outdoor exercise more difficult? Is it a behavior that is influenced by our biology? Perhaps students with high SAT scores have better eyesight, so they are better able to read the course materials in college. As these ideas are tested, more and more causes and predictors of behavior are discovered. Some of these explanations or theories will be modified, some will be discarded, and new ones will be developed.

The purpose behind explaining and understanding the causes of behavior is the final goal of psychology, *controlling* or *changing* behavior. It relates to the goal of explanation because one needs to understand what is causing a behavior in order to change or modify it. For example, let's say that the weather is a factor in health club attendance. Health clubs could offer outdoor fitness activities beginning in mid-March to prevent declining enrollment. If eyesight is a factor in SAT performance, schools could offer vision testing to high school students to solve the problem. Many psychologists go into the field in the hope of improving society. They may want to improve child care, create healthier work environments, or reduce discrimination in society. Such sentiments reflect the goal of control and underscore the potential impact of good research. Figure 2.1 summarizes the goals of psychology.

THE SCIENTIFIC METHOD

The purpose of psychological research is to test ideas about behavior. As previously stated, researchers use a prescribed method or procedure to test ideas, called the scientific method. The scientific method is a set of rules for gathering and analyzing information that enables you to test an idea or hypothesis. All scientists adhere to these same steps even though they may use different techniques within each step. The decisions the scientist makes at each step of the scientific method will ultimately affect the types of conclusions that can be made about behavior. The steps of the scientific method are as follows:

1. *Define and describe the issue to be studied.* Psychologists decide what to study and then find relevant information on that behavior through observation or through studying previous research found in scientific journals.
2. *Form a testable hypothesis.* State what you expect to find in a way that can be objectively measured—that is, in a way that another person can come along and test the same hypothesis to verify or *replicate* your results.
3. *Choose an appropriate research strategy.* This step involves many decisions. You must decide how you are going to test the hypothesis or study the behavior. What research method will best test your hypothesis? (These methods are discussed in the next section.) You must also decide where your study will be conducted. Will it be in the field (the environment where the behavior naturally occurs) or will it be in a laboratory (a more controlled setting)? You must decide who or what you will observe in your study, in other words who you will use as *participants.* Will you use animals or humans? If using humans, how will these individuals be selected? If using animals as your subjects, what species will you use?
4. *Conduct the study to test your hypothesis.* Run the study and collect the data.
5. *Analyze the data to support or reject your hypothesis.* The type of research strategy that you have chosen will in many ways determine how you can analyze the data. Analysis of data is usually conducted using statistics, which enable you to support or reject your hypothesis.

Just as you have used the conclusions of other studies to investigate your idea (Step 1), the conclusions of your study may become a source of information for developing your next hypothesis or the hypothesis of another researcher.

Now that you are aware of the steps that psychologists follow when conducting research, you may be asking yourself, how can the scientific method be used to meet the goals of psychology? Let's say that you have an interest in understanding beer drinking among college students. You want to make some predictions (a goal of psychology) about beer drinking. You use the scientific method to test this idea as outlined in Figure 2.2. First, you develop your hypothesis. You might hypothesize that college students who buy pitchers of beer tend to drink more than college students who purchase bottles of beer (a prediction). You want to see if there is a relationship between the quantity of beer consumed and the form in which the beer is purchased. The next step would be to select a research strategy, including who and what is to be measured and in what manner. So you design a study that measures how much beer is consumed by college students who buy pitchers versus the amount of beer consumed by college students who buy bottles. After collecting the data, you employ statistics to see if there is a relationship and whether support for your hypothesis was found. Geller, Russ, and Altomari (1986) actually included this prediction in a larger study on beer drinking among college students and found support for the hypothesis that buying pitchers led to larger amounts of beer being consumed.

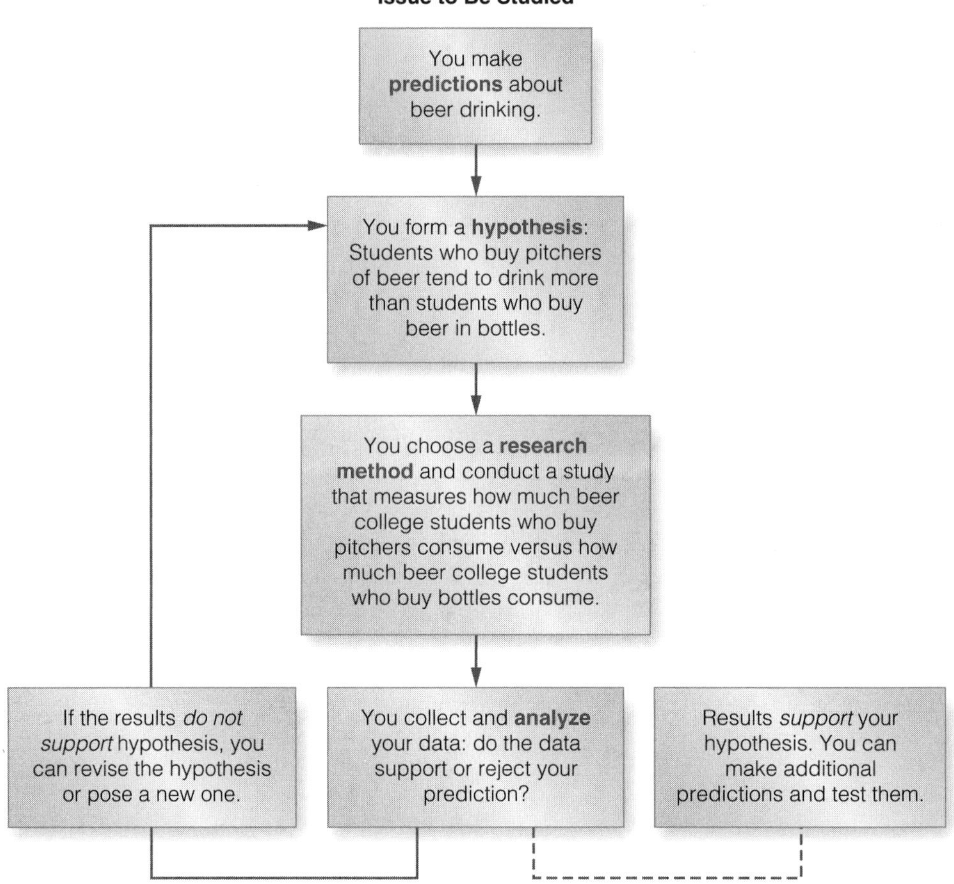

FIGURE 2.2

The Scientific Method. The scientific method enables researchers to test ideas about behavior.

No matter what goal of psychology you are addressing, the process is the same. The goal merely influences the decisions that you make when testing an idea through the scientific method. If your goal is description or prediction, your hypothesis will state what you expect to observe or what relationships you expect to find. Your research strategy then would be designed to measure observations or relationships, and your analysis of the data would employ statistics that enable you to support or refute your hypothesis. It is in this way that the scientific method allows one to test the ideas of psychology.

HYPOTHESES

What types of questions do psychologists ask when doing research? As you have seen, one of the first steps of the scientific method is to formulate a question or hypothesis about behavior. These hypotheses generally fall into one of two categories: predictive hypotheses or causal hypotheses.

Predictive Hypotheses

predictive hypothesis an educated guess about the relationships among variables.

Predictive hypotheses make a specific set of predictions about the relationships among variables. They are used to address two goals of psychology: description and prediction. The previous example on beer drinking and college youth illustrated a predictive hypothesis. Predictive hypotheses are made when the researcher measures the variables of interest but does not manipulate or control the variables in the study. For example, if we were to predict that people are more likely to experience nightmares after eating spicy food, we would measure the number of nightmares a person experiences, and then ask what he or she ate for dinner the night before. We then would see if a relationship existed between eating spicy food and having nightmares. Because the researcher does not control the variables, conclusions of research studies that test predictive hypotheses are limited. The conclusions can only state what was observed, or what variables appear to be related to one another. They cannot be used to make cause and effect conclusions. To do this, you must form and test a causal hypothesis.

Causal Hypotheses

In contrast to predictive hypotheses, **causal hypotheses** detail specifically how one variable will influence another variable. Causal hypotheses state our ideas about the causes of behavior and in many ways influence the theories that are formulated to explain behavior. Causal hypotheses can be tested only when it is possible for the researcher to control or manipulate the main variables in a study. The researcher sets up different conditions in a study and then observes whether or not there is a change in behavior because of the different conditions. For example, suppose a researcher has developed a new strategy to teach children how to read. The researcher hypothesizes that this program will cause greater gains in reading than the standard method for teaching reading. This is a causal hypothesis. Some students are assigned to the new reading program, and others are assigned to the standard program. The researcher then measures the children's gains in reading at the end of the year to see if there is a difference. As you will soon see, causal hypotheses can only be tested when an experiment is conducted. To test a causal hypothesis, a researcher must be able to conclude how one variable affects or causes a change in another variable.

causal hypothesis
an educated guess about how one variable will influence another variable.

RESEARCH METHODS

Once you have stated a hypothesis, the next step in the research process is to decide on a research strategy. The type of hypothesis you make (predictive or causal) typically determines which research methods you can employ. You are more likely to use some research methods to test predictive hypotheses and to use other methods to test cause a hypotheses.

What research methods are used to test predictive hypotheses? Several types of research methods are used to test predictive hypotheses. All of these methods are used when the researcher cannot control or manipulate the main variables in the study. Each method has its advantages and disadvantages. We will discuss three such methods: naturalistic observations, case studies, and correlational research.

Naturalistic Observations

Naturalistic observations are research studies that are conducted in the environment in which the behavior typically occurs. For example, Belsky, Woodworth, and Crnic (1996) collected naturalistic observations of parents and their toddlers around dinnertime on two occasions. Their observations enabled them to predict which families might be more troubled. The researcher in a naturalistic study is a recorder or observer of behavior who then describes or makes predictions about behavior based on what he or she has observed. Because the researcher doesn't control events in a naturalistic study, it is not possible to pinpoint the causes of

naturalistic observation
observing behavior in the environment in which the behavior typically occurs.

© Ariel Skelley/Corbis

A school playground could be an environment for naturally observing children's behaviors.

behavior. Therefore, naturalistic studies are predominately used to get at the goals of description and prediction.

Suppose you want to observe and describe childhood aggression. Would this lend itself to naturalistic observation? Where might you conduct such a study? A naturalistic environment for observing childhood aggression may be a school playground. However, not all behavior lends itself to naturalistic observation. For example, if you want to study helping behavior in an emergency situation, it would be very difficult to conduct a naturalistic study. Where would you make your observations? You could go to disaster scenes, but these observations would be taking place *after* the emergency had occurred. Even if you decided on a place, you could be waiting there a very longtime before an emergency actually occurred!

While naturalistic observation does allow a researcher to paint a picture of behavior as it normally occurs, researchers need to consider the influence of *reactivity.* Consider the example of studying childhood aggression by observing students on a school playground. What might happen if you were to simply enter the playground, sit down, and start writing about what you saw? The children might behave differently due to your presence and/or due to the awareness that they are being observed, and your observations of aggression might not be reliable or true. Consequently, when conducting a naturalistic observation, researchers attempt to minimize reactivity. In this way, they can be sure that they are observing the true behavior of their participants.

Case Studies

case study
an in-depth observation of one person.

Case studies are an in-depth observation of one subject. The subject may be an individual, an organism, or a setting such as a business or a school. Every chapter of this book opens with a brief case study. As with naturalistic observation, in case studies researchers do not control any variables but merely record or relate their observations. Oliver Sacks, a neuropsychologist doing case study research, describes the behavior of people who have been affected by various neurological disorders in his book *The Man Who Mistook His Wife for a Hat* (1985). Case studies are used to detail unusual or rare circumstances. For example, much of what we know about dissociative identity disorder, formerly called multiple personality disorder, comes from case studies that have been turned into books and films such as *Sybil, When Rabbit Howls,* and *The Three Faces of Eve.*

Case studies are valuable because they provide in-depth information on rare and unusual conditions that we may not other wise be able to study. However, the main disadvantage of the case study method is its limited applicability to other situations. It is very difficult to take one case, especially a rare case, and say that it applies to everyone. In other words, case studies lack **generalizability**; because of this, the conclusions that are drawn from case studies are limited to the topic being studied.

generalizability
how well a researcher's findings apply to other individuals and situations.

Correlational Studies

Correlational studies test the relationship, or **correlation**, between two or more variables: television watching and violent behavior, the presence of malls in a community and employment rates, or depression and gender, for example. Again, in correlational studies the researcher does not control variables but rather measures them to see if any reliable relationship exists between the two variables. For example, if we were to measure your weight (one variable), what other variable may show a relationship to your weight? Your height? Your calorie consumption? Your gender? Your age? Your life expectancy? If you were to measure all of these variables, you may find that all of them vary inrelation to weight. These relationships are correlations.

correlation
the relationship between two or more variables.

Surveys, questionnaires, and inter views often attempt to establish correlations when tabulating their results. They measure many variables and then use statistics to see if any two variables are related. If you have ever filled out a questionnaire, participated in a phone interview, or completed a survey at the mall, you have participated in a correlational study. You were probably asked many questions such as your age, income level, gender, race, and what products you buy or how you feel about a particular issue or candidate. Your responses are then sorted by these attributes to see if, for instance, men are more likely to buy a particular product or vote for acertain candidate when compared to women.

Why bother collecting all these data and what are they used for? Such data are used to make predictions and test predictive hypotheses. Knowing which people are more likely to buy a product enables a company to market its product more effectively and perhaps devise new strategies to target individuals who are not buying its products. Similarly, knowing which behaviors are related to a higher frequency of illness enables a psychologist to predict who is more at risk for physical or mental illness.

The strength of correlations are measured through a *correlation coefficient,* which is a number that tells us the strength of the relationship between two factors. Correlation coefficients range from −1.00 to +1.00. The closer the correlation coefficient is to −1.00 or +1.00, the stronger the correlation, or the more related the two variables are. The closer the correlation coefficient is to 0, the weaker the correlation—that is, one variable does not reliably predict the other variable. For example, in a study on early parent–child relationships and the degree of later problem behavior in their children, Rothbaum, Rosen, Pott, and Beatty (1995) found a −.50 correlation between the mother's attachment to the infant and later problem behavior in the child. The correlation between the father's attachment to the infant and later problem behavior was −.15. The higher correlation found with mothers suggests that the mother–child relationship is a better predictor of subsequent problem behavior than the father–child relationship. Generally, the stronger the correlation is between two variables the more accurate our predictions are, but perfect (+1.00 or −1.00) correlations never happen in psychology. Human behavior is too complex for such perfect relationships to occur.

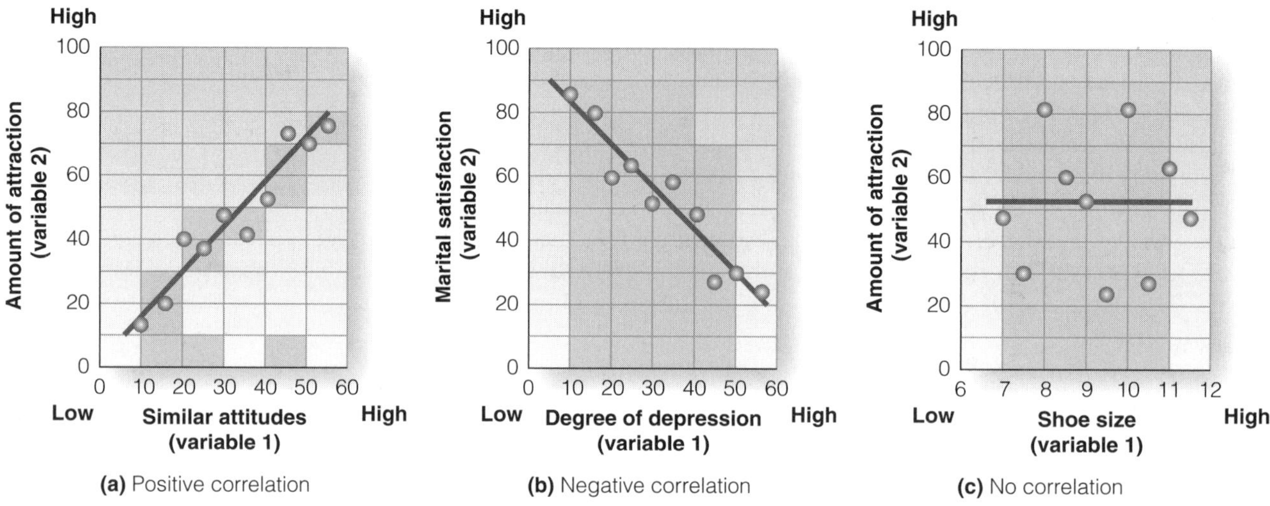

(a) Positive correlation

(b) Negative correlation

(c) No correlation

FIGURE 2.3

Correlation. Correlation, a research method used for prediction, shows how two variables are related.

positive correlation
a relationship in which increases in one variable correspond to increases in a second variable.

negative correlation
a relationship in which increases in one variable correspond to decreases in a second variable.

What do the positive and negative signs in front of the correlation mean? The sign before the correlation coefficient tells us how the variables relate to one another (Figure 2.3). A **positive correlation** means that as one variable increases the second variable also tends to increase, or as one variable decreases, the other variable tends to decrease. In both cases, the variables are changing in the *same* direction. An example of a positive correlation is marijuana use and lung cancer. As marijuana use increases, so does the likelihood of developing lung cancer (Caplan & Brigham, 1990; "Marijuanaas Medicine," 1997). Another example of a positive correlation is similarity in attitudes and attraction. The more similar two people are in attitudes, the more likely they are to be attracted to one another (Byrne, 1969).

In a **negative correlation,** as one variable increases the other variable tends to decrease in what is referred to as an *inverse* relationship. Notice that the variables are changing in *opposite* directions. An example of a negative correlation is exercise and anxiety. The more people exercise, the less anxiety they tend to experience (Morgan, 1987). Or consider the relationship between marital satisfaction and depression. As marital satisfaction increases, feelings of depression decrease (Beach, Sandeen, & O'Leary, 1990).

As stated earlier, correlational studies enable researchers to make predictions about behavior, but they do not allow us to make cause and effect conclusions. This is a point often ignored by media reports of research results. For example, suppose you hear a radio announcer say that medical research has shown that people who eat bacon are less likely to have a heart attack. From these comments, you may incorrectly conclude that bacon *causes* the risk of heart attacks to decrease. However, the study yielding the results that bacon-eaters had fewer heart attacks was a correlational study. This type of conclusion cannot be drawn. Why? Researchers do not control the main variables in a correlational study; consequently, we cannot determine which variable causes the other. Perhaps more farmers than office workers eat bacon. Farmers may get more exercise than office workers. Hence, it may be exercise rather than bacon that is influencing the functioning of the heart.

An additional example will help underscore the point that correlations do not permit cause and effect conclusions (Figure 2.4). There is a positive correlation between academic achievement and self-esteem. Students who have high academic achievement also tend to have high self-esteem. Similarly, students who have low academic achievement tend to have low self-esteem. High academic achievement

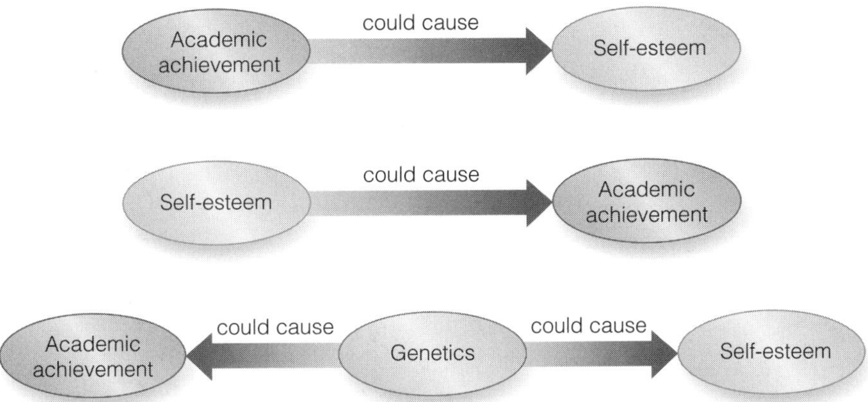

FIGURE 2.4

Correlation Does Not Mean Causation. When two variables are correlated or related, it does not mean that we know *why* they are related. It could be that high academic achievement causes high self-esteem. However, it is equally likely that high self-esteem causes high academic achievement. It is also possible that a third variable, such as genetics, causes both high self-esteem and high academic achievement, resulting in a relationship between the two variables. Correlation can only be used for making predictions, not for making cause and effect statements.

may cause an increas in self-esteem. However, it is just as likely that having high self-esteem causes one to do better academically. There may be a third variable, such as the parents' educational level or genetics, that actually causes the relationship between academic achievement and self-esteem. A correlational study does not tell us which of these explanations is correct. The only research method that permits us to make cause and effect conclusions is the experiment.

Experiments

What research method is used to test causal hypotheses? While several types of research methods are used to test predictive hypotheses, only one research method can test a causal hypothesis: the experiment. We will discuss several features of the **experiment**, including its advantages and disadvantages.

experiment
a research method that is used to test causal hypotheses.

Necessary Conditions for an Experiment Two main features characterize an experiment (Figure 2.5). First, the variables in the study are controlled or manipulated. Second, participants are randomly assigned to the conditions of the study. When these two conditions have been met, causal conclusions *may* be drawn. Let's first turn our attention to the issue of experimenter control.

The point of the experiment is to manipulate one variable and see what effect this manipulation has on another variable. These variables are termed the independent and dependent variables, respectively. The **independent variable** is the variable that the experimenter manipulates, and it is the cause in the experiment. The **dependent variable** measures any result of manipulating the independent variable, so it is the effect in the experiment. Suppose, for example, that we want to study the effects of sleep deprivation. Specifically, we hypothesize that sleep deprivation causes deficits in memory. This is a causal hypothesis that can be tested with an experiment. We decide to manipulate the amount of sleep participants receive to see if it has any effect on memory. In this example, the amount of sleep is our independent variable. Some participants will be allowed to sleep 8 hours per night for the week of our study. Others will be allowed to sleep only

independent variable
the variable in an experiment that is manipulated.

dependent variable
the variable in an experiment that measures any effect of the manipulation.

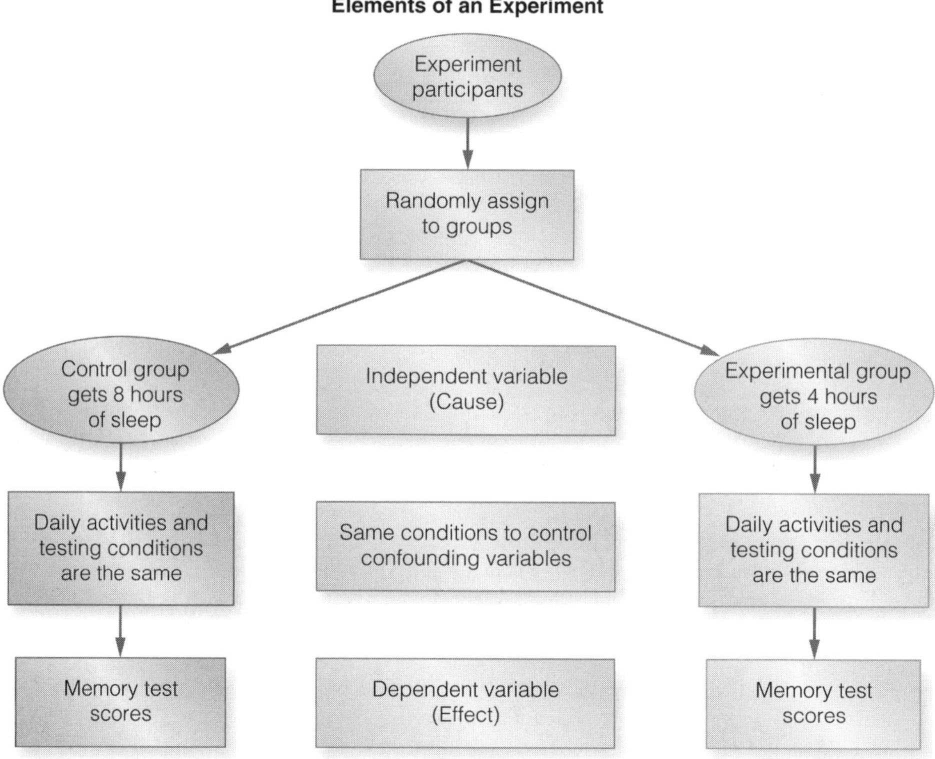

FIGURE 2.5

Elements of an Experiment. The two main ingredients of an experiment are (1) that the variables in the study are controlled or manipulated and (2) that participants are randomly assigned to the conditions of the study. When these two conditions have been met, causal conclusions *may* be drawn.

4 hours each night. The experimenter has set, or controlled, the amount of sleep (the independent variable) at two levels: 8 hours and 4 hours. Each day of our study we measure the participants' memory (the dependent variable) by having the participants complete several memory tasks. At the end of the study, we compare the memory scores of those participants who received 8 hours of sleep with those who received only 4 hours of sleep.

To be sure that it is the amount of sleep affecting memory and not something else, we need to be sure that we controlled any variable (other than the independent variable) that may influence this relationship. These potentially problematic variables are called **confounding variables**. What variables might we need to control? Maybe age influences one's memory or how one handles sleep deprivation? If either of these is true, we would want to control the age of our participants. We also would want to make sure that participants had not used any substances known to affect memory or the sleep cycle prior to their participation in the experiment. Consequently, we would control for this variable too.

confounding variable
any factor that affects the dependent measure other than the independent variable.

Both groups must be treated the same except for the amount of sleep they receive, so the researcher sets the conditions of the experiment to be the same for both groups. For example, every participant should complete the memory tasks at the same time of day, and every participant should complete the same memory tasks. The criteria for scoring the memory tasks must be the same as well. The instructions for completing the tasks must be the same. The lighting, temperature, and other physical features of the room in which the participants sleep and complete the memory tasks should be the same for all participants. Our purpose here is to design a study in which we manipulate the independent variable to see its

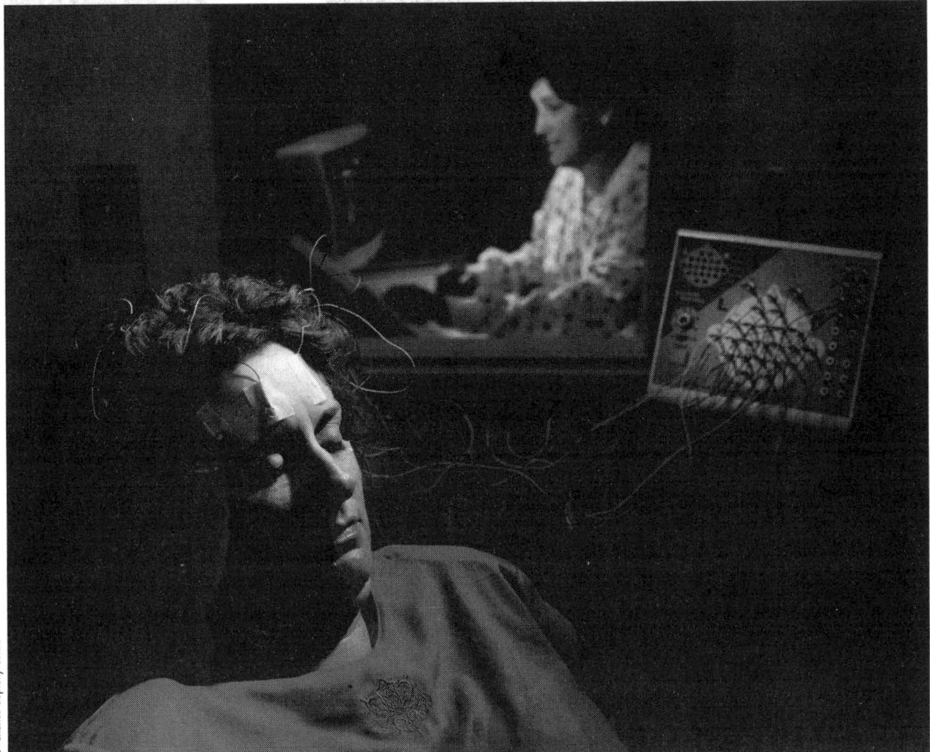

By studying behavior in a lab environment, researchers are better able to control the variables in an experiment.

effect on the dependent variable. If we control any potentially confounding variables that influence this relationship and find a difference in the dependent variable between our groups, it is most likely due to the independent variable, and we have proven a cause and effect relationship.

What if the experimenter does not control a confounding variable? We now have more than one variable that could be responsible for the change in the dependent variable: the independent variable and the confounding variable. When this occurs, the researcher is left with an alternative explanation for the results. The change in the dependent variable could have been caused by the independent variable, but it also could have been caused by the confounding variable. Consequently, causal conclusions are limited.

Let's not forget the second condition necessary for an experiment—how participants are assigned to the conditions of the independent variable. Just as we do not want any differences in the nature of our conditions other than the amount of sleep, we must be sure that there are no differences in the composition of our groups of participants. Psychologists eliminate this problem through the technique of **randomization**.

In the ideal experiment, researchers would include every person they are interested in studying. This is termed the **population of interest**. For a developmental psychologist who specializes in infant development, all infants would be the population of interest. It is impossible to test everyone, so researchers select a portion, or subset, of the population of interest called a **sample**. Because the sample will be used to make inferences or judgments about the entire population, the sample should reflect the whole population as much as possible; that is, it should be a *representative sample*. Random sampling of participants ensures a representative sample. In a *random sample,* every member of the population has an equal chance of being selected to participat in the study; thus, sampling bias is not introduced into the experiment.

randomization
when all people have an equal chance of being selected to participate in a study.

population of interest
the entire universe of animals or people that could be studied.

sample
the portion of the population of interest that is selected for a study.

Take a look around at your classmates in your general psychology course. Would this group qualify as a random sample of your college? Probably not. All of the students in the college did not have the same chance to choose the course. Registration typically is staggered such that students with more credits get to register earlier than students with fewer credits. So you are not a random sample. Would the group qualify as a representative sample of college students? Probably not. As a group, you may not represent the college student population in terms of age, race, income level, career major, geographic region, and so forth.

The more representative the sample is, the more the results will generalize to the population of interest. But random sampling is not always possible. Consequently, psychological research often uses *samples of convenience,* or groups of people who are easily accessible to the researcher. The students in your psychology course are a sample of convenience. In fact, much psychological research relies on using college students as their sample of convenience! In the United States only 24% of those over the age of 25 have college degrees, so these samples probably do not represent people from all walks of life (Snibbe, 2003).

random assignment
participants have an equal chance of being placed in any condition of the study.

Random sampling is ideal in research, but it is not a necessary condition for an experiment. It is always extremely important, however, that participants be **randomly assigned** to the conditions of the study. In our example on sleep and memory, assigning all the males in the sample to the 4-hour sleep condition and all the females to the 8-hour sleep condition would create a confounding variable. Gender differences may have an effect on memory scores. It may be that gender (the confounding variable) rather than sleep deprivation (the independent variable) is the cause of a difference in memory. To eliminate the influence of such confounding variables, experimenters randomly assign participants to conditions. Each participant has an equal chance of being placed in either condition. Males are just as likely to be assigned to the 4-hour condition as they are to the 8-hour condition, and the same is true for female participants. In this way, any participant variable that has the potential to influence the research results is just as likely to affect one group as it is the other. Without random assignment, confounding variables could affect the dependent variable. This is exactly what occurs in quasi-experiments.

quasi-experiment
a research study that is not a true experiment because participants are not randomly assigned to the conditions of the study.

A **quasi-experiment** is sort of like an experiment. The researcher manipulates the independent variable and sets the conditions of the experiment to be the same for both groups. However, the second condition necessary for an experiment—randomly assigning participants to conditions—has not been met. Quasi-experiments use existing groups of people who differ on some variable when compared to the other condition. For example, suppose you want to see if smoking cigarettes during pregnancy cause lower birth weight babies. For ethical reasons, you cannot assign some pregnant women to smoke and prevent others from smoking. Instead, for your smoking condition, you must select pregnant women who already smoke. These women may differ on other variables when compared to pregnant women who do not smoke. For example, their eating habits may differ. As a result, a confounding variable (the diet of the mothers) exists that could cause a difference in the dependent variable (the birth weigh of the offspring) other than smoking. Consider another example. You hypothesize that couples living together before marriage causes divorce. You randomly select couples for your experiment, but you cannot randomly assign them to the conditions of your study. You cannot force some of them to live together. Those couples already living together would be used as one condition, a select group of people who may differ on another variable. As you can see, quasi-experiments do not meet the conditions necessary for a "true" experiment. Consequently, causal conclusions based on quasi-experimental designs should be made cautiously.

Advantages and Disadvantages of Using Experiments Experiments have several advantages. First, it is only through experimentation that we can approach two of the goals of psychology: explaining and changing behavior. An experiment is the only research method that enables us to determine cause and effect relationships. This advantage makes interpreting research results less ambiguous. It is in the experiment that we attempt to eliminate any confounding variables either through experimenter control or random assignment of participants to groups. These techniques also foster clearer conclusions of research results.

If experiments are so great, why don't we just use them all the time? First, experiments do not address the first two goals of psychology: describing and predicting behavior. These are often the first steps in understanding behavior, and naturalistic observation and correlational studies are quite useful for doing this. Second, in an attempt to control confounding variables, experiments conducted in laboratory settings may create an artificial atmosphere. It is then difficult to know if the same result would occur in a more natural setting. This may be another reason to conduct naturalistic observations or correlational studies. Third, sometimes employing the experimental method is simply not possible due to ethical and practical considerations. As we mentioned in the case of quasi-experimental designs, we cannot force people to be randomly assigned to a condition that would harm them (such as smoking) or that does not pertain to them (such as having high blood pressure). Psychologists must follow certain ethical guidelines and practices when conducting research. We turn our attention to this topic next.

Ethical Issues in Psychological Research

Generally, psychologists affiliated with universities and colleges cannot conduct research unless their research proposal has passed review by an **Institutional Review Board (IRB)**. The function of the IRB is to ensure that the research study being proposed conforms to a set of ethical standards or guidelines. This section details who sets these standards and what the main responsibilities are for psychologists who conduct research.

Institutional Review Board (IRB)
a committee that reviews research proposals to ensure that ethical standards have been met.

Ethical Guidelines for Participants Who sets the ethical guidelines for psychological research? The American Psychological Association (APA), one of the main professional organizations for psychologists, has taken the lead in establishing ethical guidelines or professional behaviors that psychologists must follow. These guidelines, the "Ethical Principles of Psychologists and Code of Conduct" (APA, 2002), address a variety of issues including general professional responsibility, clinical practice, psychological testing, and research. Here we look at the guidelines psychologists must follow when conducting research with humans and animals.

What is the Golden Rule for conducting research on human participants? One of the main concerns of the IRB is to ensure that the proposed research has met the ethical guideline of respect and concern for the dignity and welfare of the people who participate (APA, 2002). Researchers must protect participants from any potential harm, risk, or danger as a result of their participation in a psychological study. If such effects occur, the researcher has the responsibility to remove or correct these effects. In the experiment that Watson and Raynor conducted on 9-month-old Albert, the fear that Albert developed toward white rats was never removed. Today the procedure for this experiment would be considered unethical. Watson caused harm to Albert and did not remove his fear at the end of the experiment.

A fundamental principle of ethical practice in research is **informed consent**. Researchers inform potential participants of any risks during the informed consent process wherein the researcher establishes a clear and fair agreement with research participants, prior to their participation in the research study (APA, 2002). This

informed consent
research participants agree to participate after being told about aspects of the study.

agreement clarifies the obligations and responsibilities of the participants and the researchers and includes the following information:

- The general purpose of the research study, including the experimental nature of any treatment
- Services that will or will not be available to the control group
- The manner by which participants will be assigned to treatment and control groups
- Any aspect of the research that may influence a person's willingness to participate in the research
- Compensation for or monetary costs of participating
- Any risks or side effects that may be experienced as a result of participation in the study

confidentiality
researchers do not reveal which data were collected from which participant.

Prospective participants are also informed that they may withdraw from participation in the study at any time, and they are informed of any available treatment alternatives. In addition, the researcher agrees to maintain **confidentiality**. Personal information about participants obtained by the researcher during the course of the investigation cannot be shared with others unless explicitly agreed to in advance by the participant or as required by law or court order.

Can you trick participants in an experiment? It is not always possible to fully inform participants of the details of the research, as it may change their behavior. For this reason, psychologists sometimes use *deception* in their research. For example, suppose we wanted to research student cheating. If we tell participants we are studying cheating behavior, it will likely influence their behavior. If we tell participants we are investigating student–teacher behavior, we can measure student cheating more objectively. However, the use of deception must be justified by the potential value of the research results. Moreover, deception can be used only when alternative procedures that do not use deception are unavailable.

debriefing
after an experiment, participants are fully informed of the nature of the study.

If participants have been deceived in any way during the course of a study, the researcher is obligated to debrief participants after the experiment ends. **Debriefing** consists of full disclosure by the researcher to inform participants of the true purpose of the research. Any misconceptions that the participant may hold about the nature of the research must be removed at this time. For example, suppose you volunteer to participate in a psychological experiment on attitudes toward your school. You arrive at the psychology lab at the appropriate time and are asked to wait in a room for a moment with two other participants. While in the waiting room, the other participants start talking to you. One is very pleasant and kind, but the other is rude, negative, and over bearing. The researcher then arrives and escorts you to another room in which you complete a self-esteem questionnaire. After completing the survey, you are then told that the true purpose of the study was to investigate your reaction to the people in the waiting room. The researcher is exploring how positive and negative behaviors influence another person's self-esteem. The two people in the waiting room were not really participants but *confederates,* individuals who pose as participants but who are really working for the researcher. In such an experiment, you were not physically or psychologically harmed, so the deception and subsequent debriefing were ethical. This ethical standard was not always met in the past. Consider the following research study.

In the 1960s Stanley Milgram (1963) set out to determine if the average person could be influenced to hurt others in response to orders from an authority figure. Participants were deceived into believing that they were participating in a research study on learning rather than on obedience. Participants were told that they would be playing the role of a "teacher" in the experiment. Participants were introduced to a "learner" who was then led to a separate room. The teacher's job was to administer electric shocks to the learner every time the learner made a mistake in an effort to help the learner better learn a list of words. In reality, the participant was not actually shocking the learner. The learner's responses were prerecorded on a tape, but the participants did not know this and believed they were, indeed, shocking the learner.

Despite the fact that participants believed the learner to be ill or worse, most of them continued to follow the experimenter's orders. A full 65% of the participants shocked the learner all the way up to 450 volts! During the procedure, Milgram's participants did exhibit many stress-related behaviors. Although Milgram debriefed his participants after the study, he still violated the ethical principle of psychological harm. He was criticized for exposing participants to the trauma of the procedure itself and for not leaving the participants in at least as good a condition as they were prior to the experiment (Baumrind, 1964). Because of these ethical problems, a study such as this would not be approved today.

We also must note that for years the primary focus in research was on white males. Women and minorities were not only discouraged from becoming professionals in psychology but also were largely ignored or neglected when studying psychological issues. Many minority and women psychologists as well as men have contributed to the field of psychology by addressing these shortcomings and designing research that looks specifically at the behaviors of minorities and women.

Ethical Guidelines for Animal Research Animal studies have advanced our understanding of many psychological issues including the importance of prenatal nutrition, our treatment of brain injuries, and our understanding of mental disorders (Domjan & Purdy, 1995). Psychologists must meet certain standards and follow ethical guidelines when conducting research with animals. Psychological research using animal subjects must also be approved by an IRB. Less than 10% of all psychological studies involve animal subjects, and these consist mainly of rodents and birds (APA, 1984). Animals must be treated humanely and in accord with all federal, state, and local laws and regulations. Researchers are responsible for the daily comfort, housing, cleaning, feeding, and health of animal subjects. Discomfort, illness, and pain must be kept at a minimum, and such procedures can only be used if alternative procedures are not available. Moreover, harmful or painfull procedures used on animals must be justified in terms of the knowledge that is expected to be gained from the study. Researchers also must promote the psychological well-being of some animals that are used in research, most notably primates (APA, 2002).

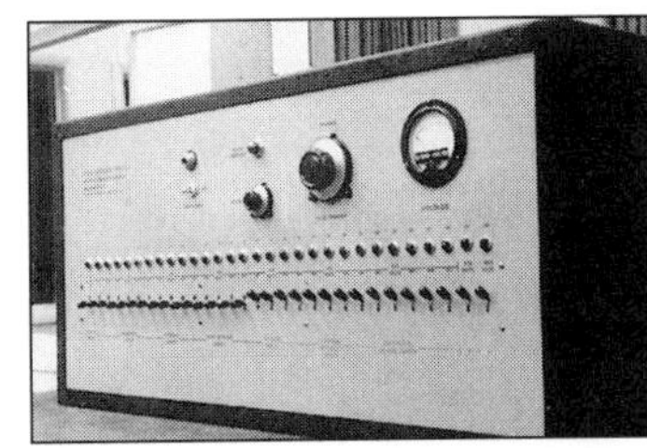
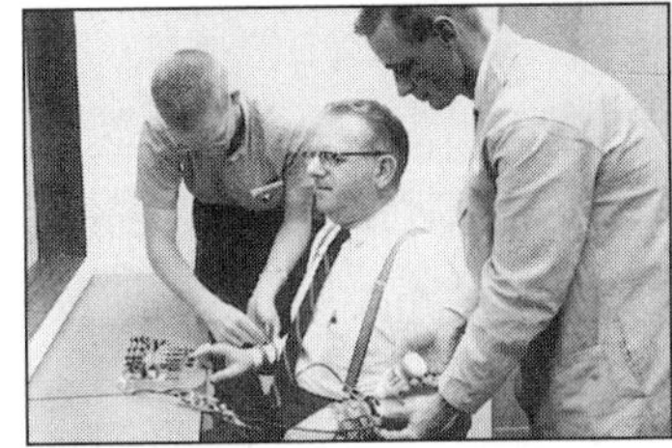
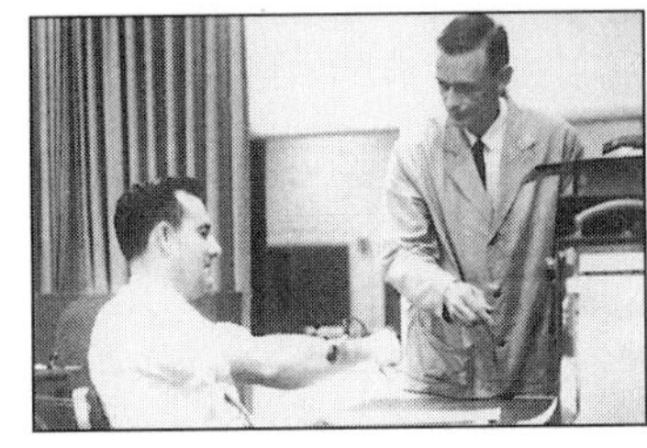

Although Stanley Milgram debriefed his participants, he still caused them psychological harm. Such a study violates current ethical standards of psychological research.

THE NATURE OF CRITICAL THINKING

Critical thinking is the conscious direction of mental processes toward representing and processing information, usually in order to find thoughtful solutions to problems, make judgments or decisions, or reason. Critical thinking is essential in psychology.

Critical thinking involves both dispositions and abilities (Ennis, 1987). *Dispositions* are how you decide to approach a problem or decision. *Abilities* are how well you approach the problem or decision. Examples of dispositions are seeking reasons for what you believe, trying to be well informed in making decisions, looking for alternative options in making decisions, being open-minded, and being sensitive to the feelings, knowledge, and viewpoints of others. Abilities are skills for solving problems. Relevant abilities include focusing on the question at hand, analyzing arguments, deciding whether a conclusion follows from the data, asking questions relevant to the problem or decision upon which you are focused, and making generalizations from past experience.

Consider an example. You find yourself thinking negatively about a group of people. You start to wonder whether your thoughts reflect critical thinking or express a prejudice. How might you decide? With respect to dispositions, you can start by asking yourself whether you have good reasons for feeling the way you do.

You might also seek information about the group. With respect to abilities, you might analyze the arguments for and against your beliefs and then decide whether the conclusions you have reached follow from the data. Critical thinking can help us overcome prejudices by making us aware of the flaws in our thinking.

When people draw the wrong conclusions from psychological (or any other kind of) research, it often is because of a failure in critical thinking. Suppose that Dr. Schlotz is convinced that speaking to plants in a soothing tone of voice helps them grow. He has 20 plants. At the beginning of a 30-day period, he carefully measures the height of each plant. Then, each day for 30 days, he speaks to them soothingly. At the end of 30 days, he compares their heights to their heights at the beginning of the 30 days. He finds that all of them have grown at least somewhat and that the difference in height is statistically significant. He concludes that talking to the plants really did help them grow.

Schlotz has shown poor critical thinking. He did not look for alternative explanations before deciding that the plants grew because he talked to them. Other factors might have caused them to grow, such as watering them, exposing them to sunlight, or just leaving them to follow their normal course of growth. If he had analyzed his argument carefully, he would have realized that his conclusion did not follow from his data. To support his conclusion, he would have needed a control group of plants. Plants would be randomly assigned to groups, and all would be treated exactly the same except that one group of plants would be talked to soothingly and the other would not. Schlotz might well have obtained a different result had he thought more critically about his experiment.

Fallacies That Prevent Critical Thinking

When people do not think critically, they often fall into traps by committing one or more of the following informal logical fallacies.

- *Irrelevant conclusion.* We commit this fallacy when our conclusion is irrelevant to the line of reasoning that led to it. For example, Tom reads an experiment by Dr. Bailey. Tom is very upset that Dr. Bailey with held food from rats so that they would run mazes in order to seek a food reward. Asked about the experiment, Tom criticizes its results as invalid because he "would never trust the results of someone who starves animals."
- *Composition.* We commit this fallacy when we reason that what is true of parts of a whole is necessarily true of the whole itself. In fact, elements (such as members of a team) may interact in ways (such as poor teamwork) that render untrue for the whole what is true for each part. For example, Jeannette reads an experiment by a team of five researchers led by Dr. Hawthorne, whom Jeannette greatly respects. Later Jeannette is asked what she thinks of the particular team of researchers that produced the article. Jeannette comments that "it is a great team," figuring that any team with Hawthorne on it must be great.
- *Personalization.* If you see yourself as the cause of some event for which you were not primarily responsible, you have committed the fallacy of personalization. Taking personally a statement that is not directed toward you is also inappropriate. For example, Mrs. Dittman criticizes a particular statistic as yielding questionable results. Mrs. Fleming has used that statistic in her research. She decides that Dittman is criticizing her personally and attacks Dittman as ignorant and incompetent.
- *False cause.* The fallacy of false cause is committed when someone concludes from the fact that two events happened in rapid succession, or have tended to happen together, that the first event caused the second. For example, one day Jack wears his fraternity T-shirt and the results of his experiment are positive.

A couple of weeks later Jack is again wearing his T-shirt and his results again work out. Jack decides that it is probably a good idea to wear his fraternity T-shirt on days when he will find out whether his results have worked out.

- *Ad hominem argument.* This kind of argument is directed "to the man" rather than the position of the person. One attempts to attack an individual personally in order to undermine the person's position. For example, Mr. Faver has been asked to comment on the research of Mr. Dunn. Faver has never liked Dunn and sees his chance to get back at what he perceives as injustices Dunn has committed toward him. Faver remarks that Dunn received his degree at a university that is not very well known and therefore people really should not trust Dunn's results.

© Spencer Grant/PhotoEdit

Critical thinking helps keep us alert to the informal fallacies to which we are all prone. For example, these two candidates seem to be blaming each other, a classic ad hominem argument in which one tries to undermine the other's position simply by saying that he or she is wrong, rather than offering evidence.

When people fail to apply critical thinking to problems—scientific or otherwise—they are likely to fall into traps that jeopardize the quality of their thinking. I have argued that even smart people can do stupid things (R. J. Sternberg, 2002). There are four traps into which smart people frequently fall. The first, *egocentrism,* occurs when an individual starts to view the world as centered around him or her. The person thinks that the important point is satisfying his or her ego rather than doing what is best. The second trap is *omniscience.* The person starts to think he or she "knows it all." The third trap is *omnipotence,* or feeling that one is all-powerful. And the fourth trap is *invulnerability,* or believing that no matter what one does, probably no one will be able to find out; or even if someone finds out, it will not matter because one has disguised one's tracks. Business executives can fall into these traps. High-level executives of major corporations severely mismanaged their companies in the late 1990s, often taking money for themselves that rightfully belonged to shareholders. This mismanagement set the stage for the sharp decline in the stock market in 2002.

These traps can also occur in science. For many years, Soviet scientists believed in *Lysenkoism,* the notion that acquired traits (such as becoming overweight by eating too much) could be inherited. In other words, if you eat too much and become obese, you may pass on your acquired obesity to your children. In fact, acquired traits cannot be inherited. A whole scientific edifice was built in the former Soviet Union around this myth. Instead of thinking critically, followers of this theory fell into traps in their thinking, perhaps believing that neither Lysenko nor they could do wrong. Scientists need to pay careful attention to critical thinking in their work to make sure they do not fall into the same traps anyone else can fall into in everyday life. The important point is to be on guard for these fallacies and to catch ourselves when we make them. In this way, we improve both our thinking and the conclusions we draw from it.

One more important issue remains before we leave this introductory discussion of psychological research methods and practices: researcher ethics.

CHAPTER 2 PRACTICE EXAM

____ 1. Hypotheses are
a. predictions
b. moot
c. answers
d. consequences

____ 2. What is the first goal of science to be done?
a. description
b. consequent
c. control
d. explanation

____ 3. To describe how college students hang out in classes, a researcher should use the ______ method.
a. naturalistic observation
b. Quasi-experimental
c. survey
d. case study

____ 4. The naturalistic observation method is best when the scientist wants to _________ behavior.
a. predict
b. explain
c. control
d. describe

____ 5. Case studies use
a. experiments of irrelevant variables.
b. The experiment on people
c. Survey research using naturalistic observation.
d. Assessing a single or several people in depth.

____ 6. If a researcher wants to learn how students like a particular professor, she should use the
a. experimental method.
b. case study method.
c. survey method.
d. naturalistic observation method.

____ 7. Precise control over the independent variable is one advantage of the _______method.
a. questionnaire, or survey
b. Quasi-case study
c. naturalistic linkage
d. experimental

____ 8. The _________ variable may be affected by the variables manipulated by the experimenter.
a. independent
b. conscious
c. dependent
d. confounding

____ 9. One group of elementary school children reads a story three times before taking a test on the story. The second group reads the story ten times before taking the test. The independent variable is the
a. number of times the story is read.
b. Grade on the test.
c. Experience of the researcher
d. The type of story being read

____ 10. Research participants who do not engage in the experimental treat are in the _________ condition.
a. dependent
b. independent
c. control
d. Wait list

____ 11. Participants in a study who are available immediately are called
a. samples of convenience.
b. representative samples.
c. uncontrolled samples.
d. Random samples.

____ 12. A scientist has _________ variables in a quasi-experimental design.
a. less freedom inside
b. less control over
c. more freedom outside
d. more control under

____ 13. Which is weakest correlation between two variables?
a. .51
b. −.82
c. −.37
d. .27

____ 14. Being a "know it all" is the trap of
a. egocentrism.
b. omniscience.
c. omnipotence.
d. invulnerability.

____ 15. __________ helps ensure that participants will not bias their responses when participating in research.
a. Informed consent
b. Debriefing
c. An Institutional Review Board
d. Deception

Answers

1. A
2. A
3. A
4. D
5. D
6. C
7. D
8. C
9. A
10. C
11. A
12. B
13. D
14. B
15. D

CHAPTER 3: MEMORY

QUESTIONS

1. What are three memory systems and examples of each system?
2. How do short-term, working, and long-term memory work? What kind of information does each store?
3. How much information is held in short-term memory?
4. What is the magic number?
5. How does chunking information help us remember?
6. What is one way to increase the odds of a memory stored in long term memory?
7. What is a suggestion for helping a person remember something, such as a name?
8. How would a student use elaborative rehearsal to remember?
9. What do most experts think about the permanence of memories?
10. How did the Loftus and Palmer (1974) study Hannigan and Reintiz studies construct memories?
11. What things help color our memories?
12. Why does hypnosis increase false memories?
13. How does a cognitive interview work in police investigations?
14. How does a network model explain memory structure?
15. What are the differences among procedural memory, declarative memory, semantic memory, and episodic memory?
16. How are recall, recognition, and relearning used to measure memory?
17. How is priming used to reveal implicit memories?
18. How did Kosslyn, Thomas, and Reiser (1978) show that memories exist as images?
19. What is the developmental course of eidetic imagery?
20. What evidence suggests exceptional memory can be learned?
21. What are some strategies exceptional memorizers' use?
22. How should a student study for a test?
23. What are the basic characteristics of the Ebbinghaus curve?
24. Why do we categorize?
25. How does short term memory operate?
26. What are some reasons disuse does not account for forgetting?
27. What is one suggestion to over come cue-dependent forgetting?
28. What are examples of state-dependent learning?
29. What are examples of retroactive and proactive interference?
30. What is the difference between repression and suppression?
31. What kinds of people are prone to repression?
32. What are two examples of false memories and two ways false memories can be created?
33. What are some characteristics of flashbulb memories?
34. How does time influence the consolidation of memories and ECS?
35. How does the hippocampus work and what happens if it is damaged?
36. Where are long term memories stored?
37. What changes occur in the cortex when memories are stored?
38. What brain mechanism is used to form lasting memories?
39. What happens to memory when memories areas of the brain are overstimulated, such as with Electroconvulsive Schock?
40. What are several ways people can improve their memory?
41. What are the basic principles of mnemonics and some examples of each?

VOCABULARY

1. Consolidation
2. Constructive processing
3. Curve of forgetting
4. Declarative memory
5. Disuse
6. Echo
7. Eidetic imagery
8. Elaborative rehearsal
9. Electroconvulsive shock (ECS)
10. Encoding
11. Encoding failure
12. Engram
13. Episodic memory
14. Explicit memory
15. Feeling of knowing
16. Flashbulb memories
17. Hippocampus
18. Icon
19. Implicit memory
20. Information bits
21. Information chunks
22. Interference
23. internal images
24. Long-term memory (LTM)
25. Maintenance rehearsal
26. Massed practice
27. Memory
28. Memory cue
29. Memory decay
30. memory task
31. Memory traces
32. Mnemonic
33. negative transfer
34. Network model
35. Positive transfer
36. Priming
37. Proactive interference
38. procedural memory
39. Recall
40. Recoding
41. Recognition memory
42. Redintegrative memories
43. Relearning
44. Repression
45. Retrieval
46. Retroactive interference
47. Sensory memory
48. Serial position effect
49. Short-term memory (STM)
50. Spaced practice
51. State-dependent learning
52. Storage
53. Suppression
54. Tip-of-the-tongue state
55. Working memory

3 Memory

Stages of Memory—Do You Have a Mind Like a Steel Trap? Or a Sieve?

Short-Term Memory—Do You Know the Magic Number?

Long-Term Memory—Where the Past Lives

Measuring Memory—The Answer Is on the Tip of My Tongue

Exceptional Memory—Wizards of Recall

Forgetting—Why We, Uh, Let's See; Why We, Uh . . . Forget!

Memory Formation—Some "Shocking" Findings

Improving Memory—Keys to the Memory Bank

Richard Heinzen/SuperStock

"What the Hell's Going on Here?"

IT'S FEBRUARY and Steven is cross-country skiing on the ice of Lake Michigan. He realizes he is very cold and decides to turn back. In a few minutes comes a new realization: He is lost. Wandering on the ice, he grows numb and very, very tired.

Put yourself in Steven's shoes, and you will appreciate the shock of what happened next. Steven clearly recalls wandering lost and alone on the ice. Immediately after that, he remembers waking up in a field. But as he looked around, Steven knew something was wrong. It was a warm spring day! In his backpack he found running shoes, swimming goggles, and a pair of glasses—all unfamiliar. As he looked at his clothing—also unfamiliar—Steven thought to himself, "What the hell's going on here?" Fourteen months had passed since he left to go skiing (Loftus, 1980). How did he get to the field? Steven couldn't say. He had lost over a year of his life to total amnesia.

As Steven's amnesia vividly shows, life without memory would be meaningless. Imagine the terror of having all your memries wiped out. You would have no identity, no knowledge, and no life history (Behrend, Beike, & Lampinen, 2004). You wouldn't recognize friends or family members. When you looked in a mirror, a stranger would stare back at you. In a very real sense, we are our memories.

This chapter discusses memory and forgeting. By reading it you'll almost certainly discover ways to improve your memory.

STAGES OF MEMORY—DO YOU HAVE A MIND LIKE A STEEL TRAP? OR A SIEVE?

Do you remember what you had for breakfast this morning? Or what happened on September 11, 2001? Of course you do. But how is it possible for us to so easily travel back in time? Let's begin with a look at basic memory systems. An interesting series of events must occur before we can say, "I remember."

Many people think of memory as "a dusty storehouse of facts." In reality, **memory** is an active system that receives, stores, organizes, alters, and recovers information (Lieberman, 2004). In some ways memory acts like a computer (Figure 3.1). Incoming information is first **encoded**, or changed into a usable form. This step is like typing data into a computer. Next, information is **stored**, or held in the system. (As we will see in a moment, human memory can be pictured as three separate storage systems.) Finally, memories must be **retrieved**, or taken out of storage, to be useful. If you're going to remember all of the 9,856 new terms on your next psychology exam, you must successfully encode, store, and retrieve them.

What are the three separate memory systems just mentioned? Psychologists have identified three stages of memory. To be stored for a long time, information must pass through all three (Figure 3.2).

memory
the mental system for receiving, encoding, storing, organizing, altering, and retrieving information.

encoding
converting information into a form in which it will be retained in memory.

storage
holding information in memory for later use.

retrieval
recovering information from storage in memory.

sensory memory
the first stage of memory, which holds an exact record of incoming information for a few seconds or less.

icon
a mental image or visual representation.

echo
a brief continuation of sensory activity in the auditory system after a sound is heard.

Sensory Memory

Let's say a friend asks you to pick up several things at a market. How will you remember them? Information first enters **sensory memory**, which can hold an exact copy of what you see or hear, for a few seconds or less. For instance, look at a flower and then close your eyes. An **icon** (EYE-kon), or fleeting mental image, of the flower will persist for about one half second. Similarly, when you hear information, sensory memory stores it as an *echo* for up to 2 seconds (Schweickert, 1993). An **echo** is a brief flurry of activity in the auditory system. In general, sensory memory holds information just long enough to move it to the second memory system (Neath, 2002).

FIGURE 3.1

In some ways, a computer acts like a mechanical memory system. Both systems process information, and both allow encoding, storage, and retrieval of data.

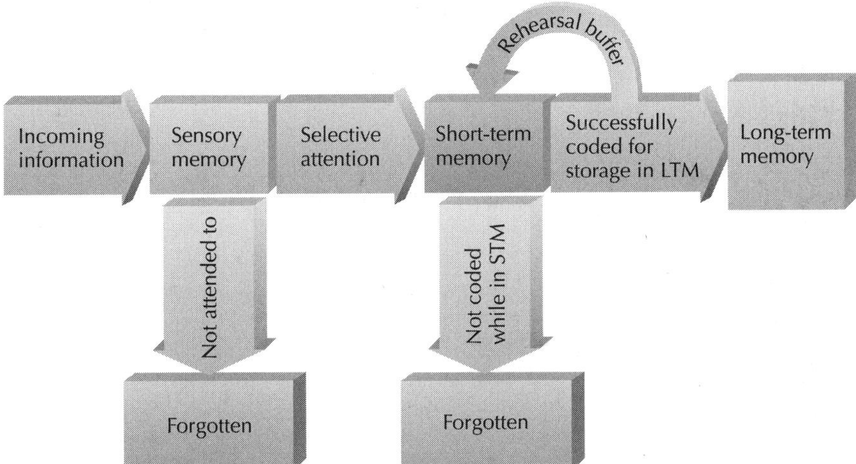

FIGURE 3.2

Remembering is thought to involve at least three steps. Incoming information is first held for a second or two by sensory memory. Information selected by attention is then transferred to temporary storage in short-term memory. If new information is not rapidly encoded or rehearsed, it is forgotten. If it is transferred to long-term memory, it becomes relatively permanent, although retrieving it may be a problem. The preceding is a useful, but highly simplified, *model* of memory; it may not be literally true of what happens in the brain (Eysenck & Keane, 1995).

Short-Term Memory

Not everything we see or hear stays in memory. Imagine that a radio is playing in the background as your friend reads her shopping list. Will you remember what the announcer says, too? Probably not, because *selective attention* (focusing on a selected portion of sensory input) controls what information moves on to short-term memory. **Short-term memory (STM)** holds small amounts of information for brief periods. By paying attention to your friend, you will place her shopping list in short-term memory (while you ignore the voice on the radio saying, "Buy Burpo Butter").

short-term memory (STM)
the memory system used to hold small amounts of information for relatively brief time periods.

How are short-term memories encoded? Short-term memories can be stored as images. But more often they are stored *phonetically* (by sound), especially in recalling words and letters (Neath, 2002). If you are introduced to Tim at a party and you forget his name, you are more likely to call him by a name that sounds like Tim (Jim, Kim, or Slim, for instance), rather than a name that sounds different, such as Bob or Mike. Your friend with the shopping list may be lucky if you don't bring home jam instead of ham and soap instead of soup!

Short-term memory briefly stores small amounts of information. When you dial a phone number or briefly remember a shopping list, you are using STM. Notice that information is quickly "dumped" from STM and forever lost. Short-term memory prevents our minds from storing useless names, dates, telephone numbers, and other trivia.

As you may have noticed when dialing a telephone, STM is very sensitive to *interruption,* or *interference.* You've probably had something like this happen: Someone leaves a phone number on your answering machine. You repeat the number to yourself as you start to dial. Then the doorbell rings and you rush to see who is there. When you return to the phone, you have completely forgotten the number. You listen to the message again and memorize the number. This time as you begin to dial, someone asks you a question. You answer, turn to the phone, and find that you have forgotten the number. Notice again that STM can handle only small amounts of information. It is very difficult to do more than one task at a time in STM (Miyake, 2001).

Working Memory Short-term memory is often used for more than just storing information. When STM is combined with other mental processes, it provides an area of **working memory** where we do much of our thinking. Working memory acts as a sort of "mental scratchpad." It briefly holds the information we need when we are thinking and solving problems (Tuholski, Engle, & Baylis, 2001). Whenever you do mental arithmetic, put together a puzzle, plan a meal, follow directions, or read a book, you are using working memory (Baddeley, 2003).

working memory
another name for short-term memory, especially when it is used for thinking and problem solving.

HUMAN DIVERSITY

Cows, Memories, and Culture

As noted, we are most likely to remember information that is personally meaningful. If you were on a farm and saw twenty cows walk by, do you think you could remember the age, color, sex, and condition of all of them? Unless you are a dairy farmer, doing so would be quite a feat of memory. However, for a Maasai person from East Africa, it would be easy. Livestock are very important in Maasai culture; wealth among the Maasai is measured by the number of cattle owned. Thus, the Maasai are prepared to code and store information about cattle that would be difficult for many people in the United States to remember.

Malcolm Linton/Liaison/Getty Images

Culture affects our memories in other interesting ways. For example, American culture emphasizes individuals, whereas Chinese culture emphasizes membership in groups. In a recent study, European-American and Chinese adults were asked to recall twenty memories from any time in their lives. As expected, American memories tended to be self-centered: Most people remembered surprising events and what they did during the events. Chinese adults, in contrast, remembered important social or historical events and their own interactions with family members, friends, and others (Wang & Conway, 2004). Thus, in the United States, personal memories tend to be about "me"; in China they tend to be about "us."

Long-Term Memory

long-term memory (LTM) the memory system used for relatively permanent storage of meaningful information.

If STM is so limited, how do we remember for longer periods of time? Information that is important or meaningful is transferred to **long-term memory (LTM),** which acts as a lasting storehouse for knowledge. LTM contains everything you know about the world—from aardvark to zucchini, math to MTV, facts to fantasy. Yet there appears to be no danger of running out of room. LTM can hold nearly limitless amounts of information. In fact, the more you know, the easier it becomes to add new information to memory. This is the reverse of what we would expect if LTM could be "filled up" (Eysenck & Keane, 1995). It is also one of many reasons for getting an education.

Are long-term memories also encoded as sounds? They can be. But typically, long-term memories are stored on the basis of *meaning,* not sound. If you make an error in LTM, it will probably be related to meaning. For example, if you are trying to recall the word *barn* from a memorized list, you are more likely to mistakenly say *shed* or *farm* than *yarn* or *darn.* If you can link information in STM to knowledge already stored in LTM, it gains meaning. This makes it easier to remember. As an example, try to memorize this story:

> With hocked gems financing him, our hero bravely defied all scornful laughter. "Your eyes deceive," he had said, "An egg, not a table, correctly typifies this unexplored planet." Now three sturdy sisters sought proof. Forging along, days became weeks as many doubters spread fearful rumors about the edge. At last from nowhere welcome winged creatures appeared, signifying momentous success. (Adapted from Dooling & Lachman, 1971)

This odd story emphasizes the impact that meaning has on memory. People given the title of the story were able to remember it far better than those not given a title. See if the title helps you as much as it did them: "Columbus Discovers America."

Dual Memory Most of our daily memory chores are handled by STM and LTM. To summarize their connection, picture short-term memory as a small desk at the front of a huge warehouse full of filing cabinets (LTM). As information enters the warehouse, it is first placed on the desk. Because the desk is small, it must be quickly cleared off to make room for new information. Unimportant items are simply tossed away. Meaningful or important information is placed in the files (LTM). When we want to use knowledge from LTM to answer a question, the information is returned to STM. Or, in our analogy, a folder is taken out of the files (LTM) and moved to the desk (STM), where it can be used.

Now that you have a general picture of memory it is time to explore STM and LTM in more detail. But first, here's a chance to rehearse what you've learned.

SHORT-TERM MEMORY—DO YOU KNOW THE MAGIC NUMBER?

To make good use of your memory, it is valuable to know more about the characteristics of STM and LTM. It's time to dig deeper into the inner workings of our primary memory systems.

How much information can be held in short-term memory? For an answer, read the following numbers once. Then close the book and write as many as you can in the correct order.

8 5 1 7 4 9 3

This is called a digit-span test. It is a measure of attention and short-term memory. If you were able to correctly repeat 7 digits, you have an average short-term memory. Now try to memorize the following list, reading it only once.

7 1 8 3 5 4 2 9 1 6 3 4

This series was probably beyond your short-term memory capacity. Psychologist George Miller found that short-term memory is limited to the "magic number" 7 (plus or minus 2) **information bits** (Miller, 1956). A bit is a single meaningful "piece" of information, such as a digit. It is as if short-term memory has 7 "slots" or "bins" into which separate items can be placed. Actually, a few people can remember up to 9 bits, and for some types of information 5 bits is the limit. Thus, an *average* of 7 information bits can be held in short-term memory (Neath, 2002).

information bits
meaningful units of information, such as numbers, letters, words, or phrases.

When all of the "slots" in STM are filled, there is no room for new information. Picture how this works at a party: Let's say your hostess begins introducing everyone who is there, "Chun, Dasia, Marco, Roseanna, Cholik, Shawn, Kyrene . . ." "Stop," you think to yourself. But she continues, "Nelia, Jay, Efren, Frank, Marietta, Jorge, Patty, Amit, Ricky." The hostess leaves, satisfied that you have met everyone. And you spend the evening talking with Chun, Dasia, and Ricky, the only people whose names you remember!

Recoding

Before we continue, test your short-term memory again, this time on letters. Read the following letters once, then look away and try to write them in the proper order.

T V I B M U S N Y M C A

Notice that there are 12 letters, or "bits" of information. This should be beyond the 7-item limit of STM. However, because the letters are in four groups, or *chunks* of information, many students are able to memorize them. **Information chunks** are made up of bits of information grouped into larger units.

information chunks
information bits grouped into larger units.

recoding
reorganizing or modifying information to assist storage in memory.

How does chunking help? Chunking **recodes** (reorganizes) information into units that are already in LTM. For example, you may have noticed that NY is the abbreviation for New York. If so, the two bits N and Y became one chunk. In an experiment that used lists like this one, people remembered best when the letters were read as familiar meaningful chunks: TV, IBM, USN, YMCA (Bower & Springston, 1970). If you recoded the letters this way, you probably remembered the entire list.

Chunking suggests that STM holds about 5 to 7 of whatever units we are using. A single chunk could be made up of numbers, letters, words, phrases, or familiar sentences (Barsalou, 1992). Picture STM as a small desk again. Through chunking, we combine several items into one "stack" of information. This allows us to place 7 stacks on the desk, where before there was only room for 7 separate items. While you are studying, try to find ways to link 2, 3, or more separate facts or ideas into larger chunks, and your memory will improve. Psychologist Nelson Cowan (2001) believes that STM may actually hold only 4 items, unless some chunking has occurred. The clear message is that creating information chunks is the key to making good use of your short-term memory.

Rehearsing Information

maintenance rehearsal
silently repeating or mentally reviewing information to hold it in short-term memory.

How long do short-term memories last? They disappear very rapidly. However, you can prolong a memory by silently repeating it, a process called **maintenance rehearsal**. You have probably briefly remembered an address or telephone number this way. In a sense, rehearsing information allows you to "hear" it many times, not just once (Nairne, 2002). The more times a short-term memory is rehearsed, the greater its chances of being stored in LTM (Barsalou, 1992).

What if rehearsal is prevented, so a memory cannot be recycled or moved to LTM? Without maintenance rehearsal, STM is incredibly brief. In one experiment, subjects heard meaningless syllables like XAR followed by a number like 67. As soon as subjects heard the number, they began counting backward by threes (to prevent them from repeating the syllable). After a delay of only 18 seconds, their memory scores fell to zero (Peterson & Peterson, 1959).

After *18 seconds* without rehearsal, the short-term memories were gone forever! Part of this rapid loss can be explained by the testing procedures used (Goldstein, 2005). In daily life, short-term memories usually last longer. Just the same, if you are introduced to someone, and the name slips out of STM, it is gone forever. To escape this awkward situation you might try saying something like, "I'm curious, how do you spell your name?" Unfortunately, the response is often an icy reply like, "B-O-B S-M-I-T-H, it's really not too difficult." To avoid embarrassment, pay careful attention to the name, repeat it to yourself several times, and try to use it in the next sentence or two—before you lose it (Neath, 2002).

elaborative rehearsal
rehearsal that links new information with existing memories and knowledge.

Elaborative rehearsal, which makes information more meaningful, is a far better way to form lasting memories. Elaborative rehearsal links new information to memories that are already in LTM. When you are studying, you will remember more if you elaborate, extend, and reflect about the meaning of information. As you read, try to frequently ask yourself "why" questions, such as, "Why would that be true?" (Willoughby et al., 1997). Also, try to relate new ideas to your own experiences and knowledge (Hartlep & Forsyth, 2000).

LONG-TERM MEMORY—WHERE THE PAST LIVES

An electrode touched the patient's brain. Immediately she said, "Yes, sir, I think I heard a mother calling her little boy somewhere. It seemed to be something happening years ago. It was somebody in the neighborhood where I live." A short time later the electrode was applied to the same spot. Again the patient said, "Yes, I hear the same familiar sounds, it seems to be a woman calling, the same lady" (Penfield, 1958). A woman undergoing brain surgery made these statements. There are no pain receptors in the brain, so the patient was awake as her brain was electrically stimulated (Figure 3.3). When activated, some brain areas seemed to produce vivid memories of long-forgotten events.

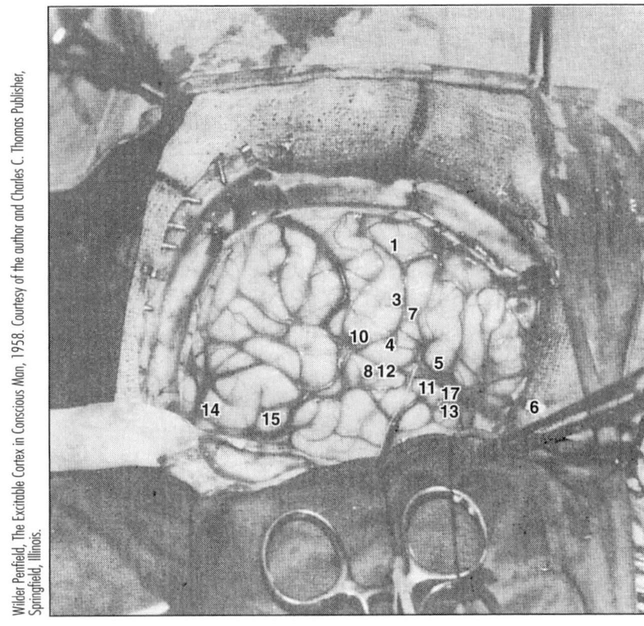

Wilder Penfield, The Excitable Cortex in Conscious Man, 1958. Courtesy of the author and Charles C. Thomas Publisher, Springfield, Illinois.

FIGURE 3.3

Exposed cerebral cortex of a patient undergoing brain surgery. Numbers represent points that reportedly produced "memories" when electrically stimulated. A critical evaluation of such reports suggests that they are more like dreams than memories. This fact raises questions about claims that long-term memories are permanent.

Permanence

Are all of our experiences permanently recorded in memory? Results like those described led neurosurgeon Wilder Penfield to claim that the brain records the past like a "strip of movie film, complete with sound track" (Penfield, 1957). But as you know, this is an exaggeration. Many events never get past short-term memory. Also, brain stimulation produces memory-like experiences in only about 3 percent of cases. Most reports resemble dreams more than memories, and many are clearly imaginary. Memory experts now believe that long-term memories are only *relatively* permanent (Barsalou, 1992). Perfect, eternal memories are a myth.

Try It Yourself: How's Your Memory?

To better appreciate the next topic, pause for a moment and read the words you see here. Read through the list once. Then continue reading the next section of this chapter.

bed dream blanket doze pillow nap snore mattress alarm clock rest slumber nod sheet bunk cot cradle groggy

Constructing Memories

There's another reason for doubting that all of our experiences are permanently recorded. As new long-term memories are stored, older memories are often updated, changed, lost, or *revised* (Lieberman, 2004). To illustrate this point, in a classic study Elizabeth Loftus and John Palmer (1974) showed people a filmed automobile accident. Afterward, some participants were asked to estimate how fast the cars were going when they "smashed" into each other. For others the words "bumped," "contacted," or "hit" replaced "smashed." One week later, each person was asked, "Did you see any broken glass?" Those asked earlier about the cars that "smashed" into each other were more likely to say yes. (No broken glass was shown in the film.) The new information ("smashed") was included in memories and altered them.

Try It Yourself: Old or New?

Now, without looking back to the list of words you read a few minutes ago, see if you can tell which of the following are "old" words (items from the list you read) and which are "new" words (items that weren't on the list). Mark each of the following words as old or new:

sofa sleep lamp kitchen

Updating memories is called **constructive processing**. Gaps in memory, which are common, may be filled in by logic, guessing, or new information

constructive processing reorganizing or updating memories on the basis of logic, reasoning, or the addition of new information.

Tom Carter/Index Stock Imagery

Eyewitness memories are notoriously inaccurate. By the time witnesses are asked to testify in court, information they learned after an incident may blend into their original memories.

(Schacter, Norman, & Koutstaal, 1998). Indeed, it is possible to have "memories" for things that never happened (such as remembering broken glass at an accident when there was none) (Loftus, 2003). In a study by Sharon Hannigan and Mark Reinitz, college students saw photographs that depicted common activities, such as shopping for groceries or eating at a restaurant. In some cases, the photos showed an unusual event. For example, in one sequence a woman at a grocery store passes a pile of oranges on the floor. Two days later, the students saw the photos again. This time, however, new photos were included that *explained* how the unusual event occurred (Figure 3.4). For instance, the woman at the market is shown pulling an orange from the bottom of a stack of oranges. Sixty-eight percent of the students were sure they remembered seeing this image (Hannigan & Reinitz, 2001).

As the preceding examples show, thoughts, inferences, and mental associations may be mistaken for true memories (Loftus, 2003). People in Elizabeth Loftus's experiments who had these *pseudo-memories* (false memories) were often quite upset to learn they had given false "testimony" (Loftus & Ketcham, 1994).

Try It Yourself: And Now, the Results

Return now and look at the labels you wrote on the "old or new" word list. If you answered as most people do, this exercise may help you appreciate how often we have false memories. All of the listed words are "new." None was on the original list!

If you thought you "remembered" that "sleep" was on the original list, you had a false memory. The word *sleep* is associated with most of the words on the original list, which creates a strong impression that you saw it before (Roediger & McDermott, 1995).

False long-term memories are a common problem in police work. For example, a witness may select a photo of a suspect from police files or see a photo in the news. Later, the witness identifies the suspect in a lineup or in court. Did the witness really remember the suspect from the scene of the crime? Or was it from the more recently seen photograph? Under some circumstances, innocent people have been "remembered" and named as criminals (Schacter, 2001).

Does new information "overwrite" existing memories? No, the real problem is that we often can't remember the *source* of a memory. This can lead witnesses to "remember" a face that they actually saw somewhere other than the crime scene (Schacter, Norman, & Koutstaal, 1998). Many tragic cases of mistaken identity occur this way.

Is there any way to avoid such problems? Forensic psychologists have tried a variety of techniques to help improve the memory of witnesses. "Telling Wrong from Right in Forensic Memory" examines research on this intriguing question.

To summarize, forming and using memories is an active, creative, highly personal process. Our memories are colored by emotions, judgments, and quirks of personality. If you and a friend were joined at the hip and you went through life side-by-side, you would still have different memories. What we remember depends on what we pay attention to, what we regarded as meaningful or important, and what we feel strongly about (Schacter, 2000).

Dennis Coon

FIGURE 3.4

Suppose you are shown a series of photographs that depict various scenes related to having lunch at the campus commons. One of the photos shows an unexpected event (the spilled soda). If you were to see all of the photos again a few days later, it's likely that you would remember seeing the image on the right, even though it wasn't in the original group of photos. When we see an unexplained event, we are very likely to think about its cause. Later, it is easy to mistake these thoughts for an actual memory (Hannigan & Reinitz, 2001).

FOCUS ON RESEARCH

Telling Wrong from Right in Forensic Memory

Imagine that you are a forensic psychologist, investigating a crime. Unfortunately, your witness can't remember much of what happened. What can you, as a "memory detective," do to help?

Could hypnosis improve the witness's memory? It might seem so. In one case in California, 26 children were abducted from a school bus and held captive for ransom. Under hypnosis, the bus driver recalled the license plate number of the kidnappers' van. This memory helped break the case. Such successes seem to imply that hypnosis can improve memory. But does it?

Research has shown that hypnosis increases false memories more than it does true ones. Eighty percent of the new memories produced by hypnotized subjects in one classic experiment were *incorrect* (Dywan & Bowers, 1983). This is in part because a hypnotized person is more likely than normal to use imagination to fill in gaps in memory. Also, if a questioner asks misleading or suggestive questions, hypnotized persons tend to weave the information into their memories (Scoboria et al., 2002). To make matters worse, even when a memory is completely false, the hypnotized person's confidence in it can be unshakable (Burgess & Kirsch, 1999). Thus, hypnosis sometimes uncovers more information, as it did with the bus driver (Schreiber & Schreiber, 1999). However, when it does, there is no sure way to tell which memories are false and which are true (Newman & Thompson, 2001).

Is there a better way to improve eyewitness memory? To help police detectives, R. Edward Geiselman and Ron Fisher created the **cognitive interview**, a technique for jogging the memory of eyewitnesses (Fisher & Geiselman, 1987). The key to this approach is recreating the crime scene. Witnesses revisit the scene in their imaginations or in person. That way, aspects of the crime scene, such as sounds, smells, and objects, provide helpful retrieval cues. Back in the context of the crime, the witness is encouraged to recall events in different orders and from different viewpoints. Every new memory, no matter how trivial it may seem, can serve as a cue to trigger the retrieval of yet more memories.

When used properly, the cognitive interview produces 35 percent more correct information than standard questioning (Davis, McMahon, & Greenwood, 2005; Geiselman et al., 1986). This improvement comes without adding to the number of false memories elicited, as occurs with hypnosis, and it is more effective in actual police work (Ginet & Py, 2001; Kebbell & Wagstaff, 1998).

A. Ramey/PhotoEdit

Some police detectives, following the advice of psychologists, recreate crime scenes to help witnesses remember what they saw. Typically, people return to the scene at the time of day the crime occurred. They are also asked to wear the same clothing they wore and go through the same motions as they did before the crime. With so many memory cues available, witnesses sometimes remember key items of information they hadn't recalled before.

Organizing Memories

Long-term memory stores huge amounts of information in a lifetime. How are we able to find specific memories? The answer is that each person's "memory index" is highly organized.

Do you mean that information is arranged alphabetically, as in a dictionary? Not a chance! If we ask you to name a black and white animal that lives on ice, is related to a chicken, and cannot fly, you don't have to go from aardvark to zebra to find the answer. You will probably only think of black and white birds living in the Antarctic. Which of these cannot fly? *Voila,* the answer is a penguin.

cognitive interview
use of various cues and strategies to improve the memory of eyewitnesses.

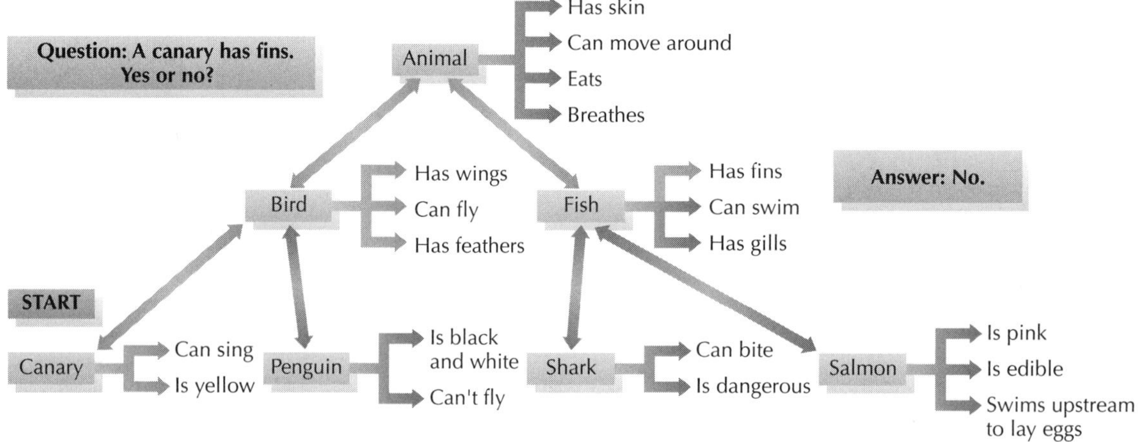

FIGURE 3.5

A hypothetical network of facts about animals shows what is meant by the structure of memory. Small networks of ideas such as this are probably organized into larger and larger units and higher levels of meaning. (Adapted from Collins & Quillian, 1969.)

Information in LTM may be arranged according to rules, images, categories, symbols, similarity, formal meaning, or personal meaning (Lieberman, 2004). In recent years, psychologists have begun to develop a picture of the *structure*, or organization, of memories. *Memory structure* refers to the pattern of associations among items of information. For example, assume that you are given two statements, to which you must answer yes or no: (1) *A canary is an animal.* (2) *A canary is a bird.* Which do you answer more quickly? Most people can say that *A canary is a bird* faster than they can recognize that *A canary is an animal* (Collins & Quillian, 1969). Why should this be so? Psychologists believe that a **network model** of memory explains why. According to this view, LTM is organized as a network of linked ideas (Figure 3.5). When ideas are "farther" apart, it takes a longer chain of associations to connect them. The more two items are separated, the longer it takes to answer. In terms of information links, *canary* is probably "close" to *bird* in your "memory files." *Animal* and *canary* are farther apart. Remember though, this has nothing to do with alphabetical order. We are talking about a system of linked meanings.

network model
a model of memory that views it as an organized system of linked information.

Redintegrative Memories Networks of associated memories may help explain a common experience: Imagine finding a picture taken on your sixth birthday or tenth Christmas. As you look at the photo, one memory leads to another, which leads to another, and another. Soon you have unleashed a flood of seemingly forgotten details. This process is called redintegration (ruh-DIN-tuh-GRAY-shun).

Redintegrative memories seem to spread through the "branches" of memory networks. Many people find that such memories are also touched off by distinctive odors out of the past—from a farm visited in childhood, Grandma's kitchen, the seashore, a doctor's office, the perfume or aftershave of a former lover, and so on. The key idea in redintegration is that one memory serves as a cue to trigger another. As a result, an entire past experience may be reconstructed from one small recollection.

redintegrative memories
memories that are reconstructed or expanded by starting with one memory and then following chains of association to other, related memories.

How many types of long-term memory are there? It is becoming clear that more than one type of long-term memory exists. Let's probe a little farther into the mysteries of memory.

Skill Memory and Fact Memory

A curious thing happens to many people who develop amnesia. Amnesic patients may be unable to learn a telephone number, an address, or a person's name. Yet the same patients can learn to solve complex puzzles in a normal amount of time (Squire & Zola-Morgan, 1988) (Figure 3.6). These and other observations have led many psychologists to conclude that long-term memories fall into at least two categories. One is called *procedural memory* (or skill memory). The other is *declarative memory* (also sometimes called fact memory).

FIGURE 3.6

The tower puzzle. In this puzzle, all the colored disks must be moved to another post, without ever placing a larger disk on a smaller one. Only one disk may be moved at a time, and a disk must always be moved from one post to another (it cannot be held aside). An amnesic patient learned to solve the puzzle in 31 moves, the minimum possible. Even so, each time he began, he protested that he did not remember ever solving the puzzle before and that he did not know how to begin. Evidence like this suggests that memories for skills are distinct from memories for facts.

Skills **Procedural memory** includes basic conditioned responses and learned actions, such as those involved in typing, driving, or swinging a golf club. Memories such as these can be fully expressed only as actions (or "know-how"). It is likely that skill memories register in "lower" brain areas, especially the cerebellum. They represent the more basic "automatic" elements of conditioning, learning, and memory (Gabrieli, 1998).

Facts **Declarative memory** stores specific factual information, such as names, faces, words, dates, and ideas. Declarative memories are expressed as words or symbols. For example, knowing that Peter Jackson directed both the *Lord of the Rings* trilogy and the latest remake of *King Kong* is a declarative memory. This is the type of memory that a person with amnesia lacks and that most of us take for granted. Declarative memory can be further divided into *semantic memory* and *episodic memory* (Tulving, 2000).

Semantic Memory Most of our basic factual knowledge about the world is almost totally immune to forgetting. The names of objects, the days of the week or months of the year, simple math skills, the seasons, words and language, and other general facts are all quite lasting. Such impersonal facts make up a part of LTM called **semantic memory**. Semantic memory serves as a mental dictionary or encyclopedia of basic knowledge.

Episodic Memory Semantic memory has no connection to times or places. It would be rare, for instance, to remember when and where you first learned the names of the seasons. In contrast, **episodic** (ep-ih-SOD-ik) **memory** is an "autobiographical" record of personal experiences. It stores life events (or "episodes") day after day, year after year. Can you remember your seventh birthday? Your first date? An accident you witnessed? What you did yesterday? All are episodic memories. Note that episodic memories are about the "what," "where," and "when" of our lives. More than a simple ability to store information, they make it possible for us to mentally travel back in time and *re-experience* events (Tulving, 2002).

Are episodic memories as lasting as semantic memories? In general, episodic memories are more easily forgotten than semantic memories. This is because new information constantly pours into episodic memory. Stop for a moment and remember where and when you first met your best friend. That was an episodic memory. Notice that you now remember that you just remembered something. You have a new episodic memory in which you remember that you remembered while reading this text! It's easy to see how much we ask of our memory.

procedural memory
long-term memories of conditioned responses and learned skills.

declarative memory
that part of long-term memory containing specific factual information.

semantic memory
a subpart of declarative memory that records impersonal knowledge about the world.

episodic memory
a subpart of declarative memory that records personal experiences that are linked with specific times and places.

How Many Types of Memory? In answer to the question posed at the beginning of this section, it is very likely that three kinds of long-term memories exist: procedural memory and two types of declarative memory, semantic and episodic (Mitchell, 1989; Squire, Knowlton, & Musen, 1993) (Figure 3.7). Although other types of memory may be discovered, it appears that some pieces of the puzzle are falling into place.

FIGURE 3.7

In the model shown here, long-term memory is divided into procedural memory (learned actions and skills) and declarative memory (stored facts). Declarative memories can be either semantic (impersonal knowledge) or episodic (personal experiences associated with specific times and places).

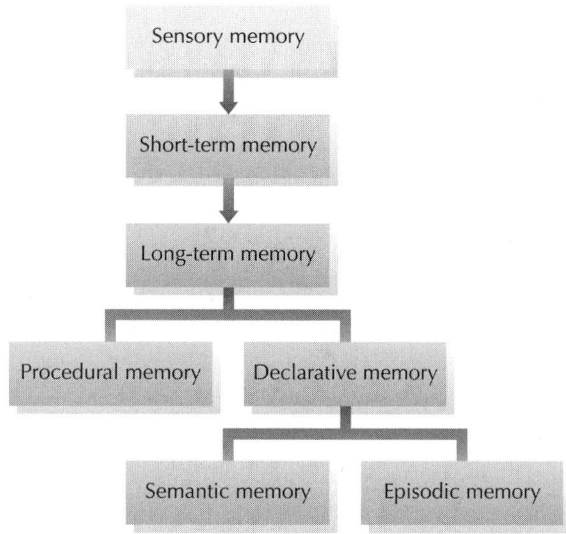

MEASURING MEMORY—THE ANSWER IS ON THE TIP OF MY TONGUE

You either remember something or you don't, right? Wrong. Partial memories are common. For instance, imagine that a clerk helps you at a clothing store. Will you remember her 6 months later? Probably not—unless you happen to see her again at the mall. If you remember her then, you will have used a type of partial memory called *recognition*.

tip-of-the-tongue state the feeling that a memory is available but not quite retrievable.

Partial memory is also demonstrated by the **tip-of-the-tongue** (TOT) **state**. This is the feeling that a memory is available, but not quite retrievable. It is as if an answer or a memory is just out of reach—on the "tip of your tongue." For instance, in one study, people listened to theme music from popular TV shows. Then they tried to name the program the tune came from. This produced TOT experiences for about one out of five tunes (Riefer, Keveri, & Kramer, 1995).

The items listed next may induce the TOT state. See if you can name the defined words. (*Answers are at the bottom of this page.)

What's on the Tip of Your Tongue?

1. A person who collects and studies postage stamps
2. To officially renounce a throne
3. A nylon strip surfaced with tiny hooks that fasten to another strip surfaced with uncut pile
4. Produced by humans rather than natural
5. The pictorial system of writing used in ancient Egypt
6. A small fish that attaches itself to a shark

In a classic TOT study, university students read the definitions of words such as *sextant, sampan,* and *ambergris.* Students who "drew a blank" and couldn't name a defined word were asked to give any other information they could. Often, they could guess the first and last letter and the number of syllables of the word they were seeking. They also gave words that sounded like or meant the same thing as the defined word (Brown & McNeill, 1966). Did any of these signs of the TOT state occur as you read the definitions above?

* 1. philatelist 2. abdicate 3. Velcro 4. artificial 5. hieroglyphics 6. remora

Closely related to the TOT state is the fact that people can often tell beforehand if they are likely to remember something. This is called the **feeling of knowing** (Nelson, 1987). Feeling-of-knowing reactions are easy to observe on TV game shows, where they occur just before contestants are allowed to answer.

feeling of knowing
a feeling that allows people to predict beforehand whether they will be able to remember something.

Because memory is not an all-or-nothing event, there are several ways of measuring it. Notice that whether you have "remembered" depends on how you are tested. Three commonly used **memory tasks** (tests of memory) are recall, recognition, and relearning. Let's see how they differ.

memory task
any task designed to test or assess memory.

Recalling Information

What is the name of the first song on your favorite CD? Who won the World Series last year? Who wrote *Hamlet?* If you can answer these questions you are using **recall**, a direct retrieval of facts or information. Tests of recall often require *verbatim* (word-for-word) memory. If you study a poem until you can recite it without looking at it, you are recalling it. If you complete a fill-in-the-blank question, you are using recall. When you answer an essay question by providing facts and ideas, you are also using recall, even though you didn't learn your essay verbatim.

recall
to supply or reproduce memorized information with a minimum of external cues.

The order in which information is memorized has an interesting effect on recall. To experience it, try to memorize the following list, reading it only once:

bread, apples, soda, ham, cookies, rice, lettuce, beets, mustard, cheese, oranges, ice cream, crackers, flour, eggs

If you are like most people, it will be hardest for you to recall items from the middle of the list. Figure 3.8 shows the results of a similar test. Notice that most errors occur with middle items of an ordered list. This is the **serial position effect**. You can remember the last items on a list because they are still in STM. The first items are also remembered well because they entered an "empty" short-term memory. This allows you to rehearse the items so they move into long-term memory (Addis & Kahana, 2004). The middle items are neither held in short-term memory nor moved to long-term memory, so they are often lost.

serial position effect
the tendency to make the most errors in remembering the middle items of an ordered list.

Recognizing Information

recognition memory
an ability to correctly identify previously learned information.

Try to write down everything you can remember learning from a class you took last year. (You have 3 minutes, which should be more than enough time!) If you actually did this, you might conclude that you had learned very little. However, a more sensitive test based on recognition could be used. In **recognition memory**, previously learned material is correctly identified. For instance, you could take a multiple-choice test on facts and ideas from the course. Because you would only have to recognize correct answers, we would probably find that you had learned a lot.

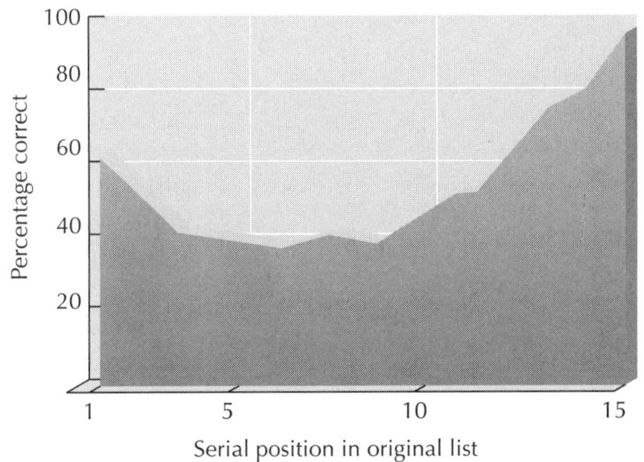

FIGURE 3.8
The serial position effect. The graph shows the percentage of subjects correctly recalling each item in a 15-item list. Recall is best for the first and last items. (Data from Craik, 1970.)

Recognition memory can be amazingly accurate for pictures and photographs. One investigator showed people 2,560 photographs at a rate of one every 10 seconds. Each person was then shown 280 pairs of photographs. Each pair included an "old" picture (from the first set of photos) and a similar "new" image. Subjects could tell 85 to 95 percent of the time which photograph they had seen before (Haber, 1970). This finding may explain why people so often say, "I may forget a name, but I never forget a face." (It's also why we rarely need to see our friends' vacation photos more than once.)

Recognition is usually superior to recall. That's why police departments use photographs or a lineup to identify criminal

SW Production/Index Stock Imagery

Police lineups make use of the sensitivity of recognition memory. However, unless great care is taken, false identifications are still possible (Wells, 2001).

suspects. Witnesses who disagree when they try to recall a suspect's height, weight, age, or eye color often agree completely when they merely need to recognize the person.

Is recognition always superior? It depends greatly on the kind of *distractors* used. These are false items included with an item to be recognized. If distractors are very similar to the correct item, memory may be poor. A reverse problem occurs when only one choice looks like it could be correct. This can produce a *false positive,* or false sense of recognition, like the false memory you had earlier when you thought you remembered seeing the word *sleep.*

There have been instances in which witnesses described a criminal as black, tall, or young. Then a lineup was held in which a suspect was the only African American among whites, the only tall suspect, or the only young person. In such cases a false identification is very likely. A better method is to have *all* the distractors look like the person witnesses described. Also, to reduce false positives, witnesses should be warned that the culprit *may not be present* (Wells et al., 1999). Many hundreds of people have been put in jail on the basis of mistaken eyewitness memories. To avoid tragic mistakes, it's far better to show witnesses one photo at a time (a sequential lineup). For each photo, the witness must decide whether the person is the culprit before another photo is shown (Wells, 2001; Wells & Olsen, 2003).

Relearning Information

In another classic experiment, a psychologist read a short passage in Greek to his son every day when the boy was between 15 months and 3 years of age. At age 8, the boy was asked if he remembered the Greek passage. He showed no evidence of recall. He was then shown selections from the passage he heard and selections from other Greek passages. Could he recognize the one he heard as an infant? "It's all Greek to me!" he said, indicating a lack of recognition (and drawing a frown from everyone in the room).

Had the psychologist stopped, he might have concluded that no memory of the Greek remained. However, the child was then asked to memorize the original quotation and others of equal difficulty. This time his earlier learning became evident. The boy memorized the passage he had heard in childhood 25 percent faster than the others (Burtt, 1941). As this experiment suggests, **relearning** is typically the most sensitive measure of memory.

relearning
learning again something that was previously learned. Used to measure memory of prior learning.

When a person is tested by relearning, how do we know a memory still exists? As with the boy described, relearning is measured by a *savings score* (the amount of time saved when relearning information). Let's say it takes you 1 hour to memorize all the names in a telephone book. (It's a small town.) Two years later you relearn them in 45 minutes. Because you "saved" 15 minutes, your savings score would be 25 percent (15 divided by 60 times 100). Savings of this type are a good reason for studying a wide range of subjects. It may seem that learning algebra, history, or a foreign language is wasted if you don't use the knowledge immediately. But when you do need such information, you will be able to relearn it quickly.

Implicit and Explicit Memories

Many memories remain outside of conscious awareness. For example, if you know how to type, it is apparent that you know where the letters are on the keyboard. But how many typists could correctly label blank keys in a drawing of a keyboard?

Many people find that they cannot directly remember such information, even though they "know" it.

Who were the last three presidents of the United States? What did you have for breakfast today? What is the title of the Black Eyed Peas latest album? Explicit memory is used in answering each of these questions. **Explicit memories** are past experiences that are consciously brought to mind. Recall, recognition, and the tests you take in school rely on explicit memories. In contrast, **implicit memories** lie outside of awareness (Roediger, 1990). That is, we are not aware that a memory exists. Nevertheless, implicit memories—such as unconsciously knowing where the letters are on a keyboard—greatly influence our behavior (Neath, 2002).

explicit memory
a memory that a person is aware of having; a memory that is consciously retrieved.

implicit memory
a memory that a person does not know exists; a memory that is retrieved unconsciously.

Priming *How is it possible to show that a memory exists if it lies outside of awareness?* Psychologists first noticed implicit memory while studying memory loss caused by brain injuries. Let's say, for example, that a patient is shown a list of common words, such as *chair, tree, lamp, table,* and so on. A few minutes later, the patient is asked to recall words from the list. Sadly, he has no memory of the words.

Now, instead of asking the patient to explicitly recall the list, we could "prime" his memory by giving him the first two letters of each word. "We'd like you to say a word that begins with these letters," we tell him. "Just say whatever comes to mind." Of course, many words could be made from each pair of letters. For example, the first item (from chair) would be the letters CH. The patient could say "child," "chalk," "chain," "check," or many other words. Instead, he says "chair," a word from the original list. The patient is not aware that he is remembering the list, but as he gives a word for each letter pair, almost all are from the list. Apparently, the letters **primed** (activated) hidden memories, which then influenced his answers.

priming
facilitating the retrieval of an implicit memory by using cues to activate hidden memories.

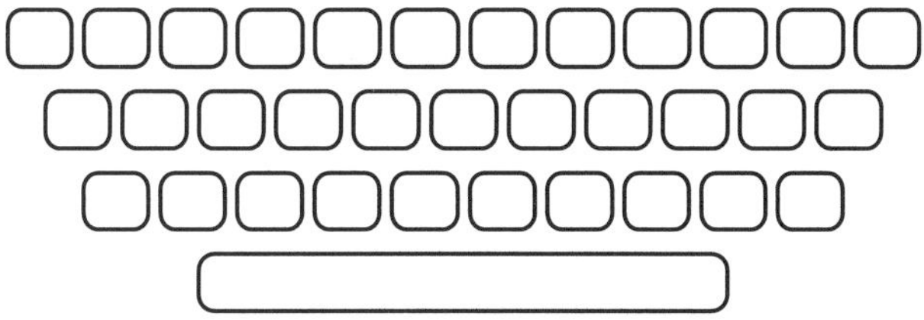

Can you label the letter keys on this blank keyboard? If you can, you probably used implicit memory to do it.

Similar effects have been found for people with normal memories. As the preceding example implies, implicit memories are often revealed by giving a person limited cues, such as the first letter of words or partial drawings of objects. Typically, the person believes that he or she is just saying whatever comes to mind. Nevertheless, information previously seen or heard affects his or her answers (Rueckl & Galantucci, 2005). Some nutritionists like to say, "You are what you eat." In the realm of memory it appears that we are what we experience—to a far greater degree than once realized.

EXCEPTIONAL MEMORY—WIZARDS OF RECALL

Can you remember how many doors there are in your house or apartment? To answer a question like this, many people form **internal images** (mental pictures) of each room and count the doorways they visualize. As this example implies, many memories are stored as mental images (Roeckelein, 2004).

internal images
mental images or visual depictions used in memory and thinking.

FIGURE 3.9

(a) "Treasure map" similar to the one used by Kosslyn, Ball, and Reiser (1978) to study images in memory. (b) This graph shows how long it took subjects to move a visualized spot various distances on their mental images of the map. (See text for explanation.)

(a)

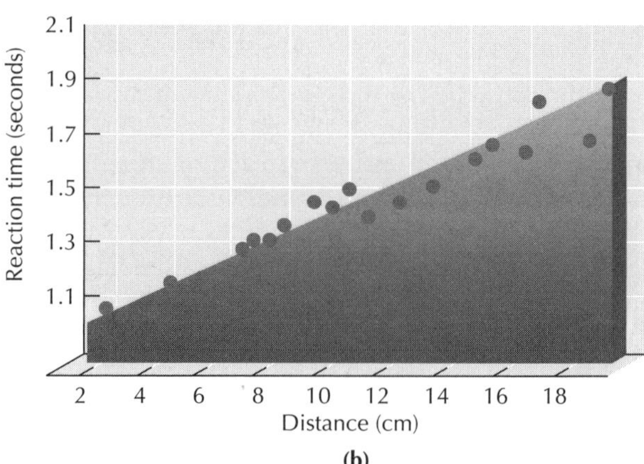

(b)

eidetic imagery
the ability to retain a "projected" mental image long enough to use it as a source of information.

Stephen Kosslyn, Thomas Ball, and Brian Reiser (1978) found an interesting way to show that memories do exist as images. Participants first memorized a sort of treasure map similar to the one shown in Figure 3.9*a*. They were then asked to picture a black dot moving from one object, such as one of the trees, to another, such as the hut at the top of the island. Did people really form an image to do this task? It seems they did. As shown in Figure 3.9*b*, the time it took to "move" the dot was directly related to actual distances on the map.

Is the "treasure map" task an example of photographic memory? In some ways, internal memory images do have "photographic" qualities. However, the term *photographic memory* is more often used to describe a type of memory called eidetic imagery.

FIGURE 3.10

A test picture like that used to identify children with eidetic imagery. To test your eidetic imagery, look at the picture for 30 seconds. Then look at a blank surface and try to "project" the picture onto it. If you have good eidetic imagery, you will be able to see the picture in detail. Return now to the text and try to answer the questions there. *(Redrawn from an illustration in Lewis Carroll's Alice's Adventures in Wonderland.)*

Eidetic Imagery

Eidetic (eye-DET-ik) **imagery** occurs when a person has visual images clear enough to be "scanned" or retained for at least 30 seconds. Internal memory images can be "viewed" mentally with the eyes closed. In contrast, eidetic images are "projected" out in front of a person. That is, they are best "seen" on a plain surface, such as a blank piece of paper. In this respect, eidetic images are somewhat like the afterimages you might have after looking at a flashbulb or a brightly lit neon sign (Kunzendorf, 1989).

Eidetic memory is most common in childhood, with about 8 children in 100 having eidetic images. In one series of tests, children were shown a picture from *Alice's Adventures in Wonderland* (Figure 3.10). To test your eidetic imagery, look at the picture and read the instructions there.

Now, let's see how much you remember. Can you say (without looking again) which of Alice's apron strings is longer? Are the cat's front paws crossed? How many stripes are on the cat's tail? After the picture was removed from view, one 10-year-old boy was asked what he saw. He replied, "I see the tree, gray tree with three limbs. I see the cat with stripes around its tail." Asked to count the stripes, the boy replied, "There are about 16" (a correct count!). The boy then went on to describe the remainder of the picture in striking detail (Haber, 1969).

Don't be disappointed if you didn't do too well when you tried your eidetic skills. Most eidetic imagery disappears during adolescence and becomes rare by adulthood (Kunzendorf, 1989). Actually, this may not be too much of a loss. The majority of eidetic memorizers have no better long-term memory than average.

Exceptional Memory

Let's return now to the concept of internal memory images. In rare instances, such images may be so vivid that it is reasonable to say that a person has "photographic memory." A notable example was reported by Aleksandr Luria (1968) in his book, *The Mind of a Mnemonist*. Luria studied a man he called Mr. S who had practically unlimited memory for visual images. Mr. S could remember almost everything that ever happened to him with incredible accuracy. Luria tried to test Mr. S's memory by using longer and longer lists of words or numbers. However, he soon discovered that no matter how long the list, Mr. S was able to recall it without error. Mr. S could memorize, with equal ease, strings of digits, meaningless consonants, mathematical formulas, and poems in foreign languages. His memory was so powerful that he had to devise ways to *forget*—such as writing information on a piece of paper and then burning it.

Mr. S's abilities might seem fantastic to any college student. However, Mr. S remembered so much that he couldn't separate important facts from trivia or facts from fantasy (Neath, 2002). For instance, if you asked him to read this chapter he might remember every word. Yet he might also recall all the images each word made him think of and all the sights, sounds, and feelings that occurred as he was reading. Therefore, finding the answer for a specific question, writing a logical essay, or even understanding a single sentence was very difficult for him. If you didn't have selective memory you would recall all the ingredients on your cereal box, every street number you've seen, and countless other scraps of information.

Few people in history have possessed memory abilities like Mr. S's. Nonetheless, you probably know at least one person who has an especially good memory. Is superior memory a biological gift? Or do excellent memorizers merely make better-than-average use of normal memory capacities? Let's investigate further.

Strategies for Remembering At first, a student volunteer named Steve could remember 7 digits—a typical score for a college student. Could he improve with practice? For 20 months Steve practiced memorizing ever-longer lists of digits. Ultimately, he was able to memorize around 80 digits, like this sample:

> 92842048050842268953990190252912807999706606574717310601080585269726
> 026357332135

How did Steve do it? Basically, he worked by chunking digits into meaningful groups containing 3 or 4 digits each. Steve's avid interest in long-distance running helped greatly. For instance, to him the first three digits above represented 9 minutes and 28 seconds, a good time for a 2-mile run. When running times wouldn't work, Steve used other associations, such as ages or dates, to chunk digits (Ericsson & Chase, 1982). It seems apparent that Steve's success was based on learned strategies. By using similar memory systems, other people have trained themselves to equal Steve's feat (Bellezza, Six, & Phillips, 1992).

Psychologist Anders Ericsson (2000) believes that exceptional memory is merely a learned extension of normal memory. As evidence, he notes that Steve's short-term memory did not improve during months of practice. For example, Steve could still memorize only 7 consonants. Steve's phenomenal memory for numbers grew as he figured out new ways to encode digits and store them in LTM.

Researchers studying Rajan Mahadevan have drawn similar conclusions about his spectacular memory for long strings of digits. In 1981 Rajan earned a place in the *Guinness Book of World Records* by reciting the first 31,811 digits of *pi!* Yet, like Steve, Rajan's memory for most other types of information is average. His exceptional memory seems to be based on highly practiced strategies for encoding and storing digits (Thompson, Cowan, & Frieman, 1993). By using similar memory systems, college students have even managed to duplicate some of Mr. S's feats, such as memorizing a 50-digit matrix in 3 minutes (Higbee, 1997).

Steve and Rajan began with normal memory for digits. Both extended their memory abilities by diligent practice. Clearly, exceptional memory can be learned (Ericsson et al., 2004). However, we still have to wonder, do some people have naturally superior memories?

Memory Champions

Each year the World Memory Championship is held in England. There, a variety of mental athletes compete to see who had the best memory. To remain in the running, each contestant has to rapidly memorize daunting amounts of information, such as long lists of unrelated words and numbers. Psychologists John Wilding and Elizabeth Valentine saw this event as an opportunity to study exceptional memory and persuaded the contestants to take some additional memory tests. These ranged from ordinary (recall a story), to challenging (recall the telephone numbers of 6 different people), to diabolical (recall 48 numerals arranged in rows and columns; recognize 14 previously seen pictures of snowflakes among 70 new photos) (Wilding & Valentine, 1994a).

Wilding and Valentine found that exceptional memorizers

- Use memory strategies and techniques
- Have specialized interests and knowledge that make certain types of information easier to encode and recall
- Have naturally superior memory abilities, often including vivid mental images

8	7	3	7	9	2	6	8
2	0	1	1	7	4	9	5
0	1	7	5	8	7	8	3
1	9	4	7	6	0	6	9
3	6	1	6	8	1	5	4
4	5	2	4	0	2	9	7

This number matrix is similar to the ones contestants in the World Memory Championship had to memorize. To be scored as correct, digits had to be recalled in their proper positions (Wilding & Valentine, 1994a).

The first two points confirm what we learned from Steve's acquired memory ability. Many of the contestants, for example, actively used memory strategies called *mnemonics* (nee-MON-iks). Specialized interests and knowledge also helped for some tasks. For example, one contestant, who is a mathematician, was exceedingly good at memorizing numbers (Wilding & Valentine, 1994a).

Several of the memory contestants were able to excel on tasks that prevented the use of learned strategies and techniques. This observation implies that superior memory ability can be a "gift" as well as a learned skill. Wilding and Valentine conclude that exceptional memory may be based on either natural ability or learned strategies. Usually it requires both. In fact, most super memorizers use strategies to augment whatever natural talents they have. Some of their strategies are described in this chapter's Psychology in Action section. Please do remember to read it.

FORGETTING—WHY WE, UH, LET'S SEE; WHY WE, UH . . . FORGET!

Forgetting is one of the more vexing aspects of memory. For example, why is it hard to remember facts you learned for a test just a week or two later? Again, the more you know about how we "lose" memories, the better you will be able to hang on to them.

Most forgetting tends to occur immediately after memorization. Herman Ebbinghaus (1885) famously tested his own memory at various time intervals after learning. Ebbinghaus wanted to be sure he would not be swayed by prior learning, so he memorized *nonsense syllables*. These are meaningless three-letter words such as CEF, WOL, and GEX. The importance of using meaningless words is shown by the fact that VEL, FAB, and DUZ are no longer used on memory tests. People who recognize these words as detergent names find them very easy to remember. This is another reminder that relating new information to what you already know can improve memory.

By waiting various lengths of time before testing himself, Ebbinghaus plotted a **curve of forgetting**. This graph shows the amount of information remembered after varying lengths of time (Figure 3.11). Notice that forgetting is rapid at first and is then followed by a slow decline. The same applies to meaningful information, but the forgetting curve is stretched over a longer time. As you might expect, recent events are recalled more accurately than those from the remote past (O'Connor et al., 2000). Thus, you are more likely to remember that *Crash* won the "Best Picture" Academy Award in 2006 than you are to remember that *American Beauty* won it in 1999.

As a student, you should note that a short delay between reviewing and taking a test minimizes forgetting. However, this is no reason for cramming. Most

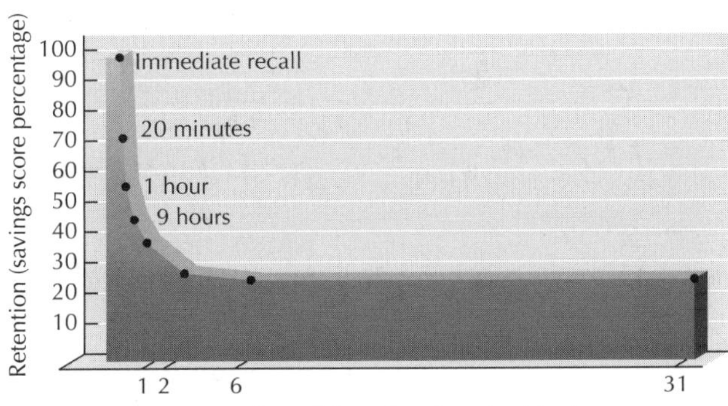

FIGURE 3.11

The curve of forgetting. This graph shows the amount remembered (measured by relearning) after varying lengths of time. Notice how rapidly forgetting occurs. The material learned was nonsense syllables. Forgetting curves for meaningful information also show early losses followed by a long, gradual decline, but overall, forgetting occurs much more slowly. (After Ebbinghaus, 1885.)

curve of forgetting
a graph that shows the amount of memorized information remembered after varying lengths of time.

DISCOVERING PSYCHOLOGY

Card Magic!

FIGURE 3.12

Pick a card from the six shown in Figure 3.12. Look at it closely and be sure you can remember which card is yours. Now, snap your fingers and look at the cards in Figure 3.13.

Poof! Only five cards remain, and the card you chose has disappeared. Obviously, you could have selected any one of the six cards in Figure 3.12. How did we know which one to remove?

This trick is based entirely on an illusion of memory. Recall that you were asked to concentrate on one card among the six cards in Figure 3.12. That prevented you from paying attention to the other cards, so they weren't stored in your memory (Mangels, Picton, & Craik, 2001). The five cards you see below are all new (none is shown in Figure 3.12). Because you couldn't find your card in the "remaining five," it looked like your card disappeared. What looked like "card magic" is actually memory magic. Now return to "When Encoding Fails" and continue reading to learn more about forgetting.

FIGURE 3.13

students make the error of *only* cramming. If you cram, you don't have to remember for very long, but you may not learn enough in the first place. If you use short, daily study sessions *and* review intensely before a test, you will get the benefit of good preparation and a minimum time lapse.

The Ebbinghaus curve shows less than 30 percent remembered after only 2 days have passed. Is forgetting really that rapid? No, not always. Meaningful information is not lost nearly as quickly as nonsense syllables. After 3 years, students who took a university psychology had forgotten about 30 percent of the facts they learned. After that, little more forgetting occurred (Conway et al., 1992). Actually, as learning grows stronger, some knowledge may become nearly permanent (Bahrick, 1984). Semantic memories and implicit memories (both mentioned earlier) appear to be very lasting (Bower, 1990).

"I'll never forget old, old . . . oh, what's his name?" Forgetting is both frustrating and embarrassing. Why *do* we forget? The Ebbinghaus curve gives a general picture of forgetting, but it doesn't explain it. For explanations we must search further. Before we do, look at "Card Magic!" where you will find an interesting demonstration.

When Encoding Fails

Whose head is on a U.S. penny? Which way is it facing? What is written at the top of a penny? Can you accurately draw and label a penny? In an interesting experiment, Ray Nickerson and Marilyn Adams (1979) asked a large group of students to draw a penny. Few could. Well then, could the students at least recognize a drawing of a real penny among fakes? (see Figure 3.14). Again, few could.

encoding failure
failure to store sufficient information to form a useful memory.

The most obvious reason for forgetting is also the most commonly overlooked. Obviously, few of us ever encode the details of a penny. In many cases, we "forget" because of **encoding failure**. That is, a memory was never formed in the first place (the card trick you just saw is another example). If you are bothered by frequent forgetting or absent-mindedness it is wise to ask yourself, "Have I been storing the information in the first place?" (Schacter, 2001). When 140 college professors were asked what they do to improve their memories, the favorite technique was to *write things down* (Park et al., 1990). Making notes prevents information from slipping out of short-term memory before you can review it and store it more **permanently**.

College Students, They're All Alike! Encoding failures also affect our memories of people. Imagine yourself in this situation: As you are walking on campus, a young man, who looks like a college student, approaches you and asks for directions. While you are talking, two workers carrying a door pass between you and the young man. While your view is blocked by the door, another man takes the place of the first. Now you are facing a different person than the one who was there just

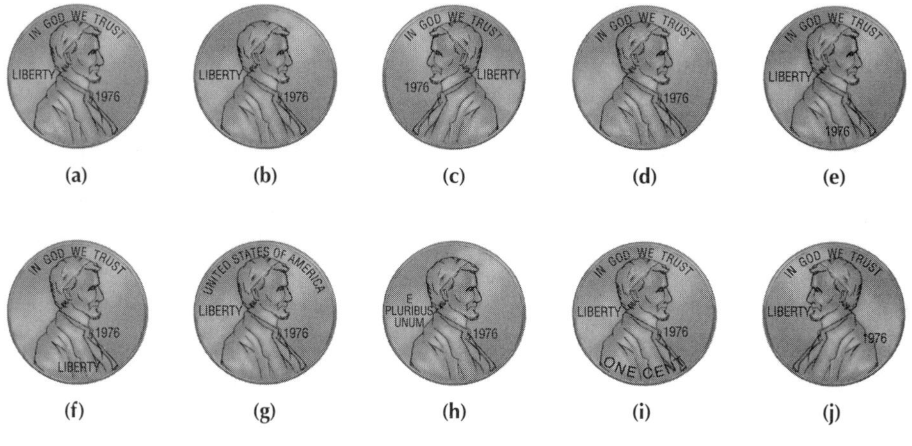

FIGURE 3.14
Some of the distractor items used in a study of recognition memory and encoding failure. Penny A is correct but was seldom recognized. Pennies G and J were popular wrong answers. (Adapted from Nickerson & Adams, 1979.)

seconds earlier. If this happened to you, do you think you would notice the change? Remarkably, only half of the people tested in this way noticed the switch (Simons & Levin, 1998)!

How could anyone fail to notice that one stranger had been replaced by another? The people who didn't remember the first man were all older adults. College students weren't fooled by the switch. Apparently, older adults encoded the first man in very general terms as a "college student." As a result, that's all they remembered about him. Because his replacement also looked like a college student, they thought he was the same person (Simons & Levin, 1998).

Actually, we all tend to categorize strangers in general terms: Is the person young or old, male or female, a member of my ethnic group or another? This tendency is one reason why eyewitnesses are better at identifying members of their own ethnic group than persons from other groups (Kassin et al., 2001). It may seem harsh to say so, but during brief social contacts, people really do act as if members of other ethnic groups "all look alike." Of course, this bias disappears when people get acquainted and learn more about one another as individuals.

Memory Decay

One view of forgetting holds that **memory traces** (changes in nerve cells or brain activity) decay (fade or weaken) over time. **Memory decay** appears to be a factor in the loss of sensory memories. Such fading also applies to short-term memory. Information stored in STM seems to initiate a brief flurry of activity in the brain that quickly dies out. Short-term memory therefore operates like a "leaky bucket": New information constantly pours in, but it rapidly fades away and is replaced by still newer information. Let's say that you are trying to remember a short list of letters, numbers, or words after seeing or hearing them once. If it takes you more than 4 to 6 seconds to repeat the list, you will forget some of the items (Dosher & Ma, 1998).

memory traces
physical changes in nerve cells or brain activity that take place when memories are stored.

memory decay
the fading or weakening of memories assumed to occur when memory traces become weaker.

Disuse Is it possible that the decay of memory traces also explains long-term forgetting? That is, could long-term memory traces fade from **disuse** (infrequent retrieval) and eventually become too weak to retrieve? There is evidence that memories not retrieved and "used" or rehearsed become weaker over time (Schacter, 2001). However, disuse alone cannot fully explain forgetting.

disuse
theory that memory traces weaken when memories are not periodically used or retrieved.

Disuse doesn't seem to account for our ability to recover seemingly forgotten memories through redintegration, relearning, and priming. It also fails to explain why some unused memories fade, whereas others are carried for life. A third contradiction will be recognized by anyone who has spent time with the elderly. People growing senile may become so forgetful that they can't remember what happened a week ago. Yet at the same time your Uncle Oscar's recent memories are fading, he may have vivid memories of trivial and long-forgotten events from the past. "Why, I remember it as clearly as if it were yesterday," he will say, forgetting that the story he is about to tell is one he told earlier the same day. In short, disuse offers no more than a partial explanation of long-term forgetting.

If decay and disuse don't fully explain forgetting, what does? Let's briefly consider some additional possibilities.

Cue-Dependent Forgetting

Often, memories appear to be *available* but not *accessible*. An example is having an answer on the "tip of your tongue." You know the answer is there, but it remains just "out of reach." This suggests that many memories are "forgotten" because **memory cues** (stimuli associated with a memory) are missing when the time comes to retrieve information. For example, if you were asked, "What were you

memory cue
any stimulus associated with a particular memory. Memory cues usually enhance retrieval.

Paul Conklin/PhotoEdit

External cues like those found in a photograph, in a scrapbook, or during a walk through an old neighborhood often aid recall of seemingly lost memories. For many veterans, finding a familiar name engraved in the Vietnam Veterans Memorial unleashes a flood of memories.

doing on Monday afternoon of the third week in September 2 years ago?" your reply might be, "Come on, how should I know?" However, if you were reminded, "That was the day the courthouse burned," or "That was the day Stacy had her automobile accident," you might remember immediately.

The presence of appropriate cues almost always enhances memory (Nairne, 2002). In theory, for instance, memory will be best if you study in the same room where you will be tested. Because this is often impossible, when you study, try to visualize the room where you will be tested. Doing so can enhance memory later (Jerabek & Standing, 1992). Similarly, people remember better if the same odor (such as lemon or lavender) is present when they study and are tested (Parker, Ngu, & Cassaday, 2001). If you wear a particular perfume or cologne while you prepare for a test, it might be wise to wear it when you take the test.

State-Dependent Learning Have you heard the story about the drunk who misplaced his wallet and had to get drunk again to find it? Although this tale is often told as a joke, it is not too farfetched. The bodily state that exists during learning can be a strong cue for later memory, an effect known as **state-dependent learning** (Neath, 2002). Being very thirsty, for instance, might prompt you to remember events that took place on another occasion when you were thirsty. Because of such effects, information learned under the influence of a drug is best remembered when the drugged state occurs again (Slot & Colpaert, 1999).

A similar effect applies to emotional states (Wessel & Wright, 2004). For instance, Gordon Bower (1981) found that people who learned a list of words while in a happy mood recalled them better when they were again happy. People who learned while they felt sad remembered best when they were sad (Figure 3.15). Similarly, if you are in a happy mood, you are more likely to remember recent happy events (Salovey & Singer, 1989). If you are in a bad mood, you will tend to have unpleasant memories (Eich et al., 1990). Such links between emotional cues and memory could explain why couples who quarrel often end up remembering—and rehashing—old arguments.

State-dependent learning
Memory influenced by one's bodily state at the time of learning and at the time of retrieval. Improved memory occurs when the bodily states match.

interference
the tendency for new memories to impair retrieval of older memories, and the reverse.

Sad mood during learning | Happy mood during learning
Percent remembered: 40, 50, 60, 70, 80
Sad | Happy | Sad | Happy
Mood while recalling words

FIGURE 3.15

The effect of mood on memory. Subjects best remembered a list of words when their mood during testing was the same as their mood was when they learned the list. (Adapted from Bower, 1981.)

Interference

Further insight into forgetting comes from a classic experiment in which college students learned lists of nonsense syllables. After studying, students in one group slept for 8 hours and were then tested for memory of the lists. A second group stayed awake for 8 hours and went about business as usual. When members of the second group were tested, they remembered *less* than the group that slept (Figure 3.16.) This difference is based on the fact that new learning can interfere with previous learning. **Interference** refers to the tendency for new memories to impair retrieval of older memories (and the reverse). It seems to apply to both short-term and long-term memory (Lustig et al., 2001; Nairne, 2002).

It is not completely clear if new memories alter existing memory traces or if they make it harder to "locate" (retrieve) earlier memories. In any case, there is no doubt that interference is a major cause of forgetting (Neath, 2002). College students who memorized 20 lists of words (one list each day) were able to recall only 15 percent of the last list. Students who learned only one list remembered 80 percent (Underwood, 1957) (Figure 3.17).

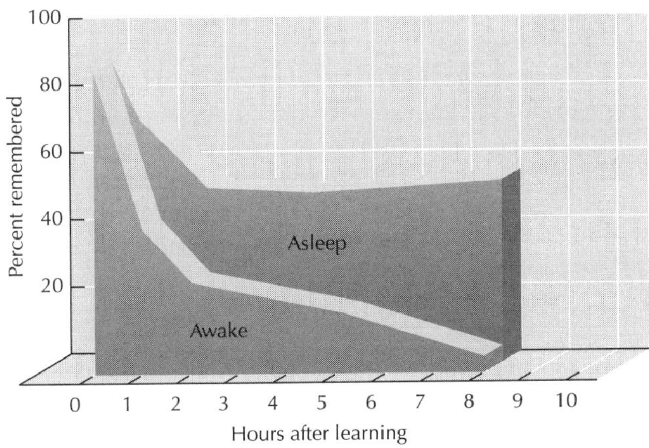

FIGURE 3.16

The amount of forgetting after a period of sleep or of being awake. Notice that sleep causes less memory loss than activity that occurs while one is awake. (After Jenkins & Dallenbach, 1924.)

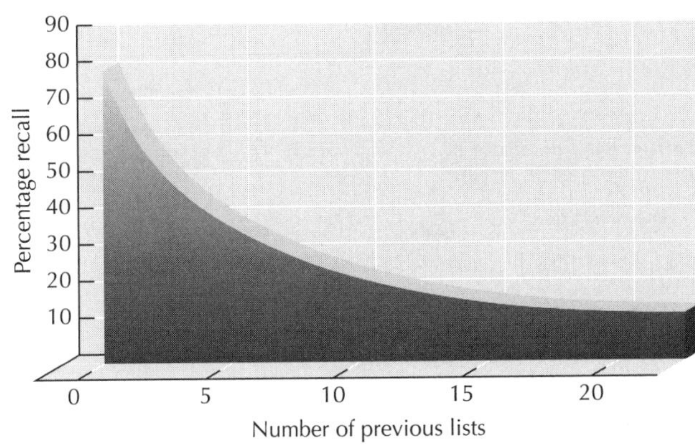

FIGURE 3.17

Effects of interference on memory. A graph of the approximate relationship between percentage recalled and number of different word lists memorized. (Adapted from Underwood, 1957.)

Order Effects The sleeping college students remembered more because retroactive (RET-ro-AK-tiv) interference was held to a minimum. **Retroactive interference** refers to the tendency for new learning to inhibit retrieval of old learning. Avoiding new learning prevents retroactive interference. This doesn't exactly mean you should hide in a closet after you study for an exam. However, you should avoid studying other subjects until the exam. Sleeping after study can help you retain memories, and reading, writing, or even watching TV may cause interference.

retroactive interference the tendency for new memories to interfere with the retrieval of old memories.

proactive interference the tendency for old memories to interfere with the retrieval of newer memories.

Retroactive interference is easily demonstrated in the laboratory by this arrangement:

Experimental group:	**Learn A**	**Learn B**	**Test A**
Control group:	**Learn A**	**Rest**	**Test A**

Imagine yourself as a member of the experimental group. In task A, you learn a list of telephone numbers. In task B, you learn a list of Social Security numbers. How do you score on a test of task A (the telephone numbers)? If you do not remember as much as the control group that learns *only* task A, then retroactive interference has occurred. The second thing learned interfered with memory of the first thing learned; the interference went "backward," or was "retroactive" (Figure 3.18).

Proactive (pro-AK-tiv) interference is a second basic source of forgetting. **Proactive interference** occurs when prior learning inhibits recall of later learning. A test for proactive interference would take this form:

Experimental group:	**Learn A**	**Learn B**	**Test B**
Control group:	**Rest**	**Learn B**	**Test B**

Let's assume that the experimental group remembers less than the control group on a test of task B. In that case, learning task A interfered with memory for task B.

Then proactive interference goes "forward"? Yes. For instance, if you cram for a psychology exam and then later the same night cram for a history exam, your memory for

Andy Reynolds/Getty Images

How could anyone lose something as large as a car? If you park your car in a different place every day you may have experienced forgetting caused by interference. Today's memory about your car's location is easily confused with memories from yesterday, and the day before, and the day before that.

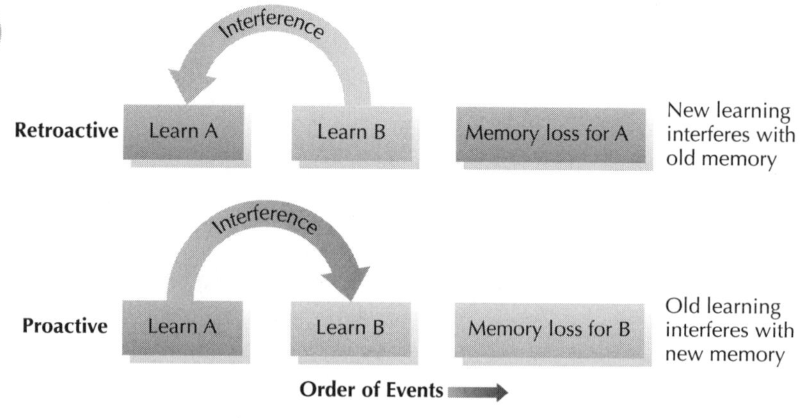

FIGURE 3.18

Retroactive and proactive interference. The order of learning and testing shows whether interference is retroactive (backward) or proactive (forward).

the second subject studied (history) will be less accurate than if you had studied only history. (Because of retroactive interference, your memory for psychology would probably also suffer.) The greater the similarity in the two subjects studied, the more interference takes place. The moral, of course, is don't procrastinate in preparing for exams. The more you can avoid competing information, the more likely you are to recall what you want to remember (Anderson & Bell, 2001).

The interference effects we have described apply primarily to memories of verbal information, such as the contents of this chapter. When you are learning a skill, similarity can sometimes be beneficial, rather than disruptive. The next section explains how this occurs.

Transfer of Training

positive transfer
mastery of one task aids learning or performing another.

negative transfer
mastery of one task conflicts with learning or performing another.

Two people begin mandolin lessons. One already plays the violin. The other is a trumpet player. All other things being equal, which person will initially do better in learning the mandolin? If you chose the violin player you have an intuitive grasp of what positive transfer is. (The strings on a mandolin are tuned the same as a violin.) **Positive transfer** takes place when mastery of one task aids mastery of a second task. Another example would be learning to balance and turn on a bicycle before learning to ride a motorcycle or motor scooter. Likewise, surfing and skateboarding skills transfer to snowboarding.

Is there such a thing as negative transfer? There is indeed. In **negative transfer**, skills developed in one situation conflict with those required to master a new task. Learning to back a car with a trailer attached to it is a good example. Normally, when you are backing a car, the steering wheel is turned in the direction you want to go, the same as when moving forward. However, when backing a trailer, you must turn the steering wheel *away* from the direction you want the trailer to go. This situation results in negative transfer, and often creates comical scenes at campgrounds and boat launching ramps.

On a more serious note, many tragic crashes caused by negative transfer finally led to greater standardization of airplane cockpits. Fortunately, negative transfer is usually brief, and it occurs less often than positive transfer. Negative transfer is most likely to occur when a new response must be made to an old stimulus. If you have ever encountered a pull-type handle on a door that must be pushed open, you will appreciate this point.

Repression and Suppression of Memories

repression
unconsciously pushing unwanted memories out of awareness.

Take a moment and scan over the events of the last few years of your life. What kinds of things most easily come to mind? Many people remember happy, positive events better than disappointments and irritations (Linton, 1979). A clinical psychologist would call this tendency **repression**, or motivated forgetting. Through repression, painful, threatening, or embarrassing memories are held out of consciousness (Anderson et al., 2004). An example is provided by soldiers who have repressed some of the horrors they saw during combat (Karon & Widener, 1997, 1998).

THE CLINICAL FILE

The Recovered Memory/False Memory Debate

Many sexually abused children develop problems that persist into adulthood. In some instances, they repress all memory of the abuse. According to some psychologists, uncovering these hidden memories can be an important step toward regaining emotional health (Palm & Gibson, 1998).

Although the preceding may be true, the search for repressed memories of sexual abuse has itself been a problem. Cases have surfaced in which families were torn apart by accusations of sexual abuse that later turned out to be completely false (Porter et al., 2003). For example, Gary Ramona lost his marriage and his $400,000-a-year job when his daughter Holly alleged that he molested her throughout her childhood. To prove to Holly that her memories were true, the therapists gave her the drug Amytal, and told her that it was a "truth drug." (Amytal is a hypnotic drug that induces a twilight state of consciousness. People do not automatically tell the truth while under its influence.) Ramona sued Holly's therapists, claiming that they had been irresponsible. After reviewing the evidence, a jury awarded Gary Ramona $500,000 in damages. In a way, Gary Ramona was lucky. Most people who are falsely accused have no way to prove their innocence (Loftus & Ketcham, 1994).

Why would anyone have false memories about such disturbing events? Several popular books and a few misguided therapists have actively encouraged people to find repressed memories of abuse. Hypnosis, guided visualization, suggestion, age regression, and similar techniques can elicit fantasies that are mistaken for real memories. As we saw earlier in this chapter, it is easy to create false memories, especially by using hypnosis (Loftus, 2003; Loftus & Bernstein, 2005).

In an effort to illustrate how easy it is to implant false memories and to publicize *false memory syndrome,* memory expert Elizabeth Loftus once even deliberately implanted a false memory in actor Alan Alda. As the host of the television series *Scientific American Frontiers,* he was scheduled to interview Loftus. Before the interview, Alda was asked to fill out a questionnaire about his tastes in food. When he arrived, Loftus told Alda that his answers revealed that he must once have gotten sick after eating hard-boiled eggs (which was false). Later that day, at a picnic, Alda would not eat hard-boiled eggs (Loftus, 2003).

Certainly, some memories of abuse that return to awareness are genuine and must be dealt with. However, there is little doubt that some "recovered" memories are pure fantasy. No matter how real a recovered memory may seem, it could be false, unless it can be verified by others, or by court or medical records (Olio, 2004).

A few years ago, an "epidemic" of recovered memories took place. Today, psychologists have developed new guidelines for therapists to minimize the risk of influencing clients' memories. Nevertheless, false claims about childhood abuse still occasionally make the news. The saddest thing about such claims is that they deaden public sensitivity to actual abuse. Childhood sexual abuse is widespread. Awareness of its existence must not be repressed.

The forgetting of past failures, upsetting childhood events, the names of people you dislike, or appointments you don't want to keep may reveal repression. People prone to repression tend to be extremely sensitive to emotional events. As a result, they use repression to protect themselves from threatening thoughts (Mendolia et al., 1996).

It's possible that some adults who were sexually abused as children have repressed memories of their mistreatment. It's also possible that such memories may surface during psychotherapy or other circumstances. However, caution is required any time accusations are made on the basis of seemingly "recovered" memories. In what appeared to be an extreme case of repression, Eileen Franklin testified in court in 1990 that her father, George Franklin, abducted, raped, and killed 8-year-old Susan Nason in 1969. Eileen testified that the memory surfaced one day as she looked into the eyes of her own young daughter. Her father was convicted solely on the basis of her

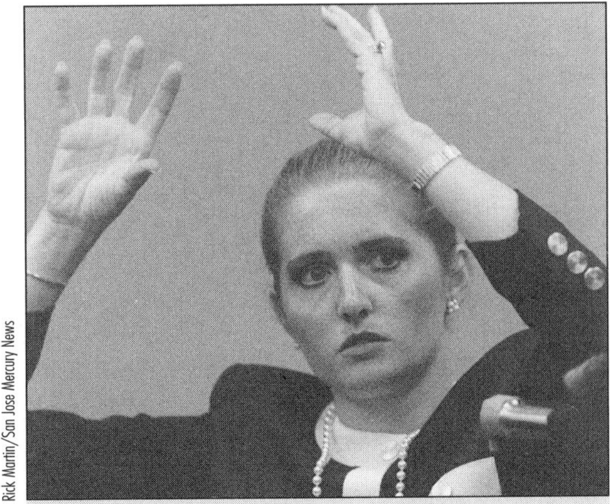

Rick Martin/San Jose Mercury News

Eileen Franklin's father was convicted on the basis of her "repressed" memories. He was later cleared by DNA testing.

AP/Wide World Photo

It is highly likely that you have a flashbulb memory about where you were when you first learned about the terrorist attack on the World Trade Center in New York. If someone alerted you about the news, you will remember that person's call and you will have clear memories about how you reacted to seeing the collapse of the towers.

suppression
a conscious effort to put something out of mind or to keep it from awareness.

"repressed" memory. However, the conviction was overturned when DNA tests cleared her father of a second murder she also accused him of committing. As the Franklin case illustrates, trying to separate true memories from fantasies is a major headache for psychologists and the courts.

If I try to forget a test I failed, am I repressing it? No. Repression can be distinguished from **suppression**, an active, conscious attempt to put something out of mind. By not thinking about the test, you have merely suppressed a memory. If you choose to, you can remember the test. Clinicians consider true repression an *unconscious* event. When a memory is repressed we may be unaware that forgetting has even occurred.

Recently, some psychologists have questioned whether repression exists (Court & Court, 2001). However, there is evidence that we can choose to actively avoid remembering upsetting information (Anderson, 2001). If you have experienced a painful emotional event, you will probably avoid all thoughts associated with it. This tends to keep cues out of mind that could trigger a painful memory. In time, your active suppression of the memory may become true repression (Anderson & Green, 2001; Bowers & Farvolden, 1996).

Flashbulb Memories

Why are some traumatic events vividly remembered, whereas others are repressed? Psychologists use the term **flashbulb memories** to describe images that seem to be frozen in memory at times of personal tragedy, accident, or other emotionally significant events (Finkenauer et al., 1998).

Depending on your age, you may have a "flashbulb" memory for the Pearl Harbor attack, the assassinations of John F. Kennedy and Martin Luther King, the *Challenger* or *Columbia* space shuttle disasters, or the terrorist attack on the World Trade Center in New York (Paradis et al., 2004). Flashbulb memories are most often formed when an event is surprising, important, or emotional (Rubin, 1985). They are frequently associated with public tragedies, but memories of positive events may also have "flashbulb" clarity.

Flashbulb memories seem to be very detailed. Often, they focus primarily on how you reacted to the event. Table 3.1 lists some memories that had "flashbulb" clarity for at least 50 percent of a group of college students. How vivid are the memories they trigger for you? (Note again that both positive and negative events are listed.)

TABLE 3.1

Bright Flashes of Memory

MEMORY CUE	PERCENTAGE OF STUDENTS WITH FLASHBULB MEMORIES
A car accident you were in or witnessed	85
When you first met your college roommate	82
The night of your high school graduation	81
The night of your senior prom (if you went or not)	78
An early romantic experience	77
A time you had to speak in front of an audience	72
When you first got your college admissions letter	65
Your first date—the moment you met him/her	57

From Rubin, 1985

The term *flashbulb memories* was first used to describe recollections that seemed to be unusually vivid and permanent. It has become clear, however, that flashbulb memories are not always accurate (Harsch & Neisser, 1989). More than anything else, what sets flashbulb memories apart is that we tend to place great *confidence* in them—even when they are wrong (Niedzwienska, 2004). Perhaps that's because we review emotionally charged events over and over and tell others about them. Also, public events such as wars, earthquakes, and assassinations reappear many times in the news, which highlights them in memory (Wright, 1993). Over time, flashbulb memories tend to crystallize into consistent, if not entirely accurate, landmarks in our lives (Schmolck, Buffalo, & Squire, 2000; Winningham, Hyman, & Dinnel, 2000).

MEMORY FORMATION— SOME "SHOCKING" FINDINGS

flashbulb memories
memories created at times of high emotion that seem especially vivid.

One possibility overlooked in our discussion of forgetting is that memories may be lost as they are being formed. For example, a head injury may cause a "gap" in memories preceding the accident. *Retrograde amnesia,* as this is called, involves forgetting events that occurred before an injury or trauma. In contrast, *anterograde amnesia* involves forgetting events that follow an injury or trauma. (An example of this type of amnesia is discussed in a moment.)

Consolidation

Retrograde amnesia can be understood if we assume that it takes a certain amount of time to move information from short-term memory to long-term memory. The forming of a long-term memory is called **consolidation** (Squire, Knowlton, & Musen, 1993). You can think of consolidation as being somewhat like writing your name in wet concrete. Once the concrete is set, the information (your name) is fairly lasting, but while it is setting, it can be wiped out (amnesia) or scribbled over (interference).

consolidation
process by which relatively permanent memories are formed in the brain.

Consider a classic experiment on consolidation, in which a rat is placed on a small platform. The rat steps down to the floor and receives a painful electric shock. After one shock, the rat can be returned to the platform repeatedly, but it will not step down. Obviously, the rat remembers the shock. Would it remember if consolidation were disturbed?

Interestingly, one way to prevent consolidation is to give a different kind of shock called **electroconvulsive shock (ECS)**. ECS is a mild electric shock to the brain. It does not harm the animal, but it does destroy any memory that is being formed. If each painful shock (the one the animal remembers) is followed by ECS (which wipes out memories during consolidation), the rat will step down over and over. Each time, ECS will erase the memory of the painful shock.

electroconvulsive shock (ECS)
an electric current passed directly through the brain, producing a convulsion.

What would happen if ECS were given several hours after the learning? Recent memories are more easily disrupted than older memories (Gold, 1987). If enough time is allowed to pass between learning and ECS, the memory will be unaffected because consolidation is already complete. That's why people with mild head injuries lose only memories from just before the accident, whereas older memories remain intact (Lieberman, 2004). Likewise, you would forget more if you studied, stayed awake 8 hours, and then slept 8 hours than you would if you studied, slept 8 hours, and were awake for 8 hours. Either way, 16 hours would pass. However, less forgetting would occur in the second instance because more consolidation would occur before interference begins (Nesca & Koulack, 1994).

Where does consolidation take place in the brain? Actually, many parts of the brain are responsible for memory, but the **hippocampus** is particularly important. The hippocampus acts as a sort of "switching station" between short-term and long-term memory (Gabrieli, 1998). The hippocampus does this, in part, by growing new neurons. New neurons probably store information by making new connections within the brain (Macklis, 2001).

hippocampus
a brain structure associated with emotion and the transfer of information from short-term memory to long-term memory.

Humans who have hippocampal damage usually show a striking inability to store new memories (Bigler et al., 1996). A patient described by Brenda Milner provides a vivid example. Two years after an operation damaged his hippocampus, a 29-year-old patient continued to give his age as 27. He also reported that it seemed as if the operation had just taken place (Milner, 1965). His memory of events before the operation remained clear, but he found forming new long-term memories almost impossible. When his parents moved to a new house a few blocks away on the same street, he could not remember the new address. Month after month, he read the same magazines over and over without finding them familiar. If you were to meet this man, he would seem fairly normal because he still has short-term memory. But if you were to leave the room and return 15 minutes later, he would act as if he had never seen you before. Years ago his favorite uncle died, but he suffers the same grief anew each time he is told of the death. Lacking the ability to form new lasting memories, he lives eternally in the present (Corkin, 2002).

The Brain and Memory

engram
a "memory trace" in the brain.

Somewhere within the 3-pound mass of the human brain lies all we know: ZIP codes, faces of loved ones, history, favorite melodies, the taste of an apple, and much, much more. Where is this information? Karl Lashley, a pioneering brain researcher, set out in the 1920s to find an **engram**, or memory trace. Lashley taught animals to run mazes and then removed parts of their brains to see how memory of the maze changed. After 30 years he had to concede defeat: Engrams are not located in any one area of the brain. It mattered little which part of the brain's cortex he removed. Only the *amount* removed was related to memory loss.

Lashley's conclusion remains true for specific memories (Squire, 2004). However, some areas of the cerebral cortex *are* more important to memory than others. Patterns of blood flow in the cerebral cortex (the wrinkled outer layer of the brain) can be used to map brain activity. Figure 3.19 shows the results of measuring blood flow while people were thinking about a semantic memory *(a)* or an episodic memory *(b)*. In the map, green indicates areas that are more active during semantic thinking. Reds show areas of greater activity during episodic thinking. The brain in view *c* shows the difference in activity between views *a* and *b*. The resulting pattern indicates that the front of the cortex is related to episodic memory. Back areas are more associated with semantic memory (Tulving, 1989, 2002).

To summarize (and simplify greatly), the hippocampus handles memory consolidation (Zola & Squire, 2001). Once long-term memories are formed, they appear to be stored in the cortex of the brain (Gabrieli, 1998; Teng & Squire, 1999).

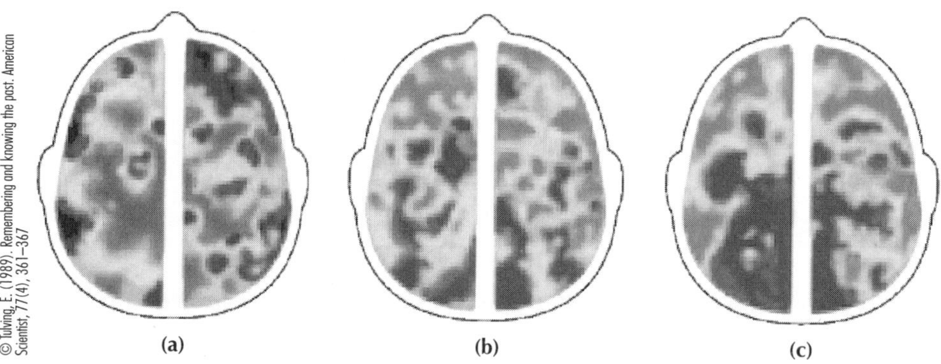

FIGURE 3.19

Patterns of blood flow in the cerebral cortex (wrinkled outer layer of the brain) change as areas become more or less active. Thus, blood flow can be used to draw "maps" of brain activity. This drawing, which views the brain from the top, shows the results of measuring cerebral blood flow while people were thinking about a semantic memory *(a)* or an episodic memory *(b)*. In the map, green indicates areas that are more active during semantic thinking. Reds show areas of greater activity during episodic thinking. The brain in view *c* shows the difference in activity between views *a* and *b*. The resulting pattern suggests that the front of the cortex is related to episodic memory. Areas toward the back and sides of the brain, especially the temporal lobes, are more associated with semantic memory (Gabrieli, 1998; Tulving, 1989, 2002).

FOCUS ON RESEARCH

The Long-Term Potential of a Memory Pill

At long last, scientists may have found the chemical "signature" that records memories in everything from snails to rats to humans. If two brain cells become more active at the same time, the connections between them grow stronger (Squire & Kandel, 2000). This process is called *long-term potentiation*. After it occurs, an affected brain cell will respond more strongly to messages from other cells. The brain appears to use this mechanism to form lasting memories (García-Junco-Clemente, Linares-Clemente, & Fernández-Chacón, 2005).

How has that been demonstrated? Electrically stimulating parts of the brain involved in memory, such as the hippocampus, can decrease long-term potentiation (Ivanco & Racine, 2000). For example, using electroconvulsive shock to overstimulate memory areas in the brains of rats interferes with long-term potentiation (Trepel & Racine, 1998). It also causes memory loss—just as it does when humans are given ECS for depression.

Will researchers ever produce a "memory pill" for people with normal memory? It's a growing possibility. Drugs that increase longterm potentiation also tend to improve memory (Shakesby, Anwyl, & Rowan, 2002). For example, rats administered such drugs could remember the correct path through a maze better than rats not given the drug (Service, 1994). Such findings suggest that memory can be and will be artificially enhanced (Schacter, 2000). However, the possibility of something like a "physics pill" or a "math pill" still seems remote.

How are memories recorded in the cortex? Scientists are beginning to identify the exact ways in which nerve cells record information. For example, Eric Kandel and his colleagues have studied learning in the marine snail *aplysia* (ah-PLEEZ-yah). Kandel found that learning in *aplysia* occurs when certain nerve cells in a circuit alter the amount of transmitter chemicals they release (Kandel, 1999). Learning also alters the activity, structure, and chemistry of brain cells. Such changes determine which connections get stronger and which become weaker. This "reprograms" the brain and records information (Abel & Lattal, 2001; Klintsova & Greenough, 1999).

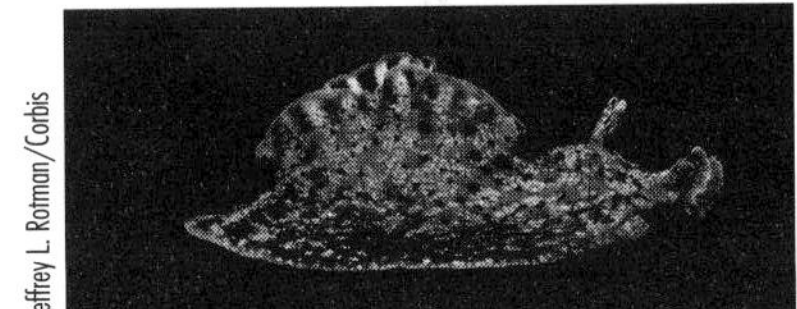

Jeffrey L. Rotman/Corbis

■ **An aplysia.** The relatively simple nervous system of this sea animal allows scientists to study memory as it occurs in single nerve cells.

Scientists continue to study various chemicals, especially neurotransmitters, that affect memory. If their research succeeds, it may be possible to help the millions of persons who suffer from memory impairment (Elli & Nathan, 2001). (See "The Long-Term Potential of a Memory Pill.")

IMPROVING MEMORY—KEYS TO THE MEMORY BANK

No matter how good your memory may be, there are probably times when you wish it were better. While we're waiting around for the arrival of a memory pill, this section describes some ways to immediately improve your memory skills.

Tatiana Cooley won a national memory contest held in New York. To win, she had to memorize long lists of words and numbers, the order of the cards in a shuffled deck, a 54-line poem, and 100 names and faces. Tatiana thinks that memorization is fun. You might expect that she would also be good at everyday memory chores. On the contrary, Tatiana describes herself as "incredibly absent-minded." When asked how many brothers and sisters she has, she replies, "Six, er seven, er six." The year she graduated from high school? She pauses for a several seconds, "1990." The elementary school grade she was in when she won a regional spelling bee? She can't remember. Ever fearful of forgetting, Tatiana keeps a daily to-do list and surrounds herself with a thicket of Post-It notes (Levinson, 1999).

Memory Strategies

What can we learn about memory from Tatiana? First, we should all be more tolerant of occasional memory lapses. Even memory champions have less than perfect memories! As we have seen in this chapter, memory is not like a tape recorder or a video camera. Information is frequently lost, and memories change as they are stored and retrieved. This can be frustrating at times, but it's also a good thing. The flexibility of human memory allows us to focus on what's important and meaningful, even though it also contributes to some inaccuracies. Tatiana's success as a "memory athlete" also suggests that making full use of memory requires effort and practice. Let's see how you can improve your memory.

Knowledge of Results Learning proceeds best when feedback, or *knowledge of results,* allows you to check your progress. Feedback can help you identify ideas that need extra practice. In addition, knowing that you have remembered or answered correctly is rewarding. A prime way to provide feedback for yourself while studying is *recitation.*

Recitation If you are going to remember something, eventually you will have to retrieve it. *Recitation* refers to summarizing aloud while you are learning. Recitation forces you to practice retrieving information. When you are reading a text, you should stop frequently and try to remember what you have just read by restating it in your own words. In one experiment, the best memory score was earned by a group of students who spent 80 percent of their time reciting and only 20 percent reading (Gates, 1958). Maybe students who talk to themselves aren't crazy after all.

Rehearsal The more you *rehearse* (mentally review) information as you read, the better you will remember it. But remember that maintenance rehearsal alone is not very effective. Elaborative rehearsal, in which you look for connections to existing knowledge, is far better. Thinking about facts helps link them together in memory. To learn college-level information, you must make active use of rehearsal strategies (Nist, Sharman, & Holschuh, 1996).

Selection The Dutch scholar Erasmus said that a good memory should be like a fish net: It should keep all the big fish and let the little ones escape. If you boil down the paragraphs in most textbooks to one or two important terms or ideas, your memory chores will be more manageable. Practice very selective marking in your texts and use marginal notes to further summarize ideas. Most students mark their texts too much instead of too little. If everything is underlined, you haven't been selective. And, very likely, you didn't pay much attention in the first place (Peterson, 1992).

Organization Assume that you must memorize the following list of words: north, man, red, spring, woman, east, autumn, yellow, summer, boy, blue, west, winter, girl, green, south. This rather difficult list could be reorganized into *chunks* as follows: north-east-south-west, spring-summer-autumn-winter, red-yellow-green-blue, man-woman-boy-girl. This simple reordering made the second list much easier to learn when college students were tested on both lists (Deese & Hulse, 1967). Organizing class notes and summarizing chapters can be quite helpful (Dickinson & O'Connell, 1990). You may even want to summarize your summaries so that the overall network of ideas becomes clearer and simpler. Summaries improve memory by encouraging better encoding of information (Hadwin, Kirby, & Woodhouse, 1999).

Whole Versus Part Learning If you have to memorize a speech, is it better to try to learn it from beginning to end? Or in smaller parts like paragraphs? Generally it is better to practice whole packages of information rather than smaller parts (*whole learning*). This is especially true for fairly short, organized information. An exception is that learning parts may be better for extremely long, complicated information. In *part learning,* subparts of a larger body of information are studied (such as sections of a textbook chapter). To decide which approach to use, remember to study the *largest meaningful amount of information* you can at one time.

For very long or complex material, try the *progressive-part method,* by breaking a learning task into a series of short sections. At first, you study part A until it is mastered. Next, you study parts A and B; then A, B, and C; and so forth. This is a good way to learn the lines of a play, a long piece of music, or a poem (Ash & Holding, 1990). After the material is learned, you should also practice by starting at points other than A (at C, D, or B, for example). This helps prevent getting "lost" or going blank in the middle of a performance.

Serial Position Whenever you must learn something in order, be aware of the serial position effect. As you will recall, this is the tendency to make the most errors in remembering the middle of a list. If you are introduced to a long line of people, the names you are likely to forget will be those in the middle, so you should make an extra effort to attend to them. You should also give extra practice to the middle of a list, poem, or speech. Try to break long lists of information into short sub-lists, and make the middle sub-lists the shortest of all.

spaced practice
a practice schedule that alternates study periods with brief rests.

massed practice
a practice schedule in which studying continues for long periods, without interruption.

Cues The best *memory cues* (stimuli that aid retrieval) are those that were present during encoding (Reed, 1996). For example, students in one study had the daunting task of trying to recall a list of 600 words. As they read the list (which they did not know they would be tested on), the students gave three other words closely related in meaning to each listed word. In a test given later, the words each student supplied were used as cues to jog his or her memory. The students recalled an astounding 90 percent of the original word list (Mantyla, 1986).

Now read the following sentence:

The fish bit the swimmer.

If you were tested a week from now, you would be more likely to recall the sentence if you were given a memory cue. And, surprisingly, the word *shark* would work better as a reminder than *fish* would. The reason for this is that most people think of a shark when they read the sentence. As a result, *shark* becomes a potent memory cue (Schacter, 2000).

The preceding examples show, once again, that it often helps to *elaborate* information as you learn. When you study, try to use new names, ideas, or terms in several sentences. Also, form images that include the new information and relate it to knowledge you already have (Pressley et al., 1988). Your goal should be to knit meaningful cues into your memory code to help you retrieve information when you need it (Figure 3.20).

Robbie Jack/Corbis

FIGURE 3.20

Actors can remember large amounts of complex information for many months, even when learning new roles in between. During testing, they remember their lines best when they are allowed to move and gesture as they would when performing. Apparently their movements supply cues that aid recall (Noice & Noice, 1999).

Overlearning Numerous studies have shown that memory is greatly improved when you **overlearn**. That is, when study is continued beyond bare mastery. After you have learned material well enough to remember it once without error, you should continue studying. Overlearning is your best insurance against going blank on a test because of being nervous.

Spaced Practice To keep boredom and fatigue to a minimum, try alternating short study sessions with brief rest periods. This pattern, called **spaced practice,** is generally superior to **massed practice,** in which little or no rest is given between learning sessions. By improving attention and consolidation, three 20-minute study sessions can produce more learning than 1 hour of continuous study. There's an old joke that goes, "How do you get to Carnegie Hall?" The answer is, "Practice, practice, practice." A better answer would be "Practice, wait awhile, practice, wait awhile, practice" (Neath, 2002).

Perhaps the best way to make use of spaced practice is to *schedule* your time. To make an effective schedule, designate times during the week before, after, and between classes when you will study particular subjects. Then treat these times just as if they were classes you had to attend.

Sleep and Memory Remember that sleeping after study reduces interference. However, unless you are a "night person," late evening may not be a very efficient time for you to study. Also, you obviously can't sleep after every study session or study everything just before you sleep. That's why your study schedule should include ample breaks between subjects, as described earlier. Using your breaks and free time in a schedule is as important as living up to your study periods.

Hunger and Memory People who are hungry almost always score lower on memory tests. So mother was right, it's a good idea to make sure you've had a good breakfast or lunch before you take tests at school (Martin & Benton, 1999; Smith, Clark, & Gallagher, 1999).

Extend How Long You Remember When you are learning new information, test yourself repeatedly. As you do, gradually lengthen the amount of time that passes before you test yourself again. For example, if you are studying German words on flash cards, look at the first card and then move it a few cards back in the stack. Do the same with the next few cards. When you get to the first "old" card, test yourself on it and check the answer. Then, move it farther back in the stack. Do the same with other "old" cards as they come up. When "old" cards come up for the third time, put them clear to the back of the stack (Cull, Shaughnessy, & Zechmeister, 1996).

Review If you have spaced your practice and overlearned, review will be like icing on your study cake. Reviewing shortly before an exam cuts down the time during which you must remember details that may be important for the test. When reviewing, hold the amount of new information you try to memorize to a minimum. It may be realistic to take what you have actually learned and add a little more to it at the last minute by cramming. But remember that more than a little new learning may interfere with what you already know.

Using a Strategy to Aid Recall Successful recall is usually the result of a planned *search* of memory (Reed, 1996). For example, one study found that students were most likely to recall names that eluded them if they made use of partial information (Reed & Bruce, 1982). The students were trying to answer questions such as, "He is best remembered as the scarecrow in the Judy Garland movie *The Wizard of Oz*." (The answer is Ray Bolger.) Partial information that helped students remember included impressions about the length of the name, letter sounds within the name, similar names, and related information (such as the names of other characters in the movie). A similar helpful strategy is to go through the alphabet, trying each letter as the first sound of a name or word you are seeking.

The *cognitive interview* described earlier in this chapter offers some further hints for recapturing context and jogging memories:

1. Say or write down *everything* you can remember that relates to the information you are seeking. Don't worry about how trivial any of it seems; each bit of information you remember can serve as a cue to bring back others.
2. Try to recall events or information in different orders. Let your memories flow out backward or out of order, or start with whatever impressed you the most.

3. Recall from different viewpoints. Review events by mentally standing in a different place. Or try to view information as another person would remember it. When taking a test, for instance, ask yourself what other students or your professor would remember about the topic.
4. Mentally put yourself back in the situation where you learned the information. Try to mentally recreate the learning environment or relive the event. As you do, include sounds, smells, details of weather, nearby objects, other people present, what you said or thought, and how you felt as you learned the information (Fisher & Geiselman, 1987).

A Look Ahead Psychologists still have much to learn about the nature of memory and how to improve it. For now, one thing stands out clearly: People who have good memories excel at organizing information and making it meaningful. With this in mind, the Psychology in Action discussion for this chapter tells how you can combine organization and meaning into a powerful method for improving memory.

mnemonic
any kind of memory system or aid.

keyword method
as an aid to memory, using a familiar word or image to link two items.

PSYCHOLOGY IN ACTION

Mnemonics—Memory Magic

Some stage performers use memory as part of their acts. Do they have eidetic imagery? Various "memory experts" entertain by memorizing the names of everyone at a banquet, the order of all the cards in a deck, long lists of words, or other seemingly impossible amounts of information. Such feats may seem like magic, but if they are, you can have a magic memory too. These tricks are performed through the use of *mnemonics* (nee-MON-iks) (Lieberman, 2004; Wilding & Valentine, 1994b). A **mnemonic** is any kind of memory system or aid. In some cases, mnemonic strategies increase recall ten-fold (Patten, 1990).

Some mnemonic systems are so common that almost everyone knows them. If you are trying to remember how many days there are in a month, you may find the answer by reciting, "Thirty days hath September . . ." Physics teachers often help students remember the colors of the spectrum by giving them the mnemonic "Roy G. Biv": **R**ed, **O**range, **Y**ellow, **G**reen, **B**lue, **I**ndigo, **V**iolet. The budding sailor who has trouble telling port from starboard may remember that port and left both have four letters or may remind herself, "I *left* port." And what beginning musician hasn't remembered the notes represented by the lines and spaces of the musical staff by learning "F-A-C-E" and "**E**very **G**ood **B**oy **D**oes **F**ine."

Mnemonic techniques are ways to avoid *rote* learning (learning by simple repetition). The superiority of mnemonic learning as opposed to rote learning has been demonstrated many times. For example, Gordon Bower (1973) asked college students to study 5 different lists of 20 unrelated words. At the end of a short study session, subjects tried to recall all 100 items. People using mnemonics remembered an average of 72 items, whereas members of a control group using rote learning remembered an average of 28.

Stage performers rarely have naturally superior memories. Instead, they make extensive use of memory systems to perform their feats (Wilding & Valentine, 1994b). Few of these systems are of practical value to you as a student, but the principles underlying mnemonics

continued

are. By practicing mnemonics you should be able to greatly improve your memory with little effort (Dretzke & Levin, 1996).

Here, then, are the basic principles of mnemonics.

1. **Use mental pictures.** Visual pictures, or images, are generally easier to remember than words. Turning information into mental pictures is therefore very helpful. Make these images as vivid as possible (Campos & Perez, 1997).
2. **Make things meaningful.** Transferring information from short-term memory to long-term memory is aided by making it meaningful. If you encounter technical terms that have little or no immediate meaning for you, *give* them meaning, even if you have to stretch the term to do so. (This point is clarified by the examples following this list.)
3. **Make information familiar.** Connect it to what you already know. Another way to get information into long-term memory is to connect it to information already stored there. If some facts or ideas in a chapter seem to stay in your memory easily, associate other more difficult facts with them.
4. **Form bizarre, unusual, or exaggerated mental associations.** Forming images that make sense is better in most situations. However, when associating two ideas, terms, or especially mental images, you may find that the more outrageous and exaggerated the association, the more likely you are to remember. Bizarre images make stored information more *distinctive* and therefore easier to retrieve (Worthen & Marshall, 1996). Imagine, for example, that you have just been introduced to Mr. Rehkop. To remember his name, you could picture him wearing a police uniform. Then replace his nose with a ray gun. This bizarre image will provide two hints when you want to remember Mr. Rehkop's name: *ray* and *cop* (Carney, Levin, & Stackhouse, 1997). This technique works for other kinds of information, too. College students who used exaggerated mental associations to remember the names of unfamiliar animals outperformed students who just used rote memory (Carney & Levin, 2001). Bizarre images mainly help improve immediate memory, and they work best for fairly simple information (Robinson-Riegler & McDaniel, 1994). Nevertheless, they can be a first step toward learning.

Ulrike Welsch

Mnemonics can be an aid in preparing for tests. However, because mnemonics help most in the initial stages of storing information, it is important to follow through with other elaborative learning strategies.

A sampling of typical applications of mnemonics should make these four points clearer to you.

Example 1

Let's say you have 30 new vocabulary words to memorize in Spanish. You can proceed by rote memorization (repeat them over and over until you begin to get them), or you can learn them with little effort by using the keyword method (Pressley, 1987). In the **keyword method** a familiar word or image is used to link two other words or items. To remember that the word *pajaro* (pronounced PAH-hah-ro) means bird, you can link it to a "key" word in English: *Pajaro* (to me) sounds like "parked car-o." Therefore, to remember that *pajaro* means bird, you might visualize a parked car jam-packed full of birds. You should try to make this image as vivid and exaggerated as possible, with birds flapping and chirping and

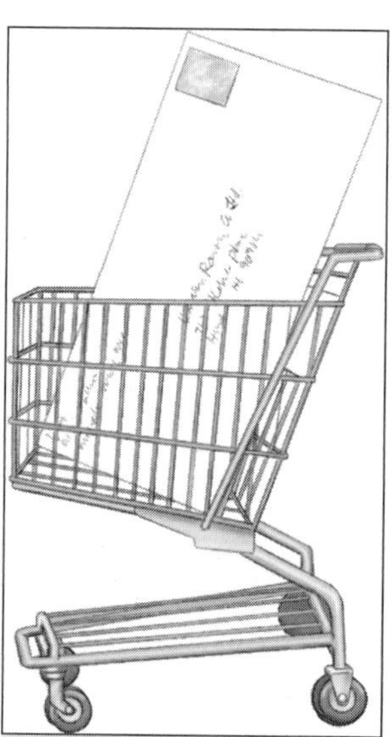

Exaggerated mental images can link two words or ideas in ways that aid memory. Here, the keyword method is used to link the English word letter with the Spanish word *carta*.

feathers flying everywhere. Similarly, for the word *carta* (which means "letter"), you might imagine a shopping *cart* filled with postal letters.

If you link similar keywords and images for the rest of the list, you may not remember them all, but you will get most without any more practice. As a matter of fact, if you have formed the *pajaro* and *carta* images just now, it is going to be almost impossible for you to ever see these words again without remembering what they mean. The keyword method is also superior when you want to work "backward" from an English word to a foreign vocabulary word (Hogben & Lawson, 1992).

What about a year from now? How long do keyword memories last? Mnemonic memories work best in the short run. Later, they may be more fragile than conventional memories. That's why it's usually best to use mnemonics during the initial stages of learning (Carney & Levin, 1998). To create more lasting memories, you'll need to use the techniques discussed earlier in this chapter.

Example 2

Let's say you have to learn the names of all the bones and muscles in the human body for biology. You are trying to remember that the jawbone is the *mandible*. This one is easy because you can associate it to a *man nibbling*, or maybe you can picture a *man dribbling* a basketball with his jaw (make this image as ridiculous as possible). If the muscle name *latissimus dorsi* gives you trouble, familiarize it by turning it into *"the ladder misses the door, sigh."* Then picture a ladder glued to your back where the muscle is found. Picture the ladder leading up to a small door at your shoulder. Picture the ladder missing the door. Picture the ladder sighing like an animated character in a cartoon.

This seems like more to remember, not less; and it seems like it would cause you to misspell things. Mnemonics are not a complete substitute for normal memory; they are an aid to normal memory. Mnemonics are not likely to be helpful unless you make extensive use of *images* (Willoughby et al., 1997). Your mental pictures will come back to you easily. As for misspellings, mnemonics can be thought of as a built-in hint in your memory. Often, when taking a test, you will find that the slightest hint is all you need to remember correctly. A mnemonic image is like having someone leaning over your shoulder who says, "Psst, the name of that muscle sounds like 'ladder misses the door, sigh.'" If misspelling continues to be a problem, try to create memory aids for spelling, too.

Here are two more examples to help you appreciate the flexibility of a mnemonic approach to studying.

Example 3

Your art history teacher expects you to be able to name the artist when you are shown slides as part of exams. You have seen many of the slides only once before in class. How will you remember them? As the slides are shown in class, make each artist's name into an object or image. Then picture the object *in* the paintings done by the artist. For example, you can picture Van Gogh as a *van* (automobile) *going* through the middle of each Van Gogh painting. Picture the van running over things and knocking things over. Or, if you remember that Van Gogh cut off his ear, picture a giant bloody ear in each of his paintings.

Example 4

If you have trouble remembering history, try to avoid thinking of it as something from the dim past. Picture each historical personality as a person you know right now (a friend, teacher, parent, and so on). Then picture these people doing whatever the historical figures did. Also, try visualizing battles or other events as if they were happening in your town or make parks and schools into countries. Use your imagination.

How can mnemonics be used to remember things in order? Here are three techniques that are helpful.

1. **Form a story or a chain.** To remember lists of ideas, objects, or words in order, try forming an exaggerated association (mental image) connecting the first item to the second, then the second to the third, and so on. To remember the following short list in order—elephant, doorknob, string, watch, rifle, oranges—picture a full-size *elephant* balanced on a *doorknob* playing with a *string* tied to him. Picture a *watch* tied to the string, and a *rifle* shooting *oranges* at the watch. This technique can be used quite successfully for lists of 20 or more items. In one test, people who used a linking mnemonic did much better at remembering lists of 15 and 22 errands (Higbee et al., 1990). Try it next time you go shopping and leave your list at home. Another helpful strategy is to make up a short story that links all of the items on a list you want to remember (McNamara & Scott, 2001).
2. **Take a mental walk.** Ancient Greek orators had an interesting way to remember ideas in order when giving a speech. Their method was to take a mental walk along a familiar path. As they did, they associated topics with the images of statues found along the walk. You can do the same thing by "placing" objects or ideas along the way as you mentally take a familiar walk (Neath, 2002).

continued

PSYCHOLOGY IN ACTION (CONTINUED)

2. **Use a system.** Many times, the first letters or syllables of words or ideas can be formed into another word that will serve as a reminder of order. "Roy G. Biv" is an example. As an alternative, learn the following: 1 is a bun, 2 is a shoe, 3 is a tree, 4 is a door, 5 is a hive, 6 is sticks, 7 is heaven, 8 is a gate, 9 is a line, 10 is a hen. To remember a list in order, form an image associating bun with the first item on your list. For example, if the first item is *frog*, picture a "frog-burger" on a bun to remember it. Then, associate shoe with the second item, and so on.

If you have never used mnemonics, you may still be skeptical, but give this approach a fair trial. Most people find they can greatly extend their memory through the use of mnemonics. But remember, like most things worthwhile, remembering takes effort.

REVIEW

Is there more than one type of memory?

- Memory is an active, computer-like system that encodes, stores, and retrieves information.
- Humans appear to have three interrelated memory systems. These are sensory memory, short-term memory (STM, also called working memory), and long-term memory (LTM).

What are the features of each type of memory?

- Sensory memory is exact but very brief. Through selective attention, some information is transferred to STM.
- STM has a capacity of about 5 to 7 bits of information, but this can be extended by chunking, or recoding. Short-term memories are brief and very sensitive to interruption, or interference; however, they can be prolonged by maintenance rehearsal.
- LTM functions as a general storehouse of information, especially meaningful information. Elaborative rehearsal helps transfer information from STM to LTM. Long-term memories are relatively permanent, or lasting. LTM seems to have an almost unlimited storage capacity.
- LTM is subject to constructive processing, or ongoing revision and updating. LTM is highly organized to allow retrieval of needed information. The pattern, or structure, of memory networks is the subject of current memory research.
- Redintegrative memories are reconstructed as each memory provides a cue for the next memory.

Is there more than one type of long-term memory?

- Within long-term memory, declarative memories for facts seem to differ from procedural memories for skills.
- Declarative memories may be further categorized as semantic memories or episodic memories.

How is memory measured?

- The tip-of-the-tongue state shows that memory is not an all-or-nothing event. Memories may therefore be revealed by recall, recognition, relearning, or priming.
- In recall, memory proceeds without explicit cues, as in an essay exam. Recall of listed information often reveals a serial position effect (middle items on the list are most subject to errors).
- A common test of recognition is the multiple-choice question.
- In relearning, "forgotten" material is learned again, and memory is indicated by a savings score.
- Recall, recognition, and relearning mainly measure explicit memories. Other techniques, such as priming, are necessary to reveal implicit memories.

What are "photographic" memories?

- Eidetic imagery (photographic memory) occurs when a person is able to project an image onto a blank surface.
- Eidetic imagery is rarely found in adults. However, many adults have internal memory images, which can be very vivid.
- Exceptional memory can be learned by finding ways to directly store information in LTM.
- Learning has no effect on the limits of STM. Some people may have exceptional memories that exceed what can be achieved through learning.

What causes forgetting?

- Forgetting and memory were extensively studied by Herman Ebbinghaus. His work shows that forgetting is most rapid immediately after learning (the curve of forgetting).

- Failure to encode information is a common cause of "forgetting."
- Forgetting in sensory memory and STM probably reflects decay of memory traces in the nervous system. Decay or disuse of memories may also account for some LTM loss.
- Often, forgetting is cue dependent. The power of cues to trigger memories is revealed by state-dependent learning and the link between moods and memory.
- Much forgetting in both STM and LTM can be attributed to interference.
- When recent learning interferes with retrieval of prior learning, retroactive interference has occurred.
- If old learning interferes with new learning, proactive interference has occurred.

How accurate are everyday memories?

- Repression is the forgetting of painful, embarrassing, or traumatic memories.
- Repression is thought to be unconscious, in contrast to suppression, which is a conscious attempt to avoid thinking about something.
- Independent evidence has verified that some recovered memories of childhood sexual abuse are true. However, others have been shown to be false.
- In the absence of confirming or disconfirming evidence, there is currently no way to separate true memories from fantasies. Caution is advised for all concerned with attempts to retrieve supposedly hidden memories.

What happens in the brain when memories are formed?

- Retrograde amnesia and the effects of electroconvulsive shock (ECS) may be explained by the concept of consolidation.
- Consolidation theory holds that engrams (permanent memory traces) are formed during a critical period after learning. Until they are consolidated, long-term memories are easily destroyed.
- The hippocampus is a brain area that has been linked with consolidation of memories. Once memories are consolidated, they appear to be stored in the cortex of the brain.
- The search within the brain for engrams has now settled on changes in nerve cells and how they interconnect.

How can memory be improved?

- Memory can be improved by using feedback, recitation, and rehearsal; by selecting and organizing information; and by using the progressive-part method, spaced practice, overlearning, and active search strategies. Effects of serial position, sleep, review, cues, and elaboration should also be kept in mind when studying or memorizing.
- Mnemonic systems use mental images and unusual associations to link new information with familiar memories already stored in LTM. Such strategies give information personal meaning and make it easier to recall.

Exploratorium: Memory Demonstrations and articles related to memory from an exceptional science museum.

False-Memory Test Use the materials in this site to induce false memories in others (for demonstration purposes).

Memories Are Made of . . . Article from *Scientific American* discusses memory-enhancing drugs for Alzheimer's patients.

Memory Techniques and Mnemonics Links to information on mnemonics.

Questions and Answers About Memories of Childhood Abuse From APA, a summary of the repressed memory issue.

Repressed and Recovered Memories Site devoted to the recovered memory controversy; has links to both sides of the controversy.

The Machinery of Thought *Scientific American* article describes research on the physiology of memory.

The Magical Number Seven, Plus or Minus Two Full text of George Miller's original article.

CHAPTER 3 PRACTICE EXAM

____ 1. Which statement best characterizes the memory?
a. an automatic way to store exact copies of events
b. a warehouse that stores facts can be retrieved when desired
c. a garage where interesting items are housed
d. a dynamic system for manipulating information

____ 2. Transforming input into a workable type is the stage called
a. storage
b. encoding.
c. retrieval
d. organization.

____ 3. Out mental to do list is stored in?
a. permanent memory
b. long-term memory
c. short-term memory
d. sensory memory

____ 4. Short-term memory is like a
a. Long term parking lot.
b. storage bins at a bookstore.
c. crypt
d. museum's archives.

____ 5. The relatively permanent storage of meaningful information is called __________ memory.
a. visual
b. short-term
c. long-term
d. sensory

____ 6. Organizing information into larger units as a way of improving the efficiency of short-term memory is called
a. chunking.
b. Categorizing
c. rethinking
d. Mnemonics

____ 7. Recoding, chunking, and rehearsal are especially important for the improvement of
a. short-term memory.
b. Mnemonic imagery.
c. Tactile memory.
d. chunking

____ 8. Silently repeating a short term memory is called
a. tacting
b. rehearsal.
c. chunking.
d. manding

____ 9. Small gaps in memory of past performances are
a. normal.
b. Early stage Alzheimer's
c. Early stage amnesia.
d. abnormal.

____ 10. The worst that happens when hypnosis is used as an aid to memory in solving a crime is that
a. the person cannot be hypnotized.
b. The person's memory is the same as when not hypnotized
c. hypnotic testimony is no admissible in court
d. False memories are produced.

____ 11. How is retention shown in tests of previous learning?
a. Multiple choice scores
b. Curving scores
c. Foregetting scores
d. Savings scores

____ 12. A memory you are aware of or can consciously retrieve is
a. explicit memory.
b. elimict memory.
c. Primordial memory
d. False memory.

____ 13. Which is true about eidetic imagery?
a. Two thirds of infants have.
b. Eeidetic skills typically are gone by adulthood.
c. It is a type of reintegrative memory.
d. eidetic learners have excellent musical skills

____ 14. The ______________ theory explains forgetting of long-term and short-term memories.
a. overload
b. behavioral
c. wave
d. interference

____ 15. A clerk rearrange faculty mailboxes by alphabet, and for several days afterwards makes mistakes sorting the mail. This is an example of
a. retroactive interference.
b. proactive interference.
c. Memory transfer.
d. memory decay.

Answers

1. D
2. B
3. C
4. B
5. C
6. A
7. A
8. B
9. A
10. D
11. D
12. A
13. B
14. D
15. B

CHAPTER 4: LEARNING

QUESTIONS

1. What is the concept of learning reserved for?
2. What are examples of behavior change that would not be considered learning?
3. What are four problems we resolve by our ability to learn?
4. What are examples of habituation and sensitization and why are they important?
5. On what factors does habituation or sensitization depend?
6. Why are habituation and sensitization examples of learning?
7. How is a connection formed between the CS and US?
8. What are three findings the information rule helps explain?
9. What is the cognitive view of classical conditioning?
10. How is second order conditioning used in advertising?
11. What are some real life examples of stimulus generalization?
12. What are some real life examples of stimulus discrimination?
13. What happens to learning in acquisition, extinction, and spontaneous recovery?
14. What are some real life examples of conditioned inhibition?
15. What is the difference between classical and operant conditioning?
16. How did Thorndike discover the Law of Effect?
17. What are some examples of discriminative stimuli?
18. Why is reinforcement not defined in terms of pleasant or rewarding or unpleasant or unrewarding consequences?
19. What is response deprivation theory and what kinds of unintuitive predictions does the theory make?
20. What do the terms positive and negative refer to with respect to reinforcement?
21. What are some examples of conditioned reinforcers?
22. What are some examples of positive and negative punishers?
23. What are some practical considerations in the use of punishment?
24. What are some real life examples of fixed-ratio, variable-ratio, fixed-interval, and variable-interval schedules of reinforcement?
25. How might you teach a dog to lie down using shaping?
26. What are some examples of shaping with humans?
27. What were some pig and raccoon examples of biological constraints on learning?
28. How do psychologists explain that humans will learn certain associations more quickly than others?
29. How does operant conditioning explain superstitious behaviors?

30. How did Skinner discover superstitious behavior conditioning?
31. How are taste aversions learned through classical conditioning?
32. What are some examples of taste aversions in animals and humans?
33. Why might it be adaptive to learn taste aversions?
34. What are some strategies for averting taste aversions in cancer patients?
35. What are some examples of observational learning in animals?
36. What are some conditions that help insure effective observational learning?
37. What is vicarious reinforcement and vicarious punishment?
38. What are self-efficacy and an example?
39. What are some positive effects of observational learning?
40. What are some negative effects of observational learning?

VOCABULARY

1. avoidance conditioning
2. classical conditioning
3. conditioned inhibition
4. conditioned reinforcer
5. conditioned response (CR)
6. conditioned stimulus (CS)
7. discriminative stimulus
8. escape conditioning
9. extinction
10. fixed-interval (FI) schedule
11. fixed-ration (FR) schedule
12. habituation
13. law of effect
14. learning
15. modeling
16. negative punishment
17. negative reinforcement
18. observational learning
19. operant conditioning
20. orienting response
21. partial reinforcement schedule
22. positive punishment
23. positive rienforcement
24. punishment
25. reinforcement
26. schedule of reinforcement
27. second-order conditioning
28. sensitization
29. shaping
30. spontaneous recovery
31. stimulus discrimination
32. stimulus generalization
33. unconditioned response (UR)
34. unconditioned stimulus (US)
35. variable-interval (VI) schedule
36. variable-ratio (VR) schedule

4 Learning

Learning About Events: Noticing and Ignoring

Learning What Events Signal: Classical Conditioning

Learning About the Consequences of Behavior: Operant Conditioning

Learning From Others: Observational Learning

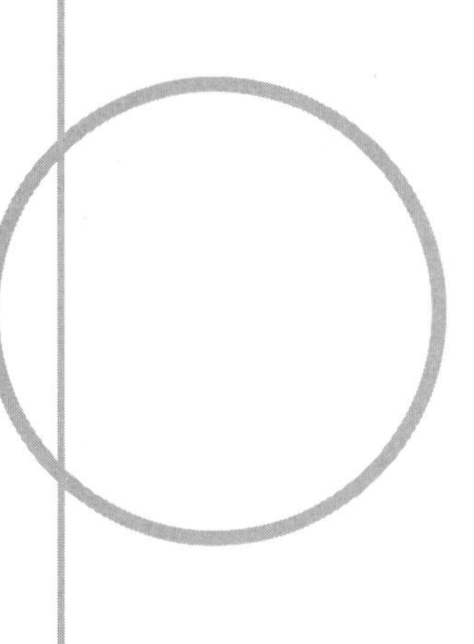

© Frank Conaway/Index Stock Imagery

HAVE YOU EVER EATEN something unusual, maybe clam pizza, and then felt sick? You're probably reluctant to sample that dish again—in fact, the mere sight of it probably makes you check for the availability of the nearest restroom. Ever taught a dog a trick, maybe to sit on command or fetch a particular toy? Researchers are studying a dog named Rico who can fetch, by name, more than 200 different toys (Kaminski et al., 2004)! Finally, do you think children are growing up more aggressive these days because of all the violence they see on TV? We've discussed this one before but like the first two examples, it's central to the topic of this chapter—learning, one of the most basic of all psychological processes.

What exactly is learning? That's an easy one—it's the process of acquiring knowledge. You go to school, you take classes, you learn how the world works. In essence, that's the same way psychologists think about learning. But, as you know, psychologists like to define concepts by how those concepts can be measured. "Knowledge" can't be measured directly—you could crack someone's head open, but all you're going to find are neurons and glial cells. Instead, **learning** is defined by behavior—more precisely, as a change in behavior, or potential behavior, that results from experience. Notice the emphasis is on *behavior,* which, unlike acquired knowledge, can be directly observed. We make inferences about learning by observing behavior and noting how it changes over time.

learning
a relatively permanent change in behavior, or potential behavior, that results from experience.

Like most definitions, this one needs a little tweaking. Sometimes behavior changes as a result of experience in ways that we wouldn't classify as learning. For example, your behavior changes as you age. Experience plays a role in development, as you know, but some changes occur purely as a result of physical development. Your behavior also changes when you get injured or sick. Suppose you're stuck in

PREVIEW

Learning From Experience

It's easy to see why psychologists are interested in learning. The ability to alter behavior over time in response to changing environments is highly adaptive. Historically, as you'll see in this chapter, psychologists have tended to focus on very simple kinds of learning processes, often using animals as subjects. We'll discuss more complex forms of learning, particularly as they relate to memory. Here our discussion revolves around four simple problems that are resolved, in part, by our ability to learn.

Noticing and Ignoring We need to recognize new events but also learn to ignore events that occur repeatedly without consequence. A baby crying, the screech of automobile brakes—these sounds demand our attention and cause us to react. Humans and animals notice sudden changes in their environment; they notice those things that are new and potentially of interest. However, our reactions to these novel events change with repeated experience, and these changes are controlled by some of the most basic and important of all learning processes.

Learning What Events Signal When does one event predict that a second event is likely to follow? Many things that happen in our world signal the occurrence of other events. For instance, you know that lightning precedes thunder and that a rattling sound can signal the presence of a venomous snake. Often you can't do anything about the co-occurrence of such events, but if you recognize the relationship, you can respond accordingly (you can take cover or move to avoid the snake).

Learning About the Consequences of Our Behavior All species, sea snails as well as people, need to learn that some behaviors have consequences. The child who flicks the tail of a cat once too often receives an unwelcome surprise. The family dog learns that if he hangs around the dinner table, an occasional scrap of food might come his way. Behaviors are instrumental in producing rewards and punishments, and it's clearly adaptive for us to learn when and how to act.

Learning From Others Often our most important teachers are not our own actions and their consequences but the actions of others. We learn by example, as does most of the animal kingdom. Observational learning has considerable adaptive significance: A teenager learns about the consequences of drunk driving, one hopes, not from direct experience but from observing others whose fate has already been sealed. A young monkey in the wild learns to be afraid of snakes not from a deadly personal encounter but from observing its mother's fear.

© Robert Rathe/Stock Boston

The bright colors and screeching sirens of a fire engine are designed to draw our attention and signal us to get out of the way.

© Stephen Krasemann/Photo Researchers, Inc.

It's clearly adaptive to learn about the signaling properties of events. A distinctive rattle on a wilderness trail signals the potential strike of the western diamondback rattlesnake.

© Anthony Wood/Stock Boston

This family dog knows about the consequences of hanging around the dinner table. She's learned that her begging behavior is instrumental in producing a tasty reward.

bed for 2 days with a high fever; your behavior is going to change—you sleep a lot more than normal—but these changes have nothing to do with learning. The concept of learning is reserved for those cases when behavior changes in a way that reflects the experience—we change our behavior, either as a reaction to the experience or as a result of practice, so we can act more sensibly in the future.

LEARNING ABOUT EVENTS: NOTICING AND IGNORING

Let's begin with the first problem: How do we learn to notice and ignore events that occur and repeat in our world? We're constantly surrounded by sights, sounds, and sensations—from the traffic outside the window, to the color of the paint on the wall, to the feel of denim jeans against our legs. As you discovered, we can't attend to all of these stimuli. Instead, because the human nervous system has limited resources, we must prioritize our mental functioning. And this is not only a human problem: Animals, too, have limited resources, and they constantly need to decide whether events in their environment are important or unimportant.

Habituation and Sensitization

People and animals are programmed from birth to notice novelty; when something new or different happens, we pay close attention. Suppose you hear a funny ticking noise in your car engine when you press the gas pedal. When you first notice the sound, it occupies your attention. You produce an **orienting response**, which means you orient toward the new sound maybe by leaning forward and listening. After driving with the problem for a while, however, your behavior changes—the ticking becomes less bothersome, and you may even stop reacting to it altogether. Your behavior in the presence of the event changes with repeated experience, which is the hallmark of learning.

orienting response
an inborn tendency to notice and respond to novel or surprising events.

habituation
the decline in the tendency to respond to an event that has become familiar through repeated exposure.

Habituation occurs when you slow or stop responding to an event that has become familiar through repeated presentation. Most birds will startle and become agitated when the shadow of a hawk passes overhead, but their level of alarm will rapidly decline if the object is presented repeatedly and there's no subsequent attack (Tinbergen, 1951). It makes sense for animals to produce a strong initial orienting response to a sudden change in their environment. If a bird fails to attend quickly to the shape of a predator, it's not likely to survive. Through the process of habituation, organisms learn to be selective about what they orient toward. They attend initially to the new and unusual but subsequently ignore events that occur repeatedly without consequence.

© Allan Roberts

It's adaptive for all living things to notice sudden changes in the environment. In this case, the unexpected appearance of a red-tailed hawk elicits distinctive orienting reactions from an opossum family.

FIGURE 4.1

Long-Term Habituation. Organisms notice sudden changes in the environment but learn to ignore those that occur repeatedly. A novel sound initially makes an eating cat panic, but if the sound is repeated daily, the cat habituates and eats without the slightest reaction.

sensitization
increased responsiveness, or sensitivity, to an event that has been repeated.

A related phenomenon, called **sensitization,** occurs when our response to an event increases rather than decreases with repeated exposure. For example, if you're exposed repeatedly to a loud noise, you're likely to become sensitized to the noise—your reactions become more intense and prolonged with repeated exposure. (This happens to me when our cat constantly yells for food.) Both habituation and sensitization are natural responses to repeated events. They help us respond appropriately to the environment. Whether repetition of a stimulus will lead to habituation or sensitization depends on several factors (Groves & Thompson, 1970). Generally, sensitization is more likely when the repeated stimulus is intense or punishing. If the stimulus is mild or modest in intensity, repeated exposure usually leads to habituation. Habituation and sensitization also depend importantly on the timing of presentations—for example, habituation typically occurs faster when the repetitions occur close together in time (Miller & Grace, 2003).

Both habituation and sensitization are examples of learning because they produce changes in behavior as a function of experience. In some cases, particularly with habituation, the learning can be quite long lasting. For example, when placed in a new environment, cats are often skittish when they eat. The slightest sound or movement is likely to send them scurrying under the nearest piece of furniture. With time the animal learns, and the adjustment is typically long lasting (see Figure 4.1).

As adaptive organisms, we rely on simple learning processes like habituation to help conserve our limited resources. The world is full of events to be noticed, far more than we can ever hope to monitor. Orienting responses guarantee that we will notice the new and unusual, but through habituation we learn to ignore those things that are repeated but are of no significant consequence. Therefore, we're able to solve a very important problem—how to be selective about the events that occur and recur in the world.

LEARNING WHAT EVENTS SIGNAL: CLASSICAL CONDITIONING

Everyone knows that a flash of lightning means a clap of thunder is likely to follow; experience has taught us to *associate* lightning with thunder. You also know that a sour smell coming from the milk means it probably won't taste very good. In both these cases, you've learned an association between two events—more specifically, you've learned that one event predicts the other. This knowledge is clearly useful because it allows you to prepare yourself for future events. You know to cover your ears or to avoid drinking the milk.

The scientific study of simple associations, like those just described, began around the turn of the century in the laboratory of a Russian physiologist named Ivan P. Pavlov (1849–1936). Pavlov developed a technique, known as **classical conditioning**, to investigate how these associations are formed. According to most accounts, Pavlov didn't start off with a burning desire to study learning. His main interest was in digestion, which included the study of how dogs salivate, or drool, in the presence of food. We salivate when food is placed in our mouth, as do dogs, because saliva contains certain chemicals that help in the initial stages of digestion. However, to his annoyance, Pavlov found that his dogs often began to drool much too soon—before the food was actually placed in their mouths. Pavlov referred to these premature droolings as "psychic" secretions, and he began to study why they occurred, in part, to avoid future contamination of his digestion experiments.

classical conditioning
a set of procedures used to investigate how organisms learn about the signaling properties of events. Classical conditioning involves learning relations between events—conditioned and unconditioned stimuli—that occur outside of one's control.

The Terminology of Classical Conditioning

Pavlov recognized immediately that "psychic" secretions developed as a result of experience. At the same time, he was keenly aware that drooling in response to food is *not* a learned response. He knew that certain stimuli, which he called **unconditioned stimuli (US)**, automatically lead to responses, which he called **unconditioned responses (UR)**. Food is an unconditioned stimulus that automatically produces salivation as an unconditioned response. Neither dogs nor humans need to be taught to drool when food is placed in their mouths; rather, this response is a reflex similar to the jerking of your leg when the doctor taps you just below the knee. The response produced to an unconditioned stimulus is *unconditioned*—that is, no learning, or conditioning, is required.

unconditioned stimulus (US)
a stimulus that automatically leads to an observable response prior to any training.

unconditioned response (UR)
the observable response that is produced automatically, prior to training, on presentation of an unconditioned stimulus.

The problem facing Pavlov was that his dogs began to drool merely at the sight of the food dish or even to the sound of an assistant entering the room. Food dishes and footsteps are not unconditioned stimuli that automatically cause a dog to salivate. Drooling in response to such stimuli is learned; it is *conditioned,* or acquired as a result of experience. For this reason, Pavlov began referring to the "psychic" secretions as **conditioned responses (CR)** and to the stimuli that produced them as **conditioned stimuli (CS)**.

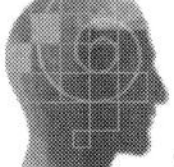

Think About It

Can you think of any reason it might be adaptive to begin the digestive processes before food actually gets into the mouth?

Let's take footsteps as an example. The sound of an approaching feeder leads to drooling because the dog has learned that the sound predicts or *signals* the appearance of the food. Footsteps and food bear a special relation to each other in time: When the footsteps are heard, the food is soon to arrive. To use Pavlov's terminology, the footsteps act as a *conditioned stimulus* that produces salivation, a *conditioned response,* in anticipation of food. This is not unlike what happens to you when your mouth begins to water as you sit down to a delicious looking meal. Conditioned stimuli typically lead to conditioned responses after the conditioned stimulus and the unconditioned stimulus have been paired together in time—the footsteps (the CS) reliably occur just before presentation of the food (the US).

conditioned response (CR)
the acquired response that is produced by the conditioned stimulus in anticipation of the unconditioned stimulus.

conditioned stimulus (CS)
the neutral stimulus that is paired with the unconditioned stimulus during classical conditioning.

Forming the CS–US Connection

What are the necessary conditions for forming an association between a conditioned stimulus and an unconditioned stimulus? It helps to remember the following general rule: A conditioned stimulus will become a signal for the unconditioned stimulus when it provides *information* about the delivery of the unconditioned stimulus (Rescorla, 1992). If a bell (CS) is struck just before the delivery of food (US),

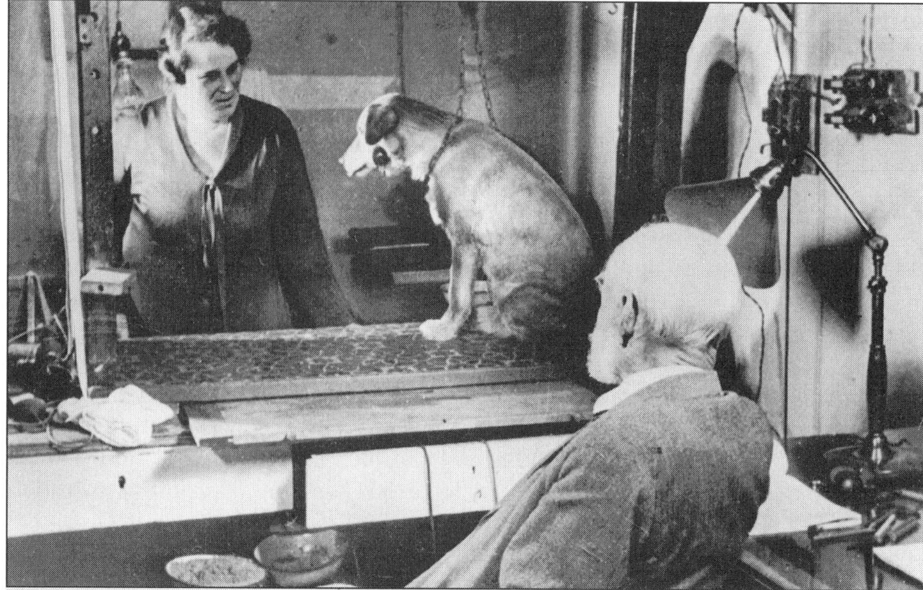

Russian physiologist Ivan Pavlov watches one of his experiments on "psychic" secretions in dogs in 1934. Notice the dog's cheek, which is fitted with a device for measuring salivation.

© Sovfoto

and these pairings are continued over time, the dog will begin to salivate (CR) whenever the bell (CS) is struck (see Figure 4.2). A connection is formed because the bell provides *information* about the delivery of the food—the dog knows that food will be arriving soon after it hears the bell. This rule helps to explain a number of experimental findings.

First, for an effective association to form, the conditioned stimulus must be presented *before* the unconditioned stimulus. If the two are presented at the same time (*simultaneous conditioning*), or if the conditioned stimulus is presented *after* the unconditioned stimulus (*backward conditioning*), not much, if any, conditioning will occur. In both cases the conditioned stimulus provides no information about when the unconditioned stimulus will appear, so conditioned responding does not develop. There are some exceptions to this general rule (Cole & Miller, 1999; Rescorla, 1980), but usually the conditioned stimulus needs to be presented first, before the unconditioned stimulus, for effective conditioning.

Second, the unconditioned stimulus needs to follow the conditioned stimulus *closely in time*. Pavlov found that if there was a long delay between when the bell (CS) was struck and the delivery of the food (US), his dogs usually didn't form a connection between the bell and the food. As the gap between presentation of the conditioned stimulus and the unconditioned stimulus increases, one becomes a less efficient signal for the arrival of the other—that is, the conditioned stimulus provides less useful information about the appearance of the unconditioned stimulus. Once again, there are important exceptions to the rule, but they need not concern us here (see Gallistel & Gibbon, 2000). (For one exception, take a look at the Practical Solutions feature.)

Think About It

Why do you think it's adaptive to learn associations only when the conditioned stimulus provides new information about the unconditioned stimulus? Can you think of any situations in which it might be useful to learn that many stimuli predict the appearance of the unconditioned stimulus?

Finally, the conditioned stimulus must provide *new* information about the unconditioned stimulus. If you already know when the unconditioned stimulus will occur, then adding another stimulus that predicts it will lead to little, if any, evidence of conditioning. Suppose you teach some rats that a tone is a reliable signal for an electric shock. Once the rats have begun to freeze when they hear the tone (a typical conditioned response to the expectation of shock), you start turning on a light at the same time as you present the tone. Both the light and the tone are then followed by the shock. Under these conditions, rats typically don't learn that the light is also a reliable signal for the shock (e.g., Kamin, 1968). This result is called *blocking* because the tone appears to prevent, or block, the animal from learning about the light. Blocking occurs because the light provides no new information

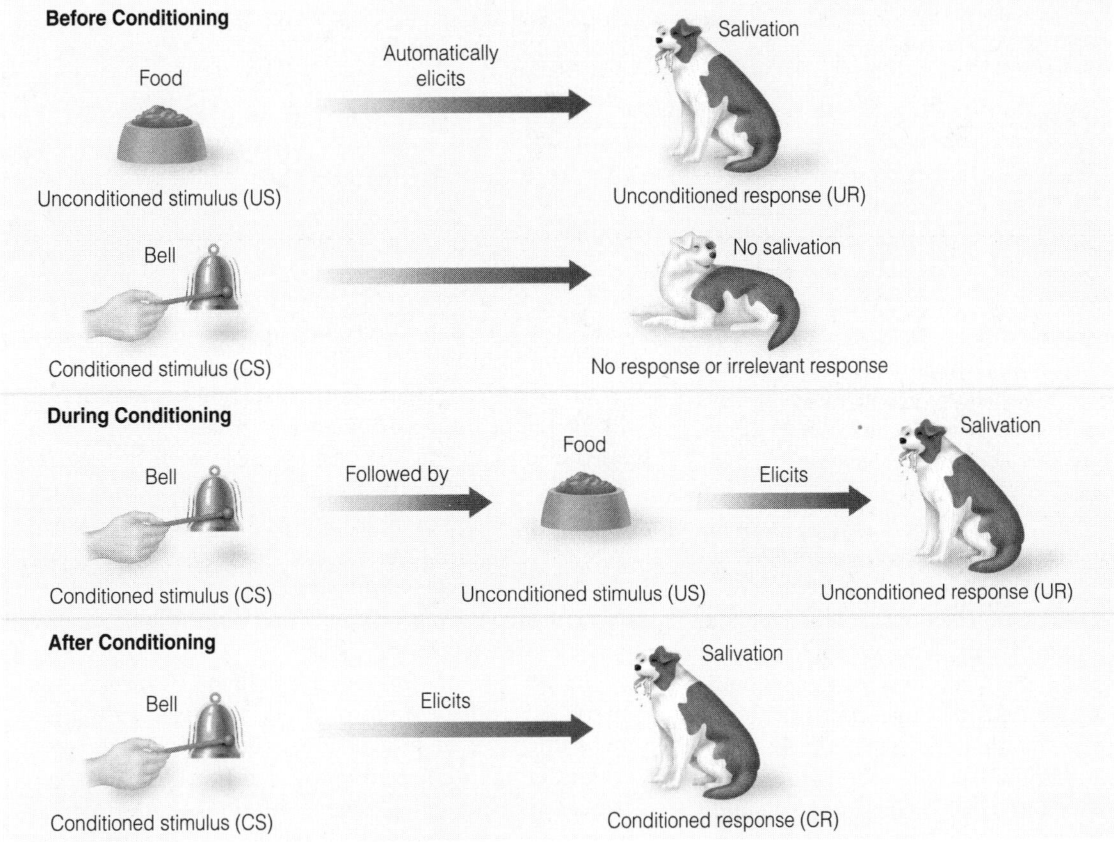

FIGURE 4.2

Classical Conditioning. Through classical conditioning, organisms learn about the signaling properties of events. The presentation of an unconditioned stimulus (US) leads to an automatic unconditioned response (UR) prior to training. A neutral stimulus is paired closely in time with a US. Eventually, the animal learns that this conditioned stimulus (CS) predicts the occurrence of the US and begins to show an appropriate conditioned response (CR) on presentation of the CS.

about the shock—the tone already tells the rat the shock is about to occur—so the animal fails to treat it as a significant signal.

Conditioned Responding: Why Does It Develop?

Forming an association between the conditioned stimulus and the unconditioned stimulus—that is, that one signals the appearance of the other—doesn't really explain conditioned responding. Why should dogs drool to a bell that signals food or rats freeze to a tone that predicts shock? One possibility is that conditioned responses prepare the organism for events that are expected to follow. Drooling readies the dog to receive food in its mouth, and "freezing" lowers the chances that any predators will see the rat. Because the conditioned stimulus tells the animal that a significant event is about to occur, it responds in a way that's appropriate for the upcoming event.

It was once commonly believed that the pairing of the conditioned stimulus and the unconditioned stimulus simply caused the unconditioned response to "shift" to the conditioned stimulus. Pavlov was convinced, for example, that the conditioned stimulus acts as a kind of substitute for the unconditioned stimulus—you respond to the conditioned stimulus as if it was essentially identical to the unconditioned stimulus. However, this suggests that the conditioned response should

PRACTICAL SOLUTIONS

Taste Aversions

On St. Thomas in the Virgin Islands, researchers Lowell Nicolaus and David Nellis encouraged captured mongooses to eat eggs laced with carbachol, a drug that produces temporary illness. After 5 days of eating eggs and getting sick, the mongooses reduced their consumption of eggs by about 37% (Nicolaus & Nellis, 1987). In a very different context, in a research program designed to combat the negative effects of chemotherapy, young cancer patients were allowed a taste of some unusually flavored ice cream just before the onset of their normal chemotherapy—a treatment that typically produces nausea and vomiting. Several weeks later, when offered the ice cream, only 21% of the children were willing to taste it again (Bernstein, 1978).

Both of these situations represent naturalistic applications of classical conditioning. Can you identify the critical features of each? First, let's look for the unconditioned stimulus—the stimulus that unconditionally produces a response prior to training. In both of these cases, the unconditioned stimulus is the illness-producing event, either the drug carbachol or the cancer-fighting chemotherapy. The response that is automatically produced, unfortunately for the participants, is stomach distress. Children don't need to learn to vomit from chemotherapy; a mongoose doesn't need to be taught to be sick after receiving carbachol. These are inevitable consequences that require no prior conditioning.

Now what is the conditioned stimulus—the event that provides information about the occurrence of the unconditioned stimulus? In these examples, it's the taste of the food, either the eggs or the ice cream, that signals the later onset of nausea. It's worth noting that the children were aware that their nausea was produced by the chemotherapy, not the ice cream, yet an association was still formed between the taste of the ice cream and a procedure that led to sickness. A conditioned response, feelings of queasiness to the food, was produced whenever the opportunity to eat was presented. Taste aversions are easy to acquire. They often occur after a single pairing of a novel food and illness.

It is extremely adaptive for people and mongooses to acquire taste aversions to potentially dangerous foods—it is in their interest to avoid those events that signal something potentially harmful. In the two studies we've just considered, the researchers investigated the aversions for a particular reason. Mongooses often eat the eggs of endangered species (such as marine turtles). By baiting the nests of mongoose prey with tainted eggs and establishing a taste aversion, scientists have been able to reduce the overall rate of egg predation. Similar techniques have also been used to prevent sheep from eating dangerous plants in the pasture (Zahorik et al., 1990).

In the case of chemotherapy, Illene Bernstein was interested in developing methods for *avoiding* the establishment of taste aversions: Cancer patients who are undergoing chemotherapy also need to eat, so it's critical to understand the conditions under which aversions are formed. Taste aversions often develop as a side effect of chemotherapy. Patients tend to avoid foods that they've consumed just before treatment,

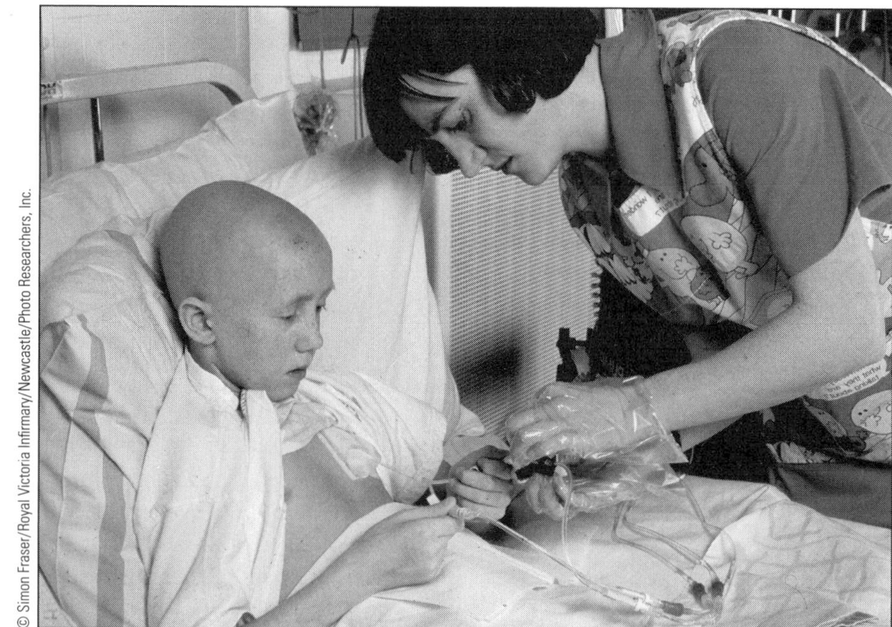

For children undergoing the rigors of chemotherapy, like this boy suffering from leukemia, it's important to prevent taste aversions from developing as a negative side effect. Broberg and Bernstein (1987) found that giving children candy with an unusual flavor just before treatment reduced the chances of a taste aversion forming.

potentially leading to weight loss that impedes recovery. Researchers have found that associations are particularly likely to form between *unusual* tastes and nausea. Broberg and Bernstein (1987) found that giving children an unusual flavor of candy just before treatment reduced the likelihood of their forming aversions to their normal diet. These children formed a taste aversion to the candy instead. Another helpful technique is to ask the patient to eat the same, preferably bland, foods before every treatment. Foods that do not have distinctive tastes and that people eat regularly (such as bread) are less likely to become aversive.

always be identical, or at least highly similar, to the unconditioned response. Dogs should always drool to a stimulus that predicts the arrival of food; rats should *jump* to a stimulus that predicts shock because they usually jump when they're actually shocked. But as you've seen, rats will freeze rather than jump to a signal predicting shock.

The form of the conditioned response depends on many factors. In general, the idea that classical conditioning turns the conditioned stimulus into a substitute for the unconditioned stimulus—or that organisms simply learn to respond to the conditioned stimulus in the same way that they automatically respond to the unconditioned stimulus—is misleading or wrong. Robert Rescorla (1988) put it this way: "Pavlovian conditioning is not the shifting of a response from one stimulus to another. Instead, conditioning involves the learning of relations among events that are complexly represented, a learning that can be exhibited in various ways" (p. 158). This perspective is known as the *cognitive view* of classical conditioning, and it remains widely accepted by current researchers (Holland & Ball, 2003).

Second-Order Conditioning

Pavlov also discovered that conditioned stimuli possess a variety of properties after conditioning. For example, he found that a conditioned stimulus could be used to condition a second signal. In **second-order conditioning**, an established conditioned stimulus, such as a tone that predicts food, is presented immediately after a new event, such as a light; the unconditioned stimulus itself is never actually presented. In such a case, pairing the tone with the light can be sufficient to produce conditioned responding to the light.

second-order conditioning a procedure in which an established conditioned stimulus is used to condition a second neutral stimulus.

An example from Pavlov's laboratory helps to illustrate the procedure. One of Pavlov's associates, Dr. Frolov, first taught a dog that the sound of a ticking metronome signaled meat powder in the mouth. The dog quickly started to drool in the presence of the ticking. A black square was then presented, followed closely by the ticking. After a number of these black square–metronome pairings, even though the ticking was never followed by food powder on these trials, the dog began to drool in the presence of the black square. The dog drooled in response to

CONCEPT SUMMARY

Factors Affecting Classical Conditioning

FACTOR	RELATION TO CONDITIONING EFFECTIVENESS
Timing relationship between CS and US	The CS should usually be presented *before* the US. The US should usually follow the CS *closely in time*.
Informativeness of CS	The CS should *uniquely* predict the US. The CS should provide *new* information about the occurrence of the US (blocking).

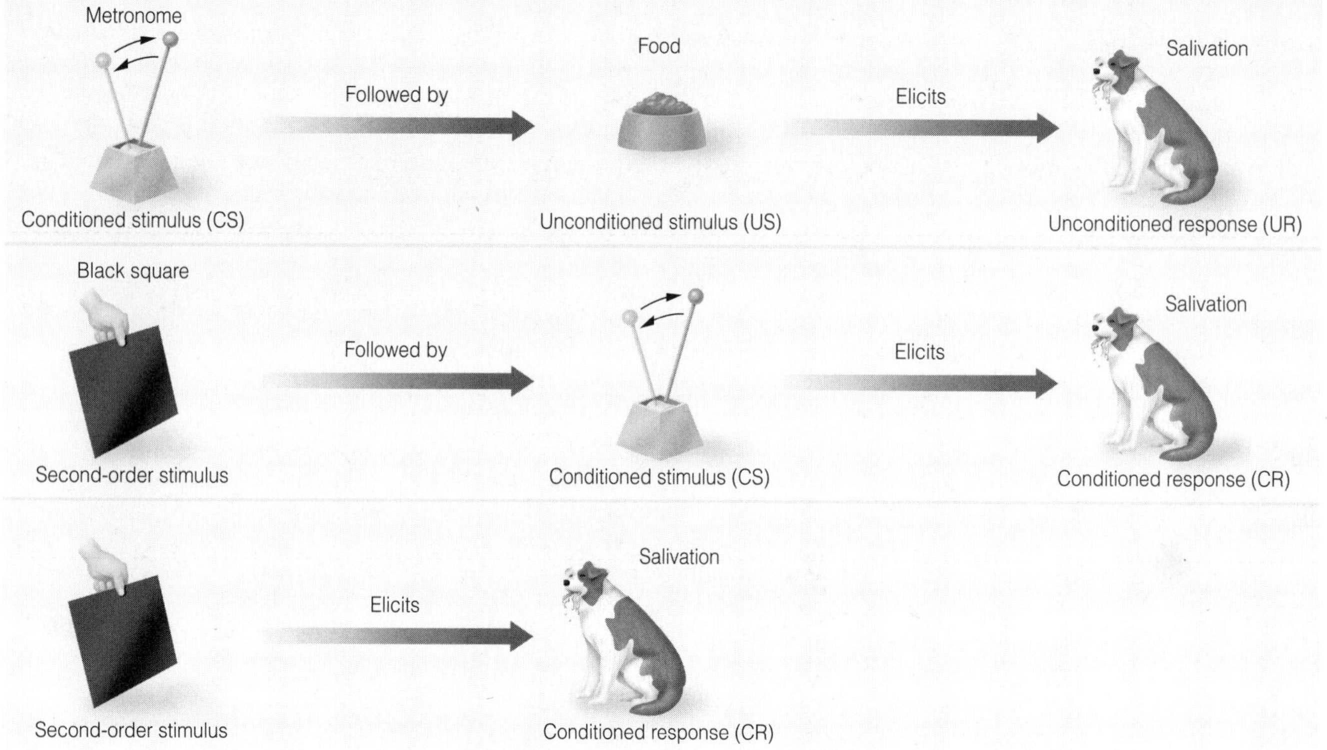

FIGURE 4.3

Second-Order Conditioning. In second-order conditioning, an established CS is used in place of a US to condition a second signal. In Dr. Frolov's experiment, a ticking metronome was first paired with food; after repeated pairings, the ticking elicited salivation as a CR. Next, a black square—which did not produce salivation initially—was paired with the ticking (no US was presented). After repeated pairings, the presentation of the black square began to produce salivation.

the square because it signaled the ticking, which the dog had previously learned signaled the food (see Figure 4.3).

The fact that conditioned stimuli can be used to condition other events greatly expands the number of situations in which classical conditioning applies. You don't need an unconditioned stimulus to be physically present to learn something about its occurrence. For example, consider the logic behind using celebrities to endorse products. Advertisers are trying to get you to form a connection between their product and feelings of pleasure or enjoyment. Most people like Tiger Woods because he's linked to something they enjoy—great skill on the golf course. If a product, such as a new automobile, is repeatedly paired with Tiger, you're likely also to associate it with pleasurable consequences—the product becomes a signal for something that leads to enjoyment. This is a kind of second-order conditioning, and it's been used for decades in the marketplace.

Stimulus Generalization

Pavlov also noticed that conditioned responses tended to generalize to other, related events. If a tone of a particular pitch was established as a signal for food, other similar-sounding tones also produced drooling—even though they had never actually been presented. When a new stimulus produces a response similar to the one produced by the conditioned stimulus, it's called **stimulus generalization**.

stimulus generalization responding to a new stimulus in a way similar to the response produced by an established conditioned stimulus.

Stimulus generalization is aptly demonstrated in a famous study by the behaviorist John Watson and his colleague Rosalie Rayner circa 1920. Watson and Rayner were interested in applying the principles of classical conditioning to a human—in this case to 11-month-old infant little Albert. They presented Albert with a white rat (the conditioned stimulus), which he initially liked, followed quickly by a very loud noise (the unconditioned stimulus), which he did not like. The loud noise, not surprisingly, produced a strong, automatic fear reaction: Albert cried (the unconditioned response). After several pairings of the rat with the noise, Albert began to pucker his face, whimper, and try to withdraw his body (all conditioned responses) immediately at the sight of the rat. (By the way, psychologists now rightly question the ethics of this experiment.) But Albert didn't just cry at the sight of the rat. His crying generalized to other stimuli—a rabbit, a fur coat, a package of cotton, a dog, and even a Santa Claus mask. These stimuli, which all contained white furry elements, had been presented to Albert before the conditioning session, and none had produced crying. Albert cried at the sight of them now because of his experience with the rat; he generalized his crying response from the white rat to the other stimuli.

Training CS
Response level before training
Intensity of Conditioned Response
Color

FIGURE 4.4

Stimulus Generalization. After conditioned responding to a CS is established, similar events will often also produce conditioned responding through stimulus generalization. For example, if a red light is trained as a CS, then similar colors that were not explicitly trained will also produce responding if tested. Notice that the less similar the test stimulus is to the training CS, the less generalization occurs.

As a rule, you'll find stimulus generalization when the newly introduced stimulus is similar to the conditioned stimulus (see Figure 4.4). If you get sick after eating clams, there's a good chance you'll avoid eating oysters; if you've had a bad experience in the dentist's chair, the sound of the neighbor's high-speed drill may make you uncomfortable. Generalization makes adaptive sense: Things that look, sound, or feel the same often share significant properties. It really doesn't matter whether it's a tiger, a lion, or a panther leaping at you—you should run all the same.

Stimulus Discrimination

Albert did notice the difference between white furry or fluffy things and things that were not white and fluffy. For example, he didn't cry when a block of wood was shoved into his crib. This is called **stimulus discrimination**; it occurs when you respond to a new stimulus in a way that's different from your response to the original conditioned stimulus. Through stimulus discrimination, you reveal that you can distinguish among stimuli, even when those stimuli share properties.

stimulus discrimination responding differently to a new stimulus than how one responds to an established conditioned stimulus.

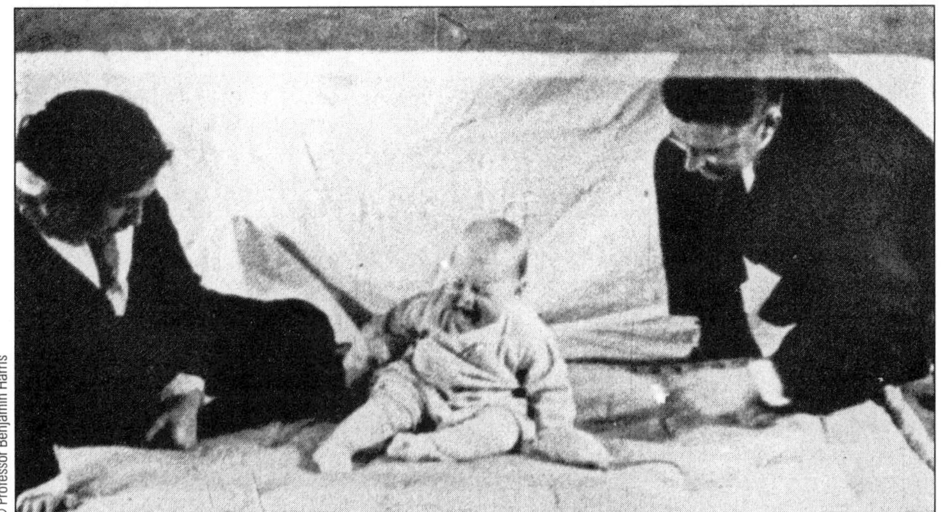

This still from a 1920 film shows little Albert reacting with dismay to a white rat that had previously been paired with a very unpleasant noise. On the right is behavioral psychologist John Watson; to the left of Albert is Watson's colleague, Rosalie Rayner.

Think About It

After reading about little Albert, can you understand why some psychologists believe that certain psychological problems, such as specific fears called phobias, might result from learning experiences?

When stimuli do share properties—for example, two tones of a similar pitch—we often need experience to teach us to discriminate. The natural tendency is to generalize, that is, to treat similar things in the same way. Albert could certainly tell the difference among rats, rabbits, and Santa Claus masks; what he needed to learn was which of those white, furry things signaled the unfortunate noise. In many cases, the development of stimulus discrimination requires that one directly experience whether or not the unconditioned stimulus will follow a particular event. If event A is followed by the unconditioned stimulus but event B is not, then you learn to discriminate between these two events and respond accordingly.

Extinction: When the CS No Longer Signals the US

extinction
presenting a conditioned stimulus repeatedly, after conditioning, without the unconditioned stimulus, resulting in a loss in responding.

spontaneous recovery
the recovery of an extinguished conditioned response after a period of nonexposure to the conditioned stimulus.

Remember our general rule: A conditioned stimulus becomes a good signal when it provides information about the occurrence of the unconditioned stimulus. But what happens if the conditioned stimulus stops signaling the appearance of an unconditioned stimulus? In the procedure of **extinction**, the conditioned stimulus is presented repeatedly, after conditioning, but it is no longer followed by the unconditioned stimulus. Under these conditions, the conditioned stimulus loses its signaling properties, and conditioned responding gradually diminishes as a result. So if a dog drools to a bell that predicts food, and we suddenly stop delivering the food after striking the bell, the dog will eventually stop drooling.

It's sensible for us to change our behavior during extinction because we're learning something new—the conditioned stimulus no longer predicts the unconditioned stimulus. Yet Pavlov discovered an interesting twist: If you wait a while after extinction and present the conditioned stimulus again, sometimes the conditioned response reappears. **Spontaneous recovery** is the recovery of an extinguished response when the conditioned stimulus is presented again, after a delay (see the far right panel in Figure 4.5). In Pavlov's case, his dogs stopped drooling

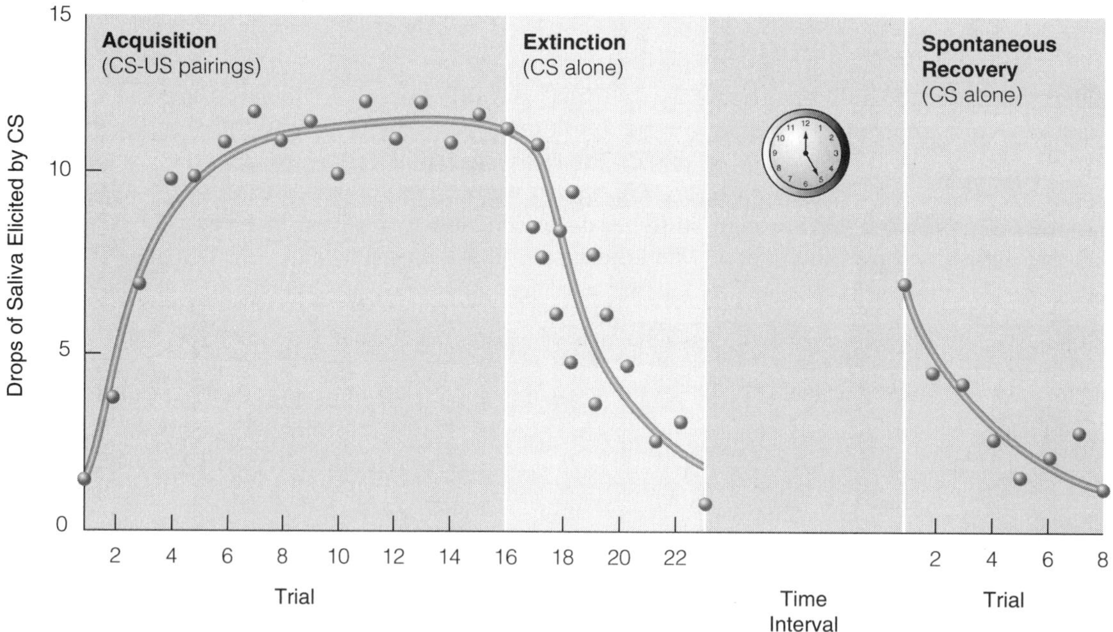

FIGURE 4.5

Training, Extinction, and Spontaneous Recovery. During training, Pavlov found that the amount of salivation produced in response to the CS initially increased and then leveled off as a function of the number of CS–US pairings. During extinction, the CS is repeatedly presented without the US, and conditioned responding gradually diminishes. If no testing of the CS occurs for a rest interval following extinction, spontaneous recovery of the CR will often occur if the CS is presented again.

if a bell signaling food was repeatedly presented alone, but when the bell was rung again the day after extinction, the conditioned response reappeared (although often not as strongly). No one is certain exactly why spontaneous recovery occurs, but it tells us that behavior, or performance, isn't always a perfect indicator of what is known or remembered. At the end of extinction, the conditioned stimulus can seem to have lost its signaling properties, but when it is tested after a delay, we see that at least some of the learning remained (Bouton, 1991; Quirk, 2002).

Conditioned Inhibition: Signaling the Absence of the US

During extinction, you learn that a conditioned stimulus no longer predicts the appearance of the unconditioned stimulus. As a result, you stop responding to a stimulus that once elicited a response because you no longer anticipate that the unconditioned stimulus will follow. You've not forgotten about the unconditioned stimulus. Instead you've learned something new: A conditioned stimulus that used to signal the unconditioned stimulus no longer does (Rescorla, 2001).

In **conditioned inhibition**, you learn that an event signals the *absence* of the unconditioned stimulus. There are a variety of ways to create an inhibitory stimulus but most involve presenting a new stimulus when the unconditioned stimulus is normally expected but is not delivered (Williams et al., 1992). For example, if dogs are currently drooling to a bell that predicts food, then putting the bell together with a light and then following this compound (bell + light) with no food will establish the light as a conditioned inhibitor for food. The animal learns that when the light is turned on, food does not follow the bell.

conditioned inhibition learning that an event signals the absence of the unconditioned stimulus.

What change in behavior is produced by a stimulus that predicts the absence of something? Inhibitory learning can be expressed in various ways, but often you get a reaction that is the *opposite* of that produced by a normal conditioned stimulus. For example, if a conditioned stimulus signaling food produces an increase in responding, then an inhibitory conditioned stimulus will lead to a decrease in the

CONCEPT SUMMARY

Major Phenomena of Classical Conditioning

PHENOMENON	DESCRIPTION	PAVLOV'S DOGS
Second-order conditioning	An established CS is presented immediately after a new event; after several pairings, this new event may come to elicit a response.	After a dog has been conditioned to salivate in response to a CS (tone), the CS is presented immediately after a new signal (e.g., a light). After several pairings, the light may come to elicit a response.
Stimulus generalization	A new stimulus produces a response similar to the one produced by the conditioned stimulus.	After a dog has been conditioned to salivate in response to a CS (e.g., a red light), the same response may be produced by a similar stimulus (e.g., an orange or purple light).
Stimulus discrimination	The response to a new stimulus is different from the response to the original CS.	After a dog has been conditioned to salivate in response to a CS (light), the response does not occur to a different stimulus, such as a ringing bell.
Acquisition	Conditioned responding becomes stronger with repeated CS–US pairings.	The more times a dog hears the stimulus (tone) paired with the US (food), the stronger the conditioned response becomes.
Extinction	Conditioned responding diminishes when the CS (after conditioning) is presented repeatedly without the US.	After a dog has been conditioned to salivate in response to a CS (tone), the tone is presented repeatedly without the US (food). The dog's response to the CS lessens.
Spontaneous recovery	Conditioned responding that has disappeared in extinction is recovered spontaneously with the passage of time.	After extinction, a dog no longer responds to the CS (tone). After a rest period, the dog will again respond when presented with the CS (tone).

FIGURE 4.6

Conditioned Inhibition. In conditioned inhibition the CS provides information about the absence of the US. Pigeons will approach and peck at a keylight CS that signals the appearance of food (upper panel), but they will withdraw from a keylight CS signaling no food (lower panel). Notice that the withdrawal response is an indication that the red light has become a conditioned inhibitor—a CS that predicts the absence of food.

normal amount of responding. Several experiments have shown that pigeons and dogs will approach a signal predicting food but will withdraw from a stimulus signaling its absence (see Figure 4.6; Hearst & Franklin, 1977; Jenkins et al., 1978).

The conditions required for establishing the presence of conditioned inhibition are complex and need not concern us here, but it's important to appreciate the value of an inhibitory signal. It's just as adaptive to know that a significant event will not occur as it is to know that the event will occur. For example, every kid knows there are bullies on the playground. The sight of troublemaker Randy might usually make Kelley quake with fear—but not if there's a teacher around. The teacher signals the absence of a negative event—Randy won't be causing any trouble while the teacher is present. Inhibitory stimuli often act as "safety signals," telling people when potentially dangerous events are likely to be absent or when dangerous conditions no longer apply.

LEARNING ABOUT THE CONSEQUENCES OF BEHAVIOR: OPERANT CONDITIONING

Classical conditioning answers an important survival question: How do we learn that certain events signal the presence or the absence of other events? Through classical conditioning, we learn to expect that certain events will or will not occur, at certain times, and we react accordingly. But our actions under these conditions typically don't have any effect on the presentation of the signal and the unconditioned stimulus. Usually, occurrences of the conditioned stimulus and the unconditioned stimulus are outside of our control. For example, you can't change the fact that thunder will follow lightning; all you can do is prepare for an event (thunder) when a prior event (lightning) tells you it's coming.

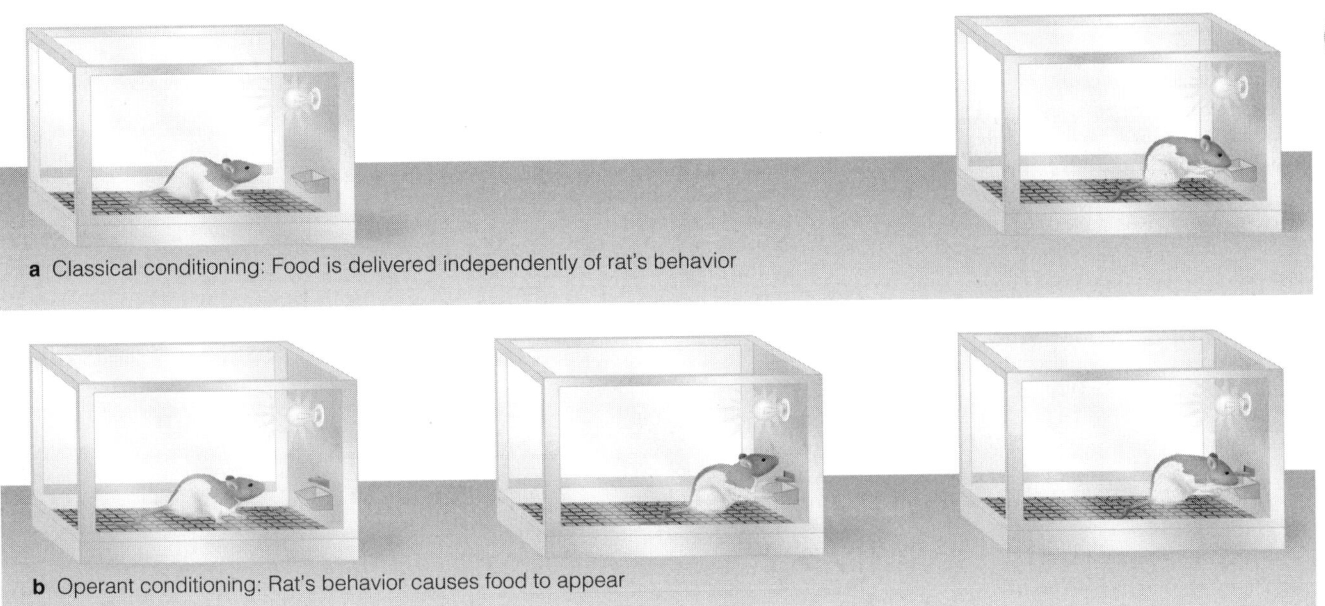

FIGURE 4.7

Classical Versus Operant Conditioning. In classical conditioning (top row), food is delivered independently of the rat's behavior. The light CS signals the automatic arrival of the food US. In operant conditioning (bottom row), the rat must press the bar in the presence of the light to get the food. The light serves as a discriminative stimulus, indicating that pressing the bar will now produce the food.

In another type of learning, studied through a procedure called **operant conditioning** (or *instrumental conditioning*), we learn that our own *actions,* rather than conditioned stimuli, lead to outcomes. If you study for hours and hours for an exam and receive an A, you learn that your behavior is *instrumental* in producing a top-notch grade; by *operating* on your environment, you have produced a pleasing consequence. Notice how classical conditioning differs from operant conditioning: In the former you learn that events signal outcomes; in the latter you learn that your own actions produce outcomes (see Figure 4.7).

operant conditioning
a procedure for studying how organisms learn about the consequences of their own voluntary actions (also called *instrumental conditioning*).

The Law of Effect

The study of operant conditioning predates Pavlov's historic work by several years. In 1895 Harvard graduate student Edward Lee Thorndike (1874–1949), working in the cellar of his mentor William James, began a series of experiments on "animal intelligence" using cats from around the neighborhood. He built a puzzle box, which resembled a kind of tiny prison, and carefully recorded the time it took for the cats to escape. The boxes were designed so that escape was possible only through an unusual response, such as tilting a pole, pulling a string, or pressing a lever (see Figure 4.8 on the next page). On release, the cats received a small amount of food as a reward.

Thorndike specifically selected escape responses that were unlikely to occur when the animals were first placed in the box. In this way he could observe how the cats learned to escape over time. Through trial and error, the cats eventually learned to make the appropriate response, but the learning process was gradual. Thorndike also found that the time it took for an animal to escape on any particular trial depended on the number of prior successful escapes. The more times the animal had successfully escaped in the past, the faster it could get out of the box on a new trial.

The relationship between escape time and the number of prior successful escapes led Thorndike to formulate the **law of effect**: If a response in a particular situation is followed by a satisfying or pleasant consequence, then the connection

law of effect
if a response in a particular situation is followed by a satisfying consequence, it will be strengthened. If a response in a particular situation is followed by an unsatisfying consequence, it will be weakened.

FIGURE 4.8

Operant Conditioning. In Thorndike's famous experiments on animal intelligence, cats learned that some kinds of unusual responses—such as pressing a lever or tilting a pole—allowed them to escape from a puzzle box. The graph shows that the time required to escape gradually diminished over learning trials. Here the cat is learning that its behavior is instrumental in producing escape. (Based on Weiten, 1995)

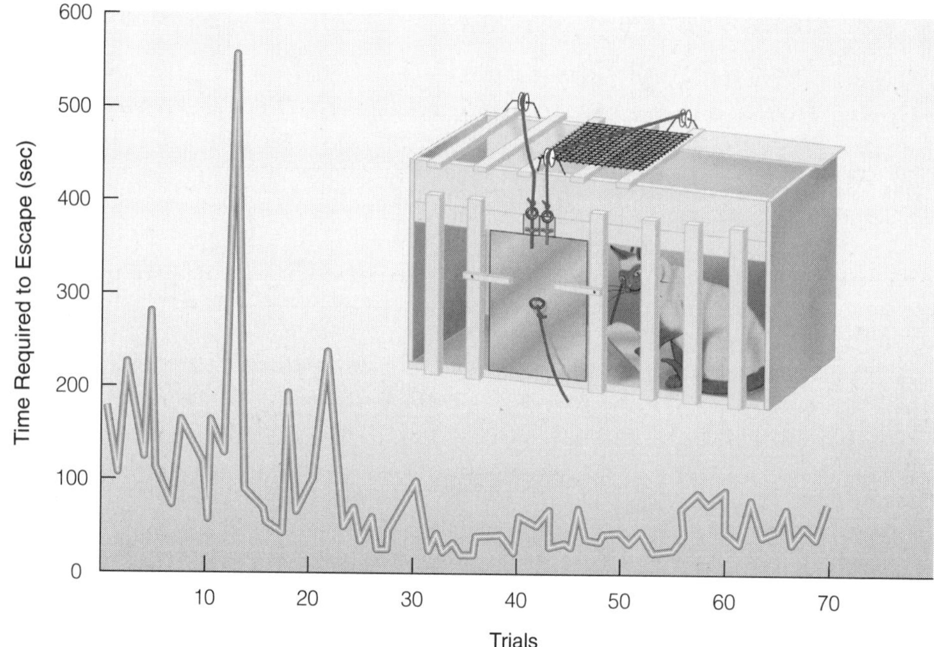

between the response and that situation will be strengthened; if a response in a particular situation is followed by an unsatisfying or unpleasant consequence, the connection will be weakened. According to the law of effect, all organisms learn to make certain responses in certain situations; the responses that regularly occur are those that have produced positive consequences in the past. If a response tends to occur initially (e.g., scratching at the walls of the cage) but is not followed by something good (such as freedom from the box), the chances of that same response reoccurring diminish.

The Discriminative Stimulus: Knowing When to Respond

It's important to understand that the law of effect applies only to responses that are rewarded in particular situations. If you are praised for raising your hand in class and asking an intelligent question, you're not likely to begin walking down the street repeatedly raising your hand. You understand that raising your hand is rewarded only in a particular situation, namely, the classroom lecture. What you really learn is the following: If some stimulus situation is present (the classroom), and you act in a certain way (raising your hand), then some consequence will follow (praise).

B. F. Skinner (1938) referred to the stimulus situation as the **discriminative stimulus**. He suggested that a discriminative stimulus "sets the occasion" for a response to be rewarded. Being in class—the discriminative stimulus—sets the occasion for question-asking to be rewarded. In some ways, the discriminative stimulus shares properties with the conditioned stimulus established in classical conditioning. For example, you often find *stimulus generalization* of a discriminative stimulus: If a pigeon is trained to peck a key in the presence of a red light, the bird will later peck the key whenever a light of a similar color is turned on. If you're rewarded for asking questions in psychology, you might naturally generalize your response to another course, such as economics, and raise your hand there. Conversely, *stimulus discrimination* also occurs, usually after experiencing reward in one situation but not in another. You may learn, for instance, that raising your hand in psychology class leads to positive consequences but that a similar behavior in your economics class is frowned on by the professor. In such a case, one setting (psychology) acts as an effective discriminative stimulus for a certain response, but another setting (economics) does not.

discriminative stimulus
the stimulus situation that sets the occasion for a response to be followed by reinforcement or punishment.

The Nature of Reinforcement

The law of effect states that responses will be strengthened if they are followed by a pleasant or satisfying consequence. By "strengthened," Thorndike meant that a response was more likely to occur in the future in that particular situation. But what defines a pleasant or satisfying consequence? This is a tricky problem because the concept of a "pleasant" or "satisfying" event is highly personal—what's pleasant for me might not be pleasant for you. Moreover, something that's pleasing at one time might not be pleasing at another. Food, for example, is "positive at the beginning of Thanksgiving dinner, indifferent halfway through, and negative at the end of it" (Kimble, 1993).

For these reasons, psychologists use a technical term—**reinforcement**—to describe consequences that *increase* the likelihood of responding. As you'll see, it's popular to distinguish between two major types of reinforcement: *positive* and *negative*.

reinforcement
response consequences that increase the likelihood of responding in a similar way again.

Positive Reinforcement When the *presentation* of an event after a response increases the likelihood of that response occurring again, it's called **positive reinforcement**. Usually, the presented event is an *appetitive stimulus*—something the organism likes, needs, or has an "appetite" for. According to Thorndike (1911), an appetitive stimulus is "one which the animal does nothing to avoid, often doing such things as to attain or preserve it" (p. 245). Food and water are obvious examples, but responses can be reinforcing too (such as sexual activity or painting a picture). Remember, though, it's not the subjective qualities of the consequence that matter—what matters in defining positive reinforcement is an increase in a tendency to respond. As long as the consequence makes the response more likely to occur again in that situation, the consequence qualifies as positive reinforcement.

positive reinforcement
an event that, when *presented* after a response, increases the likelihood of that response.

Many psychologists believe that events are reinforcing whenever they allow us to engage in desirable behaviors. We all have a certain desire to eat, drink, listen to music, play volleyball, study for school, and so on. These tendencies, or needs, vary over time depending on our experiences. If you've been deprived of eating for a while, you'll find the presentation of food to be positively reinforcing because it allows you to eat. Once you've eaten, food loses its reinforcing value because you've satisfied your need. According to the *response deprivation theory* of reinforcement, an event is reinforcing as long as it allows you to engage in a behavior that has been effectively deprived (Allison, 1989; Timberlake, 1980).

This theory sounds like common sense, but it makes an important and unintuitive prediction. It suggests that any event or response, in principle, can serve as positive reinforcement (see also Premack, 1962). If you've been deprived of responding to an event for long enough, the presentation of that event should be reinforcing. Most children, for example, would rather color than do math problems (presumably because our natural desire to color is high). However, if children are deprived of doing math problems for long enough, the opportunity to do math can actually serve as positive reinforcement (see Konarski, 1985; Timberlake, 1980).

Think About It

Can you think of a case in which presenting an unpleasant event actually increases the likelihood of the response that produces it?

Negative Reinforcement When the *removal* of an event after a response increases the likelihood of the response occurring again, it's called **negative reinforcement**. In most cases negative reinforcement occurs when a response allows you to eliminate, avoid, or escape from an unpleasant situation. For instance, you hang up the phone on someone who is criticizing you unfairly, shut off the blaring alarm clock in the morning, or walk out of a boring movie. These responses are more likely to occur again in the future, given the appropriate circumstance, because they lead to the removal of something negative—criticism, noise, or boredom. But, as you may have guessed, the event that's removed doesn't have to be unpleasant—it simply has to increase the likelihood of the "contingent" response (the response that led to the removal).

negative reinforcement
an event that, when *removed* after a response, increases the likelihood of that response occurring again.

FIGURE 4.9

Escape Versus Avoidance Conditioning. In escape conditioning (top row), a response is negatively reinforced because it ends an aversive event. The rat learns that jumping over a short barrier will terminate a mild electric shock. In avoidance conditioning (bottom row), the rat learns to make a response that prevents the aversive stimulus from occurring; here the rat learns to avoid the shock by jumping when the light comes on. Often the animal will learn first to escape from, and then to avoid, an aversive event.

escape conditioning
a situation in which a response can reduce or eliminate an unpleasant stimulus, such as when a rat escapes an ongoing shock by jumping over a barrier.

avoidance conditioning
a situation in which a response can prevent the delivery of an aversive stimulus, such as when a rat learns to jump over a barrier to avoid a shock.

Think About It

When you study for an examination, or try to do well in school, are you seeking positive reinforcement or negative reinforcement?

Researchers have historically used two kinds of learning procedures to study negative reinforcement: escape conditioning and avoidance conditioning. In **escape conditioning**, one learns that a response will end some kind of unpleasant stimulus. For example, a rat might learn that jumping over a short barrier separating one part of the cage from another will terminate a mild electric shock. The jumping response is reinforced because it allows the animal to escape from a negative situation (see the top row in Figure 4.9). In **avoidance conditioning**, the response *prevents* the negative situation from occurring. For example, if the mild electric shock is signaled by the appearance of a light, the rat might learn to jump over the barrier as soon as the light appears, thus avoiding exposure to the shock. Once again, the avoidance response is reinforced by the elimination of something negative (see the bottom row in Figure 4.9).

Students are often confused by the term "negative reinforcement" because they think negative reinforcement is a bad thing. Actually, whenever psychologists use the term "reinforcement," both positive and negative, they're referring to outcomes that increase the probability of responding. Here *positive* and *negative* simply refer to whether the response ends with the presentation of something or the removal of something. In both cases the result is rewarding, and we can expect the response that produced the reinforcement to occur again in that situation.

Conditioned Reinforcers Sometimes a stimulus can act like a reinforcer even though it seems to have little or no direct value. For example, money serves as a satisfying consequence even though it's only a well-made piece of paper marked with interesting engravings. However, having money predicts something of value—you

CONCEPT SUMMARY

Positive and Negative Reinforcement

CONSEQUENCE	DESCRIPTION	EXAMPLE
Positive reinforcement	The *presentation* of an event after a response increases the likelihood of the response occurring again.	Juan's parents reward him for cleaning his room by giving him $5. This reinforcement increases the likelihood that Juan will clean his room again.
Negative reinforcement	The *removal* of an event after a response increases the likelihood of the response occurring again.	Hannah's parents nag her continually about cleaning up her room. When she finally cleans her room, her parents stop nagging her. The removal of the nagging increases the probability that Hannah will clean her room again.

can buy things—and this is what gives it its reinforcing value. In the same way, if a stimulus or event predicts the absence or removal of something negative, then its presentation is also likely to be reinforcing. Stimuli of this type are called **conditioned reinforcers** because their reinforcing properties are acquired through learning (they are also sometimes called "secondary" reinforcers to distinguish them from more "primary" reinforcers such as food or water). These stimuli are reinforcing because they signal the presence or absence of other events.

conditioned reinforcer
a stimulus that has acquired reinforcing properties through prior learning.

Punishment: Lowering the Likelihood of a Response

Now for the dark side: *punishment.* Remember Thorndike claimed that if a response is followed by an unsatisfying or unpleasant consequence, it will be weakened. The term **punishment** is used to refer to consequences that decrease the likelihood of responding. Like reinforcement, punishment comes in two forms: *positive* and *negative.*

punishment
consequences that decrease the likelihood of responding in a similar way again.

Positive Punishment When the *presentation* of an event after a response decreases the likelihood of that response occurring again, it's called **positive punishment**. Notice, as with reinforcement, the concept is defined in terms of its effect on behavior—lowering the likelihood of responding—rather than on its subjective qualities. Often, however, positive punishment occurs when a response leads directly to the presentation of an aversive outcome. As a parent, if your child hassles the cat with her new toy, you could scold the child loudly whenever she engages in the behavior—this qualifies as positive punishment. Provided the aversive event (the scolding) is intense enough, the response that produced the punishment (hassling the cat) will tend to disappear rapidly or become *suppressed.*

positive punishment
an event that, when *presented* after a response, lowers the likelihood of that response occurring again.

Negative Punishment When the *removal* of an event after responding lowers the likelihood of that response occurring again, it's called **negative punishment**. Instead of scolding your child for hassling the cat, you could simply take her toy away. You're removing something she likes when she engages in an inappropriate behavior—this qualifies as negative punishment. Similarly, if you withhold your child's weekly allowance because his or her room is messy, you are punishing the child by removing something good—money. As with positive punishment, negative punishment is recognized as an effective training procedure for rapidly suppressing an undesirable response.

negative punishment
an event that, when *removed* after a response, lowers the likelihood of that response occurring again.

What accounts for the rapid suppression of the response that's punished? It seems likely that people simply learn the connection between their behavior and the particular outcome. You learn about the consequences of your actions—that a particular kind of behavior will lead to a relatively unpleasant consequence. In this sense, we don't really need two different explanations to account for the behavior changes produced by reinforcement and punishment; the only major difference is that behavior increases in one situation and declines in the other. In both cases you use your knowledge about behavior and its consequences to maximize gain and minimize loss in a particular situation.

Practical Considerations Punishment works—it's an effective technique for suppressing undesirable behavior. However, punishment isn't always the smartest way to change behavior. Sometimes it can be hard to gauge the appropriate strength of the punishing event. When the punishment is aggressive or violent, such as the forceful spanking of a child, you run the risk of hurting the child either physically or emotionally. At the same time, if a child feels ignored, yelling can actually be reinforcing because of the attention it provides. Children who spend a lot of time in the principal's office may be causing trouble partly because of the attention that the punishment produces. In such cases punishment leads to the exact opposite of the intended result (Martin & Pear, 1999; Wissow, 2002).

Moreover, punishment only suppresses a behavior; it doesn't teach the child how to act appropriately. Spanking your child for lying might reduce the lying, but it won't teach the child how to deal more effectively with the social situation that led to the lie. To teach the child about more appropriate forms of behavior, you need to reinforce some kind of alternative response. You must teach the child a positive strategy for dealing with situations that can lead to lying. That's the main advantage of reinforcement over punishment: Reinforcement teaches you what you

CONCEPT SUMMARY

Comparing Reinforcement and Punishment

Reinforcement: Consequences that *Increase* the Likelihood of Responding

OUTCOME	DESCRIPTION	EXAMPLE
Positive reinforcement	Response leads to the presentation of an event that increases the likelihood of that response occurring again.	Five-year-old Skip helps his mom do the dishes. She takes him to the store and lets him pick out any candy bar he wants. Letting Skip pick out a candy bar increases the likelihood that he'll help with the dishes again.
Negative reinforcement	Response leads to the removal of an event that increases the likelihood of that response occurring again.	Five-year-old Skip has been such a good helper all week that his mom tells him that next week he doesn't have to do any of his scheduled chores. Relieving Skip of his chores increases the likelihood that he'll be a good helper.

Punishment: Consequences that *Decrease* the Likelihood of Responding

OUTCOME	DESCRIPTION	EXAMPLE
Positive punishment	Response leads to the presentation of an event that decreases the likelihood of that response occurring again.	Five-year-old Skip runs nearly into the street; his mother pulls him back from the curb and gives him a brief tongue-lashing. This decreases the likelihood that Skip will run into the street.
Negative punishment	Response leads to the removal of an event that decreases the likelihood of that response occurring again.	Five-year-old Skip keeps teasing his 3-year-old sister at the dinner table. His mom sends him to bed without his favorite dessert. Withholding the dessert decreases the likelihood that Skip will tease his sister at the dinner table.

should be doing—how you should act—whereas punishment only teaches you what you shouldn't be doing.

There can also be side effects with punishment, most notably anger, resentment, and aggression. Studies with animals in the laboratory have shown that aggressive behavior is often a consequence of punishment procedures. Animals that are shocked together in the same experimental context will often attack one another throughout the shock duration (Domjan, 2003). Parents who punish their children regularly, without alternative reinforcement, invite future resentment and hurt the quality of the relationship with their child. Psychologists recognize that punishment can be an effective means for stopping a behavior, and it may even be desirable in some circumstances (e.g., when the child runs into the street or sticks a fork into an electrical outlet), but punishment alone is rarely a sufficient technique—it must be supplemented with alternative strategies for behaving that provide the opportunity for a little tender loving care (positive reinforcement).

Schedules of Reinforcement

Actions are more likely to be repeated if they're followed by positive or negative reinforcement. However, just like in classical conditioning, the development of a response in operant conditioning depends importantly on how often, and when, the reinforcements are actually delivered. People must understand that their behavior uniquely predicts the reward—if you deliver the reward in a haphazard way, or when the behavior in question has not occurred, learning can be slow or nonexistent (Miller & Grace, 2003).

A **schedule of reinforcement** is a rule used by the experimenter to determine when particular responses will be reinforced (Ferster & Skinner, 1957). If a response is followed rapidly by reinforcement every time it occurs, the reinforcement schedule is called *continuous*. If reinforcement is delivered only some of the time after the response has occurred, it's called a **partial reinforcement schedule**. There are four major types of partial reinforcement schedules: fixed-ratio, variable-ratio, fixed-interval, and variable-interval. Each produces a distinctive pattern of responding (see Figure 4.10 on the next page).

schedule of reinforcement
a rule that an experimenter uses to determine when particular responses will be reinforced.

partial reinforcement schedule
a schedule in which reinforcement is delivered only some of the time after the response has occurred.

Fixed-Ratio Schedules Ratio schedules of reinforcement require a certain *number* of responses before reinforcement is delivered. In a **fixed-ratio (FR) schedule**, the number of required responses is fixed and doesn't change from one trial to the next. Suppose you're paid a dollar for every 100 envelopes you stuff for a local marketing firm. This schedule of reinforcement is called an "FR 100" (fixed-ratio 100) because it requires 100 responses (envelopes stuffed) before the reinforcement is delivered (a dollar). You can stuff the envelopes as quickly as you like, but you must produce 100 responses before you get the reward.

Fixed-ratio schedules typically produce steady, consistent rates of responding because the relationship between the response and the reinforcement is clear and predictable. For this reason, assembly-line work in factories is often reinforced on a fixed-ratio schedule. The only behavioral quirk occurs when the number of required responses is relatively large. For example, if you have to pick 10 bushels of grapes for each monetary reward, you're likely to pause a bit in your responding immediately after the 10th bushel. This delay in responding after reinforcement is called the *postreinforcement pause*. Pausing after reinforcement is easy to understand in this situation—after all, you have to do a lot of work before you receive the next reward.

fixed-ratio (FR) schedule
a schedule in which the number of responses required for reinforcement is fixed and does not change.

Variable-Ratio Schedules A **variable-ratio (VR) schedule** also requires that you make a certain number of responses before reinforcement. (This is the defining feature of a ratio schedule.) However, with a variable-ratio schedule, the required number can change from trial to trial. Reinforcement might be delivered after the first response on trial 1, after the seventh response on trial 2, after the third response

variable-ratio (VR) schedule
a schedule in which a certain number of responses are required for reinforcement, but the number of required responses typically changes.

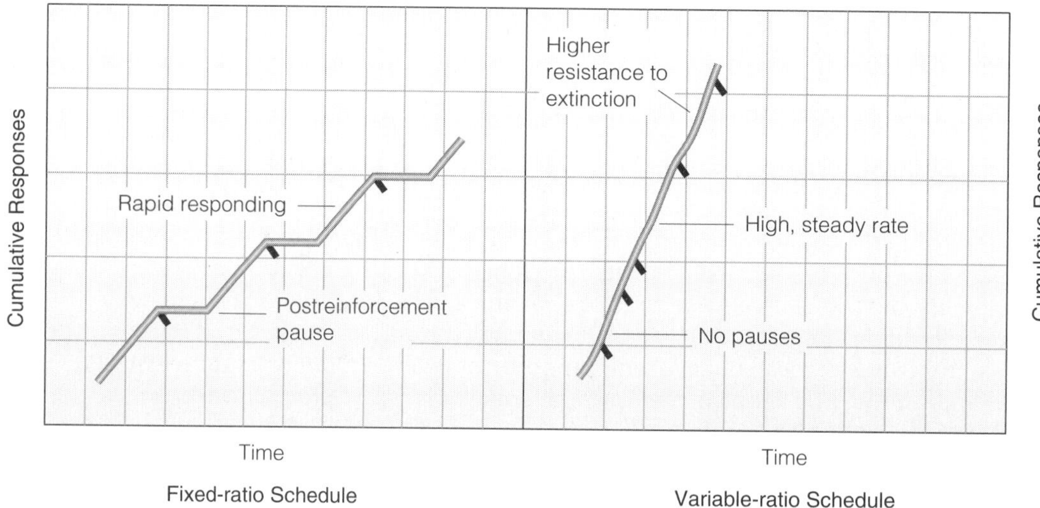

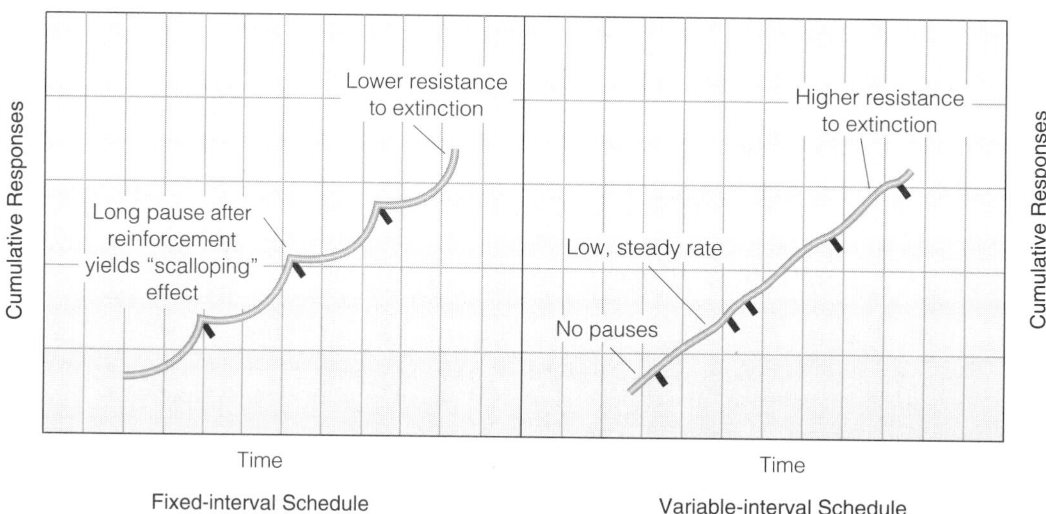

FIGURE 4.10

Schedules of Reinforcement. Schedules of reinforcement are rules that the experimenter uses to determine when responses will be reinforced. Ratio schedules tend to produce rapid rates of responding because reinforcement depends on the number of responses. Interval schedules tend to produce lower rates of responding because reinforcement is delivered only for the first response after a specified time interval. In the cumulative response functions plotted here, the total number of responses is plotted over time.

on trial 3, and so on. It's called a variable-ratio schedule because the responder doesn't know how many responses are needed to obtain the reward (that is, the number of responses varies, often in a random fashion).

In a variable-ratio schedule, unlike a fixed-ratio schedule, you can never predict which response will get you the reward. As a result, these schedules typically produce high rates of responding, and the postreinforcement pause, seen in fixed-ratio schedules, is usually absent (after all, the next response might get you the reward again). Gambling is an example of a variable-ratio schedule; because of chance factors, a gambler wins some bets and loses others, but the gambler never knows what to expect on a given bet.

The unpredictability of reward during a variable-ratio schedule makes it difficult to eliminate a response trained on this schedule when the response is no longer reinforced. Consider the typical compulsive slot machine player: Dollar after dollar goes into the machine; sometimes there's a payoff, more often not. Even if the machine breaks and further payments are never delivered (thus placing the responder on *extinction*), many gamblers would continue playing long into the night. On a variable-ratio schedule, it's hard to see that reinforcements are no longer being delivered because you can never predict when reinforcement will occur.

Fixed-Interval Schedules In interval schedules of reinforcement, the reward is delivered for the first response that occurs following a certain interval of time; in a **fixed-interval (FI) schedule,** this time period remains constant from one trial to the next. Suppose we reward a pigeon with food when it pecks a lighted response key after 2 minutes have elapsed. In this case we would be using an "FI 2 min" schedule. Note that the pigeon must still produce the response to receive the reward. (Otherwise the learning procedure would not be operant conditioning.) Pecking just doesn't do any good until at least 2 minutes have elapsed.

fixed-interval (FI) schedule a schedule in which the reinforcement is delivered for the first response that occurs following a fixed interval of time.

Fixed-interval schedules typically produce low rates of responding. There is no direct association between how much you respond and the delivery of reinforcement—you're rewarded only when you respond after the interval has passed—so it doesn't make sense to respond all the time. Another characteristic of fixed-interval schedules is that responding slows down after reinforcement and gradually increases as the end of the interval approaches. If the total number of responses is plotted over time in a cumulative response record, the net effect is a *scalloping* pattern of the type shown in Figure 4.10. Again, this makes adaptive sense—there's no point in responding immediately after reinforcement; you should only start responding when you think the interval has passed.

Variable-Interval Schedules In a **variable-interval (VI) schedule,** the critical time interval changes from trial to trial. For example, reinforcement might be

variable-interval (VI) schedule a schedule in which the allotted time before a response will yield reinforcement varies from trial to trial.

CONCEPT SUMMARY

Schedules of Reinforcement

TYPE OF SCHEDULE	DESCRIPTION	EXAMPLE	EFFECT ON BEHAVIOR
Continuous	Every response is followed rapidly by reinforcement.	Every time Duane cleans his room, his parents give him $1.	Leads to fast acquisition of response, but response is easily extinguished.
Partial	Response is followed by reinforcement only some of the time.	Sometimes Duane gets $1 after he cleans his room.	Acquisition is slower, but learned response is more resistant to extinction.
• fixed-ratio	The number of responses required for reinforcement is fixed.	Duane gets $1 every third time he cleans his room.	Duane cleans his room consistently with a pause in cleaning after each $1; he stops quickly if reward stops.
• variable-ratio	The number of responses required for reinforcement varies.	Duane gets $1 after cleaning his room a certain number of times, but the exact number varies.	Duane cleans his room consistently with few pauses; he continues to clean his room even if the reward isn't delivered for a while.
• fixed-interval	Reinforcement is delivered for the first response after a fixed interval of time.	Every Tuesday, Duane's parents give him $1 if his room is clean.	Duane doesn't do much cleaning until Tuesday is approaching; he stops quickly if reward stops.
• variable-interval	Reinforcement is delivered for the first response after a variable interval of time.	On some random weekday, Duane gets $1 if his room is clean.	Duane cleans his room consistently and doesn't stop even if the reward isn't delivered for a while.

delivered for a response occurring after 2 minutes on trial 1, after 10 minutes on trial 2, after 30 seconds on trial 3, and so on. Variable-interval schedules are common in everyday life. Suppose you're trying to reach someone on the telephone, but every time you dial you hear a busy signal. To be rewarded, you know you have to dial the number and that a certain amount of time has to elapse, but you're not sure exactly how long you need to wait.

Like variable-ratio schedules, variable-interval schedules help eliminate the pause in responding that usually occurs after reinforcement. The rate of extinction also tends to be slower because it's never clear when (or if) the next reinforcement will be delivered. For responding to cease, you need to recognize that the relationship between responding and reinforcement has changed—that's tough to do when the reinforcements aren't predictable.

Shaping: Acquiring Complex Behaviors

Reinforcement schedules are fine and good, but how do you train a response that never occurs in the first place? For example, suppose you wanted to teach your dog to sit or shake hands—how do you reward your dog for sitting if the dog never sits on command? Most people simply yell "Sit," push the dog's bottom down, and then stuff a food reward in its mouth. Under these conditions, though, you're not really establishing the proper relationship between the dog's own behavior and the delivery of a reward. You've actually set up a kind of classical conditioning procedure—the dog is taught that having his bottom pushed downward is a *signal* for an inviting unconditioned stimulus (food). This might work, but it doesn't teach the animal that its own behavior is instrumental in producing the outcome.

shaping
a procedure in which reinforcement is delivered for successive approximations of the desired response.

To solve this problem, Skinner (1938) developed a procedure called **shaping**, in which reinforcement is delivered for successive *approximations* to the desired response. Instead of waiting for the complete response—here, sitting to the command "Sit"—you reinforce some part of the response that is likely to occur initially. For instance, you might reward your dog for simply approaching when you say, "Sit." As each part of the response is acquired, you become more strict in your criterion for what constitutes a successful response sequence. Skinner and others have shown that incredibly complex sequences of behavior can be acquired using the successive approximation technique of shaping.

It is possible to produce unusual behaviors in animals through shaping—reinforcements are delivered for successive approximations of a desired behavior. These rabbits are in the early stages of training for an advertisement that featured them popping out of top hats (circa 1952).

Shaping also works quite well for modifying behavior in people. Disturbed children who can't communicate have been taught to speak by reinforcing verbal sequences with candy or cereal. Whereas the child might be reinforced initially for any kind of verbal utterance, gradually the reward is withheld until the child produces a more natural flow of sounds. The same kind of training can be used with adult patients who are suffering from severe psychological disorders. Patients with serious mental problems sometimes lack normal living skills—for example, they might lose the ability to clean or bathe themselves properly or to communicate effectively with others. Social skills can be trained, through shaping, leading to a significant improvement in the quality of the patient's life (e.g., Pratt & Mueser, 2002).

Shaping also has enormous applications for teaching, both inside and outside of the classroom. B. F. Skinner and others long advocated for the use of shaping as a technique for learning. Mastery of subject matter can be broken down into small steps accompanied by lots of positive reinforcement. Many computer programs used in schools and at home follow the shaping format—start small and gradually increase the requirements for a reward. Shaping is also a great technique for sports activities.

PRACTICAL SOLUTIONS

Superstitious Behavior

Have you ever noticed the odd behavior of a professional baseball player as he approaches the batter's box? He kicks the dirt (a fixed number of times), adjusts his helmet, hitches up his trousers, grimaces, swings toward the pitcher a few times, and adopts a characteristic crouch. Basketball players, as they prepare to make a free throw, endlessly caress the ball with their hands, bounce it a certain number of times, crouch, pause, and release. Such regular patterns are a player's signature—you can identify who's in the batter's box or up at the line by watching these ritualistic preparation patterns.

Let's analyze these behaviors from the perspective of operant conditioning. According to the law of effect, these odd patterns of behavior must have been reinforced—they occurred, perhaps by chance, and were followed by a reward (a hit or a successful free throw). But because the pairing of the behavior with its consequence was really accidental, psychologists refer to this kind of reinforcement as *accidental* or *adventitious reinforcement.* In the player's mind, however, a cause-and-effect link has been formed, and he acts in a similar fashion again. Once the player starts to perform the behavior on a regular basis, it's likely that the behavior will continue to be accidentally reinforced, although on a partial schedule of reinforcement. (Can you identify the particular schedule?) The result is called a superstitious act, and because of the partial schedule (a variable-ratio one), it is difficult to eliminate.

In 1948 B. F. Skinner developed an experimental procedure to mimic and gain control over the development of superstitious acts. He placed hungry pigeons in a chamber and delivered bits of food every 15 seconds, irrespective of what a bird happened to be doing at the time. In his own words: "In six out of eight cases the resulting responses were so clearly defined that two observers could agree perfectly in counting instances. One bird was conditioned to turn counter clockwise about the cage, making two or three turns between reinforcements. Another repeatedly thrust its head into one of the upper corners of the cage. A third developed a 'tossing' response, as if placing its head beneath an invisible bar and lifting it repeatedly" (Skinner, 1948, p. 168).

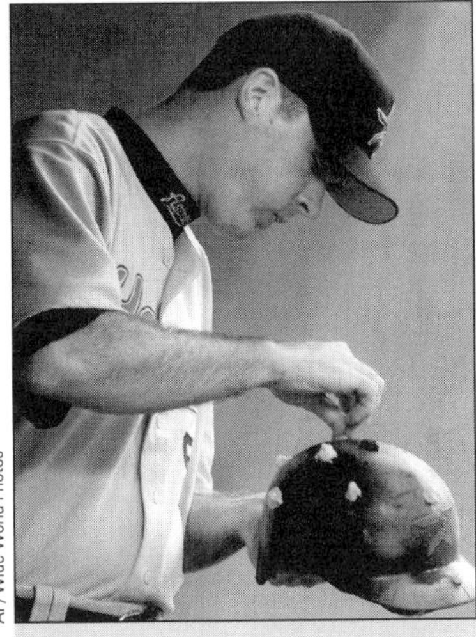

AP/Wide World Photos

Many athletes perform odd rituals on a regular basis. This professional baseball player feels the need to put his gum on a batting helmet every time before going up to the plate. A learning theorist might argue that the player's bizarre behavior was somehow accidentally reinforced in the past, forming a superstitious cause-and-effect link between gum chewing and successful performance.

Remember, from the experimenter's point of view, no cause-and-effect relationship existed between these quirky behaviors and the delivery of food. Researchers since Skinner have replicated his results, but with some added caveats (Staddon & Simmelhag, 1971). For example, many of the behaviors that Skinner noted are characteristic responses that birds make in preparation for food; therefore, some of the strange behaviors Skinner observed might have been natural pigeon reactions to the expectation of being fed rather than learned responses. Nevertheless, the point Skinner made is important to remember: From the responder's point of view, illusory connections can form between behaviors and outcomes. Once these connections have been made, if the behaviors recur, they might continue to be accidentally reinforced and thus serve as the basis for the familiar forms of superstitious acts.

To teach someone an effective golf swing, it's best to begin by rewarding simple contact between the club and the ball. Later the teacher can fine-tune the person's swing by offering praise only when the mechanics of the swing are more technically correct.

Biological Constraints on Learning

Is it really possible to teach any response, in any situation, provided you have enough time and a reinforcer that works? Probably not. Many psychologists believe there are biological constraints, perhaps based on the genetic code, that limit the responses that can be taught. Thorndike, in his early studies of cats in puzzle boxes, noted that it was basically impossible to increase the probability of yawning or of certain reflexive scratching responses in cats through the application of reinforcement.

Similar observations were reported later by animal trainers Keller and Marion Breland (1961). The Brelands, who were former students of B. F. Skinner, encountered some interesting difficulties while attempting to train a variety of species to make certain responses. In one case, they tried to train a pig to drop large wooden coins into a piggy bank (for a bank commercial). They followed the shaping procedure, where successive approximations of the desired sequence are reinforced, but they could not get the pig to complete the response. The animal would pick up the coin and begin to lumber toward the bank but would stop midway and begin "rooting" the coins along the ground. Despite applying punishment and nonreinforcement of the rooting response, the Brelands could never completely eliminate the response. They encountered similar problems trying to teach a raccoon to put coins in a bank.

> We started out by reinforcing him for picking up a single coin. Then the metal container was introduced, with the requirement that he drop the coin into the container. Here we ran into the first bit of difficulty: he seemed to have a great deal of trouble letting go of the coin. He would rub it against the inside of the container, pull it back out, and clutch it firmly for several seconds. However, he would finally turn it loose and receive his food reinforcement. Then the final contingency: we [required] that he pick up [two] coins and put them in the container.
>
> Now the raccoon really had problems (and so did we). Not only could he not let go of the coins, but he spent seconds, even minutes, rubbing them together (in a most miserly fashion) and dipping them into the container. He carried on this behavior to such an extent that the practical application that we had in mind—a display featuring a raccoon putting money into a piggy bank—simply was not feasible. The rubbing behavior became worse and worse as time went on, in spite of nonreinforcement. (Breland & Breland, 1961, p. 682)

In the cases of the pig and the raccoon, biological tendencies connected with feeding and food reinforcement interfered with the learning of certain response sequences. Pigs root in connection with feeding, and raccoons rub and dunk objects related to food (Domjan, 2003). These natural tendencies are adaptive responses for the animals—at least with respect to feeding—but they may limit what the animals can be taught.

In other cases, people and animals may be predisposed to *learn* relationships between certain stimuli and outcomes. For example, the delay between experiencing a distinctive taste (such as clam pizza) and subsequent illness can be quite long (hours), yet we're still quite likely to form an aversion to the taste (Garcia & Koelling, 1966). We may also be naturally predisposed to learn about and recognize potential predators in our environment, such as snakes. In a classical conditioning procedure, we quickly learn to associate pictures of snakes with aversive events (e.g., shock)—much more quickly, in fact, than we do to nonthreatening events, such as pictures of flowers (Öhman & Mineka, 2001). Some psychologists believe that we have special circuitry in the brain, acquired through evolution, that helps us process and learn about stimuli related to survival threats (Öhman & Mineka, 2003).

LEARNING FROM OTHERS: OBSERVATIONAL LEARNING

The world would be a very unpleasant place if you could only learn about the consequences of your behavior through simple trial and error. You could learn to avoid certain foods through positive punishment, but only after eating them and experiencing an unpleasant consequence. Through escape and avoidance conditioning, children might learn not to play in the street, provided they leap away from the oncoming traffic in time. You could learn to avoid illegal drugs, but only if you have a bad experience, such as an arrest or a risky overdose. Clearly, it's sometimes best not to undergo the actual experiences that lead to learning.

In the wild, rhesus monkeys show an adaptive fear response in the presence of snakes. Because snakes are natural predators of monkeys, it makes sense for monkeys to avoid them whenever possible. But how do you suppose that fear is originally acquired? According to a strict interpretation of the law of effect, the animal must learn its fear through some kind of direct reinforcement or punishment—that is, through trial and error. This means that a monkey would probably need to approach a snake and be bitten (or nearly bitten) before it could learn to fear the snake; unfortunately, this single learning experience is likely to be fatal much of the time. This suggests that trial-and-error learning is not always adaptive, especially when you're learning about something dangerous or potentially harmful.

Fortunately, it's possible to learn a great deal without trial and error—by simply observing the experiences of *others*. People and animals can learn by example, and this kind of learning, called **observational learning** (or *social learning*), has considerable adaptive value. In the wild, newly weaned rats acquire food habits by eating what the older rats eat (Galef, 1985); red-winged blackbirds will refuse to eat a certain food if they've observed another bird getting sick after it has eaten the food (Mason & Reidinger, 1982); chimpanzees in the wild learn how to use stone tools to crack open nuts by observing older chimpanzees eating (Inoue-Nokamura & Matsuzawa, 1997). Rhesus monkeys, it turns out, acquire their fear of snakes partly through social learning rather than through direct experience (Öhman & Mineka, 2003). They watch other monkeys in their environment showing fear in the presence of a snake and thereby acquire the tendency to show fear themselves. It's also possible to learn by observing the mistakes of others—if one bird watches another bird consistently choosing an incorrect response for food, the bird doing the observing is less likely to make the same mistake (Templeton, 1998).

observational learning
learning by observing the experience of others.

Do you think monkeys raised in captivity, such as in a zoo, will also show a strong fear of snakes?

Modeling: Learning From Others

What conditions produce effective observational learning? One important factor is the presence of a significant role model. People naturally tend to imitate, or **model**, the behavior of significant others, as do most members of the animal kingdom. You probably learned a lot of things by watching your parents or your teachers—even though you may never have been aware of doing so. Research has shown that observational learning is particularly effective if the model has positive characteristics, such as attractiveness, honesty, perceived competence, and some kind of social standing (Bandura, 1986; Brewer & Wann, 1998). It's also more likely if you observe the model being rewarded for a particular action, or if the model's behavior is particularly successful.

modeling
the natural tendency to imitate the behavior of significant others.

In one classic study, Bandura and his colleagues showed nursery-school children a film that portrayed an adult striking, punching, and kicking a large, inflatable, upright "Bobo" doll. Afterward, when placed in a room with Bobo, many of these children imitated the adult and violently attacked the doll (Bandura et al., 1963). In addition, the chances of the children kicking the doll increased if the adult was

© David Oliver/Taxi/Getty Images

We naturally tend to imitate, or model, the behavior of significant others. Modeling is adaptive because it allows us to learn things without directly experiencing consequences.

directly praised in the film for attacking Bobo ("You're the champion!"). Bandura (1986) has claimed that the responses acquired through observational learning are especially strengthened through *vicarious reinforcement,* which occurs when the model is reinforced for an action, or weakened through *vicarious punishment,* in which the model is punished for an action. A clear parallel therefore exists between the law of effect and observational learning; the difference, of course, is that the behavior of others is being reinforced or punished rather than our own.

Albert Bandura did much of the early pioneering work on observational learning. Bandura believes that much of what we learn from an experience depends on our existing beliefs and expectations. You're unlikely to learn from a model, for example, if you believe you're incapable of ever performing the model's behavior. You can watch a great pianist or singer or athlete, but you're not likely to imitate his or her behavior if you feel you're incapable of performing the task. Our beliefs about our own abilities, which Bandura refers to as "self-efficacy," significantly shape and constrain what we gain from observational learning.

Practical Considerations

Psychologists regularly use the techniques of observational learning to improve or change unwanted behaviors. Many studies have shown that observing desirable behavior can lower unwanted or maladaptive behavior. Children have been able to reduce their fear of dental visits (Craig, 1978) or impending surgery (Melamed & Siegel, 1975) by observing films of other children effectively handling their dental or surgical anxieties. Clinical psychologists now use observational learning as a technique to deal with specific fears and as a method for promoting cooperative behavior among preschoolers (Granvold, 1994).

© Richard Hutchings/Photo Researchers, Inc.

Observational learning has powerful consequences that are not always what we intend. Children imitate significant role models, even when the behavior lacks adaptive value.

At the same time, observational or social learning can have significant negative effects as well. For example, children witness thousands of reinforced acts of violence just by watching Saturday morning cartoons. Although causal connections between TV violence and personal aggression remain somewhat controversial (Freedman, 1988), the consensus among psychologists clearly supports a link (Anderson et al., 2003). In addition, it can be difficult for a society to overcome unproductive stereotypes if they're repeatedly portrayed through the behavior of others. Many gender-related stereotypes, such as submissive or helpless behavior in females, continue to be represented in TV programs and movies. By the age of 6 or 7, children have already begun to shy away from activities that are identified with members of the opposite sex. Although it's unlikely that television is entirely responsible for this trend, it's widely believed that television plays an important role (Ruble et al., 1981).

Even if people don't directly imitate or model a particular violent act, it's still likely that the observation itself influences the way they think. For instance, witnessing repeated examples of fictional violence distorts people's estimates of realistic violence—they're likely to believe, for example, that more people die a violent death than is actually the case. This can lead individuals to show irrational fear and to avoid situations that are in all likelihood safe. People who watch a lot of television tend to view the world in a way that mirrors what they see on the screen. They might think, for example, that a large proportion of the population are professionals (such as doctors or lawyers) and that few people in society are actually old (Gerbner & Gross, 1976). It's not just the imitation of particular acts we need to worry about: Television and other vehicles of observational learning can literally change or determine our everyday view of the world (Bandura, 1986; Bushman & Anderson, 2001).

Finally, suppose the link between witnessed violence and personal aggression is real, but small. Imagine, for example, that only 1% of people who watch a violent television program become more violent after watching the show. Is this a cause for concern? Remember, many millions of people watch television every day. If 10 million people watch a show, and only 1% are affected, that would still mean that 100,000 people might have an increased tendency for violence. Those are scary numbers when you consider that it only takes one or two people to terrorize a building or commit murder in a school (e.g., Columbine). Ironically, recent research suggests that when violence is shown in a television program, it may actually hurt the very industries that are sponsoring the show. Evidence collected from Bushman and Phillips (2001) indicates that television violence actually impairs subsequent memory for the brand names and product information shown in accompanying commercials.

Think About It

Given what you've learned about modeling, do you now favor the passage of laws that will control the amount of violence shown on television? Why or why not?

REVIEW

Psychology for a Reason

As we struggle to survive, our capacity to learn—that is, to change our behavior as a result of experience—represents a great strength. Psychologists have long recognized the importance of understanding how behavior changes with experience; historically, research on learning predates research on virtually all other topics, with the exception of basic sensory and perceptual processes. In this chapter we've concentrated on relatively simple learning processes. To meet the needs of changing environments, each of us must solve certain types of learning problems, and the principles of behavior you've learned about apply generally across animal species.

Learning About Events Novel or unusual events lead to an orienting response, which helps ensure that we'll react quickly to sudden changes in our environment. The sound of screeching automobile brakes leads to an immediate reaction; we don't have to stop and think about it. At the same time, no one can attend to all the stimuli that surround us, so we learn to ignore events that are of little adaptive significance. Through the process of habituation, characterized by the decline in the tendency to respond to an event that has become familiar, we become selective about responding to events that occur repeatedly in our environment.

Learning About Signals We also learn about what events *signal*—it's helpful to know, for example, that a wailing siren means an emergency vehicle is somewhere nearby. Signals, or conditioned stimuli, are established through classical conditioning. Events that provide information about the occurrence or nonoccurrence of other significant events become conditioned stimuli. A conditioned stimulus elicits a conditioned response, which is a response appropriate for anticipating the event that will follow. When we hear the siren, we anticipate the arrival of the ambulance and quickly move out of the way.

Learning About the Consequences of Behavior We also learn that our actions produce outcomes that are sometimes pleasing and sometimes not. In operant conditioning, the presentation and removal of events after responding can either increase or decrease the likelihood of responding in a similar way again. When a response is followed by reinforcement, either positive or negative, the tendency to respond similarly is strengthened. When a response is followed by punishment, either positive or negative, we are less likely to repeat the behavior. It's also important to consider the schedule of reinforcement. Schedules affect not only how rapidly we will learn and respond, but also the pattern of responding and how likely we are to change our behavior if the reinforcement stops.

Learning From Others Through observational or social learning, we imitate and *model* the actions of others, thereby learning from example rather than from direct experience. We study how other people behave and how their behavior is reinforced or punished, and we change our own behavior accordingly. Whether or not we will imitate the behavior of others depends on several factors, including the social standing of the model. Observational learning can have a number of effects, both positive and negative, on the individual and on society.

CHAPTER 4 PRACTICE EXAM

____ 1. The children automatically turned toward the window as the ball crashed through it. Automatically turning their heads is an example of:
a. a conditioned stimulus
b. operant response
c. an orienting response
d. Sensitization response

____ 2. Harold hardly notices his aunt's musty house smell now that he is living with her, but he couldn't stand it before he moved in. Harold's is showing . . .
a. habituation
b. Extinction
c. Carry over conditioning
d. Primary sensitization

____ 3. Following repeated exposure, if a response increases, then you have been:
a. habituated
b. desensitized
c. sensitized
d. Slipsized

____ 4. When Mary was six years old she became hysterical when she woke up with a snake in her bed. As an adult the sight of a toy snake makes Mary anxious. In this example the snake is the:
a. an unconditioned response
b. a conditioned stimulus
c. an unconditioned stimulus
d. a conditioned response

____ 5. Out of nowhere, Bob received a text message from a girl Bob wanted to go out amd she asked him if wanted to go to a party with her. Bob felt a surge of excitement during the call. Whenever Bob sees a text message notice, he gets that surge of excitement. The unconditioned response is:
a. the surge of excitement when he gets a text message
b. the girl asking Bob out
c. the surge of excitement when the girl asked him out
d. the ringing of a telephone

____ 6. A few seconds before your microwave oven makes a loud buzz and stops, it makes a small tick. You now turn your head after hearing the tick, but before the buzzer goes off indicating the microwave has stopped. The tick is acting as:
a. a conditioned stimulus
b. an unconditioned stimulus
c. a positive stimulus
d. a habituated stimulus

____ 7. George tried some banana margaritas once, but after the tenth margarita George became violently sick. Now George gets sick when he simply smells a banana. The conditioned response is:
a. Getting sick after the tenth margarita
b. the smell of bananas
c. the banana margaritas that George drank
d. the sickness George feels when he smells bananas

____ 8. When Mary was four years old, she was bitten by a neighborhood dog. As a teenager Mary is afraid of any small animal, including kittens and mice. Mary's fear occurred through the process of:
a. stimulus discrimination
b. stimulus generalization
c. aversive conditioning
d. conditioned inhibition

____ 9. When Wilbur was two years old, he fell off his green scooter and smashed his toes. As a three year old Wilbur is afraid to ride his green scooter but not a red one or a purple one. Wilbur has shown:
a. stimulus generalization
b. stimulus discrimination
c. aversive conditioning
d. conditioned inhibition

____ 10. Samantha takes aspirin before he plays basketball to prevent extensive knee pain. What operant conditioning principle is Samantha using:
a. avoidance conditioning
b. escape conditioning
c. observational conditioning
d. classical conditioning

____ 11. When they behave appropriately, elementary school children receive stars they can later exchange for admission to a school store to buy things. The stars are an example of:
a. Intermittent reinforcer
b. Bribery reinforcer
c. conditioned reinforcer
d. negative reinforcer

____ 12. Rues mother spanked her when she jumped down the stairs; she quit jumping down the stairs. Her mother used:
a. positive reinforcement
b. negative reinforcement
c. positive punishment
d. negative punishment

____ 13. Barb can't figure out how to work his new computer, so Alexis shows her the steps she must follow to work the computer. Barb learned how to use her computer by:
a. classical conditioning
b. operant conditioning
c. vicarious observation
d. observational learning

____ 14. Smith watched Sarah sneak into the neighbor's yard and pick some cherries. Sarah got the cherries and made a tasty pie with them. If Smith, at some later time, sneaks into the neighbor's yard for cherries, he has learned through the process known as:
a. vicarious punishment
b. vicarious reinforcement
c. negative punishment
d. positive reinforcement

____ 15. Katie observed three people get arrested for shoplifting. As a result, Katie put back on the shelf the cell phone she was planning to take. This is an example of:
a. extinction
b. conditioned inhibition
c. vicarious punishment
d. accidental reinforcement

Answers

1. C
2. A
3. C
4. C
5. C
6. A
7. D
8. A
9. B
10. B
11. C
12. C
13. D
14. A
15. C

CHAPTER 5: BIOLOGICAL PSYCHOLOGY

QUESTIONS

1. What are the parts of a neuron?
2. What is the advantage and disadvantage of an action potential over electrical conduction?
3. How does the action potential work?
4. Why should a psychologist care about action potentials?
5. What does a neuron do at a synapse?
6. What do neurotransmitters do?
7. Why is it possible to develop drugs for some behaviors and psychological conditions?
8. What did Loewi (1960) do to demonstrate that neurons communicate chemically?
9. What hypothesis does the drug L-dopa for Parkinson's disease support?
10. Why does using Ritalin for Attention Deficit Disorder muddle the hypothesis that unusual behavior is due to an excess or deficit of synaptic activity?
11. Why should psychologists care about the brain and effects of brain damage?
12. What are the major divisions of the nervous system?
13. What happens to people with occipital lobe damage?
14. What is the effect of extensive damage to the parietal region?
15. What area is damaged in and what happens in Wernicke's aphasia?
16. What is the effect of damage to the amygdala?
17. What is the only sensory information that goes directly to the cerebral cortex?
18. What is the path of touch, pain, and other skin senses?
19. What are the paths of vision, hearing, and taste?
20. What is the cerebellum important for?
21. What are the two parts of the autonomic nervous system?
22. What is some evidence for and against the hypothesis that exercising the brain makes the brain bigger?
23. What happens to a split-brain patient when they feel something with their left hand?
24. What happens when a split-brain patient sees something?
25. What are some ways the right hemisphere is different from the left hemisphere?
26. What is the generalization about the specializations of the right and left hemispheres?
27. What is the evidence for the notion that some people are right brained (i.e. creative) and left brained (i.e. logical)?

VOCABULARY

1. action potential
2. autonomic nervous system
3. axon
4. binding problem
5. central nervous system
6. cerebellum
7. cerebral cortex
8. corpus callosum
9. dendrite
10. dopamine
11. EEG
12. endocrine system
13. frontal lobe
14. fMRI
15. hemisphere
16. hormone
17. MEG
18. neuron
19. neurotransmitter
20. occipital lobe
21. parietal lobe
22. peripheral nervous system
23. PET
24. postsynaptic neuron
25. prefrontal cortex
26. reflex
27. resting potential
28. spinal cord
29. stem cells
30. synapse
31. temporal lobe
32. thalamus

5 Biological Psychology

Nervous System Cells

The Action Potential

Synapses

Neurotransmitters and Behavior

The Nervous System and Behavior

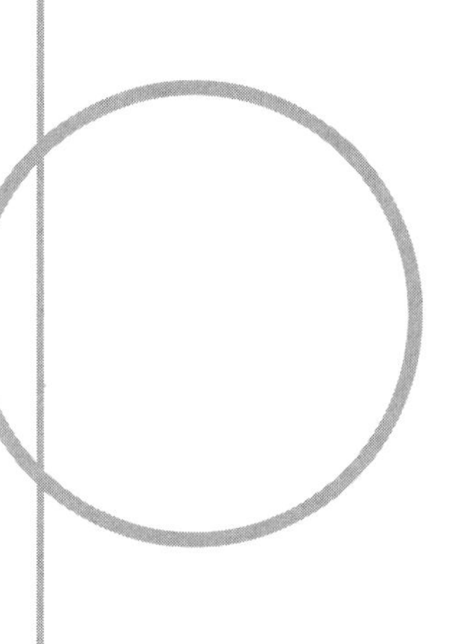

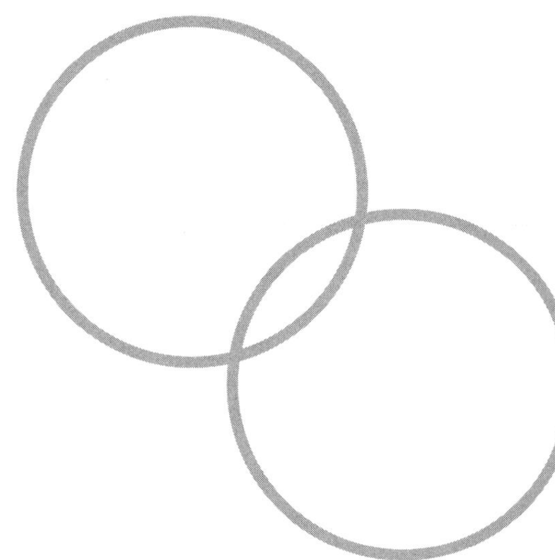

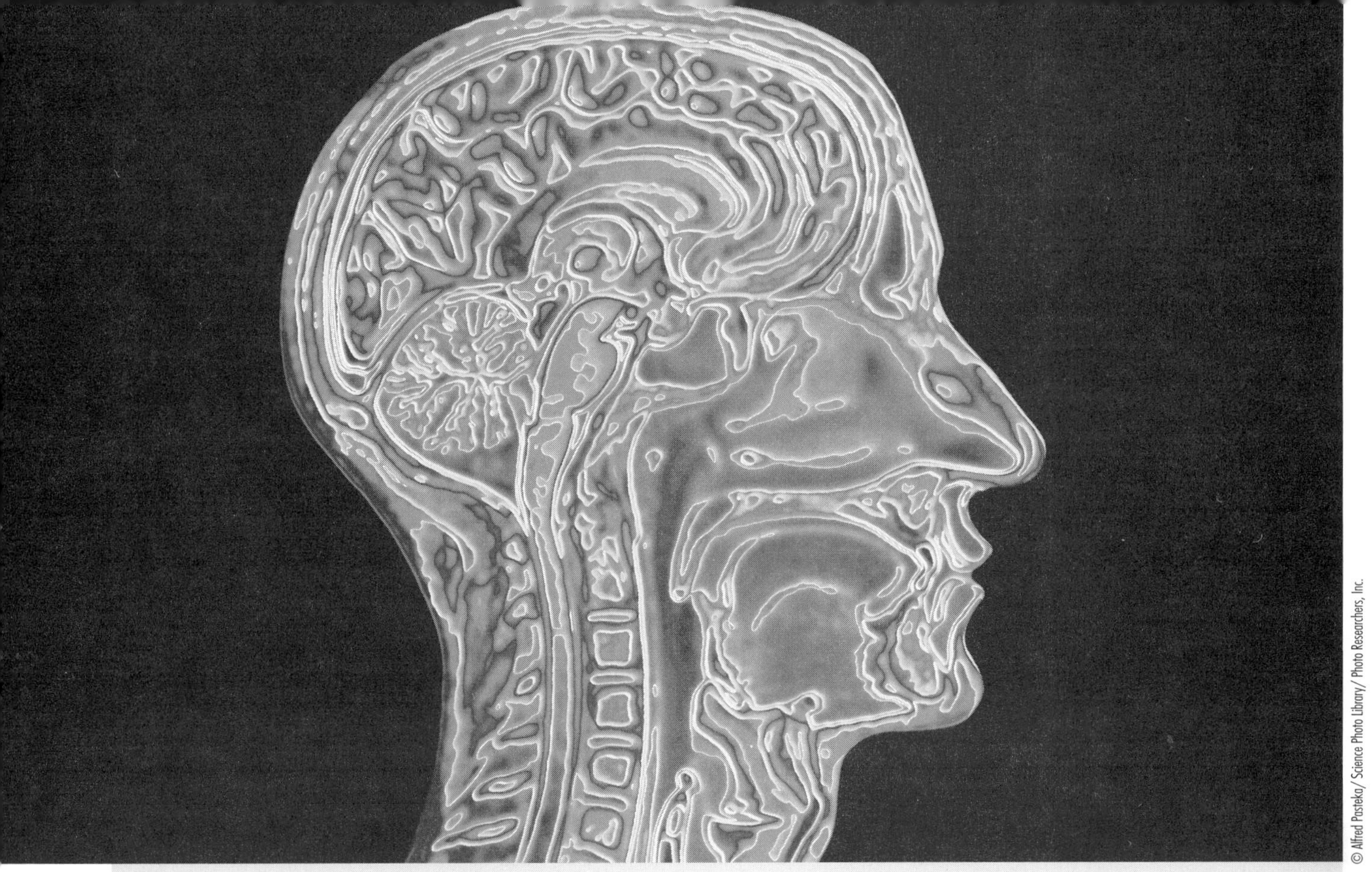

© Alfred Pasieka/Science Photo Library/Photo Researchers, Inc.

CAN WE EXPLAIN our experiences and our behavior in terms of the actions of single cells in the nervous system? One highly productive strategy in science is *reductionism*—the attempt to explain complex phenomena by reducing them to combinations of simpler components. Biologists explain breathing, blood circulation, and metabolism in terms of chemical reactions and physical forces. Chemists explain chemical reactions in terms of the properties of the elements and their atoms. Physicists explain the properties of the atom in terms of a few fundamental forces.

How well does reductionism apply to psychology? Can we explain human behavior and experience in terms of chemical and electrical events in the brain? The only way to find out is to try. Here we explore efforts to explain behavior based on single cells of the nervous system.

NERVOUS SYSTEM CELLS

You experience your "self" as a single entity that senses, thinks, and remembers. And yet neuroscientists have found that the nervous system responsible for your experiences consists of an enormous number of separate cells. The brain processes information in **neurons** (NOO-rons), or *nerve cells.* Figure 5.1 shows estimates of the numbers of neurons in various parts of the human nervous system (R. W. Williams & Herrup, 1988). The nervous system also contains another kind of cells called **glia** (GLEE-uh), *which support the neurons in many ways such as by insulating them and removing waste products.* The glia are about one tenth the size of neurons but about 10 times more numerous.

neuron
a cell of the nervous system that receives information and transmits it to other cells by conducting electrochemical impulses.

glia
a cell of the nervous system that insulates neurons, removes waste materials (e.g., dead cells), and performs other supportive functions.

FIGURE 5.1

Estimated distribution of the neurons in the adult human central nervous system. No one has attempted an exact count, and the number varies substantially from one person to another. (*Based on data of R. W. Williams & Herrup,* 1988.)

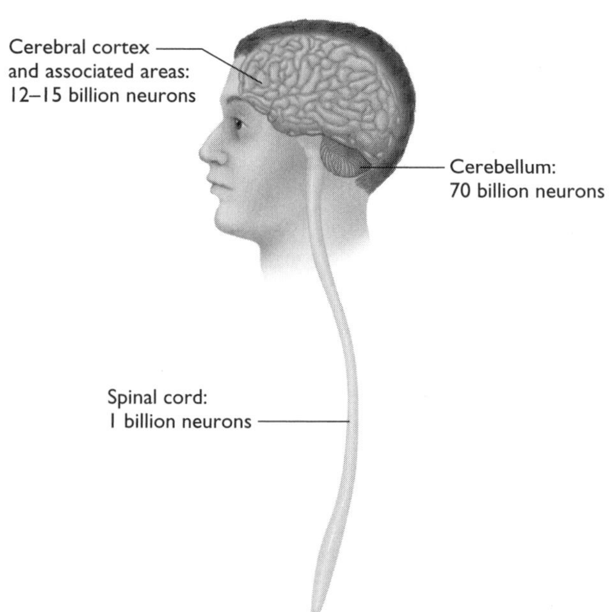

How do so many separate neurons and glia combine forces to produce the single stream of experiences that is you? The secret is communication. Each neuron receives information and transmits it to other cells by conducting electrochemical impulses. Sensory neurons carry information from the sense organs to the central nervous system, where neurons process the information, compare it to past information, and exchange information with other neurons, and ultimately, motor neurons send commands to the muscles and glands.

cell body
the part of the neuron that contains the nucleus of the cell.

dendrite
one of the widely branching structures of a neuron that receive transmissions from other neurons.

To understand our nervous system, we must first understand the properties of both the individual neurons and the connections among them. Neurons have a variety of shapes depending on whether they receive information from a few sources or many and whether they send impulses over a short or a long distance (Figure 5.2).

A neuron consists of three parts: a cell body, dendrites, and an axon (Figure 5.3). The **cell body** *contains the nucleus of the cell.* The **dendrites** (from a Greek word

FIGURE 5.2

Neurons, which vary enormously in shape, consist of a cell body and branched attachments called axons (coded blue for easy identification) and dendrites. The neurons in (a) and (b) receive input from many sources, the neuron in (c) from only a few sources, and the neuron in (d) from an intermediate number of sources. The sensory neurons (e) carry messages from sensory receptors to the brain or spinal cord. Inset: Electron micrograph showing cell bodies in brown and axons and dendrites in green. The color was added artificially; electron micrographs are made with electron beams, not light, and therefore, they show no color.

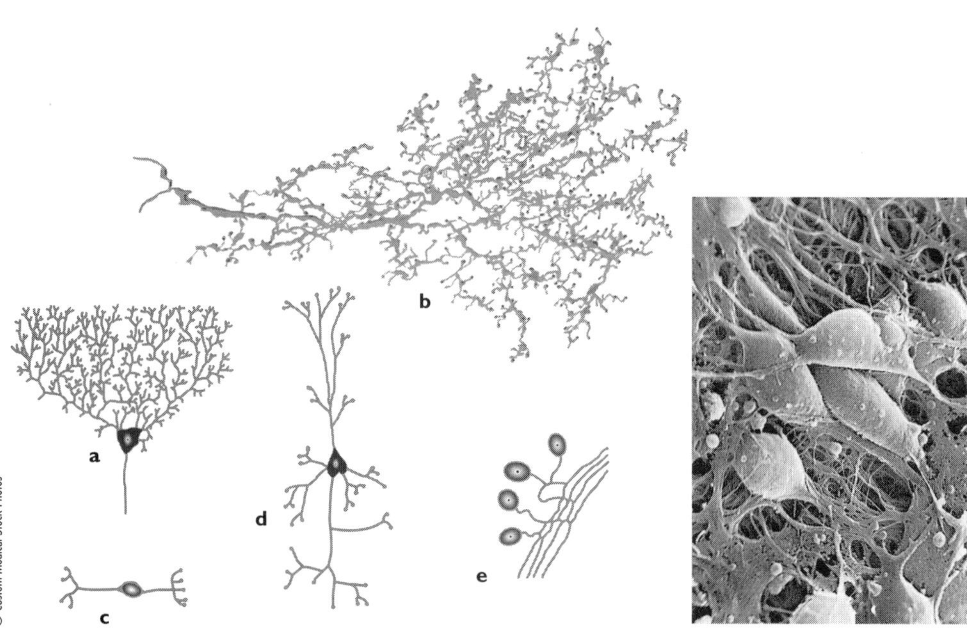

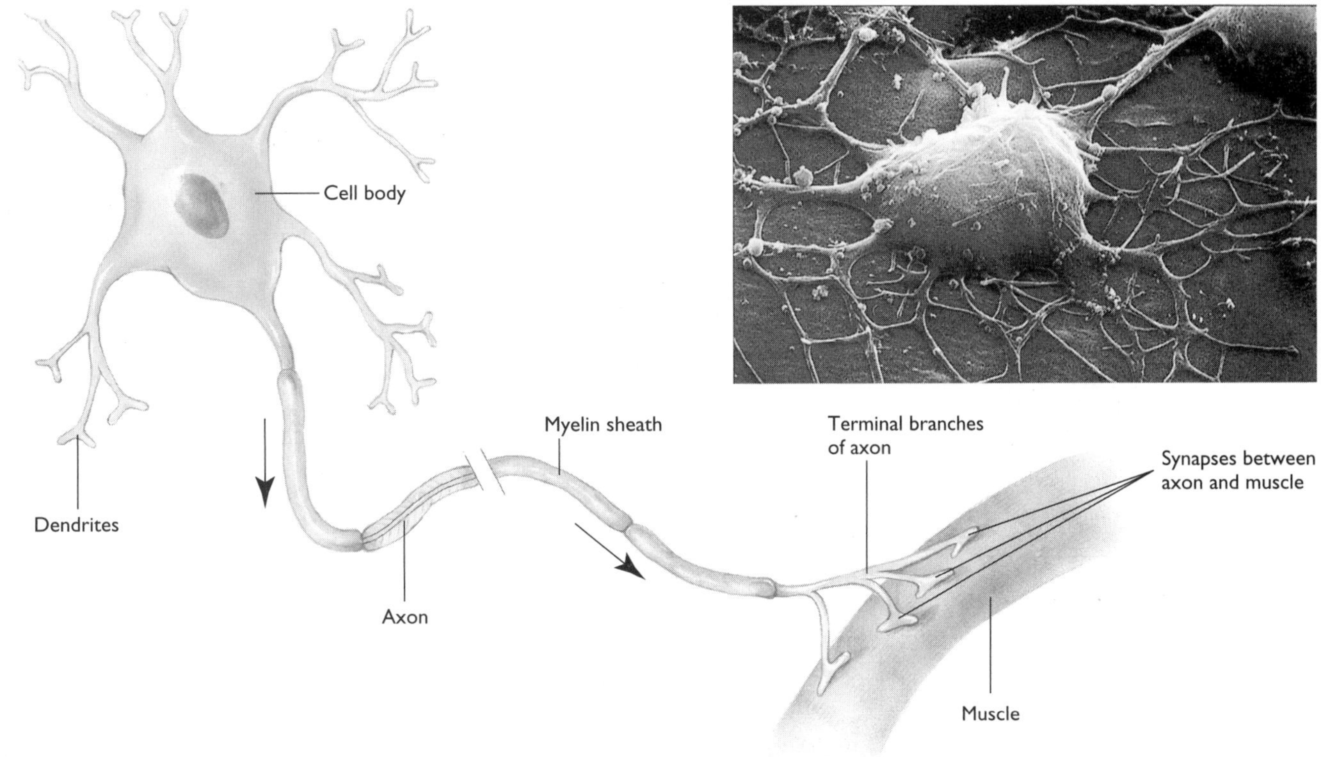

FIGURE 5.3

The generalized structure of a motor neuron shows the dendrites, the branching structures that receive transmissions from other neurons, and the axon, a single, long, thin, straight fiber with branches near its tip. Inset: A photomicrograph of a neuron.

meaning "tree") are *widely branching structures that receive transmissions from other neurons.* The **axon** is a *single, long, thin, straight fiber with branches near its tip.* Some vertebrate axons are covered with *myelin,* an insulating sheath that speeds up the transmission of impulses along an axon. As a rule an axon transmits information to other cells, and the dendrites or cell body of each cell receives that information. That information can be either excitatory or inhibitory; that is, it can increase or decrease the probability that the next cell will send a message of its own. Inhibitory messages are important for many purposes. For example, during a period of painful stimulation, your brain has mechanisms to inhibit further sensation of pain.

axon
a single, long, thin, straight fiber that transmits information from a neuron to other neurons or to muscle cells.

THE ACTION POTENTIAL

Axons are specialized to convey information over distances ranging to a meter or more. Imagine what would happen if they relied on electrical conduction: Electricity is extremely fast, but with a poor conductor such as any part of an animal body, electrical impulses weaken noticeably as they travel. The farther from your brain some information started, the less you would feel it. Short people would feel a pinch on their toes more intensely than tall people would . . . if indeed either felt their toes at all.

Instead, axons convey information by a special combination of electrical and chemical processes called an **action potential,** *an excitation that travels along an axon at a constant strength, no matter how far it must travel.* An action potential is a yes/no or on/off message, like a standard light switch. (Most switches don't let you make the light dimmer or brighter. It's either on or off.) This principle is known as the *all-or-none law.*

action potential
an excitation that travels along an axon at a constant strength, no matter how far it must travel.

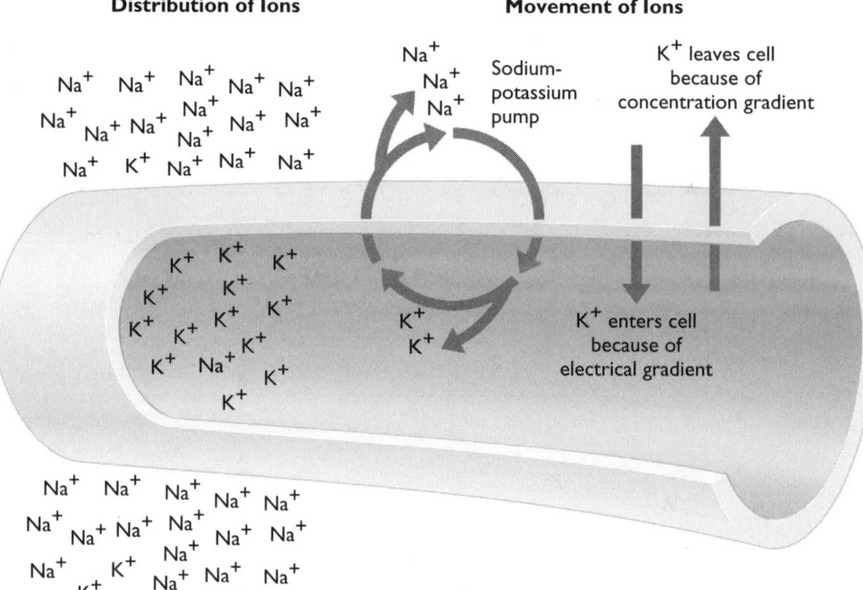

FIGURE 5.4

The sodium and potassium distribution for a resting membrane. Sodium ions (Na^+) are concentrated outside the neuron; potassium ions (K^+) are concentrated inside. Because of negatively charged proteins inside the neuron, the inside of the cell is negatively charged relative to the outside. Protein and chloride ions (not shown) bear negative charges inside the cell. At rest very few sodium ions cross the membrane except by the sodium-potassium pump. Potassium tends to flow into the cell because it is attracted by the negative charge inside the cell. It tends to flow out because it is more concentrated inside than outside.

The advantage of an action potential over simple electrical conduction is that action potentials from distant places like your toes reach your brain at full strength. The disadvantage is that action potentials are slower than electrical conduction. Your knowledge of what is happening to your toes is at least a twentieth of a second out of date. A twentieth of a second is seldom worth worrying about, but your information about different body parts is out of date by different delays. Consequently, if you are touched on two or more body parts at almost the same time, your brain cannot accurately gauge which touch came first.

resting potential electrical polarization that ordinarily occurs across the membrane of an axon that is not undergoing an action potential.

Here is a quick description of how the action potential works:

1. When the axon is not stimulated, its membrane has a **resting potential,** *an electrical polarization across the membrane (or covering) of an axon, with a negative charge inside the axon.* A typical value is –70 millivolts on the inside relative to the outside. The resting potential depends largely on negatively charged proteins inside the axon. In addition a mechanism called the sodium-potassium pump pushes sodium ions out of the axon while pulling potassium ions in. In Figure 5.4 the sodium ions are marked Na^+, and the potassium ions are marked K^+, their chemical symbols. Both have a charge of +1 unit. The result of the sodium-potassium pump is that sodium ions are more concentrated outside the axon and potassium ions are more concentrated inside.
2. An action potential starts in either of two ways: First, many axons produce spontaneous activity. Second, input from other axons can excite a neuron's membrane. In either case, when the action potential starts, sodium gates open and allow sodium ions to enter (Figure 5.5). As the sodium ions enter the axon, they drive the inside of the cell to a slightly positive charge. Whenever that charge is great enough to reach the *threshold* of the axon, it opens narrow channels that permit still more sodium ions to enter, bringing with them their positive charges. This influx of positively charged sodium ions is the action potential.

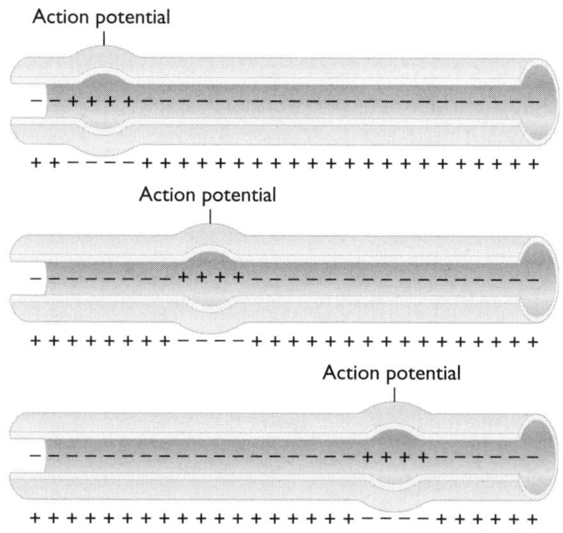

FIGURE 5.5

Ion movements conduct an action potential along an axon. At each point along the membrane, sodium ions enter the axon and alter the distribution of positive and negative charges. As each point along the membrane returns to its original state, the action potential flows to the next point.

3. After the sodium gates have been open for barely an instant, they snap shut. Then potassium gates open to allow potassium ions to leave the axon. The potassium ions each carry a positive charge, so their exit drives the inside of the axon back to its original resting potential (Figure 5.6b).
4. Eventually, the sodium-potassium pump removes the invading sodium ions and recaptures the escaping potassium ions.

You will recall that the axon does not conduct like an electrical wire. The action potential travels down the axon like a wave of energy, and the stimulation at each point excites the next point along the axon. You could imagine it like a fire burning along a string: The fire at each point ignites the next point, which in turn ignites the next point. That is, after sodium ions enter some point along an axon, some of them diffuse to the neighboring portion of the axon and thereby excite that part of the membrane enough to open its own sodium gates. The action potential spreads to this next area and so on down the axon, as shown in Figure 5.6. In this manner the action potential remains equally strong all the way to the end of the axon.

All of this information is clearly important to investigators of the nervous system, but why should a psychology student care? First, it explains why sensations on points on your fingers and toes do not fade away by the time they reach your brain. Second, an understanding of action potentials is one step toward understanding the communication between one neuron and the next. Third, certain drugs operate by blocking action potentials. For example, anesthetic drugs (e.g., Novocain) silence neurons by clogging the sodium gates. When your dentist drills a tooth, the receptors in your tooth send out the message "Pain! Pain! Pain!" But that message does not get through to the brain because a shot of Novocain has blocked the sodium gates and thereby halted the sensory messages.

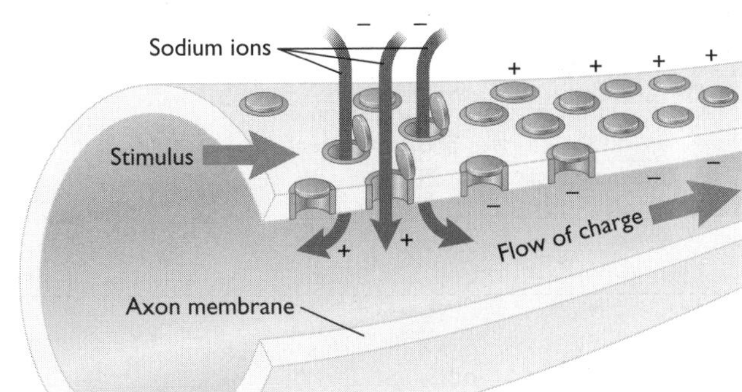

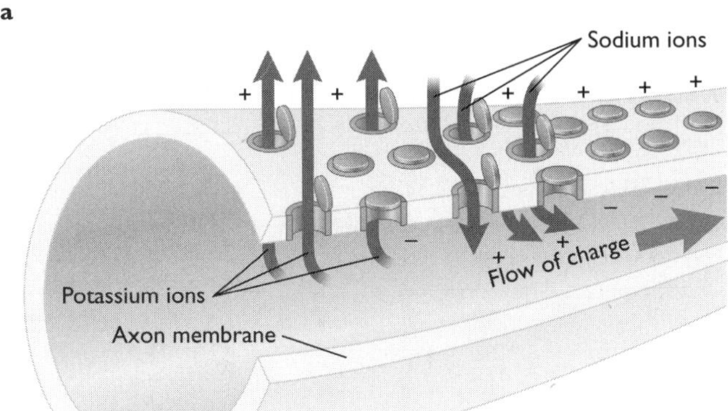

FIGURE 5.6
(a) During an action potential, sodium gates in the neuron membrane open, and sodium ions enter the axon, bringing a positive charge with them. (b) After an action potential occurs at one point along the axon, the sodium gates close at that point and open at the next point along the axon. When the sodium gates close, potassium gates open, and potassium ions flow out of the axon, carrying a positive charge with them. (*Modified from Starr & Taggart, 1992*)

SYNAPSES

Communication between one neuron and the next is not like transmission along an axon. At a **synapse** (SIN-aps), *the specialized junction between one neuron and another* (Figure 5.7), *a neuron releases a chemical that either excites or inhibits the next neuron.* That is, the chemical can make the next neuron either more or less likely to produce an action potential. At other kinds of synapses, a neuron releases a chemical that excites a muscle or gland. The events at synapses are central to everything that your nervous system does because synapses determine which cells will be active at any moment.

A typical axon has several branches, each ending with a little bulge called a *presynaptic ending,* or **terminal bouton** (or **button**), as shown in Figure 5.8. When an action potential reaches the terminal bouton, it releases molecules of a **neurotransmitter**, *a chemical that has been stored in the neuron and that can activate receptors of other neurons* (Figure 5.8). Several dozen chemicals are used as neurotransmitters in various brain areas, although any given neuron releases only one or a few of them.

synapse
the specialized junction between one neuron and another; at this point one neuron releases a neurotransmitter, which either excites or inhibits the next neuron.

terminal bouton (or button)
a bulge at the end of an axon from which the axon releases a chemical called a neurotransmitter.

neurotransmitter
a chemical that is stored in the terminal of an axon and that, when released, activates receptors of other neurons.

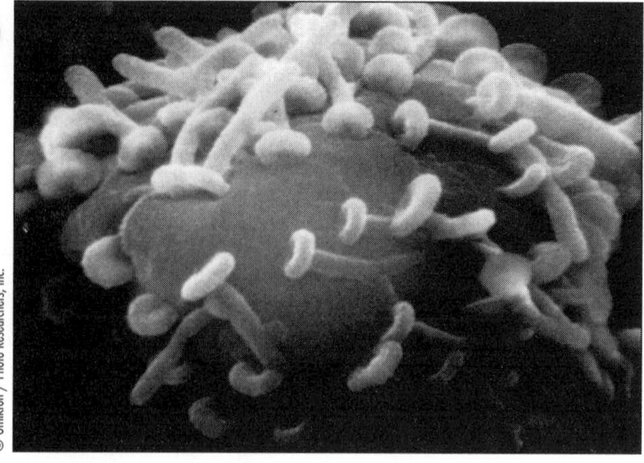

FIGURE 5.7

The tips of axons swell to form terminal boutons, which form synapses onto the surface of another cell, as shown in this electron micrograph.

postsynaptic neuron
a neuron on the receiving end of a synapse.

The neurotransmitter molecules diffuse across a narrow gap to the **postsynaptic neuron**, *the neuron on the receiving end of the synapse*. There the neurotransmitter molecules attach to receptors on the neuron's dendrites or cell body (or for special purposes on the tip of its axon). The neural communication process is summarized in Figure 5.9.

Depending on the neurotransmitter and the type of receptor, the attachment can either excite or inhibit the postsynaptic neuron. That is, it enables either positively charged or negatively charged ions to enter. The postsynaptic neuron produces an action potential of its own if the total excitation at any moment outweighs the total inhibition coming from a variety of synapses. The process resembles making a decision: When you are trying to decide whether to do something, you weigh all the pluses and minuses and act if the pluses are stronger.

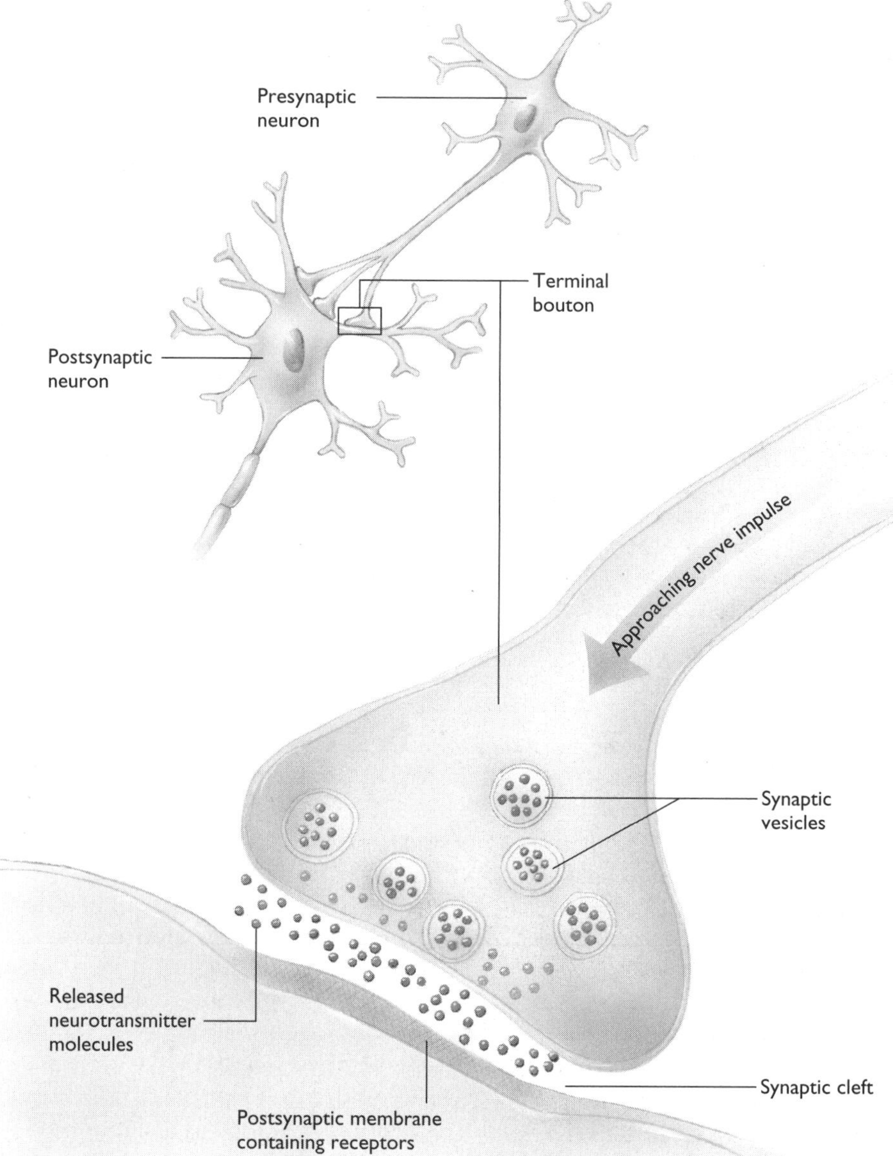

FIGURE 5.8

The synapse is the junction of the presynaptic (message-sending) cell and the postsynaptic (message-receiving) cell. At the end of the presynaptic axon is the terminal bouton, which contains many molecules of the neurotransmitter. The thick, dark area at the bottom of the cell is the synapse.

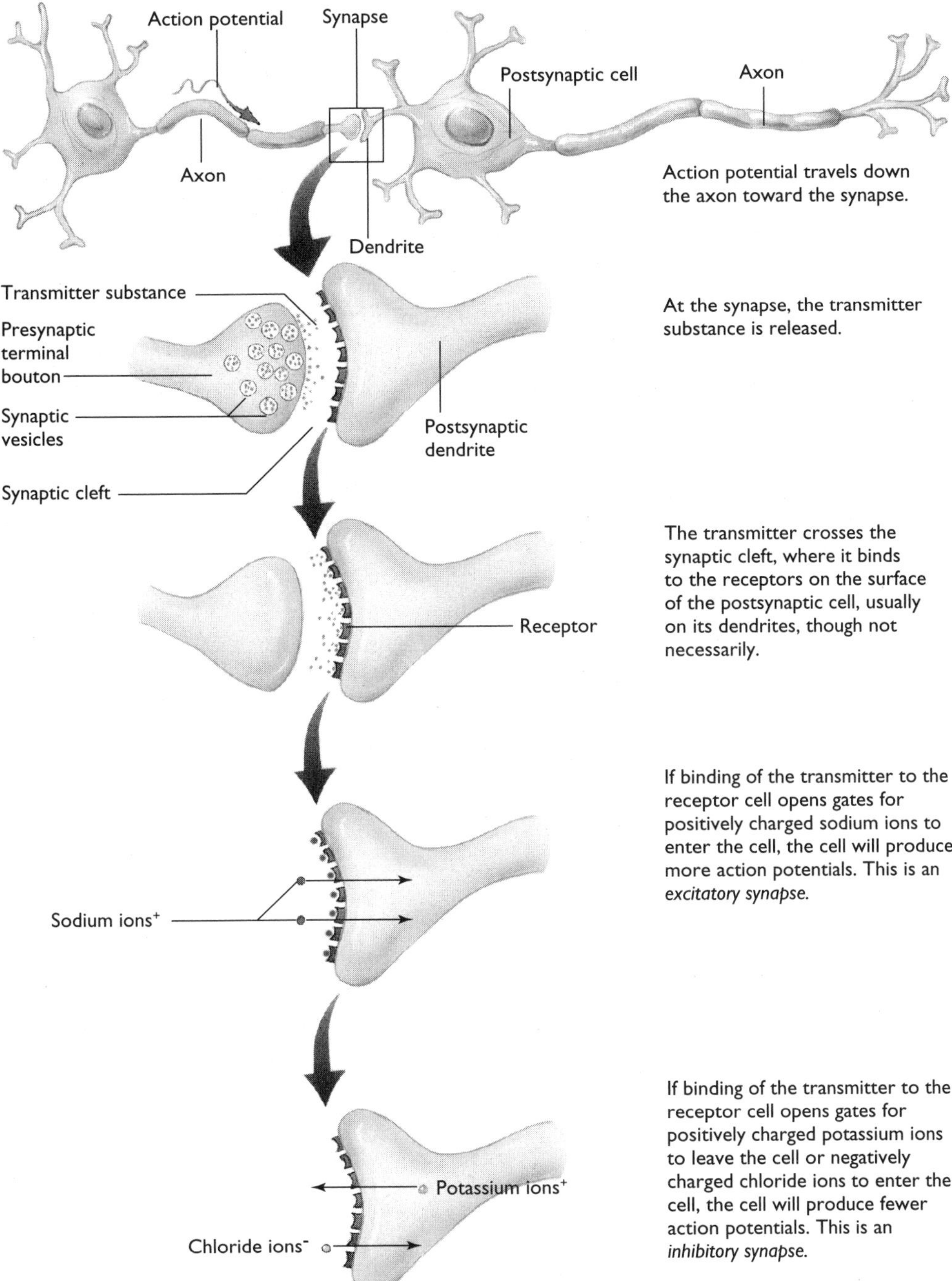

FIGURE 5.9

The complex process of neural communication takes only 1–2 milliseconds.

Inhibition is not the absence of excitation; it is like stepping on the brakes. For example, when a pinch on your foot causes you to raise it, thus contracting one set of muscles, inhibitory synapses in your spinal cord block activity in the muscles that would move your leg in the opposite direction. Those inhibitory synapses prevent messages from trying to raise your leg and extend it at the same time.

After a neurotransmitter excites or inhibits a receptor, it separates from the receptor, terminating the message. From that point on, the fate of the receptor molecule varies. It could become reabsorbed by the axon that released it (through a process called *reuptake*); it could diffuse away, get metabolized, and eventually show up in the blood or urine; or it could bounce around for a moment, return to the postsynaptic receptor, and reexcite it. Many antidepressant drugs act by blocking reuptake and therefore prolonging the effects of one transmitter or another.

Different neurotransmitters are associated with different functions, although it is misleading to assign a specific behavior (e.g., sleep or pleasure) to a specific transmitter. Any complex behavior depends on many transmitter systems, and each transmitter contributes to many aspects of behavior. Still, an alteration of a particular kind of synapse will affect some behaviors more than others. For that reason it is possible to develop drugs that decrease depression, anxiety, appetite, and so forth by increasing or decreasing activity of a certain type of synapse. However, because each transmitter has several behavioral functions, drugs intended for one purpose almost always have other results, referred to as "side effects."

Neurons Communicate Chemically

You have just learned that neurons communicate by releasing chemicals at synapses. Perhaps you are perfectly content to take my word for it and go on with something else. Still, it is advisable to pause and contemplate the evidence responsible for an important conclusion.

Today, neuroscientists have a wealth of evidence that neurons release chemicals at synapses. They can radioactively trace where chemicals go and what happens when they get there; they also can inject purified chemicals at a synapse and use extremely fine electrodes to measure the response of the postsynaptic neuron. But scientists of the 1920s had no fancy equipment, yet they still managed to establish that neurons communicate with chemicals.

Otto Loewi conducted a simple, clever experiment, as he later described in his autobiography (Loewi, 1960).

Hypothesis If a neuron releases chemicals, an investigator should be able to collect some of those chemicals, transfer them from one animal to another, and thereby get the second animal to do what the first animal had been doing. Loewi had no method of collecting chemicals released within the brain itself, so he worked with axons communicating with the heart muscle. (The communication between a neuron and a muscle is similar to that between neurons.)

Method Loewi began by electrically stimulating some axons connected to a frog's heart. These particular axons slowed down the heart rate. As he continued to stimulate those axons, he collected some of the fluid on and around that heart and transferred it to the heart of a second frog.

Results When Loewi transferred the fluid from the first frog's heart, the second frog's heart rate also slowed (Figure 5.10).

Interpretation Evidently, the stimulated axons had released a chemical that slows heart rate. At least in this case, neurons send messages by releasing chemicals.

Loewi eventually won a Nobel Prize in physiology for this and related experiments. Even outstanding experiments have limitations, however. In this case the main limitation was the uncertainty about whether axons release chemicals at most synapses, all, or only a few. Answering *that* question required technologies not available until several decades later. (The answer is that *most* communication by neurons depends on chemicals; a few synapses use electrical communication.)

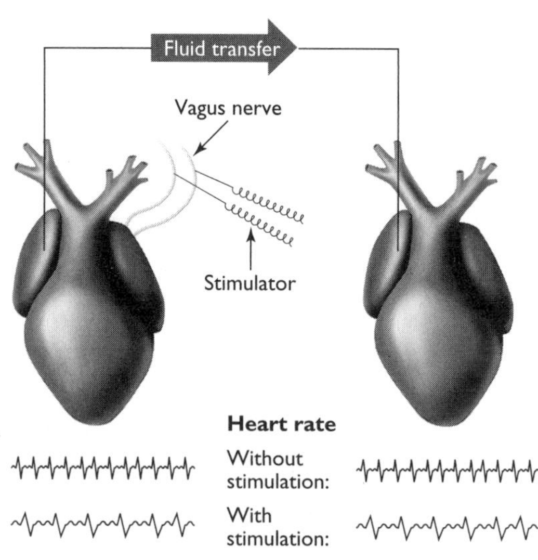

FIGURE 5.10

Otto Loewi demonstrated that axons release chemicals that can affect other cells. Using a frog, he electrically stimulated a set of axons known to decrease the heart rate. Then he collected some fluid from around the heart and transferred it to the surface of another frog's heart. When that heart slowed its beat, Loewi concluded that the axons in the first heart must have released a chemical that slows the heart rate.

NEUROTRANSMITTERS AND BEHAVIOR

The use of drugs that affect neurotransmitters has already revolutionized psychiatry, and investigating the role of these neurotransmitters has produced major theoretical implications for psychology. The brain has dozens of neurotransmitters, and each activates many kinds of receptors. For example, serotonin activates at least 15 kinds, probably more (Roth, Lopez, & Kroeze, 2000). Each receptor type controls somewhat different aspects of behavior. For example, serotonin type 3 receptors are responsible for nausea, and this fact makes it possible to develop drugs that block nausea without major effects on other aspects of behavior (Perez, 1995).

Any drug that increases or decreases the activity of a particular type of receptor produces specific effects on behavior. One hypothesis, therefore, is that any unusual behavior is due to an excess or deficiency of some kind of synaptic activity. One example is **Parkinson's disease**, *a condition that affects about 1% of people over the age of 50. The main symptoms are difficulty in initiating voluntary movement, slowness of movement, tremors, rigidity, and depressed mood.* All of these symptoms can be traced to a gradual decay of a pathway of axons that release *the neurotransmitter* **dopamine** (DOPE-uh-meen) (Figure 5.11). One common treatment is the drug L-dopa, which enters the brain, where neurons convert it into dopamine. The effectiveness of this treatment for most people with mild cases of Parkinson's disease supports our beliefs about the link between the transmitter and the disease.

An example that shows more of the difficulty of interpreting results is **attention deficit disorder (ADD)**, *a condition marked by impulsive behavior and short attention span.* ADD is usually treated with amphetamine or methylphenidate (Ritalin), and researchers know how these drugs work: Both prevent presynaptic neurons from reabsorbing (and thus recycling) the neurotransmitters dopamine and serotonin after releasing them (Volkow et al., 1998). Amphetamine also increases the release of dopamine (Giros, Jaber, Jones, Wightman, & Caron, 1996). So both drugs prolong the activity of dopamine and serotonin at their synaptic receptors. It might

Parkinson's disease
a condition that affects about 1% of people over the age of 50; the main symptoms are difficulty in initiating voluntary movement, slowness of movement, tremors, rigidity, and depressed mood.

dopamine
a neurotransmitter that promotes activity levels and facilitates movement.

attention deficit disorder (ADD)
a condition marked by impulsive behavior and short attention span.

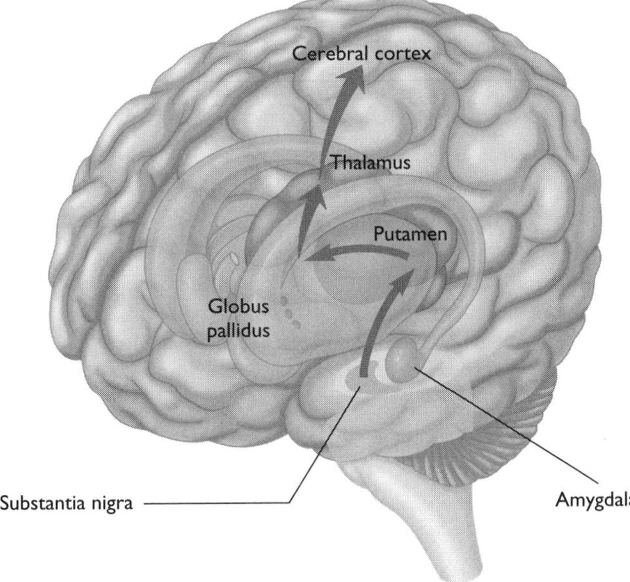

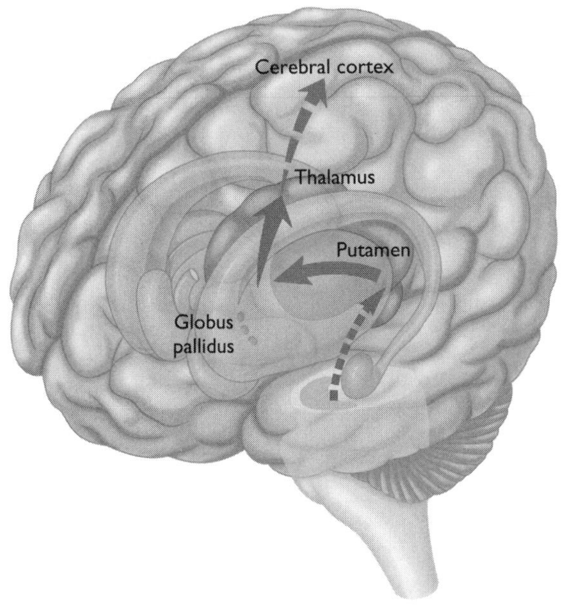

FIGURE 5.11

With Parkinson's disease, axons from the substantia nigra gradually die. (a) Normal brain. (b) Brain of person with Parkinson's disease. Green = excitatory path; red = inhibitory.

Former boxing champion Muhammad Ali developed symptoms of Parkinson's disease.

seem, therefore, that the underlying problem in ADD is either a deficiency of those transmitters or an abnormality of their receptors. However, most people with ADD have normal dopamine release and receptors, and many people with abnormal dopamine receptors do not have ADD (Faraone & Biederman, 1998; Swanson et al., 2000). Perhaps understanding the drugs that relieve the problem doesn't tell us what caused the problem. One study found that methylphenidate improves attention even for normal healthy children, who presumably have normal dopamine activity (Zahn, Rapoport, & Thompson, 1980).

Drugs that alleviate depression and schizophrenia also act on dopamine and serotonin synapses, but again the relationship between the neurotransmitters and the behavior is complex. We still have much to learn about the relationship between the elements of the nervous system and their behavioral outcomes.

THE NERVOUS SYSTEM AND BEHAVIOR

If you lose part of your brain, do you also lose part of your mind? Why should psychologists care about the brain and the effects of brain damage? The reasons are both practical and theoretical. A practical reason is to distinguish between people who act strangely because of bad experiences and people who have brain disorders. There's no point in talking to someone about deep-seated psychological conflicts if the real problem is a brain tumor.

A theoretical reason is that studying the brain helps explain the organization of behavior. In some manner behavior must be made up of component parts, but what are they? Is behavior composed of ideas? Sensations? Movements? Personality characteristics? And how do the various components combine to produce the overall pattern? One way to answer such questions is to take behavior apart, one piece at a time, and brain damage does exactly that.

A related reason is that studying the brain sheds light on the mind–brain relationship. According to brain researchers, the mind *is* brain activity. But what exactly does that statement mean? And if it is so, why is it so? And how does brain activity produce experience? We cannot answer these questions, but studies of the brain at least help us come closer to an understanding.

The Major Divisions of the Nervous System

central nervous system
the brain and the spinal cord.

peripheral nervous system
the bundles of axons that convey messages between the spinal cord and the rest of the body.

somatic nervous system
peripheral nerves that communicate with the skin and muscles.

Psychologists and biologists distinguish between the central nervous system and the peripheral nervous system. The **central nervous system** consists of *the brain and the spinal cord.* The central nervous system communicates with the rest of the body by the **peripheral nervous system**, which is composed of *bundles of axons between the spinal cord and the rest of the body.* The *peripheral nerves that communicate with the skin and muscles* are collectively called the **somatic nervous system**. Those that control the heart, stomach, and other organs are called

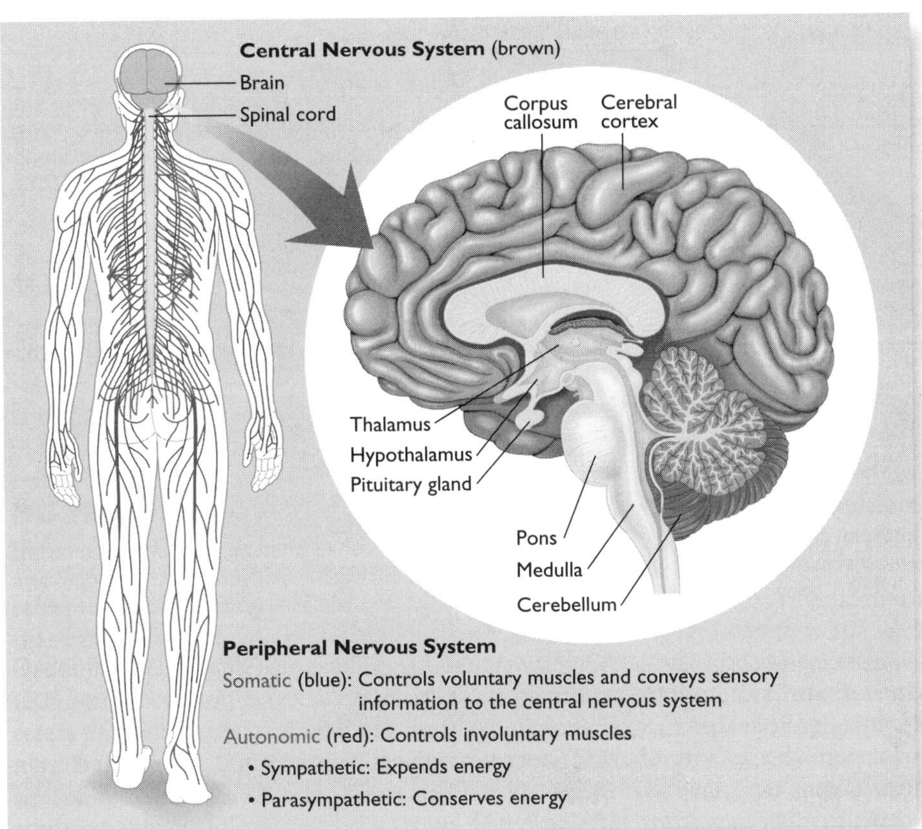

FIGURE 5.12

The nervous system has two major divisions: the central nervous system and the peripheral nervous system. Each of these has major subdivisions, as shown.

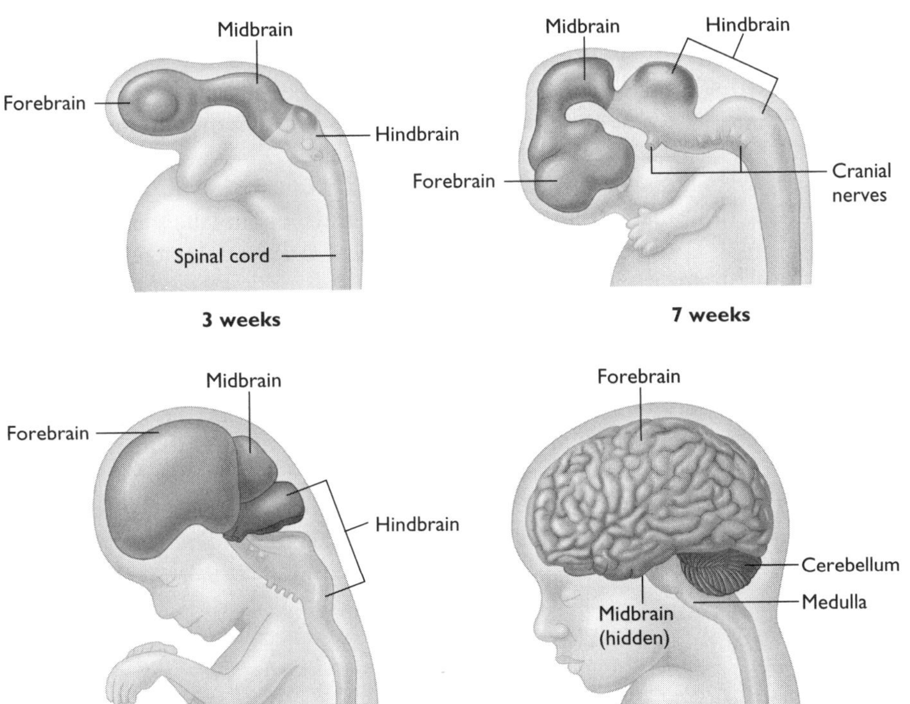

FIGURE 5.13

The human brain begins development as three lumps. By birth the forebrain has grown much larger than either the midbrain or the hindbrain, although all three structures perform essential functions.

the *autonomic nervous system.* Figure 5.12 summarizes these major divisions of the nervous system.

Early in its embryological development, the central nervous system of vertebrates, including humans, is a tube with three lumps, as shown in Figure 5.13.

FIGURE 5.14

The major divisions of the human central nervous system, as seen from the midline.

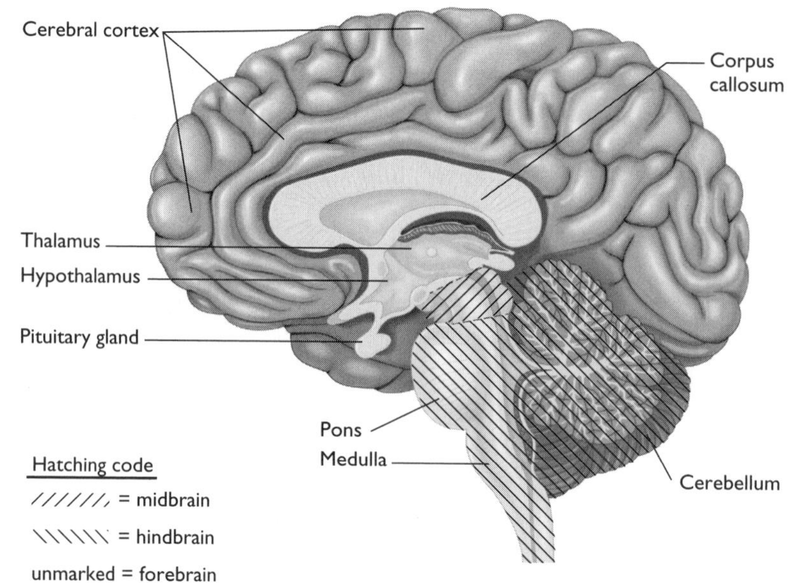

hemisphere
the left or right half of the brain; each hemisphere is responsible for sensation and motor control on the opposite side of the body.

cerebral cortex
the outer surface of the forebrain.

occipital lobe
the rear portion of each cerebral hemisphere, critical for vision.

parietal lobe
a portion of each cerebral hemisphere; the main receiving area for the sense of touch and for the awareness of one's own body and perception of location of the body in space.

These lumps develop into the *forebrain,* the *midbrain,* and the *hindbrain;* the rest of the tube develops into the spinal cord (Figure 5.14). The forebrain, which contains the cerebral cortex and other structures, is by far the dominant portion of the brain in mammals, especially in humans.

The Forebrain The forebrain consists of two **hemispheres**, *the left and right halves* (Figure 5.15). Each hemisphere is responsible for sensation and motor control on the opposite side of the body. Why does each hemisphere control the opposite side instead of its own side? People have speculated, but no one knows. We shall consider the differences between the left and right hemisphere in more detail later in this chapter.

The *outer covering of the forebrain,* known as the **cerebral cortex**, is especially prominent in humans. You have probably heard people talk about "having a lot of gray matter." Gray matter is composed of cell bodies and dendrites, which are grayer than the axons, and the cerebral cortex is by far your biggest area of gray matter. The interior of the forebrain beneath the cerebral cortex consists of axons, many of them covered with *myelin,* a white insulation. You can see areas of gray matter and white matter in Figure 5.16.

For the sake of convenience, we describe the cortex in terms of four *lobes*: occipital, parietal, temporal, and frontal, as shown in Figure 5.17. The **occipital lobe**, *at the rear of the head, is specialized for vision.* People with damage in this area have *cortical blindness*: They have no conscious vision, no object recognition, and no visual imagery (not even in dreams), although they still have visual reflexes, such as eye blinks, that do not depend on the cerebral cortex. They also tend to set their wake–sleep cycles so they wake up in the day and get sleepy at night, again because this aspect of behavior depends on subcortical brain areas, not the cerebral cortex.

The **parietal lobe**, *just anterior (forward) from the occipital lobe, is specialized for the body senses, including touch, pain, temperature, awareness of the location of body parts, and perception of location of the body in space.* The **primary somatosensory** (body-sensory) **cortex**, *a strip in the anterior portion of the parietal lobe, has neurons sensitive to touch in different body areas,* as shown in Figure 5.18. Note that in Figure 5.18a larger areas are devoted to touch in the more sensitive parts of the body, such as the lips and hands, than to less sensitive areas, such as the abdomen and the back. Damage to any part of the somatosensory cortex will impair sensation from the corresponding part of the body. Extensive damage here also interferes

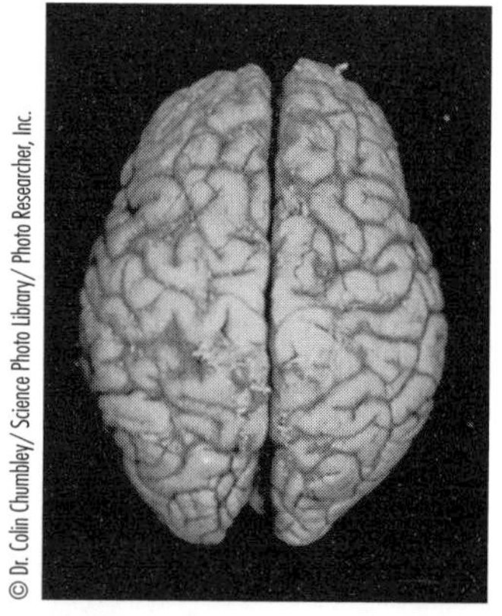

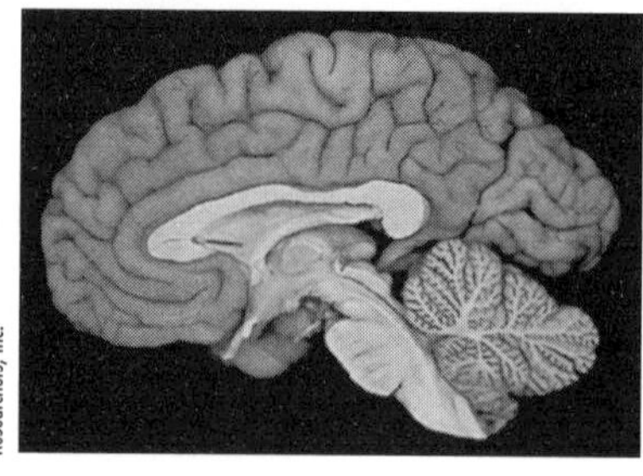

FIGURE 5.15

The human cerebral cortex: (a) left and right hemispheres; (b) inside view of a complete hemisphere. The folds greatly extend the brain's surface area.

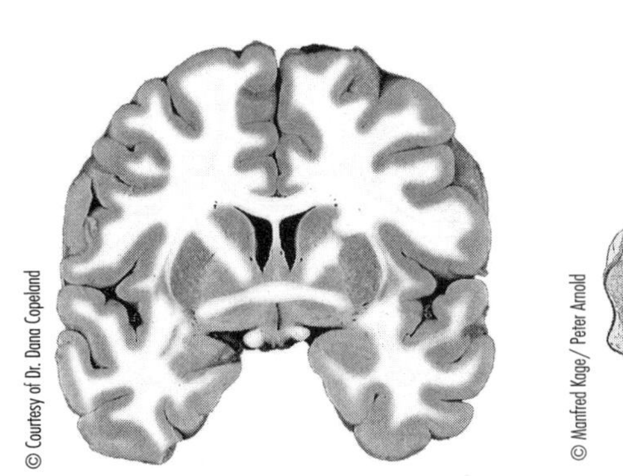

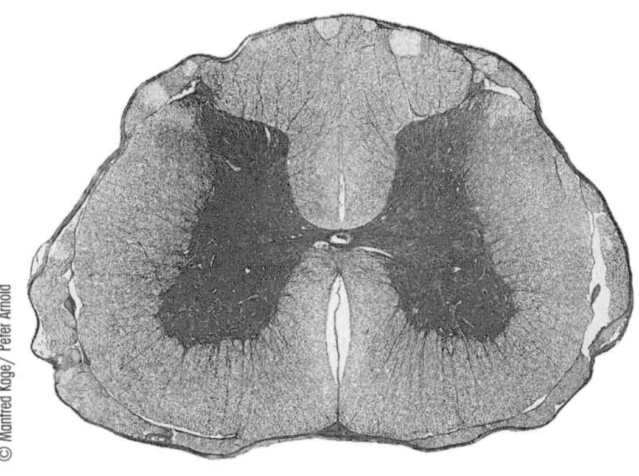

FIGURE 5.16

(a) This cross section of a human brain shows gray matter (mostly cell bodies and dendrites) and white matter (axons). The whiteness comes from myelin, a fatty sheath that surrounds many axons. (b) The H-shaped structure in the center of the spinal cord is gray matter, composed largely of cell bodies. The surrounding white matter consists of axons. (*Source: Manfred Kage/Peter Arnold, Inc.*)

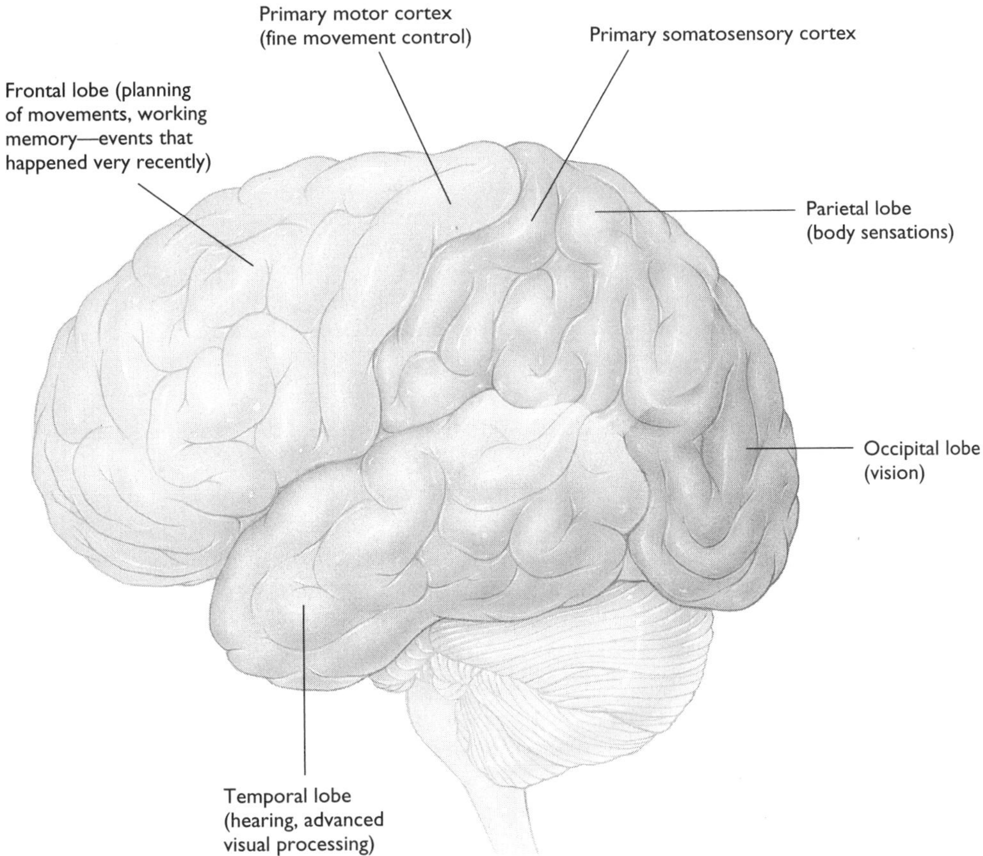

FIGURE 5.17

The four lobes of the human cerebral cortex, with indications of some of their major functions.

with spatial attention. After parietal damage, people see something but cannot decipher where it is relative to their body; consequently, they have trouble reaching toward it, walking around it, or shifting attention from one object to another. Because they cannot locate objects in space, they often confuse two objects. While looking at a yellow lemon and a red tomato, they might report seeing a yellow tomato and no lemon at all (Robertson, 2003). Most intact people can hardly imagine what the world must look like after parietal damage.

primary somatosensory cortex a strip in the anterior (forward) part of the parietal lobe that receives most touch sensations and other information about the body.

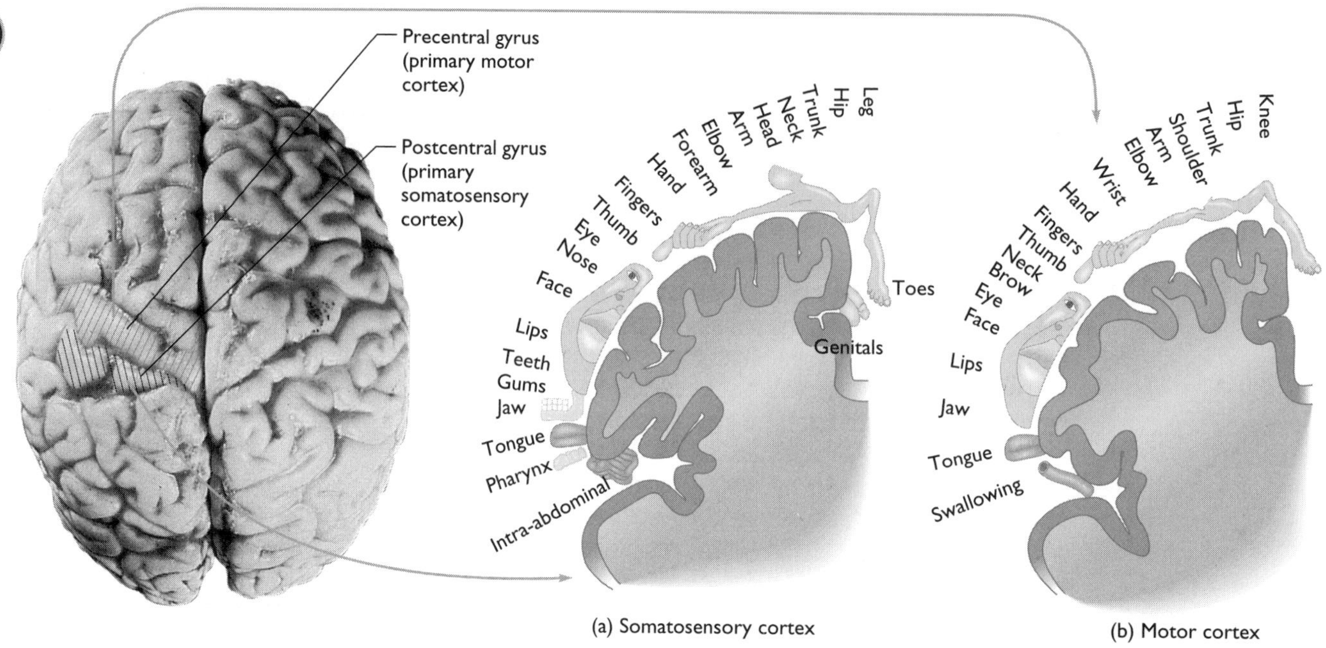

FIGURE 5.18

(a) The primary somatosensory cortex and (b) the primary motor cortex, illustrating which part of the body each brain area controls. Larger areas of the cortex are devoted to body parts that need to be controlled with great precision, such as the face and hands. (*Parts a and b adapted from* The Cerebral Cortex of Man *by W. Penfield and T. Rasmussen, Macmillan Library Reference. Reprinted by permission of Gale, a division of Cengage Learning.*)

temporal lobe
a portion of each cerebral hemisphere; the main processing area for hearing, complex aspects of vision, and certain aspects of emotional behavior.

The **temporal lobe** of each hemisphere, *located toward the left and right sides of the head, is the main processing area for hearing and some of the complex aspects of vision.* People with damage to small areas of the temporal lobe show striking and specialized deficits, such as an inability to recognize faces and other complex patterns (Tarr & Gauthier, 2000); difficulty perceiving visual motion (Zihl, von Cramon, & Mai, 1983); or difficulty recognizing melodies and other complex sounds. One area in the temporal lobe of the left hemisphere is important for language comprehension. Damage in this area produces *Wernicke's aphasia,* characterized by trouble remembering the names of objects and understanding speech, although these people do a little better if someone speaks slowly. Their own speech, largely lacking nouns and verbs, is hard to understand, and they resort to made-up expressions, as do normal people if they are pressured to talk faster than they can think of the correct words (Dick et al., 2001).

Other parts of the temporal lobe are critical for certain aspects of emotion. The *amygdala* (Figure 5.19), a structure within the temporal lobe, responds strongly to emotional situations and to facial expressions that convey emotion. People with damage to the amygdala are slow to process emotional information (Baxter & Murray, 2002). Apparently, their problem is not that they cannot feel fear, for example, but that they are not sure when to feel fear. If you were driving down a steep, winding mountain road and suddenly discovered that your brakes weren't working, how frightened would you be? On a scale from 0 to 9, almost everyone rates this situation as 9, but someone with amygdala damage rates it about 6 (Adolphs, Russell, & Tranel, 1999).

In later chapters we shall return to examine some of the structures that you see in Figure 5.19. The hypothalamus and amygdala are important for emotional and motivated behaviors.

frontal lobe
a portion of each cerebral hemisphere at the anterior pole, with sections that control movement and certain aspects of memory.

primary motor cortex
a strip in the posterior (rear) part of the frontal cortex that controls fine movements, such as hand and finger movements.

The **frontal lobe,** *at the anterior (forward) pole of the brain,* includes the **primary motor cortex,** *a structure that is important for the planned control of fine movements,* such as moving one finger at a time. As with the primary somatosensory cortex, each area of

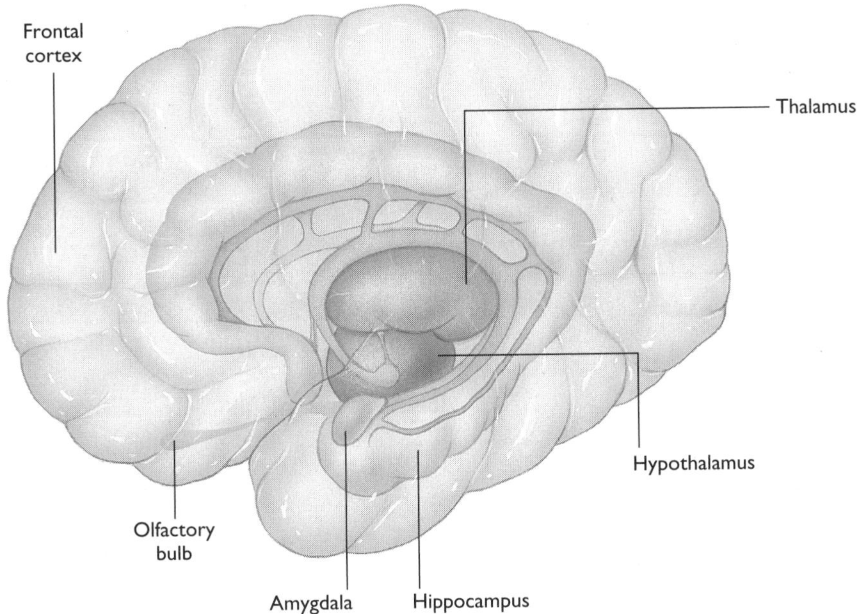

FIGURE 5.19

A view of the forebrain, showing internal structures as though the cerebral cortex were transparent.

prefrontal cortex
an area in the anterior portion of the frontal lobes, critical for planning movements and for certain aspects of memory.

thalamus
a forebrain area that relays information to the cerebral cortex.

pons
a structure adjacent to the medulla that receives sensory input from the head and controls many muscles in the head.

medulla
a structure that is located in the hindbrain and is an elaboration of the spinal cord; controls many muscles in the head and several life-preserving functions, such as breathing.

spinal cord
that part of the central nervous system that communicates with sensory neurons and motor neurons below the level of the head.

reflex
a rapid, automatic response to a stimulus.

the primary motor cortex controls a different part of the body, and larger areas are devoted to precise movements of the tongue and fingers than to, say, the shoulder and elbow muscles. The *anterior sections of the frontal lobe,* called the **prefrontal cortex,** contribute to the organization and planning of movements and to certain aspects of memory. Indeed, planning a movement depends on memory. Recall, for example, the delayed-response task: The individual must remember a signal during a delay and then make the appropriate movement. Certain areas in the left frontal lobe are essential for producing language.

How the Cerebral Cortex Communicates with the Body The only sensory information that goes directly to the cerebral cortex is olfaction (the sense of smell). Touch, pain, and other skin senses enter the spinal cord, which sends information that eventually reaches the **thalamus,** *a forebrain area that relays information to the cerebral cortex* (Figure 5.19). Vision, hearing, and taste information also goes through several synapses before reaching the thalamus and then the cerebral cortex.

The cerebral cortex does not directly control the muscles. It sends information to the **pons** and **medulla,** *which control the muscles of the head* (e.g., for chewing, swallowing, and breathing), and the **spinal cord,** *which controls the muscles from the neck down* (Figures 5.14 and 5.20). The spinal cord also controls many reflexes that do not require the forebrain. A **reflex** is a *rapid, automatic response to a stimulus,* such as unconscious adjustments of your legs while you are walking or quickly jerking your hand away from something hot.

The medulla, pons, and midbrain also contain the *reticular formation* and several other systems that send messages throughout the forebrain to regulate its arousal (Young & Pigott, 1999). A malfunction in these systems, depending on its nature and location, can render someone either persistently sleepy or persistently aroused.

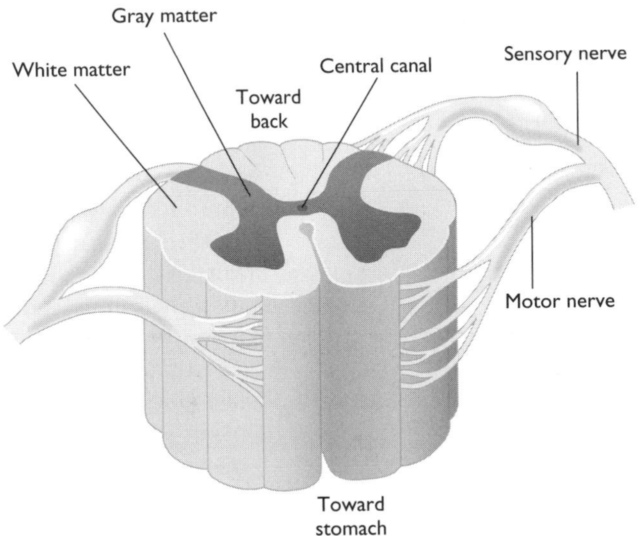

FIGURE 5.20

The spinal cord receives sensory information from all parts of the body except the head. Motor nerves in the spinal cord send messages to control the muscles and glands.

Sympathetic system	Parasympathetic system
Uses much energy	**Conserves energy**
• Pupils open	• Pupils constrict
• Saliva decreases	• Saliva flows
• Pulse quickens	• Pulse slows
• Sweat increases	• Stomach churns
• Stomach less active	
• Epinephrine (adrenaline) secreted	

FIGURE 5.21

The sympathetic nervous system prepares the body for brief bouts of vigorous activity; the parasympathetic nervous system promotes digestion and other nonemergency functions. Although both systems are active at all times, the balance can shift from a predominance of one to a predominance of the other.

The **cerebellum** (Latin for "little brain"), *another part of the hindbrain,* is important for any behavior that requires aim or timing, such as tapping out a rhythm, judging which of two visual stimuli is moving faster, and judging whether the delay between one pair of sounds is shorter or longer than the delay between another pair (Ivry & Diener, 1991; Keele & Ivry, 1990). It is also essential to learned responses that require precise timing (Krupa, Thompson, & Thompson, 1993).

The Autonomic Nervous System and Endocrine System The **autonomic nervous system,** closely associated with the spinal cord, *controls the internal organs such as the heart.* The term *autonomic* means involuntary, or automatic, in the sense that we have little voluntary control of it. We are generally unaware of its activity, although it does receive information from, and sends information to, the brain and the spinal cord.

cerebellum
(Latin for "little brain") a hindbrain structure that is active in the control of movement, especially for complex, rapid motor skills and behaviors that require precise timing.

autonomic nervous system
a system of neurons that controls the internal organs such as the heart.

endocrine system
a set of glands that produce hormones and release them into the bloodstream.

hormone
a chemical released by glands and conveyed by the blood to other parts of the body, where it alters activity.

The autonomic nervous system has two parts: (a) The *sympathetic nervous system,* controlled by a chain of neurons lying just outside the spinal cord, increases heart rate and breathing rate and readies the body for vigorous fight-or-flight activities. (b) The *parasympathetic nervous system,* controlled by neurons at the very top and very bottom levels of the spinal cord, decreases heart rate, increases digestive activities, and in general promotes activities of the body that take place during rest (Figure 5.21).

The autonomic nervous system has some control over the **endocrine system,** *a set of glands that produce hormones and release them into the blood.* Hormones controlled by the hypothalamus and pituitary gland also regulate the endocrine system. Figure 5.22 shows some of the major endocrine glands. **Hormones** are *chemicals released by glands and conveyed via the blood to alter activity in various organs.* Hormones' effects resemble those of neurotransmitters. The difference is that a neurotransmitter is released immediately adjacent to a synapse, whereas a hormone flows with the blood. Some hormonal effects are brief, such as changes in blood pressure, but others can last months, such as preparation for migration or hibernation.

Measuring Brain Activity

Up to this point, you have been reading about the functions of various brain areas, as well as those of endocrine organs and so forth. But how did we learn about these functions? For many years nearly all the conclusions came from studies of medical patients, especially brain-damaged patients, but their brain damage could not be examined until after death. Researchers can now supplement such evidence with modern techniques that examine brain anatomy and activity in living people.

electroencephalograph (EEG)
a device that uses electrodes on the scalp to record rapid changes in brain electrical activity.

magnetoencephalograph (MEG)
a device that records rapid magnetic changes during brain activity.

positron-emission tomography (PET)
a technique that provides a high-resolution image of brain activity by recording radioactivity emitted from injected chemicals.

An **electroencephalograph (EEG)** *uses electrodes on the scalp to record rapid changes in brain electrical activity* (Figure 5.23). A similar method is a **magnetoencephalograph (MEG),** *which records magnetic changes.* Both of these methods provide data on a millisecond-by-millisecond basis, so they can measure people's reactions to lights and sounds, as well as how reactions depend on instructions, previous experience, and so forth. However, because EEG and MEG record from the surface of the scalp, they provide little detail about the location of the brain activity.

Another method offers much better anatomical localization, with information on a minute-by-minute basis: **Positron-emission tomography (PET)** *records radioactivity of various brain areas emitted from injected chemicals* (Phelps &

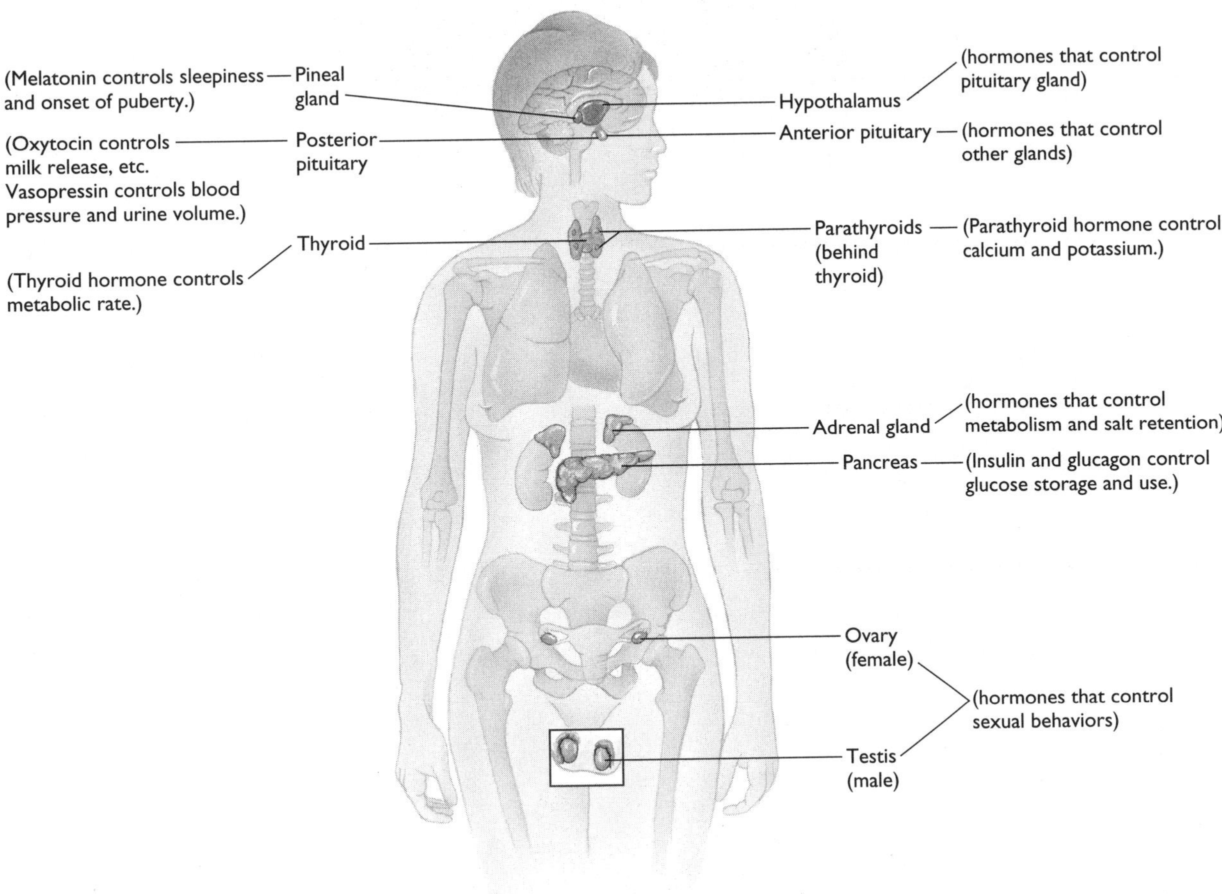

FIGURE 5.22

Glands in the endocrine system produce hormones and release them into the bloodstream. This figure shows only some of the endocrine glands and some of their most abundant hormones.

Mazziotta, 1985). First someone receives an injection of a radioactively labeled compound such as glucose. Glucose, a simple sugar that is the brain's main fuel (almost its only fuel), is absorbed mainly in the most active brain areas. Therefore, radioactivity comes primarily from those areas. Detectors around the head record the amount of radioactivity coming from each brain area and send that information to a computer, which generates an image such as the one in Figure 5.24. Red indicates areas of greatest activity, followed by yellow, green, and blue. Unfortunately, PET scans are expensive and require exposing the brain to radioactivity, a risky procedure, especially with repeated use.

Another technique, **functional magnetic resonance imaging (fMRI),** *uses magnetic detectors outside the head to compare the amounts of hemoglobin with and without oxygen in different brain areas* (J. D. Cohen, Noll, & Schneider, 1993). (Adding or removing oxygen changes the response of hemoglobin to a magnetic field.) Highly active brain areas use much oxygen and therefore decrease the oxygen bound to hemoglobin in the blood. The fMRI technique thus indicates which brain areas are currently the most active, as in Figure 5.25.

functional magnetic resonance imaging (fMRI)
a technique that uses magnetic detectors outside the head to measure the amounts of hemoglobin, with and without oxygen, in different parts of the brain and thereby provides an indication of current activity levels in various brain areas.

Brain scans are a potentially powerful research tool, but interpreting the results requires careful research. For example, suppose we want to determine which brain areas are important for recent memory. We record activity while someone is

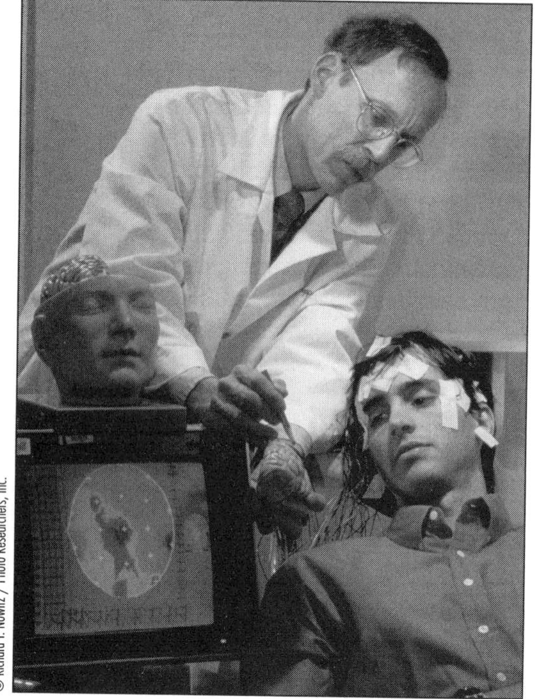

FIGURE 5.23

An EEG records momentary changes in electrical potential from the scalp, revealing an average of the activity of brain cells beneath each electrode.

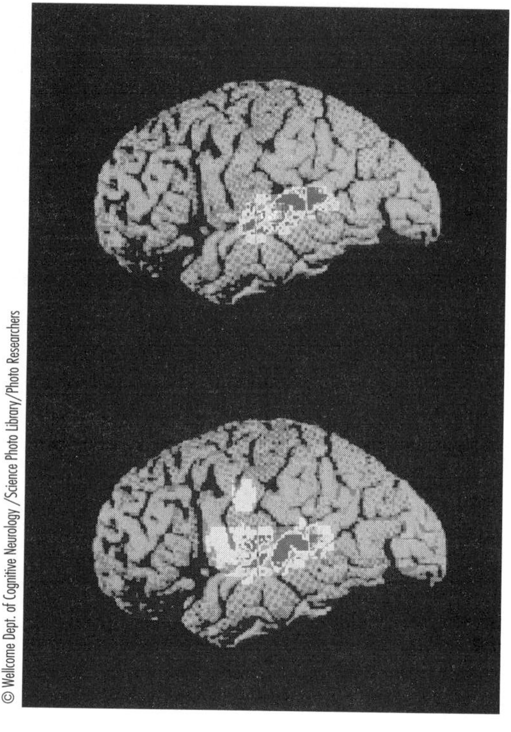

FIGURE 5.24

A PET scan of the human brain. Red shows areas of most-increased activity during some task, yellow shows areas of next most-increased activity.

engaged in a memory task and compare that activity to times when the person is doing . . . what? Doing nothing? That comparison wouldn't work; the memory task presumably includes sensory stimuli, motor responses, attention, and other processes besides memory. Researchers must design a comparison task that requires attention to the same sensory stimuli, the same hand movements, and so forth as the memory task.

Effects of Experience on Brain Structure

Several illustrations in this text have been labeled "the" human nervous system. We do not need to specify whose nervous system because the gross structure is about the same from one person to another anywhere in the world. The detailed anatomy does vary, however. For example, brain volume tends to shrink in old age (Sowell et al., 2003), and it declines sharply with Alzheimer's disease and other medical conditions. The brain also shows small beneficial changes as a result of experience. Both axons and dendrites almost constantly withdraw old branches and grow new ones, producing a periodic turnover of synapses. Dendritic changes and synaptic renewal are particularly common in young animals (and presumably humans also) and become progressively less vigorous with advancing age (Grutzendler, Kasthuri, & Gan, 2002).

Think About It

Suppose you want to determine which brain areas are active during recent memory. Try to design some task that requires memory and a comparison task that is similar in every other way except for the memory requirement.

Can you improve your brain functioning by "exercising" your brain, as you can with your muscles? People have long assumed so. In former times students were taught ancient Latin and Greek on the assumption that they would acquire mental discipline that would make them more accomplished in whatever other tasks they undertook. Today, a similar argument is sometimes offered for why

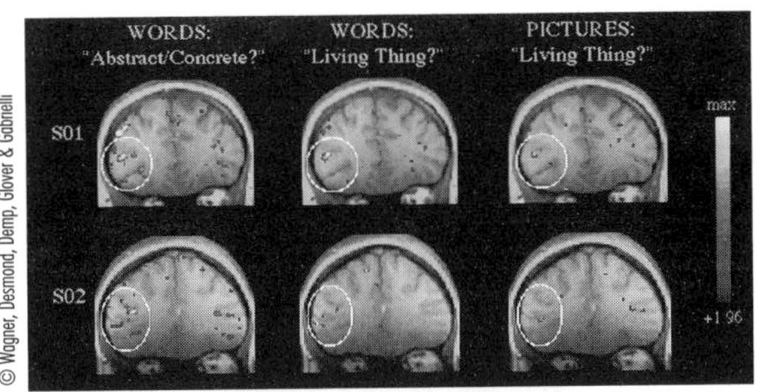

© Wagner, Desmond, Demp, Glover & Gabrielli

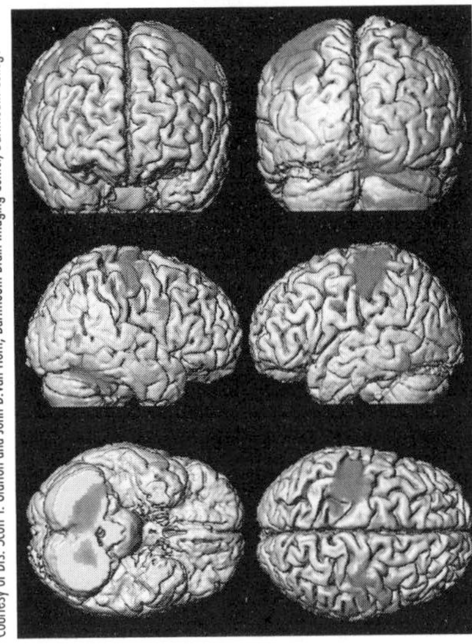

Courtesy of Drs. Scott T. Grafton and John D. Van Horn, Dartmouth Brain Imaging Center, Dartmouth College

FIGURE 5.25

(a) This brain scan was made with functional magnetic resonance imaging (fMRI). Participants looked at words or pictures and judged whether each item was abstract or concrete, living or nonliving. Yellow shows the areas most activated by this judgment; red shows areas less strongly activated. (*From Wagner, Desmond, Demb, Glover, & Gabrieli, 1997. Photo courtesy of Anthony D. Wagner*) (b) A male volunteer, using his dominant right hand, was either rotating a small cylinder or resting in alternating 30-second intervals during a 5-minute fMRI scan, yielding six perspectives in which motor areas of the left brain are highlighted.

students should study Shakespeare or calculus. But is it true? There is such a thing as learning to study, but otherwise, it is difficult to demonstrate that studying one topic carries over to unrelated topics (Barnett & Ceci, 2002). For example, practicing chess would make you better at chess but not at anything else.

When we look at brain anatomy, the result is that practicing a particular skill expands the dendritic spread and probably the cell bodies of the brain areas relevant to that skill. For example, professional musicians have a larger than average auditory cortex (Schneider et al., 2002) and expansions of several other brain areas important for timing and other musical processes (Gaser & Schlaug, 2003). The brain area representing the fingers expands in people who spend much time reading Braille (Pascual-Leone, Wasserman, Sadato, & Hallett, 1995). The longer someone has been a London taxi driver, the larger the posterior hippocampus, a brain area important for spatial memory (Maguire et al., 2000).

The hypothesis that using your brain in general expands your brain in general is harder to demonstrate. Rats that live in large cages with other rats do show brain enlargement relative to those in small individual cages (Greenough, 1975), but much or all of that effect can be attributed to increased physical activity, which increases blood flow to the head (van Praag, Kempermann, & Gage, 2000). Physical activity also benefits human brain size, especially in old age (Colcombe et al., 2003). Brain autopsies have shown that people with more education or greater mental activity in their daily lives tend to have greater branching in their dendrites (Jacobs, Schall, & Scheibel, 1993). However, we cannot draw a cause-and-effect conclusion. It is possible that education and mental activity promote brain growth but also possible that people who started with more dendritic branching succeeded well in their education and were drawn to more intellectual activities. In short, no evidence available so far indicates unambiguously that "exercising" your brain expands it anatomically.

For many decades researchers believed that all neurons formed before birth or early after it, so that beyond early infancy one could only lose neurons and never gain new ones. However, later researchers found that in a few brain areas, it is possible for *undifferentiated cells called* **stem cells** to develop into additional neurons (Gage, 2000; Graziadei & deHan, 1973; Song, Stevens, & Gage, 2002). Development of new neurons is well established in rats and songbirds, although not yet clear in humans, as the studies in humans may not have distinguished adequately between new neurons and new glia cells (Eriksson et al., 1998; Rakic, 2002). At most, however, new neurons form slowly, sporadically, and only in certain brain areas. It is not a routine matter like growing new skin cells or blood cells.

stem cells
undifferentiated cells.

The "Binding Problem"

As researchers answered certain questions about brain function, a new one arose: One part of your brain is responsible for hearing, another for touch, several other areas for various aspects of vision, and so forth, and those areas have few if any direct connections with one another. So how do you get the experience of being a single "self?" If you shake a baby's toy rattle, how do you know that the object you see is also what you hear and feel? *The question of how separate brain areas combine forces to produce a unified perception of a single object* is the **binding problem** (Treisman, 1999). The binding problem is at the heart of the profound and difficult mind–brain problem.

binding problem
the question of how separate brain areas combine forces to produce a unified perception of a single object.

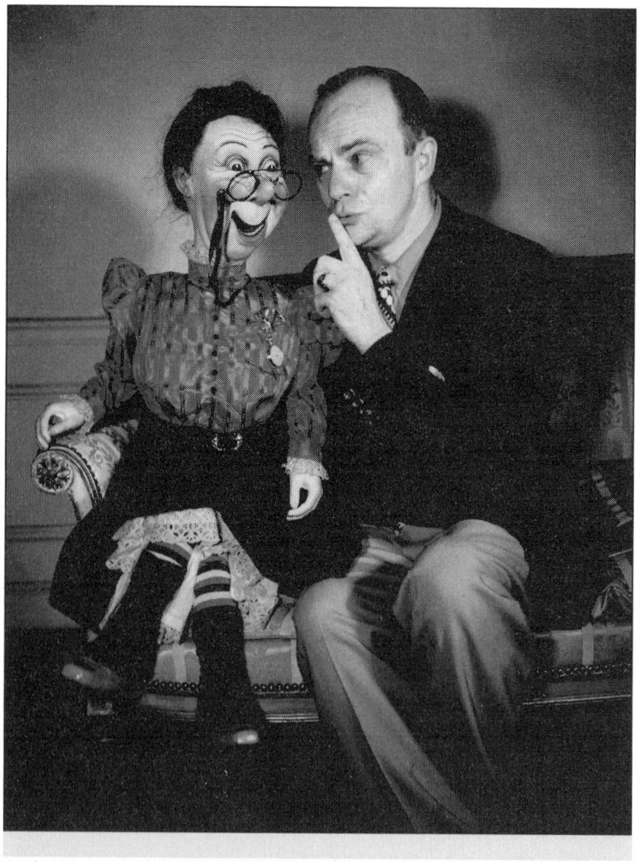

A naive explanation would be that all the various parts of the brain funnel their information to a "little person in the head" who puts it all together. Although no one takes that concept seriously, the underlying idea is hard to abandon, and brain researchers have sometimes imagined a "master area" of the brain that would serve the same purpose. Research on the cerebral cortex, however, has found no master area or central processor. Few neurons receive a combination of visual and auditory information or visual and touch information.

In fact the mystery deepens: Even in vision, different brain areas specialize in different aspects of the stimulus, such as shape, color, and movement. When you see a brown rabbit hopping, one brain area is most sensitive to the shape, another most sensitive to the movement, and another most sensitive to the brownness. The division of labor is not complete, but it is enough to make researchers wonder how we combine the different aspects, or "bind" them into a single object (Gegenfurtner, 2003).

The answer is not fully known, but part of the answer lies with the parietal cortex, important for spatial perception. Go back to shaking a toy rattle: If you can identify the location of your hand, the location of the rattle you see, and the location of the sound source, you probably can link the sensations together. If, like someone with parietal cortex damage, you cannot locate anything in space, you probably won't bind sensations into a single experience (Robertson, 2003). We also know that binding occurs only for precisely simultaneous events. Have you ever watched a film or television show in which the soundtrack is noticeably ahead of or behind

We hear the sound as coming from the dummy's mouth only if sound and movements are synchronized. In general, binding depends on simultaneity of two kinds of stimuli.

the picture? If so, you knew that the sound wasn't coming from the performers on screen. You get the same experience watching a poorly dubbed foreign-language film. However, when you watch a ventriloquist, the motion of the dummy's mouth simultaneous with the sound causes you to perceive the sound as coming from the dummy.

We also know that binding takes time. If you see a brief flash on the screen showing a red circle and a green square, you might see red, green, circle, and square but not be sure which color went with which shape. The more complex the stimulus, the longer it takes to bind its elements into a whole (Holcombe & Cavanagh, 2001). People with parietal lobe damage have trouble binding a stimulus even with prolonged exposure (Treisman, 1999; Wheeler & Treisman, 2002).

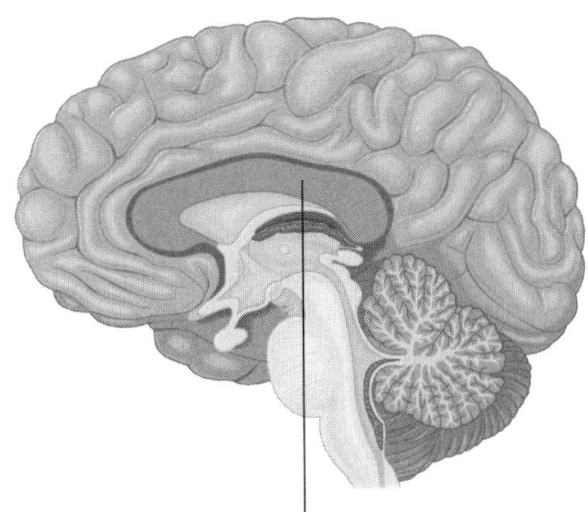

FIGURE 5.26
The corpus callosum is a large set of axons that convey information between the two hemispheres of the cerebral cortex. (a) A midline view showing the location of the corpus callosum. (b) A horizontal section showing how each axon of the corpus callosum links one spot in the left hemisphere to a corresponding spot in the right hemisphere.

The Corpus Callosum and the Split-Brain Phenomenon

What would happen if the two hemispheres of your brain could not communicate with each other? Such a situation occurs after damage to the **corpus callosum,** *a set of axons connecting the cerebral cortex of the left and right hemispheres* (Figure 5.26). Corpus callosum damage prevents someone from comparing sights seen on the left to those on the right and from comparing something felt with the left hand to something in the right. In some ways the person now has two half-brains side by side, and maybe even two spheres of consciousness.

Occasionally, brain surgeons cut the corpus callosum in an effort to relieve **epilepsy**, *a condition in which neurons somewhere in the brain emit abnormal rhythmic, spontaneous impulses.* Depending on where the abnormal impulses start and spread, epilepsy can produce varied effects. Most people with epilepsy respond well to antiepileptic drugs and live normal lives. A few, however, continue to have frequent major seizures. When all else fails, surgeons sometimes recommend cutting the corpus callosum. The original idea was that epileptic seizures would be limited to one hemisphere and therefore less incapacitating.

The operation was more successful than expected. Not only are the seizures limited to one side of the body, but they also become less frequent. A possible explanation is that the operation interrupts the feedback loop between the two hemispheres that allows an epileptic seizure to echo back and forth. However, although these split-brain patients resume a normal life, they have some interesting behavioral effects. First, we need to consider some anatomy.

Connections Between the Eyes and the Brain *Note: This section presents a concept that is contrary to most people's expectations, and the left-right–right-left connections can be confusing. So please read carefully!*

Because each hemisphere of the brain controls the muscles on the opposite side of the body, each half of the brain needs to see the opposite side of the world. This does *not* mean that your left hemisphere sees with the right eye or that your right hemisphere sees with the left eye.

Convince yourself: Close one eye, then open it, and close the other. Note that you see almost the same view with both eyes. You see each half of the world with part of your left eye and part of your right eye.

Figure 5.27, which shows the human visual system, warrants careful study. Light from each half of the world strikes receptors on the opposite side of *each* retina. (The retina is the lining in the back of each eye. The retina is lined with

corpus callosum
a large set of axons connecting the left and right hemispheres of the cerebral cortex and thus enabling the two hemispheres to communicate with each other.

epilepsy
a condition characterized by abnormal rhythmic activity of brain neurons.

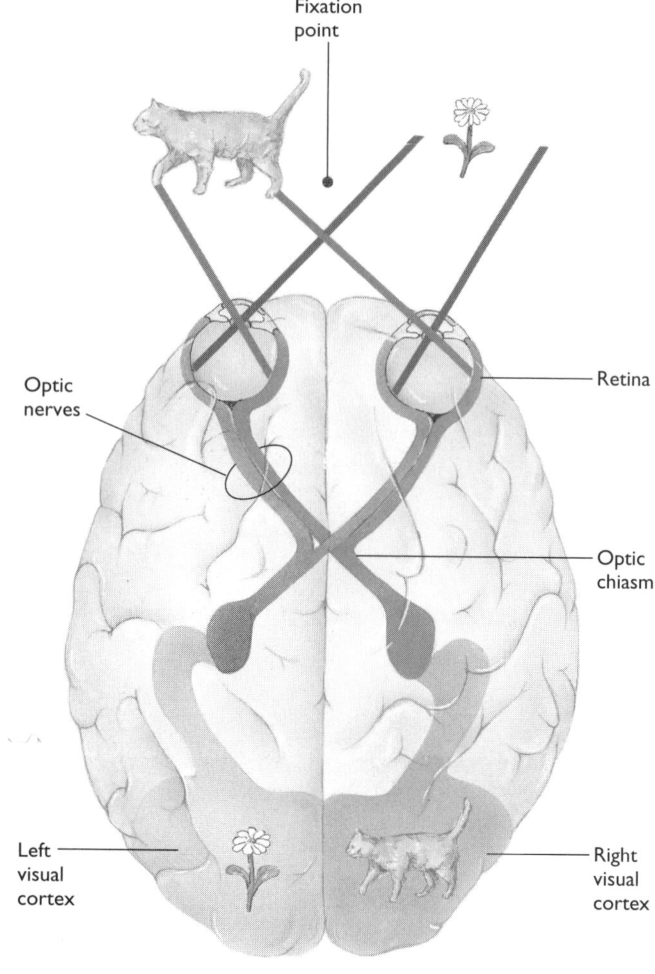

FIGURE 5.27

In the human visual system (viewed here from above), light from either half of the world crosses through the pupils to strike the opposite side of each retina. Axons from the left half of each retina travel to the left hemisphere of the brain; axons from the right half of each retina travel to the right hemisphere of the brain.

receptors.) Information from the left half of each retina travels via the *optic nerves* to the left hemisphere of the cerebral cortex; information from the right half of each retina travels via the optic nerves to the right hemisphere.

Here is one way to remember this material: *Light from each side of the world strikes the opposite side of the retina. The brain is connected to the eyes so that each hemisphere sees the opposite side of the world.* If you remember those two statements, you should be able to deduce that each hemisphere is connected to the half of each retina *on the same side,* as shown in Figure 5.27. You might also draw the diagram for yourself.

What about the very center of the retina? The cells in a thin strip down the center of each retina send axons to both sides of the brain.

Effects of Severing the Corpus Callosum For almost all right-handed people and about 60% of left-handed people, parts of the left hemisphere control speech. For most other left-handers, both hemispheres control speech. Complete right-hemisphere control of speech is rare. The right hemisphere is critical for understanding the emotional aspects of speech, however, as we shall see later.

Assuming you have left-hemisphere control of speech, can you talk about something you feel with the left hand or see in the left visual field? Yes, easily, if your brain is intact: The information enters your right hemisphere but then passes quickly across the corpus callosum to your left hemisphere.

The result is different if the corpus callosum is severed. A split-brain patient (someone whose corpus callosum has been cut) feels something with the left hand but cannot describe it because the information goes to the right (nonspeech) hemisphere (Nebes, 1974; Sperry, 1967). If asked to point to it, the person points correctly only with the left hand. In fact, while correctly pointing with the left hand, the person might say, "I have no idea what it was. I didn't feel anything." Evidently, the right hemisphere can understand the instructions and answer with the hand it controls, but it cannot talk.

Now consider what happens when a split-brain patient sees something (Figure 5.28). Ordinarily, the person moves the eyes and sees the same thing in both hemispheres. In the laboratory, however, researchers can flash information faster than the eyes can move. The person in Figure 5.28 focuses the eyes on a point in the middle of the screen. The investigator flashes a word such as *hatband* on the screen for a split second, too briefly for an eye movement, and asks for the word. The reply is, "band," which is what the left hemisphere saw. (Information from the right side, you will recall, goes to the left side of each retina and from there to the left hemisphere.) To the question of what *kind* of band it might be, the reply is, "I don't know. Jazz band? Rubber band?" However, the left hand points to a hat (which the right hemisphere saw).

Split-brain people get along reasonably well with common behaviors such as walking or even tying shoes because well-practiced behaviors don't need much input from the cerebral cortex anyway. The problem comes with unfamiliar

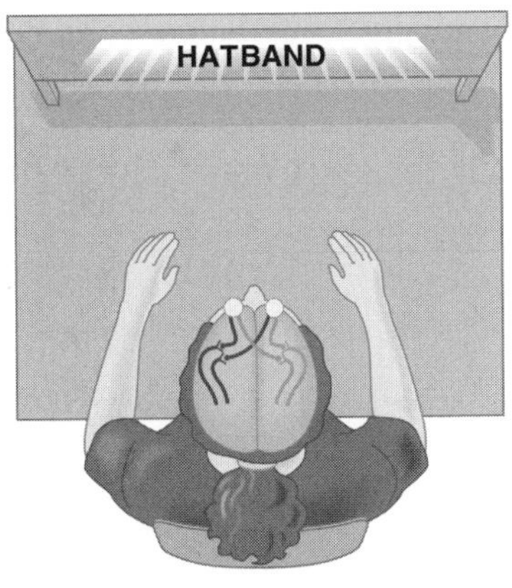

FIGURE 5.28

(a) When the word hatband is flashed on a screen, a split-brain patient reports only what the left hemisphere saw, *band* and (b) writes *band* with the right hand. However, (c) the left hand (controlled by the right hemisphere) points to a hat, which is what the right hemisphere saw.

behaviors. Two split-brain people were asked "pretend you're threading a needle" and "pretend you're attaching a fishhook to a line." The two behaviors require almost the same movements. The person who had frequently threaded a needle before the operation had no trouble threading an imaginary needle but couldn't show how to attach a fishhook. Another who had previously attached many fishhooks but never used a sewing needle had the opposite results (Franz, Waldie, & Smith, 2000).

In special circumstances the two hemispheres cooperate in clever ways. One split-brain person was looking at pictures flashed on a screen, as in Figure 5.28a. He could seldom name the objects flashed in the left visual field, but after some delay, he could name simple shapes. Here is how he did it: After seeing the object in the left visual field (with the right hemisphere), he let his eyes move around the room. (Both hemispheres control the eye muscles.) When the right hemisphere saw something with the same shape as the object it had just seen, it would stop moving the eyes. The left hemisphere just waited for the eyes to stop moving and then called out the shape of the object it saw.

The Right and Left Hemispheres How does the right hemisphere differ from the left? The right hemisphere does not speak, but it understands language, especially with short words and simple grammar. It is especially important for understanding the emotional content of speech; people with right-hemisphere damage often can't tell when a speaker is being sarcastic, and they frequently don't understand jokes (Beeman & Chiarello, 1998). The right hemisphere is also better than the left for recognizing and understanding facial expressions (Stone, Nisenson, Eliassen, & Gazzaniga, 1996) and for tasks that are hard to put into words, such as drawing pictures or arranging puzzle pieces.

Let me describe an interesting study. It will seem that I am changing the subject, but later you will see that I am not. People watched a videotape that showed each of 10 people speaking twice. In one speech they described themselves honestly, and in the other case they told nothing but lies. Do you think you could tell when someone was telling the truth? The average for MIT undergraduates was 47% correct, slightly *less* than they should have done by random guessing. Other groups did about equally badly, except for one group that managed to get 60% correct. (That's not great, but it's better than anyone else did.) Guess who could tell lies from truth. They were people with left-hemisphere brain damage! They could understand almost nothing of what people were saying, so they relied on gestures and facial expressions—which the right hemisphere understands quite well (Etcoff, Ekman, Magee, & Frank, 2000).

Split-brain surgery is rare. We study such patients not because you are likely to meet one but because they teach us something about brain organization: Although we cannot fully explain our experience of a unified consciousness, we see that it depends on communication across brain areas. If communication between the two hemispheres is lost, then each hemisphere becomes partly independent of the other.

Before closing this section, I want to caution you about a common misunderstanding. The left hemisphere is specialized for language and the right hemisphere for emotional perception and complex visuospatial tasks. Some writers have gone beyond this generalization to claim that the left hemisphere is logical and the right hemisphere is creative, so logical people are left brained and creative people are right brained. Some have even suggested that we could all become more creative if we could find a way to exercise the right hemisphere.

In fact, although certain tasks activate one hemisphere more than the other, complex tasks require both. What's the evidence that some people are left brained or that others are right brained? We have *no* evidence, except in the rare cases of people who have had damage to one hemisphere or the other. Nevertheless, the hypothesis is popular. Some people excuse themselves for thinking illogically by saying, "I'm a right-brained person," with the implication that *because* they are illogical, *therefore* they are creative!

REVIEW

- *Neuron structure.* A neuron, or nerve cell, consists of a cell body, dendrites, and an axon. The axon conveys information to other neurons.
- *The action potential.* Information is conveyed along an axon by an action potential, which is regenerated without loss of strength at each point along the axon.
- *Mechanism of the action potential.* An action potential depends on the entry of sodium into the axon. Anything that blocks this flow will block the action potential.
- *How neurons communicate.* A neuron communicates with another neuron by releasing a chemical called a neurotransmitter at a specialized junction called a synapse. A neurotransmitter can either excite or inhibit the next neuron.
- *Neurotransmitters and behavioral disorders.* An excess or a deficit of a particular neurotransmitter can lead to abnormal behavior, such as that exhibited by people with Parkinson's disease. However, understanding what happens at some kind of synapse is far removed from understanding the entire behavior pattern.
- *Central and peripheral nervous systems.* The central nervous system consists of the brain and the spinal cord. The peripheral nervous system consists of nerves that communicate between the central nervous system and the rest of the body.
- *The cerebral cortex.* The four lobes of the cerebral cortex and their primary functions are: occipital lobe, vision; temporal lobe, hearing and some aspects of vision; parietal lobe, body sensations; frontal lobe, preparation for movement. Damage in the cerebral cortex can produce specialized deficits depending on the location of damage.
- *Communication between the cerebral cortex and the rest of the body.* Information from the cerebral cortex passes to the medulla and then on into the spinal cord. The medulla and spinal cord have axons that receive sensory input from the periphery and other axons that send output to the muscles and glands.
- *Autonomic nervous system and endocrine system.* The autonomic nervous system controls the body's organs, preparing them for emergency activities or for vegetative activities. The endocrine system consists of organs that release hormones into the blood.
- *Imaging brain activity.* Modern technology enables researchers to develop images showing the structure and activity of various brain areas in living, waking people.

- *Experience and brain structure.* The anatomy of the nervous system is constantly in flux in small ways. Extensive practice of a behavior can modify brain structure, especially if the practice begins early in life.
- *The binding problem.* Brain researchers cannot yet explain how we develop a unified experience of an object even though our registers of hearing, touch, vision, and so forth occur in different brain areas that do not connect directly to one another. Even different aspects of vision depend on different brain areas.
- *Corpus callosum.* The corpus callosum is a set of axons through which the left and right hemispheres of the cortex communicate. If the corpus callosum is damaged, information that reaches one hemisphere cannot be shared with the other.
- *Connections from eyes to brain.* In humans information from the *left* visual field strikes the *right* half of both retinas, from which it is sent to the *right* hemisphere of the brain. Information from the *right* visual field strikes the *left* half of both retinas, from which it is sent to the *left* hemisphere.
- *Split-brain patients.* The left hemisphere is specialized for language in most people, so split-brain people can describe information only if it enters the left hemisphere. Because of the lack of direct communication between the left and right hemispheres in split-brain patients, such people show signs of having separate fields of awareness.

CHAPTER 5 PRACTICE EXAM

____ 1. The neuron is made up of the cell body, the ____, and the ____.
a. glia . . . dendrites
b. action potential . . . membrane
c. glia . . . axon
d. dendrites . . . axon

____ 2. Neurons communicate at the synapse via:
a. Moving onto the neuron's synapse membrane.
b. Reenergizing the movement of muscle.
c. releasing a chemical.
d. transmitting electricity.

____ 3. A neurotransmitter is?
a. a telegraphic like machine that transmits brain waves.
b. a chemical that travels across neurons.
c. a chemical that induces. somnambulism.
d. A positively charged ion that frees the cells membrane.

____ 4. Virtually all illegal and prescribed drugs do their work at
a. synapses.
b. blood neurons.
c. Neuronal targets.
d. Genetic alleles.

____ 5. Otto Loewi's experiment showed that neurons communicate
a. Via electrical charges.
b. with multiple neurons.
c. by neuronal vibration.
d. by releasing chemicals.

____ 6. Why does L-DOPA seem to work for Parkinson's disease?
a. It alleviates neuron weakness.
b. It strengthens existing neurons.
c. It increases levels of a synaptic transmitter that had declined.
d. It serves as a catalyst for growing neurons.

____ 7. Drugs that help those with attention deficit disorder lengthen the activity of dopamine and serotonin by blocking their reabsorption. What can we conclude from this drug action?
a. ADD is caused by a dopamine deficiency.
b. ADD is caused by a serotonin deficiency.
c. ADD is caused by chemical reabsorption.
d. We do not know the cause based on how drugs work.

____ 8. Nerves that transmit information from the sense organs to the spinal cord and brain, and from the spinal cord and brain to the glands and muscles, are known as the
a. central nervous system.
b. sympathetic nervous system.
c. autonomic nervous system.
d. peripheral nervous system.

____ 9. The occipital lobe's specialization is
a. vision.
b. touch.
c. hearing.
d. Smell.

____ 10. Damage to the parietal lobe would typically lead to problems with
a. hearing.
b. touch.
c. Smell.
d. vision.

____ 11. Damage to the temporal lobe would lead to problems with
a. hearing.
b. Smell.
c. Touch.
d. Vision.

____ 12. Functional magnetic resonance imaging (fMRI)
a. uses x-rays that provide images of brain anatomy.
b. Uses magnetic detectors to recording chemical movements of brain.
c. Records brain activity by using magnetic detectors to measure hemoglobin with and without oxygen.
d. Records brain activity with magnetic radiation traces.

_____ 13. The way distinct parts of the brain combine information to produce a clear perception of an object is
a. the "Binding Problem."
b. the "Bonding Problem."
c. the Natural Coalescence.
d. the Distinct Integration Issue.

_____ 14. After his brain was damaged, Mary cannot name what she sees in her left visual field. Yet, she can point to the correct answer with her left hand, and if she moves her eyes to the left, she can name the object. Mary likely has damage to the
a. occipital lobe.
b. corpus callosum.
c. temporal lobe.
d. Amygdale.

_____ 15. The popular notion that there are right brained and left brained people
a. is right since many people only use their left hemisphere.
b. is wrong because the hemispheres are combined.
c. is right because neurogenesis only occurs in the left of right hemisphere.
d. is wrong because all tasks involve both hemispheres.

Answers

1. D
2. C
3. B
4. A
5. D
6. C
7. D
8. D
9. A
10. B
11. A
12. C
13. A
14. B
15. D

CHAPTER 6: INTERPRETATION OF SENSORY INFORMATION

QUESTIONS

1. What are three things the chapter suggests subliminal perception cannot do?
2. What is one example of each of the things subliminal perception cannot do?
3. What can subliminal messages do?
4. How do we recognize people's faces?
5. What were the hypothesis, method, results, and interpretation of the Hubel and Weisel research on Feature Detection?
6. Why don't feature detectors explain perception?
7. How does Gestalt Psychology help us understand vision and hearing perception?
8. How are feature detectors and Gestalt Psychology complementary?
9. Why does an object appear stationary when you move your eyes?
10. What are two explanations for the moon illusion and why don't many psychologists accept these explanations?

VOCABULARY

1. closure
2. common fate
3. continuation
4. convergence
5. depth perception
6. feature detector
7. Gestalt psychology
8. good figure
9. induced movement
10. monocular cures
11. moon illusion
12. motion parallax
13. optical illusion
14. proximity
15. reversible figure
16. visual constancy

6 Interpretation of Sensory Information

Perception of Minimal Stimuli

Perception and the Recognition of Patterns

Perception of Movement and Depth

Optical Illusions

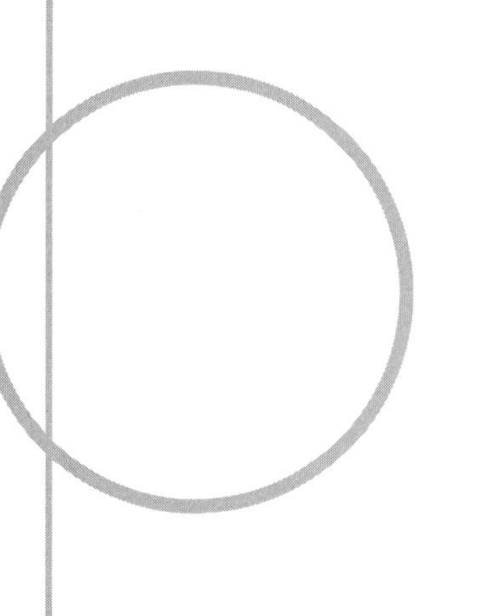

© Lynn Rogers

WHAT IS the relationship between the real world and the way we perceive it? Why are we sometimes wrong about what we think we see? No doubt you have heard the expression "a picture is worth a thousand words." If so, what is one one-thousandth of a picture worth? One word? Perhaps not even that.

Printed photographs are composed of a great many dots. Ordinarily, you will be aware of only the overall patterns and objects, but if you magnify a photo, as in Figure 6.1, you can see the individual dots. Although one dot by itself tells us almost nothing, the pattern of dots as a whole constitutes a meaningful picture.

Actually, our vision is like this all the time. Your retina includes about 126 million rods and cones, each of which sees one dot of the visual field. What you perceive is not dots, however, but lines, curves, and complex objects. In a variety of ways, your nervous system starts with an array of details and extracts the meaningful information.

PERCEPTION OF MINIMAL STIMULI

Some of the very earliest psychological researchers asked, "What is the weakest sound, the weakest light, the weakest touch, and so forth that a person can detect?" They assumed that this question would be easy to answer and therefore a good starting point for further research. As is often the case, however, a question that appeared simple became more complicated.

FIGURE 6.1

Although this photograph is composed entirely of dots, we see objects and patterns. The principles at work in our perception of this photograph are at work in all our perceptions.

Sensory Thresholds and Signal Detection

absolute sensory threshold
the intensity at which a given individual can detect a sensory stimulus 50% of the time; a low threshold indicates the ability to detect faint stimuli.

signal-detection theory
the study of people's tendencies to make hits, correct rejections, misses, and false alarms.

Imagine a typical experiment to determine the threshold of hearing—that is, the minimum intensity that one can hear: Participants are presented with tones of varying intensity in random order, and sometimes no tone occurs at all. Each time, the participants are asked to say whether they heard anything. Figure 6.2 presents typical results. Notice that no sharp line separates sounds that people hear from sounds they do not. Researchers therefore define an **absolute sensory threshold** as the *intensity at which a given individual can detect a stimulus 50% of the time*. Note, however, that people sometimes report stimuli below the threshold or fail to report stimuli above it. Note also that people sometimes report hearing a tone when none was present. We should not be surprised. Throughout the study they have been listening to faint tones and saying "yes" when they heard almost nothing. The difference between nothing and almost nothing is pretty slim.

Your threshold can change drastically from one time to another. For example, if you have been outdoors on a bright, sunny day and you now walk into a darkened movie theater, you will have trouble seeing the seats at first. After a few minutes, your threshold drops (i.e., your sensitivity increases) and you can see better. Your threshold would drop still further in a completely darkened room.

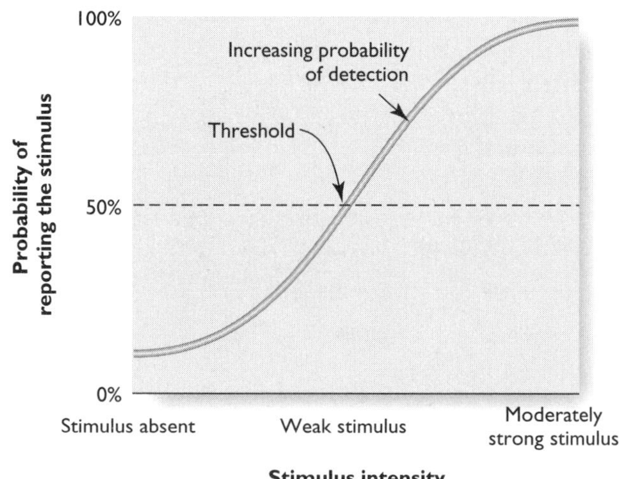

FIGURE 6.2

Typical results of an experiment to measure an absolute sensory threshold. There is no sharp boundary between stimuli that you can perceive and stimuli that you cannot perceive.

When people try to detect weak stimuli, they can be correct in two ways: reporting the presence of a stimulus (a "hit") and reporting its absence (a "correct rejection"). They can also be wrong in two ways: failing to detect a stimulus when present (a "miss") and reporting a stimulus when none was present (a "false alarm"). Figure 6.3 outlines these possibilities.

Signal-detection theory is the *study of people's tendencies to make hits, correct rejections, misses, and false alarms* (D. M. Green & Swets, 1966). (Signal-detection theory originated in engineering, where it is applied to such matters as detecting radio signals in the presence of interfering noise.) In signal-detection studies, we compare responses for stimulus-present and stimulus-absent trials. For example, suppose that someone reports a stimulus present on 80% of the trials when it is actually present. That statistic is meaningless unless we also know how often the person said it was present when it was not. For example, the person might have reported a stimulus present on 80% of trials

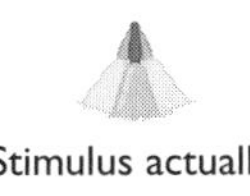

FIGURE 6.3

People can make two kinds of correct judgments (green backgrounds) and two kinds of errors (red backgrounds). Someone who too readily reports the stimulus present would get many hits but also many false alarms.

when it was absent. In that case we would conclude that the person can't tell the difference between stimulus-present and stimulus-absent.

In a signal-detection experiment, people's responses depend on their willingness to risk a miss or a false alarm. (When in doubt, you have to risk one or the other.) Suppose you are the participant and I tell you that you will receive a 10-cent reward whenever you correctly report that a light is present, but you will be fined 1 cent if you say "yes" when it is absent. When you are not sure, you will probably guess "yes," and the results will resemble those in Figure 6.4a. Then I change the rules: You will receive a 1-cent reward for correctly reporting the presence of a light, but you will suffer a 10-cent penalty and an electrical shock if you report a light when none was present. Now you will say "yes" only when you are certain, and the results will look like those in Figure 6.4b. In short, people's answers depend on the instructions they receive and the strategies they use, not just what their senses tell them.

People become cautious about false alarms for other reasons too. In one experiment participants were asked to read words that were flashed on a screen for a split second. They performed reasonably well with ordinary words such as *river* or *peach*. For emotionally loaded words such as *penis* or *bitch,* however, they generally said they were not sure what they saw. Several explanations are possible (e.g., G. S. Blum & Barbour, 1979); one is that participants hesitate to blurt out an emotionally charged word unless they are certain they are right.

The signal-detection approach is useful in many settings remote from a psychologist's laboratory. For example, the legal system is also a signal-detection situation. When

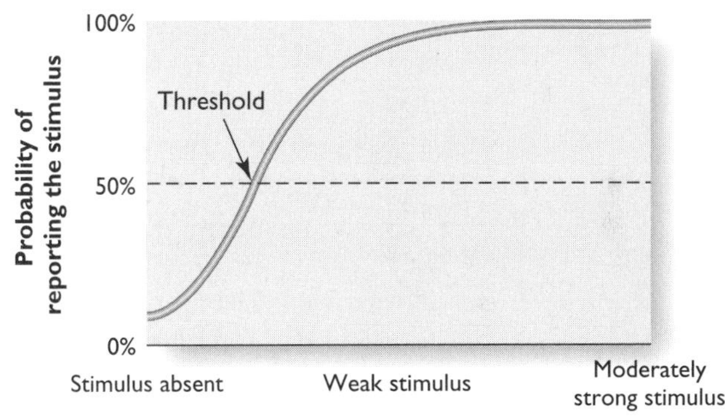

Instructions: You will receive a 10-cent reward for correctly reporting that a light is present. You will be penalized 1 cent for reporting that a light is present when it is not.

a

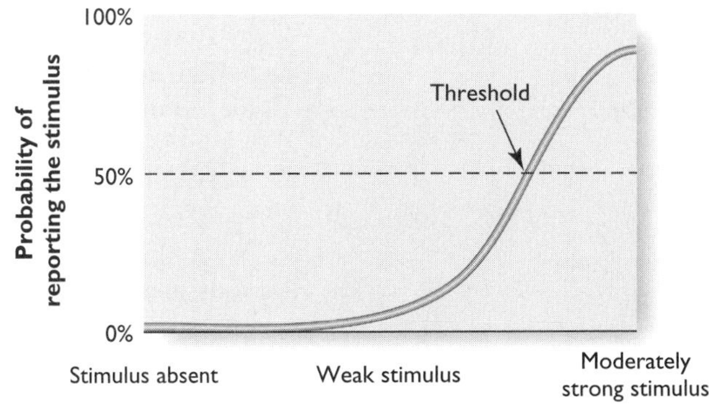

Instructions: You will receive a 1-cent reward for correctly reporting that a light is present. You will be penalized 10 cents *and* subjected to an electric shock for reporting that a light is present when it is not.

b

FIGURE 6.4

Results of experiments to measure a sensory threshold using two different sets of instructions.

we examine the evidence and try to decide whether someone is guilty or innocent, we can be right in two ways and wrong in two ways:

	Defendant is actually guilty	**Defendant is actually innocent**
Jury votes "guilty"	Hit	False alarm
Jury votes "not guilty"	Miss	Correct rejection

Most people agree it is more important to avoid false alarms (finding an innocent person guilty). Therefore, we insist on convincing evidence before convicting someone of a crime.

Subliminal Perception

subliminal perception
the ability of a stimulus to influence our behavior even when it is presented so faintly or briefly or along with such strong distracters that we do not perceive it consciously.

You have probably heard of **subliminal perception,** the idea that *a stimulus can influence our behavior even when it is presented so faintly or briefly or along with such strong distracters that we do not perceive it consciously.* (*Limen* is Latin for "threshold"; thus, subliminal means "below the threshold.") Generally, the operational definition of "not perceived consciously" is that the person reports not seeing it. Is subliminal perception powerful, meaningless, or something in between?

What Subliminal Perception Cannot Do

Many years ago claims were made that subliminal messages could control people's buying habits. For example, an unscrupulous theater owner might insert a single frame, "EAT POPCORN," in the middle of a film. Customers who were not consciously aware of the message could not resist it, so they would flock to the concession stand to buy popcorn. Despite many tests of this claim, no one found any evidence to support it (Bornstein, 1989).

Another claim is that certain rock-'n'-roll recordings contain "satanic" messages that were recorded backward and superimposed on the songs. Some people allege that listeners unconsciously perceive these messages and then follow the evil advice. The issue for psychologists is not whether any rock band ever inserted such a message. (There are a lot of rock bands, after all.) The issue is whether a backward message has any influence. If people hear a backward message, can they understand it? Even if they don't, does it influence their behavior? Researchers have recorded various messages (nothing satanic) and asked people to listen to them backward. So far, no one listening to a backward message has been able to discern what it would sound like forward, and listening to it has not influenced behavior in any detectable way (Vokey & Read, 1985). In other words even if certain music does contain messages recorded backward, we have no evidence that the messages matter.

A third unsupported claim: "Subliminal audiotapes" can help you improve your memory, quit smoking, lose weight, raise your self-esteem, and so forth. In one study psychologists asked more than 200 volunteers to listen to a popular brand of audiotape. But they intentionally mislabeled some of the tapes. That is, some tapes with self-esteem messages were labeled "memory tapes," and some tapes with memory messages were labeled "self-esteem tapes." After 1 month of listening, most who *thought* they were listening to self-esteem tapes said they had greatly improved their self-esteem; those who *thought* they were listening to memory tapes said their memory had greatly improved. What they actually heard made no difference. In other words the memory improvement was a result of people's expectations, not the tapes themselves (Greenwald, Spangenberg, Pratkanis, & Eskanazi, 1991).

What Subliminal Perception Can Do

Subliminal messages do produce effects, although they are in most cases brief, subtle, and hard to measure. For example, people in one study viewed a happy, neutral, or angry face flashed on a screen for less than one thirtieth of a second, followed immediately by a neutral face. Under these conditions no one reports seeing a happy or angry face, and even if asked to guess, people do no better than chance. However, when they see a happy face, they slightly and briefly move their facial muscles in the direction of a smile; after seeing an angry face, they tense their muscles slightly and briefly in the direction of a frown (Dimberg, Thunberg, & Elmehed, 2000).

In another study students watched a screen where they saw a word flash for one third of a second, followed by a 133-millisecond response window in which they were supposed to press one computer key if they saw a "pleasant" word (e.g., HAPPY or WARM) and a different key if they saw an "unpleasant" word (e.g., SCUM or KILL). They do see the word, but because they are forced to respond so quickly, they find the task difficult and make many mistakes. The additional element of this procedure is that prior to the flashed word, another word was also flashed *very* briefly, under conditions that made it impossible for anyone to identify it consciously. That is, it was subliminal. The full procedure is out lined as follows:

1	2
Blank screen	Masking stimulus such as KQHYTPDQFPBYL for 150 milliseconds
3	**4**
Subliminal stimulus such as FRIEND for 50 ms	Another interfering stimulus for 17 ms
5	**6**
Target stimulus such as HAPPY for 333 ms	Response window for 133 ms

Although none of the participants could identify any of the subliminal words (step 3), or even noticed them at all, they responded more accurately to the target stimulus (step 5) if both the subliminal and target stimuli were pleasant, or both were unpleasant, than if one was pleasant and the other unpleasant. In other words a pleasant subliminal word (step 3) primed them to respond better to a pleasant target word (step 5), and an unpleasant subliminal word primed them to respond to an unpleasant target word (Abrams, Klinger, & Greenwald, 2002). Other research has indicated that unpleasant subliminal words have a slightly stronger effect than pleasant ones (Dijksterhuis & Aarts, 2003).

The fact that subliminal perception affects behavior at all is theoretically interesting. It shows that we are not consciously aware of all the information we process or all the events that influence us (Greenwald & Draine, 1997). However, notice that what has been demonstrated is a small, brief facilitation of one response or another, and researchers have to average results over many participants and many trials to demonstrate any effect at all. The evidence does not indicate any powerful or long-lasting subliminal influences.

PERCEPTION AND THE RECOGNITION OF PATTERNS

How do you know what you're looking at? Take what seems like a very simple example: When you look at something, how does your brain decide how bright it is? We might guess that the answer would be simply that the more intense the light, the brighter the appearance.

brightness contrast
an increase or decrease in an object's apparent brightness because of the effects of objects around it.

However, perceived brightness depends on comparison to the surrounding objects. **Brightness contrast** *is the increase or decrease in an object's apparent brightness because of the effects of objects around it.* Consider Figure 6.5. Compare the pink bars in the middle left section to those in the middle right. The ones on the right probably look darker, but in fact they are the same. Then examine Figure 6.6.

Compare the little square in the center of the upper face of the cube to the one in the center of the front face. The one on the top face looks brown, whereas the one on the front face looks yellow or orange. Amazingly, they are physically the same (Lotto & Purves, 1999). Don't believe it? Cover everything on the page except those two squares and then compare them.

If two spots on the page reflect light the same way, why don't we see them the same? Apparently, when the brain sees something, it uses its past experience to calculate how that pattern of light probably was generated (Lotto & Purves, 1999). In Figure 6.6 the context clearly indicates that the top face is in bright light, whereas the front face is in a shadow. The square you see in the top face is seen as a dark object, brown in color. The square you see in the front face is rather bright considering that it's in a shadow, and therefore, it looks yellow or orange. Your brain calculates what the object probably *is,* not just what light strikes your retina.

Similarly, in Figure 6.5 we see what appears to be a partly clear white bar covering the center of the left half of the grid, and the pink bars look very light. The corresponding section to the right also has pink bars, but these appear to be under the red bars and on top of a white background; here the pink looks much darker. As you will have guessed by now, the pink bars on the left are the same brightness and color as those on the right.

If just perceiving brightness is that complicated, imagine how hard it is to explain something like face recognition. People are amazingly good at recognizing faces, though inept at explaining how they do it. When you someday attend your 25th high school reunion, you will probably recognize many people despite major changes in their appearance.

Can you match the high school photos in Figure 6.7 with the photos of the same people as they looked 25 years later? Probably not, but other people who had

FIGURE 6.5
Because pink bars appear to lie above the dark bars on the left and below them on the right, we see a contrast between pink and dark red on the left, pink and white on the right. Therefore, we see the pink bars on the right as darker, even though they are actually the same shade as the others.

FIGURE 6.6

The little squares in the center of the top and front faces of the left cube look very different, but they are physically identical. The cube on the right has those same squares, but the context has been removed. Try covering everything on the left cube except the two central squares, or fold the page so you can match the squares of the right cube with those of the left. (*From Lotto & Purves, 1999*)

attended that high school succeeded with a respectable 49% accuracy (Bruck, Cavanagh, & Ceci, 1991).

We recognize faces by whole patterns, and certain areas in the temporal lobe of the brain appear to be specialized for facial recognition (Farah, 1992; Kanwisher, 2000). Changing even one feature can sometimes make a face hard to recognize. Perhaps you have had the experience of seeing people who have just changed their hair style and for a moment you cannot recognize them. Can you identify the person in Figure 6.8?

The Feature-Detector Approach

Even explaining how we recognize a simple letter of the alphabet is difficult enough. According to one explanation, we begin recognition by breaking a complex stimulus into its component parts. For example, when we look at a letter of the alphabet, *specialized neurons in the visual cortex,* called **feature detectors**, *respond to the presence of certain simple features, such as lines and angles.* That is, one neuron might become active only when you are looking at a horizontal line in a particular location. That feature detector would be detecting the feature "horizontal line." Other neurons might detect horizontal lines in other locations, vertical lines, and so forth.

feature detector
a neuron in the visual system of the brain that responds to the presence of a certain simple feature, such as a horizontal line.

Feature Detectors What evidence do we have for the existence of feature detectors in the brain? We have two kinds of evidence: one from laboratory animals and one from humans.

Experiment 1

Hypothesis Neurons in the visual cortex of cats and monkeys will respond specifically when light strikes the retina in a particular pattern.

Method Two pioneers in the study of the visual cortex, David Hubel and Torsten Wiesel (1981 Nobel Prize winners in physiology and medicine), inserted thin electrodes into cells of the occipital cortex of cats and monkeys and

FIGURE 6.7

High school photos and the same people 25 years later. Can you match the photos in the two sets? (Check your answers by going online for a drag and drop version of this figure or check answer C on page 204.)

FIGURE 6.8

Who is this? We recognize people partly by hair as well as facial features. If you're not sure who it is, check answer D, page 204.

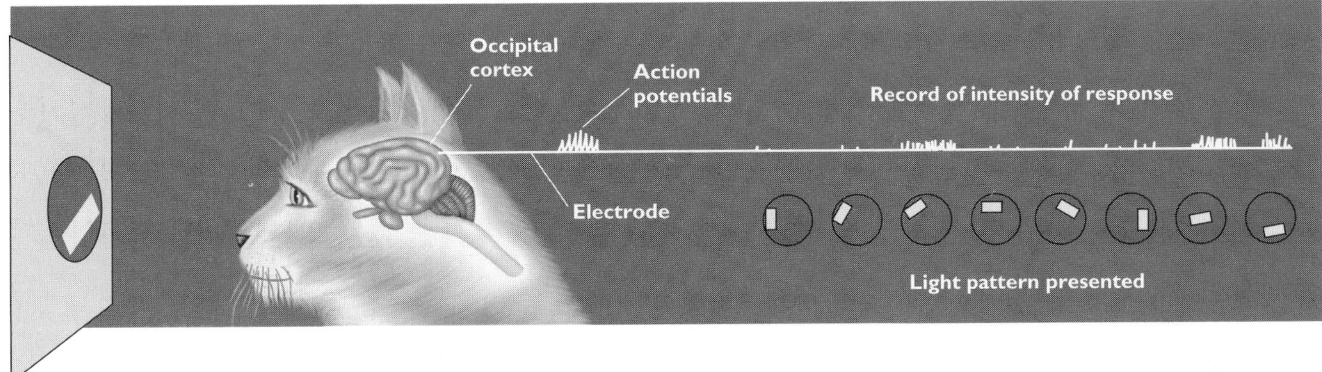

FIGURE 6.9
Hubel and Wiesel implanted electrodes to record the activity of neurons in the occipital cortex of a cat. Then they compared the responses evoked by various patterns of light and darkness on the retina. In most cases a neuron responded vigorously when a portion of the retina saw a bar of light oriented at a particular angle. When the angle of the bar changed, that cell became silent but another cell responded.

then recorded the activity of those cells when various light patterns struck the animals' retinas. At first they used mere points of light; later they tried lines (Figure 6.9).

Results They found that each cell responds best in the presence of a particular stimulus (Hubel & Wiesel, 1968). Some cells become active only when a vertical bar of light strikes a given portion of the retina. Others become active only when a horizontal bar strikes the retina. In other words such cells appear to act as feature detectors. In later experiments Hubel and Wiesel and other investigators found cells that respond to other kinds of features, such as movement in a particular direction.

Interpretation Hubel and Wiesel reported feature-detector neurons in both cats and monkeys. If the organization of the occipital cortex is similar in species as distantly related as cats and monkeys, it is likely (though not certain) to be similar in humans.

A second line of evidence is based on the following reasoning: If the human cortex does contain feature-detector cells, one type of cell should become fatigued after we stare for a time at the features that excite it. When we look away, we should see an aftereffect created by the inactivity of that type of cell.

One example of this phenomenon is the **waterfall illusion**: *If you stare at a waterfall for a minute or more and then turn your eyes to some nearby cliffs, the cliffs will appear to flow upward.* By staring at the waterfall, you fatigue the neurons that respond to downward motion. When you look away, those neurons become inactive, but others that respond to upward motion continue their normal activity. Even though the motionless cliffs stimulate those neurons only weakly, the stimulation is enough to produce an illusion of upward motion. For another example here is a demonstration that you can perform yourself.

waterfall illusion
a phenomenon in which prolonged staring at a waterfall and then looking at nearby cliffs causes those cliffs to appear to flow upward.

Experiment 2

Hypothesis After you stare at one set of vertical lines, you will fatigue the feature detectors that respond to lines of a particular width. If you then look at lines slightly wider or narrower than the original ones, they will appear to be even wider or narrower than they really are.

Method Cover the right half of Figure 6.10 and stare at the little rectangle in the middle of the left half for at least 1 minute. (Staring even longer will increase

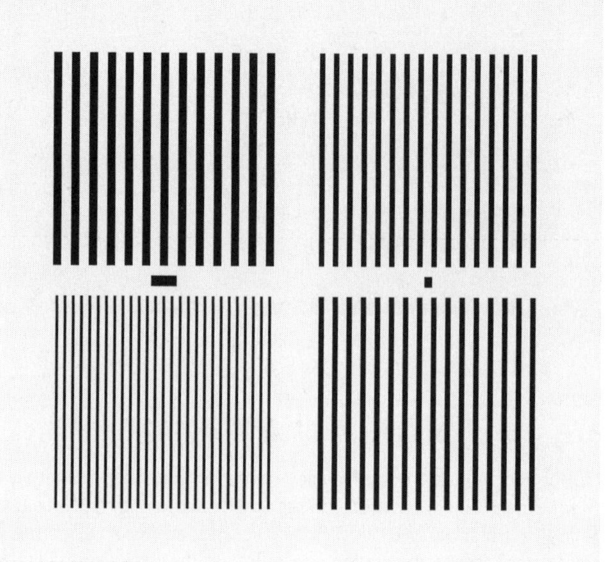

FIGURE 6.10
Use this display to fatigue your feature detectors and create an afterimage. Follow the directions in Experiment 2. (*From Blakemore & Sutton, 1969*)

the effect.) Do not stare at just one point; move your focus around within the rectangle. Then look at the square in the center of the right part of the figure and compare the spacing between the lines of the top and bottom gratings (Blakemore & Sutton, 1969).

Results What did you perceive in the right half of the figure? People generally report that the top lines look narrower and the bottom lines look wider, even though they are the same.

Interpretation Staring at the left part of the figure fatigues neurons sensitive to wide lines in the top part of the figure and neurons sensitive to narrow lines in the bottom part. Then, when you look at lines of medium width, the fatigued cells become inactive. Therefore, your perception is dominated by cells sensitive to narrower lines in the top part and to wider lines in the bottom part.

To summarize, we have two types of evidence for the existence of visual feature detectors: (a) The brains of other species contain cells with the properties of feature detectors, and (b) after staring at certain patterns, we see aftereffects that can be explained as fatigue of feature-detector cells in the brain.

The research just described was only the start of an enormous amount of activity by laboratories throughout the world; later results have led to revised views of what the earlier results mean. For example, even though certain neurons respond better to a single vertical line

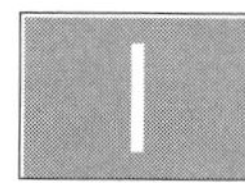

than to points or lines of other orientations, the vertical line may not be the best stimulus for exciting those neurons. Most respond even more strongly to a sine-wave grating of lines:

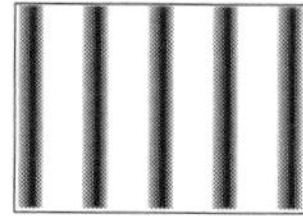

Thus, the feature that such cells detect is probably more complex than just a line. Furthermore, because each cell responds to stimuli as different as a line and a group of lines, obviously no one cell provides an unambiguous message about what someone is seeing at any moment.

One important point about scientific advances: A single line of evidence—even excellent, Nobel Prize-winning evidence—seldom provides the final answer to any question. We should always look for multiple ways to test a hypothesis; even if several kinds of evidence support a conclusion, a great many unanswered questions can still remain.

FIGURE 6.11

We perceive elements differently depending on their context. In (a) the A in CAT is the same as the H in HAT, but we perceive them differently. In (b) the central character can appear to be a B or the number 13 depending on whether we read horizontally or vertically. (*Part b from* Inversions, *by S. Kim. W. H. Freeman and Company. Copyright © 1989 by Scott Kim.*)

Do Feature Detectors Explain Perception?

The neurons I have just described are active during the early stages of visual processing. Do we simply add up the responses of a great many feature detectors so that the sum of enough feature detectors constitutes your perception of, say, your psychology professor's face?

No, feature detectors cannot provide a complete explanation even for how we perceive letters, much less faces. For example, we perceive the words in Figure 6.11a as CAT and HAT, even though the A in CAT is identical to the H in HAT, and therefore, both of them stimulate the same feature detectors. Likewise, the character in the center of Figure 6.11b can be read as either the letter B or the number 13. The early stages of visual perception use feature detectors, but the perception of a complex pattern requires more.

Gestalt Psychology

Figure 6.12, which we see as the overall shape of an airplane, is a photo of several hundred people. The plane is the overall pattern, not the sum of the parts. Recall also Figure 6.1 from earlier in this chapter: The photograph is composed of dots, but we perceive a face, not just dots.

Such observations derive from **Gestalt psychology**, a field that focuses on our ability to perceive overall patterns. *Gestalt* (geh-SHTALT) is a German word translated as "overall pattern or configuration." The founders of Gestalt psychology rejected the idea that a perception can be broken down into its component parts. A melody broken up into individual notes is no longer a melody. Their

Gestalt psychology
an approach to psychology that seeks to explain how we perceive overall patterns.

FIGURE 6.12

According to Gestalt psychology, the whole is different from the sum of its parts. Here we perceive an assembly of several hundred people as an airplane.

FIGURE 6.13

Do you see an animal in each picture? If not, check answer E on page 204. (*Part b from Dallenbach, 1951*)

a

b

slogan was, "The whole is different from the sum of its parts." According to Gestalt psychologists, visual perception is an active creation, not just the adding up of lines, dots, or other pieces. We considered an example of this principle in Figure 6.11. Here are some further examples.

In Figure 6.13 you may see animals or you may see meaningless black and white patches. You might see only patches for a while, and then one or both animals suddenly emerge. (If you give up, check answer E on page 204.) To perceive the animals, you must separate **figure and ground**—that is, you must distinguish the *object from the background.* Ordinarily, you make that distinction almost instantly; you become aware of the process only when it is difficult (as it is here).

figure and ground
an object and its background.

reversible figure
a stimulus that you can perceive in more than one way.

Figure 6.14 contains five **reversible figures,** *stimuli that can be perceived in more than one way.* In effect we test hypotheses: "Is this the front of the object or is that the front? Is the object facing left or right? Is this section the foreground or the background?" In Figure 6.14 part a is called the *Necker cube,* after the psychologist who first called attention to it. Which is the front face of the cube? If you look long enough, you will see it two ways. You can see part b either as a vase or as two profiles. In part c, with a little imagination, you might see a woman's face or a man blowing a horn. (If you need help, check answer F on page 204.) Part d shows both an old woman and a young woman. Almost everyone sees one or the other immediately, but many people lock into one perception so tightly that they cannot see the other one. Part e was drawn by an 8-year-old girl who intended it as the picture of a face. Can you find another possibility? (If you have trouble with parts d or e,

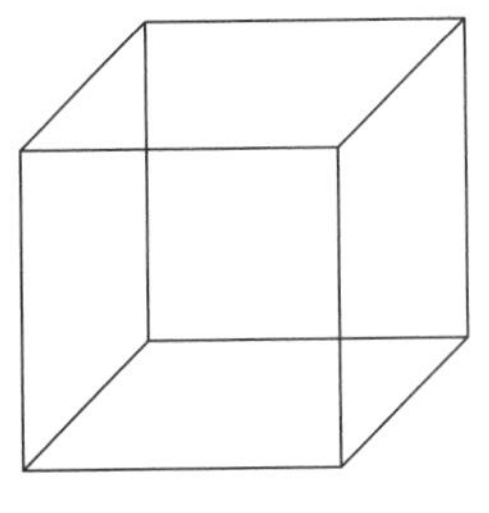
a

b

c

d

e

FIGURE 6.14

Reversible figures: (a) The Necker cube. Which is the front face? (b) Faces or a vase. (c) A sax player or a woman's face ("Sara Nader"). (d) An old woman or a young woman. (e) A face or what? (*Part c from Shepard, 1990; part d from Boring, 1930*)

check answers G and H on page 205.) Overall, the point of the reversible figures is that we perceive by imposing order on an array, not just by adding up lines and points.

The Gestalt psychologists described several principles of how we organize perceptions into meaningful wholes, as illustrated in Figure 6.15. **Proximity** is the *tendency to perceive objects that are close together as belonging to a group.* The objects in part a form two groups because of their proximity. The *tendency to perceive objects that resemble each other as forming a group* is called **similarity**. The objects in part b group into Xs and Os because of similarity. When lines are interrupted, as in part c, we may perceive **continuation**, *a filling in of the gaps.* You probably perceive this illustration as a rectangle covering the center of one very elongated hot dog.

When a familiar figure is interrupted, as in part d, we perceive a **closure** of the figure; that is, *we imagine the rest of the figure.* The figure we imagine completes what we already see in a way that is simple, symmetrical, or consistent with our past experience (Shimaya, 1997). For example, you probably see the following as

proximity
in Gestalt psychology the tendency to perceive objects that are close together as belonging to a group.

similarity
in Gestalt psychology the tendency to perceive objects that resemble each other as belonging to a group.

continuation
in Gestalt psychology the tendency to fill in the gaps in an interrupted line.

closure
in Gestalt psychology the tendency to imagine the rest of an incomplete, familiar figure.

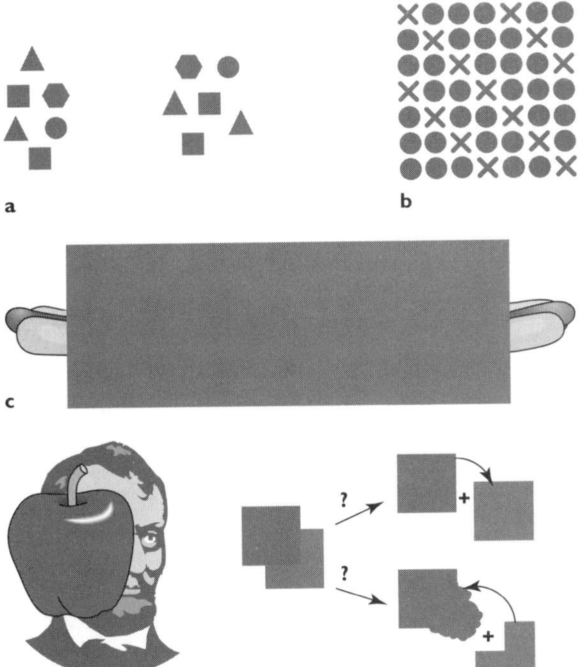

FIGURE 6.15

Gestalt principles of (a) proximity, (b) similarity, (c) continuation, (d) closure, and (e) good figure.

an orange rectangle overlapping a blue diamond, although you don't really know what, if anything, is behind the rectangle:

Of course, the principle of closure is similar to that of continuation. With a complicated pattern, however, closure takes into account more than a continuation of the lines. For example, in Figure 6.15c you fill in the gaps to perceive one long hot dog. With some additional context, you would probably perceive the same pattern as two shorter hot dogs:

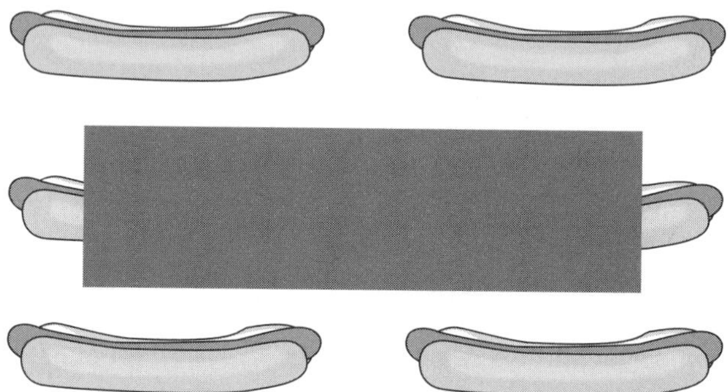

common fate
the tendency to perceive objects as being part of the same group if they change or move in similar ways at the same time.

good figure
in Gestalt psychology the tendency to perceive simple, symmetrical figures.

Yet another Gestalt principle is **common fate**: *We perceive objects as being part of the same group if they change or move in similar ways at the same time.* Suppose you see an array of miscellaneous objects differing in shape, size, and color. If some of them move in the same direction and speed, we see them as a related group. Also if some of them grow brighter or darker together, again we see them as related (Sekuler & Bennett, 2001).

In everyday life the principle of common fate is a useful tool. Imagine you see a snake's head sticking out of one hole in the ground and a tail sticking out of another. When the head starts moving forward, if the tail also moves down into the ground, you perceive it as all one snake. If the head moves and the tail doesn't, you see that you have two snakes to deal with.

Finally, when possible, we tend to perceive a **good figure**—*a simple, familiar, symmetrical figure.* Many important, familiar objects in the world are geometrically simple or close to it: The sun and moon are round, tree trunks meet the ground at almost a right angle, faces and animals are nearly symmetrical, and so forth. When we look at a complex pattern, we tend to focus on regular patterns. If we can see something as a circle, square, or straight line, we do. In Figure 6.15e the part on the left could represent a red square overlapping a green one or a green backward L overlapping a red object of irregular shape. We are powerfully drawn to the first interpretation because it includes "good," regular, symmetrical objects.

In Figure 6.16a we perceive a white triangle overlapping three ovals (Singh, Hoffman, & Albert, 1999). That perception is so convincing that you may have to look carefully to persuade yourself that there is no line establishing a border for the triangle. However, if we tilt the black objects slightly, as in Figure 6.16b, the illusion of something lying on top of them disappears. We "see" the overlapping object only if it is a symmetrical, good figure.

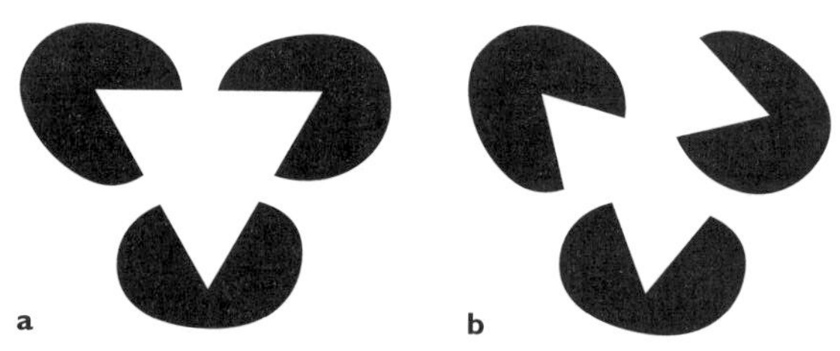

FIGURE 6.16

In (a) we see a triangle overlapping three irregular ovals. We see it because triangles are "good figures" and symmetrical. If we tilt the ovals, as in (b), they appear as irregular objects, not as objects with something on top of them. (*From "Contour Completion and Relative Depth: Petter's Rule and Support Ratio," by M. Singh, D. D. Hoffman and M. K. Albert,* Psychological Science, *1999, 10, 423–428. Copyright © 1999 Blackwell Publishers Ltd. Reprinted by permission.*)

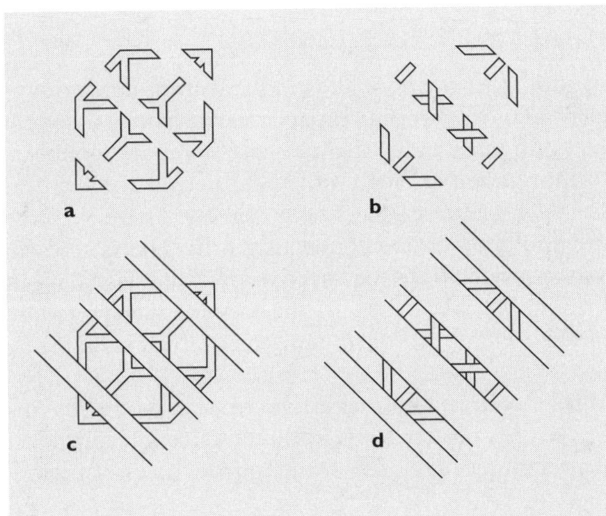

FIGURE 6.17
(a) and (b) appear to be arrays of flat objects. Introducing a context of overlapping lines causes a cube to emerge in (c) and (d). (*From* Organization in Vision: Essays on Gestalt Perception, *by Gaetano Kanizsa, pp. 7–9. Copyright © 1979 by Gaetano Kanizsa. Reproduced with permission of Greenwood Publishing Group, Westport, CT.*)

Similarities Between Vision and Hearing

The perceptual organization principles of Gestalt psychology apply to hearing as well as to vision. There are reversible figures in sound, just as there are in vision. For instance, you can hear a clock going "tick, tock, tick, tock" or "tock, tick, tock, tick." You can hear your windshield wipers going "dunga, dunga" or "gadung, gadung."

The Gestalt principles of continuation and closure work best when we see something that has interrupted something else. For example, consider Figure 6.17. In parts c and d, the context suggest objects partly blocking our view of a three-dimensional cube. In parts a and b, we are much less likely to see a cube, as nothing suggests an object occluding our view. Similarly, in Figure 6.18a we see a series of meaningless patches. In Figure 6.18b the addition of some black glop helps us see these patches as the word *psychology* (Bregman, 1981). We get continuation or closure mainly when we see that something has blocked the presumed object in the background.

The same is true in hearing. If a speech or song is broken up by periods of silence, we do not fill in the gaps and we find the utterance hard to understand. However, if the same gaps are filled by noise, we "hear" what probably occurred during those gaps; in other words we apply continuation and closure (C. T. Miller, Dibble, & Hauser, 2001; Warren, 1970).

FIGURE 6.18
Why is the word "psychology" easier to read in (b) than in (a)? (*After Bregman, 1981*)

Feature Detectors and Gestalt Psychology

The Gestalt approach to perception does not conflict with the feature-detector approach as much as it might seem. The feature-detector approach describes the first stages of perception—how the brain takes individual points of light and connects them into lines and then into more complex features. According to the feature-detector approach, the brain says, "I see these points here, here, and here, so there must be a line. I see a line here and another line connecting with it here, so there must be a letter L." The Gestalt approach describes how we combine visual input with our knowledge and expectations. According to the Gestalt interpretation, the brain says, "I see what looks like a circle, so the missing piece must be part of a circle too."

Which view is correct? Both, of course. Our perception must assemble the individual points of light or bits of sound, but once it forms a tentative interpretation of the pattern, it uses that interpretation to organize or reorganize the information.

PERCEPTION OF MOVEMENT AND DEPTH

visual constancy
the tendency to perceive objects as unchanging in shape, size, and color, despite variations in what actually reaches the retina.

As an automobile drives away from us, its image on the retina grows smaller, yet we perceive it as moving, not as shrinking. That perception illustrates **visual constancy**—our *tendency to perceive objects as keeping their shape, size, and color, even though what actually strikes our retina changes from time to time.* Figure 6.19 shows examples of two visual constancies: shape constancy and size constancy. Constancies depend on our familiarity with objects and on our ability to estimate distances and angles of view. For example, we know that a door is still rectangular even when we view it from an odd angle. But to recognize that an object keeps its shape and size, we have to perceive movement or changes in distance. How do we do so?

Perception of Movement

Moving objects capture our attention, and for a good reason. A moving object could be a person or animal, something people have made (e.g., a car), something thrown, or something that has fallen. In any case it is more likely to require our immediate attention than something stationary.

The detection of motion raises some interesting issues, including how we distinguish between our own movement and the movement of objects. Try this simple

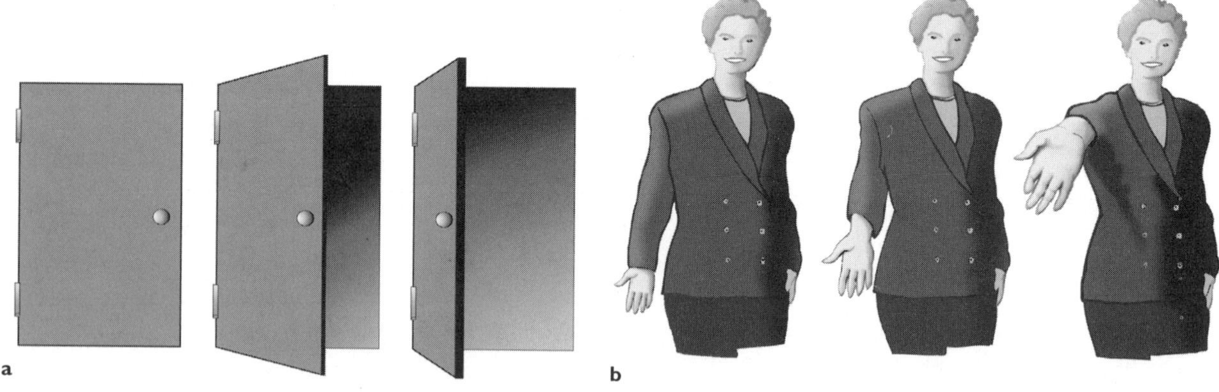

FIGURE 6.19

(a) Shape constancy: We perceive all three doors as rectangles. (b) Size constancy: We perceive all three hands as equal in size.

demonstration: Hold an object in front of your eyes and then move it to the right. Now hold the object in front of your eyes and move your eyes to the left. The image of the object moves across your retina in the same way when you move the object or move your eyes. Yet you perceive the object as moving in one case but not in the other. Why?

The object looks stationary when you move your eyes for two reasons. One is that the vestibular system informs the visual areas of the brain about your head movements. When your brain knows that your eyes have moved to the left, it interprets a change in what you see as being a result of that movement. One man with a rare kind of brain damage could not connect his eye movements with his perceptions. Whenever he moved his head or eyes, the world appeared to be moving, and frequently, he became dizzy and nauseated (Haarmeier, Thier, Repnow, & Petersen, 1997).

The second reason that the object does not appear to move is that we perceive motion when an object moves *relative to the background* (Gibson, 1968). For example, when you walk forward, stationary objects in your environment move across your retina. If something fails to move across your retina, you perceive it as moving in the same direction as you are.

What do we perceive when an object is stationary and the background is moving? That seldom happens, but when it does, we may *incorrectly perceive the object as moving against a stationary background,* a phenomenon called **induced movement**. For example, when you watch clouds moving slowly across the moon, you might perceive the clouds as stationary and the moon as moving. Induced movement is a form of *apparent movement,* as opposed to *real movement.*

induced movement
a perception that an object is moving and the background is stationary when in fact the object is stationary and the background is moving.

You have already read about the waterfall illusion (page 187), another example of apparent movement. Yet another is **stroboscopic movement**, an *illusion of movement created by a rapid succession of stationary images.* When a scene is flashed on a screen and is followed a split second later by a second scene slightly different from the first, you perceive the objects as having moved smoothly from their location in the first scene to their location in the second scene (Figure 6.20). Motion pictures are actually a series of still photos flashed on the screen.

stroboscopic movement
an illusion of movement created by a rapid succession of stationary images.

We also experience an *illusion of movement created when two or more stationary lights separated by a short distance blink on and off at regular intervals.* Your brain creates the sense of motion in what is called the **phi effect**. You may have noticed signs in front of restaurants or motels that use this effect. As the lights blink on and off, an arrow seems to move and invite you in.

phi effect
the illusion of movement created when two or more stationary lights separated by a short distance flash on and off at regular intervals.

Our ability to detect visual movement played an interesting role in the history of astronomy. In 1930 Clyde Tombaugh was searching the skies for a possible undiscovered planet beyond Neptune. He photographed each region of the sky

FIGURE 6.20
A movie consists of a series of still photographs flickering at 86,400 per hour. You perceive moving objects, however, not a series of stills. Here you see a series of stills spread out in space instead of time.

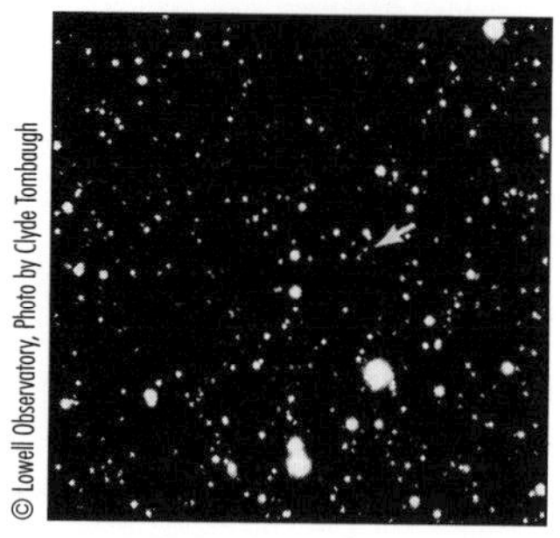

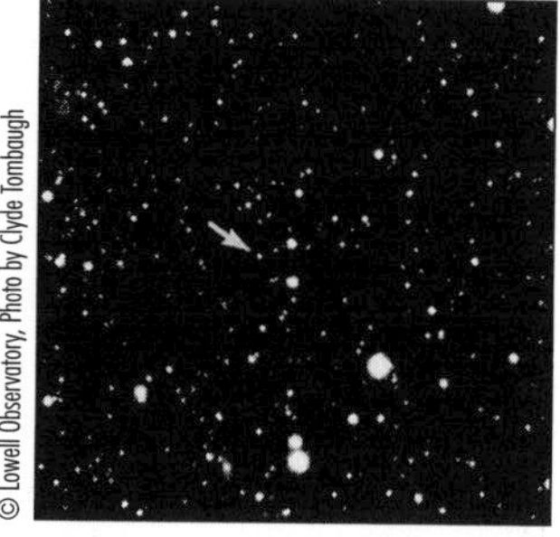

FIGURE 6.21

Clyde Tombaugh photographed each area of the sky twice, several days apart. Then he used a machine to flip back and forth between the two photos of each pair. When he came to one part of the sky, he immediately noticed one dot that moved between the two photos. That dot was the planet Pluto.

twice, several days apart. A planet, unlike a star, moves from one photo to the next. However, how would he find one dot that moved among all the countless unmoving dots in the sky? He put each pair of photos on a machine that would flip back and forth between one photo and the other. When he came to the correct pair of photos, the machine flipped back and forth between them, and he immediately noticed the one moving dot (Tombaugh, 1980). We now know that little dot as the planet Pluto (Figure 6.21).

Perception of Depth

depth perception
the perception of distance, which enables us to experience the world in three dimensions.

retinal disparity
the difference in the apparent position of an object as seen by the left and right retinas.

convergence
the degree to which the eyes turn in to focus on a close object.

Although we live in a world of three dimensions, our retinas are in effect two-dimensional surfaces. **Depth perception**, our *perception of distance,* enables us to experience the world in three dimensions. This perception depends on several factors.

One factor is **retinal disparity**—*the difference in the apparent position of an object as seen by the left and right retinas.* Try this: Hold one finger at arm's length. Focus on it with one eye and then with the other. Note that the apparent position of your finger shifts with respect to the background. Now hold your finger closer to your face and repeat the experiment. Notice that the apparent position of your finger shifts even more. The discrepancy between the slightly different views the two eyes see becomes greater as the object comes closer. We use the amount of discrepancy to gauge distance. If you watch a three-dimensional movie while wearing special glasses, the principle is that the lenses enable your two eyes to see different views of the same scene.

A second cue for depth perception is the **convergence** of the eyes—that is, the *degree to which they turn in to focus on a close object* (Figure 6.22). When you focus on a distant object, your eyes are looking in almost parallel directions. When you focus on something close, your eyes turn in, and you sense the tension of your eye muscles. The more the muscles pull, the closer the object must be.

FIGURE 6.22

Convergence of the eyes as a cue to distance. The more this viewer must converge her eyes toward each other to focus on an object, the closer the object must be.

FIGURE 6.23

We judge depth and distance in a photograph using monocular cues (those that would work even with just one eye): (a) Closer objects occupy more space on the retina (or in the photograph) than do distant objects of the same type. (b) Nearer objects show more detail. (c) Closer objects overlap certain distant objects. (d) Objects in the foreground look sharper than objects do on the horizon.

Retinal disparity and convergence are called **binocular cues** because they *depend on the action of both eyes.* **Monocular cues** enable a person to *judge depth and distance with just one eye* or when both eyes see the same image, as when you look at a picture, such as Figure 6.23. The ability to use these monocular cues to interpret an illustration depends on our experience, including specifically experiences with photographs and drawings. For example, in Figure 6.24, does it appear to you that the hunter is aiming his spear at the antelope? When this drawing was shown to African people who had seldom seen drawings, many said the hunter was aiming at a baby elephant (Hudson, 1960). Clearly, people have to learn how to judge depth in drawings.

binocular cues
visual cues that depend on the action of both eyes.

monocular cues
visual cues that are just as effective with one eye as with both.

Let's consider some of the monocular cues we use to perceive depth:

Object size: Other things being equal, a nearby object produces a larger image than a distant one. However, this cue is useful only for objects of known sizes. For example, the jogger in Figure 6.23 produces a larger image than do any of the houses, which we know are actually larger. So we see the jogger as closer. However, the mountains in the background differ in actual as well as apparent size, so we cannot assume the ones that look bigger are closer.

FIGURE 6.24

Which animal is the hunter attacking? Most readers of this text, using monocular cues to distance, will reply that the hunter is attacking the antelope. However, many African people unfamiliar with drawings thought he was attacking a baby elephant because the hunter is physically closer to the elephant in the drawing. (*From Hudson, 1960*)

If you were a passenger on this train, the ground beside the tracks would appear to pass by more quickly than the more distant elements in the landscape. In this photo's version of motion parallax, the ground is blurred and more distant objects are crisp.

Linear perspective: As parallel lines stretch out toward the horizon, they come closer and closer together. Examine the road in Figure 6.23. At the bottom of the photo (close to the viewer), the edges of the road are far apart; at greater distances they come together.

Detail: We see nearby objects, such as the jogger, in more detail than objects in the distance.

Interposition: A nearby object interrupts our view of a more distant object. For example, the closest telephone pole (on the right) interrupts our view of the closest tree, so we see that the telephone pole is closer than the tree.

Texture gradient: Notice the distance between one telephone pole and the next. At greater distances the poles come closer and closer together. The "packed together" appearance of objects gives us another cue to their approximate distance.

Shadows: Shadows help us gauge sizes as well as relative locations of objects.

Accommodation: The lens of the eye *accommodates*—that is, it changes shape—to focus on nearby objects, and your brain detects that change and thereby infers the distance to an object. Accommodation could help tell you how far away the photograph itself is, although it provides no information about the relative distances of objects in the photograph.

Motion parallax: Another monocular cue helps us perceive depth while we are moving, although it does not help with a photograph. When we are walking or riding in a car, close objects seem to pass by swiftly, while distant objects seem to pass by very slowly. *The faster an object passes by, the closer it must be.* This is the principle of **motion parallax**. Television and film crews use this principle. If the camera moves very slowly, you see closer objects move more than distant ones and get a good sense of depth.

motion parallax
the apparently swift motion of objects close to a moving observer and the apparently slow motion of objects farther away.

OPTICAL ILLUSIONS

optical illusion
a misinterpretation of a visual stimulus as being larger or smaller, or straighter or more curved, than it really is.

Many people claim to have seen ghosts, flying saucers, the Loch Ness monster, Bigfoot, or people floating in the air. Maybe they are lying, maybe they did see something extraordinary, or maybe they saw something ordinary but misinterpreted it. An **optical illusion** is a *misinterpretation of a visual stimulus.* Figure 6.25 shows a few examples.

Psychologists would like to develop a single explanation for all optical illusions. They can explain many, though not all, optical illusions from the relationship between size perception and depth perception.

The Relationship Between Depth Perception and Size Perception

If you can estimate the size of an object, you can deduce its distance. If you can estimate its distance, you can deduce its size. Figure 6.26 shows that a given image on the retina may represent either a small, close object or a large, distant object.

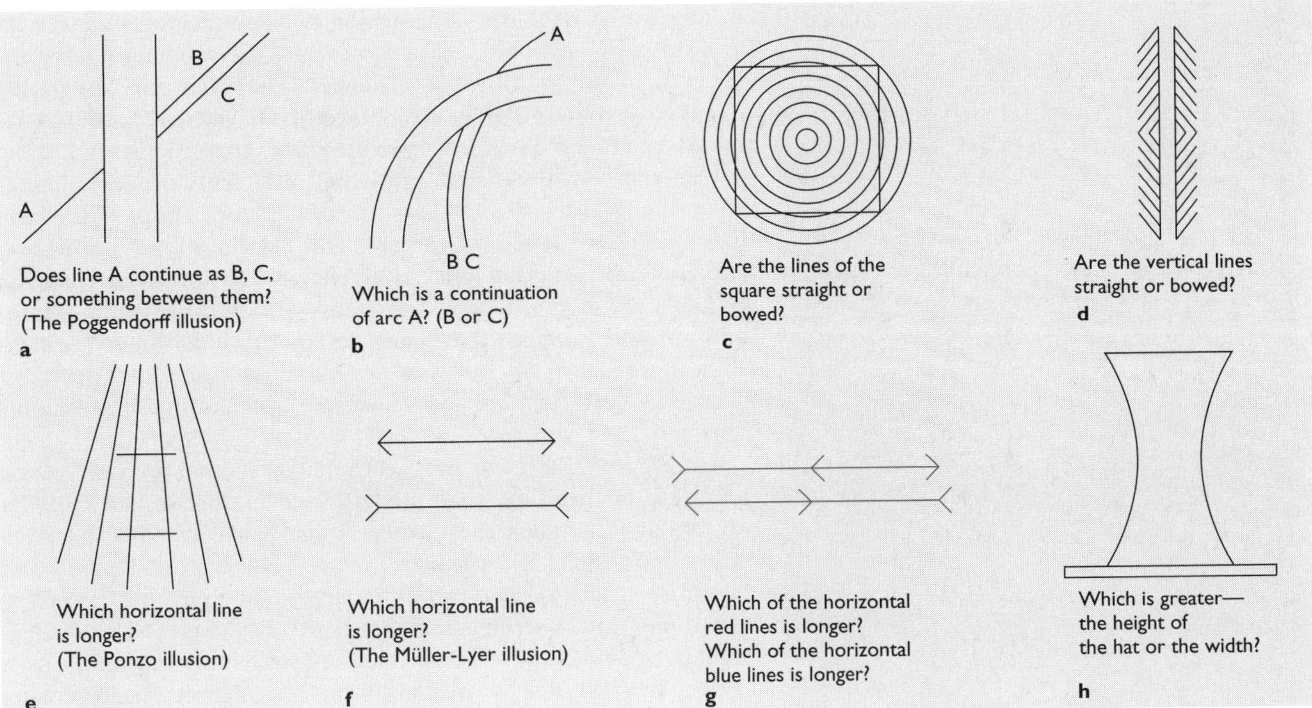

FIGURE 6.25

These geometric figures illustrate optical illusions. Answers (which you are invited to check with ruler and compass): (a) B, (b) B, (c) straight, (d) straight, (e) equal, (f) equal, (g) equal, (h) equal.

In the real world, we usually have many cues for judging the size and distance of objects. However, when you have fewer cues, you can become confused (Figure 6.27). I once saw an airplane overhead and was unsure whether it was a small, remote-controlled toy airplane or a distant, full-size airplane. Airplanes come in many sizes, and the sky has few cues to distance.

A similar issue arises in reported sightings of UFOs. When people see an unfamiliar object in the sky, they can easily misjudge its distance. If they over-estimate its distance, they also will overestimate its size and speed.

What does all this have to do with optical illusions? Whenever we misjudge distance, we misjudge size as well. For example, Figure 6.28a shows people in the Ames room (named for its designer, Adelbert Ames). The room is designed to look like a normal rectangular room, though its true dimensions are as shown in Figure 6.28b. The right corner is much closer than the left corner. The two young

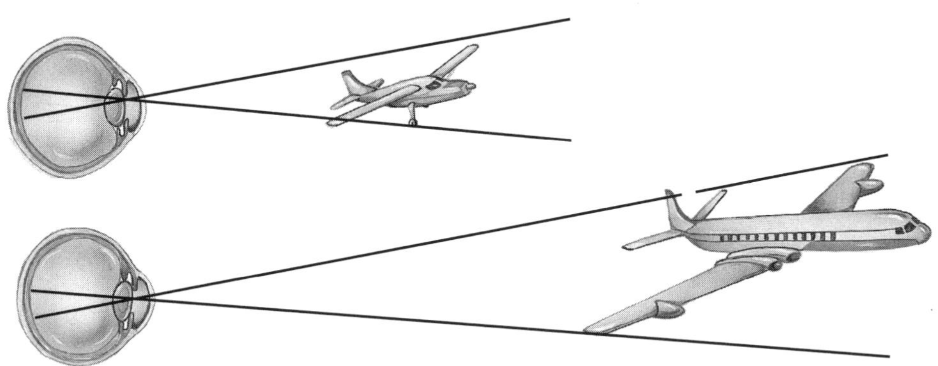

FIGURE 6.26

The trade-off between size and distance: A given image on the retina can indicate either a small, close object or a large, distant object.

FIGURE 6.27

Because fish come in many sizes, we can estimate the size of a fish only if we know how far away it is or if we can compare its size to other nearby objects. See what happens when you cover the man and then cover the hand.

women are actually the same height. If we eliminated all the background cues, we would correctly perceive the women as being the same size but at different distances. However, the apparently rectangular room provides such powerful (though misleading) cues to distance that the women appear to differ greatly in height.

Even a two-dimensional drawing on a flat surface can offer cues that lead to erroneous depth perception. People who have had much experience with photos and drawings tend to interpret two-dimensional drawings as if they were three-dimensional. Figure 6.29 shows a bewildering two-prong/three-prong device and a round staircase that seems to run uphill all the way clockwise or downhill all the way counterclockwise. Both drawings puzzle us because we try to interpret them as three-dimensional objects.

In Figure 6.30 linear perspective suggests that the right of the picture is farther away than the left. We therefore see the cylinder on the right as being the farthest away. If it is the farthest away and still produces the same size image on the retina as the other two, then it would have to be the largest. In short, by perceiving two-dimensional representations as if they were three-dimensional, we misjudge distance and consequently misjudge size. When we are somehow misled by the cues that ordinarily ensure constancy in size and shape, we experience an optical illusion (Day, 1972).

We can experience an *auditory illusion* by a similar principle: If we misestimate the distance to a sound source, we misestimate the intensity of the sound. That is, if you hear a sound that you think is coming from a distant source, you hear it as loud. (It would have to be for you to hear it so well from a distance.) If you hear the same sound but think it is coming from a source near you, it sounds softer (Kitigawa & Ichihara, 2002; Mershon, Desaulniers, Kiefer, Amerson, & Mills, 1981).

a

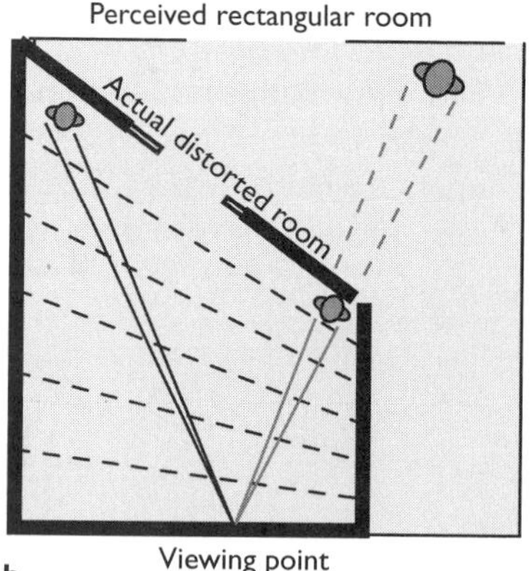

b

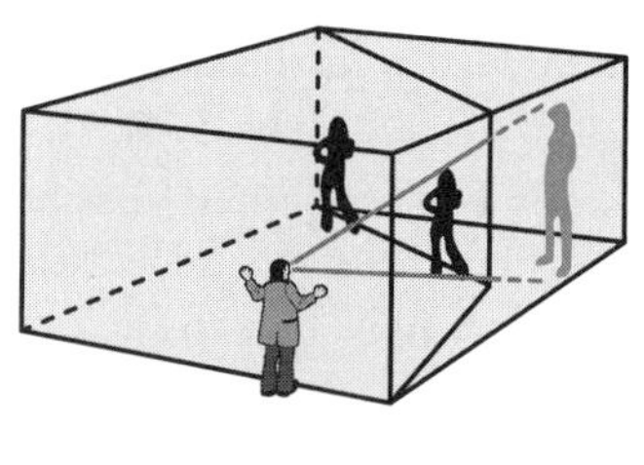

FIGURE 6.28

The Ames room is a study in deceptive perception, designed to be viewed through a peephole with one eye. (a) Both of these people are actually the same height. We are so accustomed to rooms with right angles that we can't imagine how this apparently ordinary room creates this optical illusion. (b) This diagram shows the positions of the people in the Ames room and demonstrates how the illusion of distance is created. (*Part b from J. R. Wilson et al., 1964*)

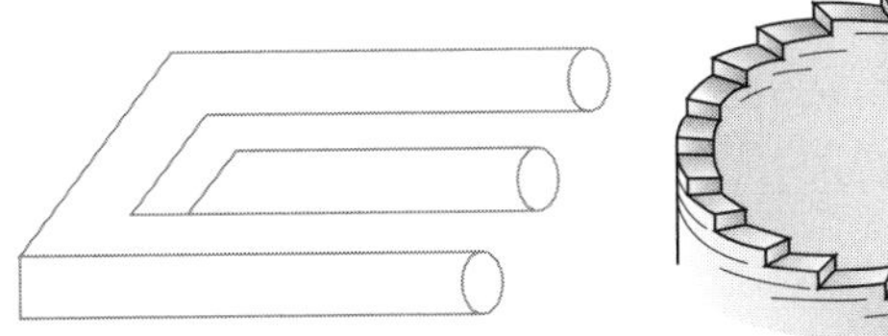

FIGURE 6.29

These two-dimensional drawings puzzle us because we try to interpret them as three-dimensional objects.

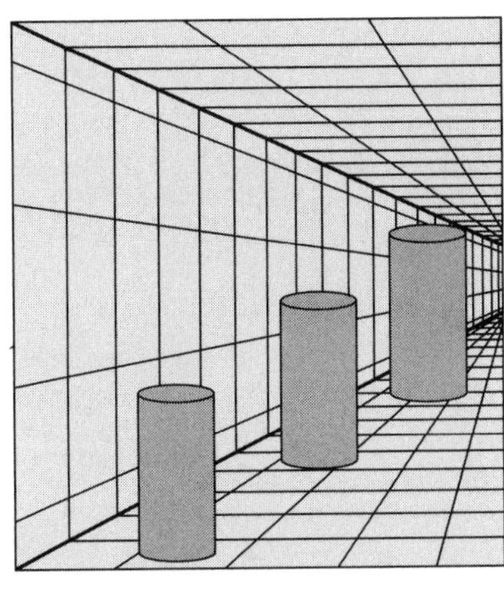

FIGURE 6.30

Many optical illusions depend on misjudging distances. The jar on the right seems larger because the context makes it appear farther away.

Further Evidence Linking Illusions to Depth Perception

The illusions occur because your brain does its best to judge distances and depths and then constructs an image of what the objects it sees *really are* (as opposed to what pattern of light strikes the retina). Let's belabor this point with two more examples. The first, shown in Figure 6.31, is the tabletop illusion (Shepard, 1990). Here, almost unbelievably, the vertical dimension of the blue table equals the horizontal dimension of the yellow table, and the horizontal dimension of the blue table equals the vertical dimension of the yellow table. (Take measurements at the center of each table. The shapes of the two tables are not exactly the same.) The blue table appears long and thin compared to the yellow one because we interpret it in depth. In effect your brain constructs what each table would have to really *be* in order to look this way (Purves & Lotto, 2003).

Now consider the Poggendorff illusion, first shown in Figure 6.25a, with a modified version in Figure 6.32. A diagonal line interrupted by something else appears

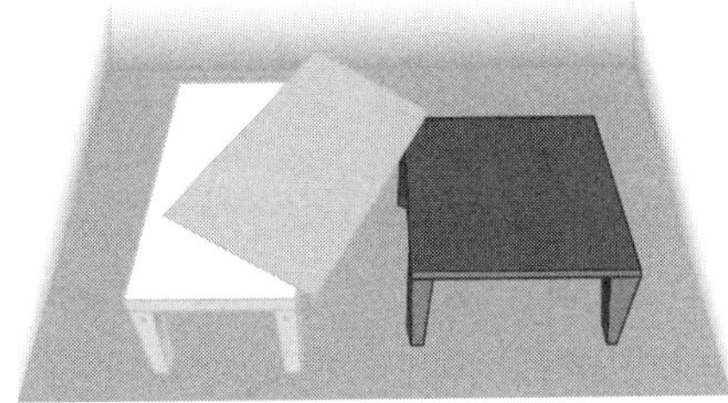

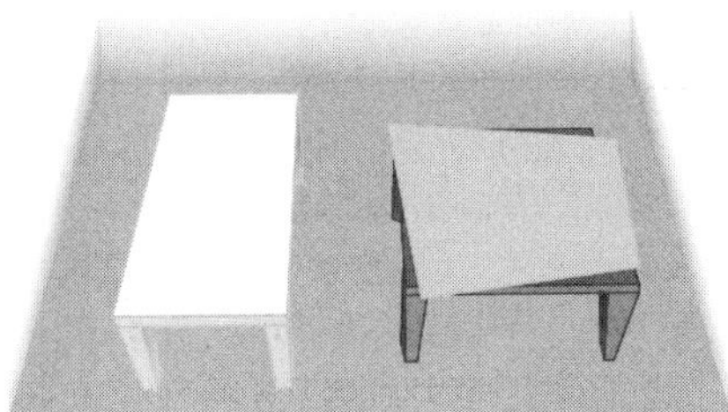

FIGURE 6.31

The tabletop illusion. The blue table is as wide as the yellow table is long, and as long as the yellow table is wide, if you measure in the middle of each table. The parts below show rotation of the blue table to overlap the yellow one.

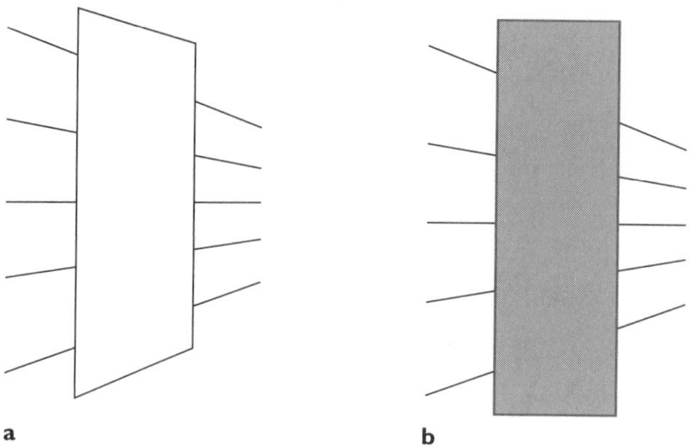

FIGURE 6.32

Variations of the Poggendorff illusion. If the interrupting bar encourages the perception of a line receding into the distance, we see the lines as continuous and straight. However, if the bar suggests the line has not receded, the lines appear distorted. (*From Spehar & Gillam, 2002*)

to be not quite straight, not quite continuous. Branka Spehar and Barbara Gillam (2002) have suggested an explanation: When we see a diagonal line, we ordinarily interpret it as a line receding into the distance, such as a path moving away from us toward the horizon. In Figure 6.32a the object that interrupts a diagonal line is consistent with that interpretation and even encourages it. In that case the illusion weakens or disappears; we see each line on the right as a continuation of the correct line on the left. However, in part b the bar provides a context that conflicts with the idea of a receding line, and we have more trouble processing the information.

The Moon Illusion

moon illusion
the apparent difference between the size of the moon at the horizon and its size when viewed higher in the sky.

To most people, the *moon close to the horizon appears about 30% larger than it appears when it is higher in the sky.* This **moon illusion** is so convincing that some people have tried to explain it by referring to the bending of light rays by the atmosphere or another physical phenomenon. The explanation, however, must depend on the observer, not the light rays. If you measure the moon image with navigational or photographic equipment, you will find that it is the same size at the horizon as it is higher in the sky. For example, Figure 6.33 shows the moon at two positions in the sky; you can measure the two images to demonstrate that they are really the same size. (The atmosphere's bending of light rays makes the moon look orange near the horizon, but it does not increase the size of the image.) However, photographs do not capture the full strength of the moon illusion as we see it in real life. In Figure 6.33 (or any similar pair of photos), the moon looks almost the same at each position; in the actual night sky, though, the moon looks enormous at the horizon.

One explanation is that the vast terrain between the viewer and the horizon provides a basis for size comparison. When you see the moon at the horizon, you can compare it to other objects you see at the horizon, which look tiny. By contrast the moon looks large. When you see the moon high in the sky, however, it is surrounded only by the vast, featureless sky, so in contrast it appears smaller (Baird, 1982; Restle, 1970).

A second explanation is that the terrain between the viewer and the horizon gives an impression of great distance. When the moon is high in the sky, we have no basis to judge distance, and perhaps we unconsciously see the overhead moon as closer than when it is at the horizon. If we see the "horizon moon" as more

FIGURE 6.33

Ordinarily, the moon looks much larger at the horizon than it does overhead. In photographs this illusion disappears almost completely, but the photographs do serve to demonstrate that the physical image of the moon is the same in both cases. The moon illusion requires a psychological explanation, not a physical one.

distant, we will perceive it as larger (Kaufman & Rock, 1989; Rock & Kaufman, 1962). This explanation is appealing because it relates the moon illusion to our misperceptions of distance, a factor already accepted as important for many other illusions.

Many psychologists are not satisfied with this explanation, however, primarily because they are not convinced that the horizon moon looks farther away than the overhead moon. If we ask people which looks farther away, many say they are not sure. If we insist on an answer, most say the horizon moon looks *closer,* contradicting the theory. Some psychologists reply that the situation is complicated: We unconsciously perceive the horizon as farther away; consequently, we perceive the horizon moon as very large; then, because of the perceived large size of the horizon moon, we secondarily and consciously say it looks closer, although we continue to unconsciously perceive it as farther (Rock & Kaufman, 1962).

One major message arises from work on optical illusions and indeed from all the research on visual perception: What we perceive is not the same as what is "out there." Our visual system does an amazing job of providing us with useful information about the world around us, but under unusual circumstances we can be very wrong about what we think we see.

REVIEW

- *Perception of minimal stimuli.* There is no sharp dividing line between sensory stimuli that can be perceived and sensory stimuli that cannot be perceived.
- *Signal detection.* To determine how accurately someone can detect a signal or how accurately a test diagnoses a condition, we need to consider not only the ratio of hits to misses when the stimulus is present but also the ratio of false alarms to correct rejections when the stimulus is absent.
- *Subliminal perception.* Under some circumstances a weak stimulus that we do not consciously identify can influence our behavior, at least weakly or briefly. However, the evidence does not support claims of powerful effects.

REVIEW (CONTINUED)

- *Face recognition.* People are amazingly good at recognizing faces.
- *Detection of simple visual features.* In the first stages of the process of perception, feature-detector cells identify lines, points, and simple movement. Visual afterimages can be interpreted in terms of fatiguing certain feature detectors.
- *Perception of organized wholes.* According to Gestalt psychologists, we perceive an organized whole by identifying similarities and continuous patterns across a large area of the visual field.
- *Visual constancies.* We ordinarily perceive the shape, size, and color of objects as constant, even though the pattern of light striking the retina varies from time to time.
- *Motion perception.* We perceive an object as moving if it moves relative to its background. We can generally distinguish between an object that is actually moving and a similar pattern of retinal stimulation that results from our own movement.
- *Depth perception.* To perceive depth, we use the retinal discrepancy between the views that our two eyes see. We also learn to use other cues that are just as effective with one eye as with two.
- *Optical illusions.* Many, but not all, optical illusions result from interpreting a two-dimensional display as three-dimensional or from other faulty estimates of depth.
- *The size-distance relationship.* Our estimate of an object's size depends on our estimate of its distance from us. If we overestimate its distance, we will also overestimate its size.

Answers to Other Questions in the Chapter

C. a. 7. b. 1. c. 5. d. 9. e. 4.

D.

E.

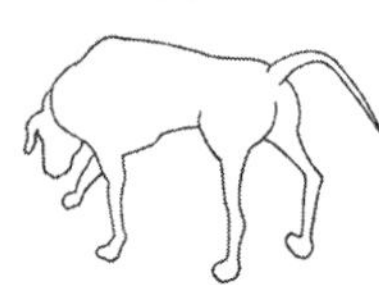

F.

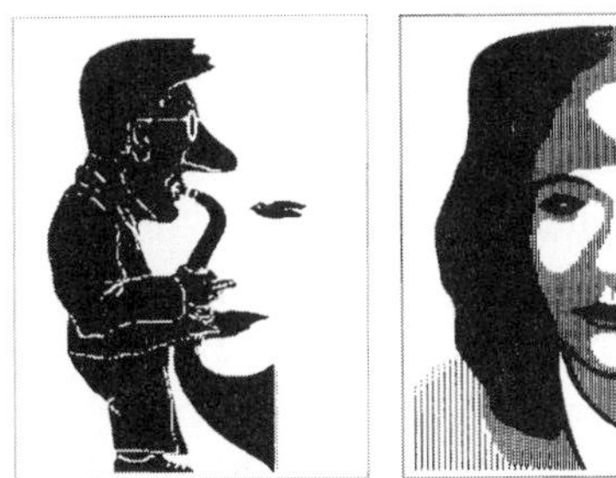

G.

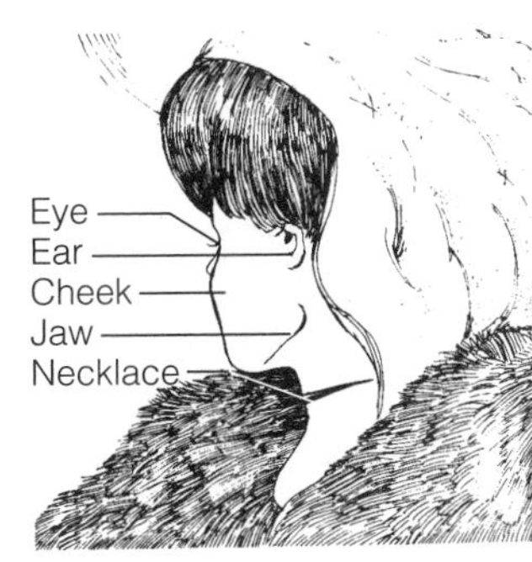

Young woman

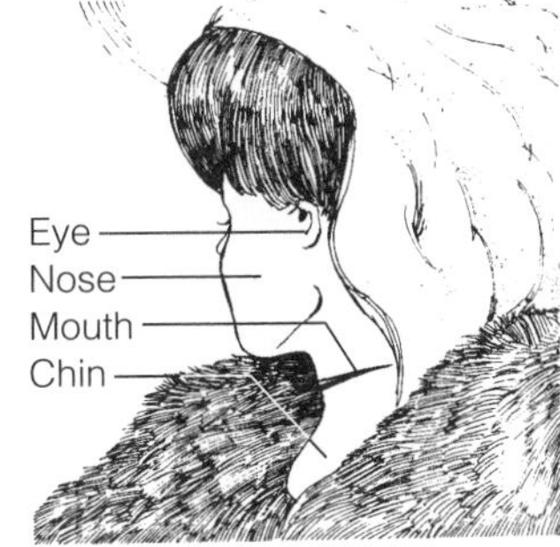

Old woman

H.

I. Line d is the same length as the one on the right. (Check it with a ruler.)

CHAPTER 6 PRACTICE EXAM

____ 1. Subliminal perception is defined as perceiving
a. stimuli weaker than the sensory threshold.
b. by attention to irrelevant stimuli.
c. Senory nformation without using sense organs.
d. Sensations that might affect perceptions.

____ 2. Psychological researchers have concluded that when rock bands included recorded backward messages
a. rock bands do not record backwards messages.
b. backwards messages influences the preconscious level of behavior.
c. Backards messages are automatically store and retrieved at a later date.
d. backwards messages have not been shown to influence behavior.

____ 3. After exposure to a subliminal visual stimulus of a happy face, people tend to
a. Become disturbed when someone smiles at them.
b. smile slightly and briefly.
c. Buy happy face stickers at the store.
d. Begin to draw pictures of happy faces.

____ 4. The brain appears to have a special module for face recognition because
a. The cortex imprints recognition features.
b. MRI shows that faces are stored in the amygdale.
c. Some brain damage can impair face recognition but not recognition of other objects.
d. Chimpanzees and humans recognize faces.

____ 5. A feature detector neuron in the visual cortex responds to
a. bright light anywhere on the fovea.
b. Shadows that move on the neuron.
c. light in a particular shape or pattern in one part of the retina.
d. Shadows from objects that are stationary.

____ 6. A neuron in the visual cortex that becomes excited whenever light of a certain shape falls on a particular part of the retina is a
a. visual constancy.
b. feature detector.
c. Neuron detector.
d. basilar membrane.

____ 7. Hubel and Wiesel's Nobel prize-winning research with monkeys and cats provided evidence for the existence of
a. signal detection.
b. Tactile receptors.
c. feature-detector cells.
d. Olfactory.

____ 8. If a person looks at wide bars for a minute, then looks at some narrower bars, the narrow bars will appear narrower than they really are because of
a. Reticular cues.
b. Moon illusion parallax.
c. feature detectors.
d. Transitional objects dectectors.

____ 9. The term "Gestalt" (as in Gestalt psychology) came from
a. a Latin word meaning gestation.
b. a German word meaning pattern.
c. An Old English word meaning gustatory.
d. A French word meaning potato.

____ 10. Gestalt psychology suggests that
a. the whole is deeper than the part.
b. the whole is less than than a few of its parts.
c. the whole is different from the sum of its parts.
d. the whole is more than none of its parts.

____ 11. Gestalt psychologists
a. Believe that experiences are perceived as components.
b. Believe that perceptions depend on overall configurations.
c. Suggest that perception is contains several parts.
d. Suggest that perceiving is an illusion.

_____ 12. Perceive objects that are close together and thinking they belonging to the same group is called
a. closeness.
b. Prolaxtion.
c. closure.
d. proximity.

_____ 13. When the moon looks like it is moving but clouds are not, is an example of
a. the moon delusion.
b. induced movement.
c. perceptual influence.
d. the psi chi illusion.

_____ 14. Which depth perception cues requires both eyes?
a. Linear vergence
b. convergence
c. interposition
d. Parallel cues

_____ 15. An example of motion parallax occurs when
a. You feel relaxed in your visual space when you thin about a pleasant scene.
b. When you fly in a plane, close objects pass by faster than distant objects.
c. Movie special effects appear real but aren't.
d. You observe an object moving when it really is.

Answers

1. A
2. D
3. B
4. C
5. C
6. B
7. C
8. C
9. B
10. C
11. B
12. D
13. B
14. B
15. B

CHAPTER 7: MOTIVATION AND EMOTION

QUESTIONS

1. What is the model of motivation introduced on the first page of the chapter?
2. What are three major categories of motives and examples of each?
3. What combination of signals to the hypothalamus indicates whether or not a person is hungry?
4. Why are weight problems begun in childhood harder to control?
5. What is the paradox of yo-yo dieting?
6. How might taste aversions be helpful or adaptive?
7. What are three possible causes of anorexia and bulimia?
8. What are the usual treatment approaches for anorexia and bulimia?
9. What ethnic and cultural groups appear less susceptible to anorexia and bulimia?
10. How are the food, air, water, sleep, and elimination drives similar?
11. What does pain prompt people to do?
12. In humans, what three things determine sexual expression?
13. How are hormones related to sex drive in men and women?
14. What do stimulus drives reflect the need for?
15. What does the inverted U function suggest about the relationship between arousal and performance?
16. What kinds of people have short or long circadian rhythms?
17. How does the opponent process theory explain a person's continuing a hazardous pursuit?
18. How do people high in nAch differ from people low in nAch?
19. What is the main key to success?
20. How can play be turned into work?
21. How can emotions be considered adaptive?
22. How does the amygdala regulate emotion?
23. What kinds of questions are asked by a lie detector examiner?
24. What is the lie detector's most common error?
25. What cultures differ with respect to expressions of anger and positive emotions?
26. What is the most easily recognized universal emotion?
27. What is the chameleon effect?
28. What are the best clues to lying?
29. What are the sequences of the three main theories of emotion?
30. What does attribution theory predict about arousal and interpersonal attraction?
31. How did Ekman demonstrate the facial feedback hypothesis?
32. In what ways were James and Lange, Cannon and Bard, and Schachter correct?
33. What are the sequences of the contemporary model of emotion?

VOCABULARY

1. anorexia nervosa
2. arousal
3. arousal theory
4. bulimia
5. circadian rhythms
6. Coolidge effect
7. drive
8. emotional expressions
9. emotional feelings
10. episodic drive
11. external eating cues
12. extracellular thirst
13. extrinsic motivation
14. facial feedback hypothesis
15. galvanic skin response
16. goal
17. homeostasis
18. incentive value
19. intracellular thirst
20. intrinsic motivation
21. inverted U function
22. leptin
23. motivation
24. need
25. need for achievement (nAch)
26. non-homeostatic
27. preadaptation
28. primary emotions
29. rate of metabolism
30. sensation seeking
31. set point
32. social motives
33. taste aversion
34. triangular theory of love
35. Yerkes-Dodson law

7 Motivation and Emotion

Mike Brinson/Getty Images

The Sun Sets Twice in Utah

SEVREN AND DENNIS had been backpacking for a week in the Unitas Mountains of Utah. Every day they enjoyed new trails, inspiring vistas, fresh air, and lots of wildlife. Best of all, neither of them wore a watch.

After a long hike one day, they reached a lake, just as darkness fell. The light was fading quickly, so they set up a tent, cooked dinner, and prepared to eat. Neither of them had an appetite, but they didn't want to wake up hungry in the middle of the night, so they ate anyway. Then they washed dishes and climbed into their tent, where they tried to get to sleep. That's when the sun came up.

Pulling back the tent flap, they looked around in amazement to discover bright sunshine outside. It was late afternoon. They had *hours* of daylight left before nightfall!

Heavy, dark clouds had covered most of the western sky when our wayward hikers first arrived at the lake. Apparently, an approaching storm blocked the sun, reducing the forest to twilight. When the storm retreated, the sun came out again. No wonder they weren't hungry or sleepy! Fortunately, no one else was there to laugh at them—although they did have a good laugh themselves.

This chapter is about the motives and emotions that underlie human behavior. As our hikers' experience suggests, even "simple" motivated activities, such as eating, are not solely under the control of the body. In many instances, external cues, expectations, learning, cultural values, and other factors influence our motives, actions, and goals (R. C. Beck, 2004).

Let's begin with basic motives, such as hunger and thirst, and then explore how emotions affect us. Although emotions can be the spice of life, they are sometimes the spice of death as well. Read on to find out why.

MOTIVATION—FORCES THAT PUSH AND PULL

What do you plan to do today? What are your goals? Why do you pursue them? How vigorously do you try to reach them? When are you satisfied? When do you give up? These are all questions about motivation, or why we act as we do. Let's begin with a basic model of motivation and an overview of types of motives.

motivation
internal processes that initiate, sustain, and direct activities.

Motivation refers to the dynamics of behavior—the ways in which our actions are *initiated, sustained, directed,* and *terminated* (Petri, 2003). Imagine that a student named Omar is studying psychology in the library. He begins to feel hungry and can't concentrate. His stomach growls and he decides to buy an apple from a vending machine. The machine is empty, so he goes to the cafeteria. Closed. Omar drives home, where he cooks a meal and eats it. At last his hunger is satisfied, and he resumes studying. Notice how Omar's food seeking was *initiated* by a bodily need. His search was *sustained* because the need was not immediately met, and his actions were *directed* by possible sources of food. Finally, achieving his goal *terminated* his food seeking.

A Model of Motivation

need
an internal deficiency that may energize behavior.

drive
the psychological expression of internal needs or valued goals. For example, hunger, thirst, or a drive for success.

response
any action, glandular activity, or other identifiable behavior.

goal
the target or objective of motivated behavior.

Many motivated activities begin with a **need**, or internal deficiency. The need that initiated Omar's search was a depletion of key substances in his body. Needs cause a **drive** (an energized motivational state) to develop. The drive was hunger, in Omar's case. Drives activate a **response** (an action or series of actions) designed to attain a **goal** (the "target" of motivated behavior). Reaching a goal that satisfies the need will end the chain of events. Thus, a simple model of motivation can be shown in this way:

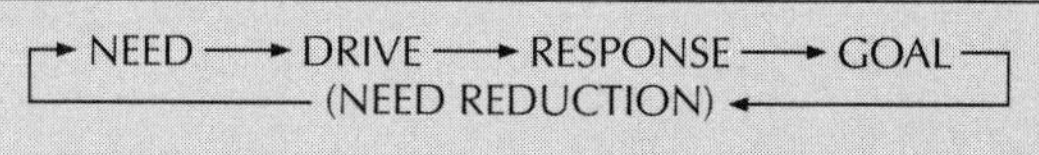

Aren't needs and drives the same thing? No, because the strength of needs and drives can differ. If you begin fasting today, your bodily need for food will increase every day. However, you would probably feel less "hungry" on the seventh day of fasting than you did on the first. Although your need for food steadily increases, the hunger drive comes and goes.

Now let's observe Omar again. It's Saturday night: For dinner, Omar has soup, salad, a large steak, a baked potato, four pieces of bread, two pieces of cheesecake, and three cups of coffee. After dinner, he complains that he is "too full to move." Soon after, Omar's roommate arrives with a strawberry pie. Omar exclaims that strawberry pie is his favorite dessert and eats three large pieces! Is this hunger? Certainly, Omar's dinner satisfied his biological needs for food.

How does that change the model of motivation? Omar's "pie lust" illustrates that motivated behavior can be energized by the "pull" of external stimuli, as well as by the "push" of internal needs.

incentive value
the value of a goal above and beyond its ability to fill a need.

Incentives The "pull" of a goal is called its **incentive value** (the goal's appeal beyond its ability to fill a need). Some goals are so desirable (strawberry pie, for example) that they can motivate behavior in the absence of an internal need. Other goals are so low in incentive value that they may be rejected even if they meet the internal need. Fresh, live grubworms, for instance, are highly nutritious. However, it is doubtful that you would eat one no matter how hungry you might be.

Usually, our actions are energized by a mixture of internal needs *and* external incentives. That's why a strong need may change an unpleasant incentive into a desired goal. Perhaps you've never eaten a grubworm, but we'll bet you've eaten

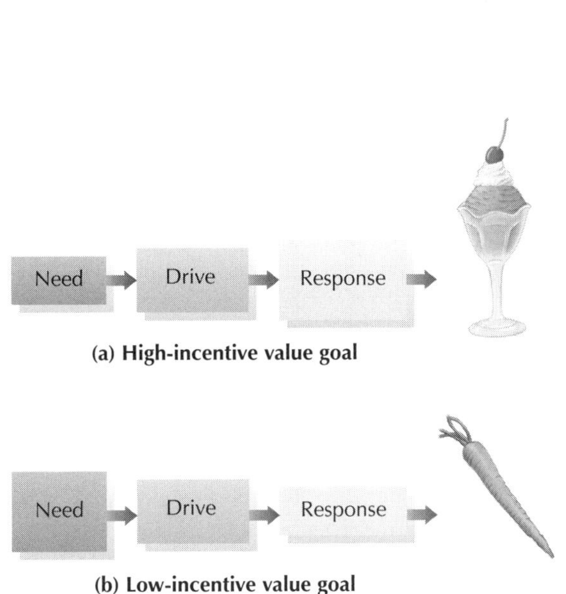

FIGURE 7.1

Needs and incentives interact to determine drive strength *(top)*. *(a)* Moderate need combined with a high-incentive goal produces a strong drive. *(b)* Even when a strong need exists, drive strength may be moderate if a goal's incentive value is low. It is important to remember, however, that incentive value lies "in the eye of the beholder" *(photo)*. No matter how hungry, few people would be able to eat the pictured grubworms.

some pretty horrible leftovers when the refrigerator was bare. The incentive value of goals also helps explain motives that don't seem to come from internal needs, such as drives for success, status, or approval (Figure 7.1).

Types of Motives For our purposes, motives can be divided into three major categories:

1. **Primary motives** are based on biological needs that must be met for survival. The most important primary motives are hunger, thirst, pain avoidance, and needs for air, sleep, elimination of wastes, and regulation of body temperature. Primary motives are innate.
2. **Stimulus motives** express our needs for stimulation and information. Examples include activity, curiosity, exploration, manipulation, and physical contact. Although such motives also appear to be innate, they are not strictly necessary for survival.
3. **Secondary motives** are based on learned needs, drives, and goals. Learned motives help explain many human activities, such as making music, creating a web page, or trying to win the skateboarding finals in the X Games. Many secondary motives are related to learned needs for power, affiliation (the need to be with others), approval, status, security, and achievement. Fear and aggression also appear to be greatly affected by learning.

primary motives innate motives based on biological needs.

stimulus motives innate needs for stimulation and information.

secondary motives motives based on learned needs, drives, and goals.

Primary Motives and Homeostasis

How important is food in your life? Water? Sleep? Air? Temperature regulation? Finding a public rest room? For most of us, satisfying biological needs is so routine that we tend to overlook how much of our behavior they direct. But exaggerate any of these needs through famine, shipwreck, poverty, near drowning, bitter cold, or drinking 10 cups of coffee, and their powerful grip on behavior becomes evident. We are, after all, still animals in many ways.

Biological drives are essential because they maintain *homeostasis* (HOE-me-oh-STAY-sis), or bodily equilibrium (Cannon, 1932).

homeostasis a steady state of bodily equilibrium.

What is homeostasis? The term **homeostasis** means "standing steady," or "steady state." Optimal levels exist for body temperature, for chemicals in the blood, for blood pressure, and so forth. When the body deviates from these "ideal" levels, automatic reactions begin to restore equilibrium (Deckers, 2005). Thus, it might help to think of homeostasis as being similar to a thermostat set at a particular temperature.

A (Very) Short Course on Thermostats

When room temperature falls below the level set on a thermostat, the heat is automatically turned on to warm the room. When the heat equals or slightly exceeds the ideal temperature, it is automatically turned off. In this way room temperature is kept in a state of equilibrium hovering around the ideal level.

The first reactions to disequilibrium in the human body are also automatic. For example, if you become too hot, more blood will flow through your skin and you will begin to perspire, thus lowering body temperature. Usually, we are not aware of such changes, unless continued disequilibrium drives us to seek shade, warmth, food, or water.

HUNGER—PARDON ME, MY HYPOTHALAMUS IS GROWLING

You get hungry, you find food, and you eat: Hunger might seem like a "simple" motive, but only recently have we begun to understand it. Hunger provides a good model of how internal and external factors direct our behavior. And, as we will see later, many of the principles that explain hunger also apply to thirst.

What causes hunger? When you feel hungry, you probably think of your stomach. That's why Walter Cannon and A. L. Washburn decided to see if stomach contractions cause hunger. In an early study, Washburn trained himself to swallow a balloon, which could be inflated through an attached tube. This allowed Cannon to record the movements of Washburn's stomach (Figure 7.2). When Washburn's stomach contracted, he reported that he felt "hunger pangs." In view of this, the two scientists concluded that hunger is nothing more than the contractions of an empty stomach (Cannon & Washburn, 1912). (Unfortunately, this proved to be an inflated conclusion.)

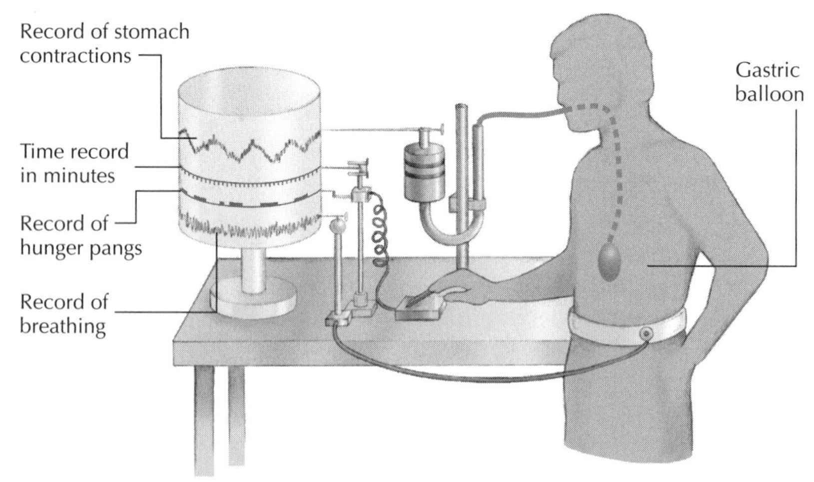

FIGURE 7.2
In Cannon's early study of hunger, a simple apparatus was used to simultaneously record hunger pangs and stomach contractions. (*After Cannon, 1934.*)

For many people, hunger produces an overall feeling of weakness or shakiness, rather than a "growling" stomach. Of course, eating *does* slow when the stomach is stretched or distended (full). (Remember last Thanksgiving?) However, we now know that the stomach is not essential for feeling hunger. Even people who have had their stomachs removed for medical reasons continue to feel hungry and eat regularly (Woods et al., 2000).

Then what does cause hunger? One important signal for hunger is lowered levels of glucose (sugar) in the blood (Campfield et al., 1996). Strange as it may seem, the liver also affects hunger.

The liver? Yes, the liver responds to a lack of bodily "fuel" by sending nerve impulses to the brain. These "messages" contribute to a desire to eat (Woods et al., 2000).

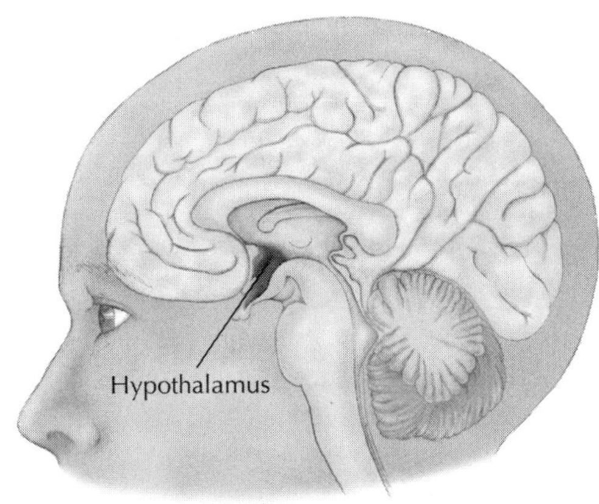

FIGURE 7.3
Location of the hypothalamus in the human brain.

Brain Mechanisms

What part of the brain controls hunger? When you are hungry, many parts of the brain are affected, so no single "hunger center" exists. However, a small area called the **hypothalamus** (HI-po-THAL-ah-mus) regulates many motives, including hunger, thirst, and the sex drive (Figure 7.3).

The hypothalamus is sensitive to levels of sugar in the blood (and other substances described in a moment). It also receives neural messages from the liver and the stomach. When combined, these signals determine if you are hungry or not (Woods et al., 2000).

One part of the hypothalamus acts as a *feeding system* that initiates eating. If the *lateral hypothalamus* is "turned on" with an electrified probe, even a well-fed animal will immediately begin eating. (The term *lateral* simply refers to the sides of the hypothalamus. See Figure 7.4.) If the same area is destroyed, the animal will never eat again.

A second area in the hypothalamus is part of a *satiety system,* or "stop mechanism" for eating. If the *ventromedial hypothalamus* (VENT-ro-MEE-dee-al) is destroyed, dramatic overeating results. (*Ventromedial* refers to the bottom middle of the hypothalamus.) Rats with such damage will eat until they balloon up to weights of 1,000 grams or more (Figure 7.5). A normal rat weighs about 180 grams. To put this weight gain in human terms, picture someone you know who weighs 180 pounds growing to a weight of 1,000 pounds.

hypothalamus
a small area at the base of the brain that regulates many aspects of motivation and emotion, especially hunger, thirst, and sexual behavior.

set point
the proportion of body fat that tends to be maintained by changes in hunger and eating.

The *paraventricular nucleus* (PAIR-uh-ven-TRICK-you-ler) of the hypothalamus also affects hunger (Figure 7.4). This area helps keep blood sugar levels steady by both starting and stopping eating. The paraventricular nucleus is very sensitive to a substance called *neuropeptide Y* (NPY). If NPY is present in large amounts, an animal will eat until it cannot hold another bite (Woods et al., 2000). Incidentally, the hypothalamus also responds to a chemical in marijuana, which can produce intense hunger (the "munchies") (Di Marzo et al., 2001).

How do we know when to stop eating? A chemical called glucagon-like peptide 1 (GLP-1) causes eating to cease. After you eat a meal, GLP-1 is released by the intestines. From there, it travels in the bloodstream to the brain. When enough GLP-1 arrives, your desire to eat ends (Nori, 1998; Turton et al., 1996). It takes at least 10 minutes for the hypothalamus to respond after you begin eating. That's why you are less likely to overeat if you eat slowly, which gives your brain time to get the message that you've had enough (Liu et al., 2000).

The substances we have reviewed are only some of the chemical signals that start and stop eating (Geary, 2004). Others continue to be discovered. In time, they may make it possible to artificially control hunger. If so, better treatments for extreme obesity and self-starvation could follow (Batterham et al., 2003; Woods et al., 2000).

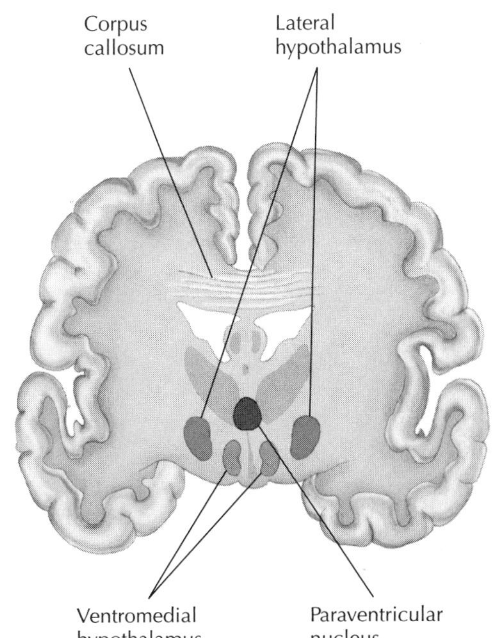

FIGURE 7.4
This is a cross section through the middle of the brain (viewed from the front of the brain). Indicated areas of the hypothalamus are associated with hunger and the regulation of body weight.

Set Point In addition to knowing when to start eating, and when a meal is over, your body needs to regulate weight over longer periods of time. This is done by monitoring the amount of fat stored in the body (Woods, Seeley, & Porte, 1998). Basically, your body has a **set point** for the proportion of fat it maintains. The set point acts like a "thermostat" for fat levels. Your own set point is the weight you maintain when you are making

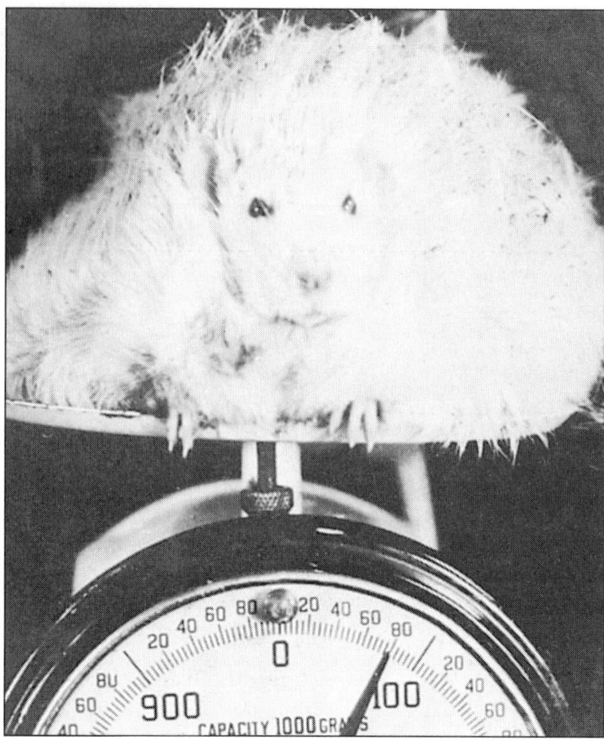

John Sholtis, Rockefeller University

FIGURE 7.5

Damage to the hunger satiety system in the hypothalamus can produce a very fat rat, a condition called hypothalamic *hyperphagia* (Hiper-FAGE-yah: overeating). This rat weighs 1,080 grams. (The pointer has gone completely around the dial and beyond.)

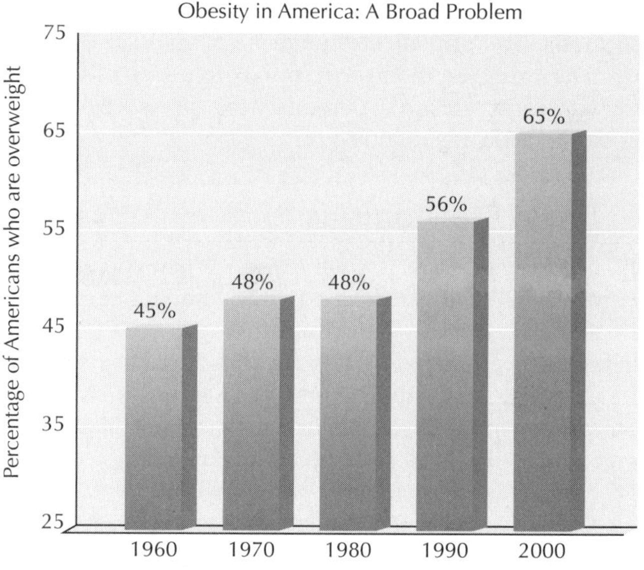

FIGURE 7.6

A near epidemic of obesity and has occurred in the United States during the last 20 years, with 65 percent of all Americans now classified as overweight (*CDC, 2003*).

no effort to gain or lose weight. When your body goes below its set point, you will feel hungry most of the time. On the other hand, fat cells release a substance called *leptin* when your "spare tire" is well inflated. Leptin is carried in the bloodstream to the brain, where it tells us to eat less (Mercer et al., 1998; Williams et al., 2004).

Set points are only one piece in a complex puzzle that's worth solving. Obesity is a major health risk and, for many, a source of social stigma and low self-esteem. Roughly 65 percent of adults in the United States are overweight (Figure 7.6). As a result, obesity is overtaking smoking as a cause of needless deaths (Murray, 2001b).

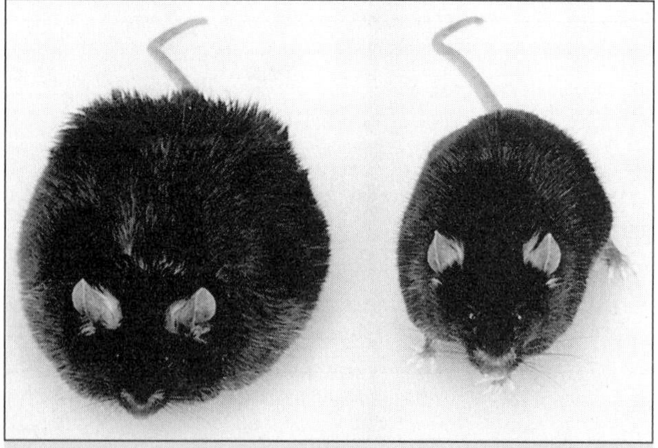

Charron Smith Amgen, Inc. John Sholtis

The mouse on the left has a genetic defect that prevents its fat cells from producing normal amounts of leptin. Without this chemical signal, the mouse's body acts as if its set point for fat storage is, shall we say, rather high.

Obesity

Why do people overeat? If internal needs alone controlled eating, fewer people would overeat. However, most of us are also sensitive to *external eating cues*. These are signs and signals linked with food. Do you tend to eat more when food is attractive, highly visible, and easy to get? If so, then external cues affect your food intake. In cultures like ours, where food is plentiful, external cues often lead to overeating (Woods et al., 2000). For example, many college freshmen gain weight rapidly during their first three months on campus (the famous "Frosh 15"). All-you-can-eat dining halls in the dorms and nighttime snacking appear to be the culprits (Levitsky et al., 2003).

Is it true that people also overeat when they are emotionally upset? Yes. People with weight problems are just as likely to eat when they are anxious, angry, or sad as when hungry (Schotte, Cools, & McNally, 1990). Furthermore, obese individuals are often unhappy in our fat-conscious culture.

DISCOVERING PSYCHOLOGY

What's Your BMI? (We've Got Your Number.)

From the standpoint of fashion, you may already have an opinion about whether you are overweight. But how do you rate from a medical perspective? Obesity is directly linked to heart disease, high blood pressure, stroke, diabetes, and premature death. But how heavy do you have to be to endanger your health? A measure called the *body mass index* (BMI) can be used to assess where you stand on the weight scale (so to speak). You can calculate your BMI by using the following formula:

$$\text{BMI} = \frac{\text{(your weight in pounds)}}{\text{(height in inches)(height in inches)}} \times 703$$

To use the formula, take your height in inches and multiply that number by itself (square the number). Then divide the result into your weight in pounds. Multiply the resulting number by 703 to obtain your BMI. For example, a person who weighs 220 pounds and is 6 feet 3 inches tall has a BMI of 27.5.

$$\frac{\text{(220 pounds)}}{\text{(75 inches)(75 inches)}} \times 703 = 27.5$$

Now, compare your BMI to the following scale:

Underweight	less than 18.5
Normal weight	18.5 to 24.9
Overweight	25 to 29.9
Obesity	30 or greater

If your BMI is greater than 25 you should be concerned. If it is greater than 30, your weight may be a serious health risk. (There are two exceptions: The BMI may overestimate body fat if you have a muscular build, and it may underestimate body fat in older persons who have lost muscle mass.) Losing weight and keeping it off can be very challenging. However, if you're overweight, lowering your BMI is well worth the effort. In the long run, it could save your life.

The result is overeating, which leads to emotional distress and still more overeating (Rutledge & Linden, 1998).

Diet A diet is not just a way to lose weight. Your current diet is defined by the types and amounts of food you regularly eat. Some diets actually encourage overeating. For instance, placing animals on a "supermarket" diet leads to gross obesity. In one classic experiment, rats were given meals of chocolate chip cookies, salami, cheese, bananas, marshmallows, milk chocolate, peanut butter, and fat. These pampered rodents gained almost three times as much weight as rats that ate only laboratory chow (Sclafani & Springer, 1976). (Rat chow is a dry mixture of several bland grains. If you were a rat, you'd probably eat more cookies than rat chow, too.)

People are also sensitive to dietary content. In general, *sweetness*, high *fat content*, and *variety* tend to encourage overeating (Lucas & Sclafani, 1990). Sadly, our culture provides the worst kinds of foods for people who suffer from obesity. For instance, restaurant food tends to be higher in fat and calories than meals made at home. The convenience-food industry also tends to promote cheap, tasty products that are loaded with fat and sugar (Brownell, 2003).

Large meals are another problem. For example, food portions at restaurants in the United States are 25 percent larger, or more, than they are in France. Far fewer people are obese in France, most likely, because they simply eat less. The French also take longer to eat a meal, which discourages overeating (Rozin et al., 2003).

An added problem faced by people who want to control their weight concerns the way evolution prepared us to store fat when food is plentiful.

Large food portions contribute to overeating. A fast food meal consisting of a hamburger, medium fries, and a medium soda averages 1,200 calories, which is over half the daily caloric need for an adult. Make that a double burger, add cheese, super-size the fries and the drink and you will consume two thirds of the food you need in a day, in just one meal. Notice, too, that people tend to eat all the food they have paid for, even if it is more than they need.

Evolution and Yo-Yo Dieting If dieting works, why are hundreds of "new" diets published each year? The answer is that although dieters do lose weight, most regain it soon after they stop dieting. In fact, many people end up weighing even more than before. Why should this be so? Dieting (starving) slows the body's rate of metabolism (the rate at which energy is used up). In effect, a dieter's body becomes highly efficient at *conserving* calories and storing them as fat (Pinel, Assanand, & Lehman, 2000).

Apparently, evolution prepared us to save energy when food is scarce and to stock up on fat when food is plentiful. Briefly starving yourself, therefore, may have little lasting effect on weight. "Yo-yo dieting," or repeatedly losing and gaining weight, is especially dangerous. Frequent changes in weight can dramatically slow the body's metabolic rate. This makes it harder to lose weight each time a person diets and easier to regain weight when the diet ends. Frequent weight changes also increase the risk of heart disease and premature death (Wang & Brownell, 2005). To avoid bouncing between feast and famine requires a permanent change in eating habits and exercise—a topic we will return to soon.

To summarize, overeating is related to internal and external influences, diet, emotions, genetics, exercise, and many other factors. We live in a culture that provides inexpensive, good-tasting food everywhere, and a brain that evolved to say, "Eat whenever food is available." We eat more when we are given more, and big portions combined with rapid eating can override a natural sense of fullness. For such reasons, scientists are still a long way from winning the "battle of the bulge." Nevertheless, many people have learned to take control of eating by applying the principles of behavioral dieting.

Behavioral Dieting

behavioral dieting weight reduction based on changing exercise and eating habits, rather than temporary self-starvation.

As we have noted, dieting is usually followed by rapid weight gains. If you really want to lose weight you must overhaul your eating habits, an approach called **behavioral dieting**. Here are some helpful behavioral techniques.

1. **Get yourself committed to weight loss.** Involve other people in your efforts. Programs such as Overeaters Anonymous or Take Off Pounds Sensibly can be a good source of social support.
2. **Exercise.** No diet can succeed for long without an increase in exercise, because exercise lowers the body's set point. Stop saving steps and riding elevators. Add activity to your routine in every way you can think of. To lose weight, you must use more calories than you take in. Burning just 200 extra calories a day can help prevent rebound weight gains. That's just 30 minutes a day of walking or light exercise. The more frequently and vigorously you exercise, the more weight you will lose (Jeffery & Wing, 2001).
3. **Learn your eating habits by observing yourself and keeping a "diet diary."** Begin by making a complete, 2-week record of when and where you eat, what you eat, and the feelings and events that occur just before and after eating. Is a roommate, relative, or spouse encouraging you to overeat? What are your most "dangerous" times and places for overeating?
4. **Learn to weaken your personal eating cues.** When you have learned when and where you do most of your eating, avoid these situations. Try to restrict your eating to one room, and do not read, watch TV, study, or talk on the phone while eating. Require yourself to interrupt what you are doing in order to eat.
5. **Count calories, but don't starve yourself.** To lose, you must eat less, and calories allow you to keep a record of your food intake. If you have trouble eating less every day, try dieting 4 days a week. People who diet intensely every other day lose as much as those who diet moderately every day (Viegener et al., 1990).
6. **Develop techniques to control the act of eating.** Begin by taking smaller portions. Carry to the table only what you plan to eat. Put all other food away before leaving the kitchen. Eat slowly, sip water between bites of food, leave

food on your plate, and stop eating before you are completely full. As mentioned earlier, you should be especially wary of the extra-large servings at fast-food restaurants. Saying "super-size me" too often can, indeed, leave you super sized (Murray, 2001b).

7. **Avoid snacks.** It is generally better to eat several small meals a day than three large ones (Assanand, Pinel, & Lehman, 1998). However, high-calorie snacks tend to be eaten *in addition to* meals. If you have an impulse to snack, set a timer for 20 minutes and see if you are still hungry then. Delay the impulse to snack several times if possible. Dull your appetite by filling up on raw carrots, bouillon, water, coffee, or tea.
8. **Chart your progress daily.** Record your weight, the number of calories eaten, and whether you met your daily goal. Set realistic goals by cutting down calories gradually. Losing about a pound per week is realistic, but remember, you are changing habits, not just dieting. Diets don't work!
9. **Set a "threshold" for weight control.** Maintaining weight loss can be even more challenging than losing weight. A study found that people who successfully maintained weight losses had a regain limit of 3 pounds or less. In other words, if they gained more than 2 or 3 pounds, they immediately began to make corrections in their eating habits and amount of exercise (Brownell et al., 1986).

Be patient with this program. It takes years to develop eating habits. You can expect it to take at least several months to change them. If you are unsuccessful at losing weight with these techniques, you might find it helpful to seek the aid of a psychologist familiar with behavioral weight-loss techniques.

Other Factors in Hunger

As research on overeating suggests, "hunger" is affected by more than bodily needs for food. Let's consider some additional factors.

Cultural Factors Learning to think of some foods as desirable and others as revolting has a large impact on what we eat. In North America we would never consider eating the eyes out of the steamed head of a monkey, but in some parts of the world they are considered a delicacy. By the same token, vegans and vegetarians think it is barbaric to eat any kind of meat. In short, cultural values (widely held beliefs about the desirability of various objects and activities) greatly affect the *incentive value* of foods.

Taste Even tastes for "normal" foods vary considerably. For example, if you are well fed, leptin dulls the tongue's sensitivity to sweet tastes (Kawai et al., 2000). That's why you may lose your "sweet tooth" when you are full. Actually, if you eat too much of any particular food, it will become less appealing. This probably helps us maintain variety in our diets. However, it also encourages obesity in societies where tasty foods are plentiful. If you overdose on fried chicken or French fries, moving on to some cookies or chocolate cheesecake certainly won't do your body much good (Pinel, Assanand, & Lehman, 2000).

taste aversion
an active dislike for a particular food.

It is easy to acquire a **taste aversion**, or active dislike, for a particular food. This can happen if a food causes sickness or if it is merely associated with nausea (Jacobsen et al., 1993). Not only do we learn to avoid such foods, but they too can become nauseating. A friend of ours, who once became ill after eating a cheese Danish (well, actually, *several*), has never again been able to come face to face with this delightful pastry.

If getting sick occurs long after eating, how does it become associated with a particular food? A good question. Taste aversions are a type of classical conditioning. A long delay between the CS and US usually prevents conditioning. However, psychologists theorize that we have a biological tendency to associate an upset stomach with foods eaten earlier. Such learning is usually protective. Yet, sadly, many cancer patients suffer taste aversions long after the nausea of their drug treatments has passed (Stockhorst, Klosterhalfen, & Steingrueber, 1998).

If you like animals, you will be interested in an imaginative approach to an age-old problem. In many rural areas, predators are poisoned, trapped, or shot by ranchers. These practices have nearly wiped out the timber wolf, and in some areas the coyote faces a similar end. How might the coyote be saved without a costly loss of livestock?

bait shyness
an unwillingness or hesitation on the part of animals to eat a particular food.

anorexia nervosa
active self-starvation or a sustained loss of appetite that has psychological origins.

bulimia nervosa
excessive eating (gorging) usually followed by self-induced vomiting and/or taking laxatives.

In a classic experiment, coyotes were given lamb tainted with lithium chloride. Coyotes who took the bait became nauseated and vomited. After one or two such treatments, they developed **bait shyness**—a lasting distaste for the tainted food (Gustavson & Garcia, 1974). If applied consistently, taste aversion conditioning might solve many predator–livestock problems. (Perhaps this technique could even be used to protect roadrunners from the Wiley Coyote!)

Taste aversions may also help people avoid severe nutritional imbalances. For example, if you go on a fad diet and eat only grapefruit, you will eventually begin to feel ill. In time, associating your discomfort with grapefruit may create an aversion to it and restore some balance to your diet.

Janet Hass/Rainbow

Like humans and other animals, coyotes develop taste aversions when food is associated with nausea.

Eating Disorders

Under the sheets of her hospital bed Krystal looks like a skeleton. If her **anorexia nervosa** (AN-uh-REK-see-yah ner-VOH-sah: self-starvation) cannot be stopped, Krystal may die of malnutrition. Victims of anorexia, who are mostly adolescent females (5 to 10 percent are male), suffer devastating weight losses from severe, self-inflicted dieting (Cooper, 2005; Polivy & Herman, 2002).

Do anorexics lose their appetite? No, many continue to feel hungry, yet struggle to starve themselves to excessive thinness. A compulsive desire to lose weight causes them to actively avoid food. However, this does not prevent them from feeling physical hunger. Often, anorexia starts with "normal" dieting that slowly begins to dominate the person's life. In time, anorexics suffer debilitating health problems. From 5 to 8 percent (more than 1 in 20) die of malnutrition (Polivy & Herman, 2002). Table 7.1 lists the symptoms of anorexia nervosa.

Bulimia nervosa (bue-LIHM-ee-yah) is a second major eating disorder. Bulimic persons gorge on food, then vomit or

TABLE 7.1 Recognizing Eating Disorders

ANOREXIA NERVOSA	BULIMIA NERVOSA
• Body weight below 85 percent of normal for one's height and age.	• Normal or above-normal weight.
• Refusal to maintain body weight in normal range.	• Recurring binge eating.
• Intense fear of becoming fat or gaining weight, even though underweight.	• Eating within an hour or two an amount of food that is much larger than most people would consume.
• Disturbance in one's body image or perceived weight.	• Feeling a lack of control over eating.
• Self-evaluation is unduly influenced by body weight.	• Purging behavior (vomiting or misuse of laxatives or diuretics).
• Denial of seriousness of abnormally low body weight.	• Excessive exercise to prevent weight gain.
• Absence of menstrual periods.	• Fasting to prevent weight gain.
• Purging behavior (vomiting or misuse of laxatives or diuretics).	• Self-evaluation is unduly influenced by body weight.

DSM-IV-TR, 2000.

take laxatives to avoid gaining weight (see Table 7.1). Like anorexia, most victims of bulimia are girls or women. Approximately 5 percent of college women are bulimic, and as many as 61 percent have milder eating problems. Bingeing and purging can seriously damage health. Typical risks include sore throat, hair loss, muscle spasms, kidney damage, dehydration, tooth erosion, swollen salivary glands, menstrual irregularities, loss of sex drive, and even heart attack.

Causes *What causes anorexia and bulimia?* Women who suffer from eating disorders are extremely dissatisfied with their bodies. Usually, they have distorted views of themselves and exaggerated fears of becoming fat. Many overestimate their body size by 25 percent or more. As a result, they think they are disgustingly "fat" when they are actually wasting away (Figure 7.7) (Gardner & Bokenkamp, 1996; Polivy & Herman, 2002). Many of these problems are related to harmful messages in the media. Girls who spend a lot of time reading teen magazines are more likely to have distorted body images and unrealistic ideas about how they compare with others (Martinez-Gonzalez et al., 2003).

Anorexic teens are usually described as "perfect" daughters—helpful, considerate, conforming, and obedient. Many seem to be seeking perfect control in their lives by being perfectly slim (Pliner & Haddock, 1996). People suffering from bulimia are also concerned with control. Typically they are obsessed with thoughts of weight, food, eating, and ridding themselves of food. As a result, they feel guilt, shame, self-contempt, and anxiety after a binge. Vomiting reduces their anxiety, which makes purging highly reinforcing (Powell & Thelen, 1996).

Treatment People suffering from eating disorders need professional help. Treatment for anorexia usually begins with giving drugs to relieve obsessive fears of gaining weight. Then a medical diet is used to restore weight and health. Next, a counselor may help patients work on the emotional conflicts that led to weight loss. For bulimia, behavioral counseling may include self-monitoring of food intake. The urge to vomit can be treated with extinction training. A related cognitive-behavioral approach focuses on changing the thinking patterns and beliefs about weight and body shape that perpetuate eating disorders (Byrne & McLean, 2002; Cooper, 2005).

AP/Wide World Photo

Anorexia nervosa is far more dangerous than many people realize. This haunting photo shows popular singer Karen Carpenter shortly before she died of starvation-induced heart failure. Many other celebrities have struggled with eating disorders, including Paula Abdul, Kirstie Alley, Fiona Apple, Victoria Beckham (Posh Spice), Princess Diana, Tracey Gold, Janet Jackson, and Mary-Kate Olsen.

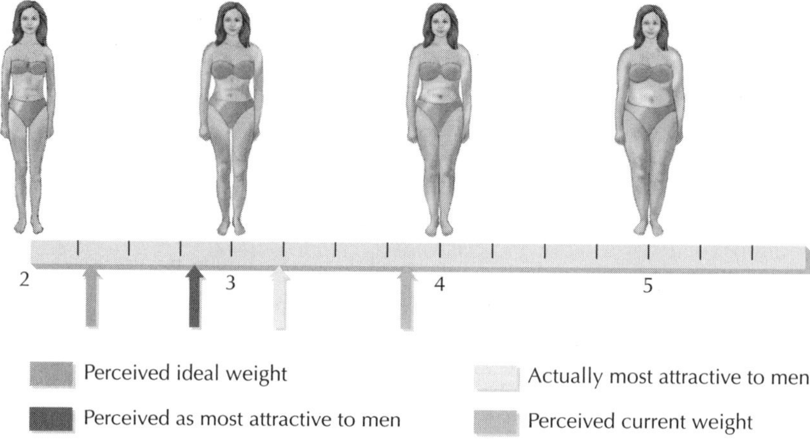

FIGURE 7.7

Women with abnormal eating habits were asked to rate their body shape on a scale similar to the one you see here. As a group, they chose ideal figures much thinner than what they thought their current weights were. (Most women say they want to be thinner than they currently are, but to a lesser degree than women with eating problems.) Notice that the women with eating problems chose an ideal weight that was even thinner than what they thought men prefer. This is not typical of most women. In this study, only women with eating problems wanted to be thinner than what they thought men find attractive (Zellner, Harner, & Adler, 1989).

Evan Agostini/Getty Images

The relentless parade of atypically thin models in the media contributes to eating disorders. People with eating disorders are much more likely to report being influenced by unrealistic body ideals in the media (Murray, Touyz, & Beumont, 1996).

Most people suffering from eating disorders will not seek help on their own. Typically, it takes strong urging by family or friends to get victims into treatment.

Culture, Ethnicity, and Dieting

Women with eating disorders are not alone in having body image problems. In Western cultures, many women learn to see themselves as "objects" that are evaluated by others. As a result, they try to shape their bodies to the cultural ideal of slimness through dieting (Fredrickson et al., 1998).

Just looking at a fashion magazine tends to leave women less satisfied with their weight and anxious to be thinner (Simpson, 2002). However, women from some cultural backgrounds appear to be less susceptible to the glorification of slimness. For example, Asian-American college students are only half as likely to diet as other college women are (Tsai, Hoerr, & Song, 1998). Within the African-American and Pacific-Islander communities there is a general preference for a fuller and shapelier figure. In these groups a larger body size is associated with high social status, health, and beauty (Flynn & Fitzgibbon, 1998; Ofosu, Lafreniere, & Senn, 1998). Clearly, what constitutes an attractive body style is a matter of opinion.

PRIMARY MOTIVES REVISITED—THIRST, SEX, AND PAIN

Most biological motives work in ways that are similar to hunger. For example, thirst is only partially controlled by dryness of the mouth. If you were to take a drug that made your mouth constantly wet, or dry, your water intake would remain normal. Like hunger, thirst is regulated by separate *thirst* and *thirst satiety* systems in the hypothalamus. Also like hunger, thirst is strongly affected by learning and cultural values.

Thirst

You may not have noticed, but there are actually two kinds of thirst. **Extracellular thirst** occurs when water is lost from the fluids surrounding the cells of your body. Bleeding, vomiting, diarrhea, sweating, and drinking alcohol cause this type of thirst (Petri, 2003). When a person loses both water and minerals in any of these ways—especially by perspiration—a slightly salty liquid may be more satisfying than plain water.

extracellular thirst
thirst caused by a reduction in the volume of fluids found between body cells.

Why would a thirsty person want to drink salty water? The reason is that before the body can retain water, minerals lost through perspiration (mainly salt) must be replaced. In lab tests, animals greatly prefer saltwater after salt levels in their bodies are lowered (Strickler & Verbalis, 1988). Similarly, some nomadic peoples of the Sahara Desert prize blood as a beverage, probably because of its saltiness. (Maybe they should try Gatorade?)

A second type of thirst occurs when you eat a salty meal. In this instance your body does not lose fluid. Instead, excess salt causes fluid to be drawn out of cells. As the cells "shrink," **intracellular thirst** is triggered. Thirst of this type is best quenched by plain water.

intracellular thirst
thirst triggered when fluid is drawn out of cells due to an increased concentration of salts and minerals outside the cell.

The drives for food, water, air, sleep, and elimination are all similar in that they are generated by a combination of activities in the body and the brain, and they are influenced by various external factors. However, the sex drive and the drive to avoid pain are more unusual.

Pain

How is the drive to avoid pain different? Hunger, thirst, and sleepiness come and go in a fairly regular cycle each day. Pain avoidance, by contrast, is an **episodic drive** (ep-ih-SOD-ik). That is, it occurs in distinct episodes when bodily damage takes place or is about to occur. Most drives prompt us to actively seek a desired goal (food, drink, warmth, and so forth). Pain prompts us to *avoid* or *eliminate* sources of discomfort.

episodic drive
a drive that occurs in distinct episodes.

estrus
changes in the sexual drives of animals that create a desire for mating; particularly used to refer to females in heat.

estrogen
any of a number of female sex hormones.

Some people feel they must be "tough" and not show any distress. Others complain loudly at the smallest ache or pain. The first attitude raises pain tolerance, and the second lowers it. As this suggests, the drive to avoid pain is partly learned. That's why members of some societies endure cutting, burning, whipping, tattooing, and piercing of the skin that would agonize most people (but apparently not devotees of piercing and "body art"). In general, we learn how to react to pain by observing family members, friends, and other role models (McMahon & Koltzenburg, 2005).

Alain Evrard/Photo Researchers, Inc.

Tolerance for pain and the strength of a person's motivation to avoid discomfort are greatly affected by cultural practices and beliefs.

The Sex Drive

Many psychologists do not think of sex as a primary motive, because sex (contrary to anything your personal experience might suggest) is not necessary for *individual* survival. It is necessary, of course, for *group* survival.

The term sex drive refers to the strength of one's motivation to engage in sexual behavior. In lower animals the sex drive is directly related to hormones. Female mammals (other than humans) are interested in mating only when their fertility cycles are in the stage of **estrus**, or "heat." Estrus is caused by a release of **estrogen** (a female sex hormone) into the bloodstream. Hormones are important in males as well. In most animals, castration will abolish the sex drive. But in contrast to females, the normal male animal is almost always ready to mate. His sex drive is primarily aroused by the behavior and scent of a receptive female. Therefore, in many species mating is closely tied to female fertility cycles.

How much do hormones affect human sex drives? Hormones affect the human sex drive, but not as directly as in animals (Crooks & Baur, 2005). The sex drive in men is related to the amount of androgens (male hormones) provided by the testes. When the supply of androgens dramatically increases at puberty, so does the male sex drive. Likewise, the sex drive in women is related to their estrogen levels (Graziottin, 1998). However, "male" hormones also affect the female sex drive. In addition to estrogen, a woman's body produces small amounts of androgens. When their androgen levels increase, many women experience a corresponding increase in sex drive (Van Goozen et al., 1995).

The link between hormones and the sex drive grows weaker as we ascend the biological scale. For example, there is no connection between female sexual activity and women's monthly menstrual cycles. In humans, mental, cultural, and emotional factors determine sexual expression. However, our liberation from hormones is not total. Human males lose their sex drive after castration, and some women lose sexual desire when taking birth control pills.

non-homeostatic drive
a drive that is relatively independent of physical deprivation cycles or bodily need states.

For now it is enough to note that the sex drive is largely **non-homeostatic** (relatively independent of bodily need states). In humans, the sex drive can be aroused at virtually any time by almost anything. It therefore shows no clear relationship to deprivation (the amount of time since the drive was last satisfied). Certainly, an increase in desire may occur as time passes. But recent sexual activity does not prevent sexual desire from occurring again. Notice, too, that people may seek to arouse the sex drive as well as to reduce it. This unusual quality makes the sex drive capable of motivating a wide range of behaviors. It also explains why sex is used to sell almost everything imaginable.

The non-homeostatic quality of the sex drive can be shown in this way: A male animal is allowed to copulate until it seems to have no further interest in sexual behavior. Then a new sexual partner is provided. Immediately the animal resumes sexual activity. This pattern is called the *Coolidge effect* after former U.S. president Calvin Coolidge. What, you might ask, does Calvin Coolidge have to do with the sex drive? The answer is found in the following story.

While touring an experimental farm, Coolidge's wife reportedly asked if a rooster mated just once a day. "No ma'am," she was told, "he mates dozens of times each day." "Tell that to the president," she said, with a faraway look in her eyes. When President Coolidge reached the same part of the tour, his wife's message was given to him. His reaction was to ask if the dozens of matings were with the same hen. No, he was told, different hens were involved. "Tell *that* to Mrs. Coolidge," the president is said to have replied.

STIMULUS DRIVES—SKYDIVING, HORROR MOVIES, AND THE FUN ZONE

Are you full of energy right now? Are you feeling tired? Clearly, the level of arousal you are experiencing is closely linked with your motivation. Are there ideal levels of arousal for different people and different activities? Let's find out.

stimulus drives
drives based on needs for exploration, manipulation, curiosity, and stimulation.

Most people enjoy a steady "diet" of new movies, novels, tunes, fashions, games, news, websites, and adventures. Yet **stimulus drives**, which reflect needs for information, exploration, manipulation, and sensory input, go beyond mere entertainment. Stimulus drives also help us survive. As we scan our surroundings, we constantly identify sources of food, danger, shelter, and other key details. Stimulus drives are readily apparent in animals as well as humans. For example, monkeys will quickly learn to solve a mechanical puzzle made up of interlocking metal pins,

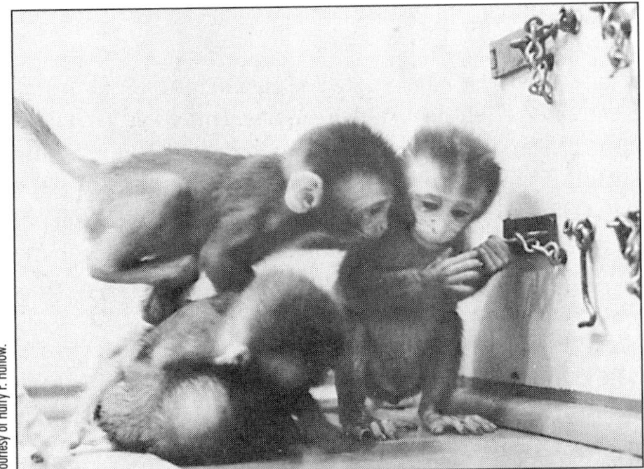

Courtesy of Harry F. Harlow.

FIGURE 7.8
Monkeys happily open locks that are placed in their cage. Because no reward is given for this activity, it provides evidence for the existence of stimulus needs.

hooks, and latches (Butler, 1954) (Figure 7.8). No food treats or other external rewards are needed to get them to explore and manipulate their surroundings. The monkeys seem to work for the sheer fun of it. The drive for stimulation can even be observed in infants. By the time a child can walk, there are few things in the home that have not been tasted, touched, viewed, handled, or, in the case of toys, destroyed!

Arousal Theory

Are stimulus drives homeostatic? Yes. According to **arousal theory** we try to keep arousal at an optimal level (Hancock & Ganey, 2003; Hebb, 1966). In other words, when your level of arousal is too low or too high, you will seek ways to raise or lower it.

arousal theory assumes that people prefer to maintain ideal, or comfortable, levels of arousal.

What do you mean by arousal? Arousal refers to activation of the body and the nervous system. Arousal is zero at death; it is low during sleep; it is moderate during normal daily activities; and it is high at times of excitement, emotion, or panic. Arousal theory assumes that we become uncomfortable when arousal is too low ("I'm bored") or when it is too high, as in fear, anxiety, or panic ("The dentist will see you now"). Most adults vary their activities to maintain a comfortable level of activation. Music, parties, sports, conversation, sleep, surfing the web, and the like are combined to keep arousal at moderate levels. The right mix of activities prevents boredom *and* overstimulation.

Sensation Seekers *Do people vary in their needs for stimulation?* Picture a city dweller who is visiting the country. Before long, she begins to complain that it is "too quiet," and seeks some "action." Now imagine a country dweller who is visiting the city. Very soon, she finds the city "overwhelming" and seeks peace and quiet. These examples are extremes, but arousal theory also suggests that people learn to seek particular levels of arousal.

Sensation seeking is a trait of people who prefer high levels of stimulation. Whether you are high or low in sensation seeking is probably based on how your body responds to new, unusual, or intense stimulation (Zuckerman, 1990, 2002). People high in sensation seeking tend to be bold and independent, and they value change. They also report more sexual partners than low scorers, they are more likely to smoke, and they prefer spicy, sour, and crunchy foods over bland foods. Low sensation seekers are orderly, nurturant, and giving, and they enjoy the company of others. Which are you? (Most people fall somewhere between the extremes. See "Xtreme!")

Levels of Arousal

Is there an ideal level of arousal for peak performance? If we set aside individual differences, most people perform best when their arousal level is *moderate*. Let's say that you have to take an essay exam. If you are sleepy or feeling lazy (arousal level too low), your performance will suffer. If you are in a state of anxiety or panic about the test (arousal level too high), you will also perform below par. Thus, the relationship between arousal and performance forms an *inverted U function* (a curve in the shape of an upside-down U) (Figure 7.9) (Hancock & Ganey, 2003).

The inverted U tells us that at very low levels of arousal you're not sufficiently energized to perform well. Performance will improve as your arousal level increases, up to the middle of the curve. Then it begins to drop off, as you become emotional, frenzied, or disorganized. For example, imagine trying to start a car stalled on a railroad track, with a speeding train bearing down on you. That's what the high-arousal end of the curve feels like.

Is performance always best at moderate levels of arousal? No, the ideal level of arousal depends on the complexity of a task. If a task is relatively simple, it is best for arousal to be high. When a task is more complex, your best performance will occur at lower levels of arousal. This relationship is called the **Yerkes-Dodson law** (see Figure 7.9). It applies to a wide variety of tasks and to measures of motivation other than arousal.

Yerkes-Dodson law a summary of the relationships among arousal, task complexity, and performance.

Some examples of the Yerkes-Dodson law might be helpful. At a track meet, it is almost impossible for sprinters to get too aroused for a race. The task is direct and uncomplicated: Run as fast as you can for a short distance. On the other hand, a basketball player making a game-deciding free throw faces a more sensitive and complex task. Excessive arousal is almost certain to hurt his or her performance. In school, most students have had experience with "test anxiety," a familiar example of how too much arousal can lower performance.

Coping with Test Anxiety *Then is it true that by learning to calm down, a person would do better on tests?* Usually, but not always. **Test anxiety** is a mixture of *heightened physiological arousal* (nervousness, sweating, pounding heart) and *excessive worry.* This combination—arousal plus worry—tends to distract students with a rush of upsetting thoughts and feelings (Gierl & Rogers, 1996). Studies show that students are typically most anxious when they don't know the material. If this is the case,

test anxiety high levels of arousal and worry that seriously impair test performance.

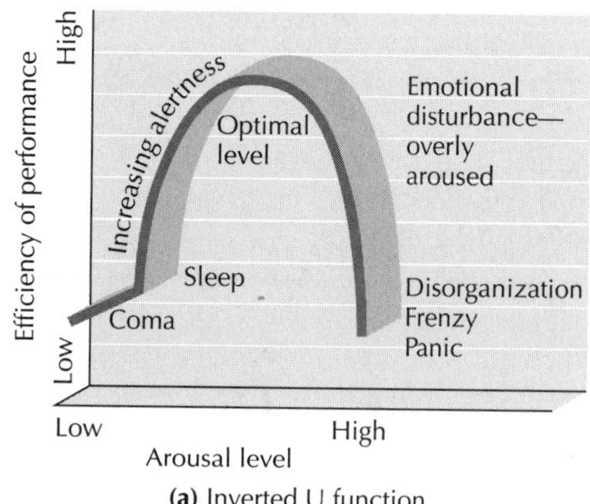

(a) Inverted U function

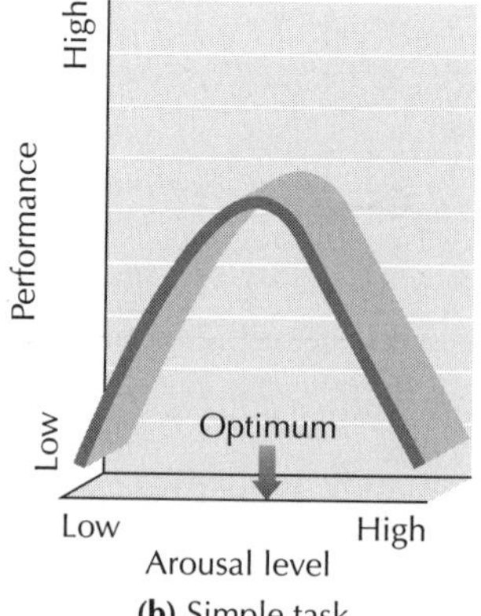

(b) Simple task

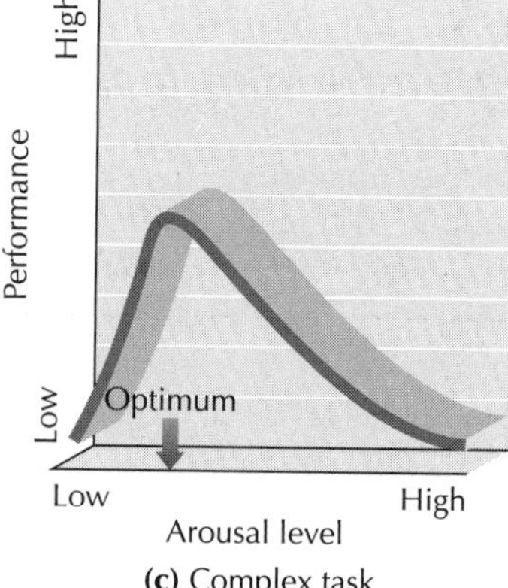

(c) Complex task

FIGURE 7.9

(a) The general relationship between arousal and efficiency can be described by an inverted U curve. The optimal level of arousal or motivation is higher for a simple task *(b)* than for a complex task *(c)*.

HUMAN DIVERSITY

Xtreme!

Where would you prefer to go on your next summer vacation? How about a week with your best friends at a cottage on a nearby lake? Or a shopping and museum trip to New York City? Better yet, how about cage diving with great white sharks in South Africa? If the shark adventure attracts you, you are probably high in sensation seeking and would be interested in a vacation that includes activities like bungee-jumping, scuba diving, skiing, surfing, sky diving, or white water rafting (Pizam et al., 2004).

Marvin Zuckerman (1990, 2000) has devised a test to measure differences in sensation seeking. His *Sensation-Seeking Scale* (SSS) includes statements like the samples shown here (from Zuckerman, 1996):

Jeffrey L. Rotman

Thrill seeking is an element of the sensation-seeking personality.

Thrill and adventure seeking

- I would like to try parachute jumping.
- I think I would enjoy the sensations of skiing very fast down a high mountain slope.

Experience seeking

- I like to explore a strange city or section of town myself, even if it means getting lost.
- I like to try new foods that I have never tasted before.

Disinhibition

- I like wild, "uninhibited" parties.
- I often like to get high (drinking liquor or smoking marijuana).

Boredom susceptibility

- I can't stand watching a movie that I've seen before.
- I like people who are sharp and witty, even if they do sometimes insult others.

So who are the potential cage divers? Perhaps it's not surprising that SSS scores tend to be higher among men and younger people (Butkovic & Bratko, 2003; Roberti, 2004). SSS scores also vary across cultures. In one study of eleven different cultures, people from America, Israel, and Ireland scored higher on the SSS than people from South Africa, Slovakia, Sicily, or Gabon (Pizam et al., 2004).

Exciting lives aside, there is a dark side to sensation seeking as well. High sensation seekers are also more likely to engage in highrisk behaviors such as substance abuse (Horvath et al., 2004) and casual unprotected sex (Gullette & Lyons, 2005).

calming down simply means you will remain calm while failing. Here are some suggestions for coping with test anxiety:

1. **Preparation.** *Hard work* is the most direct antidote for test anxiety. Many anxious students simply study too little, too late. That's why improving your study skills is a good way to reduce test anxiety (Jones & Petruzzi, 1995). The best solution is to *overprepare* by studying long before the "big day." Well-prepared students score higher, worry less, and are less likely to panic (Zohar, 1998).
2. **Relaxation.** Learning to relax is another way to lower test anxiety (Ricketts & Galloway, 1984). Emotional support also helps (Stöber, 2004). If you are test anxious, discuss the problem with your professors or study for tests with a supportive classmate.
3. **Rehearsal.** To reduce your nervousness, rehearse how you will cope with upsetting events. Before taking a test, imagine yourself going blank, running out of time, or feeling panicked. Then calmly plan how you will handle each situation—by keeping your attention on the task, by focusing on one question at a time, and so forth (Watson & Tharp, 2001).

4. **Restructuring Thoughts.** Another helpful strategy involves listing the upsetting thoughts you have during exams. Then you can learn to combat worries with calming, rational replies (Jones & Petruzzi, 1995). (These are called *coping statements;* Let's say you think, "I'm going to fail this test and everybody will think I'm stupid." A good reply to this upsetting thought would be to say, "If I prepare well and control my worries, I will probably pass the test. Even if I don't, it won't be the end of the world. My friends will still like me, and I can try to improve on the next test."

Students who cope well with exams usually try to do the best they can, even under trying circumstances. Becoming a more confident test taker can actually increase your scores, because it helps you remain calm. With practice, most people can learn to be less testy at test-taking time (Smith, 2002; Zeidner, 1995).

Circadian Rhythms

We have seen that moment-to-moment changes in activation can have a major impact on performance. What about larger cycles of arousal? Do they also affect energy levels, motivation, and performance? Scientists have long known that bodily activity is guided by internal "biological clocks." Every 24 hours, your body undergoes a cycle of changes called **circadian** (SUR-kay-dee-AN) **rhythms** (*circa:* about; *diem:* a day) (Antle & Mistlberger, 2005).

circadian rhythms cyclical changes in bodily functions and arousal levels that vary on a schedule approximating a 24-hour day.

Throughout the day, large changes take place in body temperature, blood pressure, and amino acid levels (Figure 7.10). Also affected are the activities of the liver, kidneys, and endocrine glands. These activities, and many others, peak sometime each day. Output of the hormone adrenaline, which arouses the body, is often three to five times greater during the day. Most people are more energetic and alert at the high point of their circadian rhythms (Natale & Cicogna, 1996).

People with shorter circadian rhythms are "day people," who wake up alert, peak early in the day, and fall asleep early in the evening. People with longer rhythms are "night people," who wake up groggy, peak in the afternoon or early evening, and stay up late (Duffy, Rimmer, & Czeisler, 2001). Such differences are so basic that when a day person rooms with a night person, both are more likely to give their relationship a negative rating (Carey, Stanley, & Biggers, 1988). This is easy to understand: What could be worse than having someone bounding around cheerily when you're half asleep, or the reverse?

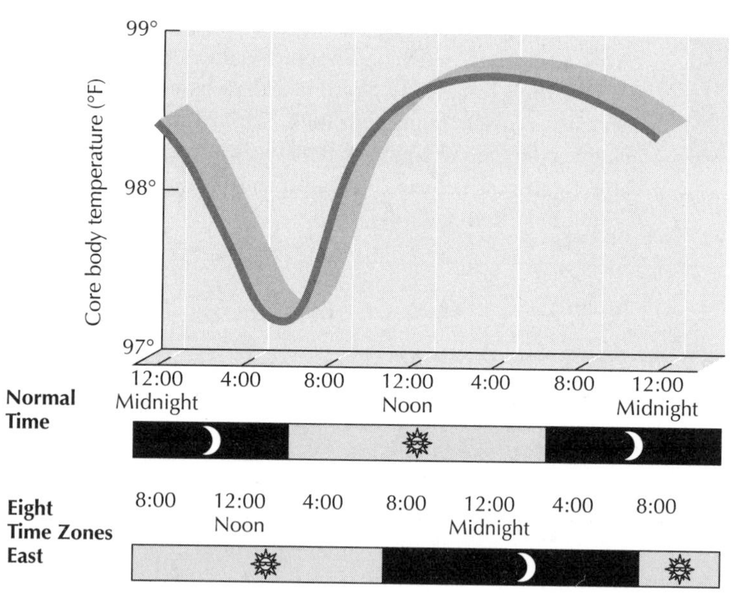

FIGURE 7.10

Core body temperature is a good indicator of a person's circadian rhythm. Most people reach a low point 2–3 hours before their normal waking time. It's no wonder that both the Chernobyl and Three-Mile Island nuclear power plant accidents occurred around 4 AM. Rapid travel to a different time zone, shift work, depression, and illness can throw sleep and waking patterns out of synchronization with the body's core rhythm. Mismatches of this kind are very disruptive (Hauri & Linde, 1990).

Shift Work and Jet Lag Circadian rhythms are most noticeable whenever there is a major shift in time schedules. Businesspersons, diplomats, athletes, and other time zone travelers tend to make errors or perform poorly when their body rhythms are disturbed (Rader & Hicks, 1987). If you travel great distances east or west, the peaks and valleys of your circadian rhythms will be out of phase with the sun and clocks. For example, you might find that you are wide awake and alert at midnight. Your low point, in contrast, occurs during the middle of the day (return to Figure 7.10). Shift work has the same effect, causing fatigue, inefficiency, irritability, upset stomach, and depression (Akerstedt, 1990).

How fast do people adapt to time shifts? For major time zone shifts (5 hours or more) it can take from several days to 2 weeks to resynchronize. Adaptation to jet lag is slowest when you stay indoors, where you can sleep and eat on "home time." Getting outdoors, where you must sleep, eat, and socialize on the new schedule, speeds adaptation. A 5-hour dose of bright sunlight early each day is particularly helpful for resetting your circadian rhythm in a new time zone (Czeisler et al., 1989). The same principle can be applied to shift work by bathing workers in bright light during their first few night shifts (Eastman et al., 1994).

The *direction* of travel also affects adaptation (Herxheimer, & Waterhouse, 2003). If you fly west, adapting is relatively easy, taking an average of 4 to 5 days. If you fly east, adapting takes 50 percent longer, or more (Figure 7.11). Why is there a difference? The answer is that when you fly east the sun comes up *earlier* (relative to your "home" time). Let's say that you live in Los Angeles and fly to New York. Getting up at 7 AM in New York will be like getting up at 4 AM in Los Angeles. If you fly west, the sun comes up later, and it is easier for most people to "advance" (stay up later and sleep in) than it is to shift backward. Likewise, work shifts that "rotate" backward (night, evening, day) are more disruptive than those that advance (day, evening, night). Best of all are work shifts that do not change: Even continuous night work is less upsetting than rotating shifts (Lac & Chamoux, 2004).

What does all of this have to do with those of us who are not shift workers or world travelers? There are few college students who have not at one time or another "burned the midnight oil," especially for final exams. During any strenuous period, it is wise to remember that departing from your regular schedule is likely to cost more than it's worth. Often, you can do as much during 1 hour in the morning as you could have in 3 hours of work after midnight. The 2-hour difference in efficiency might as well be spent sleeping. If you feel you must deviate from your normal schedule, do it gradually over a period of days.

In general, if you can anticipate an upcoming body rhythm change (when traveling, before finals week, or when doing shift work), it is best to *preadapt* to your new schedule. Preadaptation is the gradual matching of sleep–waking cycles to a new time schedule. Before traveling, for instance, you should go to sleep one hour later (or earlier) each day until your sleep cycle matches the time at your destination. If you are unable to do that, it at least helps to fly early in the day when you fly east. When you fly west, it is better to fly late. (Remember, the *E* in *east* matches the *E* in *early.*)

Studies of flight crews show that jet lag can also be minimized by a hormone called melatonin (mel-ah-TONE-in). Melatonin is normally produced at night by the pineal gland and suppressed during daylight (Sharkey & Eastman, 2002). Melatonin has a strong impact on the timing of body rhythms and sleep cycles. As far as the brain is concerned, it's bedtime when melatonin levels rise (Shanahan et al., 1999).

To reset the body's clock in a new time zone, a small amount of melatonin can be taken about an hour before bedtime. This dose is continued for as many days as necessary to ease jet lag. The same treatment can be used for rotating work shifts (Comperatore et al., 1996; Sharkey & Eastman, 2002).

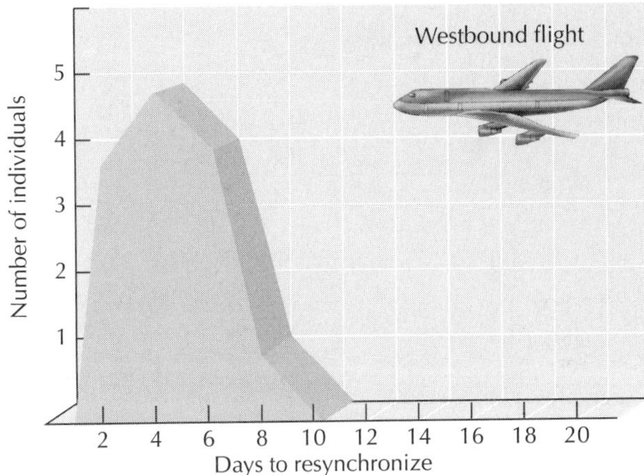

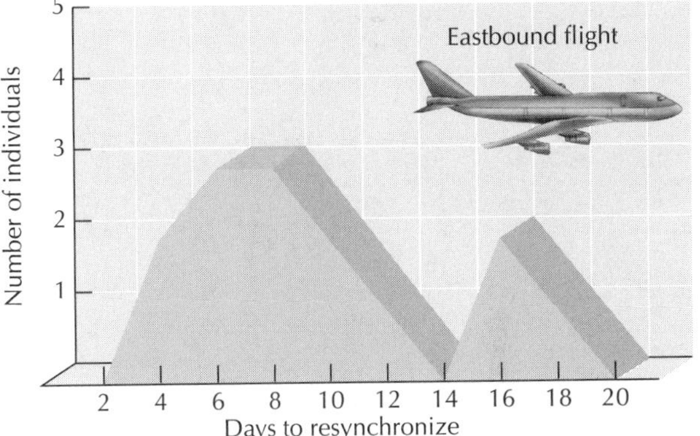

FIGURE 7.11

Time required to adjust to air travel across six time zones. The average time to resynchronize was shorter for westbound travel than for eastbound flights. (Data from Beljan et al., 1972; cited by Moore-Ede, Sulzman, & Fuller, 1982.)

David Frazier/The Image Works

Flight crews often suffer severe disruptions in their sleep cycles. For example, a crew that leaves Los Angeles at 4 PM, bound for London, will arrive in 8 hours. Crew members' bodies, which are on California time, will act as if it is 12 AM. Yet in London, it will be 8 AM. Recent studies confirm that melatonin can help people adjust more rapidly to such time-zone changes.

LEARNED MOTIVES—THE PURSUIT OF EXCELLENCE

Many motives are acquired directly. It is easy enough to see that praise, money, success, pleasure, and similar reinforcers affect our goals and desires. But how do people learn to enjoy activities that are at first painful or frightening? Why do people climb rocks, jump out of airplanes, run marathons, take sauna baths, or swim in frozen lakes? For an answer, let's examine a related situation.

When a person first tries a drug such as heroin, he or she feels a "rush" of pleasure. However, as the drug wears off, discomfort and craving occurs. The easiest way to end the discomfort is to take another dose—as most drug users quickly learn. But in time, habituation takes place; the drug stops producing pleasure, although it will end discomfort. At the same time, the after effects of the drug grow more painful. At this point, the drug user has acquired a powerful new motive. In a vicious cycle, heroin relieves discomfort, but it guarantees that withdrawal will occur again in a few hours.

Opponent-Process Theory

Psychologist Richard L. Solomon (1980) offers an intriguing explanation for drug addiction and other learned motives. According to his **opponent-process theory**, if a stimulus causes a strong emotion, such as fear or pleasure, an opposite emotion tends to occur when the stimulus ends. For example, if you are in pain, and the pain ends, you will feel a pleasant sense of relief. If a person feels pleasure, as in the case of drug use, and the pleasure ends, it will be followed by craving or discomfort. If you are in love and feel good when you are with your lover, you will be uncomfortable when she or he is absent.

What happens if the stimulus is repeated? Solomon assumes that when a stimulus is repeated, our response to it habituates, or gets weaker. First-time skydivers, for instance, are almost always terrified. But with repeated jumps, fear decreases, until finally the skydiver feels a "thrill" instead of terror (Roth et al., 1996). In contrast, emotional aftereffects get stronger with repetition. After a first jump, beginning parachutists feel a brief but exhilarating sense of relief. After many such experiences, seasoned skydivers can get a "rush" of euphoria that lasts for hours after a jump (Figure 7.12). With repetition, the pleasurable aftereffect gets stronger and the initial "cost" (pain or fear) gets weaker. The opponent-process theory thus explains how skydiving, rock climbing, ski jumping, and other hazardous pursuits become reinforcing. If you are a fan of horror movies, carnival rides, or bungee jumping, your motives may be based on the same effect. (Notice, too, the strong link between motivation and emotion in such examples. We will return to this idea later.)

opponent-process theory
states that strong emotions tend to be followed by an opposite emotional state; also the strength of both emotional states changes over time.

social motives
learned motives acquired as part of growing up in a particular society or culture.

Social Motives

Some of your friends are more interested than others in success, achievement, competition, money, possessions, status, love, approval, grades, dominance, power, or belonging to groups—all of which are *social motives* or goals. We acquire **social motives** in complex ways, through socialization and cultural conditioning. The behavior of outstanding artists, scientists, athletes, educators, and leaders is best understood in terms of such learned needs, particularly the need for achievement.

The Need for Achievement

To many people, being "motivated" means being interested in achievement. For now, let us focus on the **need for achievement** (nAch), which is a desire to meet an internal standard of excellence (McClelland, 1961). People with high needs for achievement strive to do well any time they are evaluated.

Is that like the aggressive businessperson who strives for success? Not necessarily. Needs for achievement may lead to wealth and prestige, but people who are high achievers in art, music, science, or amateur sports may excel without seeking riches. Such people typically enjoy challenges and they relish a chance to test their abilities (Puca & Schmalt, 1999).

Alex Bartel/SPL/Photo Researchers, Inc.

FIGURE 7.12

A sport parachutist takes the plunge. The typical emotional sequence for a first jump is anxiety before, terror during, and relief after the jump. After many jumps the emotional sequence becomes eagerness before, a thrill during, and exhilaration after a jump. The new sequence strongly reinforces skydiving.

Power The need for achievement differs from a **need for power**, which is a desire to have impact or control over others (McClelland, 1975). People with strong needs for power want their importance to be visible: They buy expensive possessions, wear prestigious clothes, and exploit relationships. In some ways the pursuit of power and financial success is the dark side of the American dream. People whose main goal in life is to make lots of money tend to be poorly adjusted and unhappy (Kasser & Ryan, 1993).

Characteristics of Achievers David McClelland (1917–1998) and others have probed the need for achievement. Using a simple measure, McClelland found that he could predict the behavior of high and low achievers. For instance, McClelland compared people's occupations with scores on an achievement test they took as college sophomores. Fourteen years later, those who scored high in nAch tended to have jobs that involved risk and responsibility (McClelland, 1965).

need for achievement
the desire to excel or meet some internalized standard of excellence.

need for power
the desire to have social impact and control over others.

Here's a test: In front of you are five targets. Each is placed at an increasing distance from where you are standing. You are given a beanbag to toss at the target of your choice. Target A, anyone can hit; target B, most people can hit; target C, some people can hit; target D, very few people can hit; target E is rarely if ever hit. If you hit A, you will receive $2; B, $4; C, $8; D, $16; and E, $32. You get only one toss. Which one would you choose? McClelland's research suggests that if you have a high need for achievement, you will select C or perhaps D. Those high in nAch are *moderate* risk takers. When faced with a problem or a challenge, persons high in nAch avoid goals that are too easy.

Why do they pass up sure success? They do it because easy goals offer no sense of satisfaction. They also avoid long shots because there is either no hope of success, or "winning" will be due to luck rather than skill. Persons low in nAch select sure things or impossible goals. Either way, they don't have to take any responsibility for failure.

Desires for achievement and calculated risk taking lead to success in many situations. People high in nAch complete difficult tasks, they earn better grades, and they tend to excel in their occupations. College students high in nAch attribute success to their own ability, and failure to insufficient effort. Thus, high nAch students are more likely to renew their efforts when they perform poorly. When the going gets tough, high achievers get going.

The Key to Success?

What does it take to achieve extraordinary success? Psychologist Benjamin Bloom did an interesting study of America's top concert pianists, Olympic swimmers, sculptors, tennis players, mathematicians, and research neurologists. Bloom

AP/Wide World Photo

The person with high needs for achievement strives to do well in any situation in which evaluation takes place.

(1985) found that drive and determination, not great natural talent, led to exceptional success.

The first steps toward high achievement began when parents exposed their children to music, swimming, scientific ideas, and so forth, "just for fun." At first, many of the children had very ordinary skills. One Olympic swimmer, for instance, remembers repeatedly losing races as a 10-year-old. At some point, however, the children began to actively cultivate their abilities. Before long, parents noticed the child's rapid progress and found an expert instructor or coach. After more successes, the youngsters began "living" for their talent and practiced many hours daily. This continued for many years before they reached truly outstanding heights of achievement.

The upshot of Bloom's work is that talent is nurtured by dedication and hard work (R. C. Beck, 2004). It is most likely to blossom when parents actively support a child's special interest and emphasize doing one's best at all times. Studies of child prodigies and eminent adults also show that intensive practice and expert coaching are common ingredients of high achievement. Elite performance in music, sports, chess, the arts, and many other pursuits requires at least 10 years of dedicated practice (Ericsson & Charness, 1994). The old belief that "talent will surface" on its own is largely a myth. This is especially true for talented women, who face a wide variety of social obstacles to exceptional achievement (Noble, Subotnik, & Arnold, 1996).

Self-Confidence Achieving elite performance may be reserved for the dedicated few. Nevertheless, you may be able to improve everyday motivation by increasing your self-confidence. People with self-confidence believe they can successfully carry out an activity or reach a goal. To enhance self-confidence, it is wise to do the following (Druckman & Bjork, 1994):

- Set goals that are specific and challenging, but attainable.
- Visualize the steps you need to take to reach your goal.
- Advance in small steps.
- When you first acquire a skill, your goal should be to make progress in learning. Later, you can concentrate on improving your performance, compared with other people.
- Get expert instruction that helps you master the skill.
- Find a skilled model (someone good at the skill) to emulate.
- Get support and encouragement from an observer.
- If you fail, regard it as a sign that you need to try harder, not that you lack ability.

Self-confidence affects motivation by influencing the challenges you will undertake, the effort you will make, and how long you will persist when things don't go well. You can be confident that self-confidence is worth cultivating.

MOTIVES IN PERSPECTIVE—A VIEW FROM THE PYRAMID

hierarchy of human needs Abraham Maslow's ordering of needs, based on their presumed strength or potency.

What motivates people who live fully and richly? Abraham Maslow called the full use of personal potential *self-actualization*. Maslow also described a **hierarchy of human needs**, in which some needs are more basic or powerful than others. Think about the needs that influence your own behavior. Which seem strongest? Which do you spend the most time and energy satisfying? Now look at Maslow's

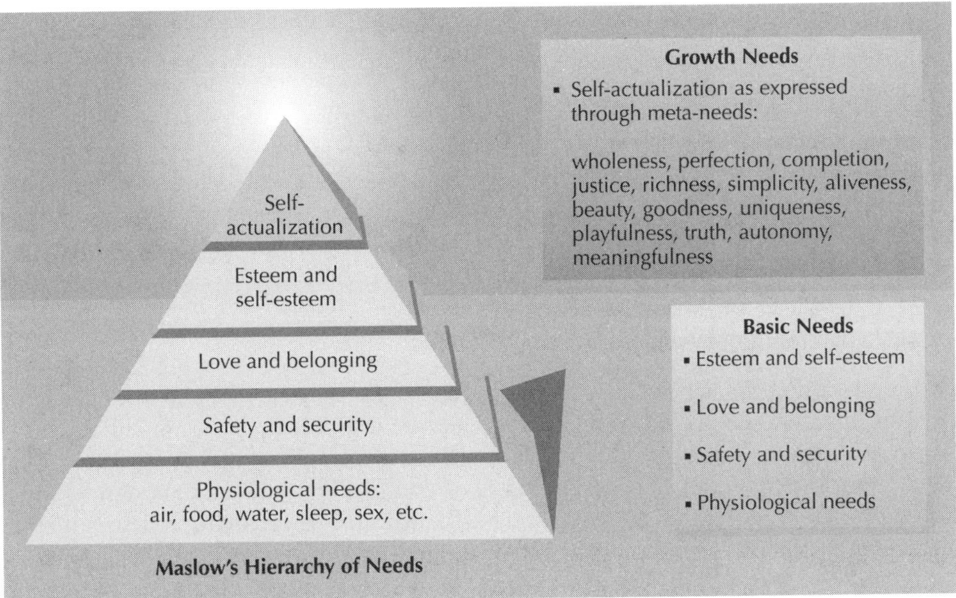

FIGURE 7.13

Maslow believed that lower needs in the hierarchy are dominant. Basic needs must be satisfied before growth motives are fully expressed. Desires for self- actualization are reflected in various metaneeds (see text).

hierarchy (Figure 7.13). Note that physiological needs are at the base of the pyramid. Because these needs must be met if we are to survive, they tend to be *prepotent,* or dominant over the higher needs. It could be said, for example, that "to a starving person, food is god."

Maslow believed that higher, more fragile needs are expressed only after we satisfy our physiological needs. This is also true of needs for safety and security. Until they are met, we may have little interest in higher pursuits. For instance, a person who is extremely thirsty might have little interest in writing poetry or even talking with friends. For this reason, Maslow described the first four levels of the hierarchy as **basic needs**. Other basic needs include love and belonging (family, friendship, caring), and needs for esteem and self-esteem (recognition and self-respect).

All of the basic needs are *deficiency* motives. That is, they are activated by a *lack* of food, water, security, love, esteem, or other basic needs. At the top of the hierarchy we find **growth needs**, which are expressed as a need for self-actualization. The need for self-actualization is not based on deficiencies. Rather, it is a positive, life-enhancing force for personal growth (Reiss & Havercamp, 2005). Like other humanistic psychologists, Maslow believed that people are basically good. If our basic needs are met, he said, we will tend to move on to actualizing our potentials.

How are needs for self-actualization expressed? Maslow called the less powerful but humanly important actualization motives **meta-needs** (Maslow, 1970). Meta-needs are an expression of tendencies to fully development your personal potentials. The meta-needs are

1. Wholeness (unity)
2. Perfection (balance and harmony)
3. Completion (ending)
4. Justice (fairness)
5. Richness (complexity)

basic needs
the first four levels of needs in Maslow's hierarchy; lower needs tend to be more potent than higher needs.

growth needs
in Maslow's hierarchy, the higher-level needs associated with self-actualization.

meta-needs
in Maslow's hierarchy, needs associated with impulses for self-actualization.

Reuters/Corbis

Wheelchair athletes engage in vigorous competition. Maslow considered such behavior an expression of the need for self-actualization.

6. Simplicity (essence)
7. Aliveness (spontaneity)
8. Beauty (rightness of form)
9. Goodness (benevolence)
10. Uniqueness (individuality)
11. Playfulness (ease)
12. Truth (reality)
13. Autonomy (self-sufficiency)
14. Meaningfulness (values)

According to Maslow, we tend to move up through the hierarchy of needs, toward the meta-needs. When the meta-needs are unfulfilled, people fall into a "syndrome of decay" marked by despair, apathy, and alienation.

Maslow's point is that mere survival or comfort is usually not enough to make a full and satisfying life. It's interesting to note, in this regard, that college students who are primarily concerned with money, personal appearance, and social recognition score lower than average in vitality, self-actualization, and general well-being (Kasser & Ryan, 1996).

Maslow's hierarchy is not well documented by research, and many questions can be raised about it. How, for instance, do we explain the actions of people who fast as a means of social protest? How can the meta-need for justice overcome the more basic need for food? (Perhaps the answer is that fasting is temporary and self-imposed.) Despite such objections, Maslow's views are a good way to understand and appreciate the rich interplay of human motives.

Are many people motivated by meta-needs? Maslow estimated that few people are primarily motivated by needs for self-actualization. Most of us are more concerned with esteem, love, or security. Perhaps this is because rewards in our society tend to encourage conformity, uniformity, and security in schools, jobs, and relationships. When was the last time you met a meta-need?

Intrinsic and Extrinsic Motivation

Some people cook for a living and consider it hard work. Others cook for pleasure and dream of opening a restaurant. For some people, carpentry, gardening, writing, photography, or jewelry making is fun. For others the same activities are drudgery they must be paid to do. How can the same activity be "work" for one person and "play" for another?

When you do something for enjoyment or to improve your abilities, your motivation is usually *intrinsic*. **Intrinsic motivation** occurs when we act without any obvious external rewards. We simply enjoy an activity or see it as an opportunity to explore, learn, and actualize our potentials. In contrast, **extrinsic motivation** stems from external factors, such as pay, grades, rewards, obligations, and approval. Most of the activities we think of as "work" are extrinsically rewarded (Baard, Deci, & Ryan, 2004; Ryan & Deci, 2000).

intrinsic motivation
motivation that comes from within, rather than from external rewards; motivation based on personal enjoyment of a task or activity.

extrinsic motivation
motivation based on obvious external rewards, obligations, or similar factors.

Turning Play into Work

Don't extrinsic incentives strengthen motivation? Yes they can, but not always. In fact, *excessive* rewards can decrease intrinsic motivation and spontaneous interest (Lepper, Keavney, & Drake, 1996; Tang & Hall, 1995). For instance, children who were lavishly rewarded for drawing with felt-tip pens later showed little interest in playing with the pens again (Greene & Lepper, 1974). Apparently, "play" can be turned into "work" by *requiring* people to do something they would otherwise enjoy. When we are coerced or "bribed" to act, we tend to feel as if we are "faking it." Employees who lack initiative and teenagers who reject school and learning are good examples of such reactions (Ryan & Deci, 2000).

Creativity People are more likely to be creative when they are intrinsically motivated. On the job, for instance, salaries and bonuses may increase the amount of work done. However, work *quality* is affected more by intrinsic factors, such as personal interest and freedom of choice (Nakamura & Csikszentmihalyi, 2003). People who are intrinsically motivated usually get personally involved in tasks, which leads to greater creativity (Ruscio, Whitney, & Amabile, 1998).

Psychologist Teresa Amabile lists the following as "creativity killers" on the job:

- Working under surveillance
- Having your choices restricted by rules
- Working primarily to get a good evaluation (or avoid a bad one)
- Working mainly to get more money

Time pressure also kills creativity. Employees are less likely to solve tricky problems and come up with innovative ideas when they work "under the gun" (Amabile, Hadley, & Kramer, 2002). When a person is intrinsically motivated, a certain amount of challenge, surprise, and complexity makes a task rewarding. A person who is extrinsically motivated wants to take the fastest, most direct route to a goal, not the most creative (Sternberg and Lubart, 1995).

How can the concept of intrinsic motivation be applied? Both types of motivation are necessary. But extrinsic motivation shouldn't be overused, especially with children. To summarize, (1) if there's no intrinsic interest in an activity to begin with, you have nothing to lose by using extrinsic rewards; (2) if basic skills are lacking, extrinsic rewards may be necessary at first; (3) extrinsic rewards can focus attention on an activity so real interest will develop; and (4) if extrinsic rewards are used, they should be small and phased out as soon as possible (Greene & Lepper, 1974). It also helps to tell children they seem to be *really interested* in drawing, playing the piano, learning a language, or whatever activity you are rewarding (Cialdini et al., 1998).

At work, it is valuable for managers to find out what each employee's interests and career goals are. People are not solely motivated by money. A chance to do challenging, interesting, and intrinsically rewarding work is often just as important (Campion & McClelland, 1993). In many situations it is important to encourage intrinsic motivation, especially when children are learning new skills.

Rick Friedman/Corbis

Gregory A. Beaumont/® The Great Arcata to Ferndale World Championship Cross Country Kinetic Sculpture Race

People who are intrinsically motivated feel free to explore creative solutions to problems. (*Left.* Dean Kaman, inventor of the Segway personal transportation device. *Right.* "Caffiends at the Beach," an entrant in the Great Arcata to Ferndale World Championship Cross Country Kinetic Sculpture Race.)

INSIDE AN EMOTION—HOW DO YOU FEEL?

Picture the faces of terrified people fleeing the collapse of the World Trade Center towers in New York and it's easy to see that motivation and emotion are closely related. Emotions shape our relationships and color our daily activities. What are the basic parts of an emotion? How does the body respond during emotion?

If a mad scientist replaced your best friend's brain with a computer, how would you know that something was wrong? An absence of emotion might be one of the first telltale signs. **Emotion** is characterized by physiological arousal, and changes in facial expressions, gestures, posture, and subjective feelings.

emotion
a state characterized by physiological arousal, changes in facial expression, gestures, posture, and subjective feelings.

The word *emotion* means "to move," and emotions do indeed move us. First, the body is physically aroused during emotion. Such bodily stirrings are what cause us to say we were "moved" by a play, a funeral, or an act of kindness. Second, we are often motivated, or moved to take action, by emotions such as fear, anger, or joy. Many of the goals we seek make us feel good. Many of the activities we avoid make us feel bad. We feel happy when we succeed and sad when we fail (Oatley & Jenkins, 1992).

Emotions are linked to many basic **adaptive behaviors**, such as attacking, fleeing, seeking comfort, helping others, and reproducing. Such behaviors help us survive and adjust to changing conditions (Plutchik, 2003). However, it is also apparent that emotions can have negative effects. Stage fright or "choking up" in sports can spoil performances. Hate, anger, contempt, disgust, and fear disrupt behavior and relationships. But more often, emotions aid survival. As social animals, it would be impossible for humans to live in groups, cooperate in raising children, and defend one another without positive emotional bonds of love, caring, and friendship (Buss, 2000).

adaptive behaviors
actions that aid attempts to survive and adapt to changing conditions.

A pounding heart, sweating palms, "butterflies" in the stomach, and other bodily reactions are a major element of fear, anger, joy, and other emotions. Typical **physiological changes** include changes in heart rate, blood pressure, perspiration, and other bodily stirrings. Most are caused by activity in the sympathetic nervous system and by the hormone **adrenaline**, which the adrenal glands release into the bloodstream.

physiological changes (in emotion)
alterations in heart rate, blood pressure, perspiration, and other involuntary responses.

adrenaline
a hormone produced by the adrenal glands that tends to arouse the body.

Emotional expressions, or outward signs of what a person is feeling, are another ingredient of emotion. For example, when you are intensely afraid, your hands tremble, your face contorts, your posture becomes tense and defensive, and your voice changes. In general, these expressions serve to tell others what emotions we are experiencing (Hortman, 2003).

emotional expression
outward signs that an emotion is occurring.

Emotional feelings (a person's private emotional experience) are a final major element of emotion. This is the part of emotion with which we are usually most familiar.

emotional feelings
the private, subjective experience of having an emotion.

Primary Emotions

Are some emotions more basic than others? Yes. Robert Plutchik (2003) has identified eight **primary emotions**. These are fear, surprise, sadness, disgust, anger, anticipation, joy, and trust (acceptance). If the list seems too short, it's because each emotion can vary in *intensity*. When you're angry, for instance, you may feel anything from rage to simple annoyance, as shown in Figure 7.14.

primary emotions
according to Robert Plutchik, the most basic emotions are fear, surprise, sadness, disgust, anger, anticipation, joy, and acceptance.

As shown in Figure 7.14, each pair of adjacent emotions can be mixed to yield a third, more complex emotion. Other mixtures are also possible. For example, 5-year-old Tupac feels both joy and fear as he eats a stolen cookie. The result? Guilt—as you may recall from your own childhood. Likewise, jealousy could be a mixture of love, anger, and fear.

A *mood* is the mildest form of emotion (Figure 7.15). **Moods** are low-intensity emotional states that can last for many hours, or even days. Moods often affect

mood
a low-intensity, long-lasting emotional state.

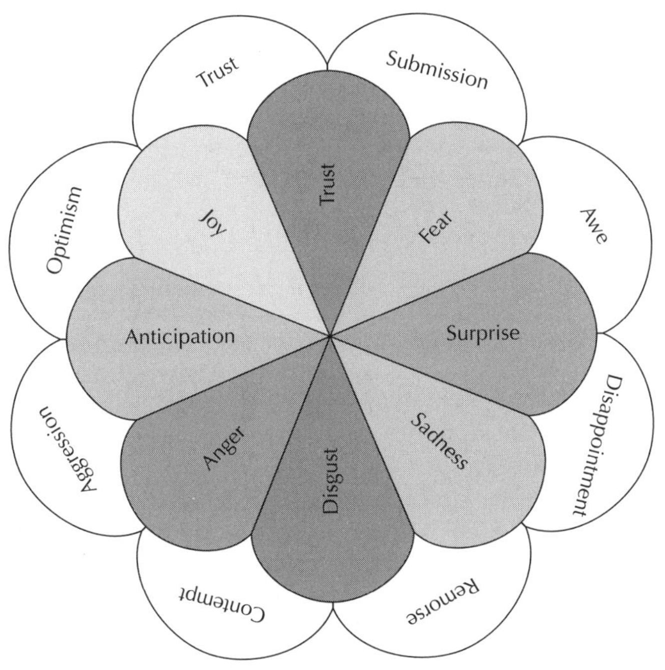

Less intense	Primary emotion	More intense
Interest	Anticipation	Vigilance
Serenity	Joy	Ecstasy
Acceptance	Trust	Admiration
Apprehension	Fear	Terror
Distraction	Surprise	Amazement
Pensiveness	Sadness	Grief
Boredom	Disgust	Loathing
Annoyance	Anger	Rage

FIGURE 7.14

Primary and mixed emotions. In Robert Plutchik's model there are eight primary emotions, as listed in the inner areas. Adjacent emotions may combine to give the emotions listed around the perimeter. Mixtures involving more widely separated emotions are also possible. For example, fear plus anticipation produces anxiety. (Adapted from Plutchik, 2003.)

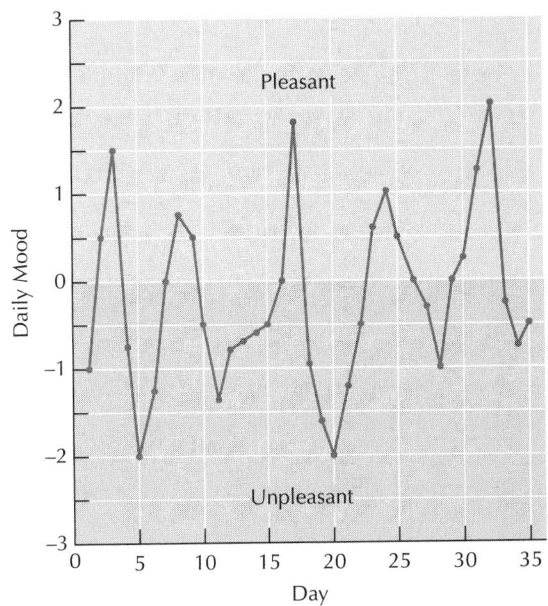

FIGURE 7.15

Folklore holds that people who work or attend school on a weekly schedule experience their lowest moods on "Blue Monday." Actually, moods tend to be generally lower for *most* weekdays than they are on weekends. The graph shown here plots the average daily mood ratings made by a group of college students over a 5-week period. As you can see, many people find that their moods rise and fall on a 7-day cycle. For most students, a low point tends to occur around Monday or Tuesday and a peak on Friday or Saturday. (Adapted from Larsen & Kasimatis, 1990.) In other words, moods are often entrained (pulled along) by weekly schedules.

day-to-day behavior by preparing us to act in certain ways. For example, when your neighbor Roseanne is in an irritable mood she may react angrily to almost anything you say. When she is in a happy mood, she can easily laugh off an insult. Happy, positive moods tend to make us more adaptable in several ways. For example, when you are in a good mood, you are likely to make better decisions and you will be more helpful, efficient, creative, and peaceful (Compton, 2005).

The Brain and Emotion

Emotions can be either positive or negative. Ordinarily, we might think that positive and negative emotions are opposites. But this is not the case. As Tupac's "cookie guilt" implies, it is possible to have positive and negative emotions at the

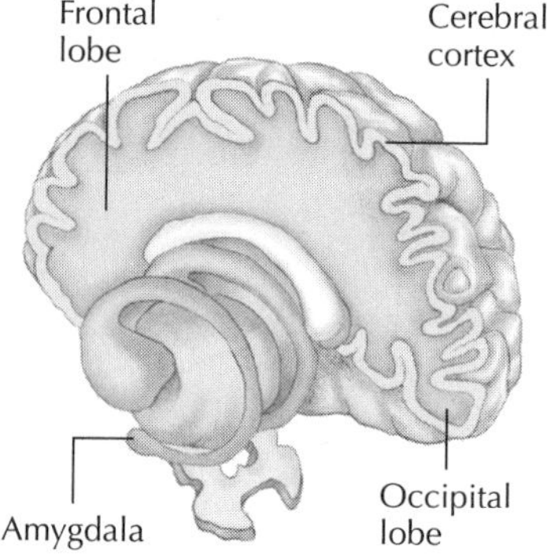

FIGURE 7.16

An amygdala can be found buried within the temporal lobes on each side of the brain. The amygdala appears to provide "quick and dirty" processing of emotional stimuli that allows us to react involuntarily to danger.

amygdala
a part of the limbic system (within the brain) that produces fear responses.

autonomic nervous system (ANS)
the system of nerves that connects the brain with the internal organs and glands.

sympathetic branch
a part of the ANS that activates the body at times of stress.

same time. How is that possible? In the brain, positive emotions are processed mainly in the left hemisphere. In contrast, negative emotions are processed in the right hemisphere. The fact that positive and negative emotions are based on different brain areas helps explain why we can feel happy and sad at the same time (Canli et al., 1998). It also explains why your right foot is more ticklish than your left foot! The left hemisphere controls the right side of the body and processes positive emotions (Smith & Cahusac, 2001). Thus, most people are more ticklish on their right side. If you really want to tickle someone, be sure to "do it right."

Scientists used to think that all emotions are processed by the cerebral cortex. However, this is not always the case. Imagine this test of willpower: Go to a zoo and place your face close to the glass in front of a rattlesnake display. Suddenly, the rattlesnake strikes at your face. Do you flinch? Even though you know you are safe, Joseph LeDoux predicts that you will recoil from the snake's attack (LeDoux, 2000).

LeDoux and other researchers have found that an area of the brain called the **amygdala** (ah-MIG-duh-la) specializes in producing fear (Figure 7.16). The amygdala receives sensory information very directly and quickly, bypassing the cortex. As a result, it allows us to respond to potential danger before we really know what's happening. This primitive fear response is not under the control of higher brain centers. The role of the amygdala in emotion may explain why people who suffer from phobias and disabling anxiety often feel afraid without knowing why (Fellous & Ledoux, 2005).

People who suffer damage to the amygdala become "blind" to emotion. An armed robber could hold a gun to the person's head and the person wouldn't feel fear. Such people are also unable to "read" or understand other people's emotions. Many lose their ability to relate normally to friends, family, and coworkers (Goleman, 1995).

Later we will attempt to put all the elements of emotion together into a single picture. But first, we need to look more closely at bodily arousal and emotional expressions.

PHYSIOLOGY AND EMOTION—AROUSAL, SUDDEN DEATH, AND LYING

An African Bushman frightened by a lion and a city dweller frightened by a prowler will react in much the same way (Mesquita & Frijda, 1992). Such encounters usually produce muscle tension, a pounding heart, irritability, dryness of the throat and mouth, sweating, butterflies in the stomach, frequent urination, trembling, restlessness, sensitivity to loud noises, and numerous other bodily changes. These reactions are nearly universal because they are innate. Specifically, they are caused by the **autonomic nervous system (ANS)** (the neural system that connects the brain with internal organs and glands). Activity of the ANS is *automatic,* rather than voluntary.

Fight or Flight

The ANS has two divisions, the sympathetic branch and the parasympathetic branch. The two branches are active at all times. Whether you are relaxed or aroused at any moment depends on the combined activity of both branches (Kalat, 2004).

What does the ANS do during emotion? In general, the **sympathetic branch** activates the body for emergency action—for "fighting or fleeing." It does this by arousing some bodily systems and inhibiting others (Figure 7.17). These changes have a purpose. Sugar is released into the bloodstream for quick energy, the heart beats faster to supply blood to the muscles, digestion is temporarily slowed, blood flow in the skin is restricted to reduce bleeding, and so forth. Such reactions improve the chances of surviving an emergency.

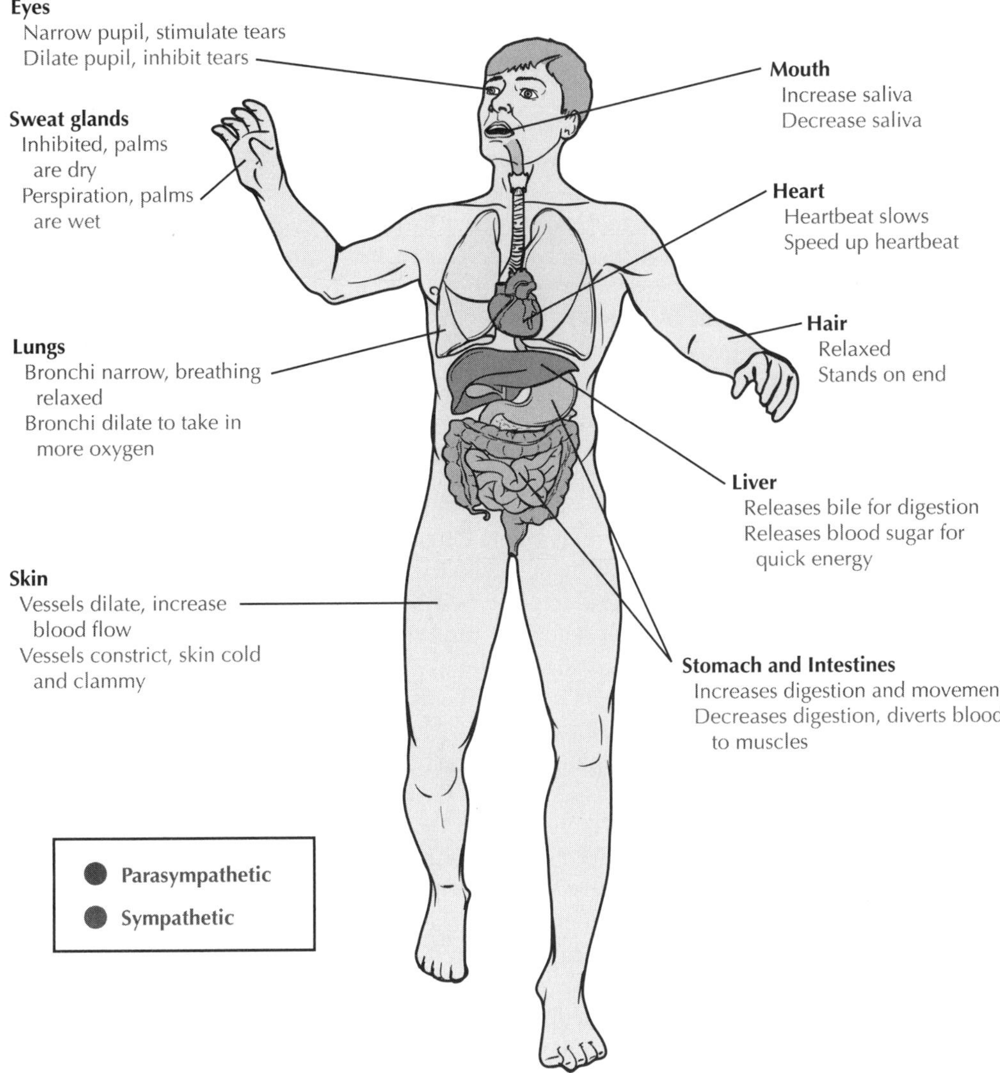

FIGURE 7.17

The parasympathetic branch of the ANS calms and quiets the body. The sympathetic branch arouses the body and prepares it for emergency action.

The **parasympathetic branch** reverses emotional arousal. This calms and relaxes the body. After a period of high emotion, the heart is slowed, the pupils return to normal size, blood pressure drops, and so forth. In addition to restoring balance, the parasympathetic system helps build up and conserve bodily energy.

parasympathetic branch a part of the autonomic system that quiets the body and conserves energy.

The parasympathetic system responds much more slowly than the sympathetic system does. That's why a pounding heart, muscle tension, and other signs of arousal don't fade for 20 or 30 minutes after you feel an intense emotion, such as fear. Moreover, after a strong emotional shock, the parasympathetic system may overreact and lower blood pressure too much. This can cause you to become dizzy or to faint after seeing something shocking, such as a horrifying accident.

Sudden Death An overreaction to intense emotion is called a **parasympathetic rebound**. If the rebound is severe, it can sometimes cause death. In times of war, for instance, combat can be so savage that some soldiers literally die of fear (Moritz & Zamchech, 1946). Apparently, such deaths occur because the parasympathetic nervous system slows the heart to a stop. Even in civilian life this is possible. In one

parasympathetic rebound excess activity in the parasympathetic nervous system following a period of intense emotion.

case, a terrified young woman was admitted to a hospital because she felt she was going to die. A backwoods midwife had predicted that the woman's two sisters would die before their 16th and 21st birthdays. Both died as predicted. The midwife also predicted that this woman would die before her 23rd birthday. She was found dead in her hospital bed the day after she was admitted. It was 2 days before her 23rd birthday (Seligman, 1989). The woman was an apparent victim of her own terror.

Is the parasympathetic nervous system always responsible for such deaths? Probably not. For older persons or those with heart problems, sympathetic effects may be enough to bring about heart attack and collapse. For example, five times more people than usual died of heart attacks on the day of a major 1994 earthquake in Los Angeles (Leor, Poole, & Kloner, 1996). In Asia, the number 4 is considered unlucky, and more heart patients die on the fourth day of the month than any other day. Because they fear they will die on an "unlucky day," their chance of dying actually increases (Phillips et al., 2001).

Lie Detectors

Was Michael Jackson guilty? Has Scott Peterson ever told the whole truth about Laci? Has a trusted employee been stealing from the business? The most popular method for detecting lies measures the bodily changes that accompany emotion. However, the accuracy of "lie detector" tests is doubtful, and they can be a serious invasion of privacy (Lykken, 2001; National Academy of Sciences, 2002).

What is a lie detector? Do lie detectors really detect lies? The lie detector is more accurately called a *polygraph,* a word that means "many writings" (Figure 7.18). A typical **polygraph** records changes in heart rate, blood pressure, breathing, and the **galvanic skin response (GSR)**. The GSR is recorded from the hand by electrodes that measure skin conductance or, more simply, sweating. Popularly known as a lie detector because it is used for that purpose by the police, the polygraph was invented in 1915 by psychologist William Marston. He also created the comic book character *Wonder Woman,* a superhero whose "magic lasso" could force people to tell the truth (Grubin & Madsen, 2005). In reality, the polygraph is not a lie detector at all. The device only records *general emotional arousal*—it can't tell the difference between lying and fear, anxiety, or excitement (Lykken, 2001).

polygraph
a device for recording heart rate, blood pressure, respiration, and galvanic skin response; commonly called a "lie detector."

galvanic skin response (GSR)
a change in the electrical resistance (or inversely, the conductance) of the skin, due to sweating.

When trying to detect a lie, the polygraph operator begins by asking irrelevant (neutral, non-emotional) questions, such as, "Is your name (person's name)?" "Did you eat lunch today?" and so forth. This establishes a "baseline" for normal emotional responses. Then the examiner asks relevant questions: "Did you murder Hensley?" Presumably, only a guilty person will become anxious or emotional if they lie when answering relevant questions.

Wouldn't a person be nervous just from being questioned? Yes, but to minimize this problem, skilled polygraph examiners ask a *series* of questions with critical items mixed among them. An innocent person may respond emotionally to the whole procedure, but only a guilty person is supposed to respond more to key questions. For example, a suspected bank robber might be shown several pictures and asked, "Was the teller who was robbed this person? Was it this person?"

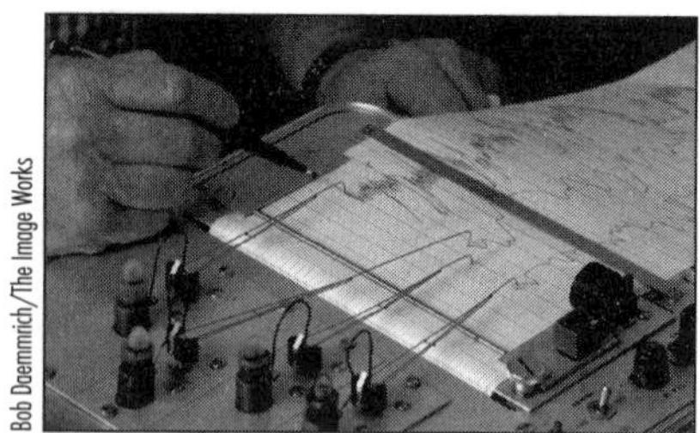
Bob Daemmrich/The Image Works

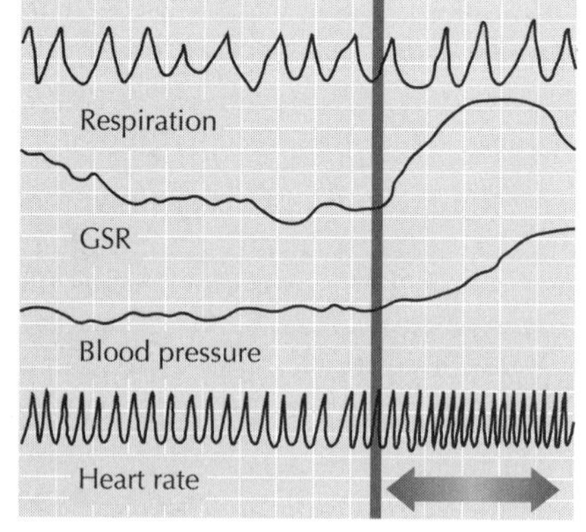

FIGURE 7.18
(left) A typical polygraph includes devices for measuring heart rate, blood pressure, respiration, and galvanic skin response. Pens mounted on the top of the machine make a record of bodily responses on a moving strip of paper. *(right)* Changes in the area marked by the arrow indicate emotional arousal. If such responses appear when a person answers a question, he or she may be lying, but other causes of arousal are also possible.

CRITICAL THINKING

To Catch a Terrorist

An airport check-in agent asks a passenger if he packed his own luggage. He says he did. But he is sitting in a booth that creates high-resolution infrared images of the heat patterns on his face. The patterns reveal stress, suggesting that he is lying. His luggage is searched and an otherwise undetectable explosive device is confiscated, averting a potential disaster.

Although this scenario is not yet a reality, it is not as far-fetched as you might think. The growing realization that polygraph tests are not very accurate could not have come at a worse time for national security (Knight, 2004). The infrared scanner is just one alternative technology currently under development. Preliminary research indicates that infrared face scans are at least as accurate as polygraphs at detecting lying (Pavlidis, Eberhardt, & Levine, 2002).

Other new techniques look directly at brain activity, thus bypassing the traditional approach of looking for indirect signs of general emotional arousal. For example, psychologist Daniel Langleben theorizes that a liar must inhibit telling the truth in order to lie (Langleben et al., 2002). Thus, extra brain areas must be activated to tell a lie, which can be seen in fMRI brain images when people are lying.

Even if new techniques are used, a problem remains: How can we avoid falsely classifying liars as truth tellers and truth tellers as liars? Until that can be done with acceptable accuracy, the new technologies may have no more value than the polygraph does.

As an alternative, subjects may be asked **control questions**, which are designed to make almost anyone anxious: "Have you ever stolen anything from your place of work?" Typically, such questions are very difficult to answer truthfully with an unqualified no. In theory they show how a person reacts to doubt or misgivings. The person's reaction to critical questions can then be compared with responses to control questions.

control questions
in a polygraph exam, questions that almost always provoke anxiety.

Even when questioning is done properly, lie detection may be inaccurate (Grubin & Madsen, 2005). For example, a man named Floyd Fay was convicted of murdering his friend Fred Ery. To prove his innocence, Fay volunteered to take a lie detector test, which he failed. Fay spent 2 years in prison before the real killer confessed to the crime. Psychologist David Lykken (1998, 2001) has documented many cases in which innocent people were jailed after being convicted on the basis of polygraph evidence.

If Floyd Fay was innocent, why did he fail the test? Put yourself in his place, and it's easy to see why. Imagine the examiner asking, "Did you kill Fred?" Because you knew Fred, and you are a suspect, it's no secret that this is a critical question. What would happen to *your* heart rate, blood pressure, breathing, and perspiration under such circumstances?

Proponents of lie detection claim it is 95-percent accurate. But in one study, accuracy was dramatically lowered when people thought about past emotional experiences as they answered irrelevant questions (Ben-Shakhar & Dolev, 1996). Similarly, the polygraph may be thrown off by self-inflicted pain, by tranquilizing drugs, or by people who can lie without anxiety (Waid & Orne, 1982). Worst of all, the test is much more likely to label an innocent person guilty, rather than a guilty person innocent. In studies involving real crimes, an average of one innocent person in five was rated as guilty by the lie detector (Lykken, 2001; Patrick & Iacono, 1989; Saxe, Dougherty, & Cross, 1985). In some instances, these false positives have caused three out of four innocent persons to be labeled guilty. Individuals who believe the polygraph is highly accurate may actually change their statements to be consistent with the test. This, too, can leave an innocent person open to false accusations (Meyer & Youngjohn, 1991). For such reasons, the National Academy of Sciences (2002) recently concluded that polygraph tests should not be used to screen employees. (See "To Catch a Terrorist.")

Despite the lie detector's unreliability, you may be tested for employment or other reasons. Should this occur, the best advice is to remain calm; then actively challenge the outcome if the machine wrongly questions your honesty.

EXPRESSING EMOTIONS—MAKING FACES AND TALKING BODIES

Next to our own feelings, the expressions of others are the most familiar part of emotion. Are emotional expressions a carryover from human evolution? Charles Darwin thought so. Darwin (1872) observed that angry tigers, monkeys, dogs, and humans all bare their teeth in the same way. Psychologists believe that emotional expressions evolved to communicate our feelings to others, which aids survival. Such messages give valuable hints about what other people are likely to do next (Ekman & Rosenberg, 1997). For instance, in a recent study, people were able to detect angry and scheming faces faster than happy, sad, or neutral faces (Figure 7.19). Presumably, we are especially sensitive to threatening faces because they warn us of possible harm (Oehman, 2002; Tipples, Atkinson, & Young, 2002.)

Facial Expressions

Are emotional expressions the same for all people? Basic expressions appear to be fairly universal (Figure 7.20). Children who are born blind have little opportunity to learn emotional expressions from others. Even so, they display joy, sadness, fear, anger, and disgust in the same way as sighted people do (Galati, Scherer, & Ricci-Bitti, 1997).

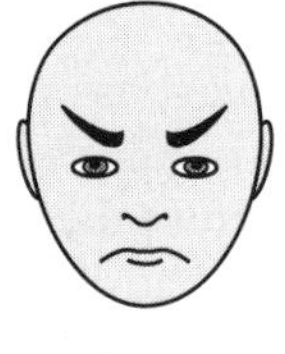

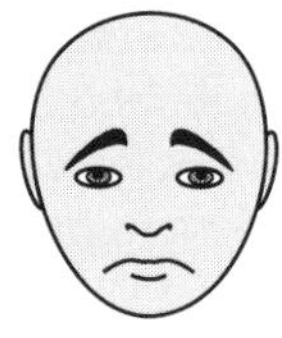

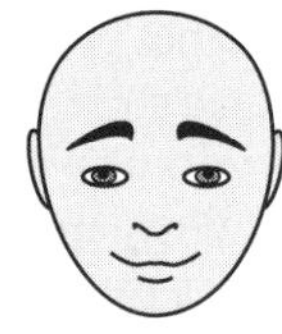

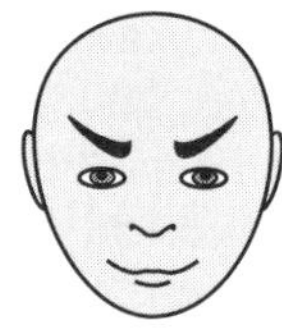

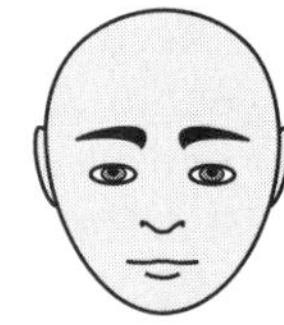

FIGURE 7.19
When shown groups of simplified faces (without labels), the angry and scheming faces "jumped out" at people faster than sad, happy, or neutral faces. An ability to rapidly detect threatening expressions probably helped our ancestors survive. (*Adapted from Tipples, Atkinson, & Young, 2002.*)

Gary Conner/PhotoEdit

FIGURE 7.20
Is anger expressed the same way in different cultures? A study of masks from 18 cultures found that those meant to be frightening or threatening were strikingly similar. Shared features included angular, diagonal, or triangular eyes, eyebrows, nose, cheeks, and chin, together with an open, downwardcurved mouth. (Keep this list in mind next Halloween.) Obviously, the pictured mask is not meant to be warm and cuddly. Your ability to "read" its emotional message suggests that basic emotional expressions have universal biological roots (Aronoff, Barclay, & Stevenson, 1988).

FOCUS ON RESEARCH

Crow's-Feet and Smiles Sweet

The next time you see an athletic contest or a beauty pageant on television, look closely at the winner's smile and the smile of the runner-up. Although both people will be smiling, it is likely that the winner's smile will be authentic and the loser's smile will be forced.

We smile for many reasons: to be polite or because of embarrassment, or sometimes to deceive (Frank, 2002; Frank & Ekman, 2004). These "social smiles" are often intentional or forced, and they only involve lifting the corners of the mouth. What does a genuine smile look like? A real smile involves not only the mouth, but also the small muscles around the eyes. These muscles lift the cheeks and make crow's-feet or crinkles in the outside corners of the eyes.

Authentic smiles are called *Duchenne smiles* (after Guilluame Duchenne, a French scientist who studied facial muscles). The muscles around the eyes are very difficult to tighten on command. Hence, to tell if a smile in authentic, or merely posed, look at the corners of a person's eyes, not the mouth (Williams et al., 2001). To put it another way, crow's-feet mean a smile is sweet.

Duchenne smiles signal genuine happiness and enjoyment (Soussignan, 2002). In a recent study, women who had authentic smiles in their college yearbook photos were contacted 6, 22, and 31 years later. At each interval, real smiles in college were associated with more positive emotions and a greater sense of competence. We can only speculate about why this is the case. However, it is likely that smiling signals that a person is helpful or nurturing. This leads to more supportive social relationships and, in a self-fulfilling manner, to greater happiness (Gladstone & Parker, 2002).

Dennis Coon

The face on the left shows a social smile; the one on the right is an authentic, or Duchenne, smile.

Some facial expressions are shaped by learning and may be found only in specific cultures. Among the Chinese, for example, sticking out the tongue is a gesture of surprise, not of disrespect or teasing. If a person comes from another culture, it is wise to remember that you may easily misunderstand his or her expressions. At such times, knowing the social *context* in which an expression occurs helps clarify its meaning (Carroll & Russell, 1996; Ekman, 1993). (Also, see "Cultural Differences in Emotion.")

Cultural Differences in Emotion How many times have you been angry this week? Once? Twice? Several times? If it was more than once, you're not unusual. Anger is a very common emotion in Western cultures. Very likely this is because our culture emphasizes personal independence and a free expression of individual rights and needs. In North America, anger is widely viewed as a "natural" reaction to feeling that you have been treated unfairly.

On the opposite side of the globe, many Asian cultures place a high value on group harmony. In Asia, expressing anger in public is less common and anger is regarded as less "natural." The reason for this is that anger tends to separate people. Thus, being angry is at odds with a culture that values cooperation (Markus, Kitayama, & VandenBos, 1996).

Culture also influences positive emotions. In America, we tend to have positive feelings such as pride, happiness, and superiority, which emphasize our role as *individuals.* In Japan, positive feelings are more often linked with membership in groups (friendly feelings, closeness to others, and respect) (Kitayama, Markus, & Kurokawa, 2000). It is common to think of emotion as an individual event. However, as you can see, emotion is shaped by cultural ideas, values, and practices.

Gender and Emotion *Women have a reputation for being "more emotional" than men. Are they?* There is little reason to think that men and women differ in their private experiences of emotion. However, in Western cultures women do tend to more openly express sadness, fear, shame, and guilt. Men more often express anger and hostility (Fischer et al., 2004). Why should this be so? The answer again lies in learning: As they are growing up, boys learn to express emotions related to power; girls learn to express emotions related to nurturing others (Wood & Eagly, 2002). For many men, an inability to express feelings is a major barrier to having close, satisfying relationships with others (Bruch, Berko, & Haase, 1998). It may even contribute to tragedies like the murders at Columbine High School in Littleton, Colorado. For many young males, anger is the only emotion they can freely express.

kinesics
study of the meaning of body movements, posture, hand gestures, and facial expressions; commonly called body language.

Universal Expressions Despite cultural differences, facial expressions of *fear, anger, disgust, sadness,* and *happiness* (enjoyment) are recognized around the world. *Contempt, surprise,* and *interest* may also be universal, but researchers are less certain of these expressions (Ekman, 1993). Notice that this list covers most of the primary emotions described earlier. It's also nice to note that a genuine smile is the most universal and easily recognized facial expression of emotion.

Sergei Karpukhgin/Reuters/Corbis

The expression of emotion is strongly influenced by learning. As you have no doubt observed, women cry more often, longer, and more intensely than men do. Men begin learning early in childhood to suppress crying—possibly to the detriment of their emotional health (Williams & Morris, 1996). Many men are especially unwilling to engage in public displays of emotion, in contrast to these women, who are grieving for the victims of a 2005 school siege in Breslan, Russia, which left hundreds of children dead.

Body Language If a friend walked up to you and said, "Hey, ugly, what are you doing?" would you be offended? Probably not, because such remarks are usually delivered with a big grin. The facial and bodily gestures of emotion speak a language all their own and add to what a person says.

Kinesics (kih-NEEZ-iks) is the study of communication through body movement, posture, gestures, and facial expressions. Informally, we call it body language. To see a masterful use of body language, turn off the sound on a television and watch a popular entertainer or politician at work.

What kinds of messages are sent with body language? Popular books on body language tend to list particular meanings for gestures. For instance, a woman who stands rigidly, crosses her arms over her chest, or sits with her legs tightly crossed is supposedly sending a "hands off" message. But experts in kinesics emphasize that gestures are rarely this fixed in meaning. The message might simply be, "This room is cold."

It is important to realize cultural learning also affects the meaning of gestures. What, for instance, does it mean if you touch your thumb and first finger together to form a circle? In North America it means "Everything is fine" or "A-okay." In France and Belgium it means "You're worth zero." In southern Italy it means "You're an ass!" (Ekman, Friesen, & Bear, 1984). Thus, when the layer of culturally defined meanings is removed, it is more realistic to say that body language reveals an overall emotional tone (underlying emotional state).

Amy Etra/PhotoEdit, Inc.

Emotions are often unconsciously revealed by gestures and body positioning.

Your face can produce some 20,000 different expressions, which makes it the most expressive part of your body. Most of these are *facial blends* (a mixture of two or more basic expressions). Imagine, for example, that you just received an F on an unfair test. Quite likely, your eyes, eyebrows, and forehead would reveal anger, while your mouth would be turned downward in a sad frown.

Most of us believe we can fairly accurately tell what others are feeling by observing their facial expressions. If thousands of facial blends occur, how do we make such judgments? The answer is that facial expressions can be boiled down to three basic dimensions: *pleasantness–unpleasantness, attention–rejection,* and *activation* (or arousal) (Schlosberg, 1954). By smiling when you give a friend a hard time, you add an emotional message of acceptance to the verbal insult, which changes its meaning. As they say in movie Westerns, it makes a big difference to "Smile when you say that, partner."

The body telegraphs other feelings. The most general "messages" involve *relaxation* or *tension,* and *liking* or *disliking.* Relaxation is expressed by casually positioning the arms and legs, leaning back (if sitting), and spreading the arms and legs. Liking is expressed mainly by leaning toward a person or object. Thus, body positioning can reveal feelings that would normally be concealed. Who do you "lean toward"?

Psychologists John Bargh and Tanya Chartrand have identified an aspect of body language they call the "chameleon effect." This refers to the fact that we often unconsciously mimic the postures, mannerisms, and facial expressions of other people as we interact with them. (We change our gestures to match our surroundings, like a chameleon changes color.) Bargh and Chartrand also found that if another person copies your gestures and physical postures, you are more inclined to like them (Chartrand & Bargh, 1999). This implies that to make a stronger connection with others, it helps to subtly mimic their gestures.

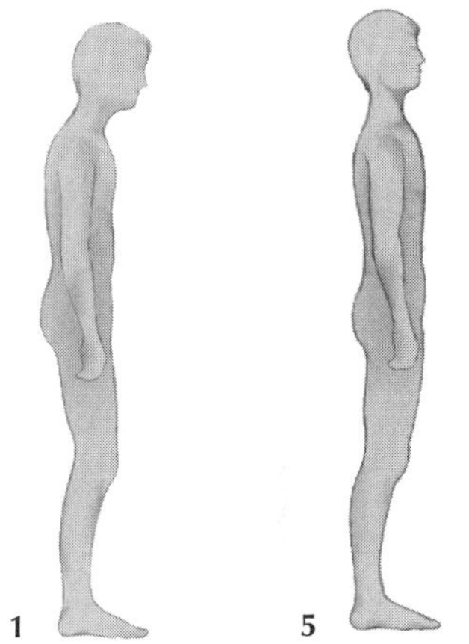

FIGURE 7.21

Posture and success. These drawings show the end points of a five-point scale used to measure erectness of posture. Success by people in various situations was found to be reflected by a more upright posture. (*Adapted from Weisfeld & Beresford, 1982.*)

Imagine that you are standing 30 yards from a classroom in which test grades are being announced. As students file out, do you think you could tell—without the aid of facial expressions—who got an A and who got an F? Actually, your task might not be too difficult. Overall *posture* can also indicate one's emotional state. Specifically, when a person is successful, his or her posture is likely to be more erect (Weisfeld & Beresford, 1982) (Figure 7.21). Psychologists debate whether this tendency is a product of evolution or is simply learned. In any case, standing tall with pride and slumping with dejection do seem to be consistent patterns.

Does body positioning or movement ever reveal lying or deception? Just as a less than genuine smile may betray a liar, so too might body language (Ekman & O'Sullivan, 1991). But the signs are subtle; seemingly obvious clues like shifty eyes, squirming, and nervous movements that involve touching one's own body (rubbing, grooming, scratching, twisting hair, rubbing hands, biting lips, stroking the chin, and so on) are not consistently related to lying (Ekman, 2001).

On the other hand, the gestures people use to illustrate what they are saying may reveal lying. These gestures, called **illustrators**, tend to *decrease* when a person is telling a lie. In other words, persons who usually "talk with their hands" may be much less animated when they are lying.

illustrators
gestures people use to illustrate what they are saying.

emblems
gestures that have widely understood meanings within a particular culture.

Other movements, called *emblems,* can also reveal lying. **Emblems** are gestures that have widely understood meanings within a particular culture. Some examples are the thumbs-up sign, the A-okay sign, the middle-finger insult, a head nod for yes, and a head shake for no. Emblems tend to *increase* when a person is lying. More important, they often reveal true feelings contrary to what the liar is saying. For example, a person might smile and say, "Yes, I'd love to try some of your homemade candied pig's feet," while slowly shaking her head from side to side.

THEORIES OF EMOTION—SEVERAL WAYS TO FEAR A BEAR

Is it possible to explain what takes place during emotion? How are arousal, behavior, cognition, expression, and feelings interrelated? Theories of emotion offer different answers to these questions. Let's investigate some prominent views. Each appears to have a part of the truth, so we will try to put them all together in the end.

The James-Lange Theory (1884–1885)

James-Lange theory
states that emotional feelings follow bodily arousal and come from awareness of such arousal.

Common sense tells us that we see a bear, feel fear, become aroused, and run (and sweat and yell). But is this the true order of events? In the 1880s, American psychologist William James (the functionalist) and Danish psychologist Carl Lange proposed that common sense had it backward. According to James and Lange, bodily arousal (such as increased heart rate) does not follow a feeling such as fear. Instead, they argued, *emotional feelings follow bodily arousal.* Thus, we see a bear, run, are aroused, and *then* feel fear as we become aware of our bodily reactions (Figure 7.22).

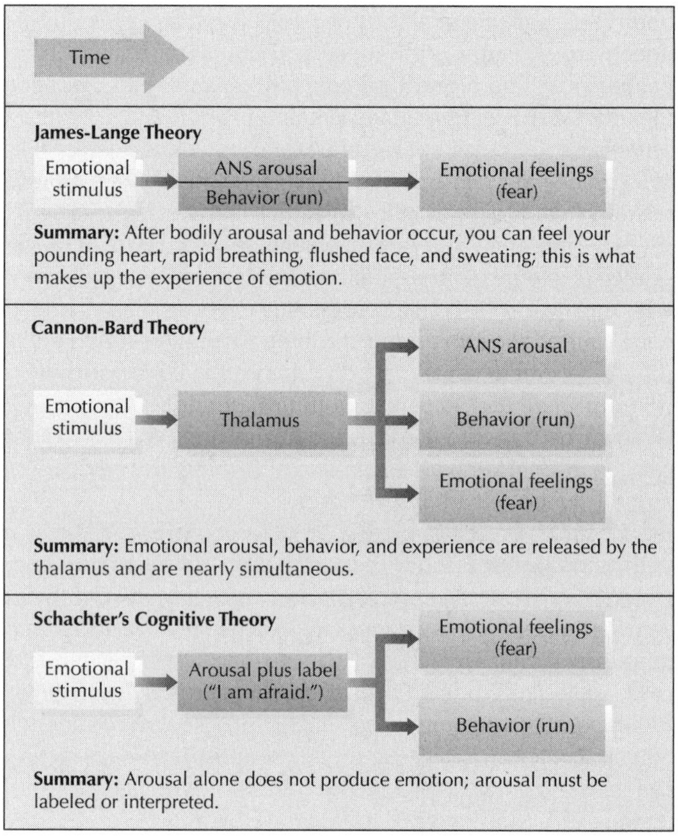

FIGURE 7.22
Theories of emotion.

To support his ideas, James pointed out that we often do not experience an emotion until after reacting. For example, imagine that you are driving. Suddenly a car pulls out in front of you. You swerve and skid to an abrupt halt at the side of the road. Only after you have come to a stop do you notice your pounding heart, rapid breathing, and tense muscles—and recognize your fear.

The Cannon-Bard Theory (1927)

Cannon-Bard theory
states that activity in the thalamus causes emotional feelings and bodily arousal to occur simultaneously.

Walter Cannon (1932) and Phillip Bard disagreed with the James-Lange theory. According to them, emotional feelings and bodily arousal *occur at the same time*. Cannon and Bard believed that seeing a bear activates the thalamus in the brain. The thalamus, in turn, alerts the cortex and the hypothalamus for action. The cortex produces our emotional feelings and emotional behavior. The hypothalamus triggers a chain of events that arouses the body. Thus, if you see a dangerous-looking bear, brain activity will simultaneously produce bodily arousal, running, and feeling fear (Figure 7.22).

Schachter's Cognitive Theory of Emotion

Schachter's cognitive theory
states that emotions occur when physical arousal is labeled or interpreted on the basis of experience and situational cues.

The previous theories are mostly concerned with our physical responses. Stanley Schachter realized that cognitive (mental) factors also enter into emotion. According to Schachter, emotion occurs when we apply a particular *label* to general physical *arousal*. Schachter believed that when we are aroused, we have a need to interpret our feelings. Assume, for instance, that someone sneaks up behind you on a dark street and says, "Boo!" No matter who the person is, your body will be aroused (pounding heart, sweating palms, and so on). If the person is a total stranger, you might interpret this arousal as fear; if the person is a close friend, the arousal may be labeled as surprise or delight. The label (such as anger, fear, or happiness) you apply to bodily arousal is influenced by your past experiences, the situation, and the reactions of others (Figure 7.22).

Support for the cognitive theory of emotion comes from an experiment in which people watched a slapstick movie (Schachter & Wheeler, 1962). Before viewing the movie, one third of the people received an arousing injection of adrenaline, one third got a placebo (salt water) injection, and one third was given a tranquilizer. People who received the adrenaline rated the movie funniest and laughed the most while watching it. In contrast, those given the tranquilizer were least amused. The placebo group fell in between.

According to the cognitive theory of emotion, individuals who received adrenaline had a stirred-up body, but no explanation for what they were feeling. Consequently, they became happy when the movie implied that their arousal was due to amusement. This and similar experiments make it clear that emotion is much more than just an agitated body. Perception, experience, attitudes, judgment, and many other mental factors also affect the emotions we feel. Schachter's theory would predict, then, that if you met a bear, you would be aroused. If the bear seemed unfriendly, you would interpret your arousal as fear, and if the bear offered to shake your "paw," you would be happy, amazed, and relieved!

Attribution We now move from slapstick movies and fear of bear bodies to appreciation of bare bodies. Researcher Stuart Valins (1967) added an interesting wrinkle to Schachter's theory of emotion. According to Valins, arousal can be attributed to various sources—a process that alters perceptions of emotion. To demonstrate **attribution**, Valins (1966) showed male college students a series of slides of nude females. While watching the slides, each subject heard an amplified heartbeat that he believed was his own. In reality, subjects were listening to a recorded heartbeat carefully designed to beat *louder* and *stronger* when some (but not all) of the slides were shown.

attribution
the mental process of assigning causes to events. In emotion, the process of attributing arousal to a particular source.

Michael Grecco/Stock, Boston/ PictureQuest

Which theory of emotion best describes the reactions of these people? Given the complexity of emotion, each theory appears to possess an element of truth.

After watching the slides, each student was asked to say which was most attractive. Students who heard the false heartbeat consistently rated slides paired with a "pounding heart" as the most attractive. In other words, when a student saw a slide and heard his heart beat louder, he attributed his "emotion" to the slide. His interpretation seems to have been, "Now that one I like!" His next reaction, perhaps, was "But why?" Later research suggests that subjects persuaded themselves that the slide really was more attractive in order to explain their apparent arousal (Truax, 1983).

That seems somewhat artificial. Does it really make any difference what arousal is attributed to? Yes. To illustrate attribution in the "real world," consider what happens when parents interfere with the budding romance of a son or daughter. Often, trying to separate a young couple *intensifies* their feelings. Meddling parents add frustration, anger, and fear or excitement (as in seeing each other "on the sly") to the couple's feelings. Because they already care for each other, they are likely to attribute all this added emotion to "true love" (Walster, 1971).

Attribution theory predicts that you are most likely to "love" someone who gets you stirred up emotionally (Foster et al., 1998). This is true even when fear, anger, frustration, or rejection is part of the formula. Thus, if you want to successfully propose marriage, take your intended to the middle of a narrow, windswept suspension bridge over a deep chasm and look deeply into his or her eyes. As your beloved's heart pounds wildly (from being on the bridge, not from your irresistible charms), say, "I love you." Attribution theory predicts that your companion will conclude, "Oh wow, I must love you too."

The preceding is not as farfetched as it may seem. In an ingenious study, a female psychologist interviewed men in a park. Some were on a swaying suspension bridge 230 feet above a river. The rest were on a solid wooden bridge just 10 feet above the ground. After the interview, the psychologist gave each man her telephone number, so he could "find out about the results" of the study. Men interviewed on the suspension bridge were much more likely to give the "lady from the park" a call (Dutton & Aron, 1974). Apparently, these men experienced heightened arousal, which they interpreted as attraction to the experimenter—a clear case of love at first fright!

The Facial Feedback Hypothesis

Schachter added thinking and interpretation (cognition) to our view of emotion, but the picture still seems incomplete. What about expressions? How do they influence emotion? As Charles Darwin observed, the face is very central to emotion—certainly it must be more than just an "emotional billboard."

Psychologist Carrol Izard (1977, 1990) was among the first to suggest that the face does, indeed, affect emotion. According to Izard and others, emotional activity causes innately programmed changes in facial expression. Sensations from the face then provide cues to the brain that help us determine what emotion we are feeling. This idea is known as the **facial feedback hypothesis** (Adelmann & Zajonc, 1989). Stated another way, it says that having facial expressions and becoming aware of them is what leads to emotional experience. Exercise, for instance, arouses the body, but we don't experience this arousal as emotion because it does not trigger emotional expressions.

facial feedback hypothesis states that sensations from facial expressions help define what emotion a person feels.

Psychologist Paul Ekman takes the idea one step further. Ekman believes that "making faces" can actually cause emotion (Ekman, 1993). In one study, participants were guided as they arranged their faces, muscle by muscle, into expressions of surprise, disgust, sadness, anger, fear, and happiness (Figure 7.23). At the same time, each person's bodily reactions were monitored.

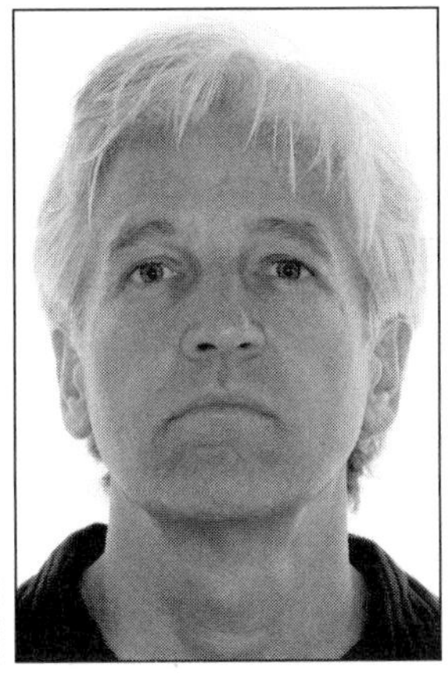

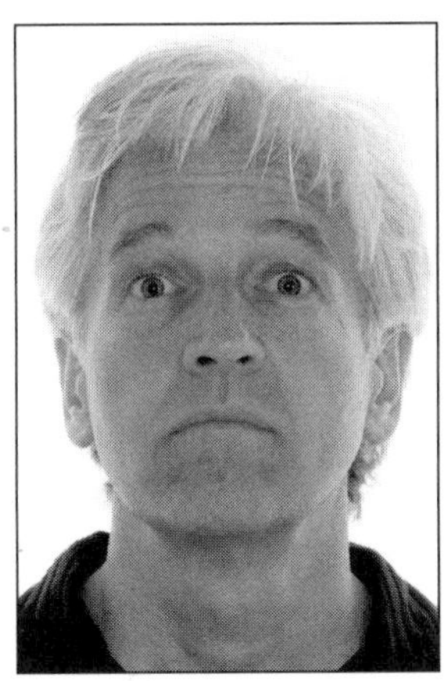

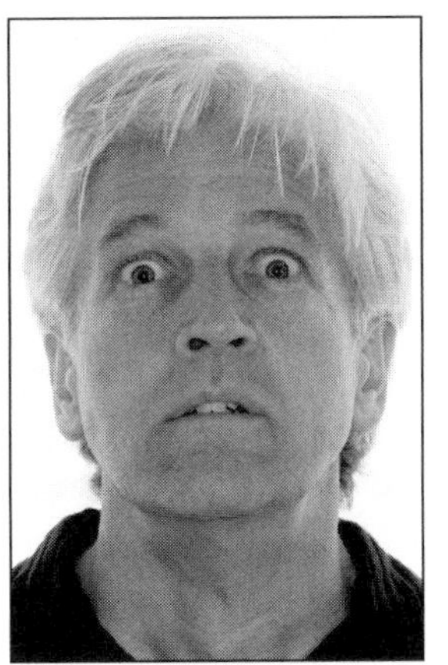

Dennis Coon

FIGURE 7.23

Facial feedback and emotion. Participants in Ekman's study formed facial expressions like those normally observed during emotion. When they did this, emotion-like changes took place in their bodily activity. (*After Ekman, Levenson, & Friesen, 1983.*)

Contrary to what you might expect, "making faces" can affect the autonomic nervous system, as shown by changes in heart rate and skin temperature. In addition, each facial expression produces a different pattern of activity. An angry face, for instance, raises heart rate and skin temperature, whereas disgust lowers both (Ekman et al., 1983). Other studies have confirmed that posed expressions alter emotions and bodily activity (Duclos & Laird, 2001; Soussignan, 2002).

In a fascinating experiment on facial feedback, people rated how funny they thought cartoons were while holding a pen crosswise in their mouths. Those who held the pen in their teeth thought the cartoons were funnier than did people who held the pen in their lips. Can you guess why? The answer is that if you hold a pen with your teeth, you are forced to form a smile. Holding it with the lips makes a frown. As predicted by the facial feedback hypothesis, emotional experiences were influenced by the facial expressions that people made (Strack, Martin, & Stepper, 1988). Next time you're feeling sad, bite a pen!

It appears, then, that not only do emotions influence expressions, but expressions influence emotions, as shown here (Adelmann & Zajonc, 1989; Duclos & Laird, 2001):

Contracted Facial Muscles	Felt Emotion
Forehead	Surprise
Brow	Anger
Mouth (down)	Sadness
Mouth (smile)	Joy

THE CLINICAL FILE

Suppressing Emotion—Is It Healthy?

Emotional life has its ups and downs. While sharing a beautiful day with friends, you can freely express your happiness. But often, we try to appear less emotional than we really are, especially when we are feeling negative emotions. Have you ever been angry with a friend in public? Embarrassed by someone's behavior at a party? Disgusted by someone's table manners or a bad joke? In such circumstances, people are quite good at suppressing outward signs of emotion. However, restraining emotion can actually increase activity in the sympathetic nervous system. In other words, hiding emotion requires a lot of effort.

Suppressing emotions can impair thinking and memory, as you devote energy to self-control. Thus, although suppressing emotion allows us to appear calm and collected on the outside, this cool appearance comes at a high cost (Richards & Gross, 2000). People who suppress emotions cope poorly with life and are prone to depression and other problems (Lynch et al., 2001). Conversely, people who express their emotions generally experience better emotional and physical health (Lumley, 2004; Pennebaker, 2004). Usually, it's better to manage emotions than it is to suppress them. You will find some suggestions for managing emotions in the upcoming Psychology in Action feature.

This could explain an interesting effect you have probably observed. When you are feeling "down," forcing yourself to smile will sometimes be followed by an actual improvement in your mood (Kleinke, Peterson, & Rutledge, 1998).

If smiling can improve a person's mood, is it a good idea to inhibit negative emotions? For an answer, see "Suppressing Emotion—Is It Healthy."

A Contemporary Model of Emotion

To summarize, James and Lange were right that feedback from arousal and behavior adds to our emotional experiences. Cannon and Bard were right about the timing of events. Schachter showed us that cognition is important. In fact, psychologists are increasingly aware that how you *appraise* a situation greatly affects your emotions (Strongman, 1996). **Emotional appraisal** refers to evaluating the personal meaning of a stimulus: Is it good/bad, threatening/supportive, relevant/irrelevant, and so on.

emotional appraisal
evaluating the personal meaning of a stimulus or situation.

In recent years many new theories of emotion have appeared. Rather than pick one "best" theory, let's put the main points of several theories together in a single contemporary model of emotion (Figure 7.24).

Imagine that a large snarling dog lunges at you with its teeth bared. A modern view of your emotional reactions goes something like this: An *emotional stimulus* (the dog) is *appraised* (judged) as a threat or other cause for emotion (Table 7.2). (You think to yourself, "Uh oh, big trouble!") Your appraisal gives rise to *ANS arousal* (your heart pounds and your body becomes stirred up). The appraisal also releases *innate emotional expressions* (your face twists into a mask of fear and your posture becomes tense). At the same time, your appraisal leads to *adaptive behavior* (you run from the dog). It also causes a change in consciousness that you recognize as the subjective experience of fear. (The intensity of this *emotional feeling* is directly related to the amount of ANS arousal taking place in your body.)

Each element of emotion—ANS arousal, adaptive behavior, subjective experience, and your emotional expressions—may further alter your appraisal of the situation, as well as your thoughts, judgments, and perceptions. Such changes affect each of the other reactions, which again alters your appraisal and interpretation of events. Thus, emotion may blossom, change course, or diminish as it proceeds. Note too that the original emotional stimulus can be external, like the attacking dog, or internal, such as a memory

TABLE 7.2

Appraisals and Corresponding Emotions

APPRAISAL	EMOTION
You have been slighted or demeaned	Anger
You feel threatened	Anxiety
You have experienced a loss	Sadness
You have broken a moral rule	Guilt
You have not lived up to your ideals	Shame
You desire something another has	Envy
You are near something repulsive	Disgust
You fear the worst but yearn for better	Hope
You are moving toward a desired goal	Happiness
You are linked with a valued object or accomplishment	Pride
You have been treated well by another	Gratitude
You desire affection from another person	Love
You are moved by someone's suffering	Compassion

Paraphrased from Lazarus, 1991b.

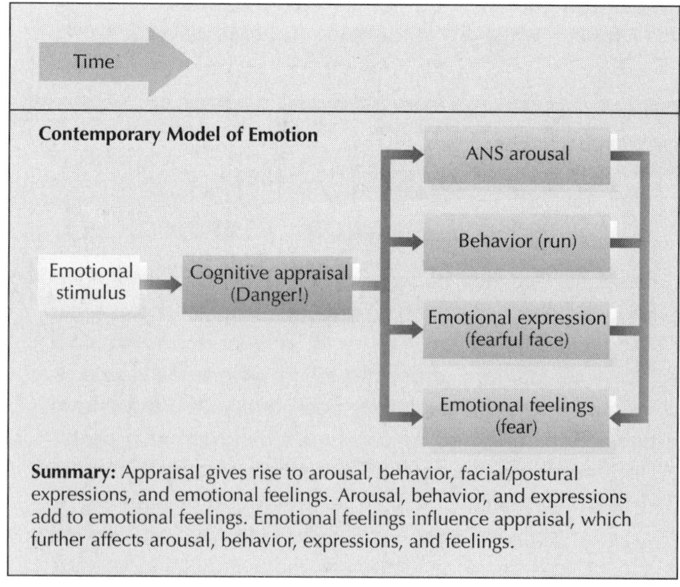

FIGURE 7.24
A contemporary model of emotion.

of being chased by a dog, rejected by a lover, or praised by a friend. That's why mere thoughts and memories can make us fearful, sad, or happy (Strongman, 1996).

Our discussion suggests that emotion is greatly influenced by how you think about an event. For example, if another driver "cuts you off" on the highway, you could become very angry. But if you do, you will add 15 minutes of emotional upset to your day. By changing your appraisal, you could just as easily choose to laugh at the other driver's childish behavior—and minimize the emotional wear-and-tear (Gross, 2001).

In this chapter we will look further at the impact of emotional appraisals through an examination of *emotional intelligence*. Before we continue, you might want to appraise your learning with the exercises that follow.

Emotional intelligence emotional competence, including empathy, self-control, self-awareness, and other skills.

PSYCHOLOGY IN ACTION

Emotional Intelligence—The Fine Art of Self-Control

The Greek philosopher Aristotle had a recipe for handling relationships smoothly. You must be able, he said, "to be angry with the right person, to the right degree, at the right time, for the right purpose, and in the right way." Psychologists Peter Salovey and John Mayer call such self-control "emotional intelligence." **Emotional intelligence** refers to a combination of skills, such as empathy, self-control, and self-awareness (Salovey & Mayer, 1997). Such skills can make us more flexible, adaptable, and emotionally mature (Bonanno et al., 2004).

People who excel in life tend to be emotionally intelligent (Fisher & Ashanasy, 2000; Mehrabian, 2000). Indeed, the costs of poor emotional skills can be high. They range from problems in marriage and parenting to poor physical health. A lack of emotional intelligence can ruin careers and sabotage achievement. Perhaps the greatest toll falls on children and teenagers. For them, having poor emotional skills can contribute to depression, eating disorders, unwanted pregnancy, aggression, violent crime, and poor academic performance (Parker et al., 2004). Thus, in many life circumstances emotional intelligence is as important as IQ (Dulewicz & Higgs, 2000).

Are there specific skills that make up emotional intelligence? Many elements contribute to emotional intelligence (Mayer et al., 2001). Descriptions of some of the most important skills follows.

Self-awareness Emotionally intelligent people are tuned in to their own feelings. For example, they are able to recognize quickly if they are angry, or envious, or feeling guilty, or depressed. This is valuable because many people have disruptive emotions without being able to pinpoint why they are uncomfortable. Those who are more self-aware are keenly sensitive to their own feelings.

Empathy Empathetic people accurately perceive emotions in others and sense what others are feeling. They are good at "reading" facial expressions, tone of voice, and other signs of emotion.

Managing emotions Emotional intelligence involves an ability to manage your own emotions and those of others. For example, you know how to calm down when you are angry and you also know how to calm others. As Aristotle noted so long ago, people who are emotionally intelligent have an ability to amplify or restrain emotions, depending on the situation (Bonanno et al., 2004).

Understanding emotions Emotions contain useful information. For instance, anger is a cue that something is wrong; anxiety indicates uncertainty; embarrassment communicates shame; depression means we feel helpless; enthusiasm tells us we're excited. People who are emotionally intelligent know what causes various emotions, what they mean, and how they affect behavior.

Using emotion People who are emotionally intelligent use their feelings to enhance thinking and decision making. For example, if you can remember how you reacted emotionally in the past, it can help you react better to new situations. Emotional intelligence also involves using emotions to promote personal growth and improve relationships with others. For instance, you may have noticed that helping someone else makes you feel better, too. Likewise, when good fortune comes their way, people who are emotionally smart share the news with others. Almost always, doing so strengthens relationships and increases emotional well-being (Gable et al., 2004).

continued

PSYCHOLOGY IN ACTION (CONTINUED)

Emotional Flexibility In general, being emotionally intelligent means accepting that emotions are an essential part of who we are and how we survive. There is a natural tendency to enjoy positive emotions like joy or love, while treating negative emotions as unwelcome misery. However, negative emotions can also be valuable and constructive. For example, persistent distress may impel a person to seek help, mend a relationship, or find a new direction in life (Plutchik, 2003).

Often, the "right" choices in life can only be defined by taking personal values, needs, and emotions into account. Extremely rational approaches to making choices can produce sensible but emotionally empty decisions. Good decisions often combine emotion with reason. In short, emotional intelligence is the ability to consciously make your emotions work for you.

Positive Psychology and Positive Emotions It's obvious that joy, interest, contentment, love, and similar emotions are pleasant and rewarding. However, as psychologist Barbara Fredrickson has pointed out, positive emotions have other benefits. Negative emotions are associated with actions that probably helped our ancestors save their skins: escaping, attacking, expelling poison, and the like. As useful as these reactions may be, they tend to narrow our focus of attention and limit our ideas about possible actions. In contrast, positive emotions tend to broaden our focus. This opens up new possibilities and builds up our personal resources. For instance, emotions such as joy, interest, and contentment create an urge to play, to be creative, to explore, to savor life, to seek new experiences, to integrate, and to grow. In short, positive emotions are not just a pleasant side effect of happy circumstances. They also encourage personal growth and social connection. A capacity for having positive emotions is a basic human strength, and cultivating good feelings is a part of emotional intelligence (Fredrickson, 2001).

Authentic Happiness Psychologists have worked hard to find ways to relieve the negative emotions that make us miserable. Recently, psychologist Martin Seligman has proposed an alternate approach. Rather than trying to fix weaknesses, he believes we are more likely to find genuine happiness by emphasizing our natural strengths. Seligman teaches that happiness can be cultivated by using the strengths we already possess—including kindness, originality, humor, optimism, and generosity. Such strengths are natural buffers against misfortune, and they can help people live more positive, genuinely happy lives (Seligman, 2002).

Becoming Emotionally Smart Understandably, many psychologists believe that schools should promote emotional competence as well as intellectual skills. The result, they think, would be greater self-control, altruism, and compassion—all basic capacities needed if our society is to thrive.

How would a person learn the skills that make up emotional intelligence? Psychologists are still unsure how to teach emotional intelligence. Nevertheless, it's clear that emotional skills can be learned. Accepting that emotions are valuable is an important first step. There are many valuable lessons to learn from paying close attention to your emotions and the emotions of others. It's a good bet that many of the people you admire the most are not just smart, but also emotionally smart. They are people who know how to offer a toast at a wedding, tell a joke at a roast, comfort the bereaved at a funeral, add to the fun at a party, or calm a frightened child. These are skills worth clutivating.

REVIEW

- Motives initiate, sustain, and direct activities. Motivation typically involves this sequence: need, drive, goal, and goal attainment (need reduction).
- Behavior can be activated either by needs (push) or by goals (pull). The attractiveness of a goal and its ability to initiate action are related to its incentive value.
- Three principal types of motives are primary motives, stimulus motives, and secondary motives. Most primary motives operate to maintain homeostasis.
- Hunger is influenced by a complex interplay between fullness of the stomach, blood sugar levels, metabolism in the liver, and fat stores in the body.
- The most direct control of eating is effected by the hypothalamus, which has areas that act like feeding and satiety systems. The hypothalamus is sensitive to both neural and chemical messages, which affect eating.
- Other factors influencing hunger are the body's set point, external eating cues, the attractiveness and variety of diet, emotions, learned taste preferences and taste aversions, and cultural values.
- Obesity is the result of a complex interplay of internal and external influences, diet, emotions, genetics, and exercise.

- Behavioral dieting is based on techniques that change eating patterns and exercise habits.
- Anorexia nervosa and bulimia nervosa are two prominent eating disorders. Both tend to involve conflicts about self-image, self-control, and anxiety.
- Like hunger, thirst and other basic motives are affected by a number of bodily factors, but are primarily under the central control of the hypothalamus. Thirst may be either intracellular or extracellular.
- Pain avoidance is unusual because it is episodic as opposed to cyclic. Pain avoidance and pain tolerance are partially learned.
- The sex drive is also unusual in that it is non-homeostatic.
- The stimulus motives include drives for exploration, manipulation, change, and sensory stimulation.
- Drives for stimulation are partially explained by arousal theory, which states that an ideal level of bodily arousal will be maintained if possible. The desired level of arousal or stimulation varies from person to person, as measured by the *Sensation-Seeking Scale*.
- Optimal performance on a task usually occurs at *moderate* levels of arousal. This relationship is described by an inverted U function. The Yerkes-Dodson law further states that for simple tasks the ideal arousal level is higher, and for complex tasks it is lower.
- Circadian rhythms of bodily activity are closely tied to sleep, activity, and energy cycles. Time zone travel and shift work can seriously disrupt sleep and bodily rhythms.
- Social motives are learned through socialization and cultural conditioning. Such motives account for much of the diversity of human motivation. Opponent-process theory explains the operation of some acquired motives.
- One of the most prominent social motives is the need for achievement (nAch). High nAch is correlated with success in many situations, with occupational choice, and with *moderate* risk taking.
- Self-confidence greatly affects motivation in everyday life.
- Maslow's hierarchy of motives categorizes needs as basic and growth oriented. Lower needs in the hierarchy are assumed to be prepotent (dominant) over higher needs. Self-actualization, the highest and most fragile need, is reflected in meta-needs.
- Higher needs in Maslow's hierarchy are closely related to the concept of intrinsic motivation. In many situations, extrinsic motivation can reduce intrinsic motivation, enjoyment, and creativity.
- Emotions are linked to many basic adaptive behaviors. Other major elements of emotion are physiological changes in the body, emotional expressions, and emotional feelings.
- The following are considered to be primary emotions: *fear, surprise, sadness, disgust, anger, anticipation, joy,* and *acceptance*. Other emotions seem to represent mixtures of the primaries.
- The left hemisphere of the brain primarily processes positive emotions. Negative emotions are processed in the right hemisphere.
- The amygdala provides a "quick and dirty" pathway for the arousal of fear that bypasses the cerebral cortex.
- Physical changes associated with emotion are caused by the action of adrenaline, a hormone released into the bloodstream, and by activity in the autonomic nervous system (ANS).
- The sympathetic branch of the ANS is primarily responsible for arousing the body, the parasympathetic branch for quieting it.
- The polygraph, or "lie detector," measures emotional arousal by monitoring heart rate, blood pressure, breathing rate, and the GSR.
- Under some circumstances, the accuracy of the lie detector can be quite low.
- Basic emotional expressions, such as smiling or baring one's teeth when angry, appear to be unlearned. Facial expressions appear to be central to emotion.
- Body gestures and movements (body language) also express feelings, mainly by communicating emotional tone. Three dimensions of facial expressions are pleasantness–unpleasantness, attention–rejection, and activation. The study of body language is known as kinesics.
- Lying can sometimes be detected from changes in illustrators or emblems and from signs of general arousal.
- The James-Lange theory says that emotional experience follows the bodily reactions. In contrast, the Cannon-Bard theory says that bodily reactions and emotional experiences are organized in the brain and occur simultaneously.
- Schachter's cognitive theory of emotion emphasizes the importance of the labels we apply to feelings of bodily arousal. In addition, emotions are affected by attribution (ascribing bodily arousal to a particular source).
- The facial feedback hypothesis holds that emotional expressions help define what emotion a person is feeling.
- Contemporary views of emotion place greater emphasis on the effects of cognitive appraisals. Also, all of the elements of emotion are seen as interrelated and interacting.
- Emotional intelligence is the ability to consciously make your emotions work for you in a wide variety of life circumstances.
- Important elements of emotional intelligence include self-awareness, empathy, an ability to manage emotions, understanding emotion, and knowing how to use emotions to enhance thinking, decision making, and relationships.
- Positive emotions are valuable because they tend to broaden our focus and they encourage personal growth and social connection.

CHAPTER 7 PRACTICE EXAM

____ 1. Motivation initiates, __________, and directs an organism's
a. Supplys
b. Sustains
c. Supines
d. Suspends

____ 2. A hungry lion does not eat when given meat covered with ice cream. The lion's reaction is related to
a. Didactic value
b. incentive value.
c. intrinsic value .
d. extrinsic value.

____ 3. An overweight adult who overate as a child, will have __________ fat cells.
a. Larger and smaller
b. more and larger
c. More and less
d. An equal number of

____ 4. Gorging on food and vomiting to avoid weight gain is
a. Behavior modification.
b. anorexia
c. Anxious eating .
d. bulimia nervosa.

____ 5. Which is true of anorexia nervosa?
a. Mortality rate is more than 1 in 5.
b. Females have it more than men.
c. Serotonin levels are nonexistent.
d. They have excess religiosity.

____ 6. Which is true of anorexia and bulimia?
a. There are extensive fears of becoming obese and misperception of normal size.
b. Most die due to malnutrition.
c. The person is of average height and weight
d. Both anorexia and bulimia are over diagnosed.

____ 7. Some cultures are do not have as many eating disorders because they prefer fuller sizes. An example is found in __________ culture.
a. Euro American
b. African American
c. Pacific Islander
d. both African American and Pacific Islander

____ 8. According to arousal theory,
a. an individual becomes uncomfortable when arousal is too low or too high.
b. there is an ideal level of arousal for various activities.
c. stimulus drives are homeostatic because they allow individuals to attain moderate levels of arousal.
d. all of these

____ 9. The inverted-U function describes the relationship between
a. deprivation and drive.
b. stimulation and response.
c. arousal and performance.
d. sex drive and deprivation.

____ 10. Lucas whines that he plays the cello wonderfully at school, but he plays horribly during concerts. What might explain his problem?
a. the Yerkes-Dodson Law.
b. the Watson-Skinner Law
c. The Verplanck-Madson law.
d. The Hammond-Madson Law

____ 11. The sleep and waking rhythms
a. Vary with the moon cycles.
b. are often shorter than 20 hours
c. are about 24 hours.
d. Are much longer than 48 hours.

____ 12. The need for achievement
a. is found only in wealthy Americans.
b. does not occur in Asian cultures.
c. is the desire to meet internalized standards of excellence.
d. is the desire to make more money than your parents

____ 13. Individuals who are high in nAch
a. do not take risks.
b. take low risks.
c. take moderate risks.
d. take high risks.

____ 14. A job seeker who applies for jobs that offer challenge and surprise more than high pays is likely someone who is __________ motivated.

a. extrinsically
b. intrinsically
c. lyrically
d. Weirdly

____ 15. Students who study only readings they are likely to be tested are

a. Have high need motivation.
b. Have low need motivation.
c. Are intrinsically motivated
d. Are extrinsically motivated

Answers

1. B
2. B
3. B
4. D
5. B
6. A
7. D
8. D
9. C
10. A
11. C
12. C
13. C
14. B
15. D

CHAPTER 8: CONSCIOUSNESS

QUESTIONS

1. What have psychologists observed about consciousness?
2. How is the brain involved in attention?
3. What parts of the brain seem to be activated during different kinds of tasks?
4. How did Cherry research the cocktail party phenomenon?
5. What did Treisman find in her research?
6. What is mindfulness?
7. What are two examples of mindlessness?
8. What is mindlessness and what does Langer suggest people do about mindlessness?
9. What are the explanations as to why the Stroop effect is difficult?
10. What are three filter theories for explaining selective attention?
11. What are attentional resource theories?
12. What do current models of selective attention emphasize?
13. How do Locke, Hume, and Dennett discuss consciousness?
14. What are the two main purposes of consciousness?
15. What are stored at the preconscious level?
16. What is the tip of the tongue phenomenon?
17. How have researchers demonstrated preconscious processes?
18. How did Krosnick, Betz, Jussim, & Lynn (1992) study a subliminal intervention?
19. What is the effect of subliminal tapes?
20. What does the subconscious level involve?
21. What is the near death experience?
22. What is the current thinking about near death experiences?
23. How does an altered state of consciousness differ from a normal state?
24. What are the common characteristics of altered states of consciousness?
25. What are two views and the evidence for why we sleep?
26. How does the sleep and wake cycle change as we age?
27. What are physiological changes that occur during the circadian rhythm?
28. What were the results of the research on allowing people to create their own schedules?
29. Why do researchers think people adjust to jet lag in one direction than another?
30. What are the effects of melatonin, trytophan, and light on sleep cycles?
31. What are the effects of sleep deprivation?
32. What are the five stages of sleep?
33. What emotions did people report during REM sleep?
34. Why is REM sleep called paradoxical sleep?
35. What are symptoms of insomnia?
36. What are problems with taking sleeping pills and sedatives for insomnia?
37. What is the pattern of narcolepsy?
38. Why is sleep apnea considered dangerous?
39. Who tends to have sleep apnea?
40. What are the characteristic symptoms and problems that occur with sleepwalking?
41. What are the most common dreams of college students?
42. According to Calkins research, how many dreams to people have a night and to what are the dreams related?
43. Why did Freud thought people dreamed and what support is there for his theory?
44. What are two research examples of the problem solving view of dreams?
45. According to McCarley and Hobson, what do our brains do when we are awake and asleep?
46. What kinds of people tend to have nightmares?
47. What is the course of night terrors?
48. What are some things hypnotized people might do?
49. What similarities and differences to people report who are hypnotized and simulating being hypnotized?
50. What are three theories of hypnosis and the evidence for each?
51. What are four factors that influence whether a person can be easily hypnotized?
52. What does current research suggest about hypnosis and memory?
53. How is meditation similar to hypnosis?
54. What is the purpose of a *koan* in Zen meditation?
55. What is the goal of opening up meditation?
56. What physiological and psychological changes occur during meditation?
57. What are the four basic categories of drugs, their effects, and names?
58. Why do people take drugs?
59. What are the effects and side effects of narcotics?
60. How does dependency to narcotics occur?
61. What happens if a person prolongs use of a narcotic?
62. What is the current thinking about psychological and physical dependence?

63. What are the symptoms of narcotic withdrawal?
64. In what ways is narcotic dependence treated?
65. What do intoxicants do to people?
66. What can high doses or overdoses of intoxicants cause?
67. What happens to a person at different levels of alcohol concentrations?
68. What helps determine the effect alcohol has on a person?
69. What did Larimer et al. (2000) and Blume, et al. (2000) find in their studies of drinking among college students?
70. What are the estimates of alcohol abuse in this country?
71. What are the effects of chronic alcoholic abuse?
72. What are the withdrawal symptoms of alcoholism?
73. How can alcoholism be treated?
74. Why are sedatives used?
75. How can chronic use of sedatives misfire?
76. How is depressant abuse treated?
77. What are the effects of central nervous system stimulants?
78. What are the effects of caffeine?
79. What are the symptoms of caffeine addiction?
80. What is the effect of amphetamines on neurotransmitters?
81. What are the effects of prolonged use of amphetamines?
82. What are the physical and psychological effects of cocaine?
83. What are the effects of prolonged cocaine use?
84. Why do recovering cocaine addicts crave cocaine?
85. What are the effects of tobacco on the body?
86. What is prolonged tobacco use linked to?
87. What are the common treatments for stimulants?
88. How do most hallucinogenics work?
89. What are the physical and psychological symptoms of taking LSD?
90. What are the short term and possible long term effects of marijuana use?
91. What does PCP do when taken?
92. What is the effect of MDMA?
93. What may happen during chronic use of hallucinogenics?
94. How do the different type of psychologist study sleep deprivation?
95. What were the findings of the sleep deprivation study by Sadeh et al. (2002)?

VOCABULARY

1. activation-synthesis hypothesis
2. acute toxicity
3. adenosine
4. amphetamines
5. ascending reticular activating system
6. Attention
7. barbiturates
8. binaural presentation
9. blindsight
10. caffeine
11. chronic toxicity
12. circadian rhythms
13. CNS depressant
14. CNS stimulant
15. cocktail party phenomenon
16. concentrative meditation
17. daydreaming
18. detoxification
19. dichotic presentation
20. dopamine
21. drug dependence
22. epiphenomenon
23. hallucinations
24. hypnosis
25. insomnia
26. K-complexes
27. Korsakoff's syndrome
28. maintenance
29. meditation
30. melatonin
31. mindfulness
32. mindlessness
33. narcolepsy
34. narcotics
35. neodissociative theory
36. night terrors
37. nightmares
38. norepinephrine
39. opening up meditation
40. overdose
41. placebo effect
42. preconscious level
43. psychoactive drugs
44. REM sleep
45. sedatives
46. selective attention
47. sensitization
48. serotonin
49. shadowing
50. simulating paradigm
51. single-pool model
52. sleep apnea
53. sleep spindles
54. sleep state misperception
55. somnambulism
56. Stroop effect
57. subconscious level
58. subliminal perception
59. tip of the tongue phenomenon
60. tolerance
61. tranquilizers
62. tryptophan
63. visual illusions
64. withdrawal symptoms

8 Consciousness

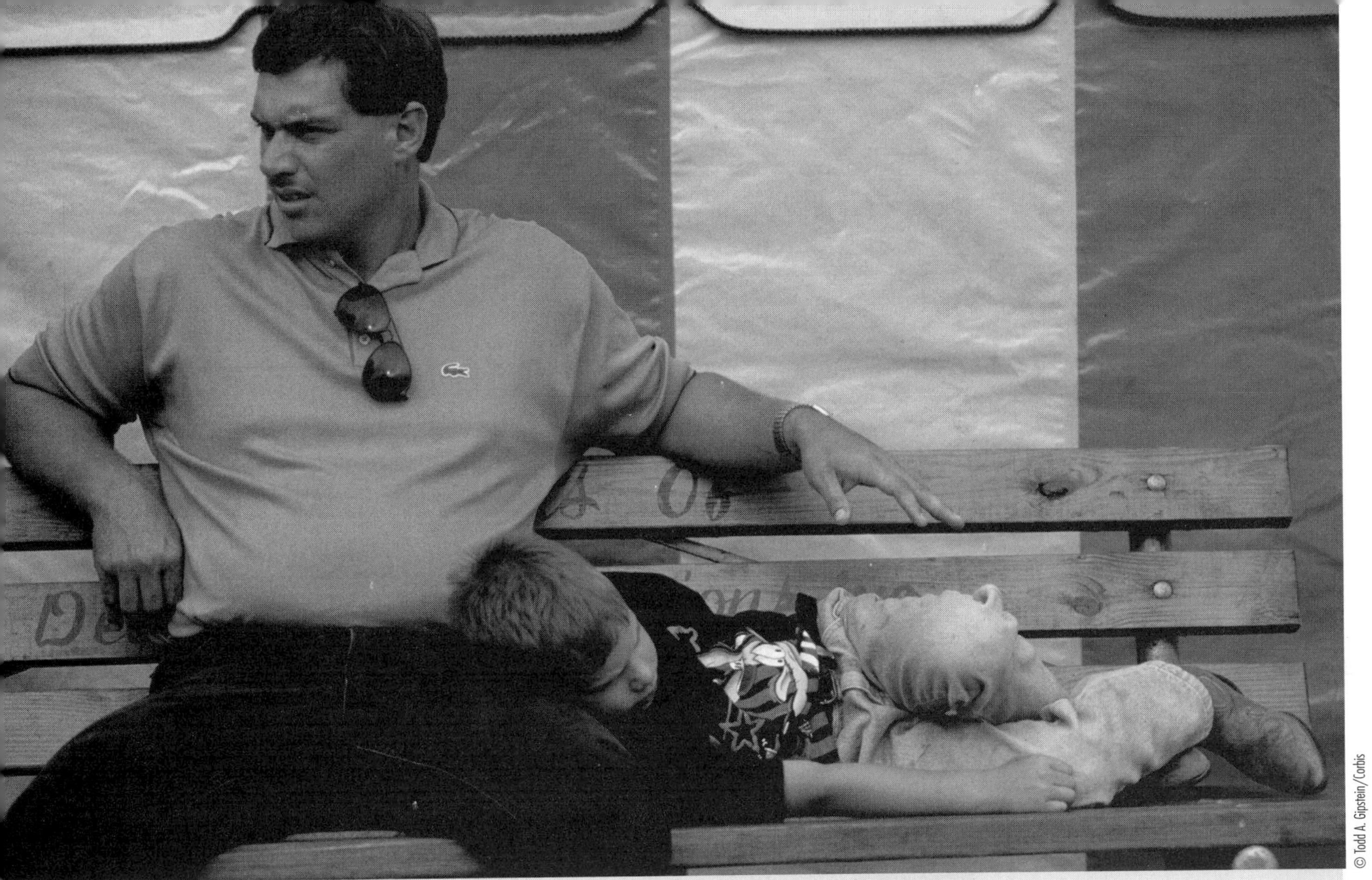

© Todd A. Gipstein/Corbis

PAYING ATTENTION

Consciousness might be overwhelming if we were unable to limit our experience of stimuli in the environment by focusing our attention. **Attention** is the link between the enormous amount of information that assails our senses and the limited amount that we actually perceive. It enables us to perceive things we need to be aware of and to ignore others (Pashler, 1998). As you read these words, you are probably paying attention to the words (figure) on the text page and disregarding all the other visual sensations (ground) reaching your retina. If you paid attention to all the sensory information available to you at any one time, you would never be able to concentrate on the important and ignore the unimportant. You may be vaguely aware of the ways your skin is being touched by your clothes, of the ambient sounds surrounding you, or even of some internal cues such as hunger or fatigue. What allows you to dismiss most of this sensory information and concentrate on reading? Pay attention and find out.

attention
the active cognitive processing of a limited amount of information from the vast amount of information available through the senses, in memory and through cognitive processes; focus on a small subset of available *stimuli*.

Attention involves mostly the interaction of diverse areas of the brain, with no specialized areas fully responsible for specific attentional functions (Cohen, Romero, Servan-Schreiber, & Farah, 1994; Farah, 1994). Certain areas of the brain do appear to be partly responsible for certain kinds of attentional processing, however (Farah, 2001; Polk & Farah, 2002; Polk et al., 2002). Michael Posner (1995, 2001) has suggested that the frontal lobe tends to be activated during tasks that require attention to verbal stimuli. The parietal lobe tends to be activated during tasks that require attention to visual and spatial stimuli (see Albright, Kandel, & Posner, 2000; Fan, McCandliss, Sommer, Raz, & Posner, 2002).

Selective Attention

Suppose you are at a banquet. It is just your luck to be seated next to this year's winner of the "Most Boring Conversationalist" award. As you are talking to this blatherer, who happens to be on your right, you become aware of the conversation of the two guests sitting on your left. Their exchange is much more interesting. So you find yourself trying to keep up the semblance of a conversation with the bore on your right while tuning in to the dialogue on your left.

© image100/Alamy Images

Attention is what enables us to focus on some stimuli and block out others. However, sometimes our attention may wander.

selective attention
a process by which an individual attempts to track one *stimulus* or one type of stimulus and to ignore another.

cocktail party phenomenon
the process of tracking one conversation in the face of the distraction of other conversations; a phenomenon often experienced at cocktail parties.

The Cocktail Party Phenomenon This vignette illustrates a naturalistic experiment in **selective attention**, in which you attempt to track one message and ignore another. This phenomenon inspired the research of E. Colin Cherry (1953) on the **cocktail party phenomenon**, in which we follow one conversation despite the distraction of other conversations.

Cherry did not actually do his research at cocktail parties. Rather, he investigated conversations in a carefully controlled setting. In an experimental task called *shadowing*, each of the ears listens to a different message and the listener is required to repeat the message that goes to one of the ears as soon as possible after hearing it. Think of a detective "shadowing" a suspect. In *dichotic presentation* each ear receives a different message. When the two ears receive the same message, it is called *binaural presentation*.

Cherry's research prompted additional work in this area. Anne Treisman (1964a, 1964b) noted that although people who shadowed the message presented to one ear heard almost nothing of the message presented to the other ear, they were not totally ignorant of the unattended message. They could hear, for example, if the voice was replaced by a tone or if a man's voice was replaced by a woman's. If the unattended message was identical to the attended one, every research participant noticed it, even if one of the messages was temporally out of synchronization with the other. When this delay effect was studied systematically, people typically recognized the two messages to be the same. In particular, they recognized the relationship between messages when the shadowed message was either as much as 4.5 seconds ahead of the unattended one or as far as 1.5 seconds behind (Treisman, 1964a, 1964b). In other words, it is easier to recognize the unattended message when it follows, rather than precedes, the attended one. Treisman also observed that some people who were fluently bilingual noticed the identity of messages if the unattended message was the translated version of the attended one.

© Paul Barton/Corbis

Have you ever thought you heard someone call your name in a crowded room? Selective attention is involved in the cocktail party phenomenon.

Mindlessness A construct related to selective attention is *mindfulness* (Langer, 1989, 1997, 2000, 2002; Moldoveanu & Langer, 2002), which is paying deliberate attention to the immediate situation at hand. Lack of mindfulness is *mindlessness*. Ellen Langer (1989) gave an example of mindlessness. In 1982, a pilot and copilot went through a routine checklist prior to takeoff, mindlessly noting that the anti-icer was "off"—as it should be under most circumstances, but not under the icy conditions for which they were preparing. The flight ended in a crash that killed 74 passengers. Fortunately for most of us, our mindlessness usually has far less fatal consequences, as when we put a carton of milk in the cupboard rather than in the refrigerator. Attention is generally a purposeful application of our consciousness. But it also operates automatically and at different levels.

Selective attention can be influenced by various psychological disorders. People with obsessive-compulsive disorder tend to be preoccupied with thoughts they cannot get out of their minds and behaviors they are unable to control. They show decreased ability selectively to attend to stimuli they want to focus on and to screen out other stimuli they wish to ignore (Clayton, Richards, & Edwards, 1999).

Theories of selective attention differ primarily in whether or not they propose that we somehow filter, and thus sort out, competing stimuli. Theories that propose a filter disagree about when filtering occurs and what it affects.

The Stroop Effect Much of the research on selective attention has focused on auditory processing. However, selective attention can also be studied visually. One of the tasks most frequently used for this purpose was formulated by John Ridley Stroop (1935), for whom the effect is named. You can try it: Quickly read aloud the following words: *brown, blue, green, red, purple*. Easy, isn't it? Now quickly name aloud the colors shown in part (a) of Figure 8.1. The ink matches the name of the color word. This task, too, is easy. Now look at part (c) of the figure, in which the colors of the inks differ from the color names that are printed with them. Again name the ink colors you see, out loud, as quickly as possible.

You probably found the last task very difficult: Your understanding of the written words interferes with naming the color of the ink. The **Stroop effect** demonstrates the psychological difficulty of selectively attending to the color of the ink and trying to ignore the word it forms. One reason the Stroop test may be particularly difficult is that, for you and most other adults, reading is an automatic process, not readily subject to your conscious control (MacLeod, 1991, 1996). You find it difficult to ignore what you read and concentrate on the color of the ink. An alternative explanation is that the output of a response occurs when the mental pathways for producing the response are activated sufficiently (MacLeod, 1991). In the Stroop test, the name of the written color activates a cortical pathway for saying the word. In contrast, the name of the color the word is written in activates a pathway for naming the color. But the activity of the first pathway interferes with the latter. In this situation, it takes longer to gather sufficient strength of activation to produce the color-naming response and not the word-reading response.

What do you think explains why you attend to some things and not to others? Why do you think you sometimes find it difficult to focus your attention?

stroop effect
difficulty in selectively attending to the colors of inks and ignoring words written in those colors (e.g., the word *green* printed in red letters).

(a) Read through this list of color names as quickly as possible. Read from right to left across each line.

Red	Yellow	Blue	Green
Blue	Red	Green	Yellow
Yellow	Green	Red	Blue

(b) Name each of these color patches as quickly as possible. Name from left to right across each line.

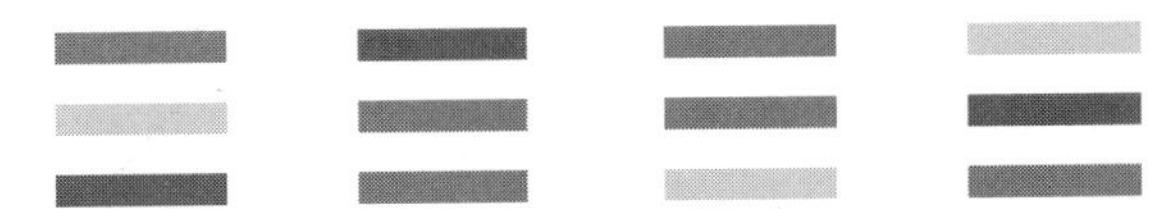

(c) Name as quickly as possible the color of ink in which each word is printed. Name from left to right across each line.

Red	Blue	Green	Yellow
Yellow	Red	Blue	Green
Blue	Yellow	Green	Red

FIGURE 8.1
The Stroop Effect. If you are like most people, you will find it more difficult to perform task (c) than either task (a) or task (b).

Filter Theories

An early theory of selective attention, proposed by Donald Broadbent (1958), suggested that we filter information right after it is registered at the sensory level. Thus, we filter out irrelevant stimuli almost as soon as we sense them, and so they never receive any top-down, higher-order processing. Subsequent research, however, indicated that Broadbent's model must be wrong. For example, participants in shadowing studies hear one particular stimulus in the unattended ear regardless of when it occurs: the sound of their own name (Moray, 1959). If we are able to recognize our own names in this way, then some higher-level processing of the information must be occurring and reaching the supposedly unattended ear. If such processing were not occurring, we would not recognize the familiar sounds. That is, if the incoming information were filtered out at the level of sensation, we would never perceive it at all.

This kind of finding led some investigators to propose a theory that places the filter later in the perceptual process, after some top-down, higher-order conceptual analysis of input has taken place (Deutsch & Deutsch, 1963; D. A. Norman, 1968). This later filtering would allow us to recognize the meaning of information that enters the unattended ear (such as the sound of our own names).

An alternative to both of these theories suggests that a filter may take the form of a signal-attenuating mechanism rather than a signal-blocking mechanism (Treisman, 1964b). Information is not totally blocked out at any level; it is just weakened. We receive some of the information that is transmitted, but in a degraded form. What gets through is determined by whether the information is more likely to be important (such as our names) or unimportant (such as idle prattle).

Attentional Resource Theories

Theorists have moved away from the notion of filters and toward attentional resources. The idea is that we have a fixed amount of attention, which we can allocate according to what the task requires. Our single pool of attentional resources can be divided up, say, among multiple tasks (Kahneman, 1973). Suppose that you were dividing your total attention among the acts of talking to a friend, surfing the Internet, and thinking about an upcoming exam. The amount of attention you could devote to each task would depend on how you allocated your single pool of attentional resources. In the *single-pool model,* allocating attention to one task always takes away attention from all other tasks.

This model now appears to be oversimplified because we are much better at dividing our attention when the competing stimuli are in different perceptual modalities (e.g., one requires seeing, the other hearing). Multiple-pool resource models specify that at least some attentional resources may be specific to the modality in which a task is presented. Thus, it is more likely that two visual tasks will interfere with each other than that a visual task will interfere with an auditory one. Competition for attentional resources also can occur as a result of overlap in the content type. For example, speech heard on a radio is more likely to interfere with your reading than instrumental music.

In sum, current models of selective attention emphasize that we bring to bear multiple attentional resources, using more than one sensory modality, on tasks that require divided attention.

LEVELS OF CONSCIOUSNESS

According to British philosopher John Locke (1632–1704), a major function of consciousness is to help us form a sense of personal identity by linking past and present events to ourselves. Consciousness is the means by which we define who we are. British philosopher David Hume (1711–1776), in contrast, believed that our sense of personal identity is a myth. It is not something we can empirically establish through any of our senses. All consciousness can do is reveal a succession of states of the world. It can never connect them. An analogy is the successive frames of a film strip. We provide the connections between what are really large numbers of rapidly moving static frames. We only imagine them to be linked together.

Psychological interest in levels of consciousness has waxed and waned over the years. Behaviorists would not give the subject any attention at all, whereas psychodynamic theorists saw it as one of the most fundamental issues in psychology.

A contemporary philosopher, Daniel Dennett (1995), believes, like Locke, that we have a sense of identity. Dennett (1997, 2001) believes our sense of identity stems not from high-level consciousness, but from low-level processing. Basing his notions on Darwin's (1859) theory of evolution, Dennett argues that our senses of self and of intentionality (what we want to do) are products of countless simple processes going on within us simultaneously.

Whether or not consciousness establishes a sense of personal identity, it clearly serves two main purposes: monitoring and controlling (Kihlstrom, 1984; Kihlstrom, Mulvaney, Tobias, & Tobis, 2000). By *monitoring,* the individual keeps track of internal mental processes, personal behavior, and the environment to maintain self-awareness in relation to the surrounding environment. If you feel depressed and try to figure out what is bothering you, you are monitoring your thinking. By *controlling,* the individual plans what to do based on the information received from the monitoring process. If you realize you are depressed because you have not had any fun all week, and you then decide it is time to do something fun, you are controlling your thinking and behavior. These two functions seem to operate, in one way or another, at various levels of consciousness. Normally, we see ourselves as being at a fully conscious level of awareness. Sometimes people seek to achieve a "higher" level of consciousness through practices like meditation and drug use. Other levels of consciousness exist as well (Lambie & Marcel, 2002). One way of classifying them is as either preconscious or subconscious.

The Preconscious Level

The **preconscious** level of consciousness contains information that could easily become conscious but that is not continuously available. For example, if prompted, you can remember what your bedroom looks like. But obviously you are not always thinking about your bedroom. Also stored at the preconscious level are *automatic behaviors*—those that require no conscious decisions about which muscles to move or which actions to take. Examples are dialing a familiar telephone number and driving a car to a familiar place.

preconscious
a part of *consciousness* that comprises information that could become conscious readily but that is not continuously available in awareness.

Tip-of-the-tongue Phenomenon Perhaps our most common experience of preconsciousness is the *tip-of-the-tongue phenomenon,* which occurs when we are trying to remember something we already know but cannot quite retrieve. If a man needs a new wallet, he might try to remember the name of the store where he bought the wallet he has. But the store is not one he patronizes frequently, and the name does not immediately come to mind. He remembers the name of the store begins with a "C." An image of a cow comes into his mind. Eventually he remembers the name of the store is "Cowley's." This phenomenon indicates that particular preconscious information, though not fully accessible, is still available in conscious thinking.

Subliminal Perception Researchers have demonstrated preconscious processing (Marcel, 1983). Research participants were shown words for just 10 milliseconds. The rate of presentation was so rapid that observers were generally unaware that they had even seen a word. When the research participants were shown a second word for a longer period of time, this new word was recognized more quickly if it was related to the first word than if it was unrelated. For example, *doctor* and *nurse* were considered to be related words, whereas *doctor* and *oven* were considered unrelated. Some kind of recognition of the rapidly presented word must have taken place; the recognition was clearly preconscious. This *subliminal perception,* a preconscious processing of information that is thus below the level of conscious awareness of that information, suggests that people have the ability to detect information without being aware they are doing so. However, situations in which subliminal perception occurs appear to be quite limited.

The effects of subliminal perception are small. Krosnick, Betz, Jussim, and Lynn (1992) studied the effects of a subliminal intervention on attitudes. Participants were shown slides designed to arouse either positive emotions (e.g., a bride and groom) or negative emotions (e.g., a skull). The exposure times of the slides were extremely brief, however—only 13/1000 second. Participants then viewed a series of slides showing an individual engaged in ordinary, everyday activities. The question was whether the subliminally presented slides would affect people's attitudes toward the individual in the slides. Krosnick and his colleagues obtained small but statistically significant effects. Their data suggested that the subliminal intervention had some effect in the expected direction, but that the effect was a small one (see also Bizer & Krosnick, 2001).

One effect that appears to be totally absent is for subliminal tapes. Indeed, a careful study of such tapes renders it questionable whether they really contain any subliminal messages at all. Even if the messages are there but well-hidden, they do not work (Greenwald, Spangenberg, Pratkanis, & Eskenazi, 1991). Many users of these tapes believe they work, however. Available data suggest that any effect they have is likely to be a *placebo effect,* whereby people's belief in the efficacy of an intervention, rather than the intervention itself, results in an improvement in behavior, health, or whatever else the intervention is supposed to affect.

blindsight
a phenomenon in which individuals can see something but are not aware of what they are seeing.

Blindsight Another example of information processing that is outside of conscious awareness is **blindsight**, a phenomenon by which individuals can see but are unaware that they are seeing (Sahraie et al., 1997; Scharli, Harman, & Hogben, 1999; Weiskrantz, Warrington, Sanders, & Marshall, 1974). This phenomenon is observed in individuals who have damage to the primary visual cortex, but whose optic nerve fibers from the eyes nevertheless are still hooked up with those parts of the brain that handle visual information. When asked whether they see an object, these patients will say no. But they can nevertheless give information about it, such as what shape or color it is. Thus, they have information about an object that they are certain they cannot see.

To summarize, automatic behaviors, tip-of-the-tongue phenomena, subliminal perception, blindsight, and other forms of preconscious knowledge generally are outside the view of our conscious minds. We engage in them without being fully aware of doing so.

subconscious
a level of *consciousness* that involves less awareness than full consciousness and either is synonymous with the *unconscious* level (according to many theorists) or is slightly more accessible to consciousness than is the unconscious level (according to a few theorists).

unconscious
a level of *consciousness* at which thoughts, wishes, and feelings are not accessible to conscious awareness (often considered synonymous with *subconscious*); an important construct of *psychodynamic theory.*

The Subconscious Level

Unlike information stored at the preconscious level, information stored at the **subconscious** or **unconscious** level is not easily accessible. The subconscious level involves less awareness than full consciousness and is either synonymous with the unconscious level (according to many theorists) or slightly more accessible to consciousness than the unconscious level (according to a few theorists). For our purposes, we make no distinction. In general, however, the term *unconscious* is usually preferred by followers of Sigmund Freud, the founder of psychoanalysis.

According to Freud, material that we find too anxiety-provoking to handle at a conscious level is often *repressed*—that is, never admitted to consciousness. Repressing the material keeps it from distressing us. Freud believed that many of our most important memories and impulses are unconscious, but they still have a

DISCOVERING PSYCHOLOGY

Near-Death Experience

In a near-death experience, an individual either comes extremely close to dying or is actually believed to be dead and then is revived before permanent brain death occurs. During this time, some people undergo unusual psychological experiences.

Near-death experiences have been reported in writings throughout history and in the lore of cultures as disparate as those of the ancient Greeks, Buddhists, and North American Indians. A variety of researchers have reviewed accounts of people who claim to have had near-death experiences (e.g., Blackmore, 1993, 1999; Serdahely, 1990; Zaleski, 1987). A large number of people of differing ages and cultural backgrounds report similar near-death sensations. They often feel peace or intense joy. Some feel that they have left their bodies or have looked at them from the outside. They often report traveling through a dark tunnel and seeing a brilliant light at the end of it. Some speak of reunions with deceased friends or relatives, and others report contact with a being that encourages them to return to life. Some report rapidly reviewing many or all of the events of their lives.

Not all people who have the near-death experience are equally likely to experience all of these phenomena. The frequency and intensity of these experiences tend to be greatest for people who are ill, lowest for people who have attempted suicide, and in between for accident victims. Interestingly, few people have reported any negative experiences.

Although there are many explanations for near-death experiences, recent thinking has converged on events produced by the brain (Blackmore, 1993, 1999; Persinger, 1999, 2001; Persinger & Richards, 1995). For example, the experience of seeing or walking through a tunnel may result from activation of the medial occipital cortexes due to insufficient blood supply, which then causes contrast between the peripheral and central visual fields, or the experiencing of a tunnel. Although such explanations are plausible, they have yet to be verified, and so near-death experience remains something of a mystery. Perhaps the most interesting news to come out of the research is that people who have such experiences typically say that their lives have changed for the better. They are less afraid of death, more appreciative of what they have, and more determined to live their lives to the fullest.

profound effect on our behavior. For example, people who experienced rejection by one of their parents (or both) are more likely to be extremely sensitive to rejection in all areas of life than are individuals who had no such early experience. However, the people who experienced rejection may be unaware of why they are more sensitive to it. Their unawareness derives from their repression of the original feelings of rejection. The process of repression is open to debate, however. Even its existence has not been conclusively documented.

Altered States of Consciousness

There are many different states of consciousness. What constitutes a "normal" state and what constitutes an "altered" state are a matter of some debate. One way to view "altered states" is as those other than our normal, waking state. In an altered state of consciousness, such as sleep and dreaming (discussed below), awareness is somehow changed from our normal, waking state. Each state of consciousness involves qualitative changes in our alertness and awareness.

Altered states of consciousness have several common characteristics (Martindale, 1981). First, cognitive processes may be more shallow or uncritical than usual. For example, during sleep, you accept unrealistic dream events as being real, although you would never accept those events as realistic while awake. Second, perceptions of self and of the world may change from what they are during wakefulness. Under the influence of hallucinogenic drugs, objects may appear to take on bizarre forms. Even objects that do not exist may be clearly perceived. Third, normal inhibitions and control over behavior may weaken. People under the influence of alcohol may do things they normally would not do in a sober state. The remainder of this chapter looks at consciousness through the lens of altered states of consciousness. We will consider sleep and dreaming, hypnosis, meditation, and chemically induced altered states.

SLEEP

The cycle of sleep and waking is one of the most basic in humans as well as other animals. In humans, the part of the brain most relevant to sleep is the reticular formation. In particular, the *ascending reticular activating system* contributes to the alternating cycle of sleep and wakefulness. Other areas of the brain are involved as well, however, so that this one area cannot be seen as "responsible for" sleep. Neurotransmitters, including norepinephrine, dopamine, and GABA, are involved in sleep. Their exact roles remain to be determined, however (B. E. Jones, 1994). Thus, there is no one neurotransmitter that is responsible for sleep.

Why Do We Sleep?

During sleep, people become relatively, but not totally, unaware of external sources of stimulation (Antrobus, 1991). Despite centuries of inquiry, scientists have yet to reach a consensus about exactly why people need to sleep (Borbely & Tononi, 2001). Two possibilities, which are not mutually exclusive, are a preservation and protection theory and a restorative theory. Although scientists do not know why we sleep, they do know that healthful sleep is one of the best predictors of longevity (Dement & Vaughan, 1999).

Preservation and Protection One view is that sleep serves an adaptive function. It protects the individual during that portion of the 24-hour day in which being awake, and hence roaming around, would place the individual at greatest risk. Animals do not require 24 hours to feed themselves and meet other necessities. From the standpoint of adaptation, therefore, they are best off staying out of harm's way.

There is some evidence to support this theory (Allison & Cicchetti, 1976; Webb, 1982). The amount of time various species sleep tends to vary with two important factors. The first is the amount of time they require to find the food they need to stay alive. The second is how well they can hide themselves when they sleep. Moreover, they sleep at times that maximize their safety, given their physical capacities and their habits. For example, animals that tend to be prey for other animals guided primarily by vision tend to sleep during the day (when they would most likely be seen if they were roaming about) and in hidden places.

According to the preservation and protection theory of sleep, day-sleeping animals maximize their safety by remaining hidden and asleep during the hours when their predators are awake.

Restoration A second view is that we sleep to restore depleted resources and dissipate accumulated wastes. In other words, the restoration view of sleep is that it may have chemical causes. Psychologists study the restoration view of why people sleep by searching specifically for sleep-causing chemicals produced in our bodies. Several substances seem to be associated with sleep, although none of them has been shown conclusively to cause sleep.

One experiment was designed to see whether chemicals in the brains of sleep-deprived goats would induce sleep in rats (Pappenheimer, Koski, Fencl, Karnovsky, & Krueger, 1975). One group of goats was deprived of sleep for several days. A control group was allowed to sleep normally. Then cerebrospinal fluid from each group of goats was injected into rats. Rats injected with fluid from the first group of goats slept more than did rats that received fluid from the control group. What was in the sleep-deprived goats' cerebrospinal fluid that caused the rats to sleep more? It was a small peptide made up of five amino acids, including muramic acid. This amino acid was recognized to be the sleep-producing compound that may have built up in the central nervous systems of the sleep-deprived goats. A second sleep-producing compound is sleep-promoting substance, or SPS (Inoue, Uchizono, & Nagasaki, 1982). A third is DSIP (delta-sleep–inducing peptide; Schroeder-Helmert, 1985). There may be many more.

Circadian Rhythms

Circadian Rhythms are biological cycles that last about 24 hours in humans and other species. In humans, circadian rhythms vary with age and individual and cultural factors.

Usually infants alternate frequently between sleep and wakefulness. They sleep for a total of about 17 hours each day. Within the first 6 months, however, their sleep patterns change to about two short naps and one long stretch of sleep at night. They are then totaling about 13 hours per day. By 5 to 7 years of age, most of us have adopted what is basically an adult pattern of sleep (Berger, 1980). We sleep about 8 hours each night and remain awake about 16 hours each day. Regardless of the average, the actual range of sleep needed varies widely across individuals. Some people require as little as an hour of sleep each day, and others need 10 to 12 hours. Studies of long sleepers (people who regularly sleep more than 9.5 hours per day) and short sleepers (who regularly sleep less than 4.4 hours per day) show no differences in their average health. People differ not only in how much they sleep but also in when they prefer to sleep. Research has shown that our intuitions are correct that people differ in the time of day when they are most alert and aroused—that there are "day people" and "night people" (B. Wallace, 1993). Culture can also affect people's circadian rhythms. People's sleep schedules can be affected by a variable as simple as the typical hour for dinner. For example, in the United States, dinner time is 3 to 5 hours earlier than it is in Spain.

The Effect of Daylight on Sleep Cycles Despite individual and cultural differences, the usual sleeping–waking pattern for most people roughly corresponds to our planet's cycle of darkness and light. Humans experience physiological changes that can be measured according to their daily rhythm. Such changes include a lowering of body temperature at night and changes in hormone levels. The rhythm is controlled by the hypothalamus (Ralph, Foster, Davis, & Menaker, 1990).

Several investigators have studied circadian rhythms (see Hobson, 1989, 2001; R. A. Wever, 1979). Participants in one study lived in a specially built underground environment in which they were deprived of all cues that are normally used for telling the time of day. These cues include the rising and setting of the sun, clocks, scheduled activities, and so on (R. A. Wever, 1979). For one month, these participants were told that they could create their own schedules. They could sleep whenever they wished. But they were discouraged from napping so that they would get on a regular sleeping–waking cycle.

The results were striking and have since been replicated many times (e.g., Mistlberger & Rusak, 1999; Welsh, 1993).

French geologist Michel Siffre was shielded from all time cues in this underground cavern for 6 months. When people have no external time cues, their natural circadian rhythms shift from a 24-hour day to a 25-hour day. When they return to a normal environment, their circadian rhythms return to a 24-hour day, cued by clocks and the daily cycle of the sun.

© Getty Images, Getty Images AsiaPac

Athletes who travel to competitions in different time zones must adjust their sleep schedules to maintain peak performance.

As people acclimated to an environment without time cues, their subjective days became longer, averaging about 25 hours. Typically, they went to bed a little bit later each night that they spent in isolation. Eventually, they drifted toward a point where they were spending slightly more awake time than they had when there were time cues. The difference could, of course, have been due in part to the departure from the normal activities of their daily lives. Participants showed stable individual rhythms. The rhythms differed somewhat from person to person, however. When returned to the normal environment, the participants reestablished a 24-hour cycle.

Anything that changes our circadian rhythm can interfere with sleep. Many of us have experienced *jet lag,* which is a disturbance in circadian rhythm caused by altering the light–dark cycle too rapidly or too slowly when we travel through time zones. Even if you have never flown out of your own time zone, you may have experienced a mild case of jet lag when you have changed to and from daylight savings time. Think about how you feel that first Sunday morning after setting your clocks forward an hour in the spring.

It sometimes is easier to adjust one's circadian rhythm when flying in one direction rather than another. Suppose someone travels from Los Angeles to New York. When it is 8:00 P.M. for native New Yorkers, it is only 5:00 P.M. for native Californians. The westerners therefore may be less tired than the easterners. One study found that visiting teams in basketball performed 4 points better, on average, when they traveled west to east rather than east to west, thereby almost nullifying the home-court advantage of the home team (Steenland & Deddens, 1997). The reason for the difference may be, at least in part, that people tend to have a natural sleeping–waking cycle of 25 rather than 24 hours, so that it is easier for them to have to go to sleep later than to go to sleep earlier.

Neurochemical Influences on Sleep Cycles Sleeping–waking cycles appear to be controlled in part by the pineal gland, which also secretes certain sleep-producing substances. *Melatonin,* a natural hormone secreted by the pineal gland, is one of several chemicals that appears to play an important role in regulating waking–sleeping cycles (Lewy, Ahmed, Jackson, & Sack, 1992; Reppert, Weaver, Rivkees, & Stopa, 1988). Small doses of melatonin—as little as a fraction of a milligram—appear to be capable of restarting the bodily clock and, especially, helping travelers who cross time zones to adjust to the changes in the clock (Arendt, Aldhous, & Wright, 1988; Tzischinsky, Pal, Epstein, Dagan, & Lavie, 1992). Melatonin supplements are now available without a prescription. People who take such supplements need to exercise caution, however, because there can be some side effects (such as drowsiness in the morning). The long-term effects of high dosages are unknown. *Tryptophan,* an amino acid that is a precursor to the neurotransmitter serotonin, also has sleep-inducing properties. Light also affects the sleeping–waking cycle. For example, bright lights have been used to help

illusion
a distorted *perception* of objects and other external *stimuli* that may be due to misleading cues in the objects themselves or to distortions of the perceptual process, such as distortions caused by altered states of consciousness or psychological disorder (see *optical illusion;* cf. *delusion*).

people get over jet lag (D. Dawson, Lack, & Morris, 1993). Computer software is now available to calculate the optimal amounts of bright light to use for different flight paths. Such software makes it possible to individualize the level of light to an actual trip (Houpt, Boulos, & Moore-Ede, 1996).

Although some chemicals that *can* cause sleep have indeed been found, the view that sleep actually *is* induced chemically has not been conclusively supported. Indeed, the restoration view presumably would predict that people who are more active on a given day would sleep more than when they are not active. A related prediction would be that people who are active in general would sleep more. But these predictions have not been upheld. Researchers have thus sought other ways to study why we sleep, such as looking at the effects of not sleeping.

hallucinations
perceptions of sensory stimulation (e.g., sounds, the most common hallucinated sensations; sights; smells; or tactile sensations) in the absence of any actual corresponding external sensory input from the physical world.

Sleep Deprivation

In sleep-deprivation experiments (e.g., Borbely, 1986; Dement, 1976), research participants usually have few problems after the first sleepless night. They appear to be relaxed and cheerful. They have more difficulty staying awake during the second night, however, and usually are severely tired by 3:00 A.M. of the next day. If they are given long test problems to solve, they will fall asleep but will often deny having done so.

After three nights without sleep, the participants appear tense. They become increasingly apathetic and are irritable when disturbed. Although they may follow the instructions of the experimenter, they do so with little energy. Their moods swing wildly. They often are unable to stay awake without special intervention. By this time, periods of *microsleep* are observed: People stop what they are doing for several seconds and stare into space. During these periods, their EEGs (electroencephalograms) show brain-wave patterns typical of sleep. People deprived of sleep for this long may start to experience visual **illusions**, distorted perceptions of objects and other external stimuli. They may also succumb to **hallucinations**, or perceptions of sensory stimuli in the absence of any actual corresponding external sensory input from the physical world. They commonly experience auditory hallucinations, such as hearing voices in the sound of running water.

Things really start to fall apart after four days without sleep. Research participants typically become paranoid, sometimes believing the experimenters are plotting against them. It is possible to keep sleep-deprived people awake for longer than four days, but prolonged sleep deprivation is clearly serious business and of questionable ethical justification.

Although research has not determined conclusively why we need to sleep, studies of circadian rhythms help us understand when and how much most people need to sleep.

Stages of Sleep

When studying circadian rhythms and other aspects of our sleeping–waking cycles, psychologists often examine people's brain-wave patterns using electroencephalograms (EEGs). EEG recordings of the brain activity of sleeping people (see Figure 8.2) have shown that sleep occurs in stages common to almost everyone, although EEG patterns vary slightly as a function of a person's age (Landolt & Borbely, 2001). During relaxed wakefulness, we exhibit

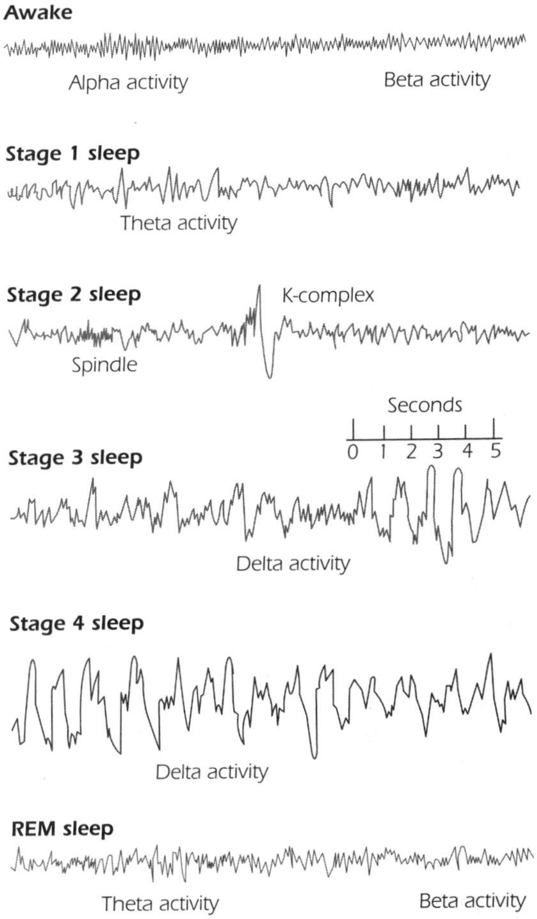

FIGURE 8.2

EEG Patterns in the Stages of Sleep. These EEG patterns illustrate changes in brain waves, which reflect changes in consciousness during REM sleep and during the four stages of N-REM sleep. (a) Alpha waves typify relaxed wakefulness. (b) More rapid, irregular brain waves typify Stage 1 of N-REM sleep. (c) During Stage 2, large, slow waves are occasionally interrupted by bursts of rapid brain waves. (d) During Stages 3 and 4, extremely large, slow brain waves (delta waves) predominate. When delta waves are 20% to 50% of all EEG waves, the sleeper is in Stage 3, whereas when delta waves are more than 50% of all EEG waves, the sleeper is in Stage 4. (e) During REM sleep, the brain waves look very much like those of the awake brain.

an *alpha-wave* EEG pattern. As we doze, the alpha-wave rhythm of the EEG gives way to smaller, more rapid, irregular waves. This pattern characterizes *Stage 1* sleep, a transitional state between wakefulness and sleep. If we are brought back to full consciousness from Stage 1 sleep, we may observe that our thoughts during this period did not make much sense, even though we may have felt fully or almost fully awake.

In *Stage 2* sleep, the stage in which we spend more than half of our sleeping time, the EEG pattern changes again. EEG waves are larger and overlap with *sleep spindles* (bursts of rapid EEG waves) and occasionally with *K-complexes* (large, slow waves). Muscle tension is markedly lower in Stage 2 than in the waking state.

In the next stages, the EEG pattern changes to *delta waves,* which are larger and slower than alpha waves. Delta waves characterize *delta sleep,* or deep sleep, which comprises both Stages 3 and 4. The distinction between Stages 3 and 4 is the proportion of delta waves. When delta waves represent 20% to 50% of the EEG waves, the sleeper is in *Stage 3.* When delta waves represent more than 50% of the EEG waves, the sleeper is in *Stage 4.*

N-REM sleep
the four stages of sleep that are not characterized by rapid eye movements (hence, the acronym for **n**on-**r**apid **e**ye **m**ovement) and that are less frequently associated with dreaming (cf. *REM sleep*).

REM sleep
the distinctive kind of sleep that is characterized by **r**apid **e**ye **m**ovements (REMs) and frequently—though not exclusively—associated with dreaming (cf. *N-REM sleep*).

The first four stages of sleep, sometimes associated with dreaming, make up **N-REM sleep**, which is non–rapid eye movement sleep. During these four stages, as the name "N-REM" implies, our eyes are not moving very much. During the next stage, however, our eyes roll around in their sockets (Kleitman, 1963). If sleepers are awakened during this eye-rolling stage of sleep, they usually report being in the midst of a dream (Dement & Kleitman, 1957).

This fifth stage has become known as **REM sleep**, the distinctive kind of sleep that is characterized by rapid eye movements (REMs) and is frequently—though not exclusively—associated with dreaming. Fosse, Stickgold, and Hobson (2001) investigated emotions experienced during dreaming in REM sleep. They found that emotions were reported 74% of the time, with roughly balanced proportions of positive and negative emotions. A total of 86% of the reports were of at least two emotions. Joy was most frequently experienced, followed by surprise, anger, anxiety/fear, and sadness. Levels of anxiety and fear were significantly less intense than those of other emotions.

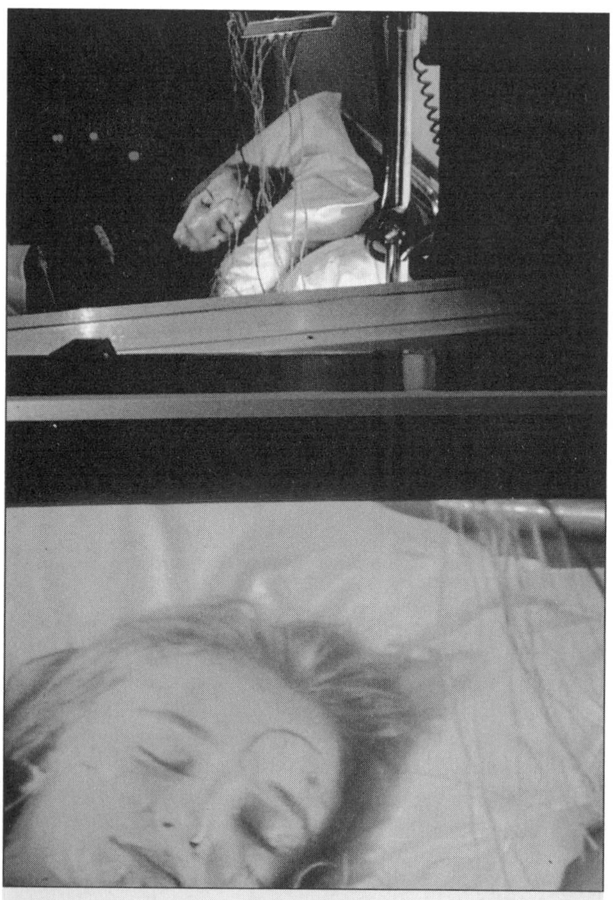

Sleep researchers monitor the patterns of brain-wave activity throughout the sleep cycles of research participants.

Dreaming frequently occurs during N-REM sleep. Dreams from N-REM sleep, however, are generally less clearly remembered upon waking than are dreams from REM sleep. Because dreaming can be associated with both REM and N-REM sleep, some investigators believe the difference is exaggerated (Antrobus, 2001). But other investigators argue that the distinction between REM and N-REM sleep is quite clear (Hobson, Pace-Schott, & Stickgold, 2000).

EEG patterns become extremely active during REM sleep, which begins about an hour after Stage 1. The EEG of REM sleep somewhat resembles the EEG of the awake brain (see Figure 8.2). REM sleep is both the most like wakefulness in EEG patterns and yet the hardest from which to wake people. For this reason, REM sleep is sometimes called "paradoxical sleep." This term is also used because at the same time that the brain is very active, the body's capacity for movement is greatly diminished.

The stages of N-REM and REM sleep alternate throughout the night, roughly in 90-minute cycles. As the night progresses, the duration and sequence of the sleep stages may vary, as shown in Figure 8.3.

Sleep Disorders

Although circadian rhythms and sleep cycles normally vary somewhat from person to person, extreme variations from the normal sleep patterns can wreak havoc on a person's life. Sleep disorders that cause problems for many people include: inability to sleep, known as *insomnia;* sudden uncontrollable sleep, called *narcolepsy;* breathing difficulties during sleep, or *sleep apnea;* talking in one's sleep, called *somniloquy;* and sleepwalking, also termed *somnambulism.*

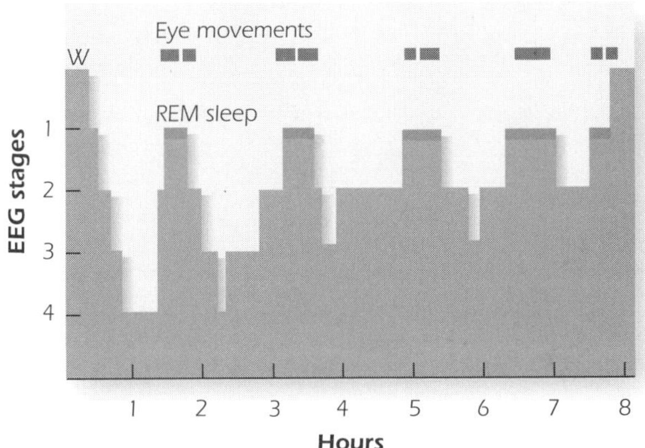

FIGURE 8.3

Sequences of States and Stages of Sleep. The sequence of REM and N-REM stages of sleep cycles alternates throughout the night. The repetitions of the REM stage are identified in red. (From Hartmann, *The Biology of Dreaming,* 1967. Courtesy of Charles C. Thomas, Publishers, Ltd., Springfield, IL.)

Insomnia **Insomnia** afflicts millions and is characterized by various disturbances of sleep. They include difficulty falling asleep, waking up during the night and being unable to go back to sleep, and waking up too early in the morning. These symptoms may vary in intensity and duration. People may experience temporary insomnia because of stress. They may suffer prolonged bouts of insomnia because of poor sleeping habits. Somewhat surprisingly, most people who suffer from insomnia usually sleep for at least a few hours, although they may not be aware of having slept. Laboratory studies have shown that insomniacs usually overestimate the amount of time it takes them to fall asleep.

insomnia
any of various disturbances of sleep, including difficulty falling asleep, waking up during the night and being unable to go back to sleep, or waking up too early in the morning, and which may vary in intensity and duration.

Although almost everybody has trouble falling asleep occasionally, in one survey, 6% of adult respondents said that they had sought medical attention because of sleeplessness. Roughly 15% of adults report serious insomnia. Another 15% report milder levels of insomnia or occasional insomnia (Bootzin, Manger, Perlis, Salvio, & Wyatt, 1993). Insomnia and most other sleep disorders are more common among women and the elderly (Borbely, 1986; Mellinger, Balter, & Uhlenhuth, 1985). Sleeping pills may help temporarily, but their side effects are troublesome. They often eventually intensify the insomnia. Prescription sleeping pills interfere with the natural sleep cycle, usually decreasing REM sleep. Moreover, sedatives often continue to work during the day, impairing cognitive and motor functions while the user is awake. Sedatives are also habit-forming, and people who rely on them may find it hard to sleep without taking medicine. For all of these reasons, physicians often recommend that their patients take the steps listed in Table 8.1 to avoid the need to take medicine (Borbely, 1986).

Some people believe they suffer from insomnia when they do not. What they are showing is a form of pseudo-insomnia, or *sleep state misperception.* Many of us have had the experience of thinking that we are awake for hours. We then check the clock, only to discover that we had tossed and turned for a much shorter time than we thought. Others have had the experience of being certain that they did not sleep all night. Then someone who observed them says they actually slept for several hours. In each case, people believe their sleep is severely disrupted when, at worst, it is only mildly disrupted. Indeed, 5% of individuals who go to insomnia clinics may suffer from pseudo-insomnia (Hauri, 1994).

About 15% of adults experience insomnia, which encompasses a number of sleep disturbances.

Narcolepsy In contrast to insomnia, **narcolepsy** is a disturbance in the pattern of wakefulness and sleep in which the narcoleptic experiences an uncontrollable urge to fall asleep periodically during the day. The afflicted individual loses consciousness for brief periods of time (usually 10 or 15 minutes). The narcoleptic can be in grave danger if the

TABLE 8.1 **How to Get a Good Night's Sleep.** The following recommendations have been suggested by numerous experts in the field of sleep research. (After Atkinson, Atkinson, Smith, & Bem, 1993)

DO	DON'T
Set a regular bedtime.	Change your schedule on the weekends.
Get up at the same time every morning.	Have caffeine 5–6 hours before bedtime.
Drink alcohol only in moderation.	Eat heavily just before bedtime.
Try warm milk or a *light* snack before bedtime.	Take sleeping pills; they can disrupt sleep cycles and leave you hung over.
Establish a relaxing evening ritual, such as reading before bed.	Attempt to wear yourself out with exercise before bedtime or when sleep won't come.
Exercise regularly.	
Stay in bed and try to relax if you're having problems sleeping.	

narcolepsy
a disturbance of the pattern of wakefulness and sleep, in which the narcoleptic person experiences an uncontrollable urge to fall asleep periodically during the day and as a result loses *consciousness* for brief periods of time (usually 10 to 15 minutes), thereby putting the narcoleptic in grave danger if the attacks occur when the person is driving or otherwise engaged in activities for which sudden sleep might be hazardous.

sleep apnea
a breathing disorder that occurs during sleep, in which the sleeper repeatedly (perhaps hundreds of times per night) stops breathing.

attacks occur while driving or engaged in activities in which sudden sleep might be hazardous. Narcolepsy actually is more accurately described as a disorder of the waking state than as a sleep disorder. Nevertheless, narcoleptics frequently experience disturbed nighttime sleep as well. Narcoleptics usually fall into REM sleep immediately, whereas a person with normal sleep patterns rarely (if ever) does so. This observation has led some scientists to suggest that, for narcoleptics, REM sleep may be insufficiently differentiated from the waking state. Narcolepsy affects 1 or 2 people in every 1,000 (Borbely, 1986). Although the cause of narcolepsy is unknown, the disorder seems to run in families and so may be inherited. Fortunately, medication can usually control the symptoms of this disorder.

Sleep Apnea Another disorder with unknown etiology and possible hereditary involvement is **sleep apnea**, a breathing disorder that occurs when the sleeper repeatedly (perhaps hundreds of times per night) stops breathing. The episodes usually last only a few seconds, but they may last as long as 2 minutes in severe cases. Sleep apnea is potentially dangerous because it deprives the body of oxygen. It most often afflicts overweight men over 40 years of age. A study of long-haul truck drivers found that men with disordered breathing during sleep were twice as likely to have accidents on the road as men with normal breathing during sleep (Stoohs, Guilleminault, Itoi, & Dement, 1994). Sleep apnea also seems to be associated with alcohol consumption. The disorder is difficult to treat in adults, although weight loss sometimes helps.

Sleep apnea occurs frequently in prematurely born infants. Infants generally outgrow the disorder, but it may be life threatening if the breathing patterns of infants at risk are not closely monitored. It has also been suggested that there may be a link between sudden infant death syndrome (SIDS) and sleep apnea. Maternal smoking has been linked to SIDS, as has the baby's sleeping on its stomach (J. A. Taylor & Sanderson, 1995). It is therefore particularly important that parents not expose their baby to smoke (even in utero) and also that they place their baby in a position other than on the stomach for sleeping.

somnambulism
sleepwalking, which combines aspects of waking and sleeping, with the sleepwalker able to see, walk, and perhaps even talk, but usually unable to remember the sleepwalking episodes; rarely accompanied by dreaming.

Sleepwalking In **somnambulism** (sleepwalking), the sleepwalker is able to see, walk, and perhaps even talk, but usually cannot remember the episodes. For many years, scientists believed that sleepwalkers were merely acting out their dreams. In fact, however, sleepwalking usually begins during Stage 3 or Stage 4 of N-REM sleep. It typically is not accompanied by dreaming. If the sleepwalking episode is short, sleepwalkers may stay in the deep sleep of Stages 3 and 4. If the episode is lengthy, EEG patterns begin to resemble either those of Stage 1 of N-REM sleep or those of the waking state.

Sleepwalking varies in severity. Some people may simply sit up in bed, mutter a few words, and then lie down again. Such episodes are no cause for concern. Other people may get out of bed, get dressed, walk around, and even leave their homes. Although sleepwalkers' eyes are open (usually with a rigid facial expression) and they can see, their perception is often impaired. They can injure themselves by mistaking one object for another, such as a window for a door.

Most sleepwalkers do not remember their episodes of sleepwalking when they awaken the next morning. They may even be surprised to find themselves asleep in some place other than their beds. Scientists have not found a cause or a cure for sleepwalking. However, sleepwalking is known to be more common in children than in adults. It usually disappears as children grow older.

DREAMS

People have always been fascinated with dreams. Dreams have been used to predict the outcomes of battles. They even have caused people to change religions. Indeed, dreams fill our heads with fantastic ideas—sometimes pleasant, sometimes frightening. Some people have experienced breakthrough insights or other creative ideas while dreaming or in a dreamlike state of mind. What is it about dreaming that may facilitate such breakthroughs?

All of us have dreams every night, whether or not we remember them (Ornstein, 1986). Dreams often occur in the form of strange fantasies that we accept as true while we sleep yet would dismiss if we were awake (Antrobus & Conroy, 1999). Common dream themes among college students are listed in Table 8.2.

Mary Whiton Calkins was one of the earliest American investigators of dreaming. She and her advisor, Edmund Sanford, collected dreams of college students. On the basis of 375 dreams studied, they concluded that people averaged four dreams per night. Calkins also argued that there is a close relationship between dreaming and waking life. She believed that dreams draw on the persons, places, and happenings of everyday life (Furumoto, 1980).

Why do we dream? There are several views. Perhaps the best-known theory of dreaming was proposed by Sigmund Freud (1900/1954). According to Freud, dreams allow us to express our unconscious wishes in a disguised way. Freud called dreams the "royal road to the unconscious" because they are one of the few ways we have of allowing the contents of the unconscious to be expressed. However, he also postulated that the contents of the unconscious would be so threatening if expressed directly and clearly that we might awaken every time we dreamed. Thus, according to Freud, we dream in symbols that both express and disguise our unconscious wishes. Because these wishes are disguised, they do not shock us into wakefulness. The empirical support for this theory is weak.

Other theorists have suggested that dreams represent everyday concerns expressed in a language that is peculiar to dreams (Foulkes, 1990, 1996, 1999) or even that dreams

TABLE 8.2

Common Dreams of College Students, in percent (Data from Schneider & Domhoff, 2003)

	MEN	WOMEN
Who and What We Dream About		
Animals	6	4
Familiar characters	45	58
Friends	31	37
Groups	31	28
Men	67	48
Women	37	52
Acts of aggression	59	51
Aggression is physical	50	34
Dreamer is aggressor	40	33
Dreamer is victim	60	67
Acts of friendliness	41	49
Dreamer befriends others	50	47
Dreamer achieves success	51	42
Bodily misfortune	29	35
Negative emotions	80	80
Where Our Dreams Are Set		
Indoors	48	61
Outdoors	52	39
Familiar place	62	79
Unfamiliar place	38	21
Percentage of Dreams with at Least One		
Act of aggression	47	44
Act of friendliness	38	42
Act of sexuality	12	4
Misfortune	36	33
Success	15	8
Failure	15	10

have no particular meaning at all (F. Crick & Mitchison, 1983, 1995)—that they represent a kind of mental housekeeping that has no deep psychological meaning whatsoever.

If dreams do indeed have meaning, the disguises of dream content are sometimes rather thin (Dement, 1976; Dement & Vaughan, 1999). In a study of the dreams of people who were deprived of liquid, many dreams were found to involve liquid consumption (p. 69): "Just as the bell went off, somebody raised a glass and said something about a toast. I don't think I had a glass."

Some theorists take a cognitive perspective on dreaming. In particular, a *problem-solving view* of dreaming suggests that dreams provide a way for us to work out our problems (Cartwright, 1977, 1993; Cartwright & Lamberg, 1992; Cartwright, Newell, & Mercer, 2001). For example, women going through a divorce are likely to dream about problems related to divorce. In fact, women who dream about divorce-related problems seem better able when they are awake to cope with the problems of divorce than are those who do not frequently dream about it (Cartwright, 1991).

activation–synthesis hypothesis a proposed perspective on dreaming that considers dreams to be the result of subjective organization and interpretation (synthesis) of neural activity (activation) that takes place during sleep; contrasting views include the Freudian view of dreams as a symbolic manifestation of wishes and the view of dreams as mental housekeeping.

According to the **activation–synthesis hypothesis**, dreams are the result of subjective organization and interpretation (synthesis) of neural activity (activation) that takes place during sleep (Hobson, 2001; McCarley & Hobson, 1981). Robert W. McCarley and J. Allan Hobson believe that we accept bizarre occurrences in dreams because of changes in brain physiology. That is, just as our brains work to organize sensory information during wakefulness, our brains also strive to organize sensory information during sleep. The brain may interpret the neural activity that occurs during dreaming. That activity, in turn, blocks motor commands as a sensation of our being chased. Our sleeping brains may interpret neural activity in the vestibular system (which controls balance) as the sensation of floating, flying, or falling.

The biological purpose or reasons for dreaming may someday be discovered. It is unlikely that scientists will ever devise a definitive model for interpreting dreams or for decoding the contents of dreams. Dreams are highly personal. To say that you could predict why people dream what they dream, you would have to be able to predict the content of a specific dream at a particular time (Hobson, 1989). Such prediction is not likely to occur.

Daydreaming can help us to creatively contemplate the information we have been studying.

Sigmund Freud and Carl Jung looked for universal symbols that would have the same meanings in every person's dreams. But people freely interpret their own dreams within the context of their current lives and past memories. They draw conclusions that seem appropriate to them. Some people find analyzing their dreams merely entertaining. Others believe the messages they find in their dreams are useful in solving the problems of waking life. Occasionally, dreams can be terrifying. Certain kinds of antidepressants that keep the serotonin system active can deprive people of dreaming and lead to a state of distress.

Nightmares are anxiety-arousing dreams that may awaken the dreamer. Sometimes we seem to wake up in order to avoid some threat in the nightmare. People who have nightmares often remember them if asked to recount them immediately after waking. Nightmares tend to increase during times of stress. Some people, however, seem to be more susceptible to them than others. Children are more susceptible, on average, than are adults. Nightmares generally require no special action, except when they are unusually severe or common or when the same nightmare repeats again and again.

Night terrors are sudden awakenings from N-REM sleep that are accompanied by feelings of intense fright or panic. These awakenings are characterized by intense arousal of the autonomic nervous system. A common symptom is greatly accelerated heart rate. People can experience night terrors at any age, but they are especially common in children from 3 to 8 years old. Often people wake up suddenly and may scream or sit upright. They usually do not remember any specific, coherent nightmare. They may, nevertheless, recall a frightening image or thought. People who experience night terrors may find that their sense of panic quickly fades. They then are able fairly rapidly to fall back asleep.

No discussion of dreaming is complete without mentioning daydreaming. **Daydreaming** is a state of consciousness somewhere between waking and sleeping that permits a shift in focus from external events toward internal thoughts and images (see J. L. Singer, 1998; J. A. Singer, Singer, & Zittel, 2000). Daydreaming can be useful in cognitive processes that involve the generation of creative ideas (D. G. Singer & Singer, 2001). It also can be disruptive, however. Anyone who has ever been questioned in class while daydreaming has learned firsthand how aggravating and even embarrassing this disruption can be.

daydreaming
a state of consciousness somewhere between waking and sleeping that permits a shift in the focus of conscious processing toward internal thoughts and images and away from external events; useful in cognitive processes that involve the generation of creative ideas, but disruptive in cognitive processes that require focused attention on environmental events.

HYPNOSIS AND MEDITATION

Most (but not all) psychologists view **hypnosis** as an altered state of consciousness that usually involves deep relaxation and extreme sensitivity to suggestion. It appears to bear some resemblance to sleep. Hypnotized people may imagine that they see or hear things when they are prompted to do so (Bowers, 1976). They may also receive a **posthypnotic suggestion,** an instruction given during hypnosis that is to be implemented after the subject wakens. Participants often have no recollection of receiving the instruction or even being hypnotized (Ruch, 1975). Hypnotized persons also may not sense things that they otherwise would sense. For example, a person may not feel pain when dipping an arm into very cold water. Hypnotized persons may be induced to remember things they had seemingly forgotten.

hypnosis
an altered state of *consciousness* that usually involves deep relaxation and extreme sensitivity to suggestion and appears to bear some resemblance to sleep (see *posthypnotic suggestion*).

posthypnotic suggestion
an instruction given to an individual during *hypnosis,* which the individual is to implement after having wakened from the hypnotic state; subjects often have no recollection of having been given the instructions or even of having been hypnotized.

Many psychologists wonder whether hypnotism is a genuine psychological phenomenon. Historically, even the man credited with introducing hypnotism, Franz Anton Mesmer (1734–1815), did not fully understand the phenomenon. Mesmer came to be viewed as a fraud, largely because he made claims for his techniques that he could not scientifically support (see Figure 8.4).

Since Mesmer's time, scientists have continued to investigate hypnotism. The **simulating paradigm** is a research technique for determining the true effects of a psychological treatment in which one group of participants is subjected to the treatment (hypnotized) and another group (a control group) is not (Orne, 1959). The control participants are then asked to behave as though they had received the treatment (in this case, been hypnotized). People must then try to distinguish between the behavior of the treatment group and the behavior of the control group.

simulating paradigm
a research technique for determining the true effects of a psychological treatment (e.g., *hypnosis*), in which one group of participants is subjected to the treatment and another group (a control group) is not, but the control participants are asked to behave as though they had received the treatment; people must then try to distinguish between the behavior of the treatment group and the behavior of the control group (most effective if the persons who make the distinction are blind about which participants are in the treatment group and which are in the control group).

As it turns out, simulators are able to mimic some, but not all, of the behavior of hypnotized participants (Gray, Bowers, & Fenz, 1970). Also, hypnotized participants in simulation experiments provide very different reports than do simulators of their subjective experiences. Simulating participants report themselves as actively faking. Hypnotized participants, in contrast, report the behavior as more or less just happening to them. Simulating participants try to figure out what the hypnotist expects from them. Hypnotized participants instead claim to be uninfluenced by the experimenter's expectations of them (Orne, 1959). Thus, hypnotized people do not appear to be faking (Kinnunen, Zamansky, & Block, 1994; Spanos, Burgess, Roncon, Wallace-Capretta, & Cross, 1993; Spanos, Burgess, Wallace-Capretta, & Ouaida, 1996).

FIGURE 8.4

Mesmerism. Franz Anton Mesmer, one of the first to experiment with hypnotism, believed that animal magnetism could cure illnesses. His patients would sit around the "magnetized" tub, wrap themselves with cord, and hold onto bent iron bars. "Magnetizers," Mesmer's helpers, would rub the patients' afflicted parts to hasten the cure. Mesmer and his method were discredited.

Theories of Hypnosis

If we accept the phenomenon of hypnosis as genuine, we still need to determine exactly what goes on during hypnosis. We discuss here only the more credible theories. One theory holds that hypnosis is a form of deep relaxation (Edmonston, 1981, 1991). This theory builds on the idea of hypnosis as a form of sleep, as suggested earlier by Ivan Pavlov, a Russian physiologist. We now know that EEG patterns shown during hypnosis are different from EEG patterns shown during sleep. Nevertheless, there may still be a close connection between hypnosis and the deep relaxation that sometimes precedes or resembles sleep.

A second theory suggests that hypnosis is an *epiphenomenon,* something that exists only as a secondary outcome of another phenomenon. Two psychologists who have taken this position are Theodore Barber (1979, 1986) and Nicholas Spanos (1986; Spanos & Coe, 1992). According to this view, hypnosis is largely a form of role-playing in response to experimenter demands. In attempting to meet the expectations of the experimenter, a person may act in particular ways.

The view of hypnosis as an epiphenomenon seems similar to the view that the behavior of hypnotized people is merely a sham, but the two ideas are not the same. According to the epiphenomenal view, the person in a hypnosis situation becomes so genuinely caught up in the role that he or she unwittingly plays the role of a hypnotized person for a brief time. Advocates of this position point out that individuals can successfully fake many of the phenomena attributed to hypnosis. More recently, it has become increasingly apparent that many of the memories seemingly miraculously retrieved under hypnosis are instead after-the-fact constructions that come from the suggestions of the hypnotist (McConkey, 1992). In other words, hypnosis did not result in people's being able to perform an astounding feat of memory. Rather they constructed memories that they believed to be ones the hypnotist wanted them to construct.

Perhaps the most widely accepted view among scientists who believe that hypnosis is a genuine phenomenon was developed by Ernest Hilgard. According to his **neodissociative theory**, some individuals can separate one part of their conscious minds from another part (*dissociation*) (Hilgard, 1977, 1992a, 1992b, 1994). In one part of the mind, the individual responds to the hypnotist's commands. In the other part of the mind, the individual becomes a hidden observer who simultaneously observes and monitors the events and actions taking place. These events and actions include some of those that the hypnotized participant appears not to be processing in the part of the conscious mind that is engaging in the actions (Hilgard, 1977, 1994).

For example, psychologists have found that while participants respond to a hypnotist's suggestion that they feel no pain and behave in ways that seem to show they are not in pain, they nevertheless are also able to describe how the pain feels. In other experiments, participants can be made to write down messages while unaware that they are doing so because they are actively engaged in another task at the same time (see Kihlstrom, 1985; Knox, Crutchfield, & Hilgard, 1975; Zamansky & Bartis, 1985). Thus, it seems that part of the person's consciousness is unself-consciously involved in the hypnosis. At the same time, another part observes and thereby knows, at some level, what is taking place.

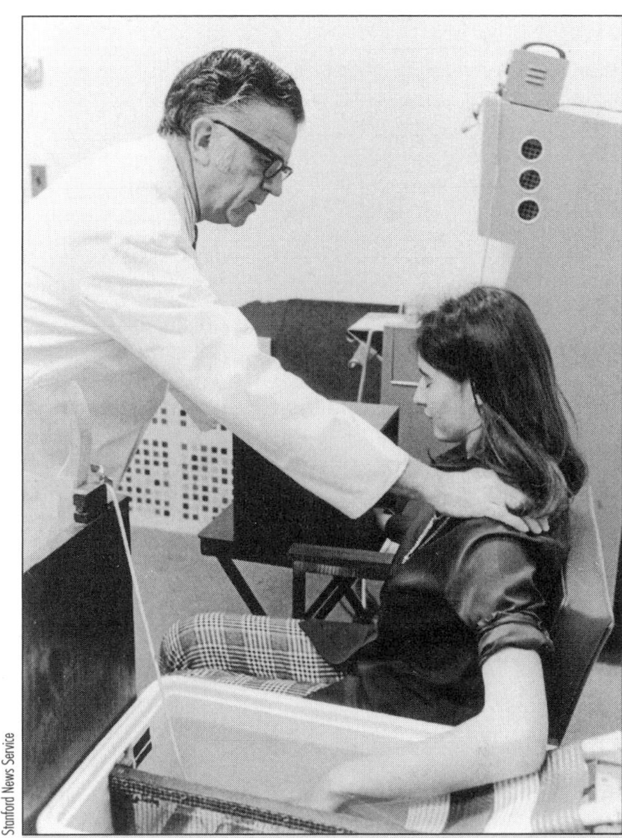

Stanford News Service

Hypnotists are able to induce a state of deep relaxation in susceptible individuals. Here, Ernest Hilgard conducts an experiment to determine the effects of hypnosis.

People differ in their susceptibility to hypnosis (Bowers, 1998; Hilgard, 1965; Oakman, Woody, & Bowers, 1996). Some people readily become deeply hypnotized, others do not. Still others appear to be relatively invulnerable to hypnotism. Four factors are hypothesized to influence whether an individual can be easily hypnotized: (1) social factors that lead the individual to cooperate and to try to conform to the wishes of the hypnotist; (2) the skill of the hypnotist and the individual's relationship with the hypnotist; (3) the effectiveness of the procedure for inducing hypnosis; and (4) what, exactly, the individual is being asked to do (Barber, 1999a, 1999b, 2000). It is not surprising that hypnosis is more successful as a clinical treatment with highly suggestible individuals.

neodissociative theory
a view of hypnosis in which it is asserted that some individuals are capable of separating one part of their conscious minds from another part; in one part, the individual responds to the hypnotist's commands, while in the other part, the individual observes and monitors the events and actions taking place, including some of the actions that the hypnotized individual appears not to be processing in the part of the conscious mind that is engaging in the actions.

Hypnosis and Memory

Some psychologists have become convinced that hypnosis can be used to dredge up old memories of events that otherwise seem to be forgotten, even memories of past lives! In one study, a third of the hypnotized college students who were instructed to remember events from previous lives were able to do so (Spanos, DuBreuil, & Gabora, 1991). While they were recalling these past lives, they were asked questions about their lives and surrounding events. Their recall cast serious doubt on the validity of their assertions. One student, for example, recalled his life as Julius Caesar in A.D. 50, when he was emperor of Rome. In fact, Caesar died in 44 B.C. and was never crowned emperor of Rome.

Evidence suggests that at least some recall may be inadvertently induced by hypnotists (L. S. Newman & Baumeister, 1994). Hypnotists' questions about events during reported abductions by extraterrestrial aliens often contain suggestions that are picked up by the hypnotized individual and "recalled" as having happened. An example is being asked whether one was injected with a needle by the extraterrestrials and then "remembering" that one was indeed injected (Fiore, 1989).

Some recollections under hypnosis may be correct (Geiselman, Fisher, MacKinnon, & Holland, 1985). But the current weight of the evidence is that memories under hypnosis need to be viewed with skepticism. Corroborating evidence for these recollections is needed before they are accepted as true memories. Hypnosis not only seems to be questionable as a technique for inducing recall of memories from the intermediate and distant past. It also is dubious as a technique for inducing recall of very recent memories. When memory for recently learned stories was compared for participants who either were or were not hypnotized, the hypnotized participants actually showed worse recall of the stories than did the nonhypnotized participants (Muzur, Fabbro, Clarici, Braun, & Bava, 1998).

At times, courts have allowed testimony from individuals who are under hypnosis, allegedly to improve their recall of past events. Research suggests that the testimony of such people is less reliable than that of people who are not hypnotized (Karlin & Orne, 1997), possibly because the people under hypnosis are so suggestible they may pick up clues about what they are expected to say.

In sum, the verdict on hypnosis is not yet in. Today, hypnosis is used in clinical settings to control smoking and to treat a variety of health-related problems, such as asthma, high blood pressure, and migraine headaches. The effects of hypnosis, however, appear to be temporary. For this reason, hypnotism generally is used in conjunction with other therapeutic techniques. Still, hypnosis appears to be more effective than other treatment techniques, whether in relieving pain or in changing behavior. Although persuasive evidence suggests that hypnosis is more than a crass simulation, psychologists have not reached consensus regarding what hypnosis is or even whether it is a genuine phenomenon.

Meditation

meditation
a set of techniques used for altering *consciousness* through focused contemplation (see *concentrative meditation, opening-up meditation*).

concentrative meditation
a form of contemplation in which the meditator focuses on an object or thought and attempts to remove all else from *consciousness* (see *meditation*).

opening-up meditation
one of the two main forms of contemplation, in which the meditator integrates *meditation* with the events of everyday life, seeking to expand awareness of everyday events, rather than to separate meditation from mundane existence; often involves an attempt to focus on becoming one with an ordinary activity, and on putting all other interfering thoughts out of *consciousness* (cf. *concentrative meditation*).

Meditation is a state of awareness that depends on techniques for altering consciousness through contemplation. It functions by "a shift away from the active, outward-oriented, linear mode and toward the receptive and quiescent mode, and often, a shift from an external focus of attention to an internal one" (Ornstein, 1977, p. 159). In its emphasis on receptivity and quiescence, meditation bears some resemblance to hypnotism. Brain-wave patterns as well as external perceptions can be altered during meditation. Meditation is viewed as slightly exotic in many Western cultures but is a normal part of life in some Eastern cultures.

Concentrative meditation is a form of contemplation in which the meditator focuses on an object or thought. The individual attempts to remove all else from consciousness. Concentrative meditation is performed in various ways. For example, meditators might focus on the whole process of breathing. They might think about the movement of the air as it reaches the nose, permeates the lungs, remains in the lungs, and then is finally expelled. The idea is to focus on a simple, repetitive, and rhythmic activity.

In Zen meditation, the meditator might contemplate the answer to a *koan*—a riddle or paradox, such as What is the sound of one hand clapping? or What is the size of the real you? These questions have no logical answers, which is just the point. You can think about the questions time and again without coming to a conclusion.

Opening-up meditation is the second of the two main forms of contemplation, in which the meditator integrates meditation with the events of everyday life, seeking to expand awareness of everyday events rather than to separate meditation from mundane existence. Yoga can take an opening-up form as well as a concentrative

© Marc Grimberg/The Image Bank-Getty Images

© Big Shots/Getty Images

Meditation and yoga can relax people and improve their mental health.

one. In one form of opening-up yoga, the individual learns to observe himself or herself as though another person. In another form of opening-up meditation, the person performs everyday actions slightly differently from the customary way. The goal is to become more aware of the routine of life.

What actually happens during meditation? What value, if any, is in the various forms of meditation? In general, respiration, heart rate, blood pressure, and muscle tension decrease (D. H. Shapiro & Giber, 1978; R. K. Wallace & Benson, 1972). Some evidence indicates that meditation can help patients who have bronchial asthma (Honsberger & Wilson, 1973). It also can decrease blood pressure in patients who are hypertensive (H. Benson, 1977). It may reduce insomnia in some people (Woolfolk, Carr-Kaffashan, McNulty, & Lehrer, 1976) and symptoms of psychiatric syndromes in others (Glueck & Stroebel, 1975). It also helps reduce addictive behavior (Marlatt, 2002), anxiety (M. E. Taylor, 2002), and irritable bowel syndrome (Keefer & Blanchard, 2002). EEG studies suggest that concentrative meditation tends to produce an accumulation of alpha waves. This is the type of brain wave associated with a state of relaxation and the beginning stages of sleep (Fenwick, 1987). Thus, concentrative meditation seems to relax people, which is of value in its own right. In addition, many practitioners of meditation believe that it enhances their overall consciousness. They think it moves them toward a more enlightened state of consciousness. (Users of various drugs also sometimes seek a similar state, more often than not with negative, and sometimes even life-threatening, results.)

PSYCHOACTIVE DRUGS

Drugs introduced into the body may destroy bacteria, ease pain, or alter consciousness. In this chapter we are concerned only with **psychoactive drugs**, which produce a significant effect on behavior, mood, and consciousness. Psychoactive drugs can be classified into four basic categories (Seymour & Smith, 1987): narcotics, central nervous system depressants, central nervous system stimulants, and hallucinogens. (See Table 8.3 for a summary of drugs in each

psychoactive drugs
chemical substances that modify mental, emotional, or behavioral functioning.

TABLE 8.3
Concept Review

Four Basic Categories of Drugs. Psychoactive drugs can be sorted into four basic categories, each of which produces distinctive psychoactive effects.

CATEGORY	EFFECT	DRUGS
Narcotics	Produce numbness or stupor, relieve pain	• Opium and its natural derivatives: morphine, heroin, and codeine • Opioids (synthetic narcotics): meperidine (Demerol®), propoxyphene (Darvon®), oxycodone (Percodan®), methadone
CNS depressants ("downers")	Slow (depress) the operation of the central nervous system	• Alcohol • Sedatives Barbiturates: secobarbital (Seconal®), phenobarbital (Dilantin®) Tranquilizers (benzodiazepines): chlorpromazine (Thorazine®), chlordiazepoxide (Librium®), diazepam (Valium®), alprazolam (Xanax®) • Methaqualone (Quaalude®) • Chloral hydrate
CNS stimulants ("uppers")	Excite (stimulate) the operation of the central nervous system	• Caffeine (found in coffee, teas, cola drinks, chocolate) • Amphetamines: amphetamine (Benzedrine®), dextroamphetamine (Dexedrine®), methamphetamine (Methedrine®) • Cocaine • Nicotine (commonly found in tobacco)
Hallucinogens (psychedelics, psychotomimetics)	Induce alterations of consciousness	• LSD • Mescaline • Marijuana • Hashish • Phencyclidine (PCP) • MDMA (ectasy) • Psilocybin ("magic" mushrooms)

category.) It is important to realize that different kinds of drugs can be used in combination, such as a "speedball," which combines a stimulant (cocaine) with a narcotic (heroin). The use of such combinations is more likely to be seriously toxic or deadly than is the use of single drugs.

With all the problems associated with psychoactive drug use, you may wonder why anybody uses drugs. The answers are as varied as people themselves. Some people take drugs to experiment, feeling confident that they are personally immune to addiction or that they will not get addicted in the short amount of time they plan to take the drugs. Others feel so unhappy in their daily lives that the risks seem worth it.

narcotic
any drug in a class of drugs derived from opium (*opiates* such as heroin, morphine, or codeine) or synthetically produced to create the numbing, stuporous effects of opium (*opioids* such as meperidine or methadone) and that lead to addiction; lead to a reduction in pain and an overall sense of well-being (from the Greek term for "numbness") (see also *central nervous system (CNS) depressant*).

opiate
a *narcotic* that is derived from the opium poppy bulb; may be injected intravenously, smoked, ingested orally, or inhaled (cf. *opioid*).

Narcotics

Narcotic, from the Greek term for "numbness," originally referred only to *opium* and to drugs derived from opium. Derivatives include drugs such as heroin, morphine, and codeine. Narcotics can be either naturally or synthetically produced to create the numbing, stuporous effects of opium. They also can lead to addiction. Narcotics derived from the opium poppy pod are **opiates**. **Opioids** are synthetically produced drugs that have similar chemical structure and effects as opiates. Examples are meperidine and methadone. When used illegally, opiates and opioids are usually injected intravenously, smoked, or inhaled. When used medically, they are either swallowed or injected intravenously. Narcotics are potent analgesics that lead to a reduction in pain and an overall sense of well-being.

Drug Actions Narcotics are highly addictive. They are usually either regulated by prescription or banned outright. Narcotics are sometimes prescribed for very brief periods to reduce postsurgical pain. In very low doses, they can relieve diarrhea. Narcotics have a constipating effect because they also depress other physiological systems, including metabolic processes.

Narcotics primarily affect the functioning of the brain and the bowel. They bring about pain relief, relaxation, and sleepiness. They help to suppress coughs (hence their use in *codeine* prescription cough medicines) and also can stimulate vomiting. Users typically notice an impaired ability to concentrate and a sense of mental fuzziness or cloudiness. For these reasons, driving under the influence of narcotics is extremely dangerous. Doing cognitively intensive work (such as studying) while under their influence is likely to be unproductive. Side effects of narcotics include contraction of the pupils, sweating, nausea, and depressed breathing.

Tolerance and Dependency Another danger of narcotic use over time is the possibility of an eventual **overdose,** in which the user ingests a life-threatening or lethal dose of drugs. Prolonged use of psychoactive drugs leads to **tolerance**, in which individuals progressively experience fewer effects for a given amount of the drug. Tolerance often prompts drug users to take increasing amounts of a given drug to achieve the same desired effect. Actually, most narcotics users find that the euphoria they felt when they initially used the drug disappears after prolonged use. They must continue to use drugs to keep from feeling ill from withdrawal from them.

Dependency occurs because, like many other drugs, narcotics mimic neurotransmitters in the way they act at synapses (see Figure 8.5). The molecular composition of opiates resembles that of endorphins, which are *endogenous morphines,* the body's natural painkilling neurotransmitters. Initial use of narcotics prompts pain relief and some of the euphoria that normally accompanies the natural release of endorphins. Prolonged use of narcotics apparently causes a drop in the body's natural production of particular endorphins. As a drug replaces the body's natural painkillers, people can develop *drug dependence,* a state in which an individual must continue to use a drug to satisfy intense physical, mental, or emotional cravings for the drug. In the past, it was common to distinguish between physical dependence, in which a person continues to use a drug to avoid physical symptoms, and psychological dependence, in which a person continues to use a drug to avoid mental or emotional symptoms. Today, however, many psychologists believe that the distinction between the two kinds of dependence is so fuzzy as to be useless (Koob & Bloom, 1988; Ray & Ksir, 1990). Dependence increases and tolerance develops because more narcotic is needed to do the job that the body gradually ceases to perform. **Withdrawal** symptoms are the temporary discomforts that result from a decreased dosage or a complete discontinuation of a psychoactive drug. A former user undergoing withdrawal may experience symptoms much like a severe case of intestinal flu, accompanied by extreme depression or anxiety. During withdrawal, the drug user's physiology and mental processes must adjust to the loss of the drug. Typical narcotic withdrawal symptoms are chills, sweating, intense stomach cramps, diarrhea, headache, and repeated vomiting. These symptoms may occur separately or in combinations.

Treatment of Narcotic Abuse Once a user has formed narcotic dependence, the form of treatment differs for *acute*

opioid
a *narcotic* that has a similar chemical structure and set of effects to those of an *opiate* but that is made synthetically through combinations of chemicals.

overdose
ingestion of a life-threatening or lethal dose of drugs, often associated with the use of *psychoactive* drugs, such as *narcotics, amphetamines,* or *sedatives;* though often linked to intentional suicide, overdoses commonly occur due to *tolerance* or *sensitization,* particularly when the users are also using street drugs, which contain many impurities and are not reliably controlled with regard to the concentrations of psychoactive elements in the drug compounds.

tolerance
a consequence of prolonged use of *psychoactive* drugs, in which the drug user stops feeling the *psychotropic* effects of a given drug at one dose and must take increasing amounts of the drug in order to achieve the effects, eventually reaching a level of nonresponse at which the current level no longer produces the desired effects, but higher levels will cause overdose; the person generally still continues to take the drugs, despite the lack of psychotropic effects, simply to avoid experiencing the unpleasant feelings associated with drug *withdrawal* (see *addiction;* see also specific drugs, e.g., *amphetamine* and *barbiturate*).

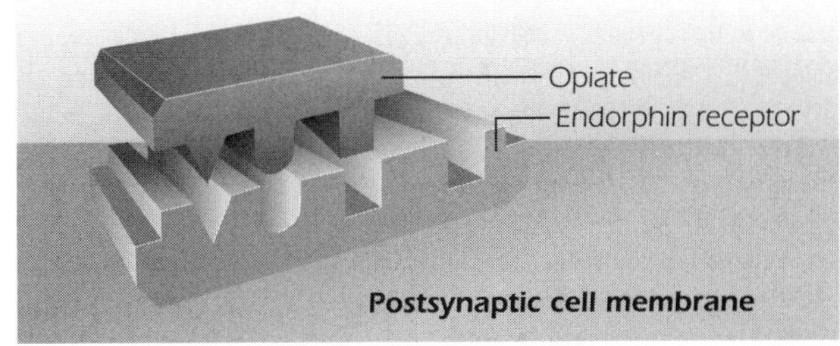

FIGURE 8.5

Molecular Similarity of Opiates and Endorphins. Opiates and endorphins have similar structures, which is why narcotics easily fit the receptor sites for endorphins.

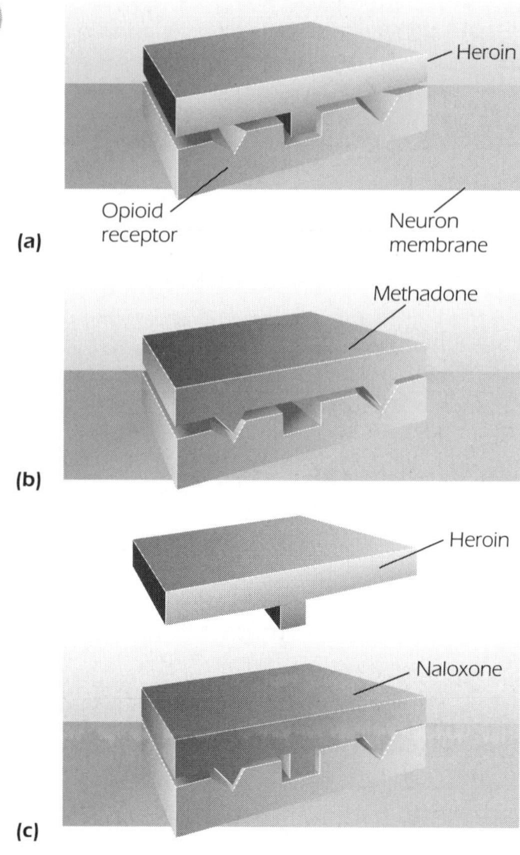

FIGURE 8.6

Molecular Similarity of Opiates, Methadone, and Naloxone. The nonnarcotic drug naloxone fits the receptor sites for endorphins so well that it can push out opiates and block them from reentering those sites, as shown in panel (c). Hence, naloxone can be used as effective temporary treatment for narcotic overdose, although its effects are short-lived. For long-term treatment, methadone is often substituted for heroin. It also fits the endorphin receptor sites, as shown in panel (b), and can reduce heroin cravings and withdrawal symptoms.

withdrawal
the temporary discomfort (which may be extremely negative, much like a severe case of intestinal flu, accompanied by extreme depression or *anxiety*) associated with a decrease in dosage or a discontinuation altogether of a *psychoactive* drug, during which the drug user's physiology and mental processes must adjust to an absence of the drug; during withdrawal from some drugs (e.g., some stimulants and some *sedatives*), the user should obtain medical supervision to avoid life-threatening complications that may arise during the readjustment to normal physiological and mental functioning.

toxicity (the damage done from a particular overdose) versus *chronic toxicity* (the damage done by long-term drug addiction). Acute toxicity is often treated with naloxone or related drugs. Naloxone (as well as a related drug, naltrexone) occupies opiate receptors in the brain better than the opiates themselves occupy those sites; thus, it blocks all effects of narcotics (see Figure 8.6). In fact, naloxone has such a strong affinity for the endorphin receptors in the brain that it actually displaces molecules of narcotics already in these receptors and then moves into the receptors itself. Naloxone is not addictive, however. Even though it binds to receptors, it does not activate them. Naloxone can be a lifesaving drug for someone who has overdosed on opiates, but its effects are short-lived. Thus, it is a poor long-term treatment for drug addiction.

Maintenance and detoxification are the primary methods of treating chronic toxicity caused by prolonged drug addiction. *Maintenance* controls an addict's use of the drug. In a maintenance program, the addict is still given the drug or a substitute, but in a controlled manner. The goal is to substitute a more controllable, less lethal, addiction—a goal considered controversial by many. *Detoxification* seeks to break the addiction both by weaning an addict off the drug to break the habit and by restoring good health habits. In narcotic detoxification, methadone often is substituted for the narcotic (typically heroin). Methadone binds to endorphin receptor sites (see panel (b) in Figure 8.6) and reduces the heroin cravings and withdrawal symptoms of addicted persons. After the substitution, gradually decreasing dosages are administered to the patient until he or she is drug-free. Unfortunately, the usefulness of methadone is limited because it is itself addictive.

Central Nervous System Depressants

Drug Actions **Central nervous system (CNS) depressant** drugs are a highly addictive class of psychoactive drugs (e.g., alcohol and the sedatives) that slow the operation of the CNS. They are often prescribed in low doses to reduce anxiety and in relatively high doses to combat insomnia. Alcohol is readily available for purchase by adults in most countries around the world. Sedatives are usually prescribed (Nishino, Mignot, & Dement, 2001). CNS depressants can be ingested orally or injected. They usually elevate mood, reduce anxiety and guilt, and relax normal inhibitions. However, such drugs may cause people to become **intoxicated**—that is, stupefied by toxins in the depressants. The individuals may also find themselves susceptible to sudden shifts in mood. Their sense of relaxation and euphoria quickly can give way to *increased* anxiety and irritability. High doses of depressants can cause slow reflexes, unsteady gait, slurred speech, and impaired judgment. Overdoses can slow physiological responses so much that they cause death.

Alcohol Abuse and Treatment *Alcohol* is the most well known and widely used CNS depressant. It is the natural result of the fermentation of fruits and grains. Alcohol is so widely promoted and consumed that people tend to ignore the fact that it is an addictive psychoactive drug.

Alcohol's effects vary with the amount consumed, the rate of consumption, and an individual's body weight, tolerance, and metabolism. Someone who sips a drink over the course of an evening is less likely to become intoxicated than someone who gulps it. Furthermore, a 300-pound person is typically less affected than a

100-pound person by the same amount of alcohol. A frequent drinker usually builds up a tolerance (similar to narcotics tolerance), however, and this tolerance can lead to increased consumption.

When concentrations of alcohol in the blood are around 0.03% to 0.05%, people often feel relaxed and uninhibited, and they have a general sense of well-being. At a blood-alcohol level of 0.10%, sensorimotor functioning is markedly impaired. Many states consider people to be legally drunk at this level. Some states use a lower level of 0.08%. People may exhibit slurred speech and grow angry, sullen, or morose. At a concentration of 0.20%, people show grave dysfunction. With concentrations of 0.40% or higher, there is a serious risk of death.

Most dosages of alcohol decrease the effectiveness of the neurotransmitter *dopamine* thus reducing motor abilities and attention. Alcohol also appears to interfere with the activities of other neurotransmitters (Hittner, 1997). At first, alcohol often seems to increase people's level of arousal, apparently because it first depresses the effects of synapses that release inhibitory neurotransmitters in the brain. People initially may feel more excited because inhibitory activity is slowed and excitatory transmissions predominate. Soon, however, alcohol depresses the effects of excitatory synapses as well, causing a general decrease in sensorimotor functioning. Interestingly, it has been found that there are strong expectancy effects for alcohol consumption, which is sometimes called the "think-drink" phenomenon. The effects one gets from alcohol are very much determined by the effects one expects to get (Stacy, Widaman, & Marlatt, 1990). If one drinks a substance that one believes to be alcoholic but that is not, one will experience some signs of inebriation. If one drinks a substance that one believes is not alcoholic but that is, one will feel fewer signs of inebriation.

Although party–goers often drink alcohol to relax and reduce inhibitions, prolonged or excessive drinking can cause stupor, damage to the brain and nervous system, and sometimes death. Is this person having fun yet?

Larimer, Anderson, Baer, and Marlatt (2000) did a study of drinking among residents of fraternities, sororities, and residence halls. They found that men who lived in a fraternity were likely to consume more alcohol than men who lived in a residence hall, with more negative consequences, even after controlling for family history, expectancies, and history of drinking in high school. A history of alcohol problems in the family produced negative consequences only for men, not for women. The results for women were quite different. Residence in a sorority was actually found to moderate the negative consequences of drinking. Heavy drinkers among women in residence halls reported more negative consequences than did heavy drinkers in sororities.

In a separate study, Blume, Marlatt, and Schmaling (2000) found reduced higher-order cognitive functioning among heavy drinkers in college. This finding suggests a possible explanation for people who become heavy drinkers. They may lack the cognitive skills to anticipate the long-term consequences of heavy drinking.

Alcoholism is the tendency to abuse alcohol to a degree that leads to social, cognitive, or occupational dysfunction. It is one of the most common afflictions in the United States. Alcoholics have great difficulty abstaining from alcohol and controlling their drinking once they start. Roughly two-thirds of adults in the United States report that they use alcohol. An estimated 10% of these people have problems related to alcohol use. An estimated 90% of all assaults, 50%–60% of all homicides, and more than 50% of rapes and sexual attacks on children are alcohol

central nervous system (CNS) depressant
a drug (e.g., alcohol and *sedatives*) that slows the operation of the *CNS* and is often prescribed in low doses to reduce *anxiety* and in relatively higher doses to combat *insomnia* (see *barbiturate, tranquilizer;* cf. *narcotic;* see also *central nervous system (CNS) stimulant*).

intoxicated
Characterized by stupefaction due to the effects of toxins such as alcohol or *sedatives.*

TABLE 8.4 **Are You an Alcoholic?** If you answer yes to any of these questions, developed by the National Institute on Alcohol Abuse and Alcoholism, alcohol may be a problem in your life. If you answer yes to several of the questions, you may be an alcoholic.

If You Can Answer Yes to Even One of These Questions, Consider Seeking Advice About Your Use of Alcohol
1. Has someone close to you sometimes expressed concern about your drinking?
2. When faced with a problem, do you often turn to alcohol for relief?
3. Are you sometimes unable to meet home or work responsibilities because of drinking?
4. Have you ever required medical attention as a result of drinking?
5. Have you ever experienced a blackout—a total loss of memory while still awake—when drinking?
6. Have you ever come in conflict with the law in connection with your drinking?
7. Have you often failed to keep the promises you have made to yourself about controlling or cutting out your drinking?

related. The costs to society of alcohol abuse are probably double those of all other types of drug abuse combined (Segal, 1988).

Chronic alcoholics may sustain permanent damage to the nervous system, pancreas, liver, and brain cells. Heavy drinking can also lead to suppression of the immune system, nutritional deficits, and general failure to be careful about health matters. These problems can eventually result in other unfortunate consequences, including increased risk of cancer (Herity, Moriarty, Daly, Dunn, & Bourke, 1982; Heuch, Kvale, Jacobsen, & Bjelke, 1983). For these and other reasons, alcoholics generally have their life expectancy shortened by an average of 10 to 12 years. Alcoholics also may experience blackouts, loss of memory, cardiac arrest, psychosis, and alcohol-induced death. They are at risk for *Korsakoff's syndrome,* a brain disorder in which learning and other cognitive functions are impaired. Alcohol use by pregnant women, even in moderate amounts, can result in *fetal alcohol syndrome.* This illness may produce permanent mental retardation, as well as facial deformities, in the children who must endure this toxic prenatal environment.

The National Institute on Alcohol Abuse and Alcoholism has developed a list of seven questions for self-diagnosis of alcoholism (see Table 8.4). A "yes" answer to even one question may suggest that alcohol is a problem. Affirmative answers to several questions should be taken as an indication that you may be an alcoholic. Most of these questions boil down to a central issue: Is your use of alcohol creating problems in other areas of your life?

Heavy drinkers experience withdrawal symptoms when they stop drinking alcohol. In withdrawal from chronic intoxication, symptoms may be severe, including convulsions, hallucinations, tremors, agitation, and even death (Seymour & Smith, 1987). Chronic alcoholism can be treated through medical intervention, through a peer counseling program such as Alcoholics Anonymous, through therapy that combines cognitive and behavioral change (Parks, Marlatt, & Anderson, 2001), or through a combination of treatments.

In withdrawal from acute intoxication, typical symptoms are headache, loss of appetite, nausea, and shakiness—in short, a hangover. Detoxification from a hangover is simply a matter of time. As time passes, the body metabolizes the alcohol and the symptoms dissipate. Drinking coffee does not reduce the effects of alcohol. Instead, it creates a wide-awake, stimulated drunk. Drinking a lot of nonalcoholic liquids can help, as can moderate exercise. Drinking more alcohol to reduce the effect of a hangover does little good. Moreover, it can lead to increased alcohol dependence.

sedative
one type of *central nervous system (CNS) depressant,* used for calming *anxiety* and relieving *insomnia* (e.g., *barbiturate, tranquilizer,* methequalone, and chloral hydrate).

Tranquilizers and Barbiturates **Sedatives** depress the CNS and are used for calming anxiety and relieving insomnia (see Table 8.3). The most widely used sedative drugs are **barbiturates**, which are prescribed to reduce anxiety through physiological inhibition of arousal. When used properly, barbiturates are effective sedatives. In low doses, barbiturates calm the user. Higher dosages inhibit neurons in arousal centers in the brain, causing sleep. Still higher dosages can cause respiratory failure. As is true of nearly all psychoactive drugs, the addictive properties of barbiturates encourage rampant abuse. Chronic use leads to increased tolerance, so that the user takes more and more of the drug to achieve the same effect. Increased dosages can misfire in several ways, however. The user may fall asleep or be groggy in situations that demand full attention. Accidents can lead to injury or even death. The user may also ingest a lethal dosage in a desperate attempt to fall asleep.

Following the development of tranquilizers (benzodiazepines, listed in Table 8.3), physicians shifted away from prescribing barbiturates as sedatives and moved toward prescribing them primarily as sleep inducers. **Tranquilizers**, another class of the sedative drugs used for combating anxiety, are considered to be safer than barbiturates because of the lower dosages required and the reduced likelihood of drowsiness and respiratory difficulties. The potential for addiction remains a problem, however. Even so, they are among the more commonly prescribed drugs in the United States (Seymour & Smith, 1987). Clearly, the potential for abuse exists.

Treatment of Depressant Abuse Treatment for addiction or overdose varies according to the sedative drug. Both psychological and physiological dependence must be addressed. Chronic toxicity may be treated through a counseling and support program or, in the case of barbiturates, through maintenance via gradual phenobarbital substitution. Whereas withdrawal from narcotic drugs is extremely uncomfortable but usually not life-threatening, withdrawal from sedative drugs can be both painful and life-threatening. Withdrawal symptoms can include anxiety, tremors, nightmares, insomnia, nausea, vomiting, fever, seizures, and delirium (Seymour & Smith, 1987).

Central Nervous System Stimulants

Drug Actions Stimulants, like the other drugs we have considered, have been around for centuries. **Central nervous system (CNS) stimulants** are drugs (e.g., caffeine, amphetamines, cocaine, and nicotine) that arouse and excite the central nervous system. They do so either by stimulating the heart or by inhibiting the actions of natural compounds that depress brain activity. (In other words, they act as "double-negatives" on brain stimulation; see Table 8.3.) Short-term effects of relatively low doses include increased stamina and alertness, reduced appetite, exuberance, and euphoria. Larger doses may cause anxiety and irritability. Problems with tolerance and addiction are linked with long-term use; problems with sensitization are tied to intermittent use. Illegal stimulants, most notably cocaine, have overtaken narcotics as a drug problem in the United States.

Caffeine **Caffeine**, a mild stimulant, is found in a number of drinks that come close to being "national drinks"—coffee in the United States, tea in the United Kingdom, *guarana* in Brazil, *maté* in Argentina. It creates fewer problems than the other drugs in this category. Chocolate and cola drinks are also sources of caffeine. An ounce of coffee typically contains 11–29 mg of caffeine, whereas tea typically contains 5–17 mg. Cola and other soft drinks vary widely in their caffeine content, depending on the brand.

barbiturates
an antianxiety drug prescribed to reduce *anxiety* through physiological inhibition of *arousal* (high dosages can even induce sleep); may lead to grogginess that may impair functioning in situations requiring alertness; chronic use leads to *tolerance* and to physiological *addiction*, and high doses can lead to respiratory failure (see also *central nervous system (CNS) depressant*).

tranquilizer
a *sedative* used for combating *anxiety;* considered to be safer than *barbiturates* because of the lower dosages required and the reduced likelihood of drowsiness and respiratory difficulties, although the potential for *addiction* remains a problem (see *central nervous system (CNS) depressants*).

central nervous system (CNS) stimulant
a drug (e.g., *caffeine, amphetamines, cocaine,* and nicotine—found in tobacco) that arouses and excites the *CNS*, either by stimulating the heart or by inhibiting the actions of natural compounds that depress brain activity (in other words, it acts as a "double-negative" on brain stimulation); short-term effects of relatively low doses include increased stamina and alertness, reduced appetite, and exuberant euphoria; higher doses may cause anxiety and irritability; problems with *tolerance* and *addiction* are linked with long-term use, and problems with *sensitization* are tied to intermittent use (cf. *central nervous system (CNS) depressant*).

Caffeine in coffee is a powerful stimulant.

caffeine
a mild *central nervous system (CNS) stimulant.*

Caffeine increases neural activity, stimulating tension in the heart and skeletal muscles. Caffeine stimulates the CNS partly by suppressing the effects of *adenosine,* a naturally occurring depressant (inhibitory chemical) in the brain. High doses of caffeine can cause anxiety, nervousness, irritability, tremulousness, muscle twitching, insomnia, rapid heart beat, hyperventilation, increased urination, and gastrointestinal disturbances. Very high doses of caffeine can increase blood pressure and possibly contribute to coronary heart disease (Lane & Williams, 1987; D. Shapiro, Lane, & Henry, 1986). It appears, though, that caffeine is dangerous for most people only in very large amounts. Someone who drinks seven or eight cups of coffee a day may be at risk, but someone who drinks a cup or two a day is not.

Although caffeine is addictive, caffeine addiction is not a major societal problem. However, the indications of addiction are similar to those of other, more destructive drugs. These indications include compulsive behavior, loss of control, and continued drug use despite adverse consequences (Seymour & Smith, 1987). Some people, for example, continue to ingest high doses of caffeine despite symptoms such as noticeable increases in heart rate, nervousness, and difficulties sleeping at night after drinking coffee or tea. Symptoms of withdrawal from caffeine include lethargy, irritability, difficulties in working, constipation, and headache.

amphetamines
a type of synthetic *central nervous system (CNS) stimulant* that is usually either ingested orally or injected; short-term effects include increased body temperature, heart rate, and endurance, as well as reduced appetite; psychological effects include stimulation of the release of *neurotransmitters,* such as norepinephrine and *dopamine* into brain *synapses,* as well as inhibition of *reuptake* of neurotransmitters, leading to a sense of euphoria and increased alertness, *arousal,* and motor activity; long-term effects are a reduction of *serotonin* and other neurotransmitters in the brain, thereby impairing neural communication within the brain; long-term use also leads to *tolerance* and intermittent use may lead to *sensitization.*

Amphetamines **Amphetamines** are a type of synthetic CNS stimulant that increases body temperature, heart rate, and endurance. They are usually either swallowed or injected. They are sometimes used by people whose jobs require long hours and sustained attention. They are also used in some diet pills to reduce appetite. In the brain, amphetamines stimulate the release of neurotransmitters such as *norepinephrine* and *dopamine* into brain synapses. The result is a euphoric "high" and increasing alertness. Amphetamines may further increase the levels of these neurotransmitters by preventing their reuptake from the synaptic gaps (Ray & Ksir, 1990). The resulting higher-than-normal concentrations of these neurotransmitters lead to increased arousal and motor activity. When amphetamines are taken over long periods of time, the levels of serotonin and other neurotransmitters in the brain may start to decrease. The result can be damage to the neural communication system within the brain.

As is true of many other drugs, the prolonged use of amphetamines creates tolerance and a resulting need for higher doses. In sufficiently large doses, amphetamines can produce odd behavior, such as repetitive searching and examining, prolonged staring at objects, chewing, and moving an object back and forth (Groves & Rebec, 1988). Overdoses produce intoxication, paranoia, confusion, and hallucinations. They also may lead to death from respiratory failure or wild fluctuations in body temperature. Withdrawal symptoms include extreme fatigue and depression. Rare or occasional use of amphetamines seems to produce the paradoxical phenomenon of *sensitization,* in which an intermittent user of a drug demonstrates heightened sensitivity to low doses of the drug.

cocaine
a powerful *central nervous system (CNS) stimulant.*

Cocaine **Cocaine** is probably the most powerful natural stimulant. It was used in religious ceremonies by the Incas in pre-Columbian times. For centuries, South Americans have chewed the leaves of the coca plant to increase their physical stamina in their rugged environment. Cocaine, commonly known as "coke," is highly addictive, especially when smoked in the form of "crack." Physiologically, cocaine increases body temperature and constricts peripheral blood vessels. It also produces spurious feelings of increased mental ability and can produce great excitement. If consumed in sufficient quantity, cocaine can cause hallucinations and seizures. Like amphetamines, cocaine appears to increase the transmission of *norepinephrine* and *dopamine* across synapses and to inhibit the reuptake of both these neurotransmitters and of *serotonin.* Increased concentrations of these neurotransmitters result in the heightened arousal and motor activity associated with amphetamines. Initially at least, cocaine also seems to stimulate acute sexual arousal. But prolonged use diminishes sexual arousability and performance (Wade & Cirese, 1991). Prolonged use also leads to lower levels of neurotransmitters and difficulties in neural transmission similar to those associated with prolonged amphetamine use.

Recovering cocaine addicts crave the drug intensely. Their prolonged use has diminished their natural brain-stimulant mechanisms, and as a result, they feel great anxiety, loss of control, depression, and lethargy.

tobacco
a plant product that contains nicotine, a *central nervous system (CNS) stimulant.*

Tobacco **Tobacco** is a plant product that contains *nicotine,* a CNS stimulant. It is legally available to adults in a variety of forms. Nevertheless, stop-smoking campaigns have emerged from widespread publicity about the health dangers of tobacco. Studies have also found harmful effects from inhaling *secondary smoke,* exhaled by smokers or otherwise released into the air by burning tobacco. The result has been increasingly restrictive laws prohibiting smoking in public places. Laws also restrict the accessibility of tobacco to young people. Still, even preadolescent children often can obtain tobacco products.

The tobacco leaf is grown throughout the world. It is usually smoked, but it is also often chewed. Nicotine is absorbed through the respiratory tract as well as the oral and nasal mucosa and the gastrointestinal tract. Most of the inhaled nicotine is absorbed by the lungs. Nicotine activates nicotinic receptors located on nerve cells and on skeletal muscles. These receptors use *acetylcholine*. Their activation thereby increases the neurotransmission of acetylcholine.

Tobacco has complex effects on the body. It can increase respiration, heart rate, and blood pressure, but decrease appetite. Intoxication is characterized by euphoria, light-headedness, giddiness, dizziness, and a tingling sensation in the extremities (Seymour & Smith, 1987). Tolerance and dependence develop relatively quickly. As a result, the intoxication effect is typically experienced only by newcomers to smoking. People who habitually use tobacco usually stabilize at some point that becomes a maintenance dosage for them.

Tobacco is now believed to be among the most addictive substances in existence. Fully 9 out of 10 people who start smoking become addicted (compared with 1 in 6 people who try crack cocaine and 1 in 10 people who experiment with alcohol). In 1996, the Food and Drug Administration recommended that nicotine be classified as a controlled

© David Cummings, Eye Ubiquitous/Corbis

The nicotine in tobacco is one of the most addictive drugs known.

© Jeremy Horner/Corbis

Coca leaves processed into cocaine become highly addictive.

substance. Smoking by pregnant women has been linked to both premature birth and low birth weight, grave risk factors for newborns. Most of the long-term adverse effects of tobacco occur after prolonged use. They include heart disease, cancers of various sorts (especially lung and mouth cancers), gum disease, eating disorders, emphysema, gastrointestinal disease, and brittle bones. Secondary smoke has been linked with many of these ailments as well. Nicotine is highly poisonous and is even used as a potent insecticide. Tobacco smoke contains other potentially harmful by-products in addition to nicotine, including tar, carbon monoxide, and hydrogen cyanide. During the 1980s, 5 million people are believed to have died because of tobacco use. In comparison, 1 million died from alcohol-related causes and 350,000 died from other addictions. Actually, nearly all of the stimulant drugs discussed here can cause death if taken in sufficient quantities. Abuse can and should be treated before it is too late.

Treatment of Stimulant Abuse Acute toxicity from stimulants must be treated medically. The exact treatment depends on the drug that was taken. For example, a massive amphetamine overdose may call for inducing bowel movements in people who are conscious. It may require stomach pumping in individuals who have lost consciousness. Overdoses of cocaine may be treated with tranquilizers and may require hospitalization.

The most common treatment for chronic addiction to stimulants is individual or group psychotherapy. Stimulant abusers need to find ways to stay off drugs. Education about the dangers of cocaine abuse and attendance at support groups are, for now, the best methods of overcoming cocaine addiction. Organizations dedicated to helping people get off drugs include Narcotics Anonymous, which helps with stimulant abuse as well, and Cocaine Anonymous.

Drug-substitution therapy is generally not used except for nicotine. For acute nicotine withdrawal, nicotine gum and epidermal patches appear to be effective when used in combination with some other form of therapy. Without additional supportive treatment, users run the risk of becoming addicted to the substitute. Stop-smoking programs (such as those offered by the American Lung Association) use a wide array of techniques, including hypnosis, acupuncture, *aversion therapy* (overdosing people with smoke or nicotine to render it repulsive), group support, and education.

Finally, let's consider the remaining major class of psychoactive drugs: hallucinogens.

Hallucinogens

hallucinogenic
a type of *psychoactive* drug (e.g., mescaline, LSD, and marijuana) that alters *consciousness* by inducing *hallucinations* and affecting the way the drug-takers perceive both their inner worlds and their external environments; often termed *psychotomimetics* (also known as "psychedelics") because some clinicians believe that these drugs mimic the effects produced by psychosis.

Drug Actions **Hallucinogenic** drugs are a type of psychoactive drug (e.g., mescaline and LSD) that alter consciousness by inducing hallucinations. They also affect the way the drug takers perceive both their inner worlds and their external environments. *Hallucinations* are experiences of sensory stimulation in the absence of any actual corresponding external sensory input. These drugs are often termed *psychotomimetics* (and are also known as "psychedelics") because some clinicians believe these drugs mimic the effects produced by psychosis. Others suggest that these hallucinations differ in kind from those produced by psychosis (see Table 8.3).

People react in very different ways to hallucinogenic drugs. Their reactions appear to be determined partly by situational factors. Physiologically, most hallucinogenic drugs, such as LSD, work by interfering with the transmission of *serotonin* in the brain (Jacobs, 1987). Serotonin-releasing neuronal systems begin in the brainstem and progress to nearly all parts of the brain. The fact that hallucinations can seem so real on so many different sensory levels may be connected to this widespread cerebral interference. Some suggest that a way to think of this mechanism is that serotonin normally blocks us from dreaming when we are awake. So the inhibition of serotonin during wakefulness allows the hallucinations associated with dreams to occur. Serotonin interference is not characteristic of marijuana, mescaline, or phencyclidine (PCP), however. The mechanisms of action for these hallucinogens are still uncertain; however, stimulation of norepinephrine neurotransmission may be a factor.

LSD The hallucinogenic effects of *lysergic acid diethylamide* (LSD, first synthesized in 1938) were discovered in 1943, when a chemist at Sandoz Pharmaceuticals in Switzerland accidentally ingested some. LSD typically causes physical symptoms such as dizziness, creeping or tingling of the skin, nausea, and tremors. It also can cause perceptual symptoms such as hallucinations and an altered sense of time. Affective (emotional) symptoms include rapid mood swings ranging from severe depression to extreme agitation and anxiety. Finally, cognitive symptoms can involve the feeling of having learned things that would have been impossible to learn without the drug (Groves & Rebec, 1988; Jacobs & Trulson, 1979).

LSD can cause people to become anxious at their inability to control the drug experience or "trip." The most dangerous time in a bad reaction to LSD occurs during hallucinations. Users may try to flee the hallucinations, which can put them into physical danger. Even LSD users who enjoy the experience can be at risk for dangerous behavior. Occasionally, users who forgot they had ingested LSD or people who were given the drug without their knowledge panic. They feel afraid the hallucinations will go on forever.

Marijuana is used by many people for relaxation, but it has adverse effects on memory and some other cognitive processes.

Marijuana The most commonly used hallucinogen, *marijuana,* is produced from the dried leaves and flowers of the cannabis plant. *Hashish* is a stronger form of marijuana made from a concentrated resin derived from the plant's flowers. Most users of marijuana or hashish either smoke the drug or ingest it as an ingredient in food.

People under the influence of marijuana typically experience a disconnected flow of ideas and altered perceptions of space and time. Some people become extremely talkative, others inarticulate. Users may experience intense food cravings and may become impulsive. Very high doses can even lead to hallucinations, although typical use of the drug does not.

Even moderate use of marijuana appears to impair some short-term learning and memory processes (C. F. Darley, Tinklenberg, Roth, Hollister, & Atkinson, 1973; Sullivan, 2000). There is disagreement about the long-term effects of marijuana use (Gunderson, Vosburg, & Hart, 2002). Some investigators claim that it damages nerve cells and the reproductive system. Other researchers have failed to replicate such findings (V. Rubin & Comitas, 1974) or have argued that the beneficial effects of marijuana for pain relief outweigh any potential negative effects.

Phencyclidine *Phencyclidine (PCP)* is popular among adolescents in some communities because of its modest price and easy accessibility. PCP somehow profoundly alters the relationship between the body's physical experiences and the mind's perceptual experiences. It causes extreme cognitive and perceptual distortions. Its effects work particularly on receptors that play a role in learning. Thus, PCP has great potential for causing serious cognitive deficits. Users should be medically treated as soon as possible.

MDMA (ecstasy) Another popular drug with similar effects is MDMA, known commonly by its street name, ecstasy. (The technical name for the drug is 3-4 methylenedioxymethamphetamine.) The use of ecstasy can cause psychological difficulties such as confusion, depression, problems in sleeping, and intense anxiety. It also can cause physical symptoms such as muscle tension, involuntary clenching of the teeth, nausea, blurred vision, increased heart rate and blood pressure, and liver damage.

Treatment of Hallucinogen Abuse Acute overdoses of hallucinogens are normally treated by a therapist attempting to talk to the user. The goal is to reduce anxiety reactions and to make the user feel as comfortable as possible ("talking the user down"). Tranquilizers are sometimes used. A final alternative is antipsychotic drugs. Chronic use of hallucinogens can lead to prolonged psychotic reactions, severe and sometimes life-threatening depression, a worsening of pre-existing psychiatric problems, and flashbacks of past drug experiences without further ingestion of the drug (Seymour & Smith, 1987). Scientists do not understand how flashbacks occur. They have not yet found any physiological mechanism that can account for them.

In sum, consciousness is our means of monitoring and evaluating the environment. Through consciousness, we come to experience the world in our own terms. Altered states of consciousness enrich our lives. Some of them, such as sleep, seem to be necessary to our survival. Other altered states, however, are produced by substances that may have considerable addictive potential. Whatever the reasons for taking addictive psychoactive drugs, people need to learn that the harmful outcomes generally outweigh any perceived benefits.

FOCUS ON RESEARCH

The Effects of Sleep Deprivation

Most of what we know about sleep is based on the results of research conducted by *psychophysiologists*. Psychophysiologists are psychologists who study behavior and emotion by measuring such physiological responses as heart and respiration rates, muscle activity, electrical skin responses, and electrical activity in the brain. Their research helps us understand changes in brain activity in people who have been deprived of sleep or engaged in intense physical exertion.

Research conducted by psychophysiologists has revealed that sleep deprivation alters normal sleep rhythms during the following night, when subjects experience increased REM sleep and less deep sleep. This result is very different from the change in sleep patterns observed in runners after they race for 20 miles or farther. The night after an extremely strenuous race, runners spend less time in REM sleep and more time in deep sleep, especially in Stage 4 (Torsvall, Akerstedt, & Lindbeck, 1984).

Psychophysiologists have examined the effects of sleep deprivation on brain activity, but not its effect on behavior. Fortunately, health psychologists, developmental psychologists, cognitive psychologists, clinical psychologists, and neuropsychologists also conduct research on the effects of sleep deprivation. For example, *health psychologists* study the relationship between sleep deprivation and traffic accidents. *Developmental psychologists* examine the effects of sleep deprivation on children's temperament, cognitive development, and academic achievement. *Cognitive psychologists* concentrate on how sleep deprivation affects attention, thinking, memory, and language skills in children and adults. *Clinical psychologists* focus on the relationship between sleep deprivation and behavioral problems in clinical populations, such as people with asthma, sleep apnea, attention-deficit/hyperactivity disorder, schizophrenia, or autism. *Neuropsychologists* measure brain functioning in people who are sleep-deprived.

Avi Sadeh and his colleagues at Tel Aviv University recently examined the cognitive and behavioral effects of sleep deprivation in 135 healthy children in the second, fourth, and sixth grades (Sadeh, Gruber, & Raviv, 2002). To assess cognitive functioning, Sadeh and his colleagues used neuropsychological tests that included a continuous performance test (in which a child watched pictures of animals that were continually shown on a computer monitor and pressed a key as quickly as possible whenever a cat appeared) and a symbol-digit substitution test (in which a child was shown nine pairs of symbols and digits on the computer monitor and typed in corresponding digits).

Sadeh and his fellow investigators also used the Child Behavior Checklist, an assessment instrument developed by clinical psychologists to measure behavioral problems in the children.

Each child's sleep was monitored for five nights with a device that measured movement. The researchers calculated the number of hours the children slept and the number of times they awakened. Children who slept for fewer hours and who woke up more often performed less well than the other children on tests that required high levels of cognitive functioning, particularly the symbol-digit substitution test and the continuous performance test. This was especially true for the second-graders, the youngest children in the study, whose cognitive performance was seriously disrupted by a lack of sleep.

According to Sadeh and his colleagues, sleep deprivation was also associated with behavior problems. Children who woke up at least three times per night, or spent at least 10% of the night awake, had significantly higher scores on assessments of behavior problems. They were observed to be significantly more delinquent and to think in significantly more disordered ways than children who slept well during the test period. Using neuropsychological and clinical tests, these cognitive psychologists were able to demonstrate a relationship between sleep deprivation and cognitive and behavioral problems in children (Sadeh, Gruber, & Raviv, 2002).

Taken as a whole, research conducted by psychophysiologists and physiological, health, developmental, cognitive, and clinical psychologists has conclusively determined that sleep deprivation affects brain activity, cognition, mood, and behavior in adults and children.

REVIEW

Paying Attention

- *Attention* is the link between the enormous amount of information that assails our senses and the limited amount that we actually perceive.
- People use *selective attention* to track one message and simultaneously ignore others (such as in the *cocktail party phenomenon* or in shadowing).
- Two theories of selective attention are filter theories, according to which information is selectively blocked out or attenuated as it passes from one level of processing to the next, and attentional resource theories, according to which people have a fixed amount of attentional resources (perhaps modulated by sensory modalities) that they allocate according to the perceived requirements of a given task.

Levels of Consciousness

- *Consciousness* is a stream of thought or awareness—the state of mind by which we compare possibilities for what we might perceive, and then select some of these possibilities and reject others.
- Some of the functions of consciousness are to aid in our species' survival, to keep track of (monitor and evaluate) the environment, to sift important from unimportant information, and to facilitate memory and planning.
- John Locke believed that consciousness is essential to establishing a sense of personal identity.
- Consciousness occurs on multiple levels. The *preconscious* level is immediately prior to or just outside of consciousness. The *unconscious* level is deeper, and we normally can gain access to it only with great difficulty or via dreams.

Sleep

- Scientists have isolated several chemical sleep substances in our bodies, although it has not been verified that any of these is fully responsible for our normal sleep.
- In the absence of typical environmental cues, people seem to settle on a daily, or *circadian, rhythm* of about 25 hours.
- If people are deprived of sleep for several days, they show increasingly severe maladaptive symptoms. By the fourth day of deprivation, they often show signs of psychopathology, such as paranoid delusions of persecution.
- There are two basic kinds of sleep: *REM sleep* and *non-REM (N-REM) sleep*. The former is characterized by rapid eye movements and is usually accompanied by dreaming. N-REM sleep is customarily divided into a series of four stages of successively deeper sleep and is seldom accompanied by dreaming.
- *Insomnia* is a condition in which an individual has trouble falling asleep, wakes up during the night, or wakes up too early in the morning. *Narcolepsy* is a syndrome characterized by the strong impulse to sleep during the day or when it is otherwise undesirable to do so. *Sleep apnea* is a syndrome in which oxygen intake is temporarily impaired during sleep. *Somnambulism* (sleepwalking) most often occurs in children. Contrary to popular belief, somnambulists are typically not dreaming while they are engaging in wakeful-seeming behaviors in their sleep.

Dreams

- Several theories of dreaming have been proposed. According to Freud, dreams express the hidden wishes of the unconscious. Another view is that dreams represent a kind of mental housekeeping. A cognitive view holds that we work out our daily problems through dreams. According to McCarley and Hobson's *activation–synthesis hypothesis,* dreams represent our subjective interpretation of nocturnal brain activity.
- *Nightmares* are anxiety-arousing dreams that may lead to a person's waking up, sometimes seemingly to avoid some threat that emerges in the nightmares. *Night terrors* are sudden awakenings from N-REM sleep that are accompanied by feelings of intense fright or panic.

Hypnosis and Meditation

- *Hypnosis* is an altered state of consciousness in which a person becomes extremely sensitive to, and often compliant with, the communications of the hypnotist. The hypnotized person accepts distortions of reality that would not be accepted in the normal waking state of consciousness.
- Some psychologists question whether hypnotism is a genuine psychological phenomenon; they suggest instead that it is an epiphenomenon, in which research participants respond to demands, pleasing the hypnotist by doing what he or she says to do.
- A *posthypnotic suggestion* is a means by which hypnotized people can be asked to do something—typically something that they would not normally do or might have difficulty doing—after the hypnotic trance is removed.
- Various theories of hypnosis have been proposed. One theory views it as a form of deep relaxation. Another theory considers hypnosis as genuine involvement in a play-acted role. A third views it as a form of split

consciousness; that is, a hidden observer in the person observes what is going on, as though from the outside, at the same time that the person responds to hypnotic suggestions.

- *Meditation* is a set of techniques to alter one's state of consciousness by shifting away from an active, linear mode of thinking toward a more receptive and quiescen mode. Meditation generally decreases respiration, heart rate, blood pressure, and muscle tension.
- Two main kinds of meditation are *concentrative,* in which the meditator focuses on an object or thought and attempts to remove all else from consciousness, and *opening-up,* in which the meditator attempts to integrate meditation with, rather than separate it from, other activities.

Psychoactive Drugs

- A person's current state of consciousness can be altered by four kinds of *psychoactive* drugs: narcotics, CNS (central nervous system) depressants, CNS stimulants, and hallucinogens.
- *Narcotics,* including natural *opiates* and synthetic *opioids,* produce some degree of numbness, stupor, often a feeling of well-being, or freedom from pain.
- *Tolerance* is a lessening of the effects of a drug with prolonged use, which can lead users to take larger amounts of the drug. *Withdrawal* is the temporary discomfort, which may be severe, following discontinuation of a psychoactive drug.
- *Depressants,* including alcohol and *sedative* drugs, slow the operation of the central nervous system. In contrast, *stimulants,* including *caffeine, nicotine, cocaine,* and *amphetamines,* speed up the operation of the central nervous system.
- *Hallucinogens,* including LSD, marijuana, PCP, and ecstasy, produce distorted perceptions of reality.

CHAPTER 8 PRACTICE EXAM

____ 1. Selective attention is when
a. you try to listen to three different conversations.
b. dishabituation occurs during a psychology lecture.
c. habituation occurs during a psychology lecture.
d. Trying to track a message while ignoring another.

____ 2. An explanation of the Stroop effect considers
a. Conscious reading.
b. the automaticity of reading.
c. the automaticity of colors.
d. Deselective reading.

____ 3. The preconscious level contains
a. Information of which a person is currently aware.
b. Information about your dreams.
c. Information that remains out of awareness permanently.
d. Information that can be returned to awareness.

____ 4. Last year Julie fell off his bike and landed on the back of his head. The accident caused blindness, but one day someone threw a ball to him and he caught the ball. Julies ability to catch the ball is
a. blindsight.
b. hindsight.
c. Surreal.
d. impossible.

____ 5. Evolutionary theory hypothesizes that humans sleep because
a. We can get rid of body poisons.
b. We will wake up rested.
c. We won't be killed by predators.
d. We won't work too long during the day.

____ 6. Bodily functions that occur over 24 hours is
a. Sacral rhythm.
b. Circadian rhythm.
c. Bavarian rhythm.
d. Harmonious rhythm.

____ 7. Hallucinations are
a. Brain lightening.
b. Illusions of daydreaming.
c. perceptions of nonexistent objects.
d. perceptions of existent objects.

____ 8. Why is REM sleep called "paradoxical sleep"?
a. People are awake during REM sleepar awake during REM.
b. The brain activity is in the Delta stage but muscle tension is very high.
c. The brain's activity resembles a waking state but the person's muscle tension is very low.
d. People wake up and do not remember their dreams.

____ 9. Sleep Apnea involves
a. Using sleeping medications.
b. sudden sleep onset.
c. breathing difficulties during sleep.
d. Breathing difficulties during wakefulness.

____ 10. The activation-synthesis theory suggests people dream in order to
a. Activate and synthesize the neural network.
b. interpret our brain's neural activity while we sleep.
c. Let us know we are still alive.
d. Realize our preconscious desires in a safe manner.

____ 11. ________ often wake a person up to avoid a threat in the dream.
a. Night terrors
b. Preconscious dreams
c. Nightmares
d. Conscious dreams

____ 12. Drugs that alter behavior, mood, and consciousness are called
a. Not good.
b. preconcious.
c. behavioral.
d. psychoactive.

_____ 13. Chronic drinking may cause
a. Increased risk of heart disease.
b. reduced risk of heart disease.
c. Korsakoff's syndrome.
d. Smirnoff's syndrome.

_____ 14. Hallucinogens can lead to
a. Flashbacks.
b. Mania.
c. Psychosis.
d. Flashforwardselief of preexisting psychiatric disorders.

_____ 15. MDMA is
a. mescaline.
b. ecstasy.
c. cannabis.
d. peyote.

Answers

1. D
2. B
3. D
4. A
5. C
6. B
7. C
8. B
9. C
10. B
11. C
12. D
13. C
14. A
15. B

CHAPTER 9: COGNITION AND LANGUAGE

QUESTIONS

1. What do cognitive psychologists study?
2. What were the Hypothesis, Method, Results, and Interpretation of the Shepard and Metzler study (1971)?
3. What is categorization by prototype?
4. How do conceptual networks and priming work?
5. How does the spreading activation principle work?
6. How does priming help reading comprehension?
7. What were the Hypothesis, Method, Results, and Interpretation of the Word Meanings and Concepts in Different Languages study?
8. What happens to attention processes in the brain when we increase out attention to something specific?
9. Attention is increasing brain responses to what stimuli?
10. What is our attention drawn to and what does it depend on?
11. What is an example of a preattentive process?
12. What is an example of an attentive process?
13. What is a practical application of distinguishing between attentive and preattentive processes?
14. What is one explanation of the Stroop effect that will not work?
15. What are we primed to attend to when we are speaking or we are pointing?
16. Under what conditions does change blindness occur?
17. What were the methods and results of the Rensink, O'Rean, & Clark (1997) study on change blindness?
18. According to Henderson and Hollingworth (2003) when are people more likely to notice a changed object?
19. What is an example of change deafness?
20. How would you summarize representation of detail in visual and auditory stimuli?
21. Under what conditions can people do two things at once?
22. What can we not plan?
23. What is talking on a cell phone while driving more dangerous than listening to the radio?
24. What does research suggest about attention and people who spend a lot of time playing video games?
25. What is an example of a way to test attentional blink?
26. What is one explanation for the attentional blink?
27. What is the main thing becoming an expert requires?
28. What are some examples of areas where practice is important?
29. What is one thing experts are able to do with respect to patterns?
30. What are the four phases of problem solving?
31. What is an example of the difference between an algorithm and a heuristic?
32. What is the failure of transfer principle and two examples?
33. What are three reasons we have difficulty solving logically similar problems?
34. What is an insight problem?
35. Are insight problems solved suddenly or gradually?
36. What were the four characteristics of the creative people Gardner studied?
37. What is a major characteristic of creative people?
38. What are the ages of creative careers?
39. When might a simple heuristic work to solve a problem?
40. How can the representativeness heuristic lead people to incorrect conclusions by incorporation of base-rate information?
41. What are some examples of the availability heuristic?
42. What do we assume about the representativeness heuristic and availability heuristic and when do they lead us astray?
43. What are three examples of the availability heuristic?
44. How do people across cultures behave when choosing attractive but unlikely outcomes?
45. What are two reasons people prefer a low probability of a high gain?
46. What are examples of the confirmation bias and functional fixedness?
47. What are examples of the framing effect?
48. What are examples of the Sunk Cost Effect?
49. Who does not show the sunk cost effect?
50. What is the difference and examples of deep structure and surface structure?
51. What is the difference between Washoe's use of American sign language and a child's talking?
52. How do Bonobo's (*pan paniscus*) use of symbols similar to human language?
53. What are three possible reasons bonobos' (*pan paniscus*) use of symbols is impressive?
54. What evidence suggests that human language is not an accidental by-product of evolution?
55. What are the effects on language in people with a gene for language and Williams Syndrome children?

56. What did Chomsky suggest as to why humans learn language so easily?
57. What were the methods and results of the study in which people learned another language with real and fake grammars?
58. What are some characteristics of parentese?
59. How do infants learn the basics of language?
60. What is the difference between Broca's aphasia and Wernicke's aphasia?
61. What other processes are critical for the brain areas to be intact?
62. What are the language stages, typical ages, and typical abilities of each stage?
63. How does exposure to a lot of language, or little language affect language development?
64. What is language course for deaf infants?
65. What are some of the first sound infants make and the interpretation of those sounds?
66. What is the importance of context when children say single words?
67. What does "learn how to learn" the meaning of words mean?
68. What are some examples of idiosyncratic negatives?
69. What are some examples of overgeneralization rules?
70. How does language appear to unfold?
71. What is the critical period for learning language over time?
72. What is the evidence from deaf children concerning language learning?
73. What are some similarities of deaf children's sign language inventions?
74. What is the importance of early development of language?
75. What are the advantages and disadvantages of bilingualism?
76. How does context affect our perception of consonants?
77. What is the importance of lip movements in understanding?
78. What were the results of the Warren (1970) study?
79. What is the importance of context for comprehending words and sentences?
80. How long can people "hold" an ambiguous sound and how does that related to context?
81. What does language comprehension depend on?
82. What happens to our understanding of embedded sentences and double and triple negatives?
83. What were the methods and results of the jar experiment (Rozin, Markwith, & Ross, 1990)?
84. What evidence suggests we overestimate listener's comprehension?
85. What were the methods and results of the Reicher (1969) and Johnston and McClelland (1974) studies on word superiority?
86. What is one explanation for the word superiority effect?
87. How do our eyes move when we read?
88. Why can't we see our eyes move in the mirror?
89. What is the character limit of reading fixations?
90. What are the character limits of readers of different languages?
91. How does previewing the next word facilitate reading?
92. What is the average number of fixations per second and the average number of words read per minute?
93. What are the limits of speed reading?

VOCABULARY

1. algorithm
2. attention
3. attentional blink
4. attentive process
5. availability heuristic
6. base-rate information
7. bilingual
8. Broca's aphasia
9. change blindness
10. cognition
11. confirmation bias
12. critical thinking
13. fixation
14. framing effect
15. functional fixedness
16. heuristics
17. language acquisition devise
18. morpheme
19. overconfidence
20. phoneme
21. preattentive process
22. productivity
23. prototype
24. representativeness heuristic
25. saccade
26. spreading activation
27. Stroop effect
28. sunk cost effect
29. transformational grammar
30. Wernicke's aphasia
31. Williams syndrome
32. word-superiority effect

9

Cognition and Language

- Methods of Research in Cognitive Psychology
- Categorization
- Cross-Cultural Studies of Concepts
- Attention
- Attention Limits over Space and Time
- Problem Solving, Expertise, and Error
- Language

© Walter Hodges/CORBIS

COGNITION MEANS *thinking, gaining knowledge, and dealing with knowledge*. Cognitive psychologists study how people think, how they acquire knowledge, what they know, how they imagine, and how they solve problems. They also deal with how people organize their thoughts into language and communicate with others.

cognition
the processes of thinking, gaining knowledge, and dealing with knowledge.

Cognitive psychology increased in popularity after computers became popular. Although brains and computers do not work the same way, computers provide a valuable way of modeling theories of cognitive processes. A researcher may say, "Imagine that cognitive processes work as follows. . . . Now let's program a computer to go through those same steps. If we then give the computer the same information that a human has, will it draw the same conclusions and make the same errors as a human?" In short, computer modeling provides a way to test theories of cognition. Today, cognitive psychologists use a variety of methods to measure mental processes and to test theories about what we know and how we know it.

METHODS OF RESEARCH IN COGNITIVE PSYCHOLOGY

Perhaps it seems that cognitive psychology should be simple. "If you want to find out what people think or what they know, why not ask them?" Sometimes psychologists do ask, but people can't always describe their own thought processes (Kihlstrom, Barnhardt, & Tataryn, 1992). Recall, implicit memory sometimes you

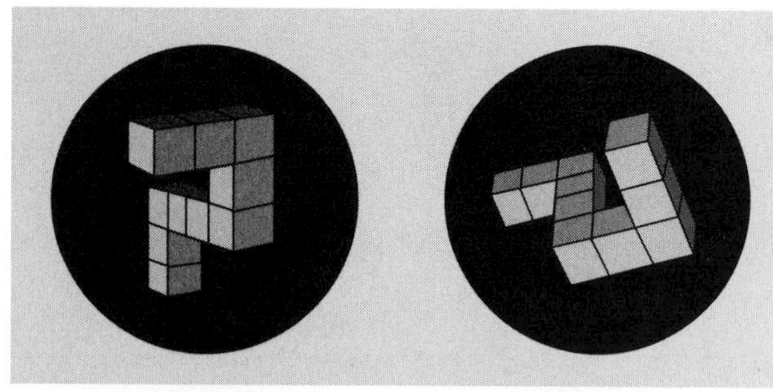

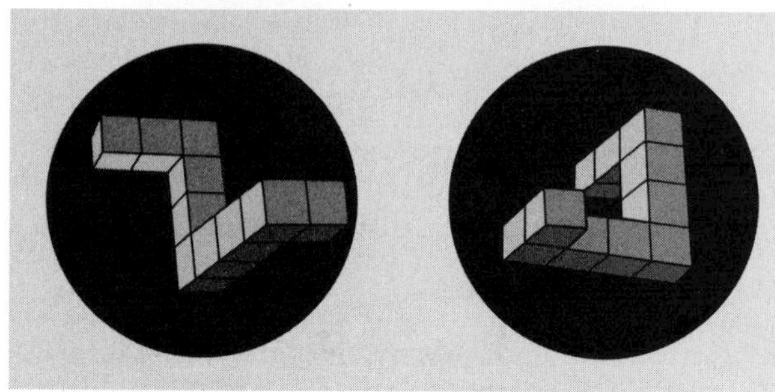

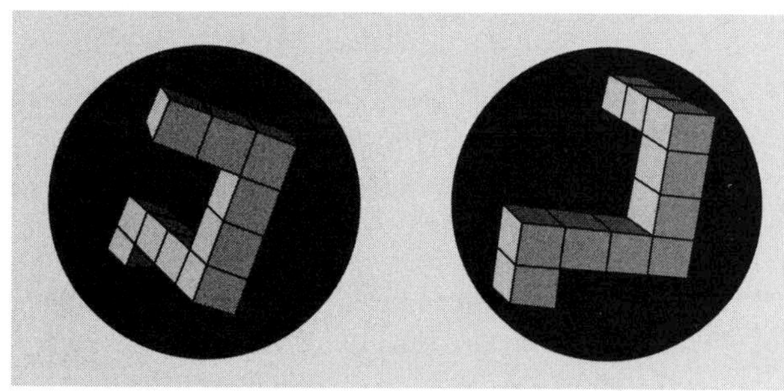

FIGURE 9.1

Examples of pairs of drawings used in an experiment by Shepard and Metzler (1971). Do the drawings for each pair represent the same object being rotated, or are they different objects? (*Reprinted with permission from "Mental Rotation of Three-Dimensional Objects," by R. N. Shepard and J. N. Metzler, Science, 1971, 171, 701–703. Copyright © 1980 American Association for the Advancement of Science.*)

see or hear something that influences your behavior without your realizing it. Similarly, we sometimes solve a problem without knowing how we did it.

Also, consider visual imagery. People often claim that they have a clear mental image of some object but then cannot correctly answer simple questions about it. To illustrate, imagine a simple cube balanced with one point (corner) on the table and the opposite point straight up. Imagine that you are holding the highest point with one finger. Now, using a finger of the opposite hand, point to all the remaining corners of the cube (not counting the one touching the table). How many corners do you touch?

You probably will say that you answered this question by "picturing" a cube in your mind as if you were actually seeing it. However, most people answer the question incorrectly, and few get it right quickly (Hinton, 1979).

In short, we cannot simply accept people's self reports about their thinking. So how *can* we measure thinking, a process that we obviously cannot observe? Physicists don't directly observe magnetic fields or electrical currents either. In each case researchers infer the unobservable processes from their effects. To illustrate, let's consider one of the classic experiments in cognitive psychology, which demonstrated a way to measure a mental process.

Mental Imagery

Roger Shepard and Jacqueline Metzler (1971) studied how humans solve visual problems. They reasoned that if people visualize mental images, then the time it takes them to rotate a mental image should be similar to the time needed to rotate a real object.

Hypothesis When people have to rotate a mental image to answer a question, the farther they have to rotate it, the longer it will take them to answer the question.

Method Participants examined pairs of drawings of three-dimensional objects, as in Figure 9.1, and indicated whether the two drawings represented one object and a rotated view of it or different objects.

People pulled one lever to indicate *same* and another lever to indicate *different.* When the correct answer was *same,* someone might determine that answer by rotating a mental image of the first picture until it matched the second. If so, the delay should depend on how far the image had to be rotated.

Results Participants answered almost 97% of the items correctly. As predicted, their reaction time when they responded *same* depended on the angular difference in orientation between the two views. For example, if the first image of a pair had to be rotated 30 degrees to match the second image, people needed a certain amount of time to pull the *same* lever. If an image had to be rotated 60 degrees to match the other, they took twice as long to pull the lever. In other words they reacted as if they were watching a model of the object rotate; the more the object needed to be rotated, the longer they took to determine the answer.

Interpretation First, viewing a mental image is at least partly like real vision. So, in this case common sense appears to be correct. Second, it is possible for researchers to infer thought processes from someone's delay in answering a question.

Some people report that they have auditory images as well as visual images. They "hear" words or songs "in their head." What kind of evidence would we need to test this claim?

CATEGORIZATION

An ancient Greek philosopher once said that you cannot step into the same river twice. He referred to the fact that the river changes, but in fact you change too from one time to the next. Nothing stays the same, and almost every concept refers to items that differ from one another. Nevertheless, to make reasonable decisions, we have to treat similar objects similarly. A major part of thinking is the formation of categories or concepts.

Ways of Describing a Category

Do we look up our concepts in a mental dictionary to determine their meaning? A few words have simple, unambiguous definitions. For example, we think of the term *bachelor* as an unmarried male. Because we would not ordinarily apply the term bachelor to a young child or to a Catholic priest, we might refine the definition to "a male who has not yet married but could." That definition pretty well explains the concept.

Many concepts are harder to define, however. Try defining *country music,* for example. Also, imagine a man who loses one hair from his head. Is he bald? Of course not. Then he loses one more hair, then another and another. Eventually, he *is* bald, so was there some point at which losing one more hair made him bald? We are forced to that absurdity if we use baldness as a yes/no category. (Similar problems arise if we try to classify everyone as depressed or not, schizophrenic or not, and alcoholic or not. Almost everything comes in degrees.)

Eleanor Rosch (1978; Rosch & Mervis, 1975) argued that many categories are best described by *familiar or typical examples* called **prototypes.** We decide whether an object belongs to a category by determining how much it resembles the prototypes of that category. For example, we define the category "vehicle" by examples: *car, bus, train, airplane, boat, truck.* Is a *blimp* also a vehicle? What about an *elevator* or *water skis*? These other items resemble the prototypes in some ways but not others, so they are marginal members of the category, which has fuzzy boundaries.

prototype
a familiar or typical example of a category.

However, some categories cannot be described by prototypes (Fodor, 1998). For example, we can talk and think about "bug-eyed monsters from outer space" without ever encountering a single prototype of that category.

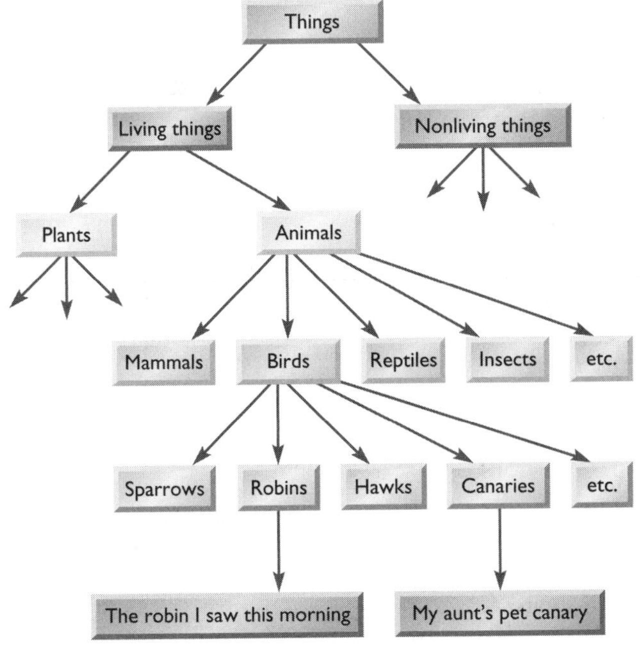

Conceptual Networks and Priming

Choose any concept and try to think about only it and nothing else. It's impossible. You can't really think about something without relating it to something else. When you think about some concept, for example *bird,* you link it to more specific terms, such as *sparrow,* more general terms, such as *animals,* and related terms such as *flight* and *eggs.*

We naturally organize items into hierarchies, such as animal as a higher level category, bird as intermediate, and sparrow as a lower level category. Researchers demonstrate the reality of this kind of hierarchy by measuring the delay for people to answer various questions (A. M. Collins &

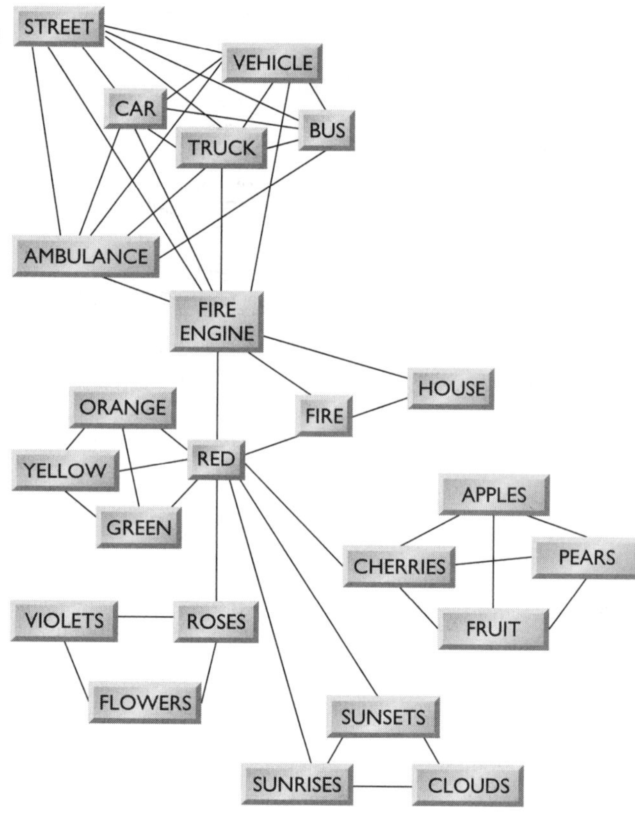

FIGURE 9.2

We link each concept to a variety of other related concepts. Any stimulus that activates one of these concepts will also partly activate (or "prime") the ones that are linked to it. (*From A. M. Collins & Loftus, 1975*)

Quillian, 1969, 1970). Answer the following true/false questions as quickly as possible:

- Canaries are yellow.
- Canaries sing.
- Canaries lay eggs.
- Canaries have feathers.
- Canaries have skin.

Presumably you answered "true" to all five items, but you may have answered some faster than others. Most people answer fastest on the *yellow* and *sing* items, slightly slower on the *eggs* and *feathers* items, and still slower on the *skin* item. Why? It is because yellowness and singing are distinctive characteristics of canaries. You probably do not think of eggs or feathers specifically as canary features; instead you reason (quickly), "Canaries are birds, and birds lay eggs. So canaries must lay eggs." Skin is not even distinctive of birds, so you have to reason, "Canaries are birds and birds are animals. Animals have skin, so canaries must have skin." Even though this way of categorizing things delays you slightly in answering whether canaries have skin, it saves you enormous effort overall. When you learn some new fact about birds or animals in general, you don't have to learn it again separately for every individual species. Reasoning in terms of categories and subcategories simplifies our memory.

We also link a word or concept to other concepts related to it. Figure 9.2 shows a possible network of conceptual links that someone might have at a particular moment (A. M. Collins & Loftus, 1975). Suppose this network describes your own concepts. *Thinking about one of the concepts shown in this figure will activate, or prime, the concepts linked to it* (A. M. Collins & Loftus, 1975). This process is called **spreading activation**. For example, if you hear *flower*, you are primed to think of *rose, violet,* and various other flowers. If you also hear *red*, the combination of *flower* and *red* strongly primes you to think of *rose*. You might think of the word spontaneously, and you would recognize it more easily than usual if it were flashed briefly on a screen or spoken very softly.

spreading activation
the process by which the activation of one concept also activates or primes other concepts that are linked to it.

Priming is important during reading. When you come to a difficult word that you barely know, you find it easier to understand if the preceding sentences were about closely related concepts (Plaut & Booth, 2000). In effect they provide hints about the meaning of the new word.

Here is an illustration that can be explained in terms of a spreading activation model. Quickly answer each of the following questions (or ask someone else):

1. How many animals of each kind did Moses take on the ark?
2. What was the famous saying uttered by Louis Armstrong when he first set foot on the moon?
3. Some people pronounce St. Louis "saint loo-iss" and some pronounce it "saint loo-ee." How would you pronounce the capital city of Kentucky?

The answers are in the footnote on this page.[1] Many people miss these questions and are then embarrassed or angry. Figure 9.3 offers an explanation in terms of

[1] Answers: 1. None. Moses didn't have an ark; Noah did. 2. Louis Armstrong never set foot on the moon; it was Neil Armstrong. 3. The right pronunciation of Kentucky's capital is "frank-furt." (Not "loo-ee-ville"!)

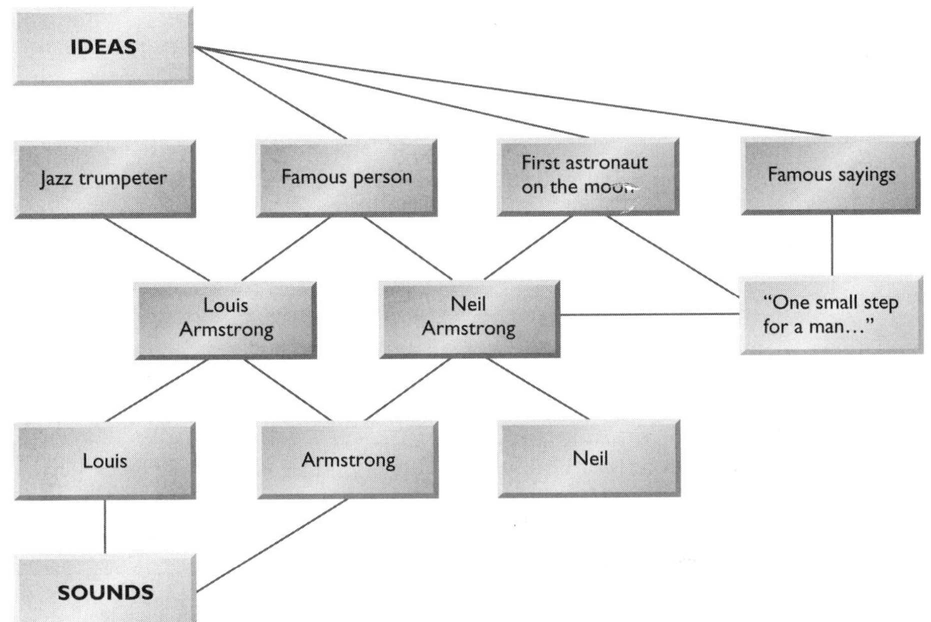

FIGURE 9.3

According to one explanation, the word *Armstrong* and the ideas *astronaut, first person on the moon,* and *famous sayings* all activate the linked saying "One small step for a man . . ." Even the word *Louis* contributes, because both Louis Armstrong and Neil Armstrong were famous people.

spreading activation (Shafto & MacKay, 2000): The question about Louis Armstrong activates a series of sounds and concepts that are linked to one another and to other items. The sound *Armstrong* and the ideas *first astronaut on the moon* and *famous sayings* are all linked to "One small step for a man . . ." Even the name *Louis Armstrong* is loosely linked to *Neil Armstrong* because both are famous people. (You probably would not respond the same way to a question about "What was the famous line uttered by Jennifer Armstrong . . .?") The combined effect of all these influences automatically triggers the answer, "One small step for a man . . ."

CROSS-CULTURAL STUDIES OF CONCEPTS

When you and I use the same term—river, vehicle, free will, or anything else—do we really have the same concept? Do people of different cultures and languages have the same concepts? People fluent in two languages sometimes remark that something gets lost in translation; a translated statement doesn't mean in English exactly the same as what it meant in Russian. Let's start with one line of research that measures differences in meaning for what are regarded as equivalent words in different languages.

Word Meanings and Concepts in Different Languages

Hypothesis Even though a word in one language is considered a translation of a word in another language, people will use them in *different* ways. For example, the English word *bottle* is considered a translation of the Spanish word *botella*, and the English word *jar* is translated as the Spanish word *frasco*. Nevertheless, they might not apply to all the same objects.

Method Researchers showed English-, Argentinean Spanish-, and Chinese-speaking people a large array of objects, including those shown in Figure 9.4 Researchers asked them what word they would use for each. They also asked people to arrange pictures of the objects into groups of "similar" objects.

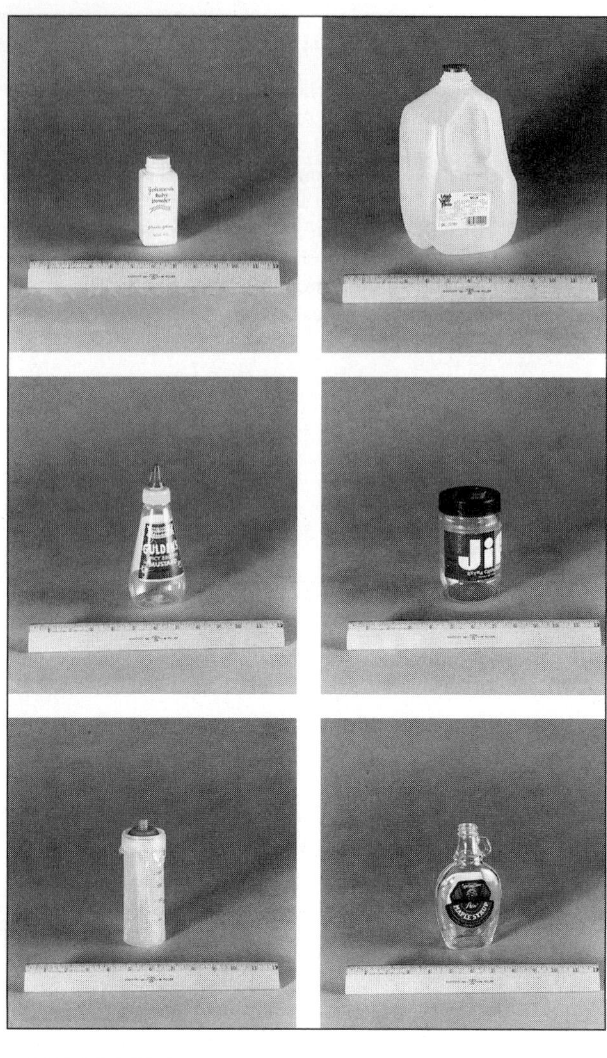

FIGURE 9.4

What word would you use for each of these objects? Would all the objects you call *bottle* translate as *botella* in Spanish? (*From Malt, Sloman, Gennari, Shi, & Wang, "Knowing vs. Naming: Similarity and the Linguistic Categorization of Artifacts,"* Journal of Memory and Language, 40, *230–262, 1999.*)

Results U.S. English speakers used seven words for the various objects—*jar, bottle, container, can, jug, tube,* and *box.* Argentinean Spanish speakers used fifteen words for the same objects, and Chinese speakers used five. Of the sixteen objects called *bottle* in English, many were called *botella* in Spanish, but a total of six other names were given to some of them. One Chinese term applied to all the objects called *jar* in English but also applied to some of the objects considered *bottles* or *containers.*

However, when people were asked to arrange pictures of objects into groups of similar items, users of the three languages made remarkably similar categories. That is, people might put several objects into the same group, even though they gave them different names (Malt, Sloman, & Gennari, 2003; Malt, Sloman, Gennari, Shi, & Wang, 1999).

Interpretation The simple conclusion is that words don't translate exactly. Generally, the items that English-speakers considered good examples (prototypes) of *bottle* were also considered good examples of *botella* in Spanish and so forth. However, people disagreed about how to label many marginal cases. On the other hand, differences in what people called objects had little apparent influence on which objects they considered similar. So, in this case the results suggest that people speaking different languages do not think very differently. (Obviously, we should not generalize too far based on this one example.)

ATTENTION

You are constantly bombarded with sights, sounds, smells, and other kinds of sensation. **Attention** is *your tendency to respond to some stimuli more than others at any given time or to remember some more than others.* Attention can shift or select. That is, you attend to different items at different times.

attention
the tendency to respond to some stimuli more than others or to remember some more than others.

To illustrate, recall that the fovea of your retina receives the most detail. Ordinarily, you remember mainly what was in your fovea, and that information has the biggest impact on your behavior. However, it is possible to direct your attention elsewhere. For example, you might not want someone to know that you are watching him or her, so you look off to the side, but you nevertheless concentrate on that person. You can demonstrate your ability to shift attention with the following. Fixate your eyes on the x in the center, and then without moving your eyes, read the letters in the circle around it clockwise:

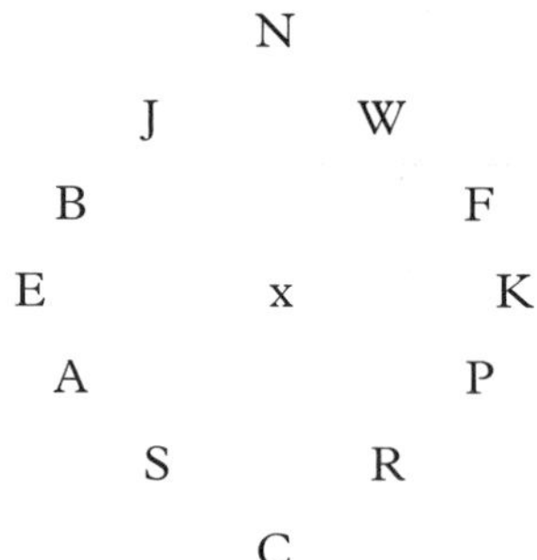

As you see, focusing your attention away from the center of your vision is difficult but possible. You can even attend to two nonadjacent spots at once—for example, the places occupied by A and F in the display above. When you increase your attention to something in your visual field, the part of your visual cortex sensitive to that area becomes more active and receives more blood flow (Müller, Malinowski, Gruber, & Hillyard, 2003). Also, if you try to pay extra attention to the color or motion of the next object to be shown on the screen, then the brain areas sensitive to color or motion become more active, even before the object appears (Driver & Frith, 2000). So attention is a process of increasing the brain's response to certain classes of stimuli. Nevertheless, explaining exactly how all this happens is a major challenge.

Preattentive and Attentive Processes

In the example just described, you deliberately shifted your attention from one letter to another. Often, however, objects grab your attention automatically when they start to move (Abrams & Christ, 2003) or because they are brightly colored or surprising in some way. I once watched an unusual costume contest. People were told to dress so distinctively that their friends or family could find them in a crowd as quickly as possible. The winner was a young man who came onto the stage naked. Although I concede that he earned the prize, there is a problem with this contest: The most distinctive clothing (or lack of it) depends on what everyone else is wearing. A naked person would be easy to spot in a shopping mall, but not quite so easy at a beach and not at all at a nudist beach. Our attention is drawn to the unusual, but what is unusual depends on the context. Ordinarily, we notice something that is flashing on and off, but if almost everything is flashing on and off, our attention is drawn to the one thing that isn't (Pashler & Harris, 2001).

To illustrate how an unusual object draws attention, look at Figure 9.5, which shows a huge flock of sandhill cranes plus one whooping crane. Find the whooping crane—the one that's different. That was easy, wasn't it? When an object differs drastically from those around it in size, shape, or color, we find it by a **preattentive process,** *meaning that it stands out immediately; we don't have to shift attention from one object to another.* Because the distinctive item jumps out preattentively, the number of sandhill cranes is irrelevant. Even if someone added or subtracted a few, you would find the whooping crane just as fast.

preattentive process
a procedure for extracting information automatically and simultaneously across a large portion of the visual field.

FIGURE 9.5
Demonstration of preattentive processes: Find the one whooping crane among the sandhill cranes. It stands out immediately. You would find the whooping crane just as fast in a much larger or much smaller flock of sandhill cranes.

FIGURE 9.6

Demonstration of attentive processes: Find the marbled godwit that is facing to the right. In this case you need an attentive process, checking the birds one at a time.

Contrast that task with Figure 9.6. Here the photo shows a flock of marbled godwits. Most of them are facing to your left; your task is to find the one that is facing to your right. Now you have to check each one separately, and the more birds present, the longer you will need, on the average, to find the one you are looking for. (You might find it quickly if you are lucky enough to start your search in the correct corner of the photograph.) You had to rely on an **attentive process**—*one that requires searching through the items in series* (Enns & Rensink, 1990; Treisman & Souther, 1985). (The *Where's Waldo* books are an excellent example of a task requiring an attentive process.) Studies of brain activity confirm that when we are searching through a complex display for an item that is hard to find, we are shifting attention (and the brain's responsiveness) from one area to another (Woodman & Luck, 2003).

The distinction between attentive and preattentive processes has practical applications. Imagine yourself as an ergonomist (human factors psychologist) designing machinery with several gauges. When the apparatus is running safely, the first gauge should read about 70, the second 40, the third 30, and the fourth 10, and any reading far from these normal values is dangerous. If you arrange the gauges as in the top row of Figure 9.7, then people using this machine must check each gauge separately to find anything dangerous. Note how the bottom row of Figure 9.7 simplifies the process: All the gauges are arranged so that the safe range is on the right. Now someone can glance at the display and quickly (preattentively) notice anything out of position.

attentive process
a procedure that extracts information from one part of the visual field at a time.

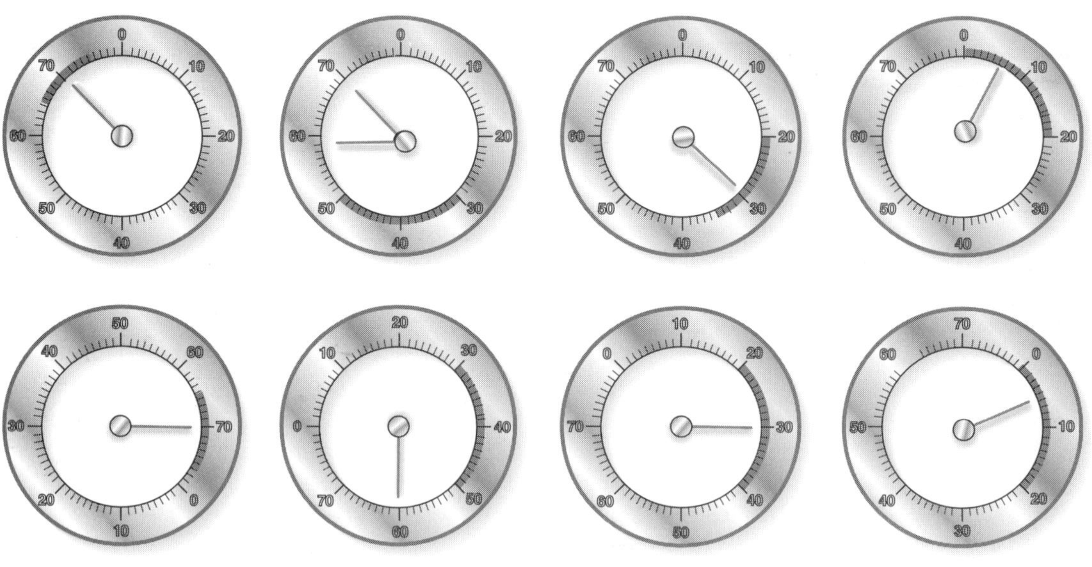

FIGURE 9.7

Each gauge represents a measurement of a different variable in a machine, such as an airplane. The top row shows one way of presenting the information. The operator must check each gauge one at a time to find out whether the reading is within the safe range for that variable. The bottom row shows the information represented in a way that is easier to read. The safe range for each variable is rotated to the same visual position. At a glance the operator can detect any reading outside the safe zone.

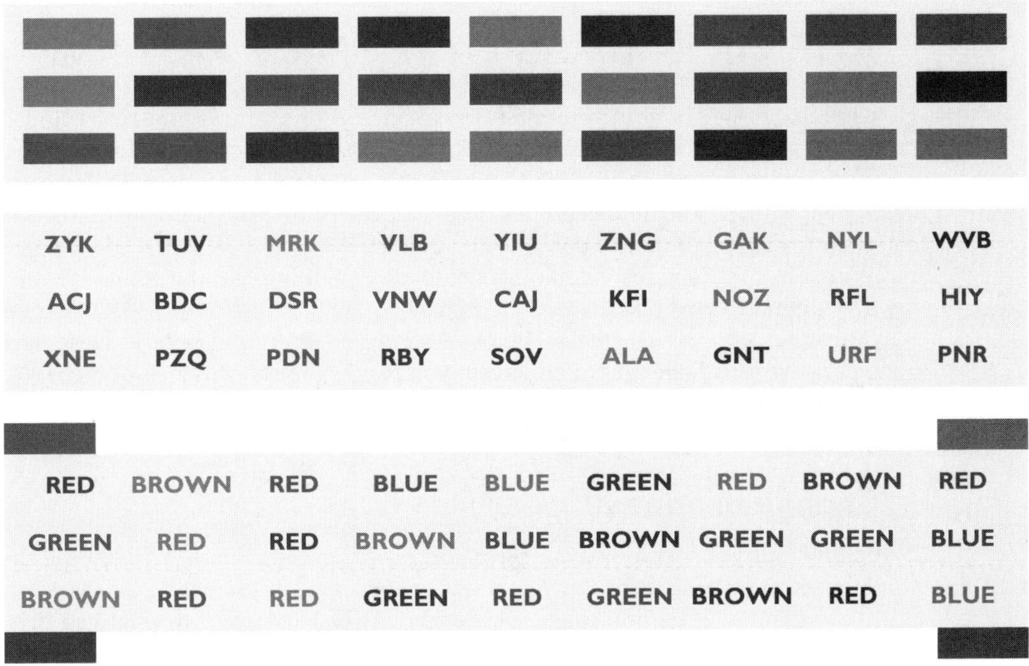

FIGURE 9.8
Read (left to right) the color of the ink in each part. Try to ignore the words themselves.

The Stroop Effect

Here is another example of something that grabs our attention automatically: Read the following instructions and then examine Figure 9.8:

> Notice the blocks of color at the top of the figure. Scanning from left to right, give the name of each color as fast as you can. Then notice the nonsense syllables printed in different colors in the center of the figure. Don't try to pronounce them; just say the color of each one as fast as possible. Then turn to the real words at the bottom. Don't read them; quickly state the color in which each one is printed.

Most people find it very difficult to ignore the words at the bottom of the figure. After all of your years of reading, you can hardly bring yourself to look at RED and say "green." *The tendency to read the word, instead of saying the color of ink as instructed,* is known as the **Stroop effect**, after the psychologist who discovered it.

stroop effect
the tendency to read a word, especially if it is a color name, in spite of instructions to disregard the word and state the color of the ink in which it is printed.

One explanation of the Stroop effect that we can discard is the idea that words always take priority over colors. Try the following: Go back to Figure 9.8 and notice the red, green, blue, and yellow patches at the four corners. This time, instead of saying anything, point to the correct color patch. First, try pointing to the color patch corresponding to the color of the ink; that is, when you come to RED, point to the blue patch in the lower left. Then try it again but point to the color corresponding to the meaning of the word. That is, when you come to RED, point to the red patch in the upper left. Try it now.

You probably found it easy to point to the patch that matches the color of the ink and harder to point to the color matching the word meaning (Durgin, 2000). When you are speaking, you are primed to read the words you see, but when you are pointing, you are more primed to attend to something nonverbal, such as ink color. In either case one response dominates, and it interferes with the less dominant response.

ATTENTION LIMITS OVER SPACE AND TIME

How much can you hold in your attention at once? For example, imagine yourself in the control room of the Three Mile Island nuclear power plant, the site of a nearly disastrous accident in 1979. Figure 9.9 shows a small portion of the room as it appeared then. You notice immediately the enormous number of knobs and gauges for what is, after all, a complicated system. What you cannot see in the picture is that in certain cases the knob controlling something and the gauge measuring it were in different places.

Since then the controls have been redesigned to simplify the task. Designing good controls is a challenge for engineers and psychologists with a combination of theoretical and applied interests. One of the main issues they face is understanding the limits of human attention.

change blindness
the tendency to fail to detect changes in any part of a scene to which we are not focusing our attention.

Change Blindness

If you look out your window, you see a scene with many objects. Do you see the whole scene at once? If a display disappears but a signal immediately calls your attention to one part of the display, you can say what had been there. So, in a sense you did see the whole scene. However, if nothing calls your attention to a particular spot, then how much did you see and how well could you recall it? If you have scanned around the scene, briefly fixating practically everything, do you now know everything in the scene?

Most people think they do, and they believe they would notice anything that changed. However, movie directors discovered long ago that they could shoot different parts of a story segment on different days, and few viewers would notice that some of the actors had changed clothes, that some of the props had moved, or that the extra actors in the background were different people (Simons & Levin, 2003).

Psychologists have named this phenomenon **change blindness**—*the frequent failure to detect changes in parts of a scene.* If anything moves or changes its appearance suddenly in any way, it automatically draws your attention. However, if a similar change occurs slowly or during an instant you are not watching, you might not notice. Have you ever seen one of those puzzles that ask you to "find ten differences between these two pictures"? The difficulty of finding them all indicates that you don't exactly "see" everything you look at.

In one experiment people looked at a screen that alternated between two views of a scene, as shown in Figure 9.10. Each view appeared for 560 milliseconds (ms), followed by a blank screen for 80 ms, and then the other view for 560 ms, with the sequence repeating until the viewer detected how the two scenes differed. Generally, viewers found differences in important features of the scene faster than changes in less central details, but on the average they took almost 11 seconds to find a difference. On some pairs of pictures the average viewer needed more than 50 seconds (Rensink, O'Regan, & Clark, 1997).

Even without an intervening blank screen, people often fail to detect a change in the scene if the change happens while they are blinking their eyes or even while moving their eyes to focus on a different area (Henderson & Hollingworth, 2003b).

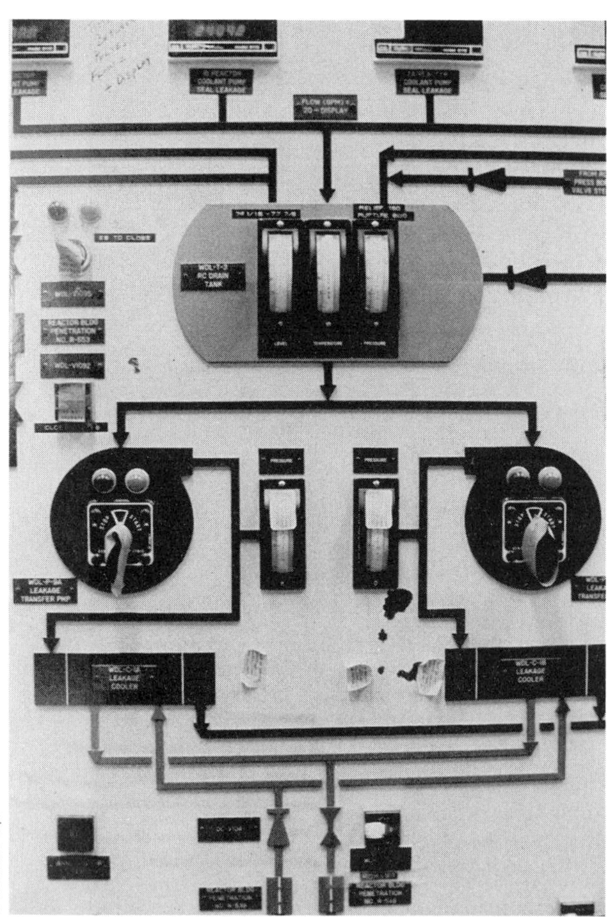

FIGURE 9.9
The Three Mile Island TMI-2 nuclear power plant had a complex and confusing control system, a small portion of which is shown here. Some of the important gauges were not easily visible, some were poorly labeled, and many alarm signals had ambiguous meanings. After the accident in 1979, the control system was redesigned and simplified.

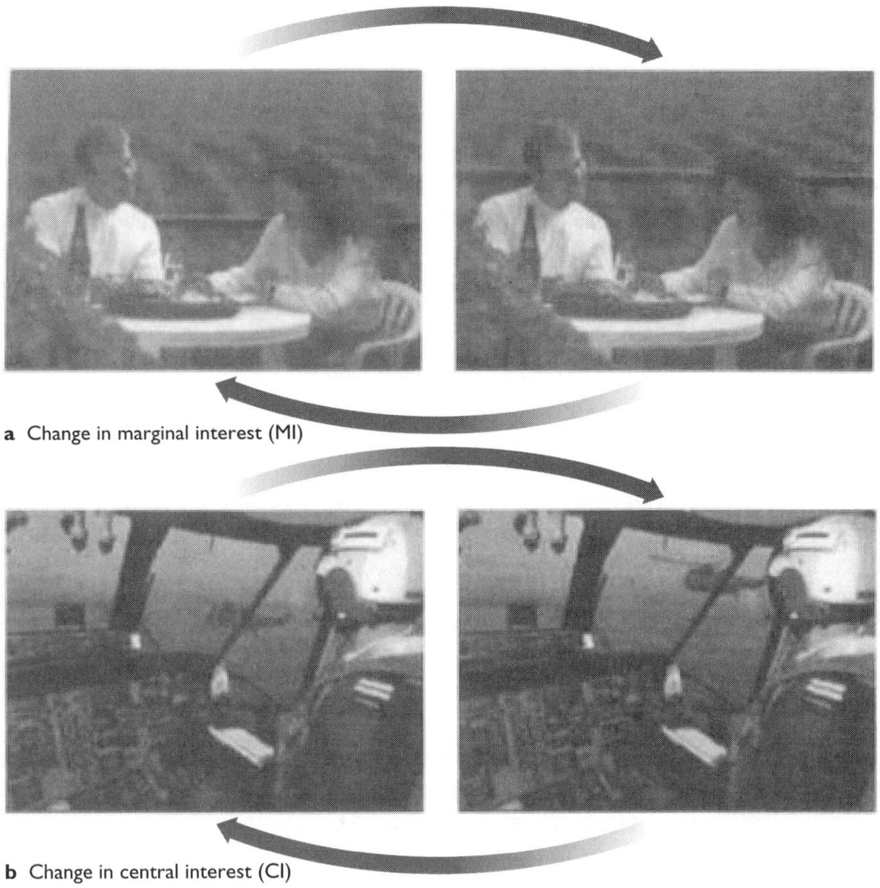

a Change in marginal interest (MI)

b Change in central interest (CI)

FIGURE 9.10

Viewers' task was to detect what was different between the two scenes, which were presented in alternation. The top scene has a change in a usually unattended detail; the lower scene has a change in a more important feature. *(Rensink, R. A., O'Regan, J. K., and Clark, J. J. (1997). "To see or not to see: The need for attention to perceive changes in scenes."* Psychological Science, 8, *368–373. Figure 2, p. 370. Reprinted with permission of Blackwell Publishing.)*

They are more likely to notice a changed object if their eyes were moving toward that object than if moving away (Henderson & Hollingworth, 2003a).

Would viewers notice a change in a display even if they had already paid attention to every part of the display? In one experiment students looked at a circular array of one-digit numbers, as shown in Figure 9.11, for 2 seconds. During that time they had to attend to each digit to answer a question such as, "What is the highest digit included?" or "What is the lowest digit *not* included?" Then the display went blank for 150 milliseconds and reappeared. The viewers' task was to say whether any of the digits had changed. They detected a change only about one third of the time (Becker & Pashler, 2002).

In sound we have change deafness, analogous to change blindness. In one study students tried to repeat the words they heard someone speak, as quickly as possible. After a 1-minute rest break, the procedure continued, but in some cases with a new voice speaking the words. Only about half of the students noticed the change (Vitevitch, 2003).

Overall, the apparent conclusion is that you do not maintain a detailed representation of what you have seen or heard. You hold a few details, but which details you hold vary from one time to another. (That's what we mean by attention.) You do retain the gist of the rest of the scene but not in detail (Becker & Pashler, 2002; Tatler, Gilchrist, & Rusted, 2003). We ordinarily remember a few details and only the gist of the rest of the story.

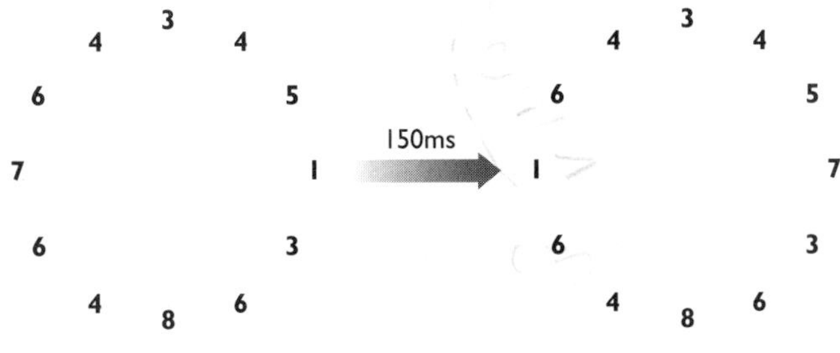

FIGURE 9.11

In the experiment by Becker and Pashler (2002), people saw a circular array of numbers for 2 seconds and then, after a 150 millisecond delay, saw the same or a changed array. People usually failed to detect the change.

Shifting Attention

Paying attention to one thing detracts from attention to something else (Pashler, 1994). Can you do two things at once? Yes, you can *do* two things at once, especially if one of them is simple or highly practiced. However, you cannot *plan* two actions at once. For example, if you have to respond to one signal that tells you something to say and another signal that tells you which computer key to press, you can't make both responses as fast as you could make just one or the other (Ruthruff, Pashler, & Hazeltine, 2003; Ruthruff, Pashler, & Klaassen, 2001).

Many years ago, when automobile radios were introduced, people worried that listening to the radio would distract drivers and cause accidents. We no longer worry about radio, but we do worry about drivers using cell phones, and some states and countries have outlawed driving while holding a cell phone. Even if you don't have to hold the phone, listening with a phone on one ear tends to shift your attention toward that side of the body instead of straight ahead (Spence & Read, 2003). Also, conversations require more attention than radio, and a cell-phone conversation is more distracting than one with a passenger in the car because most passengers pause a conversation when they see that driving conditions are difficult. Research on simulated driving finds that a cell-phone conversation decreases a driver's attention to signs and increases the risk of accidents (Stayer, Drews, & Johnston, 2003).

The way you divide your attention among tasks is not fixed from birth; you can change it—perhaps unintentionally. For example, the research indicates that people who spend much time playing complex action video games learn to divide their attention widely over the video screen. That division of attention helps while playing the games, and probably in some real-life situations too, but on the other hand, it impairs the ability to concentrate on just one item. That is, habitual video game players tend to be distracted by irrelevant stimuli in their peripheral vision that most other people ignore (C. S. Green & Bavelier, 2003). Not much is known yet about this process, but it opens the way for further research: Might certain kinds of video games be either helpful or harmful to people with, say, attention deficit disorder?

The Attentional Blink

Just as we don't attend equally to every point in space, we also don't attend equally at all points in time. It takes time to shift attention from one item to another.

The demonstration of this point is called the **attentional blink**: *During a brief time after perceiving one stimulus, it is difficult to attend to something else*. Just as you don't see anything during a brief blink of the eyes, you don't attend to something during the attentional "blink." For example, suppose you watch a screen that displays a series of letters, one at a time for 90 ms each. Every series includes one letter in blue ink, and it may or may not include the letter T. Your task is to name the blue letter and say whether or not a T appeared. Here are two series and their correct answers:

attentional blink
a brief period after perceiving a stimulus, during which it is difficult to attend to another stimulus.

D S R B **J A O E C V** "B, no."
Y L H F X G **W K T Q** "G, yes."

Most people miss the T (and say "no") if the T appears during a period about 100 to 700 ms after the blue letter. Similar results occur with many other kinds of stimuli and several variations of this procedure (Visser, Bischof, & DiLollo, 1999). It is an interesting demonstration theoretically and also a useful way of measuring how quickly various people can switch attention. For example, people with attention deficit disorder—known for their difficulty in controlling attention—have an unusually long attentional blink and often miss a target letter (T in the preceding example) even a full second after the blue letter (Hollingsworth, McAuliffe, & Knowlton, 2001). One exception: You might not notice most words if they are presented during the attentional blink, but you do notice your own name (K. L. Shapiro, Caldwell, & Sorensen, 1997).

Note that calling this phenomenon the attentional blink does not explain it. Why do we not notice a second stimulus 100 to 700 ms after the first one? "Because of the attentional blink." How do we know there is such a thing as an attentional blink? "Because we ignore a second stimulus 100 to 700 ms after the first one." Among several possible explanations that psychologists have been considering, one is that while the brain is "binding" the first stimulus into a single object, it cannot bind the second one and therefore does not fully perceive it (Raymond, 2003). Clearly, much more research is needed here.

Think About It

When you read or listen to someone talk, one word or syllable follows another with very short delays. Why doesn't the attentional blink stop you from hearing or reading some of the words?

Answers to Other Questions in the Chapter

A. The cube has six (not four) remaining corners.

© Glenn Riley

B. The objects in pair a are the same; in b they are the same; and in c they are different.

C. In the top scene, a horizontal bar along the wall has changed position. In the lower scene, the location of the helicopter has changed.

PROBLEM SOLVING, EXPERTISE, AND ERROR

On a college physics exam, a student was asked how to use a barometer to determine the height of a building. He answered that he would tie a long string to the barometer, go to the top of the building, and carefully lower the barometer until it reached the ground. Then he would cut the string and measure its length.

When the professor marked this answer incorrect, the student asked why. "Well," said the professor, "your method would work, but it's not the method I wanted you to use." When the student objected, the professor offered as a compromise to let him try again.

"All right," the student said. "Take the barometer to the top of the building, drop it, and measure the time it takes to hit the ground. Then, from the formula for the speed of a falling object, using the gravitational constant, calculate the height of the building."

"Hmmm," replied the professor. "That too would work. And it does make use of physical principles. But it still isn't the answer I had in mind. Can you think of another way?"

"Another way? Sure," he replied. "Place the barometer next to the building on a sunny day. Measure the height of the barometer and the length of its shadow. Also measure the length of the building's shadow. Then use the formula

> height of barometer ÷ height of building = length of barometer's shadow ÷ length of building's shadow

The professor was impressed but still reluctant to give credit, so the student persisted with another method: "Measure the barometer's height. Then walk up the stairs of the building, marking it off in units of the barometer's height. At the top take the number of barometer units and multiply by the height of the barometer to get the height of the building."

How would you carry 98 water bottles—all at one time, with no vehicle? When faced with a new problem, sometimes people find a novel and effective solution, and sometimes they do not.

The professor sighed: "Give me one more way—any other way—and I'll give you credit, even if it's not the answer I wanted."

"Really?" asked the student with a smile. "*Any* other way?"

"Yes, any other way."

"All right," said the student. "Go to the man who owns the building and say, 'Hey, buddy, if you tell me how tall this building is, I'll give you this cool barometer!'"

Whenever we face a new problem, we must devise a new solution instead of relying on a memorized or practiced solution. Sometimes people develop creative, imaginative solutions like the ones that the physics student proposed. Sometimes they offer less imaginative but reasonable solutions or something quite illogical or no solution at all. Psychologists study problem-solving behavior partly to understand the thought processes behind it and partly to look for ways to help people reason more effectively.

Expertise

People vary in their performance on problem-solving and decision-making tasks. In the barometer story just described, we would probably talk about the student's creativity; in other cases we might talk of expertise. Expertise is a high level of thinking and knowledge in a particular field and therefore an example of outstanding cognition.

If you want to become an expert on something, what would you have to do? Above all, you would have to learn facts . . . many, many facts. Computer programmers realized that need when they tried to develop software to answer people's questions (C. Thompson, 2001). For example, if a Web site is to advise someone on travel plans, it should be able to say, "Because you are claustrophobic, you should avoid taking the Channel Tunnel from England to France." But to do so, the program needs to be told that:

- Claustrophobic people dislike long tunnels.
- The Channel Tunnel is 31 miles long.
- In this context anything more than 50 feet is considered "long."
- 31 miles is longer than 50 feet.

To get a Web site to answer various other questions, programmers had to provide the following information:

- Water is wet.
- Every person has a mother.
- You should carry a glass of water open end up.
- When people die, they stay dead.
- If you melt a statue, it is no longer a statue.

These facts are so obvious that stating them seems humorous. The point is that even the simplest decisions require a huge array of facts, and expert decisions require even more.

Practice Makes (Nearly) Perfect Expert performance can be extremely impressive. An expert crossword puzzle solver not only completes *The New York Times* Sunday crossword—an impressive feat in itself—but tries to make it more interesting by racing against someone else. An expert bird watcher can look at a blurry photo of a bird and identify not only the species but also sometimes the subspecies and whether the bird is male or female, juvenile or adult, and in summer or winter plumage.

It is tempting to assume that experts were born with a special talent or great intelligence. Not so, say psychologists who have studied expertise. Winning contestants memorize a shuffled deck of cards in less than 40 seconds or a 300-digit number in 5 minutes. Psychologists tested 10 of the top memory performers and found that their mean IQ score was 111, as compared to a mean of 100 for the whole population (Maguire, Valentine, Wilding, & Kapur, 2003). A score of 111 is above average but hardly unusual. These people had developed their skills mainly by practicing the method of loci (page 250). They were no better than anyone else at remembering a series of photographs—a memory task they had not practiced because it is not part of the contest.

Similarly, in fields ranging from chess to sports to violin playing, the rule is that expertise requires about 10 years of concentrated practice (Ericsson & Charness, 1994; Ericsson, Krampe, & Tesch-Römer, 1993). The top violin players say they have practiced 3 to 4 hours every day since early childhood. A world-class tennis player spends hours working on backhand shots; a golfer works on chip shots. American writer John Irving is dyslexic and says it always took him longer than others to complete reading and writing assignments in school. By his own assessment, he is not a "talented" writer; he succeeded only because of long, hard work and a willingness to undertake many revisions (Amabile, 2001). In short, experts are made, not born, and they are extremely impressive only in their area of specialization. In fact, the very brightest people—the top 1% of the top 1%—seldom become experts at anything because they get bored with the repetition and want to move on to something else.

Hungarian author Laszlo Polgar set out to demonstrate his conviction that almost anyone can achieve expertise with sufficient effort. He allowed his three young daughters to explore several fields; when they showed an interest in chess, he devoted enormous efforts to nurturing their chess skills. All three became outstanding chess players, and one, Judit, was the first woman and the youngest person ever to reach grand master status.

Judit Polgar confirmed her father's confidence that prolonged effort could make her an expert in her chosen field, chess. By reaching the status of grand master at age 15 years and 5 months, she beat Bobby Fisher's previous record for being the youngest.

Some psychologists have argued that expertise *depends* entirely on practice, regardless of inborn predispositions. That claim is almost certainly an overstatement (H. Gardner, 1995). For obvious examples, short slow people will not become basketball stars, no matter how hard they practice, and blind people will not become expert photographers. Also, in any field those who show early success are most likely to devote the necessary effort to achieve expertise. The main point, however, is that even someone born with "talent" or "potential" (whatever that means) needs years of hard work to achieve expertise on any complicated task.

Would you like to become an expert at something? In fields as competitive as chess, violin, or basketball, nearly all the great performers started young. Still, you have a choice among many other fields. (For example, if you want to be an expert psychologist, you won't have to worry about competing against people who started in childhood.) However, do not underestimate the effort required. Judit Polgar became a grand master by practicing chess about 8 hours a day from age 5 to 15, missing nearly all of the usual childhood activities. Thomas Young, a great 19th-century scientist, worked 16 hours a day, 7 days a week, including the day he died. His wife complained that she could not get pregnant because her husband almost never found time for sex (Martindale, 2001).

Expert Pattern Recognition What exactly do experts do that other people do not? One important characteristic is that experts can look at a pattern and recognize its important features quickly.

a

b

FIGURE 9.12

Pieces arranged on a chessboard as they might actually occur in a game (a) and in a random manner (b). Master chess players can memorize the realistic pattern much better than others can, but they are no better than average at memorizing the random pattern.

In a typical experiment (de Groot, 1966), chess experts and beginners were shown pieces on a chessboard, as in Figure 9.12, for 5 seconds, and then asked to recall the positions of all the pieces. When the pieces were arranged as they might be in an actual game, expert players recalled 91% of the positions correctly, whereas novices recalled only 41%. When the pieces were arranged randomly, however, the expert players did no better than the novices. That is, on the average, expert chess players recognize the common chessboard patterns, but they do not have a superior overall memory. They still have to reason out the best move in a less-than-familiar situation, and even top chess players make occasional blunders when rushed for time (Chabris & Hearst, 2003), but recognizing common patterns is a huge head start.

In a wide variety of other areas from bird identification to reading x-rays to judging gymnastic competitions, experts recognize key patterns that other observers overlook (Murphy & Medin, 1985; Ste-Marie, 1999). They also know the difference between relevant and irrelevant information (Proffitt, Coley, & Medin, 2000).

Here is a quick demonstration, introduced by Herbert Simon, to show what happens when you develop expertise on a simple task where you do not need 10 years of practice. First, play this game with someone: The two of you take turns choosing a number from the set 1-2-3-4-5-6-7-8-9. When one of you chooses a number, scratch it out so that the other can't choose the same number. Continue until one of you has a set of three numbers that add to 15. For example, the combination 2, 4, 9 would win because 2 + 4 + 9 = 15.

Problem Solving

Problem solving can be described in terms of four phases (Polya, 1957): (a) understanding the problem, (b) generating hypotheses, (c) testing the hypotheses, and (d) checking the result (Figure 9.13). We shall discuss these four phases in detail.

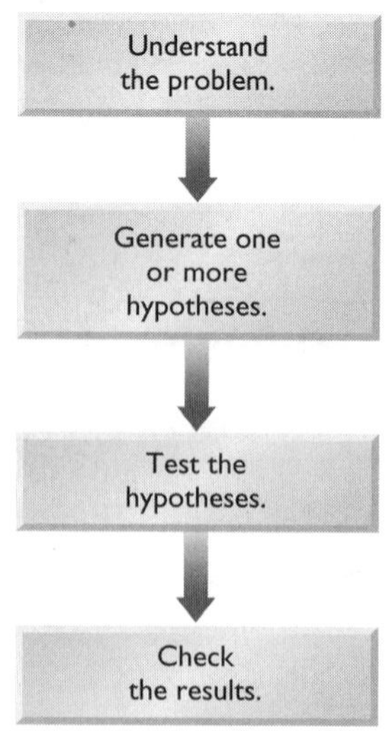

FIGURE 9.13

Four steps to solving a problem.

Understanding and Simplifying a Problem Sometimes a problem is easy to solve once we recognize it as a problem. For years airport terminals listed incoming and outgoing flights in order of time. You can imagine the struggle to find your flight: You might remember that it was supposed to depart somewhere between 10 and 10:30, but you didn't remember exactly when (and planes seldom leave exactly on time anyway), so you would have to sort through listings of many irrelevant flights to find the right one. Eventually, someone recognized the problem: People look for "the flight to San Jose," not "the flight at 10:27." Once the problem was recognized, the solution was obvious (Figure 9.14). (And then people wondered why they had overlooked the obvious for so long.)

When we recognize a problem but don't know how to solve it, a good strategy is to start with a simpler version. For example, here is what may appear to be a difficult, even impossible, problem: A professor hands back students' test papers at random. On the average how many students will accidentally receive their own paper?

Note that the problem does not specify how many students are in the class. If you don't see how to approach the problem, try the simplest cases: How many students will get their own paper back if there is only one student in the class? One, of course. What if there are two students? There is a 50% chance that both will get their own paper back and a 50% chance that neither will, for an average of one student getting the correct paper. What if there are three students? Each student then has one chance in three of getting his or her own paper. A one-third chance times

© AP/Wide World Photos

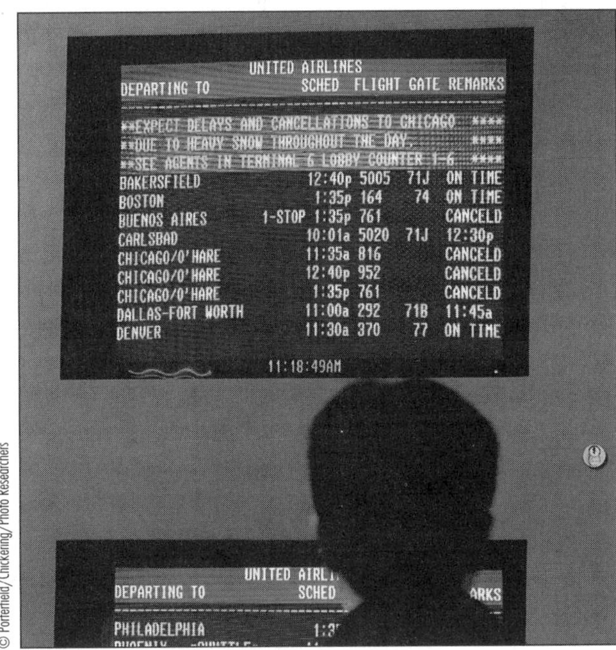

© Porterfield/Chickering/Photo Researchers

FIGURE 9.14

Switching airport terminal displays from listings by times (the old way) to listings by destinations (the new way) took little effort and had clear advantages.

three students means that on the average one student will get the correct paper. Already the pattern is clear: If there are *n* students, each student has one chance in *n* of getting his or her own paper back. No matter how many students are in the class, on the average one student will get his or her own paper back.

algorithm. a mechanical, repetitive procedure for solving a problem.

heuristics strategies for simplifying a problem or for guiding an investigation.

Generating Hypotheses After you have simplified a problem, you generate *hypotheses*—preliminary interpretations that you can evaluate or test. In some cases you can test every possible hypothesis. For example, suppose you want to connect your television set to a pair of stereo amplifiers, a VCR, and a DVD player, but you have lost the instruction manuals. You have several cables to attach, and each device has input and output channels. You could simply connect the cables by trial and error, testing every possibility until you find one that works. *A mechanical, repetitive procedure for solving a problem or testing every hypothesis* is called an **algorithm**. The rules for alphabetizing a list are one example; you check every possible item to see which one goes first, then check them all for which goes second, and so forth. You can also learn an algorithm for how to win, or at least tie, every time you play tick-tack-toe.

In many situations, however, the possible hypotheses are too numerous or vague to apply any algorithm. Consider the question, "What should I do with my life?" You could not consider every possible choice, and even if you did, you would not be sure how to evaluate them. **Heuristics** are *strategies for simplifying a problem or for guiding an investigation.* For the question about your future, you might restrict your attention to a few possible careers and then learn whatever you can about them.

To illustrate the contrast between algorithms and heuristics, consider chess. At a typical point in a game of chess, a player has about 25 legal moves, and the opponent has about 25 legal replies to each of them. To choose your

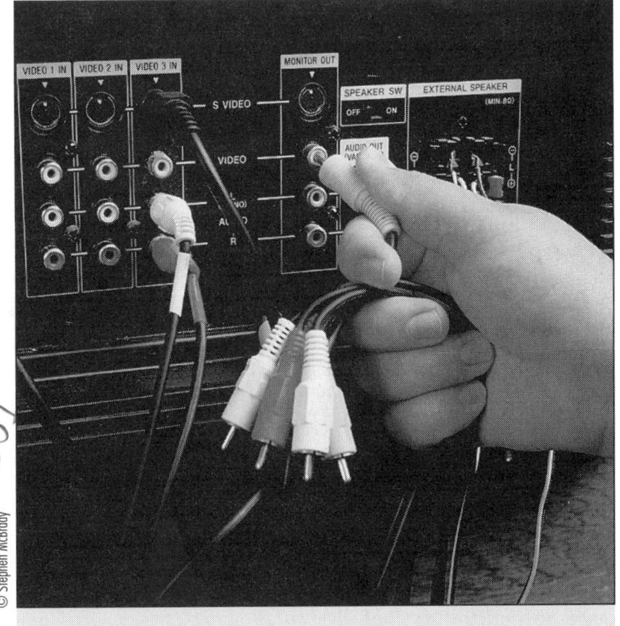

© Stephen McBrady

To find the right way to connect the lines, you could use the simple algorithm of trying every possible combination, one after the other.

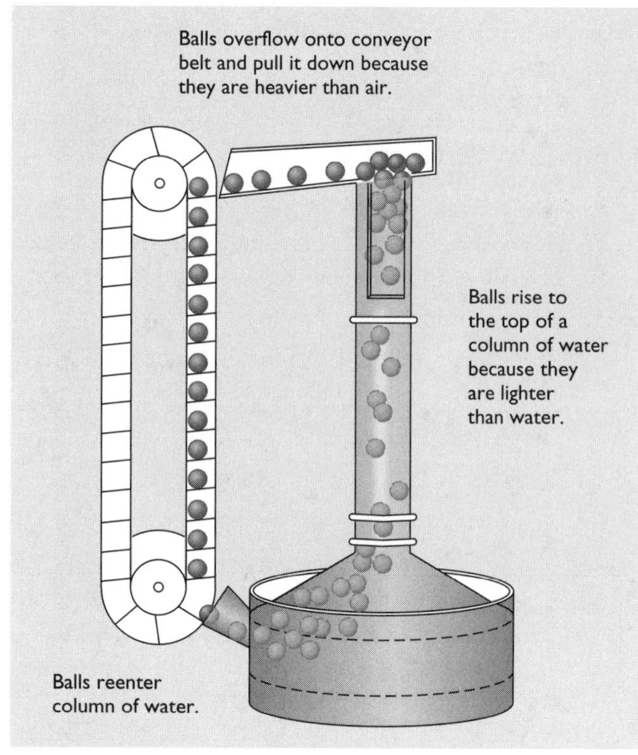

FIGURE 9.15
What is wrong with this perpetual motion machine?

best move by an algorithm, you would consider each of your possible moves, each of your opponent's possible replies, each of your next moves, and so forth, as many moves ahead as possible. Finally, you would select the move that gives you the best result, assuming that your opponent made the best possible reply at each point. Computerized chess programs do use algorithms, but human memory is more limited, so you simplify the task with heuristics: On each move you select just a few possible moves for serious consideration. You consider just a few of your opponent's likely responses, a few of your possible next moves, and so forth.

Testing Hypotheses and Checking the Results If you think you have solved a problem, test whether your idea works. Many people who think they have a great idea never bother to try it out, even on a small scale. One inventor applied for a patent on the "perpetual motion machine" shown in Figure 9.15. Rubber balls, being lighter than water, rise in a column of water and flow over the top. The balls are heavier than air, so they fall, thus moving a belt and generating energy. At the bottom they reenter the water column. Do you see why this system could never work? You would if you tried to build it.

Even if you can't physically check your idea, consider whether it is realistic. One article published in 1927 claimed that a deer botfly has a speed of 800 miles per hour (almost 1,300 kilometers per hour). Some books and Internet sources to this day list that speed as the record for the fastest species on earth. One physicist calculated that an object moving that fast would generate more than enough air pressure to squash the fly. A fly striking you at that speed would pierce you like a bullet. And the energy to move that fast would require the fly to eat 1.5 times its weight in food *per second* (May, 1999).

Generalizing Solutions to Similar Problems You might imagine that people who had just solved one problem would quickly recognize how to solve a similar problem (see Figure 9.16). Often, they do not. For example, if you have learned to use a formula in mathematics, you probably won't recognize that the same formula applies to some problem in a physics class, unless someone points out the similarity (Barnett & Ceci, 2002; Gick & Holyoak, 1980). You probably would learn faster in

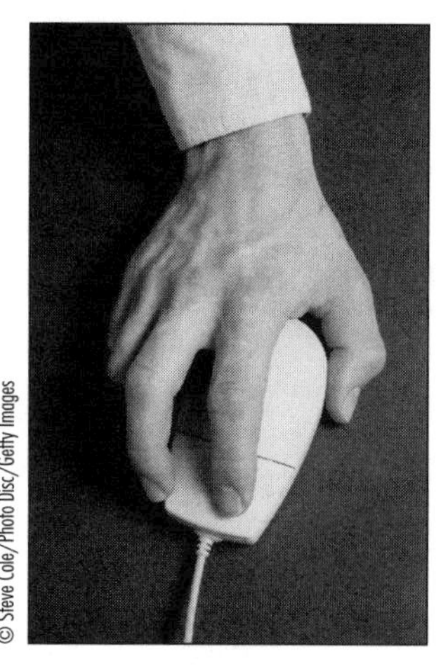
© Steve Cole/Photo Disc/Getty Images

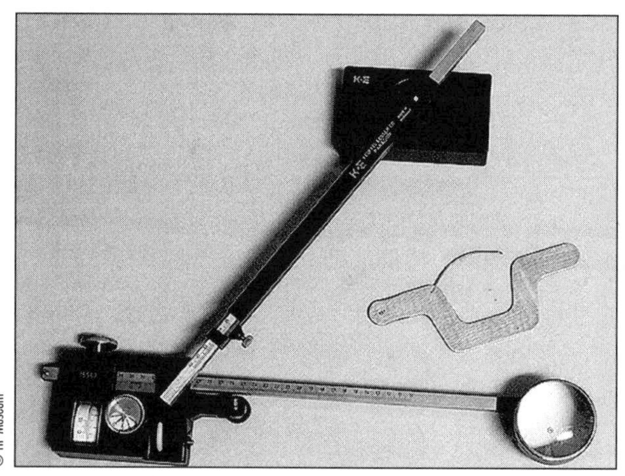
© HP Museum

FIGURE 9.16
The computer mouse was invented by a computer scientist who was familiar with an engineering device called a planimeter that he believed could be modified for use with computers. Such insights are unusual; most people do not generalize a solution from one task to another.

the new situation, so the previous training was not worthless (De Corte, 2003), but still it is noteworthy how often people apply a principle in one situation but not another.

For an example of failure to transfer principle, consider Figure 9.17a, which shows a coiled garden hose. When the water spurts out, what path will it take? (Draw it.) Figure 9.17b shows a curved gun barrel. When the bullet comes out, what path will it take? (Draw it.)

Almost everyone draws the water coming straight out of the garden hose, but most draw a bullet coming out of a gun in a curved path, as if the bullet remembered the curved path it had just taken (Kaiser, Jonides, & Alexander, 1986). The physics is the same in both situations: Except for the effects of gravity, both the water and the bullet will follow a straight path.

Here is another example in which people answer correctly one version of the problem but not another. Let's start with the harder version: You will be presented with a series of cards, each of which has a letter on one side and a number on the other. Your task is to test the hypothesis that "any card that has a vowel on one side has an even number on the other." The cards are shown below. Which cards do you need to turn over to test the hypothesis?

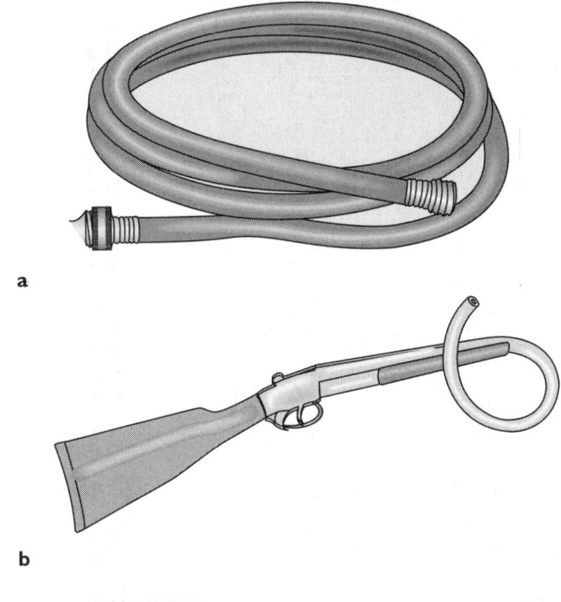

FIGURE 9.17

(a) Draw the trajectory of water as it flows out of a coiled garden hose. (b) Draw the trajectory of a bullet as it leaves a coiled gun barrel.

One choice is easy (if you understand the instructions): You have to turn over the card with an A. Most people, however, turn over the card with a 4, which is unnecessary. (Either a vowel or a consonant on the back of the 4 would be okay, according to the hypothesis.) But a vowel on the back of the 7 would contradict the hypothesis, and most people do not check the 7 (Wason, 1960).

Change the task, however, and it becomes easy. Now you are told that each card represents a person. One side indicates the person's age and the other is what kind of beverage the person is drinking. You are supposed to test the hypothesis that everyone under age 21 is drinking nonalcoholic beverages. Here are the cards; which ones do you need to turn over to check the hypothesis?

With this version the answer is obvious: Check the 18-year-old and the person drinking wine but not the other two (Cosmides, 1989).

Why was this version so much easier than the first? Some psychologists believe we are specialized to think more clearly about human social situations than about anything else. Try writing the question in some other way that pertains to realistic nonhuman events. Is your phrasing as easy as the human drinking example, as difficult as the letter–vowel example, or intermediate?

Why do we sometimes solve one problem and not another, even though they are logically similar? Part of the answer is that we sometimes apply a principle in one situation without fully understanding it or mastering it. After you have applied an approach in a few situations, you more quickly recognize its usefulness in still others (Gick & Holyoak, 1983). (This finding resembles the encoding specificity principle of memory: If you study something in just one situation, you remember it well in that one situation but probably not in others. If you study in several contexts, you remember in many.)

The other part of the answer is that, bluntly, we usually don't rely much on logical reasoning (Evans, 2002). We answer impulsively, or we look for evidence to support what we have already decided (Brownstein, 2003). In some cases people's

FIGURE 9.18

This object was made by cutting and folding an ordinary piece of cardboard with nothing left over. How was it done?

intuitions are so strong that even solid evidence and logic fail to persuade them (Arkes, 2003; Krauss & Wang, 2003).

A concept isn't something you either have or don't have. You can have it to a greater or lesser degree, find it easy or difficult to use, and use it frequently or infrequently (Siegler, 2000).

Special Features of Insight Problems

In "insight" or "aha!" problems, the correct answer occurs to you suddenly or not at all. Here is an example (M. Gardner, 1978): Figure 9.18 shows an object that was made by cutting and bending an ordinary piece of cardboard. How was it made? If you think you know, take a piece of paper and try to make it yourself.

Sudden or Gradual Insights? Solving insight problems differs from solving, say, algebra problems. Most people can look at an algebra problem and predict how quickly they will solve it if at all. As they work on it, they estimate how close they are to a solution. With insight problems, however—like the paper-folding problem just presented—people often think they are making no progress and then suddenly solve it (Metcalfe & Wiebe, 1987). Does the answer really come as suddenly as it seems?

If you were groping your way around in a dark room, you would have no idea how soon you were going to find the door, but nevertheless, you were making progress. You would have learned much about the room, including where the door was *not*. So maybe people are making more progress than they realize on insight problems. To test this possibility, psychologists gave students problems with the following form:

> The following three words are all associated with one other word. What is that word?
> color numbers oil

In this case the intended answer is paint, although you might be able to defend some other answers. As with other insight questions, participants who solved it said the answer came to them suddenly. Then the experimenters gave the students paired sets of three words each, like those shown here in Sets 1 and 2, to examine for 12 seconds. In each pair one set had a correct answer (like paint in the example just given). The other set had no correct answer. Students were asked to generate a correct answer if they could, but if not, at least to guess which set had a correct answer. Examples:

Set 1
playing credit report ***or*** **still pages music**

Set 2
town root car ***or*** **ticket shop broker**

The main result: Even students who did not know the correct answer usually guessed correctly which set had an answer (Bowers, Regehr, Balthazard, & Parker, 1990). Even when they said they had "no confidence" in their guesses, they were still right more often than not. In short, people often make progress on insight problems without realizing it.

The Characteristics of Creativity Why are some people more creative than others? Creativity is not the same as expertise. An expert gymnast goes through the same motions every time, and an expert chess player may use the same strategy in game

Howard Gardner studied the lives of seven highly creative people, including political and spiritual leader Mahatma Gandhi and dance pioneer Martha Graham, to find the features that promote creativity.

after game, but a writer, composer, or painter who kept doing the same thing again and again would not be considered creative. One hallmark of creative people is a willingness to take risks. For example, painter Claude Monet deliberately varied the style and content of his paintings instead of just producing a series of successful but similar paintings (Stokes, 2001).

Creative writers, composers, and scientists have certain features in common, such as nonconformity, risk-taking, willingness to tolerate rejection, openness to new experiences, and at least moderate intelligence (Simonton, 2000b). However, it is misleading to talk about "creative people" as if certain people are creative in everything they do. People have to know a field well before they can make creative contributions to it. That is, don't expect a creative poet to offer creative solutions to an auto-mechanics problem.

Howard Gardner (1993) studied creativity by examining the lives of seven 20th-century people who are widely regarded as creative in very different fields: Sigmund Freud (psychology), Albert Einstein (physics), Pablo Picasso (painting), Igor Stravinsky (musical composition), T. S. Eliot (poetry), Martha Graham (dance), and Mahatma Gandhi (political resistance and spirituality). Gardner found a few patterns that these people had in common, including the following:

- They worked in an atmosphere of moderate tension, sensing that the old ways of doing things were not quite right.
- They had enough background in their fields to feel confident but not so much experience that they became trapped into traditional habits.
- Early in life, each relied heavily on one or a few close friends for advice and encouragement.
- Each threw him- or herself wholeheartedly into the work, at the expense of family and friendships. Even Gandhi, a famous advocate for love and justice, had trouble developing close relationships.

Creative careers, however, are extremely variable (Simonton, 1997). As a rule poets are recognized for their greatness early in life, generally in their 20s,

Creative problem solving, evident in this temporary bridge made of old railroad cars, has two elements: novelty and social value.

In 2002 Princeton psychologist Daniel Kahneman (left) won the Nobel Prize for Economics. (There is no Nobel Prize in psychology.) Although others have won Nobel Prizes for research related to psychology, Kahneman was the first winner who had a PhD in psychology.

whereas the greatest, most creative historians seldom do their best work before their 40s or 50s. Within any field some people start early and quit early and others bloom late. Some—such as Bach, Picasso, and Edison—produce enormous quantities of good work, whereas others produce only one or two great works.

Reasoning by Heuristics

Heuristics, you will recall, are methods of simplifying a problem. We all have limited knowledge, limited memory, and limited time to collect information and reason out an answer. Frequently, we have to make very quick decisions with almost no time to weigh the evidence and consider alternatives. Therefore, heuristics are often an excellent guide, if not a necessity.

Furthermore, simple heuristics sometimes produce surprisingly good results. For example, people are given pairs of U.S. cities, such as San Diego and San Antonio, and pairs of German cities, such as Munich and Cologne. For each pair they are asked to pick the one with the larger population. Oddly, Americans guess more accurately with the German cities and Germans guess more accurately with American cities (Goldstein & Gigerenzer, 2002). Almost everyone relies on the heuristic, "The city I've heard of probably has more people." That heuristic works fine for a country you know a little about, but less well for your own country, where both cities are familiar. So the heuristic works best if you don't know too much!

However, heuristics can lead us astray if we use them habitually even when we have an opportunity to weigh the evidence logically. Economists generally assume that people are more or less rational. That is, they follow their own best interests as well as they can; they make decisions based on the facts; and they buy and sell products at prices that match their real values. In 2002 Daniel Kahneman won the Nobel Prize for Economics for research demonstrating that people often make illogical decisions based on heuristics, emotions, and biases.

Ducksaying

representativeness heuristic the tendency to assume that, if an item is similar to members of a particular category, it is probably a member of that category itself.

base-rate information data about the frequency or probability of a given item.

The Representativeness Heuristic and Base-Rate Information Perhaps you have heard the saying: "If something looks like a duck, waddles like a duck, and quacks like a duck, chances are it's a duck." This saying is an example of the **representativeness heuristic**, *the tendency to assume that, if an item resembles members of a particular category, it is probably a member of that category itself.*

The assumption is usually correct, but research by Kahneman and others has shown how it leads us astray when we deal with uncommon events. For example, if you see something that looks, walks, and sounds like some rare bird, you may indeed have found a rarity, but you should check carefully to make sure it isn't some similar, more common species. In general, to decide whether something belongs in one category or another, you should consider how closely it resembles the two categories but also the **base-rate information**—that is, *how common the two categories are.*

When people apply the representativeness heuristic, they frequently overlook base-rate information. For example, consider the following question (modified from Kahneman & Tversky, 1973):

> Psychologists have interviewed 30 engineers and 70 lawyers. One of them, Jack, is a 45-year-old married man with four children. He is generally conservative, cautious, and ambitious. He shows no interest in political and social issues and spends most of his free time on home carpentry, sailing, and solving mathematical puzzles. What is the probability that Jack is one of the 30 engineers in the sample of 100?

Most people estimate a rather high probability—perhaps 80 or 90%—because the description sounds more representative of engineers than lawyers. That estimate isn't really wrong, as we have no logical way to determine the true probability. The interesting point is that if some people are told the sample included 30 engineers and 70 lawyers, and others are told it included 70 engineers and 30 lawyers, both groups make about the same estimate for Jack (Kahneman & Tversky, 1973). Certainly, the base-rate information should have some influence.

Here is another example of misuse of the representativeness heuristic. Read the following description and then answer the questions following it:

> Linda was a philosophy major. She is 31, bright, outspoken, and concerned about issues of discrimination and social justice.

What would you estimate is the probability that Linda is a bank teller? What is the probability that she is a feminist bank teller? (Answer before you read on.)

The true probabilities, hard to estimate, are not the point. The interesting result is that most people estimate a higher probability that Linda is a *feminist* bank teller than the probability that she is a bank teller (A. Tversky & Kahneman, 1983). However, she could clearly not be a feminist bank teller without being a bank teller. Apparently, people regard this description as fairly typical for a feminist and thus for a feminist bank teller (or feminist anything else) but not typical for bank tellers in general (Shafir, Smith, & Osherson, 1990).

"K" example

The Availability Heuristic When we estimate how common something is, we generally start by trying to think of examples. Try this question: In the English language, are there more words that start with *k* or more words with *k* as the third letter? Most people guess that more words start with *k*. They start by trying to think of words that start with *k*: "king, kitchen, kangaroo, key, knowledge, . . ." Those were pretty easy. Then they try to think of words with *k* as the third letter: "ask, ink, . . . uh . . ." They rely on the **availability heuristic**, *the strategy of assuming that how easily one can remember examples of some kind of event indicates how common the event itself is* (Table 9.1). Because it is easier to think of words that start with *k* than words with *k* as the third letter, people assume that more words start with *k*. In fact, however, many more words have *k* as the third letter.

availability heuristic
the strategy of assuming that how easily one can remember examples of some kind of event indicates how common the event actually is.

Because the news media tend to emphasize the spectacular, our use of the availability heuristic leads us to overestimate some dangers and underestimate others. For example, would you guess that more people die from tornadoes or lightning? From diabetes or homicide? From stomach cancer or automobile accidents? A tornado that kills 10 people gets national publicity, whereas a bolt of

TABLE 9.1 The Representativeness Heuristic and the Availability Heuristic.

	A TENDENCY TO ASSUME THAT	LEADS US ASTRAY WHEN	EXAMPLE OF ERROR
Representativeness Heuristic	An item that resembles members of a category probably belongs to that category.	Something resembles members of a rare category.	Something looks like it might be a UFO, so you decide it is.
Availability Heuristic	The more easily we can think of members of a category, the more common the category is.	One category gets more publicity than another or is more memorable.	You remember more reports of airplane crashes than car crashes so you think air travel is more dangerous.

lightning that kills one person may not even make the local news show. Therefore, we assume tornado deaths are more common, although in fact lightning kills more people. Similarly, diabetes and stomach cancer kill far more people than homicide or automobile accidents but get little publicity. If you guessed that homicide and automobile accidents kill more, probably you were using the availability heuristic (Ruscio, 2000).

Another example: Would you rate yourself a better than average, average, or worse than average driver? Most people rate themselves above average, although statistically it is impossible for more than half to be above average. When people try to imagine other people's driving, it is easy to remember times when you saw someone driving extremely badly—much worse than you ever would, right?—but hard to remember anyone driving especially better than you. Similarly, almost all people say they have less than average racial prejudice. Extremely prejudiced people stand out in your memory more than people with less prejudice.

Other Common Errors in Human Cognition

critical thinking
the careful evaluation of evidence for and against any conclusion.

Common human errors include inappropriate use of the representativeness heuristic and availability heuristic but also include many other tendencies. Although we humans pride ourselves on our intelligence and our ability to solve problems, we sometimes make embarrassing mistakes. For decades college professors have talked about the importance of **critical thinking**, *the careful evaluation of evidence for and against any conclusion.* However, even the sincerest advocates of critical thinking sometimes find that they have been repeating nonsense that they should have questioned. For example, I myself used to repeat the rumors—only I didn't know they were rumors; I thought they were facts—that "glass flows as a very slow liquid," that "when the lemming population gets very high, some of them jump off cliffs," and that "Thomas Crapper invented the flush toilet." I later learned that all these claims were false. (The story about Thomas Crapper was started by Wallace Reyburn, who wrote the book *Flushed with Pride,* a partly true, partly fictitious biography of Crapper, who manufactured toilets, but didn't invent them. Everyone might have continued to believe Reyburn's hoax if he hadn't followed it with a less plausible book, *Bust Up,* a biography of Otto Titzling, allegedly the inventor of the bra!)

Why do intelligent people sometimes come to false conclusions or accept conclusions without adequate evidence? The reasons are many; here we consider just a few.

Overconfidence Let's start with a demonstration. Ten questions follow. Few people know any of the answers exactly, but I'm asking for only an approximation. For each question answer with a 90% confidence range; that is, give a range within which you are 90% sure the correct answer lies. For example, consider this question: In the 2000 summer Olympics in Sydney, Australia, how many silver medals did China win? You might decide that you would be surprised if they won fewer than 5 or more than 25, so you guess "5 to 25." If so, you would be right because China won 16 silver medals. Okay, that's the idea. Now fill in your answers:

Your estimate (as a 90% confidence range)

1. How old was Martin Luther King, Jr., at the time of his death? __ to __
2. How long is the Nile River? __ to __
3. How many countries belong to OPEC? __ to __
4. How many books are in the Old Testament? __ to __

5. What is the diameter of the moon? __ to __
6. What is the weight of an empty Boeing 747? __ to __
7. In what year was Mozart born? __ to __
8. What is the gestation period of an Asian elephant? (in days) __ to __
9. How far is London from Tokyo? __ to __
10. What is the deepest known point in the ocean? (in feet or meters) __ to __

How many of your ranges included the correct answer? Because you said you were 90% confident of each answer, you should be right on about nine of ten. However, most people miss more than half. That is, they were **overconfident**; *they believed their estimates were more accurate than they actually were.* These were, of course, very difficult questions. On extremely easy questions, the trend is reversed and people tend to be underconfident (Erev, Wallsten, & Budescu, 1994; Juslin, Winman, & Olsson, 2000).

overconfidence
the belief that one's opinions or predictions are highly correct when in fact they are not.

Philip Tetlock (1994) conducted a study of government officials and consultants, foreign policy professors, newspaper columnists, and others who make their living by analyzing and predicting world events. He asked them to predict world events over the next several years—such as what would happen in Korea, the Middle East, Eastern Europe, and Cuba—and to state their confidence in their predictions (such as 70%). Five years later he compared predictions to actual results and found very low accuracy, especially among those who were the most confident and those with a strong liberal or conservative point of view. That is, those who saw both sides of a question were more likely to be right.

Most people are overconfident of their understanding of complex physical processes. In one study college students were asked to rate how well they understood how various devices work, including a speedometer, zipper, flush toilet, cylinder lock, helicopter, quartz watch, sewing machine, and others. Then the researchers asked them in fact to explain four of the devices and answer questions about them, such as "How could someone pick a cylinder lock?" and "How does a helicopter go from hovering to forward flight?" After producing what were obviously weak answers, nearly all students lowered their ratings of understanding for these four phenomena (Rozenblit & Keil, 2002). However, curiously, some insisted that except for the four devices that the experimenters happened to choose, they really did understand all the other devices pretty well!

Attractiveness of Valuable but Very Unlikely Outcomes If people are faced with choices A and B, and on the average A is worth $1 and on the average B is also worth $1, then theoretically, people should like both choices equally. In reality, people don't behave that way.

Which would you rather have:

- $100,000 for sure or a 10% chance of winning $1 million?
- $10,000 or a 1% chance at $1 million?
- $1,000 or a 0.1% chance at $1 million?
- $100 or a 0.01% chance at $1 million?
- $10 or a 0.001% chance at $1 million?
- $1 or a 0.0001% chance at $1 million?

If you are like most people, you chose the $100,000 over a 10% chance at a million and $10,000 over a 1% chance. But at some point, you switched from the sure profit to the gamble. Especially if the sure profit is $10 or less, most people prefer a chance at winning a million. In fact almost half of college students said they would forego $10 to have even one chance in a million of winning a million—a

© Susan Ashukian

FIGURE 9.19a

People who form a hypothesis based on the first photo look at succeeding photos to find evidence that they are right. Because their first guess is generally wrong, they don't do as well as people who look at the later photos before making any preliminary guesses. Try to guess what this shows. Then examine parts b and c as shown below.

gamble of very bad odds (Rachlin, Siegel, & Cross, 1994). A later study, using an Internet sample of thousands of people from 44 countries, confirmed this tendency to prefer a long-shot bet over a small but sure gain (Birnbaum, 1999), so it is not something unique to one culture.

Why do people prefer a slim chance at a fortune to a small but sure gain? First, for most people $10 is not going to raise your standard of living. A million dollars would. Second, although you understand the difference between a 10% chance and a 1% chance, it is hard to grasp the difference between a 0.001% chance and a 0.0001% or even a 0.000001% chance. They blur together as "unlikely but not impossible," and we think, "Someone is going to win, and it might be me." In fact the unlikeliness of winning is part of the appeal: People report more pleasure from a surprising gain than from one they expected (Mellers, Schwartz, Ho, & Ritov, 1997). That is, a surprising gambling win is a bigger thrill than money you knew you were going to gain.

confirmation bias
the tendency to accept one hypothesis and then look for evidence to support it, instead of considering other possibilities.

Confirmation Bias Often, we make mistakes by *accepting one hypothesis and then looking for evidence to support it, instead of considering other possibilities.* This tendency is known as the **confirmation bias**. For example, examine the poorly focused photo in Figure 9.19a and guess what it depicts. Then see Figures 9.19b and 9.19c. Many people find that seeing the extremely out-of-focus photo makes it harder to identify the items in the better focused photo. When they saw the first photo, they formed a hypothesis, probably a wrong one, which interfered with correctly perceiving the later photo (Bruner & Potter, 1964).

Peter Wason (1960) asked students to discover a certain rule he had in mind for generating sequences of numbers. One example of the numbers the rule might generate, he explained, was "2, 4, 6." He told the students that they could ask about other sequences, and he would tell them whether or not those sequences fit his

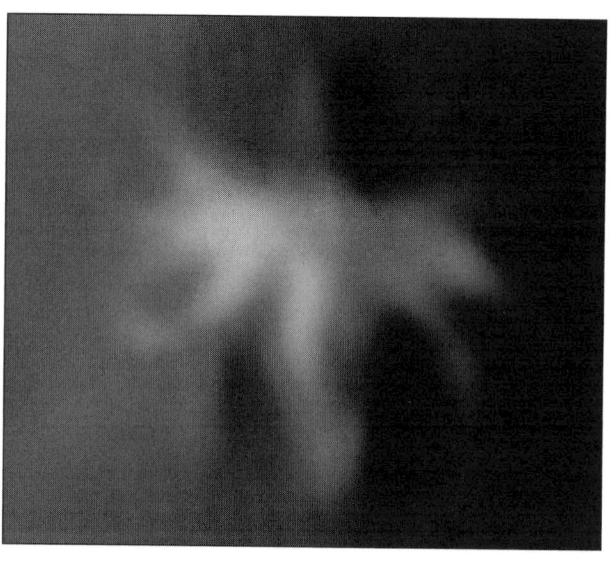
© Susan Ashukian

FIGURE 9.19b

© Susan Ashukian

FIGURE 9.19c

rule. They should tell him as soon as they thought they knew the rule.

Most students started by asking, "8, 10, 12?" When told "yes," they proceeded with "14, 16, 18?" Each time, they were told, "Yes, that sequence fits the rule." Soon most of them guessed, "The rule is three consecutive even numbers." "No," came the reply. "That is not the rule." Many students persisted, trying "20, 22, 24?" "26, 28, 30?" "250, 252, 254?" Note that they were testing sequences that fit their rule, ignoring other possibilities. The rule Wason had in mind was, "Any three positive numbers of increasing magnitude." For instance, 1, 2, 3, would be acceptable, and so would 21, 25, 24, 601.

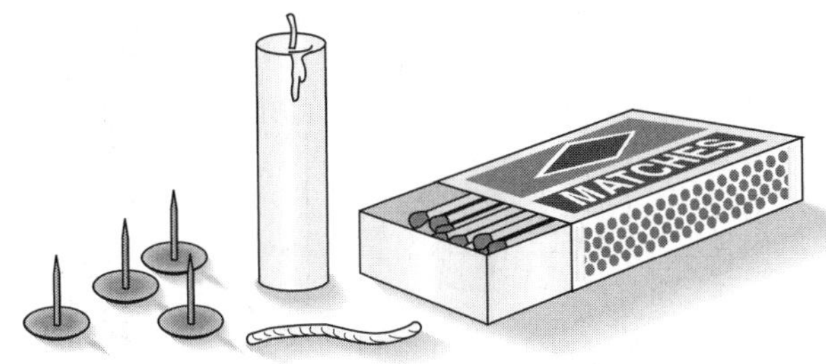

FIGURE 9.20

You are provided with a candle, a box of matches, some thumbtacks, and a tiny piece of string. What is the best way, using no other equipment, to attach the candle to a wall so that it could be lit?

A special case of confirmation bias is **functional fixedness**, *the tendency to adhere to a single approach or a single way of using an item.* Here are three examples:

functional fixedness
the tendency to adhere to a single approach to a problem or a single way of using an item.

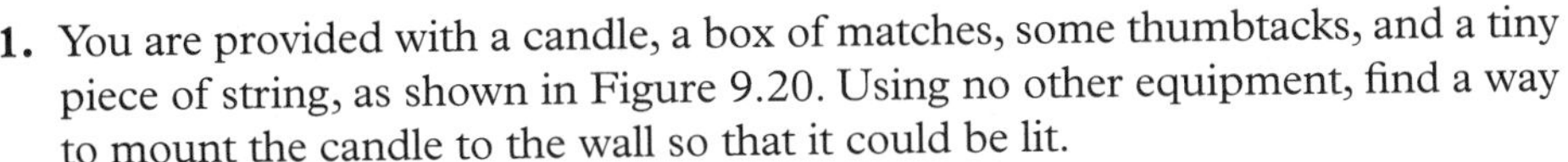

1. You are provided with a candle, a box of matches, some thumbtacks, and a tiny piece of string, as shown in Figure 9.20. Using no other equipment, find a way to mount the candle to the wall so that it could be lit.

2. Consider an array of nine dots:

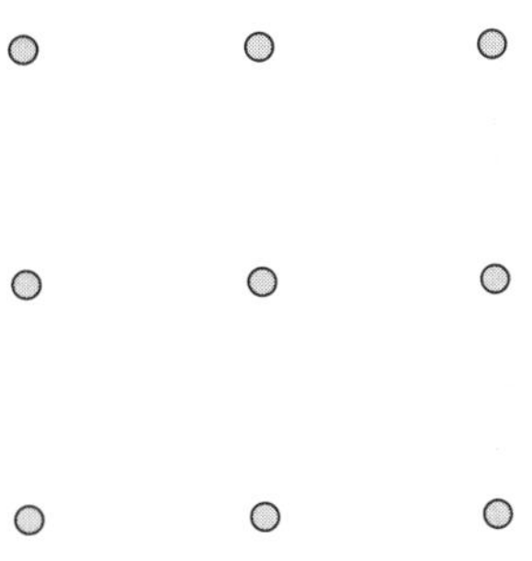

Connect all nine dots with a series of connected straight lines, such that the end of one line is the start of the next. For example, one way would be:

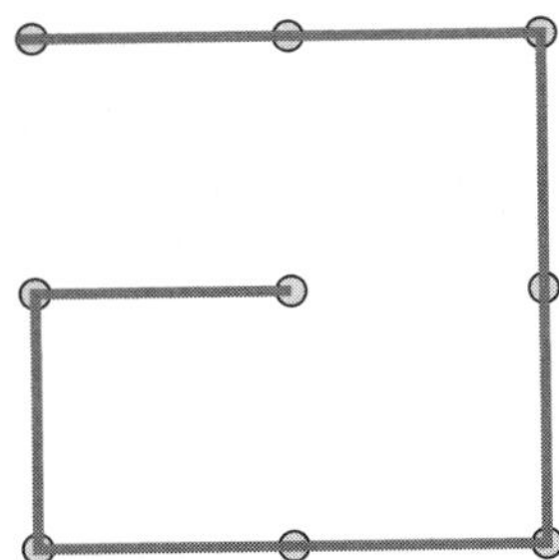

But use the fewest lines possible.

3. There are some students in a room. All but two of them are psychology majors, all but two are chemistry majors, and all but two are history majors. How many students are in the room, and what are their majors? (If your first impulse is to say "two of each," try it out: It doesn't work.) Now here's the interesting part: There are two possible solutions. After you have found one solution, discard it and find another.

Question 1 was difficult because most people think of the matchbox as simply a container for matches, not as a potential tool on its own. The box is "functionally fixed" for one way of using it. Question 2 was difficult because most people assume that the lines must remain within the area defined by the nine dots. On question 3 it is difficult to think of even one solution, and after thinking of it, it is hard to abandon it to think of an entirely different approach.

Framing Questions A truly logical person would give the same answer to a question no matter how it was worded. In fact most people answer questions differently depending on how they are phrased.

For example, answer the following: "What's the probability that Sunday will be hotter than every other day next week?" (Please answer before you read on.)

Many people answer "50%" because it seems there are two possibilities—it will be hotter, or it won't. But now consider this rewording: "What's the probability that next week, the hottest day of the week will be Sunday?" With this wording, most people switch to the correct answer, one seventh, because they see that there are seven days with an equal chance of being the hottest (Fox & Rottenstreich, 2003).

For another example, suppose you have been appointed head of the Public Health Service, and you need to choose a plan to deal with a disease that has endangered the lives of 600 people. If you adopt plan A, you will save the lives of 200 people. If you adopt plan B, there is a 33% chance that you will save all 600 and a 67% chance that you will save no one. *Choose plan A or B before reading further.*

Now another disease breaks out; again you must choose between two plans. If you adopt plan C, 400 people will die. If you adopt plan D, there is a 33% chance that no one will die and a 67% chance that 600 will die. *Choose plan C or D now.*

Figure 9.21 shows the choices that more than 150 people made. Most chose A over B and D over C. However, note that plan A is exactly the same as C (200 live, 400 die), and plan B is exactly the same as D. Why then did so many people choose both A and D? The reason, according to Tversky and Kahneman (1981), is that most people avoid taking a risk to gain something (like saving

Plan	How question was framed	Plan preferred by	Outcome
A	Save 200 people	72%	200 live, 400 die
C	400 people will die	22%	
B	33% chance of saving all 600; 67% chance of saving no one	28%	33% chance 600 live or 67% chance 600 die
D	33% chance no one will die; 67% chance all 600 will die	78%	

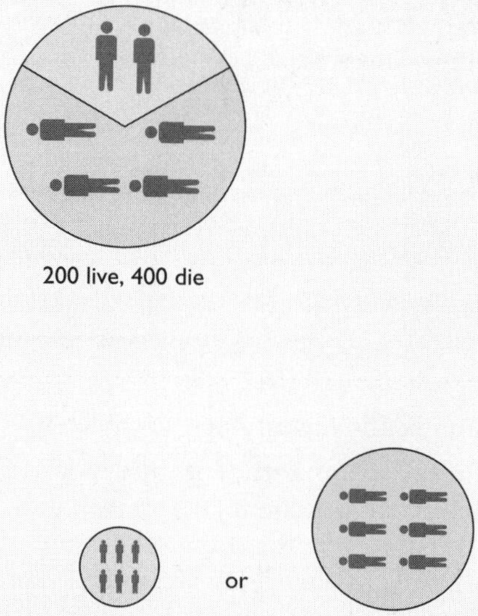

FIGURE 9.21

Most people chose plan A over B, and D over C, although A produces the same result as C and B produces the same result as D. Amos Tversky and Daniel Kahneman (1981) proposed that most people play it safe to gain something but accept a risk to avoid a loss.

lives) but willingly take a risk to avoid loss (like not letting people die). *The tendency to answer a question differently when it is framed (phrased) differently* is called the **framing effect**.

framing effect
the tendency to answer a question differently when it is framed (phrased) differently.

The Sunk Cost Effect

The sunk cost effect is a special case of the framing effect, but let's start with some examples:

- You have bought a $200 plane ticket to Wonderfulville and a $500 ticket to Marvelousville. Too late, you realize that they are both for the same weekend, and both are nonrefundable. You think you would prefer Wonderfulville, but you paid more for the ticket to Marvelousville. Where will you go?
- Months ago you bought an expensive ticket to a football game, but the game is today and the weather is miserably cold. You wish you hadn't bought the ticket. Do you go to the game?

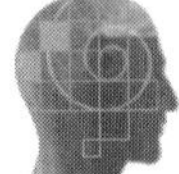

Think About It

Recall the discussion about how the phrasing of a question influences people's answers. For example, most people will take more risks to avoid a loss than to increase a gain. Can you use this principle to explain why many gamblers on a losing streak will continue betting, sometimes increasing their bets? Is there a different way to think about the situation to decrease the temptation to continue gambling?

Many people say they would go to Marvelousville instead of Wonderfulville because the Marvelousville ticket was more expensive and they don't want to waste the money. Many also say they will go to the football game in the bad weather, again because they don't want to waste the money. These examples illustrate the **sunk cost effect**, *the willingness to do something we wouldn't otherwise choose to do because of money or effort already spent* (Arkes & Ayton, 1999). This tendency arises in many situations. Someone gambles weekly on the state lottery, losing huge sums, but keeps betting because to quit without winning it back would admit that all the previous bets were a mistake. A company invests vast amounts of money in a project that now appears to be a mistake but doesn't want to cancel the project and admit it has wasted so much money. A professional sports team gives someone a huge signing bonus, and later finds the player's performance disappointing, but keeps using that player anyway to avoid wasting the money.

sunk cost effect
the willingness to do something we wouldn't otherwise choose to do because of money or effort already spent.

Curiously, young children never show the sunk cost effect. The fact that they have already wasted much time or money doesn't induce them to waste still more. No one has ever demonstrated the sunk cost effect in nonhuman animals either in spite of repeated efforts (Arkes & Ayton, 299). Apparently, you have to be fairly intelligent to do something this stupid.

Answers to Other Questions in the Chapter

D. At first you probably had no idea what strategy to use. As shown below, the game is equivalent to tick-tack-toe. If you know the correct strategy for tick-tack-toe, you now know what strategy to use for the numbers-adding-to-15 game.

2	7	6
9	5	1
4	3	8

E. The water in the tube would leak out of the hole in the bottom. Any membrane heavy enough to keep the water in would also keep the rubber balls out.

F. This illustration shows how to cut and fold an ordinary piece of paper or cardboard to match the figure with nothing left over.

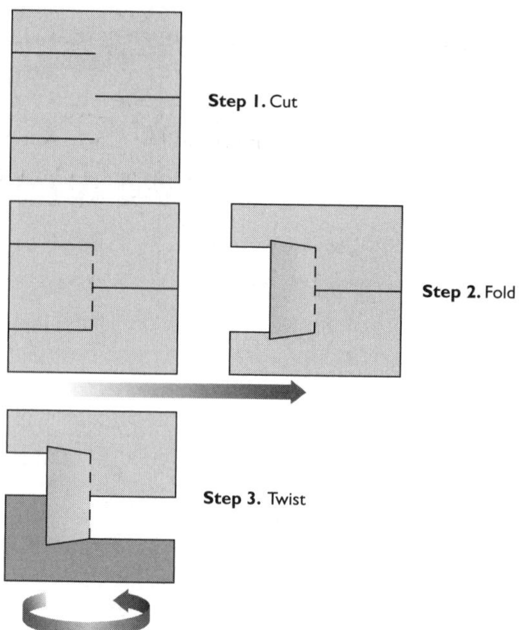

G. Set 1: The words *playing, credit,* and *report* are all associated with *card.* Set 2: The words *ticket, shop,* and *broker* are all associated with *pawn.*

H. (1) 39 years. (2) 4,187 miles, or 6,738 kilometers. (3) 13 countries. (4) 39 books. (5) 2,160 miles, or 3,476 kilometers. (6) 390,000 pounds, or 177,000 kilograms. (7) 1756. (8) 645 days. (9) 5,959 miles, or 9,590 kilometers. (10) 36,198 feet, or 11,033 meters.

I. (1) The best way to attach the candle to the wall is to dump the matches from the box and thumbtack the side of the box to the wall, as shown in this picture. The tiny piece of string is irrelevant.

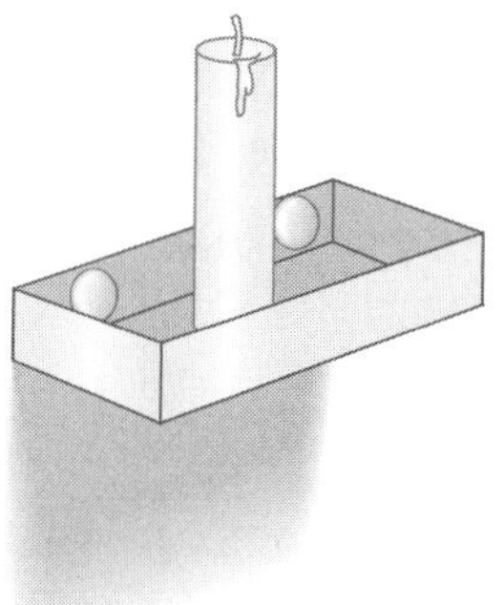

(2) The dots can be connected with four lines:

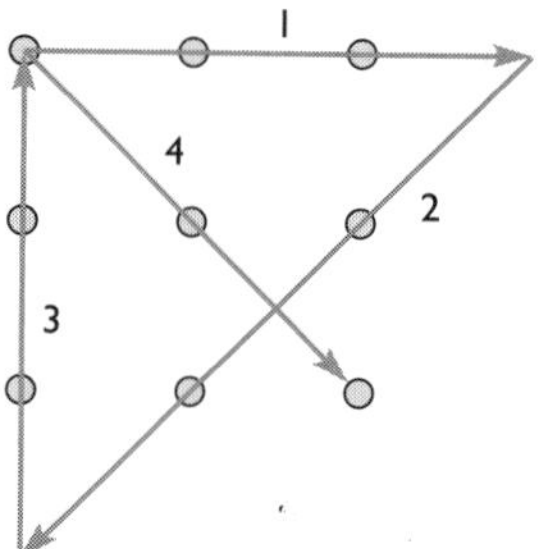

(3) One answer is three students: one psychology major, one chemistry major, and one history major. The other possibility is two students who are majoring in something else—music, for example. (If there are two music majors, all but two of them are indeed majoring in psychology etc.)

LANGUAGE

Language is a complicated and impressive product of human cognition. It enables us to learn from the experiences of people who lived at other times and places and thereby enables education and advances in technology. Thinking and language are not synonymous, but they are certainly related closely. It sometimes seems that people speak without thinking, but presumably, their speech represented *some* kind of thinking, even if it wasn't careful thinking. Furthermore, when adult humans think about something, they usually do so in words.

Language is an extremely versatile system. Other species signal one another in various ways, but only human languages have the property of **productivity**, *the ability to express new ideas.* Every day we say and hear a few stock sentences like "Nice weather we're having," or "I can't find my keys," but we also invent new sentences that no one has ever said before. The productivity of language enables humans to communicate an ever-changing array of ideas.

productivity
the ability to express new ideas.

transformational grammar
a system for converting a deep structure of a language into a surface structure.

You might ask, "How do you know that no one has ever said that sentence before?!" Well, of course, no one can be certain that a particular sentence is new, but we can be confident that many sentences are new (without specifying which ones) because of the vast number of possible ways to rearrange words. Imagine this exercise (but don't really try it unless you have nothing else to do with your life): Pick a sentence of more than 10 words from any book you choose. How long would you need to keep reading, in that book or any other, until you found the exact same sentence again?

In short, we do not memorize all the sentences we use. Not even infants do. Instead, we learn rules for making and understanding sentences. The famous linguist Noam Chomsky (1980) described those rules as a **transformational grammar**, *a system for converting a deep structure into a surface structure.* The deep structure is the underlying logic or meaning of a sentence. The surface structure is the sequence of words as they are actually spoken or written (Figure 9.22). According to this theory, whenever we speak, we transform the deep structure of the language into a surface structure.

FIGURE 9.22
According to transformational grammar, we can transform a sentence with a given deep structure into any of several other sentences with different surface structures.

Two surface structures can resemble each other without representing the same deep structure, or conversely, they can represent the same deep structure without resembling each other. For example, "John is easy to please" has the same deep structure as "pleasing John is easy" and "it is easy to please John." These sentences all represent the same underlying idea.

In contrast consider the sentence, "Never threaten someone with a chain saw." The surface structure of that sentence maps into two quite different deep structures, as shown in Figure 9.23.

Deep Structure No. 1:
You are holding a chain saw. Don't threaten to use it to attack someone!

Deep Structure No. 2:
Some deranged person is holding a chain saw. Don't threaten him!

FIGURE 9.23
The sentence "Never threaten someone with a chain saw" has one surface structure but two deep structures, corresponding to different meanings.

Language researcher Terrence Deacon once presented a brief talk about language to his 8-year-old's elementary school class. One child asked whether other animals have their own languages. Deacon explained that other species communicate but without the productivity of human language. The child persisted, asking whether other animals had at least a *simple* language, perhaps one with only a few words and short sentences. No, he replied, they do not have even a simple language.

Then another child asked, "Why not?" (Deacon, 1997, p. 12). Deacon paused, and then paused some more. Why not, indeed. He realized that this 8-year-old had asked a profound question. If language is so extremely useful to humans, why haven't other species evolved at least a little of it? And what makes humans so good at learning language?

Nonhuman Precursors to Language

One way to examine humans' language specialization is to ask how far another species could progress toward language with sufficient training. Beginning in the 1920s, several psychologists reared chimpanzees in their homes and tried to teach them to talk. The chimpanzees learned many human habits (Figure 9.24) but understood only a little of language.

a

b

c

d

e

© Courtesy of Ann Premack

FIGURE 9.24

Psychologists have tried to teach chimpanzees to communicate with gestures or visual symbols. (a) One of the Premacks' chimps arranges plastic chips to request food. (b) Viki in her human home, helping with the housework. After years with the Hayeses, she could make only a few sounds similar to English words. (c) Kanzi, a bonobo, presses symbols to indicate words. Among the primates bonobos have shown the most promising ability to acquire language. (d) A chimp signing *toothbrush*. (e) Roger Fouts with Alley the chimp, who is signing *lizard*.

Chimpanzees' vocal cords are poorly adapted to making voice sounds. The sounds they do make are mostly during inhaling, not exhaling. (Try to speak while inhaling!) However, chimpanzees do make hand gestures in nature. R. Allen Gardner and Beatrice Gardner (1969) taught a chimpanzee named Washoe to use the sign language of the American deaf (Ameslan). Washoe eventually learned the symbols for about 100 words.

How much do these gestures resemble language? Washoe and other chimpanzees trained in this way used their symbols almost exclusively to make requests, not to describe, and rarely in new, original combinations (Pate & Rumbaugh, 1983; Terrace, Petitto, Sanders, & Bever, 1979; C. R. Thompson & Church, 1980). By contrast a human child with a vocabulary of 100 words or so starts linking them into original combinations and short sentences and frequently uses words to describe.

The results have been different, however, for another species, *Pan paniscus*, sometimes known as the pygmy chimpanzee (a misleading term because these animals are almost as large as common chimpanzees) and sometimes known as the bonobo. Bonobos' social behavior resembles that of humans in several regards: Males and females form strong attachments; females are sexually responsive throughout the month, not just during their fertile period; males contribute to infant care; and adults often share food with one another.

Several bonobos have used symbols in impressive ways. They occasionally use the symbols to name and describe objects that they are not requesting. They sometimes use the symbols to describe past events. (One with a cut on his hand explained that his mother had bit him.) Also, they frequently make original, creative requests, such as asking one person to chase another.

The most proficient bonobos seem to comprehend symbols about as well as a 2- to $2^1/_2$-year-old child understands language (Savage-Rumbaugh et al., 1993). They have also shown considerable understanding of spoken English, following even such odd commands such as "bite your ball" and "take the vacuum cleaner outside" (Savage-Rumbaugh, 1990; Savage-Rumbaugh, Sevcik, Brakke, & Rumbaugh, 1992). They also passed the test of responding to commands issued over earphones, eliminating the possibility of unintentional "Clever Hans"-type signals (Figure 9.25).

The explanation for this impressive success pertains partly to species differences: Apparently, bonobos have greater language capacities than common chimpanzees. Another part of the explanation pertains to the method of training: Learning by observation and imitation promotes better understanding than the formal training methods that were used in previous studies (Savage-Rumbaugh et al., 1992). People, after all, learn language by imitation. Finally, the bonobos began their language experience early in life. Humans learn language more easily when they are young, and the same may be true for bonobos.

FIGURE 9.25

Kanzi, a bonobo, points to answers on a board in response to questions he hears through earphones. Experimenter Rose Sevcik sits with him but does not hear the questions, so she cannot signal the correct answer.

Human Specializations for Learning Language

Is the glass half full or half empty? Should we be impressed that bonobos understand language almost as well as a $2\frac{1}{2}$-year-old child or wonder why they do not progress further? Humans are clearly specialized to learn language in a way that no other species can.

Language and General Intelligence Did we evolve language as an accidental by-product of evolving big brains and great intelligence? The idea sounds appealing, but several observations argue strongly against it. Dolphins and whales have larger brains than humans have but do not develop language. (Yes, they communicate, but not in a flexible system resembling human language.) Some people with massive brain damage have less total brain mass than a chimpanzee but continue to speak and understand language.

Also, people in one family, all having a particular gene, develop normal intelligence except for language (Fisher, Vargha-Khadem, Watkins, Monaco, & Pembrey, 1998; Lai, Fisher, Hurst, Vargha-Khadem, & Monaco, 2001). Their pronunciation is poor and they do not fully master even simple rules, such as how to form plurals of nouns. So normal human brain size and normal intelligence do not automatically produce language.

Williams syndrome
a genetic condition characterized by mental retardation in most regards but skillful use of language.

At the opposite extreme, consider **Williams syndrome,** *a genetic condition characterized by mental retardation in most regards but skillful use of language.* Before the discovery of Williams syndrome, psychologists would have confidently said that good language was impossible without normal intelligence. One 14-year-old with Williams syndrome could write good creative stories and songs, but in other ways she performed like a 5- to 7-year-old and could not be left alone without a baby-sitter. Another child with Williams syndrome, when asked to name as many animals as he could think of, started with "ibex, whale, bull, yak, zebra, puppy, kitten, tiger, koala, dragon . . ." Another child could sing more than 1,000 songs in 22 languages (Bellugi & St. George, 2000). However, these children prefer 50 pennies to 5 dollars and, when asked to estimate the length of a bus, give answers such as "3 inches or 100 inches, maybe" (Bellugi, Lichtenberger, Jones, Lai, & St. George, 2000). Again, the conclusion is that language ability is not synonymous with overall intelligence.

Language Learning as a Specialized Capacity Susan Carey (1978) calculated that children between the ages of 1½ and 6 learn an average of nine new words per day. But how do they infer the meanings of all those words? Suppose you are in Japan and someone points to a pillow and says "makura." You therefore conclude that *makura* is the Japanese word for *pillow*. But logically, it could have meant "soft thing," "throwable thing," or even "*this particular* pillow." How did you make the correct inference that the word probably referred to the category *pillow*? More important, how did you know it meant anything at all? All you observed was that someone made a sound and pointed; you inferred the intention to communicate. That inference comes naturally to humans, but not to other species.

Noam Chomsky has argued that people learn language so easily that they must not be learning in the usual way. Children must begin with some preconceptions. The simplest and perhaps most important is the idea that words *mean* something. Children also make essential distinctions, such as between actors and actions (i.e., nouns and verbs), actors and recipients of action, singular and plural, same and different, and so forth. They have to learn how to express those relationships in their particular language, but they do not have to learn concepts like singular and plural themselves. Chomsky and his followers therefore suggest that people are born with a **language acquisition device** or "language instinct," *a built-in mechanism for acquiring language* (Pinker, 1994).

language acquisition device
a built-in mechanism for acquiring language.

Doubts and controversies remain, however, about exactly what is built in. Are we really born with concepts, distinctions, and a primitive grammar, or just with the ability to learn them? If we are born with a predisposition to learn language, what is the nature of that predisposition? The predisposition could be far removed from the details of language itself (Deacon, 1997; Seidenberg, 1997).

Here is one study suggesting an innate predisposition: Adult German speakers were asked to learn a little of Italian or Japanese, which were unfamiliar to them before the experiment. In all cases the experimenters used real Italian or Japanese words, but they taught some people real grammatical rules (which are unlike those of German) and other people some made-up rules unlike those of any known language. For example, one made-up rule was, "to make a sentence negative, add the negative word (*no* in Italian, *nai* in Japanese) after the third word of the sentence, whatever that word may be." Another fake rule was "to make a statement into a question, say the words in reverse order." So, "*Paolo mangia la pera"* (the Italian for "Paul eats the pear") would become "*Pera la mangia Paolo?*" ("Does Paul eat the pear?"). Those who learned either Italian or Japanese with real grammar showed increased activity in the brain areas usually associated with language. Those learning with the fake rules showed increased activity in other brain areas but not in the circuits usually important for language (Musso et al., 2003). Evidently, some grammars seem "natural" even when they are unfamiliar, whereas other grammars are recognized as "not real language."

But what conclusion do we draw? It would be a vast overstatement to say that we are literally born knowing the grammars of all possible languages. A more reasonable conclusion is that we are predisposed to learn some relationships more easily than others (Saffran, 2003). For example, making interrogatives by inverting the order of entire sentences would be difficult. Learning the rule itself would be easy, but applying it would be a difficult memory task when dealing with a long sentence.

Is it possible that infants learn all the complexities of word meanings and grammar from the apparently meager information they receive? Perhaps the information is better than we imagined. Parents throughout the world simplify the language-learning task by speaking to their infants in "parentese." I am not talking about silly "goo-goo" baby talk, but a pattern of speech that emphasizes and prolongs the vowels, making clearer than usual the difference between words such as *cat* and *cot* (Kuhl et al., 1997). Infants listen more intently to parentese than to normal speech and learn more from it. We also speak slowly, distinctly, and in simple words to someone who barely understands our language. To those who know the language well, we can speak rapidly, mumble, or speak in a noisy environment and still expect decent understanding (Calvin & Bickerton, 2000).

Several studies have found that even infants younger than 1 year old detect the regularities of the language they hear (Marcus, Vijayan, Rao, & Vishton, 1999; Saffran, 2003). For example, when adults speak they usually run all their words together without pausing between them: "Lookattheprettybaby." The infant detects which sounds go together as words by statistical relations. For example, the infant frequently hears the two-syllable combination "pretty" and frequently hears "ba-by" but less often hears the combination "ty-ba" and concludes that the word break comes between *pretty* and *baby.* We can infer that infants draw this conclusion because infants react to "ty-ba" as a new, attention-getting sound and don't react the same way to "pretty" or "baby" (Saffran, Aslin, & Newport, 1996). In short, infants learn the basics of language from regularities in what they hear.

Adults go through much the same process when trying to learn a foreign language (Cutler, Demuth, & McQueen, 2002). If you heard someone say, "vogubarilatusomatafikogovogurasu . . ." you would infer that the first word is either "vo," "vog," "vogu," or something longer because no word in any language is shorter than one syllable. (Whether we are born with that assumption or learn it is not known.) Because "vogu" was repeated already, but "voguba" was not, you would probably infer that "vogu" is one word of this language.

Language and the Human Brain What aspect of the human brain enables us to learn language so easily? Studies of people with brain damage have long pointed to two brain areas as particularly important for language. People with damage in the frontal cortex, including *Broca's area* (Figure 9.26), develop **Broca's aphasia,** *a condition characterized by inarticulate speech and by difficulties with both using and understanding grammatical devices—prepositions, conjunctions, word endings, complex sentence structures, and so forth.* For example, one patient who was asked about a dental appointment slowly mumbled, "Yes . . . Monday . . . Dad and Dick . . . Wednesday

Broca's aphasia
a condition characterized by inarticulate speech and by difficulties with both using and understanding grammatical devices—prepositions, conjunctions, word endings, complex sentence structures, and so forth.

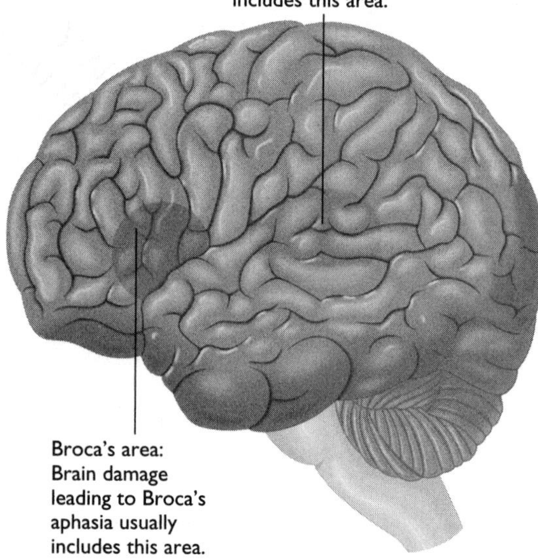

FIGURE 9.26

Brain damage that produces major deficits in language usually includes the left-hemisphere areas shown here. However, the deficits are severe only if the damage is more extensive, including these areas but extending to others as well. Many areas of the human brain contribute to language comprehension and production.

nine o'clock . . . 10 o'clock . . . doctors . . . and . . . teeth" (Geschwind, 1979, p. 186). These people do not really lose all grammatical understanding; they merely find it much more difficult to use and understand language, much as other people do when they are extremely distracted (Blackwell & Bates, 1995).

People with damage in the temporal cortex, including *Wernicke's area* (Figure 9.26), develop **Wernicke's aphasia,** *a condition marked by difficulty recalling the names of objects and impaired comprehension of language.* Because these people do not remember names, their speech is nonsensical even when it is grammatical. For example, one patient responded to a question about his health, "I felt worse because I can no longer keep in mind from the mind of the minds to keep me from mind and up to the ear which can be to find among ourselves" (Brown, 1977, p. 29).

However, language did not evolve simply by adding a language module to a chimpanzee brain. The brain areas important for language are critical for many other processes as well, including music (Patel, 2003) and some aspects of memory (Tyler et al., 2002). Brain damage that seriously impairs language always extends well beyond Broca's or Wernicke's area. Indeed, the nature of the language deficit varies from one person to another, and the location of the damage does accurately predict the language problems. Evidently, each person's language cortex is organized somewhat differently from everyone else's. Furthermore, PET scans or other brain recordings show widespread activation during speech (Just, Carpenter, Keller, Eddy, & Thulborn, 1996). It is hardly an exaggeration to say that the whole human brain is specialized to make language possible.

Wernicke's aphasia
a condition marked by difficulty recalling the names of objects and impaired comprehension of language.

Stages of Language Development Table 9.2 lists the average ages at which children reach various stages of language ability (Lenneberg, 1969; Moskowitz, 1978). Progression through these stages depends largely on maturation, not just extra

TABLE 9.2 Stages of Language Development.

AGE	TYPICAL LANGUAGE ABILITIES (MUCH INDIVIDUAL VARIATION)
3 months	Random vocalizations.
6 months	More distinct babbling.
1 year	Babbling that resembles the typical sounds of the family's language; probably one or more words including "mama"; language comprehension much better than production.
$1\frac{1}{2}$ years	Can say some words (mean about 50), mostly nouns; few or no phrases.
2 years	Speaks in two-word phrases.
$2\frac{1}{2}$ years	Longer phrases and short sentences with some errors and unusual constructions. Can understand much more.
3 years	Vocabulary near 1,000 words; longer sentences with fewer errors.
4 years	Close to adult speech competence.

experience (Lenneberg, 1967, 1969). Parents who expose their children to as much language as possible find that they can increase the children's vocabulary, but they hardly affect the rate of progression through language stages (Figure 9.27). At the other extreme, hearing children of deaf parents are exposed to much less spoken language, and at first they start "babbling" with rhythmic hand gestures (Petitto, Holowka, Sergio, & Ostry, 2001), but with even modest exposure to spoken language, their language development progresses on schedule.

© Stephen Rapley

FIGURE 9.27

Some overeager parents try to teach their children language at a very early age. The child may enjoy the attention, but the activity is unlikely to accelerate the child's progress in language development.

Deaf infants babble as much as hearing infants do for about the first 6 months and then start to decline. At first, hearing infants babble only haphazard sounds, but soon they start repeating the sounds that are common in the language they have been hearing. Thus, a 1-year-old babbles a variety of sounds that resemble French, Chinese, or whatever other language the family speaks (Locke, 1994).

One of the first sounds an infant can make is *muh*, and *muh, muh-muh*, or something similar has been adopted by most of the world's languages to mean "mother." Infants also make the sounds *duh, puh*, and *buh*. In many languages the word for father is similar to *dada* or *papa*. *Baba* is the word for grandmother in several languages. In effect infants tell their parents what words to use for important concepts. Indeed, Deacon (1997) has argued that children do not evolve to learn language; languages evolve to be easy for children to learn.

By age 1½ most toddlers have a vocabulary of about 50 words, but they seldom link words together. Thus, a toddler will say "Daddy" and "bye-bye" but not "Bye-bye, Daddy." In context parents can usually discern considerable meaning in these single-word utterances. *Mama* might mean, "That's a picture of Mama," "Take me to Mama," "Mama went away and left me here," or "Mama, I'm hungry." At this age toddlers understand language far better than they can produce it. In a sense they "learn how to learn" the meanings of words. If they are given careful practice with the idea that names refer to the shapes of objects—for example, being taught that *box* always refers to a particular shape, regardless of the color or size—they start increasing their vocabulary faster, particularly their vocabulary of the names of objects (L. B. Smith, Jones, Landau, Gershkoff-Stowe, & Samuelson, 2002).

By age 2, children start producing "telegraphic" phrases of two or more words, including combinations such as "more page," "allgone sticky," and "allgone outside" to indicate "read some more," "my hands are now clean," and "someone has closed the door," respectively. Note the originality of such phrases; it is unlikely that the parents ever said "allgone sticky"!

By age 2½ to 3 years, most children are generating full sentences, though each child maintains a few peculiarities. For example, many young children have their own rules for forming negative sentences. A common one is to add *no* or *not* to the beginning or end of a sentence, such as, "No I want to go to bed!" One little girl formed her negatives just by saying something louder and at a higher pitch; for instance, if she shrieked, "I want to share my toys!" she really meant, "I do *not* want to share my toys." Presumably, she had learned this "rule" by remembering that people screamed at her when they told her not to do something. My son Sam made negatives for a while by adding the word *either* to the end of a sentence: "I want to eat lima beans either." Apparently, he had heard people say, "I don't want to do that either" and had decided that the word *either* at the end of the sentence made it an emphatic negative.

Young children act as if they were applying grammatical rules. (I say "as if" because they cannot state the rules. By the same token, baseball players chasing a high fly ball act "as if" they understood calculus.) For example, a child may learn the word *feet* at an early age and then, after learning other plurals, abandon *feet* in favor of *foots*. Later, the child begins to compromise by saying "feets," "footses," or "feetses" before eventually returning to "feet." Children at this stage say many things they have never heard anyone else say, such as "the womans goed and doed something." Clearly, they are applying rules for how to form plurals and past tenses, although they *overregularize* or *overgeneralize* the rules. My son David invented the word *shis* to mean "belonging to a female." (He had apparently generalized the rule "He–his, she–shis.") Note that all these inventions imply that children are learning rules, not just repeating word combinations.

The progression of language stages suggests that language is a developmental process that unfolds, much like growth. Do we have a "critical period" for learning language early in life? Adults can learn the vocabulary of a second language faster than children can, but children learn the pronunciation better, as well as difficult aspects of the grammar. Even those who overheard another language in childhood without paying much attention to it learn it more easily later in life (Au, Knightly, Jun, & Oh, 2002). However, researchers find no sharp age cutoff for when language becomes more difficult. That is, starting a second language is easier for 2-year-olds than 4-year-olds, but also somewhat easier for 13-year-olds than 16-year-olds (Hakuta, Bialystok, & Wiley, 2003; Harley & Wang, 1997). So the results do not support a "critical period" with a cutoff date; we have a gradual tendency toward learning quicker when younger and gradually worsen with age (as with many other kinds of learning as well).

Children Exposed to No Language or Two Languages Would children who were exposed to no language at all make up their own? In rare cases an infant who was accidentally separated from other people grew up in a forest without human contact until discovered years later. Such children not only fail to show a language of their own but also fail to learn much language after they are given the chance (Pinker, 1994). However, their development is so abnormal and their early life so unknown that we should hesitate to draw conclusions.

The best evidence comes from studies of children who are deaf. Children who cannot hear well enough to learn speech and who are not taught sign language invent their own sign language, which they teach to other deaf children and so far as possible to their parents. As they grow older, they make the system more complex, linking signs together into sentences with fairly consistent word order and grammatical rules—for example, "Mother, twist open the jar, blow a bubble, so I can clap it" (Goldin-Meadow, McNeill, & Singleton, 1996; Goldin-Meadow & Mylander, 1998). Observations of sign language in Nicaragua found that the language had evolved over the decades, becoming more complex and richer in information. Thus, the younger deaf people, who had learned the richer language from their early childhood, had in many ways more expressive signs than older deaf people, who had originally learned the less complex version (Senghas & Coppola, 2001).

Although each deaf child invents a different system, most systems share some interesting similarities. For example, most include some sort of marker to indicate the difference between a subject that is doing something to an object ("the mouse eats the cheese") and a subject that is doing something without an object ("the mouse is moving"). The sign languages invented by children in Taiwan resemble those of children in the United States, even though the spoken languages of those countries—Chinese and English—have very different grammars (Goldin-Meadow & Mylander, 1998).

If a deaf child starts to invent a sign language and no one responds to it, because the child meets no other deaf children and the adults fail to or refuse to learn, the child gradually abandons it and becomes totally without language. If such a child is exposed to sign language much later, such as age 12, he or she struggles to develop even weak signing skills and never catches up with those who started earlier (Harley & Wang, 1997; Mayberry, Lock, & Kazmi, 2002). This observation is our best evidence for the importance of early development in language learning: A child who doesn't learn a language while young is permanently impaired at learning one.

Some children grow up in a **bilingual** environment, *learning two languages about equally well.* Bilingualism is especially common among immigrant children, who are generally bicultural as well, learning both their parents' customs and those of their new country. The areas of brain activity during language use are the same in bilingual people as in those with only one language (Paradis, 1990; Solin, 1989). If the brain representations are so similar, how do bilingual people keep their two languages separate? The answer is that they do not, at least not completely (Francis, 1999).

bilingual
able to use two languages about equally well.

Bilingualism has two disadvantages: Children take longer to master two languages than to master one (of course), and even adult bilinguals occasionally confuse words from the two languages. The primary advantage is obvious: If you learn a second language, you can communicate with more people. A second advantage is subtle: A bilingual person gains extra cognitive flexibility by learning that there are different ways of expressing the same idea. For example, children younger than 6 years old who speak only one language apparently believe that every object has only one name. If an adult gestures toward a cup and a gyroscope and says, "Please bring me the gyroscope," a child who knows the word *cup* will immediately bring the gyroscope, assuming that if one object is the cup, the other one must be the gyroscope. But the child would also fetch the gyroscope if asked to bring the *vessel,* the *chalice,* or any other synonym for *cup* that the child did not know. A bilingual child, however, is more likely to hesitate or to ask for help, understanding that an unfamiliar word could refer to the cup just as easily as the other object (Davidson, Jergovic, Imami, & Theodos, 1997).

Understanding Language

On a trip to Norway some years ago, I consulted my Norwegian phrase book and asked directions to the men's room: "Hvor er toalettet?" When the man answered—in Norwegian, of course—I suddenly realized the problem: It doesn't do me any good to speak the language unless I understand the answers!

Understanding a Word We customarily describe the word *cat* as being composed of three sounds, *kuh, ah,* and *tuh.* However, the first sound in *cat* is not quite the same as the consonant sound in *kuh;* the *a* and *t* sounds are changed also. Each letter changes its sound depending on the other sounds that precede and follow it. What we hear also depends on the context and our expectations. For example, a researcher computer-modified a sound to be halfway between a normal *s* sound and a normal *sh* sound. When this intermediate sound replaced the *s* sound at the end of the word *embarrass,* people heard it as an *s* sound, but when the same sound replaced the *sh* at the end of *abolish,* people heard the same sound as *sh* (Samuel, 2001).

We also use lipreading more than we realize to understand what we hear. If lip movements do not match the sound, we sometimes "hear" something that is neither what we saw nor what we heard, but a compromise between them (McGurk & MacDonald, 1976).

In another study students listened to a tape recording of a sentence with one sound missing (Warren, 1970). The sentence was, "The state governors met with their respective legislatures convening in the capital city." However, the sound of the first *s* in the word *legislatures,* along with part of the adjacent *i* and *l,* had been replaced by a cough or a tone. The students were asked to listen to the recording and try to identify the location of the cough or tone. None of the 20 students identified the location correctly, and half thought the cough or tone interrupted one of the other words on the tape. They all claimed to have heard the *s* plainly. In fact even those who had been told that the *s* sound was missing still insisted that they had heard the sound. Apparently, the brain uses the context to fill in the missing sound.

Many English words have different meanings in different contexts. *Rose* can refer to a flower, or it can be the past tense of the verb *to rise*. *Dove* can refer to a bird related to pigeons, or it can be the past tense of the verb *to dive*. Consider the word *mean* in this sentence: "What did that mean old statistician mean by asking us to find the mean and mode of this distribution?" Just as we hear the word *legislatures* as a whole, not as a string of separate letters, we interpret a sequence of words as a whole, not one at a time. For example, suppose you hear a tape-recorded word that is carefully engineered to sound halfway between *dent* and *tent*. If you simply hear it and are asked to say what you heard, you might reply "dent," "tent," or "something sort of intermediate between dent and tent." But now suppose you hear that same sound in context:

1. When the *ent in the fender was well camouflaged, we sold the car.
2. When the *ent in the forest was well camouflaged, we began our hike.

   Most people who hear sentence 1 report the word *dent*. Most who hear sentence 2 report *tent*. Now consider two more sentences:

3. When the *ent was noticed in the fender, we sold the car.
4. When the *ent was noticed in the forest, we stopped to rest.

For sentences 3 and 4, the context comes too late to help. People are as likely to report hearing *dent* in one sentence as in the other (Connine, Blasko, & Hall, 1991). Think for a moment what this means: In the first two sentences, the fender or forest showed up three syllables after *ent. In the second pair, the fender or forest appeared six syllables later. Evidently, when you hear an ambiguous sound, you can hold it in a temporary "undecided" state for about three syllables for the context to help you understand it. Beyond that point it is too late; you hear it one way or the other and stick with your decision, regardless of the later context.

Although a long-delayed context cannot help you hear an ambiguous word correctly, it can help you understand its meaning. Consider the following sentence from Karl Lashley (1951):

> Rapid righting with his uninjured hand saved from loss the contents of the capsized canoe.

If you hear this sentence spoken aloud, so that spelling is not a clue, you are likely at first to interpret the second word as *writing*, until you reach the final two words of the sentence. Suddenly, the phrase *capsized canoe* changes the whole scenario; now we understand that *righting* meant "pushing with a paddle." In summary only the immediate context can influence what you hear, but even a delayed context can change the word's meaning.

Understanding Sentences Making sense of language requires knowledge about the world. For example, consider the following sentences (from Just & Carpenter, 1987):

- That store sells horse shoes.
- That store sells alligator shoes.

You interpret *horse shoes* to mean "shoes for horses to wear," but you don't interpret *alligator shoes* as "shoes for alligators to wear." Your understanding of the sentences depended on your knowledge of the world, not just the syntax of the sentences.

Here is another example:

- I'm going to buy a pet hamster at the store, if it's open.
- I'm going to buy a pet hamster at the store, if it's healthy.

Nothing about the sentence structure told you that *it* refers to the store in the first sentence and the hamster in the second sentence. You understood because you know that stores but not hamsters can be open, whereas hamsters but not stores can be healthy.

In short, you don't base your sentence understanding just on the sentence itself. Language comprehension depends on your knowledge of the world and all the assumptions that you share with the speaker or writer of the sentence. Sometimes you even have to remember where you are because the meaning of a word differs from one place to another (Figure 9.28).

FIGURE 9.28

In England a *football coach* is a bus full of soccer fans. In the United States it's the person who directs a team of American football players.

Now consider this sentence: *While Anna dressed the baby played in the crib.* Quickly: Whom did Anna dress? And who played in the crib? The addition of a comma would simplify the sentence, but even without it, English grammar prohibits "baby" from being both the object of *dressed* and the subject of *played*. If the baby played in the crib (as you no doubt answered), Anna must have dressed herself. Nevertheless, many people misunderstand and think Anna dressed the baby (Ferreira, Bailey, & Ferraro, 2002). Remember the example from earlier in the chapter about how many animals Moses took on the ark? That was another example in which many people overlook the details of the sentence and construct a "good enough" interpretation of the sentence's meaning based on their knowledge and reasonable expectations. That strategy occasionally misleads us, but it proves valuable in far more cases, such as those about the alligator shoes or buying a hamster at the store.

Limits to Our Language Understanding Some sentences that follow the rules of grammar are nevertheless nearly incomprehensible. One example is a doubly embedded sentence—a sentence within a sentence within a sentence. A singly embedded sentence is understandable, though not simple:

The dog the cat saw chased a squirrel.

The squirrel the dog chased climbed the tree.

In the first sentence, "the cat saw the dog" is embedded within "the dog chased a squirrel." In the second, "the dog chased the squirrel" is embedded within "the squirrel climbed the tree." So far, so good, but now consider a doubly embedded sentence:

The squirrel the dog the cat saw chased climbed the tree.

Doubly embedded sentences overburden our memory. In fact, if your memory is already burdened with other matters, you may have trouble understanding even a singly embedded sentence (Gordon, Hendrick, & Levine, 2002).

Double negatives are also difficult to understand. "I would not deny that . . ." means that I agree. "It is not false that . . ." means that something is true. People can understand such sentences, but with difficulty. Have you ever seen a multiple-choice test item that asks "Which of the following is not true . . ." and then one of the choices has a *not* in it? When that happens, confusion is almost certain.

Triple negatives are, of course, still worse. Consider the following sentence, which includes *four* (!) negatives (emphasis added): "If you do *not* unanimously find from your consideration of all the evidence that there are *no* mitigating factors sufficient to *preclude* the imposition of a death sentence, then you should sign the verdict requiring the court to impose a sentence *other than* death." In Illinois a judge reads those instructions to a jury in a capital punishment case to explain how to decide between a death penalty and life in prison. (Do you think many jurors will understand?)

Even single negatives are sometimes confusing. Suppose you are trying to decide whether to buy a product at the supermarket. You notice on the package, "Contains no cyanide or rat pieces!" Does that notice encourage you to buy the product? Hardly! It is as if you do not fully believe the "no." (After all, why would the manufacturer even mention the absence of something unless it might be present?) I was once on an airplane that turned around shortly after departure because one of its two engines failed. The attendant told the passengers what was happening, but until she said "Please don't panic," we didn't realize there was any reason to panic.

In one clever experiment, students watched an experimenter pour sugar into two jars. The students were then told to label one jar "sucrose, table sugar" and the other "not sodium cyanide, not poison." Then the experimenter made two cups of Kool-Aid, one from each jar of sugar, and asked the students to choose one cup to drink (Figure 9.29). Of those who expressed a preference, 35 of 44 wanted Kool-Aid made from the jar marked "sucrose," not from the one that denied cyanide and poison (Rozin, Markwith, & Ross, 1990).

Monitoring Understanding Earlier, we encountered the sentence "Never threaten someone with a chain saw." Another ambiguous sentence is "The daughter of the man and the woman arrived." Who arrived—one person (the man and woman's daughter)—or two people (the man's daughter plus some other woman)? If you said something like this, you would presumably know which meaning you intended, and your listener might know too because of the context or because of your pauses, intonations, and gestures. But might you overestimate your listener's understanding?

In one study people were asked to read aloud a series of ambiguous sentences, such as, "The daughter of the man and the woman arrived." In each case the speaker was told which of the two meanings was correct and was instructed to say the sentence to convey that meaning. After each sentence the speaker estimated the probability that a listener would correctly understand. On the average, speakers estimated correct understanding 72% of the time, whereas the listeners understood only 61% (Keysar & Henly, 2002). Remember from earlier in this chapter people's general tendency to be overconfident of themselves. Here we see another example.

Good writers try to avoid ambiguous or confusing sentences, and their copy editors try to catch any confusion the writer hadn't noticed. Still, some badly worded sentences make it to print. For example, a student newspaper once included this gem of a sentence: *He said Harris told him she and Brothers told French that grades had been changed.* When good readers find a sentence like that, they stop and reread it until they understand. Poorer readers tend to read everything at about a steady speed, regardless of how confusing it is.

FIGURE 9.29

Most students preferred Kool-Aid made with sugar labeled "sugar" instead of sugar labeled "not cyanide," even though they had placed the labels themselves. Evidently, people do not fully believe the word "not." (*Based on results of Rozin, Markwith, & Ross, 1990*)

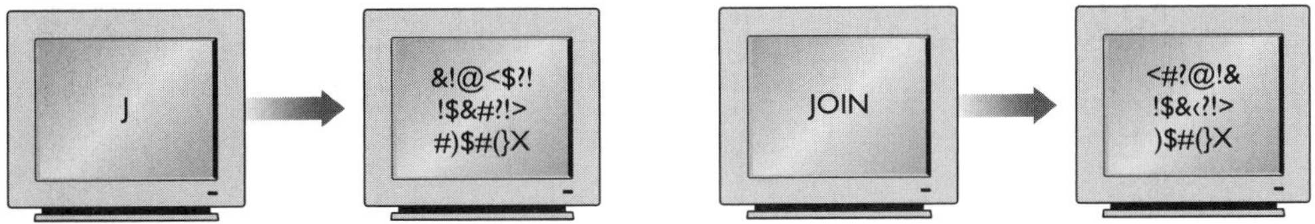

FIGURE 9.30

Either a word or a single letter flashed on a screen and then an interfering pattern. The observers were asked, "Which was presented: *C* or *J*?" More of them identified the letter correctly when it was part of a word.

Reading

As you will recall from earlier in this chapter, expertise achieved after 10 or so years of intensive practice enables one to recognize complex patterns at a glance. You have intensively practiced reading for more than the last 10 years, so in that regard you qualify as an expert reader. You may not think of yourself as an expert because we usually reserve the term *expert* for someone who is far more skilled than others. Nevertheless, your years of reading enable you to recognize words instantaneously, like an expert who recognizes chess patterns at a glance.

Word Recognition Consider the following experiment: The investigator flashes one letter on a screen for less than a quarter of a second and then shows an interfering pattern and asks, "Was the letter C or J?" Then the experimenter flashes an entire word on the screen for the same length of time and asks, "Was the first letter of the word C or J?" (Figure 9.30). Which question do you think would be easier to answer? Most people can *identify the letter more accurately when it is part of a whole word than when it is presented by itself* (Reicher, 1969; Wheeler, 1970). This is known as the **word-superiority effect**.

word-superiority effect identifying a letter with greater ease when it is part of a whole word than when it is presented by itself.

In further research James Johnston and James McClelland (1974) briefly flashed words on the screen and asked students to identify one letter (whose position was marked) in each word (Figure 9.31). On some trials the experimenters told the students to focus on the center of the area where the word would appear and to try to see the whole word. On other trials they showed the students exactly where the critical letter would appear on the screen and told them to focus on that spot and ignore the rest of the screen. Most students identified the critical letter more successfully when they looked at the whole word than when they focused on just the letter itself. This benefit occurs only with a real word, like COIN, not with a nonsense combination, like CXQF (Rumelhart & McClelland, 1982).

You may have experienced the word-superiority effect yourself. To pass time on long car trips, people sometimes try to find every letter of the alphabet on the billboards. It is usually easier to spot a letter by reading complete words than by checking letter by letter.

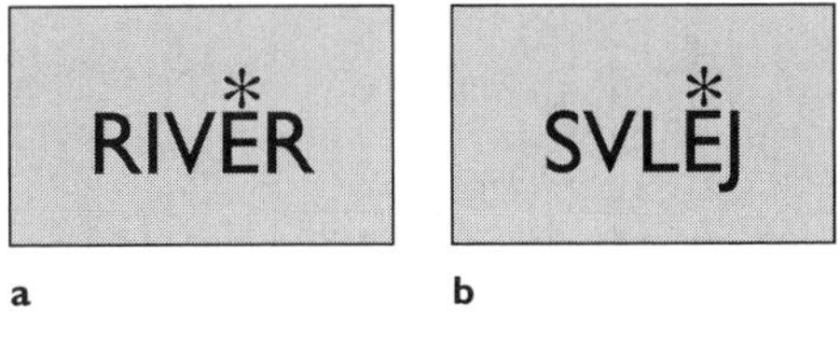

FIGURE 9.31

Students identified an indicated letter better when they focused on an entire word (a) than on a single letter in a designated spot (b).

What accounts for the word-superiority effect? According to one model (J. L. McClelland, 1988; Rumelhart, McClelland, & the PDP Research Group, 1986), our perceptions and memories are represented by vast numbers of connections among "units," presumably corresponding to sets of neurons. Each unit is connected to other units (Figure 9.32). Each unit, when activated, excites some of its neighbors and inhibits others. Suppose that, at a given moment, units corresponding to the letters C, O, I, and N are moderately active. They excite a higher order unit corresponding to the word COIN. Although none of the four letter units sends a strong message by itself, the collective impact is strong (J. L. McClelland & Rumelhart,

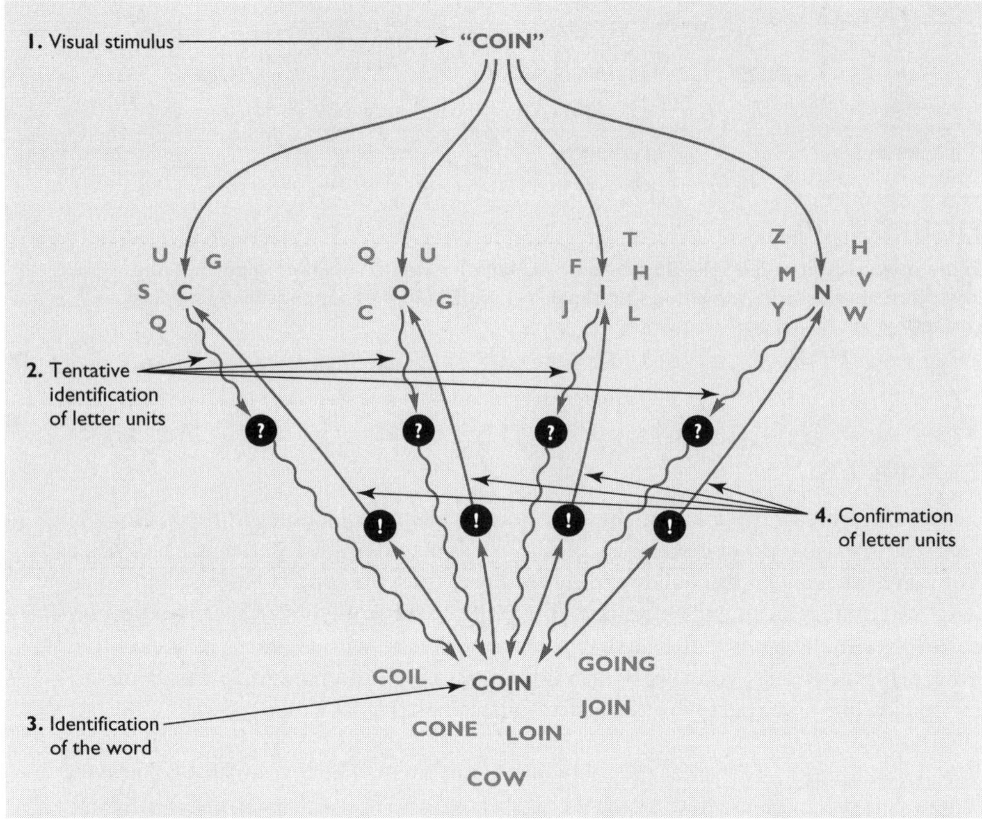

FIGURE 9.32

According to one model, a visual stimulus activates certain letter units, some more strongly than others. Those letter units then activate a word unit, which in turn strengthens the letter units that compose it. For this reason we recognize a whole word more easily than a single letter.

1981). This higher level perception COIN then feeds excitation back to the individual letter-identifying units and confirms their tentative identifications.

This model helps explain our perception of Figure 9.33. Why do you see the top word in that figure as *RED* instead of *PFB*? After all, in the other words, those letters do look like *P*, *F*, and *B*. But in the top word, one ambiguous figure activates some *P* units and some *R* units; the next figure activates *E* and *F* units, and the

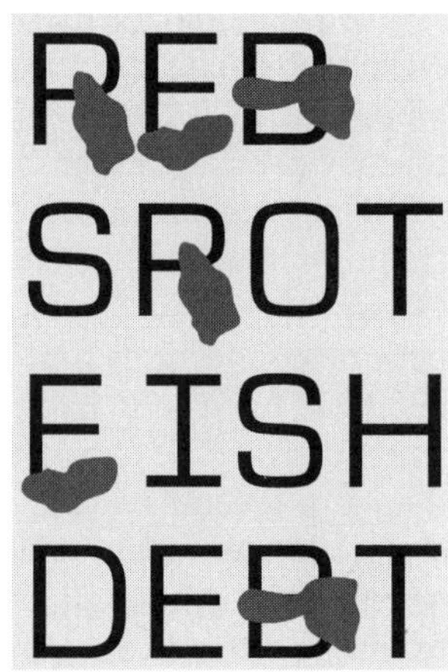

FIGURE 9.33

The combination of possible letters enables us to identify a word; word recognition in turn helps to confirm the letter identifications. Although each of the letters in the top word is ambiguous, a whole word—RED—is perceived. (*"Parallel Distributed Processing: Explorations in the Microstructures of Cognition,"* Vol. 1: Foundations *by David E. Rumethan et al., p. 8, figure 2. Series in Computational Models of Cognition and Perception. Copyright 1986 by MIT Press. Used with permission of the publisher.*)

third figure activates *D* and *B* units. All of those units in turn activate other more complex units corresponding to *RFB, PFB, PFD,* and *RED.* As you tentatively perceive the word as *RED* (the only English word among those choices), the feedback strengthens the activity of the *R, E,* and *D* units.

Reading and Eye Movements In an alphabetical language such as English, the printed page consists of letters that form familiar clusters that in turn form words and sentences. One kind of cluster is a **phoneme**, *a unit of sound.* A phoneme can be a single letter (such as *f*) or a combination of letters (such as *sh*). Good reading requires mastering phonics—the relationship between letters and sounds (Rayner, Foorman, Perfetti, Pesetsky, & Seidenberg, 2001). Another kind of cluster is a **morpheme**, *a unit of meaning.* For example, the noun *thrills* has two morphemes (*thrill* and *s*). The final *s* is a unit of meaning because it indicates that the noun is plural (see Figure 9.34).

phoneme
a unit of sound.

morpheme
a unit of meaning.

When we read, do we ordinarily read one letter, one phoneme, one morpheme, or one or more words at a time? And do we move our eyes in a steady or jerky fashion? The movements are fast, and we are ordinarily not aware of them. Psychologists have arranged devices to monitor eye movements during reading. Their first discovery was that a reader's eyes move in a jerky fashion. You can move your eyes steadily to follow a moving object, but when you are scanning a stationary object, such as a page of print, you alternate between **fixations**, *when your eyes are stationary,* and *quick eye movements called* **saccades** (sa-KAHDS) *that take your eyes from one fixation point to another.*

fixation
a period when the eyes are steady.

saccade
a quick jump in the focus of the eyes from one point to another.

You read during your fixations but you are virtually blind during the saccades. To illustrate this point, try the following demonstration: Look at yourself in the mirror and focus on your left eye. Then move your focus to the right eye. Can you see your eyes moving in the mirror? (Go ahead; try it.) People generally agree that they do not see their eyes move.

"Oh, but wait," you say. "That movement in the mirror was simply too quick and too small to be seen." Wrong. Try again, but this time get someone else to look at your left eye and then shift his or her gaze to your right eye. Now you do see the other person's eye movement, so the movement itself is not too fast or too small to be seen. Go back and try your own eyes in the mirror again and observe the difference. You can see someone else's eyes moving, but you cannot see your own eyes moving in the mirror.

There are two explanations: First, certain areas in the parietal cortex monitor impending eye movements and send a message to the primary visual cortex, in effect telling the visual cortex, "The eyes are about to move, so shut down activity for a moment." Even if you are in total darkness, the visual cortex decreases its activity during saccadic eye movements (Burr, Morrone, & Ross, 1994; Paus, Marrett, Worsley, & Evans, 1995). Second, the stationary view at the end of a saccade interferes with the blurry view you saw during the saccade (Matin, Clymer, & Matin, 1972).

FIGURE 9.34
The word *shamelessness* has nine phonemes (units of sound) and three morphemes (units of meaning).

The consequence is that we see during fixations and not during saccades. An average adult reading a magazine article fixates on each point for about 200 to 250 milliseconds (ms). Good readers generally have briefer fixations than poor readers do, and everyone has briefer fixations on familiar words like *girl* than on harder words like *ghoul*. We also tend to pause a little longer on words with more than one meaning, like *bark* or *lie* (Rodd, Gaskell, & Marslen-Wilson, 2002). After each fixation, the next saccade lasts 25 to 50 ms. Thus, most readers have about four fixations per second (Rayner, 1998).

(In the attentional blink experiments discussed earlier, a letter that is flashed on the screen interferes with another letter that is flashed 200 ms later. So why doesn't one fixation interfere with another one when you are reading? The main explanation is that the flashes are very brief in the attentional blink experiments. The other explanation relates to the word-superiority effect: It is easier to read whole words in a meaningful context than to identify isolated letters.)

How much can a person read during one fixation? Many people believe they see quite a bit of the page at each instant. However, research indicates that we read only about 11 characters—one or two words—at a time. To demonstrate this limitation, focus on the letter *i* marked by an arrow (↓) in the two sentences below.

↓

1. This is a sentence with no misspelled words.

↓

2. Xboc tx zjg rxunce with no mijvgab zucn.

If you permit your eyes to wander back and forth, you quickly notice that sentence 2 is mostly gibberish. But as long as you dutifully keep your eyes on the fixation point, the sentence looks all right. You can read the letter on which you fixated plus about three or four characters (including spaces) to the left and about seven to the right; the rest is a blur. Therefore, you see *—ce with no m—*, or possibly *—nce with no mi—*.

This limit of about 11 letters depends partly on the lighting; in faint light your span decreases to as little as 1 or 2 letters, and your reading ability suffers accordingly (Legge, Ahn, Klitz, & Luebker, 1997). The limit does not depend on how much fits into the fovea of your eyes. In the following display, again focus on the letter *i* in each sentence and check how many letters you can read to its left and right:

↓
This is a sentence with no misspelled words.

↓
This is a sentence with no misspelled words.

↓
is a sentence with no misspelled

If your reading span were limited by how many letters can fit into the fovea of your retina, you should be able to read more letters in the top sentence and fewer as the letters get larger. In fact you do at least as well, maybe even better, with a larger print sentence (up to a point).

What we can see at a glance also depends on our habits of reading. In Japanese, where each character conveys more information than English letters do, readers see fewer letters per fixation (Rayner, 1998). And in Hebrew and Farsi, which are written right to left, readers read more letters to the left of fixation and fewer to the right (Brysbaert, Vitu, & Schroyens, 1996; Faust, Kravetz, & Babkoff, 1993; Malamed & Zaidel, 1993).

Often, our 11-character window of reading includes one word plus a fragment of another. For example, suppose you have fixated on the point shown by an arrow in the following sentence:

↓
The government made serious mistakes.

Readers can see the word *serious* plus about the first three letters of *mistakes*. Three letters do not identify the word; from what the reader knows, the next word could be *misspellings, misbehavior, missiles, mishmash,* or any of a number of other *mis*-things that a government might make.

Does the preview of the next word facilitate reading? Yes. In one study college students again read passages on a computer screen while a machine monitored their eye movements. The computer correctly displayed the word the student fixated on plus the next zero, three, or four letters. So the display might look like this:

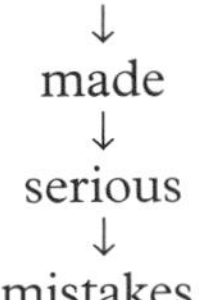

↓
made
↓
serious
↓
mistakes.

or like this:

↓
made ser
↓
serious mis
↓
mistakes.

Students who could preview the first three or four letters of the next word read significantly faster than those who could not (Inhoff, 1989). Evidently, while we are reading one word, we are previewing the next. Our preview helps guide the next eye movement and gives us a head start on identifying the next word (Inhoff, Radach, Eiter, & Juhasz, 2003).

You might wonder what speed-readers do differently from normal readers. An average adult reader has about four or five fixations per second with occasional backtracks, for an overall rate of about 200 words per minute. Speed-readers have briefer fixations with fewer backtracks. With practice people can double or triple their reading speed with normal comprehension. Some claim that they see more than 11 characters per fixation, and unfortunately, researchers haven't done enough studies to test this possibility. However, unless they increase their span enormously, reading speed has some physical limits. Each saccadic eye movement lasts 25 to 50 ms, and reading does not occur during saccades. Thus, it would be impossible to exceed 20 to 40 fixations per second, even if each fixation lasted no time at all! If we make the generous estimate that people might be able to average 2 words per fixation, the theoretical maximum would be 20 to 80 words per second, or 1,200 to 4,800 words per minute. And remember, this calculation unrealistically assumes a fixation time of zero. Yet some people claim to read 5,000 to 10,000 words per minute. In fact they are fixating on some words and guessing the rest. A combination of reading and guessing can produce very fast reading and adequate comprehension of books with predictable content, like a James Bond novel. However, the speed-reader does miss details. When speed-readers read college textbooks, they either slow their reading (Just & Carpenter, 1987) or fail the tests (Homa, 1983).

REVIEW

- *Research methods in cognitive psychology.* Researchers cannot directly observe thinking or knowledge, but they can make inferences from observations such as people's delays in answering various questions.
- *Mental imagery.* Mental images resemble vision in certain respects. For example, the time required to answer questions about a rotating object depends on how far the object would actually rotate between one position and another.
- *Categorization.* People use many categories that are hard to define; we determine whether something fits the category by how closely it resembles familiar examples. Many items are marginal examples of a category, so we cannot insist on a yes/no decision.
- *Conceptual networks.* We represent words or concepts with links to related concepts. Hearing or thinking about one concept will temporarily prime the linked concepts, and hearing several concepts can strongly prime another.
- *Cross-cultural studies of concepts.* A word in one language may not correspond exactly to a word in another language; however, the similarities people see across objects do not depend on the words they use to name them.
- *Attentive and preattentive processes.* We notice unusual items or items that have started to move almost at once, preattentively, regardless of potential distracters. Noticing less distinct items requires more careful attention to one possible target after another.
- *The Stroop effect.* Sometimes it is difficult to avoid attending to certain stimuli; for example, it is difficult to state the color of the ink in which words are written while ignoring the words themselves (especially if they are color names).
- *Attention limits.* Ordinarily, we notice only a small portion of a scene, perceiving and remembering just a vague gist of the rest. We often fail to detect changes in a scene if they occur slowly or during an eye blink or eye movement. We also frequently fail to detect a stimulus that appears 100 to 700 ms after a first stimulus that required some attention.
- *Shifting attention.* Attending to one stimulus or activity detracts from attention to another. However, repeated practice, such as from playing video games, alters the degree to which someone divides attention across objects.
- *Becoming an expert.* Experts are made, not born. Becoming an expert requires years of practice and effort.
- *Expert pattern recognition.* Experts recognize and memorize familiar and meaningful patterns more rapidly than less experienced people do.
- *Steps for solving a problem.* Problem solving can be described as a series of steps: understanding the problem, generating hypotheses, testing the hypotheses, and checking the result.
- *Algorithms and heuristics.* People solve problems by using algorithms (repetitive means of checking every possibility) or heuristics (ways of simplifying the problem to get a reasonable solution).
- *Generalizing.* People who have learned how to solve a problem often fail to apply that solution to a similar problem.
- *Insight.* With insight problems people have trouble estimating how close they are to a solution. However, they may be making more progress than they realize.
- *Creativity.* Creative people work in a field in which they have knowledge and self-confidence; no one is creative in all fields. Many highly creative people go through a period in which they rely on a small group of friends, perhaps just one, for support and encouragement. They dedicate their lives to their work, often to the exclusion of all else.
- *Thinking by heuristics.* Heuristics simplify complex problems and help us find quick answers that are correct most of the time. However, overreliance on them or inappropriate use of them can lead to errors.
- *Representativeness heuristic and base-rate information.* If something resembles members of some category, we usually assume it too belongs to that category. However, that assumption is risky if the category is a rare one.
- *Availability heuristic.* We generally assume that the more easily we can think of examples of some category, the more common that category is. However, some rare items are easy to think of because they get much publicity or because they stand out emotionally.
- *Critical thinking.* Even people who try conscientiously to evaluate the evidence for every claim sometimes find themselves repeating a nonsensical statement that they know they should have doubted.
- *Reasons for errors.* People tend to be overconfident about their own judgments, especially on difficult questions. They are attracted to high-payoff gambles even when the chance of winning is extremely low. They tend to look for evidence that supports their hypothesis instead of evidence that might reject it. They answer the same question differently when it is phrased differently. They sometimes take unpleasant actions to avoid admitting that previous actions were a waste of time or money.
- *Language productivity.* Human languages enable us to create new words and phrases to express new ideas.

- *Language training in nonhumans.* Bonobos, and to a lesser extent other chimpanzees, have learned certain aspects of language. Human evolution evidently elaborated on potentials found in our apelike ancestors but developed that potential further.
- *Language and intelligence.* It is possible to have intelligence without language or language without other aspects of intelligence. Therefore, many psychologists regard language as a specialized capacity, not just a by-product of overall intelligence.
- *Rapid language learning in children.* Children learn language at an amazing rate, considering the unsystematic training they receive. In some way children are born with a predisposition to learn language easily.
- *Brain organization and aphasia.* Brain damage, especially in the left hemisphere, can impair people's ability to understand or use language. However, many brain areas contribute to language in varied ways.
- *Stages of language development.* Children advance through several stages of language development, probably reflecting maturation of brain structures necessary for language and not just the total amount of experience. From the start children's language is creative, using the rules of language to make new word combinations and sentences.
- *Children exposed to no language or two.* If deaf children are not exposed to language, they invent a sign language of their own. However, a deaf child who has no opportunity to use sign language in childhood will be impaired on learning it or any other language later. Children in a bilingual environment sometimes have trouble keeping the two languages separate but gain the ability to converse with many people and in certain ways show extra cognitive flexibility.
- *Understanding language.* Much of speech is ambiguous; we understand words and sentences in context by applying the knowledge we have about the world in general.
- *Limits to our language understanding.* Many sentences are difficult to understand, especially those with embedded clauses or more than one negative. Difficult grammar places a burden on our working memory.
- *Reading.* When we read, we have fixation periods separated by eye movements called saccades. We read during the fixations, not the saccades. Even good readers can read only about 11 letters per fixation; people increase their speed of reading by increasing the number of fixations per second.

CHAPTER 9 PRACTICE EXAM

____ 1. In a study by Shepard and Metzler's when students had to decide if two drawings of blocks were the same or different, students
   a. Accuractely responded to same and different.
   b. took longer to say "same" when the objects were many degrees different in orientation
   c. took longer to say "same" when the objects were closely aligned.
   d. Inaccurately responded to same and different.

____ 2. The prototype concept suggests that
   a. Categorical spatial concepts are the same.
   b. Different cultures respond to prototypes by categorizing.
   c. An object is compared to typical exemplars of the object.
   d. An object is compared to every other member of the category.

____ 3. Based on the results of the cross cultural research in which participants from different cultures were asked to describe objects, the following is true.
   a. All cultures use the same number of words.
   b. All speakers used different languages and the same number of words.
   c. Chinese used more words than everyone else.
   d. Spanish speakers use more words than anyone else.

____ 4. If all but one person is wearing the same color clothes, people are likely to notice the different one immediately because of what process?
   a. Motivational process.
   b. Comparson process comparing each student to every other student.
   c. Preattentive process.
   d. Hypervigilant process.

____ 5. The Stroop Effect is when people find it easier to
   a. remember events about other people.
   b. Recall a story after ten minutes of listening to music
   c. read a word than to say the color of its ink.
   d. read a whole word pages of different colors.

____ 6. Becoming an expert on requires
   a. inborn talent in an area.
   b. A high IQ
   c. Emotional intelligence.
   d. Concentrated practice for ten years.

____ 7. Which one of the following is NOT one of the four phases in solving a problem?
   a. Coming up with an example representative sample
   b. understanding the problem
   c. generating one or more hypotheses
   d. testing the hypotheses

____ 8. A "heuristic" is a
   a. question that is worded in a confusing way.
   b. repetitive, mechanical procedure for trying all possible alternatives.
   c. way of simplifying a problem.
   d. possible answer that was considered but then rejected.

____ 9. High levels of creativity seem a
   a. highly heritable.
   b. Useful set of various skills
   c. Concept that does not exist.
   d. tied to knowing a lot about a particular topic.

____ 10. George sees a person who looks like a rock star and assumes it is the rock star, but George forgets that 1% of all women look somewhat like the rock star. George has made what error? famous movie actor. He assumes it really is the actor and overlooks the fact that about 1% of all adult men look a little like that actor. What error has Zeke made?
   a. failure of the the availability heuristic
   b. failure of cognitive mapping
   c. failure to consider base-rate information
   d. Failure of the Stroop effect

____ 11. Noam Chomsky called the rules for making and interpreting sentences ______ grammar.
a. transformational
b. lexical
c. Deep structural
d. Surface paradoxical

____ 12. Bonobos have shown in language progress development than common chimpanzees perhaps because their training
a. began very early in life and relied primarily on imitation.
b. Began early and used and both rewards and punishments.
c. used positive reinforcement and negative punishment.
d. used conditioned simuli and unconditioned reinforcers.

____ 13. Sofia had a stroke and has a hard time remembering the names of objects and has lost some language comprehension. She has what type of aphasia?
a. Wernicke's
b. Pavlov's
c. Skinner's
d. Occipital

____ 14. When 2- to 3-year-old children speak, they
a. Listen more clearly than they understand.
b. Generalize sentences they have heard others say.
c. overgeneralize grammatical rules.
d. Overgeneralize article usage.

____ 15. The basic unit of sound in a language is a
a. grammar.
b. syntax.
c. phoneme.
d. morpheme.

Answers

1. B
2. C
3. D
4. C
5. C
6. D
7. A
8. C
9. D
10. C
11. A
12. A
13. A
14. C
15. C

CHAPTER 10: INTELLIGENCE

QUESTIONS

1. What do psychologists studying intelligence attempt to do?
2. What are the three problems that face intelligence researchers?
3. Why is focusing on adaptation important but what doesn't adaptation tell us?
4. How did Galton attempt to conceptualize and measure intelligence?
5. What was the importance of factor analysis to intelligence?
6. Why did Thurstone reject Spearman's single *g*?
7. How do most modern psychometric theories explain intelligence?
8. What are some examples of fluid and crystallized intelligence?
9. Why is the fluid crystallized intelligence distinction important?
10. Why might neural speed transmission be important to intelligence?
11. What did Reed and Jensen (1992) believe about neural transmission speed and what were their research results?
12. Why can't we draw any definite conclusions from the Reed and Jensen research?
13. How would psychometric theorists discuss Larry's intelligence?
14. How did Walters and Gardner (1986) define intelligence?
15. How do people from around the world describe intelligence?
16. How does Gardner study intelligence?
17. What are Gardner's eight kinds of intelligence?
18. Why do researchers disagree with Gardner?
19. How did Sternberg conceptualize intelligence?
20. What are the three types of intelligence in the triarchic model and an example of each?
21. What is the difference between and achievement test and an aptitude test?
22. What are the three characteristics of a good test?
23. What is one kind of reliability?
24. What are three types of validity and an example of each?
25. Why is standardization of a test important and what is a norm group?
26. What is the history of the IQ test?
27. How did Binet and Simon calculate mental age?
28. Why is the IQ score useful?
29. What is the major problem with defining IQ as a ratio?
30. How is the deviation IQ different from the ratio IQ?
31. What is average and standard deviation of IQ scores in the normal distribution?
32. What are some causes of mental retardation?
33. What is adaptation potential of each of the four level retardation classifications?
34. What did Terman find in his longitudinal study of gifted people?
35. Why should causal relationships between IQ and success be interpreted with caution?
36. What are examples of savants?
37. What are the most widely used IQ tests?
38. How valid are IQ tests for predicting school achievement?
39. What do critics of IQ point out concerning the validity of intelligence tests?
40. What are most intelligence tests designed to do?
41. What are some tests of the WAIS?
42. What are some examples of problems with labeling?
43. How had creativity been measured?
44. What is the correspondence between creativity and intelligence?
45. Why might emotional intelligence be important?
46. How is tacit knowledge acquired?

47. What is the relationship between tacit knowledge and IQ?
48. What conclusions can be drawn about the research on having babies listen to Mozart and the popular press?
49. What are two explanations for how differences in intelligence might occur?
50. Why is it difficult to get accurate measurements of intelligence before 3 or 4 years of age?
51. When do IQ scores become stable?
52. How was the Seattle Longitudinal Study conducted and what are the results thus far?
53. What does the Flynn effect describe?
54. What are some explanations for the Flynn effect?
55. Why are IQ tests renormed and what might be some unintended consequences of renorming?
56. Why are family tree arguments about inherited intelligence not very convincing?
57. Who started the "nature versus" nurture phrase?
58. How can a genetic basis for intelligence be established?
59. How are twin studies conducted?
60. What relationships have been found between identical twins reared together, identical twins reared apart, fraternal twins reared together and apart?
61. In general, what can be concluded from the twin research on intelligence?
62. How is the heritability index expressed and to whom does it apply and not apply?
63. In general, what are the average racial, ethnic, and socioeconomic group IQ group differences?
64. Why is it important to understand that ethnic and racial IQ differences are group differences?
65. Why are the importance of economic differences and intelligence?
66. What are some test biases that might contribute to group IQ differences?
67. How did Steele and Aronson (1995) conduct a study and stereotype threat and what were their results?
68. What can be concluded about the interracial adoption IQ studies?
69. How can the plant analogy explain group IQ differences?
70. How is the interaction of nature and nurture a two way street?

VOCABULARY

1. achievement tests
2. aptitude tests
3. creativity
4. crystallized intelligence
5. deviation IQ
6. emotional intelligence
7. factor analysis
8. fluid intelligence
9. g (general intelligence)
10. gifted
11. heritability
12. hierarchical models
13. intelligence
14. intelligence quotient (IQ)
15. mental age
16. mental retardation
17. multiple intelligences
18. psychometrics
19. reaction range
20. reliability
21. s (specific intelligence)
22. standardization
23. tacit knowledge
24. triarchic theory
25. validity

10 Intelligence

Conceptualizing Intelligence

Measuring Individual Differences

Discovering the Sources of Intelligence

© Cleve Bryant/PhotoEdit, Inc.

ON A SATURDAY MORNING IN OCTOBER, Jefferson Tarpy drops down his yellow number 2 pencil and glances about the room with a cocky grin. Around him, working feverishly, sit dozens of others, similar in age and general appearance, but with pencils raised and sweat collecting on furrowed brows. Jefferson has finished early, as is his custom, and he's just aced the most important standardized test of his life. Next stop: medical school, a top residency, a lifetime of security.

Meanwhile, outside in a park across the street, Larry Steinway has also dropped his yellow pencil. But he doesn't notice. He'll need to rely on his attendant to recover it. Although physically 22, Larry Steinway's mind drifts in a world occupied by a 4-year-old's thoughts and impulses. He uses language haltingly; his hopes for an elementary school education are limited. Still, he responds quickly when his attendant asks him to calculate the number of seconds elapsing in 65 years, 14 days, and 15 hours. His answer includes the correct number of leap years and arrives in slightly under a minute and a half.

Overhead, unknown to Larry Steinway, flies a single nutcracker in search of a place to deposit his recently harvested supply of pine seeds. On this particular trip, one of many over the past few months, the bird will store its 25,000th seed. Across miles of terrain lie thousands of secret caches, all attributable to this one bird, scattered among the storage locations of other nutcrackers. Over the coming winter months, this bird will successfully revisit its own hiding places, ignoring others, and recover some 80% of the hidden seeds.

Each of these sketches demonstrates behavior that *might* be characterized as intelligent. What do you think? Certainly we can agree that Jefferson Tarpy fits the

© Bettmann/Corbis

Most of us have no trouble accepting that Balamurati Krishna Ambati is "intelligent"— after all, at age 12 he was a third-year premed student at New York University.

© Bettmann/Corbis

Ten-year-old savant Eddie Bonafe was born with severe physical and mental handicaps; but before he learned to walk he could play on the piano every hymn he heard sung in church. Would you call Eddie "intelligent"?

© Maurizio Lanini/Corbis

This little bird, Clark's Nutcracker, can remember the locations of thousands of seeds scattered across miles of confusing terrain. Wouldn't you call this a form of "intelligent" behavior?

description—ace performer on standardized tests, self-assured; he probably gets all A's and is popular in school. But what about Larry Steinway—someone who is poor at language, who operates at a mental level far below his physical age? Definitely not intelligent, you say; but then how do you explain his extraordinary calculating skills? Isn't "lightning calculation" an odd but nevertheless intelligent form of behavior? Finally, consider the nutcracker. It can't do geometry or calculus, but could you remember where you put 25,000 seeds scattered across miles of confusing terrain? Don't you think this remarkable ability to adapt to the harshness of winter is a prime example of intelligent behavior?

PREVIEW

The Study of Intelligence

It probably won't surprise you to learn that psychologists can't agree on a definition of intelligence. As you've seen, the term can have a variety of meanings. Practically, when psychologists talk about **intelligence**, they're usually referring to individual differences—specifically, the differences people show in their ability to perform tasks. People clearly differ in ability, and the measurement of these differences is used to infer the capacity called "intelligence."

Think about it: If everyone had the same ability to solve math problems or devise creative ideas, the label "intelligent" would lose its meaning. Psychologists who study intelligence attempt to measure the differences among people and then determine how and why those differences occur. One of the important goals is to use individual differences to predict things like job performance and success in school. In this chapter, we'll focus on three fundamental problems facing the intelligence researcher: conceptualizing, measuring, and discovering the source of individual differences in intellectual ability.

Conceptualizing Intelligence Many people talk of intelligence as if it's some "thing" that's possessed by a person, such as blue eyes, long fingers, or a slightly crooked gait. Yet we can't see intelligence, nor measure it directly with a stick. Intelligence may not even be best viewed as a single capacity; it may be better seen as a collection of separate abilities. It's possible that we have multiple intelligences ranging from the more traditional verbal and math skills to musical ability, mechanical ability, or even athletic ability. We'll discuss how psychologists have attempted to conceptualize intelligence over the years and where the brunt of opinion lies today.

Measuring Individual Differences Regardless of how we may choose to conceptualize intelligence, there's still the practical problem of measuring individual differences. For any particular task, such as performing well in school, there will be a distribution of abilities. Some people will perform extremely well; others will struggle. If these abilities can be measured accurately, through the use of psychological tests, then it should be possible to tailor your activities to fit your skills. You can be advised not to enter cartography school if your spatial abilities are weak, or you can be steered toward a career as a writer or journalist if your verbal abilities are strong. We'll discuss how intelligence is typically measured and some of the characteristics of effective tests.

Discovering the Sources of Intelligence Does intelligent behavior come primarily from your genetic background or from life experiences? People do differ in ability, but it's not immediately obvious whether these differences are largely inborn or due simply to peculiarities in one's environmental history. Is poor map reading a permanent condition, resulting from a lack of the right kind of genes, or can a superior ability to read maps be taught? Because of the wiring in my brain, am I doomed to forever have trouble fixing that leaky faucet in my kitchen, or can I be taught mechanical skills? We'll discuss the origins of intelligence from the perspective of nature and nurture and address some of the controversies that still surround the study of individual differences.

CONCEPTUALIZING INTELLIGENCE

intelligence
an internal capacity or ability that accounts for individual differences in mental test performance and enables us to adapt to ever-changing environments.

From the perspective of the adaptive mind, it certainly makes sense to talk about the adaptive characteristics of intelligence. For example, you might be considered intelligent if you can solve the problems unique to your environment. It turns out this is a fairly common way for psychologists to think about intelligence (Cosmides & Tooby, 2002; Kanazawa, 2004). Adaptive accounts of intelligence present many advantages. For one thing, focusing on adaptation prevents us from thinking that human thoughts and abilities are the only proper measuring sticks for intelligent behavior. The fact that nutcrackers can efficiently hide and relocate thousands of seeds is certainly intelligent from the standpoint of adapting to the harshness of winter (Kamil & Balda, 1990). Recognizing that different species (and people) face different survival problems virtually guarantees that we'll need to establish a wide range of criteria for what it means to be intelligent.

However, conceptualizing intelligence simply in terms of adaptability does not tell us much about what accounts for individual differences. People (and nutcrackers) differ in their ability to fit successfully into their environments, even when they're faced with similar problems. We need to understand the factors that produce individual differences. In this section of the chapter, we'll consider several ways of generally conceptualizing intelligence.

Think About It

Based on this discussion, how reasonable do you think it is to compare the intelligence of people from one culture to another?

Psychometrics: Measuring the Mind

We begin with the psychometric approach, which proposes that intelligence is a mental capacity that can be understood by analyzing performance on mental tests. The word **psychometric** literally means "to measure the mind." Intelligence is determined by administering a variety of tests that measure specific mental skills, such as verbal comprehension, memory, or spatial ability. The results are then analyzed statistically and conclusions are drawn about underlying mental abilities.

psychometrics
the use of psychological tests to measure the mind and mental processes.

One of the first systematic attempts to treat intelligence in this way was developed in the 19th century by Englishman Sir Francis Galton (1822–1911). Galton

Archives, History of American Psychology, University of Akron, OH

Archives, History of American Psychology, University of Akron, OH

Sir Francis Galton (1822–1911) and his "anthropometric" laboratory, where he measured intellectual ability.

was a half-cousin of Charles Darwin, and like his famous relative, he was deeply committed to the idea of "survival of the fittest." Galton (1869) believed individual differences in ability had their basis in heredity and could be measured through a series of tests of sensory discrimination and reaction time. For a small fee, visitors to Galton's laboratory were given a variety of psychological and physical tests, measuring such things as visual acuity, grip strength, and reaction time to sounds. At the end of the test session, they were handed a card with a detailed record of their scores (Hilgard, 1987; Johnson et al., 1985).

Galton believed he was measuring intelligence through performance on his battery of tests. He based his belief partly on the fact that there often appeared to be relationships among the various scores received by a particular individual. If a person tended to score high on a certain test, such as sensory acuity, he or she tended to score high on other measures as well. This pattern suggested to Galton that each of the separate tests might be tapping into some general ability—a general intelligence that contributed in some way to each of the different measured skills.

As it turned out, Galton's laboratory investigations into the measurement of intelligence were unsuccessful. His measurements were crude, and his tests were later shown to be poor predictors of actual intellectual performance, such as academic success (Wissler, 1901). For these and other reasons, his contributions are primarily of histor- ical rather than scientific interest. But his methods captured the attention of other researchers, who went on to develop the psychometric approach in a more rigorous way. Among the more influential of those who carried on the Galton tradition was a mathematically inclined psychologist named Charles Spearman (1863–1945).

factor analysis
a statistical procedure that groups together related items on tests by analyzing the correlations among test scores.

Spearman and Factor *g* Charles Spearman's principal contribution was the development of a mathematical technique called **factor analysis**, which is a procedure for analyzing the relationships, or correlations, among test scores. Its purpose is to isolate the various factors that can account for test performance. For example, as Galton suggested, it's possible that each of us has a single underlying ability—intelligence—that helps to explain our performance on mental tests. Alternatively, there could be multiple factors involved—we might be intelligent in one way, such as in an ability to remember, and not very intelligent in another, such as in spatial reasoning. Spearman's technique enabled researchers to study these possibilities in a systematic way.

To get an idea of how factor analysis works, think about star athletes who excel in several sports. It's natural to assume that good athletes have general athletic ability that reveals itself in a number of ways. If you were to correlate performance across a variety of skills, you should be able to predict how well they'll perform on one measure of skill, given that you know how well they perform on others. Good athletes, for instance, should run fast, jump high, and have quick reflexes. Correlations exist because presumably an underlying ability—athletic skill—is tapped by each of the individual performance measures. Similar logic applies to intelligence: Someone who is high (or low) in intelligence should perform well (or poorly) on many different kinds of ability tests. If there is general intelligence, you should be able to predict performance on one type of test (such as math) if you know how well the person performs on other tests (such as verbal comprehension or spatial ability).

When Spearman (1904) applied factor analysis to the testing of mental ability, he discovered evidence for general intellectual ability. A single factor in the analysis, which he called ***g*** for *general intelligence,* helped to explain performance on a wide variety of mental tests. At the same time, it wasn't possible to explain individual test scores entirely by referring to *g*. The correlations among the test scores were high, but not perfect. He found, for example, that someone who performed extremely well on a test of verbal comprehension did not necessarily excel on a test of spatial ability. He argued, therefore, that it's necessary to take *specific* abilities into account, reflected in ***s***, that are *unique* to each individual test (see Figure 10.1). To predict performance on a test of verbal comprehension, for example, you need a measure of ability that is specific to verbal comprehension in addition to *g*.

g (general intelligence) according to Spearman, a general factor, derived from factor analysis, that underlies or contributes to performance on a variety of mental tests.

s (specific intelligence) according to Spearman, a specific factor, derived from factor analysis, that is unique to a particular kind of test.

© Craig Jones/Allsport/Getty Images

© Reuters NewMedia, Inc./Corbis

Deion Sanders performed at the highest levels in professional football and professional baseball. Do his skills support the existence of a factor tapping "general athletic ability"?

Hierarchical Models of Intelligence As you might expect, Spearman's two-factor analysis of intelligence was quite influential in its time, and it remains influential

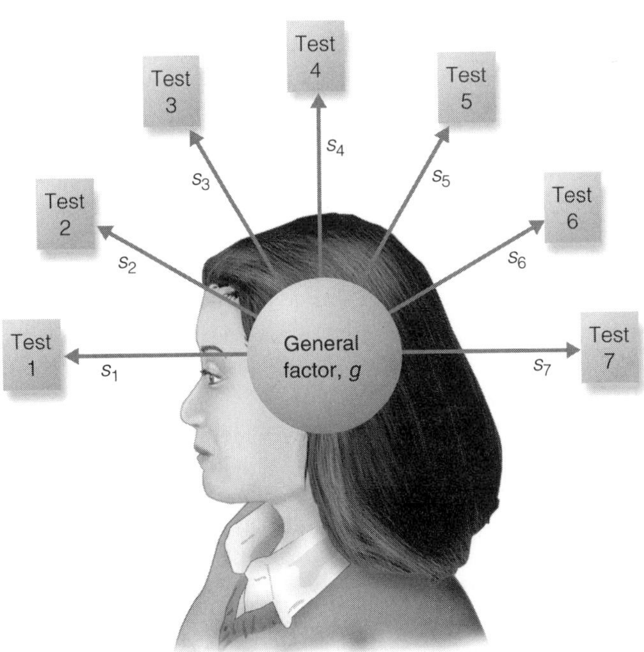

FIGURE 10.1

Spearman's General and Specific Factors. Spearman discovered that to explain performance on a variety of mental tests it was necessary to consider (1) a common factor, called *g* for general intelligence, that contributes to performance on all of the tests, and (2) specific factors—labeled as s_1 through s_7—that are specific to the particular tests.

Think About It

How well does the notion of general intelligence describe you? If you're good at one subject, does that predict how well you do in others?

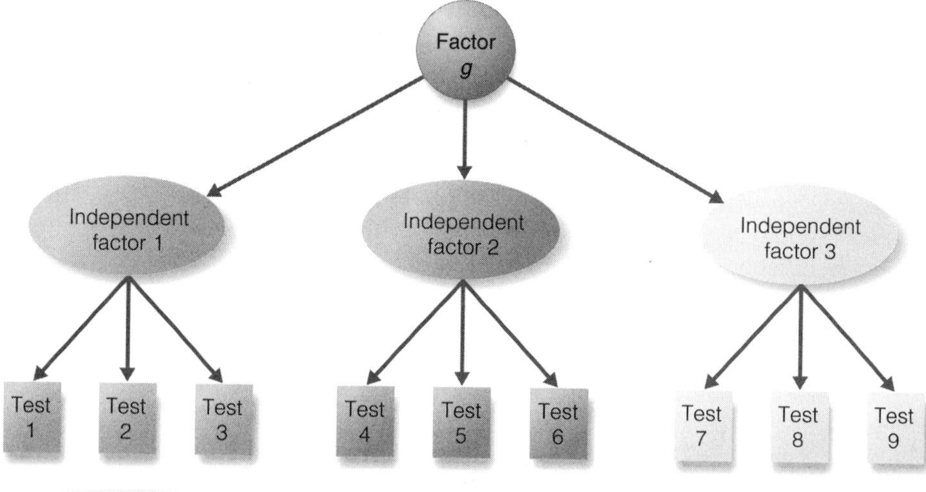

FIGURE 10.2

Hierarchical Models. Many psychologists now propose hierarchical models of intelligence that include elements found in the theories of both Spearman and Thurstone. Like Thurstone, hierarchical models propose separate factors that contribute independently to certain types of tests (for example, factor 1 contributes to tests 1–3, but not to tests 4–9). Like Spearman, these models also assume that each of the separate factors is influenced by an overall *g*.

today (Sternberg, 2003). But over the years his conclusions have been challenged, especially the overarching concept of *g*. Psychologist L. L. Thurstone (1938), for example, applied a somewhat different version of factor analysis, as well as a more extensive battery of tests, and discovered evidence for seven "primary mental abilities": verbal comprehension, verbal fluency, numerical ability, spatial ability, memory, perceptual speed, and reasoning. Thurstone rejected Spearman's notion of a single general intelligence, *g*, because his analysis indicated that these seven primary abilities are largely independent—just because someone is good at verbal reasoning doesn't mean he or she will be good at memory or show perceptual speed. If performance on one type of test tells us little or nothing about performance on a second test, it's unlikely that the two tests are measuring the same general underlying ability.

Psychologists have argued for decades about (a) the proper way to apply factor analysis, (b) the particular kinds of ability tests that should be used, and (c) whether single or multiple factors are needed to explain the data (Jensen & Weng, 1994). But the evidence for a central *g* is hard to dismiss completely, at least when intelligence is defined by performance on tests of mental ability. For this reason, most modern psychometric theories retain the concept of general intelligence but propose more of a hierarchical structure, such as that shown in Figure 10.2. General intelligence, *g*, occupies a position at the top of the hierarchy, and various subfactors (or abilities) that may or may not operate independently from one another sit at the lower levels. This represents a compromise of sorts between Thurstone's view—that there is more than one primary mental ability—and Spearman's concept of general intelligence or *g*.

Fluid and Crystallized Intelligence

fluid intelligence
the natural ability to solve problems, reason, and remember; fluid intelligence is thought to be relatively uninfluenced by experience.

Many psychologists accept the idea of general intelligence but argue that it should be further analyzed into separate components. For example, Raymond Cattell and John Horn have suggested that *g* contains two distinct components: *fluid* intelligence and *crystallized* intelligence (Cattell, 1963, 1998; Horn & Cattell, 1966). **Fluid intelligence** is a measure of your ability to solve problems, reason, and remember in ways that are relatively uninfluenced by experience. It's the type of intelligence that is probably determined primarily by biological or genetic factors. **Crystallized intelligence**, on the other hand, measures acquired knowledge and ability. You learn things about the world, such as how to solve arithmetic problems, and develop abilities based on level of schooling and other cultural influences.

crystallized intelligence the knowledge and abilities acquired as a result of experience (as from schooling and cultural influences).

In most cases, intelligent behavior relies on both fluid and crystallized intelligence. For example, as you know from earlier chapters, people differ in their ability to perform several tasks at the same time. If I ask you to solve math problems while remembering a list of words, your ability to perform this dual task correlates reasonably well with standard measures of intelligence (Engle, 2000). It's likely that you're born with a certain amount of conscious capacity (or mental resources), which is linked to fluid intelligence, but your performance also depends on what you've learned from experience. If you've learned to chunk or rehearse effectively then your performance on the dual task will improve. These acquired strategies reflect crystallized intelligence, which develops with experience.

The distinction between fluid and crystallized intelligence is important because it helps to explain how mental abilities change with age and across different cultures (Horn & Noll, 1997; Parkin & Java, 2001). As you'll see later in the chapter, fluid and crystallized intelligence should change in somewhat different ways as we age. There are also striking differences in performance on psychometric tests of mental ability across different cultures and socioeconomic classes. These differences can't be easily explained from the perspective of general intelligence, unless we assume that an important part of general intelligence is acquired from experience. Distinguishing between fluid and crystallized intelligence can help explain how people who are born with the same amount of natural (fluid) intelligence can end up performing quite differently on tests of mental ability.

Which do you think contributes the most to performance on an essay exam: fluid or crystallized intelligence?

The Speed of Neural Transmission

If individual differences in general intelligence come partly from innate abilities—such as a small or large mental capacity—what biological processes are actually involved? A number of psychologists have suggested that intelligence is related to the speed of transmission among the neurons in the brain (see Hunt, 1985; Jensen, 1993; Vernon, 1983). Specifically, the faster the brain communicates internally, the greater your intelligence. The reason communication speed might be important is that the brain has limited resources and must quickly allocate, or divide, its processing to perform efficiently. Indeed, a number of studies have found significant correlations between measures of neural communication speed and performance on mental tests of intelligence (Reed & Jensen, 1992; Vernon & Mori, 1992).

It's relatively easy to record the gross electrical activity of the brain. The procedure requires only that several electrodes be attached temporarily to locations on the scalp. Depending on the placement of the electrodes, electrical activity from different parts of the brain can then be recorded. To obtain a measure of the speed of neural processing, Reed and Jensen (1992) attached electrodes to scalp locations that are sensitive to the appearance of visual events. People were seated in a dark room and were presented with a black-and-white checkerboard pattern on a video monitor. Approximately 100 milliseconds after presentation of the stimulus, the brain generates an electrical signal—known as P100—that can be measured in scalp areas over the primary visual cortex.

Reed and Jensen (1992) were not simply interested in the appearance of the P100 signal but rather in the *latency*, or time of appearance, of the signal. People differ in the amount of time it takes for this signal to appear, which was assumed by Reed and Jensen to provide an indirect measure of the speed of information processing in the brain. They believed that short latencies reflected fast processing in the brain and long latencies indicated relatively slower processing. The main question of interest was whether P100 latency could then be used to predict performance on an intelligence test. Indeed, they found that a relationship did exist between latency and performance on the intelligence test. The shorter the latency—that is, the faster the processing in the brain—the higher the intelligence score (see also Reed et al., 2004).

Does this mean that smarter brains are faster brains, as the data might imply? Not necessarily. It's important to remember that conclusions about cause and effect can't be drawn from correlational studies such as the one conducted by Reed and Jensen. We may be able to predict intelligence scores to some extent by measuring neural processing speed, but that doesn't mean processing speed is the underlying cause of intelligence. Moreover, the predictive ability of the P100 latencies was far from perfect; they explained only a small proportion of the subject differences found in intelligence scores. The Reed and Jensen data are interesting, but they can't tell us what neurological processes actually underlie the capacity of intelligence (McRorie & Cooper, 2004). More research is needed.

multiple intelligences
the notion proposed by Howard Gardner that people possess a set of separate and independent "intelligences" ranging from musical to linguistic to interpersonal ability.

Multiple Intelligences: Gardner's Case Study Approach

Before turning to another way of conceptualizing intelligence—the multiple-intelligences approach—let's pause momentarily and return to Larry Steinway, that fictional lightning calculator we met in the opening to the chapter. After reading the previous sections, what do you think psychologists with a psychometric bent would have to say about Larry's intelligence? How does someone with a highly specialized skill—lightning calculation—but with otherwise impaired mental abilities fit into these conceptualizations of intelligence? In some respects Larry has a fast brain, but it's highly doubtful he could read a map very well, or solve a complicated analogy problem. We can be sure that Larry will not perform well on a standardized battery of tests, which means that his assigned value of *g* will be far lower than average.

Consider also the gifted athlete, who soars high above the basketball rim but has trouble reading his daughter's nursery rhymes. Or the respected mathematical wizard, full professor at a major university, who has trouble matching her shoes, let alone her socks, in the morning. The point to be made about Larry Steinway, or the athlete or the professor, is that people sometimes show specialized skills or abilities that stand alone and are not representative of a general ability. Spectacular skill can be shown in one area accompanied by profound deficits in another. Perhaps more important, these selective skills are often in areas not traditionally covered by the verbal and analytical battery of commonly used intelligence tests.

© Rick Rickman/NewsSport/Corbis

© AP/Wide World Photos

Tony Hawk seems to possess a high level of bodily-kinesthetic intelligence; Maya Angelou rates highly in linguistic intelligence.

Howard Gardner (1983, 1993) argues that traditional conceptions of intelligence need to be broadened to include special abilities or talents. He rejects the idea that intelligence can be adequately conceptualized through the analysis of test performance (as used by the psychometric approach). Rather than searching for a single ability called intelligence, we should understand that human behavior is rich in selective talents and abilities: We need a theory of **multiple intelligences**, not a method for discovering a single underlying *g*. An *intelligence* (rather than "the" intelligence) is defined as the ability to solve problems that matter in a specific cultural setting (Walters & Gardner, 1986). Although Gardner believes each of these separate intelligences may be rooted in the biology of the brain, each can manifest itself in a variety of ways, depending on one's culture. When average people around the world are asked to talk about their personal conceptions of intelligence, they almost always describe intelligence in terms of multiple factors or dimensions (Sternberg & Kaufman, 1998).

Rather than studying intelligent behavior in the laboratory, Gardner uses a case study approach. He studies reports of particular individuals with special abilities or talents, such as superior musicians, poets, scientists, and *savants* like Larry Steinway. He's also looked extensively at the effects of damage to the brain. He's noted, for example, instances in which brain damage affects one kind of ability, such as reasoning and problem solving, yet leaves other abilities, such as musical skill, intact. Based on his research, Gardner (1999) has identified what he believes to be at least eight distinct kinds of intelligence.

1. *Musical intelligence:* the type of ability displayed by gifted musicians or child prodigies
2. *Bodily-kinesthetic intelligence:* the type of ability shown by gifted athletes, dancers, or surgeons who have great control over body movements
3. *Logical-mathematical intelligence:* the type of ability displayed by superior scientists and logical problem solvers
4. *Linguistic intelligence:* the type of ability shown by great writers or poets who can express themselves verbally
5. *Spatial intelligence:* the type of ability shown by those with superior navigation skills or an ability to visualize spatial scenes
6. *Interpersonal intelligence:* the type of ability shown by those who can easily infer other people's moods, temperaments, or intentions and motivations
7. *Intrapersonal intelligence:* the ability shown by someone who has great insight into his or her own feelings and emotions
8. *Naturalist intelligence:* the ability to observe and interact with diverse species in nature; the type of ability shown by a biologist or environmentalist

Do you think the average person on the street believes superior artistic or athletic ability qualifies as a type of intelligence?

Notice that some forms of intelligence, as described by Gardner, are covered well by conventional tests of mental ability. Psychometric approaches focus extensively on logical-mathematical intelligence and to some extent on linguistic and spatial intelligence. Moreover, as discussed earlier, some researchers who use the psychometric approach, including Thurstone, have argued that it's important to distinguish among distinct and independent types of intelligence. But researchers who conceptualize intelligence in this way rarely, if ever, concentrate on intelligences such as musical ability or great athletic skill. The multiple-intelligences approach considerably broadens the conceptualization of intelligence.

Multiple Intelligences: Sternberg's Triarchic Theory

Intelligence researchers are beginning to agree about the need for a multipronged attack on intelligence. Not everyone accepts Howard Gardner's classification scheme, although his framework has been applied successfully in many educational settings (see Shearer, 2004). Some say Gardner is really talking about multiple talents rather than intelligences, and his theory remains primarily descriptive without much evidence beyond single case studies (Sternberg, 2003). But the majority of psychologists agree with Gardner that intelligence should be broadly conceived—it's not simply performance on a battery of primarily verbal-linguistic or sensory tests.

triarchic theory
Robert Sternberg's theory of intelligence; it proposes three types of intelligence: analytic, creative, and practical.

Robert Sternberg's **triarchic theory** of intelligence is a good example of a recent eclectic approach (meaning it's made up of different elements). Sternberg was trained as a cognitive psychologist. As a result, he's convinced it's important to understand the mental operations behind the planning and execution of specialized tasks. But he also believes any complete account of intelligence needs to address behavior outside of the laboratory. For example, what is the form of intelligence that enables people to apply their mental processes creatively to problems that arise in everyday life? Furthermore, how does intelligence relate to the practical experience of the individual? Consequently, he accepts the idea that there may be multiple kinds of intelligence. Triarchic means roughly "ruled by threes," and not

CONCEPT SUMMARY

Views of Intelligence

APPROACH	EXAMPLE(S)	INTELLIGENCE IS . . .
Psychometric	Spearman's factor g Hierarchical models	A mental capacity that can be understood by analyzing performance on mental tests.
Biological	Mental speed Fluid intelligence	Reflected in the speed of mental processing and in performance that is relatively uninfluenced by experience.
Multiple intelligence	Gardner's multiple intelligences	Eight proposed abilities that permit an individual to solve problems or fashion products that are of consequence in a particular cultural setting.
Triarchic theory	Analytic intelligence Creative intelligence Practical intelligence	The ability to process information analytically; the ability to cope with novel tasks; the ability to solve problems posed by unique cultural surroundings.

surprisingly, Sternberg's conceptualization of intelligence is divided into three major parts (Sternberg, 1985, 1988b).

Analytical Intelligence Sternberg believes that any complete theory of intelligence must refer in some way to basic analytic skills. Some people are simply better than others at processing information—they're good at representing (or seeing) problems in the right way and can generate effective strategies for solutions. People with high degrees of *analytical intelligence* tend to perform well on conventional tests that tap reasoning and logical-mathematical ability (such as the SAT). Because most psychometric tests of intelligence require these kinds of abilities, people who are high in analytic intelligence tend to be assigned a high *g*, for general intelligence. If you know someone who performs well in school, or who claims to be highly intelligent based on a standardized test, he or she is likely to score high on analytic intelligence.

Creative Intelligence Sternberg proposes a second kind of intelligence, *creative intelligence*, that expresses how well people are able to cope with new or novel tasks. Being analytic and processing information well does not guarantee creativity or the ability to apply the skills you've mastered in a new context. The world is full of people who are good in school, or who perform well on assigned tasks, but can't seem to think their way out of a paper bag. They lack creativity and seem to have trouble applying what they've learned (Sternberg, 1985).

Practical Intelligence Finally, people differ in *practical intelligence*, a measure of how well they fit into their environment. People with lots of practical intelligence solve the problems that are uniquely posed by their cultural surroundings. They mold themselves well into existing settings, and they can select new environments, if required, that provide a better fit for their talents. In a nutshell, these individuals have "street smarts"—they size up situations well and act accordingly. You probably know someone who seems to lack analytic skills—who fails school or drops out—but still manages to succeed in life.

Sternberg's triarchic theory has helped to broaden the concept of intelligence. Like Howard Gardner's approach, his theory deals with behaviors and skills that aren't normally covered by the standard psychometric approach. Triarchic theory, like Gardner's theory, can also be applied successfully in classroom settings where particular types of intelligence can be nurtured and developed (Sternberg, 1998; Sternberg et al., 1998). But breadth is not gained without some cost—concepts such as practical and creative intelligence can be difficult to measure and test (Brody, 2003; Gottfredson, 2003). Moreover, even if it is desirable to broaden our conceptualization of intelligence, that doesn't mean that psychometric approaches to intelligence have no value. As you'll see in the next section, psychometric tests are often useful in predicting future performance, even though they may be measuring only narrow dimensions of intelligence.

MEASURING INDIVIDUAL DIFFERENCES

We've now discussed some of the ways psychologists try to conceptualize intelligence. However, we have yet to discuss how individual differences are actually measured. People differ. Pick just about any attribute—height, weight, friendliness, intelligence—and you're going to find a scattering, or distribution, of individual values. Some people are tall, some are short; some people are friendly, some are not. As discussed in the previous section, the study of individual differences is important because many psychological concepts, including intelligence and personality, are defined and measured by individual differences.

If we can measure how you compare to others on a psychological dimension, we can then assess your current and future capabilities. For example, **achievement tests** measure your current knowledge or competence in a particular subject (such as math or reading). Researchers or teachers can use the results of an achievement test to gauge the effectiveness of a learning procedure or a curriculum in a school. It's also possible to use individual differences to make predictions about the future, such as how well you can be expected to do in your chosen profession or whether you're likely to succeed in college. **Aptitude tests** measure the ability to learn in a particular area, to acquire the knowledge needed for success in a given domain. Aptitude test results can be used to help choose a career path or even to decide whether to take up something as a hobby, such as car mechanics or the violin.

achievement tests
psychological tests that measure your current level of knowledge or competence in a particular subject.

aptitude tests
psychological tests that measure your ability to learn or acquire knowledge in a particular subject.

The Components of a Good Test

What are the characteristics of a "good" test—that is, a test that can be expected to provide a good measure of individual differences? Given we recognize the need to measure these differences, it's crucial that the measurement device provide information that is scientifically useful. Researchers generally agree on the three characteristics needed for a good test: *reliability, validity,* and *standardization.* Please note that these are characteristics of the test, not of the person taking the test.

Reliability The first test characteristic, **reliability**, is a measure of the *consistency* of the test results. Reliable tests produce similar scores from one administration to the next. Suppose we want to measure creativity, and we design a test that produces a score from 0 to 100 on a creativity scale. We measure Alan, and he gets a score of 13; we measure Cynthia, and she tops out at 96. Clearly, we conclude, Cynthia is more creative than Alan. But is she really? To be sure about the results, we administer the test again and find that the scores reverse. Sadly, our creativity test lacks reliability—it doesn't produce consistent scores from one administration to the next.

reliability
a measure of the consistency of test results; reliable tests produce similar scores or indices from one administration to the next.

It's important for a test to be reliable so we can draw firm conclusions from the results. Cynthia might be more creative than Alan, but the difference in scores could also be due to an artifact, or failing, of the test. On this particular administration Cynthia scored higher, but that's no guarantee tomorrow's results will produce the same conclusion. One way to measure a test's reliability is to give it to the same group of individuals on two separate occasions. *Test-retest reliability* is then calculated by comparing the scores across the repeated administrations. Often, a correlation coefficient is computed that indicates how well performance on the second test can be predicted from performance on the first. The closer the test-retest correlation comes to a perfect +1.00, the higher the reliability of the test.

validity
an assessment of how well a test measures what it is supposed to measure. *Content validity* assesses the degree to which the test samples broadly across the domain of interest; *predictive validity* assesses how well the test predicts some future criterion; *construct validity assesses* how well the test taps into a particular theoretical construct.

Validity The second test characteristic, **validity**, tells us how well a test measures what it's supposed to measure. A test can yield reliable data—consistent results across repeated administrations—yet not truly measure the psychological characteristic of interest. If a test of creativity actually measures shoe size, then the data are likely to be reliable but not valid. Shoe size isn't going to change much from one measurement to the next, but it has little to do with creativity.

Actually, there are several different forms of validity. *Content validity* measures the degree to which the content of a test samples broadly across the domain of interest. If you're trying to get a general measure of creativity, your test should not be limited to one kind of creativity, such as artistic creativity. For the test to have a high degree of content validity, it should probably measure artistic, verbal, mechanical, mathematical, and other kinds of creativity.

Tom McCarthy/PhotoEdit, Inc.

Students regularly take standardized tests that measure aptitude or achievement.

Sometimes psychologists are interested in designing a test that predicts some future outcome, such as job performance or success in school. For a test to have *predictive validity,* it must predict this outcome adequately. The SAT is a well-known case in point. The SAT is designed to predict success in college. So to assess its predictive validity, we need to ask whether the SAT predicts college performance as expressed through a measure such as college grade point average. Various studies have shown that the correlation between SAT scores and the grade point averages of college freshmen is somewhere between +0.40 and +0.50 (Donlon, 1984; Willingham et al., 1990). Statistically, this means that we can predict college performance with the SAT to some degree, but our predictive abilities are not perfect.

Another kind of validity, *construct validity,* measures how well a test applies to a particular theoretical scheme or construct. Suppose we have a theory of creativity that's developed well enough to generate a wide variety of predictions—how creative people act, the kinds of books they read, their susceptibility to mental disorders, and so on. To have high construct validity, our test must predict performance on each of these separate indices of creativity, rather than on just one. If a test has high construct validity, its scores tend to vary in ways that are predicted by the theory. So if the theory predicts that creative people are more likely to suffer from depression, then people who score high on the creativity test should have a greater likelihood of being depressed.

Think About It

Pick one of your classes in school. Do you think the tests that you've taken so far have been valid? What specific kind of validity are you using as a basis for your answer?

Standardization The third characteristic of a good test of individual differences is **standardization.** When you take a test such as the SAT, or any national aptitude or achievement test, you quickly learn that the testing procedures are extremely rigid. You can break the test seal only at a certain time, the instructions are spoken in a monotone by a very serious administrator, and your yellow number 2 pencil must be put down at an exact tick of the clock. These tests are *standardized,* which means the testing, scoring, and interpretation procedures remain the same across administrations of the test. Standardization is important because it guarantees that all test takers will be treated the same.

standardization
keeping the testing, scoring, and interpretation procedures similar across all administrations of a test.

In fact, the proper interpretation of a test score absolutely demands standardization. Remember, we're concerned with individual differences—it doesn't make much sense to compare two or more scores if different instructions or scoring procedures have been used across the test sessions. A person's score on a test of individual differences can be understood only with respect to a reference group, often called a *norm group,* and everyone within the group must receive the same test and administration procedures. We'll return to this notion of a norm reference group momentarily when we consider the concept of the IQ.

Alfred Binet (with an unidentified child) was commissioned by the French government to develop a test that would help teachers identify students who might have a difficult time grasping academic concepts.

IQ: The Intelligence Quotient

The most famous index of intelligence is the **IQ**, or **intelligence quotient**. The IQ is a single number, derived from performance on a test, and it may well be the most widely applied psychological measure in the world. Yet how can a single number be used to measure intelligence? This might strike you as odd given our earlier discussion about multiple intelligences and the need to establish a wide variety of criteria for what it means to be intelligent. The key to appreciating the IQ, and to understanding why it is so widely applied, is in the concept of *validity:* What is the IQ designed to measure, and how successfully does it achieve its goal? As you'll see momentarily, it turns out that IQ does a reasonably good job of predicting what it was designed to predict.

intelligence quotient (IQ)
mental age divided by chronological age and then multiplied by 100.

The historical roots of the intelligence quotient trace back about a hundred years to the work of the French psychologist Alfred Binet and his associate Théopile Simon. In 1904 Binet and Simon were commissioned by the French government to develop a test that would identify children who were considered "dull"—specifically, children who would have a difficult time grasping concepts in school. It was the French government's intention to help these children, once they were identified, through special schooling. Thus the mission of the test was primarily practical, not theoretical; the charge was to develop a test that would accurately measure individual differences in future academic performance.

Mental Age Not surprisingly, Binet and Simon designed their test to measure the kinds of skills that are needed in school—such as memory, reasoning, and verbal comprehension. The goal was to determine the **mental age**—or what Binet and Simon called the *mental level*—of the child, which was defined as the chronological

mental age
the chronological age that best fits a child's level of performance on a test of mental ability.

CONCEPT SUMMARY

Components of a Good Test

COMPONENT	DESCRIPTION	EXAMPLE
Reliability	Consistency of test results	Taking a test twice should yield similar scores each time.
Validity	Does the test measure what it's supposed to?	
—Content	—The degree to which a test samples broadly across the domain of interest.	The items on a test of creativity should cover different types of creativity, such as artistic, mathematical, and verbal.
—Predictive	—The degree to which a test predicts some future outcome	Performance on the American College Test (ACT) should correlate with later performance in college classes.
—Construct	—The degree to which a test taps into a particular theoretical construct	Performance on a creativity test should correlate with other characteristics or indices thought to be associated with creativity.
Standardization	Testing, scoring, and interpretation procedures are the same across all administrations of the test.	Everyone who takes the SAT receives the same instructions, uses a number 2 pencil and standard answer sheet, and has to complete the test within the same specified period of time.

age that best fit the child's current level of intellectual performance. Mental age is typically calculated by comparing a child's test score with the average scores for different age groups. For example, let's suppose that an average 8-year-old is able to compare two objects from memory, recognize parts of a picture that are missing, count backward from 20 to 0, and give the correct day and time. An average 12-year-old might be able to define abstract words, name 60 words in 3 minutes, and discover the meaning of a scrambled sentence. If Jenny, who is 8, is able to solve the problems of the typical 12-year-old, she would be assigned a mental age of 12.

Notice that mental age and chronological age do not have to be the same, although they will be on average (an average 8-year-old should solve problems at the average 8-year-old level). Because intelligence tests are given to lots of children, it's possible to determine average performance for a given age group and then to determine the appropriate mental age for a particular child. By using mental age, Binet and Simon (1916/1973) were able to identify the slow and quick learners and to recommend appropriate curriculum adjustments.

In the first two decades of the 20th century, Binet and Simon's intelligence test was revised several times and was ultimately translated into English for use in North America. The most popular American version was developed by psychologist Lewis Terman at Stanford University; this test later became known as the *Stanford-Binet* test of intelligence. It was also Terman who popularized the idea of an intelligence quotient (based on an idea originally proposed by German psychologist William Stern), which is defined as follows:

$$\text{Intelligence quotient (IQ)} = \frac{\text{Mental age}}{\text{Chronological age}} \times 100$$

The IQ is a useful measure because it establishes an easy-to-understand baseline for "average" intelligence—people of average intelligence will have an IQ of 100 because their mental age will always be equal to their chronological age. People with IQs greater than 100 will be above average in intelligence; those below 100 will be below average in intelligence.

Deviation IQ Defining IQ simply in terms of the *ratio* of mental age to chronological age has some problems. For one thing, it's hard to compare the meaning of the

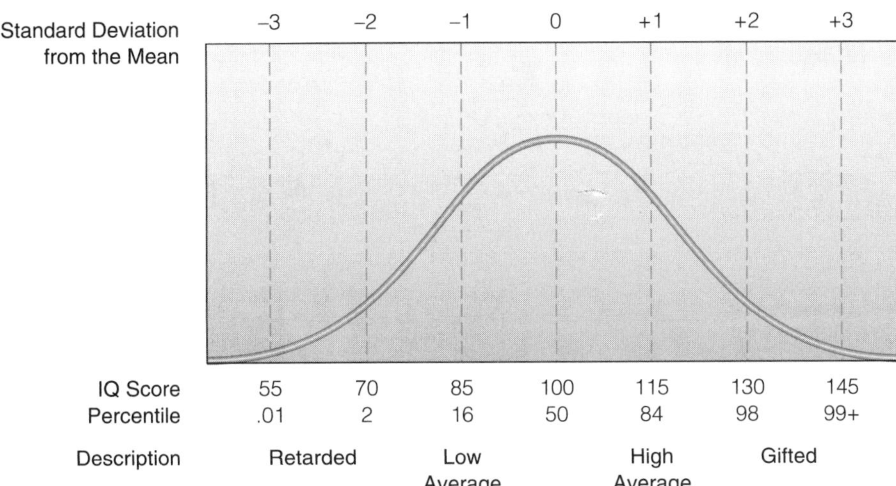

FIGURE 10.3

The Distribution of IQ Scores. IQ scores for a given age group are typically distributed in a bell-shaped, or normal, curve. The average and most frequently occurring IQ score is defined as 100. Roughly 68% of the test takers in this age group receive IQ scores between 115 and 85, one *standard deviation* above and below the mean. People labeled "gifted," with an IQ of 130 and above, or "retarded," with an IQ of 70 or below, occur infrequently in the overall population.

ratio across different ages. If a 5-year-old performed like a 7-year-old, she would be given an IQ of 140 (7/5 × 100 = 140). But if a 10-year-old scored at the level of a 12-year-old, his IQ would be only 120 (12/10 × 100 = 120). Both are performing at levels 2 years above their chronological age, but they receive very different IQs. Moreover, how much sense does it make to argue that a 30-year-old who performs comparably to a 60-year-old should be given a vastly higher IQ (60/30 × 100 = 200)?

To overcome this problem, most modern intelligence tests retain the term IQ but define it in terms of a *deviation,* or difference, rather than as a ratio. A **deviation IQ** still uses 100 as a baseline average, but a 100 IQ is redefined as the average score in the distribution of scores for people of a certain age. A particular person's IQ is then calculated by determining where his or her test score "sits," relative to the average score, in the overall distribution of scores. (Note that *age* is the "norm group" used for defining the concept of intelligence.) Figure 10.3 shows a frequency distribution of scores that might result from administering a test such as the Stanford-Binet to large groups of people. The average of the distribution is 100, and approximately half of the test takers will produce scores above 100 and the other half below 100.

deviation IQ
an intelligence score that is derived from determining where your performance sits in an age-based distribution of test scores.

One of the characteristics of modern intelligence tests is their tendency to produce very regular and smooth distributions of scores. With most intelligence tests, for example, not only will the most common score be 100 (by definition), but roughly 68% of the people who take the test will receive an IQ score between 85 and 115. With a distribution like the one shown in Figure 10.3, we can easily calculate the percentage of the population likely to receive a particular IQ score. You will find, for example, that approximately 98% of the people who take the test will receive a score at or below 130. Notice once again that IQ in this case is defined in terms of how a score compares to the scores of other people in the same age group.

Think About It

Do you see any similarities between the way deviation IQ is interpreted and the way you normally interpret your test scores in a class?

Extremes of Intelligence

Tests such as the Stanford-Binet or the related Wechsler Adult Intelligence Scale have been given to thousands and thousands of people. Consequently, we know a great deal about how IQ scores are distributed in the population. Most people fall within a normal or average range, which covers scores from about 70 to about 130. Individuals who fall above or below this range represent *extremes* in intelligence.

Mental Retardation A score of 70 or below on a standard IQ test often leads to a diagnosis of **mental retardation**, although other factors (such as daily living

mental retardation
a label generally assigned to someone who scores below 70 on a standard IQ test although other factors, such as one's ability to adapt to the environment, are also important.

TABLE 10.1 **Types of Mental Retardation**

TYPE	APPROXIMATE IQ RANGE	ADAPTATION POTENTIAL
Mild	50–70	May develop academic skills comparable to a sixth-grade educational level; with assistance, may develop significant social and vocational skills and be self-supporting.
Moderate	35–50	Unlikely to achieve academic skills over the second-grade level; may become semi-independent.
Severe	20–35	Speech skills will be limited, but communication is possible; may learn to perform simple tasks in highly structured environments.
Profound	Below 20	Little or no speech is possible; requires constant care and supervision.

skills) contribute to the diagnosis (Fredericks & Williams, 1998). The disability must also be diagnosed prior to age 18, which means that limitations in intellectual functioning arising during adulthood—for example, from brain damage—don't lead to the diagnosis (American Association of Mental Retardation, 2002). A four-level classification scheme has been developed for mental retardation, which is shown in Table 10.1. This table indicates how each category level for retardation is defined—in terms of IQ—and lists some of the skills that can be expected for individuals who meet the diagnostic criteria.

What causes mental retardation? There are many possible causes, some genetic and some environmental. Down syndrome, for example, is typically associated with low IQ scores and is caused by a genetic abnormality—usually an extra chromosome. Another genetic condition is phenylketonuria (PKU), a metabolic disorder associated with a defective enzyme that can lead to retardation if not corrected early in development. Environmental factors during development, such as inadequate nutrition or illness, can also contribute to mental retardation. You may remember about the potentially damaging effects of teratogens, such as excessive use of alcohol or other drugs, on the intellectual capacity of the developing fetus. There are probably hundreds of potential causes for extremely low IQ scores and, once again, a low IQ score does not guarantee a diagnosis of mental retardation.

Although mental retardation is assumed to affect somewhere between 1% and 3% of the population, the vast majority of these people (perhaps 85%) are only mildly affected. With the proper support, most are able to lead independent lives and may not even be recognized by the community as having any serious mental deficiencies. By no means does retardation imply an inability to learn or prosper. Even the roughly 15% of cases who are diagnosed as moderate to profoundly retarded can lead satisfying and fulfilling lives. Moreover, numerous agencies such as the American Association for Mental Retardation provide useful information and help to support ongoing research.

gifted
a label generally assigned to someone who scores above 130 on a standard IQ test.

Giftedness At the other end of the IQ scale are those considered **gifted**, with IQs at or above approximately 130. Many studies have tracked the intellectual and social accomplishments of gifted children, partly as a means of checking on the validity of the IQ measure. One of the most famous of these studies was begun in the 1920s by Lewis Terman (1925; Terman & Ogden, 1947). Terman was interested in whether children identified early in life as gifted would be likely to achieve success throughout their lives. The answer, on average, was "Yes"—Terman's gifted subjects earned more college degrees than average, made more money, wrote more books, generated more successful patents, and so on. Similar results have been found in other studies, most recently for adolescents with exceptional mathematical or verbal reasoning ability (Lubinski et al., 2001).

Interestingly, the kids studied by Terman (often known collectively as the "Termites") turned out to be emotionally stable and socially skilled as well, which is surprising given the bookworm stereotype that people have of highly intelligent people. Many had successful marriages, and their divorce rate was lower than the general population (Terman, 1954). A more recent study examining gifted children who skipped high school and moved directly to college also found evidence for excellent social adjustment (Nobel et al., 1993). On the other hand, Ellen Winner (1997) found that profoundly gifted children, those with IQ scores above 180, were more likely to suffer emotional problems, to become socially isolated, and they often ended up as "ordinary" adults (Winner, 2000). In each of these cases, however, the connection between IQ and success is correlational, so it's best to exercise caution in drawing conclusions. In such studies there are apt to be many potentially confounding factors. To list just one example, high-IQ children tend to come from economically privileged households, which might help account for later success and emotional stability (Tomlinson-Keasey & Little, 1990).

Finally, there are *savants,* who may show limited intellectual or social functioning overall but exhibit tremendous "gifts" in a particular domain. Calendrical savants, for example, have the amazing ability to name the weekday corresponding to a particular date, often in a matter of seconds (Cowan et al., 2003). Psychologists have studied savants, and tracked their abilities over time, but remain uncertain about the origins of their remarkable abilities. There's some evidence that the ability is innate, produced by some kind of atypical brain organization or genetic information (Nurmi et al., 2003), but no firm cause has yet been established. Savants are more likely to be male, and savant skills are often associated with disorders such as childhood autism (Heaton & Wallace, 2004). Experience may play a role in their development, but many of these specific skills appear not to have been explicitly taught (Cowan et al., 2004).

The Validity of Intelligence Testing

How valid is IQ as a measure of intellectual ability? Does it truly tap some hidden but powerful feature of the mind that accounts for individual differences? Does it adequately measure the ability to adapt and solve the problems of survival? Remember, here we use "validity" in the technical sense: How well does the test measure the thing that it's supposed to measure? To assess the validity of the IQ, then, we must ask: How well do the tests that produce IQ scores predict their criterion of interest?

The most widely applied intelligence tests today are the Stanford-Binet, the Wechsler Adult Intelligence Scale (WAIS), and the Wechsler Intelligence Scale for Children (WISC). These are not the only tests, of course; in fact, if we combine intelligence tests with measures of scholastic aptitude, more than a hundred different tests are currently in use. Often these tests are given for the same reason that originally motivated Binet and Simon—to predict some kind of academic performance, usually grades in high school or college. From this perspective, IQ passes the validity test with flying colors: IQ, as measured by Stanford-Binet or the Wechsler tests, typically correlates about +0.50 or higher with school grades (Ceci, 1991; Murray & Wren, 2003). Notice that the correlation isn't perfect, but it's reasonably high when you consider all of the uncontrolled factors that can affect grades in school (motivation, home environment, participation in extracurricular activities, and so on).

Test	Description	Example
Wechsler Adult Intelligence Scale (WAIS)		
Verbal scale		
Information	Taps general range of information.	On what continent is France?
Comprehension	Tests understanding of social conventions and ability to evaluate past experience.	Why are children required to go to school?
Arithmetic	Tests arithmetic reasoning through verbal problems.	How many hours will it take to drive 150 miles at 50 miles per hour?
Performance scale		
Block design	Tests ability to perceive and analyze patterns by presenting designs that must be copied with blocks.	Assemble blocks to match this design:
Picture arrangement	Tests understanding of social situations through a series of pictures that must be arranged in the right sequence to tell a story.	Put the pictures in the right order: 1 2 3
Object assembly	Tests ability to deal with part-to-whole relationships by presenting puzzle pieces that must be assembled to form a complete object.	Assemble the pieces into a complete object:

FIGURE 10.4

Examples from the WAIS. The Wechsler Adult Intelligence Scale measures both verbal and nonverbal aspects of intellectual ability. Included here are samples of the various question types. (From Weiten, 1995)

Critics of IQ often point out that it fails to provide a broad index of intelligence. As we discussed earlier, it's proper to define intelligence broadly—there are many ways that people can fit successfully into their environments—and it's certain that not all forms of multiple intelligence are measured by traditional paper-and-pencil IQ tests. This criticism has been recognized for years by the community of intelligence test researchers, and efforts have been made to develop tests that measure a variety of abilities. The influential tests of David Wechsler, for example, were developed in part to measure nonverbal aspects of intellectual ability. The Wechsler tests include not only verbal-mathematical questions of the type traditionally found on the Stanford-Binet test but also nonverbal questions requiring things such as the completion or rearrangement of pictures (see Figure 10.4). Performance is then broken down into a verbal IQ, a nonverbal (or "performance") IQ, and an overall IQ based on combining the verbal and nonverbal measures.

Think About It

Do you think it makes sense for elementary schools to use "tracking" systems—that is, to divide children early on into different classes based on performance on standardized tests?

Again, most intelligence tests are designed to accomplish some specific end, such as predicting future academic performance, not to provide an all-encompassing index of true intellectual ability. So if you develop a test to predict college performance, it probably isn't reasonable to expect it to predict creativity, originality, or the ability for deep thought. As we'll discuss later, this also means that intelligence tests can suffer from cultural limitations—a test designed to measure the abilities of high school students in suburbia may not be valid for students in the barrio or from a different region of the world. This doesn't mean that intelligence tests aren't useful—you just need to be aware of what the tests were designed to measure.

Labeling Effects Another potentially serious criticism of IQ concerns the effects of labeling. You take a test as a child, your IQ is calculated by comparing your performance with that of other kids your age, and the score becomes part of your continuing academic record. Once the IQ label is applied—you're smart, you're below average, and so on—expectations are generated in those who have access to your score. A number of studies have shown that intelligence labels influence how teachers interact with their students in the classroom. There is a kind of "rich get richer" and "poor get poorer" effect—the kids with the "smart" label are exposed to more educational opportunities and are treated with more respect. Things are held back from the "slow" kids, so they're less likely to be exposed to factors that might nurture academic growth (Oakes, 1985; Rosenthal & Jacobson, 1968).

© Bettmann/Corbis

Within 24 hours of arriving at Ellis Island, immigrants were subjected to a variety of mental and physical examinations. Unfortunately, these exams were sometimes used to discriminate unfairly among population groups; at the time, administrators were simply not sensitive to the influence of cultural factors on test performance.

Labeling effects were particularly serious in the early decades of the 20th century when intelligence tests were in their formative stages of development. Tests were widely administered—for example, to newly arriving immigrants and to all Army recruits—before the impact of cultural and educational factors on test performance were well understood. As we'll discuss later, people can perform poorly on an intelligence test because the test has certain built-in biases with respect to language and cultural lifestyle. Imagine, for example, that as part of an intelligence test I ask you to identify the vegetable broccoli. Easy, but not if you were raised in a culture that did not include broccoli as part of its diet. In such a case you would probably get the question wrong, but it wouldn't say anything about your intellectual or academic potential.

Researchers were not very sensitive to these concerns when the early intelligence tests were developed. The result was that certain population groups, such as immigrants from southern and eastern Europe, generally performed poorly on these tests. Some psychologists even went so far as to label these immigrant groups "feeble minded" or "defective" based on their test performance. Immigration laws enacted in the 1920s discriminated against poorly performing groups by reducing immigration quotas. In modern times psychologists are more aware of test bias and have worked very hard to reduce its influence on test performance.

Individual Differences Related to Intelligence

To end our discussion of the measurement of individual differences, we'll briefly consider three psychological characteristics that are often aligned with the topic of intelligence: creativity, emotional intelligence, and tacit knowledge. None is necessarily related to *g* (general intelligence), but each is an adaptive characteristic that can potentially increase our ability to succeed or even survive.

Creativity The term **creativity** refers to the ability to generate ideas that are original and novel. Creative thinkers think in unusual ways, which means they can look at the usual and express it in an unusual way. Creative thinkers tend to see the "big picture" and are able to find connections among things that others might not see. Importantly, however, it's not just the generation of new and different ideas that makes one creative; those ideas must also be useful and relevant—they must potentially have adaptive value.

creativity
the ability to generate ideas that are original, novel, and useful.

How is creativity measured? Psychologists have devised a number of ways to measure individual differences in creative ability (Cooper, 1991; Cropley, 1996). One popular technique is to supply a group of unrelated words, or unrelated objects in a picture, and ask a person to generate as many connections among the items as possible (Mednick, 1962; Torrance, 1981). Try it yourself: Take these words—food, catcher, hot—and try to think of a fourth word (or words) that relates to all three. It turns out that measures such as these reveal individual differences among people—some find this task to be quite easy, others find it extremely hard. Moreover, performance on these creativity tests can then be correlated with other abilities, such as IQ or job success, to see if there is a connection.

What's the relation between creativity and intelligence? When intelligence is conceptualized in a broad way, creativity fits in nicely as a part of general intellectual ability. (You'll remember, for instance, that Sternberg's triarchic theory includes the concept of creative intelligence.) However, there isn't a straightforward relationship between creativity and IQ. Correlations between them are usually low (Horn, 1976; MacKinnon, 1962), although positive correlations have been found between creativity and some measures of verbal intelligence (Harris, 2004). Traditional IQ tests don't really measure creative thinking, so perhaps it's not surprising that the correlations are often low.

emotional intelligence
the ability to perceive, understand, and express emotion in ways that are useful and adaptive.

Emotional Intelligence The second psychological characteristic, emotional intelligence, has recently gained some popularity among psychologists and is worthy of brief note. **Emotional intelligence** is essentially the ability to perceive, understand, and express emotion (Mayer & Salovey, 1997; Salovey & Mayer, 1990). The concept applies to perceiving and understanding the emotions of others, as well as to understanding and controlling one's own emotions. Emotions, play a large role in behavior, so it's clearly adaptive to manage and express them appropriately.

People who score high on emotional intelligence can read others' emotions well and tend to be empathetic as a result. They're good at managing conflict, both their own and the conflicts of others. Not surprisingly, emotional intelligence is believed to be an excellent predictor of success in career and social settings; in fact, some have argued that emotional intelligence may be a more important predictor of success in life than more traditional conceptions of intelligence (Goleman, 1995; but see Barchard, 2003). There's clearly overlap between emotional intelligence and the broad conceptions of intelligence proposed by others (e.g., Gardner and Sternberg), but the similarities and differences have yet to be worked out in a systematic way. Research on emotional intelligence is in its infancy, but the concept is proving useful to psychologists (Salovey & Pizzaro, 2003) and is widely applied in the workplace (Zeidner et al., 2004).

tacit knowledge
unspoken practical knowledge about how to perform well on the job.

Tacit Knowledge Finally, most intelligence tests contain questions that are specific and well defined. You must have certain knowledge to perform well; there are right and wrong answers for each question. There's also usually only one method for solving the problem. But to succeed in many areas, such as on a job, you often need knowledge and abilities that are not so cut and dried—unspoken rules and strategies that are rarely, if ever, taught formally. This kind of unspoken practical "know-how" is called **tacit knowledge**, and some psychologists believe it will turn out to be an even better predictor of job performance than *g* (Wagner & Sternberg, 1985).

Tacit knowledge is rarely assessed on standardized tests of intelligence. It's a kind of knowledge that isn't written in books, and it's not usually taught. Instead, it comes primarily from experience—from watching and analyzing the behavior of others. Moreover, people clearly differ in their grasp of job-relevant tacit knowledge. Some managers understand the rules for maximizing the performance of their subordinates better than others do. When tacit knowledge is actually measured, by asking people on the job to make ratings about imaginary job scenarios,

PRACTICAL SOLUTIONS

Can Mozart's Music Make You Smarter?

People are always looking for ways to boost intelligence. This is particularly true of new parents, who want to do everything possible to improve their newborn's cognitive functioning. Recently, you may have seen media reports claiming that the music of Mozart can make you smarter, or at least improve your functioning on cognitive tasks. Some years ago, the governor of Georgia actually budgeted money for cassettes of classical music, which could be given to the parents of each new infant born in the state. Other states have considered mandating that classical music be played in all elementary schools. Most agree that Mozart was a genius, but can his music really make you smarter?

Mozart was a musical genius, but can his music really make you smarter?

The answer is "Yes and No." In initial work on this topic, undergraduates showed a significant increase in their average spatial-reasoning scores, an ability that is measured on most intelligence tests, after listening to 10 minutes of Mozart's *Sonata for Two Pianos in D Major.* Control undergraduates, who spent the same amount of time in silence or listening to relaxation tapes, failed to show similar improvements (Rauscher et al., 1993, 1995). Some researchers have had trouble repeating this so-called "Mozart Effect" (Steele et al., 1999), but a number of laboratories have now confirmed the basic finding (see Chabris, 1999, for a review). If you spend time listening to some elegant classical music, rather than sitting in silence, you're likely to perform slightly better on some measures of cognitive ability.

What causes the improvement? One possibility is that Mozart's music, because of its creative and innovative structure, activates the same portions of the brain that handle spatial-reasoning tasks (Rauscher et al., 1995). On the other hand, maybe people simply enjoy listening to music and are therefore in a better mood, or more alert, when they're asked to perform the reasoning tasks. To conclude that Mozart is responsible for the improvement would require experiments to rule out alternative interpretations. In fact, it turns out that listening to a Stephen King short story can also produce a Mozart-like Effect, as long as it's enjoyable to the listeners (Nantais & Schellenberg, 1999). Moreover, slow and sad selections of classical music fail to produce improvements in spatial reasoning, suggesting that it's indeed an enhancement in mood or arousal that is responsible for the effect (Thompson et al., 2001).

The Mozart Effect is a classic example of how psychological findings can be overblown, or misused, by the popular press. Although the original findings probably have some scientific validity, the improvements were always relatively small and lasted only for brief periods. Moreover, the improvements were only shown on particular kinds of spatial-reasoning tasks and not on others. There's certainly no evidence to suggest that listening to 10 minutes of Mozart, or Stephen King, produces lasting improvements in general intelligence. Listening to something you enjoy simply makes you feel better and you're likely to perform better on certain tasks, but it doesn't really make you smarter in any lasting or significant way.

At the same time, evidence is accumulating that music *lessons* might, in fact, help. In a recent study, children were randomly assigned to groups receiving either music lessons (keyboard or voice), drama lessons, or no lessons for a period of one year. At the end of the year, IQ was measured and the kids who received the music lessons showed more of an increase than those in the drama or no lesson control groups (Schellenberg, 2004). The IQ boost wasn't large, but it was consistent. Again, it's tough to know what to conclude from this study because researchers have yet to isolate the components of the experience that really matter. Even so, it's intriguing—maybe those hated piano lessons you took as a child really did matter.

it seems to do a reasonably good job of predicting job performance. Sternberg and Wagner (1993) found that tacit knowledge correlates significantly with salary, performance ratings, and the prestige of the business or institution where the person is employed. Moreover, tacit knowledge improves with work experience, which is what you would expect. However, tacit knowledge seems to bear little relation to general ability, as measured by *g*. There's almost never a significant correlation with IQ. In fact, in some cultures negative correlations have been reported—the higher the index of tacit knowledge, the lower the measure of *g*—suggesting that practical knowledge is sometimes emphasized at the expense of academic skills (Sternberg & Hedlund, 2002).

The idea that it's useful to develop and use multiple strategies to perform successfully is almost certain to be true. The adaptive mind soaks up knowledge where it can, and as we've seen in earlier chapters, modeling others is an important vehicle for guiding behavior. As it stands now, however, the concept of tacit knowledge, while intuitively plausible, remains somewhat slippery scientifically. Critics have questioned whether tacit knowledge is really anything different from job knowledge (Schmidt & Hunter, 1993). It may not tap some human ability, like *g*, that can be scaled by an appropriate test; instead, measurements of tacit knowledge may simply be indices of what's been learned on the job.

DISCOVERING THE SOURCES OF INTELLIGENCE

We've seen that people differ, and we've considered some of the ways to measure those differences. We've also discussed methods for conceptualizing the differences theoretically—there may be differences in *g*, differences in the speed of brain cells, or people may lack one or more of the special "talents" needed for intelligent performance. But what accounts for these differences in the first place? Why is one person's *g* higher or lower than another person's *g*? Can anything be done about these differences, or are they fixed in stone?

There are essentially two ways to explain how differences in intelligence might arise. First, you can appeal to biological processes, particularly the internal *genetic code*—those strands of DNA that determine eye color, thickness of hair, and possibly *g*. According to this view, intellectual potential is established at conception through some particularly fortunate (or unfortunate) combination of genes. Alternatively, you can appeal to an external cause, specifically the *environment*. Variations in *g* might be attributable to one's past history—perhaps Jefferson Tarpy scores high on IQ tests because he was reinforced for intellectual pursuits or went to excellent schools; perhaps Larry Steinway performs poorly because as a child he was exposed to toxins (such as lead paint). In this section, we'll frame this classic nature–nurture debate and consider the evidence relevant to each position. But first we have a practical issue to consider—how stable is the IQ measure itself?

The Stability of IQ

One way to answer questions about the origins of intelligence is to ask whether IQ changes significantly over a lifetime. If intelligence is caused by a "fast brain," we might expect intellectual ability to change very little over time or at least remain stable throughout normal adulthood. On the other hand, if intelligence is determined mainly by the environment, we would probably expect to find changes over time: IQ might rise and fall depending on experience or environmental setting. Neither of these arguments is airtight—for instance, your environment might remain constant over time, or the genetic code might express itself throughout your lifetime; it might also be the case that IQ is determined by early experience and remains fixed after a certain point in development. Even so, examining the stability of IQ seems like a reasonable place to start the search.

When intelligence is measured in the standard way, through performance on a battery of tests, its stability depends on when the measuring process begins. Before the age of about 3 or 4, it's difficult to get an accurate assessment of intellectual ability. Infants can't talk or show lasting attention, so conventional testing procedures can't be used. Investigators resort to indirect measures, such as recording whether babies choose to look at old or new pictures presented on a screen. There's some evidence that babies who quickly habituate, or lose interest, in response to repeated presentations of the same picture, and who prefer to look at novel pictures when they're shown, score higher on intelligence tests later in childhood (Bornstein, 1989; Kavsek, 2004). But in general it's widely believed that you can't get reliable assessments of IQ until somewhere between ages 4 and 7; from that point onward, IQ scores tend to predict performance on later IQ tests reasonably well (Honzik et al., 1948; Sameroff et al., 1993).

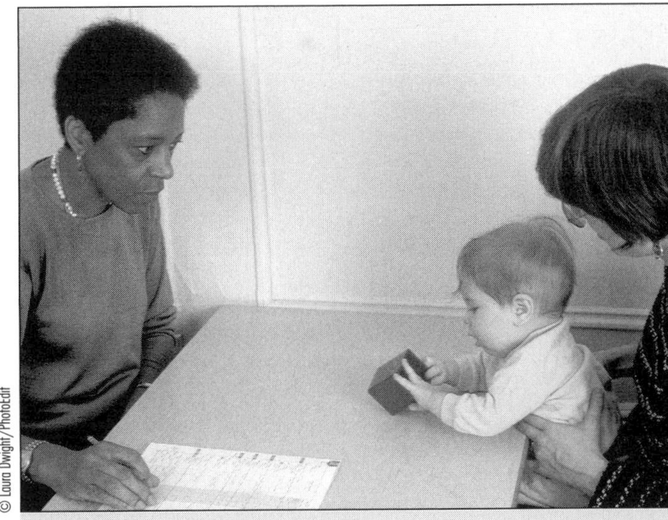

Although tests are available for measuring intelligence in small children, it's difficult to obtain reliable results before age 4.

Longitudinal Studies One of the best ways to measure the stability of IQ is through a longitudinal study, which involves testing the same people repeatedly as they age. The most widely known investigation of the stability of adult intelligence is the Seattle Longitudinal Study, which has examined mental test performance for approximately 5,000 adults ranging in age from 25 through 88 (Schaie, 1983, 1989, 1993). The participants have been tested in 7-year cycles, dating back to 1956, using a battery of tests to assess such things as verbal fluency, inductive reasoning, and spatial ability. Schaie and his colleagues have found great stability in intellectual ability throughout adulthood. From age 25 to about age 60, there appears to be no uniform decline in general intellectual ability, as measured through the test battery (see Figure 10.5 on the next page). After age 60, abilities begin to decline, although the losses are not great. There are also large individual differences—some people show excellent test performance in their 80s, whereas others do not (Schaie, 1998).

It's difficult to interpret changes in IQ with age because many factors change along with age. Elderly people are more likely to have physical problems, for example, that can affect performance. Declines in intelligence with age also depend on the type of intellectual ability measured. Earlier we discussed the distinction between fluid intelligence, which reflects basic reasoning and processing skills, and crystallized intelligence, which reflects acquired knowledge. The current thinking is that fluid intelligence may decline with age—perhaps because the biology of the brain changes—whereas crystallized intelligence remains constant, or perhaps even increases, until late in adulthood (Kaufman & Horn, 1996; Schretlen et al., 2000). The brain may become a bit slower with age, but people continue to add knowledge and experiences that are invaluable in their efforts to solve the problems of everyday life.

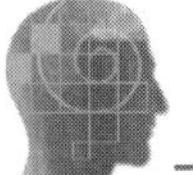

Think About It

Elderly people are often said to possess wisdom. In what ways do you think the label "wise" differs from the label "intelligent"?

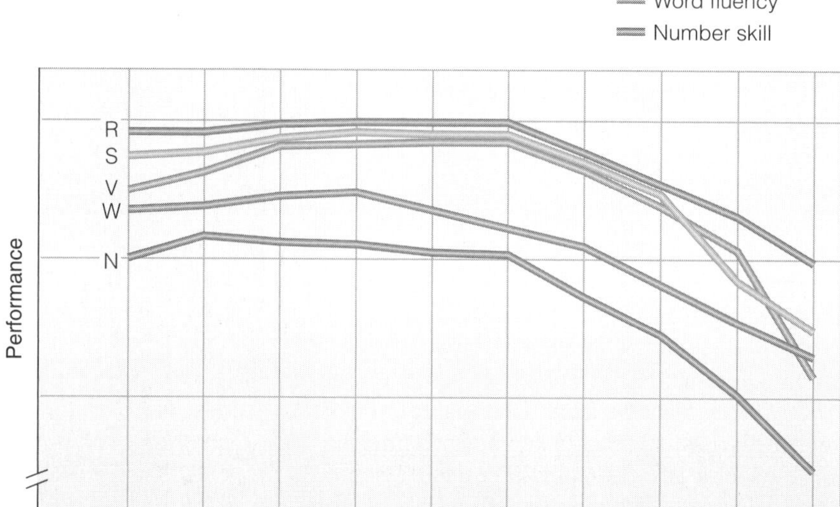

FIGURE 10.5

The Stability of Intellectual Ability. Data from the Seattle Longitudinal Study show how performance changes on a variety of mental tasks between the ages of 25 and 88. Notice that average performance is remarkably stable up to about age 60, when some declines are seen. (Data from Schaie, 1983)

The Flynn Effect Another curious fact about the stability of IQ, although it applies more to populations than to individuals, is that performance on IQ tests seems to be rising steadily and consistently over time. On average, people who take standardized intelligence tests today perform slightly better than people who took similar tests a decade ago, and the same general decade-by-decade increases have been seen since the 1930s (Flynn, 1987, 1999). This trend, known as the *Flynn effect,* has been documented worldwide, but it remains largely unexplained. Most psychologists believe the environment must be responsible because the world's gene pool is unlikely to have changed much in the past 70 years.

Most explanations of the Flynn effect appeal to factors such as increased nutrition or better schooling (Neisser, 1998; Williams, 1998). Better nutrition and health care can certainly lead to better brain functioning, although increases in brain "speed" probably can't account for the trend (Nettelbeck & Wilson, 2004). We're also exposed to new technologies, which, in turn, could help develop abstract thinking. (Think about how sophisticated we are about using cell phones and the Internet.) In addition, more and more children are placed in day care or preschool, and these experiences might contribute to better performance on standardized tests as well.

Because of the Flynn effect, IQ tests are periodically "renormed" to adjust for the fact that scores are rising. The average score is reset to 100 (remember our earlier discussion of deviation IQ), which means you now need to do "better" on the test, relative to how the test was scored in the past, to receive a given IQ. Some psychologists believe this rescoring process is having unintended effects. For example, suppose scores are rising less rapidly for people with borderline intellectual functioning (those with IQ scores around 70). Under the new scoring guidelines, significantly more individuals are apt to be diagnosed with mental retardation than in the past. Many other classification decisions are based, in part, on IQ—everything from eligibility for military service to application of the death penalty—so understanding the Flynn effect is likely to remain a priority for psychologists in the future (Kanaya et al., 2003).

Nature: The Genetic Argument

A number of early pioneers in intelligence testing, including Galton, believed strongly that individual differences in mental ability are inherited. After all, Galton argued, it's easy to demonstrate that intellectual skill runs through family lines (remember, his cousin was Charles Darwin, and his grandfather was another famous evolutionist, Erasmus Darwin). But family-tree arguments, used in isolation, aren't very convincing. Environmental factors, such as social and educational opportunities, can explain why members of the same family might show similar skills. Growing up in a family that places value on intellectual pursuits determines to some extent what sort of behaviors will be rewarded in a child, or the particular type of role models that will be available. In fairness to Galton, he realized that both inherited and environmental factors are needed to explain mental ability fully—in fact, it was Galton (1869, 1883) who coined the phrase "nature versus nurture."

© Russell Einhorn/Getty Images Entertainment

Some kinds of abilities tend to run in families, such as artistic ability in the Judd family. It's difficult, though, to separate the influences of nature and nurture.

To establish a genetic basis for a psychological or physical characteristic, it's necessary to control for the effects of the environment. In principle, if two people are raised in exactly the same environment and have exactly the same experiences, we can attribute any differences in IQ to inherited factors (nature). In this case, you've held any nurturing effects of the environment constant, so any differences must be due to genetics. Alternatively, if two people are born with exactly the same genes but end up with quite different intelligence scores, it must be the environment, not genes, that is responsible (nurture). We can't perform these kinds of experimental manipulations in the laboratory, for obvious reasons, but we can look for relevant natural comparisons.

Twin Studies Psychologists often study identical twins, who share nearly complete genetic overlap, to tease apart the nature and nurture components of mind and behavior. In twin studies, researchers search for identical twins who have been raised together in the same household or who have been separated at birth through adoption (Bouchard & McGue, 1981; Bouchard et al., 1990). The effects of the environment are assumed to be similar for the twins raised together but quite different, at least on average, for twins raised apart. If intelligence comes primarily from genetic factors, we would expect identical twins to have very similar intelligence scores, regardless of the environments in which they've been raised. One way to measure similarity is by correlation. More specifically, you can attempt to predict the IQ of one twin given the IQ of the other.

Think About It

Do you think it's possible to tease apart the relative contributions of nature and nurture to intelligence by studying animals in the laboratory?

If genes are largely responsible for intelligence, we would expect to get a strong positive correlation between IQ scores for identical twins. We wouldn't necessarily expect it to be exactly +1.00 because of measurement error or other uncontrolled factors. In reviewing the research literature on this issue, Bouchard and McGue (1981) found strong evidence for the genetic position: The IQ scores of identical twins are indeed quite similar, irrespective of the environment in which the twins have been reared. As shown in Figure 10.6 on the next page, the IQ scores for twins reared together showed an average correlation of .86; when reared apart, the average correlation remained strongly positive at .72 (Bouchard & McGue, 1981).

Researchers who conduct twin studies are actually interested in many different comparisons. For instance, it's useful to compare intelligence scores for fraternal twins (who are genetically no more similar than normal siblings) and among

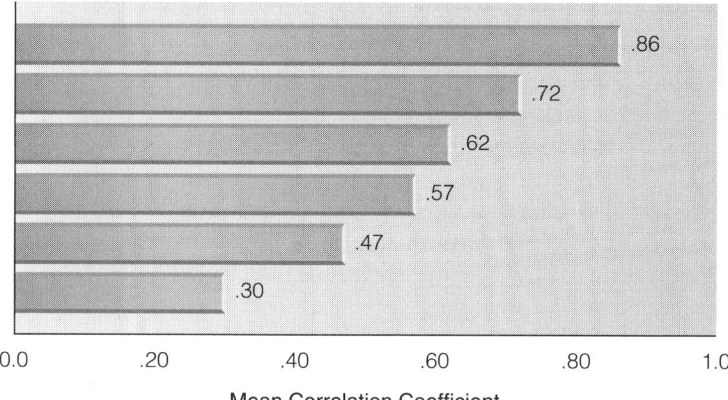

FIGURE 10.6

Nature Versus Nurture. The horizontal bars show the mean correlation coefficients for pairs of people with differing amounts of genetic overlap who have been reared in similar or different environments. For example, the top bar shows the average correlation for identical twins who have been reared together in the same environment, and the bottom bar shows the correlation coefficient for adopted siblings reared together. Higher correlations mean that the measured IQ scores are more similar. (Data from Bouchard & McGue, 1981)

unrelated people who have been reared together or apart. In general, the impressive finding is that the closer the overlap in genes, the more similar the resulting IQs. Notice, for example, that the average correlation for adopted siblings who have been reared together (.30) is much lower than the average correlation for identical twins reared apart (.72). Similarity in environmental history is not as strong a predictor of intelligence as similarity in genetic background. Data such as these suggest that genetic history plays an important role in intelligence, at least when intelligence is measured through conventional IQ testing (see also Plomin et al., 1997).

heritability
a mathematical index that represents the extent to which IQ differences in a particular population can be accounted for by genetic factors.

Heritability Intelligence researchers often use the concept of heritability to describe the influence of genetic factors on intelligence. **Heritability** is a mathematical index that represents the extent to which IQ differences within a population can be accounted for by genetic factors. For any group of people, you will find individual differences in IQ scores—heritability measures the role genetic factors play in producing these differences. It's expressed as a percentage, so if the heritability of intelligence was 100%, all differences in measured IQ could be explained genetically. Most estimates of the heritability of intelligence, derived from twin studies, hover at around 50%, which means that approximately half of the differences in IQ have a genetic basis (Sternberg & Kaufman, 1998). Other researchers propose values that are higher, perhaps closer to 70% (Bouchard et al., 1990).

It's important to understand that estimates of heritability apply only to groups, not to individuals. A heritability estimate of 70% does not mean that 70% of someone's intelligence is due to his or her genes. To see why, imagine two groups of people with the same genetic histories. Group A is placed in a rigidly controlled environment where everyone is treated exactly the same. In group B the environment is allowed to vary. If IQ scores are influenced by the environment in any way, we would expect the heritability values to be quite different for these two groups, even though the groups' genetic backgrounds are identical. Because the environment is held constant in group A, all of the differences in measured IQ will be due to genes. In group B, the heritability index will be lower because some of the differences in IQ will be due to environmental effects. Heritability tells us only that for a given group a certain percentage of the differences in intelligence can be explained by genetic factors.

Nurture: The Environmental Argument

Most psychologists agree that intelligence is influenced by genetic factors. But did you notice in Figure 10.6 that identical twins reared together have IQs that are more similar than do twins reared apart? This means that individual differences in intelligence can't be explained completely through genetic background; it's not even close—the environment clearly plays an important role.

In this section, we'll consider some environmental influences on IQ by addressing a controversial topic in the study of intelligence: group differences in IQ. The majority of intelligence researchers agree that there are stable differences in IQ across racial, ethnic, and socioeconomic groups. For example, Asian Americans tend to score 4 or 5 IQ points higher on standardized intelligence tests, on average, than White European Americans. White Americans, on average, score 10 to 15 points higher than African Americans and Hispanic Americans (Brody, 1992; Lynn, 1994).

It's important to understand that group differences in IQ, although stable, reflect average *group* differences. Not every Asian American scores high on an intelligence test, nor does every African American score low. In fact, the differences among IQ scores within a population (African Americans, Asian Americans, and so on) are much larger than the average differences between groups. This means that a large number of African Americans will score higher than the average White score, just as many Asian Americans will have scores below the average for Whites. The average population differences cannot be applied to single individuals, but the group differences are real and should be explained. How can we account for these differences? Although some psychologists have suggested that evolutionary and genetic factors are responsible for IQ differences among racial and ethnic groups (Rushton, 2000), most psychologists favor environmental explanations of the type we'll discuss next.

Economic Differences Significant economic differences continue to exist among racial/ethnic groups that could contribute to performance, and which make interpretation of the IQ differences difficult. For example, African Americans and Hispanic Americans are more likely to live at or below the poverty level in the United States. Poverty is often associated with poor nutrition, difficulties in gaining proper health care, and may hurt one's chances to enter adequate schools. African Americans and Hispanic Americans are also much more likely than Whites to suffer racial discrimination. The impact of these factors on intelligence testing is not completely understood although they almost certainly play an important role. African Americans, Whites, and Hispanic Americans tend to live in very different and somewhat isolated worlds. As a consequence, it's extremely difficult to disentangle the effects of the environment from any genetic differences that might contribute to intelligence.

Test Bias It's also possible that test biases contribute to group differences in IQ scores (Bernal, 1984). Racial/ethnic group differences depend, to a certain extent, on the type of intelligence test administered (Brody, 1992). Most traditional IQ tests are written, administered, and scored by White, middle-class psychologists. This raises the very real possibility that cultural biases might be contaminating some of the test questions. For example, if I ask you a question such as "Who wrote *Faust*?" (which once appeared on a Wechsler test), your ability to answer correctly will depend partly on whether your culture places value on exposure to such information. African American psychologist Robert L. Williams has shown that when an intelligence test is used that relies heavily on African American terms and expressions, White students who have had limited experience with African American culture perform poorly.

Do you think it's possible to eliminate cultural influences completely from a psychological test?

However, psychologists have worked hard to remove bias from standard intelligence and achievement tests (Raven et al., 1985); in some cases, the development

© Paul Chesley/Stone/Getty Images

Most psychologists agree that cultural background plays an important role in the measurement and interpretation of intelligence.

of "culture fair" tests has reduced racial differences in measured ability. However, significant group differences usually remain even after culture-bound questions have been altered or removed. Consequently, bias can contribute to test performance in some instances, but it's unlikely to be a major determinant of group differences in IQ (Cole, 1981; Kaplan, 1985).

Stereotype Threat The content of intelligence tests may no longer be biased, but situational factors remain a concern. When people take intelligence tests, they have certain expectations about how they'll perform; these expectations, in turn, can significantly affect the final score. If you're nervous, or expect to bomb the test, you're less likely to do well. Psychologist Claude Steele and his colleagues argue that African Americans, who understand the negative stereotypes people hold about their intelligence, often feel pressured or threatened by stereotypes and perform poorly as a result.

In support of this conclusion, Steele and Aronson (1995) found that African Americans performed more poorly on a verbal test when they thought the test was measuring intelligence rather than general problem solving. Everyone in the experiment took exactly the same test, but they were led to believe, through instructions, that it was either an intelligence or problem-solving test. Presumably the label "intelligence test" activated the negative stereotype, creating pressure and anxiety, and performance suffered as a result. Whether this pressure can account for the differences found between groups on intelligence tests remains uncertain (Sackett et al., 2004; Steele & Aronson, 2004), but stereotype threat is clearly an important factor to consider.

Adoption Studies A more direct test of environmental explanations of racial/ ethnic differences comes from IQ studies of African American children who have been reared in White homes. If the average African American childhood experience leads to skills that do not transfer well to standard tests of intelligence (for whatever reason), then we would expect African American children raised in White, middle-class homes to produce higher IQ scores. In general, this assumption is supported by the data. Scarr and Weinberg (1976) investigated interracial adoptions in Minnesota and found that the average IQ for African American children reared in economically advantaged White households was significantly higher than the national African American mean score. This finding was confirmed again in later follow-up studies (Waldman et al., 1994; Weinberg et al., 1992). You shouldn't conclude from this finding that White, middle-class households are somehow better than other households. The results simply imply that certain cultural experiences give one an advantage on the kinds of tests currently being used to assess intelligence.

The Interaction of Nature and Nurture

So what are we to conclude about the relative contributions of genetics and the environment to intelligence? Nature–nurture issues are notoriously difficult to resolve, and this is especially true in the politically sensitive area of intelligence. It's extremely difficult to control for the effects of either the environment or genetics. Consider the twin studies—how reasonable is it to assume that twins who have been reared apart have had unrelated environmental experiences? Are children who are adopted really representative of the racial or ethnic populations from which they have been drawn? It's difficult to answer these questions because neither the environment nor genetic structure can be manipulated directly in the laboratory (at least for humans).

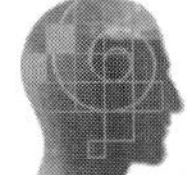

Think About It

Suppose we broaden the concept of intelligence to include athletic and artistic ability. Would it bother you to think that these abilities are influenced primarily by genetic factors?

The most reasonable position to take at the present time is that your intelligence, like many other psychological attributes, is determined by a mixture of genes and environment. The genes you inherit from your parents place upper and lower bounds on intellectual ability. Genes may importantly determine how your brain is wired, and possibly the speed of neural transmission, but the expression of your genetic material is strongly influenced by the environment. Nature always works via nurture and vice versa—one can't happen without the other (Ridley, 2003).

Recall that geneticists use the term "genotype" to refer to the genetic message itself and "phenotype" to refer to the observable characteristics that actually result from genetic expression. An analogy of the genotype/phenotype relationship that is sometimes used by intelligence researchers compares the development of intelligence to the nurturing of flowering plants (Lewontin, 1976). Imagine that we have a packet of virtually identical seeds, and we toss half into a pot containing fertile soil and half into a pot of barren soil (see Figure 10.7 on the next page). The seeds tossed into the poor soil will undoubtedly grow, but their growth will be stunted relative to that of the group planted in the rich soil. Because these are virtually identical groups of seeds, containing similar distributions of genetic information, any differences in growth between the pots are due entirely to the environment (the soil). So, too, with intelligence—two people can be born with similar genetic potential, but the degree to which their intellectual potential will "blossom" will depend critically on the environment.

Consider as well that within each handful of seeds there will be variations in genetic information. Some plants will grow larger than others, regardless of the soil in which they've been thrown. A similar kind of result would be expected for intelligence—variations in the genetic message will produce individual differences in IQ that cannot be adequately explained by environmental variables. In fact, after analyzing the differences within a pot, we might conclude that all of the differences are due to inherited factors. But even if the differences within a group are due to genes, the differences between groups would still be due to the environment (fertile or barren soil). This kind of insight can help account, in part, for the racial/ethnic differences in IQ discussed earlier. Even though genes may exert a strong influence within a population, between-population differences may still be determined primarily by the environment (Eysenck & Kamin, 1981; Lewontin, 1976).

FIGURE 10.7

Between- and Within-Group Variation. In the plant analogy, all variation in plant height within one pot is due to genetics, but the overall height difference between plants in one pot and plants in the other is attributable to the differing environments (rich soil versus poor soil).

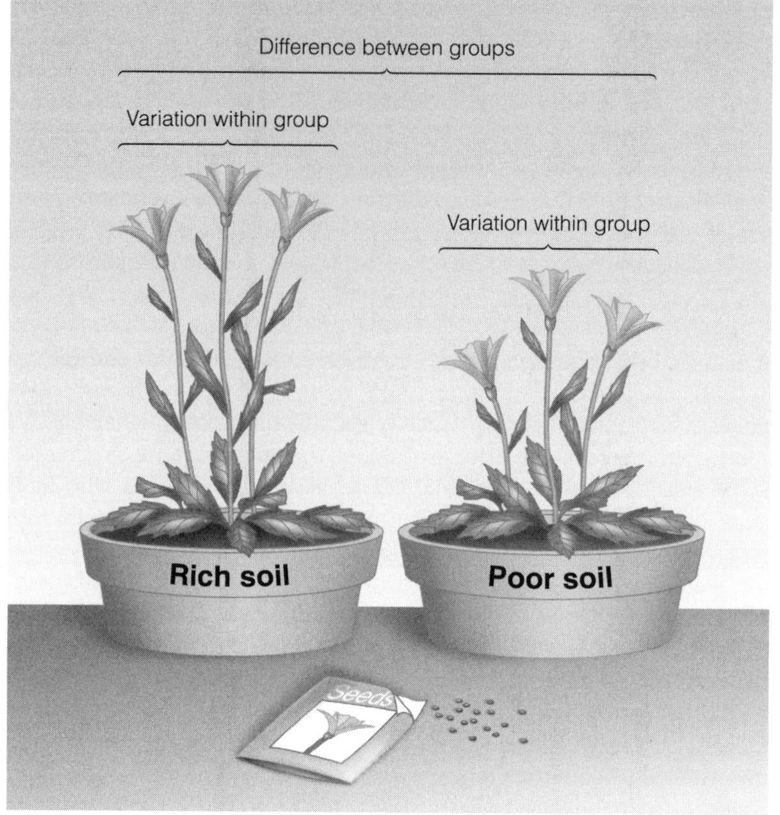

One other feature of the interaction between nature and nurture is worth noting . . . yet again. Environmental experiences do not occur independent of inherited factors. It's a two-way street. The environment will partly determine how genetic information is expressed, but so too will genetic information determine experience. If you're born with three arms, because of some odd combination of inherited factors, your interactions with the world will be quite different from those of a person with two arms. The fact that you have three arms will color your environment—it will determine how you are treated and the range of opportunities to which you are exposed. If you're born with "smart" genes, then early on you're likely to be exposed to opportunities that will help you realize your full intellectual potential; conversely, if you're born "slow," the environment is likely to shape you away from intellectually nurturing experiences (see Figure 10.8). Such is the way of life and of the world.

FIGURE 10.8

Reaction Range. Each person may have genes that set limits for intellectual potential (sometimes called a reaction range). In this case, Tom inherited an IQ potential anywhere between 80 and about 112. The IQ that Tom actually obtains (shown as the dark bar) is determined by the kind of environment in which he is reared. Notice that Miguel inherited a greater IQ potential than Tom, but if Tom is raised in an enriched environment his IQ may actually turn out to be higher than Miguel's.

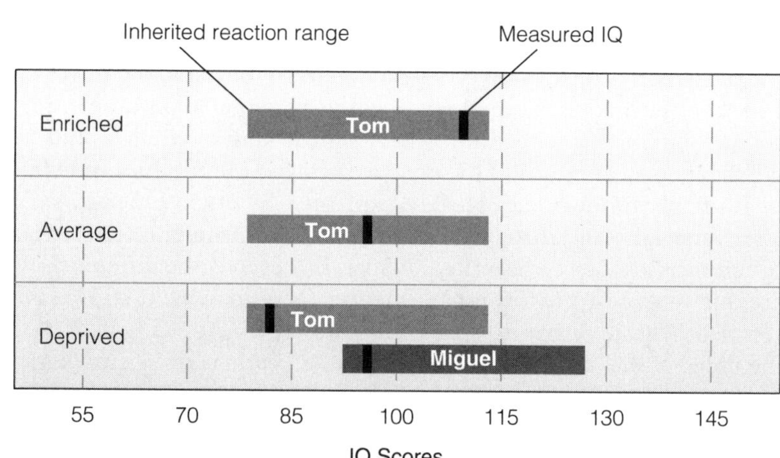

REVIEW

Psychology for a Reason

What is intelligence? You've seen in this chapter that the concept of intelligence comes primarily from the study of individual differences. People differ, and we can try to develop tests that measure these differences effectively. From an analysis of individual variability, psychologists have tried to develop theories of intellectual functioning: What kinds of mental processes underlie intelligent thought? We've seen that one way to characterize intelligence is by the adaptability of behavior. What makes one species member intelligent, and another not, may be dictated by how well organisms adapt to rapidly changing environments and solve the problems of survival. From this perspective, the nutcracker, in its successful search for a cache of seeds, fits the adaptive view of intelligence just as well as the cocky student who aces the SAT. In this chapter our discussion revolved around three problems that face researchers of intelligence.

Conceptualizing Intelligence Researchers have attempted to conceptualize intelligence in a number of ways. Proponents of psychometric approaches map out fundamental aspects of the mind by analyzing performance on a battery of mental tests. They traditionally draw distinctions between a general factor of intelligence, *g*, which applies broadly, and specific factors, *s*, which measure separate abilities. The idea that intelligence must be broken down into several, or multiple, kinds of ability remains popular today, although researchers disagree as to how many or what types of intelligence need to be included.

There's some evidence to suggest that performance on traditional tests of mental ability might be related to the speed of processing among neurons in the brain. The multiple-intelligences approach of Howard Gardner and the triarchic theory of Robert Sternberg both suggest that the concept of intelligence must be defined broadly. We cannot rely entirely on academic ability to define intelligence—everyday intelligence and "street smarts" also enhance our ability to adapt.

Measuring Individual Differences Concepts like intelligence really have little meaning outside of the study of individual differences—it's how the mental ability of Sam differs from the mental ability of Jennifer that makes the concept of intelligence meaningful. A good test of intelligence has three main characteristics: reliability, validity, and standardization. Understanding the concept of test validity is crucial because it holds the key to appreciating the widespread use of standardized measures such as IQ or tests such as the SAT. Researchers who study individual differences are often primarily interested in using the resulting measurements to make predictions about future success. Will Jennifer perform well in school? Will Sam make it as a graduate student in psychology? As you've seen, the IQ test itself was originally developed to measure academic ability, not as some ultimate measure of mental capacity.

Discovering the Sources of Intelligence There are two primary ways to explain how measured differences in intelligence might arise: genetics and the environment. Twin studies provide convincing evidence that at least some kinds of mental ability are inherited, although how much remains controversial. However, the role of the environment in determining IQ—cultural background, economic status, stereotype threat, and even built-in test biases—cannot be discounted. Intelligence, like many psychological attributes, grows out of an interaction between nature and nurture.

CHAPTER 10 PRACTICE EXAM

____ 1. The idea that intelligence can be measured by performance on mental tests is consistent with:
a. the psychometric approach
b. the cognitive approach
c. multiple intelligences
d. triarchic intelligence

____ 2. The idea intelligence models need to include special talents is with:
a. the psychometric approach
b. Howard Gardner's theory
c. the cognitive approach
d. Sternberg's triarchic theory

____ 3. The triarchic theory of intelligence suggests that:
a. intelligence can be measured by analyzing performance
b. intelligence models must address behavior that occurs in the real world
c. intelligence needs mental processes
d. traditional conceptions of intelligence include special abilities

____ 4. According to the triarchic theory, someone who can adapt very well to new or novel tasks, has high
a. analytic intelligence
b. creative intelligence
c. practical intelligence
d. Leitmotif intelligence

____ 5. Achievement tests measure
a. current level of knowledge in a particular field or area
b. ability to acquire the knowledge
c. ability to think in creative ways
d. ability to manipulate new information

____ 6. Tests that measure an individual's ability to acquire knowledge are called
a. aptitude tests
b. achievement tests
c. standardized tests
d. Personality inventory tests

____ 7. Valid tests:
a. produce similar scores
b. accurately measure
c. have testing that vary across different administrations
d. produce different results each time

____ 8. When all people given a test are took the test under exactly the same condition, the test is
a. reliable
b. standardized
c. valid
d. Quasi experimental

____ 9. An individual with a mental age greater than his or her chronological age would have:
a. an IQ greater than 100
b. an IQ less than 100
c. an IQ equal to 100
d. nowhere near 100

____ 10. What is the IQ of a 4 year old who scores like a 5 year old?
a. 80
b. 100
c. 101
d. 125

____ 11. When the deviation score is reported, what percent of people have an IQ between 70 and 130?
a. 68%
b. 10%
c. 96%
d. 50%

____ 12. Creativity appears to be the ability to:
a. acquire the knowledge in a given area
b. perform well on conventional tests
c. generate original, and novel yet useful ideas
d. Solve unique problems

____ 13. How do fluid and crystallized intelligence change across the life span?
   a. fluid intelligence remains stable
   b. fluid and crystallized intelligence increase
   c. fluid and crystallized intelligence decrease
   d. fluid intelligence decreases

____ 14. Heritability is an index that represents:
   a. the predicted IQ score for a child
   b. the extent to which genetic factors account for IQ differences within a population
   c. the predicted IQ score for an infant
   d. the proportion of each person's IQ

____ 15. Observed variations in IQ scores seem to result from:
   a. the interaction between genetic and environmental factors
   b. genetic differences alone
   c. environmental differences alone
   d. Vagaries of the test given

Answers

1. A
2. B
3. B
4. B
5. A
6. A
7. B
8. B
9. A
10. D
11. C
12. C
13. D
14. B
15. A

CHAPTER 11: PERSONALITY

QUESTIONS

1. What is the difference between the idiosyncratic and nomothetic approaches to personality?
2. What are states and traits?
3. What is the point of the trait approach to personality?
4. How is personality often measured?
5. What do reliability and validity mean regarding personality tests?
6. What is one way to check the validity of a personality test?
7. What were the results of the two studies that checked the validity of personality questionnaires?
8. What were the results of the research on raising self-esteem?
9. What are some problems with measuring self-esteem?
10. What did Allport and Odbert (1936) do to derive a list of personality traits?
11. How does factor analysis work and what is an example?
12. What is the case for the Big Five personality traits?
13. Which are the two biggest of the big five traits?
14. What were the results of the study on neuroticism (Gunthert, Cohem & Armeli, 1999)?
15. What were the results of the extraversion studies?
16. What are three criticisms of the big five model?
17. What does the research indicate about the validity of the Big Five traits across cultures?
18. How should the Big Five model be evaluated?
19. What do the results of twin studies suggest about the heritability of personality?
20. What do the results of biological and adopted children suggest about the heritability of personality?
21. How does our personality change as we age?
22. What are some explanations for why our personalities change as we age?
23. What evidence suggests personalities might change across generations?
24. Why did people agree with the false personality profile?
25. What should be included in a standardized test?
26. What is the reliability and validity of personality tests in magazines and newspapers?
27. How was the MMPI developed?
28. How was the MMPI-2 restandardized?
29. Why should psychologists be cautious about interpreting MMPI results for ethnic minorities?
30. How is deception detected in the MMPI?
31. What is the MMPI used for?
32. What do projective tests allow the person to do?
33. How was the Rorschach Inkblot test developed?

34. How is the Rorschach administered?
35. What is the main problem with interpreting the Rorschach?
36. What is Exner's scoring system?
37. What are five continuing problems with the Rorschach?
38. What is the point of critics of the Rorschach?
39. How was the Thematic Apperception Test (TAT) developed?
40. What is the assumption of the TAT?
41. What is the story told about a man clinging to a rope?
42. How do psychologists use the TAT?
43. What is the reliability of the TAT which makes it good for what?
44. What is a criticism of the TAT that is similar to the Rorschach?
45. What is the relationship between handwriting and personality?
46. What are implicit personality tests?
47. What is the emotional Stroop test?
48. What were the hypothesis, method, results, and interpretation of the study with people who had attempted suicide (Becker, Strohbach, & Rinek, 1999)?
49. How does the Implicit Association Test work?
50. What is Implicit Association Test currently good for?
51. How should personality tests be used?
52. How can personality tests be misused?
53. How accurate is criminal profiling?

VOCABULARY

1. agreeableness
2. Barnum effect
3. big five personality traits
4. conscientiousness
5. Emotional Stroop Test
6. external locus of control
7. extraversion
8. ideographic approach
9. Implicit Association Test
10. internal locus of control
11. Minnesota Multiphasic Personality Inventory (MMPI)
12. MMPI-2
13. nomothetic approach
14. personality
15. Rorschach Inkblots
16. self-concept
    social interest
17. standardized test
18. state
19. Thematic Apperception Test (TAT)
20. trait
21. trait approach to personality
22. unshared environment

11 Personality

Personality Traits and States

The Search for Broad Personality Traits

The Big Five Model of Personality

The Origins of Personality

Personality Assessment

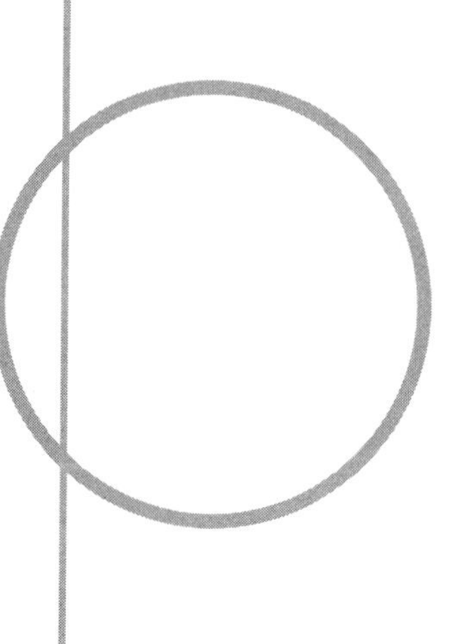

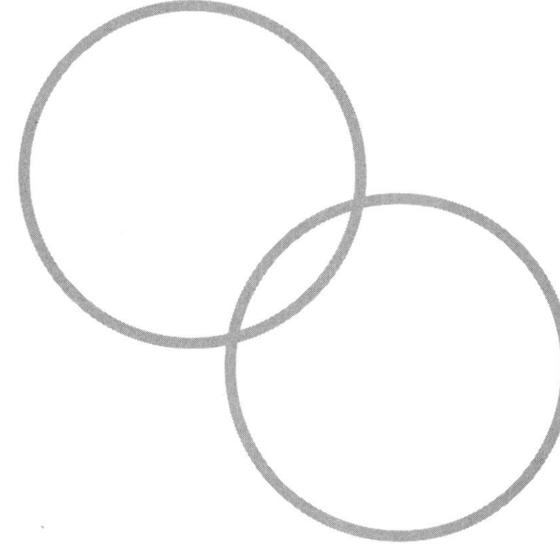

© Photo Edit

WHAT TRAITS PROVIDE the best description of personality? Why do people differ in their personalities? With regard to human personality, which would you say?

a. Every person is different from every other.

b. Way down deep, we're all the same.

c. It depends.

I vote for "it depends." The answer depends on our purposes. By analogy, in some ways every rock is unique. If you want to know the fair market value of a rock, you cannot treat diamonds the same as granite, and if you want to predict how well a rock will conduct electricity or how easily you could break it, you need to know a good deal about the content of the rock. However, if you want to predict how fast a rock will fall if you drop it or what will happen when you throw it against a window, one kind of rock is about the same as another.

Similarly, people resemble one another in some ways but not others. Psychologists study personalities in two ways, called the nomothetic and the idiographic approaches. The word *nomothetic* (NAHM-uh-THEHT-ick) comes from the Greek *nomothetes*, meaning "legislator," and the **nomothetic approach** *seeks general laws about various aspects of personality*, based on studies of large groups of people. For example, we might make the nomothetic statement that people vary in a trait called *extraversion*, and the more extraverted someone is, the more likely that person will introduce himself or herself to a stranger.

In contrast the word *idiographic* is based on the root *idio-*, meaning "individual." The **idiographic approach** concentrates on *intensive studies of individuals*

nomothetic approach
an approach to the study of individual differences that seeks general laws about how an aspect of personality affects behavior.

idiographic approach
an approach to the study of personality differences that concentrates on intensive studies of individuals.

(Allport, 1961). For example, a psychologist might study one person in detail, trying to understand that person's goals, moods, and reactions. The conclusions would apply only to this person and anyone else who is very similar.

PERSONALITY TRAITS AND STATES

Meteorologists distinguish between climate (the usual conditions) and weather (the current conditions). For example, the climate in Scotland is moister and cooler than the climate in Texas, but on a given day, the weather could be warm in Scotland and cool in Texas. Similarly, psychologists distinguish between long-lasting personality conditions and temporary fluctuations.

A consistent, long-lasting tendency in behavior, such as shyness, hostility, or talkativeness, is known as a **trait**. In contrast a **state** is *a temporary activation of a particular behavior.* For example, being afraid at a particular moment is a state; being nervous most of the time is a trait. Being quiet in a library is a state; being quiet habitually is a trait. A trait, like a climate condition, manifests itself as an average over time, though not at every moment. For example, someone who is usually quiet will have an occasional talkative moment, and someone who is usually outgoing may be shy in special circumstances.

trait
a consistent, long-lasting tendency in behavior.

state
a temporary activation of a particular behavior.

internal locus of control
the belief that one is largely in control of the events of one's life.

external locus of control
the belief that external forces are largely in control of the events of one's life.

Note that both traits and states are descriptions of behavior, not explanations. To say that someone is nervous and quiet does not explain anything; it merely tells us what we are trying to explain.

THE SEARCH FOR BROAD PERSONALITY TRAITS

The point of the **trait approach to personality** is the idea that *people have consistent personality characteristics that can be measured and studied.* Psychologists have described, studied, and measured a great many personality traits, such as honesty, friendliness, authoritarianism, and nervousness.

Some of the research deals with traits that are not familiar descriptions in everyday life. For example, people who *believe they are largely in control of their lives* are said to have an **internal locus of control**. Those who *believe they are controlled mostly by external forces* are said to have an **external locus of control** (Rotter, 1966). Table 11.1 lists some items from a questionnaire designed to measure locus of control. Generally, people with an internal locus of control like to choose tasks where they believe they can control the outcome, and then they persist at these tasks. At the end they take the credit or blame for the outcome.

Like this man playing the role of a woman in Japanese Kabuki theater, actors can present personalities that are very different from their private ones. All of us occasionally display temporary personalities that are different from our usual selves.

Issues in Personality Measurement

In past chapters, particularly in the discussions of intelligence and emotion, we have dealt with difficulties of measurement. Progress in any field depends on good measurement, and in personality research measurement is particularly difficult. The problem is that we care about how someone acts *in general* (the person's traits), but behavior fluctuates substantially from one moment to another. The same is true to some extent for any aspect of psychology: Your memory varies from one time to another, and so do your intelligence and even your vision and hearing. But those fluctuations are small compared to fluctuations in personality: You might be very friendly and outgoing at

TABLE 11.1

Sample Items from the Internal–External Scale

For each item, choose the statement you agree with more.

1. a. Without the right breaks, one cannot be an effective leader.
   b. Capable people who fail to become leaders have not taken advantage of their opportunities.
2. a. Becoming a success is a matter of hard work; luck has little or nothing to do with it.
   b. Getting a good job depends mainly on being in the right place at the right time.
3. a. As far as world affairs are concerned, most of us are the victims of forces we can neither understand nor control.
   b. By taking an active part in political and social affairs, people can control world events.
4. a. Many times I feel that I have little influence over the things that happen to me.
   b. It is impossible for me to believe that chance or luck plays an important role in my life.

Source: Rotter, 1966, pp. 11–12.

one time or in one situation but much less so an hour later. Theoretically, a researcher could observe your behavior nonstop for days or weeks to get an adequate sample, but by far the most common procedure is to ask you, or someone who knows you well, to report about your personality with a questionnaire.

Devising and evaluating a useful questionnaire are more difficult than you might think. Reliability means repeatability or consistency of scores; validity means usefulness of the scores for predicting something else. Determining the reliability of a personality questionnaire is the first step; if the reliability is low, then some of the questions may be unclear or confusing, or different questions may be measuring different aspects of personality. Validity is more difficult. When people rate their own personality, can we trust them to be accurate? For example, most Americans describe their own intelligence as well above average, whereas the British are more modest, and the Japanese are still more modest, although on actual IQ tests the British do at least as well as Americans and the Japanese usually do better (Furnham, Hosoe, & Tang, 2002). On personality questionnaires also, presumably people vary in how accurately they describe themselves.

One way to check the validity of a personality questionnaire is to compare questionnaire results to behaviors recorded in diary form. In one study 170 college students filled out questionnaires about several personality dimensions including aggressiveness and spontaneity. Then they kept daily records of such behaviors as yelling at someone (aggression) and buying something on the spur of the moment (spontaneous behavior). Both kinds of data rely on self-reports, but the daily behavior records are more detailed, closer in time to the actual events, and presumably more accurate. The questionnaire results correlated about .4 with reports of aggressive behavior, but less well with reports of spontaneous acts (Wu & Clark, 2003). That is, the questionnaire results were moderately accurate measurements.

In another study 10- to 11-year-old girls filled out a questionnaire about conscientiousness (tendency to follow the rules and keep one's promises), and a year later reported whether they had engaged in any risky sexual behaviors. Conscientiousness correlated –.42 with risky sexual behaviors; that is, those girls low in conscientiousness were the most likely to engage in risky sexual activities (Markey, Markey, & Tinsley, 2003). Again, it appears that the personality questionnaire is measuring an important aspect of behavior—not perfectly, but moderately well.

An Example of Measurement Problems: Self-Esteem

For some years a popular goal among both psychologists and the general public was to raise people's self-esteem. The belief was that low self-esteem led to self-destructive activities and violence toward others, whereas high self-esteem led to satisfaction, productivity, and a host of other good outcomes. That belief was only a hypothesis, however, and researchers needed data to test it. Psychologists developed several questionnaires to measure self-esteem and devised programs to help people raise their self-esteem. However, research results were mixed and often disappointing. On the plus side, as people increase their self-esteem, they are less likely to feel depressed (Watson, Suls, & Haig, 2002). However, raising people's self-esteem generally has little effect on aggressive behavior and in many cases leads to *decreased* performance in school or on the job (Baumeister, Campbell, Krueger, & Vohs, 2003). Evidently, if we convince people that "you're doing great," they see little need to try harder!

Part of the problem is that self-esteem means many things, and different questionnaires measure it differently. Consider some example questions on self-esteem questionnaires (Blascovich & Tomaka, 1991). Here is one set of examples:

- I feel that I have a number of good qualities.
- I am able to do things as well as most other people.
- At times I think I'm no good at all.
- I'm a failure.

An answer of "true" to the first two or "false" to the second two would count as points toward a high self-esteem score. Contrast those to the following items from a different self-esteem questionnaire, on which you are to answer from 1 (rarely or never) to 5 (usually or always):

- I feel that I am a beautiful person.
- I think that I make a good impression on others.
- I think that I have a good sense of humor.
- I feel that people really like me very much.

Would you call those items "self-esteem" or "self-evaluation"? Certainly, they highlight a different aspect of self-regard. For example, you might think you have "a number of good qualities" as in the first set of items but not describe yourself as "beautiful."

Now consider these additional true–false items:

- There are lots of things about myself I'd change if I could.
- I'm often sorry for the things I do.
- I'm not doing as well in school as I'd like.
- I wish I could change my physical appearance.

A "true" answer on any of those items would count as a point toward low self-esteem. But do the answers really indicate low self-esteem or high goals? Someone who says "true" is presumably striving for self-improvement. Someone who says "false" is satisfied with current performance, whatever that might be. In short, a self-esteem questionnaire might not be measuring what we want to measure.

Here is an additional problem: Most Americans rate themselves above average in intelligence, personality, and self-esteem. Therefore, if you rate yourself "average," you are considered to have *below-average* self-esteem! Next a survey asks what you think of minority groups or foreigners. Most Americans claim to have a "very high" opinion of minority groups and foreigners, so if you rate them "about average," you are considered to have a *below-average* opinion of them. Using these methods some studies have reported that "people with low self-esteem tend to be prejudiced," when a better statement of the data would be "people who rate themselves average rate other people average too" (Baumeister et al., 2003). As emphasized before, to evaluate anyone's conclusions, we need to examine the evidence carefully, especially the measurement methods.

THE BIG FIVE MODEL OF PERSONALITY

Psychologists have devised questionnaires to measure locus of control, self-esteem, aggressiveness, and hundreds of other traits. Measuring hundreds of traits is impractical; the goal should be a simple system listing no more traits than necessary. Remember the principle of parsimony: If we can adequately describe personality with, say, five or ten traits, we do not need to measure more.

One way to begin is by examining our language. Many psychologists assume that any human language probably has a word for every important personality trait. Although this assumption is not a logical necessity, it seems reasonable considering how much attention people pay to other people's personalities.

Gordon Allport and H. S. Odbert (1936) plodded through an English dictionary and found almost 18,000 words that might be used to describe personality. They deleted from this list words that were merely evaluations, such as *nasty,* and terms referring to temporary states, such as *confused.* (At least we hope that being confused is temporary.) In the remaining list, they looked for clusters of synonyms, such as *affectionate, warm,* and *loving,* and kept only one of these terms. When they found opposites, such as *honest* and *dishonest,* they also kept just one of them. (*Honesty* and *dishonesty* are different extremes of one dimension, not separate traits.) After eliminating synonyms and antonyms, Raymond Cattell (1965) narrowed the original list to 35 traits.

Derivation of the Big Five Personality Traits

Although some of the 35 personality traits that Cattell identified are not exactly synonyms or antonyms of one another, many of them overlapped. To determine which traits correlate with one another, psychologists use a method called *factor analysis.* For example, if measurements of warmth, gregariousness, and assertiveness correlate strongly with one another, we can cluster them together as a single trait. But if this combined trait does not correlate highly with self-discipline, then self-discipline (and anything that correlates strongly with it) is a separate trait.

Using this approach researchers found major clusters of personality traits, which they call the **big five personality traits**: *neuroticism, extraversion, agreeableness, conscientiousness, and openness to new experience* (McCrae & Costa, 1987). The case for these five traits is that (a) each correlates with many personality dimensions for which our language has a word and (b) none of these five traits correlates highly with any of the other five, so they are not measuring the same thing.

big five personality traits
five traits that account for a great deal of human personality differences: neuroticism, extraversion, agreeableness, conscientiousness, and openness to new experience.

The big five dimensions are described in the following list (Costa, McCrae, & Dye, 1991). Note that the first two, neuroticism and extraversion, are the "biggest" of the big five. Even psychologists who are skeptical of the big five model agree that neuroticism and extraversion are powerful traits that influence much of human behavior (Block, 1995).

Courtesy of Morimura Yasumasa

The Japanese artist Morimura Yasumasa re-creates famous paintings, substituting his own face for the original. Some people love his work; others dislike it or object to the whole idea. People high in "openness to experience" delight in new, unusual forms of art, literature, and music.

Neuroticism is *a tendency to experience unpleasant emotions relatively easily.* Neuroticism correlates positively with anxiety, hostility, depression, and self-consciousness. In one study college students kept a diary in which they recorded the most stressful event of the day. Students who scored high on a neuroticism questionnaire were more likely than other students to identify their most stressful event as some conflict they had with another person. They were also more likely than other students to rate the experience as highly distressing, and they were less likely than others to deal effectively with their stressful events (Gunthert, Cohen, & Armeli, 1999).

Extraversion is *a tendency to seek stimulation and to enjoy the company of other people.* The opposite of extraversion is introversion. Extraversion is associated with warmth, gregariousness, assertiveness, impulsiveness, and a need for excitement. Extraverted people tend to be risk-takers, and the unpleasant side of extraversion is an increased risk of alcohol abuse and similar problems (Martsh & Miller, 1997). The pleasant side is that extraverts tend to be happy most of the time (Francis, Brown, Lester, & Philipchalk, 1998). In one study participants reported five times a day for 2 weeks what they had been doing and how they were feeling. Generally, they reported feeling happy at the same times when they had been talkative, energetic, and adventuresome. Furthermore, when people were *instructed* to act in an extraverted way, they reported feeling happier afterward, and when instructed to act in an introverted way, they reported decreased happiness, regardless of whether they were usually extraverted or introverted (Fleeson, Malanos, & Achille, 2002). These results imply that active, outgoing behavior leads to happiness, although it is also likely that happiness leads to active, outgoing behavior.

Agreeableness is *a tendency to be compassionate toward others.* It implies a concern for the welfare of other people and is closely related to Adler's concept of social interest. People high in agreeableness generally trust other people and expect other people to trust them.

Conscientiousness is *a tendency to show self-discipline, to be dutiful, and to strive for achievement and competence.* People high in conscientiousness tend to show a strong work motivation (Judge & Ilies, 2002). They are likely to complete the tasks they say they will perform. If you were giving a speech or making some other kind of performance, would you prefer to have your performance rated by someone high in agreeableness or conscientiousness? As you might guess, people high in conscientiousness generally give lower, presumably more honest, ratings, whereas people high in agreeableness give higher, more generous ratings (Bernardin, Cooke, & Villanova, 2000).

Openness to experience, the big five trait that is usually the least variable and hardest to observe, is *a tendency to enjoy new intellectual experiences and new ideas.* Someone high in this trait would be likely to enjoy modern art, unusual music, thought-provoking films and plays, and so forth. People open to experience enjoy meeting different kinds of people and exploring new ideas and opinions (McCrae, 1996).

neuroticism
the tendency to experience unpleasant emotions relatively easily.

extraversion
the tendency to seek stimulation and to enjoy the company of other people.

agreeableness
the tendency to be compassionate toward others and not antagonistic.

conscientiousness
the tendency to show self-discipline, to be dutiful, and to strive for achievement and competence.

openness to experience
the tendency to enjoy new intellectual experiences, the arts, fantasies, and anything that exposes a person to new ideas.

Criticisms and Problems

You may already have thought about one peculiarity of the research so far: Almost none of the research behind the big five model depended on observing people's behavior. The research was based entirely on a study of personality words in the English language and people's answers to questionnaires. Questionnaire results are moderately good predictors of real behavior, but they are far from perfect.

The research methods could overlook certain personality traits just because of quirks of the English language. For example, we identify extraversion–introversion as a big factor because it relates to so many words in the English language—sociability, warmth, friendliness, adventuresomeness, gregariousness, happiness, and so forth. Religiousness would not emerge as a major personality trait because the language has few synonyms for it. Critics of the big five approach have identified nine personality dimensions that the big five model seems to have overlooked (Paunonen & Jackson, 2000). These nine are religiousness, manipulativeness, honesty, sexiness, thriftiness, conservativeness, masculinity–femininity, snobbishness, and sense of humor. None of these correlates very strongly with any of the others or with the big five.

Other critics raise the opposite objection that five is more traits than we need. Openness to experience has a modest positive correlation with extraversion, and conscientiousness correlates negatively with neuroticism, so perhaps we could get by with just three factors: neuroticism, extraversion, and agreeableness (Eysenck, 1992).

Cross-cultural studies offer partial, but only partial, support to the big five approach. Some studies have used translations of English words or an array of personality descriptions from other languages. Others have shown pictures of people in various activities and asked, "How likely would you be to do this?" The picture approach makes it easy to test people of various cultures without first thoroughly studying their language (Paunonen, Zeidner, Engvik, Oosterveld, & Maliphant, 2000). Many studies have found results approximately consistent with the big five model (McCrae & Costa, 1997).

However, some studies did find important cross-cultural differences. For example, in many traditional cultures, almost everyone is low in what Westerners call "openness to experience" (Mastor & Cooper, 2000; Saggino, 2000; Silverthorne, 2001). A study in China identified four big traits corresponding approximately to extraversion, neuroticism, conscientiousness, and "loyalty to Chinese traditions" (Cheung et al., 1996).

Overall, how should we evaluate the five-factor description? The answer depends on our purposes. If we are interested in a theoretical understanding of personality, it is premature at best to call the five-factor description a fact of nature (as some have done). The five-factor description accounts for enough of the variability in human behavior to be useful, although for some purposes three factors may be enough and for other purposes more may be necessary. It depends on how much precision we want in describing and predicting people's behavior.

THE ORIGINS OF PERSONALITY

A description of personality differences is not an explanation. What makes some people more extraverted, neurotic, agreeable, conscientious, or open to experience than other people are?

Heredity and Environment

If you want evidence that heredity can influence personality, you need look no further than the nearest pet dog. For centuries people have selectively bred dogs for

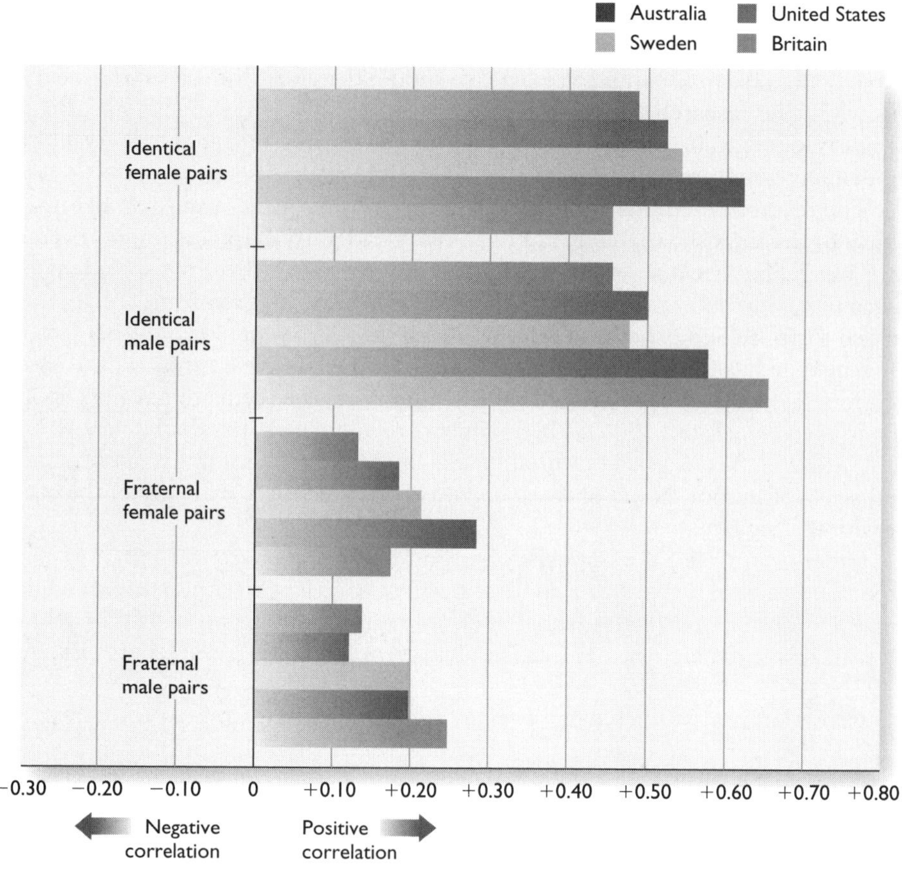

FIGURE 11.1

Five studies—conducted in Great Britain, the United States, Sweden, Australia, and Finland—found larger correlations between the extraversion levels of identical (monozygotic) twins than those of fraternal (dizygotic) twins. (*Based on data summarized by Loehlin, 1992*)

the personalities they desired, ranging from the tamest and friendliest lap dogs to those that are capable of attacking ferociously.

To measure the influences of heredity and environment on human personality, researchers have relied mostly on the same kinds of data as in other areas of psychology (Bouchard & McGue, 2003). First, they compare the similarities between identical twins and fraternal twins. As Figure 11.1 shows, five studies conducted in separate locations indicated much greater similarities in extraversion between identical pairs than fraternal pairs (Loehlin, 1992). Studies in Australia and the United States found a similar pattern for neuroticism, with identical twins resembling each other much more than fraternal twins, who resembled each other no more than brothers or sisters born at different times (Lake, Eaves, Maes, Heath, & Martin, 2000).

Modern methods make it possible to search for specific genes linked to particular personality traits. Several studies have identified genes apparently linked to neuroticism or to the specific aspect of neuroticism known as *harm avoidance* or anxiety-proneness (Fullerton et al., 2003; Zohar et al., 2003). However, each of the genes identified so far makes only a small contribution, and researchers have not yet established the route by which any gene acts.

Second, researchers compare the personalities of parents, their biological children, and their adopted children. As Figure 11.2 shows, parents' extraversion

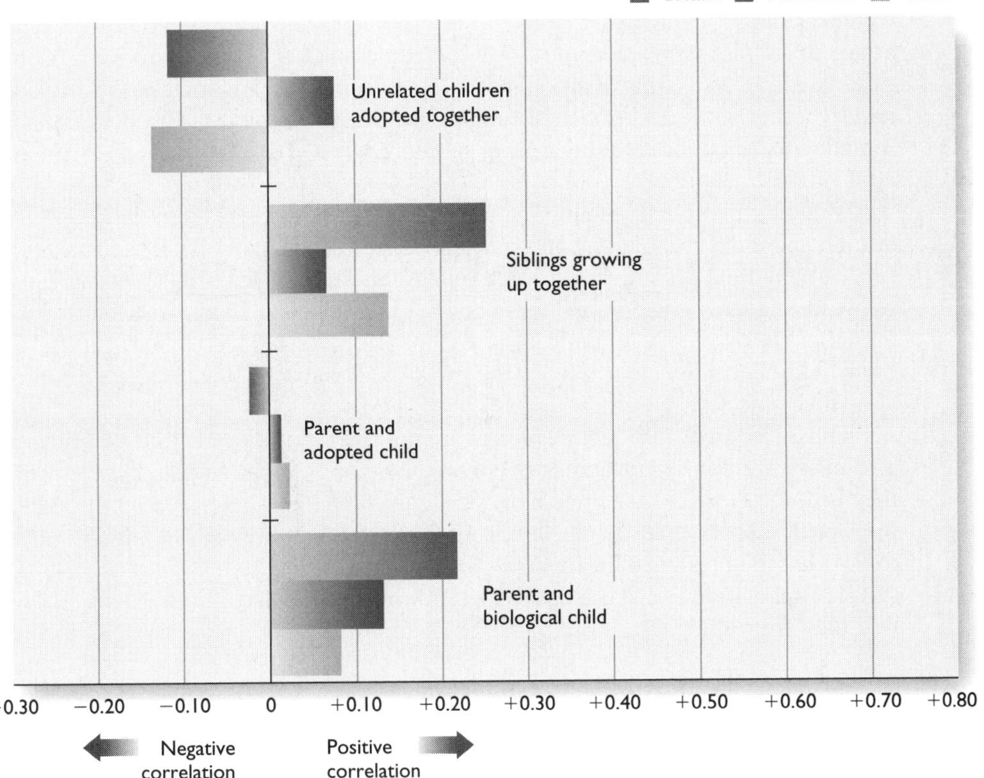

FIGURE 11.2

Studies in Britain, Minnesota, and Texas measured extraversion in members of hundreds of families. Each found moderate positive correlations between parents and their biological children and between pairs of biologically related brothers and sisters. However, all found low or even negative correlations between parents and adopted children and among adopted children living in the same family. (*Based on data summarized by Loehlin, 1992*)

levels correlate moderately with those of their biological children but hardly at all with their adopted children. Similarly, biologically related brothers or sisters growing up together resemble each other moderately in personality, and unrelated children adopted into the same family do not (Loehlin, 1992). The results shown in Figures 11.1 and 11.2 pertain to extraversion; similar studies provide a largely similar pattern for neuroticism and other personality traits (Heath, Neale, Kessler, Eaves, & Kendler, 1992; Loehlin, 1992; Viken, Rose, Kaprio, & Koskenvuo, 1994).

The low correlations between adopted children and adoptive parents imply that children learn rather little of their personalities by imitating their parents. Many researchers believe that much of the variation among people's personalities relates to the **unshared environment**, *the aspects of environment that differ from one individual to another, even within a family.* Unshared environment includes the effects of a particular playmate, a particular teacher, an injury or illness, or any other isolated experience. Because of its idiosyncratic nature, unshared environment is difficult to investigate.

unshared environment
the aspects of environment that differ from one individual to another, even within a family.

Influences of Age and Historical Era

Do you think your personality now resembles what it was in childhood? In some aspects it probably does. In one study investigators observed the behavior of

3-year-old children and followed them longitudinally until age 26. Children who were fearful and easily upset at age 3 were more nervous and inhibited than others at age 26. Those who were impulsive and restless at age 3 tended to have been in trouble with others from then on and to feel alienated from society. On the other hand, those who were confident, friendly, and eager to explore their environment at 3 tended to be confident adults, eager to take charge of events (Caspi, Harrington, et al., 2003).

Will your personality change much in the next few years? According to the research, the older people get, the more consistent their personalities remain over time. In childhood, answers on a personality questionnaire correlate a modest .34 between two tests given 6 or 7 years apart. By college age the correlation is .54. It increases to .64 at age 30 and .74 at age 60 (Roberts & DelVecchio, 2000). Why personality becomes more fixed as we grow older is not known, but you can probably imagine a few hypotheses.

The differences that occur over age are not large, but they are fairly predictable, and many are consistent across cultures. One trend is that as people grow older, they become more conscientious. In every culture that has been studied throughout the world, middle-aged people are more likely to be highly conscientious—that is, to do what they promise they will do—than are teenagers (McCrae et al., 2000). A simple explanation is that adults are forced, whether they like it or not, to hold a job, pay the bills, repair the house, care for children, and take responsibility in other ways.

As people age, they also tend to become less extraverted, especially less sensation seeking. Again this trend is found cross-culturally (Labouvie-Vief, Diehl, Tarnowksi, & Shen, 2000). Older people also tend to be less neurotic—that is, less prone to anxieties and unpleasant mood swings—and slightly more agreeable (Cramer, 2003; McCrae et al., 2000). In the United States, young people on the average score higher on openness to new experience than older people. This trend is no surprise; we see that young people enjoy new types of music, new kinds of food, new styles of clothing, and so forth (Sapolsky, 1998), whereas older people stay with old habits. In some other cultures, however, openness to experience shows no clear trend over age (McCrae et al., 2000).

Finally, does personality change from one generation to the next? Remember the Flynn effect: Over the years people's performance on IQ tests has gradually increased so that each generation does better on the tests than the previous generation. Researchers have also found generational differences in personality. For example, over the years, beginning in the 1950s, measurements of anxiety have steadily increased (Twenge, 2000). On the Child Manifest Anxiety Scale, the mean score in the 1950s was 15.1, and the mean for children in mental hospitals was 20.1. By the 1980s the mean for *all* children was 23.3! Do we really have that much more anxiety than in past generations? It is possible that people's answers do not mean exactly the same as what they used to. The more disturbing possibility is that we really do live in an age of anxiety despite our increases in health and wealth and the decreased probability of nuclear war. Compared to past generations, more children today have to live through their parents' divorce, and fewer live in a neighborhood with many friends and relatives. Might those social changes have raised the average anxiety level to what used to characterize the top 10%? The answer is uncertain, but now researchers need to worry about why people worry so much.

Answer to Other Question in the Chapter

A. Choices 1b, 2a, 3b, and 4b indicate internal locus of control; the other choices indicate external locus of control. Your answers to a longer list of such items could more accurately assess your locus of control.

PERSONALITY ASSESSMENT

What inferences can we safely draw from the results of a personality test? A new P. T. Barnum Psychology Clinic has just opened at your local shopping mall and is offering a grand opening special on personality tests. You have always wanted to know more about yourself, so you sign up. Here is Barnum's true–false test:

Questionnaire for Universal Assessment of Zealous Youth (QUAZY)

1.	I have never met a cannibal I didn't like.	T	F
2.	Robbery is the only felony I have ever committed.	T	F
3.	I eat "funny mushrooms" less frequently than I used to.	T	F
4.	I don't care what people say about my nose-picking habit.	T	F
5.	Sex with vegetables no longer disgusts me.	T	F
6.	This time I am quitting glue-sniffing for good.	T	F
7.	I generally lie on questions like this one.	T	F
8.	I spent much of my childhood sucking on telephone cords.	T	F
9.	I find it impossible to sleep if I think my bed might be clean.	T	F
10.	Naked bus drivers make me nervous.	T	F
11.	I spend my spare time playing strip solitaire.	T	F

You turn in your answers. A few minutes later, a computer prints out your individual personality profile:

> You have a need for other people to like and admire you, and yet you tend to be critical of yourself. While you have some personality weaknesses, you are generally able to compensate for them. You have considerable unused capacity that you have not turned to your advantage. Disciplined and self-controlled on the outside, you tend to be worrisome and insecure on the inside. At times, you have serious doubts as to whether you have made the right decision or done the right thing. You prefer a certain amount of change and variety and become dissatisfied when hemmed in by restrictions and limitations. You also pride yourself as an independent thinker and do not accept others' statements without satisfactory proof. But you have found it unwise to be too frank in revealing yourself to others. At times you are extraverted, affable, and sociable, while at other times you are introverted, wary, and reserved. Some of your aspirations tend to be rather unrealistic. (Forer, 1949, p. 120)

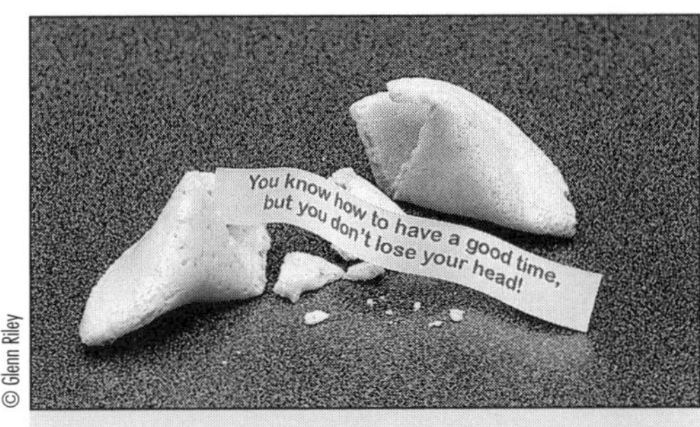

People tend to accept almost any personality assessment that someone offers them, especially if it is stated in vague, general terms that each person can interpret to fit himself or herself.

Do you agree with this assessment? Several experiments have been conducted along these lines with psychology classes (Forer, 1949; Marks & Kammann, 1980; Ulrich, Stachnik, & Stainton, 1963). Students started by filling out a questionnaire that looked fairly reasonable, not something as preposterous as the QUAZY. Several days later, each student received a sealed envelope with his or her name on it. Inside was a "personality profile," supposedly based on the student's answers to the questionnaire. The students were asked, "How accurately does this profile describe you?" About 90% rated it as good or excellent. Some expressed amazement at its accuracy: "I didn't realize until now that psychology was an exact science." None of them realized that everyone had received exactly the same personality profile—the same one you just read.

The students accepted this personality profile partly because it vaguely describes almost everyone, much like newspaper horoscopes do, and partly because people tend to accept almost *any* statement that a psychologist makes about them (Marks

Barnum effect
the tendency to accept and praise vague statements about our personality.

& Kammann, 1980). *This tendency to accept and praise vague statements about our personality is known as the* **Barnum effect,** named after P. T. Barnum, the circus owner who specialized in fooling people out of their money.

The conclusion: Psychological testing must be done carefully. If we want to know whether a particular test measures a particular person's personality, we cannot simply ask that person's opinion. Many people will praise as "highly accurate" even the results of a worthless test. To devise a psychological test that not only *appears* to work but also actually *does* work, psychologists need to design the test carefully and determine its reliability and validity.

Standardized Personality Tests

standardized test
a test that is administered according to specified rules and its scores are interpreted in a prescribed fashion.

Psychologists have devised a great variety of personality tests. A **standardized test** is *one that is administered according to exact rules that specify how to interpret the results.* One important step for standardizing a test is to determine the distribution of scores. We need to know the mean score and the range of scores for a representative sample of the population and how they differ for special populations, such as people with severe depression. Given such information, we can determine whether a particular score on a personality test is within the normal range or whether it is more typical of people with some disorder.

Most of the tests published in popular magazines have never been standardized. A magazine may herald an article: "Test Yourself: How Good Is Your Marriage?" or "Test Yourself: How Well Do You Control the Stress in Your Life?" After you take the test and compare your answers to the scoring key, the article may tell you that "if your score is greater than 80, you are doing very well . . . if it is below 20, you need to work on improving yourself!"—or some such nonsense. Unless the magazine states otherwise, you can safely assume that the author pulled the scoring norms out of thin air and never even bothered to make sure that the test items were clearly stated.

Over the years psychologists have developed an enormous variety of tests to measure both normal and abnormal personality. We shall examine a few prominent examples and explore some creative possibilities for future personality measurement.

An Objective Personality Test: The Minnesota Multiphasic Personality Inventory

Some of the most widely used personality tests are based on simple pencil-and-paper responses. We now consider in detail the MMPI, the most widely used of all personality tests (Piotrowski & Keller, 1989).

Minnesota Multiphasic Personality Inventory (MMPI)
a standardized test consisting of true–false items and intended to measure various personality dimensions and clinical conditions such as depression.

MMPI–2
the modernized edition of the MMPI.

The **Minnesota Multiphasic Personality Inventory** (mercifully abbreviated **MMPI**) consists of *a series of true–false questions intended to measure certain personality dimensions and clinical conditions such as depression.* The original MMPI, developed in the 1940s and still in use, has 550 items; *the second edition,* **MMPI–2,** published in 1990, has 567. Typical items are "my mother never loved me" and "I think I would like the work of a pharmacist." (The items stated in this text are rewordings of the actual items.)

The MMPI was devised *empirically*—that is, based on evidence rather than theory (Hathaway & McKinley, 1940). The authors wrote hundreds of true–false questions that they thought might be useful for measuring personality. They put these questions to people who were known to be suffering from various psychological disorders and to a group of hospital visitors, who were assumed to be psychologically normal. The researchers selected those items that most of the people in a given clinical group answered differently from most of the normal people. They assumed, for example, that if you answer many questions as most people with depression do, you probably are depressed also. The MMPI had scales for reporting depression, paranoia, schizophrenia, and others. The result was a test that worked, and still works, moderately well in practice. For example, most people with scores above a certain level on the Depression scale are in fact depressed.

Some of the items on the MMPI made sense theoretically; others did not. For example, some items on the Depression scale asked about feelings of helplessness or worthlessness, which are an important part of depression. But two other items were "I attend religious services frequently" and "occasionally I tease animals." If you answered *false* to either of those items, you would get a point on the Depression scale! These items were included simply because more depressed people than others answered *false*. Why is not obvious. (Perhaps people with depression do not tease animals because they do hardly anything just for fun.)

Revisions of the Test The MMPI was standardized in the 1940s. As time passed the meaning of certain items, or at least of certain answers, changed. For example, how would you respond to the following item?

I believe I am important. T F

In the 1940s fewer than 10% of all people marked this item *true*. At the time the word "important" meant about the same thing as "famous," and people who called themselves important were thought to have an inflated view of themselves. Today, we stress that every person is important.

What about this item?

I like to play drop the handkerchief. T F

Drop the handkerchief, a game similar to tag, dropped out of popularity in the 1950s. Most people born since then have never even heard of it, much less played it.

To bring the MMPI up to date, a group of psychologists rephrased some of the items, eliminated some, and added others to deal with drug abuse, suicidal thoughts, and other issues that did not concern psychologists in the 1940s (Butcher, Graham, Williams, & Ben-Porath, 1990). Then they tried out the new MMPI–2 on a large representative sample of the U.S. population. In other words they restandardized the test. Psychologists also developed a new form, the MMPI–A, intended for use with adolescents.

The MMPI–2 has 10 clinical scales, as shown in Table 11.2. The various scales have 32 to 78 items each, scattered throughout the test rather than clustered. Most

TABLE 11.2 **The Ten MMPI-2 Clinical Scales.**

SCALE	TYPICAL ITEM
Hypochondria (Hs)	I have chest pains several times a week. (T)
Depression (D)	I am glad that I am alive. (F)
Hysteria (Hy)	My heart frequently pounds so hard I can hear it. (T)
Psychopathic Deviation (Pd)	I get a fair deal from most people. (F)
Masculinity–Femininity (Mf)	I like to arrange flowers. (T = female)
Paranoia (Pa)	There are evil people trying to influence my mind. (T)
Psychasthenia (Obsessive–Compulsive) (Pt)	I save nearly everything I buy, even after I have no use for it. (T)
Schizophrenia (Sc)	I see, hear, and smell things that no one else knows about. (T)
Hypomania (Ma)	When things are dull I try to get some excitement started. (T)
Social Introversion (Si)	I have the time of my life at parties. (F)

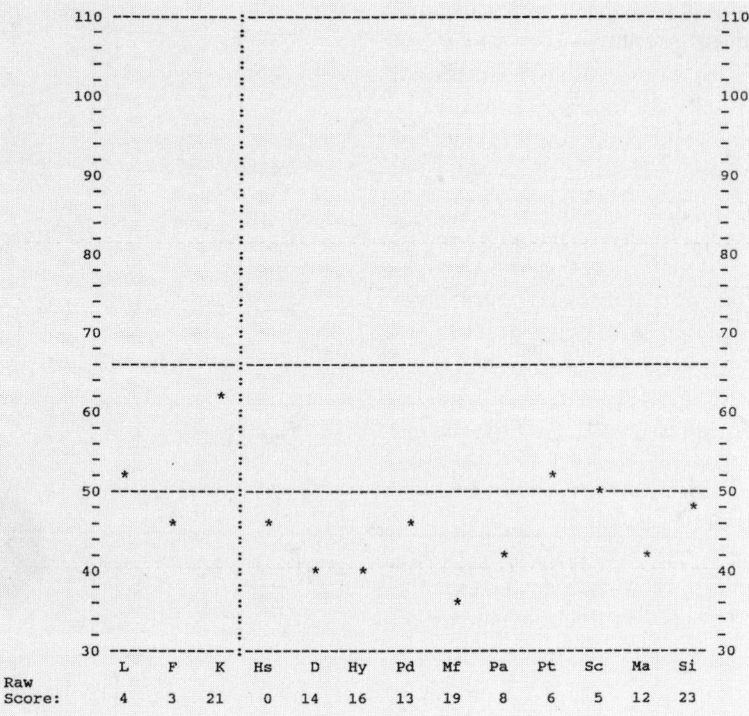

FIGURE 11.3

For the MMPI–2's 10 clinical scales, a score is plotted to profile an individual. This is the profile of a middle-aged man with no psychological problems. A person with a disorder such as hypochondria or paranoia would have scores in the range of 65 or higher on those scales. (*Minnesota Multiphasic Personality Inventory–2, © by the Regents of the University of Minnesota. Data courtesy of R. J. Huber.*)

people get at least a few points on each scale; a score above a certain level indicates a probable difficulty. Figure 11.3 shows how MMPI–2 scores are plotted.

Generalizability of the MMPI Can a single test measure personality for all kinds of people? In particular, is the MMPI (or MMPI–2 or MMPI–A) a fair measure of personality for people of different ethnic and cultural backgrounds?

This is a difficult question to answer. In general, the means and ranges on each scale are about the same for many ethnic groups, even after translation into different languages (Negy, Leal-Puente, Trainor, & Carlson, 1997). However, differences do occur. For example, Mexicans are more likely than U.S. people to say *true* to "Life is a constant strain for me." Presumably, the reason is that life really is more difficult for many people who live in Mexico. On several scales of the MMPI–2, the means for Mexicans differ from the U.S. means (Lucio, Ampudia, Durán, León, & Butcher, 2001). Consequently, the scoring standards for a personality test should differ from one country to another. Even within a country, psychologists need to be cautious in interpreting scores for ethnic minorities (Gynther, 1989).

Detection of Deception If you were taking the MMPI or another personality test, could you lie to make yourself look mentally healthier than you really are? Yes. Could someone catch your lies? Probably.

The designers of the MMPI and MMPI–2 included items designed to identify lying (Woychyshyn, McElheran, & Romney, 1992). For example, consider the items "I like every person I have ever met" and "occasionally I get angry at someone." If you answer *true* to the first question and *false* to the second, you are either a saint or a liar. The test authors, convinced that liars outnumber saints, would give you 1 point for each of these answers on a scale to measure lies. If you get too many points on that scale, a psychologist will distrust your answers to the other items. Strangely enough, some people lie on the test to try to make themselves look bad. The MMPI includes items to detect that kind of faking also.

A similar method detects deception on other questionnaires. For example, many employers ask job applicants about their experience with job-related skills. Suppose some employer's questionnaire asked you how much experience you have had at "determining myopic weights for periodic tables." You're not sure what that means, but you really want the job. Do you claim to have had extensive experience? If so, your claimed expertise will count *against* you because "determining myopic weights for periodic tables" is nonsense. The employer asked about it just to see whether you were exaggerating your qualifications on other items. According to the results of one study, almost half of all job applicants claimed to have experience with one or more nonexistent tasks (Anderson, Warner, & Spencer, 1984). Some claimed they had not only performed these tasks but had also trained others! The more skill an applicant claims to have on nonexistent tasks, the more the employer discounts that applicant's claims about real tasks.

Could you use this strategy in other situations? Suppose a political candidate promises to increase aid to college students. You are skeptical. How could you use the candidate's statements on other issues to help you decide whether to believe this promise?

Uses of the MMPI The MMPI is useful for personality assessment and for research on personality. It also helps clinical psychologists learn something about a client before therapy or measure a client's personality changes during therapy. The MMPI has better reliability and validity than many other personality tests (Garb, Florio, & Grove, 1998). However, to a client, the MMPI results are seldom surprising. For example, suppose you gave the following answers:

I doubt that I will ever be successful.	True
I am glad that I am alive.	False
I have thoughts about suicide.	True
I am helpless to control the important events in my life.	True

A psychologist analyzes your answer sheet and tells you that your results show indications of depression. Yes, of course. You already knew that. But even in a case like this, the results can be useful for comparing *how* depressed you are now and later.

Projective Techniques

The MMPI and similar personality tests are easy to score and easy to handle statistically, but they restrict how a person can respond to a question. In hopes of learning more, psychologists ask open-ended questions that permit an unlimited range of responses.

However, to the inquiry "tell me about yourself," many people are reluctant to confide embarrassing information. Many people find it easier to discuss their problems in the abstract than in the first person. For instance, they might say, "I have a friend with this problem. Let me tell you my friend's problem and ask what my friend should do." They then describe their own problem. They are "projecting" their problem onto someone else, in Freud's sense of the word—that is, attributing it to someone else.

Rather than discouraging projection, psychologists often make use of it. They use **projective techniques**, which are *designed to encourage people to project their personality characteristics onto ambiguous stimuli.* This strategy helps people reveal themselves more fully than they normally would. Let's consider the best-known projective techniques: the Rorschach Inkblots and the Thematic Apperception Test.

projective techniques
procedures designed to encourage people to project their personality characteristics onto ambiguous stimuli.

Rorschach Inkblots
a projective personality technique; people are shown 10 inkblots and asked what each might be depicting.

The Rorschach Inkblots The **Rorschach Inkblots**, *a projective technique based on people's interpretations of 10 ambiguous inkblots,* is the most famous and most widely used projective personality technique. It was created by Hermann Rorschach (ROAR-shock), a Swiss psychiatrist, who showed people inkblots and asked them to say whatever came to mind (Pichot, 1984). Rorschach was impressed that his patients' interpretations of the blots differed from his own. In a book published in 1921 (English translation 1942), he presented the 10 symmetrical inkblots that still constitute the Rorschach Inkblot Technique. (Originally, he had used a larger number, but the publisher insisted on cutting the number to 10 to reduce printing costs.) As other psychiatrists and psychologists began using these blots, they gradually developed the Rorschach into the projective technique we know today.

Administering the Rorschach The Rorschach Inkblot Technique consists of cards similar to the one in Figure 11.4. Five are in black and white and five are in color. A psychologist administering this procedure hands you a card and asks, "What might this be?" The instructions are intentionally vague on the assumption that everything you do in an ill-defined situation reveals something significant about your personality.

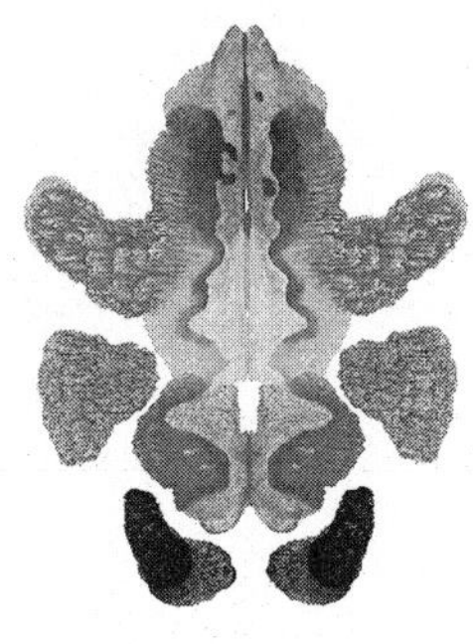

FIGURE 11.4

In the Rorschach Inkblot Technique, people study an abstract pattern and say what it looks like. The idea is that in an ambiguous situation personality will be revealed by anything that someone does and says.

Sometimes people's answers are revealing, either immediately or in response to a psychologist's probes. Here is an example (Aronow, Reznikoff, & Moreland, 1995):

Client: (looking at Card 5) Some kind of insect; it's not pretty enough to be a butterfly.
Psychologist: Any association to that?
Client: It's an ugly black butterfly, no colors.
Psychologist: What does that make you think of in your own life?
Client: You probably want me to say "myself." Well, that's probably how I thought of myself when I was younger—I never thought of myself as attractive—my sister was the attractive one. I was the ugly duckling—I did get more attractive as I got older.

Evaluation of the Rorschach It is true that personality makes a bigger difference in an ill-defined, ambiguous situation than in one where everyone is asked to do something specific. The question is how accurately a psychologist can interpret the responses in that ambiguous situation. When I describe what I see in a picture, I sometimes see how my answer relates to a past experience or current concern. But would anyone else guess the connection?

In the 1950s and 1960s, certain psychologists made exaggerated claims, even calling the Rorschach "an x-ray of the mind." Those claims provoked vigorous criticism. The main problem was that different psychologists drew different conclusions from the same answer depending on their theoretical expectations. For example, a man with depression described one blot, "It looks like a bat that has been squashed on the pavement under the heel of a giant's boot" (Dawes, 1994, p. 149). Psychologist Robyn Dawes initially was impressed with how the Rorschach had revealed the client's sense of being overwhelmed and crushed by powers beyond his control. However, Dawes later realized that he had already known the client was depressed. If a client with a history of violence had made the same response, he would have focused on the aggressive nature of the giant's foot stomp. For a hallucinating or paranoid client, he would have made still other interpretations. Psychologists often believe the Rorschach gave them some insight, when in fact they already knew it before administering the test (Wood, Nezworski, Lilienfeld, & Garb, 2003).

James Exner (1986) developed methods for interpreting Rorschach responses that were intended to standardize the interpretations. Using Exner's system, a psychologist counts the number of times a client mentions certain kinds of themes, such as aggression, how often the response refers to the whole blot or just part of it, and several other reasonably objective measurements. From comparison to standards that presumably represent normal people, a psychologist derives measures of certain kinds of mental disturbance.

However, serious problems with the Rorschach remain (Lilienfeld, Wood, & Garb, 2000; Wood et al., 2003):

- The standardization sample must have been strange because the test identifies *most* people as psychologically disturbed.
- People are asked to give as many answers as they wish on each blot, but psychologists count the *total number* of aggressive, depressive, or otherwise pathological answers. Highly intelligent or talkative people give more answers than other people do, and the more total answers you give, the more likely you are to say something that counts as "disturbed."
- Different ethnic groups have certain characteristic ways of responding that differ from the standardization group, and the test may be inappropriate for use with some groups.
- The interrater reliability of the test is only about .85. That is, different psychologists listening to the same answers do not fully agree on their counts of aggressive themes, depressive themes, and so forth. A reliability around .85 is acceptable for research purposes but is risky for making decisions about an individual.

- Many of the individual scales have doubtful validity. For example, the supposed measures of depression, anxiety, and hostility have low correlations with depressive, anxious, or hostile behavior.
- Finally and most important, the Rorschach rarely gives information that could not be obtained more easily in other ways. For example, psychologists who are given biographical and MMPI information about someone usually make the same personality judgments as psychologists who are given the same information plus the Rorschach results. In fact adding the Rorschach results sometimes makes their judgments *less* accurate.

Critics of the Rorschach stop short of calling it completely invalid. Their point is that it is not valid enough to make decisions about an individual and that it seldom provides information that a psychologist could not get more easily in other ways. For example, Rorschach results are reasonably valid for determining that someone's thinking is severely disturbed (schizophrenic), but psychologists can usually recognize a severe disturbance from a brief conversation with the person. In its defense some users of the Rorschach say they use it not for diagnosis or decisions but only as a way of starting a conversation and getting clients to talk more freely about topics they might be reluctant to discuss (Aronow et al., 1995). Of course, if used in that way, it is no longer a personality test, and its results should not be reported. Some psychologists continue to use Rorschach results to recommend to the courts which parent should get custody of a child, which prisoners should get parole, and so forth. Using the results for those purposes should require solid evidence of validity, and that evidence is lacking (Wood et al., 2003).

FIGURE 11.5
In the Thematic Apperception Test, people tell a story about what is going on in a picture such as this one. Most people include material that relates to current concerns in their lives.

The Thematic Apperception Test The **Thematic Apperception Test (TAT)** consists of pictures like the one shown in Figure 11.5. *The person is asked to make up a story for each picture, describing what is happening, what events led up to the scene, and what will happen in the future.* The test was devised by Christiana Morgan and Henry Murray as a means of measuring people's needs; it was revised and published by Murray (1943) and later revised by others. It includes 31 pictures in all, including some showing women, some showing men, some with both or neither, and one that is totally blank. Originally, it was intended that a psychologist would select 20 cards for use with a given client, but in actual practice most psychologists use fewer (Lilienfeld et al., 2000).

Thematic Apperception Test (TAT) a projective personality technique; a person is asked to tell a story about each of 20 pictures.

The assumption behind the TAT is that when you tell a story about a person in the drawing, you probably identify with the person and so the story is really about yourself. You might describe events and concerns in your own life, including some that you might be reluctant to discuss openly. For example, one young man told the following story about a picture of a man clinging to a rope:

> This man is escaping. Several months ago he was beat up and shanghaied and taken aboard ship. Since then, he has been mistreated and unhappy and has been looking for a way to escape. Now the ship is anchored near a tropical island and he is climbing down a rope to the water. He will get away successfully and swim to shore. When he gets there, he will be met by a group of beautiful native women with whom he will live the rest of his life in luxury and never tell anyone what happened. Sometimes he will feel that he should go back to his old life; but he will never do it. (Kimble & Garmezy, 1968, pp. 582–583)

This young man had entered divinity school, mainly to please his parents, but was unhappy there. He was wrestling with a secret desire to escape to a new life with greater worldly pleasures. In his story he described someone doing what he wanted to do.

Psychologists use the TAT in several ways. Many therapists use it unsystematically. They use different cards and different numbers of cards with different clients, and they interpret the results according to their "clinical judgment," without any clear rules. The results may be reasonable in some cases, but under these circumstances it is impossible to collect adequate data to estimate the reliability or validity of the test.

If you took the TAT with two psychologists, they might reach different conclusions about you. As with the Rorschach, the interrater reliability is about .85—good enough for research purposes but not for making important decisions about an individual (Cramer, 1996). When someone retakes the test a few weeks later, the test–retest reliability is generally lower, usually less than .5 (Cramer, 1996). As with the Rorschach, one criticism is that the test seldom provides information that goes beyond what we could get in other ways (Lilienfeld et al., 2000).

On the other hand, the TAT is sometimes used to measure people's need for achievement by counting all the times that they mention achievement. The test is similarly used to measure power and affiliation needs. These results are useful for many research purposes, although not necessarily for making decisions about an individual (Lilienfeld et al., 2000).

Handwriting as a Projective Technique Based on the theory that your personality affects everything you do, some psychologists (and others) have tried analyzing people's handwriting. For example, perhaps people who dot their i's with a dash—*i*—are especially energetic, or perhaps people who draw large loops above the line—as in *allow*—are highly idealistic. Carefully collected data, however, show only random relationships between handwriting and personality (Tett & Palmer, 1997).

Possible Implicit Personality Tests

The research has failed to support any of the projective tests, but the motivation behind them remains: Psychologists would like to measure personality aspects that people cannot or will not discuss openly. So the search for another kind of personality test continues.

Recall the distinction between explicit and implicit memory. If you listen to a list of words and then try to repeat them, what you recall is explicit memory. If you unknowingly use words from the list in your later conversation, your use of those words constitutes implicit memory. Implicit memory occurs even when you are not aware of remembering something.

Many researchers are trying to develop an implicit personality test—that is, one that measures some aspect of your personality without your awareness. No one knows yet whether these methods will succeed. We shall consider two examples: the Emotional Stroop Test and the Implicit Association Test.

The Emotional Stroop Test Recall the Stroop effect from Chapter 9: People are asked to look at a display like this and read the color of the ink instead of reading the words:

purple brown green blue yellow purple yellow red brown

Emotional Stroop Test
a procedure in which someone tries to say the color of ink for a number of words, some of which might pertain to a source of worry or concern.

In the **Emotional Stroop Test,** *someone examines a list of words, some of which relate to a possible source of worry or concern to the person, and tries to say the color of the ink of each word.* For example, in the following display, say the color of the ink of each word as fast as possible:

cancer venom defeat hospital rattler failure fangs blood
loser slither nurses bite jobless cobra inadequate disease

If you had a snake phobia, might you pause longer when you try to read the color of snake-related words—*venom, rattler, fangs, slither, bite, cobra?*

Let's examine a representative study. The Emotional Stroop Test is sometimes called the Personal Stroop Test because the items are individualized to concerns that some person might have. In this case the research dealt with people who had attempted suicide (Becker, Strohbach, & Rinck, 1999).

Hypothesis It is always somewhat difficult to look at a word and say the color of ink instead of reading the word. It may be especially difficult if the word has a strong emotional meaning. In this case the hypothesis is that people who have attempted suicide will be slower than other people to read the color of words that relate to suicide.

Method The experimenters asked 31 suicide attempters and 31 other people to look at four cards with 12 words each and say the color of ink for each word. One card had words with *positive* connotations, such as *talent* and *love*. Another card had words with *negative* connotations, such as *jail* and *stupidity*. A third card had words with *neutral* connotations, such as *ankle bone* and *square*. The final card had *suicide-related* words such as *grave, coldness,* and *darkness*. Different people looked at the cards in different orders. The experimenters timed how long each person took to say the ink colors of words on each card.

Results Previous suicide attempters took slightly longer to read the suicide-related words. Other people took about equal times with all four cards. Here are the means for the two groups:

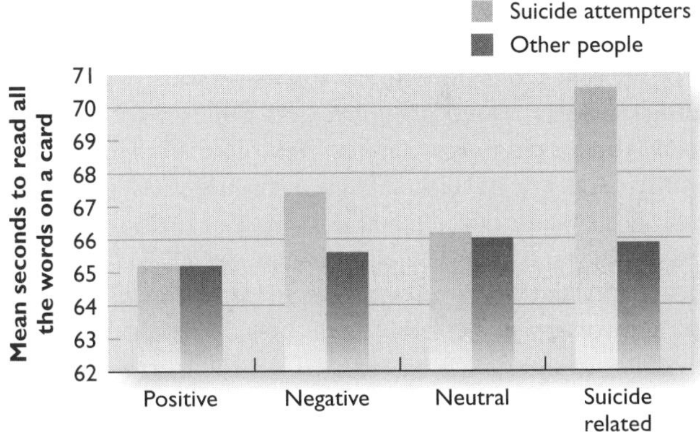

Interpretation The previous suicide attempters apparently were distracted by the suicide-related words. The difference was not large, however. In its present form, the Emotional Stroop Test can report differences between groups, but it is not accurate enough to make decisions about any individual.

The Emotional Stroop Test has similarly shown that violent offenders have long delays on words like *anger* and *hate* (P. Smith & Waterman, 2003), that pain sufferers respond slowly for words related to pain (Crombez, Hermans, & Adriaensen, 2000), and so forth. However, an extra delay on a word does not necessarily mean that the word reflects a fear or worry. In one study pessimistic people were slow to read the colors of unpleasant words like *germ, loser,* and *failure,* whereas optimistic people were slower with pleasant words like *joy, smile,* and *accomplish* (Segerstrom, 2001). Evidently, people were slow with words that grabbed their attention for whatever reason.

The Implicit Association Test Recall the idea of priming: Immediately after reading or hearing a word, such as *red,* you are quicker than usual to identify a related word, such as *cherry*. The fact that you are quicker indicates that you see the two words as related. Similarly, the **Implicit Association Test** *measures whether you respond faster to a category that combines some topic with pleasant words or with unpleasant words.* The results have implications for whether you find that category pleasant or unpleasant.

Implicit Association Test
a procedure that measures how fast someone responds to a category that combines a topic with pleasant words or with unpleasant words.

To illustrate, imagine this example: You rest your left and right forefingers on a computer keyboard. When the experimenter reads a word, you are to press with your left finger if it is an unpleasant word, such as *blunder, fail,* or *shame,* and press with your right finger if it is a pleasant word, such as *joy, nice,* or *success*. Once you have mastered this procedure, we change the instructions. Now you should press the left key if you hear either an unpleasant word or a word relating to insects, and the right key if you hear either a pleasant word or one relating to flowers. Some other people have the reverse instructions: The left key means either an unpleasant word or a flower; the right key means either a pleasant word or an insect. Most people respond faster if they pair flowers with pleasant and insects with unpleasant than if they have to pair flowers with unpleasant and insects with pleasant. The conclusion is that most people like flowers and dislike insects. In this case the procedure seems more trouble than it is worth, as people could readily tell us that they like flowers more than insects. However, we can use the method to measure preferences that people did not want to admit, perhaps not even to themselves.

For example, people in one study were given the following instructions: When they saw a word in UPPERCASE letters, they should press one key if the word was pleasant (like *FRIEND*) and another key if it was unpleasant (like *UGLY*). When they saw a word in lowercase letters, they should press one key for violent words (like *kill*) and the other key for nonviolent words (like *clock*). The rule periodically changed so that sometimes pleasant was paired with violent (and unpleasant with nonviolent), and sometimes pleasant was paired with nonviolent (and unpleasant with violent). Most people responded faster when the key for pleasant words was the same as the key for nonviolent words, implying that they considered violence unpleasant. However, a group of 13 murderers responded equally fast under both conditions, implying that for them, violence was neither pleasant nor unpleasant (Gray, MacCulloch, Smith, Morris, & Snowden, 2003).

Unfortunately, the Implicit Association Test, like the Emotional Stroop Test, produces measures accurate enough for research purposes but not for classifying individuals. Research on implicit personality tests continues, though, because of the potential advantages. Mainly, it is hard for people to "fake" their results. They can try to conceal their personalities in an interview or on the MMPI, but they cannot accurately control their reaction times on the Stroop test or an association test.

Uses and Misuses of Personality Tests

Before any drug company can market a new drug in the United States, the Food and Drug Administration (FDA) requires that it be carefully tested. If the FDA finds the drug safe and effective, it approves the drug for certain purposes but requires a warning label stating how it is to be used. After the drug is approved, however, the FDA cannot prevent a physician from prescribing it for unapproved purposes.

Personality tests are a little like prescription drugs: They should be used with caution and only for the purposes for which they have demonstrable usefulness. They are, at a minimum, helpful to psychologists as an interviewing technique to help "break the ice" and begin a good conversation. Tests can also be useful as an aid in personality assessment by a clinical psychologist. However, a test score by itself can be misleading if it is interpreted without caution. For example, suppose someone has an MMPI personality profile that resembles the profile typical for schizophrenia. Identifying schizophrenia or any other unusual condition is a signal-detection problem—a problem of reporting a stimulus when it is present without falsely reporting it when it is absent. Suppose (realistically) that people without schizophrenia outnumber people with schizophrenia by 100 to 1. Suppose further that a particular personality profile on the MMPI–2 is characteristic of 95% of people with schizophrenia and only 5% of other people. As Figure 11.6 shows, 5% of the normal population is a *larger* group than 95% of the schizophrenic population. Thus, if we labeled as "schizophrenic" everyone with a high score, we would be wrong more often than right. (Recall the representativeness heuristic and the issue of base-rate information, discussed in Chapter 9: Someone who seems "representative" of people in a rare category does not necessarily belong to that category.) Therefore, a conscientious psychologist will look for other evidence beyond the test score before drawing a firm conclusion. The same, of course, should be said of any test, including IQ tests.

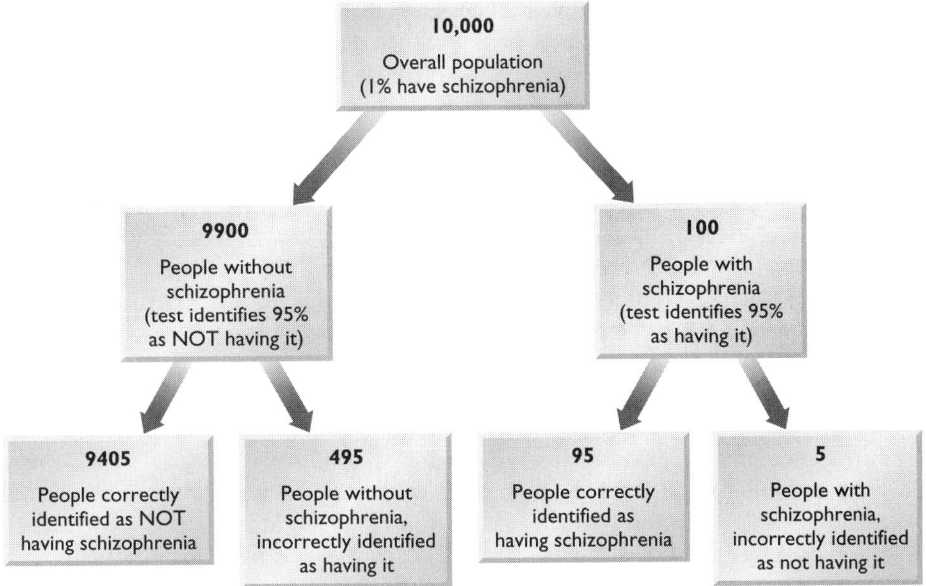

FIGURE 11.6

Assume that a certain profile occurs in 95% of people with schizophrenia and 5% of other people. If we relied entirely on this test, we would correctly identify 95 schizophrenic people, but we would also misidentify 495 normal people.

Personality Tests in Action: Criminal Profiling

Although you might not have thought of it this way, psychological profiling of criminals is an application of personality testing. The idea is that a psychologist or experienced police investigator examines the crime scene and other information about a crime and then surmises the personality, emotions, and motivations of whoever committed the crime. Constructing such a profile presupposes that someone who commits a crime has nearly the same personality as other people who have committed similar crimes in the past.

Many movies and popular television shows have featured psychological profilers almost as superheroes. In 2003, a colleague and I informally surveyed our university's freshman psychology majors about their career plans and discovered to our amazement that about one fourth said they aspired to become forensic psychologists who would construct criminal profiles to help the police. We tried to explain that the number of freshmen at this university aspiring to be criminal profilers was probably greater than the number of people currently employed as profilers in the entire country.

How accurate are criminal profiles? Can a psychologist look at the evidence of a crime and infer the criminal's personality and background in enough detail to aid a police investigation? If so, we should be amazed, even stunned. As you have seen in this chapter, personality testing is far from an exact science, even when psychologists spend hours testing and interviewing the most cooperative people.

Even skeptics do concede the possibility of a limited degree of criminal profiling (Alison, Bennell, & Mokros, 2002; Scott, Lambie, Henwood, & Lamb, 2003). For example, most criminals live or work near the location of their crimes. Also, obviously, a rapist is more likely to be a young man than a child or an old man. Less obviously, but also less consistently, a rapist who removes all trace of his semen from the scene of the crime evidently knows something about police investigative techniques and may have been arrested for similar crimes in the past. The question is whether profilers can go beyond such general statements to infer anything about a specific individual who committed a specific crime.

a

© AP/Wide World Photos

b

© AP/Wide World Photos

When two snipers shot a series of people in the Washington, D.C., area, psychological profilers said to look for a White man acting alone. That description fit most previous serial killers but was wrong this time. John Allen Muhammad (a) and Lee Boyd Malvo (b) were convicted of the killings.

A few studies have tried to collect data about the relationship between the crime and the criminal. For example, one study of sex-related murders categorized some crimes as deliberate and cruel, some as motivated more by sex than violence, others as "furious" and possibly revenge-based, and still others as antisocial and perverse. The kinds of people who committed one kind of murder differed on the average from those who committed other kinds. However, most of the crimes the researchers examined did not fit neatly into any of these categories, and those that did fit were so few that the apparent links to personal characteristics could have been due to chance (Kocsis, Cooksey, & Irwin, 2002).

Another study examined 100 cases of stranger rape (as opposed to acquaintance rape). Researchers rated the degree of similarity among crimes and also the degree of similarity among convicted offenders. They found no consistent relationship. That is, men who had committed apparently similar crimes were no more likely than others to be similar in age, ethnic group, education, marital status, employment records, or criminal records (Mokros & Alison, 2002). If, indeed, people who commit similar crimes do not resemble one another, the prospects for criminal profiling are limited.

A few studies have directly measured the ability of profilers to infer the characteristics of people who committed specific crimes. Unfortunately, sample sizes have been small because most profilers have declined to be tested. In one study five professional profilers as well as larger numbers of police officers, psychologists, college students, and self-declared psychics were given extensive details about a murder case, including photos of the crime scene, information about the victim, and various laboratory reports. Then they were asked 30 multiple-choice questions about the probable criminal—sex, height, weight, age, marital status, religion, violent fantasies, and so forth. The results were compared to what was known about the actual murderer (who had in fact been caught, although the participants did not know about him). The number of choices per multiple-choice item varied from 2 to 9; overall, random guessing would produce 8.1 correct answers out of the 30 items. However, even an uninformed person should do better than chance, just by knowing, for example, that more crimes are committed by men than women and by guessing some common religion instead of a rare one. Of the tested groups, the profilers in fact did the best, at 13.8 correct, and the psychics did the worst, at 11.3, but the differences were small and none of the groups did well (Kocsis, Irwin, Hayes, & Nunn, 2000). Even for this modest success, we do not know that the profilers based their guesses on any information about the crime. Maybe they just have more accurate stereotypes of the "average criminal" than other people do.

A similar study compared police officers with varying levels of experience and college students with no relevant experience at all. In this case the college students outperformed the police officers, although even the students averaged only 12.4 correct out of 30. Again, the differences among groups were small (Kocsis, Hayes, & Irwin, 2002).

We should not conclude that criminal profiling is impossible. However, as it is currently practiced, the results are certainly unimpressive. After all, 13.8 correct answers out of a possible 30, where 8.1 is random, means that profilers would give the police mostly wrong information.

Why, then, do so many police investigators insist that they find criminal profiles useful? Recall the Barnum effect mentioned in the introduction to this module: People tend to accept almost any statement about their own personality, especially vague statements that can be interpreted to fit the facts. A similar process applies here. Most actual (as opposed to television) profiles of criminals include vague or untestable statements that would apply to many people: The criminal is about the same age as the victim . . . average appearance . . . does not look out of context in the area . . . possibly unemployed . . . has a pornography collection . . . probably a very confused person . . . (Alison, Smith, & Morgan, 2003). In one study researchers gave police officers a criminal profile that an FBI profiler had prepared for the investigation of a particular murder, plus a description of the actual murderer (who had been caught), and asked the officers how well the profile fit the actual criminal. Most called it a good fit, rating it between 5 and 6 on a 1-to-7 scale. The researchers then gave a different group of police officers the same profile, plus a completely different, fictional description of the murderer, changing his age, relationship to the victim, childhood history, and everything else. Most of this group also called the profile a good fit, again rating it between 5 and 6 (Alison et al., 2003). In short, the actual facts about the criminal made little difference to how highly the police rated the profile.

REVIEW

- *Nomothetic and idiographic research.* Nomothetic studies examine large numbers of people briefly, whereas idiographic studies examine one or a few individuals intensively.
- *Traits and states.* Traits are personality characteristics that persist over time; states are temporary tendencies in response to particular situations.
- *Measurement problems.* Personality researchers rely mostly on self-reports, which are not entirely accurate. Many people misrepresent themselves, either knowingly or unintentionally.
- *Five major traits.* Much of personality can be explained by these five traits: neuroticism, extraversion, openness to new experience, agreeableness, and conscientiousness. However, several other important dimensions may have been overlooked.
- *Determinants of personality.* Studies of twins and adopted children indicate that heredity contributes to the observed differences in personality. Family environment evidently contributes rather little. Much of the variation in personality may be due to unshared environment, the special experiences that vary from one person to another even within a family.
- *Changes over time.* Compared to younger people, older people tend to be higher in conscientiousness and agreeableness. They are somewhat lower in extraversion and neuroticism. Openness to experience decreases with age in the United States, but several other countries do not show this trend.
- *Changes over historical era.* Measurements of anxiety have gradually increased over the decades so that normal people now report anxiety levels that used to characterize people in mental hospitals.
- *People's tendency to accept personality test results.* Because most people accept almost any interpretation of their personality based on a personality test, tests must be carefully scrutinized to ensure that they are measuring what they claim to measure.
- *Standardized personality tests.* A standardized test is administered according to explicit rules, and its results are interpreted in a prescribed fashion based on the norms for the population.
- *The MMPI.* The MMPI, a widely used personality test, consists of a series of true–false questions selected in an effort to distinguish among various personality types. The MMPI–2 is a modern version.
- *Detection of lying.* The MMPI and certain other tests guard against lying by including items on which most people admit common faults or deny rare virtues. Denying common faults or claiming rare virtues is probably a lie. An unusual number of lying answers will invalidate the results.
- *Projective techniques.* A projective technique, such as the Rorschach Inkblots or the Thematic Apperception Test, lets people describe their concerns indirectly while talking about the person in the picture or about other ambiguous stimuli. The results from projective techniques are difficult to interpret and have unimpressive validity for making decisions about any individual.
- *Implicit personality tests.* The Emotional Stroop Test measures people's delays in naming the color of ink on the assumption that they will pause longer if the word has emotional meaning to them. The Implicit Association Test asks people to give one response to a particular combination of categories (e.g., social words and happy outcomes) and a different response to a different combination (e.g., nonsocial words and unhappy outcomes). So far, such tests are useful for research but not for decisions about an individual.
- *Uses and misuses of personality tests.* Personality tests can be used as an aid for assessing personality, but their results should be interpreted cautiously and in conjunction with other evidence.
- *Criminal profiling.* Some psychologists and police officers try to aid police investigations by constructing personality profiles of the kind of person who would probably commit a certain crime. There has been little research, but what has been conducted casts doubt on the accuracy of these profiles.

CHAPTER 11 PRACTICE EXAM

____ 1. The study of individual differences that looks for general laws about how personality affects behavior is what approach?
   a. idiosyncratic
   b. reliability
   c. nomothetic
   d. validity

____ 2. A state is relatively
   a. permanent.
   b. valid.
   c. traitlike.
   d. temporary.

____ 3. A personality measure in which the scores are relatively consistent can be called a ________ measure.
   a. valid
   b. Reliable
   c. Utilitilitarian
   d. Semantic

____ 4. One use of factor analysis is to
   a. find traits that cause behavior.
   b. identify highly correlated traits.
   c. identify all behaviors that might be considered traits.
   d. Discover states that people use to answer personality questionnaires.

____ 5. What are the big five personality dimensions?
   a. neuroticism, extraversion, openness to new experiences, agreeableness, and conscientiousness.
   b. locus of control, authoritarianism, independence, dishonesty, and honesty.
   c. masculinity, femininity, extraversion, ambitiousness, and state.
   d. self, argumentativeness, locus of control, ambitiousness, and honesty.

____ 6. Which two traits seem to be the most powerful?
   a. Honesty and locus of control
   b. neuroticism and extraversion
   c. conscientiousness and agreeableness
   d. openness to experience and extraversion

____ 7. People who are extraverted tend to
   a. Be unhappy most of the time.
   b. Look forward to meditative experiences.
   c. enjoy the company of others.
   d. Are undisciplined and low achievers.

____ 8. Compassion towards people is part of
   a. Openness to experience.
   b. intoversion.
   c. agreeableness.
   d. conscientiousness.

____ 9. A criticism of the Big Five is that
   a. it was started by neuroscientists.
   b. it was analyzed on a faulty statistical test.
   c. it is based entirely on questionnaires.
   d. Data are only collected from English speaking people.

____ 10. The personality of an adopted child correlates _______ with that of the adoptive parents.
   a. strongly
   b. moderately
   c. middling
   d. weakly

____ 11. As we get older, personality seems to get more _________ .
   a. honest
   b. conscientious
   c. consistent
   d. extroverted

____ 12. The _____________ aspect of personality has shown an increase over the 40 years?
   a. extroversion
   b. honesty
   c. anxiety
   d. introversion

____ 13. The most widely used personality test is the
   a. Rorschach Inkblot Test.
   b. Sondi.
   c. MMPI.
   d. Thematic Apperception Test.

____ 14. What is purpose of the MMPI?
   a. to recover motivation
   b. to diagnose therapeutic influences on behavior
   c. to assess tendency in personality
   d. to measure the Big Five

____ 15. Items were selected to be included on the MMPI
   a. by trial and error, involving giving a large number of questions to people with and without various personality disorders.
   b. from Freud's theory.
   c. from Jung's theory.
   d. from Skinner's theory.

Answers

1. C
2. D
3. B
4. B
5. A
6. B
7. C
8. C
9. C
10. D
11. C
12. C
13. C
14. C
15. A

CHAPTER 12: PSYCHOLOGICAL DISORDERS

QUESTIONS

1. How did the Ancient Greeks and people in the Middle Ages view psychological disorders?
2. How do psychologists explain psychological disorders?
3. What are six criteria that are suggestive of psychological disorders?
4. Why is classification important?
5. What is the classification system of the DSM-IV-TR?
6. What does Szaz believe psychological disorders are?
7. What was the controversy about listing sexual orientation as a psychological disorder?
8. What disorders do gay males and lesbians more prone to have and what might be some reasons why?
9. What the five types of anxiety disorders?
10. How do different psychology theories explain different anxiety disorders?
11. What are three types of dissociative disorders?
12. How do different theories explain dissociative disorders?
13. Why is there some skepticism as to whether dissociative disorders really exist?
14. What are some examples of conversion disorders?
15. How do psychologists explain conversion disorders?
16. What are the differences between feeling depressed and major depressive disorder?
17. What are some reasons psychologists think women seem more likely to be diagnosed with depression?
18. What are some external events that bring on depression?
19. How do psychodynamic theorists view depression?
20. How did Seligman demonstrate learned helplessness with dogs?
21. How do cognitive psychologists explain depression?
22. How do different attributional styles relate to depression?
23. Why might too much self-blame make us physically sick?
24. What biological factors appear related to depression?
25. Why did emergency room staff think Jennifer might be schizophrenic?
26. Why do some think schizophrenia is the worst disorder that affects people?
27. What are some problems schizophrenics have?
28. What are some characteristics of paranoid, disorganized, and catatonic schizophrenics?
29. What are the psychodynamic, learning theory, parenting, and social/cultural factor explanations for schizophrenia?
30. What parts of the brain are affected in schizophrenics?
31. What are some biological risk factors for schizophrenia?
32. What are some other factors besides heredity that seem to make people susceptible to schizophrenia?
33. How does the dopamine theory seek to explain schizophrenia?
34. What is the history of the M'Naughten rule?
35. What percent of cases use the insanity defense?
36. What are the similarities and differences between the personality disorders?
37. How do psychodynamic and learning theorists explain personality disorders?
38. What is the evidence for genetic factors being involved in personality disorders?
39. How many people each year commit suicide?

40. What are four areas of psychological problems for adolescents?
41. What are exit life events and there relationship to suicide?
42. What are some other contributors to adolescent suicidal behavior?
43. What are three facts about suicide?
44. How do suicide rates differ according to gender and ethnicity?
45. How do African Americans and European Americans tend to explain their problems?
46. What are some myths about suicide?
47. What are some common warning signs for suicide?
48. What are eight things one can do if a person tells you they are considering suicide?

VOCABULARY

1. acrophobia
2. acute stress disorder
3. agoraphobia
4. Antisocial personality disorder
5. Attributional style
6. Avoidant personality disorder
7. Benzodiazepines
8. Bipolar disorder
9. Borderline personality disorder
10. Catatonic schizophrenia
11. claustrophobia
12. compulsion
13. concordance
14. Conversion disorder
15. Delusions
16. Disorganized Schizophrenia
17. dissociative amnesia
18. Dissociative disorders
19. Dissociative fugue
20. dissociative identity disorder
21. gamma-aminobutryic acid (GABA)
22. generalized anxiety disorder
23. glutamate
24. hallucination
25. hypochondriasis
26. ideas of persecution
27. insanity
28. Labelle indifference
29. Learned helplessness
30. major depressive disorder
31. Manic
32. multiple personality disorder
33. Mutism
34. Neuroticism
35. obsession
36. panic disorder
37. Paranoid disorder
38. Paranoid schizophrenia
39. Personality disorders
40. posttraumatic stress disorder (PTSD)
41. psychological disorders
42. Psychomotor retardation
43. Rapid flight of ideas
44. Schizoid personality disorder
45. schizophrenia
46. Schizotypal personality disorder
47. social phobia
48. Somatoform disorders
49. specific phobia
50. Stupor
51. Waxy flexibility

12 Psychological Disorders

© Everett Collection

DURING ONE LONG FALL SEMESTER, the Ohio State campus lived in terror. Four college women were abducted, forced to cash checks or obtain money from automatic teller machines, and then raped. A mysterious phone call led to the arrest of a 23-year-old drifter—let's call him "William"—who had been dismissed from the Navy.

William was not the boy next door.

Psychologists and psychiatrists who interviewed William concluded that 10 personalities—8 male and 2 female—resided within him (Scott, 1994). His personality had been "fractured" by an abusive childhood. His several personalities displayed distinct facial expressions, speech patterns, and memories. They even performed differently on psychological tests.

Arthur, the most rational personality, spoke with a British accent. Danny and Christopher were quiet adolescents. Christine was a 3-year-old girl. Tommy, a 16-year-old, had enlisted in the Navy. Allen was 18 and smoked. Adelena, a 19-year-old lesbian personality, had committed the rapes. Who had made the mysterious phone call? Probably David, 9, an anxious child.

The defense claimed that William's behavior was caused by a psychological disorder termed **dissociative identity disorder** (also referred to as **multiple personality disorder**). Several distinct identities or personalities dwelled within him. Some of them were aware of the others. Some believed that they were unique. Billy, the core identity, had learned to sleep as a child in order to avoid his father's abuse. A psychiatrist asserted that Billy had also been "asleep," or in a "psychological coma," during the abductions. Billy should therefore be found not guilty by reason of **insanity**.

dissociative identity disorder
a disorder in which a person appears to have two or more distinct identities or personalities that may alternately emerge.

multiple personality disorder
the previous term for *dissociative identity disorder*.

insanity
a legal term descriptive of a person judged to be incapable of recognizing right from wrong or of conforming his or her behavior to the law.

William was found not guilty. He was committed to a psychiatric institution and released six years later.

In 1982, John Hinckley was also found not guilty of the assassination attempt on President Reagan's life, although the shooting was witnessed on television by millions. Expert witnesses testified that he should be diagnosed with **schizophrenia**. Hinckley, too, was committed to a psychiatric institution.

schizophrenia
a psychotic disorder characterized by loss of control of thought processes and inappropriate emotional responses.

psychological disorders
patterns of behavior or mental processes that are connected with emotional distress or significant impairment in functioning.

Dissociative identity disorder and schizophrenia are examples of **psychological disorders**. If William and Hinckley had lived in Salem, Massachusetts, in 1692, just 200 years after Columbus set foot in the New World, they might have been hanged as witches. At that time, most people assumed that the strange behaviors that were associated with psychological disorders were caused by possession by the devil. A score of people were executed in Salem that year for allegedly practicing the arts of Satan.

Throughout human history people have attributed unusual behavior and psychological disorders to demons. The ancient Greeks believed that the gods punished humans by causing confusion and madness. An exception was the physician Hippocrates, who made the radical suggestion that psychological disorders are caused by an abnormality of the brain. The notion that biology could affect thoughts, feelings, and behavior was to lie dormant for about 2,000 years.

■ **Exorcism.** This medieval woodcut represents the practice of exorcism, in which a demon is expelled from a person who has been "possessed."

During the Middle Ages in Europe, as well as during the early period of European colonization of Massachusetts, it was generally believed that psychological disorders were signs of possession by the devil. Possession could stem from retribution, in which God caused the devil to possess a person's soul as punishment for committing certain kinds of sins. Agitation and confusion were ascribed to such retribution. Possession was also believed to result from deals with the devil, in which people traded their souls for earthly gains. Such individuals were called witches. Witches were held responsible for unfortunate events ranging from a neighbor's infertility to a poor harvest. In Europe, as many as 500,000 accused witches were killed during the next two centuries (Hergenhahn, 2001). The goings on at Salem were trivial by comparison.

A document authorized by Pope Innocent VIII, *The Hammer of Witches,* proposed ingenious "diagnostic" tests to identify those who were possessed. The water-float test was based on the principle that pure metals sink to the bottom during smelting. Impurities float to the surface. Suspects were thus placed in deep water. Those who sank to the bottom and drowned were judged to be pure. Those who managed to keep their heads above water were assumed to be "impure" and in league with the devil. Then they were in real trouble. This ordeal is the origin of the phrase, "damned if you do, and damned if you don't."

Few people in the United States today would argue that unusual or unacceptable behavior is caused by demons. Still, we continue to use "demonic" language. How many times have you heard the expressions "Something got into me" or "The devil made me do it"?

Throughout history, as noted, most people have explained disorders like those of William and Hinckley from a demonological perspective. Today, however, psychologists and other health professionals tend to explain psychological disorders from various psychological perspectives: the evolutionary and biological perspectives, the cognitive perspective, the humanistic–existential perspective, the psychodynamic perspective, and the learning perspective.

We will see how these various perspectives explain each of the disorders covered in the chapter. In many cases we will see that there is an *interaction* between perspectives, such as the biological perspective and the cognitive perspective. We will also frequently find an interaction between the biological *nature* of the individual and his or her life experiences, or *nurture*. The origins of psychological disorders are often complex. We cannot pretend that they are simple, but we can present them clearly.

WHAT ARE PSYCHOLOGICAL DISORDERS?

Psychology is the study of behavior and mental processes. Psychological disorders are behaviors or mental processes—like those of "William" and John Hinckley—that are connected with various kinds of distress or disability. However, they are not predictable responses to specific events.

Some psychological disorders are characterized by anxiety, but many people are anxious now and then without being considered disordered. It is appropriate to be anxious before an important date or on the eve of a midterm exam. When, then, are feelings like anxiety deemed to be abnormal or signs of a psychological disorder? For one thing, anxiety may suggest a disorder when it is not appropriate to the situation. It is inappropriate to be anxious when entering an elevator or looking out of a fourth-story window. The magnitude of the problem may also suggest disorder. Some anxiety is usual before a job interview. However, feeling that your heart is pounding so intensely that it might leap out of your chest—and then avoiding the interview—are not usual.

Behavior or mental processes are suggestive of psychological disorders when they meet some combination of the following criteria:

1. *They are unusual.* Although people with psychological disorders are a minority, uncommon behavior or mental processes are not abnormal in themselves. Only one person holds the record for running or swimming the fastest mile. That person is different from you and me but is not abnormal. Only a few people qualify as geniuses in mathematics, but mathematical genius is not a sign of a psychological disorder.

   Rarity or statistical deviance may not be sufficient for behavior or mental processes to be labeled abnormal, but it helps. Most people do not see or hear things that are not there. "Seeing things" and "hearing things," as Hinckley did, are abnormal. We must also consider the situation. Although many of us feel "panicked" when we realize that a term paper or report is due the next day, most of us do not have panic attacks "out of the blue." Unpredictable panic attacks thus are suggestive of psychological disorder.
2. *They suggest faulty perception or interpretation of reality.* Our society considers it normal to be inspired by religious beliefs but abnormal to believe that God is literally speaking to you. "Hearing voices" and "seeing things" are considered **hallucinations**. Similarly, **ideas of persecution**, such as believing that the Mafia or the FBI are "out to get you," are considered signs of disorder. (Unless, of course, they are out to get you.) Hinckley's view, that he would be impressing a popular actress with his behavior, was delusional.
3. *They suggest severe personal distress.* Anxiety, exaggerated fears, and other psychological states cause personal distress, and severe personal distress may be considered abnormal. William and Hinckley were in distress—although, of course, they victimized other people. Anxiety, of course, may be an appropriate response to a situation, as when a big test or a big date is coming up.
4. *They are self-defeating.* Behavior or mental processes that cause misery rather than happiness and fulfillment may suggest psychological disorder. Chronic drinking that impairs work and family life and cigarette smoking that impairs health may therefore be deemed abnormal.
5. *They are dangerous.* Behavior or mental processes that are hazardous to the self or others may be considered suggestive of psychological disorders. People who threaten or attempt suicide may be considered abnormal, as may people who threaten or attack others, like William and Hinckley. Yet criminal behavior or aggressive behavior in sports need not imply a psychological disorder.

hallucination
a perception in the absence of sensory stimulation that is confused with reality.

ideas of persecution
erroneous beliefs that one is being victimized or persecuted.

6. *The individual's behavior is socially unacceptable.* We must consider the cultural context of a behavior pattern in judging whether or not it is normal (Lopez & Guarnaccia, 2000). In the United States, it is deemed normal for males to be aggressive in sports and in combat. In other situations, warmth and tenderness are valued. Many people in the United States admire women who are self-assertive, yet Latino and Latina American, Asian American, and "traditional" European American groups may see outspoken women as disrespectful.

Classifying Psychological Disorders

Toss some people, apes, seaweed, fish, and sponges into a room—preferably a well ventilated one. Stir slightly. What do you have? It depends on how you classify this hodgepodge.

Classify them as plants versus animals and you lump the people, chimpanzees, fish, and, yes, sponges together. Classify them as stuff that carries on its business on land or underwater, and we throw in our lot with the chimps and none of the others. How about those that swim and those that don't? Then the chimps, the fish, and some of us are grouped together.

Classification is at the heart of science. Without classifying psychological disorders, investigators would not be able to communicate with each other and scientific progress would come to a standstill. The most widely used classification scheme for psychological disorders[1] is the *Diagnostic and Statistical Manual (DSM)* of the American Psychiatric Association (2000).

The current edition of the *DSM*—the *DSM-IV-TR*—provides information about a person's overall functioning, not just a diagnosis (see Table 12.1). People may receive diagnoses for clinical syndromes or personality disorders, or a combination of the two.

■ **Hallucinations.** Hallucinations are a feature of schizophrenia. They are perceptions that occur in the absence of external stimulation, as in "hearing voices" or "seeing things." Hallucinations cannot be distinguished from real perceptions. Are the cats in this Sandy Skoglund photograph real or hallucinatory?

[1] The American Psychiatric Association refers to psychological disorders as *mental disorders.*

TABLE 12.1 **The Classification System of the *DSM-IV–TR*.**

TYPE OF INFORMATION	COMMENTS
1. Clinical syndromes	Includes psychological disorders that impair functioning and are stressful to the individual (a wide range of diagnostic classes, such as substance-related disorders, anxiety disorders, mood disorders, schizophrenia, somatoform disorders, and dissociative disorders)
2. Personality disorders	Includes deeply ingrained, maladaptive ways of perceiving others and behaviors that are stressful to the individual or to persons who relate to that individual
3. General medical conditions	Includes chronic and acute illnesses, injuries, allergies, and so on, that affect functioning and treatment
4. Psychosocial and environmental problems	Enumerates stressors that occurred during the past year that may have contributed to the development of a new mental disorder or the recurrence of a prior disorder, or that may have exacerbated an existing disorder
5. Global assessment of functioning	An overall judgment of the current functioning and the highest level of functioning in the past year according to psychological, social, and occupational criteria

General medical conditions include physical disorders or problems that may affect people's functioning or their response to psychotherapy or drug treatment. Psychosocial and environmental problems include difficulties that may affect the diagnosis, treatment, or outcome of a psychological disorder. The global assessment of functioning allows the clinician to rate the client's current level of functioning and her or his highest level of functioning prior to the onset of the psychological disorder. The purpose is to help determine what kinds of psychological functioning are to be restored through therapy.

The *DSM–IV–TR* groups disorders on the basis of observable behaviors or symptoms. However, early editions of the *DSM,* which was first published in 1952, grouped many disorders on the basis of assumptions about their causes. Because Freud's psychodynamic theory was widely accepted at the time, one major diagnostic category contained so-called neuroses.[2] According to Freud, all neuroses—no matter how differently people with various neuroses might behave—were caused by unconscious neurotic conflict. Each neurosis was thought to reflect a way of coping with the unconscious fear that primitive impulses might break loose. As a result, sleepwalking was included as a neurosis (psychoanalysts assumed that sleepwalking reduced unconscious fear by permitting partial expression of impulses). Now that the focus is on observable behaviors, sleepwalking is classified as a sleep disorder, not a neurosis. The psychological disorders discussed in the chapter are summarized in the nearby Concept Review.

Some professionals, such as psychiatrist Thomas Szasz, believe that the categories described in the *DSM* are really "problems in living" rather than "disorders." At least, they are not disorders in the sense that high blood pressure, cancer, and the flu are disorders. Szasz argues that labeling people with problems in living as being "sick" degrades them and encourages them to evade their personal

[2] The neuroses included what are today referred to as anxiety disorders, dissociative disorders, somatoform disorders, mild depression, and some other disorders, such as sleepwalking.

CONCEPT SUMMARY

Psychological Disorders

	ANXIETY DISORDERS	DISSOCIATIVE DISORDERS	SOMATOFORM DISORDERS
CLASS	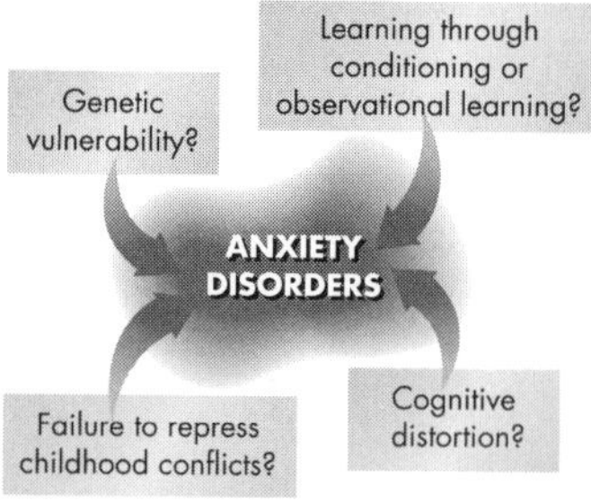	 © Rousseau/The Image Works	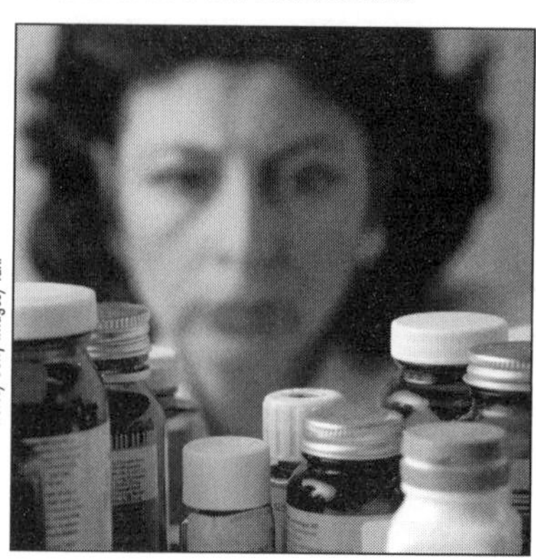 © Bald Headed Pictures/Getty Images/Taxi
MAJOR SUBTYPES	• Phobic disorder • Panic disorder • Generalized anxiety disorder • Obsessive–compulsive disorder • Stress disorders	• Dissociative amnesia • Dissociative fugue • Dissociative identity disorder (multiple personality)	• Conversion disorder • Hypochondriasis
SYMPTOMS	• Worrying • Fear of the worst happening • Fear of losing control • Nervousness • Inability to relax	• Separation of mental processes such as thoughts, emotions, identity, memory, or consciousness	• Complaints of physical problems such as paralysis or pain • Persistent belief that one has a serious disease in the absence of medical findings
POSSIBLE ORIGIN	• Phobias symbolize conflicts originating in childhood (psychodynamic theory) • Phobias may have been acquired in early childhood by conditioning or observational learning (learning theory) • People with anxiety disorders may be biased toward attending too much to threats (cognitive theory) • Genetic factors are implicated • Phobias may have contributed to survival of human species (evolutionary perspective) • Receptor sites in the brain may not be sensitive enough to the neurotransmitter GABA, which quells anxiety reactions (neurological perspective)	• People with dissociative disorders use massive repression to prevent recognition of improper impulses or ugly memories (psychodynamic) • People learn not to think about improper impulses or ugly memories, as of childhood sexual abuse (learning)	• Capacity to focus on imagined physical problems, a form of self-hypnosis • Especial sensitivity to bodily symptoms

and social responsibilities. Because sick people are encouraged to obey doctors' orders, Szasz (1999, 2000) also contends that labeling people as "sick" accords too much power to health professionals. Instead, he believes, troubled people need to be encouraged to take greater responsibility for solving their own problems.

One of the historic controversies in psychology has been whether or not a gay male or lesbian sexual orientation is a psychological disorder. We explore that issue next.

MOOD DISORDERS	SCHIZOPHRENIA	PERSONALITY DISORDERS
 © Peter Cade/Getty Images/Stone	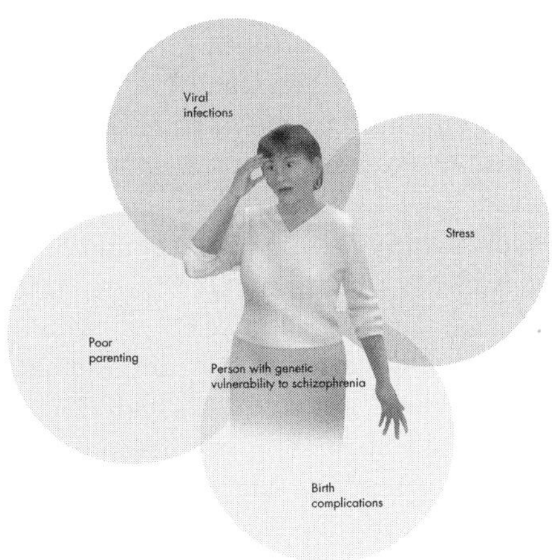 	 © Tinette Reed/CORBIS
• Major depression • Bipolar disorder	• Paranoid schizophrenia • Disorganized schizophrenia • Catatonic schizophrenia	• Paranoid • Schizotypal • Schizoid • Antisocial • Avoidant
• Disturbance in expressed emotions	• Disturbances in language and thought (e.g., delusions, loose associations), attention and perception (e.g., hallucinations) • Disturbances in motor activity • Disturbances in mood • Withdrawal and absorption in daydreams or fantasy	• Inflexible and maladaptive patterns of behavior • Impairment in personal or social functioning • Providing a source of distress to oneself or others
• Depression may be anger turned inward due to holding in rather than expressing feelings of anger; bipolar disorder may be due to alternate domination by the ego and superego (psychodynamic) • In depression, people learn that they are helpless to change their situations (learning) • Perfectionism, rumination, and attributional style—internal, stable, and global attributions for failures and shortcomings—lead to depression (cognitive) • Depression connected with neuroticism, which is believed to be heritable (genetic) • Depression connected with underutlization of neurotransmitter serotonin (neurological)	• Ego may be overwhelmed by the id (psychodynamic) • Schizophrenic behavior can be imitated in the hospital setting and reinforced by staff attention (learning) • Poor parenting, poverty, complications during pregnancy and birth contribute to schizophrenia (situational) • Schizophrenia runs in families, with a high concordance rate among MZ twins (genetic) • People with schizophrenia may have larger ventricles, smaller prefrontal cortexes, and fewer synapses than others; overutlization of neurotransmitter dopamine (neurological)	• Faulty resolution of Oedipus complex (psychodynamic) • Children learn maladaptive ways of relating to other people (learning) • Antisocial individuals misinterpret other people's behavior as threatening (cognitive) • Exaggerated personality traits, which are partly heritable (genetic) • Antisocial individuals may have less gray matter, which might lower arousal and thus feelings of guilt and the effects of punishment (neurological)

Until 1973, a gay male or lesbian sexual orientation was considered to be a psychological disorder (or "mental disorder") by the American Psychiatric Association and was listed as such in the *DSM*. But in that year, the members of the association voted to drop a gay male or lesbian sexual orientation from its list of mental disorders, although a diagnostic category for people who are *distressed* about their sexual orientation remains in place (American Psychiatric Association, 2000). Many members of the organization objected to the vote on the grounds that it was politically motivated. After all, could the American Medical Association vote to drop cancer as a physical disorder, they asked? Thus many psychiatrists continued to believe that homosexuality itself was a disorder despite the majority vote.

That was the superficial answer, but there is also the question as to whether gay males and lesbians have more psychological disorders than heterosexuals. If they do, it will still not mean that homosexuality itself is a disorder, but it may suggest that the psychological health of gay males and lesbians merits more attention from psychologists. Recent, carefully controlled studies do in fact find that gay males and lesbians are more likely than heterosexuals to experience feelings of anxiety and depression, and that they are more prone to suicide (Bagley & D'Augelli, 2000; Cochran et al., 2003; Meyer, 2003).

J. Michael Bailey (1999, 2003b) and Ilan Meyer (2003) have carefully reviewed the issues surrounding homosexuality and have concluded that societal oppression is largely responsible for the higher incidence of depression and suicidality we find among gay males and lesbians. "Surely," writes Bailey, "it must be difficult for young people to come to grips with their homosexuality in a world where homosexual people are often scorned, mocked, and feared." Bailey acknowledges the possibility that homosexuality reflects a departure from typical development and could thus be associated with other differences, some of which could be connected with anxiety and depression. However, it is difficult if not impossible to tease out such potential factors in a society where "stigma, prejudice, and discrimination create a hostile and stressful social environment that causes mental health problems" (Meyer, 2003).

Let us now consider the kinds of psychological disorders. Some of them, like anxiety disorders, are common. Others, like dissociative identity disorder (the disorder with which William was diagnosed), are rare.

ANXIETY DISORDERS: REAL LIFE "FEAR FACTORS"?

Imagine allowing spiders to crawl all over your body or clinging to a beam swinging hundreds of feet above the ground. These are the types of experiences to which many people have been exposed on the "reality TV" show *Fear Factor.* What makes the show so riveting to some viewers? Perhaps the fact that many of us, perhaps most of us, could not imagine participating in such activities, for nearly any amount of fame or fortune. Fear of spiders and fear of heights are examples of phobias, which are a type of anxiety disorder.

Anxiety has psychological and physical features. Psychological features include worrying, fear of the worst things happening, fear of losing control, nervousness, and inability to relax. Physical features reflect arousal of the sympathetic branch of the autonomic nervous system. They include trembling, sweating, a pounding or racing heart, elevated blood pressure (a flushed face), and faintness. Anxiety is an appropriate response to a real threat. It can be abnormal, however, when it is excessive or when it comes out of nowhere—that is, when events do not seem to warrant it. There are different kinds of anxiety disorders, but all of them are characterized by excessive or unwarranted anxiety.

Types of Anxiety Disorders

The anxiety disorders include phobias, panic disorder, generalized anxiety, obsessive–compulsive disorder, and stress disorders.

specific phobia persistent fear of a specific object or situation.

Phobias There are several types of phobias, including specific phobias, social phobia, and agoraphobia. Some of them, such as social phobia, can be highly detrimental to one's quality of life (Stein & Kean, 2000). **Specific phobias** are excessive, irrational fears of specific objects or situations, such as spiders, snakes, or heights.

One specific phobia is fear of elevators. Some people will not enter elevators despite the hardships they incur as a result (such as walking up six flights of steps). Yes, the cable *could* break. The ventilation *could* fail. One *could* be stuck in midair waiting for repairs. These problems are uncommon, however, and it does not make sense for most people to walk up and down several flights of stairs to elude them. Similarly, some people with a specific phobia for hypodermic needles will not have injections, even to treat profound illness. Injections can be painful, but most people with a phobia for needles would gladly suffer an even more painful pinch if it would help them fight illness. Other specific phobias include **claustrophobia** (fear of tight or enclosed places), **acrophobia** (fear of heights), and fear of mice, snakes, and other creepy-crawlies. (Fear of spiders is technically referred to as *arachnophobia*.) Fears of animals and imaginary creatures are common among children.

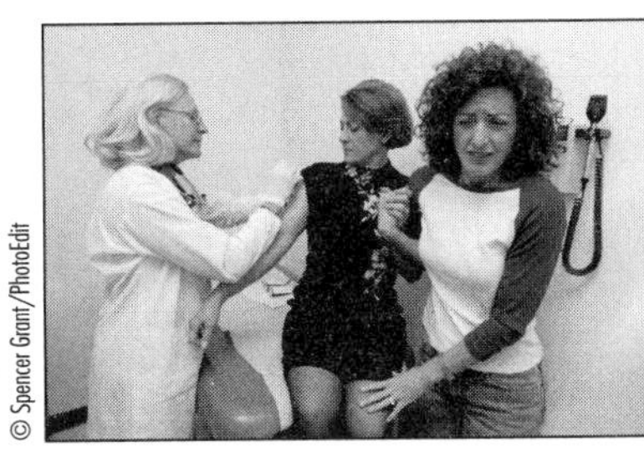
© Spencer Grant/PhotoEdit

A Person with a Phobia. Phobias are excessive, irrational fears that can interfere with the person's functioning. A phobia for needles can prevent a person from seeking needed medical assistance.

Social phobias are persistent fears of scrutiny by others or of doing something that will be humiliating or embarrassing. Fear of public speaking is a common social phobia.

Agoraphobia is also widespread among adults. Agoraphobia is derived from the Greek words meaning "fear of the marketplace," or fear of being out in open, busy areas. Persons with agoraphobia fear being in places from which it might be difficult to escape or in which help might not be available if they get upset. In practice, people who receive this diagnosis often refuse to venture out of their homes, especially by themselves. They find it difficult to hold a job or to maintain an ordinary social life.

claustrophobia
fear of tight, small places.

acrophobia
fear of high places.

social phobia
an irrational, excessive fear of public scrutiny.

agoraphobia
fear of open, crowded places.

Panic Disorder

> *My heart would start pounding so hard I was sure I was having a heart attack. I used to go to the emergency room. Sometimes I felt dizzy, like I was going to pass out. I was sure I was about to die.*
>
> Kim Weiner

Panic disorder is an abrupt attack of acute anxiety that is not triggered by a specific object or situation. People with panic disorder have strong physical symptoms such as shortness of breath, heavy sweating, tremors, and pounding of the heart. Like Kim Weiner (1992), they are particularly aware of cardiac sensations (Wilhelm et al., 2001). It is not unusual for them to think they are having a heart attack. Saliva levels of cortisol (a stress hormone) are elevated during attacks (Bandelow et al., 2000). Many fear suffocation. People with the disorder may also experience choking sensations; nausea; numbness or tingling; flushes or chills; and fear of going crazy or losing control. Panic attacks may last minutes or hours. Afterwards, the person usually feels drained.

panic disorder
the recurrent experiencing of attacks of extreme anxiety in the absence of external stimuli that usually elicit anxiety.

Many people panic now and then. The diagnosis of panic disorder is reserved for those who undergo a series of attacks or live in fear of attacks.

Panic attacks seem to come from nowhere. Thus, some people who have had them stay home for fear of having an attack in public. They are diagnosed as having panic disorder with agoraphobia.

Generalized Anxiety Disorder The central feature of **generalized anxiety disorder** is persistent anxiety. As with panic disorder, the anxiety cannot be attributed to a phobic object, situation, or activity. Rather, it seems to be free floating. The core of the disorder appears to be pervasive worrying about numerous stressors (Aikins & Craske, 2001). Features of the disorder include motor tension (shakiness, inability to relax, furrowed brow, fidgeting); autonomic overarousal (sweating, dry mouth, racing heart, light-headedness, frequent urinating, diarrhea); and excessive vigilance, as shown by irritability, insomnia, and a tendency to be easily distracted.

generalized anxiety disorder
feelings of dread and foreboding and sympathetic arousal of at least 6 months' duration.

Obsessive–Compulsive Disorder **Obsessions** are recurrent, anxiety-provoking thoughts or images that seem irrational and beyond control. They are so compelling and recurrent that they disrupt daily life. They may include doubts about whether

obsession
a recurring thought or image that seems beyond control.

one has locked the doors and shut the windows, or images such as one mother's repeated fantasy that her children had been run over on the way home from school. One woman became obsessed with the idea that she had contaminated her hands with Sani-Flush and that the chemicals were spreading to everything she touched. A 16-year-old boy found "numbers in his head" when he was about to study or take a test.

compulsion
an irresistible urge to repeat an act or engage in ritualistic behavior like hand washing.

Compulsions are thoughts or behaviors that tend to reduce the anxiety connected with obsessions. They are seemingly irresistible urges to engage in specific acts, often repeatedly, such as elaborate washing after using the bathroom. The impulse is recurrent and forceful, interfering with daily life. The woman who felt contaminated by Sani-Flush spent 3 to 4 hours at the sink each day and complained, "My hands look like lobster claws."

Stress Disorders Darla, who lives in Oregon, dreamed that she was trapped in a World Trade Center tower when it was hit by an airplane on September 11, 2001. Kelly, a Californian, dreamed of a beautiful bald eagle that was suddenly transformed into a snarling bird with glowing red eyes ("Sleepers Suffer WTC Nightmares," 2001).

The all-too-real nightmare of the events of September 11th have caused many people to have bad dreams. Such dreams are part of the experience of posttraumatic stress disorder.

posttraumatic stress disorder (PTSD)
a disorder that follows a distressing event outside the range of normal human experience and that is characterized by features such as intense fear, avoidance of stimuli associated with the event, and reliving of the event.

Posttraumatic stress disorder (PTSD) is characterized by a rapid heart rate and feelings of anxiety and helplessness that are caused by a traumatic experience. Such experiences may include a natural or human-made disaster, a threat or assault, or witnessing a death. PTSD may occur months or years after the event. It frequently occurs among firefighters, combat veterans, and people whose homes and communities have been swept away by natural disasters or who have been victims of accidents or interpersonal violence (Blanchard et al., 2003; Vasterling et al., 2002; Waelde et al., 2001; Weinstein et al., 2001).

The traumatic event is revisited in the form of intrusive memories, recurrent dreams, and flashbacks—the sudden feeling that the event is recurring (Rutkowski, 2001; Yehuda, 2002). People with PTSD typically try to avoid thoughts and activities

■ **A Traumatic Experience.** Traumatic experiences like the terrorist attack on the World Trade Center can lead to posttraumatic stress disorder (PTSD). PTSD is characterized by intrusive memories of the experience, recurrent dreams about it, and the sudden feeling that it is, in fact, recurring (as in "flashbacks").

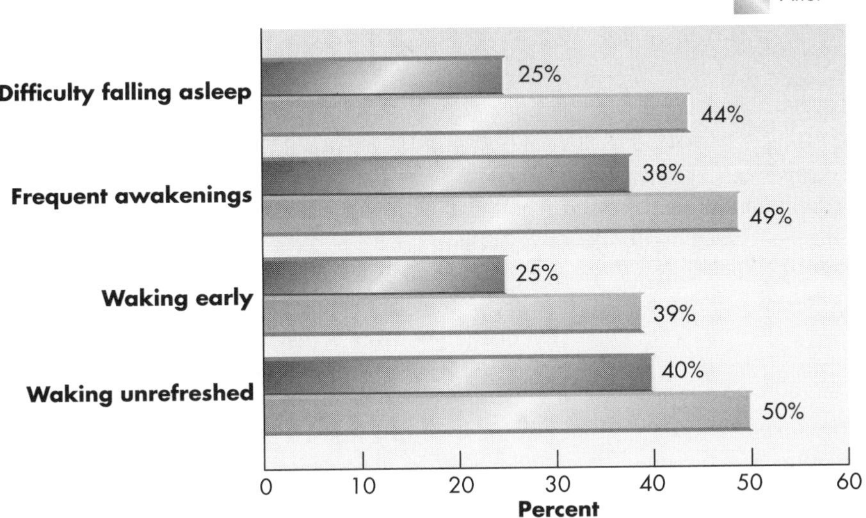

FIGURE 12.1

Sleep Problems among Americans before and Two Months after September 11, 2001. Insomnia is one of the symptoms of stress disorders. A poll by the National Sleep Foundation found that Americans had a greater frequency of sleep problems after the terrorist attacks of September 11.

connected to the traumatic event. They may also find it more difficult to enjoy life (Beckham et al., 2000) and have sleep problems (Lavie, 2001), irritable outbursts, difficulty concentrating, extreme vigilance, and an intensified "startle" response (Shayley et al., 2000). The terrorist attacks of September 11, 2001, took their toll on sleep. According to a poll taken by the National Sleep Foundation (2001) two months after the attacks, nearly half of Americans had difficulty falling asleep, as compared with about one-quarter of Americans before the attacks (Figure 12.1). Women respondents were more likely than men to report sleep problems, for example, difficulty falling asleep (50% vs. 37%).

Acute stress disorder, like PTSD, is characterized by feelings of anxiety and helplessness that are caused by a traumatic event. However, PTSD can occur 6 months or more after the traumatic event and tends to persist. Acute stress disorder occurs within a month of the event and lasts from 2 days to 4 weeks. Women who have been raped, for example, experience acute distress that tends to peak in severity about 3 weeks after the assault (Davidson & Foa, 1991; Rothbaum et al., 1992). Yet the same women frequently go on to experience PTSD (Koss et al., 2002; Street et al., 2003).

acute stress disorder
a disorder, like PTSD, that is characterized by feelings of anxiety and helplessness and caused by a traumatic event. Acute stress disorder occurs within a month of the event and lasts from 2 days to 4 weeks.

Mark Schuster and his colleagues (2001) conducted a telephone survey of a nationally representative sample of 560 American adults—not just those who lived near the attacks—three to five days following the terrorist attacks on September 11, 2001. They found that 90% of respondents reported at least one stress-related symptom, and 44% reported more severe symptoms of stress. Respondents coped by seeking social support, as in talking with others (98%) or participating in group activities (60%), by turning to religion (90%), and by making donations (36%). The great majority of parents of children aged 5 to 18 (84%) reported that they had talked with their children about the attacks for at least an hour, and about one-third (34%) restricted their children's exposure to television coverage of the attacks.

Theoretical Views

There are thus several kinds of anxiety disorders.

Psychological Views According to the psychodynamic perspective, phobias symbolize conflicts originating in childhood. Psychodynamic theory explains generalized anxiety as persistent difficulty in repressing primitive impulses. Obsessions are explained as leakage of unconscious impulses, and compulsions are seen as

THE CLINICAL FILE

Little Hans

Do you want to talk about conflict? Do you want to talk about drama? Do you want to talk about raw, unnerving fear? Well, forget about aliens from outer space. Forget about income taxes and things that go bump in the night. For there in turn of the century Vienna, that flourishing European capital of the arts, horses were biting people in the streets. Or so thought one petrified 5-year-old boy by the name of Hans.

In 1908 Hans's distraught father sought Sigmund Freud's advice. Freud went on to write one of his most famous case studies, "Analysis of a Phobia in a 5-Year-Old Boy." Freud concluded that the horses were symbols that represented Hans's father. Being bitten symbolized being castrated. In other words, Hans unconsciously feared that his father would castrate him. Why? Because Hans was his father's rival in a contest for the affection of his mother. Hans, that is, was in the throes of the Oedipus complex.

Freud's analysis has been criticized on many grounds. For one thing, Freud carried out Hans's psychoanalysis from a distance—by mail with the boy's father! For another, other interpretations of the boy's fear of horses are possible. Historically speaking, however, the case of Little Hans laid much of the groundwork for the psychoanalytic belief that phobic objects symbolize unconscious conflicts that date from early childhood.

acts that allow people to keep such impulses partly repressed. For example, fixation in the anal stage is theorized to be connected with development of traits such as excessive neatness of the sort that could explain some cases of obsessive–compulsive disorder.

Some learning theorists—particularly behaviorists—consider phobias to be conditioned fears that were acquired in early childhood. Therefore, their origins are beyond memory. Avoidance of feared stimuli is reinforced by the reduction of anxiety.

Other learning theorists—social cognitive theorists—note that observational learning plays a role in the acquisition of fears (Basic Behavioral Science Task Force, 1996b). If parents squirm, grimace, and shudder at the sight of mice, blood, or dirt on the kitchen floor, children might assume that these stimuli are awful and imitate their parents' behavior.

Cognitive theorists suggest that anxiety is maintained by thinking that one is in a terrible situation and helpless to change it. People with anxiety disorders may be cognitively biased toward paying a good deal of attention to threats (Fox et al., 2001; Sookman et al., 2001). Psychoanalysts and learning theorists agree that compulsive behavior reduces anxiety.

Cognitive theorists note that people's appraisals of the magnitude of threats help determine whether they are traumatic and can lead to PTSD (Folkman & Moskowitz, 2000a; Koss et al., 2002). People with panic attacks tend to misinterpret bodily cues and to view them as threats. Obsessions and compulsions may serve to divert attention from more frightening issues, such as "What am I going to do with my life?" When anxieties are acquired at a young age, we may later interpret them as enduring traits and label ourselves as "people who fear __________" (you fill it in). We then live up to the labels. We also entertain thoughts that heighten and perpetuate anxiety such as "I've got to get out of here," or "My heart is going to leap out of my chest." Such ideas intensify physical signs of anxiety, disrupt planning, make stimuli seem worse than they really are, motivate avoidance, and decrease self-efficacy expectations. The belief that we will not be able to handle a threat heightens anxiety. The belief that we are in control reduces anxiety (Bandura et al., 1985).

Biological Views Biological factors play a role in anxiety disorders. Genetic factors are implicated in most psychological disorders, including anxiety disorders (Kendler et al., 2001; Nestadt et al., 2000; Schmidt et al., 2000). For one thing, anxiety disorders tend to run in families. Twin studies find a higher **concordance**

concordance agreement.

rate for anxiety disorders among identical twins than among fraternal twins (Kendler et al., 2001). Studies of adoptees who are anxious similarly show that the biological parent places the child at risk for anxiety and related traits.

Evolutionary psychologists suggest that anxiety may reflect natural selection. Susan Mineka (Oehman & Mineka, 2001) suggests that humans (and nonhuman primates) are genetically predisposed to fear stimuli that may have posed a threat to their ancestors. Evolutionary forces would have favored the survival of individuals who were predisposed toward acquiring fears of large animals, spiders, snakes, heights, entrapment, sharp objects, and strangers. Thus the individuals who fearlessly encounter potentially harmful stimuli such as we see on shows like *Fear Factor* may be at a disadvantage, evolutionarily speaking, rather than at an advantage.

Perhaps a predisposition toward anxiety—in the form of a highly reactive autonomic nervous system—can be inherited. What might make a nervous system "highly reactive"? In the case of panic disorder, faulty regulation of levels of serotonin and norepinephrine may be involved. Other anxiety disorders may involve the excitatory neurotransmitter **glutamate**, and receptor sites in the brain may not be sensitive enough to **gamma-aminobutyric acid (GABA)**, an inhibitory neurotransmitter that may counterbalance glutamate (Kalin, 2003; Lydiard, 2003; Stroele et al., 2002). The **benzodiazepines**, a class of drugs that reduce anxiety, may work by increasing the sensitivity of receptor sites to GABA.

glutamate
an excitatory neurotransmitter that is involved in anxiety reactions.

gamma-aminobutyric acid (GABA)
an inhibitory neurotransmitter that is implicated in anxiety reactions.

benzodiazepines
a class of drugs that reduce anxiety; minor tranquilizers.

In many cases anxiety disorders may reflect the interaction of biological and psychological factors. In panic disorder, biological imbalances may initially trigger attacks. However, subsequent fear of attacks—and of the bodily cues that signal their onset—may heighten discomfort and give one the idea there is nothing one can do about them (Craske & Zucker, 2001). Feelings of helplessness increase fear. People with panic disorder therefore can be helped by psychological methods that provide ways of reducing physical discomfort—including regular breathing—and show them that there are, after all, things they can do to cope with attacks (Craske & Zucker, 2001).

DISSOCIATIVE DISORDERS: SPLITTING CONSCIOUSNESS

William's disorder, described at the beginning of the chapter, was a dissociative disorder. In the **dissociative disorders** there is a separation of mental processes such as thoughts, emotions, identity, memory, or consciousness—the processes that make the person feel whole.

dissociative disorders
disorders in which there are sudden, temporary changes in consciousness or self-identity.

Types of Dissociative Disorders

The *DSM* lists several dissociative disorders. Among them are dissociative amnesia, dissociative fugue, and dissociative identity disorder (also termed multiple personality).

Dissociative Amnesia In **dissociative amnesia** the person is suddenly unable to recall important personal information (that is, explicit episodic memories). The loss of memory cannot be attributed to organic problems such as a blow to the head or alcoholic intoxication. It is thus a psychological dissociative disorder and not an organic one. In the most common example, the person cannot recall events for a number of hours after a stressful incident, as in warfare or in the case of an uninjured survivor of an accident. In generalized amnesia, people forget their entire lives. Amnesia may last for hours or years.

dissociative amnesia
a dissociative disorder marked by loss of memory or self-identity; skills and general knowledge are usually retained. Previously termed *psychogenic amnesia*.

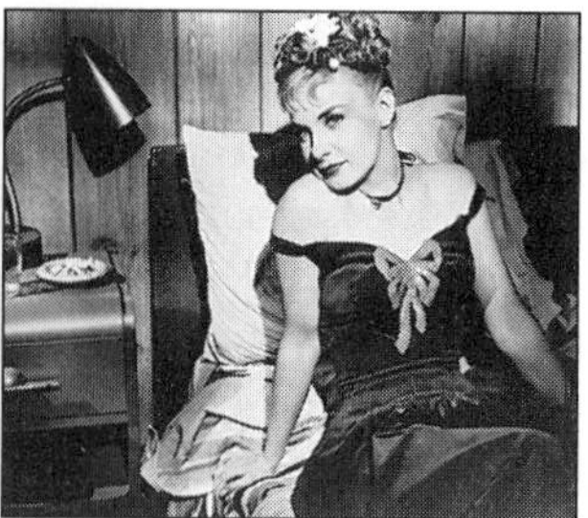

© Museum of Modern Art/Film Stills Archive.

■ **Dissociative Identity Disorder.** In the film *The Three Faces of Eve,* Joanne Woodward played three personalities in the same woman: the shy, inhibited Eve White (lying on couch); the flirtatious, promiscuous Eve Black (in dark dress); and a third personality (Jane) who could accept her sexual and aggressive impulses and still maintain her sense of identity.

dissociative fugue
a dissociative disorder in which one experiences amnesia and then flees to a new location. Previously termed *psychogenic fugue.*

Dissociative Fugue In **dissociative fugue**, the person abruptly leaves his or her home or place of work and travels to another place, having lost all memory of his or her past life. While at the new location the person either does not think about the past or reports a past filled with invented memories. The new personality is often more outgoing and less inhibited than the "real" identity. Following recovery, the events that occurred during the fugue are not recalled.

Dissociative Identity Disorder Dissociative identity disorder (formerly termed *multiple personality disorder*) is the name given to William's disorder. In dissociative identity disorder, two or more identities or personalities, each with distinct traits and memories, "occupy" the same person. Each identity may or may not be aware of the others or of events experienced by the others (Huntjens et al., 2003).

The identities of people with dissociative identity disorder can be very different from one another. They might even have different eyeglass prescriptions (Braun, 1988). Braun reports cases in which assorted identities showed different allergic responses. In one person, an identity named Timmy was not sensitive to orange juice. But when other identities gained control over him and drank orange juice, he would break out with hives. Hives would also erupt if another identity emerged while the juice was being digested. If Timmy reappeared when the allergic reaction was present, the itching of the hives would cease and the blisters would start to subside. In other cases reported by Braun, different identities within a person might show various responses to the same medicine. Or one identity might exhibit color blindness while others have normal color vision.

A few celebrated cases of this disorder have been portrayed in the popular media. One of them became the subject of the film *The Three Faces of Eve.* A timid housewife named Eve White harbored two other identities. One was Eve Black, a sexually aggressive, antisocial personality. The third was Jane, an emerging identity who was able to accept the existence of her primitive impulses yet engage in socially appropriate behavior. Finally the three faces merged into one—Jane. Ironically, later on, Jane (Chris Sizemore in real life) reportedly split into 22 identities. Another well-publicized case is that of Sybil, a woman with 16 identities who was portrayed by Sally Field in the film *Sybil.*

Theoretical Views

The dissociative disorders are some of the odder psychological disorders.

Psychologists of different theoretical persuasions have offered hypotheses about the origins of dissociative identity disorder and other dissociative disorders. According to psychodynamic theory, for example, people with dissociative disorders use massive repression to prevent them from recognizing improper impulses or remembering ugly events (Vaillant, 1994). In dissociative amnesia and fugue, the person forgets a profoundly disturbing event or impulse. In dissociative identity disorder, the person expresses unacceptable impulses through alternate identities.

According to learning theorists, people with dissociative disorders have learned *not to think* about bad memories or disturbing impulses in order to avoid feelings of anxiety, guilt, and shame. Both psychodynamic and learning theories suggest that dissociative disorders help people keep disturbing memories or ideas out of mind. Of what could such memories be? Research suggests that many—perhaps most—cases involve memories of sexual or physical abuse during childhood, usually by a relative or caretaker (Banyard et al., 2003; Martinez-Taboas & Bernal, 2000; Migdow, 2003). Yet some studies find no connection between dissociative disorders in adulthood and abuse in childhood (Elzinga et al., 2002).

As noted, dissociative disorders are quite odd, and it may be that some claim to have dissociative disorders in order to avoid responsibility for misbehavior. Therefore, it should come as no surprise that some professionals question whether they exist at all.

There is a good deal of skepticism about whether dissociative disorders exist (Thomas, 2001). For example, there were about 50 known cases of dissociative identity disorder before the public learned about "Sybil." By the 1990s, however, this number had mushroomed to more than 20,000 ("Tapes raise new doubts," 1998). Moreover, psychologists who have listened carefully to tapes of Sybil's therapy have raised the possibility that some of her psychiatrists may have "coached" her into reporting the symptoms. Sybil herself is reported to have vacillated as to whether or not her story was true ("Tapes raise new doubts," 1998). It is possible that many or even most people who are diagnosed with dissociative amnesia or dissociative identity disorder are faking. The technical term for faking in order to obtain some benefit—such as being excused from responsibility for a crime or from family obligations—is *malingering.*

somatoform disorders
disorders in which people complain of physical (somatic) problems even though no physical abnormality can be found.

conversion disorder
a disorder in which anxiety or unconscious conflicts are "converted" into physical symptoms that often have the effect of helping the person cope with anxiety or conflict.

la belle indifférence
a French term descriptive of the lack of concern sometimes shown by people with conversion disorders.

hypochondriasis
persistent belief that one is ill despite lack of medical findings.

SOMATOFORM DISORDERS: WHEN THE BODY EXPRESSES STRESS

People with **somatoform disorders** complain of physical problems such as paralysis, pain, or a persistent belief that they have a serious disease. Yet no evidence of a physical abnormality can be found. In this section we discuss two somatoform disorders: conversion disorder and hypochondriasis.

Types of Somatoform Disorders

Conversion disorder is characterized by a major change in, or loss of, physical functioning, although there are no medical findings to explain the loss of functioning. The behaviors are not intentionally produced. That is, the person is not faking. Conversion disorder is so named because it appears to "convert" a source of stress into a physical difficulty.

If you lost the ability to see at night, or if your legs became paralyzed, you would understandably show concern. But some people with conversion disorder show indifference to their symptoms, a remarkable feature referred to as **la belle indifférence**.

During World War II, some bomber pilots developed night blindness. They could not carry out their nighttime missions, although no damage to the optic nerves was found. In rare cases, women with large families have been reported to become paralyzed in the legs, again with no medical findings. More recently, a Cambodian woman who had witnessed atrocities became blind as a result.

Another more common type of somatoform disorder is **hypochondriasis** (also called *hypochondria*). People with this disorder insist that they are suffering from a serious physical illness, even though no medical evidence of illness can be found. They become preoccupied with minor physical sensations and continue to believe that they are ill despite the reassurance of physicians that they are healthy. They may run from doctor to doctor, seeking the one who will find the causes of the sensations. Fear of illness may disrupt their work or home life.

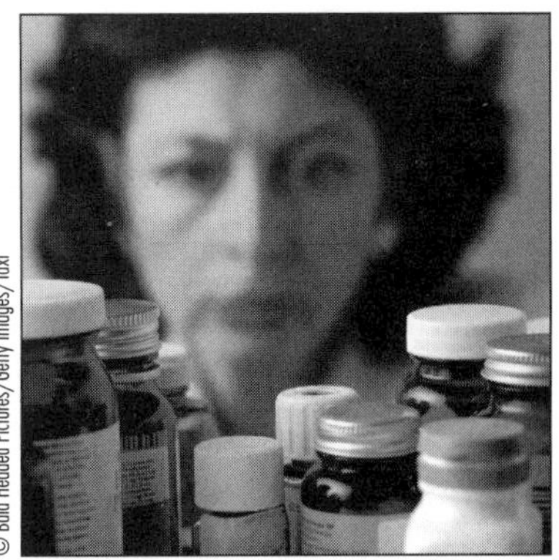

■ **Hypochondriasis.** People with hypochondriasis are irrationally concerned that they have contracted illnesses. Such people appear to be unusually sensitive to physical sensations. Do they also focus on their physical symptoms as an alternative to dealing with the social and other problems in their lives?

Theoretical Views

There is evidence that people with conversion disorder are susceptible to being hypnotized. In fact, some investigators consider conversion disorder to be a form of self-hypnosis (Roelofs et al., 2002). The idea here would seem to be that individuals with conversion disorder bring themselves to focus intently on an imaginary physical problem, to the point where they exclude conflicting information.

There is research evidence that people who develop hypochondriasis are particularly sensitive to bodily sensations and tend to ruminate about them (Lecci & Cohen, 2002). However, the history of the name of the somatoform disorders affords us insight into an interesting former sexist explanation of them. Consistent with psychodynamic theory, early versions of the *DSM* labeled somatoform disorders as "hysterical neuroses."

"Hysterical" derives from the word *hystera,* the Greek word for uterus or womb. Like many other Greeks, Hippocrates believed that hysteria was a sort of female trouble that was caused by a wandering uterus. It was erroneously thought that the uterus could roam through the body—that it was not anchored in place! As the uterus meandered, it could cause pains and odd sensations almost anywhere. The Greeks also believed that pregnancy anchored the uterus and ended hysterical complaints. What do you think Greek physicians prescribed to end monthly aches and pains? Good guess.

Even in the earlier years of the 20th century, it was suggested that strange sensations and medically unfounded complaints were largely the province of women. Moreover, viewing the problem as a neurosis suggested that it stemmed from unconscious childhood conflicts. The psychodynamic view of conversion disorders is that the symptoms protect the individual from feelings of guilt or shame or from another source of stress. Conversion disorders, like dissociative disorders, often seem to serve a purpose. For example, the "blindness" of the World War II pilots may have enabled them to avoid feelings of fear of being literally shot down or of guilt for killing civilians. The night blindness of the pilots shows that conversion disorders are not the special province of women—whether they were once labeled hysterical or not.

MOOD DISORDERS: UP, DOWN, AND AROUND

Mood disorders are characterized by disturbance in expressed emotions. The disruption generally involves sadness or elation. Most instances of sadness are normal, or "run-of-the-mill." If you have failed an important test, if you have lost money in a business venture, or if your closest friend becomes ill, it is understandable and fitting for you to be sad about it. It would be odd, in fact, if you were *not* affected by adversity.

Types of Mood Disorders

In this section we discuss two mood disorders: major depression and bipolar disorder.

Major Depression Depression is the common cold of psychological problems. People with run-of-the-mill depression may feel sad, blue, or "down in the dumps." They may complain of lack of energy, loss of self-esteem, difficulty concentrating, loss of interest in activities and other people (Nezlek et al., 2000), pessimism, crying, and thoughts of suicide.

These feelings are more intense in people with **major depressive disorder (MDD)**. According to a nationally representative sample of more than 9,000 adults

major depressive disorder a serious to severe depressive disorder in which the person may show loss of appetite, psychomotor retardation, and impaired reality testing.

in the United States, MDD affects 6% to 7% of us within any given year, and one person in six over the course of our lives (Kessler et al., 2003). About half of those with MDD experience severe symptoms such as poor appetite, serious weight loss, and agitation or **psychomotor retardation.** They may be unable to concentrate and make decisions. They may say that they "don't care" anymore and in some cases attempt suicide. A minority may display faulty perception of reality—so-called psychotic behaviors. These include delusions of unworthiness, guilt for imagined wrongdoings, even the notion that one is rotting from disease. There may also be delusions, as of the devil administering deserved punishment, or hallucinations, as of strange bodily sensations.

psychomotor retardation
slowness in motor activity and (apparently) in thought.

Bipolar Disorder It is true that feeling "up" is not always a good thing. People with **bipolar disorder**, formerly known as *manic–depressive disorder,* have mood swings from ecstatic elation to deep depression. The cycles seem to be unrelated to external events. In the elated, or **manic** phase, the person may show excessive excitement or silliness, carrying jokes too far. The manic person may be argumentative. He or she may show poor judgment, destroying property, making huge contributions to charity, or giving away expensive possessions. People often find manic individuals abrasive and avoid them. They are often oversexed and too restless to sit still or sleep restfully. They often speak rapidly (showing "pressured speech") and jump from topic to topic (showing **rapid flight of ideas**). It can be hard to get a word in edgewise.

Depression is the other side of the coin. People with bipolar depression often sleep more than usual and are lethargic. People with major (or unipolar) depression are more likely to have insomnia and agitation. Those with bipolar depression also exhibit social withdrawal and irritability. Some people with bipolar disorder attempt suicide when the mood shifts from the elated phase toward depression (Jamison, 2000). They will do almost anything to escape the depths of depression that lie ahead.

bipolar disorder
a disorder in which the mood alternates between two extreme poles (elation and depression). Also referred to as *manic–depression.*

manic
elated, showing excessive excitement.

rapid flight of ideas
rapid speech and topic changes, characteristic of manic behavior.

The Case of Women and Depression

Women are about two times more likely to be diagnosed with depression than men (Greenberger et al., 2000; Kessler, 2003). This gender difference begins to emerge during adolescence, at about the age of 13 (Hankin & Abramson, 2001).

Many people assume that biological gender differences largely explain why women are more likely to become depressed. Low levels of estrogen are widely seen as the culprit. Estrogen levels plummet prior to menstruation. How often do we hear degrading remarks such as "It must be that time of the month" when a woman expresses feelings of anger or irritation? But part of the gender difference may be due to the fact that men are less likely than women to admit to depression or seek treatment for depression. "I'm the John Wayne generation," admitted one man, a physician. "'It's only a flesh wound'; that's how you deal with it. I thought depression was a weakness—there was something disgraceful about it. A real man would just get over it" (cited in Wartik, 2000).

Still in any given year, about 12% of women and 7% of men in the United States are estimated to be diagnosable with depression (Depression Research, 2000). It was once assumed that depression was most likely to accompany menopause in women, because women could no longer carry out their "natural" function of childbearing. However, women are more likely to encounter severe depression during the childbearing years (Depression Research, 2000).

Yes, hormonal changes during adolescence, the menstrual cycle, and childbirth may contribute to depression in women (Cyranowski et al., 2000; McGrath et al., 1990). The bodies and brains of males, on the other hand, are stoked by testosterone during adolescence. High testosterone levels are connected with feelings of self-confidence, high activity levels, and aggressiveness, a cluster of traits and

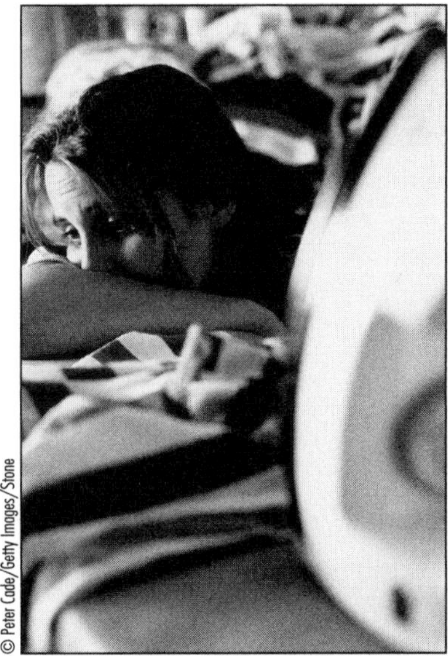

■ Women and Depression. Women are much more likely than men to be diagnosed with depression. Does the gender difference reflect biases among the mental-health professionals who make the diagnoses, women's (frequent) status as second-class citizens, the fact that women are often expected to take care of the family as well as earn a living, hormonal and other biological differences between women and men, other factors—or all of the above or some of the above?

behaviors that are more connected with elation (even if sometimes misplaced) than with depression (H. G. Pope et al., 2000; Sullivan, 2000).

However, some theorists suggest that women may also have a "cognitive vulnerability" to depression as well, connected, for example, with greater tendencies than men to ruminate about stresses and other negative events (Hankin & Abramson, 2001).

A panel convened by the American Psychological Association attributed most of the gender difference to the greater stresses placed on women, which tend to be greatest when they are trying to meet the multiple demands of childbearing, child rearing, and financial support of the family (McGrath et al., 1990). Women are more likely to experience physical and sexual abuse, poverty, single parenthood, and sexism. Single mothers, in particular, have lower socioeconomic status than men, and depression and other psychological disorders are more common among poor people (Cairney & Wade, 2002). Women are also more likely than men to help other people who are under stress. Supporting other people heaps additional caregiving burdens on themselves. A part of "therapy" for depressed women, then, is to modify the overwhelming demands that are placed on women today (Comas-Diaz, 1994). The pain may lie in the individual, but the cause often lies in society.

Women may be more likely than men to encounter depression, but men also become depressed. Let us now consider theoretical views of depression that apply both to men and women.

Theoretical Views

Although the mood disorders are connected with processes within the individual, let us begin by noting that many kinds of situations are also connected with depression. For example, depression may be a reaction to losses and stress (Cowen, 2002; Mazure et al., 2000). Sources of chronic strain such as marital discord, physical discomfort, incompetence, and failure or pressure at work all contribute to feelings of depression. We tend to be more depressed by things we bring on ourselves, such as academic problems, financial problems, unwanted pregnancy, conflict with the law, arguments, and fights (Greenberger et al., 2000). However, some people recover from depression less readily than others. People who remain depressed have lower self-esteem (Andrews, 1998; Sherrington et al., 2001), are less likely to be able to solve social problems (Reinecke et al., 2001), and have less social support.

What are the origins of depression?

Psychological Views Psychoanalysts suggest various explanations for depression. In one, people who are at risk for depression are overly concerned about hurting other people's feelings or losing their approval. As a result, they hold in feelings of anger rather than expressing them. Anger is turned inward and experienced as misery and self-hatred. From the psychodynamic perspective, bipolar disorder may be seen as alternating states in which the personality is first dominated by the superego and then by the ego. In the depressive phase of the disorder, the superego dominates, producing exaggerated ideas of wrongdoing and associated feelings of guilt and worthlessness. After a while the ego asserts supremacy, producing the elation and self-confidence often seen in the manic phase. Later, in response to the excessive display of ego, feelings of guilt return and plunge the person into depression once again.

Many learning theorists suggest that depressed people behave as though they cannot obtain reinforcement. For example, they appear to be inactive and apathetic. Many people with depressive disorders have an external locus of control. That is, they do not believe they can control events so as to achieve reinforcements (Tong, 2001; Weinmann et al., 2001).

learned helplessness a model for the acquisition of depressive behavior, based on findings that organisms in aversive situations learn to show inactivity when their operants go unreinforced.

Research conducted by learning theorists has also found links between depression and **learned helplessness**. In classic research, psychologist Martin Seligman taught dogs that they were helpless to escape an electric shock. The dogs were prevented from leaving a cage in which they received repeated shocks. Later, a barrier to a safe compartment was removed, offering the animals a way out. When they were shocked again, however, the dogs made no effort to escape. They had apparently learned that they were helpless. Seligman's dogs were also, in a sense, reinforced for doing nothing. That is, the shock *eventually* stopped when the dogs were showing helpless behavior—inactivity and withdrawal. "Reinforcement" might have increased the likelihood of repeating the "successful behavior"—that is, doing nothing—in a similar situation. This helpless behavior resembles that of people who are depressed.

© Karim Shamsi-Basha/The Image Works

Why Did He Miss That Tackle? This football player is compounding his feelings of depression by attributing his shortcomings on the field to factors that he cannot change. For example, he tells himself that he missed the tackle out of stupidity and lack of athletic ability. He ignores the facts that his coaching was poor and his teammates failed to support him.

Other cognitive factors also contribute to depression. For example, perfectionists set themselves up for depression by making irrational demands on themselves. They are likely to fall short of their (unrealistic) expectations and to feel depressed as a result (Flett & Hewitt, 2002; Flett et al., 2002).

Cognitive psychologists also note that people who ruminate about feelings of depression are more likely to prolong them (Nolen-Hoeksema, 2000; Spasojevic & Alloy, 2001; A. Ward et al., 2003). Women are more likely than men to ruminate about feelings of depression (Nolen-Hoeksema, 2001). Men seem more likely to try to fight off negative feelings by distracting themselves. Men are also more likely to distract themselves by turning to alcohol (Nolen-Hoeksema, 2001). They thus expose themselves and their families to further problems.

Still other cognitions involve the ways in which people explain their failures and shortcomings to themselves. Seligman (1996) suggests that when things go wrong we may think of the causes of failure as either *internal* or *external, stable* or *unstable, global* or *specific*. These various **attributional styles** can be illustrated using the example of having a date that does not work out. An internal attribution involves self-blame, as in "I really loused it up." An external attribution places the blame elsewhere (as in "Some couples just don't take to each other," or, "She was the wrong sign for me"). A stable attribution ("It's my personality") suggests a problem that cannot be changed. An unstable attribution ("It was because I had a head cold") suggests a temporary condition. A global attribution of failure ("I have no idea what to do when I'm with other people") suggests that the problem is quite large. A specific attribution ("I have problems making small talk at the beginning of a relationship") chops the problem down to a manageable size. Research has shown that people who are depressed are more likely to attribute the causes of their failures to internal, stable, and global factors—factors that they are relatively powerless to change (Lewinsohn et al., 2000b; Riso et al. 2003; Ziegler & Hawley, 2001).

attributional style
the tendency to attribute one's behavior to internal or external factors, stable or unstable factors, and so on.

Let's add one remarkable note about attributional styles and the mind–body connection. Shelley Taylor and her colleagues (2000a) found that self-blame for negative events is connected with poorer functioning of the immune system. Too much self-blame, in other words, is not only depressing; it can also make us physically ill.

Biological Factors Researchers are also searching for biological factors in mood disorders. Depression, for example, is often associated with the trait of **neuroticism**, which is heritable (Mulder, 2002). Anxiety is also connected with neuroticism, and mood and anxiety disorders are frequently found in the same person (Mulder, 2002).

neuroticism
a personality trait characterized largely by persistent anxiety.

Genetic factors appear to be involved in major depression and bipolar disorder (Jamison, 2000; Lewinsohn et al., 2000b; Nurnberger et al., 2001; P. F. Sullivan et al., 2000). Support for a role for genetic factors in bipolar disorder is found in twin and adoption studies (Craddock & Jones, 2001).

Research into depression focuses on underutilization of the neurotransmitter serotonin in the brain (Yatham et al., 2000; Young et al., 2003). It has been shown, for example, that learned helplessness is connected with lower serotonin levels in rats' brains (Wu et al., 1999). Moreover, people with severe depression often respond to drugs that heighten the action of serotonin.

Relationships between mood disorders and biological factors are complex and under intense study. Even if people are biologically predisposed toward depression, self-efficacy expectations and attitudes—particularly attitudes about whether one can change things for the better—may also play a role.

SCHIZOPHRENIA: WHEN THINKING RUNS ASTRAY

Jennifer was 19. Her husband David brought her into the emergency room because she had cut her wrists. When she was interviewed, her attention wandered. She seemed distracted by things in the air, or something she might be hearing. It was as if she had an invisible earphone.

She explained that she had cut her wrists because the "hellsmen" had told her to. Then she seemed frightened. Later she said that the hellsmen had warned her not to reveal their existence. She had been afraid that they would punish her for talking about them.

David and Jennifer had been married for about one year. At first they had been together in a small apartment in town. But Jennifer did not want to be near other people and had convinced him to rent a bungalow in the country. There she would make fantastic drawings of goblins and monsters during the days. Now and then she would become agitated and act as if invisible things were giving her instructions.

"I'm bad," Jennifer would mutter. "I'm bad." She would begin to jumble her words. David would then try to convince her to go to the hospital, but she would refuse. Then the wrist-cutting would begin. David thought he had made the cottage safe by removing knives and blades. But Jennifer would always find something.

Then Jennifer would be brought to the hospital, have stitches put in, be kept under observation for a while, and medicated. She would explain that she cut herself because the hellsmen had told her that she was bad and must die. After a few days she would deny hearing the hellsmen, and she would insist on leaving the hospital.

David would take her home. The pattern continued.

When the emergency room staff examined Jennifer's wrists and heard that she believed she had been following the orders of "hellsmen," they suspected that she could be diagnosed with schizophrenia. Schizophrenia is a severe psychological disorder that touches every aspect of a person's life. It is characterized by disturbances in thought and language, perception and attention, motor activity, and mood, and withdrawal and absorption in daydreams or fantasy.

Schizophrenia has been referred to as the worst disorder affecting human beings. It afflicts nearly 1% of the population worldwide. Its onset occurs relatively early in life, and its adverse effects tend to endure.

People with schizophrenia have problems in memory, attention, and communication. Their thinking and communication ability becomes unraveled (Kerns & Berenbaum, 2002). Unless we are allowing our thoughts to wander, our thinking is normally tightly knit. We start at a certain point, and associated thoughts tend to be logically connected. But people with schizophrenia often think illogically. Their speech may be jumbled. They may combine parts of words into new words or make meaningless rhymes. They may jump from topic to topic, conveying little useful information. They usually do not recognize that their thoughts and behavior are abnormal.

delusions
false, persistent beliefs that are unsubstantiated by sensory or objective evidence.

Many people with schizophrenia have **delusions**—for example, delusions of grandeur, persecution, or reference. In the case of delusions of grandeur, a person may believe that he is a famous historical figure such as Jesus, or a person on a special mission. He may have grand, illogical plans for saving the world. Delusions tend to be unshakable even in the face of evidence that they are not true. People with delusions of persecution may believe that they are sought by the Mafia, CIA, FBI, or some other group. A woman with delusions of reference said that news stories contained coded information about her. A man with such delusions complained that neighbors had "bugged" his walls with "radios." Other people with schizophrenia have had delusions that they have committed unpardonable sins, that they were rotting away from disease, or that they or the world did not exist.

It is true that people with schizophrenia may see and hear things that are not really there. Their perceptions often include hallucinations—imagery in the absence of external stimulation that the person cannot distinguish from reality. In Shakespeare's *Macbeth,* for example, after killing King Duncan, Macbeth apparently experiences a hallucination:

Is this a dagger which I see before me,
The handle toward my hand? Come, let me clutch thee:
I have thee not, and yet I see thee still.
Art thou not, fatal vision, sensible
To feeling as to sight? or art thou but
A dagger of the mind, a false creation,
Proceeding from the heat-oppressed brain?

Jennifer apparently hallucinated the voices of "hellsmen." Other people who experience hallucinations may see colors or even obscene words spelled out in midair. Auditory hallucinations are the most common type.

In individuals with schizophrenia, motor activity may become wild or so slowed that the person is said to be in a **stupor**—that is, a condition in which the senses, thought, and movement are inhibited. There may be strange gestures and facial expressions. The person's emotional responses may be flat or blunted, or inappropriate—as in giggling upon hearing bad news. People with schizophrenia tend to withdraw from social contacts and become wrapped up in their own thoughts and fantasies.

stupor
a condition in which the senses, thought, and movement are dulled.

paranoid schizophrenia
a type of schizophrenia characterized primarily by delusions—commonly of persecution—and by vivid hallucinations.

disorganized schizophrenia
a type of schizophrenia characterized by disorganized delusions and vivid hallucinations.

catatonic schizophrenia
a type of schizophrenia characterized by striking motor impairment.

Types of Schizophrenia

All types of schizophrenia involve a thought disorder. However, three major types of schizophrenia—paranoid, disorganized, and catatonic schizophrenia—all have distinct features.

Paranoid Type People with **paranoid schizophrenia** have systematized delusions and, frequently, related auditory hallucinations. They usually have delusions of grandeur and persecution, but they may also have delusions of jealousy, in which they believe that a spouse or lover has been unfaithful. They may show agitation, confusion, and fear, and may experience vivid hallucinations that are consistent with their delusions. People with paranoid schizophrenia often construct complex or systematized delusions involving themes of wrongdoing or persecution. John Nash, the character in the true story *A Beautiful Mind,* believed that the government was recruiting him to decipher coded messages by our Cold War enemies.

Everett Collection

■ Schizophrenia in *A Beautiful Mind.* In the film *A Beautiful Mind,* Russell Crowe played the role of the mathematician John Forbes Nash, Jr. Nash struggled with schizophrenia for more than three decades and was eventually awarded a Nobel Prize for work he had done as a graduate student decades earlier.

Disorganized Type People with **disorganized schizophrenia** show incoherence, loosening of associations, disorganized behavior, disorganized delusions, fragmentary delusions or hallucinations, and flat or highly inappropriate emotional responses. Extreme social impairment is common. People with this type of schizophrenia may also exhibit silliness and giddiness of mood, giggling, and nonsensical speech. They may neglect their appearance and personal hygiene and lose control of their bladder and bowels.

Catatonic Type Catatonic schizophrenia is one of the most unusual psychological disorders (Taylor & Fink, 2003). People with **catatonic schizophrenia** show striking impairment in motor activity. It is characterized by a slowing of activity into a stupor that may suddenly change into an agitated phase. Catatonic individuals may maintain unusual, even difficult postures for hours, even as their limbs grow

■ **Catatonic Schizophrenia.** People with catatonic schizophrenia show striking motor impairment and may hold unusual positions for hours.

waxy flexibility
a feature of catatonic schizophrenia in which people can be molded into postures that they maintain for quite some time.

mutism
refusal to talk.

swollen or stiff. A striking feature of this condition is **waxy flexibility**, in which the person maintains positions into which he or she has been manipulated by others. Catatonic individuals may also show **mutism**, but afterward they usually report that they heard what others were saying at the time.

Schizophrenia is thus characterized by extremely unusual behavior.

Theoretical Views

Psychologists have investigated various factors that may contribute to schizophrenia. They include psychological and biological factors.

Psychological Views According to the psychodynamic perspective, schizophrenia occurs because the ego is overwhelmed by sexual or aggressive impulses from the id. The impulses threaten the ego and cause intense inner conflict. Under this threat, the person regresses to an early phase of the oral stage in which the infant has not yet learned that it and the world are separate. Fantasies become confused with reality, giving rise to hallucinations and delusions. Yet critics point out that schizophrenic behavior is not the same as infantile behavior.

Most learning theorists have explained schizophrenia in terms of conditioning and observational learning. They have suggested that people engage in schizophrenic behavior when it is more likely to be reinforced than normal behavior. This may occur when a person is reared in a socially unrewarding or punitive situation. Inner fantasies then become more reinforcing than social realities. Patients in a psychiatric hospital may learn what is "expected" by observing others. Hospital staff may reinforce schizophrenic behavior by paying more attention to patients who behave bizarrely. This view is consistent with folklore that the child who disrupts the class attracts more attention from the teacher than the "good" child.

Although quality of parenting is connected with the development of schizophrenia (Buckley et al., 2000), critics note that many people who are reared in socially punitive settings are apparently immune to the extinction of socially appropriate behavior. Other people develop schizophrenic behavior without having had opportunities to observe other people with schizophrenia.

Many investigators have considered whether and how social and cultural factors such as poverty, discrimination, and overcrowding contribute to schizophrenia—especially among people who are genetically vulnerable to the disorder. Classic research in New Haven, Connecticut, showed that the rate of schizophrenia was twice as high in the lowest socioeconomic class as in the next-higher class on the socioeconomic ladder (Hollingshead & Redlich, 1958). It appears that poor-quality housing contributes to psychological disorders (Evans et al., 2000b). Some sociocultural theorists therefore suggest that treatment of schizophrenia requires alleviation of poverty and other social ills, rather than changing people whose behavior is deviant.

Critics of this view suggest that low socioeconomic status may be a result, rather than a cause, of schizophrenia. People with schizophrenia may drift toward low social status because they lack the social skills and cognitive abilities to function at higher social class levels. Thus, they may wind up in poor neighborhoods in disproportionately high numbers.

Evidence for the hypothesis that people with schizophrenia drift downward to lower socioeconomic status is mixed. Many people with schizophrenia do drift downward occupationally in comparison with their fathers' occupations. Many others, however, were reared in families in which the father came from the lowest socioeconomic class. Because the stresses of poverty may play a role in the development of schizophrenia, many researchers are interested in the possible interactions between psychosocial stressors and biological factors (Buckley et al., 2000; Sawa & Snyder, 2002).

Biological Views Schizophrenia appears to be a brain disorder (Egan et al., 2001). Many studies have been done to determine how the brains of schizophrenic people differ from those of others. Studies have focused on the amount of gray matter in the brain, the size of ventricles (hollow spaces), activity levels in the brain, and brain chemistry (e.g., neurotransmitters).

One avenue of brain research connects the major deficits we find in schizophrenia—problems in attention, working memory, abstract thinking, and language—with dysfunction in the prefrontal cortex of the brain. Imaging of the brain has shown that people with schizophrenia have less gray matter than other people (Kasai et al., 2003). For example, they have smaller brains and, in particular, a smaller prefrontal region of the cortex (Flashman et al., 2000; Selemon et al., 2002, 2003; Staal et al., 2000). They also tend to have larger ventricles in the brain than other people (Keller et al., 2003; Wright et al., 2000). PET scans reveal that people with schizophrenia also tend to have a lower level of activity in the frontal region of the brain (Kim et al., 2000; Meyer-Lindenberg et al., 2001; Lahti, et al., 2001). Still other research connects the lower activity levels with a loss in synapses (the structures that permit communication between neurons) in the region (Glantz & Lewis, 2000; McGlashan & Hoffman, 2000; Selemon et al., 2002, 2003) or white matter (Wolkin et al., 2003).

What might account for differences in brain structure and functioning? Research evidence suggests that there are a number of biological risk factors for schizophrenia, such as heredity, complications during pregnancy and birth, and birth during winter (Andreasen, 2003; Buckley et al., 2000; Jablensky & Kalaydjieva, 2003; Sawa & Snyder, 2002). Schizophrenia, like many other psychological disorders, runs in families (Conklin & Iacono, 2002; Hwu et al., 2003). People with schizophrenia constitute about 1% of the population. Yet children with one parent who has been diagnosed with schizophrenia have about a 10% chance of being diagnosed with schizophrenia themselves. Children with two such parents have about a 35% to 40% chance of being so diagnosed (Gottesman, 1991; Straube & Oades, 1992). Twin studies also find about a 45% concordance rate for the diagnosis among pairs of identical (MZ) twins, whose genetic codes are the same, compared with a 17% rate among pairs of fraternal (DZ) twins (Plomin & Crabbe, 2000). Moreover, adoptee studies find that the biological parent typically places the child at greater risk for schizophrenia than the adoptive parent—even though the child has been reared by the adoptive parent (Gottesman, 1991). Sharing genes with relatives who have schizophrenia apparently places a person at risk of developing the disorder. Many studies have been carried out to try to isolate the gene or genes involved in schizophrenia. Some studies find locations for multiple genes on several chromosomes.

But heredity is not the only factor that creates a vulnerability to schizophrenia. It also turns out that many people with schizophrenia have undergone complications during pregnancy and birth (Rosso et al., 2000). For example, the mothers of many people with schizophrenia had the flu during the sixth or seventh month of pregnancy (Brown & Susser, 2002). Poor maternal nutrition has also been implicated (Hulshoff et al., 2000; Pol et al., 2000). Complications during childbirth, especially prolonged labor, seem to be connected with the larger ventricles we find among people with schizophrenia (McNeil et al., 2000). People with schizophrenia are also somewhat more likely to have been born during winter than would be predicted by chance (Pol et al., 2000; Suvisaari et al., 2002). Alcohol abuse may also lead to differences in brain structures among people with schizophrenia (E. V. Sullivan et al., 2000). On the other hand, research evidence is mixed as to whether viral infections in childhood are connected with schizophrenia (Suvisaari et al., 2003). But taken together, these biological risk factors suggest that schizophrenia involves atypical development of the central nervous system. Problems in the nervous system may involve brain chemistry as well as brain structures, and research along these lines has led to the dopamine theory of schizophrenia.

FIGURE 12.2

A Multifactorial Model of Schizophrenia. According to the multifactorial model of schizophrenia, people with a genetic vulnerability to the disorder experience increased risk for schizophrenia when they encounter problems such as viral infections, birth complications, stress, and poor parenting. People without the genetic vulnerability would not develop schizophrenia despite such problems.

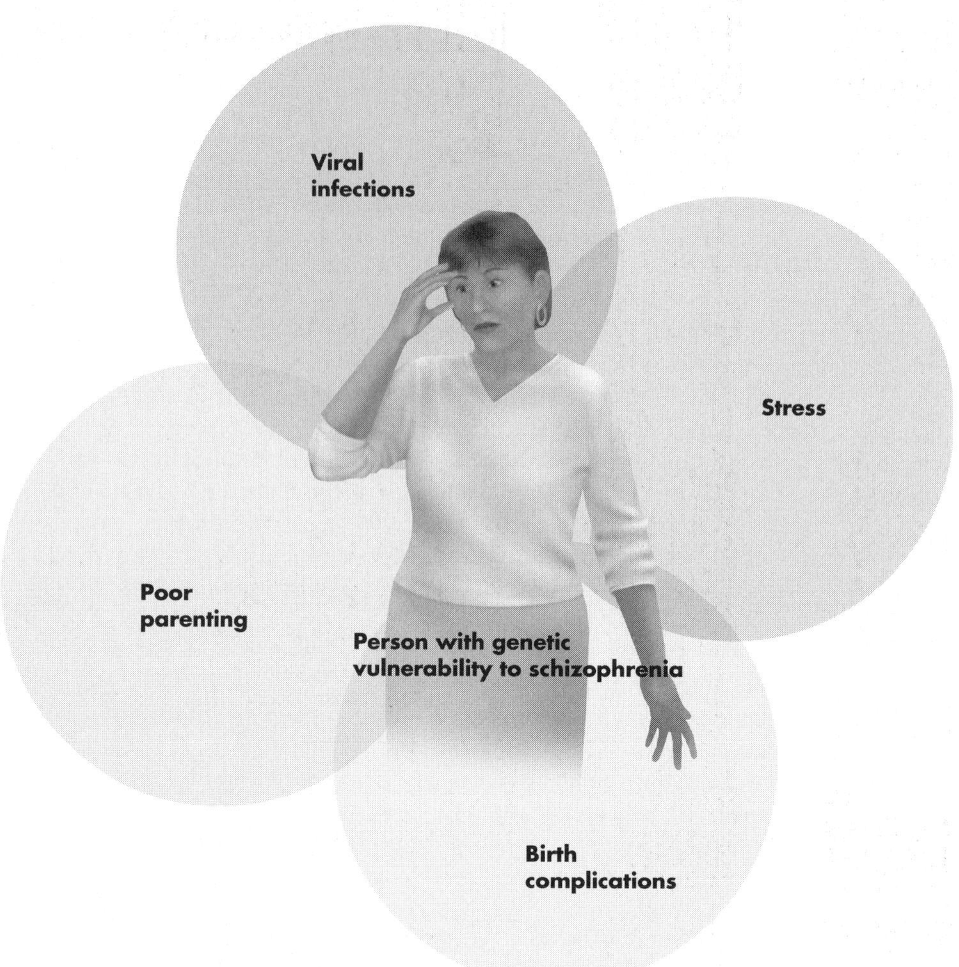

The Dopamine Theory of Schizophrenia Numerous chemical substances have been suspected of playing a role in schizophrenia, and much research has focused on the neurotransmitter dopamine. According to the dopamine theory of schizophrenia, people with schizophrenia overutilize dopamine (use more of it than other people do) although they may not produce more of it (Gijsman et al., 2002; Tsai & Coyle, 2002). Why? Research suggests that they have increased concentrations of dopamine at the synapses in the brain and also larger numbers of dopamine receptors (Butcher, 2000). It's a sort of "double hit" of neural transmission that may be connected with the confusion that characterizes schizophrenia.

Because many psychological and biological factors have been implicated in schizophrenia, most investigators today favor a *multifactorial* model. According to this model, genetic factors create a predisposition toward schizophrenia (see Figure 12.2). Genetic vulnerability to the disorder interacts with other factors, such as complications of pregnancy and birth, stress, and quality of parenting, to give rise to the disorder (Buckley et al., 2000; Sawa & Snyder, 2002).

Because the perceptions and judgment of people with schizophrenia are impaired, the diagnosis is sometimes associated with the insanity plea in the criminal courts.

Forensic psychologists apply psychological knowledge in the evaluation of people who commit crimes. They testify about defendants' competence to stand trial or participate in their own defense, as well as about whether defendants should be found not guilty by reason of insanity. For example, John Hinckley was found not guilty of a 1981 assassination attempt on President Ronald Reagan by reason of insanity. Hinckley was diagnosed with schizophrenia and committed to a psychiatric institution rather than given a prison term. He remains there to this day.

In pleading insanity, lawyers use the M'Naghten rule, named after Daniel M'Naghten, who tried to assassinate the British prime minister, Sir Robert Peel, in 1843. M'Naghten had delusions that Peel was persecuting him, and he killed Peel's secretary in the attempt. The court found M'Naghten not guilty by reason of insanity, referring to what has become the M'Naghten rule. It states that the accused did not understand what she or he was doing at the time of the act, did not realize it was wrong, or was succumbing to an irresistible impulse. Today the insanity plea tends to be used in much the same way—when the person accused of the crime could not understand that the criminal act was illegal or wrong, or when he or she could not control his or her behavior (Follingstad & McCormick 2002).

Many people would like to ban the insanity plea (DeAngelis, 1994b). Such banning "is an attempt to deal with a perception that the world is getting more violent," notes psychologist/lawyer Donald Bersoff (1994, p. 28). "That's combined with the perception that people are literally getting away with murder because of the insanity defense."

Practically speaking, there may not be all that much cause for concern, however. Although the public estimates that the insanity defense is used in about 37% of felony cases, it is actually raised in only 1% (Silver, 1994). Moreover, the insanity plea may be no bargain for people who use it. People found to be not guilty by reason of insanity are institutionalized for indefinite terms—supposedly until they are no longer insane. If it can be difficult to prove that someone is insane, it can also be difficult to prove that he or she is no longer insane. Hinckley remains institutionalized more than two decades after he attempted to kill President Reagan. If he had been convicted of attempted murder, he might already have completed a specific sentence.

PERSONALITY DISORDERS: MAKING ONESELF OR OTHERS MISERABLE

Personality disorders, like personality traits, are characterized by enduring patterns of behavior. Personality disorders, however, are inflexible and maladaptive. They impair personal or social functioning and are a source of distress to the individual or to other people.

personality disorders
enduring patterns of maladaptive behavior that are sources of distress to the individual or others.

Types of Personality Disorders

There are a number of personality disorders. They include the paranoid, schizotypal, schizoid, antisocial, and avoidant personality disorders. The defining trait of the **paranoid personality disorder** is a tendency to interpret other people's behavior as threatening or demeaning. People with the disorder do not show the grossly disorganized thinking of paranoid schizophrenia. However, they are mistrustful of others, and their relationships suffer for it. They may be suspicious of coworkers and supervisors, but they can generally hold a job.

paranoid personality disorder
a personality disorder characterized by persistent suspiciousness but not involving the disorganization of paranoid schizophrenia.

Schizotypal personality disorder is characterized by peculiarities of thought, perception, or behavior, such as excessive fantasy and suspiciousness, feelings of being unreal, or odd usage of words. The bizarre behaviors that characterize schizophrenia are absent, so this disorder is schizo*typal,* not schizophrenic.

schizotypal personality disorder
a personality disorder characterized by oddities of thought and behavior but not involving bizarre psychotic behaviors.

The **schizoid personality** is defined by indifference to relationships and flat emotional response. People with this disorder are "loners." They do not develop warm, tender feelings for others. They have few friends and rarely maintain long-term relationships. Some people with schizoid personality disorder do very well on the job provided that continuous social interaction is not required. They do not have hallucinations or delusions.

schizoid personality disorder
a personality disorder characterized by social withdrawal.

© Bettmann/CORBIS

A Person with Borderline Personality Disorder? Many well-known individuals such as Marilyn Monroe (seen here with her husband, playwright Arthur Miller) and Lawrence of Arabia may have had borderline personality disorder. The disorder is characterized by instability in relationships, self-image, and mood, and by problems in impulse control.

borderline personality disorder a personality disorder characterized by instability in relationships, self-image, mood, and lack of impulse control.

antisocial personality disorder The diagnosis given a person who is in frequent conflict with society, yet who is undeterred by punishment and experiences little or no guilt and anxiety.

People with **borderline personality disorder** show instability in their relationships, self-image, and mood, and lack of control over impulses (Yen et al., 2002). They tend to be uncertain of their values, goals, loyalties, careers, choices of friends, sometimes even their sexual orientations (Sokolova et al., 2002). Instability in self-image or identity may leave them with feelings of emptiness and boredom. Many cannot tolerate being alone and make desperate attempts to avoid feelings of abandonment. They may be clinging and demanding in social relationships, but clinging often pushes away the people on whom they depend. They alternate between extremes of adulation in their relationships (when their needs are met) and loathing (when they feel scorned). They tend to view other people as all good or all bad, shifting abruptly from one extreme to the other (Butler et al., 2002). As a result, they may flit from partner to partner in brief and stormy relationships. People whom they had idealized are treated with contempt when they feel the other person has failed them.

Instability of moods is a central characteristic of borderline personality disorder. Moods run the gamut from anger and irritability to depression and anxiety, with each lasting from a few hours to a few days. People with the disorder have difficulty controlling anger and are prone to fights or smashing things. They often act on impulse, like eloping with someone they have just met. This impulsive and unpredictable behavior is often self-destructive and linked to a risk of suicidal attempts and gestures. It may involve spending sprees, gambling, drug abuse, engaging in unsafe sexual activity, reckless driving, binge eating, or shoplifting. People with the disorder may also engage in self-mutilation, such as scratching their wrists or burning cigarettes on their arms (Sachsse et al., 2002). Self-mutilation is sometimes a means of manipulating others, particularly in times of stress. Frequent self-mutilation is also associated with suicide attempts.

It is true that some people can kill or maim others with no feelings of guilt at all. When these people also persistently violate the rights of others and are in repeated conflict with the law, they may be diagnosed with **antisocial personality disorder** (see Table 12.2). People with antisocial personality disorder often show a superficial charm and are at least average in intelligence. They fail to learn to improve their behavior from punishment, and they do not form meaningful bonds with other people (Levenston et al., 2000; Romero et al., 2001). Though they are often heavily punished by their parents and rejected by peers, they continue in their impulsive, careless styles of life. Women are more likely than men to have

TABLE 12.2 Characteristics of People Diagnosed with Antisocial Personality Disorder.

KEY CHARACTERISTICS	OTHER COMMON CHARACTERISTICS
History of delinquency and truancy	Lack of loyalty or of formation of enduring relationships
Persistent violation of the rights of others	Failure to maintain good job performance over the years
Impulsiveness	Failure to develop or adhere to a life plan
Poor self-control	Sexual promiscuity
Lack of remorse for misdeeds	Substance abuse
Lack of empathy	Inability to tolerate boredom
Deceitfulness and manipulativeness	Low tolerance for frustration
Irresponsibility	Irritability
Glibness; superficial charm	
Exaggerated sense of self-worth	

Sources: Levenston et al., 2000; Romero et al., 2001.

anxiety and depressive disorders. Men are more likely than women to have antisocial personality disorder (K. G. Anderson et al., 2001).

People with **avoidant personality disorder** are generally unwilling to enter a relationship without some assurance of acceptance because they fear rejection and criticism. As a result, they may have few close relationships outside their immediate families. Unlike people with schizoid personality disorder, however, they have some interest in, and feelings of warmth toward, other people.

avoidant personality disorder
a personality disorder in which the person is unwilling to enter relationships without assurance of acceptance because of fears of rejection and criticism.

Theoretical Views

Many theoretical explanations of personality disorders are derived from the psychodynamic model. Traditional Freudian theory focuses on Oedipal problems as the source of many psychological disorders, including personality disorders. Faulty resolution of the Oedipus complex might lead to lack of guilt, because conscience, or superego, is thought to depend on proper resolution of the complex. Although lack of guilt may occur more often among children who are rejected and punished by parents rather than given affection (Denham et al., 2000; Hastings et al., 2000), the view that such treatment causes Oedipal problems is speculative.

Learning theorists suggest that childhood experiences can contribute to maladaptive ways of relating to others in adulthood—that is, can lead to personality disorders. Cognitive psychologists find that antisocial adolescents encode social information in ways that bolster their misdeeds. For example, they tend to interpret other people's behavior as threatening, even when it is not (Crick & Dodge, 1994; Lochman, 1992). Aggressive individuals often find it difficult to solve social problems in useful ways (McMurran et al., 2002). Cognitive therapists have encouraged some antisocial adolescents to view social provocations as problems to be solved rather than as threats to their "manhood," with some favorable initial results (Lochman, 1992).

Genetic factors are apparently involved in some personality disorders (Eaves et al., 2000; Rutter & Silberg, 2002). Personality traits are to some degree heritable (Plomin, 2000), and many personality disorders seem to be extreme variations of normal personality traits. An analysis of 51 twin and adoption studies estimated that genetic factors were the greatest influences on antisocial behavior (Rhee & Waldman, 2002). Referring to the five-factor model of personality, people with schizoid personalities tend to be highly introverted (Ross et al., 2002; Widiger & Costa, 1994). People with avoidant personalities tend to be both introverted and emotionally unstable (neurotic) (Ross et al., 2002; Widiger & Costa, 1994).

Perhaps the genetics of antisocial personality involve the prefrontal cortex of the brain, a part of the brain connected with emotional responses. There is some evidence that people with antisocial personality, as a group, have less gray matter (associative neurons) in the prefrontal cortex of the brain than other people (Damasio, 2000; Raine et al., 2000). The lesser amount of gray matter could lessen the level of arousal of the nervous system. As a result, it would be more difficult to condition fear responses (Blair & James, 2001, 2003). People with the disorder would then be unlikely to show guilt for their misdeeds and would seem to be unafraid of punishment. But a biological factor such as a lower-than-normal level of arousal might not in itself cause the development of an antisocial personality (Rutter & Silberg, 2002). Perhaps a person must also be reared under conditions that do not foster the self-concept of a law-abiding citizen.

The label of borderline personality has been applied to people as diverse as Marilyn Monroe and Lawrence of Arabia. Some theorists believe we live in fragmented and alienating times that tend to create the problems in forming a stable identity and stable relationships. "Living on the edge," or border, can be seen as a metaphor for an unstable society.

PRACTICAL SOLUTIONS

Understanding and Preventing Suicide

In January 2002, 15-year-old Charles Bishop flew his small airplane into the side of a bank building in Tampa, Florida. It was no accident. He left a suicide note expressing sympathy for what terrorists had done four months earlier, flying passenger jets into the towers of the World Trade Center in New York and the Pentagon, outside Washington, DC. His teachers and friends expressed shock and dismay.

Terrorist examples and politics aside, his teachers and friends were trying to understand how Charles could have intentionally flown into the side of an—in this case—extremely unforgiving skyscraper. After all, he, like so many people, had "so much to live for." Didn't he? Apparently Charles didn't think so. Neither do the other thousands of other Americans who take their own lives each year.

About 30,000 people each year take their lives in the United States (CDC, 2000c). Suicide is the third or fourth leading cause of death among older teenagers (National Center for Health Statistics, 2002). What prompts people to take their own lives? Who is most at risk of attempting or committing suicide?

Risk Factors in Suicide Most suicides are linked to feelings of depression and hopelessness (Beautrais, 2003; Leslie et al., 2002; Sampaio et al., 2001). My daughter Jill Rathus and her colleagues (Miller et al., 2000; Velting et al., 2000) have found that suicidal adolescents experience four areas of psychological problems: (1) confusion about the self, (2) impulsiveness, (3) emotional instability, and (4) interpersonal problems. Some suicidal teenagers, like suicidal adults, are highly achieving, rigid perfectionists who have set impossibly high expectations for themselves (Miller et al., 2000; Wu et al., 2001). Many people throw themselves into feelings of depression and hopelessness by comparing themselves negatively with others, even when the comparisons are inappropriate (Barber, 2001). ("No, you didn't get the promotion, but you got a raise, and the person who received the promotion has been with the company longer.")

Suicide attempts are more common following stressful life events, especially "exit events" (Beautrais, 2003). Exit events entail loss of social support, as in the death of a parent or friend, divorce, or a family member's leaving home. These exit events result in what Shneidman (2001) refers to as psychological pain, or "psychache." Other contributors to suicidal behavior among adolescents include concerns over sexuality, grades in school, problems at home, and substance abuse (Beautrais, 2003; Miller et al., 2000; Wu et al., 2001). It is not always a stressful event itself that precipitates suicide but the individual's anxiety or fear of being "found out" about something, such as failing a course or getting arrested (Marttunen, 1998). Problem-solving ability—or lack of it—is connected with suicide. People who consider suicide are apparently less capable of solving problems, especially their social problems, than others (Miller et al., 2000; Townsend et al., 2001). People contemplating suicide are thus less likely to find productive ways of changing the stressful situation. They have borne the "psychache"; now they want a magical solution to problems that require work, or else a quick way out (Shneidman, 2001).

There is a tendency for suicide to run in families (Bongar, 2002; Joiner, 2002; Qin et al., 2003). Many suicide attempters have family members with serious psychological problems, and about 25% have family members who have taken their lives (Segal & Roy, 2001; Sorensen & Rutter, 1991). The causal connections are unclear, however. Do people who attempt suicide inherit disorders that can lead to suicide? Does the family environment subject family members to feelings of hopelessness? Does the suicide of a family member give a person the idea of committing suicide or create the impression that he or she is somehow fated to commit suicide? Perhaps these possibilities and others—such as poor problem-solving ability—form a complex web of contributing factors.

Sociocultural Factors in Suicide Suicide is connected not only with feelings of depression and stressful events, but also with age, educational status, ethnicity, and gender. Consider some facts about suicide:

- Suicide is the third leading cause of death among young people aged 15 to 24 (National Center for Health Statistics, 2002). More teenagers and young adults die from suicide than from cancer, heart disease, AIDS, birth defects, stroke, pneumonia and influenza, and chronic lung disease combined (National Center for Health Statistics, 2002).
- Suicide is more common among college students than among people of the same age who do not attend college. Each year about 10,000 college students attempt suicide.
- Although teenage suicides loom large in the media spotlight, older people are actually more likely to commit suicide (National Center for Health Statistics, 2002). The suicide rate among older people who are unmarried or divorced is double that of older people who are married (CDC, 2000c).

Rates of suicide and suicide attempts also vary among different ethnic groups and according to gender. For example, about one in every six Native Americans (17%) has attempted suicide—a rate higher than that of other Americans (Blum et al., 1992). About one in eight Latino and Latina Americans has attempted suicide and three in ten have considered it (National Center for Health Statistics, 2002). European Americans are next, with 8% attempting and 28% contemplating suicide. African Americans are least likely to attempt suicide (6.5%) or to think about it (20%). The actual suicide rates for African Americans are only about two-thirds of those for European Americans, despite the fact that African Americans are more likely to live in poverty and suffer from discrimination (National Center for Health Statistics, 2002). How can we explain this "disconnect" between hope for the future and suicide rates? One possibility is that some suicidal African American males may engage in risk-taking behaviors that lead to early death by homicide or accident. Another possibility is that cultural factors such as the support offered by extended families and the important role of religion may have a protective effect. Yet another possibility is that when African Americans are feeling low, they tend to blame social circumstances, including discrimination. Many European Americans, on the other hand, may feel that there is no one to blame but themselves.

About three times as many females as males attempt suicide, but about five times as many males succeed (National Center for Health Statistics, 2002). In part, males are more likely to "succeed" because of the methods they choose. The methods preferred by males are more deadly and more rapid: Males are more likely to shoot or hang themselves; females more often use drugs, such as overdoses of tranquilizers or sleeping pills, or poisons. Females often do not take enough of these chemicals. It also takes a while for them to work, giving people the opportunity to find them and intervene.

Now let us consider some myths about suicide.

Myths about Suicide You may have heard that individuals who threaten suicide are only seeking attention. Those who are serious just do it. Actually, it is not true that people who threaten suicide are only seeking attention. Most people who commit suicide give warnings about their intentions (Jackson & Nuttall, 2001; Waters, 2000).

Some believe that those who fail at suicide attempts are only seeking attention. But many people who commit suicide have made prior attempts (Jackson & Nuttall, 2001; Waters, 2000). Contrary to widespread belief, discussing suicide with a person who is depressed does not prompt the person to attempt suicide (CDC, 1995). Extracting a promise not to commit suicide before calling or visiting a helping professional seems to prevent some suicides.

Some believe that only "insane" people (meaning people who are out of touch with reality) would take their own lives. However, suicidal thinking is not necessarily a sign of psychosis, neurosis, or personality disorder. Instead, people may consider suicide when they think they have run out of options (Nock & Kazdin, 2002; Townsend et al., 2001).

Warning Signs of Suicide The great majority of people who commit suicide send out a variety of signals about their impending act (Bongar, 2002; Hendin et al., 2001). Sad to say, these signals often are overlooked, sometimes because other people do not recognize them, sometimes because other people do not have adequate access to health care (MacDonald, 1999; Wu et al., 2001). Sometime people do not receive help until they actually attempt suicide, and sometimes not even then (Gili-Planas et al., 2001; Wu et al., 2001). Here are some clues that a person may be at risk of committing suicide (Bongar, 2002; Hendin et al., 2001):

- Changes in eating and sleeping patterns.
- Difficulty concentrating on school or the job.
- A sharp decline in performance and attendance at school or on the job.
- Loss of interest in previously enjoyed activities.
- Giving away prized possessions.
- Complaints about physical problems when no medical basis for the problems can be found.
- Withdrawal from social relationships.
- Personality or mood changes.
- Talking or writing about death or dying.
- Abuse of drugs or alcohol.
- An attempted suicide.
- Availability of a handgun.
- A precipitating event such as an argument, a broken romantic relationship, academic difficulties, problems on the job, loss of a friend, or trouble with the law.
- In the case of adolescents, knowing or hearing about another teenager who has committed suicide (which can lead to so-called "cluster" suicides).
- Threatening to commit suicide.

What Can You Do? Imagine that you are having a heart-to-heart talk with Jamie, one of your best friends. Things haven't been going well. Jamie's grandmother died a month ago, and they were very close. Jamie's course work has been suffering, and things have also been going

continued

PRACTICAL SOLUTIONS (CONTINUED)

downhill with the person Jamie has been seeing. But you are not prepared when Jamie looks you in the eye and says, "I've been thinking about this for days, and I've decided that the only way out is to kill myself."

If someone tells you that he or she is considering suicide, you may become frightened and flustered or feel that an enormous burden has been placed on you. You are right: It has. In such a case your objective should be to encourage the person to consult a health care provider, or to consult one yourself, as soon as possible. But if the person refuses to talk to anyone else and you feel that you can't break free for a consultation, there are a number of things you can do (Hendin et al., 2001; Omer & Elitzur, 2001; Shneidman, 2001):

1. **Keep talking.** Encourage the person to talk to you or to some other trusted person (Los Angeles Unified School District, 2000). Draw the person out with questions like "What's happening?" "Where do you hurt?" "What do you want to happen?" Questions like these may encourage the person to express frustrated needs and provide some relief. They also give you time to think.
2. **Be a good listener.** Be supportive with people who express suicidal thoughts or feel depressed, hopeless, or worthless. They may believe their condition is hopeless and will never improve, but let them know that you are there for them and willing to help them get help. Show that you understand how upset the person is. Do *not* say, "Don't be silly."
3. Suggest that something other than suicide might solve the problem, even if it is not evident at the time. Many suicidal people see only two solutions—either death or a magical resolution of their problems. Therapists try to "remove the mental blinders" from suicidal people.
4. Emphasize as concretely as possible how the person's suicide would be devastating to you and to other people who care.
5. Ask how the person intends to commit suicide. People with concrete plans and a weapon are at greater risk. Ask if you might hold on to the weapon for a while. Sometimes the answer is yes.
6. Suggest that the person go *with you* to obtain professional help *now.* The emergency room of a general hospital, the campus counseling center or infirmary, or the campus or local police station will do. Some campuses have hotlines you can call. Some cities have suicide prevention centers with hotlines that people can use anonymously.
7. Extract a promise that the person will not commit suicide before seeing you again. Arrange a specific time and place to meet. Get professional help as soon as you are apart.
8. Do *not* tell people threatening suicide that they're silly or crazy. Do *not* insist on contact with specific people, such as parents or a spouse. Conflict with these people may have led to the suicidal thinking in the first place.

Resources You can also check out the following resources:

- The national suicide hotline: 1-800-SUICIDE (1-800-784-2433).
- American Association of Suicidology: Their Web site, www.suicidology.org, provides information on ways to prevent suicide. You will also find a list of crisis centers.
- American Foundation for Suicide Prevention: Their Web site, www.afsp.org, offers information about suicide and links to other suicide and mental health sites.

REVIEW

- Psychological disorders are characterized by unusual behavior, socially unacceptable behavior, faulty perception of reality, personal distress, dangerous behavior, or self-defeating behavior.
- The most widely used classification scheme is found in the *Diagnostic and Statistical Manual (DSM)* of the American Psychiatric Association. The current edition of the *DSM*—the *DSM-IV-TR*—groups disorders on the basis of observable symptoms and no longer uses the category of neuroses.
- Anxiety disorders are characterized by motor tension, feelings of dread, and overarousal of the sympathetic branch of the autonomic nervous system. These disorders include irrational, excessive fears, or phobias; panic disorder, characterized by sudden attacks in which people typically fear that they may be losing control or going crazy; generalized or pervasive anxiety; obsessive–compulsive disorder, in which people are troubled by intrusive thoughts or impulses to repeat some activity; and stress disorders, in which a

stressful event is followed by persistent fears and intrusive thoughts about the event. Posttraumatic stress disorder can occur 6 months or more after the event, whereas acute stress disorder occurs within a month.

- The psychodynamic perspective tends to view anxiety disorders as representing difficulty in repressing primitive impulses. Many learning theorists view phobias as conditioned fears. Cognitive theorists focus on ways in which people interpret threats. Some people may also be genetically predisposed to acquire certain kinds of fears. Anxiety disorders tend to run in families. Some psychologists suggest that biochemical factors—which could be inherited—may create a predisposition toward anxiety disorders. One such factor is faulty regulation of neurotransmitters.
- Dissociative disorders are characterized by sudden, temporary changes in consciousness or self-identity. They include dissociative amnesia; dissociative fugue, which involves forgetting plus fleeing and adopting a new identity; and dissociative identity disorder (multiple personality), in which a person behaves as if more than one personality occupies his or her body.
- Many psychologists suggest that dissociative disorders help people keep disturbing memories or ideas out of mind. These memories may involve episodes of childhood sexual or physical abuse.
- People with somatoform disorders exhibit or complain of physical problems, although no medical evidence of such problems can be found. The somatoform disorders include conversion disorder and hypochondriasis. In conversion disorder, stress is converted into a physical symptom, and the individual may show la belle indifférence (indifference to the symptom).
- Conversion disorders were once called "hysterical neuroses" and expected to be found more often among women. However, they are also found among men and may reflect the relative benefits of focusing on physical symptoms rather than fears and conflicts.
- Mood disorders involve disturbances in expressed emotions. Major depression is characterized by persistent feelings of sadness, loss of interest, feelings of worthlessness or guilt, inability to concentrate, and physical symptoms that may include disturbances in regulation of eating and sleeping. Feelings of unworthiness and guilt may be so excessive that they are considered delusional. Bipolar disorder is characterized by dramatic swings in mood between elation and depression; manic episodes include pressured speech and rapid flight of ideas.
- Research emphasizes possible roles for learned helplessness, attributional styles, and underutilization of serotonin in depression. People who are depressed are more likely than other people to make internal, stable, and global attributions for failures. Genetic factors involving regulation of neurotransmitters may also be involved in mood disorders. For example, bipolar disorder has been linked to inappropriate levels of the neurotransmitter glutamate. Moreover, people with severe depression often respond to drugs that heighten the action of serotonin.
- Schizophrenia is a most severe psychological disorder that is characterized by disturbances in thought and language, such as loosening of associations and delusions; in perception and attention, as found in hallucinations; in motor activity, as shown by a stupor or by excited behavior; in mood, as in flat or inappropriate emotional responses; and in social interaction, as in social withdrawal and absorption in daydreams or fantasy.
- The major types of schizophrenia are paranoid, disorganized, and catatonic. Paranoid schizophrenia is characterized largely by systematized delusions; disorganized schizophrenia by incoherence; and catatonic schizophrenia by motor impairment.
- Schizophrenia is connected with smaller brains, especially fewer synapses in the prefrontal region, and larger ventricles in the brain. According to the multifactorial model, genetic vulnerability to schizophrenia may interact with other factors, such as stress, complications during pregnancy and childbirth, and quality of parenting, to cause the disorder to develop. According to the dopamine theory of schizophrenia, people with schizophrenia *use* more dopamine than other people do, perhaps because they have more dopamine in the brain along with more dopamine receptors than other people.
- Personality disorders are inflexible, maladaptive behavior patterns that impair personal or social functioning and cause distress for the individual or others. The defining trait of paranoid personality disorder is suspiciousness. People with schizotypal personality disorders show oddities of thought, perception, and behavior. Social withdrawal is the major characteristic of schizoid personality disorder. People with antisocial personality disorders persistently violate the rights of others and are in conflict with the law. They show little or no guilt or shame over their misdeeds and are largely undeterred by punishment. People with avoidant personality disorder tend to avoid entering relationships for fear of rejection and criticism.
- Psychodynamic theory connected many personality disorders with hypothesized Oedipal problems. Genetic factors may be involved in some personality disorders. Antisocial personality disorder may develop from some combination of genetic vulnerability (less gray matter in the prefrontal cortex of the brain, which may provide lower-than-normal levels of arousal), inconsistent discipline, and cynical processing of social information.

CHAPTER 12 PRACTICE EXAM

____ 1. Bob is afraid that his neighbors are discussing how to burn his house down. He thinks they have coffee every morning at the gas station. Bob is showing which criterion for a psychological disorder?
a. Atypicalness
b. personal unhappiness
c. faulty perceptions
d. self aggrandizing behavior

____ 2. DSM stands for:
a. Diagnostic, standards, and medicine
b. Diagnostic standards manual
c. Diagnostic and statistical manual
d. Diagnostic standards of medicine

____ 3. Thomas Szasz believes that mental disorders are really:
a. social destructions.
b. problems in living.
c. caused by alleles.
d. just related to early puberty.

____ 4. Which one is a *psychological* aspect that goes along with anxiety?
a. Decreased heart rate
b. Lowered blood pressure
c. Perspiration
d. nervousness

____ 5. The primary thing that differentiates a phobia from a regular fear is:
a. what the person fears.
b. when the fear manifests in everyday life.
c. how the fear interferes with the person's life.
d. whether the fear begins in adolescence.

____ 6. Obsessions are __________ and compulsions are __________.
a. behaviors; thoughts
b. thoughts; behaviors
c. illusions; real
d. Real; illusions

____ 7. Which one below supports a biological conception of anxiety disorders?
a. People have the same fears about dieing.
b. Men report more anxiety than women.
c. Punishment of behaviors causes anxiety to occur irregularly.
d. There is a high concordance rate for anxiety disorders among identical twins.

____ 8. Conversion disorders occur when:
a. a person converts pleasure into pain.
b. a person converts stress into a physical symptom.
c. A person converts physical wounds into psychological problems.
d. a person converts an imagined handicap into anxiety.

____ 9. Barry is upset, very angry, and cannot control his aggression. His speech is rapid and he just kicked out the toilet because his cable TV went out. It appears Barry is in the __________ phase of a bipolar disorder.
a. manic
b. hyper
c. depressed
d. converted

____ 10. Psychoanlysis suggests what about bipolar disorder?
a. The id sublimates to the ego and superego.
b. personality is first dominated by the superego then the ego.
c. Personality is taken over by the ego and id.
d. Conscious conflicts occur between pre and un consciouis ideation

____ 11. Which is an unstable attribution?
a. "I can't hum."
b. "I am very nice to children."
c. "I failed the test because I was sick all the time"
d. "I really messed up."

____ 12. Depression is to __________ as schizophrenia is to __________.
a. Psychology; biology
b. myelin; neurons

c. mood; thinking
d. Thinking; mood

____ 13. The most common types of hallucinations are:
a. auditory.
b. sensory.
c. visual.
d. olfactory.

____ 14. People with the following symptoms are likely to be diagnosed as_______. systematized delusions, auditory hallucinations, delusions of grandeur and jealousy, and may show agitation.
a. paranoid schizophrenia
b. disorganized schizophrenia
c. catatonic schizophrenia
d. chronic schizophrenia

____ 15. Psychoanalysts think that schizophrenic people use what mechanism to return to the oral stage?
a. rationalization
b. repression
c. regression
d. suppression

Answers

1. C
2. C
3. B
4. D
5. C
6. B
7. D
8. B
9. A
10. B
11. C
12. C
13. A
14. A
15. A

CHAPTER 13: METHODS OF THERAPY

QUESTIONS

1. What are the four essentials of psychotherapy?
2. How has treatment of psychological problems changed through history?
3. Who was Dorthea Dix?
4. According to psychodynamic therapies, what do psychological problems reflect?
5. According to Freud, what happens to internal conflicts?
6. What does Freud's psychodynamic therapy aim to modify?
7. What are the goals of psychoanalysis?
8. How is traditional psychoanalysis conducted?
9. Why is transference considered a key aspect of psychoanalysis?
10. What did Freud believe about dreams?
11. How do contemporary psychodynamic therapies differ from traditional psychoanalysis?
12. What do humanistic therapies focus on?
13. What did Carl Rogers believe about choices we make and where do psychological problems come from?
14. What does client-centered therapy aim to do?
15. What are the qualities of an effective client-centered therapist?
16. Where is client centered therapy often practiced?
17. What are the assumptions of Gestalt therapy?
18. What is a major difference between client-centered and Gestalt therapy?
19. What are three exercises used in Gestalt therapy?
20. How did Perls view dreams?
21. What does behavior therapy focus on?
22. What do behavior therapists help people do?
23. How do behavior therapists help clients gain insight?
24. How does systematic desensitization work?
25. What are self-efficacy expectations?
26. What does modeling rely on?
27. How does aversive conditioning work?
28. How does a token economy work?
29. What is an example of the method of successive approximations?
30. What behaviors has social skills training been used for?
31. What kinds of behaviors has biofeedback training been used?
32. What are the purposes and characteristics of a functional analysis of behavior?
33. What does cognitive therapy focus on and aim to change?
34. What does Beck's cognitive therapy encourage clients to do?
35. What are four cognitive errors that contribute to clients' miseries?
36. How did cognitive therapy help the engineer?
37. What behaviors did Beck change in himself?
38. What is the cognitive triad of depression?
39. How does Ellis confront his clients?
40. What are two of the most important irrational beliefs?
41. According to Ellis, what do people need less of and more of?
42. What are six advantages of group therapy?
43. What does couples therapy try to do?
44. What does family therapy try to teach?
45. What are five problems in conducting psychotherapy research?
46. What percentage of clients improved in Smith and Glass (1977) study depending on the type of therapy?
47. What kinds of people do best with psychodynamic and client-centered therapy?

48. With what kinds of disorders did therapy not work for?
49. What types of clients is behavior and cognitive therapy effective?
50. How does cognitive behavior therapy compare with drug therapy in treating anorexia and bulimia?
51. What questions should be asked about therapy effectiveness?
52. What are some reasons for lower rates of therapy participation among ethnic minorities?
53. What competence do therapists need to develop?
54. Why are African Americans, Asian Americans, and Latinos often reluctant to seek therapy?
55. On what body systems do antianxiety drugs work?
56. How do we know antianxiety drugs induce physical dependence?
57. What do antipsychotic drugs do to a person with schizophrenia?
58. How are antidepressant drugs believed to work?
59. What is Lithium used for and why do people discontinue its use?
60. What is ECT controversial?
61. What is the history and effects of prefrontal lobotomies?
62. What are the research findings comparing cognitive therapy and drugs on various disorders?
63. What are four methods cognitive behavior therapists suggest we can do to reverse the characteristics of depression?

VOCABULARY

1. antidepressant
2. asylum
3. aversive conditioning
4. behavior rehearsal
5. behavior therapy
6. biofeedback training
7. catharsis
8. client-centered therapy
9. cognitive therapy
10. ego analyst
11. electroconvulsive therapy (ECT)
12. empathic understanding
13. encounter group
14. family therapy
15. feedback
16. frame of reference
17. free association
18. functional analysis
19. genuineness
20. Gestalt therapy
21. hierarchy
22. interpretation
23. latent content
24. manifest content
25. meta-analysis
26. modeling
27. phallic symbol
28. prefrontal lobotomy
29. psychoanalysis
30. psychotherapy
31. rapid smoking
32. rational emotive behavior therapy
33. rebound anxiety
34. resistance
35. sedative psychosurgery
36. selective serotonin reuptake inhibitors (SSRIs)
37. self-monitoring
38. successive approximations
39. systematic desensitization
40. token economy
41. transference
42. unconditional positive regard
43. wish fulfillment

13 Methods of Therapy

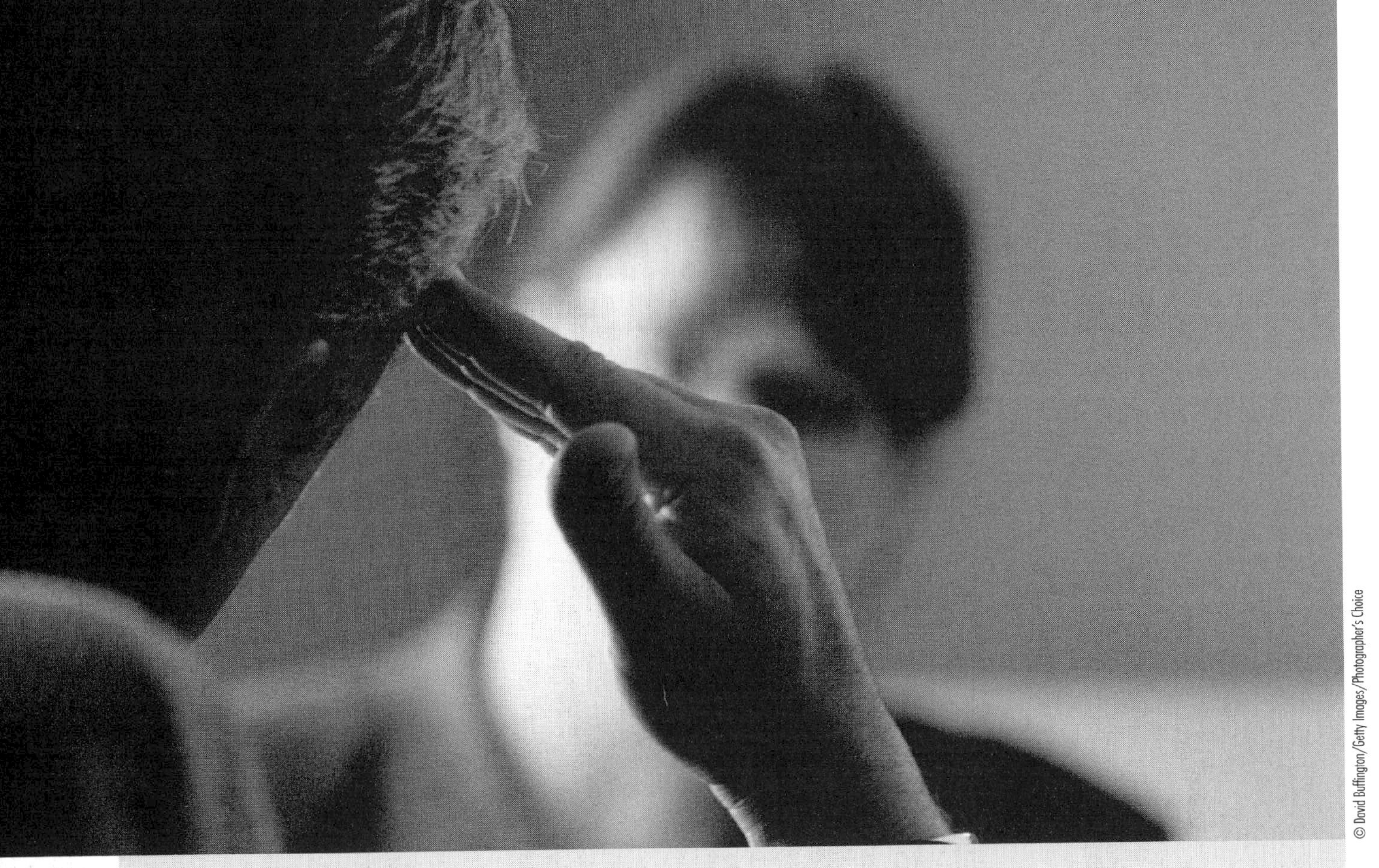
© David Buffington/Getty Images/Photographer's Choice

JASMINE IS A 19-year-old college sophomore. She has been crying almost without letup for several days. She feels that her life is falling apart. Her college dreams are in a shambles. She has brought shame upon her family. Thoughts of suicide have crossed her mind. She can barely drag herself out of bed in the morning. She is avoiding her friends. She can pinpoint some sources of stress in her life: a couple of poor grades, an argument with a boyfriend, friction with roommates. Still, her misery seemed to descend on her out of nowhere.

Jasmine is depressed—so depressed that her family and friends have finally prevailed on her to seek professional help. Had she broken her leg, her treatment by a qualified professional would have followed a fairly standard course. Yet treatment of psychological problems and disorders like depression may be approached from very different perspectives (Manji, 2003). Depending on the therapist Jasmine sees, she may be doing the following:

- Lying on a couch talking about anything that pops into her awareness and exploring the possible meaning of a recurrent dream.
- Sitting face to face with a warm, gentle therapist who accepts Jasmine as she is and expresses faith in Jasmine's ability to make the right decisions for herself.
- Listening to a frank, straightforward therapist assert that Jasmine is depressing herself with her self-defeating attitudes and perfectionist beliefs.
- Taking antidepressant medication.
- Participating in some combination of these approaches.

These methods, although different, all represent methods of therapy. In this chapter we explore various methods of psychotherapy and biological therapy.

WHAT IS THERAPY? THE SEARCH FOR A "SWEET OBLIVIOUS ANTIDOTE"[1]?

psychotherapy
a systematic interaction between a therapist and a client that brings psychological principles to bear on influencing the client's thoughts, feelings, or behavior to help that client overcome abnormal behavior or adjust to problems in living.

There are many kinds of psychotherapy, but they all have certain common characteristics. **Psychotherapy** is a systematic interaction between a therapist and a client that applies psychological principles to affect the client's thoughts, feelings, or behavior in order to help the client overcome psychological disorders, adjust to problems in living, or develop as an individual.

Quite a mouthful? True. But note the essentials:

1. *Systematic interaction:* Psychotherapy is a systematic interaction between a client and a therapist. The therapist's theoretical point of view interacts with the client's to determine how the therapist and client relate to each other.
2. *Psychological principles:* Psychotherapy is based on psychological theory and research in areas such as personality, learning, motivation, and emotion.
3. *Thoughts, feelings, and behavior:* Psychotherapy influences clients' thoughts, feelings, and behavior. It can be aimed at any or all of these aspects of human psychology.
4. *Psychological disorders, adjustment problems, and personal growth:* Psychotherapy is often used with people who have psychological disorders. Other people seek help in adjusting to problems such as shyness, weight problems, or loss of a spouse. Still other clients want to learn more about themselves and to reach their full potential as individuals, parents, or creative artists.

The History of Therapies

Historically speaking, "treatments" of psychological disorders often reflected demonological thinking. Because of this belief, treatment tended to involve cruel practices such as exorcism and death by hanging or burning. Some people who could not meet the demands of everyday life were tossed into prisons. Others begged in the streets, stole food, or became prostitutes. A few found their way to monasteries or other retreats that offered a kind word and some support. Generally speaking, they died early.

asylum
(uh-SIGH-lum). An institution for the care of the mentally ill.

Asylums **Asylums** originated in European monasteries. They were the first institutions meant primarily for people with psychological disorders. But their function was warehousing, not treatment. Their inmate populations mushroomed until the stresses created by noise, overcrowding, and disease aggravated the problems they were meant to ease. Inmates were frequently chained and beaten.

The word *bedlam* derives from St. Mary's of *Bethlehem,* the London asylum that opened its gates in 1547. Here unfortunate people with psychological disorders were chained, whipped, and allowed to lie in their own waste. And here the ladies and gentlemen of the British upper class might stroll on a lazy afternoon to be amused by the inmates' antics. The price of admission was one penny.

Humanitarian reform movements began in the 18th century. In Paris, the physician Philippe Pinel unchained the patients at La Bicêtre. Rather than run amok, as had been feared, most patients profited from kindness and freedom. Many eventually reentered society. Later movements to reform institutions were led by the Quaker William Tuke in England and by Dorothea Dix in America.

Mental Hospitals In the United States mental hospitals gradually replaced asylums. In the mid-1950s more than a million people resided in state, county, Veterans Administration, or private facilities. The mental hospital's function is treatment, not

[1]The phrase is from Shakespeare's *Macbeth.*

■ **The Unchaining of the Patients at La Bicêtre.** Philippe Pinel sparked the humanitarian reform movement by unchaining the patients at this asylum in Paris.

THE CLINICAL FILE

Dorothea Dix

Dorothea Dix (1802–1887) could be said to have spent much of her adult life cutting against the grain. In the field of psychology, Dix is best known for her efforts to create a decent mental hospital system, primarily in New Jersey. At the time, 160 years ago, there were no such hospitals, and individuals with severe psychological disorders were locked up in jails or poorhouses or placed with anyone who was willing to care for them.

In 1844 Dix traveled the state to document the squalor in which troubled people were forced to live. People lived in filth, were chained and beaten. At the Morris County Poor House, they were locked up in the cellar. In Essex County, they were thrown into jail with their children. The keeper at the Salem Country Poor House boasted of how he handled one inmate:

"I knew I must master him now or never: I . . . caught a stick of wood . . . and laid upon him until he cried for quarters: I beat him long enough to make him know I was his master, and now he is too much afraid of a thrashing to attack me; but you had better stand off ma'am, for he won't fear you."

Dix's report touched off a hot debate in the state legislature. She prevailed, and the state's first mental hospital was built in Ewing Township, where it stands to this day.

Dix is as well known in the field of nursing, which was her profession. When the Civil War broke out, she volunteered at the age of 59 and was placed in charge of all women nurses at Union army hospitals. Female nurses were not widely accepted at the time, and Dix sought to prove that women could do the job as well as men. She recruited nurses to counter the stereotype of female nurses as young women who were seeking to marry patients or doctors. For that reason, she chose plain-looking women who were at least 30 years old. She required that they dress in modest brown or black skirts without hoops, which were the fashion of the day. She also forbade jewelry. She came to be called "Dragon Dix" by her superiors because she frequently fought with the military bureaucracy and would obtain nursing supplies anywhere she could find them, from the army or not.

It may seem ironic today that a "reformer" caused her nursing staff to dress so modestly and avoided hiring young, attractive women. However, Dix's methods were important in opening the gates of the nursing profession to women. Today, of course, the great majority of nurses in the United States are women–women of all ages and appearance.

After the war, Dix returned to fight for the welfare of people with psychological disorders.

warehousing. Still, because of high patient populations and understaffing, many patients received little attention. Even today, with somewhat improved conditions, one psychiatrist may be responsible for the welfare of several hundred residents on a weekend when other staff members are absent.

The Community Mental Health Movement Since the 1960s, efforts have been made to maintain people with serious psychological disorders in their communities. Community mental health centers attempt to maintain new patients as outpatients and to serve patients who have been released from mental hospitals. Today most people with chronic psychological disorders live in the community, not the hospital. Social critics note that many people who had resided in hospitals for decades were suddenly discharged to "home" communities that seemed foreign and forbidding to them. Many do not receive adequate follow-up care. Many join the ranks of the homeless (Drury, 2003; Gulcur et al., 2003).

PSYCHODYNAMIC THERAPIES: DIGGING DEEP WITHIN

Psychodynamic therapies are based on the thinking of Sigmund Freud, the founder of psychodynamic theory. They assume that psychological problems reflect early childhood experiences and internal conflicts. According to Freud, these conflicts involve the shifting of psychic, or libidinal, energy among the three psychic structures—the id, ego, and superego. These shifts of psychic energy determine our behavior. When primitive urges threaten to break through from the id or when the superego floods us with excessive guilt, defenses are established and distress is created. Freud's psychodynamic therapy method—psychoanalysis—aims to modify the flow of energy among these structures, largely to bulwark the ego against the torrents of energy loosed by the id and the superego. With impulses and feelings of guilt and shame placed under greater control, clients are freer to develop adaptive behavior.

Traditional Psychoanalysis: "Where Id Was, There Shall Ego Be"

Canst thou not minister to a mind diseas'd,
Pluck out from the memory a rooted sorrow,
Raze out the written troubles of the brain,
And with some sweet oblivious antidote
Cleanse the stuff'd bosom of that perilous stuff
Which weighs upon the heart?
Shakespeare, *Macbeth*

In this passage, Macbeth asks a physician to help Lady Macbeth after she has gone mad. In the play, her madness is caused partly by events—namely, her role in murders designed to seat her husband on the throne of Scotland. There are also hints of mysterious, deeply rooted problems, such as conflicts about infertility.

If Lady Macbeth's physician had been a traditional psychoanalyst, he might have asked her to lie on a couch in a slightly darkened room. He would have sat behind her and encouraged her to talk about anything that came to mind, no matter how trivial, no matter how personal. To avoid interfering with her self-exploration, he might have said little or nothing for session after session. That would have been par for the course. A traditional **psychoanalysis** can extend for months, even years.

psychoanalysis
Freud's method of psychotherapy.

Psychoanalysis is the clinical method devised by Freud for plucking "from the memory a rooted sorrow," for razing "out the written troubles of the brain." It aims to provide *insight* into the conflicts that are presumed to lie at the roots of a person's problems. Insight means many things, including knowledge of the experiences that lead to conflicts and maladaptive behavior, recognition of unconscious feelings and conflicts, and conscious evaluation of one's thoughts, feelings, and behavior.

Psychoanalysis also aims to help the client express feelings and urges that have been repressed. By so doing, Freud believed that the client spilled forth the psychic energy that had been repressed by conflicts and guilt. He called this spilling forth **catharsis**. Catharsis would provide relief by alleviating some of the forces assaulting the ego.

catharsis
(cuh-THAR-sis) In psychoanalysis, the expression of repressed feelings and impulses to allow the release of the psychic energy associated with them.

Freud was also fond of saying, "Where id was, there shall ego be." In part, he meant that psychoanalysis could shed light on the inner workings of the mind. He also sought to replace impulsive and defensive behavior with coping behavior. In this way, for example, a man with a phobia for knives might discover that he had been repressing the urge to harm someone who had taken advantage of him. He might also find ways to confront the person verbally.

Free Association Early in his career as a therapist, Freud found that hypnosis allowed his clients to focus on repressed conflicts and talk about them. The relaxed "trance state" provided by hypnosis seemed to allow clients to "break through" to topics of which they would otherwise be unaware. Freud also found, however, that many clients denied the accuracy of this material once they were out of the trance. Other clients found them to be premature and painful. Freud therefore turned to **free association**, a more gradual method of breaking through the walls of defense that block a client's insight into unconscious processes.

free association
in psychoanalysis, the uncensored uttering of all thoughts that come to mind.

In free association, the client is made comfortable—for example, lying on a couch—and asked to talk about any topic that comes to mind. No thought is to be censored—that is the basic rule. Psychoanalysts ask their clients to wander "freely" from topic to topic, but they do not believe that the process occurring *within* the client is fully free. Repressed impulses clamor for release.

The ego persists in trying to repress unacceptable impulses and threatening conflicts. As a result, clients might show **resistance** to recalling and discussing threatening ideas. A client about to entertain such thoughts might claim, "My mind is blank." The client might accuse the analyst of being demanding or inconsiderate. He or she might "forget" the next appointment when threatening material is about to surface.

resistance
the tendency to block the free expression of impulses and primitive ideas—a reflection of the defense mechanism of repression.

■ **A View of Freud's Consulting Room.** Freud would sit in a chair by the head of the couch while a client free-associated. The basic rule of free association is that no thought is censored. Freud did not believe that free association was really "free"; he assumed that significant feelings would rise to the surface and demand expression.

The therapist observes the dynamic struggle between the compulsion to utter certain thoughts and the client's resistance to uttering them. Through discreet remarks, the analyst subtly tips the balance in favor of utterance. A gradual process of self-discovery and self-insight ensues. Now and then the analyst offers an **interpretation** of an utterance, showing how it suggests resistance or deep-seated feelings and conflicts.

interpretation
an explanation of a client's utterance according to psychoanalytic theory.

transference
responding to one person (such as a spouse or the psychoanalyst) in a way that is similar to the way one responded to another person (such as a parent) in childhood.

Transference Freud believed that clients not only responded to him as an individual but also in ways that reflected their attitudes and feelings toward other people in their lives. He labeled this process **transference**. For example, a young woman client might respond to him as a father figure and displace her feelings toward her father onto Freud, perhaps seeking affection and wisdom. A young man could also see Freud as a father figure, but rather than wanting affection from Freud, he might view Freud as a rival, responding to Freud in terms of his own unresolved Oedipal complex.

Analyzing and working through transference has been considered a key aspect of psychoanalysis. Freud believed that clients reenact their childhood conflicts with their parents when they are in therapy. Clients might thus transfer the feelings of anger, love, or jealousy they felt toward their own parents onto the analyst. Childhood conflicts often involve unresolved feelings of love, anger, or rejection. A client may interpret a suggestion by the therapist as a criticism and see it as a devastating blow, transferring feelings of self-hatred that he had repressed because his parents had rejected him in childhood. Transference can also distort clients' relationships with other people here and now, such as relationships with spouses or employers. The following therapeutic dialogue illustrates the way in which an analyst may interpret a client's inability to communicate his needs to his wife as a function of transference. The purpose is to provide his client, a Mr. Arianes, with insight into how his relationship with his wife has been colored by his childhood relationship with his mother:

Arianes: I think you've got it there, Doc. We weren't communicating. I wouldn't tell [my wife] what was wrong or what I wanted from her. Maybe I expected her to understand me without saying anything.

Therapist: Like the expectations a child has of its mother.

Arianes: Not my mother!

Therapist: Oh?

Arianes: No, I always thought she had too many troubles of her own to pay attention to mine. I remember once I got hurt on my bike and came to her all bloodied up. When she saw me she got mad and yelled at me for making more trouble for her when she already had her hands full with my father.

Therapist: Do you remember how you felt then?

Arianes: I can't remember, but I know that after that I never brought my troubles to her again.

Therapist: How old were you?

Arianes: Nine, I know that because I got that bike for my ninth birthday. It was a little too big for me still, that's why I got hurt on it.

Therapist: Perhaps you carried this attitude into your marriage.

Arianes: What attitude?

Therapist: The feeling that your wife, like your mother, would be unsympathetic to your difficulties. That there was no point in telling her about your experiences because she was too preoccupied or too busy to care.

Arianes: But she's so different from my mother. I come first with her.

Therapist: On one level you know that. On another, deeper level there may well be the fear that people—or maybe only women, or maybe only women you're close to—are all the same, and you can't take a chance at being rejected again in your need.

Arianes: Maybe you're right, Doc, but all that was so long ago, and I should be over that by now.

Therapist: That's not the way the mind works. If a shock, or a disappointment is strong enough it can permanently freeze our picture of ourselves and our expectations of the world. The rest of us grows up—that is, we let ourselves learn about life from experience and from what we see, hear, or read of the experiences of others, but that one area where we really got hurt stays unchanged. So what I mean when I say you might be carrying that attitude into your relationship with your wife is that when it comes to your hopes of being understood and catered to when you feel hurt or abused by life, you still feel very much like that nine-year-old boy who was rebuffed in his need and gave up hope that anyone would or could respond to him. (Basch, 1980, pp. 29–30)

Dream Analysis It is true that some therapists interpret clients' dreams. Freud often asked clients to jot down their dreams upon waking so that they could discuss them in therapy. Freud considered dreams the "royal road to the unconscious." He believed that the content of dreams is determined by unconscious processes as well as by the events of the day. Unconscious impulses tend to be expressed in dreams as a form of **wish fulfillment**.

But unacceptable sexual and aggressive impulses are likely to be displaced onto objects and situations that reflect the client's era and culture. These objects become symbols of unconscious wishes. For example, long, narrow dream objects might be **phallic symbols**, but whether the symbol takes the form of a spear, rifle, stick shift, or spacecraft partially reflects the dreamer's cultural background.

In Freud's theory, the perceived content of a dream is called its visible, or **manifest content**. Its presumed hidden or symbolic content is its **latent content**. If a man dreams he is flying, flying is the manifest content of the dream. Freud usually interpreted flying as symbolic of erection, so concerns about sexual potency might make up the latent content of the dream.

wish fulfillment
a primitive method used by the id to attempt to gratify basic instincts.

phallic symbol
a sign that represents the penis.

manifest content
in psychodynamic theory, the reported content of dreams.

latent content
in psychodynamic theory, the symbolized or underlying content of dreams.

Modern Psychodynamic Approaches

Some psychoanalysts adhere faithfully to Freud's techniques. They engage in protracted therapy that continues to rely heavily on free association, interpretation of dreams, and other traditional methods. In recent years, however, more modern forms of psychodynamic therapy have been devised. Modern psychodynamic therapy is briefer and less intense and makes treatment available to clients who do not have the time or money for long-term therapy. Many modern psychodynamic therapists do not believe that prolonged therapy is needed or justifiable in terms of the ratio of cost to benefits.

Some modern psychodynamic therapies continue to focus on revealing unconscious material and breaking through psychological defenses. Nevertheless, they differ from traditional psychoanalysis in several ways (Prochaska & Norcross, 2003). One is that the client and therapist usually sit face to face (the client does not lie on a couch). The therapist is usually directive. That is, modern therapists often suggest helpful behavior instead of focusing on insight alone. Finally, there is usually more focus on the ego as the "executive" of personality and less emphasis on the id. For this reason, many modern psychodynamic therapists are considered **ego analysts**.

ego analyst
a psychodynamically oriented therapist who focuses on the conscious, coping behavior of the ego instead of the hypothesized, unconscious functioning of the id.

Many of Freud's followers, the "second generation" of psychoanalysts—from Jung and Adler to Horney and Erikson—believed that Freud had placed too much emphasis on sexual and aggressive impulses and underestimated the role of the ego. For example, Freud aimed to establish conditions under which clients could spill forth psychic energy and eventually shore up the ego. Erikson, in contrast, spoke to clients directly about their values and concerns, encouraging them to develop desired traits and behavior patterns. Even Freud's daughter, the psychoanalyst Anna Freud (1895–1982), was more concerned with the ego than with unconscious forces and conflicts.

HUMANISTIC THERAPIES: STRENGTHENING THE SELF

Psychodynamic therapies focus on internal conflicts and unconscious processes. Humanistic therapies focus on the quality of the client's subjective, conscious experience (Cain & Seeman, 2002). Traditional psychoanalysis focuses on early childhood experiences. Humanistic therapies usually focus on what clients are experiencing "here and now."

These differences, however, are mainly a matter of emphasis. The past has a way of influencing current thoughts, feelings, and behavior. Carl Rogers, the originator of client-centered therapy, believed that childhood experiences gave rise to the conditions of worth that troubled his clients here and now. He and Fritz Perls, the originator of Gestalt therapy, recognized that early incorporation of other people's values often leads clients to "disown" parts of their own personalities.

Client-Centered Therapy: Removing Roadblocks to Self-Actualization

Rogers believed that we are free to make choices and control our destinies, despite the burdens of the past. He also believed that we have natural tendencies toward health, growth, and fulfillment. Psychological problems arise from roadblocks placed in the path of self-actualization—that is, what Rogers believed was an inborn tendency to strive to realize one's potential. If, when we are young, other people only approve of us when we are doing what they want us to do, we may learn to disown the parts of ourselves to which they object. We may learn to be seen but not heard—not even by ourselves. As a result, we may experience stress and discomfort and the feeling that we—or the world—are not real.

client-centered therapy Carl Rogers's method of psychotherapy, which emphasizes the creation of a warm, therapeutic atmosphere that frees clients to engage in self-exploration and self-expression.

Client-centered therapy aims to provide insight into the parts of us that we have disowned so that we can feel whole. It creates a warm, therapeutic atmosphere

THE CLINICAL FILE

Carl Rogers

He spent his early years in a wealthy Chicago suburb, where he attended school with Ernest Hemingway and Frank Lloyd Wright's children. His family, with its six children, was religious and close-knit. His father viewed such activities as smoking, drinking, playing cards, and going to the movies as questionable. It was all right to be tolerant of them, but relationships with those who engaged in them were discouraged. When Carl Rogers was 12, his family moved to a farm farther from the city to protect the children from such unwholesome influences.

Rogers (1902–1987) took refuge in books and developed an interest in science. His first college major was agriculture. During a student visit to Peking in 1922, he was exposed for the first time to people from different ethnic backgrounds. He wrote his parents to proclaim his independence from their conservative views. Shortly thereafter he developed an ulcer and had to be hospitalized.

Rogers then attended New York's Union Theological Seminary with the goal of becoming a minister. At the same time he took courses in psychology and education across the street at Columbia University. After a couple of years he came to believe that psychology might be a better way of helping people, so he transferred to Columbia. Perhaps in response to his parents' efforts to "protect" him from other ways of thinking, Rogers developed a form of therapy–client-centered therapy–intended to help people get in touch with their genuine feelings and pursue their own interests, regardless of other people's wishes.

that encourages self-exploration and self-expression. The therapist's acceptance of the client is thought to foster self-acceptance and self-esteem. Self-acceptance frees the client to make choices that develop his or her unique potential.

Client-centered therapy is nondirective. It is true that the client takes the lead, stating and exploring problems. An effective client-centered therapist has several qualities:

- ***Unconditional positive regard:*** Respect for clients as human beings with unique values and goals.
- ***Empathic understanding:*** Recognition of the client's experiences and feelings. Therapists view the world through the client's **frame of reference** by setting aside their own values and listening closely.
- ***Genuineness:*** Openness and honesty in responding to the client. Client-centered therapists must be able to tolerate differentness because they believe that every client is different in important ways.

unconditional positive regard
acceptance of the value of another person, although not necessarily acceptance of everything the person does.

empathic understanding
(em-PATH-ick). Ability to perceive a client's feelings from the client's frame of reference. A quality of the good client-centered therapist.

frame of reference
one's unique patterning of perceptions and attitudes, according to which one evaluates events.

genuineness
recognition and open expression of the therapist's own feelings.

The following excerpt from a therapy session shows how Carl Rogers uses empathetic understanding and paraphrases a client's (Jill's) feelings. His goal is to help her recognize feelings that she has partially disowned:

Jill: I'm having a lot of problems dealing with my daughter. She's 20 years old; she's in college; I'm having a lot of trouble letting her go. . . . And I have a lot of guilt feelings about her; I have a real need to hang on to her.

C.R.: A need to hang on so you can kind of make up for the things you feel guilty about. Is that part of it?

Jill: There's a lot of that. . . . Also, she's been a real friend to me, and filled my life. . . . And it's very hard. . . . a lot of empty places now that she's not with me.

C.R.: The old vacuum, sort of, when she's not there.

Jill: Yes. Yes. I also would like to be the kind of mother that could be strong and say, you know, "Go and have a good life," and this is really hard for me, to do that.

C.R.: It's very hard to give up something that's been so precious in your life, but also something that I guess has caused you pain when you mentioned guilt.

Jill: Yeah. And I'm aware that I have some anger toward her that I don't always get what I want. I have needs that are not met. And, uh, I don't feel I have a right to those needs. You know. . . . she's a daughter; she's not my mother. Though sometimes I feel as if I'd like her to mother me . . . it's very difficult for me to ask for that and have a right to it.

■ **Client-Centered Therapy.** By showing the qualities of unconditional positive regard, empathic understanding, genuineness, and congruence, client-centered therapists create an atmosphere in which clients can explore their feelings.

C.R.: So, it may be unreasonable, but still, when she doesn't meet your needs, it makes you mad.

Jill: Yeah I get very angry, very angry with her.

C.R.: (*Pauses*) You're also feeling a little tension at this point, I guess.

Jill: Yeah. Yeah. A lot of conflict. . . . (C.R.: M-hm.) A lot of pain.

C.R: A lot of pain. Can you say anything more about what that's about? (Farber et al., 1996, pp. 74–75)

Client-centered therapy is practiced widely in college and university counseling centers, not just to help students experiencing, say, anxieties or depression but also to help them make decisions. Many college students have not yet made career choices or wonder whether they should become involved with particular people or in sexual activity. Client-centered therapists do not tell clients what to do. Instead, they help clients arrive at their own decisions.

Gestalt Therapy: Getting It Together

gestalt therapy
Fritz Perls's form of psychotherapy, which attempts to integrate conflicting parts of the personality through directive methods designed to help clients perceive their whole selves.

Gestalt therapy was originated by Fritz Perls (1893–1970). Like client-centered therapy, Gestalt therapy assumes that people disown parts of themselves that might meet with social disapproval or rejection. People also don social masks, pretending to be things that they are not. Therapy aims to help individuals integrate conflicting parts of their personality. Perls used the term *Gestalt* to signify his interest in giving the conflicting parts of the personality an integrated form or shape. He aimed to have his clients become aware of inner conflict, accept the reality of conflict rather than deny it or keep it repressed, and make productive choices despite misgivings and fears. People in conflict frequently find it difficult to make choices, and Perls firmly challenged them to do so.

Courtesy The Gestalt Journal Press

■ **Fritz Perls.** Known to friends, clients, and peers alike as "Fritz," Perls put clients through structured experiences to help them understand how their feelings might be in conflict. He believed that people had to accept responsibility for making choices in their lives.

Although Perls's ideas about conflicting personality elements owe much to psychodynamic theory, his form of therapy, unlike psychoanalysis, focuses on the here and now. In Gestalt therapy, clients perform exercises to heighten their awareness of their current feelings and behavior, rather than exploring the past. Perls also believed, along with Rogers, that people are free to make choices and to direct their personal growth. But the charismatic and forceful Perls was unlike the gentle and accepting Rogers in temperament (Prochaska & Norcross, 2003). Thus, unlike client-centered therapy, Gestalt therapy is highly directive. The therapist leads the client through planned experiences.

There are a number of Gestalt exercises and games, including the following:

1. *The dialogue:* In this game, the client undertakes verbal confrontations between opposing wishes and ideas to heighten awareness of internal conflict. An example of these clashing personality elements is "top dog" and "underdog." One's top dog might conservatively suggest, "Don't take chances. Stick with what you have or you might lose it all." One's frustrated underdog might then rise up and assert, "You never try anything. How will you ever get out of this rut if you don't take on new challenges?" Heightened awareness of the elements of conflict can clear the path toward resolution, perhaps through a compromise of some kind.
2. *I take responsibility:* Clients end statements about themselves by adding, "and I take responsibility for it."
3. *Playing the projection:* Clients role-play people with whom they are in conflict, expressing, for example, the ideas of their parents.

Body language also provides insight into conflicting feelings. Clients might be instructed to attend to the ways in which they furrow their eyebrows and tense their facial muscles when they express certain ideas. In this way, they often find that their body language asserts feelings they have been denying in their spoken statements.

The following excerpt from a therapy session with a client named Max shows how Perls would make clients take responsibility for what they experience. One of his techniques is to show how clients are treating something they are doing (a "verb") like something that is just out there and beyond their control (a "noun"):

Max: I feel the tenseness in my stomach and in my hands.
Perls: *The* tenseness. Here we've got a noun. Now *the* tenseness is a noun. Now change the noun, the thing, into a verb.
Max: I am tense. My hands are tense.
Perls: Your hands are tense. They have nothing to do with you.
Max: I am tense.
Perls: You are tense. How are you tense? What are you doing?
Max: I am tensing myself.
Perls: That's it. (Perls, 1971, p. 115)

Once Max understands that he is tensing himself and takes responsibility for it, he can choose to stop tensing himself. The tenseness is no longer something out there that is victimizing him; it is something he is doing to himself.

Psychodynamic theory views dreams as the "royal road to the unconscious." Perls saw the content of dreams as representing disowned parts of the personality. Perls would often ask clients to role-play elements of their dreams in order to get in touch with these parts of their personality.

BEHAVIOR THERAPY: ADJUSTMENT IS WHAT YOU DO

Psychodynamic and humanistic forms of therapy tend to focus on what people think and feel. Behavior therapists tend to focus on what people do. **Behavior therapy**—also called *behavior modification*—applies principles of learning to directly promote desired behavioral changes (Rachman, 2000). Behavior therapists rely heavily on principles of conditioning and observational learning. They help clients discontinue self-defeating behavior patterns such as overeating, smoking, and phobic avoidance of harmless stimuli. They also help clients acquire adaptive behavior patterns such as the social skills required to start social relationships or say no to insistent salespeople. In both cases, they may use specific procedures—telling their clients what to do.

behavior therapy systematic application of the principles of learning to the direct modification of a client's problem behaviors.

Behavior therapists may help clients gain "insight" into maladaptive behavior in the sense of fostering awareness of the circumstances in which it occurs. They do not foster insight in the psychoanalytic sense of unearthing the childhood origins of problems and the symbolic meanings of maladaptive behavior. Behavior therapists, like other therapists, may also build warm, therapeutic relationships with clients, but they see the efficacy of behavior therapy as deriving from specific, learning-based procedures (Rachman, 2000). They insist that their methods be established by experimentation and that the outcomes be assessed in terms of measurable behavior. In this section we consider some frequently used behavior-therapy techniques.

Fear-Reduction Methods

Many people seek therapy because of fears and phobias that interfere with their functioning. This is one of the areas in which behavior therapy has made great inroads. These include flooding, systematic desensitization, and modeling.

Systematic Desensitization Adam has a phobia for receiving injections. His behavior therapist treats him as he reclines in a comfortable padded chair. In a state of deep muscle relaxation, Adam observes slides projected on a screen. A slide of a nurse holding a needle has just been shown three times, 30 seconds at a time. Each time Adam has shown no anxiety. So now a slightly more discomforting slide is shown: one of the nurse aiming the needle toward someone's bare arm. After 15 seconds, our armchair adventurer notices twinges of discomfort and raises a finger as a signal (speaking might disturb his relaxation). The projector operator turns off the light, and Adam spends 2 minutes imagining his "safe scene"—lying on a beach beneath the tropical sun. Then the slide is shown again. This time Adam views it for 30 seconds before feeling anxiety.

systematic desensitization Wolpe's method for reducing fears by associating a hierarchy of images of fear-evoking stimuli with deep muscle relaxation.

hierarchy an arrangement of stimuli according to the amount of fear they evoke.

Adam is in effect confronting his fear while lying in a recliner and relaxing. Adam is undergoing **systematic desensitization**, a method for reducing phobic responses originated by psychiatrist Joseph Wolpe (1915–1997). Systematic desensitization is a gradual process in which the client learns to handle increasingly disturbing stimuli while anxiety to each one is being counterconditioned. About 10 to 20 stimuli are arranged in a sequence, or **hierarchy**, according to their capacity to elicit anxiety. In imagination or by being shown photos, the client travels gradually up through this hierarchy, approaching the target behavior. In Adam's case, the target behavior was the ability to receive an injection without undue anxiety.

Wolpe developed systematic desensitization on the assumption that anxiety responses, like other behaviors, are learned or conditioned (Rachman, 2000). He reasoned that they can be unlearned by means of counterconditioning or extinction. In counterconditioning, a response that is incompatible with anxiety is made to appear under conditions that usually elicit anxiety. Muscle relaxation is incompatible with anxiety. For this reason, Adam's therapist is teaching him to relax in the presence of (usually) anxiety-evoking slides of needles.

Remaining in the presence of phobic imagery, rather than running away from it, is also likely to enhance self-efficacy expectations (Galassi, 1988). Self-efficacy expectations are negatively correlated with levels of adrenaline in the bloodstream (Bandura et al., 1985). Raising clients' self-efficacy expectations thus may help lower their adrenaline levels and reduce their feelings of nervousness.

Overcoming Fear of Flying. One way behavior therapists help clients overcome phobias is by having them gradually approach the feared object or situation while they remain relaxed. This woman is gradually reducing her fear of being in an airplane and flying.

Modeling **Modeling** relies on observational learning. In this method clients observe, and then imitate, people who approach and cope with the objects or situations that the clients fear. Bandura and his colleagues (1969) found that modeling worked as well as systematic desensitization—and more rapidly—in reducing fear of snakes. Like systematic desensitization, modeling is likely to increase self-efficacy expectations in coping with feared stimuli.

modeling
a behavior-therapy technique in which a client observes and imitates a person who approaches and copes with feared objects or situations.

Aversive Conditioning

Many people also seek behavior therapy because they want to break bad habits, such as smoking, excessive drinking, nail biting, and the like. One behavior-therapy approach to helping people do so is **aversive conditioning**. Aversive conditioning is a controversial procedure in which painful or aversive stimuli are paired with unwanted impulses, such as desire for a cigarette or desire to engage in antisocial behavior, in order to make the impulse less appealing. For example, to help people control alcohol intake, tastes of different alcoholic beverages can be paired with drug-induced nausea and vomiting or with electric shock.

aversive conditioning
a behavior-therapy technique in which undesired responses are inhibited by pairing repugnant or offensive stimuli with them.

Aversive conditioning has been used with problems as diverse as cigarette smoking, sexual abuse, and retarded children's self-injurious behavior. **Rapid smoking** is an aversive-conditioning method designed to help smokers quit. In this method, the would-be quitter inhales every 6 seconds. In another method the hose of a hair dryer is hooked up to a chamber containing several lit cigarettes. Smoke is blown into the quitter's face as he or she also smokes a cigarette. A third method uses branching pipes so that the smoker draws in smoke from several

rapid smoking
an aversive conditioning method for quitting smoking in which the smoker inhales every 6 seconds, thus rendering once-desirable cigarette smoke aversive.

THE CLINICAL FILE

And What If a (Virtual) Spider Sat Down Beside Her? Use of Virtual Reality in Desensitization

Some psychologists are now conducting desensitization to phobic stimuli by means of virtual reality. In the case of using virtual reality, clients don goggles and headphones such that they perceive themselves to be in the fearful setting, although they are "safe" in the office or laboratory of the therapist. Barbara Rothbaum and her colleagues (2001, 2002) have used the method to treat clients with problems such as post-traumatic stress due to combat and fear of flying. David Ready, one of Rothbaum's colleagues, notes that "You're not watching something, you're in something. All you see is what's in the goggles and all you hear is what's on the headphones" (cited in Robbins, 2000).

Virtual reality was also used to help desensitize Joanne Cartwright, who had a debilitating phobia for spiders. "I washed my truck every night before I went to work in case there were webs," says Cartwright (cited in Robbins, 2000). "I put all my clothes in plastic bags and taped duct tape around my doors so spiders couldn't get in. I thought I was going to have a mental breakdown. I wasn't living." Twelve sessions of desensitization by means of virtual reality apparently changed her life. "I'm amazed," notes Cartwright, "because I am doing all this stuff I could never do—camping, hunting and hiking."

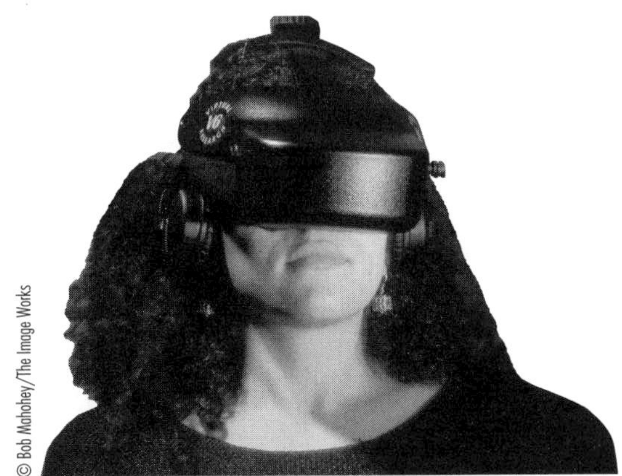

© Bob Mahoney/The Image Works

■ **Use of Virtual Reality in Psychotherapy.** Psychologists are using virtual reality to help clients cope with pain, fears, and other psychological problems. This woman's "reality" is what she sees through her goggles and what she hears in her headphones. She is being gradually desensitized to a series of images that represent her phobia.

© Lester Sloan/Woodfin Camp & Associates

■ **Aversive Conditioning.** In aversive conditioning, unwanted behaviors take on a noxious quality as a result of being repeatedly paired with aversive stimuli. Overexposure is making cigarette smoke aversive to this smoker.

cigarettes at the same time. In these methods, overexposure makes once-desirable cigarette smoke aversive. The quitter becomes motivated to avoid, rather than seek, cigarettes. Therefore, smoking can be a way to stop smoking. However, interest in aversive conditioning for quitting smoking has waned because of side effects such as raising blood pressure and the availability of nicotine-replacement techniques.

In one study of aversive conditioning in the treatment of alcoholism, 63% of the 685 people treated remained abstinent for one year afterward, and about a third remained abstinent for at least 3 years (Wiens & Menustik, 1983). It may seem ironic that punitive aversive stimulation is sometimes used to stop children from punishing themselves, but people sometimes hurt themselves in order to obtain sympathy and attention. If self-injury leads to more pain than anticipated and no sympathy, it might be discontinued.

Operant Conditioning Procedures

We usually prefer to relate to people who smile at us rather than ignore us and to take courses in which we do well rather than fail. We tend to repeat behavior that is reinforced. Behavior that is not reinforced tends to become extinguished. Behavior therapists have used these principles of operant conditioning with psychotic patients as well as with clients with milder problems.

The staff at one mental hospital was at a loss about how to encourage withdrawn schizophrenic patients to eat regularly. Ayllon and Haughton (1962) observed that staff members were making the problem worse by coaxing patients into the dining room and even feeding them. Staff attention apparently reinforced the patients' lack of cooperation. Some rules were changed. Patients who did not arrive at the dining hall within 30 minutes after serving were locked out. Staff could not interact with patients at mealtime. With uncooperative behavior no longer reinforced, patients quickly changed their eating habits. Then patients were required to pay one penny to enter the dining hall. Pennies were earned by interacting with other patients and showing other socially appropriate behaviors. These target behaviors also became more frequent.

Health professionals are concerned as to whether people who are, or have been, dependent on alcohol can exercise control over their drinking. One study showed that rewards for remaining abstinent from alcohol can exert a powerful effect (Petry et al., 2000). In the study, one group of alcohol-dependent veterans was given a standard treatment while another group received the treatment *plus* the chance to win prizes for remaining alcohol-free, as measured by a Breathalyzer test. By the end of the 8-week treatment period, 84% of the veterans who could win prizes remained in the program, as compared with 22% of the standard treatment group. The prizes had an average value of $200, far less than what alcohol-related absenteeism from work and other responsibilities can cost.

token economy
a controlled environment in which people are reinforced for desired behaviors with tokens (such as poker chips) that may be exchanged for privileges.

The Token Economy Many psychiatric wards and hospitals now use **token economies** in which patients must use tokens such as poker chips to purchase TV viewing time, extra visits to the canteen, or a private room (Comaty et al., 2001). The tokens are reinforcements for productive activities such as making beds, brushing teeth, and socializing. Token economies have not eliminated all symptoms of schizophrenia but have enhanced patient activity and cooperation. Tokens have also been used to modify the behavior of children with conduct disorders.

successive approximations
in operant conditioning, a series of behaviors that gradually become more similar to a target behavior.

Successive Approximations The operant conditioning method of **successive approximations** is often used to help clients build good habits. Let us use a (not uncommon!) example: You want to study 3 hours each evening but can concentrate for only half an hour. Rather than attempting to increase your study time all at once, you could do so gradually by adding, say, 5 minutes each evening. After every hour or so of studying, you could reinforce yourself with 5 minutes of people-watching in a busy section of the library.

Social Skills Training In social skills training, behavior therapists decrease social anxiety and build social skills through operant-conditioning procedures that employ **self-monitoring**, coaching, modeling, role-playing, **behavior rehearsal**, and **feedback**. Social skills training has been used to help formerly hospitalized mental patients maintain jobs and apartments in the community. For example, a worker can rehearse politely asking a supervisor for assistance or asking a landlord to fix the plumbing in an apartment.

Social skills training is effective in groups. Group members can role-play important people—such as parents, spouses, or potential dates—in the lives of other members.

self-monitoring
keeping a record of one's own behavior to identify problems and record successes.

behavior rehearsal
practice.

feedback
in assertiveness training, information about the effectiveness of a response.

Biofeedback Training Through **biofeedback training (BFT)**, therapists help clients become more aware of, and gain control over, various bodily functions. Therapists attach clients to devices that measure bodily functions such as heart rate. "Bleeps" or other electronic signals are used to indicate (and thereby reinforce) changes in the desired direction—for example, a slower heart rate. (Knowledge of results is a powerful reinforcer.) One device, the electromyograph (EMG), monitors muscle tension. It has been used to augment control over muscle tension in the forehead and elsewhere, thereby alleviating anxiety, stress, and headaches.

biofeedback training (BFT)
the systematic feeding back to an organism of information about a bodily function so that the organism can gain control of that function.

BFT also helps clients voluntarily regulate functions once thought to be beyond conscious control, such as heart rate and blood pressure. Hypertensive clients use a blood pressure cuff and electronic signals to gain control over their blood pressure. The electroencephalograph (EEG) monitors brain waves and can be used to teach people how to produce alpha waves, which are associated with relaxation. Some people have overcome insomnia by learning to produce the kinds of brain waves associated with sleep.

Self-Control Methods

Do mysterious forces sometimes seem to be at work in your life? Forces that delight in wreaking havoc on New Year's resolutions and other efforts to put an end to your bad habits? Just when you go on a diet, that juicy pizza stares at you from the TV set. Just when you resolve to balance your budget, that sweater goes on sale.

Functional Analysis of Behavior Behavior therapists usually begin with a **functional analysis** of the problem behavior. In this way, they help determine the stimuli that trigger the behavior and the reinforcers that maintain it. Then clients are taught how to manipulate the antecedents and consequences of their behavior and how to increase the frequency of desired responses and decrease the frequency of undesired responses. You can use a diary to jot down each instance of a problem behavior. Note the time of day, location, your activity at the time (including your thoughts and feelings), and reactions (yours and others'). Functional analysis serves a number of purposes. It makes you more aware of the environmental context of your behavior and can increase your motivation to change. For these reasons, keeping a record of where and when you engage in "bad habits" can help you end them and may occasionally be all that you need to end them.

functional analysis
a systematic study of behavior in which one identifies the stimuli that trigger problem behavior and the reinforcers that maintain it.

Brian used functional analysis to master his nail biting. Table 13.1 on the next page shows a few items from his notebook. He discovered that boredom and humdrum activities seemed to serve as triggers for nail biting. He began to watch out for feelings of boredom as signs to practice self-control. He also made some changes in his life so that he would feel bored less often. There are numerous self-control strategies aimed at the stimuli that trigger behavior, the behaviors themselves, and reinforcers.

TABLE 13.1 Excerpts from Brian's Diary of Nail Biting for April 14

INCIDENT	TIME	LOCATION	ACTIVITY (THOUGHTS, FEELINGS)	REACTIONS
1	7:45 a.m.	Freeway	Driving to work, bored, not thinking	Finger bleeds, pain
2	10:30 a.m.	Office	Writing report	Self-disgust
3	2:25 p.m.	Conference	Listening to dull financial report	Embarrassment
4	6:40 p.m.	Living room	Watching evening news	Self-disgust

Note: A functional analysis of problem behavior like nail biting increases awareness of the environmental context in which it occurs, spurs motivation to change, and, in highly motivated people, might lead to significant behavioral change.

COGNITIVE THERAPIES: ADJUSTMENT IS WHAT YOU THINK (AND DO)

There is nothing either good or bad, but thinking makes it so.
Shakespeare, *Hamlet*

In this line from *Hamlet*, Shakespeare did not mean to suggest that injuries and misfortunes are painless or easy to manage. Rather, he meant that our appraisals of unfortunate events can heighten our discomfort and impair our coping ability. In so doing, Shakespeare was providing a kind of motto for cognitive therapists.

cognitive therapy
a form of therapy that focuses on how clients' cognitions (expectations, attitudes, beliefs, etc.) lead to distress and may be modified to relieve distress and promote adaptive behavior.

Cognitive therapy focuses on changing the beliefs, attitudes, and automatic types of thinking that create and compound their clients' problems (Beck, 1993; Ellis & Dryden, 1996). Cognitive therapists, like psychodynamic and humanistic therapists, aim to foster self-insight, but they aim to heighten insight into *current cognitions* as well as those of the past. Cognitive therapists also aim to directly change maladaptive cognitions in order to reduce negative feelings, provide insight, and help the client solve problems.

You may have noticed that many behavior therapists incorporate cognitive procedures in their methods. For example, techniques such as systematic desensitization, covert sensitization, and covert reinforcement ask clients to focus on visual imagery. Behavioral methods for treating bulimia nervosa focus on clients' irrational attitudes toward their weight and body shape as well as foster healthful eating habits. Let us look at the approaches and methods of some major cognitive therapists.

Cognitive Therapy: Correcting Cognitive Errors

Cognitive therapy is the name of a general approach to therapy as well as Aaron Beck's specific methods. Beck (1991, 1993) focuses on clients' cognitive distortions. Beck encourages clients to become their own personal scientists and challenge beliefs that are not supported by evidence.

Beck questions people in a way that encourages them to see the irrationality of their ways of thinking. For example, depressed people tend to minimize their accomplishments and to assume that the worst will happen. Both distortions heighten feelings of depression. Cognitive distortions can be fleeting and automatic, difficult to detect (Persons et al., 2001). Beck's therapy methods help clients become aware of distortions and challenge them.

Beck notes how cognitive errors contribute to clients' miseries:

1. Clients may *selectively perceive* the world as a harmful place and ignore evidence to the contrary.

2. Clients may *overgeneralize* on the basis of a few examples. For example, they may perceive themselves as worthless because they were laid off at work or as unattractive because they were refused a date.
3. Clients may *magnify,* or blow out of proportion, the importance of negative events. They may catastrophize failing a test by assuming they will flunk out of college or catastrophize losing a job by believing that they will never find another one and that serious harm will befall their family as a result.
4. Clients may engage in *absolutist thinking,* or looking at the world in black and white rather than in shades of gray. In doing so, a rejection on a date takes on the meaning of a lifetime of loneliness; an uncomfortable illness takes on life-threatening proportions.

The concept of pinpointing and modifying errors may become clearer from the following excerpt from a case in which a 53-year-old engineer obtained cognitive therapy for severe depression. The engineer had left his job and become inactive. As reported by Beck and his colleagues, the first goal of treatment was to foster physical activity—even things like raking leaves and preparing dinner—because activity is incompatible with depression. Then:

> [The engineer's] cognitive distortions were identified by comparing his assessment of each activity with that of his wife. Alternative ways of interpreting his experiences were then considered.
>
> In comparing his wife's résumé of his past experiences, he became aware that he had (1) undervalued his past by failing to mention many previous accomplishments, (2) regarded himself as far more responsible for his "failures" than she did, and (3) concluded that he was worthless since he had not succeeded in attaining certain goals in the past. When the two accounts were contrasted, he could discern many of his cognitive distortions. In subsequent sessions, his wife continued to serve as an "objectifier."
>
> In midtherapy, [he] compiled a list of new attitudes that he had acquired since initiating therapy. These included:
>
> 1. "I am starting at a lower level of functioning at my job, but it will improve if I persist."
> 2. "I know that once I get going in the morning, everything will run all right for the rest of the day."
> 3. "I can't achieve everything at once."
> 4. "I have my periods of ups and downs, but in the long run I feel better."
> 5. "My expectations from my job and life should be scaled down to a realistic level."
> 6. "Giving in to avoidance [e.g., staying away from work and social interactions] never helps and only leads to further avoidance."
>
> He was instructed to reread this list daily for several weeks even though he already knew the content. (Rush et al., 1975)

The engineer gradually became less depressed and returned to work and an active social life. Along the way, he learned to combat inappropriate self-blame for problems, perfectionist expectations, magnification of failures, and overgeneralization from failures.

Becoming aware of cognitive errors and modifying catastrophizing thoughts helps us cope with stress. Internal, stable, and global attributions of failure lead to depression and feelings of helplessness. Cognitive therapists also alert clients to cognitive errors such as these so that the clients can change their attitudes and pave the way for more effective overt behavior.

Rational Emotive Behavior Therapy: Overcoming "Musts" and "Shoulds"

In **rational emotive behavior therapy (REBT),** Albert Ellis (2002) points out that our beliefs *about* events, not only the events themselves, shape our responses

rational emotive behavior therapy (REBT)
Albert Ellis's form of therapy that encourages clients to challenge and correct irrational expectations and maladaptive behaviors.

THE CLINICAL FILE

Aaron Beck and Albert Ellis

Aaron Beck and Albert Ellis are two of the preeminent cognitive therapists in the United States. Aaron Beck used cognitive and behavioral techniques on himself before he became a psychiatrist. In fact, one of the reasons Aaron Beck went into medicine was to confront his own fear of blood. He had had a series of operations as a child, and from then on the sight of blood had made him feel faint. During his first year of medical school, he forced himself to watch operations. In his second year, he became a surgical assistant. Soon the sight of blood became normal to him. Later he essentially argued himself out of an irrational fear of tunnels. He convinced himself that the tunnels did not cause the fear because the symptoms of faintness and shallow breathing would appear before he entered them.

As a psychiatrist, Beck first practiced psychoanalysis. However, he could not find scientific evidence for psychoanalytic beliefs. Psychoanalytic theory explained depression as anger turned inward, so that it is transformed into a need to suffer. Beck's own clinical experiences led him to believe that it is more likely that depressed people experience cognitive distortions such as the *cognitive triad.* That is, they expect the worst of themselves ("I'm no good"), the world at large ("This is an awful place"), and their future ("Nothing good will ever happen"). Beck's approach to therapy is active. Beck encourages clients to challenge beliefs that are not supported by evidence. Beck also challenges his own points of view. "I am a big self-doubter," Beck (2000) admits. "I always doubt what I do, which is one of the reasons I do so much research and encourage research." Beck teaches health professionals his form of therapy—and scientific skepticism—at the University of Pennsylvania.

Photograph by Michael Fenichel, www.fenichel.com

Psychologist Albert Ellis, like Aaron Beck, was originally trained in psychoanalysis but became frustrated with the slow rate of progress made by clients. He also found himself uncomfortable with the psychoanalyst's laid-back approach and took to engaging in sometimes heated discussions with his clients about their irrational and self-defeating ways of viewing themselves and other people. Ellis can be even more argumentative than Beck with his clients. He confronts them with the ways in which their irrational beliefs, especially those that give rise to excessive needs for social approval and perfect performance, make them miserable.

Ellis has been a workaholic and a prolific writer, having the ability to connect both with professionals and the public. Just a few of his dozens of mass-market books include *A Guide to Rational Living, How to Live with a Neurotic, How to Keep People from Pushing Your Buttons, Optimal Aging: Getting Over Getting Older,* and *Sex without Guilt.* Never resting, Ellis recently revised his *Sex without Guilt,* which was originally written half a century ago. The 2003 version is called *Sex without Guilt in the 21st Century.*

to them. Moreover, many of us harbor a number of irrational beliefs that can give rise to problems or magnify their impact. Two of the most important ones are the belief that we must have the love and approval of people who are important to us and the belief that we must prove ourselves to be thoroughly competent, adequate, and achieving.

Albert Ellis, like Aaron Beck, began as a psychoanalyst. But he became disturbed by the passive role of the analyst and by the slow rate of obtaining results—if they were obtained at all. Still, Ellis finds a role for Freud's views: "One of the main things [Freud] did was point out the importance of unconscious thinking. Freud pointed out that when people are motivated to do things, that they unconsciously think, and even feel, certain things. We use that concept," Ellis (2000) admits, "although Freud, as usual, ran it into the ground."

Ellis's REBT methods are active and directive. He does not sit back like the traditional psychoanalyst and occasionally offer an interpretation. Instead, he urges clients to seek out their irrational beliefs, which can be unconscious, though not as deeply buried as Freud believed. Nevertheless, they can be hard to pinpoint without some direction. Ellis shows clients how those beliefs lead to misery and challenges clients to change them. When Ellis sees clients behaving according to irrational beliefs, he may refute the beliefs by asking "Where is it written that you must . . . ?" or "What evidence do you have that . . . ?" According to Ellis, we need less misery and less blaming in our lives, and more action.

Ellis straddles behavioral and cognitive therapies. He originally dubbed his method of therapy *rational–emotive therapy,* because his focus was on the cognitive—irrational beliefs and how to change them. However, Ellis has also always promoted behavioral changes to cement cognitive changes. In keeping with his broad philosophy, he recently changed the name of rational–emotive therapy to rational emotive *behavior* therapy.

Many theorists consider cognitive therapy to be a collection of techniques that are part of the overall approach known as behavior therapy, which is discussed in the following section. Some members of this group use the term "cognitive–*behavioral* therapy." Others argue that the term *behavior therapy* is broad enough to include cognitive techniques. Many cognitive therapists and behavior therapists differ in focus, however. Behavior therapists deal with client cognitions in order to change *overt* behavior. Cognitive therapists also see the value of tying treatment outcomes to observable behavior, but they believe that cognitive change is a key goal in itself.

GROUP THERAPIES

When a psychotherapist has several clients with similar problems—anxiety, depression, adjustment to divorce, lack of social skills—it often makes sense to treat them in a group rather than in individual sessions. The methods and characteristics of the group reflect the needs of the members and the theoretical orientation of the leader. In group psychoanalysis, clients might interpret one another's dreams. In a client-centered group, they might provide an accepting atmosphere for self-exploration. Members of behavior therapy groups might be jointly desensitized to anxiety-evoking stimuli or might practice social skills together.

Group therapy has the following advantages:

1. It is economical (Prochaska & Norcross, 2003). It allows the therapist to work with several clients at once.
2. Compared with one-to-one therapy, group therapy provides more information and life experience for clients to draw upon.
3. Appropriate behavior receives group support. Clients usually appreciate an outpouring of peer approval.
4. When we run into troubles, it is easy to imagine that we are different from other people or inferior to them. Affiliating with people with similar problems is reassuring.
5. Group members who show improvement provide hope for other members.
6. Many individuals seek therapy because of problems in relating to other people. People who seek therapy for other reasons also may be socially inhibited. Members of groups have the opportunity to practice social skills in a relatively nonthreatening atmosphere. In a group consisting of men and women of different ages, group members can role-play one another's employers, employees, spouses, parents, children, and friends. Members can role-play asking one another out on dates, saying no (or yes), and so on.

CONCEPT SUMMARY

Methods of Therapy

PSYCHODYNAMIC THERAPIES

Assume disorders stem from unresolved unconscious conflict

© Freud Museum, London

Freud's consulting room.

HUMANISTIC THERAPIES

Assume that disorders reflect feelings of alientation from one's genuine beliefs and feelings.

Stephen Frisch/Stock Boston, LLC

Client-centered therapists provide a warm atmosphere in which clients feel free to explore their genuine feelings.

BEHAVIOR THERAPIES

Assume disorders reflect learning of maladaptive responses (such as maladaptive fear responses, or phobias) or failure to acquire adaptive responses (such as social skills).

Teresa Zabala/Uniphoto

One way behavior therapists help clients overcome phobias is to have them gradually approach the feared object or situation while they remain relaxed.

GOALS

Psychodynamic therapies: To strengthen the ego; to provide self-insight into unconscious conflict

Humanistic therapies: To help clients get in touch with parts of themselves that they have "disowned" and actualize their unique desires and abilities

Behavior therapies: To use principles of learning to help clients engage in adaptive behavior and discontinue maladaptive behavior

METHODS

Psychodynamic therapies: Traditional psychoanalysis is lengthy and nondirective and involves methods such as free association and dream analysis.

Humanistic therapies: Client-centered therapy is nondirective. It provides an atmosphere of "unconditional positive regard" from the therapist in which clients can engage in self-exploration without fear. Gestalt therapy uses highly directive methods to help clients integrate conflicting parts of the personality into a healthy "Gestalt," or whole.

Behavior therapies: Behavior therapy is directive and uses fear-reduction methods (including systematic desensitization) to overcome phobias such as fear of flying, aversive conditioning (to help clients discontinue bad habits), operant conditioning procedures (e.g., social skills training), and self-control methods (beginning with functional analysis of behavior).

COMMENTS

Psychodynamic therapies: Most effective with verbal, "upscale" clients. Modern ego-analytic approaches are briefer and more directive than traditional psychoanalysis.

Principle proponent: Sigmund Freud (1856–1939) formulated his psychodynamic theory of personality a century ago. His method of therapy, psychoanalysis, achieved greatest prominence in the 1940s and 1950s.

© Bettmann/CORBIS

Sigmund Freud

Humanistic therapies: Client-centered therapy is practiced widely in college and university counseling centers to help students make academic and personal decisions.

Principle proponents: Carl Rogers (1902–1970) developed client-centered therapy in the mid-20th century. Fritz Perls (1893–1970) originated Gestalt therapy, which reached its greatest prominence in the 1960s.

© Bettmann/CORBIS

Carl Rogers

Courtesy The Gestalt Journal Press

Fritz Perls

Behavior therapies: Behavior therapists have developed treatment for problems (e.g., smoking, phobias, sexual dysfunctions) for which there previously were no effective treament methods.

Principle proponents: Joseph Wolpe (1915–1997) introduced systematic desensitization in the late 1950s. Albert Bandura integrated behavioral and cognitive factors in forming his therapeautic methods, such as modeling.

Courtesy Dr. Joseph Wolpe

Joseph Wolpe

Courtesy of Albert Bandura

Albert Bandura

COGNITIVE THERAPIES

Assume disorders reflect cognitive errors such as excessive self-blame, pessimism, and selective focus on negative events.

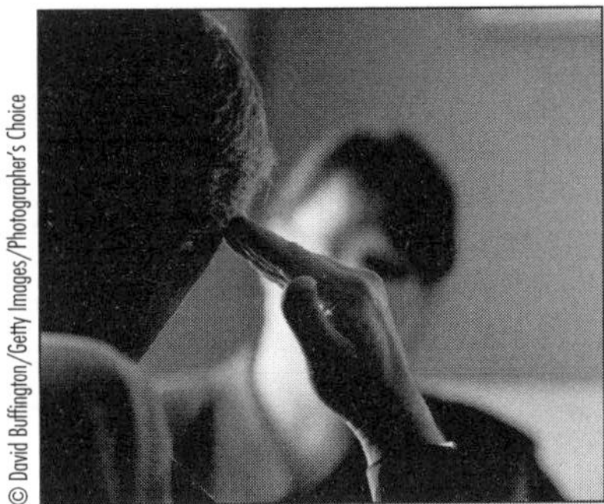
© David Buffington/Getty Images/Photographer's Choice

The therapist seeks to guide the client to correct cognitive errors and recognize irrational beliefs.

To make clients aware of the beliefs, attitudes, and automatic types of thinking that create and compound their problems; to help them correct these kinds of thinking to reduce negative feelings and solve problems

Aaron Beck's cognitive therapy helps people recognize and correct cognitive errors such as selective perception, overgeneralization, magnification of negative events, and absolutist thinking. Rational emotive behavior therapists show clients how irrational beliefs catastrophize events and make them miserable.

Many theorists consider cognitive therapy to be part of behavior therapy, and some call it cognitive–*behavioral* therapy.

Priniciple proponents: Aaron Beck introduced his approach, "cognitive therapy," in the 1960s. Albert Ellis first developed what he called "rational–emotive therapy" (RET) in the late 1950s and 1960s. More recently, he changed the name to "rational emotive behavior therapy" (REBT).

Photograph by Michael Fenichel, www.fenichel.com

Aaron Beck and Albert Ellis

BIOLOGICAL THERAPIES

Assume that disorders reflect the interaction of genetic vulnerability with other factors, such as imbalances of neurotransmitters or hormones or situational stressors; for example, depression may reflect interaction of genetic vulnerability with low levels of serotonin and with a personal failure.

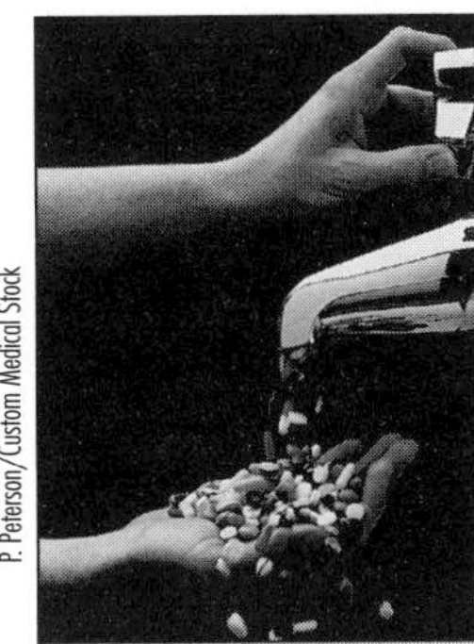
P. Peterson/Custom Medical Stock

Many drugs have been used to combat psychological disorders.

To decrease anxiety, alleviate depression, lessen mood swings in bipolar disorder, eliminate or lessen symptoms of schizophrenia

Antianxiety drugs (also known as *anxiolytic* drugs or "minor tranquilizers"), antidepressant drugs, lithium and other drugs for treatment of bipolar disorder, antipsychotic drugs ("major tranquilizers"), electroconvulsive shock therapy (ECT) for treatment of depression that is unresponsive to drug therapy, psychosurgery

Most psychologists prefer psychotherapy to biological therapies as being more helpful in developing strategies for solving problems. There is controversy as to whether cognitive therapy is as effective as biological therapy for depression. Most psychologists agree that biological therapies may be appropriate when disorders are severe and unresponsive to psychotherapy.

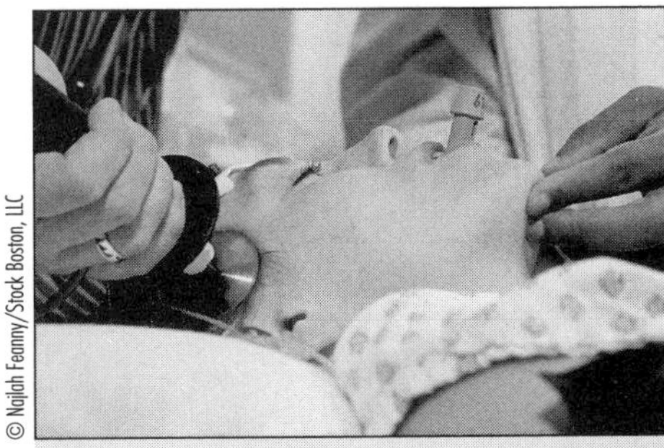
© Najlah Feanny/Stock Boston, LLC

Electroconvulsive therapy is used mainly in cases of major depression where other therapies have failed

But group therapy is not for everyone. Some clients fare better with individual treatment. Many prefer not to disclose their problems to a group. They may be overly shy or want individual attention. It is the responsibility of the therapist to insist that group disclosures be kept confidential, to establish a supportive atmosphere, and to ensure that group members obtain the attention they need.

Many types of therapy can be conducted either individually or in groups. Encounter groups and family therapy are conducted only in groups.

Encounter Groups

encounter group
a type of group that aims to foster self-awareness by focusing on how group members relate to each other in a setting that encourages open expression of feelings.

Encounter groups are not appropriate for treating serious psychological problems. Rather, they are intended to promote personal growth by heightening awareness of one's own needs and feelings and those of others. This goal is sought through intense confrontations, or encounters, between strangers.

Like ships in the night, group members come together out of the darkness, touch one another briefly, then sink back into the shadows of one another's lives. But something is gained from the passing.

Encounter groups stress interactions between group members in the here and now. Discussion of the past may be outlawed. Interpretation is out. However, expression of genuine feelings toward others is encouraged. When group members think a person's social mask is phony, they may descend en masse to rip it off.

Encounter groups can be damaging when they urge overly rapid disclosure of intimate matters or when several members attack one member. Responsible leaders do not tolerate these abuses and try to keep the group moving in a growth-enhancing direction.

Couple Therapy

Couple therapy helps couples enhance their relationship by improving their communication skills and helping them manage conflict (Prochaska & Norcross, 2003). There are often power imbalances in relationships, and couple therapy helps individuals find "full membership" in the couple. Correcting power imbalances increases happiness and can decrease the incidence of domestic violence. Ironically, in situations of domestic violence, the partner with *less* power in the relationship is usually the violent one. Violence sometimes appears to be a way of compensating for inability to share power in other aspects of the relationship (Rathus & Sanderson, 1999).

Today the main approach to couple therapy is cognitive–behavioral (Rathus & Sanderson, 1999). It teaches couples communications skills (such as how to listen and how to express feelings), ways of handling feelings like depression and anger, and ways of solving problems.

Family Therapy

family therapy
a form of therapy in which the family unit is treated as the client.

Family therapy is a form of group therapy in which one or more families constitute the group. Family therapy may be undertaken from various theoretical viewpoints. One is the systems approach, in which family interaction is studied and modified to enhance the growth of individual family members and of the family unit as a whole (Prochaska & Norcross, 2003).

Family members with low self-esteem often cannot tolerate different attitudes and behaviors in other family members. Faulty communication within the family also creates problems. In addition, it is not uncommon for the family to present an "identified patient"—that is, the family member who has *the* problem and is *causing* all the trouble. Yet family therapists usually assume that the identified patient is a scapegoat for other problems within and among family members. It is a sort of myth: Change the bad apple—or identified patient—and the barrel—or family—will be functional once more.

The family therapist—often a specialist in this field—attempts to teach the family to communicate more effectively and encourage growth and autonomy in each family member.

DOES PSYCHOTHERAPY WORK?

In 1952, the British psychologist Hans Eysenck published a review of psychotherapy research—"The Effects of Psychotherapy"—that sent shock waves through the psychotherapy community. On the basis of his review of the research, Eysenck concluded that the rate of improvement among people in psychotherapy was no greater than the rate of "spontaneous remission"—that is, the rate of improvement that would be shown by people with psychological disorders who received no treatment at all. Eysenck was not addressing people with schizophrenia, who typically profit from biological forms of therapy, but he argued that whether or not people with problems such as anxiety and depression received therapy, two of three reported substantial improvement within two years.

That was half a century ago. Since that time, sophisticated research studies—many of them employing a statistical averaging method called **meta-analysis**—have strongly suggested that psychotherapy is, in fact, effective.

meta-analysis
a method for combining and averaging the results of individual research studies.

Before we report on the research dealing with the effectiveness of therapy, let us review some of the problems of this kind of research (Shadish, 2002).

Problems in Conducting Research on Psychotherapy

It is not an easy matter to evaluate the effectiveness of psychotherapy. Many problems bedevil the effort.

Problems in Running Experiments on Psychotherapy The ideal method for evaluating a treatment—such as a method of therapy—is the experiment (Chambless & Hollon, 1998; Shadish, 2002). However, experiments on therapy methods are difficult to arrange and control. The outcomes can be difficult to define and measure.

Consider psychoanalysis. In well-run experiments, people are assigned at random to experimental and control groups. A true experiment on psychoanalysis would require randomly assigning people seeking therapy to psychoanalysis and to a control group or other kinds of therapy for comparison. But a person may have to remain in traditional psychoanalysis for years to attain beneficial results. Could we create control treatments that last as long? Moreover, some people seek psychoanalysis per se, not psychotherapy in general. Would it be ethical to assign them at random to other treatments or to a no-treatment control group? Clearly not.

In an ideal experiment, subjects and researchers are "blind" with regard to the treatment the subjects receive. Blind research designs allow researchers to control for subjects' expectations. In an ideal experiment on therapy, individuals would be blind regarding the type of therapy they are obtaining—or whether they are obtaining a placebo. However, it is difficult to mask the type of therapy clients are obtaining (Seligman, 1995). Even if we could conceal it from clients, could we hide it from therapists?

Problems in Measuring Outcomes of Therapy Consider the problems we run into when measuring outcomes of therapy (Shadish, 2002). Behavior therapists define their goals in behavioral terms—such as a formerly phobic individual being able to obtain an injection or look out of a 20th-story window. Therefore, behavior therapists do not encounter many problems in this area. But what about the client-centered therapist who fosters insight and self-actualization? We cannot directly measure these qualities. The psychoanalytic process is educational as well as therapeutic, and some argue that different standards must be applied in evaluating what the client gains from treatment (Strupp, 2001).

Are Clinical Judgments Valid? Because of problems like these, many clinicians believe that important clinical questions cannot be answered through research (Silberschatz, 1998). For them, clinical judgment is the basis for evaluating the effectiveness of therapy. Unfortunately, therapists have a stake in believing that their clients profit from treatment. They are not unbiased judges, even when they try to be.

Does Therapy Help Because of the Method or Because of "Nonspecific Factors"? Even when psychotherapy helps, we're often not sure why (Marks, 2002). Sorting out the benefits of therapy per se from other aspects of the therapy situation is a staggering task. These other aspects are termed *nonspecific factors.* They refer to features that are found in most therapies, such as the client's relationship with the therapist. Most therapists, regardless of theoretical outlook, show warmth and empathy, encourage exploration, and instill hope (Perlman, 2001; Scaturo, 2001). People in therapy also often learn to present themselves to their therapists in a positive light, and creating favorable impressions can help boost one's self-concept in therapy as in everyday life (Arkin & Hermann, 2000; Kelly, 2000). Many of the benefits of therapy could stem from interactions such as these. In such cases, the method itself might have little more value than a "sugar pill" in combating physical ailments.

What Is the Experimental Treatment in Psychotherapy Outcome Studies? We may also ask, what exactly is the experimental "treatment" being evaluated? Various therapists may say that they are practicing psychoanalysis, but they differ both as individuals and in their training. It is therefore difficult to specify just what is happening in the therapeutic session.

Analyses of the Effectiveness of Psychotherapy

Despite these evaluation problems, research on the effectiveness of therapy has been encouraging (Luborsky et al., 2002; Shadish et al., 2000). Some of this research has relied on meta-analysis. Meta-analysis combines and averages the results of individual studies. Generally speaking, the studies included in the analysis address similar issues in a similar way. Moreover, the analysts judge them to have been conducted in a valid manner.

In their classic early use of meta-analysis, Mary Lee Smith and Gene Glass (1977) analyzed the results of dozens of outcome studies of various types of therapies. They concluded that people who obtained psychodynamic therapy showed greater well-being, on the average, than 70% to 75% of those who did not obtain treatment. Similarly, nearly 75% of the clients who obtained client-centered therapy were better off than people who did not obtain treatment. Psychodynamic and client-centered therapies appear to be most effective with well-educated, verbal, strongly motivated clients who report problems with anxiety, depression (of light to moderate proportions), and interpersonal relationships. Neither form of therapy appears to be effective with people with psychotic disorders such as major depression, bipolar disorder, and schizophrenia. Smith and Glass (1977) found that people who obtained Gestalt therapy showed greater well-being than about 60% of those who did not obtain treatment. The effectiveness of psychoanalysis and client-centered therapy thus was reasonably comparable. Gestalt therapy fell behind.

Smith and Glass (1977) did not include cognitive therapies in their meta-analysis because at the time of their study many cognitive approaches were relatively new. Because behavior therapists also incorporate many cognitive techniques, it can be difficult to sort out which aspects—cognitive or otherwise—of behavioral treatments are most effective. However, many meta-analyses of cognitive–behavioral therapy have been conducted since the early work of Smith and Glass. Their results are encouraging.

THE CLINICAL FILE

Ethnicity and Psychotherapy

The United States, they are a-changing. The numbers of African Americans, Asian Americans, and Latino and Latina Americans are growing rapidly (U.S. Bureau of the Census, 2003), yet most of the "prescriptions" for psychotherapy discussed in this chapter were originated by, and intended for use with, Europeans and European Americans (Dana, 2002).

Americans from ethnic minority groups are less likely than European Americans to seek therapy (Kim & Omizo, 2003; Sue & Sue, 2002). Reasons for their lower participation rate include:

- Unawareness that therapy would help (Sue & Sue, 2002).
- Lack of information about the availability of professional services or inability to pay for them (Dana, 2002).
- Distrust of professionals, particularly European American professionals and (for women) male professionals (Whaley, 2001; Wong et al., 2003).
- Language barriers (American Psychological Association, 1993).
- Reluctance to open up about personal matters to strangers—especially strangers who are not members of one's own ethnic group (Whaley, 2001; Wong et al., 2003).
- Cultural inclinations toward other approaches to problem solving, such as religious approaches and psychic healers (Baez & Hernandez, 2001; de Rios, 2002; Olson, 2003).
- Negative experiences with professionals and authority figures (Whaley, 2001).

There are thus many reasons that clinicians need to be sensitive to the cultural heritage, language, and values of the people they see in therapy (American Psychological Association, 1993; Comas-Diaz, 1994). That is, they need to develop *multicultural competence* (Sue & Sue, 2002). Let us consider some of the issues involved in conducting psychotherapy with African Americans, Asian Americans, Latino and Latina Americans, and Native Americans.

African Americans often are reluctant to seek psychological help because of cultural assumptions that people should manage their own problems and because of mistrust of the therapy process (Jackson & Greene, 2000; Whaley, 2001). They tend to assume that people are supposed to solve their own problems. Signs of emotional weakness such as tension, anxiety, and depression are stigmatized. Many African Americans are also suspicious of their therapists—especially when the therapist is a European American. They may withhold personal information because of the society's history of racial discrimination (Dana, 2002; Whaley, 2001).

Asian Americans tend to stigmatize people with psychological disorders. As a result, they may deny problems and refuse to seek help for them (Kim & Omizo, 2003). Asian Americans, especially recent immigrants, also may not understand or believe in Western approaches to psychotherapy. For example, Western psychotherapy typically encourages people to express their feelings openly. This mode of behavior may conflict with the Asian tradition of restraint in public. Many Asians also experience and express psychological problems as physical symptoms (Kim & Omizo, 2003; Sue & Sue, 2002). Rather than thinking of themselves as being anxious, they may focus on physical features of anxiety such as a pounding heart and heavy sweating. Rather than thinking of themselves as depressed, they may focus on fatigue and low energy levels.

Therapists need to be aware of potential conflicts between the traditional Latino and Latina American value of interdependency in the family and the typical European American belief in independence and self-reliance (Baez & Hernandez, 2001; de Rios, 2002).

Many psychological disorders experienced by Native Americans involve the disruption of their traditional culture caused by European colonization (Olson, 2003).

© Bill Aron/PhotoEdit

■ **Is Psychotherapy for Everyone?** Why are members of some ethnic groups more willing to seek therapy than members of other ethnic groups? Do members of all ethnic groups have the same kinds of needs in therapy? Must therapists be from the same ethnic group as their clients? Can therapists from the dominant culture be sensitive to the life issues of people from ethnic minority groups?

continued

THE CLINICAL FILE (CONTINUED)

Loss of cultural identity and social disorganization have set the stage for problems such as alcoholism, substance abuse, and depression. Efforts to prevent psychological disorders should focus on strengthening Native American cultural identity, pride, and cohesion.

Psychotherapy is most effective when therapists attend to and respect people's sociocultural as well as individual differences. Although it is the individual who experiences psychological anguish, the fault often lies in the cultural setting and not the individual.

A meta-analysis of 90 studies by William R. Shadish and his colleagues (2000) concurred that psychotherapy is generally effective. Generally speaking, the more therapy the better; that is, people who have more psychotherapy tend to fare better than people who have less of it. Therapy also appears to be more effective when the outcome measures reflect the treatment (e.g., when the effects of treatment aimed at fear-reduction are measured in terms of people's ability to approach fear-inducing objects and situations).

Studies of cognitive therapy have shown that modifying irrational beliefs of the type described by Albert Ellis helps people with problems such as anxiety and depression (Engels et al., 1993; Haaga & Davison, 1993). Modifying self-defeating beliefs of the sort outlined by Aaron Beck also frequently alleviates anxiety and depression (Butler & Beck, 2001; Frank & Kupfer, 2003). Cognitive therapy may help people with severe depression, who had been thought responsive only to biological therapies (Hollon & Shelton, 2001; Simons et al., 1995). Cognitive therapy has also helped people with personality disorders (Beck et al., 2001; Trull et al., 2003).

Behavioral and cognitive therapies have provided strategies for treating anxiety disorders, social skills deficits, and problems in self-control (DeRubeis & Crits-Christoph, 1998). These therapies—which are often integrated as *cognitive–behavioral therapy*—have also provided empirically supported methods for helping couples and families in distress (Baucom et al., 1998), and for modifying behaviors related to health problems such as headaches (Blanchard, 1992), smoking, chronic pain, and bulimia nervosa (Agras et al., 2000; Compas et al., 1998). Cognitive–behavioral therapists have also innovated treatments for sexual dysfunctions for which there previously were no effective treatments. One meta-analysis of psychodynamic therapy and cognitive–behavioral therapy found both treatments to be effective with personality disorders (Leichsenring & Leibing, 2003). It is perhaps of interest that of hundreds of studies reviewed, the researchers found only 14 psychodynamic studies and 11 cognitive–behavioral studies that were rigorous enough to be included in the meta-analysis.

Cognitive–behavioral therapy has been used to help anorexic and bulimic individuals challenge their perfectionism and their attitudes toward their bodies. It has also been used to systematically reinforce appropriate eating behavior. Studies that compare the effectiveness of cognitive–behavioral therapy and antidepressants find them to be comparably effective, with cognitive–behavioral therapy frequently showing a slight advantage (e.g., Jacobi et al., 2002). Drugs, after all, do not directly "attack" people's perfectionist attitudes and their distorted body images. They ease the presence of negative feelings and may help individuals enlist their own psychological resources, but pills do not contain advice or even a sympathetic ear.

Cognitive therapy has helped many people with schizophrenia (who are also using drug therapy) modify their delusional beliefs (Chadwick & Lowe, 1990). Behavior therapy has helped to coordinate the care of institutionalized patients, including people with schizophrenia and mental retardation (Spreat & Behar, 1994). However, there is little evidence that psychological therapy alone is effective in treating the quirks of thought exhibited in people with severe psychotic disorders.

Thus, it is not enough to ask which type of therapy is most effective. We must ask which type is most effective for a particular problem and a particular patient. What are its advantages? Its limitations? Clients may successfully use systematic desensitization to overcome stage fright, as measured by ability to speak to a group of people. If clients also want to know *why* they have stage fright, however, behavior therapy alone will not provide the answer.

As we see in the nearby "The Clinical File" on ethnicity and psychotherapy, we must also consider the sociocultural features of clients in determining how to make therapy most effective. Failure to do so leaves many people who would profit from therapy on the wayside. And in some cases, inappropriate methods of therapy may do more harm than good.

BIOLOGICAL THERAPIES

The kinds of therapy we have discussed are psychological in nature—forms of *psycho*therapy. Psychotherapies apply *psychological* principles to treatment, principles based on psychological knowledge of matters such as learning and motivation. People with psychological disorders are also often treated with biological therapies. Biological therapies apply what is known of people's *biological* structures and processes to the amelioration of psychological disorders. For example, they may work by altering events in the nervous system, as by changing the action of neurotransmitters. In this section, we discuss three biological, or medical, approaches to treating people with psychological disorders: drug therapy, electroconvulsive therapy, and psychosurgery.

Drug Therapy: In Search of the Magic Pill?

In the 1950s Fats Domino popularized the song "My Blue Heaven." Fats was singing about the sky and happiness. Today "blue heavens" is one of the street names for the 10-milligram dose of the antianxiety drug Valium. Clinicians prescribe Valium and other drugs for people with various psychological disorders.

Antianxiety Drugs Most antianxiety drugs (also called *minor tranquilizers*) belong to the chemical class known as *benzodiazepines*. Valium (diazepam) is a benzodiazepine. Other benzodiazepines include chlordiazepoxide (for example, Librium), oxazepam (Serax), and alprazolam (Xanax). Antianxiety drugs are usually prescribed for outpatients who complain of generalized anxiety or panic attacks, although many people also use them as sleeping pills. Valium and other antianxiety drugs depress the activity of the central nervous system (CNS). The CNS, in turn, decreases sympathetic activity, reducing the heart rate, respiration rate, and feelings of nervousness and tension.

Many people come to tolerate antianxiety drugs very quickly. When tolerance occurs, dosages must be increased for the drug to remain effective.

Sedation (feelings of being tired or drowsy) is the most common side effect of antianxiety drugs. Problems associated with withdrawal from these drugs include **rebound anxiety**. That is, some people who have been using these drugs regularly report that their anxiety becomes worse than before once they discontinue them. Antianxiety drugs can induce physical dependence, as evidenced by withdrawal symptoms such as tremors, sweating, insomnia, and rapid heartbeat.

rebound anxiety
anxiety that can occur when one discontinues use of a tranquilizer.

Antipsychotic Drugs People with schizophrenia are often given antipsychotic drugs (also called *major tranquilizers*). In most cases these drugs reduce agitation, delusions, and hallucinations. Many antipsychotic drugs, including phenothiazines (for example, Thorazine) and clozapine (Clozaril) are thought to act by blocking dopamine receptors in the brain (Buckley et al., 2000; Sawa & Snyder, 2002). Research along these lines supports the theory that schizophrenia is connected with overactivity of the neurotransmitter dopamine.

antidepressant
(ant-eye-dee-PRESS-ant). Acting to relieve depression.

Antidepressants People with major depression often take so-called **antidepressant** drugs. These drugs are also helpful for some people with eating disorders, panic disorder, obsessive–compulsive disorder, and social phobia (Bacaltchuk et al., 2000; Barlow et al., 2000; McElroy et al., 2000; Santonastaso et al., 2001). Problems in the regulation of noradrenaline and serotonin may be involved in eating and panic disorders as well as in depression. Antidepressants are believed to work by increasing levels of one or both of these neurotransmitters, which can affect both depression and the appetite (Schneider et al., 2003; C. L. White et al., 2000). However, as noted in the section on the effectiveness of psychotherapy, cognitive–behavioral therapy addresses irrational attitudes concerning weight and body shape, fosters normal eating habits, and helps people resist the urges to binge and purge, often making this form of therapy more effective with people with bulimia than antidepressants (Wilson et al., 2002). But when cognitive–behavioral therapy does not help people with bulimia nervosa, drug therapy may (Walsh et al., 2000).

There are various antidepressants. Each increases the concentration of noradrenaline or serotonin in the brain (Frank & Kupfer, 2003). *Monoamine oxidase (MAO) inhibitors* block the activity of an enzyme that breaks down noradrenaline and serotonin. *Tricyclic and tetracyclic antidepressants* prevent the reuptake of noradrenaline and serotonin by the axon terminals of the transmitting neurons. **Selective serotonin-reuptake inhibitors (SSRIs)** such as Prozac, Zoloft, and Effexor also block the reuptake of serotonin by presynaptic neurons. As a result, serotonin remains in the synaptic cleft longer, influencing receiving neurons. SSRIs appear to be more effective than other antidepressants (Bech et al., 2000).

selective serotonin-reuptake inhibitors (SSRIs)
antidepressant drugs that work by blocking the reuptake of serotonin by presynaptic neurons.

Antidepressant drugs must usually build up to a therapeutic level over several weeks. Because overdoses can be lethal, some people stay in a hospital during the buildup to prevent suicide attempts. There are also side effects, some of which are temporary, such as nausea, agitation, and weight gain.

Lithium The ancient Greeks and Romans were among the first to use the metal lithium as a psychoactive drug. They prescribed mineral water—which contains lithium—for people with bipolar disorder. They had no inkling as to why this treatment sometimes helped. A salt of the metal lithium (lithium carbonate), in tablet form, flattens out cycles of manic behavior and depression in most people. Lithium can also be used to strengthen the effects of antidepressant medication (Bauer et al., 2000). It is not known exactly how lithium works, although it affects the functioning of neurotransmitters.

People with bipolar disorder may have to use lithium indefinitely, as a person with diabetes must use insulin to control the illness. Lithium also has been shown to have side effects such as hand tremors, memory impairment, and excessive thirst and urination (Kleindienst & Greil, 2003). Memory impairment is reported as the main reason why people discontinue lithium.

Electroconvulsive Therapy

electroconvulsive therapy (ECT)
treatment of disorders like major depression by passing an electric current (that causes a convulsion) through the head.

Electroconvulsive therapy (ECT) is a biological form of therapy for psychological disorders that was introduced by the Italian psychiatrist Ugo Cerletti in 1939. Cerletti had noted that some slaughterhouses used electric shock to render animals unconscious. The shocks also produced convulsions. Along with other European researchers of the period, Cerletti erroneously believed that convulsions were incompatible with schizophrenia and other major psychological disorders.

ECT was originally used for a variety of psychological disorders. Because of the advent of antipsychotic drugs, however, it is now used mainly for people with major depression who do not respond to antidepressants (Thase & Kupfer, 1996).

People typically obtain one ECT treatment three times a week for up to 10 sessions. Electrodes are attached to the temples and an electrical current strong enough to produce a convulsion is induced. The shock causes unconsciousness, so

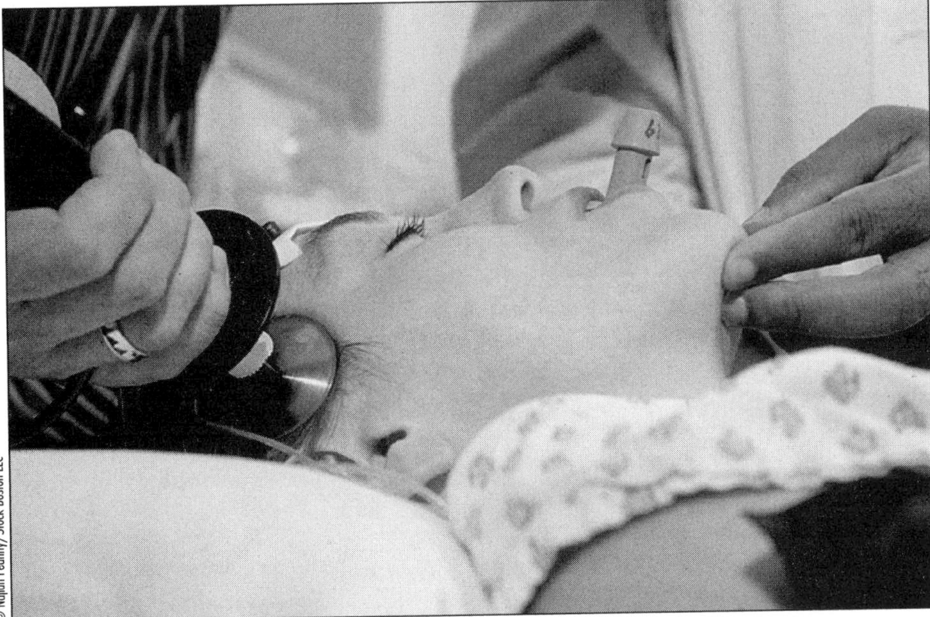

■ **Electroconvulsive Therapy.** In ECT, electrodes are placed on each side of the patient's head and a current is passed between them, inducing a seizure. ECT is used mainly in cases of major depression when antidepressant drugs and psychotherapy are not sufficient.

the patient does not recall it. Nevertheless, patients are given a **sedative** so that they are asleep during the treatment.

sedative
a drug that relieves nervousness or agitation or puts one to sleep.

ECT is controversial for many reasons, such as the fact that many professionals are distressed by the thought of passing an electric shock through a patient's head and producing convulsions. But there are side effects, including memory problems in the form of retrograde amnesia (Lisanby et al., 2000; Weiner, 2000). (Some researchers argue that stronger shock to one side of the head may be as effective yet have fewer side effects as compared with weaker shock to both sides of the head [Sackeim et al., 2000].) However, research suggests that for most people, cognitive impairment tends to be temporary (Eranti & McLoughlin, 2003). One study followed up 10 adolescents who had received ECT an average of 3½ years earlier. Six of the 10 had complained or memory impairment immediately after treatment, but only one complained of continued problems at the follow-up. Nevertheless, psychological tests did not reveal any differences in cognitive functioning between severely depressed adolescents who had received ECT and others who had not (Cohen et al., 2000).

Psychosurgery

Psychosurgery is more controversial than ECT. The best-known modern technique, **prefrontal lobotomy**, has been used with people with severe disorders. In this method, a picklike instrument severs the nerve pathways that link the prefrontal lobes of the brain to the thalamus. This method was pioneered by the Portuguese neurologist Antonio Egas Moniz and was brought to the United States in the 1930s. The theoretical rationale for the operation was vague and misguided and Moniz's reports of success were exaggerated. Nevertheless, by 1950 prefrontal lobotomies had been performed on more than a thousand people in an effort to reduce violence and agitation. Anecdotal evidence of the method's unreliable outcomes is found in an ironic footnote to history: One of Dr. Moniz's "failures" shot the doctor, leaving a bullet lodged in his spine and paralyzing his legs. It is true that the originator of a

psychosurgery
surgery intended to promote psychological changes or to relieve disordered behavior.

prefrontal lobotomy
the severing or destruction of a section of the frontal lobe of the brain.

surgical technique intended to reduce violence learned that it was not always successful . . . when one of his patients shot him.

Prefrontal lobotomy also has a host of side effects, including hyperactivity and distractibility, impaired learning ability, overeating, apathy and withdrawal, epileptic-type seizures, reduced creativity, and, now and then, death. Because of these side effects, and because of the advent of antipsychotic drugs, this method has been largely discontinued in the United States.

Does Biological Therapy Work?

There are thus a number of biological approaches to the therapy of psychological disorders.

There is little question that drug therapy has helped many people with severe psychological disorders. For example, antipsychotic drugs largely account for the reduced need for the use of restraint and supervision (padded cells, straitjackets, hospitalization, and so on) with people diagnosed with schizophrenia. Antipsychotic drugs have allowed hundreds of thousands of former mental hospital residents to lead largely normal lives in the community, hold jobs, and maintain family lives. Most of the problems related to these drugs concern their side effects. Therefore, people with psychological disorders should *not* always say no to drugs.

But many comparisons of psychotherapy (in the form of cognitive therapy) and drug therapy for depression suggest that cognitive therapy is as effective as, or more effective than, antidepressants (Antonuccio, 1995; Muñoz et al., 1994). For one thing, cognitive therapy provides coping skills that reduce the risk of recurrence of depression once treatment ends (Hollon & Shelton, 2001). Then again, at least one study suggests that a combination of cognitive therapy and antidepressant medication is superior to either treatment alone with chronically depressed people (Keller et al., 2000). On the other hand, SSRIs may also help prevent subsequent heart attacks in depressed people who have had prior heart attacks (Writing Committee for the ENRICHD Investigators, 2003). The chapter's "Life Connections" section discusses cognitive–behavioral methods for tackling depression.

A similar story holds for experiments comparing the effectiveness of cognitive–behavioral therapy and "antidepressant" medication in the treatment of panic disorder and bulimia nervosa. The first study found that cognitive–behavioral therapy and the antidepressant imipramine are both helpful in treating panic disorder, but a combination of the psychological and biological treatments appears to be somewhat more helpful in the long run (Barlow et al., 2000). The second study found that cognitive–behavioral therapy, antidepressant medication, and the combination of the two were all helpful in treating bulimia nervosa. At least in this study, cognitive–behavioral therapy was the most helpful of the three treatments, superior even to the combination of cognitive–behavioral therapy and the medicine (Jacobi et al., 2002).

Many psychologists and psychiatrists are comfortable with the short-term use of antianxiety drugs in helping clients manage periods of unusual anxiety or tension. However, many people use antianxiety drugs routinely to dull the arousal stemming from anxiety-producing lifestyles or interpersonal problems. Rather than make the often painful decisions required to confront their problems and change their lives, they prefer to take a pill.

One study found that both tranquilizers and cognitive–behavioral therapy (stress management training plus imagined exposure to the fearful stimuli) helped phobic people get through a dental session. However, 70% of those who received cognitive–behavioral therapy continued to go for dental treatment, as compared with only 20% of those who took the tranquilizer (Thom et al., 2000). The cognitive–behavioral therapy apparently taught the individuals in the study coping skills, whereas the tranquilizers afforded only temporary relief.

Despite the controversies surrounding ECT, it helps many people who do not respond to antidepressant drugs (Thase & Kupfer, 1996). ECT, that is, may be a useful "last resort" when other treatment methods are of no avail.

In sum, drug therapy and perhaps ECT seem to be effective for some disorders that do not respond to psychotherapy alone. Yet common sense and research evidence suggest that psychotherapy is preferable for problems such as anxiety and mild depression. No chemical can show a person how to change an idea or solve an interpersonal problem.

PRACTICAL SOLUTIONS

Alleviating Depression: Getting out of the Dumps

Be not afraid of life. Believe that life is worth living and your belief will help create the fact.

William James

We began the chapter with the case of a depressed college sophomore, Jasmine. We noted that various kinds of therapist might treat her depression in different ways.

Depression is characterized by inactivity, feelings of sadness, and cognitive distortions. When we suspect that our feelings may fit the picture of a major depressive episode or bipolar disorder, it may be helpful to talk things over with our instructor or visit the college counseling or health center. Some of us may also want to try to get at the deep-seated roots of our feelings of depression, and doing so in some cases might require long-term talk therapy. On the other hand, cognitive–behavioral therapists have pointed out that there are many things we can do on our own to cope with milder feelings of depression. These methods attempt to directly reverse the characteristics of depression. They include:

- Engaging in pleasant events.
- Thinking rationally.
- Exercising.
- Asserting ourselves.

Engaging in Pleasant Events There is a relationship between our moods and what we do. Losses, failures, and tension can trigger feelings of depression. Pleasant events can generate feelings of happiness and joy. You may be able to use pleasant events to lift your mood purposefully by taking the following steps:

1. Check off items in Table 13.2 that appeal to you.
2. Engage in at least three pleasant events each day.
3. Record your activities in a diary. Add other activities and events that strike you as pleasant, even if they are unplanned.
4. Toward the end of each day, rate your response to each activity, using a scale like this one:

   +3 Wonderful
   +2 Very nice
   +1 Somewhat nice
   0 No particular response
   −1 Somewhat disappointing
   −2 Rather disappointing
   −3 The pits

5. After a week or so, check the items in the diary that received positive ratings.
6. Repeat successful activities and experiment with new ones.

Thinking Rationally

Public opinion is a weak tyrant compared with our own private opinion. What a man thinks of himself, that it is which determines . . . his fate.

Henry David Thoreau, *Walden*

Depressed people tend to blame themselves for failures and problems, even when they are not at fault. They *internalize* blame and see their problems as *stable* and *global*—as all but impossible to change. Depressed people also make cognitive errors such as *catastrophizing* their problems and *minimizing* their accomplishments.

Column 1 in Table 13.3 illustrates a number of irrational, depressing thoughts. How many of them have you had? Column 2 indicates the type of cognitive error being

■ **Tackling Depression or Just Having Fun?** Many cognitive–behavioral therapists tackle depression directly, by focusing on what depressed people do (or don't do) and think. Depressed people are often inactive, withdrawn from the activities that typically delighted them. Therefore, cognitive–behavioral therapists may prescribe such activities as part of the treatment for depression.

continued

PRACTICAL SOLUTIONS (CONTINUED)

TABLE 13.2 **A Catalog of Pleasant Events**

1. Being in the country
2. Wearing expensive or formal clothes
3. Making contributions to religious, charitable, or political groups
4. Talking about sports
5. Meeting someone new
6. Going to a rock concert
7. Playing baseball, softball, football, or basketball
8. Planning trips or vacations
9. Buying things for yourself
10. Being at the beach
11. Doing art work (painting, sculpture, drawing, moviemaking, etc.)
12. Rock climbing or mountaineering
13. Reading the Scriptures
14. Playing golf
15. Rearranging or redecorating your room or house
16. Going naked
17. Going to a sports event
18. Going to the races
19. Reading stories, novels, poems, plays, magazines, newspapers
20. Going to a bar, tavern, club
21. Going to lectures or talks
22. Creating or arranging songs or music
23. Boating
24. Restoring antiques, refinishing furniture
25. Watching television or listening to the radio
26. Camping
27. Working in politics
28. Working on machines (cars, bikes, radios, television sets)
29. Playing cards or board games
30. Doing puzzles or math games
31. Having lunch with friends or associates
32. Playing tennis
33. Driving long distances
34. Woodworking, carpentry
35. Writing stories, novels, poems, plays, articles
36. Being with animals
37. Riding in an airplane
38. Exploring (hiking away from known routes, spelunking, etc.)
39. Singing
40. Going to a party
41. Going to church functions
42. Playing a musical instrument
43. Snow skiing, ice skating
44. Wearing informal clothes, "dressing down"
45. Acting
46. Being in the city, downtown
47. Taking a long, hot bath
48. Playing pool or billiards
49. Bowling
50. Watching wild animals
51. Gardening, landscaping
52. Wearing new clothes
53. Dancing
54. Sitting or lying in the sun
55. Riding a motorcycle
56. Just sitting and thinking
57. Going to a fair, carnival, circus, zoo, amusement park
58. Talking about philosophy or religion
59. Gambling
60. Listening to sounds of nature
61. Dating, courting
62. Having friends come to visit
63. Going out to visit friends
64. Giving gifts
65. Getting massages or backrubs
66. Photography
67. Collecting stamps, coins, rocks, etc.
68. Seeing beautiful scenery
69. Eating good meals
70. Improving your health (having teeth fixed, changing diet, having a checkup, etc.)
71. Wrestling or boxing
72. Fishing
73. Going to a health club, sauna
74. Horseback riding
75. Protesting social, political, or environmental conditions
76. Going to the movies
77. Cooking meals
78. Washing your hair
79. Going to a restaurant
80. Using cologne, perfume
81. Getting up early in the morning
82. Writing a diary
83. Giving massages or backrubs
84. Meditating or doing yoga
85. Doing heavy outdoor work
86. Snowmobiling, dune buggying
87. Being in a body-awareness, encounter, or "rap" group
88. Swimming
89. Running, jogging
90. Walking barefoot
91. Playing Frisbee or catch
92. Doing housework or laundry, cleaning things
93. Listening to music
94. Knitting, crocheting
95. Making love
96. Petting, necking
97. Going to a barber or beautician
98. Being with someone you love
99. Going to the library
100. Shopping
101. Preparing a new or special dish
102. Watching people
103. Bicycling
104. Writing letters, cards, or notes
105. Talking about politics or public affairs
106. Watching attractive women or men
107. Caring for houseplants
108. Having coffee, tea, or Coke, etc., with friends
109. Beachcombing
110. Going to auctions, garage sales, etc.
111. Water skiing, surfing, diving
112. Traveling
113. Attending the opera, ballet, or a play
114. Looking at the stars or the moon
115. Surfing the Net
116. Playing videogames

Source: Adapted from D. J. MacPhillamy & P. M. Lewinsohn, *Pleasant Events Schedule, Form III-S,* University of Oregon, Mimeograph, 1971.

made (such as internalizing or catastrophizing), and column 3 shows examples of rational alternatives.

You can pinpoint irrational, depressing thoughts by identifying the kinds of thoughts you have when you feel low. Look for the fleeting thoughts that can trigger mood changes. It helps to jot them down. Then challenge their accuracy. Do you characterize difficult situations as impossible and hopeless? Do you expect too much from yourself and minimize your achievements? Do you internalize more than your fair share of blame?

You can use Table 13.3 to classify your cognitive errors and construct rational alternatives. Write these next to each irrational thought. Review them from time to time. When you are alone, you can read the irrational thought aloud. Then follow it by saying to yourself firmly, "No, that's irrational!" Then read the rational alternative aloud twice, *emphatically.*

After you have thought or read aloud the rational alternative, think, "That makes more sense! That's a more accurate view of things! I feel better now that I have things in perspective."

Exercising Exercise not only fosters physical health. It can enhance psychological well-being and help us cope with depression. Depression is characterized by inactivity and feelings of helplessness. Exercise is, in a sense, the opposite of inactivity. Exercise might also help alleviate feelings of helplessness. In one experiment, 156 adult volunteers who were depressed were randomly assigned to four months of either aerobic exercise, antidepressant medication, or a combination of the two (Babyak et al., 2000). Following treatment, all three groups showed comparable relief from depression. But at a further 6-month follow-up, subjects from the exercise groups who had continued to exercise showed the greatest improvement. Other experiments also find that exercise alleviates feelings of depression (Jorm et al., 2002; Tkachuk & Martin, 1999). Exercise has also been shown to decrease anxiety and hostility and to boost self-esteem (Hansen et al., 2001; Norvell & Belles, 1993).

TABLE 13.3 Irrational, Depressing Thoughts and Rational Alternatives

IRRATIONAL THOUGHT	TYPE OF THOUGHT	RATIONAL ALTERNATIVE
"There's nothing I can do."	Catastrophizing (the size of the problem), minimizing (one's coping ability), stabilizing	"I can't think of anything to do right now, but if I work at it, I may."
"I'm no good."	Internalizing, globalizing, stabilizing	"I did something I regret, but that doesn't make me evil or worthless as a person."
"This is absolutely awful."	Catastrophizing	"This is pretty bad, but it's not the end of the world."
"I just don't have the brains for college."	Stabilizing, globalizing	"I guess I really need to go back over the basics in that course."
"I just can't believe I did something so disgusting!"	Catastrophizing	"That was a bad experience. Well, I won't be likely to try that again soon."
"I can't imagine ever feeling right."	Stabilizing, catastrophizing	"This is painful, but if I try to work it through step by step, I'll probably eventually see my way out of it."
"It's all my fault."	Internalizing	"I'm not blameless, but I wasn't the only one involved. It may have been my idea, but he went into it with his eyes open."
"I can't do anything right."	Globalizing, stabilizing, catastrophizing, minimizing	"I sure screwed this up, but I've done a lot of things well, and I'll do other things well."
"I hurt everybody who gets close to me."	Internalizing, globalizing, stabilizing	"I'm not totally blameless, but I'm not responsible for the whole world. Others make their own decisions, and they have to live with the results, too."
"If people knew the real me, they would have it in for me."	Globalizing, minimizing (the positive in yourself)	"I'm not perfect, but nobody's perfect. I have positive as well as negative features, and I am entitled to self-interests."

Many of us create or compound feelings of depression because of cognitive errors such as those in this table. Have you had any of these irrational, depressing thoughts? Are you willing to challenge them?

continued

PRACTICAL SOLUTIONS (CONTINUED)

Asserting Ourselves: Stand Up! We humans are social creatures, and social interactions are important to us. Unassertive behavior patterns are linked to feelings of depression. Learning to express our feelings and relate to others has been shown to alleviate feelings of depression (Hersen et al., 1984). Assertive behavior permits more effective interactions with family members, friends, coworkers, and strangers. In this way we remove sources of frustration and expand our social support. Expressions of positive feelings—saying you love someone or simply saying "Good morning" cheerfully—help reduce feelings of hostility and pave the way toward further social involvement.

Assertive behavior involves the expression of one's genuine feelings, standing up for one's legitimate rights, and refusing unreasonable requests. It means resisting undue social influences, disobeying *arbitrary* authority figures, and resisting conformity to *arbitrary* group standards. But many feelings such as love and admiration are positive, so assertive behavior also means expressing positive feelings ("That was great!" "You're wonderful!").

Assertive people also influence others to join them in worthwhile social and political activities. They may become involved in political campaigns, consumer groups, conservationist organizations, and other groups to advance their causes.

Alternatives to assertive behavior include submissive, or *unassertive,* behavior and *aggressive* behavior. When we are submissive, our self-esteem plummets. Unexpressed feelings sometimes smolder as resentments and then catch fire as socially inappropriate outbursts. Aggressive behavior includes physical and verbal attacks, threats, and insults. Sometimes we get our way through aggression, but we also earn the condemnation of others. And, unless we are unfeeling, we condemn ourselves for bullying others. You may wish to take the nearby questionnaire to gain insight into how assertive you are as part of the process of deciding whether to become more assertive.

Perhaps you can't become completely assertive overnight, but you can decide *now* that you have been unassertive long enough and plan to change. There may be times when you want to quit and revert to your unassertive ways. Expressing your genuine beliefs may lead to some immediate social disapproval. Others may have a stake in your remaining a doormat, and the people we wind up confronting are sometimes those who are closest to us: parents, spouses, supervisors, and friends.

Perhaps the strategies presented here will work for you. If they don't, why not talk things over with your professor or visit the college health or counseling center?

REVIEW

- Psychotherapy is a systematic interaction between a therapist and a client that uses psychological principles to help the client overcome psychological disorders or adjust to problems in living.
- Mostly badly. It has been generally assumed that psychological disorders represented possession due to witchcraft or divine retribution, and cruel methods such as exorcism were used to try to rid the person of evil spirits. Asylums were the first institutions for people with psychological disorders, and eventually mental hospitals and the community mental health movement came into being.
- The goals of psychoanalysis are to provide self-insight, encourage the spilling forth (catharsis) of psychic energy, and replace defensive behavior with coping behavior. The main method is free association, but dream analysis and interpretations are used as well. For example, a psychoanalyst may help clients gain insight into the ways in which they are transferring feelings toward their parents onto a spouse or even onto the analyst.
- Modern approaches are briefer and more directive, and the therapist and client usually sit face to face.
- Client-centered therapy uses nondirective methods to help clients overcome obstacles to self-actualization. The therapist shows unconditional positive regard, empathic understanding, and genuineness.
- Perls's highly directive method aims to help people integrate conflicting parts of their personality. He aimed to make clients aware of conflict, accept its reality, and make choices despite fear.
- Behavior therapy relies on psychological learning principles (for example, conditioning and observational learning) to help clients develop adaptive behavior patterns and discontinue maladaptive ones.
- These include flooding, systematic desensitization, and modeling. Flooding exposes a person to fear-evoking stimuli without aversive consequences until fear is extinguished. Systematic desensitization counterconditions fears by gradually exposing clients to a hierarchy of fear-evoking stimuli while they remain relaxed.

Modeling encourages clients to imitate another person (the model) in approaching fear-evoking stimuli.

- This is a behavior-therapy method for discouraging undesirable behaviors by repeatedly pairing clients' self-defeating goals (for example, alcohol, cigarette smoke, deviant sex objects) with aversive stimuli so that the goals become aversive rather than tempting.
- These are behavior therapy methods that foster adaptive behavior through principles of reinforcement. Examples include token economies, successive approximation, social skills training, and biofeedback training.
- Behavior-therapy methods for adopting desirable behavior patterns and breaking bad habits begin with a functional analysis to determine the antecedents and consequences of the problem behavior, along with the details of the behavior itself. They then focus on modifying the antecedents (stimuli that act as triggers) and consequences (reinforcers) of behavior and on modifying the behavior itself.
- Cognitive therapies aim to give clients insight into irrational beliefs and cognitive distortions and replace these cognitive errors with rational beliefs and accurate perceptions.
- Aaron Beck notes that clients develop emotional problems such as depression because of cognitive errors that lead them to minimize accomplishments and catastrophize failures. He found that depressed people experience cognitive distortions such as the cognitive triad; that is, they expect the worst of themselves, the world at large, and the future. Beck teaches clients how to scientifically dispute cognitive errors.
- Albert Ellis originated rational emotive behavior therapy, which holds that people's beliefs *about* events, not only the events themselves, shape people's responses to them. Ellis points out how irrational beliefs, such as the belief that we must have social approval, can worsen problems. Ellis literally argues clients out of irrational beliefs.
- Group therapy is more economical than individual therapy. Moreover, group members benefit from the social support and experiences of other members. However, some clients cannot disclose their problems in the group setting or risk group disapproval. They need individual attention.
- Encounter groups attempt to foster personal growth by heightening awareness of people's needs and feelings through intense confrontations between strangers. Encounter groups can be harmful when they urge too rapid disclosure of personal matters or when several members attack an individual.
- In family therapy, one or more families make up the group. Family therapy undertaken from the "systems approach" modifies family interactions to enhance the growth of individuals in the family and the family as a whole.
- It is difficult and perhaps impossible to randomly assign clients to therapy methods such as traditional psychoanalysis. Moreover, clients cannot be kept blind as to the treatment they are receiving. Further, it can be difficult to sort out the effects of nonspecific therapeutic factors such as instillation of hope from the effects of specific methods of therapy.
- Statistical analyses such as meta-analysis show that people who obtain most forms of psychotherapy fare better than people who do not. Psychodynamic and client-centered approaches are particularly helpful with highly verbal and motivated individuals. Cognitive and behavior therapies are probably most effective. Cognitive therapy appears to be as effective as drug therapy in the treatment of depression.
- Antipsychotic drugs help many people with schizophrenia by blocking the action of dopamine receptors. Antidepressants often help people with severe depression, apparently by raising levels of serotonin available to the brain. Lithium often helps people with bipolar disorder, apparently by regulating levels of glutamate. The use of antianxiety drugs for daily tensions and anxieties is not recommended because people who use them rapidly build tolerance for the drugs. Also, these drugs do not solve personal or social problems, and people attribute their resultant calmness to the drug and not to self-efficacy.
- In ECT an electrical current is passed through the temples, inducing a seizure and frequently relieving severe depression. ECT is controversial because of side effects such as loss of memory and because nobody knows why it works.
- Psychosurgery is a controversial method for alleviating agitation by severing nerve pathways in the brain. The best-known psychosurgery technique, prefrontal lobotomy, has been largely discontinued because of side effects.
- There is controversy as to whether psychotherapy or drug therapy should be used with people with anxiety disorders or depression. Drugs do not teach people how to solve problems and build relationships. Having said that, antidepressants are apparently advisable when psychotherapy does not help people with depression; furthermore, ECT appears to be helpful in some cases in which neither psychotherapy nor drug therapy (antidepressants) is of help. Psychosurgery has been all but discontinued because of questions about whether it is effective and because of side effects. Most health professionals agree that antipsychotic drugs are of benefit to large numbers of people with schizophrenia.

CHAPTER 13 PRACTICE EXAM

____ 1. The first mental institutions were in
a. monasteries.
b. hospitals.
c. homes.
d. ships.

____ 2. Pychodynamic treatment seeks to
a. Change behavior.
b. Modify the self.
c. Change neurons.
d. Achieve insight.

____ 3. A client does not want to talk about her mother. When psychoanalyst asks about the mother, the client says it was nice. The client is experiencing
a. Counter transference.
b. Resistance.
c. Lexicon.
d. free meals.

____ 4. Psychodynamic therapists will make comments to clients when the therapist wants to
a. Correct an error.
b. make an interpretation.
c. Make the client uncomfortable.
d. Ease the tension.

____ 5. In client-centered therapy, the therapist attempts to view the world through the client's
a. frame of reference.
b. catharsis.
c. Id.
d. family.

____ 6. Client-centered and Gestalt therapy focus on
a. the childhood.
b. the here and now.
c. The preconscious unconscious.
d. Past relationships.

____ 7. A client who expresses opposing thoughts on a topic is using a ________ according to Gestalt therapy.
a. Conscientiousness
b. Dialogue
c. Introjection
d. Goal directedness

____ 8. Behavior therapy uses __________ principles to change behavior.
a. Analytic
b. Dynamic
c. Client centeredavoidance
d. Learning

____ 9. A divorcee is having problems with communicating with people. What type of therapist would establish to program to increase the person's social skills through reinforcement?
a. psychoanalytic
b. psychodynamic
c. Gestalt
d. behavior

____ 10. The procedure in which a client watches another person engage in the feared behavior is called __________
a. imitation.
b. psychoanalysis.
c. modeling.
d. gingivitis.

____ 11. Token economies are based on __________ learning concepts.
a. aversive
b. classical
c. latent
d. operant

____ 12. In behavioral techniques, __________ are critical for treatment to succeed.
a. Dynamic ideas
b. Practice and repetition
c. Analytic analogues
d. Introversions

____ 13. Which is not an advantage of group therapy?
a. it is less expensive than individual sessions.
b. there are opportunities to try out new behaviors with group members.
c. the individual doesn't feel alone.
d. feedback is always positive.

____ 14. Which therapys has shown wide applicability and success?
a. psychodynamic
b. psychoanalytic
c. client-centered
d. cognitive-behavioral

____ 15. "Minor tranquilizer" is another term for
a. antipsychotic drug.
b. antianxiety drug.
c. analgesic.
d. antidepressant.

Answers

1. A
2. D
3. B
4. B
5. A
6. B
7. B
8. D
9. D
10. C
11. D
12. B
13. D
14. D
15. B

CHAPTER 14: SOCIAL BEHAVIOR

QUESTIONS

1. What does research suggest about the correlation between personality and physical attractiveness?
2. What is the relationship between the perception of physical attractiveness and competence?
3. Why do people depend on social schemas?
4. What are common gender, age, ethnic, and occupational stereotypes?
5. What is the problem with stereotyping people based on probabilities?
6. How did Cohen's (1981) study find evidence supporting confirmatory bias?
7. How do evolutionary psychologists explain bias in person perception?
8. What are examples of the effect internal and external attributions can have on perceptions of people?
9. What is Weiner's model of attributions for success and failures?
10. Why do people tend to overestimate personal qualities as opposed to situational factors?
11. What is the generality about actors and observers and attributions?
12. What are examples of defensive attribution?
13. What are examples of the self-serving bias?
14. What cultures tend to be individualistic or collectivist?
15. What is the single prominent factor in dating relationships?
16. What is an example of the matching hypothesis?
17. What does research suggest about illusions and romantic relationships?
18. What did Hazan and Shave (1987) discover about love and attachment relationships?
19. What are the relationships between attachment style and adjustment?
20. What are differences between marriages in individualistic cultures and collectivist cultures?
21. What are the most documented findings on the evolutionary bases of heterosexual attraction?
22. What are the three crucial dimensions of attitudes?
23. How are two reasons for the inconsistent relationship between attitudes and behavior?
24. What factors does the persuasion process boil down to?
25. How do credibility, trustworthiness, and likeability influence persuasion?
26. How do the message variables of argument sides, argument strength, message repetition, and fear arousal increase and decrease persuasion?
27. How do the receiver factors of forewarning, disconfirmation bias, attitude strength, and prior knowledge influence the effect of a message?
28. How might operant conditioning work in attitude formation and change?
29. How might observational learning work in attitude formation and change?
30. What were the procedures and results of Festinger and Carlsmith (1959) study on cognitive dissonance?
31. What is cognitive dissonance thought to create?
32. What are two reasons dissonance effects are not very reliable?
33. When is self-perception in attitude change at work?
34. What is the traditional view and the self-perception view of attitude change?

35. What is the relationship between group size and conformity?
36. When the pressure is on, what do people tend to do?
37. Who were the subjects, what were the procedures, and what were the results of Milgram's study on obedience?
38. What were two criticisms of Milgram's research on obedience?
39. What does research in collectivist cultures suggest about conformity?
40. What is one enduring insight about behavior in groups?
41. What are three factors that may account for the bystander effect?
42. Under what conditions does social loafing occur?
43. Under what conditions is social loafing less likely to occur?
44. What are two reasons group polarization occurs?
45. What is an example of the three components of prejudice as an attitude?
46. What are two reasons stereotypes are resistant to change?
47. What are four questions one should ask when evaluating the credibility of information and an example of each?

VOCABULARY

1. attitudes
2. attributions
3. bystander effect
4. cognitive dissonance
5. collectivism
6. conformity
7. counterattitudinal behavior
8. defensive attribution
9. diffusion of responsibility
10. discrimination
11. effort justification
12. ethnocentrism
13. external attributions
14. foot-in-the-door technique
15. fundamental attribution error
16. group
17. group cohesiveness
18. group polarization
19. groupthink
20. hindsight bias
21. illusory correlation
22. individualism
23. ingroup
24. internal attributions
25. interpersonal attraction
26. lowball technique
27. matching hypothesis
28. outgroup
29. person perception
30. prejudice
31. reciprocity
32. reciprocity norm
33. self effacing bias
34. self serving bias
35. social loafing
36. social schemas
37. spotlight effect
38. stereotypes

14 Social Behavior

© Dennis Stock/Magnum Photos

WHEN MUFFY, "the quintessential yuppie," met Jake, "the ultimate working-class stiff," her friends got very nervous.

Muffy is a 28-year-old stockbroker and a self-described "snob" with a group of about ten close women friends. Snobs all. They're graduates of fancy business schools. All consultants, investment bankers, and CPAs. All "cute, bright, fun to be with, and really intelligent," according to Muffy. They're all committed to their high-powered careers, but they all expect to marry someday, too.

Unfortunately, most of them don't date much. In fact, they spend a good deal of time "lamenting the dearth of 'good men'" Well, lucky Muffy actually met one of those "good men." Jake is a salesman. He comes from a working-class neighborhood. His clothes come from Sears.

He wasn't like the usual men Muffy dated. He treats Muffy the way she's always dreamed of being treated. He listens; he cares; he remembers. "He makes me feel safe and more cherished than any man I've ever known," she says.

So she decided to bring him to a little party of about 30 of her closest friends. . . .

Perhaps it was only Jake's nerves that caused him to commit some truly unforgivable faux pas that night. His sins were legion. Where do we start? First of all, he asked for a beer when everyone else was drinking white wine. He wore a worn turtleneck while everyone else had just removed the Polo tags from their clothing. He smoked. . . .

"The next day at least half of the people who had been at the party called to give me their impressions. They all said that they felt they just had to let me know that they thought Jake 'lacked polish' or 'seemed loud' or 'might not be a suitable match,'" Muffy says.

Now, you may think that Muffy's friends are simply very sensitive, demanding people. But you'd be wrong. Actually, they've been quite accepting of some of the other men that Muffy has brought to their little parties. Winston, for example, was a great favorite.

"He got drunk, ignored me, and asked for other women's phone numbers right in front of me. But he was six-foot-four, the classic preppie, with blond hair, horn-rimmed glasses, and Ralph Lauren clothes."

So now Muffy is confused. "Jake is the first guy I've been out with in a long time that I've really liked. I was excited about him and my friends knew that. I was surprised by their reaction. I'll admit there's some validity in all their comments, but it's hard to express how violent it was. It made me think about what these women really want in a man. Whatever they say, what they really want is someone they can take to a business dinner. They want someone who comes with a tux. Like a Ken doll."

Muffy may have come to a crossroads in her young life. It's clear that there's no way she can bring Jake among her friends for a while.

"I don't want their reaction to muddy my feelings until I get them sorted out," she says.

The preceding account is a real story, taken from a book about contemporary intimate relationships (Lavin, & Kavesh, 1988, pp. 118–121). Muffy is on the horns of a difficult dilemma. Romantic relationships are important to most people, but so are friendships, and Muffy may have to choose between the two. Muffy's story illustrates the significance of social relations in people's lives. It also foreshadows each of the topics that we'll cover in this chapter, as we look at behavior in its social context.

social psychology
the branch of psychology concerned with the way individuals' thoughts, feelings, and behaviors are influenced by others.

Social psychology is the branch of psychology concerned with the way individuals' thoughts, feelings, and behaviors are influenced by others. Our coverage of social psychology will focus on six broad topics highlighted in Muffy's story:

- *Person perception.* The crux of Muffy's problem is that Jake didn't make a very good impression on her friends, primarily because her friends have preconceived views of "working-class stiffs." To what extent do people's expectations color their impressions of others?
- *Attribution processes.* Muffy is struggling to understand her friends' rejection of Jake. When she implies that Jake's rejection is due to their snotty elitism, she's engaging in attribution, making an inference about the causes of her friends' behavior. How do people use attributions to explain social behavior?
- *Interpersonal attraction.* Jake and Muffy are different in many important ways—is it true that opposites attract? Why does Jake's lack of similarity to Muffy's friends lead to such disdain?
- *Attitudes.* Muffy's girlfriends have negative attitudes about working-class men. How are attitudes formed? What leads to attitude change? How do attitudes affect people's behavior?
- *Conformity and obedience.* Muffy's friends discourage her from dating Jake, putting her under pressure to conform to their values. What factors influence conformity? Can people be coaxed into doing things that contradict their values?
- *Behavior in groups.* Muffy belongs to a tight-knit group of friends who think along similar lines. Do people behave differently when they are in groups as opposed to when they are alone? Why do people in groups often think alike?

Social psychologists study how people are affected by the actual, imagined, or implied presence of others. Their interest is not limited to individuals' interactions with others, as people can engage in social behavior even when they're alone. For instance, if you were driving by yourself on a deserted highway and tossed your trash out your car window, your littering would be a social action. It would defy social norms, reflect your socialization and attitudes, and have repercussions (albeit, small) for other people in your society. Social psychologists often study individual behavior in a social context. This interest in understanding individual behavior should be readily apparent in our first section, on person perception.

PERSON PERCEPTION: FORMING IMPRESSIONS OF OTHERS

Can you remember the first meeting of your introductory psychology class? What impression did your professor make on you that day? Did your instructor appear to be confident? Easygoing? Pompous? Open-minded? Cynical? Friendly? Were your first impressions supported or undermined by subsequent observations? When you interact with people, you're constantly engaged in **person perception**, the process of forming impressions of others. People show considerable ingenuity in piecing together clues about others' characteristics. However, impressions are often inaccurate because of the many biases and fallacies that occur in person perception. In this section we consider some of the factors that influence, and often distort, people's perceptions of others.

person perception the process of forming impressions of others.

Effects of Physical Appearance

"You shouldn't judge a book by its cover." "Beauty is only skin deep." People know better than to let physical attractiveness determine their perceptions of others' personal qualities. Or do they? Studies have shown that judgments of others' personality are often swayed by their appearance, especially their physical attractiveness. People tend to ascribe desirable personality characteristics to those who are good looking, seeing them as more sociable, friendly, poised, warm, and well adjusted than those who are less attractive (Eagly et al., 1991; Wheeler & Kim, 1997). In reality, research findings suggest that little correlation exists between attractiveness and personality traits (Feingold, 1992). Why do we inaccurately assume that a connection exists between good looks and personality? One reason is that extremely attractive people are vastly overrepresented in the entertainment media, where they are mostly portrayed in a highly favorable light (Smith, McIntosh, & Bazzini, 1999).

You might guess that physical attractiveness would influence perceptions of competence less than perceptions of personality, but the data suggest otherwise. A recent review of the relevant research found that people have a surprisingly strong tendency to view good-looking individuals as more competent than less attractive individuals (Langlois et al., 2000). This bias literally pays off for good-looking people, as they tend to secure better jobs and earn higher salaries than less attractive individuals (Collins & Zebrowitz, 1995; Frieze, Olson, & Russell, 1991). For example, research on attorneys whose law school class photos were evaluated by independent raters found that physical attractiveness boosted their actual income by 10%–12% (Engemann & Owyang, 2005). Fortunately, not all trait inferences are influenced by physical attractiveness. For instance, good looks seem to have relatively little impact on perceptions of honesty and integrity (Eagly et al., 1991).

"Beauty is life's E-Z Pass."

Observers are also quick to draw inferences about people based on how they move, talk, and gesture—that is, their style of nonverbal expressiveness—and these inferences tend to be fairly accurate (Ambady & Rosenthal, 1993; Borkenau et al., 2004). For example, based on a mere 10 seconds of videotape, participants can guess strangers' sexual orientation (heterosexual-homosexual) with decent accuracy (Ambady, Hallahan, & Conner, 1999). It is also widely believed that it is reasonable to draw inferences about someone's personality based on his or her handshake. Surprisingly little research has been conducted on handshaking and person perception, but preliminary evidence suggests that a firm, vigorous handshake is associated with relatively favorable first impressions (Chaplin et al., 2000).

Cognitive Schemas

Even though every individual is unique, people tend to categorize one another. For instance, in our opening story, Muffy is characterized as "the quintessential yuppie," and Jake as a "working-class stiff." Such labels reflect the use of cognitive schemas in person perception. As we discussed in the chapter on memory, *schemas* are cognitive structures that guide information processing. Individuals use schemas to organize the world around them—including their social world. **Social schemas** are organized clusters of ideas about categories of social events and people. People have social schemas for events such as dates, picnics, committee meetings, and family reunions, as well as for certain categories of people, such as "dumb jocks," "social climbers," "frat rats," and "wimps" (see Figure 14.1). Individuals depend on social schemas because the schemas help them to efficiently process and store the wealth of information that they take in about others

social schemas
organized clusters of ideas about categories of social events and people.

FIGURE 14.1
Examples of social schemas. Everyone has social schemas for various "types" of people, such as sophisticated professionals or working-class stiffs. Social schemas are clusters of beliefs that guide information processing.

in their interactions. Hence, people routinely place one another in categories, and these categories influence the process of person perception (Macrae & Bodenhausen, 2000).

Stereotypes

Some of the schemas that individuals apply to people are unique products of their personal experiences, while other schemas may be part of their shared cultural background. **Stereotypes** are special types of schemas that fall into the latter category. *Stereotypes* are widely held beliefs that people have certain characteristics because of their membership in a particular group.

stereotypes
widely held beliefs that people have certain characteristics because of their membership in a particular group.

The most common stereotypes in our society are those based on sex, age, and membership in ethnic or occupational groups. People who subscribe to traditional *gender stereotypes* tend to assume that women are emotional, submissive, illogical, and passive, while men are unemotional, dominant, logical, and aggressive. *Age stereotypes* suggest that elderly people are slow, feeble, rigid, forgetful, and asexual. Notions that Jews are mercenary, Germans are methodical, and Italians are passionate are examples of common *ethnic stereotypes. Occupational stereotypes* suggest that lawyers are manipulative, accountants are conforming, artists are moody, and so forth.

Stereotyping is a normal cognitive process that is frequently automatic and that saves on the time and effort required to get a handle on people individually (Devine & Monteith, 1999; Operario & Fiske, 2001). Stereotypes save energy by simplifying our social world. However, this conservation of energy often comes at some cost in terms of accuracy (Wigboldus, Dijksterhuis, & Knippenberg, 2003). Stereotypes tend to be broad overgeneralizations that ignore the diversity within social groups and foster inaccurate perceptions of people (Hilton & von Hippel, 1996). Obviously, not all males, Jews, and lawyers behave alike. Most people who subscribe to stereotypes realize that not all members of a group are identical. For instance, they may admit that some men aren't competitive, some Jews aren't mercenary, and some lawyers aren't manipulative. However, they may still tend to assume that males, Jews, and lawyers are *more likely* than others to have these characteristics. Even if stereotypes mean only that people think in terms of slanted *probabilities,* their expectations may lead them to misperceive individuals with whom they interact. As we've noted in previous chapters, perception is subjective, and people often see what they expect to see.

Subjectivity in Person Perception

Stereotypes and other schemas create biases in person perception that frequently lead to confirmation of people's expectations about others. If someone's behavior is ambiguous, people are likely to interpret what they see in a way that's consistent with their expectations (Olson, Roese, & Zanna, 1996). Thus, after dealing with a pushy female customer, a salesman who holds traditional gender stereotypes might characterize the woman as "emotional." In contrast, he might characterize a male who exhibits the same pushy behavior as "aggressive."

People not only see what they expect to see, they also tend to overestimate how often they see it (Johnson & Mullen, 1994; Shavitt et al., 1999). **Illusory correlation** occurs when people estimate that they have encountered more confirmations of an association between social traits than they have actually seen. People also tend to underestimate the number of disconfirmations they have encountered, as illustrated by statements like "I've never met an honest lawyer."

illusory correlation
a misperception that occurs when people estimate that they have encountered more confirmations of an association between social traits than they have actually seen.

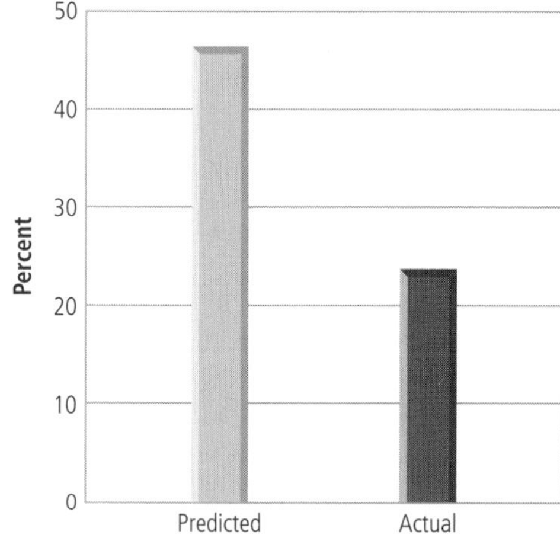

FIGURE 14.2

The spotlight effect. In a study of the spotlight effect, Gilovich, Medvec, and Savitsky (2000) induced college students to wear an embarrassing T-shirt while interacting with other participants. The shirt depicted Barry Manilow, a singer who was characterized by the authors as "not terribly popular among college students." The subjects who wore the Manilow shirt were asked to predict what percentage of the other participants would notice the shirt. As you can see, their predictions far exceeded the actual number of participants who noticed the embarrassing shirt.
Source: Adapted from Gilovich, T., Medvec, V. H., & Savitsky, K. (2000). The spotlight effect in social judgment: An egocentric bias in estimates of the salience of one's own actions and appearance. *Journal of Personality and Social Psychology, 78,* 211–222. Copyright © 2000 by the American Psychological Association. Used by permission of the publisher and author.

Memory processes can contribute to confirmatory biases in person perception in a variety of ways. Often, individuals selectively recall facts that fit with their schemas and stereotypes (Fiske, 1998; Quinn, Macrae, & Bodenhausen, 2003). Evidence for such a tendency was found in a study by Cohen (1981). In this experiment, participants watched a videotape of a woman, described as either a waitress or a librarian, who engaged in a variety of activities, including listening to classical music, drinking beer, and watching TV. When asked to recall what the woman did during the filmed sequence, participants tended to remember activities consistent with their stereotypes of waitresses and librarians. For instance, subjects who thought the woman was a waitress tended to recall her beer drinking, while subjects who thought she was a librarian tended to recall her listening to classical music.

Further evidence for the subjectivity of social perception comes from a phenomenon called the *spotlight effect*—people's tendency to assume that the social spotlight shines more brightly on them than it actually does (Gilovich & Savitsky, 1999). Recent studies show that people often overestimate the degree to which others pay attention to their appearance and behavior. For example, in one study some college students were induced to wear an embarrassing Barry Manilow T-shirt in interactions with other participants and were subsequently asked to estimate the percentage of the other subjects who had noticed the shirt. Their estimates were over twice as high as the actual percentage of subjects who noticed the embarrassing T-shirt (see Figure 14.2; Gilovich, Medvec, & Savitsky, 2000). The bad news about the spotlight effect is that it occurs in moments of triumph as well as moments of embarrassment, so our successes and accomplishments often garner less attention from others than we believe they do. The good news is that our blunders and failures are less salient to others than we think they are and that people's inferences about us based on these blunders are not as harsh as widely assumed (Savitsky, Epley, & Gilovich, 2001).

An Evolutionary Perspective on Bias in Person Perception

Why is the process of person perception riddled with bias? Evolutionary psychologists argue that many of the biases seen in social perception were adaptive in humans' ancestral environment (Krebs & Denton, 1997). For example, they argue that person perception is swayed by physical attractiveness because attractiveness was associated with reproductive potential in women and with health, vigor, and the accumulation of material resources in men.

What about the human tendency to automatically categorize others? Evolutionary theorists attribute this behavior to our distant ancestors' need to quickly separate friend from foe. They assert that humans are programmed by evolution to immediately classify people as members of an **ingroup**—a group that one belongs to and identifies with, or as members of an **outgroup**—a group that one does not belong to or identify with. This crucial categorization is thought to structure subsequent perceptions. As Krebs and Denton (1997) put it, "It is as though the act of classifying others as ingroup or outgroup members activates two quite different brain circuits" (p. 27). In-group members tend to be viewed in a favorable light, whereas outgroup members tend to be viewed in terms of various negative stereotypes. According to Krebs and Denton, these negative stereotypes ("They are inferior; they are all alike; they will exploit us") move outgroups out of our domain of empathy, so we feel justified in not liking them or discriminating against them.

ingroup
the group that people belong to and identify with.

outgroup
people who are not part of the ingroup.

Thus, evolutionary psychologists ascribe much of the bias in person perception to cognitive mechanisms that have been shaped by natural selection. Their speculation is thought provoking, but empirical work is needed to test their hypotheses.

ATTRIBUTION PROCESSES: EXPLAINING BEHAVIOR

It's Friday evening and you're sitting around at home feeling bored. You call a few friends to see whether they'd like to go out. They all say that they'd love to go, but they have other commitments and can't. Their commitments sound vague, and you feel that their reasons for not going out with you are rather flimsy. How do you explain these rejections? Do your friends really have commitments? Are they worn out by school and work? When they said that they'd love to go, were they being sincere? Or do they find you boring? Could they be right? Are you boring? These questions illustrate a process that people engage in routinely: the explanation of behavior. *Attributions* play a key role in these explanatory efforts, and they have significant effects on social relations.

What are attributions? **Attributions** are inferences that people draw about the causes of events, others' behavior, and their own behavior. If you conclude that a friend turned down your invitation because she's overworked, you have made an attribution about the cause of her behavior (and, implicitly, have rejected other possible explanations). If you conclude that you're stuck at home with nothing to do because you failed to plan ahead, you've made an attribution about the cause of an event (being stuck at home). If you conclude that you failed to plan ahead because you're a procrastinator, you've made an attribution about the cause of your own behavior. People make attributions mainly because they have a strong need to understand their experiences. They want to make sense out of their own behavior, others' actions, and the events in their lives. In this section, we'll take a look at some of the patterns seen when people make attributions.

attributions
inferences that people draw about the causes of events, others' behavior, and their own behavior.

internal attributions
ascribing the causes of behavior to personal dispositions, traits, abilities, and feelings.

external attributions
ascribing the causes of behavior to situational demands and environmental constraints.

Internal Versus External Attributions

Fritz Heider (1958) was the first to describe how people make attributions. He asserted that people tend to locate the cause of behavior either *within a person,* attributing it to personal factors, or *outside a person,* attributing it to environmental factors.

Elaborating on Heider's insight, various theorists have agreed that explanations of behavior and events can be categorized as internal or external attributions (Jones & Davis, 1965; Kelley, 1967; Weiner, 1974). **Internal attributions** ascribe the causes of behavior to personal dispositions, traits, abilities, and feelings. **External attributions** ascribe the causes of behavior to situational demands and environmental constraints. For example, if a friend's business fails, you might attribute it to his or her lack of business acumen (an internal, personal factor) or to negative trends in the nation's economic climate (an external, situational explanation). Parents who find out that their teenage son has just banged up the car may blame it on his carelessness (a personal disposition) or on slippery road conditions (a situational factor).

Internal and external attributions can have a tremendous impact on everyday interpersonal interactions. Blaming a friend's business failure on poor business acumen as opposed to a poor economy will have a great impact on how you view your

■ **Fritz Heider.** "Often the momentary situation which, at least in part, determines the behavior of a person is disregarded and the behavior is taken as a manifestation of personal characteristics."

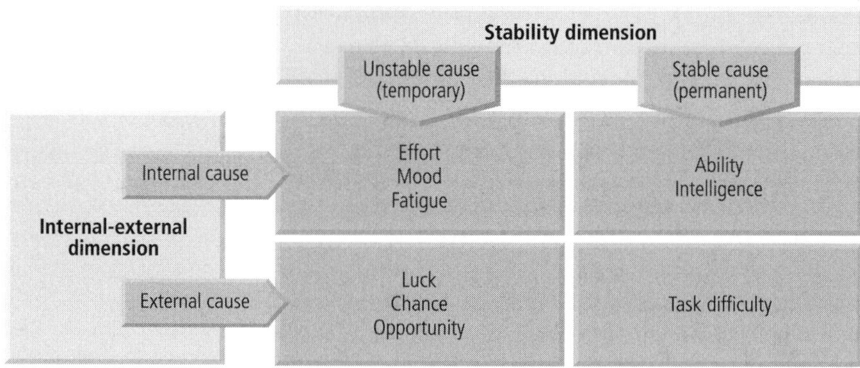

FIGURE 14.3

Weiner's model of attributions for success and failure. Weiner's model assumes that people's explanations for success and failure emphasize internal versus external causes and stable versus unstable causes. Examples of causal factors that fit into each of the four cells in Weiner's model are shown in the diagram. *Source:* Weiner, B., Friese, I., Kukla, A., Reed, L., & Rosenbaum, R. M. (1972). Perceiving the causes of success and failure. In E. E. Jones, D. E. Kanouse, H. H. Kelley, R. E. Nisbett, S. Valins, & B. Weiner (Eds.), *Perceiving the causes of behavior.* Morristown, NJ: General Learning Press. Used by permission of Bernard Weiner.

friend. Likewise, if parents attribute their son's automobile accident to slippery road conditions, they're likely to deal with the event very differently than if they attribute it to his carelessness.

Attributions for Success and Failure

Some psychologists have sought to discover additional dimensions of attributional thinking besides the internal-external dimension. After studying the attributions that people make in explaining success and failure, Bernard Weiner (1980, 1986, 1994) concluded that people often focus on the *stability* of the causes underlying behavior. According to Weiner, the stable-unstable dimension cuts across the internal-external dimension, creating four types of attributions for success and failure, as shown in Figure 14.3.

Let's apply Weiner's model to a concrete event. Imagine that you're contemplating why you failed to get a job that you wanted. You might attribute your setback to internal factors that are stable (lack of ability) or unstable (inadequate effort to put together an eye-catching résumé). Or you might attribute your setback to external factors that are stable (too much outstanding competition) or unstable (bad luck). If you got the job, your explanations for your success would fall into the same four categories: internal-stable (your excellent ability), internal-unstable (your hard work to assemble a superb résumé), external-stable (lack of top-flight competition), and external-unstable (good luck).

Bias in Attribution

Attributions are only inferences. Your attributions may not be the correct explanations for events. Paradoxical as it may seem, people often arrive at inaccurate explanations even when they contemplate the causes of *their own behavior.* Attributions ultimately represent *guesswork* about the causes of events, and these guesses tend to be slanted in certain directions. Let's look at the principal biases seen in attribution.

Actor-Observer Bias Your view of your own behavior can be quite different from the view of someone else observing you. When an actor and an observer draw inferences about the causes of the actor's behavior, they often make different attributions. A common form of bias seen in observers is the **fundamental attribution error,** which refers to observers' bias in favor of internal attributions in explaining others' behavior. Of course, in many instances, an internal attribution may not be an "error." However, observers have a curious tendency to overestimate the likelihood that an actor's behavior reflects personal qualities rather than situational factors (Krull, 2001). Why? One reason is that situational pressures may not be

fundamental attribution error
observers' bias in favor of internal attributions in explaining others' behavior.

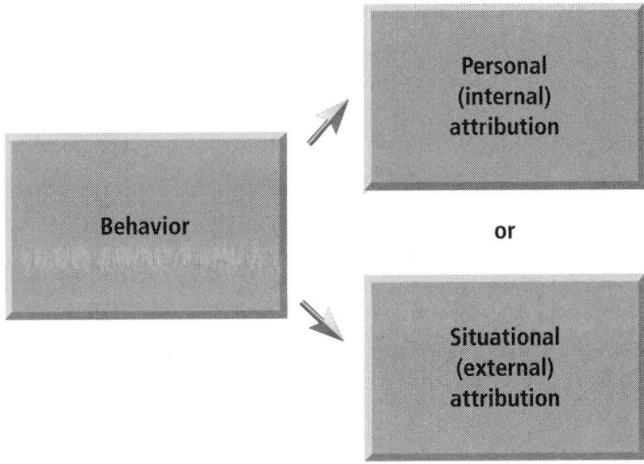

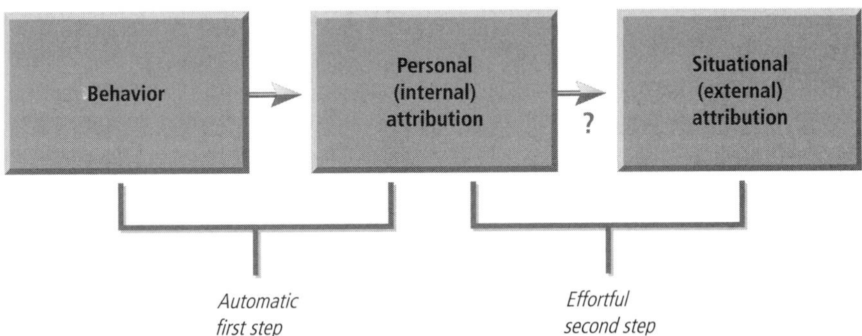

FIGURE 14.4

An alternative view of the fundamental attribution error. According to Gilbert (1989) and others, the nature of attribution processes favors the *fundamental attribution error.* Traditional models of attribution assume that internal and external attributions are an either-or proposition requiring equal amounts of effort. In contrast, Gilbert posits that people tend to automatically make internal attributions with little effort, and then they *may* expend additional effort to adjust for the influence of situational factors, which can lead to an external attribution. Thus, external attributions for others' behavior require more thought and effort, which makes them less common than personal attributions.

readily apparent to an observer. As Gilbert and Malone (1995) put it, "When one tries to point to a situation, one often stabs empty air" (p. 25). It is not that people assume that situational factors have little impact on behavior (Gawronski, 2004). Rather, it's that attributing others' behavior to their dispositions is a relatively effortless, almost automatic process, whereas explaining people's behavior in terms of situational factors requires more thought and effort (see Figure 14.4; Krull & Erickson, 1995). Another factor favoring internal attributions is that many people feel that few situations are so coercive that they negate all freedom of choice (Forsyth, 2004).

To illustrate the gap that often exists between actors' and observers' attributions, imagine that you're visiting your bank and you fly into a rage over a mistake made on your account. Observers who witness your rage are likely to make an internal attribution and infer that you are surly, temperamental, and quarrelsome. They may be right, but if asked, you'd probably attribute your rage to the frustrating situation. Perhaps you're normally a calm, easygoing person, but today you've been in line for 20 minutes, you just straightened out a similar error by the same bank last week, and you're being treated rudely by the teller. Observers are often unaware of historical and situational considerations such as these, so they tend to make internal attributions for another's behavior (Gilbert, 1998).

In contrast, the circumstances that have influenced an actor's behavior tend to be more salient to the actor. Hence, actors are more likely than observers to locate the cause of their behavior in the situation. In general, then, *actors favor external attributions for their behavior, whereas observers are more likely to explain the same behavior with internal attributions* (Jones & Nisbett, 1971; Krueger, Ham, & Linford, 1996).

A common example of defensive attribution is the tendency to blame the homeless for their plight.

Defensive Attribution In attempting to explain the calamities and setbacks that befall other people, an observer's tendency to make internal attributions may become even stronger than normal. Let's say that a friend gets mugged and severely beaten. You may attribute the mugging to your friend's carelessness or stupidity ("He should have known better than to be in that neighborhood at that time") rather than to bad luck. Why? Because if you attribute your friend's misfortune to bad luck, you have to face the ugly reality that it could just as easily happen to you. To avoid such disturbing thoughts, people often attribute mishaps to victims' negligence (Salminen, 1992; Thornton, 1984, 1992).

defensive attribution
the tendency to blame victims for their misfortune, so that one feels less likely to be victimized in a similar way.

Defensive attribution is a tendency to blame victims for their misfortune, so that one feels less likely to be victimized in a similar way. *Hindsight bias* probably contributes to this tendency, but blaming victims also helps people maintain their belief that they live in a just world, where they're unlikely to experience similar troubles (Lerner & Goldberg, 1999). The bias toward making defensive attributions can have unfortunate consequences. Blaming victims causes them to be seen in a negative light, and undesirable traits are unfairly attributed to them. Thus, it is assumed that burglary victims must be careless, that people who get fired must be incompetent, that poor people must be lazy, that rape victims must be seductive ("She probably asked for it"), and so on. As you can see, defensive attribution can lead to unwarranted derogation of victims of misfortune.

To some extent, such attributional tendencies are influenced by people's political ideology (Skitka et al., 2002). Conservatives tend to attribute poverty, homelessness, and criminal behavior to individuals' personal shortcomings. In contrast, liberals are more likely to attribute these social problems to institutional failures and unjust social practices. Research suggests that this disparity is mainly due to differences in peoples' willingness to consider situational factors that might contribute to poverty, homelessness, and other social problems (Skitka et al., 2002).

Self-Serving Bias The self-serving bias in attribution comes into play when people attempt to explain success and failure. This bias may either strengthen or weaken one's normal attributional tendencies, depending on whether one is trying to explain positive or negative outcomes (Campbell & Sedikides, 1999; Mezulis et al., 2004). The **self-serving bias** is the tendency to attribute one's successes to personal factors and one's failures to situational factors. Interestingly, this bias grows stronger as time passes after an event, so that people tend to take progressively more credit for their successes and less responsibility for their failures (Burger, 1986).

self-serving bias
the tendency to attribute one's successes to personal factors and one's failures to situational factors.

In explaining *failure,* the usual actor-observer biases are apparent. Actors tend to make external attributions, blaming their failures on unfavorable situational factors, while observers are more likely to attribute the same failures to the actors' personal shortcomings. Thus, if you fail an exam, you may place the blame on the poorly constructed test items, lousy teaching, distractions in the hallway, or a bad week at work (all external attributions). However, an observer is more likely to attribute your failure to your lack of ability or lack of study (both internal attributions). *In explaining success, the usual actor-observer differences are reversed to some degree.* Thus, if you get a high exam score, you'll probably make an internal attribution and point to your ability or your hard work, whereas observers are more likely to assume that the test was easy.

Culture and Attributional Tendencies

Do the patterns of attribution observed in subjects from Western societies transcend culture? More research is needed, but the preliminary evidence suggests not. Some interesting cultural disparities have emerged in research on attribution processes.

According to Harry Triandis (1989, 1994, 2001), cultural differences in **individualism** versus **collectivism** influence attributional tendencies as well as other aspects of social behavior. *Individualism* involves putting personal goals ahead of group goals and defining one's identity in terms of personal attributes rather than group memberships. In contrast, *collectivism* involves putting group goals ahead of personal goals and defining one's identity in terms of the groups one belongs to (such as one's family, tribe, work group, social class, caste, and so on). In comparison to individualistic cultures, collectivist cultures place a higher priority on shared values and resources, cooperation, mutual interdependence, and concern for how one's actions will affect other group members. Childrearing patterns in collectivist cultures emphasize the importance of obedience, reliability, and proper behavior, whereas individualistic cultures emphasize the development of independence, self-esteem, and self-reliance.

individualism
putting personal goals ahead of group goals and defining one's identity in terms of personal attributes rather than group memberships.

collectivism
putting group goals ahead of personal goals and defining one's identity in terms of the groups one belongs to.

A variety of factors influence whether societies cherish individualism as opposed to collectivism. Among other things, increases in a culture's affluence, education, urbanization, and social mobility tend to foster more individualism (Triandis, 1994). Many contemporary societies are in transition, but generally speaking, North American and Western European cultures tend to be individualistic, whereas Asian, African, and Latin American cultures tend to be collectivistic (Hofstede, 1980, 1983, 2001) (see Figure 14.5).

How does individualism versus collectivism relate to patterns of attribution? The evidence suggests that collectivist cultures may promote different attributional biases than individualistic cultures. For example, people from collectivist societies appear to be less prone to the *fundamental attribution error* than those from individualistic societies (Choi, Nisbett, & Norenzayan, 1999; Triandis, 2001). In Western cultures, people are viewed as autonomous individuals who are responsible for their actions. Endorsing beliefs such as "You can do anything you put your mind to" or "You have no one to blame but yourself," Westerners typically explain

FIGURE 14.5

Individualism versus collectivism around the world. Hofstede (1980, 1983, 2001) used survey data from over 100,000 employees of a large, multinational corporation to estimate the emphasis on individualism versus collectivism in 50 nations and 3 regions. His large, diverse international sample remains unequaled to date. In the figure, cultures are ranked in terms of how strongly they embraced the values of individualism. As you can see, Hofstede's estimates suggest that North American and Western European nations tend to be relatively individualistic, whereas more collectivism is found in Asian, African, and Latin American countries. *Source:* Adapted from Hofstede, G. (2001). *Culture's consequences* (2nd Ed., p. 215). Thousand Oaks, CA: Sage. Copyright © 2001 Sage Publications. Adapted by permission of Dr. Geert Hofstede.

Hofstede's rankings of national cultures' individualism

Individualistic cultures	Intermediate cultures	Collectivist cultures
1. United States	19. Israel	37. Hong Kong
2. Australia	20. Spain	38. Chile
3. Great Britain	21. India	40. Singapore
4. Canada	22. Argentina	40. Thailand
4. Netherlands	22. Japan	40. West Africa region
6. New Zealand	24. Iran	42. El Salvador
7. Italy	25. Jamaica	43. South Korea
8. Belgium	26. Arab region	44. Taiwan
9. Denmark	26. Brazil	45. Peru
10. France	28. Turkey	46. Costa Rica
11. Sweden	29. Uruguay	47. Indonesia
12. Ireland	30. Greece	47. Pakistan
13. Norway	31. Philippines	49. Colombia
14. Switzerland	32. Mexico	50. Venezuela
15. West Germany	34. East Africa region	51. Panama
16. South Africa	34. Portugal	52. Ecuador
17. Finland	34. Yugoslavia	53. Guatemala
18. Austria	36. Malaysia	

behavior in terms of people's personality traits and unique abilities. In contrast, collectivists, who value interdependence and obedience, are more likely to assume that one's behavior reflects adherence to group norms.

Although the *self-serving bias* has been documented in a variety of cultures, it is particularly prevalent in individualistic, Western societies, where an emphasis on competition and high self-esteem motivates people to try to impress others, as well as themselves (Mezulis et al., 2004). In contrast, Japanese subjects exhibit a *self-effacing bias* in explaining success (Akimoto & Sanbonmatsu, 1999; Markus & Kitayama, 1991), as they tend to attribute their successes to help they receive from others or to the ease of the task, while downplaying the importance of their ability. When they fail, Japanese subjects tend to be more self-critical than subjects from individualistic cultures (Heine & Renshaw, 2002). It is not that self-enhancement motives are absent in collectivist cultures. Cultural disparities in attributional bias reflect the fact that people from individualist and collectivist cultures cherish and value different traits (Sedikides, Gaertner, & Toguchi, 2003). People from individualistic cultures exhibit attributional biases (such as the self-serving bias) that help them to feel independent, competent, and self-reliant. In contrast, people from collectivist cultures display attributional biases that help them to feel loyal, cooperative, and respectful. People from both types of cultures show distortions in attribution that are intended to enhance their feelings of self-esteem, but the distortions are different because self-esteem is derived from different virtues.

CLOSE RELATIONSHIPS: LIKING AND LOVING

"I just don't know what she sees in him. She could do so much better for herself. I suppose he's a nice guy, but they're just not right for each other." Can't you imagine Muffy's friends making these comments in discussing her relationship with Jake? You've probably heard similar remarks on many occasions. These comments illustrate people's interest in analyzing the dynamics of attraction. **Interpersonal attraction** refers to positive feelings toward another. Social psychologists use this term broadly to encompass a variety of experiences, including liking, friendship, admiration, lust, and love. In this section, we'll analyze key factors that influence attraction and examine some theoretical perspectives on the mystery of love.

interpersonal attraction
positive feelings toward another.

Key Factors in Attraction

Many factors influence who is attracted to whom. Here we'll discuss factors that promote the development of liking, friendship, and love. Although these are different types of attraction, the interpersonal dynamics at work in each are largely similar.

Physical Attractiveness Although people often say that "beauty is only skin deep," the empirical evidence suggests that most people don't really believe that homily (Fitness, Fletcher, & Overall, 2003). The importance of physical attractiveness was demonstrated in a study in which unacquainted men and women were sent off on a "get-acquainted" date (Sprecher & Duck, 1994). The investigators were mainly interested in how communication might affect the process of attraction, but to put this factor in context they also measured subjects' perceptions of their date's physical attractiveness and similarity to themselves. They found that the quality of communication during the date did have some effect on females' interest in friendship, but the key determinant of romantic attraction for both sexes was the physical attractiveness of the other person. Many other studies have demonstrated the singular prominence of physical attractiveness in the initial stage of dating and have shown that it continues to influence the course of commitment as dating relationships evolve (Hendrick & Hendrick, 1992). In the realm of romance, being physically attractive appears to be more important for females than males (Regan, 2003). For example, in a study of college students (Speed & Gangestad, 1997), the correlation between romantic popularity (assessed by peer ratings) and physical attractiveness was higher for females (.76) than for males (.47). Not surprisingly, those who are handsome or beautiful know that they are attractive (Marcus & Miller, 2003).

matching hypothesis
the idea that males and females of approximately equal physical attractiveness are likely to select each other as partners.

Although people prefer physically attractive partners in romantic relationships, they may consider their own level of attractiveness in pursuing dates. What people want in a partner may be different from what they are willing to settle for (Regan, 1998). The **matching hypothesis** proposes that males and females of approximately equal physical attractiveness are likely to select each other as partners. The matching hypothesis is supported by evidence that married couples tend to be very similar in level of physical attractiveness (Feingold, 1988b). Interestingly, people expect that individuals who are similar in attractiveness will be more satisfied as couples and less likely to break up (Garcia & Khersonsky, 1996).

© Jack Hollingsworth/Getty Images

According to the matching hypothesis, males and females who are similar in physical attractiveness are likely to be drawn together. This type of matching may also influence the formation of friendships.

Similarity Effects Is it true that "birds of a feather flock together," or do "opposites attract"? Research provides far more support for the former than the latter. Married and dating couples tend to be similar in age, race, religion, social class, education, intelligence, physical attractiveness, values, and attitudes (Kalmijn, 1998; Watson et al., 2004). Similarity in personality appears to be

"It would never work out between us, Tom—we're from two totally different tiers of the upper middle class."

modest at best (Luo & Klohnen, 2005). Similarity is also seen among friends. For instance, adult friends tend to be relatively similar in terms of income, education, occupational status, ethnicity, and religion (Blieszner & Adams, 1992).

The most obvious explanation for these correlations is that similarity causes attraction. Laboratory experiments on *attitude similarity,* conducted by Donn Byrne and his colleagues, suggest that similarity *does* cause attraction (Byrne, 1997; Byrne, Clore, & Smeaton, 1986). However, research also suggests that attraction can foster similarity (Anderson, Keltner, & John, 2003). For example, Davis and Rusbult (2001) found that dating partners gradually modify their attitudes in ways that make them more congruent, a phenomenon they called *attitude alignment.* Moreover, people in stable, satisfying intimate relationships tend to subjectively overestimate how similar they and their partners are (Murray et al., 2002). Wanting to believe that they have found a kindred spirit, they tend to assume that their partners are mirrors of themselves.

■ **Ellen Berscheid.** "The emotion of romantic love seems to be distressingly fragile. As a 16th-century sage poignantly observed, 'the history of a love affair is the drama of its fight against time.'"

Reciprocity Effects People often attempt to gain others' liking by showering them with praise and flattery. However, we've all heard that "flattery will get you nowhere." What does the research show? The evidence suggests that flattery will get you somewhere, with some people, some of the time. In interpersonal attraction, **reciprocity** involves liking those who show that they like you. In general, research indicates that we tend to like those who show that they like us and that we tend to see others as liking us more if we like them. Thus, it appears that liking breeds liking and loving promotes loving (Sprecher, 1998). Reciprocating attraction generally entails providing friends and intimate partners with positive feedback that results in a *self-enhancement* effect—in other words, you help them feel good about themselves (Sedikides & Strube, 1997). However, studies suggest that people are also interested in *self-verification*—that is, they seek feedback that matches and supports their self-concepts (Bosson & Swann, 2001).

reciprocity
liking those who show that they like you.

Romantic Ideals In the realm of romance, people want their partner to measure up to their ideals. These ideals spell out the personal qualities that one hopes to find in a partner, such as warmth, good looks, loyalty, high status, a sense of humor, and so forth. According to Simpson, Fletcher, and Campbell (2001), people routinely evaluate how close their intimate partners come to matching these ideal standards, and these evaluations influence how relationships progress. Consistent with this theory, research shows that the more closely individuals' perceptions of their partners match their ideals, the more satisfied they tend to be with their relationship—both in the early stages of dating (Fletcher, Simpson, & Thomas, 2000) and in stable, long-term relationships (Fletcher et al., 1999). Moreover, the size of the discrepancy between ideals and perceptions predicts whether a dating relationship will continue or dissolve (Fletcher et al., 2000).

Of course, these evaluations of how one's partner compares to one's ideals are subjective, leaving room for distortion. When people are highly invested in a relationship they can reduce the discrepancy between their ideals and their perceptions either by lowering their standards or by making charitable evaluations of their partners. Research suggests that the latter strategy is more common. For example, in a study of 180 couples, Murray, Holmes, and Griffin (1996) found that most participants viewed their partners more favorably than the partners viewed themselves. Individuals' perceptions of their romantic partners seemed to reflect their ideals for a partner more than reality. Moreover, the data showed that people were happier in their relationship when they idealized their partners and when their partners idealized them. Another study found that individuals who are satisfied with their romantic relationships tend to focus on their partners' virtues and to minimize and rationalize their partners' faults (Murray & Holmes, 1999). This line of research suggests that small, positive illusions about one's partner may foster happier and more resilient romantic relationships (Murray, 2001). That said, when people come to important choice points in their relationships, they are often motivated to be more objective about their partner's strengths and weaknesses (Gagne & Lydon, 2004).

Courtesy of Elaine Hatfield

■ **Elaine Hatfield.** "Passionate love is like any other form of excitement. By its very nature, excitement involves a continuous interplay between elation and despair, thrills and terror."

Perspectives on the Mystery of Love

Love has proven to be an elusive subject of study. It's difficult to define, difficult to measure, and often difficult to understand. Nonetheless, psychologists have begun to make some progress in their study of love. Let's look at their theories and research.

Passionate and Companionate Love Two early pioneers in research on love were Elaine Hatfield (formerly Walster) and Ellen Berscheid (Berscheid, 1988; Berscheid & Walster, 1978; Hatfield & Rapson, 1993). They have proposed that romantic relationships are characterized by two kinds of love: passionate love and companionate love. **Passionate love** is a complete absorption in another that includes tender sexual feelings and the agony and ecstasy of intense emotion. **Companionate love** is warm, trusting, tolerant affection for another whose life is deeply intertwined with one's own. Passionate and companionate love *may* coexist, but they don't necessarily go hand in hand. Research suggests that, as a general rule, companionate love is more strongly related to relationship satisfaction than passionate love (Fehr, 2001).

The distinction between passionate and companionate love has been further refined by Robert Sternberg (1988a), who suggests that love has three facets rather than just two. He subdivides companionate love into intimacy and commitment. **Intimacy** refers to warmth, closeness, and sharing in a relationship. **Commitment** is an intent to maintain a relationship in spite of the difficulties and costs that may arise. Sternberg has mapped out the probable relations between the passage of time and the three components of love, as shown in Figure 14.6. Like Hatfield and Berscheid, he suspects that passion reaches its zenith in the early phases of love and then erodes. He believes that intimacy and commitment increase with time, although at different rates.

passionate love
a complete absorption in another that includes tender sexual feelings and the agony and ecstasy of intense emotion.

companionate love
warm, trusting, tolerant affection for another whose life is deeply intertwined with one's own.

intimacy
warmth, closeness, and sharing in a relationship.

commitment
an intent to maintain a relationship in spite of the difficulties and costs that may arise.

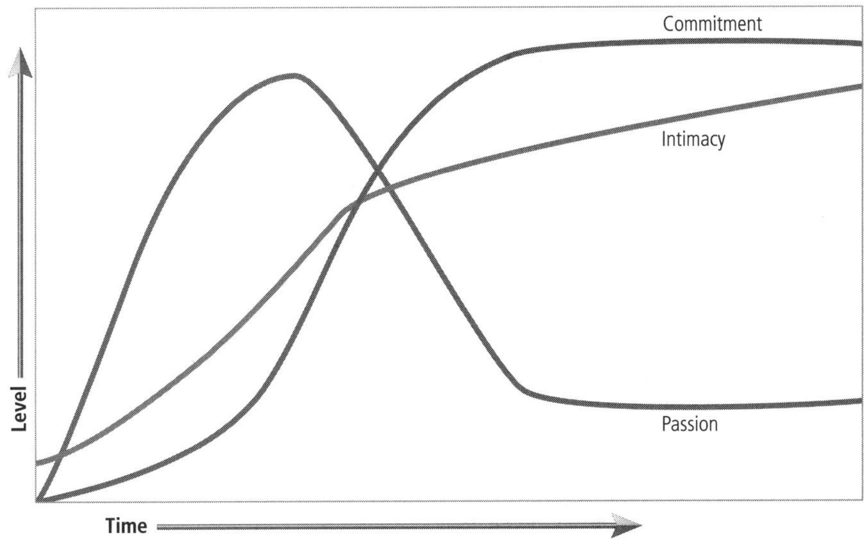

FIGURE 14.6

Sternberg's view of love over time. In his theory of love, Robert Sternberg (1988a) hypothesizes that the various elements of love progress in different ways over the course of time. According to Sternberg, passion peaks early in a relationship, whereas intimacy and commitment typically continue to build gradually. (Graphs adapted from Trotter, 1986)

Research suggests that commitment is a crucial facet of love that is predictive of relationship stability. For example, declining commitment is associated with an increased likelihood of infidelity in dating relationships (Drigotas, Safstrom, & Gentilia, 1999). In another study of dating couples who were followed for four years, Sprecher (1999) found that participants' feelings of commitment were more predictive of whether they broke up than their ratings of their overall love. Interestingly, the participants who broke up indicated that their love had remained reasonably stable, but their commitment and satisfaction had declined.

Love as Attachment In another groundbreaking analysis of love, Cindy Hazan and Phillip Shaver (1987) looked not at the components of love but at similarities between love and *attachment relationships* in infancy. We noted in our chapter on human development that infant-caretaker bonding, or attachment, emerges in the first year of life. Early attachments vary in quality, and *most* infants tend to fall into one of three groups, which depend in part on parents' caregiving styles (Ainsworth et al., 1978). A majority of infants develop a *secure attachment.* However, some are very anxious when separated from their caretaker, a syndrome called *anxious-ambivalent attachment.* A third group of infants, characterized by *avoidant attachment,* never bond very well with their caretaker (see Figure 14.7).

According to Hazan and Shaver, romantic love is an attachment process, and people's intimate relationships in adulthood follow the same form as their attachments in infancy. According to their theory, a person who had an anxious-ambivalent attachment in infancy will tend to have romantic relations marked by anxiety and

Parents' caregiving style	Infant attachment	Adult attachment style
Warm/responsive She/he was generally warm and responsive; she/he was good at knowing when to be supportive and when to let me operate on my own; our relationship was almost always comfortable, and I have no major reservations or complaints about it.	**Secure attachment** An infant-caregiver bond in which the child welcomes contact with a close companion and uses this person as a secure base from which to explore the environment	**Secure** I find it relatively easy to get close to others and am comfortable depending on them and having them depend on me. I don't often worry about being abandoned or about someone getting too close to me.
Cold/rejecting She/he was fairly cold and distant, or rejecting, not very responsive; I wasn't her/his highest priority, her/his concerns were often elsewhere; it's possible that she/he would just as soon not have had me.	**Avoidant attachment** An insecure infant-caregiver bond, characterized by little separation protest and a tendency of the child to avoid or ignore the caregiver	**Avoidant** I am somewhat uncomfortable being close to others; I find it difficult to trust them, difficult to allow myself to depend on them. I am nervous when anyone gets too close, and often love partners want me to be more intimate than I feel comfortable being.
Ambivalent/inconsistent She/he was noticeably inconsistent in her/his reactions to me, sometimes warm and sometimes not; she/he had her/his own agenda, which sometimes got in the way of her/his receptiveness and responsiveness to my needs; she/he definitely loved me but didn't always show it in the best way.	**Anxious/ambivalent attachment** An insecure infant-caregiver bond, characterized by strong separation protest and a tendency of the child to resist contact initiated by the caregiver, particularly after a separation	**Anxious/ambivalent** I find that others are reluctant to get as close as I would like. I often worry that my partner doesn't really love me or won't want to stay with me. I want to merge completely with another person, and this desire sometimes scares people away.

FIGURE 14.7

Infant attachment and romantic relationships. According to Hazan and Shaver (1987), people's romantic relationships in adulthood are similar in form to their attachment patterns in infancy, which are determined in part by parental caregiving styles. The theorized relations between parental styles, attachment patterns, and intimate relations are outlined here. (Data for parental caregiving styles and adult attachment styles based on Hazan and Shaver, 1986, 1987; infant attachment patterns adapted from Shaffer, 1985) ambivalence in adulthood. In other words, people relive their early bonding with their parents in their adult romantic relationships.

Hazan and Shaver's (1987) initial survey study provided striking support for their theory. They found that adults' love relationships could be sorted into groups that paralleled the three patterns of attachment seen in infants. *Secure adults* (56% of the subjects) found it relatively easy to get close to others, described their love relations as trusting, rarely worried about being abandoned, and reported the fewest divorces. *Anxious-ambivalent adults* (20% of the subjects) reported a preoccupation with love accompanied by expectations of rejection and described their love relations as volatile and marked by jealousy. *Avoidant adults* (24% of the subjects) found it difficult to get close to others and described their love relations as lacking intimacy and trust. Consistent with their theory, Hazan and Shaver (1987) found that the percentage of adults falling into each category was roughly the same as the percentage of infants in each comparable category—a finding that was subsequently replicated with a nationally representative sample of American adults (Mickelson, Kessler, & Shaver, 1997). Also, subjects' recollections of their childhood relations with their parents were consistent with the idea that people relive their infant attachment experiences in adulthood.

Understandably, Hazan and Shaver's theory has attracted considerable interest. In fact, it has generated thousands of studies on the effects of attachment style. For example, research has shown that securely attached individuals have more committed, satisfying, interdependent, well-adjusted, and longer-lasting relationships compared to people with either anxious-ambivalent or avoidant attachment styles (Feeney, 1999). Moreover, studies have shown that attachment patterns are reasonably stable over time (Fraley, 2002) and that people with different attachment styles are predisposed to think, feel, and behave differently in their relationships (Collins & Allard, 2001). For example, anxious-ambivalent people tend to report more intense emotional highs and lows in their romantic relationships. They also report having more conflicts with their partners, that these conflicts are especially stressful, and that these conflicts often have a negative impact on how they feel about their relationship (Campbell et al., 2005). In a similar vein, attachment anxiety promotes *excessive reassurance seeking*—the tendency to persistently ask for assurances from partners that one is worthy of love (Shaver, Schachner & Mikulincer, 2005).

Attachment style is also related to the motivations that underlie people's sexual interactions. People high in attachment anxiety report that they tend to have sex to reduce their feelings of insecurity and to enhance the closeness in their relationships, whereas avoidant individuals tend to engage in more casual sex in an effort to impress their peer group (Schachner & Shaver, 2004). Reactions to romantic breakups also tend to vary depending on attachment style. People who are high in attachment anxiety have much more difficulty than others in dealing with the dissolution of romantic relationships. They report greater emotional and physical distress, greater preoccupation with the former partner, more attempts to regain the lost partner, more angry and vengeful behavior, and more maladaptive coping responses, such as using alcohol and drugs to cope with the loss (Davis, Shaver, & Vernon, 2003).

Studies have further suggested that attachment patterns may have far-reaching repercussions that extend into many aspects of people's lives besides their romantic relationships. For instance, people with secure attachments tend to have high self-esteem and to be relatively well adjusted. In contrast, people with avoidant or anxious-ambivalent attachments tend to be overrepresented in groups suffering from depression, eating disorders, and other types of psychopathology (Crowell, Fraley, & Shaver, 1999). Attachment security promotes compassionate feelings and values and more helping behavior when people are in need (Mikulincer & Shaver, 2005). Researchers have also found correlations between attachment styles and gender roles (Schwartz, Waldo, & Higgins, 2004), religious beliefs (Kirkpatrick, 2005), attitudes about work (Shaver & Hazan, 1993, 1994), health habits (Huntsinger & Luecken, 2004), styles of coping with stress (Howard & Medway, 2004), and vulnerability to burnout (Pines, 2004). Thus, Hazan and Shaver's innovative ideas about the long-term effects of infant attachment experiences have triggered an avalanche of thought-provoking research.

Culture and Close Relationships

Relatively little cross-cultural research has been conducted on the dynamics of close relationships. The limited evidence suggests both similarities and differences between cultures in romantic relationships (Hendrick & Hendrick, 2000; Schmitt, 2005). For the most part, similarities have been seen when research has focused on what people look for in prospective mates. David Buss (1989, 1994a) has collected data on mate preferences in 37 divergent cultures and found that people all over the world value mutual attraction, kindness, intelligence, emotional stability, dependability, and good health in a mate. Buss also found that gender differences in mating priorities are nearly universal, with males placing more emphasis on physical attractiveness and females putting a higher priority on social status and financial resources.

Cultures vary, however, in their emphasis on love—especially passionate love—as a prerequisite for marriage. Love as the basis for marriage is an 18th-century invention of Western culture (Stone, 1977). As Hatfield and Rapson (1993) note, "Marriage-for-love represents an ultimate expression of individualism" (p. 2). In contrast, marriages arranged by families and other go-betweens remain common in cultures high in collectivism, including India (Gupta, 1992), Japan (Iwao, 1993), and China (Xiaghe & Whyte, 1990). This practice is declining in some societies as a result of Westernization, but in collectivist societies people contemplating marriage still tend to think in terms of "What will my parents and other people say?" rather than "What does my heart say?" (Triandis, 1994). Studies show that attitudes about love in collectivist societies reflect these cultural priorities. For example, in comparison to Western participants, subjects from Eastern countries report that romantic love is less important for marriage (Levine et al., 1995; Medora et al., 2002).

Marriages based on romantic love are the norm in Western cultures, whereas arranged marriages prevail in collectivist cultures.

An Evolutionary Perspective on Attraction

Evolutionary psychologists have a great deal to say about heterosexual attraction. For example, they assert that physical appearance is an influential determinant of attraction because certain aspects of good looks can be indicators of sound health, good genes, and high fertility, all of which can contribute to reproductive potential (Soler et al., 2003; Sugiyama, 2005). Consistent with this analysis, recent research has found that some standards of attractiveness are more consistent across cultures than previously believed (Sugiyama, 2005). For example, *facial symmetry* seems to be a key element of attractiveness in highly diverse cultures (Fink & Penton-Voak, 2002). Facial symmetry is thought to be valued because a host of environmental insults and developmental abnormalities are associated with physical asymmetries, which may serve as markers of relatively poor genes or health (Jones et al., 2001). Another facet of appearance that may transcend culture is *women's waist-to-hip ratio.* Around the world, men seem to prefer women with a moderately low waist-to-hip ratio (in comparison to other women in that society), which appears to be a meaningful correlate of females' reproductive potential (Hughes & Gallup, 2003; Sugiyama, 2005).

The most thoroughly documented findings on the evolutionary bases of heterosexual attraction are those on gender differences in humans' mating preferences. Consistent with the notion that humans are programmed by evolution to behave in ways that enhance their reproductive fitness, evidence indicates that men generally are more interested than women in seeking youthfulness and physical attractiveness in their mates because these traits should be associated with greater reproductive potential. On the other hand, research shows that women place a greater premium on prospective mates' ambition, social status, and financial potential because these traits should be associated with the ability to invest material resources in children (Shackelford, Schmitt, & Buss, 2005; Li et al., 2002). The degree to which these trends transcend history and culture was driven home by a recent study that examined the mate preferences apparent in 658 traditional folktales drawn from the ancient oral traditions of 48 different cultures (Gottschall et al., 2004). The analyses showed that the characters in these extremely old and diverse stories showed the same gender differences seen in contemporary research: Male characters tended to place a greater emphasis on potential mates' physical attractiveness, while female characters showed more interest in potential mates' wealth and social status.

Does the gender gap in mating priorities influence the tactics people actually use in pursuing romantic relationships? Research suggests that the answer is yes. Buss (1988) asked 208 newlywed individuals to describe the things they did when they first met their spouse, and during the remainder of their courtship, to make themselves more appealing to their partner. He found that men were more likely than women to emphasize their material resources by doing such things as flashing lots of money, buying nice gifts, showing off expensive possessions, and bragging about their importance at work (see Figure 14.8). In contrast, women were more likely than men to work at enhancing their appearance by dieting, wearing stylish clothes, trying new hairstyles, and getting a tan.

The tactics used by both sexes may include efforts at deception. Research shows that many men and women would be willing to lie about their personality,

FIGURE 14.8

Similarities and differences between the sexes in tactics of attraction. Buss (1988) asked newlywed subjects to rate how often they had used 23 tactics of attraction to make themselves more appealing to their partner. The tactics used by one sex significantly more often than the other are listed in the first two sections of the figure. Although there were significant differences between the sexes, there were also many similarities. The 11 tactics used most frequently by each sex (those above the median) are boldfaced, showing considerable overlap between males and females in the tactics they use most. (Note: Higher means in the data reflect higher frequency of use, but the numbers do not indicate frequency per day or week.) *Source:* Adapted from Buss, D. M. (1988). The evolution of human intrasexual competition: Tactics of mate attraction. *Journal of Personality and Social Psychology, 54,* 616–628. Copyright © 1988 by the American Psychological Association. Adapted by permission of the publisher and author.

Tactics of attraction	Mean frequency ($N = 102$)	Mean frequency ($N = 106$)
Tactics used significantly more by males	*Men*	*Women*
Display resources	0.67	0.44
Brag about resources	0.73	0.60
Display sophistication	**1.18**	0.88
Display strength	0.96	0.44
Display athleticism	**1.18**	0.94
Show off	0.70	0.47
Tactics used significantly more by females	*Men*	*Women*
Wear makeup	0.02	**1.63**
Keep clean and groomed	**2.27**	**2.44**
Alter appearance—general	0.39	**1.27**
Wear stylish clothes	**1.22**	**2.00**
Act coy	0.54	0.73
Wear jewelry	0.25	**2.21**
Wear sexy clothes	0.68	0.91
Tactics for which no significant sex differences were found	*Men*	*Women*
Act provocative	0.77	0.90
Flirt	**2.13**	**2.09**
Keep hair groomed	**2.20**	**2.31**
Increase social exposure	0.89	0.90
Act nice	**1.77**	**1.86**
Display humor	**2.42**	**2.28**
Act promiscuous	0.30	0.21
Act submissive	**1.24**	**1.11**
Dissemble (feign agreement)	**1.26**	1.09
Touch	**2.26**	**2.16**

income, past relationships, and career skills to impress a prospective date who was attractive (Rowatt, Cunningham, & Druen, 1999). Consistent with evolutionary theory, women report that they are most upset when men exaggerate their social status, their financial resources, or the depth of their romantic commitment to the woman, whereas men are most upset when women conceal a history of "promiscuity" (Haselton et al., 2005). Females anticipate more deception from prospective dates than males do (Keenan et al., 1997). Perhaps this is the reason women tend to underestimate the strength of men's relationship commitment (Haselton & Buss, 2000). Men do not appear to show a similar bias, but they do show a tendency to overestimate women's sexual interest. These cognitive biases seem to be designed to reduce the probability that ancestral women would consent to sex and then be abandoned and to minimize the likelihood that ancestral men would overlook sexual opportunities (Buss, 2001).

Deception lies at the heart of *mate poaching,* a phenomenon that has recently attracted the interest of evolutionary psychologists. Mate poaching occurs when someone tries to attract another person who is already in a relationship. Although it presents some extra challenges and risks, this strategy is not rare, as 50%–60% of undergraduates report that they have attempted to poach someone (Schmitt & Buss, 2001). Mate poaching has probably occurred throughout history and is universally seen across cultures, although its prevalence varies some from one culture to another (Schmitt et al., 2004). Men are somewhat more likely than women to make poaching attempts, but the gap is modest and poaching by women is common (Schmitt et al., 2004). The tactics employed in poaching efforts overlap considerably with the normal tactics of attraction, except the tactics are more likely to be executed in a disguised and secretive manner. Poaching is a two-way street, as people often try to entice others into poaching them by expressing boredom about their current relationship, complaining about their partner, or asking for "advice" about their relationship (Schmitt & Shackelford, 2003).

ATTITUDES: MAKING SOCIAL JUDGMENTS

In our chapter-opening story, Muffy's friends exhibited decidedly negative attitudes about working-class men. Their example reveals a basic feature of attitudes: they're evaluative. Social psychology's interest in attitudes has a much longer history than its interest in attraction. Indeed, in its early days social psychology was defined as the study of attitudes. In this section we'll discuss the nature of attitudes, efforts to change attitudes through persuasion, and theories of attitude change.

What are attitudes? **Attitudes** are positive or negative evaluations of objects of thought. "Objects of thought" may include social issues (capital punishment or gun control, for example), groups (liberals, farmers), institutions (the Lutheran church, the Supreme Court), consumer products (yogurt, computers), and people (the president, your next-door neighbor).

attitudes
orientations that locate objects of thought on dimensions of judgment.

Components and Dimensions of Attitudes

Social psychologists have traditionally viewed attitudes as being made up of three components: a cognitive component, an affective component, and a behavioral component. However, it gradually became apparent that many attitudes do not include all three components (Fazio & Olson, 2003), so it is more accurate to say that *attitudes may include up to three types of components.* The *cognitive component* of an attitude is made up of the beliefs that people hold about the object of an attitude. The *affective component* of an attitude consists of the *emotional feelings* stimulated by an object of thought. The *behavioral component* of an attitude consists of *predispositions to act* in certain ways toward an attitude object. Figure 14.9 on the next page provides concrete examples of how someone's attitude about gun control might be divided into its components.

Attitudes vary along several crucial dimensions, including their *strength, accessibility,* and *ambivalence* (Olson & Maio, 2003). Definitions of *attitude strength* differ, but strong attitudes are generally seen as ones that are firmly held (resistant to change), that are durable over time, and that have a powerful impact on behavior (Petty, Wheeler, & Tormala, 2003). The *accessibility* of an attitude refers to how often one thinks about it and how quickly it comes to mind. Highly accessible attitudes are quickly and readily available (Fabrigar, MacDonald, & Wegener, 2005). Attitude accessibility is correlated with attitude strength, as highly accessible attitudes *tend* to be strong, but the concepts are distinct and there is no one-to-one correspondence. *Ambivalent attitudes* are conflicted evaluations that include both positive and negative feelings about an object of thought (Fabrigar, MacDonald, & Wegener, 2005). Like attitude strength, attitude ambivalence has been measured in various ways (Priester & Petty, 2001). Generally speaking, ambivalence increases as the ratio of positive to negative evaluations gets closer to being equal. When ambivalence is high, an attitude tends to be less predictive of behavior and more pliable in the face of persuasion (Armitage & Conner, 2000).

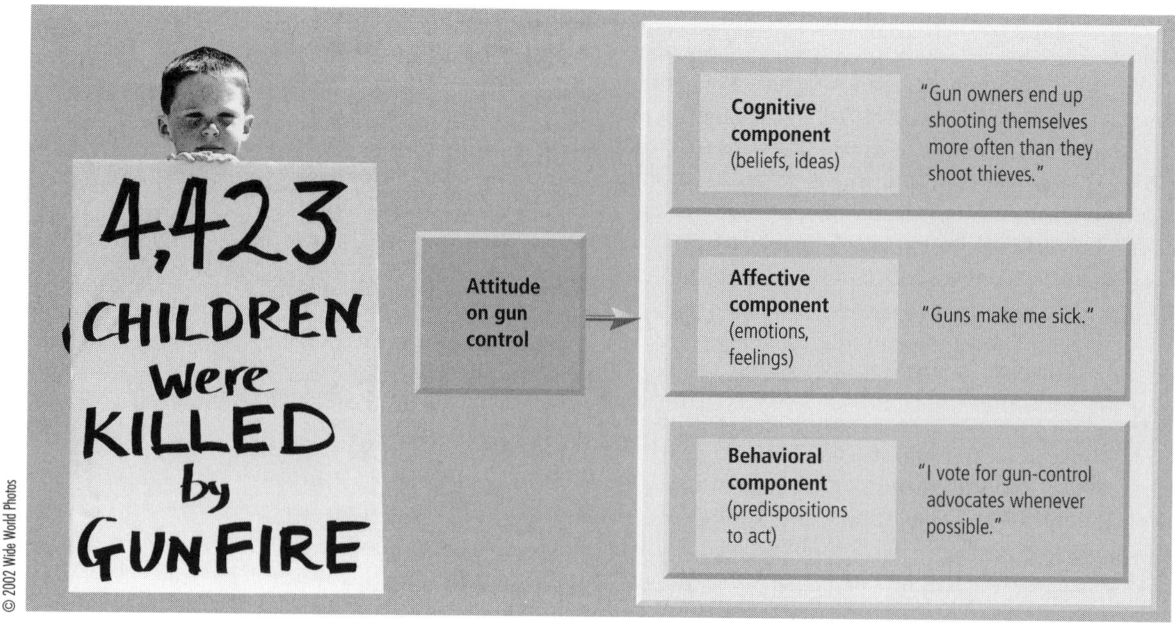

FIGURE 14.9

The possible components of attitudes. Attitudes may include cognitive, affective, and behavioral components, as illustrated here for a hypothetical person's attitude about gun control.

Attitudes and Behavior

In the early 1930s, when prejudice against Asians was common in the United States, Richard LaPiere journeyed across the country with a Chinese couple. He was more than a little surprised when they weren't turned away from any of the restaurants they visited in their travels—184 restaurants in all. About six months after his trip, LaPiere surveyed the same restaurants and asked whether they would serve Chinese customers. Roughly half of the restaurants replied to the survey, and over 90% of them indicated that they would not seat Chinese patrons. Thus, LaPiere (1934) found that people who voice prejudicial attitudes may not behave in discriminatory ways. Since then, theorists have often asked: Why don't attitudes predict behavior better?

Admittedly, LaPiere's study had a fundamental flaw that you may already have detected. The person who seated LaPiere and his Chinese friends may not have been the same person who responded to the mail survey sent later. Nonetheless, numerous follow-up studies, using more sophisticated methods, have repeatedly shown that attitudes are mediocre predictors of people's behavior (Ajzen & Fishbein, 2005; McGuire, 1985). That's not to say that attitudes are irrelevant or meaningless. Kraus (1995) reviewed 88 attitude-behavior studies and found that the average correlation between attitudes and behavior was .38. That figure is high enough to justify Eagly's (1992) conclusion that researchers have identified "many conditions under which attitudes are substantial predictors of behavior" (p. 697). But on the whole, social psychologists have been surprised by how often a favorable attitude toward a candidate or product does not translate into a vote or a purchase.

Why aren't attitude-behavior relations more consistent? One consideration is that until recently researchers failed to take variations in *attitude strength, accessibility, and ambivalence* into account. Accumulating evidence indicates that these factors influence the connection between attitudes and behavior, but they have generally been left uncontrolled in decades of research on attitudes (Olson & Maio, 2003). Another consideration is that attitudes are often measured in a *general, global* way that isn't likely to predict *specific* behaviors (Bohner & Schwarz, 2001). Although you may express favorable feelings about protecting civil liberties (a very general, abstract concept), you may not be willing to give $100 to the American Civil Liberties Union (a very specific action). Another reason for attitude-behavior inconsistency is that many behaviors occur spontaneously and are not the product of thoughtful deliberation about one's attitudes (Fazio & Olson, 2003).

Finally, inconsistent relations between attitudes and behavior are seen because behavior depends on situational constraints—especially your subjective perceptions of how people expect you to behave (Ajzen & Fishbein, 2000, 2005). Attitudes interact with situational norms to shape people's intentions, which then determine their behavior. Although you may be strongly opposed to marijuana use, you may not say anything when friends start passing a joint around at a party because you don't want to turn the party into an argument. However, in another situation governed by different norms, such as a class discussion, you may speak out forcefully against marijuana use. If so, you may be trying to change others' attitudes, the process we'll discuss next.

Trying to Change Attitudes: Factors in Persuasion

The fact that attitudes aren't always good predictors of a person's behavior doesn't stop others from trying to change those attitudes. Indeed, every day you're bombarded by efforts to alter your attitudes. To illustrate, let's trace the events of an imaginary morning. You may not even be out of bed before you start hearing radio advertisements intended to influence your attitudes about specific mouthwashes, computers, athletic shoes, and telephone companies. When you unfurl your newspaper, you find not only more ads but quotes from government officials and special interest groups, carefully crafted to shape your opinions. When you arrive at school, you encounter a group passing out leaflets that urge you to repent your sins and join them in worship. In class, your economics professor champions the wisdom of free markets in international trade. At lunch, the person you've been dating argues about the merits of an "open relationship." Your discussion is interrupted by someone who wants both of you to sign a petition. "Doesn't it ever let up?" you wonder. When it comes to persuasion, the answer is "no." As Anthony Pratkanis and Elliot Aronson (2000) put it, we live in the "age of propaganda." In light of this reality, let's examine some of the factors that determine whether persuasion works.

The process of persuasion includes four basic elements: source, receiver, message, and channel (see Figure 14.10). The **source** is the person who sends a

source
the person who sends a communication.

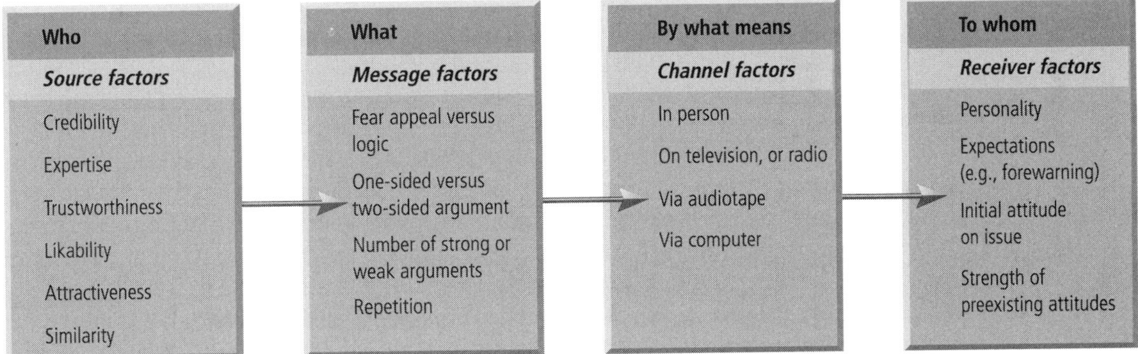

FIGURE 14.10

Overview of the persuasion process. The process of persuasion essentially boils down to *who* (the source) communicates *what* (the message) *by what means* (the channel) *to whom* (the receiver). Thus, four sets of variables influence the process of persuasion: source, message, channel, and receiver factors. The diagram lists some of the more important factors in each category (including some that are not discussed in the text due to space limitations). (Adapted from Lippa, 1994)

receiver
the person to whom a message is sent.

message
the information transmitted by a source.

channel
the medium through which a message is sent.

communication, and the **receiver** is the person to whom the message is sent. Thus, if you watch a presidential news conference on TV, the president is the source, and you and millions of other viewers are the receivers. The **message** is the information transmitted by the source, and the **channel** is the medium through which the message is sent. Although the research on communication channels is interesting, we'll confine our discussion to source, message, and receiver variables, which are most applicable to persuasion.

Source Factors Occasional exceptions to the general rule are seen, but persuasion tends to be more successful when the source has high *credibility* (Pornpitakpan, 2004). What gives a person credibility? Either expertise or trustworthiness. *Expertise* tends to be more influential when arguments are ambiguous (Chaiken & Maheswaran, 1994). People try to convey their expertise by mentioning their degrees, their training, and their experience or by showing an impressive grasp of the issue at hand.

Expertise is a plus, but *trustworthiness* can be even more important. Many people tend to accept messages from trustworthy sources with little scrutiny (Priester & Petty, 1995, 2003). If you were told that your state needs to reduce corporate taxes to stimulate its economy, would you be more likely to believe it from the president of a huge corporation in your state or from an economics professor from out of state? Probably the latter. Trustworthiness is undermined when a source, such as the corporation president, appears to have something to gain. In contrast, trustworthiness is enhanced when people appear to argue against their own interests (Hunt, Smith, & Kernan, 1985). This effect explains why salespeople often make remarks like, "Frankly, my snowblower isn't the best. They have a better brand down the street. Of course, you'll have to spend quite a bit more . . ."

Likability also increases the effectiveness of a persuasive source (Johnson, Maio, & Smith-McLallen, 2005), and some of the factors at work in attraction therefore have an impact on persuasion. Thus, the favorable effect of *physical attractiveness* on likability can make persuasion more effective (Shavitt et al., 1994). We also respond better to sources who share *similarity* with us in ways that are relevant to the issue at hand (Mackie, Worth, & Asuncion, 1990).

Message Factors If you were going to give a speech to a local community group advocating a reduction in state taxes on corporations, you'd probably wrestle with a number of questions about how to structure your message. Should you look at both sides of the issue, or should you present just your side? Should you use all of the arguments at your disposal, or should you concentrate on the stronger arguments? Should you deliver a low-key, logical speech? Or should you try to strike fear into the hearts of your listeners? These questions are concerned with message factors in persuasion.

Let's assume that you're aware that there are two sides to the taxation issue. On the one hand, you're convinced that lower corporate taxes will bring new companies to your state and stimulate economic growth. On the other hand, you realize that reduced tax revenues may hurt the quality of education and roads in your state (but you think the benefits will outweigh the costs). Should you present a *one-sided argument* that ignores the possible problems for education and road quality? Or should you present a *two-sided argument* that acknowledges concern about education and road quality and then downplays the probable magnitude of these problems? The optimal strategy depends on a variety of considerations, but overall, two-sided arguments tend to be more effective (Petty & Wegener, 1998). Just mentioning that there are two sides to an issue can increase your credibility with an audience.

In presenting your side, should you use every argument you can think of, or should you focus on the stronger points? One study suggests that it is wise to concentrate on your strong arguments (Friedrich et al., 1996). The investigators exposed students to a variety of weak and strong arguments advocating a new senior comprehensive exam at their school. They found that adding strong arguments paid off but that adding weak arguments hurt rather than helped. It appears that weak arguments may actually raise doubts rather than add to your case.

On the other hand, raw repetition of a message does seem to be an effective strategy. The *validity effect* refers to the finding that simply repeating a statement causes it to be perceived as more valid or true. It doesn't matter whether the statement is true, false, or clearly just an opinion; if you repeat something often enough, some people come to believe it (Boehm, 1994).

Persuasive messages frequently attempt to arouse fear. Opponents of nuclear power scare us with visions of meltdowns. Antismoking campaigns emphasize the threat of cancer, and deodorant ads highlight the risk of embarrassment. You could follow their lead and argue that if corporate taxes aren't reduced, your state will be headed toward economic ruin and massive unemployment. *Do appeals to fear work?* Yes—if they are successful in arousing fear. Research reveals that many messages intended to induce fear fail to do so. However, studies involving a wide range of issues (nuclear policy, auto safety, dental hygiene, and so on) have shown that messages that are effective in arousing fear tend to increase persuasion (Ruiter, Abraham, & Kok, 2001). Fear appeals are most likely to work when your listeners view the dire consequences that you describe as exceedingly unpleasant, fairly probable if they don't take your advice, and avoidable if they do (Das, de Wit, & Stroebe, 2003).

Receiver Factors What about the receiver of the persuasive message? Are some people easier to persuade than others? Undoubtedly, but researchers have not found any personality traits that are reliably associated with susceptibility to persuasion (Petty & Wegener, 1998). Other factors, such as the forewarning a receiver gets about a persuasive effort and the receiver's initial position on an issue, generally seem to be more influential than the receiver's personality.

An old saying suggests that "to be forewarned is to be forearmed." The value of *forewarning* applies to targets of persuasive efforts (Wood & Quinn, 2003). When you shop for a new TV, you *expect* salespeople to work at persuading you, and to some extent this forewarning reduces the impact of their arguments. Considerations that stimulate counterarguing in the receiver tend to increase resistance to persuasion (Jain, Buchanan, & Maheswaran, 2000).

A receiver's resistance to persuasion will depend in part on the nature of the attitude or belief that the source is trying to change. Obviously, resistance is greater when you have to advocate a position that is incompatible with the receiver's existing attitudes or beliefs. In general, people display a *disconfirmation bias* in evaluating arguments (Edwards & Smith, 1996). Arguments that are in conflict with one's prior attitudes are scrutinized longer and subjected to more skeptical analysis than arguments that are consistent with one's prior beliefs.

Furthermore, studies show that *stronger attitudes are more resistant to change* (Eagly & Chaiken, 1998). Strong attitudes may be tougher to alter because they tend to be embedded in networks of beliefs and values that might also require change (Erber, Hodges, & Wilson, 1995). Finally, *resistance can promote resistance.* That is, when people successfully resist persuasive efforts to change specific attitudes, they often become more certain about those attitudes (Tormala & Petty, 2002, 2004).

Our review of source, message, and receiver variables has shown that attempting to change attitudes through persuasion involves a complex interplay of factors—and we haven't even looked beneath the surface yet. How do people acquire attitudes in the first place? What dynamic processes within people produce attitude change? We turn to these theoretical issues next.

Theories of Attitude Formation and Change

Many theories have been proposed to explain the mechanisms at work in attitude change, whether or not it occurs in response to persuasion. We'll look at four theoretical perspectives: learning theory, dissonance theory, self-perception theory, and the elaboration likelihood model.

Learning Theory We've seen repeatedly that *learning theory* can help explain a wide range of phenomena, from conditioned fears to the acquisition of sex roles to the development of personality traits. Now we can add attitude formation and change to our list.

The affective, or emotional, component in an attitude can be created through a special subtype of *classical conditioning,* called evaluative conditioning (Olson & Fazio, 2001, 2002). *Evaluative conditioning* consists of efforts to transfer the emotion attached to a UCS to a new CS (Kruglanski & Stroebe, 2005; Schimmack & Crites, 2005). Advertisers routinely try to take advantage of evaluative conditioning by pairing their products with stimuli that elicit pleasant emotional responses, such as extremely attractive models, highly likable spokespersons, and cherished events, such as the Olympics (Till & Priluck, 2000). This conditioning process is diagrammed in Figure 14.11.

Operant conditioning may come into play when you openly express an attitude, such as "I believe that husbands should do more housework." Some people may endorse your view, while others may jump down your throat. Agreement from other people generally functions as a reinforcer, strengthening your tendency to express a specific attitude (Bohner & Schwarz, 2001). Disagreement often functions as a form of punishment, which may gradually weaken your commitment to your viewpoint.

Another person's attitudes may rub off on you through *observational learning* (Oskamp, 1991). If you hear your uncle say, "Republicans are nothing but puppets of big business" and your mother heartily agrees, your exposure to your uncle's attitude and your mother's reinforcement of your uncle may influence your attitude toward the Republican party. Studies show that parents and their children tend to have similar political attitudes (Sears, 1975). Observational learning presumably

■ **Leon Festinger.** "Cognitive dissonance is a motivating state of affairs. Just as hunger impels a person to eat, so does dissonance impel a person to change his opinions or his behavior."

CS
Products
(e.g., autos, foods)
UCS
Likable
celebrity
CR
Pleasant emotional
response
UCR

FIGURE 14.11

Classical conditioning of attitudes in advertising. Advertisers routinely pair their products with likable celebrities in the hope that their products will come to elicit pleasant emotional responses. This special type of classical conditioning is called *evaluative conditioning.*

accounts for much of this similarity. The opinions of teachers, coaches, co-workers, talk-show hosts, rock stars, and so forth are also likely to sway people's attitudes through observational learning.

Dissonance Theory Leon Festinger's *dissonance theory* assumes that inconsistency among attitudes propels people in the direction of attitude change. Dissonance theory burst into prominence in 1959 when Festinger and J. Merrill Carlsmith published a famous study of counterattitudinal behavior. Let's look at their findings and at how dissonance theory explains them.

Festinger and Carlsmith (1959) had male college students come to a laboratory, where they worked on excruciatingly dull tasks such as turning pegs repeatedly. When a subject's hour was over, the experimenter confided that some participants' motivation was being manipulated by telling them that the task was interesting and enjoyable before they started it. Then, after a moment's hesitation, the experimenter asked if the subject could help him out of a jam. His usual helper was delayed and he needed someone to testify to the next "subject" (really an accomplice) that the experimental task was interesting. He offered to pay the subject if he would tell the person in the adjoining waiting room that the task was enjoyable and involving.

This entire scenario was enacted to coax participants into doing something that was inconsistent with their true feelings—that is, to engage in *counterattitudinal behavior.* Some participants received a token payment of $1 for their effort, while others received a more substantial payment of $20 (an amount equivalent to about $80–$90 today, in light of inflation). Later, a second experimenter inquired about the subjects' true feelings regarding the dull experimental task. Figure 14.12 summarizes the design of the Festinger and Carlsmith study.

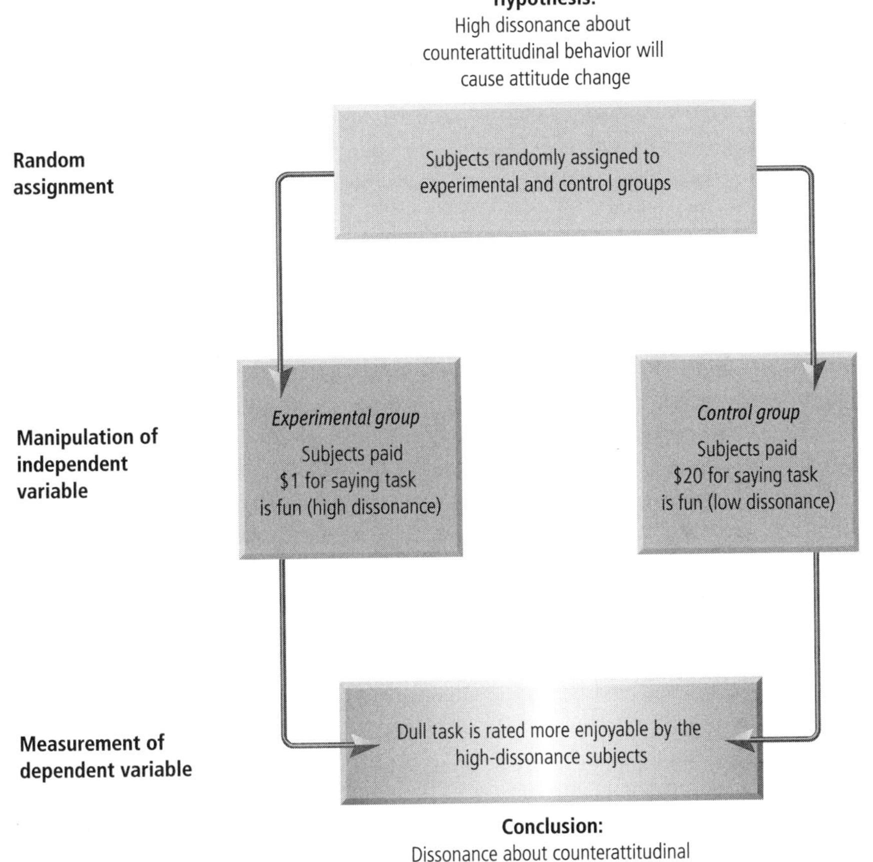

FIGURE 14.12

Design of the Festinger and Carlsmith (1959) study. The sequence of events in this landmark study of counterattitudinal behavior and attitude change is outlined here. The diagram omits a third condition (no dissonance), in which subjects were not induced to lie. The results in the nondissonance condition were similar to those found in the low-dissonance condition.

Who do you think rated the task more favorably—the subjects who were paid $1 or those who were paid $20? Both common sense and learning theory would predict that the subjects who received the greater reward ($20) should come to like the task more. In reality, however, the subjects who were paid $1 exhibited more favorable attitude change—just as Festinger and Carlsmith had predicted. Why? Dissonance theory provides an explanation.

cognitive dissonance
a psychological state that exists when related cognitions are inconsistent.

According to Festinger (1957), **cognitive dissonance** exists when related cognitions are inconsistent—that is, when they contradict each other. Cognitive dissonance is thought to create an unpleasant state of tension that motivates people to reduce their dissonance—usually by altering their cognitions. In the study by Festinger and Carlsmith, the subjects' contradictory cognitions were "The task is boring" and "I told someone the task was enjoyable." The subjects who were paid $20 for lying had an obvious reason for behaving inconsistently with their true attitudes, so these subjects experienced little dissonance. In contrast, the subjects paid $1 had no readily apparent justification for their lie and experienced high dissonance. To reduce it, they tended to persuade themselves that the task was more enjoyable than they had originally thought. Thus, dissonance theory sheds light on why people sometimes come to believe their own lies.

Cognitive dissonance is also at work when people turn attitudinal somersaults to justify efforts that haven't panned out, a syndrome called *effort justification.* Aronson and Mills (1959) studied effort justification by putting college women through a "severe initiation" before they could qualify to participate in what promised to be an interesting discussion of sexuality. In the initiation, the women had to read obscene passages out loud to a male experimenter. After all that, the highly touted discussion of sexuality turned out to be a boring, taped lecture on reproduction in lower animals. Subjects in the severe initiation condition experienced highly dissonant cognitions ("I went through a lot to get here" and "This discussion is terrible"). How did they reduce their dissonance? Apparently by changing their attitude about the discussion, since they rated it more favorably than subjects in two control conditions. Effort justification may be at work in many facets of everyday life. For example, people who wait in line for an hour or more to get into an exclusive restaurant often praise the restaurant afterward even if they have been served a mediocre meal.

Dissonance theory has been tested in hundreds of studies with mixed, but largely favorable, results. The dynamics of dissonance appear to underlie many important types of attitude changes (Draycott & Dabbs, 1998; Keller & Block, 1999; Petty et al., 2003). Research has largely supported Festinger's claim that dissonance involves genuine psychological discomfort and even physiological arousal (Visser & Cooper, 2003; Devine et al., 1999). However, dissonance effects are not among the most reliable phenomena in social psychology. Researchers have had difficulty specifying the conditions under which dissonance will occur, and it has become apparent that people can reduce their dissonance in quite a variety of ways besides changing their attitudes (Olson & Stone, 2005; Visser & Cooper, 2003).

Self-Perception Theory After taking a close look at studies of counterattitudinal behavior, Daryl Bem (1967) concluded that self-perception, rather than dissonance, explains why people sometimes come to believe their own lies. According to Bem's *self-perception theory,* people often *infer* their attitudes from their behavior. Thus, Bem argued that in the study by Festinger and Carlsmith (1959), the subjects paid $1 probably thought to themselves, "A dollar isn't enough money to get me to lie, so I must have found the task enjoyable."

This thinking isn't much different from what dissonance theory would predict. Both theories suggest that people often think, "If I said it, it must be true." But the two theories propose that similar patterns of thought unfold for entirely different reasons. According to dissonance theory, subjects think along these lines because they're struggling to reduce tension caused by inconsistency among their cognitions. According to self-perception theory, subjects are engaged in normal attributional

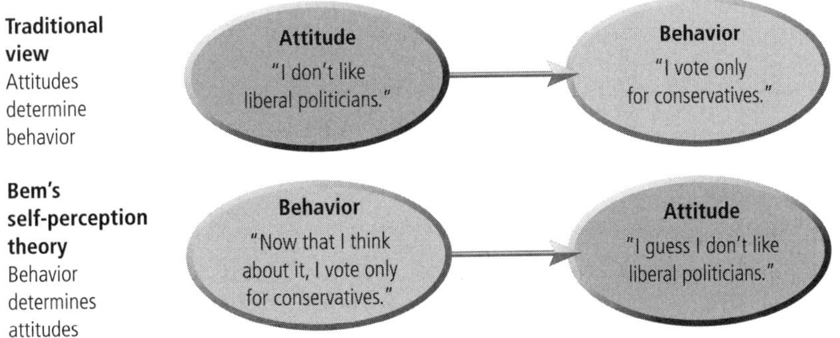

FIGURE 14.13

Bem's self-perception theory. The traditional view is that attitudes determine behavior. However, Bem stood conventional logic on its head when he proposed that behavior often determines (or causes people to draw inferences about) their attitudes. Subsequent research on attribution has shown that sometimes people *do* infer their attitudes from their behavior.

efforts to better understand their own behavior. Bem originally believed that most findings explained by dissonance were really due to self-perception. However, studies eventually showed that self-perception is at work primarily when subjects do not have well-defined attitudes regarding the issue at hand (Olson & Roese, 1995). Although self-perception theory did not replace dissonance theory, Bem's work demonstrated that attitudes are sometimes inferred from one's own behavior (Olson & Stone, 2005; see Figure 14.13).

Elaboration Likelihood Model The *elaboration likelihood model* of attitude change, originally proposed by Richard Petty and John Cacioppo (1986), asserts that there are two basic "routes" to persuasion (Petty & Wegener, 1999). The *central route* is taken when people carefully ponder the content and logic of persuasive messages. The *peripheral route* is taken when persuasion depends on nonmessage factors, such as the attractiveness and credibility of the source, or on conditioned emotional responses (see Figure 14.14). For example, a politician who campaigns by delivering carefully researched speeches that thoughtfully analyze complex issues is following the central route to persuasion. In contrast, a politician who depends on marching bands, flag waving, celebrity endorsements, and emotional slogans is following the peripheral route.

Both routes can lead to persuasion. However, according to the elaboration likelihood model, the durability of attitude change depends on the extent to which people elaborate on (think about) the contents of persuasive communications. Studies suggest that the central route to persuasion leads to more enduring attitude change than the peripheral route and that attitudes changed through central processes predict behavior better than attitudes changed through peripheral processes (Kruglanski & Stroebe, 2005; Petty & Wegener, 1998).

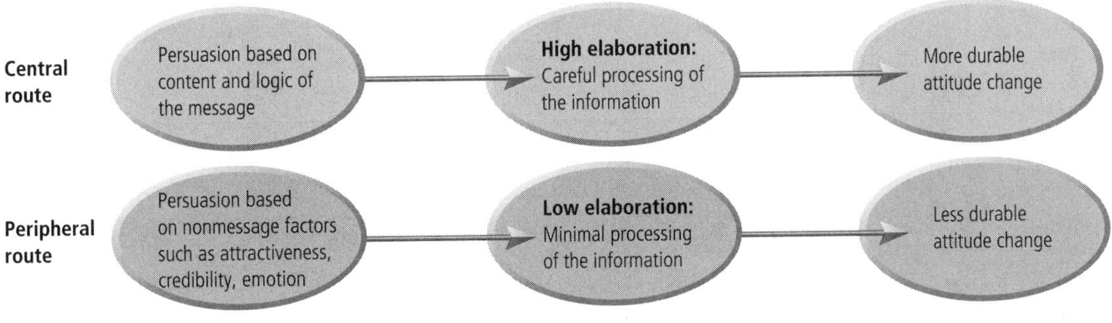

FIGURE 14.14

The elaboration likelihood model. According to the elaboration likelihood model (Petty & Cacioppo, 1986), the central route to persuasion leads to more elaboration of message content and more enduring attitude change than the peripheral route to persuasion.

CONFORMITY AND OBEDIENCE: YIELDING TO OTHERS

A number of years ago, the area that I lived in experienced a severe flood that required the mobilization of the National Guard and various emergency services. At the height of the crisis, a young man arrived at the scene of the flood, announced that he was from an obscure state agency that no one had ever heard of, and proceeded to take control of the emergency. City work crews, the fire department, local police, municipal officials, and the National Guard followed his orders with dispatch for several days, evacuating entire neighborhoods—until an official thought to check and found out that the man was just someone who had walked in off the street. The imposter, who had had small armies at his beck and call for several days, had no training in emergency services, just a history of unemployment and psychological problems.

After news of the hoax spread, people criticized red-faced local officials for their compliance with the imposter's orders. However, many of the critics probably would have cooperated in much the same way if they had been in the officials' shoes. For most people, willingness to obey someone in authority is the rule, not the exception. In this section, we'll analyze the dynamics of social influence at work in conformity and obedience.

Conformity

conformity
the tendency for people to yield to real or imagined social pressure.

If you keep a well-manicured lawn, are you exhibiting conformity? According to social psychologists, it depends on whether your behavior is the result of group pressure. **Conformity** occurs when people yield to real or imagined social pressure. For example, if you maintain a well-groomed lawn only to avoid complaints from your neighbors, you're conforming to social pressure. However, if you maintain a nice lawn because you genuinely prefer a nice lawn, that's *not* conformity.

In the 1950s, Solomon Asch (1951, 1955, 1956) devised a clever procedure that reduced ambiguity about whether subjects were conforming, allowing him to investigate the variables that govern conformity. Let's re-create one of Asch's (1955) classic experiments, which have become the most widely replicated studies in the history of social psychology (Markus, Kitayama, & Heiman, 1996). The subjects are male undergraduates recruited for a study of visual perception. A group of seven subjects are shown a large card with a vertical line on it and are then asked to indicate which of three lines on a second card matches the original "standard line" in length (see Figure 14.15). All seven subjects are given a turn at the task, and they announce their choice to the group. The subject in the sixth chair doesn't know it, but everyone else in the group is an accomplice of the experimenter, and they're about to make him wonder whether he has taken leave of his senses.

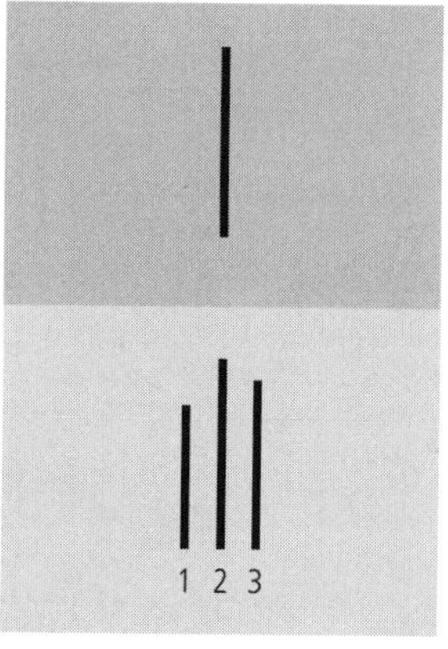

FIGURE 14.15
Stimuli used in Asch's conformity studies. Subjects were asked to match a standard line (top) with one of three other lines displayed on another card (bottom). The task was easy—until experimental accomplices started responding with obviously incorrect answers, creating a situation in which Asch evaluated subjects' conformity.
Source: Adapted from Asch, S. (1955). Opinion and social pressure. *Scientific American, 193* (5), 31–35. Based on illustrations by Sara Love.

The accomplices give accurate responses on the first two trials. On the third trial, line number 2 clearly is the correct response, but the first five "subjects" all say that line number 3 matches the standard line. The genuine subject is bewildered and can't believe his ears. Over the course of 15 trials, the accomplices all give the same incorrect response on 12 of them. How does the real subject respond? The line judgments are easy and unambiguous. So, if the participant consistently agrees with the accomplices, he isn't making honest mistakes—he's conforming.

Averaging across all 50 participants, Asch (1955) found that the young men conformed on 37% of the trials. The subjects varied considerably in their tendency to conform, however. Of the 50 participants, 13 never caved in to the group, while 14 conformed on more than half the trials. One could argue that the results show that people confronting a unanimous majority generally tend to *resist* the pressure to conform, but given how clear and easy the line judgments were, most social scientists viewed the findings as a dramatic demonstration of humans' propensity to conform (Levine, 1999).

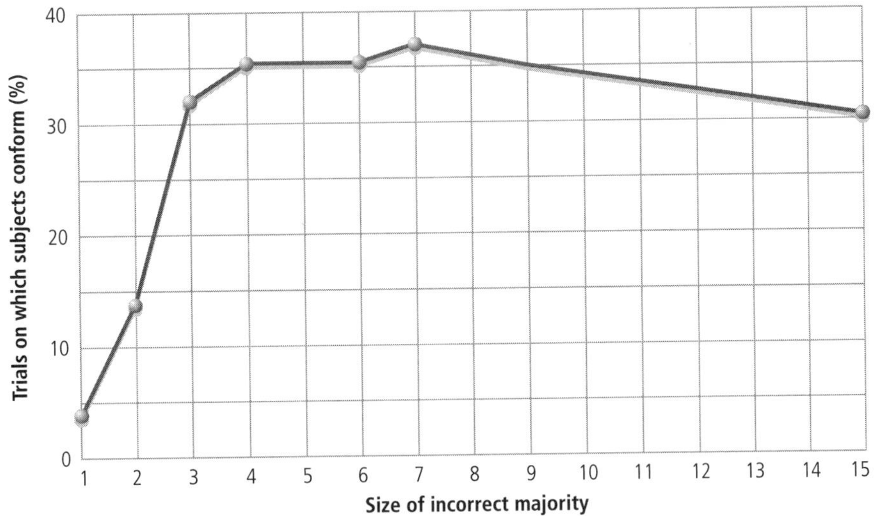

FIGURE 14.16

Conformity and group size. This graph shows the percentage of trials on which participants conformed as a function of group size in Asch's research. Asch found that conformity became more frequent as group size increased up to about four, and then the amount of conformity leveled off. *Source:* Adapted from Asch, S. (1955). Opinion and social pressure. *Scientific American, 193* (5), 31–35. Based on illustrations by Sara Love. Copyright © 1955 by Scientific American, Inc. All rights reserved.

In subsequent studies, Asch (1956) found that *group size* and *group unanimity* are key determinants of conformity. To examine the impact of group size, Asch repeated his procedure with groups that included from 1 to 15 accomplices. Little conformity was seen when a subject was pitted against just one person, but conformity increased rapidly as group size went up to 4, and then leveled off (see Figure 14.16). Thus, Asch reasoned that as groups grow larger, conformity increases—up to a point, a conclusion that has been echoed by other researchers (Cialdini & Trost, 1998).

However, group size made little difference if just one accomplice "broke" with the others, wrecking their unanimous agreement. The presence of another dissenter lowered conformity to about one-quarter of its peak, even when the dissenter made *inaccurate* judgments that happened to conflict with the majority view. Apparently, the subjects just needed to hear someone else question the accuracy of the group's perplexing responses. The importance of unanimity in fostering conformity has been replicated in subsequent research (Nemeth & Chiles, 1988).

Courtesy of Solomon Asch

Solomon Asch. "That we have found the tendency to conformity in our society so strong that reasonably intelligent and well-meaning young people are willing to call white black is a matter of concern."

Obedience

Obedience is a form of compliance that occurs when people follow direct commands, usually from someone in a position of authority. To a surprising extent, when an authority figure says, "Jump!" many people simply ask, "How high?"

obedience
a form of compliance that occurs when people follow direct commands, usually from someone in a position of authority.

Milgram's Studies Stanley Milgram wanted to study this tendency to obey authority figures. Like many other people after World War II, he was troubled by how readily the citizens of Germany had followed the orders of dictator Adolf Hitler, even when the orders required morally repugnant actions, such as the slaughter of millions of Jews. Milgram, who had worked with Solomon Asch, set out to design a standard laboratory procedure for the study of obedience, much like Asch's procedure for studying conformity. The clever experiment that Milgram devised became one of the most famous and controversial studies in the annals of psychology. It has been hailed as a "monumental contribution" to science and condemned as "dangerous, dehumanizing, and unethical research" (Ross, 1988). Decades after the research was conducted, it still generates spirited debate (Berkowitz, 1999; Lutsky, 1995). Because of its importance, it's our Featured Study for this chapter.

After his initial demonstration, Milgram (1974) tried about 20 variations on his experimental procedure, looking for factors that influence participants' obedience. In one variation, Milgram moved the study away from Yale's campus to see if the prestige of the university was contributing to the subjects' obedience. When the study was run in a seedy office building by the "Research Associates of Bridgeport," only a small decrease in obedience was observed (48% of the subjects gave all the shocks).

FOCUS ON RESEARCH

"I Was Just Following Orders"

"I was just following orders." That was the essence of Adolf Eichmann's defense when he was tried for his war crimes, which included masterminding the Nazis' attempted extermination of European Jews. Milgram wanted to determine the extent to which people are willing to follow authorities' orders. In particular, he wanted to identify the factors that lead people to follow commands that violate their ethics, such as commands to harm an innocent stranger.

Method The participants were a diverse collection of 40 men from the local community, recruited through advertisements to participate in a study at Yale University. When a subject arrived at the lab, he met the experimenter and another subject, a likable, 47-year-old accountant, who was actually an accomplice of the experimenter. The "subjects" were told that the study would concern the effects of punishment on learning. They drew slips of paper from a hat to get their assignments, but the drawing was fixed so that the real subject always became the "teacher" and the accomplice the "learner."

The participant then watched as the learner was strapped into an electrified chair through which a shock could be delivered to the learner whenever he made a mistake on the task (left photo in Figure 14.17). The subject was told that the shocks would be painful but "would not cause tissue damage," and he was then taken to an adjoining room that housed the shock generator that he would control in his role as the teacher. This elaborate apparatus (right photo in Figure 14.17) had 30 switches designed to administer shocks varying from 15 to 450 volts, with labels ranging from "Slight shock" to "Danger: severe shock" and "XXX." Although the

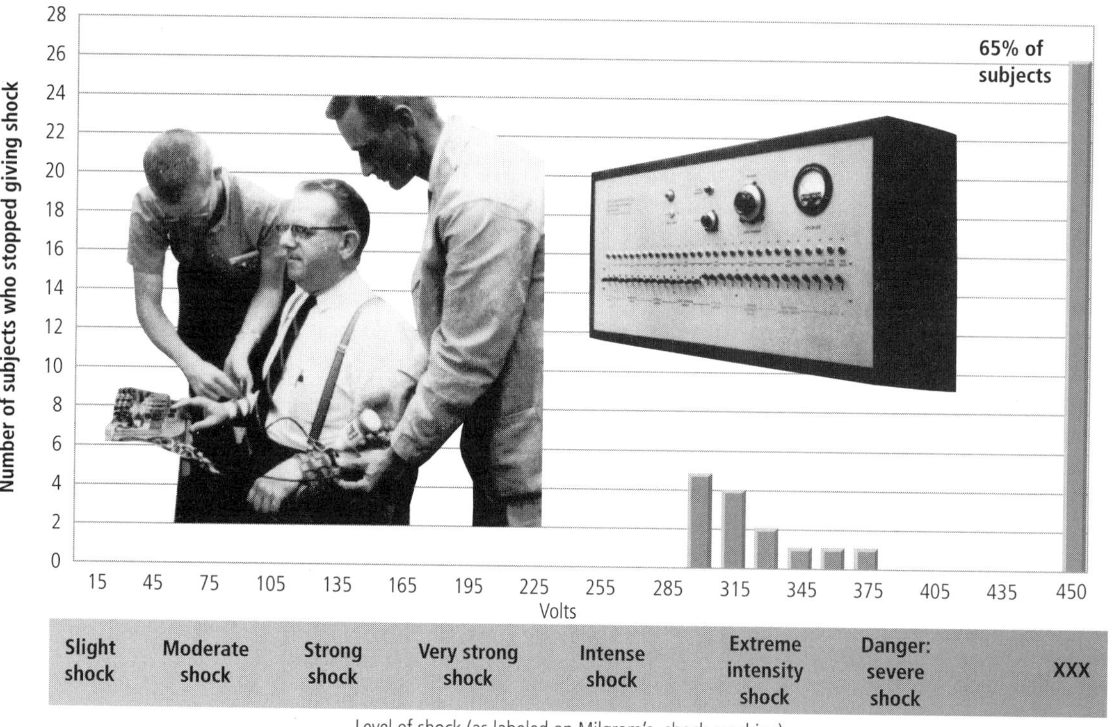

FIGURE 14.17

Milgram's experiment on obedience. The photo on the left shows the "learner" being connected to the shock generator during one of Milgram's experimental sessions. The photo on the right shows the fake shock generator used in the study. The surprising results of the Milgram (1963) study are summarized in the bar graph. Although subjects frequently protested, the vast majority (65%) delivered the entire series of shocks to the learner. *Source:* Photos copyright © 1965 by Stanley Milgram. From the film *Obedience,* distributed by The Pennsylvania State University. Reprinted by permission of Alexandra Milgram.

apparatus looked and sounded realistic, it was a fake, and the learner was never shocked.

As the "learning experiment" proceeded, the accomplice made many mistakes that necessitated shocks from the teacher, who was instructed to increase the shock level after each wrong answer. At "300 volts," the learner began to pound on the wall between the two rooms in protest and soon stopped responding to the teacher's questions. At this point, participants ordinarily turned to the experimenter for guidance. The experimenter, a 31-year-old male in a gray lab coat, firmly indicated that no response was the same as a wrong answer and that the teacher should continue to give stronger and stronger shocks to the now silent learner. If the participant expressed unwillingness to continue, the experimenter responded sternly with one of four pre-arranged prods, such as, "It is absolutely essential that you continue."

When a participant refused to obey the experimenter, the session came to an end. The dependent variable was the maximum shock the participant was willing to administer before refusing to cooperate. After each session, the true purpose of the study was explained to the subject, who was reassured that the shock was fake and the learner was unharmed.

Results No participant stopped cooperating before the learner reached the point of pounding on the wall, but 5 quit at that point. As the graph in Figure 14.17 shows, only 14 out of 40 subjects defied the experimenter before the full series of shocks was completed. Thus, 26 of the 40 subjects (65%) administered all 30 levels of shock. Although they tended to obey the experimenter, many participants voiced and displayed considerable distress about harming the learner. The horrified subjects groaned, bit their lips, stuttered, trembled, and broke into a sweat, but they continued administering the shocks.

Discussion Based on these results, Milgram concluded that obedience to authority is even more common than he or others had anticipated. Before the study was conducted, Milgram had described it to 40 psychiatrists and had asked them to predict how much shock subjects would be willing to administer to their innocent victims.

Photo by Eric Kroll, courtesy of Alexandra Milgram

■ **Stanley Milgram.** "The essence of obedience is that a person comes to view himself as the instrument for carrying out another person's wishes, and he therefore no longer regards himself as responsible for his actions."

Most of the psychiatrists had predicted that fewer than 1% of the subjects would continue to the end of the series of shocks!

In interpreting his results, Milgram argued that strong pressure from an authority figure can make decent people do indecent things to others. Applying this insight to Nazi war crimes and other travesties, Milgram asserted that some sinister actions may not be due to actors' evil character so much as to situational pressures that can lead normal people to engage in acts of treachery and violence. Thus, he arrived at the disturbing conclusion that given the right circumstances, anyone might obey orders to inflict harm on innocent strangers.

Comment In itself, obedience is not necessarily bad or wrong. Social groups of any size depend on obedience to function smoothly. Life would be chaotic if orders from police, parents, physicians, bosses, generals, and presidents were routinely ignored. However, Milgram's study suggests that many people are overly willing to submit to the orders of someone in command.

If you're like most people, you're probably confident that you wouldn't follow an experimenter's demands to inflict harm on a helpless victim. But the empirical findings indicate that you're probably wrong. After many replications, the results are deplorable, but clear: Most people can be coerced into engaging in actions that violate their morals and values. This finding is disheartening, but it sharpens our understanding of moral atrocities, such as the Nazi persecutions of Jews.

In another version of the study, Milgram borrowed a trick from Asch's conformity experiments and set up teams of three teachers that included two more accomplices. When they drew lots, the real subject was always selected to run the shock apparatus in consultation with his fellow teachers. When both accomplices accepted the experimenter's orders to continue shocking the learner, the pressure increased obedience a bit. However, if an accomplice defied the experimenter and supported the subject's objections, obedience declined dramatically (only 10% of the subjects gave all the shocks), just as conformity had dropped rapidly when dissent surfaced in Asch's conformity studies. Dissent from another "teacher" turned out to be one of the few variations that reduced participants' obedience appreciably. As a whole, Milgram was surprised at how high subjects' obedience remained as he changed various aspects of his experiment.

The Ensuing Controversy Milgram's study evoked a controversy that continues through today. Some critics argued that Milgram's results couldn't be generalized to apply to the real world (Baumrind, 1964; Orne & Holland, 1968). They maintained that participants went along only because they knew it was an experiment and "everything must be okay." Or they argued that subjects who agree to participate in a scientific study *expect to obey* orders from an experimenter. Milgram (1964, 1968) replied by arguing that if subjects had thought "everything must be okay," they wouldn't have experienced the enormous distress that they clearly showed.

As for the idea that research participants expect to follow an experimenter's commands, Milgram pointed out that so do real-world soldiers and bureaucrats who are accused of villainous acts performed in obedience to authority. "I reject Baumrind's argument that the observed obedience doesn't count because it occurred where it is appropriate," said Milgram (1964). "That is precisely why it *does* count." Overall, the evidence supports the generalizability of Milgram's results, which were consistently replicated for many years, in diverse settings, with a variety of subjects and procedural variations (Blass, 1999; Miller, 1986).

Critics also questioned the ethics of Milgram's procedure (Baumrind, 1964; Kelman, 1967). They noted that without prior consent, subjects were exposed to extensive deception that could undermine their trust in people and to severe stress that could leave emotional scars. Moreover, most participants also had to confront the disturbing fact that they caved in to the experimenter's commands to inflict harm on an innocent victim.

Milgram's defenders argued that the brief distress experienced by his subjects was a small price to pay for the insights that emerged from his obedience studies. Looking back, however, many psychologists seem to share the critics' concerns about the ethical implications of Milgram's work. His procedure is questionable by contemporary standards of research ethics, and no replications of his obedience study have been conducted in the United States since the mid-1970s (Blass, 1991)—a bizarre epitaph for what may be psychology's best-known experiment.

Cultural Variations in Conformity and Obedience

Are conformity and obedience unique to American culture? By no means. The Asch and Milgram experiments have been repeated in many societies, where they have yielded results roughly similar to those seen in the United States. Thus, the phenomena of conformity and obedience seem to transcend culture.

The replications of Milgram's obedience study have largely been limited to industrialized nations similar to the United States. Comparisons of the results of these studies must be made with caution because the composition of the samples and the experimental procedures have varied somewhat. But many of the studies have reported even higher obedience rates than those seen in Milgram's American samples. For example, obedience rates of over 80% have been reported for samples from Italy, Germany, Austria, Spain, and Holland (Smith & Bond, 1994). Thus, the surprisingly high level of obedience observed by Milgram does not appear to be peculiar to the United States.

The Asch experiment has been repeated in a more diverse range of societies than the Milgram experiment. Like many other cultural differences in social behavior, variations in conformity appear to be related to the degree of *individualism versus collectivism* seen in a society. Various theorists have argued that collectivistic cultures, which emphasize respect for group norms, cooperation, and harmony, probably encourage more conformity than individualistic cultures

(Schwartz, 1990) and have a more positive view of conformity (Kim & Markus, 1999). As Matsumoto (1994) puts it, "To conform in American culture is to be weak or deficient somehow. But this is not true in other cultures. Many cultures foster more collective, group-oriented values, and concepts of conformity, obedience, and compliance enjoy much higher status" (p. 162). Consistent with this analysis, studies *have* found higher levels of conformity in collectivistic cultures than in individualistic cultures (Bond & Smith, 1996; Smith, 2001).

The Power of the Situation: The Stanford Prison Simulation

The research of Asch and Milgram provided dramatic demonstrations of the potent influence that situational factors can have on social behavior. The power of the situation was underscored once again, about a decade after Milgram's obedience research, in another landmark study conducted by Philip Zimbardo, who, ironically, was a high school classmate of Milgram's. Zimbardo and his colleagues designed the Stanford Prison Simulation to investigate why prisons tend to become abusive, degrading, violent environments (Haney, Banks, & Zimbardo, 1973; Zimbardo et al., 1973). Like Milgram, Zimbardo wanted to see how much the power of the situation would shape the behavior of normal, average subjects.

The participants were college students recruited for a study of prison life through a newspaper ad. After giving 70 volunteers an extensive battery of tests and interviews, the researchers chose 24 students who appeared to be physically healthy and psychologically stable to be the subjects. A coin flip determined which of them would be "guards" and which would be "prisoners" in a simulated prison setup at Stanford University. The prisoners were "arrested" at their homes, handcuffed, and transported to a mock prison on the Stanford campus. Upon arrival, they were ordered to strip, sprayed with a delousing agent, given prison uniforms (smocks), assigned numbers as their identities, and locked up in iron-barred cells. The subjects assigned to be guards were given khaki uniforms, billy clubs, whistles, and reflective sunglasses. They were told that they could run their prison in whatever way they wanted except that they were not allowed to use physical punishment.

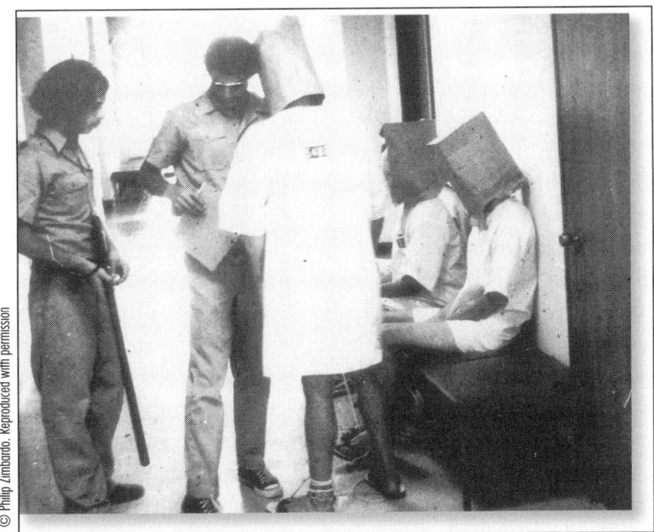

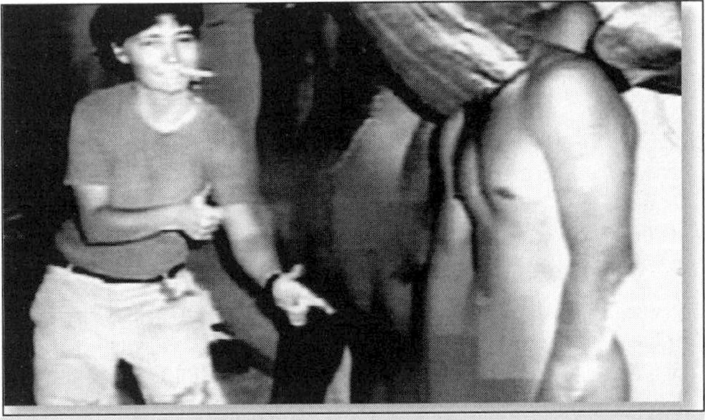

The recent Abu Ghraib prison scandal in Iraq has sparked renewed interest in the Stanford Prison Simulation. Some of the photos taken of the abuse at Abu Ghraib (right) are stunningly similar to photos from the Stanford study (left). For instance, in both cases, the guards "dehumanized" their prisoners by placing bags over their heads.

What happened? In short order, confrontations occurred between the guards and prisoners, and the guards quickly devised a variety of sometimes cruel strategies to maintain total control over their prisoners. Meals, blankets, and bathroom privileges were selectively denied to some prisoners to achieve control. The prisoners were taunted, humiliated, called demeaning names, and forced to beg for opportunities to go to the bathroom. Pointless, petty rules were strictly enforced and difficult prisoners were punished with hard labor (doing pushups and jumping jacks, cleaning toilets with their bare hands). The guards harassed the prisoners by waking them up in the middle of the night to assemble and count off. And the guards creatively turned a 2-foot by 2-foot closet into a "hole" for solitary confinement of rebellious prisoners. Although there was some variation among the guards, collectively they became mean, malicious, and abusive in fulfilling their responsibilities. How did the prisoners react? A few showed signs of emotional disturbance and had to be released early, but they mostly became listless, apathetic, and demoralized. The study was designed to run two weeks, but Zimbardo decided that he needed to end it prematurely after just six days because he was concerned about the rapidly escalating abuse and degradation of the prisoners. The subjects were debriefed, offered counseling, and sent home.

social roles
widely shared expectations about how people in certain positions are supposed to behave.

Courtesy of Philip Zimbardo

■ **Phil Zimbardo.** "But in the end, I called off the experiment not because of the horror I saw out there in the prison yard, but because of the horror of realizing that *I* could have easily traded places with the most brutal guard or become the weakest prisoner full of hatred at being so powerless."

How did Zimbardo and his colleagues explain the stunning transformations of their subjects? First, they attributed the participants' behavior to the enormous influence of social roles. **Social roles** are widely shared expectations about how people in certain positions are supposed to behave. We have role expectations for salespeople, waiters, ministers, medical patients, students, bus drivers, tourists, flight attendants, and, of course, prison guards and prisoners. The participants had a rough idea of what it meant to act like a guard or a prisoner and they were gradually consumed by their roles (Haney & Zimbardo, 1998). Second, the researchers attributed their subjects' behavior to the compelling power of situational factors. Before the study began, the tests and interviews showed no measureable differences in personality or character between those randomly assigned to be guards versus prisoners. The stark differences in their behavior had to be due to the radically different situations that they found themselves in. As Haney and Zimbardo (1998, p. 719) put it, the study "demonstrated the power of situations to overwhelm people and elicit from them unexpectedly cruel, yet 'situationally appropriate' behavior." As a result, Zimbardo, like Milgram before him, concluded that situational pressures can lead normal, decent people to behave in sinister, repugnant ways.

The results of the Stanford Prison Simulation were eye-opening, to say the least. Within a short time, subjects with no obvious character flaws became tyrannical, sadistic, brutal guards. If this transformation can occur so swiftly in a make-believe prison, one can only imagine how the much stronger situational forces in real prisons readily promote abusive behavior. Although the Stanford Prison Simulation was conducted over 30 years ago, renewed interest in the study was sparked by the recent Abu Ghraib prison scandal in Iraq. American military personnel with little or no experience in running prisons were found to have engaged in "sadistic, blatant, and wanton criminal abuses" of their Iraqi prisoners (Hersh, 2004). Some of the photos taken of the abuse at Abu Ghraib are eerily reminiscent of photos from the Stanford simulation. The U.S. government blamed these horrific abuses on "a few bad apples" who were presumed to be pathological or morally deficient, writing off the incident as an aberration. Yet the evidence from the Stanford Prison Simulation clearly suggests otherwise. Phil Zimbardo (2004, 2005) argues, and has testified as an expert witness, that it is far more likely that situational pressures led normal, average Americans to commit morally reprehensible abuses. This explanation does *not* absolve the brutal guards of responsibility for their behavior. However, Zimbardo emphasizes that making scapegoats out of a handful of guards does not solve the real problem, which lies in the system. He maintains that abuses in prisons are more likely than not and can only be reduced if authorities provide extensive training and strong supervision for guards, enact explicit sanctions for abuses, and maintain clear accountability in the chain of command.

BEHAVIOR IN GROUPS: JOINING WITH OTHERS

Social psychologists study groups as well as individuals, but exactly what is a group? Are all the divorced fathers living in Baltimore a group? Are three strangers moving skyward in an elevator a group? What if the elevator gets stuck? How about four students from your psychology class who study together regularly? A jury deciding a trial? The Boston Celtics? The U.S. Congress? Some of these collections of people are groups and others aren't. Let's examine the concept of a group to find out which of these collections qualify.

In social psychologists' eyes, a **group** consists of two or more individuals who interact and are interdependent. The divorced fathers in Baltimore aren't likely to qualify on either count. Strangers sharing an elevator might interact briefly, but they're not interdependent. However, if the elevator got stuck and they had to deal with an emergency together, they could suddenly become a group. Your psychology classmates who study together are a group, as they interact and depend on each other to achieve shared goals. So do the members of a jury, a sports team such as the Celtics, and a large organization such as the U.S. Congress. Historically, most groups have interacted on a face-to-face basis, but advances in telecommunications are changing that reality. In the era of the Internet, people can interact, become interdependent, and develop a group identity without ever meeting in person (Bargh & McKenna, 2004; McKenna & Bargh, 1998).

group
two or more individuals who interact and are interdependent.

Groups vary in many ways. Obviously, a study group, the Celtics, and Congress are very different in terms of size, purpose, formality, longevity, similarity of members, and diversity of activities. Can anything meaningful be said about groups if they're so diverse? Yes. In spite of their immense variability, groups share certain features that affect their functioning. Among other things, most groups have *roles* that allocate special responsibilities to some members, *norms* about suitable behavior, a *communication structure* that reflects who talks to whom, and a *power structure* that determines which members wield the most influence (Forsyth, 1999).

Thus, when people join together in a group, they create a social organism with unique characteristics and dynamics that can take on a life of its own. One of social psychology's enduring insights is that in a given situation you may behave quite differently when you're in a group than when you're alone. To illustrate this point, let's look at some interesting research on helping behavior.

Behavior Alone and in Groups: The Case of the Bystander Effect

Imagine that you have a precarious medical condition and that you must go through life worrying about whether someone will leap forward to provide help if the need ever arises. Wouldn't you feel more secure when around larger groups? After all, there's "safety in numbers." Logically, as group size increases, the probability of having a "good Samaritan" on the scene increases. Or does it?

We've seen before that human behavior isn't necessarily logical. When it comes to helping behavior, many studies have uncovered an apparent paradox called the **bystander effect**: People are less likely to provide needed help when they are in groups than when they are alone. Evidence that your probability of getting help *declines* as group size increases was first described by John Darley and Bibb Latané (1968), who were conducting research on the determinants of helping behavior. In the Darley and Latané study, students in individual cubicles connected by an intercom participated in discussion groups of three sizes. (The separate cubicles

bystander effect
a paradoxical social phenomenon in which people are less likely to provide needed help when they are in groups than when they are alone.

allowed the researchers to examine each individual's behavior in a group context, a technique that minimizes confounded variables in individual-group comparisons.) Early in the discussion, a student who was an experimental accomplice hesitantly mentioned that he was prone to seizures. Later in the discussion, the same accomplice feigned a severe seizure and cried out for help. Although a majority of subjects sought assistance for the student, the tendency to seek help *declined* with increasing group size.

Similar trends have been seen in many other experiments, in which over 6000 subjects have had opportunities to respond to apparent emergencies, including fires, asthma attacks, faintings, crashes, and flat tires, as well as less pressing needs to answer a door or to pick up objects dropped by a stranger (Latané & Nida, 1981). Many of the experiments have been highly realistic studies conducted in subways, stores, and shopping malls, and many have compared individuals against groups in face-to-face interaction. Pooling the results of this research, Latané and Nida (1981) estimated that subjects who were alone provided help 75% of the time, whereas subjects in the presence of others provided help only 53% of the time. They concluded that the only significant limiting condition on the bystander effect is that it is less likely to occur when the need for help is unambiguous.

What accounts for the bystander effect? A number of factors may be at work. Bystander effects are most likely in ambiguous situations because people look around to see whether others think there's an emergency. If everyone hesitates, their inaction suggests that there's no real need for help. The *diffusion of responsibility* that occurs in a group is also important. If you're by yourself when you encounter someone in need of help, the responsibility to provide help rests squarely on your shoulders. However, if other people are present, the responsibility is divided among you, and you may all say to yourselves, "Someone else will help." A reduced sense of responsibility may contribute to other aspects of behavior in groups, as we'll see in the next section.

Group Productivity and Social Loafing

Have you ever driven through a road construction project—at a snail's pace, of course—and become irritated because so many workers seem to be just standing around? Maybe the irony of the posted sign "Your tax dollars at work" made you imagine that they were all dawdling. And then again, perhaps not. Individuals' productivity often *does* decline in larger groups (Karau & Williams, 1993). This fact is unfortunate, as many important tasks can only be accomplished in groups. Group productivity is crucial to committees, sports teams, firefighting crews, sororities, study groups, symphonies, and work teams of all kinds, from the morning crew in a little diner to the board of directors of a Fortune 500 company.

Two factors appear to contribute to reduced individual productivity in larger groups. One factor is *reduced efficiency* resulting from the *loss of coordination* among workers' efforts. As you put more people on a yearbook staff, for instance, you'll probably create more and more duplication of effort and increase how often group members end up working at cross purposes.

social loafing
a reduction in effort by individuals when they work in groups as compared to when they work by themselves.

The second factor contributing to low productivity in groups involves *effort* rather than efficiency. **Social loafing** is a reduction in effort by individuals when they work in groups as compared to when they work by themselves. To investigate social loafing, Latané and his colleagues (1979) measured the sound output produced by subjects who were asked to cheer or clap as loud as they could. So they couldn't see or hear other group members, subjects were told that the study concerned the importance of sensory feedback and were asked to don blindfolds and put on headphones through which loud noise was played. This maneuver permitted a simple deception: Subjects were *led to believe* that they were working alone or in a group of two or six, when in fact *individual* output was actually measured.

When participants *thought* that they were working in larger groups, their individual output declined. Since lack of coordination could not affect individual output, the subjects' decreased sound production had to be due to reduced effort. Latané and his colleagues also had the same subjects clap and shout in genuine groups of two and six and found an additional decrease in production that was attributed to loss of coordination. Figure 14.18 shows how social loafing and loss of coordination combined to reduce productivity as group size increased.

The social-loafing effect has been replicated in numerous studies in which subjects have worked on a variety of tasks, including cheering, pumping air, swimming in a relay race, solving mazes, evaluating editorials, and brainstorming for new ideas (Karau & Williams, 1995; Levine & Moreland, 1998). Social loafing and the bystander effect appear to share a common cause: diffusion of responsibility in groups (Comer, 1995; Latané, 1981). As group size increases, the responsibility for getting a job done is divided among more people, and many group members ease up because their individual contribution is less recognizable. Thus, social loafing occurs in situations where individuals can "hide in the crowd" (Karau & Williams, 1993).

Social loafing is *not* inevitable. For example, people with high achievement motivation are less likely to exhibit social loafing than those who are low in achievement motivation (Hart et al., 2004). Social loafing is also less likely when group members are convinced that individual performance is crucial to group performance and that excellent group performance will lead to valued outcomes (Shepperd & Taylor, 1999). And social loafing is reduced when people work in smaller and more cohesive groups (Liden et al., 2004). Cultural factors may also influence the likelihood of social loafing. Studies with subjects from Japan, China, and Taiwan suggest that social loafing may be less prevalent in collectivistic cultures, which place a high priority on meeting group goals and contributing to one's ingroups (Karau & Williams, 1995; Smith, 2001).

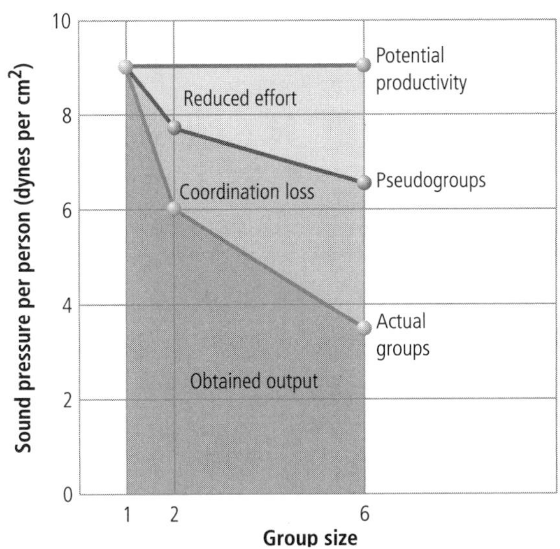

FIGURE 14.18

The effect of loss of coordination and social loafing on group productivity. The amount of sound produced per person declined noticeably when people worked in actual groups of two or six (orange line). This decrease in productivity reflects both loss of coordination and social loafing. Sound per person also declined when subjects merely thought they were working in groups of two or six (purple line). This smaller decrease in productivity is due to social loafing. *Source:* Adapted from Latané, B., Williams, K., & Harkins, S. (1979). Many hands make light the work: The causes and consequences of social loafing. *Journal of Personality and Social Psychology, 37,* 822–832. Copyright © 1979 by the American Psychological Association. Adapted by permission of the publisher and author.

Decision Making in Groups

Productivity is not the only issue that commonly concerns groups. When people join together in groups, they often have to make decisions about what the group will do and how it will use its resources. Whether it's your study group deciding what type of pizza to order, a jury deciding on a verdict, or Congress deciding on whether to pass a bill, groups make decisions.

Evaluating decision making is often more complicated than evaluating productivity. In many cases, the "right" decision may not be readily apparent. Who can say whether your study group ordered the right pizza or whether Congress passed the right bills? Nonetheless, social psychologists have discovered some interesting tendencies in group decision making. We'll take a brief look at *group polarization* and *groupthink*.

Group Polarization Who leans toward more cautious decisions: individuals or groups? Common sense suggests that groups will work out compromises that cancel out members' extreme views. Hence, the collective wisdom of the group should yield relatively conservative choices. Is common sense correct? To investigate this question, Stoner (1961) asked individual subjects to give their recommendations on tough decisions and then asked the same subjects to engage in group discussion to arrive at

FIGURE 14.19

Group polarization. Two examples of group polarization are diagrammed here. The positions of the people on the horizontal scales reflect their positive or negative attitudes regarding an idea before and after group discussion. In the first example (top) a group starts out mildly opposed to an idea, but after discussion sentiment against the idea is stronger. In the second example (bottom), a group starts out with a favorable disposition toward an idea, and this disposition is strengthened by group discussion.

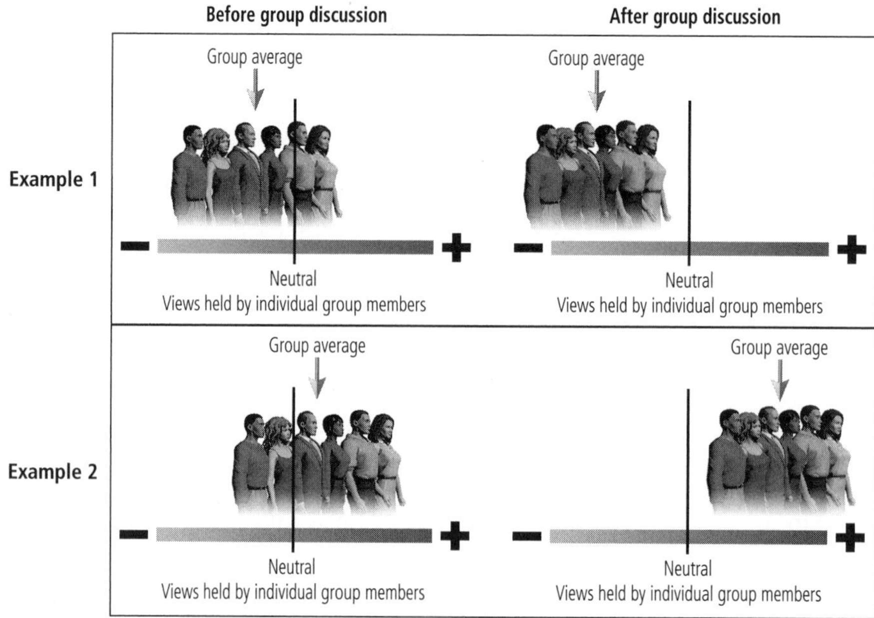

joint recommendations. When Stoner compared individuals' average recommendation against their group decision generated through discussion, he found that groups arrived at *riskier* decisions than individuals did. Stoner's finding was replicated in other studies (Pruitt, 1971), and the phenomenon acquired the name *risky shift.*

However, investigators eventually determined that groups can shift either way, toward risk or caution, depending on which way the group is leaning to begin with (Friedkin, 1999). A shift toward a more extreme position, an effect called *polarization,* is often the result of group discussion (Tindale, Kameda, & Hinsz, 2003). Thus, **group polarization** occurs when group discussion strengthens a group's dominant point of view and produces a shift toward a more extreme decision in that direction (see Figure 14.19). Group polarization does *not* involve widening the gap between factions in a group, as its name might suggest. In fact, group polarization can contribute to consensus in a group, as we'll see in our discussion of groupthink.

group polarization
a phenomenon that occurs when group discussion strengthens a group's dominant point of view and produces a shift toward a more extreme decision in that direction.

groupthink
a process in which members of a cohesive group emphasize concurrence at the expense of critical thinking in arriving at a decision.

Groupthink In contrast to group polarization, which is a normal process in group dynamics, groupthink is more like a "disease" that can infect decision making in groups. **Groupthink** occurs when members of a cohesive group emphasize concurrence at the expense of critical thinking in arriving at a decision. As you might imagine, groupthink doesn't produce very effective decision making. Indeed, groupthink can lead to major blunders that may look incomprehensible after the fact. Irving Janis (1972) first described groupthink in his effort to explain how President John F. Kennedy and his advisers could have miscalculated so badly in deciding to invade Cuba at the Bay of Pigs in 1961. The attempted invasion failed miserably and, in retrospect, seemed remarkably ill-conceived.

Applying his many years of research and theory on group dynamics to the Bay of Pigs fiasco, Janis developed a model of groupthink, which is summarized in Figure 14.20. When groups get caught up in groupthink, members suspend their critical judgment and the group starts censoring dissent as the pressure to conform increases. Soon, everyone begins to think alike. Moreover, "mind guards" try to shield the group from information that contradicts the group's view.

Many types of groups have to arrive at collective decisions. The social dynamics of group decisions are complicated, and a variety of factors can undermine effective decision making.

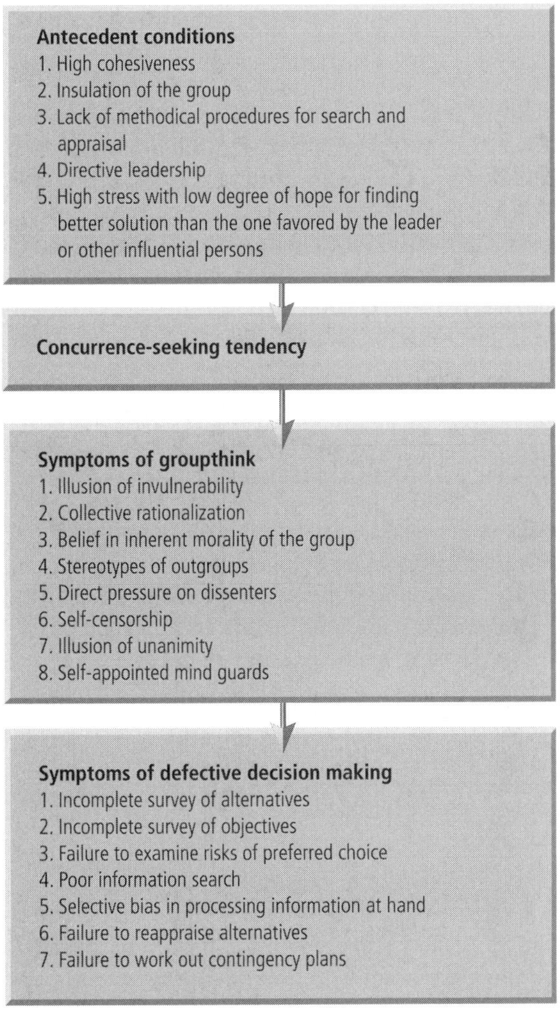

Antecedent conditions
1. High cohesiveness
2. Insulation of the group
3. Lack of methodical procedures for search and appraisal
4. Directive leadership
5. High stress with low degree of hope for finding better solution than the one favored by the leader or other influential persons

↓

Concurrence-seeking tendency

↓

Symptoms of groupthink
1. Illusion of invulnerability
2. Collective rationalization
3. Belief in inherent morality of the group
4. Stereotypes of outgroups
5. Direct pressure on dissenters
6. Self-censorship
7. Illusion of unanimity
8. Self-appointed mind guards

↓

Symptoms of defective decision making
1. Incomplete survey of alternatives
2. Incomplete survey of objectives
3. Failure to examine risks of preferred choice
4. Poor information search
5. Selective bias in processing information at hand
6. Failure to reappraise alternatives
7. Failure to work out contingency plans

FIGURE 14.20

Overview of Janis's model of groupthink. The antecedent conditions, symptoms, and resultant effects of groupthink postulated by Janis (1972) are outlined here. His model of groupthink has been very influential, but practical difficulties have limited research on the theory. The antecedent conditions outlined here do not always lead to groupthink. *Source:* Adapted from Janis, I. L., & Mann, L. (1977). *Decision making: A psychological analysis of conflict, choice and commitment.* New York: Free Press. Adapted with permission of The Free Press, a Division of Simon & Schuster. Copyright © 1977 by The Free Press.

If the group's view is challenged from outside, victims of groupthink tend to think in simplistic "us versus them" terms. Members begin to overestimate the ingroup's unanimity, and they begin to view the outgroup as the enemy. Groupthink also promotes incomplete gathering of information. Like individuals, groups often display a confirmation bias, as they tend to seek and focus on information that supports their initial views (Schulz-Hardt et al., 2000).

Recent research has uncovered another factor that may contribute to groupthink—individual members often fail to share information that is unique to them (Postmes, Spears, & Cihangir, 2001). Sound decision making depends on group members combining their information effectively (Winquist & Larson, 1998). However, when groups discuss issues, they have an interesting tendency to focus mainly on the information that the members already share as opposed to exchanging information unique to individual members (Stasser, Vaughn, & Stewart, 2000).

What causes groupthink? According to Janis, a key precondition is high group cohesiveness. **Group cohesiveness** refers to the strength of the liking relationships linking group members to each other and to the group itself. Members of cohesive groups are close-knit, are committed, have "team spirit," and are loyal to the group. Cohesiveness itself isn't bad. It can facilitate group productivity (Mullen & Copper, 1994) and help groups achieve great things. But Janis maintains that the danger of groupthink is greater when groups are highly cohesive. Groupthink is also more likely when a group works in relative isolation, when the group's power structure is dominated by a strong, directive leader, and when the group is under stress to make a major decision (see Figure 14.20). Under these conditions, group discussions can easily lead to group polarization, strengthening the group's dominant view.

group cohesiveness
the strength of the liking relationships linking group members to each other and to the group itself.

A relatively small number of experiments have been conducted to test Janis's theory, because the antecedent conditions thought to foster groupthink—such as high decision stress, strong group cohesiveness, and dominating leadership—are difficult to create effectively in laboratory settings (Aldag & Fuller, 1993). The studies that have been conducted have yielded mixed results in that high cohesiveness and strong leadership do not *necessarily* produce groupthink (Kerr & Tindale, 2004). Thus, the evidence on groupthink consists mostly of retrospective case studies of major decision-making fiascos (Eaton, 2001). In light of this situation, Janis's model of groupthink should probably be characterized as an innovative, sophisticated, intuitively appealing theory that needs to be subjected to much more empirical study (Esser, 1998).

REFLECTING ON THE CHAPTER'S THEMES

Our discussion of social psychology has provided a final embellishment on three of our seven unifying themes. One of these is the value of psychology's commitment to empiricism—that is, its reliance on systematic observation through research to arrive at conclusions. The second theme that stands out is the importance of cultural factors in shaping behavior, and the third is the extent to which people's experience of the world is highly subjective. Let's consider the virtues of empiricism first.

It's easy to question the need to do scientific research on social behavior, because studies in social psychology often seem to verify common sense. While most people wouldn't presume to devise their own theory of color vision, question the significance of REM sleep, or quibble about the principal causes of schizophrenia, everyone has beliefs about the nature of love, how to persuade others, and people's willingness to help in times of need. Thus, when studies demonstrate that credibility enhances persuasion, or that good looks facilitate attraction, it's tempting to conclude that social psychologists go to great lengths to document the obvious, and some critics say, "Why bother?"

You saw why in this chapter. Research in social psychology has repeatedly shown that the predictions of logic and common sense are often wrong. Consider just a few examples. Even psychiatric experts failed to predict the remarkable obedience to authority uncovered in Milgram's research. The bystander effect in helping behavior violates cold-blooded mathematical logic. Dissonance research has shown that after a severe initiation, the bigger the letdown, the more favorable people's feelings are. These principles defy common sense. Thus, research on social behavior provides dramatic illustrations of why psychologists put their faith in empiricism.

Our coverage of social psychology also demonstrated once again that, cross-culturally, behavior is characterized by both variance and invariance. Thus, we saw substantial cultural differences in patterns of attribution, the role of romantic love in marriage, attitudes about conformity, the tendency to obey authority figures, and the likelihood of social loafing. Although basic social phenomena such as stereotyping, attraction, obedience, and conformity probably occur all over the world, cross-cultural studies of social behavior show that research findings based on American samples may not generalize precisely to other cultures.

Research in social psychology is also uniquely well suited for making the point that people's view of the world is highly personal and subjective. In this chapter we saw how physical appearance can color perception of a person's ability or personality, how social schemas can lead people to see what they expect to see in their interactions with others, how pressure to conform can make people begin to doubt their senses, and how groupthink can lead group members down a perilous path of shared illusions.

The subjectivity of social perception will surface once again in our Applications for the chapter. The Personal Application focuses on prejudice, a practical problem that social psychologists have shown great interest in, whereas the Critical Thinking Application examines aspects of social influence.

UNDERSTANDING PREJUDICE

Answer the following "true" or "false."

____ **1** Prejudice and discrimination amount to the same thing.

____ **2** Stereotypes are always negative or unflattering.

____ **3** Ethnic and racial groups are the only widespread targets of prejudice in modern society.

____ **4** People see members of their own ingroup as being more alike than the members of outgroups.

James Byrd Jr., a 49-year-old black man, was walking home from a family gathering in the summer of 1998 when he was offered a ride by three white men, one of whom he knew. Shortly thereafter, pieces of Byrd's savagely beaten body were found strewn along a rural road in Texas. Apparently, he had been beaten, then shackled by his ankles to the back of the truck and dragged to death over 2 miles of road. Police say that Byrd was targeted simply because he was black. Thankfully, such tragic events are relatively rare in the United States. Nonetheless, they remind us that prejudice and discrimination still exist.

Prejudice is a major social problem. It harms victims' self-concepts, suppresses their potential, creates enormous stress in their lives, and promotes tension and strife between groups (Dion, 2003). The first step toward reducing prejudice is to understand its roots. Hence, in this Application, we'll try to achieve a better understanding of why prejudice is so common. Along the way, you'll learn the answers to the true-false questions at the beginning of this application.

Prejudice and discrimination are closely related concepts, and the terms have become nearly interchangeable in popular use. Social scientists, however, prefer to define their terms precisely, so let's clarify which is which. **Prejudice** is a negative attitude held toward members of a group. Like many other attitudes, prejudice can include three components (see Figure 14.21): beliefs ("Indians are

prejudice
a negative attitude held toward members of a group.

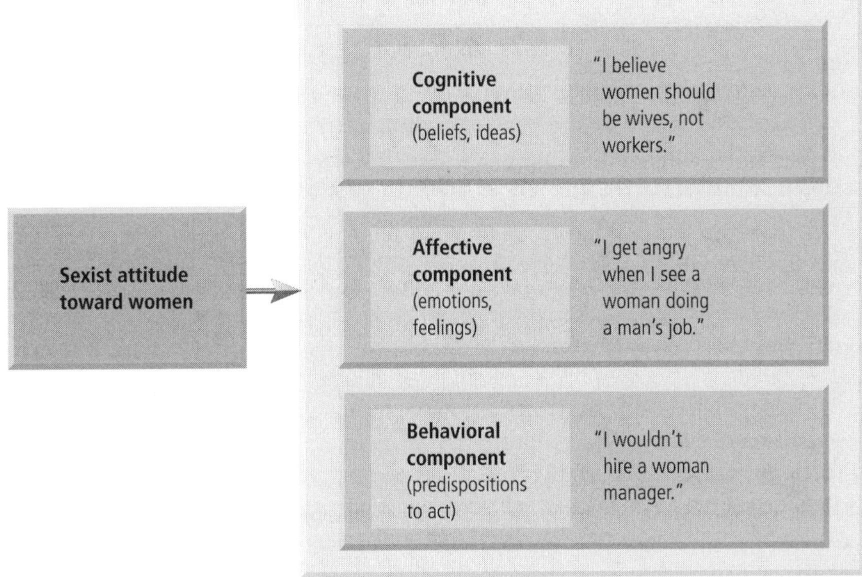

FIGURE 14.21
The three potential components of prejudice as an attitude. Attitudes can consist of up to three components. The tricomponent model of attitudes, applied to prejudice against women, would view sexism as negative beliefs about women (cognitive component) that lead to a feeling of dislike (affective component), which in turn leads to a readiness to discriminate against women (behavioral component).

Members of many types of groups are victims of prejudice. Besides racial minorities, others that have been stereotyped and discriminated against include gays and lesbians, women, the homeless, and those who are overweight.

mostly alcoholics"), emotions ("I despise Jews"), and behavioral dispositions ("I wouldn't hire a Mexican"). Racial prejudice receives the lion's share of publicity, but prejudice is *not* limited to ethnic groups. Women, homosexuals, the aged, the disabled, and the mentally ill are also targets of widespread prejudice. Thus, many people hold prejudicial attitudes toward one group or another, and many have been victims of prejudice.

discrimination
behaving differently, usually unfairly, toward the members of a group.

Prejudice may lead to **discrimination**, which involves behaving differently, usually unfairly, toward the members of a group. Prejudice and discrimination tend to go hand in hand, but as LaPiere's (1934) pioneering study of discrimination in restaurant seating showed, attitudes and behavior do not necessarily correspond (Hogg & Abrams, 2003; see Figure 14.22). In our discussion, we'll concentrate primarily on the attitude of prejudice. Let's begin by looking at processes in person perception that promote prejudice.

		Prejudice	
		Absent	Present
Discrimination	Absent	No relevant behaviors	A restaurant owner who is bigoted against gays treats them fairly because he needs their business.
	Present	An executive with favorable attitudes toward blacks doesn't hire them because he would get in trouble with his boss.	A professor who is hostile toward women grades his female students unfairly.

FIGURE 14.22

Relationship between prejudice and discrimination. As these examples show, prejudice can exist without discrimination and discrimination without prejudice. In the green cells, there is a disparity between attitude and behavior.

Stereotyping and Subjectivity in Person Perception

Perhaps no factor plays a larger role in prejudice than *stereotypes*. That's not to say that stereotypes are inevitably negative. For instance, it's hardly insulting to assert that Americans are ambitious or that the Japanese are industrious. Unfortunately, many people do subscribe to derogatory stereotypes of various ethnic groups. Although studies suggest that negative racial stereotypes have diminished over the last 50 years, they're not a thing of the past (Madon et al., 2001; Mellor, 2003). According to a variety of investigators, modern racism has merely become more subtle (Devine, Plant, & Blair, 2001; Dovidio & Gaertner, 1999, 2000). Many people carefully avoid overt expressions of prejudicial attitudes but covertly continue to harbor negative views of racial minorities. These people endorse racial equality as an abstract principle but often oppose concrete programs intended to promote equality, on the grounds that discrimination is no longer a problem (Wright & Taylor, 2003). Recent studies suggest that modern sexism has become subtle in much the same way as racism (Swim & Campbell, 2001).

Research indicates that stereotypes are so pervasive and insidious they often operate automatically (Amodio et al., 2004; Fiske, 2000). Prejudicial stereotypes are highly accessible cognitive schemas that can be activated automatically, even in people who truly renounce prejudice. Thus, a man who rejects prejudice against homosexuals may still feel uncomfortable sitting next to a gay male on a bus, even though he regards his reaction as inappropriate.

Unfortunately, stereotypes are highly resistant to change. When people encounter members of a group that they view with prejudice who deviate from the stereotype of that group, they often discount this evidence by assuming that the atypical group members constitute a distinct subtype of that group, such as wealthy African Americans or conservative homosexuals (Kunda & Oleson, 1995, 1997). Consigning deviants to a subtype that is viewed as unrepresentative of the group allows people to preserve their stereotype of the group.

Stereotypes also persist because the *subjectivity* of person perception makes it likely that people will see what they expect to see when they actually come into contact with groups that they view with prejudice (Dunning & Sherman, 1997). For example, Duncan (1976) had white subjects watch and evaluate interaction on a TV monitor that was supposedly live (it was actually a videotape) and varied the race of a person who gets into an argument and gives another person a slight shove. The shove was coded as "violent behavior" by 73% of the subjects when the actor was black but by only 13% of the subjects when the actor was white. As we've noted before, people's perceptions are highly subjective. Because of stereotypes, even "violence" may lie in the eye of the beholder.

Memory biases are also tilted in favor of confirming people's prejudices (Ybarra, Stephan, & Schaberg, 2000). For example, if a man believes that "women are not cut out for leadership roles," he may dwell with delight on his female supervisor's mistakes and quickly forget about her achievements. Thus, the *illusory correlation effect* can contribute to the maintenance of prejudicial stereotypes (Berndsen et al., 2002).

Biases in Attribution

Attribution processes can also help perpetuate stereotypes and prejudice (Maass, 1999). Research taking its cue from Weiner's (1980) model of attribution has shown that people often make *biased attributions for success and failure*. For example, men and women don't get equal credit for their successes (Swim & Sanna, 1996). Observers often discount a woman's success by attributing it to good luck, sheer effort, or the ease of the task (except on traditional feminine tasks). In comparison, a man's success is more likely to be attributed to his outstanding ability

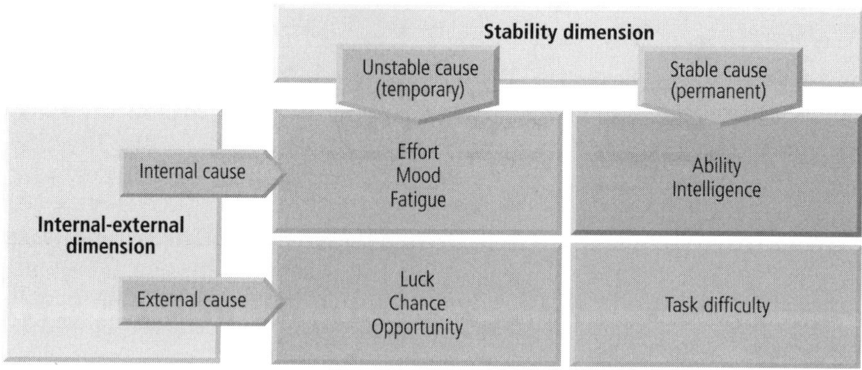

FIGURE 14.23

Bias in the attributions used to explain success and failure by men and women. Attributions about the two sexes often differ. For example, men's successes tend to be attributed to their ability and intelligence (blue cell), whereas women's successes tend to be attributed to hard work, good luck, or low task difficulty (green cells). These attributional biases help to perpetuate the belief that men are more competent than women.

(see Figure 14.23). These biased patterns of attribution help sustain the stereotype that men are more competent than women. Similar patterns of bias have been seen in attributional explanations of ethnic minorities' successes and failures (Jackson, Sullivan, & Hodge, 1993; Kluegel, 1990). Generally, when minorities experience stereotype-inconsistent success, their success is discounted by attributing it to external factors or to unstable, internal causes.

Recall that the *fundamental attribution error* is a bias toward explaining events by pointing to the actor's personal characteristics as causes (internal attributions). Research suggests that people are particularly likely to make this error when evaluating targets of prejudice (Hewstone, 1990). Thus, when people take note of ethnic neighborhoods dominated by crime and poverty, the personal qualities of the residents are blamed for these problems, whereas other explanations emphasizing situational factors (job discrimination, poor police service, and so on) are downplayed or ignored. The old saying "They should be able to pull themselves up by their bootstraps" is a blanket dismissal of how situational factors may make it especially difficult for minorities to achieve upward mobility.

Defensive attribution, which involves unjustly blaming victims of misfortune for their adversity, can also contribute to prejudice. A prominent example in recent years has been the assertion by some people that homosexuals brought the AIDS crisis on themselves and so deserve their fate (Anderson, 1992). By blaming AIDS on gays' alleged character flaws, heterosexuals may be unknowingly seeking to reassure themselves that they're immune to a similar fate.

Forming and Preserving Prejudicial Attitudes

If prejudice is an attitude, where does it come from? Many prejudices appear to be handed down as a legacy from parents (Ponterotto & Pedersen, 1993). Prejudicial attitudes can be found in children as young as ages 4 or 5 (Aboud & Amato, 2001). Research suggests that parents' racial attitudes often influence their children's racial attitudes (Sinclair, Dunn, & Lowery, 2004). This transmission of prejudice across generations presumably depends to some extent on *observational learning.* For example, if a young boy hears his father ridicule homosexuals, his exposure to his father's attitude is likely to affect his attitude about gays. If the young boy then goes to school and makes disparaging remarks about gays that are reinforced by approval from peers, his prejudice will be strengthened through *operant conditioning.* Of course, prejudicial attitudes are not acquired only through direct experience. Stereotypic portrayals of various groups in the media can also foster prejudicial attitudes (Herrett-Skjellum & Allen, 1996; Williams & Giles, 1998).

Competition Between Groups

One of the oldest and simplest explanations for prejudice is that competition between groups can fuel animosity. If two groups compete for scarce resources, such as good jobs and affordable housing, one group's gain is the other's loss. *Realistic group conflict theory* asserts that intergroup hostility and prejudice are a natural outgrowth of fierce competition between groups.

A classic study at Robbers' Cave State Park in Oklahoma provided support for this theory many years ago (Sherif et al., 1961). The subjects were 11-year-old white boys attending a three-week summer camp at the park, who did not know that the camp counselors were actually researchers (their parents knew). The boys were randomly assigned to one of two groups. During the first week, the boys got to know the other members of their own group through typical camp activities and developed a group identity, choosing to call themselves the Rattlers and the Eagles. In the second week, the Rattlers and Eagles were put into a series of competitive situations, such as a football game, a treasure hunt, and a tug of war, with trophies and other prizes at stake. As predicted by realistic group conflict theory, hostile feelings quickly erupted between the two groups, as food fights broke out in the mess hall, cabins were ransacked, and group flags were burned.

If competition between innocent groups of children pursuing trivial prizes can foster hostility, you can imagine what is likely to happen when adults from very different backgrounds battle for genuinely important resources. Research has repeatedly shown that conflict over scarce resources can fuel prejudice and discrimination (Bourhis & Gagnon, 2001). Even the mere *perception* of competition can breed prejudice (Zarate et al., 2004).

Dividing the World into Ingroups and Outgroups

As noted in the main body of the chapter, when people join together in groups, they sometimes divide the social world into "us versus them," or *ingroups versus outgroups.* As you might anticipate, people tend to evaluate outgroup members less favorably than ingroup members (Krueger, 1996; Reynolds, Turner, & Haslam, 2000). People also tend to think simplistically about outgroups. They tend to see diversity among the members of their own group but to overestimate the homogeneity of the outgroup (Oakes, 2001). At a simple, concrete level, the essence of this process is captured by the statement "They all look alike." The illusion of homogeneity in the outgroup makes it easier to sustain stereotypic beliefs about its members (Rothbart, 2001). This point disposes of our last unanswered question from the list that opened the Application. Just in case you missed one of the answers, the statements were all false.

Threats to Social Identity

According to the *social identity perspective,* self-esteem depends on both one's *personal* identity and one's *social* identity (Tajfel & Turner, 1979; Turner et al., 1987). *Social identity* refers to the pride individuals derive from their membership in various groups, such as ethnic groups, religious denominations, occupational groups, neighborhoods, country clubs, and so forth. The theory further proposes that self-esteem can be undermined by either threats to personal identity (you didn't get called for that job interview) or social identity (your football team loses a big game). Threats to both personal and social identity may motivate efforts to restore self-esteem, but threats to social identity are more likely to provoke responses that foster prejudice and discrimination.

When social identity is threatened, individuals may react in two key ways to bolster it (see Figure 14.24). One common response is to show *ingroup favoritism*—for example, tapping an ingroup member for a job opening or rating the performance

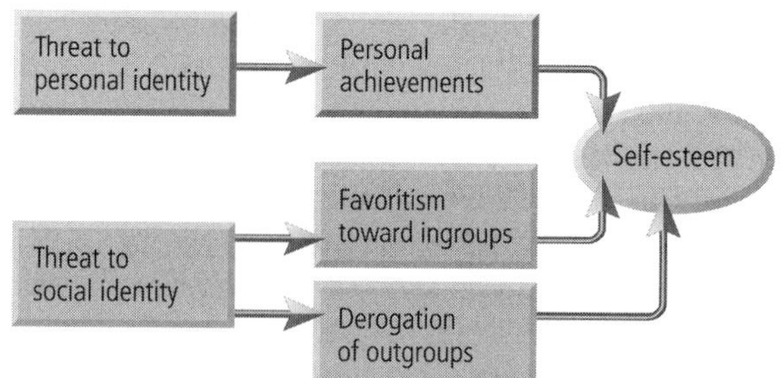

FIGURE 14.24

Threats to social identity and prejudie. According to Tajfel (1982) and Turner (1987), Individuals have both a personal identity (based on a unique sense of self) and a social identity (based on group memberships). When social identity is threatened, people are motivated to restore self-esteem by either showing favoritism to ingroup members or derogating members of outgroups. These tactics contribute to prejudice and discrimination. (Adapted from Brehm & Kassin, 1993)

of an ingroup member higher than that of an outgroup member (Capozza & Brown, 2000). A second common reaction is to engage in *outgroup derogation*—in other words, to "trash" outgroups that are perceived as threatening. Outgroup derogation is more likely when people identify especially strongly with the threatened ingroup (Levin et al, 2003; Schmitt & Maes, 2002). When people derogate an outgroup, they tend to feel superior as a result, and this feeling helps affirm their self-worth (Fein & Spencer, 1997). These unfortunate reactions are *not* inevitable, but threats to social identity represent yet another dynamic process that can foster prejudice (Turner & Reynolds, 2001).

Our discussion has shown that a plethora of processes conspire to create and maintain personal prejudices against a diverse array of outgroups. Most of the factors at work reflect normal, routine processes in social behavior. Thus, it is understandable that most people—whether privileged or underprivileged, minority members or majority members—probably harbor some prejudicial attitudes. Our analysis of the causes of prejudice may have permitted you to identify prejudices of your own or their sources. Perhaps it's wishful thinking on my part, but an enhanced awareness of your personal prejudices may help you become a little more tolerant of the endless diversity seen in human behavior. If so, that alone would mean that my efforts in writing this book have been amply rewarded.

foot-in-the-door technique
getting people to agree to a small request to increase the chances that they will agree to a larger request later.

lowball technique
getting someone to commit to an attractive proposition before revealing the hidden costs.

reciprocity norm
the rule that people should pay back in kind what they receive from others.

REVIEW

- People tend to attribute desirable characteristics to those who are good looking. Perceptions of people are also influenced by their style of nonverbal expressiveness.
- Stereotypes are widely held social schemas that lead people to expect that others will have certain characteristics because of their membership in a specific group. In interacting with others, stereotypes may lead people to see what they expect to see and to overestimate how often they see it.
- Internal attributions ascribe behavior to personal traits, whereas external attributions locate the cause of behavior in the environment. Weiner's model proposes that attributions for success and failure be analyzed in terms of the stability of causes as well as along the internal-external dimension.
- Observers favor internal attributions to explain another's behavior (the fundamental attribution error), while actors favor external attributions to explain their own behavior. Cultures vary in their emphasis on individualism as opposed to collectivism, and these differences appear to influence attributional tendencies.
- People tend to like and love others who are similar, who reciprocate expressions of affection, and who are

physically attractive. In intimate relationships, romantic ideals influence the progress of relationships.

- Berscheid and Hatfield have distinguished between passionate and companionate love. Sternberg builds on their distinction by dividing companionate love into intimacy and commitment. Hazan and Shaver's theory suggests that love relationships in adulthood mimic attachment patterns in infancy.
- The characteristics that people seek in prospective mates are much the same around the world. However, cultures vary considerably in their emphasis on passionate love as a prerequisite for marriage.
- According to evolutionary psychologists, certain aspects of good looks influence attraction because they are indicators of reproductive fitness. Consistent with evolutionary theory, gender differences in mating preferences appear to transcend culture. People's courtship tactics vary by sex in ways that make evolutionary sense. These tactics may include deception. Mate poaching is common and appears to be universal across cultures.
- Attitudes may be made up of cognitive, affective, and behavioral components. Attitudes vary in strength, accessibility, and ambivalence. Attitudes and behavior aren't as consistent as one might assume.
- A source of persuasion who is credible, expert, trustworthy, likable, and physically attractive tends to be relatively effective. Two-sided arguments, repetition, and fear arousal are effective elements in persuasive messages.
- Attitudes may be shaped through classical conditioning, operant conditioning, and observational learning. Festinger's dissonance theory asserts that inconsistent attitudes cause tension and that people alter their attitudes to reduce cognitive dissonance.
- Self-perception theory posits that people may infer their attitudes from their behavior. The elaboration likelihood model of persuasion holds that the central route to persuasion tends to yield longer-lasting attitude change than the peripheral route.
- Asch found that conformity becomes more likely as group size increases, up to a group size of four, and then levels off. If a small group isn't unanimous, conformity declines rapidly.
- In Milgram's study of obedience, subjects showed a remarkable tendency to follow orders to shock an innocent stranger. The generalizability of Milgram's findings has stood the test of time, but his work also helped to stimulate stricter ethical standards for research.
- The Asch and Milgram experiments have been replicated in many cultures. These replications have uncovered modest cultural variations in the propensity to conform or to obey an authority figure.
- The Stanford Prison Simulation demonstrated that social roles and other situational pressures can exert tremendous influence over social behavior. Like Milgram, Zimbardo showed that situational forces can lead normal people to exhibit surprisingly callous, abusive behavior.
- The bystander effect occurs primarily because a group creates diffusion of responsibility. Individuals' productivity often declines in larger groups because of loss of coordination and because of social loafing.
- Group polarization occurs when discussion leads a group to shift toward a more extreme decision in the direction the group was already leaning. In groupthink, a cohesive group suspends critical judgment in a misguided effort to promote agreement in decision making.
- Our study of social psychology illustrated the value of empiricism, the cultural limits of research based on American samples, and the subjectivity of perception.
- Prejudice is supported by selectivity and memory biases in person perception and stereotyping. Stereotypes are highly resistant to change. Attributional biases, such as the tendency to assume that others' behavior reflects their dispositions, can contribute to prejudice.
- Negative attitudes about groups are often acquired through observational learning and strengthened through operant conditioning. Realistic group conflict theory posits that competition between groups fosters prejudice. The propensity to see outgroups as homogenous serves to strengthen prejudice. Threats to social identity can lead to ingroup favoritism and outgroup derogation.
- Useful criteria in judging credibility include whether a source has vested interests or appropriate credentials. One should also consider the method of analysis used in reaching conclusions and why information might not coincide with conventional wisdom.
- To resist manipulative efforts, it helps to be aware of social influence tactics, such as the **foot-in-the-door technique**, misuse of the **reciprocity norm**, the **lowball technique**, and feigned scarcity.

CHAPTER 14 PRACTICE EXAM

_____ 1. Person perception is
a. forming impressions
b. developing a personality theory
c. predicting others
d. monitoring impressions y

_____ 2. Widely held beliefs people based on group membership defines
a. cognitive planning
b. cultural redirection
c. stereotypes
d. stigmatizing

_____ 3. Bill has only met four actresses who were blonds, and he met four actresses who were redheads but Bill continues to believe the most actresses are blonds. His belief concerns
a. an regression to the mean
b. an illusory correlation
c. a fundamental correlation
d. An irreducible conceptual error

_____ 4. Sarah is in a sorority and she is the only one not to vote for a person who wants be in the sorority. Sarah's sorority sisters should consider her
a. as a member of their ingroup
b. A member of the sorority bias
c. as a member of their outgroup
d. A not managing good judgment

_____ 5. What is the effect used when a political party repeats a message which causes the message to be considered true whether or not it is?
a. validity effect
b. contrast effect
c. exposure effect
d. reiteration effect

_____ 6. In Milgram's obedience research, what did the teacher think the consequences were for the learner if the learner made an error?
a. receive a shock
b. be negatively reinforced
c. be asked to change places
d. The experiment was ended

_____ 7. Higher levels of conformity are found in
a. collectivistic cultures
b. individualistic cultures
c. industrialized cultures
d. autonomous

_____ 8. Four college students all watched a serious accident but made no effort to call the police or see if anyone was injured. These four students were exhibiting
a. social loafing
b. a individualism
c. group antipathy
d. the bystander effect

_____ 9. The bystander effect is
a. greater when there are more people in the group
b. less when there are fewer people in the group
c. The same whether the group is large or small
d. Only occurs in groups of one individual

_____ 10. Diffusion of responsibility is defined as
a. Assuming someone besides you will take responsibility in a crisis
b. Is a genetic prosocial disorder
c. halo effect
d. Blaming the other person

_____ 11. Social loafing is defined as
a. increases in socializing to smaller groups
b. the reduction of effort by individuals when they work in groups
c. Not having a leader in a group
d. Becoming the victim in a large group

_____ 12. Polarizing ingroup and outgroup is a basic feature of ?
a. social loafing
b. group polarization
c. social diffusion
d. groupthink

_____ 13. _____________ means that psychology is committed to systematic observation through research to arrive at conclusions.

a. empiricism
b. objectivity
c. subjectivity
d. functionalism

_____ 14. Denying a person equal social treatment based on his or her group membership defines

a. discrimination
b. chauvinism
c. prejudice
d. social scaling

_____ 15. The fundamental attribution error leads observers to attribute the crime and poverty of urban ethnic neighborhoods to the

a. personal qualities
b. job discrimination
c. poor police protection
d. crowded living conditions

Answers

1. A
2. C
3. B
4. C
5. A
6. A
7. A
8. D
9. A
10. A
11. B
12. D
13. A
14. A
15. A

Glossary

absolute sensory threshold The intensity at which a given individual can detect a sensory stimulus 50% of the time; a low threshold indicates the ability to detect faint stimuli.

accommodation The process through which we change or modify existing schemata to accommodate new experiences.

achievement tests Psychological tests that measure your current level of knowledge or competence in a particular subject.

acrophobia Fear of high places.

action potential An excitation that travels along an axon at a constant strength, no matter how far it must travel.

activation–synthesis hypothesis A proposed perspective on dreaming that considers dreams to be the result of subjective organization and interpretation (synthesis) of neural activity (activation) that takes place during sleep; contrasting views include the Freudian view of dreams as a symbolic manifestation of wishes and the view of dreams as mental housekeeping.

acute stress disorder A disorder, like PTSD, that is characterized by feelings of anxiety and helplessness and caused by a traumatic event. Acute stress disorder occurs within a month of the event and lasts from 2 days to 4 weeks.

adaptive behaviors Actions that aid attempts to survive and adapt to changing conditions.

adrenaline A hormone produced by the adrenal glands that tends to arouse the body.

ageism Discrimination or prejudice against an individual based on physical age.

agoraphobia Fear of open, crowded places.

agreeableness The tendency to be compassionate toward others and not antagonistic.

algorithm A mechanical, repetitive procedure for solving a problem.

amphetamines A type of synthetic *central nervous system (CNS) stimulant* that is usually either ingested orally or injected; short-term effects include increased body temperature, heart rate, and endurance, as well as reduced appetite; psychological effects include stimulation of the release of *neurotransmitters,* such as norepinephrine and *dopamine* into brain *synapses,* as well as inhibition of *reuptake* of neurotransmitters, leading to a sense of euphoria and increased alertness, *arousal,* and motor activity; long-term effects are a reduction of *serotonin* and other neurotransmitters in the brain, thereby impairing neural communication within the brain; long-term use also leads to *tolerance* and intermittent use may lead to *sensitization.*

amygdala A part of the limbic system (within the brain) that produces fear responses.

anorexia nervosa Active self-starvation or a sustained loss of appetite that has psychological origins.

antidepressant Acting to relieve depression.

antisocial personality disorder The diagnosis given a person who is in frequent conflict with society, yet who is undeterred by punishment and experiences little or no guilt and anxiety.

aptitude tests Psychological tests that measure your ability to learn or acquire knowledge in a particular subject.

arousal theory Assumes that people prefer to maintain ideal, or comfortable, levels of arousal.

assimilation The process through which we fit—or assimilate—new experiences into existing schemata.

asylum An institution for the care of the mentally ill.

attachments Strong emotional ties formed to one or more intimate companions.

attention deficit disorder (ADD) A condition marked by impulsive behavior and short attention span.

attention The active cognitive processing of a limited amount of information from the vast amount of information available through the senses, in memory and through cognitive processes; focus on a small subset of available *stimuli.*

attention The tendency to respond to some stimuli more than others or to remember some more than others.

attentional blink A brief period after perceiving a stimulus, during which it is difficult to attend to another stimulus.

attentive process A procedure that extracts information from one part of the visual field at a time.

attitudes Orientations that locate objects of thought on dimensions of judgment.

attribution The mental process of assigning causes to events. In emotion, the process of attributing arousal to a particular source.

attributional style The tendency to attribute one's behavior to internal or external factors, stable or unstable factors, and so on.

attributions Inferences that people draw about the causes of events, others' behavior, and their own behavior.

autonomic nervous system (ANS) The system of nerves that connects the brain with the internal organs and glands.

autonomic nervous system A system of neurons that controls the internal organs such as the heart.

availability heuristic The strategy of assuming that how easily one can remember examples of some kind of event indicates how common the event actually is.

aversive conditioning A behavior-therapy technique in which undesired responses are inhibited by pairing repugnant or offensive stimuli with them.

avoidance conditioning A situation in which a response can prevent the delivery of an aversive stimulus, such as when a rat learns to jump over a barrier to avoid a shock.

avoidant personality disorder A personality disorder in which the person is unwilling to enter relationships without assurance of acceptance because of fears of rejection and criticism.

axon A single, long, thin, straight fiber that transmits information from a neuron to other neurons or to muscle cells.

bait shyness An unwillingness or hesitation on the part of animals to eat a particular food.

barbiturates An antianxiety drug prescribed to reduce *anxiety* through physiological inhibition of *arousal* (high dosages can even induce sleep); may lead to grogginess that may impair functioning in situations requiring alertness; chronic use leads to *tolerance* and to physiological *addiction,* and high doses can lead to respiratory failure (see also *central nervous system (CNS) depressant*).

barnum effect The tendency to accept and praise vague statements about our personality.

base-rate information Data about the frequency or probability of a given item.

basic needs The first four levels of needs in Maslow's hierarchy; lower needs tend to be more potent than higher needs.

behavior rehearsal Practice.

behavior therapy Systematic application of the principles of learning to the direct modification of a client's problem behaviors.

behavioral dieting Weight reduction based on changing exercise and eating habits, rather than temporary self-starvation.

benzodiazepines A class of drugs that reduce anxiety; minor tranquilizers.

big five personality traits Five traits that account for a great deal of human personality differences: neuroticism, extraversion, agreeableness, conscientiousness, and openness to new experience.

bilingual Able to use two languages about equally well.

binding problem The question of how separate brain areas combine forces to produce a unified perception of a single object.

binocular cues Visual cues that depend on the action of both eyes.

biofeedback training (BFT) The systematic feeding back to an organism of information about a bodily function so that the organism can gain control of that function.

bipolar disorder A disorder in which the mood alternates between two extreme poles (elation and depression). Also referred to as *manic–depression.*

blindsight A phenomenon in which individuals can see something but are not aware of what they are seeing.

borderline personality disorder A personality disorder characterized by instability in relationships, self-image, mood, and lack of impulse control.

brightness contrast An increase or decrease in an object's apparent brightness because of the effects of objects around it.

broca's aphasia A condition characterized by inarticulate speech and by difficulties with both using and understanding grammatical devices—prepositions, conjunctions, word endings, complex sentence structures, and so forth.

bulimia nervosa Excessive eating (gorging) usually followed by self-induced vomiting and/or taking laxatives.

bystander effect A paradoxical social phenomenon in which people are less likely to provide needed help when they are in groups than when they are alone.

caffeine A mild *central nervous system (CNS) stimulant.*

Cannon-Bard theory States that activity in the thalamus causes emotional feelings and bodily arousal to occur simultaneously.

case study An in-depth observation of one person.

catatonic schizophrenia A type of schizophrenia characterized by striking motor impairment.

catharsis In psychoanalysis, the expression of repressed feelings and impulses to allow the release of the psychic energy associated with them.

causal hypothesis An educated guess about how one variable will influence another variable.

cell body The part of the neuron that contains the nucleus of the cell.

central nervous system (CNS) depressant A drug (e.g., alcohol and *sedatives*) that slows the operation of the CNS and is often prescribed in low doses to reduce anxiety and in relatively higher doses to combat *insomnia* (see *barbiturate, tranquilizer;* cf. *narcotic;* see also *central nervous system (CNS) stimulant).*

central nervous system (CNS) stimulant A drug (e.g., *caffeine, amphetamines, cocaine,* and nicotine—found in tobacco) that arouses and excites the *CNS,* either by stimulating the heart or by inhibiting the actions of natural compounds that depress brain activity (in other words, it acts as a "double-negative" on brain stimulation); short-term effects of relatively low doses include increased stamina and alertness, reduced appetite, and exuberant euphoria; higher doses may cause anxiety and irritability; problems with *tolerance* and *addiction* are linked with long-term use, and problems with *sensitization* are tied to intermittent use (cf. *central nervous system (CNS) depressant).*

central nervous system The brain and the spinal cord.

cerebellum (Latin for "little brain") A hindbrain structure that is active in the control of movement, especially for complex, rapid motor skills and behaviors that require precise timing.

cerebral cortex The outer surface of the forebrain.

change blindness The tendency to fail to detect changes in any part of a scene to which we are not focusing our attention.

channel The medium through which a message is sent.

circadian rhythms Cyclical changes in bodily functions and arousal levels that vary on a schedule approximating a 24-hour day.

classical conditioning A set of procedures used to investigate how organisms learn about the signaling properties of events. Classical conditioning involves learning relations between events—conditioned and unconditioned stimuli—that occur outside of one's control.

claustrophobia Fear of tight, small places.

client-centered therapy Carl Rogers's method of psychotherapy, which emphasizes the creation of a warm, therapeutic atmosphere that frees clients to engage in self-exploration and self-expression.

closure In Gestalt psychology the tendency to imagine the rest of an incomplete, familiar figure.

cocaine A powerful *central nervous system (CNS) stimulant.*

cocktail party phenomenon The process of tracking one conversation in the face of the distraction of other conversations; a phenomenon often experienced at cocktail parties.

cognition The processes of thinking, gaining knowledge, and dealing with knowledge.

cognitive dissonance A psychological state that exists when related cognitions are inconsistent.

cognitive interview Use of various cues and strategies to improve the memory of eyewitnesses.

cognitive therapy A form of therapy that focuses on how clients' cognitions (expectations, attitudes, beliefs, etc.) lead to distress and may be modified to relieve distress and promote adaptive behavior.

collectivism Putting group goals ahead of personal goals and defining one's identity in terms of the groups one belongs to.

commitment An intent to maintain a relationship in spite of the difficulties and costs that may arise.

common fate The tendency to perceive objects as being part of the same group if they change or move in similar ways at the same time.

companionate love Warm, trusting, tolerant affection for another whose life is deeply intertwined with one's own.

compulsion An irresistible urge to repeat an act or engage in ritualistic behavior like hand washing.

concentrative meditation A form of contemplation in which the meditator focuses on an object or thought and attempts to remove all else from *consciousness* (see *meditation*).

concordance Agreement.

concrete operational period Piaget's third stage of cognitive development, lasting from ages 7 to 11. Children acquire the capacity to perform a number of mental operations but still lack the ability for abstract reasoning.

conditioned inhibition Learning that an event signals the absence of the unconditioned stimulus.

conditioned reinforcer A stimulus that has acquired reinforcing properties through prior learning.

conditioned response (CR) The acquired response that is produced by the conditioned stimulus in anticipation of the unconditioned stimulus.

conditioned stimulus (CS) The neutral stimulus that is paired with the unconditioned stimulus during classical conditioning.

confidentiality Researchers do not reveal which data were collected from which participant.

confirmation bias The tendency to accept one hypothesis and then look for evidence to support it, instead of considering other possibilities.

conformity The tendency for people to yield to real or imagined social pressure.

confounding variable Any factor that affects the dependent measure other than the independent variable.

conscientiousness The tendency to show self-discipline, to be dutiful, and to strive for achievement and competence.

consolidation Process by which relatively permanent memories are formed in the brain.

constructive processing Reorganizing or updating memories on the basis of logic, reasoning, or the addition of new information.

continuation In Gestalt psychology the tendency to fill in the gaps in an interrupted line.

control questions In a polygraph exam, questions that almost always provoke anxiety.

conventional level In Kohlberg's theory of moral development, the stage in which actions are judged to be right or wrong based on whether they maintain or disrupt the social order.

convergence The degree to which the eyes turn in to focus on a close object.

conversion disorder A disorder in which anxiety or unconscious conflicts are "converted" into physical symptoms that often have the effect of helping the person cope with anxiety or conflict.

corpus callosum A large set of axons connecting the left and right hemispheres of the cerebral cortex and thus enabling the two hemispheres to communicate with each other.

correlation The relationship between two or more variables.

creativity The ability to generate ideas that are original, novel, and useful.

critical thinking The careful evaluation of evidence for and against any conclusion.

cross-sectional design A research design in which people of different ages are compared at the same time.

crystallized intelligence The knowledge and abilities acquired as a result of experience (as from schooling and cultural influences).

curve of forgetting A graph that shows the amount of memorized information remembered after varying lengths of time.

daydreaming A state of consciousness somewhere between waking and sleeping that permits a shift in the focus of conscious processing toward internal thoughts and images and away from external events; useful in cognitive processes that involve the generation of creative ideas, but disruptive in cognitive processes that require focused attention on environmental events.

debriefing After an experiment, participants are fully informed of the nature of the study.

declarative memory That part of long-term memory containing specific factual information.

defensive attribution The tendency to blame victims for their misfortune, so that one feels less likely to be victimized in a similar way.

delusions False, persistent beliefs that are unsubstantiated by sensory or objective evidence.

dementia Physically based losses in mental functioning.

dendrite One of the widely branching structures of a neuron that receive transmissions from other neurons.

dependent variable The variable in an experiment that measures any effect of the manipulation.

depth perception The perception of distance, which enables us to experience the world in three dimensions.

development The age-related physical, intellectual, social, and personal changes that occur throughout an individual's lifetime.

deviation IQ An intelligence score that is derived from determining where your performance sits in an age-based distribution of test scores.

discrimination Behaving differently, usually unfairly, toward the members of a group.

discriminative stimulus The stimulus situation that sets the occasion for a response to be followed by reinforcement or punishment.

disorganized schizophrenia A type of schizophrenia characterized by disorganized delusions and vivid hallucinations.

dissociative amnesia A dissociative disorder marked by loss of memory or self-identity; skills and general knowledge are usually retained. Previously termed *psychogenic amnesia.*

dissociative disorders Disorders in which there are sudden, temporary changes in consciousness or self-identity.

dissociative fugue A dissociative disorder in which one experiences amnesia and then flees to a new location. Previously termed *psychogenic fugue*.

dissociative identity disorder A disorder in which a person appears to have two or more distinct identities or personalities that may alternately emerge.

disuse Theory that memory traces weaken when memories are not periodically used or retrieved.

dopamine A neurotransmitter that promotes activity levels and facilitates movement.

drive The psychological expression of internal needs or valued goals. For example, hunger, thirst, or a drive for success.

echo A brief continuation of sensory activity in the auditory system after a sound is heard.

ego analyst A psychodynamically oriented therapist who focuses on the conscious, coping behavior of the ego instead of the hypothesized, unconscious functioning of the id.

egocentrism The tendency to see the world from one's own unique perspective only; a characteristic of thinking in the preoperational period of development.

eidetic imagery The ability to retain a "projected" mental image long enough to use it as a source of information.

elaborative rehearsal Rehearsal that links new information with existing memories and knowledge.

electroconvulsive shock (ECS) An electric current passed directly through the brain, producing a convulsion.

electroconvulsive therapy (ECT) Treatment of disorders like major depression by passing an electric current (that causes a convulsion) through the head.

electroencephalograph (EEG) A device that uses electrodes on the scalp to record rapid changes in brain electrical activity.

emblems Gestures that have widely understood meanings within a particular culture.

embryonic period The period of prenatal development lasting from implantation to the end of the 8th week.

emotion A state characterized by physiological arousal, changes in facial expression, gestures, posture, and subjective feelings.

emotional appraisal Evaluating the personal meaning of a stimulus or situation.

emotional expression Outward signs that an emotion is occurring.

emotional feelings The private, subjective experience of having an emotion.

emotional intelligence Emotional competence, including empathy, self-control, self-awareness, and other skills.

emotional intelligence The ability to perceive, understand, and express emotion in ways that are useful and adaptive.

emotional stroop test A procedure in which someone tries to say the color of ink for a number of words, some of which might pertain to a source of worry or concern.

empathic understanding Ability to perceive a client's feelings from the client's frame of reference. A quality of the good client-centered therapist.

encoding failure Failure to store sufficient information to form a useful memory.

encoding Converting information into a form in which it will be retained in memory.

encounter group A type of group that aims to foster self-awareness by focusing on how group members relate to each other in a setting that encourages open expression of feelings.

endocrine system A set of glands that produce hormones and release them into the bloodstream.

engram A "memory trace" in the brain.

epilepsy A condition characterized by abnormal rhythmic activity of brain neurons.

episodic drive A drive that occurs in distinct episodes.

episodic memory A subpart of declarative memory that records personal experiences that are linked with specific times and places.

escape conditioning A situation in which a response can reduce or eliminate an unpleasant stimulus, such as when a rat escapes an ongoing shock by jumping over a barrier.

estrogen Any of a number of female sex hormones.

estrus Changes in the sexual drives of animals that create a desire for mating; particularly used to refer to females in heat.

experiment A research method that is used to test causal hypotheses.

explicit memory A memory that a person is aware of having; a memory that is consciously retrieved.

external attributions Ascribing the causes of behavior to situational demands and environmental constraints.

external locus of control The belief that external forces are largely in control of the events of one's life.

extinction Presenting a conditioned stimulus repeatedly, after conditioning, without the unconditioned stimulus, resulting in a loss in responding.

extracellular thirst Thirst caused by a reduction in the volume of fluids found between body cells.

extraversion The tendency to seek stimulation and to enjoy the company of other people.

extrinsic motivation Motivation based on obvious external rewards, obligations, or similar factors.

facial feedback hypothesis States that sensations from facial expressions help define what emotion a person feels.

factor analysis A statistical procedure that groups together related items on tests by analyzing the correlations among test scores.

family therapy A form of therapy in which the family unit is treated as the client.

feature detector A neuron in the visual system of the brain that responds to the presence of a certain simple feature, such as a horizontal line.

feedback In assertiveness training, information about the effectiveness of a response.

feeling of knowing A feeling that allows people to predict beforehand whether they will be able to remember something.

fetal period The period of prenatal development lasting from the 9th week until birth.

figure and ground An object and its background.

fixation A period when the eyes are steady.

fixed-interval (FI) schedule A schedule in which the reinforcement is delivered for the first response that occurs following a fixed interval of time.

fixed-ratio (FR) schedule A schedule in which the number of responses required for reinforcement is fixed and does not change.

flashbulb memories Memories created at times of high emotion that seem especially vivid.

fluid intelligence The natural ability to solve problems, reason, and remember; fluid intelligence is thought to be relatively uninfluenced by experience.

foot-in-the-door technique Getting people to agree to a small request to increase the chances that they will agree to a larger request later.

formal operational period Piaget's last stage of cognitive development; thought processes become adult-like, and people gain mastery over abstract thinking.

frame of reference One's unique patterning of perceptions and attitudes, according to which one evaluates events.

framing effect The tendency to answer a question differently when it is framed (phrased) differently.

free association In psychoanalysis, the uncensored uttering of all thoughts that come to mind.

frontal lobe A portion of each cerebral hemisphere at the anterior pole, with sections that control movement and certain aspects of memory.

functional analysis A systematic study of behavior in which one identifies the stimuli that trigger problem behavior and the reinforcers that maintain it.

functional fixedness The tendency to adhere to a single approach to a problem or a single way of using an item.

functional magnetic resonance imaging (fMRI) A technique that uses magnetic detectors outside the head to measure the amounts of hemoglobin, with and without oxygen, in different parts of the brain and thereby provides an indication of current activity levels in various brain areas.

fundamental attribution error Observers' bias in favor of internal attributions in explaining others' behavior.

***g* (general intelligence)** According to Spearman, a general factor, derived from factor analysis, that underlies or contributes to performance on a variety of mental tests.

galvanic skin response (GSR) A change in the electrical resistance (or inversely, the conductance) of the skin, due to sweating.

gamma-aminobutyric acid (GABA) An inhibitory neurotransmitter that is implicated in anxiety reactions.

gender roles Specific patterns of behavior that are consistent with how society dictates makes and females should act.

generalizability How well a researcher's findings apply to other individuals and situations.

generalized anxiety disorder Feelings of dread and foreboding and sympathetic arousal of at least 6 months' duration.

genuineness Recognition and open expression of the therapist's own feelings.

germinal period The period in prenatal development from conception to implantation of the fertilized egg in the wall of the uterus.

gestalt psychology An approach to psychology that seeks to explain how we perceive overall patterns.

gestalt therapy Fritz Perls's form of psychotherapy, which attempts to integrate conflicting parts of the personality through directive methods designed to help clients perceive their whole selves.

gifted A label generally assigned to someone who scores above 130 on a standard IQ test.

glia A cell of the nervous system that insulates neurons, removes waste materials (e.g., dead cells), and performs other supportive functions.

glutamate An excitatory neurotransmitter that is involved in anxiety reactions.

goal The target or objective of motivated behavior.

good figure In Gestalt psychology the tendency to perceive simple, symmetrical figures.

group cohesiveness The strength of the liking relationships linking group members to each other and to the group itself.

group polarization A phenomenon that occurs when group discussion strengthens a group's dominant point of view and produces a shift toward a more extreme decision in that direction.

group Two or more individuals who interact and are interdependent.

groupthink A process in which members of a cohesive group emphasize concurrence at the expense of critical thinking in arriving at a decision.

growth needs In Maslow's hierarchy, the higher-level needs associated with self-actualization.

habituation The decline in responsiveness to a stimulus that is repeatedly presented.

habituation The decline in the tendency to respond to an event that has become familiar through repeated exposure.

hallucination A perception in the absence of sensory stimulation that is confused with reality.

hallucinations *Perceptions* of sensory stimulation (e.g., sounds, the most common hallucinated sensations; sights; smells; or tactile sensations) in the absence of any actual corresponding external sensory input from the physical world.

hallucinogenic A type of *psychoactive* drug (e.g., mescaline, LSD, and marijuana) that alters *consciousness* by inducing *hallucinations* and affecting the way the drug-takers perceive both their inner worlds and their external environments; often termed *psychotomimetics* (also known as "psychedelics") because some clinicians believe that these drugs mimic the effects produced by psychosis.

hemisphere The left or right half of the brain; each hemisphere is responsible for sensation and motor control on the opposite side of the body.

heritability A mathematical index that represents the extent to which IQ differences in a particular population can be accounted for by genetic factors.

heuristics Strategies for simplifying a problem or for guiding an investigation.

hierarchy of human needs Abraham Maslow's ordering of needs, based on their presumed strength or potency.

hierarchy An arrangement of stimuli according to the amount of fear they evoke.

hippocampus A brain structure associated with emotion and the transfer of information from short-term memory to long-term memory.

homeostasis A steady state of bodily equilibrium.

hormone A chemical released by glands and conveyed by the blood to other parts of the body, where it alters activity.

hypnosis An altered state of *consciousness* that usually involves deep relaxation and extreme sensitivity to suggestion and appears to bear some resemblance to sleep (see *posthypnotic suggestion*).

hypochondriasis Persistent belief that one is ill despite lack of medical findings.

hypothalamus A small area at the base of the brain that regulates many aspects of motivation and emotion, especially hunger, thirst, and sexual behavior.

icon A mental image or visual representation.

ideas of persecution Erroneous beliefs that one is being victimized or persecuted.

idiographic approach An approach to the study of personality differences that concentrates on intensive studies of individuals

illusion A distorted *perception* of objects and other external *stimuli* that may be due to misleading cues in the objects themselves or to distortions of the perceptual process, such as distortions caused by altered states of consciousness or psychological disorder (see *optical illusion;* cf. *delusion*).

illusory correlation A misperception that occurs when people estimate that they have encountered more confirmations of an association between social traits than they have actually seen.

illustrators Gestures people use to illustrate what they are saying.

Implicit Association Test A procedure that measures how fast someone responds to a category that combines a topic with pleasant words or with unpleasant words.

implicit memory A memory that a person does not know exists; a memory that is retrieved unconsciously.

incentive value The value of a goal above and beyond its ability to fill a need.

independent variable The variable in an experiment that is manipulated

individualism Putting personal goals ahead of group goals and defining one's identity in terms of personal attributes rather than group memberships.

induced movement A perception that an object is moving and the background is stationary when in fact the object is stationary and the background is moving.

information bits Meaningful units of information, such as numbers, letters, words, or phrases.

information chunks Information bits grouped into larger units.

informed consent Research participants agree to participate after being told about aspects of the study.

ingroup The group that people belong to and identify with.

insanity A legal term descriptive of a person judged to be incapable of recognizing right from wrong or of conforming his or her behavior to the law.

insomnia Any of various disturbances of sleep, including difficulty falling asleep, waking up during the night and being unable to go back to sleep, or waking up too early in the morning, and which may vary in intensity and duration.

Institutional Review Board (IRB) A committee that reviews research proposals to ensure that ethical standards have been met.

intelligence quotient (IQ) Mental age divided by chronological age and then multiplied by 100.

intelligence An internal capacity or ability that accounts for individual differences in mental test performance and enables us to adapt to ever-changing environments.

intelligence An internal capacity or ability that accounts for individual differences in mental test performance and enables us to adapt to ever-changing environments.

interference The tendency for new memories to impair retrieval of older memories, and the reverse.

internal attributions Ascribing the causes of behavior to personal dispositions, traits, abilities, and feelings.

internal images Mental images or visual depictions used in memory and thinking.

internal locus of control The belief that one is largely in control of the events of one's life.

interpersonal attraction Positive feelings toward another.

interpretation An explanation of a client's utterance according to psychoanalytic theory.

intimacy Warmth, closeness, and sharing in a relationship.

intoxicated Characterized by stupefaction due to the effects of toxins such as alcohol or *sedatives.*

intracellular thirst Thirst triggered when fluid is drawn out of cells due to an increased concentration of salts and minerals outside the cell.

intrinsic motivation Motivation that comes from within, rather than from external rewards; motivation based on personal enjoyment of a task or activity.

James-Lange theory States that emotional feelings follow bodily arousal and come from awareness of such arousal.

keyword method As an aid to memory, using a familiar word or image to link two items.

kinesics Study of the meaning of body movements, posture, hand gestures, and facial expressions; commonly called body language.

la belle indifférence A French term descriptive of the lack of concern sometimes shown by people with conversion disorders.

language acquisition device A built-in mechanism for acquiring language.

latent content In psychodynamic theory, the symbolized or underlying content of dreams.

law of effect If a response in a particular situation is followed by a satisfying consequence, it will be strengthened. If a response in a particular situation is followed by an unsatisfying consequence, it will be weakened.

learned helplessness A model for the acquisition of depressive behavior, based on findings that organisms in aversive situations learn to show inactivity when their operants go unreinforced.

learning A relatively permanent change in behavior, or potential behavior, that results from experience.

longitudinal design A research design in which the same people are studied or tested repeatedly over time.

long-term memory (LTM) The memory system used for relatively permanent storage of meaningful information.

lowball technique Getting someone to commit to an attractive proposition before revealing the hidden costs.

magnetoencephalograph (MEG) A device that records rapid magnetic changes during brain activity.

maintenance rehearsal Silently repeating or mentally reviewing information to hold it in short-term memory.

major depressive disorder A serious to severe depressive disorder in which the person may show loss of appetite, psychomotor retardation, and impaired reality testing.

manic Elated, showing excessive excitement.

manifest content In psychodynamic theory, the reported content of dreams.

massed practice A practice schedule in which studying continues for long periods, without interruption.

matching hypothesis The idea that males and females of approximately equal physical attractiveness are likely to select each other as partners.

meditation A set of techniques used for altering *consciousness* through focused contemplation (see *concentrative meditation, opening-up meditation*).

medulla A structure that is located in the hindbrain and is an elaboration of the spinal cord; controls many muscles in the head and several life-preserving functions, such as breathing.

memory cue Any stimulus associated with a particular memory. Memory cues usually enhance retrieval.

memory decay The fading or weakening of memories assumed to occur when memory traces become weaker.

memory task Any task designed to test or assess memory.

memory traces Physical changes in nerve cells or brain activity that take place when memories are stored.

memory The mental system for receiving, encoding, storing, organizing, altering, and retrieving information.

menopause The period during which a woman's menstrual cycle slows down and finally stops.

mental age The chronological age that best fits a child's level of performance on a test of mental ability.

mental retardation A label generally assigned to someone who scores below 70 on a standard IQ test although other factors, such as one's ability to adapt to the environment, are also important.

message The information transmitted by a source.

meta-analysis A method for combining and averaging the results of individual research studies.

meta-needs In Maslow's hierarchy, needs associated with impulses for self-actualization.

Minnesota Multiphasic Personality Inventory (MMPI) A standardized test consisting of true–false items and intended to measure various personality dimensions and clinical conditions such as depression.

MMPI–2 The modernized edition of the MMPI.

mnemonic Any kind of memory system or aid.

modeling A behavior-therapy technique in which a client observes and imitates a person who approaches and copes with feared objects or situations.

modeling The natural tendency to imitate the behavior of significant others.

monocular cues Visual cues that are just as effective with one eye as with both.

mood A low-intensity, long-lasting emotional state.

moon illusion The apparent difference between the size of the moon at the horizon and its size when viewed higher in the sky.

morality The ability to distinguish between appropriate and inappropriate actions.

morpheme A unit of meaning.

motion parallax The apparently swift motion of objects close to a moving observer and the apparently slow motion of objects farther away.

motivation Internal processes that initiate, sustain, and direct activities.

multiple intelligences The notion proposed by Howard Gardner that people possess a set of separate and independent "intelligences" ranging from musical to linguistic to interpersonal ability.

multiple personality disorder The previous term for *dissociative identity disorder.*

mutism Refusal to talk.

narcolepsy A disturbance of the pattern of wakefulness and sleep, in which the narcoleptic person experiences an uncontrollable urge to fall asleep periodically during the day and as a result loses *consciousness* for brief periods of time (usually 10 to 15 minutes), thereby putting the narcoleptic in grave danger if the attacks occur when the person is driving or otherwise engaged in activities for which sudden sleep might be hazardous.

narcotic Any drug in a class of drugs derived from opium (*opiates* such as heroin, morphine, or codeine) or synthetically produced to create the numbing, stuporous effects of opium (*opioids* such as meperidine or methadone) and that lead to addiction; lead to a reduction in pain and an overall sense of well-being (from the Greek term for "numbness") (see also *centra nervous system (CNS) depressant*).

naturalistic observation Observing behavior in the environment in which the behavior typically occurs.

need for achievement The desire to excel or meet some internalized standard of excellence.

need for power The desire to have social impact and control over others.

need An internal deficiency that may energize behavior.

negative correlation A relationship in which increases in one variable correspond to decreases in a second variable.

negative punishment An event that, when *removed* after a response, lowers the likelihood of that response occurring again.

negative reinforcement An event that, when *removed* after a response, increases the likelihood of that response occurring again.

negative transfer Mastery of one task conflicts with learning or performing another.

neodissociative theory A view of hypnosis in which it is asserted that some individuals are capable of separating one part of their conscious minds from another part; in one part, the individual responds to the hypnotist's commands, while in the other part, the individual observes and monitors the events and actions taking place, including some of the actions that the hypnotized individual appears not to be processing in the part of the conscious mind that is engaging in the actions.

network model A model of memory that views it as an organized system of linked information.

neuron A cell of the nervous system that receives information and transmits it to other cells by conducting electrochemical impulses.

neuroticism A personality trait characterized largely by persistent anxiety.

neuroticism The tendency to experience unpleasant emotions relatively easily.

neurotransmitter A chemical that is stored in the terminal of an axon and that, when released, activates receptors of other neurons.

nomothetic approach An approach to the study of individual differences that seeks general laws about how an aspect of personality affects behavior.

non-homeostatic drive A drive that is relatively independent of physical deprivation cycles or bodily need states.

N-REM sleep The four stages of sleep that are not characterized by rapid eye movements (hence, the acronym for **non-rapid eye movement**) and that are less frequently associated with dreaming (cf. *REM sleep*).

obedience A form of compliance that occurs when people follow direct commands, usually from someone in a position of authority.

object permanence The ability to recognize that objects still exist when they're no longer in sight.

observational learning Learning by observing the experience of others.

obsession A recurring thought or image that seems beyond control.

occipital lobe The rear portion of each cerebral hemisphere, critical for vision.

opening-up meditation One of the two main forms of contemplation, in which the meditator integrates *meditation* with the events of everyday life, seeking to expand awareness of everyday events, rather than to separate meditation from mundane existence; often involves an attempt to focus on becoming one with an ordinary activity, and on putting all other interfering thoughts out of *consciousness* (cf. *concentrative meditation*).

openness to experience The tendency to enjoy new intellectual experiences, the arts, fantasies, and anything that exposes a person to new ideas.

operant conditioning A procedure for studying how organisms learn about the consequences of their own voluntary actions (also called *instrumental conditioning*).

opiate A *narcotic* that is derived from the opium poppy bulb; may be injected intravenously, smoked, ingested orally, or inhaled (cf. *opioid*).

opioid A *narcotic* that has a similar chemical structure and set of effects to those of an *opiate* but that is made synthetically through combinations of chemicals.

opponent-process theory States that strong emotions tend to be followed by an opposite emotional state; also the strength of both emotional states changes over time.

optical illusion A misinterpretation of a visual stimulus as being larger or smaller, or straighter or more curved, than it really is.

orienting response An inborn tendency to notice and respond to novel or surprising events.

outgroup People who are not part of the ingroup.

overconfidence The belief that one's opinions or predictions are highly correct when in fact they are not.

overdose Ingestion of a life-threatening or lethal dose of drugs, often associated with the use of *psychoactive* drugs, such as *narcotics, amphetamines,* or *sedatives;* though often linked to intentional suicide, overdoses commonly occur due to *tolerance* or *sensitization,* particularly when the users are also using street drugs, which contain many impurities and are not reliably controlled with regard to the concentrations of psychoactive elements in the drug compounds.

panic disorder The recurrent experiencing of attacks of extreme anxiety in the absence of external stimuli that usually elicit anxiety.

paranoid personality disorder A personality disorder characterized by persistent suspiciousness but not involving the disorganization of paranoid schizophrenia.

paranoid schizophrenia A type of schizophrenia characterized primarily by delusions—commonly of persecution—and by vivid hallucinations.

parasympathetic branch A part of the autonomic system that quiets the body and conserves energy.

parasympathetic rebound Excess activity in the parasympathetic nervous system following a period of intense emotion.

parietal lobe A portion of each cerebral hemisphere; the main receiving area for the sense of touch and for the awareness of one's own body and perception of location of the body in space.

Parkinson's disease A condition that affects about 1% of people over the age of 50; the main symptoms are difficulty in initiating voluntary movement, slowness of movement, tremors, rigidity, and depressed mood.

partial reinforcement schedule A schedule in which reinforcement is delivered only some of the time after the response has occurred.

passionate love A complete absorption in another that includes tender sexual feelings and the agony and ecstasy of intense emotion.

peripheral nervous system The bundles of axons that convey messages between the spinal cord and the rest of the body.

person perception The process of forming impressions of others.

personal identity A sense of who one is as an individual and how well one measures up against peers.

personality disorders Enduring patterns of maladaptive behavior that are sources of distress to the individual or others.

phallic symbol A sign that represents the penis.

phi effect The illusion of movement created when two or more stationary lights separated by a short distance flash on and off at regular intervals.

phoneme A unit of sound.

physiological changes (in emotion) Alterations in heart rate, blood pressure, perspiration, and other involuntary responses.

polygraph A device for recording heart rate, blood pressure, respiration, and galvanic skin response; commonly called a "lie detector."

pons A structure adjacent to the medulla that receives sensory input from the head and controls many muscles in the head.

population of interest The entire universe of animals or people that could be studied.

positive correlation A relationship in which increases in one variable correspond to increases in a second variable.

positive punishment An event that, when *presented* after a response, lowers the likelihood of that response occurring again.

positive reinforcement An event that, when *presented* after a response, increases the likelihood of that response.

positive transfer Mastery of one task aids learning or performing another.

positron-emission tomography (PET) A technique that provides a high-resolution image of brain activity by recording radioactivity emitted from injected chemicals.

postconventional level Kohlberg's highest level of moral development, in which moral actions are judged on the basis of a personal code of ethics that is general and abstract and that may not agree with societal norms.

posthypnotic suggestion An instruction given to an individual during *hypnosis,* which the individual is to implement after having wakened from the hypnotic state; subjects often have no recollection of having been given the instructions or even of having been hypnotized.

postsynaptic neuron A neuron on the receiving end of a synapse.

posttraumatic stress disorder (PTSD) A disorder that follows a distressing event outside the range of normal human experience and that is c haracterized by features such as intense fear, avoidance of stimuli associated with the event, and reliving of the event.

preattentive process A procedure for extracting information automatically and simultaneously across a large portion of the visual field.

preconscious A part of *consciousness* that comprises information that could become conscious readily but that is not continuously available in awareness.

preconventional level In Kohlberg's theory, the lowest level of moral development, in which decisions about right and wrong are made primarily in terms of external consequences.

predictive hypothesis An educated guess about the relationships among variables.

prefrontal cortex An area in the anterior portion of the frontal lobes, critical for planning movements and for certain aspects of memory.

prefrontal lobotomy The severing or destruction of a section of the frontal lobe of the brain.

prejudice A negative attitude held toward members of a group.

preoperational period Piaget's second stage of cognitive development, lasting from ages 2 to about 7; children begin to think symbolically but often lack the ability to perform mental operations such as conservation.

primary emotions According to Robert Plutchik, the most basic emotions are fear, surprise, sadness, disgust, anger, anticipation, joy, and acceptance.

primary motives Innate motives based on biological needs.

primary motor cortex A strip in the posterior (rear) part of the frontal cortex that controls fine movements, such as hand and finger movements.

primary somatosensory cortex A strip in the anterior (forward) part of the parietal lobe that receives most touch sensations and other information about the body.

priming Facilitating the retrieval of an implicit memory by using cues to activate hidden memories.

principle of conservation The ability to recognize that the physical properties of an object remain the same despite superficial changes in the object's appearance.

proactive interference The tendency for old memories to interfere with the retrieval of newer memories.

procedural memory Long-term memories of conditioned responses and learned skills.

productivity The ability to express new ideas.

projective techniques Procedures designed to encourage people to project their personality characteristics onto ambiguous stimuli.

prototype A familiar or typical example of a category.

proximity In Gestalt psychology the tendency to perceive objects that are close together as belonging to a group.

psychoactive drugs Chemical substances that modify mental, emotional, or behavioral functioning.

psychoanalysis Freud's method of psychotherapy.

psychological disorders Patterns of behavior or mental processes that are connected with emotional distress or significant impairment in functioning.

psychometrics The use of psychological tests to measure the mind and mental processes.

psychomotor retardation Slowness in motor activity and (apparently) in thought.

psychosurgery Surgery intended to promote psychological changes or to relieve disordered behavior.

psychotherapy A systematic interaction between a therapist and a client that brings psychological principles to bear on influencing the client's thoughts, feelings, or behavior to help that client overcome abnormal behavior or adjust to problems in living.

puberty The period during which a person reaches sexual maturity and is potentially capable of producing offspring.

punishment Consequences that decrease the likelihood of responding in a similar way again.

quasi-experiment A research study that is not a true experiment because participants are not randomly assigned to the conditions of the study.

random assignment Participants have an equal chance of being placed in any condition of the study.

randomization When all people have an equal chance of being selected to participate in a study.

rapid flight of ideas Rapid speech and topic changes, characteristic of manic behavior.

rapid smoking An aversive conditioning method for quitting smoking in which the smoker inhales every 6 seconds, thus rendering once-desirable cigarette smoke aversive.

rational emotive behavior therapy (REBT) Albert Ellis's form of therapy that encourages clients to challenge and correct irrational expectations and maladaptive behaviors.

rebound anxiety Anxiety that can occur when one discontinues use of a tranquilizer.

recall To supply or reproduce memorized information with a minimum of external cues.

receiver The person to whom a message is sent.

reciprocity norm The rule that people should pay back in kind what they receive from others.

reciprocity Liking those who show that they like you.

recoding Reorganizing or modifying information to assist storage in memory.

recognition memory An ability to correctly identify previously learned information.

redintegrative memories Memories that are reconstructed or expanded by starting with one memory and then following chains of association to other, related memories.

reflex A rapid, automatic response to a stimulus.

reinforcement Response consequences that increase the likelihood of responding in a similar way again.

relearning Learning again something that was previously learned. Used to measure memory of prior learning.

reliability A measure of the consistency of test results; reliable tests produce similar scores or indices from one administration to the next.

REM sleep The distinctive kind of sleep that is characterized by **r**apid **e**ye **m**ovements (REMs) and frequently—though not exclusively—associated with dreaming (cf. *N-REM sleep*).

representativeness heuristic The tendency to assume that, if an item is similar to members of a particular category, it is probably a member of that category itself.

repression Unconsciously pushing unwanted memories out of awareness.

resistance The tendency to block the free expression of impulses and primitive ideas—a reflection of the defense mechanism of repression.

response Any action, glandular activity, or other identifiable behavior.

resting potential Electrical polarization that ordinarily occurs across the membrane of an axon that is not undergoing an action potential.

retinal disparity The difference in the apparent position of an object as seen by the left and right retinas.

retrieval Recovering information from storage in memory.

retroactive interference The tendency for new memories to interfere with the retrieval of old memories.

reversible figure A stimulus that you can perceive in more than one way.

rorschach inkblots A projective personality technique; people are shown 10 inkblots and asked what each might be depicting.

s (specific intelligence) According to Spearman, a specific factor, derived from factor analysis, that is unique to a particular kind of test.

saccade A quick jump in the focus of the eyes from one point to another.

sample The portion of the population of interest that is selected for a study.

Schachter's cognitive theory States that emotions occur when physical arousal is labeled or interpreted on the basis of experience and situational cues.

schedule of reinforcement A rule that an experimenter uses to determine when particular responses will be reinforced.

schemata Mental models of the world that we use to guide and interpret our experiences.

schizoid personality disorder A personality disorder characterized by social withdrawal.

schizophrenia A psychotic disorder characterized by loss of control of thought processes and inappropriate emotional responses.

schizotypal personality disorder A personality disorder characterized by oddities of thought and behavior but not involving bizarre psychotic behaviors.

secondary motives Motives based on learned needs, drives, and goals.

second-order conditioning A procedure in which an established conditioned stimulus is used to condition a second neutral stimulus.

sedative A drug that relieves nervousness or agitation or puts one to sleep.

sedative One type of *central nervous system (CNS) depressant,* used for calming *anxiety* and relieving *insomnia* (e.g., *barbiturate, tranquilizer,* methequalone, and chloral hydrate).

selective attention A process by which an individual attempts to track one *stimulus* or one type of stimulus and to ignore another.

selective serotonin-reuptake inhibitors (SSRIs) Antidepressant drugs that work by blocking the reuptake of serotonin by presynaptic neurons.

self-monitoring Keeping a record of one's own behavior to identify problems and record successes.

self-serving bias The tendency to attribute one's successes to personal factors and one's failures to situational factors.

semantic memory A subpart of declarative memory that records impersonal knowledge about the world.

sensitization Increased responsiveness, or sensitivity, to an event that has been repeated.

sensorimotor period Piaget's first stage of cognitive development, lasting from birth to about 2 years of age; schemata revolve around sensory and motor abilities.

sensory memory The first stage of memory, which holds an exact record of incoming information for a few seconds or less.

serial position effect The tendency to make the most errors in remembering the middle items of an ordered list.

set point The proportion of body fat that tends to be maintained by changes in hunger and eating.

shaping A procedure in which reinforcement is delivered for successive approximations of the desired response.

short-term memory (STM) The memory system used to hold small amounts of information for relatively brief time periods.

signal-detection theory The study of people's tendencies to make hits, correct rejections, misses, and false alarms.

similarity In Gestalt psychology the tendency to perceive objects that resemble each other as belonging to a group.

simulating paradigm A research technique for determining the true effects of a psychological treatment (e.g., *hypnosis*), in which one group of participants is subjected to the treatment and another group (a control group) is not, but the control participants are asked to behave as though they had received the treatment; people must then try to distinguish between the behavior of the treatment group and the behavior of the control group (most effective if the persons who make the distinction are blind about which participants are in the treatment group and which are in the control group).

sleep apnea A breathing disorder that occurs during sleep, in which the sleeper repeatedly (perhaps hundreds of times per night) stops breathing.

social loafing A reduction in effort by individuals when they work in groups as compared to when they work by themselves.

social motives Learned motives acquired as part of growing up in a particular society or culture.

social phobia An irrational, excessive fear of public scrutiny.

social psychology The branch of psychology concerned with the way individuals' thoughts, feelings, and behaviors are influenced by others.

social roles Widely shared expectations about how people in certain positions are supposed to behave.

social schemas Organized clusters of ideas about categories of social events and people.

somatic nervous system Peripheral nerves that communicate with the skin and muscles.

somatoform disorders Disorders in which people complain of physical (somatic) problems even though no physical abnormality can be found.

somnambulism Sleepwalking, which combines aspects of waking and sleeping, with the sleepwalker able to see, walk, and perhaps even talk, but usually unable to remember the sleepwalking episodes; rarely accompanied by dreaming.

source The person who sends a communication.

spaced practice A practice schedule that alternates study periods with brief rests.

specific phobia Persistent fear of a specific object or situation.

spinal cord That part of the central nervous system that communicates with sensory neurons and motor neurons below the level of the head.

spontaneous recovery The recovery of an extinguished conditioned response after a period of nonexposure to the conditioned stimulus.

spreading activation The process by which the activation of one concept also activates or primes other concepts that are linked to it.

standardization Keeping the testing, scoring, and interpretation procedures similar across all administrations of a test.

standardized test A test that is administered according to specified rules and its scores are interpreted in a prescribed fashion.

state A temporary activation of a particular behavior.

state-dependent learning Memory influenced by one's bodily state at the time of learning and at the time of retrieval. Improved memory occurs when the bodily states match.

stem cells Undifferentiated cells.

stereotypes Widely held beliefs that people have certain characteristics because of their membership in a particular group.

stimulus discrimination Responding differently to a new stimulus than how one responds to an established conditioned stimulus.

stimulus drives Drives based on needs for exploration, manipulation, curiosity, and stimulation.

stimulus generalization Responding to a new stimulus in a way similar to the response produced by an established conditioned stimulus.

stimulus motives Innate needs for stimulation and information.

storage Holding information in memory for later use.

strange situation test Gradually subjecting a child to a stressful situation and observing his or her behavior toward the parent or caregiver. This test is used to classify children according to type of attachment—secure, resistant, avoidant, or disorganized/disoriented.

stroboscopic movement An illusion of movement created by a rapid succession of stationary images.

stroop effect Difficulty in selectively attending to the colors of inks and ignoring words written in those colors (e.g., the word *green* printed in red letters).

stroop effect The tendency to read a word, especially if it is a color name, in spite of instructions to disregard the word and state the color of the ink in which it is printed.

stupor A condition in which the senses, thought, and movement are dulled.

subconscious A level of *consciousness* that involves less awareness than full consciousness and either is synonymous with the *unconscious* level (according to many theorists) or is slightly more accessible to consciousness than is the unconscious level (according to a few theorists).

subliminal perception The ability of a stimulus to influence our behavior even when it is presented so faintly or briefly or along with such strong distracters that we do not perceive it consciously.

successive approximations In operant conditioning, a series of behaviors that gradually become more similar to a target behavior.

sunk cost effect The willingness to do something we wouldn't otherwise choose to do because of money or effort already spent.

suppression A conscious effort to put something out of mind or to keep it from awareness.

sympathetic branch A part of the ANS that activates the body at times of stress.

synapse The specialized junction between one neuron and another; at this point one neuron releases a neurotransmitter, which either excites or inhibits the next neuron.

systematic desensitization Wolpe's method for reducing fears by associating a hierarchy of images of fear-evoking stimuli with deep muscle relaxation.

tacit knowledge Unspoken practical knowledge about how to perform well on the job.

taste aversion An active dislike for a particular food.

temperament A child's general level of emotional reactivity.

temporal lobe A portion of each cerebral hemisphere; the main processing area for hearing, complex aspects of vision, and certain aspects of emotional behavior.

teratogens Environmental agents—such as disease organisms or drugs—that can potentially damage the developing embryo or fetus.

terminal bouton (or button) A bulge at the end of an axon from which the axon releases a chemical called a neurotransmitter.

test anxiety High levels of arousal and worry that seriously impair test performance.

thalamus A forebrain area that relays information to the cerebral cortex.

thematic apperception Test (TAT) A projective personality technique; a person is asked to tell a story about each of 20 pictures.

tip-of-the-tongue state The feeling that a memory is available but not quite retrievable.

tobacco A plant product that contains nicotine, a *central nervous system (CNS) stimulant.*

token economy A controlled environment in which people are reinforced for desired behaviors with tokens (such as poker chips) that may be exchanged for privileges.

tolerance A consequence of prolonged use of *psychoactive* drugs, in which the drug user stops feeling the *psychotropic* effects of a given drug at one dose and must take increasing amounts of the drug in order to achieve the effects, eventually reaching a level of nonresponse at which the current level no longer produces the desired effects, but higher levels will cause overdose; the person generally still continues to take the drugs, despite the lack of psychotropic effects, simply to avoid experiencing the unpleasant feelings associated with drug *withdrawal* (see *addiction;* see also specific drugs, e.g., *amphetamine* and *barbiturate*).

trait A consistent, long-lasting tendency in behavior.

tranquilizer A *sedative* used for combating *anxiety;* considered to be safer than *barbiturates* because of the lower dosages required and the reduced likelihood of drowsiness and respiratory difficulties, although the potential for *addiction* remains a problem (see *central nervous system (CNS) depressants*).

transference Responding to one person (such as a spouse or the psychoanalyst) in a way that is similar to the way one responded to another person (such as a parent) in childhood.

transformational grammar A system for converting a deep structure of a language into a surface structure.

triarchic theory Robert Sternberg's theory of intelligence; it proposes three types of intelligence: analytic, creative, and practical.

unconditional positive regard Acceptance of the value of another person, although not necessarily acceptance of everything the person does.

unconditioned response (UR) The observable response that is produced automatically, prior to training, on presentation of an unconditioned stimulus.

unconditioned stimulus (US) A stimulus that automatically leads to an observable response prior to any training.

unconscious A level of *consciousness* at which thoughts, wishes, and feelings are not accessible to conscious awareness (often considered synonymous with *subconscious*); an important construct of *psychodynamic theory.*

unshared environment The aspects of environment that differ from one individual to another, even within a family.

validity An assessment of how well a test measures what it is supposed to measure. *Content validity* assesses the degree to which the test samples broadly across the domain of interest; *predictive validity* assesses how well the test predicts some future criterion; *construct validity* assesses how well the test taps into a particular theoretical construct.

variable-interval (VI) schedule A schedule in which the allotted time before a response will yield reinforcement varies from trial to trial.

variable-ratio (VR) schedule A schedule in which a certain number of responses are required for reinforcement, but the number of required responses typically changes.

visual constancy The tendency to perceive objects as unchanging in shape, size, and color, despite variations in what actually reaches the retina.

waterfall illusion A phenomenon in which prolonged staring at a waterfall and then looking at nearby cliffs causes those cliffs to appear to flow upward.

waxy flexibility A feature of catatonic schizophrenia in which people can be molded into postures that they maintain for quite some time.

Wernicke's aphasia A condition marked by difficulty recalling the names of objects and impaired comprehension of language.

Williams syndrome A genetic condition characterized by mental retardation in most regards but skillful use of language.

wish fulfillment A primitive method used by the id to attempt to gratify basic instincts.

withdrawal The temporary discomfort (which may be extremely negative, much like a severe case of intestinal flu, accompanied by extreme depression or *anxiety*) associated with a decrease in dosage or a discontinuation altogether of a *psychoactive* drug, during which the drug user's physiology and mental processes must adjust to an absence of the drug; during withdrawal from some drugs (e.g., some stimulants and some *sedatives*), the user should obtain medical supervision to avoid life-threatening complications that may arise during the readjustment to normal physiological and mental functioning.

word-superiority effect Identifying a letter with greater ease when it is part of a whole word than when it is presented by itself.

working memory Another name for short-term memory, especially when it is used for thinking and problem solving.

Yerkes-Dodson Law A summary of the relationships among arousal, task complexity, and performance.

zygote The fertilized human egg, containing 23 chromosomes from the father and 23 chromosomes from the mother.